BRITISH POETRY

19TH CENTURY

WILLIAM FLESCH

The Facts On File Companion to British Poetry, 19th Century

Facts On File, Inc.
An imprint of Infobase Publishing
132 West 31st Street
New York NY 10001

Library of Congress Cataloging-in-Publication Data

Flesch, William, 1956–
The Facts on File companion to 19th century British poetry / William Flesch.
p. cm.—(Companion to literature)
Includes bibliographical references and index.
ISBN 978-0-8160-5896-9 (alk. paper)
1. English poetry—19th century—History and criticism. I. Flesch, William, 1956– II. Title. III. Title: Companion to 19th century British poetry.
PR591.F54 2009
821'.809—dc22 2008032028

Facts On File books are available at special discounts when purchased in bulk quantities for businesses, associations, institutions, or sales promotions. Please call our Special Sales Department in New York at (212) 967-8800 or (800) 322-8755.

You can find Facts On File on the World Wide Web at http://www.factsonfile.com

Text design adapted by James Scotto-Lavino
Cover design by Salvatore Luongo

Printed in the United States of America

VB Hermitage 10 9 8 7 6 5 4 3 2 1

This book is printed on acid-free paper and contains 30 percent postconsumer recycled content.

To my parents

CONTENTS

ABOUT THIS BOOK

This book offers accounts of a number of major poems as well as significant minor ones, from *Adonais* (major) to *The Zilver-Weed* (minor), by the very many major and significant minor poets of the 19th century. During the period, Britain probably produced more good poems than any other country in any other comparable period, and it is a pleasure to read them and to introduce them to other readers.

Just to say so is to risk sounding polemical, so I should also say, straight out, that the book does have what might be taken, in the current climate, as a polemical purpose. I follow the American legal philosopher Ronald Dworkin's maxim that every work of art, and thus every poem, should be interpreted so as to make it as good as it possibly can be. Of course, notions of what makes a poem "good" are subjective, but, nevertheless, the aim should be to understand what makes these poems valuable in themselves. Fortunately, 19th-century poetry is easy to value very highly because it is so indubitably marvelous. It also often treats the question of what makes poetry a good in itself in a world in which military conflict and science and industry are rapidly transforming cultures beyond recognition, and so it asks to be read according to some such maxim as Dworkin's.

Because most of the poems I discuss are probably included in anthologies, I should mention those I think are the best: Harold Bloom and Lionel Trilling's sections on British romantic literature and Victorian literature in the *Oxford Anthology of English Literature;* Valentine Cunningham's *The Victorians: An Anthology of Poetry and Poetics;* Christopher Ricks's *New Oxford Book of Victorian Verse;* and Isobel Armstong, Joseph Bristow, and Cath Sharrock's *Nineteenth Century Women Poets: An Oxford Anthology.*

The online *Oxford Dictionary of National Biography* is the first place to go for biographical information about the poets profiled here. Though not always perfectly accurate (it was a pleasure to send in minor corrections to dozens of entries, as I am sure it will be painful to receive dozens of minor corrections to this volume), it gives a very sound first impression of the figures it treats; it is also very worthwhile going to the archive from the original *Dictionary of National Biography* to which each entry provides a link.

This is a book of many debts, which I can repay here only in the most partial manner: to Isobel Armstrong, Stephen Brown, John Burt, Stephen Burt, Daniel Flesch, Debra Fried, Hannah Ginsborg, Nick Halpern, Neil Hertz, Herb Marks, Robin Feuer Miller, Jeff Nunokawa, Adela Pinch, Laura Quinney, Christopher Ricks, Joseph Solman, Paul Solman, Willard Spiegelman, Karen Swann, Gordon Teskey, and Helen Vendler. Adam Rutledge was a superb research assistant and saved me from many inaccuracies, both of fact and of interpretation. Jeff Soloway, who commissioned this volume, was endlessly patient.

William Flesch
Arlington, Massachusetts

INTRODUCTION

This book covers the major British poets and poems of the 19th century. If the readings here make a single argument, that would be that 19th-century poetry, whatever else it is about, is about the nature, meaning, fate—the essence—of what poetry is. Different kinds of urgency attend this question as the century unfolds—urgencies that arise from larger historical, economic, social, political, and literary contexts. The larger literary context is the most convenient for a quick account of the through-lines of 19th-century poetry, because poetry is a part of the history of literature.

Nineteenth-century poetry starts with poetry at the center of British literary culture, because the romantic poets and their satellites make up the most important literary movement of the beginning of the century. But by mid-century, and certainly at the end of the century, poetry no longer commands an exclusive position at the center of literary culture and, indeed, evinces in incipient form some of the marginalization that characterizes the study and practice of poetry today. Poetry was still widely read, and poets were still thought of as cultural heroes at the end of the century (certainly a decade before its end, when Lord Tennyson and Robert Browning died). But the historical trajectory of 19th-century English literature is best traced as the history of what has come to be called the rise of the novel; that rise began in the 18th century (with Henry Fielding and Samuel Richardson, preeminently) but may be said to culminate in the Victorian era. A list of that era's great novelists would be an unusually long one, probably as long as that of all the other great English-language novelists put together, and would include at or near the top Charles Dickens, William Makepeace Thackeray, George Eliot, Emily Brontë, Charlotte Brontë, Anthony Trollope, George Meredith, Thomas Hardy, and Henry James.

While it is noteworthy that six of the nine members of this list are also accomplished poets (Thackeray, Eliot, the Brontës, Meredith, and Hardy), of these, only Hardy is a great poet. The great Victorian poets are not nearly as widely read now as the Victorian novelists, but they would include, preeminently, Tennyson and Browning, as well as Hardy and the early William Butler Yeats. Expanding this list to include the near great, we would add Elizabeth Barrett Browning, both Dante Gabriel Rossetti and Christina Rossetti, and William Morris. Of this set of poets, it could only be argued of Yeats and Christina Rossetti that they did not go beyond their romantic forebears in the line of long and quasi-novelistic narrative.

Of course the romantics did a lot of storytelling in their poems as well. The very idea of a ballad, even if lyrical (as in William Wordsworth and Samuel Taylor Coleridge's revolutionary 1798 book *Lyrical Ballads*) is that it tells a story. William Blake's great epics also tell stories, more or less. Though their narrative mode is unimaginably far from that of *Lyrical Ballads* they share with Wordsworth and Coleridge's poetry, Percy Bysshe Shelley's drama, John Keats's own retelling of various myths and tales, Sir Walter Scott's and Thomas Moore's tales in verse, and even Lord Byron's incessantly inventive *Don Juan,* a source in John Milton's *Paradise Lost,* whose great legacy to English literary thought is intense meditation on solitary human subjectivity. There is great commitment to ethical and social life among the romantics, but their conception of the mind is one of intense and often abject isolation, what has been called "the loneliness of the soul" or "the self-disappointed self." The standard caricature of the romantic poet, bidding farewell to his friends "with as much affection as his lacerated spirit could feel for anything" (as Thomas Love Peacock puts it in his parodic novel *Nightmare Abbey*) contains a large element of truth. The romantics found in Milton's Satan a portrait of thrown, fallen, abandoned, lonely human subjectivity. Satan is a model for characters as different (and as similar) as the narrator of Wordsworth's *Prelude,* Coleridge's Ancient Mariner, Blake's Los, Byron's Childe Harold (and Manfred), Scott's Marmion, Shelley's Prometheus, Keats's Hyperion, and Mary Shelley's monster in *Frankenstein* and survives in the prose fiction of the Victorian age in such figures (partly through cross-fertilization with a gothic tradition that also has its roots in *Paradise Lost*) as Heathcliff (in Emily Brontë's *Wuthering Heights*) and Rochester (in Charlotte Brontë's *Jane Eyre*).

Victorian storytelling is different, and we could say that if romantic poetry is Miltonic, Victorian prose fiction is Shakespearean. Shakespeare was the writer that the greatest of the Victorians, Charles Dickens, knew best and most modeled himself on. Thomas Carlyle, reflecting much critical opinion, tended to associate Goethe with Shakespeare, as poets and dramatists more concerned with the possibility of human souls overcoming separation or recognizing that separation is not the condition of the soul, except when it becomes blind to its true nature and possibility. The most famous line of Carlyle's *Sartor Resartus,* in the climactic chapter "The Everlasting Yea," is the self-exhortation to "Close thy *Byron;* open thy *Goethe.*" The difference between them, for Carlyle, is the difference between what he insists is a selfish soul avid only for its own happiness (though how fair this is to Byron may be questioned) and the soul that feels the infinite within itself just as much as Byron does but devotes itself to making the world flourish. This is the difference between Goethe's Shakespearean *Faust* (a play which quotes Hamlet, even while admiring Byron) and Christopher Marlowe's *Doctor Faustus,* whose characters are a source for Milton's Satan. Such a transformation might be taken to be a Shakespearean transmutation of romanticism (a good description of Goethe would be a romantic transmutation of Shakespeare), one that will ultimately embrace the social destiny of human life rather than seeing humans as irretrievably separated from one another.

There is a sense in which Elizabeth Barrett Browning's *Aurora Leigh* may be taken as a milestone in the history of English poetry's relation to and displacement by the novel. When the poem came out in 1856, reviewers immediately commented on the way that it sought to combine poetic with novelistic ambitions. In general, they preferred the poetic aspects of the poem, so that the wonderfully stringent critic and parodist W. E. Aytoun complains of the awkward intermingling of the two modes: "All poetical characters, all poetical situations, must be idealized. The language is not that of common life, which belongs essentially to the domain of prose. Therein lies the distinction between a novel and poem." George Eliot, too, disparaged the narrative aspects of *Aurora Leigh,* while praising its poetry, and Coventry Patmore had much the same criticism.

One point of the poem, though, was to attempt to reconcile modernity with poetic ambition. Such a reconciliation would ask modernity (as Aurora does) to keep faith with the things of poetry: the commitment to subjectivity or spirituality, that is, to art and beauty. But poetry, too, would have to acknowledge, as she does, and as Browning herself does, the intensely urban and social character of life during and after the Industrial Revolution. (This is the subject of the poetic movement known as Chartism as well, but there were no very estimable Chartist poets.) This social life and its institutions, church and Parliament and the legal system, became all the more important with the rise of a

Darwinian understanding of the geological record, a record that stunned so many Victorian poets, including Tennyson and the Brownings, away from any easy recourse to the faith that the beauty or sublimity of nature could be read as evidence of the existence, let alone the goodness, of God.

If *Aurora Leigh* fails as a novel (it almost succeeds, but cannot possibly sustain comparison with any of the memorable novels of the age), it signals at least an important new development in the now somewhat more minor history of poetry as well as the more major history of the novel: the pluralization, as one might call it, of the subjectivity that was the focus of romanticism. The difference between the Victorian poets and the romantic poets, so palpable in the Victorian turn to narrative, can be summarized by saying that the Victorians (and all the English poets who followed them) took as one of their prime elements the social fact of the history of poetry. The Victorian poets represent themselves and their characters as readers and not only as thinkers or brooders. Their experience of poetry is an experience of other minds, many other minds, as well as the experience of their own minds. If Shelley, in his *Defence of Poetry,* called the poet a nightingale singing to cheer his own solitude while an audience overheard these songs, the Victorian poets recognized and put stock in the possibility that human social experience could be one in which even at their most intensely inward moments, poets could recognize that their sense of solitude was shared and sharable. Such sharing is always an achievement: Robert Browning's *Childe Roland* manages through an inward quest to join the company of other absolutely solitary questers for the Dark Tower; Tennyson manages in *In Memoriam* to return to the world which Arthur Henry Hallam's absence leaves a shadow. Algernon Charles Swinburne's poems complain of their own solitude. The romantics would never even have thought it remarkable that poetic solitude feels lonely.

The increased sociality of the Victorians should in no way be understood as a disparagement of romantic inwardness. It was just this inwardness that the Victorians needed to find in others to see that there was a relation between their own inwardness and that of others. Victorian poets saw reading poetry as one of the most intense and important of private human experiences. To see this, they had to have intense and intensely private poetry to read, and the romantics provided them with this poetry.

The romantics also provided the Victorian novel with the poetry its characters needed, so that Lizzie Eustace, in Trollope, goes about memorizing Shelley, and Dickens makes Leigh Hunt and Walter Savage Landor into characters in *Bleak House,* while James makes a version of Byron the central object of biographical interest in *The Aspern Papers.* In the descriptive passages of her novels, George Eliot is almost a prose Wordsworth. Partly because novelistic narrative was successfully poetic in its conception of human subjectivity, late Victorian poetry can be seen (as I have already implied) as a return to the more solitary concerns of the romantics: thus Yeats, Hardy, and Gerard Manley Hopkins all went to poetry as a medium of intense self-expression rather than to poetry as narrative (though Rudyard Kipling is a near-great exception to this claim). But they thought of themselves, in a far more empirical and real-world mode than the romantics, as offering this meditation and expression to others. They actively sought to do for society around them what the earlier Victorians registered the romantics as having done for them, whether intentionally or not.

We could, therefore, summarize the history of 19th-century poetry as a history that allowed poetry to live on through the 20th century and beyond: The romantics invented or discovered the modern poetic subject or self; the high Victorians affirmed the importance of this discovery even or especially in an urban, industrial, scientific, and narrative age; and the late Victorians showed how to return to romantic lyricism from Victorian narrative in the new world that arrived after the 20th century's destruction of Victorian piety and faith in the permanence of social structure.

A

ADONAIS PERCY BYSSHE SHELLEY **(1821)** In 1820 PERCY BYSSHE SHELLEY invited JOHN KEATS to come to live in Pisa's more salubrious climate after Keats had been struck with consumption (tuberculosis). Keats only got as far as Rome, where he died on February 23, 1821. Although Shelley did not know Keats well, he admired him intensely as a poet (as he says in his preface to *Adonais,* his elegy to Keats) and hated the vicious treatment that Keats's poetry was subjected to by the anonymous reviewers of the English literary magazines. In particular, the *Quarterly Review* had been very severe about Keats's first major long poem, *Endymion,* and the story was that Keats was so upset by the review as to collapse under its cruelty and develop the tuberculosis to which he would eventually succumb. In fact, Keats had contracted the disease while caring for his brother, who died of it, and Shelley knew that it was contagious, praising Keats's friend, the artist Joseph Severn, for caring for Keats in his last illness in disregard of the dangers to his own health. LORD BYRON (who disliked Keats but conceded his talent) memorably deflated the idea that Keats had died of a broken heart caused by the attack in the *Quarterly Review* when he wrote in *DON JUAN*: "'Tis strange the mind, that very fiery particle, / Should let itself be snuff'd out by an article" (XI, ll. 479–480).

Of course, Shelley did not believe this (even if he did not quite disbelieve it). The idea, however, makes it possible for him to treat the death of Keats as the death of a *poet* rather than the more accidental death of the person who wrote the poetry. The deep mourning that the poem displays for the death of Adonais is mourning for the poetic talent that brought him to this grief (since it was as a poet that Keats was exposed to the review and as a poet that he was attacked), which makes it possible for the elegy to become what poetic elegies tend to be: a lament for the makers, a lament for all poets in their mortality.

This is a characteristic of elegy. When a poet writes an elegy for another poet, the elegy by its nature must acknowledge that poets die, and therefore it solicits the same attention from later poets as well. Poets are known through their laments, both the laments they make and the laments made for them. In English poetry the locus classicus of this idea or theme is John Milton's *Lycidas,* whose speaker imagines that someone will write an elegy for him just as he is doing for Lycidas. In *Adonais,* which echoes *Lycidas* throughout, Shelley laments not only Keats but the great poets who preceded him into "the gulph of death" (l. 35), in particular Milton, "the third among the sons of light" (l. 36), after Homer and Dante. This makes *Adonais* one of the poems answering the elegist's prayer in *Lycidas,* even as it elevates Keats to Miltonic status by placing him, too, among the sons of light.

Shelley does this as well by invoking the same muse, Urania—for Keats and for himself—whom Milton invokes at the beginning of book 7 of *Paradise Lost.* Urania is the muse of heavenly love, of the transcendent world to which Shelley imagines Keats aspiring and attaining at the end of the poem. Milton calls upon her in contrast to Calliope, muse of epic poetry and mother of the greatest of earthly poets, Orpheus. In Milton, Calliope is unable to save Orpheus from death, and he mourns her failure, turning to Urania instead: "So fail not thou, who thee implores, / For thou art Heav'nlie, shee an empty dreame" (book 7, ll. 38–39). But the Urania of *Adonais* is not able to defend him. Rather, she comes to mourn him when it is too late.

The poem echoes *Lycidas* throughout, particularly in the way it works through the hopelessly repeated entreaty to "Weep for Adonais" to a poetic recovery that is the subject of the final movement of the poem, beginning in the 39th of the Spenserian stanzas that make up the poem—"Mourn not for Adonais" (l. 362)—since he has become a part of nature and a part of its transcendent beauty. This absorption into nature is anticipated by the way *Lycidas* reimagines the absence of the dead poet. Thus, Milton's poem also traces the trajectory from an opening in which its speaker must "Yet once more" (l. 1) mourn the loss of a friend, but that *Yet once more* modulates at the end of the poem into "Weep no more / For *Lycidas* your sorrow is not dead" (ll. 165–166). He is not dead because he has become "the Genius of the shore" (l. 183), absorbed into the very substance of the world from which he has been so poignantly absent.

These and other echoes of *Lycidas* frame the most important revision of that poem, in Urania's inability to save Adonais. In *Paradise Lost* she is to save her poet-son as Calliope has failed to do so, and Calliope's failure is also an important element in the grief expressed in *Lycidas:* "Where were ye Nymphs when the remorseless deep / Clos'd o're the head of your lov'd Lycidas? . . ./ Ay me, I fondly dream! / Had ye bin there—for what could that have don?/ What could the Muse her self that Orpheus bore, / The Muse her self, for her inchanting son. . . ?" (ll. 50–59). This question, which Milton has his speaker pose to Calliope, is posed to Urania herself in *Adonais.* "Where wert thou mighty Mother, when he lay, / When thy son lay, pierced by the shaft which flies / In darkness? where was lorn Urania / When Adonais died?" (ll. 9–12). She was unable to help him, just as the nymphs were unable to help Lycidas, just as Calliope was unable to help Orpheus. For Shelley, unlike Milton, Urania cannot save the mortal poet.

Where was Urania? It is always important, reading Shelley, to give him credit for the coherence of his thought and imagery, and the question here is not just a rhetorical one (as it is in Milton). We find out that she was lost in a reverie, listening to the echoes of Keats's poetry. She was absorbed, more or less, in the beauties of "ODE TO A NIGHTINGALE" and the synesthetic way its nightingale's plaintive and flowery anthem fades: She listens to "all the fading melodies . . . like flowers" (ll. 16–17). The beauty of Keats's poetry is not to be distinguished from its own tendency toward death. In "Ode to a Nightingale," Keats describes himself as "half in love with easeful death" (l. 52). Shelley echoes this line in the preface to the poem when he describes the Protestant cemetery in Rome: "It might make one in love with death, to think that one should be buried in so sweet a place."

Indeed, Shelley's young son William was buried there, as his own ashes would be when he drowned a year later. Shelley alludes to William's death toward the end of the poem, where despite the recovery the elegy attempts, he acknowledges the sorrow he cannot think himself beyond: "Here pause: these graves are all too young as yet / To have outgrown the sorrow which consigned / Its charge to each" (ll. 451–453). The sorrow is real, the recovery from it energetic and willful, and perhaps not entirely convincing.

Urania's grief for Adonais is modeled on the grief Saturn displays in Keats's *Hyperion* poems (see HYPERION and *The* FALL OF HYPERION) when Thea seeks to rouse him from his sorrows. There is nothing to be done about what has happened, and although in Keats's fragments the Titans do attempt to rise again, we know that this attempt is doomed to failure. We should therefore understand that the movement of thought in *Adonais* is not triumphal. Shelley represents himself, both within the poem and again at its very end, in two different modes, and we should consider how that self-representation changes. In the 31st stanza he lists "one frail Form" who joins the parade of mourning poets, "A phantom among men," and following this we get a memorable self-portrait of Shelley's melancholy.

It makes sense that following this self-portrait, the poem moves into its mode of recovery. The structure of its argument is fairly clear and is to be found in *Lycidas* as well: The world from which Adonais is absent is a grim and cheerless one (as the frail Form's own melancholy helps register). But why would we want him to be alive in this grim, cheerless, melancholy world? He is better where he is, absorbed into the beautiful, "a portion of the loveliness / Which once he made more lovely" (ll. 379–380). He contributed to its loveliness—did that contribution survive him? Or was the loveliness in the poetry he wrote, and not in the ideal beauty the poetry was about? The lines are ambiguous but share the poem's sense that it is poetic description that finds beauty in the world, a beauty that in finding, it in fact creates. (Compare stanza 42 to Shelley's use of the word *find* at the end of "The Two Spirits: An Allegory.") And by a corresponding collapse of dichotomy, Shelley can say that at least Adonais does not belong to this world, which is a good thing since it has no intrinsic loveliness in it; it is empty and poor and undesirable now that he is gone.

The loveliness to which Adonais belongs, then, is the loveliness of poetic desire—not an ideal realm or place or world but an aspiration to the beauty of an ideal which is by its nature "Unapparent" (l. 399) since it does not exist. It is a hope or beacon or desire: It is what gives poetry the beauty of its evocations of darkness, but it is not a place one could actually come to. The memory of his son William's death reminds Shelley that there is nothing beyond sorrow, but that sorrow itself gives poetry its intensity. Thus, the beautiful last stanza of *Adonais,* with its evocation of the end of *Alastor,* gives us Shelley in the first person: "I am borne darkly, fearfully, afar" (l. 492). "The soul of Adonais, like a star, Beacons" (ll. 494–495), but he is not drawn upward into platonic certainty, but further into the wilds of beauty and darkness. Poetry is a beacon and an orientation in this journey, but not salvation. It is what sorrow can offer us instead of salvation.

BIBLIOGRAPHY

Bloom, Harold. *Genius: A Mosaic of One Hundred Exemplary Creative Minds.* New York: Warner, 2002.

———. *Shelley's Mythmaking.* New Haven, Conn.: Yale University Press, 1959.

———. *The Visionary Company: A Reading of English Romantic Poetry.* Garden City, N.Y.: Doubleday, 1961.

Burke, Kenneth. *Grammar of Motives.* Berkeley: University of California Press, 1969.

Chernaik, Judith. *The Lyrics of Shelley.* Cleveland: Press of Case Western Reserve University, 1972.

Duffy, Edward. *Rousseau in England: The Context for Shelley's Critique of the Enlightenment.* Berkeley: University of California Press, 1979.

Hogle, Jerrold E. *Shelley's Process: Radical Transference and the Development of His Major Works.* New York: Oxford University Press, 1988.

Keach, William. *Shelley's Style.* New York: Methuen, 1984.

Leavis, F. R. *Revaluation: Tradition & Development in English Poetry.* New York: Norton, 1963.

Leighton, Angela. *Shelley and the Sublime: An Interpretation of the Major Poems.* New York: Cambridge University Press, 1984.

Notopolous, James A. *The Platonism of Shelley: A Study of Platonism and the Poetic Mind.* Durham, N.C.: Duke University Press, 1949.

Quinney, Laura. *The Poetics of Disappointment: Wordsworth to Ashbery.* Charlottesville: University Press of Virginia, 1999.

Wasserman, Earl. *Shelley: A Critical Reading.* Baltimore: Johns Hopkins Press, 1971.

———. *Subtler Language: Critical Readings of Neoclassic and Romantic Poems.* Baltimore: Johns Hopkins Press, 1968.

AEOLIAN HARP The Aeolian harp is a central metaphor in a number of romantic poems, especially Samuel Taylor Coleridge's "The Eolian Harp" and "Dejection: An Ode," Percy Bysshe Shelley's "Hymn to Intellectual Beauty" and "Ode to the West Wind," Sir Walter Scott's *The Lady of the Lake* and Thomas Hardy's "The Darkling Thrush." Originally a Greek invention (Aeolus was the Greek god of the winds), it became popular in Europe in the 17th century, and the romantics were fascinated by it because of the way it exemplified a simultaneously natural and lyrical response to natural phenomena.

The harp worked something like a modern windchime. It would be set in a window, and the air passing over and through it would set its strings resonating, producing sound in response to the air. An image of it may be seen on the following Web site: http://freespace.virgin.net/music.magic/aeolianharp.htm.

Coleridge thought of the harp as a powerful emblem for the mind's relation to the world in which it was embedded. The harp could help reconcile his early propensity toward pantheism, the idea that God was everywhere, in all things, with human individuation and individual expressiveness. If the harp represents the poet's soul, then the soul would be an instrument woken into its own particular sound by the wind of nature blowing on it or through it. In his poem "The Eolian Harp," Coleridge describes the Eolian harp to his fiancée, Sara Fricker:

> And that simplest Lute,
> Placed length-ways in the clasping casement,
> hark!
> How by the desultory breeze caressed,
> Like some coy maid half yielding to her lover,
> It pours such sweet upbraiding, as must needs
> Tempt to repeat the wrong! . . .

The lute responds to the wind as a lover responds to a caress: The sexual stimulation comes from outside but awakens desire within; erotic experience is both internal and external, an instinct to respond to another outside oneself. It is not surprising that Coleridge should read the metaphor this way, within a poem addressed to his beloved, but what interests us here—and what interests him as well—is the unified structure of the world, which extends to all modes of the mind's responsiveness, whether erotic, philosophical, or poetic. He sees in the harp a symbol of the unity of world and mind:

> O! the one Life within us and abroad,
> Which meets all motion and becomes its soul,
> A light in sound, a sound-like power in light,
> Rhythm in all thought, and joyance everywhere—
> Methinks, it should have been impossible
> Not to love all things in a world so filled;
> Where the breeze warbles, and the mute still air
> Is Music slumbering on her instrument.

That instrument, he will go on to say, is the poet's brain; but so unified are the origins of harmony, wind, and harp, that Coleridge will allow the metaphor to alternate, so that the mind may not only be the lute over which the wind of nature plays but the air itself, sometimes a singing breeze, sometimes mute and still, which can awaken from an indolent sleep and play over the objects it perceives and makes music of its expression of these perceptions:

> And thus, my Love! as on the midway slope
> Of yonder hill I stretch my limbs at noon,
> Whilst through my half-closed eyelids I behold
> The sunbeams dance, like diamonds, on the
> main,
> And tranquil muse upon tranquility:
> Full many a thought uncalled and undetained,
> And many idle flitting phantasies,
> Traverse my indolent and passive brain,
> As wild and various as the random gales
> That swell and flutter on this subject Lute!

Coleridge is making a philosophical point here, one that fascinated the romantic poets. The mind does not passively perceive the world, as the English philosopher John Locke had argued in his *Essay Concerning Human Understanding*. It adds its own categories in order to transmute perception into experience. This was the German philosopher Immanuel Kant's argument, and it was one the romantic poets found very congenial. Shelley would make a similar claim in the first line of his 1817 poem "MONT BLANC": "The everlasting universe of things . . ."

Note that as with Coleridge, there is an interchange between mind and world where the correspondences of the metaphor can shift. Sometimes the mind is like the cavern the universe flows through; sometimes the mind inhabits that cavern, which is the universe. As with Coleridge, the very fact that the metaphor can be so fluid is itself metaphorical of the fluid relation of world and mind.

Although in "Mont Blanc" Shelley does not use the image of the natural world playing upon an instrument and eliciting sound from it, he will use just this idea in "Ode to the West Wind." He asks the wind to "make me thy lyre, even as the forest is!"—so that the lute would be both a natural object, the forest, and the human mind perceiving natural objects. At the end of the poem, he alters the metaphor slightly, imagining himself as the trumpet through which the wind would blow a prophecy. The image was central to Shelley himself. He also uses it at the end of "A Defence of Poetry," in which he describes the mind as responsive to the winds that come from the outside world: "The mind in creation is like a fading coal that a fitful and inconstant wind awakens into a transitory brightness. . . ."

Coleridge returned to the Aeolian harp in his great, despairing poem "Dejection: An Ode," where he describes the outer weather which—appropriately—matches his inner feeling of despairing anxiety:

> Well! If the Bard was weather-wise, who made
> The grand old ballad of Sir Patrick Spence,
> This night, so tranquil now, will not go hence
> Unroused by winds, that ply a busier trade
> Than those which mould yon cloud in lazy flakes,
> Or the dull sobbing draft, that moans and rakes
> Upon the strings of this Æolian lute,
> Which better far were mute.

The idea is one that WILLIAM WORDSWORTH uses as well. In "TINTERN ABBEY," in lines heavily influenced by "The Eolian Harp," Wordsworth describes his response to the natural world:

> And I have felt . . . 93
> A motion and a spirit, that impels 100
> All thinking things, all objects of all thought,
> And rolls through all things. Therefore am I still
> A lover of the meadows and the woods,
> And mountains; and of all that we behold
> From this green earth; of all the mighty world
> Of eye, and ear,—both what they half create,
> And what perceive; well pleased to recognise
> In nature and the language of the sense,
> The anchor of my purest thoughts, the nurse,
> The guide, the guardian of my heart, and soul 110
> Of all my moral being.

Shelley picks this up in "Mont Blanc" when he talks about how his separate fantasy "now renders and receives fast influencings" (l. 38).

In Wordsworth, the eye and ear perceive and, while perceiving, half-create because they are a part of the world they perceive, and their creations are part of what that world creates. At his best, as here, Wordsworth knew himself better than the English essayist William Hazlitt credited him for doing. Of Wordsworth, Hazlitt was to say: "His powers have been mistaken by the age, nor does he exactly understand them himself. He cannot form a whole. He has not the constructive faculty. He can give only the fine tones of thought, drawn from his mind by accident or nature, like the sounds drawn from the Aeolian harp by the wondering gale. He is totally deficient in all the machinery of poetry."

Hazlitt was referring here to *The Excursion* (1814), but he did not know Wordsworth's greatest long poem, *The PRELUDE*, not published until after the poet's death in 1850 (and 20 years after Hazlitt's death). In the later poem Wordsworth recognizes the sources of his power. *The Prelude* begins with lines probably influenced by the idea of the Aeolian harp:

> O there is blessing in this gentle breeze,
> A visitant that while it fans my cheek
> Doth seem half-conscious of the joy it brings
> From the green fields, and from yon azure sky.

The half-conscious awareness of the breeze is like the half-creating awareness of the perceptive mind in "Tintern Abbey," and it again shows the familiar alternation between mind and world in the very imagery of the mind's relation to the world. The breeze is conscious of the consciousness it works upon, as though consciously responds to consciousness, as consciousness responds to the breeze.

Whether Wordsworth is thinking about the Aeolian harp here or not, he certainly has it in mind a few lines later in the "glad preamble" to *The Prelude* when he writes:

> I, methought, while the sweet breath of heaven
> Was blowing on my body, felt within

> A correspondent breeze, that gently moved
> With quickening virtue, but is now become
> A tempest, a redundant energy,
> Vexing its own creation.

The "correspondent breeze" is like the responsiveness of the harp, and here Wordsworth is showing the possibilities of disharmony in this responsiveness as well. For if the harp produces its own music in *distinction* from that of the world it responds to, the response may end up reflecting not the union but the separation between self and world which is the darkest and deepest theme of romanticism. The expressive self may find that the world which impels expression is a world not consonant with what the soul or mind or self or subject is brought to see, and it is brought primarily to see its distinctness from the world. This is the final meaning of the image in Wordsworth, as well as in Coleridge and Shelley, and it is made explicit again in the broken strings of the forest in Hardy's "The Darkling Thrush." Whatever may contribute to the harmony of the world may also separate itself from that harmony, and the story of this separation is the universal theme of romantic accounts of finding oneself more and more estranged from the natural world with which the soul began in harmony.

See also "Harp that once through Tara's Halls, The."

BIBLIOGRAPHY

Bidney, Martin. "The Aeolian Harp Reconsidered: Music of Unfulfilled Longing in Tjutchev, Mōriche, Thoreau, and Others." *Comparative Literature Studies* 22, no. 3 (1985): 329–343.

Brown, Andrew. *The Aeolian Harp in European Literature, 1591–1892.* Cambridge, England: Bois de Boulogne, 1970.

Grigson, Geoffrey. *The Harp of Aeolus: and Other Essays on Art, Literature & Nature.* London: Routledge, 1948.

Hazlitt, William. *Lectures on the English Poets.* New York: Dodd, Mead, 1892.

"AFTER READING AESCHYLUS" DIGBY MACKWORTH DOLBEN (ca. 1867)

Digby Mackworth Dolben's poetry often feels like the portrait of the artist as a young genius, perhaps the portrait of the artist as John Keats, and his lovely seven-line epigram on reading Aeschylus is his version, perhaps, of Keats's sonnet "On Sitting Down to Read King Lear Once Again." Keats did not know Greek, as is obvious from the famous sonnet Dolben is also thinking of, "On First Looking into Chapman's Homer," and Dolben did. His poem on the greatest of Greek playwrights, Aeschylus, is one of poetic vocation or election, a mode he learned from Keats and appropriate to a poet who feels the pride of extreme freshness and youth. (Dolben met Gerard Manley Hopkins through his cousin Robert Bridges, both of whom were four years older than he was, but both of whom treated him as a peer.)

Dolben's poem is more or less in iambic pentameter, but its brilliance lies in the way he manages the stresses. Iambic pentameter is a uniquely flexible meter in English, allowing for what Hopkins called a counterpoint between the metrical substrate and its phenomenalization, in which the actual stresses interact in complex and musical ways with the expected stresses. Hopkins's idea of counterpoint is an apt one since it is possible to get two different rhythms, even two different meters, into the same set of words, and to hear or anticipate both of them simultaneously and in relation to each other. This is what Dolben does here, overlaying a loose dactylic meter over the iambic pentameter. The dactylic meter is the meter of Aeschylus's plays—both his choruses and his speeches. This is the meter that is ringing in Dolben's mind as he composes his poem about not writing any more of his "little puny songs" (l. 1), and the meter that makes possible the metrical experiment he undertakes here.

This is how it works: The first line is a sing-song pentameter, representing just the kind of puniness of meter that Dolben abjures. But in the last two lines he declares his decision to lie still "And let the multitudinous music of the Greek / Pass into me, till I am musical." Here, his meter becomes more complex and grave. *Multitudinous* is a word that contains an inescapably dactylic foot in its last three syllables, which counterpoint the preliminary scansion by which *tud* would be the stressed second syllable of an iamb. The word itself cannot appear in a good iambic line, but it does appear here, appropriately so, and leads to the dactylic foot that follows it, *music of* or even *music of the.* The line immediately preceding also provides a fine example of the metrical complexity of the poem, with *passiveness* able to be scanned as part of the iambic pentameter but describing itself more appropriately if pronounced more naturally and quietly as a dactyl. That pronunciation affects how we stress the last words of the line. The last foot should probably be a spondee (*líe still*), which can substitute for a dactyl in dactylic meter.

The point is that Dolben shows himself musical (the last word is almost certainly an echo of John Milton's *Il Penseroso*) in the way he has allowed himself to merge with "the music of the Greek" (l. 6)—both the language and Aeschylus, the Greek playwright, whom the language stands for—and in becoming musical he becomes, like Keats, the elected poet, joining with the great poets of the past.

BIBLIOGRAPHY

Bridges, Robert. *The Poems of Digby Mackworth Dolben.* New York: Oxford University Press, 1911.

———. *Three Friends: Memoirs of Digby Mackworth Dolben, Richard Watson Dixon, Henry Bradley.* Westport, Conn.: Greenwood Press, 1975.

Cohen, Martin, ed. *Uncollected Poems of Digby Mackworth Dolben.* Reading, England: Whiteknights Press, 1973.

Cunningham, Valentine. Headnote to selection of Dolben in *The Victorians: An Anthology of Poetry & Poetics.* Malden, Mass.: Blackwell, 2000.

Dolben, Digby Mackworth. *The Poems and Letters of Digby Mackworth Dolben, 1848–1867.* Edited by M. Cohen. Amersham, England: Avebury, 1981.

Najarian, James. *Victorian Keats: Manliness, Sexuality and Desire.* New York: Palgrave, 2002.

White, Norman. *Hopkins: A Literary Biography.* New York: Oxford University Press, 1992.

"ALBUM MUTOR IN ALITEM" JAMES HENRY (1854) JAMES HENRY's little squib (in characteristically subtle trochaic tetrameter) on WILLIAM WORDSWORTH ("the bard of Ambleside," l. 5) is interesting (and delightful) as an example of the reaction that certain minor but exquisitely accomplished Victorian poets had to ROMANTICISM's invention of extreme subjectivity. In this they followed LORD BYRON, who preferred Horace and classicism to Wordsworthian romanticism, much as Byron also set up himself as a figure of unparalleled subjective suffering. Like many of the best minor Victorians, Henry refused expressive poetry the central position it attained in the life of the poet as romanticism conceived such a life was lived. Henry's poetry is observational, occasional, pointed, but not in any way vocational. He writes not as a poet communicating the experience of being a poet, but as a normal person who expresses his subtle observations well and, as it happens, in verse.

In "Album mutes in alitem" Henry contrasts Horace to Wordsworth. The title of the poem is from Horace's *Odes* (II.20.10); Horace is telling his friend Maecenas that he will be immortal after death, turned metaphorically into a swan by his own poetry. This is not really the boast that it appears to be, however. It is Horace describing his own experience of normal human life in this world, and the idea that he will live on in his poetry is consciously wishful; it is the expression of a fine wistfulness. Henry grants Horace his immortality, saying that he has in fact "continued to sing on" (l. 4).

Henry then turns his attention to Wordsworth. He repeats a joke out of Pope: Wordsworth follows Horace's example. How?—by dying (just as Pope anticipates that when he dies people will compare him to Homer, who "died three thousand years ago"). But this is about as far as Wordsworth follows Horace's example. Wordsworth *had* died "in bed" four years before the night Henry composed this poem, but his soul has not entered the body of a swan but of a goose. His poetry, Henry says, is pure gabbling: "gak, gak, gak" (l. 9). Partly this is a comment on what Henry takes to be Wordsworth's insipid rhymes (in *Lyrical Ballads*, especially), as opposed to the more surprising rhyme with which Henry reports Wordsworth's incoherence: *knack / gak*. It should be noted that Wordsworth, too, is "faithful to the ancient knack" (l. 9). Far from being a modern, far from innovating, he is an ancient, but so are geese.

Henry was a classicist, and he is no doubt thinking of the famous geese who (according to Livy) saved Rome from a surprise attack by the Gauls in 390 B.C.E.; geese became sacred to Rome for that reason. So Wordsworth is a kind of sacred relic, a throwback even to Aristophanes and his famous onomotopoiea of the sounds of the frogs in *The Frogs:* "Brekekex." Wordsworth makes meaningless sounds as well, and in saying that he does so, Henry contrasts him with the less-primitive urbanity of Horace—an urbanity that Henry emulated in his own poetry, which learned from Wordsworth the goal of being skillfully observant of ordinary life, but which took a much more urbane perspective on what was ordinary. Henry draws a moral contrast between his intentionally unpretentious poetry and that of the romantics.

BIBLIOGRAPHY

Cunningham, Valentine, ed. *The Victorians: An Anthology of Poetry and Poetics.* Malden, Mass.: Blackwell, 2000.

Henry, James. *Selected Poems of James Henry.* Edited by Christopher Ricks. New York: Handsel, 2002.

Ricks, Christopher, ed. *The New Oxford Book of Victorian Verse.* New York: Oxford University Press, 1987.

Rogoff, Jay. "First Fruits." *Southern Review* 40, no. 3 (2004): 602–628.

ALLINGHAM, WILLIAM (D. POLLEX, PATRICIUS WALKER) (1824–1889)

William Allingham (who also published under the pseudonyms D. Pollex and Patricius Walker) is remembered now for one poem, "The FAIRIES," which is representative of a mode that he did much to advance, the recovery or invention of an ancient and beautiful Ireland of legend and mystery. WILLIAM BUTLER YEATS, who edited a volume of Allingham's poems, called him a "minor immortal" and a strong influence on his own poetry, especially the early highly lyrical poetry Yeats was writing in the 19th century.

Allingham was born in Ballyshannon, Donegal, Ireland. Like Yeats, he was a Protestant but committed to the old Ireland, whose ballads he collected and imitated in his own writing. In 1843 he traveled to London, where he met LEIGH HUNT and became a contributor to *Leigh Hunt's London Journal.* In 1850 he also contributed to the first number of the journal Charles Dickens began publishing, the famous *Household Words.* Allingham expanded his acquaintanceship in the British literary circle, eventually becoming an intimate of ALFRED, LORD TENNYSON; ROBERT BROWNING; THOMAS CARLYLE; DANTE GABRIEL ROSSETTI; COVENTRY PATMORE; WILLIAM MAKEPEACE THACKERAY; and the great English historian James Anthony Froude, from whom Allingham took over the editorship of *Fraser's Magazine* in 1874. Tennyson was impressed by Allingham's poetry and would sometimes read it aloud; Allingham later became very close to Tennyson, as is attested in his highly popular diary, published two decades after their deaths. The diary has become an invaluable source for biographers not only of Tennyson, whose opinions of his contemporaries Allingham recorded, but of many other of Allingham's friends.

Alligham's first book, which contains "The Fairies," sold poorly on its publication in 1850. A second book, *Day and Night Songs,* was published in 1854; a year later a new edition came out, illustrated by Rossetti, John Everett Millais, and Arthur Hughes. Two decades later, in 1874, he married Helen Patterson, who became an important watercolorist, still admired today. (She illustrated the serial publication of THOMAS HARDY's *Far from the Madding Crowd.*)

In 1865 Allingham edited and introduced an anthology of British ballads, *The Ballad Book* (part of the series inaugurated by Francis Turner Palgrave's *Golden Treasury of English Songs and Lyrics*). This was shortly after the publication of what he himself regarded as his major work, *Laurence Bloomfield in Ireland,* first published serially in *Fraser's* in 1863 and then as a book edited by Froude in 1864. The title character is a good-hearted landlord who helps ameliorate the state of his tenants and others in Ireland. This book, like GEORGE CRABBE's *Village* (also written in heroic couplets), provides often powerful descriptions of the state of the poor, especially the rural poor after the Irish potato famine. The Russian novelist Ivan Turgenev praised the work for helping him understand Ireland, and Gladstone quoted it on the floor of the House of Commons, but Yeats thought it was too local and too idealized.

Of more lasting importance is *The Ballad Book.* What Allingham writes in the preface gives insight not only into the ballads but into his own most suggestive and enduring poetry: "'The Old Ballads' suggests as distinct a set of impressions as the name of Shakespeare, Spenser, or Chaucer; but on looking close we find ourselves puzzled; . . . the mountain chain so definite on the horizon is found to be a disunited and intricate region." Yet he can still assign a set of names to this kind of poem: Thomas Percy (for his *Reliques* [1765]), and SIR WALTER SCOTT, for example. These names can be misleading, and it is important to Allingham that "the text of an old ballad is of an obscure and evasive kind," but that the obscurity coexists with detailed intricacy. To be lost in their pure poetry—the sort of poetry that Allingham himself attempted and in which Yeats would follow him—did not mean to dispense with detail, but to attend to it with all the greater intensity.

See also "BOY FROM HIS BEDROOM-WINDOW, THE"; "IN SNOW."

BIBLIOGRAPHY

Allingham, H., and E. Baumer Williams, eds. *Letters to William Allingham.* London: Longmans & Co., 1911.

Allingham, William. *William Allingham: A Diary.* Edited by H. Allingham and D. Radford. London: Macmillan & Co., 1907.

———, ed. *The Ballad Book.* London: Macmillan, 1907.

Hill, George Birkbeck, ed. *Letters of Dante Gabriel Rossetti to William Allingham, 1854–1870.* London: T. Fisher Unwin, 1897.

***AMOURS DE VOYAGE* ARTHUR HUGH CLOUGH (1858)** This poem ends with an envoi through which ARTHUR HUGH CLOUGH speaks: "I was written in a Roman chamber, / When from Janiculan heights thundered the cannon of France" (V, ll. 223–224). Indeed, though it was published years later, Clough wrote this long, meditative narrative poem while he was living in Rome in 1849, during the public events that it describes. The short-lived Roman Republic lasted only a few months before the French conquered it and restored the pope (Pius IX). Claude, the poem's main character, tells Eustace of the original French attack in April 1849, the gallantry of the Roman defenders who drove the French back under the great revolutionary leader and patriot Giuseppe Garibaldi, and the ill-advised vacillations of Giuseppe Mazzini, who allowed the French to regroup and eventually take Rome. Clough tells a similar story in his own letters from Rome.

There are three main speakers (or writers) in the poem: Claude, a young English aristocrat with intellectual pretensions who is writing to his friend Eustace from Italy; Mary Trevellyn, a young English woman who is also visiting Italy with her wealthy but bourgeois family; and the voice of the poet himself, represented in italics at the beginning and end of each canto. That italicized voice maintains a certain ironic distance from the story he tells—partly by reflecting on the story itself and the choices that it offers him. There is nothing postmodern about this, however. The self-reflections are those of a poet thinking about what he wants to describe in his poetry, but the descriptions furnish the main substance of the poem, not the self-reflections. This can be noted most efficiently by noting that the name *Claude* is an echo of *Clough,* and that he is largely engaged in self-analysis in depicting Claude's own self-analysis. (This identifies Eustace as Matthew—MATTHEW ARNOLD, Clough's closest friend and his elegist—via the reversal of assonance in their names: *Eu[st]a[ce]* turns into *[M]a[tth]ew.*) The ironic distance makes him *like* Claude, capable of a certain dispassionate clarity about himself, and clarity as well about its costs.

The poem is written in a loose dactylic hexameter, the classical meter appropriate to the setting in the ruins of ancient Rome, and one congenial to Clough's taste. He called it "anglo-savage," probably in self-deprecation, but the *savage* part of the pun also indicates that he has succeeded in a kind of archaism of tone or feeling in the poem (not unlike WILLIAM MORRIS's poetry) rather than an archaism of vocabulary or subject.

The story the poem tells is intentionally slight, and its very slightness makes the fact that it does not end happily a surprise. Claude finds himself thrown into the company of the Trevellyns in Rome, being a friend to a young man who is going to marry Mary's sister. He is ambivalent about the company, and in particular he and Mary take a kind of wary dislike to each other, not unlike Beatrice and Benedick in Shakespeare's *Much Ado about Nothing* (whose feckless young man Claudio might also be in Clough's mind). Claude shows himself at his best in protecting the Trevellyns during the first French attack, and making it possible for them to escape from Rome during a period of calm. We discover this mainly in Mary's letters—the whole poem, except for the italicized frames, is epistolatory—since Claude is too refined a character to boast. Claude sees terrible violence in the streets, violence we can guess Clough himself has witnessed, and agrees to go to Florence with the Trevellyns, but due to a fatal lack of subtlety on the part of his friend, who wants to know when he will declare his intentions to Mary, he decides to stay. This is all a pity—a comic pity, despite the grave tone of the poem—because in fact he and Mary love each other, despite their reticence and dignity, and Mary wants nothing more than for Claude to accompany them.

When each is properly reassured that the other is interested, Claude pursues Mary and the Trevellyns, but due to some more quasi-comic business with lost letters and miscommunications, he never finds her. At what should be the climactic resolution to these troubles, they both give up on the other, Mary returning "to England" and Claude traveling farther afield, in a parallel line never to meet Mary's, "to Egypt" (V, ll. 205, 216).

These missed opportunities allow Clough scope for reflection. Claude is essentially a passive figure, since he is a skeptic and does not believe in action—does not believe in *belief.* Love for him would be just the kind of idealization about which he is skeptical, an idealization whose source is actually in biological instinct. Clough, like ALFRED, LORD TENNYSON, had a proto-Darwinian intuition (based in part on the fossil record that had recently been discovered and deciphered) that humans were better analyzed as animals than as spirits. Clough had been attracted *away* from the Anglicanism in which he had been raised, to John Henry (later Cardinal) Newman's Anglo-Catholicism, whose very difficulties and demands offered succor to so many clear-sighted English literary figures of the 19th century (from COVENTRY PATMORE to GERARD MANLEY HOPKINS to ALICE MEYNELL), but he went beyond that to another sort of religion—clear-sighted atheism, which is more demanding still, as Claude represents it, than Catholicism. This is what he finds in a Rome emptied of supernatural belief and the pope expelled just as surely (though not for very long) as the ancient gods. It is the material shell of belief that is of interest to Claude as a materialist aesthete and atheist.

In what is perhaps the most interesting moment in the poem, Claude concedes that at the moment of his death he will very probably seek spiritual comfort: "I shall entreat thee then, though now I dare to refuse thee, . . . Well, I will see thee again, and while I can I will repel thee" (V, ll. 110–112). The word *repel* is a complex one in the poem, but it is used consistently to mean something like intellectual antipathy even in the face of instinctive attraction. Claude is articulating atheism as a difficult faith, one that he seeks to hold onto because it is the truth, the knowledge that survives (counter St. Paul) faith, hope, and charity (V, l. v).

Clough's refusal of a happy ending is a commitment to the material details of the world as against the spiritual uplift that both Mary and Claude are skeptical of—a skepticism to which their union would be untrue. Claude thinks a great deal about the concept of *juxtaposition* (see III, ll. vi and vii), and it is in juxtaposition, rather than the "affinity" that Eustace seems to have offered as a concept to replace it, that the truth is to be found. That is the truth of the world without illusion, the world as seen in its material reality, and which only voyaging can give you. The title of the poem is a pun: "Amours de voyage" mean people we fall in love with, or think we do, when traveling. But it also means the various loves we have for journey, which teaches us only that traveling or staying in one's chamber and thinking (I, l. 8) are similar ways of not falling into the illusion that instinct projects about friends and religion. As we have seen, the way Clough does it is to stay in his chamber in Rome.

BIBLIOGRAPHY

Clough, Arthur Hugh. *Oxford Diaries of Arthur Hugh Clough.* Edited by Anthony Kenny. New York: Oxford University Press, 1990.

Hofmann, Michael. "Arthur Hugh Clough: 1819–1861." *Poetry* 187, no. 6 (March 2006): 495–496.

Kenny, Anthony. *Arthur Hugh Clough: A Poet's Life.* New York: Continuum, 2005.

Sutherland, Gillian, *Faith, Duty, and the Power of Mind: The Cloughs and Their Circle, 1820–1960.* London: Cambridge University Press, 2006.

"ANGEL, THE" WILLIAM BLAKE (1789) "The Angel" is one of the most compelling and enigmatic of WILLIAM BLAKE's *Songs of Experience* (see *SONGS OF INNOCENCE AND OF EXPERIENCE*). Blake's illustration of this poem shows a child angel holding the hand and arm of an adult woman lying on her side and looking moodily away from him, either in distraction or in refusal.

In order to assess the poem, we can begin with the question that the child-angel and adult human suggest: How old is the dreamer of the poem? At the end she says, "For the time of youth was fled / And grey hairs were on my head" (ll. 15–16). The poem is certainly appropriate to *Songs of Experience* since it narrates the end of the time of childish innocence and the onset and experience of adulthood. But we do not know whether the dreamer is a child dreaming of adulthood or an adult recapitulating the process that made her experienced and bitter.

Part of the answer to this issue of the speaker's age depends on whether the question in the first line of the poem—"I dreamt a dream! What can it mean?"—is rhetorical or genuine. If it is genuine, then the speaker still trusts in an external authority to whom she can appeal. Thus, if the question is genuine, then the person to answer it is someone like the angel himself. But if it is rhetorical—if it means something like: *No one can answer this because the question it poses is unanswerable* or *has a perfectly and grimly obvious answer*—then there is no point in trusting the angel to guard her from the disasters of the world any longer.

The dream itself is ambiguous, partly sexualized and partly not, which leads to one further question: Who was "ne'er beguil'd" in the fourth line? The angel or the dreamer (or at least her dream avatar as maiden queen)? The reference to beguilement (like the "disguise" that ends the *Experience* version of the "NURSE'S SONG") suggests that sexuality is an issue, as does the speaker's explicit description of herself as a "maiden Queen," a virgin like Thel in "THE BOOK OF THEL," with which this poem should be compared.

The angel comes and guards the dreamer and comforts her in her grief—presumably the innocent grief of childhood, which (experience knows) is not without sorrow. The dreamer takes more pleasure in the angel's comfort than in pain of her grief, and so she becomes willfully sad, weeping so that he will comfort her and hiding the erotic pleasure ("heart's delight") she takes in it. But he recognizes this and leaves, either out of fear or out of reproach, and the blush of the mourning is a symbol at once of the innocence of sexuality and of the shame and guilt that attaches to it in a world of repression. Her response is to resent what she is sure is the angel's reproach (a reproach her hypocrisy would deserve) and to prevent his return.

For he does return, either to love or to guard her, but she spurns him. She spurns him either because she is now old and bitter, or she becomes old and bitter because she has attempted to beguile him and to arm herself against him.

The thing to notice is that the poem means essentially the same thing whether you see the dreamer as young or old. Even the so-called innocents (as the Nurse will lament in the *Experience* version of the "Nurse's Song") already know about sexuality and about the repression and hypocrisy that society creates concerning issues of sexuality. The young girl already has within her the seeds of bitter middle age, and is already willing to manipulate the boy who loves her. But one could also say that if the speaker is indeed old, then her dream is a wistful and regretful memory of how she came to the pass she laments to find herself in, which would mean that even in the bitterness of old age she longs for the purity of love and trust that was glimpsed in innocence. Blake's *Songs of Innocence and of Experience* do not recommend innocence as the superior state; rather, innocence is a token of how we can transcend experience, through memory, poetry, and aspiration toward a higher form where innocence can be fulfilled. (Blake's prophetic books are about the struggles for this kind of transcendence.)

BIBLIOGRAPHY

Bloom, Harold. *Blake's Apocalypse: A Study in Poetic Argument.* Ithaca, N.Y.: Cornell University Press, 1970.

———. *Poetry and Repression: Revisionism from Blake to Stevens.* New Haven, Conn.: Yale University Press, 1976.

Damrosch, Leopold. *Symbol and Truth in Blake's Myth.* Princeton, N.J.: Princeton University Press, 1980.

Erdmann, David V. *Blake, Prophet against Empire: A Poet's Interpretation of the History of His Own Times.* Princeton, N.J.: Princeton University Press, 1977.

Fry, Northrop. *Fearful Symmetry: A Study of William Blake.* Princeton, N.J.: Princeton University Press, 1974.

Gilchrist, Alexander. *Life of William Blake, with Selections from His Poems and Other Writings.* Totowa, N.J.: Rowman and Littlefield, 1973.

Hollander, John. "Blake and the Metrical Contract." In *From Sensibility to Romanticism,* edited by Frederick Hilles and Harold Bloom, New York: Oxford, 1965. 213–310. Reprinted in John Hollander, *Vision and Resonance: Two Senses of Poetic Form,* 187–211. New Haven, Conn.: Yale University Press, 1985.

Ostriker, Alicia. "Desire Gratified and Ungratified: William Blake and Sexuality." *Blake: An Illustrated Quarterly* 16 (1982–83): 156–165.

Quinney, Laura. *Literary Power and the Criteria of Truth.* Gainesville: University Press of Florida, 1995.

Raine, Kathleen. *Blake and Antiquity.* Princeton, N.J.: Princeton University Press, 1977.

Thompson, E. P. *Witness against the Beast: William Blake and the Moral Law.* New York: Cambridge University Press, 1993.

ARNOLD, MATTHEW (1822–1888) Matthew Arnold was perhaps the most important of Victorian cultural critics. His most famous book, *Culture and Anarchy* (1869), is still highly influential today, living on in such works as Samuel Huntington's *The Clash of Civilizations and the Remaking of World Order* (1996). Arnold was a major source for the thinking of mid-20th century literary lions, such as Lionel Trilling, who consciously or unconsciously modeled their notion of what it meant to be a public intellectual on his example. Arnold also bequeathed to us the distinction between Hebraic and Hellenistic culture as forming the two central strands in our own aesthetics. He saw both strands as important and as aiming at a similar end: human perfection. But he regretted that what he called Hellenism was in the blinkered, superstitious, and philistine culture of the time a servant of Hebraism, and he sought a reversal: "The uppermost idea with Hellenism is to see things as they really are; the uppermost idea with Hebraism is conduct and obedience" (*Culture and Anarchy*). Seeing things as they really are was for Arnold the goal of all critical thinking. For Arnold there was too much religious Hebraism (under which category he placed Christianity as well) in contemporary culture, and he preferred the "sweetness and light" (the phrase from Swift he made famous through incessant repetition) of Hellenism and the cultural amplitude and free play of consciousness that it made possible. He also liked its openness to "the best which has been thought and known in the world," so that "culture is, or ought to be, the study and pursuit of perfection; and . . . of perfection as pursued by culture, beauty and intelligence, or, in other words, sweetness and light, are the main characters" (*Culture and Anarchy*).

Arnold was the son of Thomas Arnold, the famous headmaster of Rugby School, and he was therefore brought up in one of the prime sources of Victorian academic and cultural values. (His close friend ARTHUR HUGH CLOUGH was a student at Rugby.) He adopted and amplified those values in his own work and was one of the great champions of romantic literature, especially WILLIAM WORDSWORTH (and Goethe in German), while being highly critical of JOHN KEATS and PERCY BYSSHE SHELLEY (whom he famously and inaccurately called "a beautiful *and ineffectual* angel, beating in the void his luminous wings in vain" (*Essays in Criticism*). Arnold thought Shelley lacked a sense of humor and for this reason was angelic but not quite sane, either in life or in his poetry. For Arnold, sanity was everything—it was what made cultures healthy.

As a poet, Arnold's reputation rests on the laboriously worked poems that he wrote almost entirely before the age of 40 (such as "DOVER BEACH" and "The SCHOLAR-GYPSY." He famously complained of his waning powers in 1853, the year that he published the first edition of his collected poems: "I am past thirty and three parts iced over." He had pretty much stopped writing poetry when he was elected to the Oxford professorship of poetry in 1857, though one notable exception was "THYRSIS," his elegy on Clough, written in 1864 or so. There his shepherd-speaker laments the falling-off of his own powers: "Ah me! this many a year / My pipe is lost, my shepherd's holiday" (ll. 36–37), so that Clough's literal death reminds him of his own figurative death as a poet. Arnold spent most of the rest of his life as a school inspector, a role in which he put into practice his commitment to general education and enlightenment, but one which stood for the kind of unimaginative earnestness with which his name has come to be synonymous.

Arnold's most famous poem is probably "DOVER BEACH," a poetic version of the warning against anarchy—the ignorant armies that battle by night—which exercised him so much throughout his career. It is a poem much parodied but also much loved, and one that deserves both parody and love.

See also "GROWING OLD"; "HAWORTH CHURCHYARD"; "PHILOMELA"; "TO MARGUERITE—CONTINUED."

BIBLIOGRAPHY

Arnold, Matthew. *Culture and Anarchy*. Edited by Samuel Lipman. New Haven, Conn.: Yale University Press, 1994.

———. *Essays in Criticism, Second Series, 1903*. London: Macmillan Press, 1903.

———. Preface to *Poems*. London: Longman, Brown, Green, and Longmans, 1853.

Miller, J. Hillis. *Disappearance of God: Five Nineteenth-Century Writers*. Cambridge, Mass.: Harvard University Press, 1975.

Trilling, Lionel. *Matthew Arnold*. New York: Columbia University Press, 1949.

"AS KINGFISHERS CATCH FIRE"

GERARD MANLEY HOPKINS (ca. 1882) This sonnet is one of GERARD MANLEY HOPKINS's great paeans to God through a celebration of what he has created—the dazzling, unending local detail of the world. (For an account of Hopkins's celebration of such specificity see the entry on "BINSEY POPLARS.") Its grammar is a little difficult, but that is because its meaning is somewhat unexpected. It is helpful to examine the first few lines: "Dragonflies draw flame in the same way the kingfishers catch fire," which is to say that they are both vital elements of the general fact (as he puts it in a much later poem), "THAT NATURE IS A HERACLITEAN FIRE"). The flame dragonflies draw is that which we can see shimmering on their diaphanous wings; the kingfishers catch fire by diving into the dazzling refractions of the waves and no doubt by emerging with the dazzling, fiery-scaled fish they catch. This is a simile where both sides of the comparison are vivid and also equivalent. Usually similes compare what they wish to describe to something already familiar and which needs no description. But for Hopkins, God's creation is all novel, all fresh, never familiar, and therefore the simile is very close to a simple, Whitmanian catalogue (Walt Whitman was Hopkins's favorite American poet): Kingfishers catch fire; dragonflies draw flame; and yet these specifics are linked since they do these things in the same way, as absolutely specific elements of the divine, all-linking similitude whose substrate is God.

The grammar of the second clause (beginning with the second line) is an intensification of that of the first: "Stones ring the way they ring when they are tumbled over the rims of wells," which is to say kingfishers are like dragonflies and stones sound like . . . stones. The ringing of the stone has become a simile for itself. This extreme compression and saturation of meaning should be compared to the kind of portmanteau word that Hopkins uses in "I WAKE AND FEEL THE FELL OF DARK," where *fell* is a kind of single-word compression of what Hopkins habitually produces out of concatenation (like the great word *heaven-haven* in *The WRECK OF THE DEUTSCHLAND*). The compressed simile then becomes one of the many to which the sound of a "tucked," or plucked, string may be compared. That sound is "like each" of the things already mentioned, and like them, too, the tongue of the bell flings out its sounds.

What do all these things have in common? What is the similarity that the similes indicate? The second quatrain of the octet spells it out: each one "Selves" (l. 7)—that is, persists in the blind and vital production of its own being. This is an idea Hopkins would have found in Plato's *Symposium* originally, but he combines it with the answer God gives Moses out of the burning bush in Exodus when Moses asks him his name: "I am that am. . . . Tell them I AM sent you." To exist as a self is an active, not a stative verb. Being perpetuates itself through its own instinctive drive. (Hopkins was also thinking of Darwin here.)

That idea of "selving" will be a source of great and grim despair in the later "terrible sonnet" "I Wake and Feel the Fell of Dark," with its awful evocation of the "scourge" by which the lost are condemned "to be their sweating selves" (l. 14) driven to perceive their own drive to remain what they are. "As kingfishers catch fire" is more hopeful, since it sees the possibility of extending the activity already present in "selving." If one can "selve"—(l. 7) and all selves do—one can do more. One can also "justice" (l. 9)—that is, be one who "Acts in God's eye what in God's eye he is" (l. 11). It is the nature of the self to act, since its existence is action, and that action can be that of doing justice and keeping grace. What is one in God's eye? Christ himself, we learn, because the father sees the image of Christ in all humans (as Genesis has taught). We "selve" because we have the divine power to create ourselves afresh every moment, just to persist in our being, and this ability makes us godlike, and therefore makes of ourselves the thing that God recognizes as Christ.

This ubiquity of Christ, who "plays in ten thousand places" (l. 12) finally clarifies the extent of divine similitude: Christ is everywhere, and all faces are similitudes of each other and of Christ himself. This pressure on simile is explained by the philosophical or theological claim all but explicit in the poem, a claim whose structure is like that of the simile we examined in the second line. We should be just to others because they are all images of Christ, and what makes us able to be just to others is that we, too, are an image of Christ. The self "justices" or should "justice" because it is surrounded by other selves who also "justice" or should "justice." All are similes for each other and for the *fact* that Christ makes us a simile for him, and himself a simile for us.

BIBLIOGRAPHY

Bridges, Robert. Preface *to Notes* in *Poems of Gerard Manley Hopkins.* Edited with additional poems, notes, and a biographical introduction by W. H. Gardner, 94–101. New York: Oxford University Press, 1948.

Gardner, W. H. *Gerard Manley Hopkins (1844–1889): A Study of Poetic Idiosyncrasy in Relation to Poetic Tradition.* New Haven, Conn.: Yale University Press, 1949.

———, ed. Introduction to *Poems and Prose of Gerard Manley Hopkins.* xiii–xxxvi. Harmondsworth, Middlesex, England: Penguin, 1953.

Hartman, Geoffrey. *The Unmediated Vision: An Interpretation of Wordsworth, Hopkins, Rilke, and Valery.* New Haven, Conn.: Yale University Press, 1954.

Hopkins, Gerard Manley. *Gerard Manley Hopkins: Selected Letters.* Edited by Catherine Phillips. New York: Oxford University Press, 1990.

Miller, J. Hillis. "Gerard Manley Hopkins." In *The Disappearance of God: Five Nineteenth-Century Writers.* 270–359. Cambridge, Mass.: Belknap Press of Harvard University Press, 1963.

White, Norman. *Hopkins: A Literary Biography.* New York: Oxford University Press, 1992.

ATALANTA IN CALYDON **ALGERNON CHARLES SWINBURNE (1865)** The most daring parts of ALGERNON CHARLES SWINBURNE's classical tragedy are the choral odes. Swinburne excelled in meditation and lamentation while action was suspended, and the unities of time and place, as well as the use the great Greek tragedians made of these unities, were perfect for Swinburne, since none of the action occurs on stage, only discussion of the action. Those who like his poetry admire *Atalanta in Calydon*'s long and sonorous linguistic brooding and its mode of repetition to the point of saturation. Its choral odes, as well as monologues of lamentation such as those that Althea and Meleager produce in the last third of the play, are the perfect classical analogue for Swinburne's lyricism.

Atalanta in Calydon should be regarded as a kind of extension and sometimes an objection to PERCY BYSSHE SHELLEY, in particular to the celebration of love in Shelley's *PROMETHEUS UNBOUND.* For the always sadomasochistic Swinburne, love is part of the debate that structures *Atalanta in Calydon:* the debate first of all between Althea and her son Meleager about his feelings for Atalanta, the virgin warrior devoted to Artemis, chaste goddess of the hunt, who kills the boar that Artemis has sent to punish Calydon and its king (Oenus, Meleager's father) for failing to sacrifice to her. For Shelley, love is the great law of the universe, the transcendent and transcendently beautiful repudiation of the fact that we live in a world of death; fate is finally on the side of love, because the very painfulness of life sensitizes us to the pain, and therefore the humanity, of others. In Shelley's darkly optimistic vision, sorrow leads to love.

Swinburne's more genuinely classical perspective sees fate as destroying all love. *Atalanta in Calydon* is in a sense *Prometheus Unbound* with Prometheus losing and Jupiter (or Zeus) winning—not that Zeus appears in person in the play, but the chorus acknowledges that it is impossible to escape fate or "the bitter jealousy of God" (l. 1,838). The story of Althea and Meleager (Atalanta is really only a catalyst, or MacGuffin, for the plot, and says almost nothing in the play) provides him with a perfect occasion to show the tragic collapse of love into sorrow. Before Meleager's birth, Althea dreams that she gives birth to a burning brand of wood: When her son is born, the Fates tell her that his life will last as long as a brand then burning in the fire. She snatches the brand out of the fire and extinguishes it completely. But now Meleager is full-grown, a glory to her and to his country, but in love with Atalanta. For Swinburne this already gives rise to Althea's jealousy, in a kind of reversed oedipal drama ("What dost thou, / Following strange loves?" she demands of him [ll. 692–693]), and that sets the stage for what follows: Meleager kills Althea's brothers when they attempt to wrest the boar away that Meleager and Atalanta have killed. In the mode of Aeschylus's *Oresteia,* Swinburne is interested in the tragic consequences of divided blood loyalties: Althea's loyalty to her brothers and to her own mother, who has borne them too. The very mother love she owes Meleager is also the love of her dead mother for her own sons; then Meleager turns away from her and toward Atalanta. Similarly, in Aeschylus's play, Clytemnestra—Althea's niece (and sister of Helen of Troy), as Meleager points out—kills her husband Agamemnon because he has sacrificed their daughter, and her son Orestes kills his mother (blood murder) to avenge the death of his father (blood revenge). Swinburne's story is set when Clytemnestra and Helen are little girls, as though to give himself a kind of priority over Aeschylus, and in his story the Clytemnestra figure, Althea, kills her own son by setting fire to the palace and thus burning the brand within it, in a scene highly allusive of Clytemnestra's murder of Agamemnon in the first play of the *Oresteia.*

Althea's great lamentation, after which she sustains complete silence, is matched by Meleager's swan song and the sad fate of the love between mother and son. Part of Meleager's lament is that he should wither away with the brand that represents and sustains him, rather than die gloriously in battle. But Swinburne's point is to make everyday death—death through wasting disease—tragic as well. The Victorians, partly under the influence of the new vision of nature and natural history provided by Charles Darwin and Sir Charles Lyell, were struck to the heart by the ambivalence of motherhood, in which the mother introduces the child she loves most in the world into the cycles of natural decay and destruction. Thus, ALICE MEYNELL saw the mother as giving death with the life she gave; and WILLIAM BUTLER YEATS became obsessed with the mother's vision of her child at 60 (in *Among School-Children*). Thus, too, the chorus in *Atalanta in Calydon* describes the birth of Aphrodite or of love, for the world of living things and repeated in the life of each living thing, as an event in which living beings "knew thee for mother of love, / And knew thee not mother of death" (ll. 760–761). The ambivalence about motherhood is something Swinburne almost always represents from his own point of view, that of the child for whom the mother in the end will mean death; as Meleager says, "there is nothing terribler to men / Then the sweet face of mothers" (ll. 710–711). Partly, she means death because she is so much vaster than the child for whom she is everything but who feels that for her he is nearly nothing. Even in "ITYLUS," which is told from the point of view of the women who kill their nephew and son, the mother's point of view is not represented. But in *Atalanta in Calydon* it is, and it is to Swinburne's credit, as to Aeschylus's, that he can enter into her own tragic perspective. Of course, he then ends by shifting to Meleager's (the son's) perspective, but there is a deep sense in which they understand each other and are finally brought more fully together in their deep understanding of how they have drifted apart as he has grown up.

Growing up means becoming sexually mature, but it also means growing toward death, wasting away as the brand wastes away. Swinburne characteristically uses the imagery of the brand both metaphorically and literally, as when Meleager laments how "all my ashen life burns down" (l. 2,233), just as Althea has observed how Meleager's face is ashen (l. 1,925) in her great, guilty lament to her dying son. There she feels on her cheek, she says, "the burning of a brand" (l. 1,911), which means both her stigmatization as the murderer of her own son and the pain that she feels at his death since he is the burning brand, which burns into her as well. The brand is the link by which the mother gives her child both life and death, and dedicates her own life and death to the child, "the bitter and the rooted love / That burns between us" (ll. 689–690). But that link between mother and child, by which the mother is both the mother of love and of death, stands for the passage of time and wasting away of life, as God "Bids day waste night as fire devours a brand" (l. 1,149).

Shelley thought beauty as powerful as death and imagined how darkness made a dying flame more beautiful. It is this capacity for human apprehension that eventually triumphs over God—Jupiter, or Milton's God, at any rate, in *Prometheus Unbound.* But Swinburne sees day destroying even the nourishment of darkness, and he sees in this the unshakable sway of "The supreme evil, God" (l. 1,151). Beauty in Swinburne is part compensation, part bait, or perhaps it would be better to see the compensation for the very fact that it is also a bait. Love destroys, and destruction leads to a transcendent, and transcendently tragic, need for love.

BIBLIOGRAPHY

Louis, Margot Kathleen. *Swinburne and His Gods: The Roots and Growth of an Agnostic Poetry.* Kingston, Ontario: McGill-Queen's University Press, 1990.

McGann, Jerome J. *Swinburne: An Experiment in Criticism.* Chicago: University of Chicago Press, 1972.

Rutland, William R. *Swinburne: A Nineteenth Century Hellene.* Oxford: Blackwell, 1931.

AURORA LEIGH **ELIZABETH BARRETT BROWNING (1857)** *Aurora Leigh* is Browning's most ambitious work. Both its very high poetic quality, when the poem is at its best, and its sometimes turgid moralizing, when it is at its worst, were noted by contemporary reviewers like GEORGE ELIOT, COVENTRY PATMORE, and W. E. AYTOUN, as well as by friends and correspondents of the Brownings, like John Ruskin. The poem is rightly called a novel in verse, but it is important to stress the *verse* part of that definition: It is full of extremely intense poetry as well as of novelistic interaction, and is in fact about the relation between the kinds of things of interest to a poet and the kinds of things of interest to a novelist. Indeed it stages a debate between these two kinds of interests—a debate that consciously and explicitly updates the debate between poets and philosophers in Plato.

In *Aurora Leigh* that debate takes place between the narrator of the poem, Aurora herself, and her cousin Romney Leigh, who has extremely high ambitions as a social reformer in the mode of Charles Fourier. The kind of literature that he would like if he liked literature is the socially conscious and tendentious (but great) fiction of Charles Dickens (5.403), whom he discusses with Aurora just before undertaking a Dickensian marriage with a poor and down-trodden but morally dazzling young woman who could easily be a character out of Dickens's *Tale of Two Cities.* Aurora, however, has aspirations for the soul-addressing beauties of poetry and is skeptical of her cousin's technocratic elevation of political economy above all else.

These two attitudes are explicitly couched in feminist terms. Romney believes that poetry is effeminate; poetry by a woman all the more so, and while he has all the respect in the world for Aurora (their relationship is handled with much subtlety and tact by Browning), he does not respect her vocation as she does. Since Aurora is in large part an autobiographical figure (though her father dies instead of anathematizing her the way Browning's own father had), the stirring encomiums to vocation that Browning puts into Aurora's mouth are her own defenses of poetry, and consciously and powerfully feminist defenses at that.

In the structure of the story and the development of human relationship that it depicts, Marianne Erle, the abject young woman whom Romney wishes to marry after Aurora has refused him, but whom he does not love, represents the possibility and indeed the necessity for both Romney and Aurora to concede the rightness of each other's commitments. Marianne, Dickensian in all her sentimental but heartbreaking splendor and goodness, represents a powerful appeal to sustained commitment to the spiritual and immaterial, vivid in her single mother's love for the child conceived through rape (here, also, Browning put her own experience as a mother into Marianne's attitude and feeling), a commitment that poetry mediates (far from being the imitation of an imitation, as Plato said, poetry for Aurora allows clearer contact with what is outside the cave of the material world), while also showing the necessity of working to ameliorate the oppressions of the earth that leave its Marianne Erles so vulnerable and many others so tortured into their own modes of pettiness and evil. (Thus, Marianne's father strikes Romney a vicious blow that ends up blinding him, while simultaneously offering him the

Miltonic sight that allows him at last to see Aurora for what she is.)

The fact that we get this all from Aurora's point of view makes her the opposite of a standard story depicting an anxious, overambitious hero—a Plantagenet Palliser or Phineas Finn, for example, saved through the ministrations of an oppressed but loyal woman who returns at the end to find fulfillment in rescuing him. Rescue him she does, but the poem depicts her changing values, not his, and only summarizes his moral development in the last book retrospectively. The changes Aurora undergoes are of the sort that could commit a poet who began with Wordsworthian balladry (Aurora dismisses the ballads she used to write) to the novelistic perspectives of the contemporary moment, which is why the last books of *Aurora Leigh* are formally contemporaneous, written in a journalistic mode and not the autobiographical mode of the retrospective account she gives of her life before she comes upon Marianne Erle again. As the poem moves into the present, it takes on the unpoetic social horrors of the present, most particularly rape and abandonment of women. (It should be noted that Browning's relation to Wordsworth includes an expansion of the very line of subjects for poetry that he had inaugurated.) The novelistic subject matter reflects the strong social and political ambitions in Browning's work akin to Dickens's (whom she cites in the poem), but overtly feminist, while its poetic form simultaneously shows its aspiration towards permanence. Romney and Aurora stand for these two modes, and Browning means their powerful and moving reconciliation at the end, therefore, to demonstrate how humanist and feminist demands in the political sphere manifest as well the spiritual aspiration to the enlargement of the human soul and not only the material aspiration to economic and social equality.

If *Aurora Leigh* presents poetry as feminine in its concern for beauty and in its emphasis on individual sorrow, the fact that feminism is a radical and growing movement makes both Aurora's and Browning's feminism, and their poetry, just as political as Romney's political economy. The poem finally declares for modern times and modern concerns, but for a modernity inflected by the insights into the actual individual experience of human psychology and human suffering that poetry affords. Feminism is a feature of modernity, and to be truly progressive would mean to be feminist as well. Romney would not disagree, perhaps, but what he fails to see at the start is that if poetry has now (as Romney, but Aurora above all, insist) become the province of women, then feminism will have to be part of the new and advanced order of things because poetry by its nature will have to be part of the new and advanced order of things. Without poetry, Browning insists, there can only be failed social engineering: Poetry reminds one of God. Conversely, since feminism is part of the new order, so is the poetry that Aurora defends in her intellectual arguments with Romney. Thus, the political argument of *Aurora Leigh* could be summarized this way: There can be no genuine progress without the inclusion of feminist concerns, which are important not only for women but for everyone. Those concerns include poetry; if women are now going to be writing the important poetry of the day—important not least because of its political ambition—then there will be no genuine progress without feminist poetry that makes this very point.

Poetry survives in *Aurora Leigh* because women make it survive, so that at the end of the poem generosity and greatness of heart go with feminism and political modernity, and all of them go with being a poet. By combining feminism with poetic vocation, Browning strengthens them both and paves the way for the great women poets who would succeed her. And at her best, though she has neither their consistency nor their range, she challenges and bears comparison with any of the other Victorian poets. (Indeed *Aurora Leigh* is a kind of answer to ALFRED, LORD TENNYSON's mild skepticism about women's ambitions for higher education in his long poem *The Princess.*) Aurora could achieve the highest cultural height, and so could her creator, as the moving and deep character she has created makes clear.

"AVE ATQUE VALE" ALGERNON CHARLES SWINBURNE (1868) This poem in memory of the French poet Charles Baudelaire (1821–67), author of *Les Fleurs du Mal,* is one of the great elegies in English, exceeded only by John Milton's *Lycidas,* PERCY BYSSHE

SHELLEY'S *ADONAIS,* and ALFRED, LORD TENNYSON'S *IN MEMORIAM A.H.H.* ALGERNON CHARLES SWINBURNE and Baudelaire never met, but they did correspond, and Swinburne saw in Baudelaire the model for the poet he wished to be, captivated by a ephemeral beauty that has nothing to do with transcendence. This elegy is, like all true elegies (as Samuel Beckett says), for the elegist himself. As we know from Milton and Shelley, when one poet elegizes another, he weeps his or her own fate in that of the other.

The title itself suggests this. "Ave atque vale" are the famous last words of the Latin poet Catullus's elegy for his brother: "Now and forever, brother, hail and farewell." It is as a brother that Swinburne addresses Baudelaire (l. 2)—that is to say, as a brother poet. The poem begins with an epigraph from Baudelaire that it will attempt to live up to. The epigraph (from the poem "La servante au grand coeur dont vous étiez jalouse") may be translated: "Yet still to him we should come bearing flowers; / The dead, the poor dead—whose sorrows exceed ours, / When October, despoiler of old trees, blows / Its melancholy wind round the marble tombs of those / Who lie there—must find the living all ungrateful." In the original, the ambiguous French word *lui* refers to a woman, but Swinburne makes it refer to her elegist. His quotation ends without providing a line to rhyme for its last line, which contributes to the sorrowful incompletion of the quotation itself (which I hope my translation helps suggest).

Swinburne, accordingly, begins his elegy with the thought of bringing flowers to Baudelaire, and he lists them in the first stanza. Such a list has been common to English elegy since Ophelia in *Hamlet* brought flowers to her father's grave; it suggests a way for poetry to occupy the mourning mind through its search for flowers, whose names with their metrical and rhyming arrangement provide a correlative to the arrangement of flowers themselves that a mourner might undertake (see, for example, AMY LEVY'S "TO VERNON LEE"). They are particularly appropriate for the grave of Baudelaire whose flowers of evil or disease grow from the inextricability of beauty and death. What Swinburne loved in Baudelaire was his attraction to the kinds of flowers that grow in "The GARDEN OF PROSERPINE" (as Swinburne puts it in another poem), and not those that grow in Paradise—that is, an attraction to the loveliness of "lovely leaf-buds poisonous" (l. 25). He returns to these flowers in the dazzling description of the "mournful garden" (l. 180) whose "sick flowers of secrecy and shade" (l. 182), the human passions, were depicted by Baudelaire, "gardener of strange flowers" (l. 68).

Swinburne himself is characteristically attracted less to flowers than to imagery of the sea as a place where beauty and death come together, and therefore he compares Baudelaire to Sappho, "the supreme head of song" (l. 18), who drowned herself out of disappointed love (see also LETITIA ELIZABETH LANDON'S "SAPPHO'S SONG"). It is there where he might be able to find the sleep his poetic speakers consistently crave, and which Baudelaire has already achieved.

We should recognize that Swinburne's Baudelaire is almost another JOHN KEATS, who has found the "easeful death" ("ODE TO A NIGHTINGALE") he seeks. Keats, too, was obsessed with flowers and with ceasing or dying painlessly, and it is no surprise that Swinburne, lover of Shelley that he was, should rewrite Shelley's elegy on Keats, *Adonais.* At any rate, he alludes to Keats throughout the poem, referring to *The Fall of Hyperion* (in stanza 6, which more overtly alludes to Baudelaire's sonnet "La Géante" [The Giantess]) as well as to all of Keats's major odes.

The references to Keats as well as to Baudelaire make it possible for Swinburne to think through the relationship of the poetry that survives to the dead poet who has written it. The peace to be found in oblivion is one in which—to reverse Keats's lament in "Ode to a Nightingale"—the high requiem survives even when its maker has become sod, and it is still available to the "communion" (l. 104) that the living Swinburne craves. Such communion does not threaten the dead poet who is safely at peace, so the sorrow of the song no longer implies that the poet, too, is sorrowful. The achievement of his death is to make his sorrow a universal thing, available in its beauty to all who experience it, even as the death that it represents and may be said to lament is a universal thing.

Of course, such representation comes after the poet's death, in general. But this is partly Swinburne's point: He is anticipating his own death, in mourning for himself before the fact, and in mourning for what he will be after the fact. The pagan gods that both Swinburne and Baudelaire (and Keats as well) so praised are not real, except in their poetry. But they are all that are left to mourn their makers—they and the songs that cite them. Swinburne knows the sorrow of these songs will not "make death clear or make life durable" (l. 172) since it is just this incapacity which the songs themselves are made to express.

The poem ends reiterating that the sorrow it expresses is detached from the person the sorrow is for. It is now Swinburne who weaves the garland (l. 189) for Baudelaire, who need not fear any more the grievous experiences of life. The nothingness offered by death is a synthesis of all he loved. It is a synthesis in the mode of privation, true. But the privation is just the form that abstraction takes (abstraction being a privation of the individual and concrete). It is for this reason that the great last lines can offer a synthesis that describes nothingness but makes it feel like the culmination of all Baudelaire's imagery. He is now one for whom "all winds are quite as the sun / All waters as the shore" (ll. 197–198), which returns us to the imagery of the world to which Baudelaire (and later Swinburne) is oblivious, using that imagery in its sheer and sorrowful abstraction as just the way that oblivion represents itself, and therefore saving the songs of oblivion from their own knowledge, which is transfigured instead into mournful beauty.

BIBLIOGRAPHY

Louis, Margot Kathleen. *Swinburne and His Gods: The Roots and Growth of an Agnostic Poetry*. Kingston, Ontario: McGill-Queen's University Press, 1990.

McGann, Jerome J. *Swinburne: An Experiment in Criticism*. Chicago: University of Chicago Press, 1972.

Rutland, William R. *Swinburne: A Nineteenth Century Hellene*. Oxford: Blackwell, 1931.

AYTOUN, WILLIAM EDMONSTOUNE (1813–1865)

William Edmonstoune Aytoun was a Scottish lawyer who lived in Edinburgh, where he had been born; his mother was a friend of Sir WALTER SCOTT's. He is chiefly (and justly) remembered today as a parodist, most of his parodies appearing in *Blackwood's Magazine*, to which he contributed most of his adult life. But he also wrote wildly popular imitations of the Scottish ballads (*Lays of the Scottish Cavaliers*), in the style of Scott, and some other serious historical poetry, of which *Bothwell*, a dramatic monologue set in the 16th century, had the most success. He also published a collection of genuine Scottish ballads, and he was a translator of the poet and dramatist Johann Wolfgang von Goethe, whose work he began reading seriously when he was a student in Germany; with his friend Theodore Martin, he published a translation of Goethe's ballads, in 1858. He and Martin were also hugely popular for their parodies, published in their final form in 1855 as the *Bon Gaultier Ballads*.

Aytoun' greatest and most entertaining work was his parody of those he called the "Spasmodic Poets," particularly SYDNEY DOBELL (from whose preface to Part I of his long poem *Balder* he took the term, originally applied by Thomas Carlyle to LORD BYRON) and Scottish poet Alexander Smith. (Dobell moved to Edinburgh a few years later and became a friend of Aytoun's.) In 1854, after *Balder* came out, Aytoun published in *Blackwell's* a parody review, complete with ample quotation, of a nonexistent book: *Firmilian: or, The Student of Badajoz: a Tragedy. By T. Percy Jones. Printed for Private Circulation,* full of extravagant praise for the Spasmodic School. So successful was the parody that he followed it up with the book itself, *Firmilian . . . a Spasmodic Tragedy,* the same year.

Besides being hilarious on its own, *Firmilian* has great value, as parodies often do, in underlining the kinds of language that aspire to high poetic diction. Thus, we hear how a drunk mariner clutches at "the wild incongruity of ropes," a phrase that is just and perfectly overdone, powerfully but nonsensically evocative. Aytoun knows that perfect parody requires something very close to the talents of the writer being parodied. He is (like A. E. HOUSMAN after him) a superb stylist and therefore a superb example of the signal achievements of the minor Victorian poets (such as WALTER SAVAGE LANDOR and WILLIAM JOHNSON CORY): not the originality of the truly great poets that dares failure in its aspirations, but the absolute control of the language and medium they have invented.

This can be seen in "La Mort d'Arthur," his 1849 spoof of ALFRED, LORD TENNYSON's "MORTE D'ARTHUR"

(1842), which sends up the wild incongruity of linking Victorian commercialism with Tennyson's deep (and complex) poetic nostalgia. Aytoun's lines probably respond to Tennyson's incongruous linking of the modern frame (with its fireplace flues) with the medieval subject and sound exactly Tennysonian until the punch line about his armor: "Whereon no canker lighted, for they bore / The magic stamp of Mechi's Silver Steel" (ll. 15–16). "Silver steel" was a fine steel alloy with a little silver in it, invented by the great scientist Michael Faraday, and as John Holland said in his 1834 *Treatise on the . . . Manufactures in Metal,* it became popular partly because of the euphony of its name. (John Joseph Mechi was among many other things one of the leading cutlers of London.) Aytoun's shrewdness (which James Joyce would echo in *Ulysses*) was to see the connection between poetic euphony and that of commercial advertisement.

BIBLIOGRAPHY

Aytoun, William Edmonstoune. *Firmilian: A "Spasmodic" Tragedy*. New York: Redfield, 1854.

———. "Review" of *Firmilian*. In *The Victorians: An Anthology of Poetry and Poetics,* edited by Valentine Cunningham, 389–406. Malden, Mass.: Blackwell, 2000.

Boos, Florence S. "'Spasm' and Class: W. E. Aytoun, George Gilfillan, Sydney Dobell, and Alexander Smith." *Victorian Poetry* 42, no. 4 (2004): 553–583.

Weinstein, Mark A. *William Edmondstoune Aytoun and the Spasmodic Controversy*. New Haven, Conn.: Yale University Press, 1968.

B

BAILLIE, JOANNA (1762–1851) Joanna Baillie was one of the most popular playwrights of her time, publishing a series of verse dramas on the passions between 1798 and 1836. They first appeared anonymously and were attributed to Sir WALTER SCOTT (who also, like many writers of the day, published anonymously). Baillie shared Scott's Scottish origins (she was born in Bothwell, on the River Clyde, on September 11, 1762), and in fact claimed direct descent from the great Scottish hero William Wallace (d. 1305), who sought to free Scotland from English suzerainty. One of her best poems, "The GHOST OF FADON," recounts a supernatural incident in the life of Wallace.

After the death of her father in 1783, Baillie and her family settled in London, where she spent the rest of her long life, living with her sister Agnes (who died in 1860, age 100). In 1790 Baillie published a volume of *Poems* on "nature and rustic manners," which does not survive, but many of the poems from that book were reprinted in her augmented 1840 book *Fugitive Verses,* with what alterations we cannot know.

The preface to the 1798 publication of Baillie's first verse drama, *Plays on the Passions,* has recently been claimed as highly influential on WILLIAM WORDSWORTH's 1800 preface to *Lyrical Ballads* by Wordsworth and SAMUEL TAYLOR COLERIDGE. (Wordsworth and Baillie were to become friends a decade or so later). In the preface, Baillie introduces her projected series of plays and notes that she sees "the task . . . peculiarly belonging to tragedy—unveiling the human mind under the dominion of those strong and fixed passions which, seemingly unprovoked by outward circumstances, will from small beginnings brood within the breast till all the better dispositions, all the fair gifts of nature, are borne down before them." Tragedies should accordingly "open to our view the nature and portraitures of those great disturbers of the human breast with whom we are all, more or less, called upon to contend." Wordsworth was after something quite different from this when he wrote in his preface of his choosing rural subjects and people in *Lyrical Ballads* "because, in that condition, the essential passions of the heart find a better soil in which they can attain their maturity." Wordsworth was interested in the passions common to all, the passions that make us human; whereas Baillie concerned herself with pathological, life-ruining passion. What they shared, however, was an interest in acute psychological subtlety, in examining the universal depths of the human mind, and this interest is manifest in all of Baillie's work.

Plays on the Passions had a mixed success, both on stage (where the leading actors of the day performed them) and with the reading public. They were sometimes wildly praised and sometimes damned as by the Scottish critic Francis Jeffrey, who panned Baillie in 1803 in the *Edinburgh Review*; later they became friends.

As a poet, Baillie wrote in a variety of modes, from innovative, geographically (or loco-) descriptive poems like "LONDON" to love songs to poems written in the Scots dialect (a mode originated by Robert Burns and Scott). She was admired by contemporaries such as Scott, who was particularly enthusiastic about her; LORD BYRON; ANNA LAETITIA BARBAULD, who, in "EIGHTEEN HUNDRED AND ELEVEN," thinks of her as one of the few people remembered from the wreck of English culture; and HARTLEY COLERIDGE, who, like Barbauld, praised her in his own poetry.

See also "KITTEN, THE"; "SONG (GOOD NIGHT)"; "SONG: WOO'D AND MARRIED AND A'."

BIBLIOGRAPHY

Baillie, Joanna. *Dramatic and Poetical Works of Joanna Baillie.* London: Longman, Brown, Green, and Longmans, 1851.

Forbes, A. "'Sympathetic Curiosity' in Joanna Baillie's Theater of the Passions." *European Romantic Review* 14, no. 1 (January 2003): 31–48.

McMillan, Dorothy, ed. The Association for Scottish Literary Studies, ASLS Annual Volume 29: 1999: *The Scotswoman at Home and Abroad,* Glasgow (contains excerpts from Baillie's unpublished "Memoir written to please my nephew, William Baillie," and "Recollections written for Miss Berry," both in English archives.)

Wordsworth, Jonathan. *Ancestral Voices: Fifty Books from the Romantic Period.* New York: Woodstock, 1996.

"BALLADE OF BLUE CHINA" ANDREW LANG (1880) The troubadour form of the ballade, resuscitated by ALGERNON CHARLES SWINBURNE and DANTE GABRIEL ROSSETTI turned out to be especially good for comic or light verse in English. (For more about the form, see the entry on ANDREW LANG's more serious ballade, "ON CALAIS SANDS.") This is because the repetitions of rhyme and refrain in the ballade require ambiguity or at least substantial and surprising range of meaning to prevent them from being obvious and without function.

This ballade gave Lang the title of two of his books, both *XXII* and *XXXII Ballades in Blue China,* both because it is perfect in its kind and because it captures something about Lang more generally—his curious and voraciously aesthetic antiquarianism. The blue china from the reign of Emperor Hwang (pronounced—incorrectly—*wang* in this poem, not the correct *wong*) would be nearly 5,000 years old. The emperor Hwang Tsi was mythological; he was said to have invented pottery making. The china Lang is looking at fills him, then, with two kinds of joy: the fictive joy of having ancient china from the dawn of history; and the joy of pastische—that is, of the myth that blue china comes from the dawn of history and that he is looking at a scene already painted in biblical times. Remember that Lang was most popular for his retelling of ancient fairy tales in the series of *Fairy Books* he put out.

If the first stanza is about something real, the pottery itself, the second is about something unreal, the dragons depicted on it. But both the real pot and the things that it depicts date from the reign of Hwang, and so the myth and the material object are merged together. The third stanza describes a real scene on the pottery—the bench and the park—and tells the story of this conventional scene: Koong-Shee eloped with her lover Chang; the gods saved them from their pursuers by turning them into doves.

This legend, as Lang knew, was in fact a Victorian fabrication of the English pottery makers. The scene designed certainly was fabricated, and the wit of the last full stanza consists in the fact that the "tale is undoubtedly true / In the reign of the Emperor Hwang," and only there, so not true at all, since Hwang is a myth.

But the beauty of the pottery comes from its patina of antiquity, which is what Lang sought in his own writing, and simultaneously, undercut and wittily justified in poems like this. The carping critic of the envoi, who knows that the blue china is of recent manufacture, might snarl at the speaker's "ecstatsies" or madness, but he answers with a punning quotation from Shakespeare's *Tempest* (2.2.50)—*tang* would be a pun on the Tang dynasty (618–907 C.E.), which was real and a high point of Chinese civilization. (The pun also suggests the wittily suppressed rhyme on Lang's own name in the rhymes.) Lang's response is to prefer the times when sages did not listen to critics—alas, only the mythological times of Emperor Hwang.

For some interesting images, see the California Academy of Sciences Web page on blue and white crockery at http://www.calacademy.org/research/anthropology/kitchen/crockery.html.

BIBLIOGRAPHY

Beerbohm, Max. "Two Glimpses of Andrew Lang." *Life and Letters* 1, no. 1 (June, 1928): 1–11.

Cocq, Antonius Petrus Leonardus de. *Andrew Lang, a Nineteenth Century Anthropologist.* Tilburg, Netherlands: Zwijsen, 1968.

Green, Roger Lancelyn. *Andrew Lang: A Critical Biography with a Short-Title Bibliography of the Works of Andrew Lang.* Leicester, England: E. Ward, 1946.

Gross, John. *Rise and Fall of the Man of Letters: Aspects of English Literary Life since 1800.* London: Weidenfeld & Nicolson, 1969.

Orel, Harold. *Victorian Literary Critics: George Henry Lewes, Walter Bagehot, Richard Holt Hutton, Leslie Stephen, Andrew Lang, George Saintsbury, and Edmund Gosse.* London: Macmillan Press, 1984.

Webster, A. Blyth. *Andrew Lang's Poetry, by A. Blyth Webster, being the Andrew Lang Lecture Delivered before the University of St. Andrews 20 October 1937.* London: Oxford University Press, 1937.

"BALLAD OF BOUILLABAISSE" WILLIAM MAKEPEACE THACKERAY (1856)

WILLIAM MAKEPEACE THACKERAY's ballads are in their way as delightful as those moments in his novels (especially *Vanity Fair*) where the narrator engages in some winningly self-deprecatory wryness at his own expense. Thackeray's great tonal mode is to say serious things without ever being hampered by humorlessness, and the "Ballad of Bouillabaisse" is a perfect example of that mode.

Bouillabaisse is a French (specifically Provençal) fish stew that contains, as Thackeray puts it, a "hotchpotch of all sorts of fishes" (l. 11). The hodgepodge comes together to make "a rich and savory stew" and to stand as well for the poem that can freely itemize its ingredients—the poem we are reading. The praise of bouillabaisse is a praise as well for a kind of poetic form open to all the different and interesting elements to be met in a life filled with gusto. Such gusto is for poetic delight, including delight in how much the ballad can delight in. Thackeray's ballads are verbally inventive, and it is that invention for which the bouillabaisse is a metaphor.

One can feel that inventiveness in Thackeray's delight in what is called *mosaic rhyme,* a form of rhyme which usually has a comic effect in English. Mosaic rhyme consists of rhyming a single polysyllabic word with other, separated words. The poem begins with a mosaic rhyme, *famous / name is,* and there are examples in about half the other stanzas. The effect of mosaic rhyme is to make the reader feel the arbitrariness of the connection, as though rhyme itself just throws things together. It does, and therefore the bouillabaisse rhymed here is the perfect subject since it allows the rhymer to go anywhere to find his rhymes.

The poem is more than a celebration of the heterogeneity that makes it possible. In typical Thackerayean fashion, it also becomes a melancholy dirge for the loss of some of the things a life lived with gusto has yielded—the loss of ways of life and of friends whom time has taken away. Loss is the inevitable other side of gusto since the more you love, the more you will lose. The poem modulates brilliantly into a catalogue of loss, through the speaker's discovery that the original proprietor of the restaurant where he so loved to eat bouillabaisse in Paris, and to which he is now returned, has died (l. 36).

The death of the purveyor of bouillabaisse puts the poet in mind of all the other people who have died since the days he now recollects. The sadness of this catalogue leads finally to the penultimate stanza, the only one which does not rhyme on bouillabaisse; Thackeray's extraordinary and effortless invention has been such that every other stanza has ended with the word.

The brilliant turn of the poem is this: Bouillabaisse has reminded him of the times that are gone and filled him with sadness, but that sadness requires a cure, and that cure is a hot tureen of bouillabaisse. Catalyst of sorrow and antidote to the sorrow it catalyzes, it still stands for and feeds the same gusto as that which animates Thackeray's lines, and therefore it returns as the last word of the last stanza, and thus of the poem.

BIBLIOGRAPHY

Peters, Catherine. *Thackeray's Universe: Shifting Worlds of Imagination and Reality.* London: Faber and Faber, 1987.

Ray, Gordon N. *Thackeray: The Age of Wisdom, 1847–1863.* New York: McGraw-Hill, 1957.

———. *Thackeray: The Uses of Adversity, 1811–1846.* New York: McGraw-Hill, 1955.

Shillingsburg, Peter L. *William Makepeace Thackeray: A Literary Life.* New York: Palgrave, 2001.

"BALLAD OF EAST AND WEST, THE"

RUDYARD KIPLING (1889) This is one of RUDYARD KIPLING's half-dozen most famous and most quoted poems. It is more or less typical of Kipling at his best in the complexity of its attitude (a complexity that has room for a great deal of sentimentality), the extremely high technical sheen, the light touch of its versification and language, and the absorbing interest of the story it tells.

The interest of the poem's story is far more important than the details of its setting or its characters, but it is still helpful to know, especially at the beginning of the 21st century, that the story takes place on the border between India and Afghanistan, near the Khyber Pass—the northwest corner of India under British administration and guarded by British troops is in what is now (after 1947) Pakistan and no longer India.

Kamal is an Afghan warrior and raider, and the poem tells the story of a memorable raid he made on a horse belonging to an English colonel. He crosses the border, steals the colonel's mare, and rides away, back to his own territories over the "border-line." Kamal is one of the two strong men, the man who comes from the eastern end of the earth in the ballad's famous proem (preface); the other is the colonel's son, who pursues Kamal past all reason and reasonableness. The colonel's son leads "a troop of the Guides"—that is, a troop belonging to a regiment headquartered near the border and protecting the frontier, Queen Victoria's Own Corps of Guides. Most of its members were not British but native, like Mohammed Kahn, the son of the ressaldar, or native commander of a troop of horse, who informs the colonel's son of Kamal's practices and methods. This is an important point for understanding what Kamal has in mind at the end when he sends his son back with the colonel's son. He warns the colonel's son against going beyond the frontiers of Bonair and the Abazai, but the colonel's son ignores those warnings in his pursuit of Kamal.

The story is beautifully structured: The horse of the colonel's son cannot match his father's horse, which is now being ridden by Kamal, and there is something of an oedipal struggle going on here as the colonel's son seeks to prove himself to his father (as Kamal shrewdly intuits) by getting his mare back. That she is a mare, and the colonel's pride, is not irrelevant, nor is Kamal's praise of the mother of the colonel's son, later on, as a "Dam of lances" (l. 62)—that is, a mother of the fiercest warriors.

Because his horse cannot keep up with his father's, the colonel's son finally finds himself thrown, and Kamal returns to help him. The colonel's son shows defiant scorn toward Kamal, who replies with a sublime confirmation of all that Mohammed Kahn has said about the danger he might have been to the colonel's son. But the colonel's son is equally sublime in his lighthearted courage, and he impresses Kamal as much as Kamal impresses him. It is here that Kamal praises his mother's fierceness, and that we learn that the colonel's son is Scottish, not English: "I hold by the blood of my clan." The Scottish clans that harried the English on the Anglo-Scottish border until the 18th century parallel the Afghan tribal clans to which Kamal and his followers belong.

If Kamal is impressed by the courage of the colonel's son, the latter is just as impressed by Kamal's. The fact that Kamal treats him as an equal, neither enraged nor humiliated by the insult that the colonel's son spits at him, induces him to a spontaneous gesture of friendship, and his most sublime moment occurs when he offers the mare as a gift to Kamal. At this moment he takes on his father's authority and offers the sign of that authority, "the Colonel's pride," to Kamal.

The spontaneous and almost nonchalant offer of a tremendous gift in highly fraught life-and-death circumstances is a perfect example of the deep significance of the gift-giving practices that have been studied extensively by anthropologists in the 20th century. The colonel's son's gesture is one that demonstrates greatness of spirit: generosity mingled with supreme self-confidence. Kamal matches that greatness of spirit in his reply when the mare runs to the colonel's son. To either take or refuse the gift would be a concession, but when he follows and confirms the mare's choice by paralleling himself with the colonel's son, their friendship is sealed.

Kamal makes a matching gift to the colonel's son, and he calls it a "dower," which is to say that the two of them see the return of the mare as a gift on Kamal's part, and indeed a gift like that of the father giving away the bride. But in addition to giving the colonel's son the mare, and the gear that Kamal has treasured, he also gives him his own son to be a member of the Guides. Here, too, we can see what Sigmund Freud would call the theme of oedipal rivalry: Kamal sees his son as rising to ressaldar even as he will meet the likely fate of all the tribal outlaws who go up against the British. But by doing so, he also does two things: He sets himself up as again sublimely more courageous and courteous than the offstage colonel himself; and he sets up his son as a parallel to the colonel's son and therefore he sets himself up as a truer father, a more equal, more capable father than the colonel is. His son is subordinate to the colonel's, but that means he and the colonel's son have become equals as they come face to face. They understand each other; they have become brothers in blood, and something passes between the wolf and grey wolf that transcends political or cultural differences.

It is far too easy to see the homoerotic bonding going on between these two men, and the reading I have given should clarify the existence of that bond. But one should also recognize that the bond is itself a metaphor for something else—for the possibility of a sublime transcultural or omnicultural moment of communication and understanding of just the kind of powerful gesture that the poem itself makes vivid for its readers everywhere. It is perfectly legitimate to say that this is in fact a Western attitude, and that the claim the poem makes to universalize it when East and West meet as equals is in fact a ruse of imperialism to assimilate the subaltern. Nevertheless, one should remember that Kipling was there, and that he was insisting on the general bloodiness of history and the general capacity for sublimity among some of its figures.

BIBLIOGRAPHY

Durand, Ralph. *A Handbook to the Poetry of Rudyard Kipling.* London: Hodder & Stoughton, 1914.

Mauss, Marcel. *The Gift: Forms and Functions of Exchange in Archaic Societies,* Translated by Ian Cunnison. New York: Norton, 1967.

Said, Edward. *Culture and Imperialism.* New York: Knopf, 1993.

***BALLAD OF READING GAOL, THE* OSCAR WILDE (1898)** At its best, *The Ballad of Reading Gaol* bears comparison to SAMUEL TAYLOR COLERIDGE's *THE RIME OF THE ANCIENT MARINER,* the poem that most strongly influences it. At its worst, it descends into somewhat incoherent moralism as well as maudlin excess, and OSCAR WILDE acknowledged, even as he defended, what he called the propagandistic ending of the poem. (Wilde thought of the ballad as more in the mode of RUDYARD KIPLING than of Coleridge, but this is true mainly of the propagandistic parts, though the repetition of the phrase "the man who had to swing" is indeed in the mode of Kipling.)

In 1895 Wilde was sentenced to two years' hard labor for gross indecency arising out of his relationship with LORD ALFRED DOUGLAS, and he spent most of that time (November 1895–May 1897) in Reading Gaol (the British spelling of the American *jail*). In the poem, the gaol's inmate is memorably represented by the archetypes of "the fool, the fraud, the knave" (l. 261); Wilde, of course, was the fool, the person who had been betrayed by excessive and unwise love into this torture. He describes the hard labor quite memorably in the ballad, particularly in lines 217–226, where he emphasizes the sheer and sadistic pointlessness of the work imposed. On its publication, the poem was ascribed only to C.3.3—that is, to the number of the prison cell where Wilde was confined ("my numbered tomb" [l. 246]), which is part of its self-denying point. Wilde was no longer the figure who had nothing to declare but his genius: He was anonymous, one of the outlaws and outcasts in Reading Gaol.

But worse still was the fate of the "C.T.W." in memory of whom the poem is inscribed: *"Obit H.M. Prison, Reading, Berkshire, July 7, 1896."* This is Charles Thomas Wooldridge, a trooper of the Royal Horse Guards, who was executed for cutting his wife's throat in what seems to have been a fit of insanity brought on by both personal turmoil and unfortunate circumstances. He stood at attention on the scaffold and was buried in an unmarked grave within the walls of the prison.

The best part of the poem by far is the description of the night of horror spent by the other prisoners as they wait for the morning of Wooldridge's execution, which took place promptly at 8:00 A.M. (It was the first execution in Reading Gaol in 18 years, and the executioners seem to have been giddy with excitement.) Wilde's account of that night recalls and in some ways surpasses the Ancient Mariner's description of being becalmed on the ocean, dying of thirst, and being haunted by his dead shipmates. Wilde and his fellow prisoners are haunted by "the crooked shapes of Terror" (l. 285); everyone's "tongue was thick with thirst" (l. 377), and the night of unrelenting terror goes on endlessly (l.326). But unlike Coleridge, Wilde has had the actual experience he describes. As with the Ancient Mariner, he returns to the living; through his own experience of the desperate effects of being outlawed, he knows more than any of the socially acceptable people he now confronts the awfulness of the punishment society imposes on its outcasts. The poetry is not as good as Coleridge's, but it is probably more unbearable to read because we know that it is describing what really happened.

The worst part of the poem is probably its overquoted aphorism (twice repeated from earlier in the poem as its conclusion: "And all men kill the thing they love . . . / The coward does it with a kiss, / The brave man with a sword!" (ll. 648–654). When Douglas asked Wilde what these lines meant, Wilde replied "*You* ought to know." This suggests that Douglas was the coward who killed Wilde; but to say only that would be overly simplistic since the lines are so clearly self-lacerating. It also suggests Wilde's guilt at what was essentially his abandonment of his own wife, Constance Mary Lloyd, whom he did love and who was dying. In his autobiography, WILLIAM BUTLER YEATS reports that Wilde said that "his vice was not the crime itself, but that he should have brought such misery upon his wife and children." In 1898, before she died Constance read and was deeply moved by the ballad. Wilde probably felt guilt as well (less appropriate this time) about his treatment of the much younger Douglas. At any rate, the praise of the brave man seems overdone, but the poem shows why it was that Wilde should have been so overwrought from his grim and brutal experiences at Reading Gaol.

BIBLIOGRAPHY

Douglas, Alfred Bruce, Lord. *Oscar Wilde and Myself.* New York: Duffield and Co., 1914.

Ellmann, Richard. *Oscar Wilde.* New York: Knopf, 1988.

Harris, Frank. *Oscar Wilde. His Life and Confessions.* Garden City, N.Y.: Garden City Publishing Co., 1932.

Morrison, Paul. *The Explanation for Everything: Essays on Sexual Subjectivity.* New York: New York University Press, 2001.

Nunokawa, Jeff. *The Tame Passions of Wilde: Styles of Manageable Desire.* Princeton, N.J.: Princeton University Press, 2003.

Whittington-Egan, Richard, "Oscar Wilde: A Centennial Wreath of Memories." *Contemporary Review* (November 1, 2000). Available online. URL: http://www.encyclopedia.com/doc/1G1-68157978.html. Accessed on January 15, 2008.

Wilde, Oscar. *Complete Works of Oscar Wilde.* New York: HarperCollins, 1989.

———. *Three Trials of Oscar Wilde.* Edited and introduced by H. Montgomery Hyde. New York: University Books, 1956.

BARBAULD, ANNA LAETITIA (ANNA LETITIA BARBAULD) (1743–1825) Anna Laetitia Barbauld was one of the preeminent writers and leaders of literary culture, primarily in the 1790s, the period which might be thought of as the transition between the 18th-century age of Enlightenment and the succeeding era of ROMANTICISM. She was admired by the lexicographer and author Samuel Johnson, who would have hated romanticism; and by WILLIAM WORDSWORTH and SAMUEL TAYLOR COLERIDGE, the distinguished romantic poets who rightly saw in her work a forerunner of their own. In the 1790s Barbauld edited editions of the preromantic poets Mark Akenside and William Collins, and edited the letters of the novelist Samuel Richardson; she also published a 50-volume edition of *The English Novelists,* each volume including an introduction. These introductions were meant to be for novelists what Johnson's *Lives of the Poets* was for British poetry. Barbauld's work was central to the promotion of the status of the novel to the rank of serious literature.

Barbauld was the daughter of a Dissenting (nonconformist) schoolmaster, the Reverend John Aikin. A brilliant child, she involved herself completely in the philosophical and literary issues of the day. At the age of 29, at the behest of her brother John, she published her first book of poems, which was a great success. The next year, she married Rochemont Barbauld, a Dissenting clergyman and student of her father's, and, following in her father's footsteps, they opened a school together in Suffolk. Her poetry shows her strongly committed to social virtues, education primary among them, and while running the school she wrote an enormous amount for children, in prose and poetry. Of such writing she said: "The task is humble but not mean; for to lay the first stone of a noble building, and to plant the first idea in a human mind, can be no dishonour to any hand" (advertisement to *Lessons for Children*). It is perhaps a similar cast of mind that made her admire Coleridge's *The Rime of the Ancient Mariner* while complaining that its chief defects were that "it was improbable, and had no moral." (Coleridge, of course, disagreed: He thought it had too much of a moral.)

One reason that she might have been so good with children is, paradoxically, that she had none of her own (although the Barbaulds adopted her brother John's son Charles). This meant that her relationship to children was that of an ex-child, as one might say, rather than an authoritative parent. She understood children because she remembered with great intensity what it was like to be a child, and that intense memory also prefigures Wordsworth's Intimations Ode ("Intimations of Immortality from Recollections of Early Childhood"), which would be at the heart of the romantic sense of subjectivity. Such prefigurations may be seen in her poem "Washing Day" as well as the philosophical "Life! I know not what thou art."

Rochemont Barbauld was mentally unstable; he tried to convince Barbauld to take her own life and on another occasion attacked her with a knife. She escaped by jumping out a window. Eventually he attempted suicide, and was confined for the rest of his life to an asylum, where he died in 1808. Barbauld continued writing for the rest of her life, becoming something of a mentor and something of a scourge to the new generation of romantics.

Many consider "Eighteen Hundred and Eleven" to be Barbauld's most important poem; certainly the visionary grandeur and ferocity of this critique of England in 1811 make it a powerful work. When it was published, it was roundly criticized by less radical writers, notably by John Wilson Croker in the *Quarterly Review*. Croker was a conservative MP who would also review John Keats viciously. She never published again, but kept on writing, as her complete poetical works, published just after her death in 1825, proved. For a while, Barbauld was considered the leading poet of her age, and certainly her work in all spheres, including that of poetry, make her one of the grand figures of the late 18th and early 19th centuries. Her poems are powerful and original, and their reevaluation is an important development in recent critical history.

See also "To a Little Invisible Being Who Is Expected Soon to Become Visible," "To Mr Coleridge."

BIBLIOGRAPHY

Armstrong, Isobel. "The Gush of the Feminine: How Can We Read Women's Poetry of the Romantic Period?" In *Romantic Women Writers: Voices and Countervoices*, edited by Paula R. Feldman and Theresa M. Kelley, 13–32. Hanover, N.H.: University Press of New England, 1995.

Armstrong, Isobel, and Virginia Blain, eds. *Women's Poetry in the Enlightenment: The Making of a Canon, 1730–1820.* New York: St. Martin's Press, 1999.

Barbauld, Anna Letitia. *Poems, 1792.* New York: Woodstock, 1993.

Keach, William. *Arbitrary Power: Romanticism, Language, Politics.* Princeton, N.J.: Princeton University Press, 2004.

Mellor, Anne K. *Romanticism & Gender.* New York: Routledge, 1993.

Stabler, Jane. *Burke to Byron, Barbauld to Baillie, 1790–1830.* New York: Palgrave, 2001.

Wordsworth, Jonathan. *Bright Work Grows: Women Writers of the Romantic Age.* Washington, D.C.: Woodstock Books, 1997.

BARNES, WILLIAM (1801–1886) Born in North Dorset on February 22, 1801, William Barnes may be the best 19th century poet to suffer persistent omission from anthologies and surveys. He is often compared to John Clare, and in some modes his work rivals and anticipates great poems by Thomas Hardy, Gerard Manley Hopkins (especially "Binsey Poplars"), and A. E. Housman. He is in some ways a poet's poet (Philip Larkin wrote a wonderful appreciation of him), but that is because he is a dialect poet, and his dialect makes him seem somewhat amateurish at first glance.

However, Barnes may be the best dialect poet in English, better even than Robert Burns, JOANNA BAILLIE, and later Hugh MacDiarmid. In 1918 Hardy regretted that "The veil of a dialect . . . is disconcerting to many, and to some distasteful," and he was not sure that Barnes should have spelled his words as he did. Nevertheless Barnes's quasi-phonetic spelling has a certain charm, and most probably made him relish and feel his own sonorities more than the standard spelling would have done.

As his contemporaries knew, nothing is further from the truth than the idea that Barnes was an amateur: Hardy rightly called him "an academic poet, akin to the school of Gray and Collins," whose work is "as studied as the so-called simple Bible-narratives are studied." The son of a Dorset farmer, he became one of the most learned men of his time. Like Housman, he combined a very deeply felt sense of place with great and original philological knowledge. He taught classical languages and read something like 60 different languages, including Sanskrit; Welsh; Hebrew; and Persian, whose poetry strongly influenced his own. He was an expert draftsman and wrote a book, still in print, on perspectival drawing. He also wrote historical grammars of various dialects of English. In the obituary that Hardy wrote of Barnes in the *Atheneaum,* he said Barnes was "not only a lyric writer of a high order of genius, but probably the most interesting link between present and past forms of rural life that England possessed." (In addition to the obituary, Hardy wrote "The LAST SIGNAL" as an elegy to Barnes, and he later edited and introduced a selection of his poetry.)

WILLIAM ALLINGHAM, who collected ballads and praised the sense of evocative strangeness to be found in them, invited Barnes to visit him in 1865. Allingham describes in his diary "B's old-fashioned ways, his gaiters, his long knitted purse which he ties up in a knot, broad brimmed hat, homely speech." He brought Barnes to visit ALFRED, LORD TENNYSON, who also admired Barnes; they had a hilarious discussion about Darwin and the significance of evolution. Tennyson said much about what he was thinking of in *IN MEMORIAM A.H.H.:* "Time is nothing. Are we not all part of Deity?" Barnes, a bachelor of divinity and rector of Winterborne Came, tried to keep up his part of the conversation, suggesting, probably with a kind of anxiety at the temptation it represented, "Pantheism?" Tennyson responded darkly, "Well! I think I believe in Pantheism, of a sort," and later told Allingham that Barnes "is not accustomed to strong views theologic."

That was because for Barnes time was *not* nothing. For Barnes, time passes and with it passes one's early life, and those one knew in the past. Pantheism is a temptation to him in his poetry, a sense that at least the natural world does not change, even as our relationship to it does. The natural world allows us to measure in sadness and regret how far we have changed, but also what it continues to offer to our children. We can take an intense vicarious pleasure in their relation to a world which is still there for them to respond to as we once did but no longer do.

There is a sense in which the near-pantheism of Barnes is like that of WILLIAM WORDSWORTH, at least the Wordsworth of "TINTERN ABBEY." But Barnes is very much unlike Wordsworth in his completely unsolipsistic temperament. He is lonely much of the time in his poetry, but that loneliness is not Wordsworthian solitude. It is a sense of the loss of those who have grown or died, including one son who died at three, and his beloved wife, Julia Miles, who died at 47 in 1852 of breast cancer. Some of his best poetry arises out of his lifelong sense of missing her, such as "The WIFE A-LOST." Where Wordsworth makes others elements in the natural world to which he learns his own unique relation, Barnes fully acknowledges their reality and expresses his love for them. His poems are often gifts to their addressees, invitations to a shared experience.

For Barnes that experience is partly the experience of the local language he so relished. He published three books of poems "in the Dorset dialect," as well as books in "common English." Sometimes he would write two versions of the same poem, and in every case it is easy to see that the dialect poem was the first version, the standard English poem a rendering of the dialect. There is a strong sense that writing in a mother tongue was, for him, the link with the past and the world that he loved so much. His philology is a way of seeing the persistence of the past even in a present whose language has become more self-consciously "adult." There is great pleasure in reading Barnes's dialect poetry, not only the pleasure of losing oneself in the world it preserves; it is the pleasure of being invited to do so, being invited to join a genius like Barnes in the pleasures of recollecting what is timeless even as we experience the depredations of time.

That invitation feels particularly strong because the dialect is not framed, as it is in Hardy's novels, by standard English. The poems present themselves as they are: deeply sophisticated in their construction and the subtlety of their thought, but without a knowingly sophisticated intelligence presenting them as a kind of pastoral slumming that we can enjoy. (Francis Turner Palgrave, a month after Barnes's death, called him a "true idyllist" for whom pastoral never descended into the artificial.) For Barnes the language of the poems was exactly what made it such a pleasure to write them, and the pleasure was total. It was for him, too, a link to the past that otherwise passes away.

See also "CHILDHOOD"; "LWONESOMENESS"; "POLLY BE-EN UPSIDES WI' TOM"; "TURNSTILE, THE"; "VAÏCES THAT BE GONE, THE; ZILVER-WEED THE."

BIBLIOGRAPHY

Allingham, William. *William Allingham: A Diary*. Edited by H. Allingham and D. Radford. New York: Penguin, 1985.

Hardy, Thomas. Review of *Poems of Rural Life in the Dorset Dialect*. *New Quarterly Magazine* (October 1879). Reprinted in *Thomas Hardy's Personal Writings: Prefaces, Literary Opinions, Reminiscences*, edited by Harold Orel. 94–100. London: Macmillan, 1990.

Levy, William Turner. *William Barnes: The Man and the Poems*. Dorchester, England: Longmans, 1960.

Parias, James W. *William Barnes*. Boston: Twayne Publishers, 1984.

Scott, Leader. *The Life of William Barnes: Poet and Philologist, by his Daughter, Lucy Baxter* ("Leader Scott"). 1887. Reprint, St. Clair Shores, Mich.: Scholarly Press, 1971.

"BATTLE OF BLENHEIM, THE" ROBERT SOUTHEY (1798) This is one of the most famous of the myriad poems ROBERT SOUTHEY published in the *Morning Post*, with which he had a contract to contribute verse regularly, and derives from the period in which (under the influence of William Godwin) he still fancied himself a political radical. The poem retains a grim power not unlike that of the *Lyrical Ballads* that WILLIAM WORDSWORTH and Southey's close friend SAMUEL TAYLOR COLERIDGE published the same year. However, it is more characteristic of Southey in its allusion to an actual historical event and in the topically parodic tone with which it skewers those who support British power against the possibilities of peace and freedom that had been promised by the French Revolution, of which Southey, like Coleridge, had been an enthusiastic supporter.

"The Battle of Blenheim" might be compared to *Lyrical Ballads* in its structure and in the simplicity of its language. A farmer and his grandchildren are resting at the end of the day, and the poem consists largely of conversation between them in simple language. The farmer, Kaspar, is the straight man, perhaps knowingly, and his granddaughter Wilhelmine plays the role of the wise child, like the little girl in Wordsworth's "We Are Seven." Her young brother finds a skull as he is playing by a stream, and Kaspar takes it from him, remarking that he finds skulls frequently. They belong to the soldiers who died at the Battle of Blenheim, of which Kaspar professes to understand very little, but which we can summarize as follows. It was fought on August 13, 1704, by the forces of England and her allies, in particular the Austrian commander Prince Eugene of Savoy, under the leadership of the duke of Marlborough, against the French and Bavarian troops who were seeking control of Bavaria (now southern Germany) to pursue their goal of the unifying the great Catholic powers of France and Spain, essentially under the rule of the great French king Louis XIV. After the Glorious Revolution of 1688, England was a nervously Protestant country under the reign of William and Mary, and at William's death (1702), Queen Anne sought to counter the establishment of France as a preeminent Catholic power. William had suspected that Marlborough had Catholic, pro-Jacobite sympathies, but he proved himself loyal to Anne and to England's Protestant cause. He was the greatest military genius in English history, and the Battle of Blenheim was a famous victory, perhaps the decisive battle of the war which ended up preventing the unification of France and Spain.

In "The Battle of Blenheim," Southey laments Britain's traditional francophobia, now intensified by the fear that France will export revolution. The poem expresses anger that the lives of ordinary people, whose fates will not be affected by the outcome of any war, except perhaps for the worse, should be sacrificed to the calculations of those with political power. Kaspar's skulls belong to some of the "many thousand men . . . slain in that great victory" (ll. 23–24), a figure he gives accurately, since the number slain that single day was more than 20,000, out of a combined total of about 112,000, or nearly 20 percent of the soldiers. Twenty thousand more were wounded.

It is left to Wilhelmine and to some extent, Peterkin, Kaspar's grandchildren, to wonder of what use was this battle seen by their great-grandfather. Kaspar has no answer to this question, since to them it was essentially no use at all. It nevertheless became a rallying cry in England for jingoistic demagoguery after the duke of Marlborough decisively and stunningly defeated the French and Bavarian forces threatening Vienna. It is to this the poem objects, with passion and power—enough passion and power, indeed, that the young PERCY BYSSHE SHELLEY thought of Southey as a kindred spirit, as can be seen in some of Shelley's far greater poems of parodic rage, such as "The Mask of Anarchy."

BIBLIOGRAPHY

Bromwich, David. "Of the Mule Breed." *London Review of Books* (May 21, 1998). Available online by subscription. URL: www.lrb.com.uk/v20/n10/brom01_.html. Accessed March 16, 2009.

Butler, Marilyn. *Romantics, Rebels, and Reactionaries: English Literature and Its Background, 1760–1830.* New York: Oxford University Press, 1982.

De Quincey, Thomas. *Recollections of the Lakes and the Lake Poets.* Edited with an introduction by David Wright. Harmondsworth, England: Penguin, 1970.

Hazlitt, William. *Spirit of the Age; or, Contemporary Portraits.* London: Oxford University Press, 1970.

Perry, Seamus. "Southey's Genius for Repression." *London Review of Books* (January 26, 2006). Available online by subscription. URL: www.lrb.com.uk/v28/n02/perr01_.html. Accessed March 16, 2009.

Storey, Mark. *Robert Southey: A Life.* New York: Oxford University Press, 1997.

BEACHY HEAD CHARLOTTE TURNER SMITH (1807)

Beachy Head was published posthumously and is unfinished, but it is one of CHARLOTTE TURNER SMITH's best poems. Smith was one of the most important of immediate influences on WILLIAM WORDSWORTH and SAMUEL TAYLOR COLERIDGE, and in *Beachy Head* she produces a meditative blank verse that allows her to think things through by free-associating on landscape—exactly as Wordsworth was doing in poems like *The PRELUDE* (which Smith would almost certainly not have known) and "TINTERN ABBEY" (which she would have), as well as in Wordsworth's very early poem "An Evening Walk" in which he quotes the phrase "a happy child" from her poem "To the South Downs." *Beachy Head* is not Smith's first ambitious poem in blank verse, but it is her greatest, and it repays comparison and contrast with Wordsworth.

In one of her extensive notes on the poem, mainly concerned with the details of the natural history she describes, Smith corrects Shakespeare, who "describes cuckoo buds as being yellow. He probably meant the numerous ranunculi, or Marsh marigolds (*caltha palustris*) . . . but poets have never been botanists" (note at l. 591; the allusion is to a song in *Love's Labour's Lost*). There is some asperity in her irony here, since her own botanical expertise would seem to deny her the title of being a poet. But it is better to see the novelty that she is claiming for herself in *Beachy Head,* a novelty that consists in the minute and accurate representation of nature in all its extraordinary detail. (Sir WALTER SCOTT was among the admirers of her descriptive powers.) Smith is here a major forerunner of JOHN CLARE; GERARD MANLEY HOPKINS, who also devoted himself to extremely fine studies of natural phenomena; and THOMAS HARDY; as well as such 20th-century poets of minute natural observation as May Swenson and A. R. Ammons, and she is implicitly, if lightly, rebuking Erasmus Darwin, whose 1789 *Loves of the Plants* allows rhetoric to add artificial luster to an interest that nature itself should supply.

Darwin tends to use the wonderful strangeness of nature as a caricature of human beings; his nature brings Charles Dickens to mind. But Smith follows the lead of John Aikin (brother of ANNA LAETITIA BARBAULD), whose 1777 book *An Essay on the Application of Natural History to Poetry,* which she footnotes, complains about the tendency in poetry to rely on "a too cursory and general survey of objects, without exploring their minuter distinctions and mutual relations; [which] is only to be rectified by accurate and attentive observation, conducted upon somewhat of a scientific plan" (p. 10). Smith's footnote alludes to Aikin's complaint (pp. 7–9) that every poet likes to follow Shakespeare and Milton in describing evening as associated with the hum of the beetle, but in her poem she instead describes the far more unusual "nightjar chasing fern-flies" (l. 514), an image she proceeds to explain, and which is one of the many "all unlike the poet's fabling dreams / Describing Arcady" (ll. 209–210; here she is describing human behavior in the real natural world).

These minute particulars coexist in *Beachy Head* with the largest and most comprehensive view of England, both present and past. The poem belongs to the genre called the topographic, or loco-descriptive, poem; its invention as a genre goes back to John Denham's 1642 poem *Cooper's Hill*. In Smith's hands it becomes deeply and intensely romantic (see ROMANTICISM). She represents herself as standing or sitting on Beachy Head, which juts out into the English Channel, and gazing on the land, water, boats, and landscapes about her. The poem begins at sunrise, but noon and sunset follow soon after, and it becomes clear that she has been lost in descriptive reverie all day long. After dark falls, she begins thinking about the history of the place and the history of England from before the Norman Conquest to the present day. She returns to the present to think about the people around her in the landscape, but also about other landscapes in England, brought to mind in her associative meditation. Her prospect and her knowledge are perspicacious: She can know that the different types of people who inhabit the world around her will misjudge each other's fortune and happiness, and this leads her to a meditation on happiness (ll. 255ff.), which in turn leads to autobiographical reflection on her lost childhood and the places to which she has since been compelled to go. She calls herself "An early worshipper at Nature's shrine" (l. 346), a phrase which could be from Wordsworth's *The Prelude*.

Unlike Wordsworth, however, Smith does not take nature as an allegory or a spur to pure introspection. What she does instead is to infuse the landscape around her with every intense and accurate perception that is important to her. Smith loves to quote, just as she loves to footnote, and what she does at Beachy Head is to make her surroundings a kind of support for restlessly observant accumulations: She sees the significance of everything—the history, biology, geology (she is fascinated by the appearance of seashells well inland and is ready to accept the geological metamorphoses that the fossils record; she even writes about what turn out to be mammoth skeletons), social customs, and modes of labor of the world she observes. And she sees the appositeness of quotation, from Virgil, Milton, Shakespeare, and a host of contemporary or near-contemporary writers.

These quotations do not veil the reality that Smith is observing; rather, it is the reality that gives the quotations more sense than they might have had in their original, more "poeticized" use. Her vision is intense and clarifying, in ways that Wordsworth put to use for much longer interior meditations. But there is something bracing about Smith's strenuous vividness of vision that makes *Beachy Head* a nearly perfect poem of its kind, a kind of demonstration that nature is as interesting as the great poetry that describes it. Smith, even more than Wordsworth, gives nature its due.

BIBLIOGRAPHY

Aikin, John. *An Essay on the Application of Natural History to Poetry*. 1777. Reprint, New York: Garland, 1970.

Fletcher, Loraine. *Charlotte Smith: A Critical Biography*. New York: St. Martin's Press, 1998.

Labbe, Jacqueline M. *Charlotte Smith: Romanticism, Poetry, and the Culture of Gender*. New York: Palgrave, 2003.

Smith, Charlotte. *The Poems of Charlotte Smith*. Edited by Stuart Curran. New York: Oxford University Press, 1993.

Quinney, Laura. *Poetics of Disappointment: Wordsworth to Ashbery*. Charlottesville: University Press of Virginia, 1999.

Zimmerman, Sarah MacKenzie. *Romanticism, Lyricism, and History*. New York: State University of New York Press, 1999.

BEDDOES, THOMAS LOVELL (1803–1849) In 1876, ROBERT BROWNING missed being appointed professor of poetry at Oxford (as a Congregationalist, he had not attended Oxford, and though he had an honorary degree from Oxford, he was still not eligible for the post). The world therefore lost its chance for his proposed inaugural lecture on "Beddoes: A Forgotten Oxford Poet." Thomas Lovell Beddoes, intensely shy, irascible, gay, politically radical, had died a suicide in Basel, Switzerland, 27 years earlier, having more or less abandoned England in 1825 to study anatomy with the great Johann Friedrich Blumenbach in Göttingen, Germany. Blumenbach was one of the first anatomists to see humans as part of an evolutionary system (unfortunately, it was he who propounded the doctrine of the different races that we still live with today), and as such was part of the great scientific revolution that culminated in Charles Darwin's earth-shattering *Origin of Species* in 1859. He described Beddoes as the best student he had ever taught. Beddoes was eventually appointed professor of medicine in Zurich, where he went when his radical writings made him persona non grata in Germany, but he was too radical for the climate there as well.

Beddoes himself was fascinated by the evidence for evolution (which was evident well before Darwin, whose theory explained *how* it happened), and he saw in it one way of approaching the great question that animates his poetry: whether there is any possible transcendence of biological existence. This question is, of course, central to the single work to which he devoted his most intense poetic ambition, the pseudo-Jacobean, pseudo-Goethean drama *Death's Jest Book,* from which editors and anthologists have drawn Beddoes's best-known lyrics and songs. That work is subtitled *The Fool's Tragedy,* and it is in the mode of the Jacobean revenge tragedies that had obsessed Beddoes from his childhood. The play is set in Egypt and Silesia at the end of the 13th century; the fool Isbrand is the avenger, and life therefore is a tale told not quite by Macbeth's idiot but at least by Shakespeare's fool. The best parts of this wild and undisciplined work are the songs, especially "The Ghost's Moonshine," sung as part of the violent denouement.

Beddoes's other obsession was PERCY BYSSHE SHELLEY; indeed, he was a guarantor of the publication of Shelley's posthumous poems in 1824 and one of the first people outside Shelley's own circle to champion his poetry. (Beddoes's interest in science is also Shelleyan and forms a connection between him and Browning, who was also obsessed with Shelley. Beddoes later became friends with Mary Shelley and WALTER SAVAGE LANDOR. He was intensely shy and self-destructive. A native morbidity was intensified by his medical studies (and by the fact that he contracted septicimia through infection by a cadaver he was examining), though his suicide ultimately seems to have been precipitated by the breakup of a romantic relationship with a young German actor.

Beddoes did not make friends easily, but he was championed in his own day by contemporaries like GEORGE DARLEY and later revived by Browning and Sir Edmund Gosse. It should also be noted that some of his poems are hilariously funny. He is one of the most interesting and intense of the poets in the canon of minor English poetry, and his best poems are nearly perfect.

See also "PHANTOM WOOER, THE"; "SONG"; "SONG OF THE STYGIAN NAIADES."

BIBLIOGRAPHY

Beddoes, Thomas Lovell. *Complete Works of Thomas Lovell Beddoes, edited with a memoir by Sir Edmund Gosse and decorated by the Dance of Death of Hans Holbein.* London: Fanfrolico Press, 1928.

Bradshaw, Michael. *Resurrection Songs: The Poetry of Thomas Lovell Beddoes.* Burlington, Vt.: Ashgate Press, 2001.

Donner, Henry Wolfgang. *Thomas Lovell Beddoes: The Making of a Poet.* Oxford: Blackwell, 1935.

"BEER" CHARLES STUART CALVERLEY (1861)

"Beer" is a poem in praise of drinking, in the Horatian mode that CHARLES STUART CALVERLEY loved and imitated, especially the great ode "Nunc est bibendum" ("Now it is time to drink"). Every educated poet loved Horace, considered the greatest and most urbane of Latin lyricists, and Calverley reminds one most of LORD BYRON in his imitations of Horace. The way he imitates is Byronic as well, which is to say that he loves quoting other poets whose language he considers too stylized, arch, or archaic, and turning those quotations to comic use. The effect is that of the mild and cheering tipsiness that comes from relishing poetic language without allowing it to become emotionally taxing—the tipsiness that beer offers as well. He can relish and offer us the chance to relish the language of the poetic tags that he quotes and make us feel that the stateliness or even portliness of language itself guarantees the same sense of *exemption* that the end of the poem offers, where he conveys a sense of post-prandial satisfaction in thinking that fate cannot touch him, for he is replete.

Calverley is probably thinking of the famous speech in act 3, scene 1 of Shakespeare's *Measure for Measure,* where Duke Vincentio tells a condemned man not to worry about his approaching death: "Thou hast nor youth nor age; / But, as it were, an after-dinner's sleep, / Dreaming on both." This is the truth he accedes to and therefore "soothly says" it, a phrase he quotes from the Bible but also uses in his own translation of Theocritus's 24th idyll, where it is applied to the good dinner that Herakles (Hercules) has eaten.

The praise of beer in the poem is in a tradition that in English will remind one of THOMAS HOOD's poems of human satisfaction. Byron also wrote about drinking, but in Byron it is always excessive; in Calverley it is part of a general account of what satisfaction and happiness can look like. Byron also liked to quote, as he says in *DON JUAN,* but does not seem to make it an object of happiness itself. Calverley does, as he says in the passage where he explains at hilarious length why he is quoting William Cowper's poem "John Gilpin" accurately despite the fact that it does not quite apply. (The quotations will all be found to come from what were the chestnuts of the 19th century; "in language quant and olden," for example, comes from Henry Wadsworth Longfellow.)

So what is it that makes Calverley happy? The answer is essentially: the contemplation of social pleasures, including the pleasures of contemplation itself. (This is true in his poems on such pleasures as tobacco, "Ode to Tobacco"; and on reading the newspaper, "PEACE: A STUDY.") Quoting poetry is an essential part of this kind of happiness, which helps us to see the natural extension of such happiness in the *writing* of poetry about being happy. "Beer" is an example of a happy poem, a poem its poet was happy to write and that (like beer itself) affords happiness to its readers. It follows the advice that it quotes from an ode of Horace's addressed to Virgil: "Dulce est desipere in loco"—"It is sweet even to the wise sometimes to be foolish" (that is, to be tipsy).

BIBLIOGRAPHY

Auden, W. H. Introduction to *The Oxford Book of Light Verse.* New York: New York Review of Books, 2004. xxii–xxxii.

Babington, Percy Lancelot. *Browning & Calverley; or, Poem and Parody.* London: John Castle, 1925.

Ince, Richard Basil. *Calverley and Some Cambridge Wits of the Nineteenth Century.* London: G. Richards and H. Toulmin at the Cayme Press, 1929.

"BINSEY POPLARS" GERARD MANLEY HOPKINS (1879) GERARD MANLEY HOPKINS was a very subtle and observant naturalist, as his poetry and his journals attest. He loved both nature and the God of nature, and he saw nature as the sign of God. In 1870, in his journal, replete as it already was with amazing, detailed description of natural scenery, he wrote of a bluebell: "I know the beauty of the Lord by it." For Hopkins, nature signifies God because it is so momentous and unexpected a creation, and it is "charged with the grandeur of God," as he had put it just two years earlier, in "GOD'S GRANDEUR."

"Binsey Poplars" should be seen as a kind of counterweight to that poem, since here the emphasis is on the fragility of the natural world and not on its holy inexhaustibility. Hopkins's reading of the late medieval philosopher and theologian Duns Scotus had focused him on the bare particular *thisness* (haecceity) of every individual thing in the world, every one of which is therefore "especial" (l. 24). (Hopkins's 1879 poem "Duns Scotus's Oxford," written within a week or two of "Binsey Poplars," about Scotus's 1301 visit to the town where Hopkins had been an undergraduate and was now serving as assistant to the parish priest, celebrates the bare particularity of the things—"*this* air . . . *these* leaves and water, *these* walls" (emphasis added)—that they both perceive and which therefore bind them across the centuries.)

These two aspects are, of course, complementary. The fact that nature matters everywhere means both that it is everywhere and that it can be harmed everywhere. For Hopkins, nature is the place the soul or self can flow into to feel God's omnipresence, and it therefore represents not only God's overwhelming and overwhelmingly generous ubiquity but also the place where the soul can feel in the presence of God. Any harm done to its least aspect, then, is harm also done to God's presence.

That presence is persistently felt in Hopkins as a kind of intense pulsating rhythm in the way the world accommodates itself to language. Language is also a natural richness, and it is for this reason that Hopkins's intense prosody can represent, embody, or exemplify the human soul's response to the world—to a world shaped like the soul that belongs to it or to the grandeur of God.

"Binsey Poplars" is a remarkable exploration of these themes, or rather a remarkable enactment of them. Binsey was a small town near Oxford, and the poplars (as the subtitle tells us) were felled in 1879. Hopkins undoubtedly wrote the poem the day he perceived their absence, on March 13. The poem, like all poems of grief or mourning, seeks to find in its own language a substitute for the thing it mourns. (In Hopkins's poems of praise, the poet seeks to find something answering the fullness it seeks to represent; these are two sides of the same coin.) The row of poplars finds a kind of ghostly avatar in the poem's repetitions, its rhymes and alliterations. The complexity of their crowns, their "airy cages," is caught by the complexity of the poetic form, in particular by the cagelike alliterations that allow meaning to come through the airy forms of consonants framing different sets of vowels ("Quelled or quenched" [l. 2]).

And yet the poplars have suffered the blow of the ax, and the lamentable repetition of its striking can be heard in the third line, describing the poplars now: "All felled, felled, are all felled," as they are by only "ten or twelve, only ten or twelve / Strokes of havoc" (ll. 20–21). (Where alliteration and rhyme do not carry through the poem, assonance and off-rhyme do, as in the relation of the sounds in *felled* and *twelve*.) Their beautiful forms and shadows are in the past, the openness of the shadows of their branches running across meadow and river and bank. Now things are flat and uniform. This allows for the moral of the second stanza, which asks us, like WILLIAM WORDSWORTH, to touch "with gentle hand / For there is a spirit in the woods" ("NUTTING"). The moral indeed alludes to the Crucifixion, which was so deep an object of Hopkins's meditations. "O if we knew what we do," he laments, and that lamentation alludes to Christ's words on the cross: "Forgive them, father, for they know not what they do."

If the poem had ended with this second stanza, it would have pointed a powerful moral lesson. But Hopkins goes much further still, and what makes it a great poem is its last stanza. In consenting to injure nature and to try to reshape it to our materialist ends, we consent to the way the "Strokes of havoc unselve / The sweet especial scene." *Unselve* is a deep word here: it does not mean merely, or primarily, that we destroy the natural landscape. Rather, we destroy its relation to our own self. Our selves are hid in nature with God, and in destroying the scene we are destroying ourselves, destroying the place where a part of our self lives and has its being.

It is for this reason that Hopkins must end the poem with the tremendous last lines, the nursery-rhyme repetitions of its ending. The poplars are gone, and he is like a little child, comforting himself in his misery with the repetitions of what is lost, with the words that are all that are left of the memory, and all that are left for him to hold onto.

BIBLIOGRAPHY

Bridges, Robert. Preface to *Notes in the Poems of Gerard Manley Hopkins.* Edited with additional poems, notes, and a biographical introduction by W. H. Gardner, 94–101. New York: Oxford University Press, 1948.

Gardner, W. H. *Gerard Manley Hopkins (1844–1889): A Study of Poetic Idiosyncrasy in Relation to Poetic Tradition.* New Haven, Conn.: Yale University Press, 1949.

———. Introduction to *Poems and Prose of Gerard Manley Hopkins.* Edited by W. H. Gardner, xiii–xxxvi. Harmondsworth, Middlesex, England: Penguin, 1963.

Hartman, Geoffrey. *The Unmediated Vision: An Interpretation of Wordsworth, Hopkins, Rilke, and Valery.* New Haven, Conn.: Yale University Press, 1954.

Hopkins, Gerard Manley. *Gerard Manley Hopkins: Selected Letters.* Edited by Catherine Phillips. New York: Oxford University Press, 1990.

Miller, J. Hillis. "Gerard Manley Hopkins." In *The Disappearance of God: Five Nineteenth-Century Writers,* 270–359. Cambridge, Mass.: Belknap Press of Harvard University Press, 1963.

White, Norman. *Hopkins: A Literary Biography.* New York: Oxford University Press, 1992.

BLAKE, WILLIAM (1757–1827) A couple of years before his "official" death, William Blake signed himself in an autograph album belonging to William Upcott, "WILLIAM BLAKE / one who is very much delighted with being in good Company // Born 28 NOVr 1757 in London & has died several times since." Blake's obituary writers quoted this piece of whimsicality as evidence of his madness—the madness that made him claim that among the good company he had loved to be in was that of various biblical figures such as the prophets Ezekiel and Isaiah and King Saul. But Blake was not mad, however fierce he was in his commitment to his own vision. To ask whether Blake "really" believed that he saw and conversed with the figures he described is to mistake what Blake would have meant by such words as *really, belief,* and *saw.* As one of his "Proverbs of Hell" puts it: "The fool sees not the same tree that a wise man sees." Vision is not the registration of what is in the empirical world but a power of the imaginative mind, and it is this which makes it possible "To see a world in a grain of sand" ("Auguries of Innocence"). So Blake's autograph in Upcott's album is not entirely whimsical, and indeed he commented about it that no artist could simply write an autograph "helter skelter," and therefore the humor in it has some point. *Died* probably has its slang meaning (as in Shakespeare and elsewhere) of sexual climax. For Blake, the connection between death and sexuality is the opposition they both meant to the empirical universe in which all living beings are "closed" to each other, radically separated by an atomistic individuality counter to all things spiritual, transcendent, and imaginative in human life. Good company for Blake meant something very important as well: As he says in the "Proverbs of Hell," "The most sublime act is to set another before you." "Before you" here means both to give precedence and (perhaps more importantly) to interact with another person, to take another as being as fully human as yourself.

For Blake, "fully human," means holy and divine. The English diarist Henry Crabb Robinson shrewdly assessed Blake as hard to fix "between Christianity, Platonism, and Spinozism." In conversation, as they were walking home together one night in December of 1825, Crabb Robinson (who was at the center of the literary social network of romantic and early Victorian literature) was skeptical of Blake's self-proclaimed Christianity, and according to Crabb Robinson, Blake replied, "'He is the only God. But then,' he added, 'and so am I, and so are you.'" ALGERNON CHARLES SWINBURNE, who wrote the first serious book about Blake, quoted approvingly Blake's unexpected appreciation of Voltaire. Voltaire was for Blake one of the prime representatives of the Enlightenment rationalism that he thought of as seeing the universe as a complicated, externalized, dead machine—"a mill with complicated wheels" as he puts it in his page-long prose tract "There is No Natural Religion." But later Blake claimed that he had seen Voltaire in a vision in which the French philosophe had said to him, "I blasphemed the Son of Man and it shall be forgiven me; but my enemies blasphemed the Holy Ghost in me, and it shall not be forgiven them."

This is the heart of Blake's political as well as his poetical commitment; the two join in his sense of poetic prophecy. Christianity, Platonism, and Spinozism come together in Blake's transcendent sense that Christianity calls upon all of us to see that everything that lives is holy, that all are Jesus Christ, and that all have the Holy Ghost within them. For this reason Blake denied to Crabb Robinson that there were any purely evil: "That was the fault of Plato—he knew nothing but of the Virtues and Vices And good & evil. There is nothing in all that. Everything is good in God's eyes." Crabb Robinson was surprised that this view coexisted with Blake's saying that all beings are impure, not only Dante but even heavenly beings, and he reported Blake asking: "Do you think there is any purity in God's eyes? The angels in heaven are no more so than we." Crabb Robinson added that Blake "extended this to the Supreme Being. He is liable to error too." Crabb Robinson was baffled by "these metaphysical speculation[s] so nearly allied to the most opposite systems." Thus, Blake could not only compare himself to Plato's major philosophical avatar, Socrates (who Crabb Robinson noted also conversed with a spirit), but say, "I was Socrates," adding, as if correcting himself, "A sort of brother."

What Crabb Robinson understood as "the most opposite systems" should be seen from the perspective of Blake's central claim that "opposition is true friendship," and from his doctrine of contraries: "Without Contraries is no progression. Attraction and Repulsion, Reason and Energy, Love and Hate, are necessary to Human existence. From these contraries spring what the religious call Good & Evil. Good is the passive that obeys Reason. Evil is the active springing from Energy. Good is Heaven. Evil is Hell." So both are necessary, since "Energy is eternal delight," and this is what makes possible the "Marriage of Heaven and Hell" (the Blake book from which these remarks are drawn).

It is not surprising that Crabb Robinson could not quite make sense of Blake. Like everyone else who had taken notice of him before the time that WILLIAM BUTLER YEATS undertook an intensive study of Blake's prophetic books, Crabb Robinson thought of Blake primarily as an artist—engraver, draughtsman, and occasional watercolorist—who had written some stunning lyrics when he was younger but whose poetical work had devolved into incomprehensibility by the time he came to what are now described as the "Prophetic Books." In particular, Blake's *SONGS OF INNOCENCE AND OF EXPERIENCE* impressed CHARLES LAMB, WILLIAM WORDSWORTH, SAMUEL TAYLOR COLERIDGE, and William Hazlitt. The latter two did not like his graphic art but loved the poems. Hazlitt, in particular, understood Blake's essential perspective and wrote to Crabb Robinson, "They are beautiful & only too deep for the vulgar: he has no sense of the ludicrous & to a God a worm crawling in a privy is as worthy an object as any other, all being to him indifferent, so to Blake the Chimney Sweeper &c." In a letter from 1818, Coleridge called Blake "a man of Genius . . . certainly, a mystic *emphatically*. You perhaps smile at *my* calling another poet, a *Mystic;* but verily I am in the very mire of commonplace common-sense compared with Mr Blake, apo- or rather anacalyptic Poet, and Painter!" (quoted in Bentley *Critical Heritage* 1975, 54).

Yet what reputation Blake had in his lifetime was that of a graphic artist. Apprenticed as a boy, he became an engraver and it was as an engraver that he read an enormous number of books and heard a prodigious quantity of conversation among the artists, writers, and craftsmen who were producing their works. Much of his autodidactic education derived from the hints he gleaned from these conversations and reading. In his lifetime he would undertake to illustrate *Paradise Lost, The Divine Comedy, The Canterbury Tales,* and *The Book of Job,* as well as a large number of other works, major and minor—including, of course, his own. Blake's view of Enlightenment materialism was partly that of a craftsman who worked very closely with the material world, the world of "mechanical reproduction" (as the literary critic and essayist Walter Benjamin was to call it), which ushered in the Industrial Revolution and the new distinctions between the working-class left-wing movement that Blake participated in and a prosperous mercantile class whose wealth derived in large part from the endless labor of the working class. For Blake, poetry, prophecy, and vision were liberating.

Interestingly, materially, this meant that he invented a new mode of etching—the negative of the standard procedure. In Blake's practice, the *rest* of the plate was corroded away and the writing and designs that he had protected by wax on the surface of the plate remained. Thus, vision arises from the purgation of the material context that makes it invisible. Blake produced his beautiful books, both the writing and the illustration, through this method. And his books were beautiful enough that he was regarded, by the end of his life, as an important painter by some of the major artists of his day.

As a painter, then, he had disciples, though his refusal ever to compromise with authorities on matters of principle made it certain that he would never be financially comfortable (he was even tried for treason for kicking a British soldier out of the garden of the house he was renting). As a poet he was admired for a handful of early poems. But even Swinburne and Alexander Gilchrist (his first and most important biographer) saw only incoherent madness in the prophetic books such as *Urizen* and *Jerusalem.* This was partly, perhaps, because as a poet Blake was writing for himself and could work out his own mythology without needing to compromise (again) with his readers. He expected very few. It was only in the 20th century that assiduous (and continuing) efforts to make sense of that mythology began to yield real insight, most notably in the work of Northrop Frye, and since then in that of Harold Bloom and Laura Quinney.

The outline of Blake's mythology as presented in the prophetic books is clear, it is consistent with the picture of Blake that Crabb Robinson drew. Urizen is the creator of the universe, a godlike figure but also the figure who binds it to material existence. He both represents and finds himself unable to sustain the utter imaginative freedom that infuses life, and so he falls into limitation, first off the Newtonian limitation of sheer rationality. His name is, in fact, his fallen name: Urizen suggests "Ur-horizon," first hemming in of the world. Urizen might be said to impose Newtonian, materialistic, empirical laws on the world of Spirit. Various figures chafe against these laws, most notably Orc, but every movement toward freedom requires the defeat of an enslaver, and therefore we have the repetition of defeat and binding, so that Orc keeps recapitulating Urizen. Even John Milton, greatest of English poets for Blake, succumbs to this dynamic. These contraries are also mirrored in the fruitful opposition between male and female principles within all people, sometimes described as specter (male) and emanation (female). The grandest exposition of these ideas is in *The Four Zoas,* where "Zoa" means something like a life principle. It will help to approximate the four principles more or less as follows: They are forms of gigantic life once unified in Albion (the soul of England and the world), the unfallen essence of humanity, fallen into a material world. Urizen will essentially stand for rational limitation; Luvah (an avatar of Orc) embodies the principle of love his name suggests and attempts to transcend these limitations; while Tharmas is pure natural instinct, and Urthona (an avatar of Los) stands for a lost and fallen creativity within the soul. These are the male specters whose emanations Ahania, Vala, Enion, and Enitharmon, respectively, stand for the fallen aspect of the things each Zoa has lost: the future, the beauty of the world, a sense of wholeness, and fullness (more or less respectively again).

All of this is very rough and will only become meaningful with a reading of the poems. The best way, therefore, into Blake's prophetic books is to read them slowly, feeling the power of each line and passage before trying to make sense of them as wholes. They will make sense, but the same kind of sense that life makes, not the sense of rational and enlightenment reconstructions of life. Blake's poetry is the work of a lifetime, and it should be that for readers, too.

See also "ANGEL, THE"; "BOOK OF THEL, THE"; "CHIMNEY-SWEEPER, THE"; "LAMB THE"; "LONDON"; "NURSE'S SONG"; "TO THE EVENING STAR" "TYGER, THE."

BIBLIOGRAPHY

Bentley, G. E., Jr. *William Blake: The Critical Heritage.* London: Routledge Press, 1975.

Bloom, Harold. *Blake's Apocalypse: A Study in Poetic Argument.* Ithaca, N.Y.: Cornell University Press, 1970.

———. *Poetry and Repression: Revisionism from Blake to Stevens.* New Haven, Conn.: Yale University Press, 1976.

———. *The Visionary Company: A Reading of English Romantic Poetry.* Garden City, N.Y.: Doubleday, 1961.

Damrosch, Leopold. *Symbol and Truth in Blake's Myth.* Princeton, N.J.: Princeton University Press, 1980.

Erdman, David V. *Blake, Prophet against Empire: A Poet's Interpretation of the History of His Own Times.* Princeton, N.J.: Princeton University Press, 1954.

Frye, Northrop. *Fearful Symmetry: A Study of William Blake.* Princeton, N.J.: Princeton University Press, 1947.

Gilchrist, Alexander. *Life of William Blake, with Selections from His Poems and Other Writings.* Totowa, N.J.: Rowman and Littlefield, 1973.

Levinson, Marjorie. "The Book of Thel by William Blake: A Critical Reading." *ELH: English Literary History* 47 (1980): 287–303.

Quinney, Laura. *Literary Power and the Criteria of Truth.* Gainesville: University Press of Florida, 1995.

Swinburne, Algernon Charles. *William Blake: A Critical Essay.* New York: Dutton, 1906.

Thompson, E. P. *Witness against the Beast: William Blake and the Moral Law.* New York: Cambridge University Press, 1993.

"BLESSED DAMOZEL, THE" DANTE GABRIEL ROSSETTI (1847)

This is one of DANTE GABRIEL ROSSETTI's earliest poems, as well as one of his greatest and best known. A quarter of a century after writing it at 18, Rossetti depicted its subject in one of his most famous Pre-Raphaelite paintings. The bottom of the painting (now at the Fogg Museum at Harvard University) has the relevant part of the poem captioned underneath it.

Rossetti was not thinking of any particular person when he wrote the poem. He wanted to rewrite Edgar Allan Poe's "The Raven," or "Annabel Lee" from the point of view of the dead woman, not the surviving man. But that is not quite what he did. Instead he has imagined the woman in heaven and what she would say, and he laments, as mourner, both what has happened and the sad truth that what his imagination hopes is not real.

The imagery is from Rossetti's namesake, the Italian poet Dante. In *The Divine Comedy,* the blessed damozel would be Beatrice, who supervises Dante's journey from hell through purgatory to paradise and then guides him through the fantastic and overwhelming visual phantasmogoria of heaven to where God sits enthroned. No rival to Dante's constantly self-exceeding vision of heaven is imaginable, but it is at least within that tradition that Rossetti writes. He gives us the perspective of the woman, who sees earth from an unimaginable distance. The largeness of space is made palpable by the smallness of Earth, engulfed in a vastness at her Dantesque command, but overwhelming for human contemplation. It is this contrast between her dizzyingly heavenly perspective and the speaker's earth-bound one that makes the poem so powerful. But it is not powerful so much for the grandeur that it imagines but for the way that grandeur is persistently brought back to a terrestrial perspective.

Throughout the poem, the speaker contrasts his experience with the woman's. She has been dead for 10 years, as we know from the perspective of her survivors; but to her, from the perspective of eternity, the 10 years seem scarcely a single day. On the other hand, to the speaker, they seem "ten years of years," so that the converse of the way 10 years reduces to a single day for her is the way a single day seems on the scale of a year to him, and the 10 years more like millennia.

We learn this, crucially, in a parenthetical stanza, and it is within the parentheses where we get the speaker's perspective in full and come to realize that the rest of the poem represents the speaker's wish, not the thing that the poem itself is claiming. It is crucial to see that the poem is claiming to represent what the speaker wants, not (as in Dante) what is true in the world of heaven.

That first parenthesis shows us the truth of things:

> (To one it is ten years of years.
> . . . Yet now, and in this place,
> Surely she leaned o'er me—her hair
> Fell all about my face . . .
> Nothing: the autumn-fall of leaves.
> The whole year sets apace.)

The one to whom it is 10 years of years is, of course, the speaker himself. After that reticent, self-effacing entrance, though, he speaks in his own voice, using the first-person singular. And we see the situation in which he is uttering these words: It is autumn, and the autumn leaves have brushed his face and made him want to think that he felt her hair. Notice the skill with which Rossetti contrasts the complaint about the near-eternity of the speaker's experience of loss with his recognition that time is passing as swiftly as ever: The whole year sets the fall of leaves apace.

The next parenthetical stanza similarly contrasts wishful fantasy from a heavenly perspective with the truth from the earthly perspective of her adoring survivor:

> Her voice was like the voice the stars
> Had when they sang together.
>
> (Ah, sweet! Even now, in that bird's song,
> Strove not her accents there,
> Fain to be harkened? When those bells
> Possess'd the mid-day air,
> Strove not her steps to reach my side
> Down all the echoing stair?)

As the fall of leaves had reminded him of time, which in the poet's wishful imagination he transmuted into eternity, so too does the sound of birdsong make him think that she is speaking and that her voice is like the music of the spheres. But the parenthesis tells us the reality from which the fantasy derives. The speaker hears the song of a bird and the chiming of bells and imagines that they are the distant echoes or representatives of her heavenly presence.

The third parenthetical stanza marks an advance in the speaker's self-understanding, as he realizes that even his most ecstatic, wishful, hopeful fantasies of where she is just then and what she is doing are not enough. He has imagined her praying to God for the time to come when "'We two will stand'" beside the shrine of God, the time to come when

> "We two will lie i' the shadow of
> That living mystic tree
> Within whose secret growth the Dove
> Is sometimes felt to be,
> While every leaf that His plumes touch
> Saith His Name audibly."

But this hope already has too much of despair and impossibility in it, as the parenthetical response shows:

> (Alas! We two, we two, thou say'st!
> Yea, one wast thou with me
> That once of old. But shall God lift
> To endless unity
> The soul whose likeness with thy soul
> Was but its love for thee?)

> "We two," she said, "will seek the groves
> Where the lady Mary is. . . .

The speaker feels that his distance from her is unbridgeable. She is Beatrice-like and divine: The only thing he shares with her is the love she embodies and inspires. But when she was alive, he did feel at one with her; now he thinks this can never happen again. He laments the words he has imagined for her, the first-person plural that looks like community and union but is not. And she does not hear his parenthesis, since her next line insists on the phrase he has wished to repudiate: "We two, thou say'st!" he has lamented, but "'We two,' she *said*" is how the poem insists she continues her speech.

She continues her hopeful account of what their love will be like together in the afterlife, but by now we know that this account is also impossible. It is impossible because the speaker knows that she belongs to the realm of an extravagant imagination appropriate for her but beyond the wildest hopes of the human who is imagining the impossible. The last two parentheses, punctuating the last stanza, make this vivid. In the speaker's imagination, his beloved becomes aware that her ecstatic prophecy is as much about someone lost in the gulfs of space and time as his imagination of her is. If, like Poe, he is describing the absolute gap between life and death, only from her point of view, that gap is no less absolute for that. This is what the last two stanzas realize, as he imagines her finally becoming aware of that gap:

> "There will I ask of Christ the Lord
> Thus much for him and me—
> Only to live as once on earth
> With Love—only to be,
> As then awhile, for ever now,
> Together, I and he."

> She gazed and listen'd and then said,
> Less sad of speech than mild—
> "All this is when he comes." She ceased.
> The light thrilled toward her, filled
> With angels in strong, level flight.
> Her eyes prayed, and she smiled.

> (I saw her smile.) But soon their path
> Was vague in distant spheres;
> And then she cast her arms along
> The golden barriers,
> And laid her face between her hands,
> And wept. (I heard her tears.)

She listens and apparently hears nothing, which is why she responds with a mildness verging on sadness. But what is she listening for? Christ to answer her prayer? Or the voice of the speaker? Whatever it is, her prayer is not answered, and she must now exhibit the impossible patience that is his lament throughout the poem. The angels approach her but then disappear, and presumably she must go with them, sooner or later. For this reason she smiles with hope but weeps with knowledge, and the speaker recognizes in those parentheses in the last stanza his imagination of her recognition of the sad truth—that they will never live as once in earth, with love.

It is fascinating to see not only how Rossetti's punctuation, especially the parentheses, but also his versification contribute to the meaning of the poem. Take, for example, the stanza quoted above, beginning "We two will lie. . . ." Like all the six-line stanzas in the poem, its rhyme scheme is *xaxaxa* (where only the even-numbered lines rhyme). This is a strong rhyme scheme, focusing attention on the rhyme, and most people will have the sense of the poem as rhyming *ababab,* although it does not. (For another example, see also LEWIS CARROLL'S "THE MAD GARDENERS'S SONG.") In that stanza, though, it comes close to doing so, since *of* rhymes with *Dove.* This sets up the obvious concluding rhyme *love* for line 5, but instead we get the assonant half-rhyme *touch* (see also echo of these rhymes in lines 115–120, where the assonant *dumb* half-rhymes with *love* and *approve*). The word brings us up short, makes us realize that what will have happened between them is the heartbreaking ephemerality of human contact, of touch, and not the permanence of the Dantesque love ("which moves the sun and other stars," as the last line of the *Divine Comedy* puts it), which the speaker desires and imagines his love desiring.

See also PRE-RAPHAELITE POETRY.

BIBLIOGRAPHY

Ash, Russell. *Dante Gabriel Rossetti.* New York: Harry N. Abrams, 1995.

McGann, Jerome J. *Dante Gabriel Rossetti and the Game That Must Be Lost.* New Haven, Conn.: Yale University Press, 2000.

Rossetti, Dante Gabriel. *Correspondence of Dante Gabriel Rossetti.* Edited by William E. Fredeman. Rochester, N.Y.: D. S. Brewer, 2002.

"BOOK OF THEL, THE" **WILLIAM BLAKE (1789–1790)** "The Book of Thel" is the first in a series of illuminated books that constitute WILLIAM BLAKE'S major work and most sustained exploration of the travails and adventures of the human soul. (This series also includes the abandoned *The Four Zoas,* which Blake never printed.) The style of "Thel" sets the tone for the style of the rest of Blake's prophetic books, written over the next 15 years or so: the long 14-syllable lines written below, above, and around Blake's own illustration. (Several different versions can be seen at http://www.blakearchive.org/cgi-bin/nph-dweb/blake/Illuminated-Book/THEL/.) Written at about the same time as *Songs of Innocence,* that is to say substantially before the Songs of Experience were appended to them (see *Songs of Innocence and of Experience*)—"Thel" casts light on both the virtues and the limitations of innocence in a world of passion, aspiration, and despair.

Thel's motto, with which the poem opens, shows that the symbol for the experience that the poem's eponymous heroine desires and fears is sexuality itself. The silver cord and the golden bowl are sexualized allusions to the biblical book of bitter experience, Ecclesiastes. There we are warned to remember the Creator in the days of our youth, before evil days come, the daughters of music are brought low, man goes to his long home the grave, desire fails, the silver cord is loosened, the golden bowl is broken, and we return to dust and spirit (Ecclesiastes 12:1–7). The desire Ecclesiastes mentions is not only sexual desire but any interest in the world or hope for its future. This is the desire that Thel's name (from the Greek for *wish*) refers to, the desire that Blake writes about as well in his short pamphlet "There Is No Natural Religion" (1788). There he analyzes desire as the desire for what exceeds accumulation or repetitive possession. The fact that our desires transcend what earth seems to offer us is itself evidence for our own transcendent destiny, since desire is commensurate with its objects and the absolute nature of our desire implies an equivalently absolute realm where it will find satisfaction.

Just as it would be wrong to understand Thel's name as meaning only sexual desire, it would be quite wrong to take sexuality as the meaning of experience, as opposed to innocence. Rather, sexuality represents all the energies of desire, anxiety, confusion, and anarchy, which only lead to corruption but also potentially to transcendence of the fugitive and cloistered, and therefore repressive, state of innocence. This is a transcendence that Thel does not manage to attain but the poem does, at least momentarily, in the intensity of its climax. Thel does not attain it because she lacks the courage to meet the demands her own desire places on her: She retreats to the dubious safety of the Vales of Har at the end of the poem rather than risking all on transcendence.

Still, Thel asks the right questions within her Edenic home. For in that home, death also exists, and Thel knows, with the preacher who utters the words of

Ecclesiastes, that she will die, that she will become nothing, just as the rainbow and transient day and music disappear (as the daughters of music are brought low in Ecclesiastes). She questions the natural transient beings around her about how they can face up to their mortality, but she finds that their answers, while beautiful, do not satisfy her. Their being is all directed toward others, and they participate in a cycle, or reciprocity, that is beautiful but leaves no room for the subjectivity that defines the human spirit. They are always directed elsewhere, but Thel has an inwardness that they necessarily lack.

At last she is led to the Clod of Clay—the most material of beings within the Vales of Har—who allows her to enter the realms of earth itself, the "long home," or underworld, which represents the grave or the afterlife, or the truth of the material world—or all three; at any rate, certainly, the "long home" that we will all enter. What happens next is puzzling: She sees the grim post-Edenic world as it is—that is to say, the world of *Songs of Experience*. She has entered the house of the Clod of Clay, and there she finds her own grave and hears a voice of sorrow rising from it. Her grave is described as a "hollow pit" (Plate 6, l. 10), like the "pit" in Thel's motto that the mole and not the eagle knows. Her grave, therefore, is coincident with her confrontation of sexuality: The grave and the sexual organs go together, or at least they do for Thel, who locates both in the realm of grim and uncontrollable Experience.

The voice from the grave asks a series of rhetorical questions that are somewhat hard to coordinate with each other. But they make the most sense if one considers them as rebukes of deceitful sexuality and praise instead of pure commitment to the impulse of the will: "Why a little curtain of flesh on the bed of our desire?" (Plate 6, l. 20) the youthful burning boy asks, referring both to the hymen as a sign of virginity and to the limitations of the material human body. Desire is *our desire:* It does not belong to Thel alone but to the mutual and intensely subjective reciprocation (unlike the pure selflessness of the beings Thel has questioned in the Vales of Har), a reciprocation which sexual love symbolizes and which might make transcendence possible. But it is possible only on condition of an embrace of experience, not out of despair but out of a sense of the power to overcome its limitations. The limitations of innocence, of the Vales of Har, are less obvious but are what drove Thel into the world the Clod of Clay opened for her. Her fearful return to the Vales of Har show that she cannot make her way through the forests of the night to a higher unity or synthesis. She needs protection but cannot become one of the protectors, and ultimately she comes to represent helpless innocence rather than the prophetic militancy Blake always aimed at. Her story is very beautiful, but the beauty is partial—or it might be better to say that beauty is itself only part of the truth and this is one of the lessons that "The Book of Thel" seeks to teach.

BIBLIOGRAPHY

Bloom, Harold. *Blake's Apocalypse: A Study in Poetic Argument.* Ithaca, N.Y.: Cornell University Press, 1970.

———. *Poetry and Repression: Revisionism from Blake to Stevens.* New Haven, Conn.: Yale University Press, 1976.

Damrosch, Leopold. *Symbol and Truth in Blake's Myth.* Princeton, N.J.: Princeton University Press, 1980.

Erdmann, David V. *Blake, Prophet against Empire: A Poet's Interpretation of the History of His Own Times.* Princeton, N.J.: Princeton University Press, 1977.

Fry, Northrop. *Fearful Symmetry: A Study of William Blake.* Princeton, N.J.: Princeton University Press, 1974.

Gilchrist, Alexander. *Life of William Blake, with Selections from His Poems and Other Writings.* Totowa, N.J.: Rowman and Littlefield, 1973.

Levinson, Marjorie. "The Book of Thel by William Blake: A Critical Reading." *ELH: English Literary History* 47 (1980): 287–303.

Hollander, John. "Blake and the Metrical Contract." In *From Sensibility to Romanticism,* edited by Frederick Hilles and Harold Bloom, 293–310. New York: Oxford, 1965. Reprinted in John Hollander, *Vision and Resonance: Two Senses of Poetic Form,* 187–211. New Haven, Conn.: Yale University Press, 1985.

Ostriker, Alicia. "Desire Gratified and Ungratified: William Blake and Sexuality." *Blake: An Illustrated Quarterly* 16 (1982–83): 156–165.

Raine, Kathleen. *Blake and Antiquity.* Princeton, N.J.: Princeton University Press, 1977.

Thompson, E. P. *Witness against the Beast: William Blake and the Moral Law.* New York: Cambridge University Press, 1993.

"BOTANIST'S VISION, THE" SYDNEY DOBELL **(1856)** This poem is from the second book of poems that SYDNEY DOBELL published about the Crimean War (1854–56), which ended when the allied forces of England and France took Sebastapol from Russia. At the time, Dobell was living in Scotland (where he had brought his wife for medical treatment), and here he represents himself as a botanist—not a scientist but a person curious about flora—walking through the town of Breadalbane on the banks of the lake and the Tay river when news comes that Sebastapol has fallen. (For more about the war, see the entry on Dobell's sonnet "The WOUNDED," from the book of sonnets on the war he and Alexander Smith had published the year before.)

To understand the psychological subtlety and complexity of this poem, it helps to analyze the situation. It is the evening of September 11, and the speaker is watching the sunset as a crowd of people are out for a walk. It is a beautiful day in late summer when people get the news of Sebastapol, conveyed immediately by telegraph and shouted out into the streets. The poet turns away from the cry to look back, not at the sunset but at the intricate detail of the mold and mildew on the stone wall by the lake. He loses himself in that intricacy, focuses all his consciousness and awareness on it, in order not to think about what he has just heard. Why is the news so traumatic? The war is over—as he knows—and the news is therefore welcome. But the news of success now completes the balance sheet of the war. It was for this, and only for this, that there was so much carnage. This is what he does not want to think about: that death and destruction are violent and painful even if very far away, remote in both space and now in time, as the mold and mildew continue unchanged.

The poet's intense awareness of detail is at once a flight from the overwhelming and universal horror of the war he has been imagining and an intensification of that horror since the mind, which can fill itself with detail, makes the scale of the horror half a world away thousands of times more tremendous than what he is focusing on now. (The 20th-century American poet Robert Frost achieved the same effect in, for example, his poem about the Civil War, "Rangefinding;" and Dobell also does it in "Grass from a Battlefield," to which this poem is a kind of pendant.)

The poem knows the trauma it is expressing through its own severe restraint. Dobell knows that we know why his hands are hot and his head throbbing. He thinks of all the living and the dead; they march through his mind, which is unable to synthesize them into a fact of history but is aware instead of each one as a fact of individual pain and horror. His vision is not prophetic but intense and microscopic, and the sheer quantity of perception such microscopic awareness implies in the individual human reminds us of what died with every human being that died in the Crimean War.

BIBLIOGRAPHY

Boos, Florence S. "'Spasm' and Class: W. E. Aytoun, George Gilfillan, Sydney Dobell, and Alexander Smith." *Victorian Poetry* 42, no. 4 (2004): 553–583.

Dobell, Sydney. *The Life and Letters of Sydney Dobell.* Edited by E. Jolly. London: Smith, Elder & Co., 1878.

Preyer, Robert. "Sydney Dobell and the Victorian Epic." *University of Toronto Quarterly* 30 (January 1961): 163–178.

Westwater, Martha. *The Spasmodic Career of Sydney Dobell.* Lanham, Md.: University Press of America, 1992.

"BOY FROM HIS BEDROOM-WINDOW, THE" WILLIAM ALLINGHAM **(1877)** This is one of WILLIAM ALLINGHAM's most moving experiments in the play of perspective in which he excelled, and probably an important influence on ROBERT LOUIS STEVENSON's *A Child's Garden of Verses* eight years later, especially its moving last poem, "TO ANY READER." Allingham describes a boy looking out of his window, and we think that we are going to get a narrative based on the boy's reaction to what he has seen, to the beautiful and haunting scene that the ballad-like poem describes. The town is a place of the ordinary, but behind it is spookier upland, which suggests the adventure to come. A sudden gleam of moonlight reveals a tarn, or small mountain pool, and the scene is set; it is made especially eerie by the suggestion that the boy may be entering into the world of dreams.

But the poem turns out to describe his departure from that world, for in the third stanza we discover that the boy has become the speaker of the poem. He was not the speaker, but he has *become* the speaker, because the speaker is a man—William Allingham—and not the almost anonymous, or typical but unique, boy of the opening lines. He grows into ordinariness. And it is the man who suggests that the tarn in the moorland may have been a dream, because he cannot find the tarn anywhere in the world as he searches in vain through the lands in which he grew up.

The last stanza combines the boy and man together under the pronoun *I*. As a boy, he glimpsed many fine things and anticipated finding them as a man; but as a man, he does not know where he glimpsed them: in the world or within himself. This question is slightly more complex than it looks, since the man knows that the "fine things" he glimpsed are not *now* to be found in the outside world. What he does not know is whether what he saw as a boy survives at all. If it does, it survives in his memory and in the intensity of his love for what he glimpsed as a boy and thought was in the world.

But from the third stanza we already know the only place where "that midnight pool" might abide: in "the Land of Memory." The poem, like Allingham's "The Fairies" and in a very different way his "In Snow," has come to understand that poetic vision is not a matter of seeing where one wants to go but of seeing that there is another, always elusive perspective on the place or event or object that one might think one wanted direct access to. That elusiveness is what poetic suggestiveness comprises. Suggestiveness itself is the most intense experience that poetry can offer, but it can only be intense if one does not insist on having more, on breaking through to some hoped-for but inexistent reality. The poem's speaker is not the boy any longer—the boy is, as Stevenson will put it, "a child of air"—but the memory of what the boy saw is what the poem can revive.

BIBLIOGRAPHY

Allingham, H., and E. Baumer Williams, eds. *Letters to William Allingham.* London: Longmans & Co., 1911.

Allingham, William. *William Allingham: A Diary.* Edited by H. Allingham and D. Radford. London: Macmillan, 1907.

Hill, George Birkbeck, ed. *Letters of Dante Gabriel Rossetti to William Allingham 1854–1870.* London: T. Fisher Unwin, 1897.

BRADLEY, KATHARINE HARRIS See Field, Michael.

"BRIDGE OF SIGHS, THE" Thomas Hood (1844) Like "The Song of the Shirt" "The Bridge of Sighs" was published in *Punch,* during the magazine's most radical days. Thomas Hood knew that he was near the end of his life when he wrote these and similar poems of social distress. This one was prompted by the newspaper account of a woman's suicide, and Hood laments her terror and despair in powerful and compelling lines.

They are powerful and compelling partly because of the odd tension between their form and their content. The poem is written in short, somewhat irregular lines, but the general meter is dactylic dimeter (two dactyls per line). Dactyls are an unnatural and therefore vividly noticed form in English (which tends rather toward iambic meter), but their presence is meaningful since classical elegiac verse was dactylic. To write dactylic verse in English is thus to announce a desire to give the dignity of the classical elegy to one's subject. Matthew Arnold's "Haworth Churchyard," his elegy on Charlotte Brontë, is also written in very irregular dactyls, in trimeter in Arnold's case. The difference between Arnold's tone and Hood's is instructive.

Arnold's poem does not rhyme (nor do the classical antecedents; rhyme only became a general feature of European poetry after about 1000 C.E.), and it has a kind of spare and stately dignity. Hood's poem not only rhymes; most of its stanzas alternate polysyllabic and monosyllabic rhymes. The polysyllabic ones are vividly noticeable (*Unfortunate/importunate, tenderly/slenderly, scornfully/mournfully, scrutiny/mutiny, undutiful/beautiful,* and the mosaic rhyme *pitiful/city full,* etc.). They are dactyls themselves, so the sobriety of classical elegy is combined with an energy that seems to provide a dramatic contrast.

In English poetry, polysyllables are almost always comic. This is because they are ideal for comic timing, for the sudden surprise readers feel when they realize that a line is already rhyming, earlier than they expected it to. The great 19th-century master of such comic rhymes is Lord Byron (for example, in *Don Juan*), but the observation is generally true. Hood, who was a wonderful comic writer, here uses the comic form in an unexpected way. The woman who drowns herself—yet another unfortunate—does not have the dignity of any individuality. She is therefore perfect fodder for the broad strokes, the bravura rhymes of comic verse, and in a sense to understand this is to limn her tragedy. There is nothing more to say or know about her: The clownish accidents of language are sufficient to describe everything that can be understood about her, her motivations, or her despair. ("The Bridge of Sighs" is the name of the bridge in Venice that convicts about to be imprisoned for life crossed over and from which they got their last glimpse of daylight. Here, though, the bridge on which the woman is sighing is over the Thames.)

The poem therefore requires an enormous act of sympathy from its readers. We have to overcome our tendency to caricature, abetted by the poem's form, and make the effort to understand what it would instead be so easy to laugh at. The most extraordinary lines in the poem come in the 12th stanza (ll. 63–71), especially the contrast between the bleak March wind, which makes the woman tremble and shiver, and the dark river into which she plunges. Her suicide combines despair and courage: The river that makes *us* tremble does not do the same to her, and we are given at once a sense of the depth of the despair that would make her hurl herself into it and a sense of the extreme, inscrutable courage it required for her to kill herself.

The poem is sentimental, as is much of the great meliorist (belief that society can be improved by human intervention) literature of the 19th century (which is why the German socialist Friedrich Engels had such contempt for Hood's readers). But the sentimentality had a strong effect: It humanized the poor for the more affluent, made them seem more real, and made the fact that they were anonymous and faceless in a "city full" of people part of their tragedy and part of what his readers would begin to pay attention to.

BIBLIOGRAPHY

Hood, Thomas. *Memorials of Thomas Hood: Collected, Arranged, and Edited by His Daughter, with a Preface and Notes by His Son. Illustrated with Copies From His Own Sketches.* London: E. Moxon, 1860.

———. *Poetical Works of Thomas Hood, with a Critical Memoir by William Michael Rossetti.* New York: G. Routledge, 1874.

BRIDGES, ROBERT (1844–1930)

ANDREW LANG (the great literary compiler, reviewer, critic, and poet) wrote a review of ROBERT BRIDGES's first volume of poems (1873) in January 1874 in the *Academy*. Lang knew nothing about Bridges but liked the poems, which appealed to his own sense of the ancient purity of English verse: "It could scarcely be gathered from his book that he has ever read Mr. Tennyson or Mr. Swinburne; and he sees things as clearly, speaks as simply, feels as truly, as if the modern demand for research and subtlety had never been heard." This was enough for GERARD MANLEY HOPKINS, who had been at Oxford with Bridges, to recognize his long-lost friend (Bridges had been traveling in the Middle East and had returned to family disasters, including the murders of his sister, her husband, and their newborn baby), despite the fact that he did not know Bridges had become a poet. Hopkins, who was now a Jesuit (Bridges was a high Anglican), wrote to him, and thus began one of the most important literary correspondences in English literary history, devoted to many things but largely to the new metrical ideas that both Hopkins and Bridges were exploring.

Hopkins was the more radical of the two, discovering or reinventing SPRUNG RHYTHM, but Bridges outlived him by 45 years. He eventually became poet laureate and, more than 30 years after Hopkins's death, published his work when World War I and the modernity that was the world's cultural reaction to the war made literary culture more receptive to Hopkins's innovations. Bridges made a powerful and convincing case for Hopkins because of his own constant study of English prosody, especially in his great and many-times-augmented book on *Milton's Prosody*. Bridges and Hopkins thought in terms of the play between stress and concatenations of syllables, rather than seeing syllables as the matrix by which stressed and unstressed syllables would alternate with predictable regularity. But where Hopkins liked to jam stresses together, using as few unstressed syllables as possible, Bridges wrote in the more natural style that Lang praised for its truth and simplicity, even when he began experimenting in sprung rhythm following his reading of Hopkins's "The WRECK OF THE DEUTSCHLAND" in 1878.

Bridges's father died when he was nine; four of his seven siblings died in the next two decades; his beloved cousin, the boy genius DIGBY MACKWORTH DOLBEN, drowned at 19; and his mother (whom he supported at his house) was widowed twice. He trained as a physician and practiced with extraordinary dedication until he was struck by pneumonia in 1881, probably as a consequence of his exposure to his patients. When he recovered, he married, continued to support his mother, and decided to devote himself to the study and practice of poetry, which he did for the rest of his life, becoming poet laureate in 1913 and publishing his best-known work, *The Testament of Beauty* on his 85th birthday, the year before he died.

Bridges is an important minor poet and a highly influential and insightful critic, especially when it comes to matters of poetic form, and perhaps most important as the correspondent, publisher, and promoter of his friend Hopkins, whose work was almost entirely unpublished until Bridges's 1918 edition of his poems. Bridges is a model for what a life devoted to literature in all its forms can be. He shows us what it is like both to be a writer and to be a reader.

See also "LONDON SHOW," "ON A DEAD CHILD."

BIBLIOGRAPHY

Phillips, Catherine. *Robert Bridges: A Biography*. New York: Oxford University Press, 1992.

Ritz, Jean-Georges. *Robert Bridges and Gerard Hopkins 1863–1889: A Literary Friendship*. New York: Oxford University Press, 1960.

White, Norman. *Hopkins: A Literary Biography*. New York: Oxford University Press, 1992.

"BRIGHT STAR" JOHN KEATS (ca. 1819)

"Bright Star," one of JOHN KEATS's most beautiful sonnets, is about Fanny Brawne, the great passion of his life, although its date is somewhat uncertain. It was written on a blank page of his copy of Shakespeare's poems, facing "A Lover's Complaint," which may therefore have helped inspire it. A Shakespearean sonnet, it very beautifully manages the subtlety of perspective in Shakespeare's own complaints about love. Thus, it is a love poem, though it is not addressed to Fanny Brawne, the beloved, but to a star in the heavens, seen from the earth.

In his most intense work, Keats would give himself over to multiple perspectives within a single scene. He talked in his letters of the chameleon poet who can be like all the things in the surrounding world. In his own method, this is manifested as a need to inhabit all the figures in a scene, to embrace them in a kind of unity (like the pictorial unity he so admired), synthesized out of and into his own multifaceted subjectivity. Such rapid mobility of perspective aims at totality, here called steadfastness, but the two can be hard to reconcile. In "Bright Star," Keats imagines what the Earth looks like from the vantage point of the steadfast star, presumably the polar star that never moves (and which Shakespeare alludes to in Sonnet 116: "the ever fixed mark [which is a] star to every wandering bark"). Keats imagines the living Earth from the standpoint of the star, and he imagines the various natural phenomena of Earth—its shores, waters, and all-covering snows. The star sees "earth's human shores," a lovely phrase which means the shores where humans live and which they make significant, but also the shores of being human, the place where nature extends far beyond into its inhuman places of ocean and night. (Keats's recurrence to this image is everywhere; see, for example, "WHEN I HAVE FEARS . . . " *HYPERION* and *THE FALL OF HYPERION*. From the vertical perspective of the star, then, Keats imagines the horizontally extended perspective of snow and sea and water.

The negative that governs the first eight lines, when he says that he wants to be steadfast like the star but not lone like it, suggests the widening motion of the Earth the star looks at, where all things blend into each other rather than being hung in lone splendor. This prepares for the last six lines, where he contrasts the almost rigid, solitary motionlessness of the star to the steadfastness that he wishes for himself: to have his head cradled on her breast. Fanny Brawne becomes the last and most focused of the series of earthly things he turns to from the doubled perspective of the star before returning to his own perspective, pillowed on her breast. There the star's rigid steadfastness is modulated into the "sweet unrest" of rising and falling with her breathing. But this unrest is not the opposite of steadfastness: It is its culmination and complete reconciliation, since *unrest* does not only mean endless motion but also being "Awake forever" (l. 12), just as the star too is "sleepless" (l. 4).

This is one of Keats's many poems in which he expresses fear of death as fear of rigidity, and he tries to reconcile the idea of death and breathing—of dying by having death take into the air his quiet breath, as he puts it in "ODE TO A NIGHTINGALE." Here he imagines the solution and dissolution of all opposites: steadfastness and restlessness, waking and swooning, height and breadth, and finally life and death, all under the sign of tenderness and love. But it should be noted that the poem represents this as a wistful desire. He wishes he could be steadfast, but he is not—except perhaps to the wish itself.

BIBLIOGRAPHY

Bate, Walter Jackson. *John Keats.* Cambridge, Mass.: Harvard University Press, 1963.

Bloom, Harold. *Poetry and Repression: Revisionism from Blake to Stevens.* New Haven, Conn.: Yale University Press, 1976.

———. *The Visionary Company: A Reading of English Romantic Poetry.* Garden City, N.Y.: Doubleday, 1961.

De Man, Paul. *The Rhetoric of Romanticism.* New York: Columbia University Press, 1984.

Flesch, William. "The Ambivalence of Generosity: Keats Reading Shakespeare." *ELH: English Literary History* 62, no. 1 (Spring 1995): 149–169.

McFarland, Thomas. *The Masks of Keats: The Endeavour of a Poet.* New York: Oxford University Press, 2000.

Wasserman, Earl. *The Finer Tone: Keats' Major Poems.* Baltimore: Johns Hopkins Press, 1953.

BRONTË, EMILY (1818–1848) Emily Brontë is now largely remembered as the author of one of the greatest novels of the 19th century, *Wuthering Heights.* So it is interesting to observe that she spent far more time writing poetry than she devoted to her novel, which was intended (like the first novels of her sisters Charlotte and Anne) to make money rather than establish her place in the canon of literature. Yet her poems were not aspirations to canonical authority either. Like the slightly younger Emily Dickinson (who loved the Brontës' novels), Emily Brontë wrote for the sake of writing. She was shocked when her older sister Charlotte found and read her poems, though eventually she acquiesced to their publication, along with Charlotte's and Anne's, in the 1846 volume of *Poems* of Currer, Ellis and Acton Bell (their pseudonyms for a long time, even after their authorship was known).

Not that Brontë was not a natural storyteller: Many of the poems were actually written for the elaborate narrative world that she and Anne, primarily, established between them as children and kept up as adults, the world of Gondal. A large number of her earlier poems derive from this world, though they were reworked and decontextualized for publication. But this is a way of saying that narrative was for Brontë a way to provide a context for the poems it presented. None of the Gondal writing survives (it was probably destroyed by Charlotte after the deaths of her sisters), but we can guess from the uncompromising accounts of nature on the moors in *Wuthering Heights* that it provided a background for poems that matched its severity. *Wuthering Heights* is set on the Yorkshire moors, in a place very like Haworth, where Brontë lived almost her entire life and which she hated leaving; so, too, are the natural descriptions in her poems reminiscent of the severe and barren Yorkshire moors.

It should be remembered that Heathcliff in *Wuthering Heights* is based largely on LORD BYRON, one of the great romantic nature poets, at least in the later parts of *CHILDE HAROLD'S PILGRIMAGE.* But as a poet of nature, Brontë should be compared with WILLIAM WORDSWORTH (whom she revered and who outlived her) on one hand, and with THOMAS HARDY on the other. Brontë's nature reflects a kind of emptiness that stands for a lost other life. The intensity of its emptiness is ultimately an intensity greater than the thing that has left it void and empty: love or the loved person who has died (and Brontë saw plenty of death—her mother died when she was a little girl and two of her sisters died within weeks of each other, as she was to die within months of her brother Branwell and her sister Anne). That intensity is somehow at Brontë's command, as though she is able to live up to it, respond to it, meet it with an answering intensity. Her nature is not Wordsworthian; it is cold and distant. But it is still *intentional:* It still lends itself to personification and therefore to the personification of the dead. Hardy's nature by contrast is dead, a corpse, and even its intensities are deceptive. For Brontë those intensities are real, and the great power in her verse is in their uncompromising acceptance of things as they are, including the fact that they once were otherwise.

Hardy and Brontë are both great novelists who are also poets of embittered emptiness, but Brontë makes that emptiness into her own achievement, as Hardy does not, and into a place where she can live. "How still, how happy! these are words / That once would scarce agree together," she begins one poem describing how now the world makes a wasteland, but she calls it peace: "my heart loves December's smile / As much as July's golden beam." Compare the last words of *Wuthering Heights,* after its three great principal characters, embodiments of ungovernable passion, have died and the narrator stands by their graves: "I lingered round them, under that benign sky; watched the moths fluttering among the heath, and hare-bells; listened to the soft wind breathing through the grass; and wondered how anyone could ever imagine unquiet slumbers, for the sleepers in that quiet earth."

Like her sisters, Emily Brontë died too young, just after the death of her younger brother, the wild and dissolute Branwell, and also of the tuberculosis that took away almost everyone in her family. But she left behind one of the greatest of all novels and a set of poems which are as intense in their way of evoking an entire world and its psychological analogues as anything in the novel.

See also "NO COWARD SOUL IS MINE," "REMEMBRANCE."

BIBLIOGRAPHY

Barker, Juliet. *The Brontës.* New York: St. Martin's Press, 1994.

Bristow, Joseph, ed. *Victorian Women Poets: Emily Bronte, Elizabeth Barrett Browning, Christina Rossetti.* Basingstoke, England: Macmillan, 1995.

Gezari, Janet. "Fathoming 'Remembrance'; Emily Bronte in Context." *ELH: English Literary History* 66, no. 4 (1999): 965–984.

Homans, Margaret. *Women Writers and Poetic Identity: Dorothy Wordsworth, Emily Brontë, and Emily Dickinson.* Princeton, N.J.: Princeton University Press, 1980.

Mason, Emma. *Women Poets of the Nineteenth Century.* Tavistock, Devon, England: Northcote House Publishers, 2006.

Nestor, Pauline. *Female Friendships and Communities: Charlotte Bronte, George Eliot, Elizabeth Gaskell.* New York: Oxford University Press, 1985.

"BROTHER AND SISTER" GEORGE ELIOT **(1874)** Except perhaps for the fact that the brother is named Will (the sister is unnamed), this poem is an autobiography of a feeling or a sensibility. GEORGE ELIOT (born Mary Ann Evans) was very close to her brother Isaac as a child, but relations with both her father and her brother grew strained under the pressure of her freethinking and nonconformity (which also elicited her father's stern disapproval). They eventually collapsed when Isaac learned that she was not married to G. H. Lewes, with whom she was to live for 24 years, because Lewes was unable to obtain a divorce from his wife. Isaac also convinced her other sisters to renounce her, but after Lewes's death and Eliot's marriage to Johnnie Cross in 1880, they reconciled.

Eliot was far too principled to renounce a relationship under both societal and family pressure, but the pain of separation can be seen in "Brother and Sister," written 20 years after her brother's break with her. (It can also be seen in her great novel *The Mill on the Floss,* where Maggie Tulliver's brother, the deeply loved but frightening, demanding, and unforgiving Tom, is based on Isaac.) "Brother and Sister" is by no means a great poem, but its high interest is due to far more than its biographical content. The poem—a sonnet sequence comprising 11 sonnets—develops its sense of the growth and expansion of the human mind very subtly, and it relates the mind's discovery of what the world is really like to its hopes about the world as seen from the perspective of "a little sister." It should be noted that there is no mention of the other siblings: What counted was the relation between this brother and sister, to the exclusion of all else.

The poem was written under the strong influence of WILLIAM WORDSWORTH's accounts of the freshness of nature's aspect in childhood. Eliot's prose was highly influenced by Wordsworth, and by the iterated theme in Wordsworth of the way life will disappoint the promises it makes when the world seems beautiful and new. But where Wordsworth describes the solitude of his own early childhood (and makes no mention of his sister Dorothy), Eliot remembers her own as intensely involved with that of her brother (he was three years older than she). The poem begins with the plangent Wordsworthian phrase "I cannot choose but think upon the time" when she and her brother were close. In Wordsworth the phrase is "cannot choose but feel," and what we cannot choose but feel is that everything the mind creates will perish (*The* PRELUDE, 5, l. 21); but at the climax of *The Prelude,* such inevitable feeling becomes a glory: All people, no matter how insensitive, are endowed with feeling (14, l. 86).

Both Wordsworth and Eliot are thinking of Shakespeare. In the passage from book 5 cited above, Wordsworth actually quotes from sonnet 64: "This thought is as a death which cannot choose / But weep to have that which it fears to lose," and Eliot's own tortured ambivalence about remembering her brother's love can be compared to Shakespeare's agony in thinking of what time will do to his love. Perhaps just as central is Ophelia's complaint after the death of her father in Shakespeare's *Hamlet,* when she laments: "I hope all will be well. We must be patient, but I cannot choose but weep to think they would lay him i' th' cold ground. My brother shall know of it" (4.5.68). Eliot feels like Ophelia to her brother's Laertes, and her own poem is a lamentation over the death of her childhood and the aloofness of that brother. Indeed, the stanza continues with an allusion to a famous passage in *A Midsummer Night's Dream* when she says that she and her brother were like "two buds that kiss," like the "two lovely berries on one stem" (3.2.220) that the sisterly Hermia and Helena grew before the dissension between them that sexuality introduced into their lives.

Eliot's poem takes the form of thinking upon and remembering that happy time, in particular the Wordsworthian expeditions she took with her brother, gathering flowers, nutting, and fishing. One memorable line talks about the intensity of perception that belongs to freshness and youth, a perception that arises from an intense capacity to love which is lost when "those blest hours of infantine content" (l. 24) are gone. To the child, unlike the adult, reasons for love can be seen everywhere "thick as the stars above" (l. 52; compare Wordsworth's "I WANDERED LONELY AS A CLOUD"). But love must see those reasons, and to the blindness of maturity, they are like light to a blind person: "Day is but Number to the darkened sight" (l. 54).

Eliot's memory of those days is not general only but exemplified by particular scenes, and she tells the story of a moment of anger overcome. Her brother had asked her to "mind the rod" with which they were fishing. Although we need not insist on it, it is not overreading to note the phallic symbolism here, since Isaac's break with Eliot originated in her insistence on making her way in whatever manner it took in a male world, including her taking on a male literary identity. She is interested in watching the barges move down the canal (in her novels she is always interested in boats), and she neglects the line that one barge is about to run down. (The sudden appearance of the barge and its pitch-black prow should be compared to the the boat-stealing scene in *The Prelude,* to which it directly alludes.) Her brother flashes in anger at her, but suddenly—"lo!"—she catches a perch at the last moment, and her "guilt" is turned to "merit," and she is praised even by the "gardener" in this wishful memory of a reversal of the biblical story of the Fall (sonnet 8).

All this would make for a moving expression of wistful memory if it were not for the unexpected and powerful transition that the sequence makes in its last three sonnets. Sonnet 9 describes how her presence was good for Will; he is named here because it is her presence that teaches him how to curb his *will* and make room for the needs and desires of others—that is, of her. He learns the "nobler mastery" of self-restraint, discerns in the widening vision of his life a "separate life"—hers—and therefore "a Self that self restrains." When she reflects that "His years with others must the sweeter be / For those brief days he spent in loving me," the painfulness of the reflection—he loved her only briefly—is mitigated by what that love did for him in his own life, despite the fact that he has disowned her. She has been as important to him as he is to her because she is the self whose existence restrained his own self. She is the form that his conscience took and internalized. Self-restraint means how one restrains one's own impulses, but the restraining self, as opposed to the self restrained, is modeled not on her but on her presence.

This acute and subtle psychological insight is matched by what follows it: the self-restraint he learns, the nobility of self-mastery which is due to her presence and his love for her, gives rise to her own admiration of him as a person and entices her out of her own absolute and childlike self-absorption. She ceases to live in the narcissistic fantasies we are all born into, and that all the heroines and heroes in her books seem to be born into as well, more or less, and discovers, like them, the total and independent being of others. It is her brother who makes her discover this, and he does so because of what she has made him, or because of *his* discovery of her independence. They are separate selves, and to learn this is a considerable moral advance.

But it is also the beginning of a decline in happiness, since it is her first inkling of the separation and ultimate indifference of the world. Soon they will be separated for good: "School parted us," she writes, and we should take that both figuratively and literally—figuratively in that learning about the world is learning that people are fundamentally apart from each other; the hard lesson that the school of life teaches is this essential separation; literally because when she was five and Isaac was eight, he was sent off to boarding school and she started school herself, and they never became close again. Their souls are divorced from one another, and she is embarked upon the pitiless and dire years that bring only change and not security. Their love has prepared them to cope with these years, but it has done so only because by its very nature it taught them to acknowledge their fundamental separateness as a prelude to separation.

The last lines are the most moving. If there is to be an afterlife, "another childhood world," she would be reborn as a little sister—that is, as *his* little sister. Such a world would be like that in Wordsworth's INTIMATIONS ODE, a repetition of all that is fine and intense in memory (see also ANNA LAETITIA BARBAULD's "LIFE!"), not the Christian heaven that her brother believed in. In imagining her brother's reaction to this poem, she is no doubt hoping to show him what heaven really is: the joy they had together in their innocent childhood when the gardener praised them and when they could be moral beacons to each other. Alas that her brother ended up so much more conventional than she.

BIBLIOGRAPHY

Bodenheimer, Rosemarie. *The Real Life of Mary Ann Evans: George Eliot, Her Letters and Fiction.* Ithaca, N.Y.: Cornell University Press, 1994.

Bonaparte, Felicia. *The Triptych and the Cross: The Central Myths of George Eliot's Poetic Imagination.* New York: New York University Press, 1979.

Haight, Gordon. *George Eliot: A Biography.* New York: Oxford University Press, 1968.

———, ed. *The George Eliot Letters.* New Haven, Conn.: Yale University Press, 1954.

Hertz, Neil. *George Eliot's Pulse.* Stanford, Calif.: Stanford University Press, 2003.

Woolf, Virginia. "George Eliot." *Times Literary Supplement,* November 20, 1919. Available online. URL: http://digital.library.upenn.edu/women/woolf/VW-Eliot.html. Accessed on February 1, 2008.

BROWNING, ELIZABETH BARRETT (1806–1861)

Elizabeth Barrett Browning tended to publish over her initials, EBB, even before she met and married ROBERT BROWNING, the "EBB" originally standing for *Elizabeth Barrett Barrett.* "EBB" has become more or less conventional, partly to honor her explicitly feminist independence from those whose names she shared: first her father and then her husband. (Similarly, her semiautobiographical heroine Aurora Leigh has the same last name as her father, and as the cousin she finally marries, but is always very much her own person.) EBB is the most consciously feminist of the leading poets of the English canon up to her own time. The eldest and most brilliant of 12 children, she was precocious as a reader and poet, and much doted upon by her parents, who encouraged her in every way. She learned Latin and Greek starting at about age 10, working with her brother's tutor. A sickly teenager, she spent much of her time in bed reading widely in English and classical literature (her devotion to Greek literature and mythology was lifelong); she also read Mary Wollstonecraft's great feminist tract, the *Vindication of the Rights of Women,* published in 1792. (Wollstonecraft was Mary Shelley's mother.) EBB's first poems were published when she was 15 years old, with the strong encouragement and support of her parents, though her father, Edward Barrett Barrett, became more and more irascible, a character trait that was to become tragically oppressive when her mother died in 1828. Edward Barrett Barrett, after the serious financial reversals to his interests in Jamaica when the slave trade was abolished, insisted on keeping his children with him and would not hear of his daughters' marrying—an attitude that testifies to the overbearing and oppressive intensity of his love for them.

EBB's poetry was now being widely published and celebrated, and Robert Browning wrote her some fan letters. She admired his poetry too (he was five years younger than she was), and despite being an invalid, partly no doubt because of the oppressive demands made on her in her father's house, she eventually agreed to meet him. After an intense series of visits and letters (some of her feelings for him are chronicled in her secretly written *SONNETS FROM THE PORTUGUESE,* which she only showed him after they got married), she eloped with him, and they went to Italy, whose climate was much better for her lungs (her invalidism may have been tubercular). Her father never spoke to her or acknowledged her again, except to disinherit her.

The devotion, respect, admiration, and encouragement of Robert Browning, who thought her the greatest poet of her time, contrasted strongly with her father's oppressiveness and gave her space for her feminist and somewhat radical political engagement. She was strongly against slavery (and felt guilty about the source of some of her family's fortune), and Frederick Douglass admired her antislavery poems. The best account of her life is probably *AURORA LEIGH,* a daring first-person narrative about a poet who learns how serious the poetic vocation can be, and how it can be both true to itself and politically engaged. Political reformation, to which EBB was committed, is predicated on the humanity of those who are oppressed, and it is poetry that can best express that humanity. As semiautobiography, the poem is striking for the grief that it shows over Aurora's dead father, though EBB's own father was not to die until after its publication. Aurora eventually marries her cousin Romney Leigh, but only after he learns the importance of what she has to teach, just as she learns the importance of his political commitments. One can see in that poem the model of a feminist writer, contributing to and engaging with the world around her as an equal.

EBB and Robert had one child, and the account of motherhood in *Aurora Leigh* shows her experience as a mother, an experience vividly and explicitly separated from that of being a wife: EBB saw maternal devotion as one of the great experiences of human life, but did not confuse it with subjection to patriarchy.

Although she and Robert were married for 15 years after they eloped, EBB never entirely overcame her lung disease and died in Florence in 1861. Robert's grief and devotion was lifelong, and perhaps his greatest tribute to her was *The RING AND THE BOOK,* which memorialized their life together, especially in Florence, to which he never returned. EBB is probably not the greatest female poet of the century (that honor should probably go to CHRISTINA ROSSETTI in England, or, in the English language, to Emily Dickinson, who admired EBB). She was, however, certainly the poet who did most to get the world to take women seriously as poets and writers, partly through persuasion, partly through example, and she certainly counts as one of the leading poets of the Victorian era.

See also ""MUSICAL INSTRUMENT, A."

BIBLIOGRAPHY

Forster, Margaret. *Elizabeth Barrett Browning: A Biography.* New York: Doubleday, 1989.

Karlin, Daniel. *The Courtship of Robert Browning and Elizabeth Barrett.* Oxford: Oxford University Press, 1985.

Markus, Julia. *Dared and Done: The Marriage of Elizabeth Barrett and Robert Browning.* New York: Knopf, 1995.

Mermin, Dorothy. *Elizabeth Barrett Browning: The Origins of a New Poetry.* Chicago: University of Chicago Press, 1989.

BROWNING, ROBERT (1812–1889) Robert Browning's greatest poem is *The RING AND THE BOOK,* he found the book of its title in an outdoor bazaar in Florence in June 1860 (as he explains in the poem's first book). He worked on the poem from 1864 to 1868, but after 1861 he left Florence for ever. His wife and the great love of his life, ELIZABETH BARRETT BROWNING, had died there on June 29, just a year after he found the book, and he could not bear to go back. It is in the poem that he sustains a kind of nostalgic sense of the ambience of Florence (many significant events take place in Arezzo, which was under Florentine law), an ambience which makes the poem an idealized elegy of Barrett Browning to a not insignificant extent.

The Ring and the Book consists of 12 dramatic monologues, the form that Browning wrote in to the virtual exclusion of all others. The first and last are more or less in his own voice, and in it he recalls the happier times when he found the book, even as he gazes at the ring which is a reminder of the past. The others are in the voices of all the characters whose interactions make up the story the work tells—each monologue urging a particular perspective on that story. One of the speakers is the dying Pompilia, and the beauty of both her language and her moral character clearly identify her as Browning's loving and loyal portrait of the dead Elizabeth, whose carefully engineered elopement with him in September 1846 (the invalid poet, more or less confined to her house by her father, had allowed Browning to meet her after a long correspondence in which he expressed his admiration for her writing; she also admired his) left the print of its anxiety on his account of Pompilia's escape with the virtuous priest who spirits her away from her tyrannical and abusive husband, modeled in some ways on Barrett Browning's father. (The writing of the book about these long-dead people is itself, among many other things, an act of supreme loyalty)

The diction of Pompilia's monologue presents a direct, lovely, luminous contrast to the diction of most of the other characters in *The Ring and the Book,* which is in one way or another gnarled or impacted or crammed full of fusty legal Latinisms of all sorts. The grotesquery of style that Browning has been accused of almost from the start of his career is on full display in *The Ring and the Book*. It is a grotesquery that still makes him the object of such derisive anthologies as the great *Stuffed Owl* (edited by C. Day Lewis), which are paeans to memorable misfires. The charge of grotesquery was leveled most notoriously by Walter Bagehot in his 1864 essay "Wordsworth, Tennyson and Browning or Pure, Ornate and Grotesque Art in English Poetry" (the adjectives apply respectively to the three poets), although Bagehot registered himself among Browning's admirers. Bagehot says of Browning that "He puts together things which no one else would have put together"; his poetry is realistic and the product of "a hard strong intellect" belonging to a "great mind" and coping with the incongruities of brute reality through a matching incongruity of style.

Interestingly, Bagehot instances Browning's great dramatic monologue "CALIBAN UPON SETEBOS," published in May 1864 (in *Dramatis Personae*), as an example of the failures to which grotesquery is liable: "a quarry of ideas . . . in such a jagged, ugly, useless shape that [one] can hardly bear them." But "Caliban upon Setebos" is (among other things, some specified in the entry in this book) a kind of *ars poetica*—a self-portrait of the poet in a Darwinian world which is *constitutively* grotesque. Bagehot's account of Browning is very like the one Caliban gives of Setebos and also of himself, in whose image he imagines Setebos. Setebos is "rougher than His handiwork, be sure!" (l. 111). That roughness is the roughness not of the work of art (whose purified beauty Browning will always suspect comes at the cost of true human feeling: the murderous Duke of Ferrara in "MY LAST DUCHESS" is the greatest aesthete in his poetry) but of the creating mind: Setebos's, Caliban's, Browning's. It is the roughness of thought, and again we can see how explicitly Browning means Caliban as a self-portrait (like all the other damaged artist-figures of his poetry) in Caliban's painful, needy observation that "'Tis solace making baubles, ay, and sport" (l. 149) as he tries himself to create artistic and literary objects like those of Prospero: Caliban, like his god Setebos, "taketh his mirth with make-believes" (l. 168) and "tasteth, himself, no finer good i' the world . . . Than trying what to do with wit and strength" (ll. 187–191). These make-believes are vast variations on human personality: Browning imagines a Caliban imagining himself both like and unlike a Setebos who imagines the experiences of those both like and unlike himself. Setebos creates characters to experience through them what he cannot experience directly, and we may say the same of Browning.

A listing of the titles of some of Browning's most central collections makes the point: *Dramatic Lyrics* (1842), *Dramatic Romances and Lyrics* (1845), *Dramatis Personae* (1864), and the two volumes *of Dramatic Idylls* (1879), to say nothing of such books as *Men and Women.* Browning persistently imagine other voices—not only from the outside but from the inside; he imagines the thought of those vastly unlike himself and makes us imagine the thought of those vastly unlike ourselves, whoever we are. This all comes down to saying that

Browning's roughness and ruggedness (as his friend John Ruskin described his style) comes out of the extraordinary heterogeneity of the world and its inhabitants to which he was just as extraordinarily alert.

An outsider from the start—a Congregationalist in a conformist culture, rejected by the British public until his late 50s, and unable to attend Oxford or Cambridge or to take up the post of Oxford professor of poetry for which he was considered because he was a nonconformist—Browning was uniquely fitted to explore the world on his own terms. He was an accomplished musician and draftsman (the Brownings' only child, their son Pen, became a minor but highly competent painter in his own right) and an immensely learned thinker. That learning made informed and forceful his refusal to accept the pieties of such mandarins as MATTHEW ARNOLD, whose views on culture as ultimately the domain of sweetness and light Browning ridiculed. In the end, following the tremendous success of *The Ring and the Book,* it won him the adulation that his integrity had prevented him from courting earlier on, including an audience with Queen Victoria, who was an admirer. His style was often crabbed and cranky, but it was crabbed because it included everything within it, even spaciousness and elegance and ease.

Browning is the great Victorian poet who most demonstrates the romantic sensibility. He shows how poetic power can sustain itself through the most heterogeneous knowledge of all the productions of an age that challenged poetry itself. If he is often grotesque, so are Gothic cathedrals, and it is well to remember his own line from his greatest poem, "CHILDE ROLAND TO THE DARK TOWER CAME": "Seldom went such grotesqueness with such woe" (l. 82)—the woe that gives depth to poetry, no matter how grotesque the world it measures and measures up to. Browning's grotesqueness of style is an achievement of heterogeneity. His greatest exemplar was PERCY BYSSHE SHELLEY, whose style is either lyrical or urbane, and Browning wrote in Shelleyan modes at every stage of his career. But he wrote in every other mode as well, and it bespeaks a narrowness of intellect to lump them all together as grotesque.

See also "HOME THOUGHTS, FROM ABROAD"; "MEMORABILIA"; ROMANTICISM; "SOLILOQUY IN A SPANISH CLOISTER"; "THAMURIS MARCHING"; "TOCCATA OF GALUPPI'S, A."

BIBLIOGRAPHY

Bloom, Harold. *A Map of Misreading.* New York: Oxford University Press, 2003.

DeVane, William C. *A Browning Handbook.* New York: Appleton-Century-Crofts, 1955.

Gest, John Marshall. *The Old Yellow Book: Source of Browning's The Ring and the Book, a new translation with explanatory notes and critical chapters upon the poem and its source.* Boston: Chipman Law Publishing Co., 1925.

Langbaum, Robert Woodrow. *The Modern Spirit: Essays on the Continuity of Nineteenth- and Twentieth-Century Literature.* New York: Oxford University Press, 1970.

Markus, Julia. *Dared and Done: The Marriage of Elizabeth Barrett and Robert Browning.* New York: Random House, 1995.

Parker, Derek. *Roman Murder Mystery: The True Story of Pompilia.* Stroud, England: Sutton, 2001.

Raymond, William O. *The Infinite Moment, and Other Essays in Robert Browning.* Toronto: University of Toronto Press, 1965.

"BURDENS" EDWARD DOWDEN (1876) This strange and intense poem may be EDWARD DOWDEN'S best. (It is the one Christopher Ricks chose to represent Dowden in *The Oxford Book of Victorian Verse.* [1987]) It is most striking for its last line, which seems both powerful and abrupt—which is just the effect that Dowden desired.

The title is intentionally ambiguous, although the ambiguity seems resolved soon enough. In poetry a *burden* is a refrain, and the title suggests a song of refrains, in the Marvellian mode that Dowden was sometimes seen as resurrecting. The burdens, however, immediately turn out to be the fardels, as Hamlet calls them, that weigh down our lives. The first stanza is a short summary of the difficulties of human life and, again, puts one in mind of Hamlet's "To be or not to be" soliloquy. We find out at the end of the first stanza that it is written in the second stanza: *You* deem such burdens hard to bear. That *you* is generalized. Anyone reading the poem, anyone living a normal human life, will complain of its difficulties when he or she comes to consider them. But that is Dowden's point. We "deem" such burdens hard to bear when we have leisure to complain. The very way the stanza takes a generalizing attitude, a kind of perspicacious distance on the life it judges, shows it as a product of leisure and not an immediate response to the experiences it deplores. The poeticizing of the stanza is a part of that generalization: Natural ruin and decay are emblems of the burdens of human life, but as in GERARD MANLEY HOPKINS's "SPRING AND FALL," they make possible a kind of pleasurable protest.

The second stanza of "Burdens" is strikingly different. The perspective here is the immediate one of the speaker and not the general one of any potential happener on the poem. And *burden* is made surprisingly synonymous with *delight* (l. 7). The "dreadful joys" (l. 8) that the stanza goes on to enumerate are both burden and delight: delight because they are sublime and exalting; burdensome and dreadful because the human frame is not used to such experiences; we are more easily attracted to the indolent complaint of the first stanza. The second is about pure passion and lists, in terms as conventional as the first stanza is conventional by design, the experience of sudden, surprising, and total exaltation. The language of this stanza is not supposed to be wholly original. The "rent veils cast aside" (l. 10) is an allusion to both PERCY BYSSHE SHELLEY and GEORGE ELIOT (Dowden wrote memorably on both of them); but we should see this as an allusion as well to poetry proper, so that one of the dreadful joys here is that of poetry itself—the human expression commensurate with those joys. This is one meaning of the way one strong soul is rendered up to another (l. 11); both souls are strong—that of the poet and that of the reader. But the more obvious erotic meaning is equally present, describing a mutuality in love and passion between two souls. That mutuality is physical as well, as the subtly more graphic image of the last line makes clear with "silence filling like a cup." Or perhaps we should say of the last line that it is subtly *less* graphic. The rendering up of souls is over, and the silence is postcoital. But the cup is still filling as it has (in another way) during the passion itself.

The silence the poem ends on is the silence that comes after the poem. The abruptness of the ending is perfect: The simple word *cup* has received the succession of rhymes that bring the poem to its closure, and it is as though the sounds of the poem, now made indistinguishable from the silence it ends with, are what fill up the word. Dowden manages this partly because *cup* contains the word it rhymes with (*up*), so that we feel the abrupt conclusion not only as abrupt but as a conclusion as well, one which lasts into the silence that succeeds it.

Why is this experience a burden? We could say that it has the burden of the absolute immediacy of the experience the second stanza describes. The poet is feeling it as he writes, and it is much more present than any of the burdens of sorrows the first stanza lists.

Most poems assume that sorrows are more intense than joys, and so sorrow tends to be the stock-in-trade of the poet seeking intensity. Even joyful poems derive their joys by contrast with sorrow. But Dowden here makes joy the more intense experience—and this is what makes the poem so original.

BIBLIOGRAPHY

Murphy, William M. "Yeats, Quinn, and Edward Dowden." In *John Quinn: Selected Irish Writers from His Library*, edited by Janis and Richard Londraville, 71–108. West Cornwall, Conn.: Locust Hill Press, 2001.

Yeats, W. B. (William Butler). *Autobiography of William Butler Yeats: Consisting of Reveries over Childhood and Youth, The Trembling of the Veil, and Dramatis Personae.* Garden City, N.Y.: Doubleday Anchor Books, 1958.

BYRON, GEORGE GORDON BYRON, LORD (1788–1824) Lord Byron was (with PERCY BYSSHE SHELLEY) one of the two exemplars of what the poet laureate ROBERT SOUTHEY called the "Satanic School of poetry." Southey did not mean this as a compliment, but Byron received it as one. Throughout the 19th century, and throughout Europe, Byron was the very model of the romantic poet: brilliantly embittered, passionate, contemptuous of conformity, and committed to making life an experience of maximum intensity. Heavily influenced in his writing by the German poet and dramatist Johann Wolfgang von Goethe, the dominant literary genius of the age, he was also an impressive enough figure to feature in the older poet's own work. And not only Goethe: Byron probably appears as a character in the works of others more often than any other writer of the 19th century (under his own name, most recently perhaps in *Lord Byron's Novel* [2005] by John Crowley, or under thinly veiled disguises, most prominently Heathcliff in EMILY BRONTË's *Wuthering Heights*).

All of this suggests that Byron's prominence is more as a romantic hero than as a romantic poet. This is not an assessment he would necessarily have disagreed with: In his greatest work, *DON JUAN,* he remarks with genuine amusement that every 10 years, taste challenges the previous evaluation of "the greatest living poet," who is treated like the temporary world champion of boxing. He, too, he says, "Was reckon'd a considerable time, / The grand Napoleon of the realms of rhyme" (XI, ll. 433–440). For Byron as for his contemporaries, NAPOLEON BONAPARTE was a gigantic lesson in the futility of attempting to sit where others "durst not sore" (as John Milton's Satan puts it in *Paradise Lost.*): Byron was against him in success but strongly attracted to him in failure and ruin. Indeed, Byron's poem about Napoleon—"On the 'Star of the Legion of Honour,'" written after Napoleon's last defeat at Waterloo—so outraged public opinion, already at the breaking point because of Byron's scandalous divorce from Annabelle Milbunke (and the public did not even know that the divorce was catalyzed by Byron's affair with his half sister Augusta), that he left Tory England, for which he now felt complete contempt forever. The futility of Napoleonic ambition, whether in poetry, in theology, or in politics, is one of the things that makes it great, but since that greatness only comes at the cost of accepting its futility, Byron must and does affect to treat poetry as an avocation, not as a vocation, as in the lines just quoted. As he says in a letter to Sir WALTER SCOTT, "After having seen Napoleon begin like Tamerlane and end like Bajazet in our own time, we have not the same interest in what would otherwise have appeared important history," a fact about which Byron felt ambivalent. (Bajazet was one of the kings that Tamerlane famously used to pull his carriage like a horse.) His point was that there is more to history than Napoleon, and more people than the one great poet of the times, and yet all fade into insignificance, even as Napoleon does.

The image Byron cultivated with assiduous care was one of aristocratic, careless indifference to his own image. Byron presented himself as a figure sublimely unconcerned about his public, but he was more concerned about that public than any of the other great romantics. Shelley's close friend Thomas Love Peacock, in *Nightmare Abbey,* his wonderful parody of Byron, Shelley, and a host of their contemporaries, has his Byron character, Mr. Cypress, take his final leave of England with an assurance to his friends that to their memory he "should always look back with as much affection as his lacerated spirit could feel for anything" (chapter 11). Peacock captures the Byronic pose perfectly, and yet to do him justice, it is a pose that only a Byron (or a Hamlet) could pull off.

This is partly because Byron had such an admiring public to whom he could display his indifference (Scott did as well, but he graciously conceded Byron's superiority as a poet and turned to the historical novels for which he is now most famous). In Byron's own famous words after the publication of the first two cantos of *CHILDE HAROLD'S PILGRIMAGE,* "I awoke one morning and found myself famous." This was in 1812, when he was just 24, having returned from a tour of the Mediterranean, including many dangerous regions at a time when Britain was engaged against Napoleon in the Peninsular Wars. *Childe Harold* is a sort of diary pegged to a story with almost no incidents about Harold's travels through the Iberian Peninsula and then east to Albania, Turkey, and Greece, some of the locales in which Byron was the first Englishman to set foot.

After his divorce from his wife, Anne Isabella ("Annabella"), Byron went first to Switzerland, where he met Shelley, his best friend and the greatest intellectual and poetic influence of his life. They lived as neighbors in a kind of extended family on Lake Geneva. Mary Shelley gives a picture of their lives together in her prefatory description of the writing of her novel *Frankenstein.* Later, both households moved to Italy, where Byron lived on and off in Venice for most of the rest of his life. Shelley describes Byron in his great poem *JULIAN AND MADDALO: A CONVERSATION,* in his depiction of Count Maddalo. It is worth quoting several sentences from the description of Maddalo in the preface to that poem:

> He is a person of the most consummate genius, and capable, if he would direct his energies to

> such an end, of becoming the redeemer of his degraded country. But it is his weakness to be proud. He derives, from a comparison of his own extraordinary mind with the dwarfish intellects that surround him, an intense apprehension of the nothingness of human life. His passions and his powers are incomparably greater than those of other men; and, instead of the latter having been employed in curbing the former, they have mutually lent each other strength. His ambition preys upon itself, for want of objects which it can consider worthy of exertion. I say that Maddalo is proud, because I can find no other word to express the concentred and impatient feelings which consume him; but it is on his own hopes and affections only that he seems to trample, for in social life no human being can be more gentle, patient and unassuming than Maddalo. He is cheerful, frank and witty. His more serious conversation is a sort of intoxication; men are held by it as by a spell. He has travelled much; and there is an inexpressible charm in his relation of his adventures in different countries.

Later, in the poem itself, the narrator, Julian, says of Maddalo/Byron that he (Julian) "Argued against despondency, but pride / Made my companion take the darker side. / The sense that he was greater than his kind / Had struck, methinks, his eagle spirit blind / By gazing on its own exceeding light" (ll. 48–52).

Under Shelley's influence and tutelage, Byron read WILLIAM WORDSWORTH carefully and profoundly, and the last canto of *Childe Harold* (as Wordsworth himself complained) was highly influenced by such poems as "TINTERN ABBEY." Byron showed himself a friend to SAMUEL TAYLOR COLERIDGE, intervening to get some of Coleridge's poetry published, even as he began to turn away from his own more passionately serious composition and to write *Don Juan*, which would occupy the rest of his life. *Don Juan* is facetiously dedicated to Southey, and it contains much mirth at the expense of the LAKE POETS (Southey, Wordsworth, and Coleridge). But the strictures on Coleridge and Wordsworth had to do with their later work, not so much with the great work of their youth, which both Shelley and Byron continued to admire. The older generation of Lake Poets had, alas, turned "Tory at / Last," and Byron continued to be committed to freedom and liberation.

In 1823 Byron's aid was solicited for the Greek partisans fighting to liberate Greece from the centuries-old Ottoman domination he and Shelley had complained of in their poetry for years. Byron devoted both wealth and action to the cause. Byron's fame was such that his presence among the Greek partisans was inspirational. He spent early 1824 hoping to experience battle, but events kept frustrating him. He was violently ill several times, and finally died of a fever on April 19. His death was regarded as heroic, and he became a mythical inspiration in the struggle for Greek freedom: He is remembered today in Greece as one of that country's great heroes. In the end, Byron earned his fine superiority to his own vocation as well.

See also *MANFRED;* ROMANTICISM; "SHE WALKS IN BEAUTY"; "SO, WE'LL GO NO MORE A-ROVING"; "STANZAS FOR MUSIC."

BIBLIOGRAPHY

Addison, Catherine. "Ottava Rima and Novelistic Discourse." *Journal of Narrative Theory* 34, no. 2 (2004): 133–145.

Bloom, Harold. *The Visionary Company: A Reading of English Romantic Poetry.* Garden City, N.Y.: Doubleday, 1961.

Duffy, Edward. *Rousseau in England: The Context for Shelley's Critique of the Enlightenment.* Berkeley: University of California Press, 1979.

Hazlitt, William. *Spirit of the Age; or, Contemporary Portraits.* London: Oxford University Press, 1970.

Marchand, Leslie A. *Byron: A Portrait.* New York: Knopf, 1970.

McGann, Jerome. *Byron and Romanticism.* New York: Cambridge University Press, 2002.

Moore, Doris. *Late Lord Byron: Posthumous Dramas.* New York: Harper and Row, 1977.

Saintsbury, George. *History of English Prosody, from the Twelfth Century to the Present Day.* New York: Russell & Russell, 1961.

Thorslev, Peter Larsen. *The Byronic Hero: Types and Prototypes.* Minneapolis, University of Minnesota Press, 1962.

C

"CALIBAN UPON SETEBOS" ROBERT BROWNING (1864) This is one of the dramatic monologues in ROBERT BROWNING's book *Dramatis Personae* and one of the poems that brought him great popular success. It is put into the mouth of Caliban, the half-monster in William Shakespeare's *The Tempest,* and picks up from a few hints dropped in the play (just as "CHILDE ROLAND TO THE DARK TOWER CAME" derives from a fragment in Shakespeare's *King Lear*). The poem has Browning's trademark roughness of language, but of course, the audience here felt the appropriateness of that roughness to Caliban, the speaker, who often speaks the same way in his grumbling and cursing complaints in *The Tempest.*

The poem is considerably easier to follow if one keeps a few principles in mind. The way Caliban represents himself in his own grammatical formulations is somewhat like a child or primitive (as the Victorian age understood them, partly from having to communicate with natives of far-flung outposts of the British Empire through a kind of crude lingua franca). He has not fully risen to the kind of social self-possession and parity with others that enables him to be comfortable saying "I." He identifies with his own superego and therefore tends to speak of himself in the third person, usually without the actual pronoun. He *is* the source of all the language throughout the poem, but the bracketed opening and closing show the extent to which he is aware of himself speaking in the body of the poem, so he is speaking for himself; that is, he is speaking for his own superego, accepting and explaining the legitimacy of the regime of random pain and torment which he finds his life to be. It is as though he is testing what someone like Setebos might overhear if he is unfortunate. Setebos will always receive a capital *H* in the pronouns that refer to Him, so following the typography will enable a reader to follow the poem.

Setebos, we know from *The Tempest,* is his "dam's god"—that is, the god his mother Sycorax, a foul witch, worshipped. Sycorax (we learn) had been a foul witch in Algiers, banished for some terrible depravity—probably the depravity by which she became pregnant with Caliban—to the obscure Mediterranean island that is the setting of the play. She gives birth to Setebos on the island and imprisons Ariel, the great spirit of the air in *The Tempest* because (Shakespeare hints) he would not satisfy her sexual desires. She dies, and Prospero, banished from Milan, uses his magic to rescue Ariel and force Caliban to servitude after he returns Prospero's kindness with violence (in particular sexual violence toward his daughter Miranda). And yet Caliban has great depth of character, depth which torments him more than the shallowness of the other clownish figures in the play with whom he comes to associate.

In the play, Caliban is forced to acknowledge that Prospero's powers are greater even than Setebos's. But Browning's dramatic monologue is set before the events that the play covers. This needs a little explanation, since Browning's sense of story allows for a kind of reversal where the telling of the story in Shakespeare becomes itself the story told in Browning. The opening of *The Tempest* takes place many years after Prospero and Miranda come to the island, but in Browning's poem it is telescoped with their arrival, so that the storm that gives the play its title becomes in Browning the harbinger of the arrival of Prospero and Miranda. The poem ends as the tempest begins, and we know what will happen next, although Caliban does not.

Browning follows Shakespeare in balancing Caliban's qualities. He is a survivalist monster, barely staying alive by living like an animal, but he also thinks very deeply about the fact that he is living like an animal even as he believes in a god. His dilemma represents the dilemma of many would-be believers after the publication of Charles Darwin's *On the Origin of Species* in 1859, the culmination of the era's discovery that the world was not made for humans and that many species and types of animals had come and gone in a world in which (as ALFRED, LORD TENNYSON put it in *IN MEMORIAM A.H.H.*), Nature cares nothing even for species, let alone individuals: "From scarped cliff and quarried stone / She cries, 'A thousand types are gone; / I care for nothing, all shall go" (stanza 55). Tennyson wrote that before Darwin; Browning, writing after, had an even greater challenge to the meaningfulness of human experience to face. He does face it, both in "Caliban upon Setebos" and in the pope's monologue in *The RING AND THE BOOK*.

Caliban's "natural theology" (to allude to the poem's subtitle, "or, Natural theology in the Island") anthropomorphizes the god it tries to understand. This was a move made in the 18th century in order to argue for the existence of a god, one now associated with the theologian and philosopher William Paley at the turn of the 19th century, but already mocked by the Scottish philosopher David Hume a few decades later. Browning is of Hume's opinion on the merits of the argument: Natural theology allows for any kind of god at all, or at least any god for which one can find a human analogue. Caliban's god is as vicious, arbitrary, and incapable of sympathy as Caliban himself. Caliban repeatedly draws the analogy with the words "So He:"—which is to say that Setebos acts in his sphere toward Caliban as Caliban acts in his own toward crabs and insects and rank things in nature. Caliban lives in the Darwinian update of the world Thomas Hobbes described as a war of all against all where only the fittest survive. He is not entirely correct, however, in imagining himself like Setebos: Setebos does not spend any time tormenting himself with painful theological speculation, as Caliban does.

This aspect of his superiority is what enables Caliban to imagine something transcending Setebos even as Setebos transcends him, the thing he dimly imagines as the Quiet. The fact that Caliban can imagine this further reach and region, and imagine it more subtly and more powerfully than Setebos would, shows that Caliban represents more than Setebos—or conversely that Setebos does not represent a projection of everything there is in Caliban. This idea is one that Browning will have the Pope develop further in *The Ring and the Book:* the idea that the natural world and natural theology cannot account for everything to be found in the human spirit—even in the spirit to be found in Caliban.

BIBLIOGRAPHY

Bloom, Harold. *A Map of Misreading*. New York: Oxford University Press, 2003.

———. *Poetry and Repression: Revisionism from Blake to Stevens*. New Haven, Conn.: Yale University Press, 1976.

Browning, Robert. *Essay on Percy Bysshe Shelley*. London: Published for the Shelley Society by Reeves and Turner, 1888.

DeVane, William C. *A Browning Handbook*. New York: Appleton-Century-Crofts, 1955.

Langbaum, Robert Woodrow. *The Modern Spirit: Essays on the Continuity of Nineteenth- and Twentieth-Century Literature*. New York: Oxford University Press, 1970.

Raymond, William O. *The Infinite Moment, and Other Essays in Robert Browning*. Toronto: University of Toronto Press, 1965.

CALVERLEY, CHARLES STUART (CHARLES STUART BLAYDS) (1831–1884) Charles Stuart Calverley was a gifted parodist and, with WINTHROP MACKWORTH PRAED and LEWIS CARROLL, one of the great writers of light verse in the 19th century, and often considered the greatest (not least by Virginia Woolf's father, Leslie Stephen). He takes after THOMAS HOOD in the delightful way he combines perfect expressive command with the ability to produce a sudden and unexpected turn that makes everything fall into hilarious place. But his effects are not quite so random as Hood's and add up to a more integrated and fluid whole. Where Hood produces a series of gags, Calverley's wit is continuous and sustained.

Light verse (as W. H. Auden observed) is technically much more difficult to write than serious poetry. There can be no poetic license in light verse since the delight it offers is that of perfection, not of depth. (Calverley is thus in a sense the opposite of his highly irregular contemporary ROBERT BROWNING, whose *THE RING AND THE BOOK* he parodied in "The Cock and the Bull.") Light verse requires constant and felicitous fluidity, and this was a quality Calverley had in abundance, winning the Chancellor's Prize for Latin verse at Oxford in 1851 with a poem he ad-libbed. The extraordinary facility with Latin that this demonstrates fits with Calverley's love of Horace, whose mode Calverley's own poems emulate in English; his first book contained dazzling translations of famous English poems into Latin. His prize-winning success did not prevent him from having to leave Oxford as a consequence of some unseemly behavior in those stricter times, and so he went to Cambridge, where again he won the Chancellor's Prize, the only person ever to do so at both universities.

Calverley was born Charles Stuart Blayds, but his family reassumed the name Calverley, which had been changed by his grandfather. After graduation from Cambridge, he taught, married, and became a lawyer, but 10 years later (in 1866) he suffered a terrible concussion in an ice-skating accident and never recovered the ability for sustained concentration necessary for him to practice. His youthful experience of indolent, brilliant, improvisatory fluidity served him well, though, and he continued translating and writing original poetry; his 1872 translation of the Greek pastoral poet Theocritus is particularly noteworthy.

Calverley's later, post-concussive poetry, such as "CHANGED," (1872) might be seen as displaying a struggle against the depression that characterized his years as a semi-invalid. Certainly if one takes the sentiments of that poem seriously, he is no longer the brilliant poetic soul he once was. But what is characteristic in Calverley is the representation of happiness in his verse and the way he tries to use verse to make people happy. This is the moral stance of his poetry: It should be a document and instrument of happiness. His poetry depicts social pleasures such as charades (that is, the riddling poems that he wrote), tobacco, beer, newspapers, holidays—in a word (or rather the title of an 1872 poem), "Contentment: in the manner of Horace." The happiness Calverley offers and that he takes is that of social interaction. It makes him happy to make others happy, and it makes him happy to write poetry about making others happy.

See also "BEER," "PEACE: A STUDY."

BIBLIOGRAPHY

Auden, W. H. Introduction to *The Oxford Book of Light Verse.* New York: Oxford University Press, 1973.

Babington, Percy Lancelot. *Browning & Calverley; or, Poem and Parody.* London: John Castle, 1925.

Ince, Richard Basil. *Calverley and Some Cambridge Wits of the Nineteenth Century.* London: G. Richards and H. Toulmin at the Cayme Press, 1929.

"CARRION COMFORT" GERARD MANLEY HOPKINS (1885) ROBERT BRIDGES gave this poem its title (from its first line) when he published Hopkins's work in 1918. Hopkins had described one of his sonnets to Bridges as "written in blood," and Bridges thought it must have been this one.

"Carrion Comfort" belongs to the set of seven poems written in 1885 that Hopkins's friend and teacher R. W. Dixon called the "terrible sonnets"—"terrible" as in responsive to and expressive of terror. They are sometimes also called the "sonnets of desolation," and the terror or desolation whence they arise seems to be the psychological despair that Hopkins endured after moving to Dublin to become a professor of classics in 1884. It was in his poetry that Hopkins sought to cope with the despair that came close to overwhelming him.

In this poem, his despair offers itself as comfort—the comfort of suicidal despair and the feeling that there is nothing left to lose so no reason not to die. This is a great theme in English poetry, most vividly articulated by another English poet in Ireland, Edmund Spenser, in book 1 of *The Faerie Queene,* where the allegorical figure of Despayre tempts the hero to suicide; and by Shakespeare's Richard II, who sees no comfort but in "the sweet way I was in to despair." *Comfort* is a crucial word in Hopkins, especially in the "terrible sonnets," since it is the Holy Ghost (great solacer in "GOD'S GRANDEUR") who is supposed to bring comfort when Christ has departed. The Comforter (or Paraclete) is the Holy Ghost (John 14:26), and the departure of Christ makes possible the coming of the Spirit who will console us for his departure: "It is expedient for you that I go away: for if I go not away, the Comforter will not come unto you; but if I depart, I will send him unto you" (John 16:7). In "NO WORST, THERE IS NONE" (written on the same sheet of paper that contains the final draft of "Carrion Comfort"), Hopkins despairs "Comforter, where, where is your comforting?" (l. 3), while his great late poem "THAT NATURE IS A HERACLITEAN FIRE" anticipates "the *comfort* of the resurrection" (as the remainder of the title puts it).

In "Carrion Comfort" Hopkins finds strength only in the energy of the despair he wishes to feast on. Despair is attractive because it offers a last burst of human action, but Hopkins uses that burst to resist it. As is always true of Hopkins, his prosody here is remarkable. The poem has some features of SPRUNG RHYTHM, but it is mainly in what Hopkins calls "running rhythm"—that is, iambic meter, although the lines are of variable length, from 12 to 18 syllables. (All the lines can perhaps be counted as having six main stresses, but if so this is not easy to hear or distinguish.) The variable length allows for a play of internal rhyme that *sounds* conclusive, even when it is not, since we do not know how to anticipate how long a line will be. For example, the *me* in the third line sounds like it is the rhyme we are expecting for *thee* at the end of line 1 (we do not yet know the octet is written in a Petrarchan form, with the rhymes proceeding *abba abba*).

Hopkins represents even more powerfully his cry of despair *"I can no more"* (l. 3), which we hear as rhyming with the emphasized *or* earlier in the line. But it turns out that cry (modeled on Hopkins's great 17th-century original, George Herbert's poem "Denial") is not the end of the line. The truth is in the first two syllables of the cry, syllables repeated at the end of the line to contradict the cry: "I can." This retrospectively makes us see that the crucial rhyme is on *man,* and that Hopkins somehow manages to reject the comfort that would involve his laying aside his divinely imaged life as a human being. He can continue to do something—he may not know what, but just continuance is what his Christian vocation calls him to now.

But it is God and not Death that makes him feel so miserable—this is the strange thing that his faith makes him feel. Why should God (the "terrible" being he addresses in the second stanza) do this to him when he loved God so much, and loved his vocation so much? God is testing and winnowing him, even though he has already kissed the rod, or *seemed* to have kissed it (l. 10). He now realizes that he had kissed the rod to avoid the great struggle of faith and vocation. He had not wrestled with God as Jacob does in Genesis; it is in this wrestling that he can see his own abasement and his own exaltation as well, just in seeing the abasement. The poem itself seems to gasp with the realization that he has fought God even in seeking not to fight him, or that as with Jacob, God has come to wrestle with him and he has shown his understanding of the seriousness of the encounter when finally he fought back. But it is this that makes him cry out "my God!" (l. 14), just as he realizes that he has been fighting with "my God." That realization echoes the two "I cans" in l. 3, as though a difference has snapped shut and all is tight again. The year of darkness and despair has reduced him wholly to the need for God, and it is in the utter intensity of that need that the poet finds him.

The immense prosodic difficulty of the poem makes prosody or versification a proxy for psychological difficulty. The saving utterance that concludes it, then, makes the poem itself into the scene of Calverley's wrestling with God, and of the breakthrough and termination of that context, as the poem and the despair it chronicles end together.

BIBLIOGRAPHY

Bridges, Robert. Preface to *Poems of Gerard Manley Hopkins.* Edited by W. H. Gardner, 94–101. New York: Oxford University Press, 1948.

Gardner, W. H. *Gerard Manley Hopkins (1844–1889): A Study of Poetic Idiosyncrasy in Relation to Poetic Tradition.* New Haven, Conn.: Yale University Press, 1949.

———, ed. Introduction to *Poems and Prose of Gerard Manley Hopkins*. Harmondsworth, Middlesex, England: Penguin, 1963.

Hartman, Geoffrey. *The Unmediated Vision: An Interpretation of Wordsworth, Hopkins, Rilke, and Valery*. New Haven, Conn.: Yale University Press, 1954.

Hopkins, Gerard Manley. *Gerard Manley Hopkins: Selected Letters*. Edited by Catherine Phillips. New York: Oxford University Press, 1990.

Miller, J. Hillis. "Gerard Manley Hopkins." In *The Disappearance of God: Five Nineteenth-Century Writers*. 270–359. Cambridge, Mass.: Belknap Press of Harvard University Press, 1963.

White, Norman. *Hopkins: A Literary Biography*. New York: Oxford University Press, 1992.

CARROLL, LEWIS (CHARLES LUTWIDGE DODGSON) (1832–1898)

One way to distinguish the spirit of VICTORIAN POETRY from that of the ROMANTICISM which preceded it—one way, that is, to insist that the best feature of Victorian poetry as a whole is its commitment to being superb and perfect *minor* poetry—is to observe how much Victorian poetry is designed with its readers in mind. This may sound like a truism, but in fact we might say (borrowing a distinction of Samuel Beckett's) that romantic poetry is expressive and Victorian poetry communicative. This is nowhere better seen than in Victorian parody—rarely vicious (unlike, say, LORD BYRON's parodies of ROBERT SOUTHEY), always intelligent and often better than the poem being parodied. The greatest parodist of the age was CHARLES STUART CALVERLEY, but his contemporary, Lewis Carroll, combined parody with nonsense verse (along with EDWARD LEAR, Carroll is the inventor of the genre) to evoke a world in an afternoon, a lifetime in a dream.

This is one of the reasons that the great 20th-century philosopher Ludwig Wittgenstein so admired Carroll and pegged one of his most important philosophical points to a nonsense joke from *Alice in Wonderland*: "We call him tortoise because he taught us." Nonsense, for Wittgenstein, is what happens when "Language goes on holiday." But holidays are pleasures and public pleasures the pleasure of being with others. Parody assumes on the part of its readership familiarity with the original being parodied (this is Calverley's mode); but to this Carroll adds the idea that his readership might not know or care about the original. The poems are wonderful either way. They are wonderful because they aim at shared absurdity, shared laughter, a sense that everyone likes a character—as children do—and this is because every adult *is* a character. But every adult also remembers his or her own childish interest in the diversity of adult eccentricity—Carroll most of all.

Certainly the central idea in all of Carroll's narrative, prose and poetry, is one of vivid characteristics, and those narratives are populated with a child's garden of Dickensian personalities. We can distinguish two sorts of poems that Carroll wrote: the nonsense verse that appears in his prose fiction, like the *Alice* books; and the longer nonsense narratives in poetry, like *The Hunting of the Snark*. Both sorts of work suggest the extent to which his own characters take pleasure in the nonsensical texture of their words (see Humpty Dumpty for an obvious example)—a pleasure that they rightfully expect others to share. The only sin in Carroll is intolerant seriousness. Thus, nonsense and parody in his hands are world-embracing pleasures, and they are as tolerant of their originals (WILLIAM WORDSWORTH, for example, who is the "Aged man a-sitting on a gate" in Carroll's parody of a Wordsworth poem) as of their addressees.

It is probably no accident that Wittgenstein shared with Carroll an intense background in logic, which aims to tame the diversity of the world. Both discovered that the world was richer than their efforts to codify it. And if Carroll was influential for Wittgenstein he was even more influential for James Joyce, whose *Finnegans Wake* is in many respects a rewriting of Carroll's work, with Humpty Dumpty and Alice as central figures within that great nonsensical history of the world.

Too much has been made of Carroll's supposed pedophilia—the obvious pleasure he took in photographing young girls (like the original Alice Liddell) and their elders (like ALFRED, LORD TENNYSON) and in spending time writing them poems and telling them stories. In a Freudian age it would be incorrect to say that these pleasures were "innocent," but more correct to say that whatever pleasure he took was of the nature of a childish crush brought forward to adulthood and yet still experienced as childish, not as salacious or prurient. Those who are critical of Carroll's interest in girls are in fact the salacious ones. Another way to put this is to say that Carroll probably had no sense of his pleasure in their company as sexual, and that he did no harm either to himself or others. What he loved about children was their sense of the richness of the world, and it is this sense that makes his literary work, poetry and prose, so enchanting.

See also "JABBERWOCKY"; "MAD GARDENER'S SONG, THE."

BIBLIOGRAPHY

Bloom, Harold, ed. *Lewis Carroll.* New York: Chelsea House, 1987.

Kelly, Richard. *Lewis Carroll.* Boston: Twayne Publishers, 1990.

Lehmann, John. *Lewis Carroll and the Spirit of Nonsense.* Nottingham, England: University of Nottingham Press, 1974.

"CASABIANCA" FELICIA HEMANS (1829) This is one of FELICIA HEMANS's most famous poems, memorized in scores of schoolrooms and revivified by Elizabeth Bishop's use of it in her own poem "Casabianca." It is much mocked but demonstrates some of Hemans's virtues, including her ability to disarm objections to sentimentality, largely through the sympathy she shows to those whose interests diverge from those of Britain's. Hemans's well-known note to the poem reads that "Young Casabianca, a boy about thirteen years old, son to the Admiral of the Orient, remained at his post (in the Battle of the Nile) after the ship had taken fire, and all the guns had been abandoned, and perished in the explosion of the vessel, when the flames had reached the powder." (She probably read the story in ROBERT SOUTHEY's wildly and perennially popular *Life of Nelson.*)

The Battle of the Nile took place on August 1, 1798, just eight weeks before Hemans's own fifth birthday; it lasted past midnight into August 2. The British fleet, under the command of Horatio Nelson, demolished the French ships that were defending Alexandria (15 miles away) and their Egyptian conquests. The British checked NAPOLEON BONAPARTE's conquest of North Africa and established the clear naval superiority that would set a limit to his power for the rest of his career.

"The Orient" to which Hemans refers in the poem was the French flagship *L'Orient,* under the command of Luc-Julien-Joseph Casabianca. It blew up at 11:00 P.M., killing both Casabianca and his 12-year-old son, Giocante, who was on watch. The explosion was so powerful that it could be felt in Alexandria.

Hemans could not, of course, know what happened on the ship, and her version of the story is an imaginative reconstruction. It is all the more powerful for that. She imagines the boy's despair at his predicament, and the fact that his father is unable to protect him. What else *could* the boy be thinking? His own helplessness is almost a given, as a boy among men on a naval flagship. But the parent's care is the natural counterbalance to any child's condition of helplessness. It is his father's helplessness that must be the new and fatal fact here—his father's inability to protect him.

Indeed, the poem represents something of a critique of the father for putting him in this position to begin with. It is not a critique the boy would have recognized, and it is only implicit. The father, struck unconscious in the battle, is unaware of what he has done to his son. But we recognize this unconsciousness as moral and not merely physical. And for this reason, the reader's concern for the boy—helpless though our concern is—substitutes for the father's.

But our concern is helpless, and what must happen instead is that the boy has to become an adult, has to live his own life or take responsibility for his own death in the minutes that remain to him. And this is just what he does. His father has abandoned him—physically and morally—but he does not abandon his father. He has become what his father failed to, and it is therefore his heart that is the noblest that perished at the battle, not his father's and not that of any other casualty, whether British or French. In her later poem, Bishop quite rightly paraphrases Hemans's moral: "Love's the boy stood on the burning deck."

BIBLIOGRAPHY

Armstrong, Isobel. *Victorian Poetry: Poetry, Poetics and Politics.* New York: Routledge, 1993.

Armstrong, Isobel, and Virginia Blain, eds. *Women's Poetry in the Enlightenment: The Making of a Canon, 1730–1820.* New York: St. Martin's Press, 1999.

Southey, Robert. *Life of Horatio, Lord Nelson.* London: Society for Promoting Christian Knowledge, 1851.
Sweet, Nanora. *Felicia Hemans: Reimagining Poetry in the Nineteenth Century.* New York: Palgrave, 2001.

"CATARACT OF LODORE, THE" ROBERT SOUTHEY **(1820)** In her monologue at the end of James Joyce's great novel *Ulysses,* Molly Bloom remembers the lines "O how the waters come down at Lodore." This is a slight misquotation of ROBERT SOUTHEY's memorable experiment in a kind of semantic onomatopoeia. Southey had eight children (one of whom died in infancy, and two more of whom predeceased him, to his unspeakable sorrow). He wrote this poem down after the time he must have improvised the doggeral description of a waterfall for them. Indeed, it is a record of that improvisation.

In the poem, Southey's son asks him to describe the cataract (waterfall) at Lodore. The son who asks him this must be more or less based on Herbert (1807–16), since Charles (1819–88) was only a year old at the time, and knowing that Herbert died four years prior to the poem's composition must make us feel the sadness to which it is in part a response (like WILLIAM WORDSWORTH's "SURPRISED BY JOY"). The waterfall at Lodore falls into Borrowdale by Derwent Water in the Lake District so dear to the LAKE POETS—Wordsworth, SAMUEL TAYLOR COLERIDGE, and Southey. When in spate, the Lodore falls are very impressive, but in the summer they tend to be meager. Hence, his sons want to hear about it "As many a time / They had seen it before" (ll. 15–16)—that is, they want to have his account of it correspond to a memory that the falls themselves do not always live up to. Impressive or meager though the falls may be, the pleasure of the poem is in the poet's inventiveness, and it was this pleasure that his children sought from their father, and that he now remembers with pleasure.

His pleasure and their own coincide in the brilliant resourcefulness of the rhyming: "So I told them in rhyme / For of rhymes I had store" (ll. 17–18). The poem's appearance on the page shows the copious store of rhymes available to him and also makes a kind of ideogram of the waterfall itself. The description of the cataract proper begins at line 24, but the first verbs describing what it does appear at line 30: "It runs and it creeps." These verbs will begin modulating into the present participle form that will be the major throughline of the poem nine lines later: "And thence at departing, / Awakening and starting / It runs through the reeds" (ll. 33–35). Those participles announce their full blast after the two hobson-jobson words (as they are called), "Helter-skelter / Hurry-scurry" (ll. 41–42), which will set up the later rhymes: "Here it comes sparkling" (l. 43). The section comprising lines 56–69 is composed of paired participles, two per line, with the second ones rhyming: "Rising and leaping, / Sinking and creeping" (ll. 56–57), for example.

After a kind of violent, ledge-like pause, the next section (ll. 71–99) contains 29 couplets, again composed of paired participles, but here the participles in each *line* rhyme: "Collecting, projecting, / Receding and speeding" (ll. 71–72), for example. This rush of paired rhymes picks up from the hobson-jobson rhymes just mentioned and makes a long drop down the page, a drop which gathers into the *triple* participial rhymes that comprise the final section (ll. 100–119)—for example, "Dividing and gliding and sliding / And falling and brawling and sprawling" (ll. 100–101). A two-line summary ends the poem, but we are stunned by the sound it describes and enacts.

Where Southey's pleasure and his children's do not coincide is in his sense of them as a kind of cataract as well, rushing on him and asking for the rhymes. Southey makes the *water* of Lodore rhyme with *daughter* (ll. 8, 12), and makes *brother* rhyme with *another* daughter (ll. 9, 11), so that his children are all brought into the cataract of rhyme that represents the cataract they wish to hear about. The rhymes stand for the falls, then, and the falls stand for the children, because it was they who wanted to hear the rhymes about the falls.

Finally writing the poem down was a way for Southey to write a lovely memorial for the pure rush of life that he had experienced in his young children and which was now threatening to dry up as they, and he, got older (two having already died). Its great good humor and boundless energy and freshness make the poem a signal success. Some lovely shots of the Falls at Lodore may be seen at http://www.visitcumbria.com/kes/lodore.htm.

BIBLIOGRAPHY

Bromwich, David. "Of the Mule Breed." *London Review of Books,* (May 21, 1998). Available online. URL: www.lrb.co.uk/v20/n10/bvomo1_html. Accessed March 16, 2009.

Butler, Marilyn. *Romantics, Rebels, and Reactionaries: English Literature and Its Background, 1760–1830.* New York: Oxford University Press, 1982.

De Quincey, Thomas. *Recollections of the Lakes and the Lake Poets.* Edited by David Wright. Harmondsworth, England: Penguin, 1970.

Hazlitt, William. *Spirit of the Age; or, Contemporary Portraits.* London: Oxford University Press, 1970.

Perry, Seamus. "Southey's Genius for Repression," *London Review of Books,* (January 24, 2006). Available online by subscription. URL: www. lrb.co.uk/v28/no2/perr01_.html. Accessed March 16, 2009.

Storey, Mark. *Robert Southey: A Life.* New York: Oxford University Press, 1997.

"CHANGED" **CHARLES STUART CALVERLEY (1872)** "Changed" is another one of CHARLES STUART CALVERLEY's comic poems, one that parodies its first-person speaker. The parody is not so much for his pretension as for his lack of pretension, for the unconscious anticlimax that marks everything he says and does. Calverley is particular good at managing the meters of anticlimax. In general, those meters are truncated—the anticlimactic line surprises by how quickly it ends, as though it has little to say. This can have a powerful and uplifting effect, as at the end of LEIGH HUNT's "RONDEAU" ("JENNY KISSED ME") or ROBERT BROWNING's "MEMORABILIA," or in the tradition of echo poems from Ovid to Sidney and Herbert and beyond. But the effect can often be deflating, and Calverley uses it to deflate. He does so by ending every quatrain with a monometer, a single foot. Technically, the poem is in octets, not quatrains, but they break down into two quatrains. By using the longer stanza, Calverley makes the truncated line surprising: We keep reading final lines before we are ready for them, mid-octet.

The short lines are all the better for being pointlessly unexpected. They continue over enjambents that seem to promise genuine meaning, analysis, or explanation, and each time we fail to get the meaning we expect. Calverley promises to tell us what he knows, but it turns out that all he knows is what he has just said (ll. 3–4); he tells us an account of the time that he was socially engaging, but now he cannot engage us at all in reminding us of that time (ll. 7–8); we expect that he had nearly learned to love or to be a poet or to see into the life of things, but it turns out that he has only come close to learning to have a minimal response to the poetry that seems to ennoble him (ll. 11–12); the "until" of the end of the second stanza seems to promise an account of how far he had proceeded in his passion for the romance of legend, but it turns out he has not gone far, only until the whole thing became "a bore"; we think that his failure of memory will be Wordsworthian, an account of the tragedy with which the soul forgets how she felt, but it is only the songs he used to know that he has forgotten (ll. 19–20); he offers us a sense of dancing that will ascend into flight, but then it turns out not that he *could* but that no one ever could fly; and so on, so that at the end of the poem he describes not how he will attempt again to fight the fates that disappoint him but why he is ending the poem: He really has nothing to say.

So what has changed? The speaker has, but unlike the change in WILLIAM WORDSWORTH's INTIMATIONS ODE, where the intensity with which loss is experienced is itself a kind of compensation, Calverley's speaker can barely register the change, so stultified and uninvolved has he become. Wordsworth's lamentations of loss are great; the speaker of Calverley's poem cannot measure how much he has lost and therefore is in no way ennobled by that loss, and the witty anticlimax with which Calverley expresses this common and perhaps unavoidable fate is what makes the poem so entertaining.

BIBLIOGRAPHY

Auden, W. H. Introduction to *The Oxford Book of Light Verse.* New York: Oxford University Press, 1973.

Babington, Percy Lancelot. *Browning & Calverley; or, Poem and Parody.* London: John Castle, 1925.

Ince, Richard Basil. *Calverley and Some Cambridge Wits of the Nineteenth Century.* London: G. Richards and H. Toulmin at the Cayme Press, 1929.

"CHARGE OF THE LIGHT BRIGADE, THE" **ALFRED, LORD TENNYSON (1854)** This is one of ALFRED, LORD TENNYSON's most popular poems.

In Virginia Woolf's *To the Lighthouse,* Mr. Ramsay quotes from "The Charge of the Light Brigade" as part of his incantatory sense of the world. The poem allows Woolf to show how powerful language can hypnotize its hearers and bring them into a kind of concentrated trance where nothing else matters.

This was Tennyson's theme in general. Of the Victorians, he and ALGERNON CHARLES SWINBURNE were most interested in reflecting on the nature of poetry. Poetry was for them a reflection on the intensity of its own forms, an intensity that trumps its official theme or content. But with "The Charge of the Light Brigade" the direction of interest is reversed. The poem becomes an analogue to the charge, rather than the charge's being an analogue to the poem.

The Charge of the Light Brigade took place in the Crimean War, during the climactic Battle of Balaclava, on October 25, 1854. The English and the Russians were battling with mixed success, and on the previous day, the English had neglected to press home an advantage. Tempers ran very high among the English officers, many of whom felt others were incompetent. Much of the animosity was due to class differences, the professionals thinking the aristocratic officers naïve, and those officers distrusting the experience of the nonaristocrats.

Lines of communication were very poor, and the much-loathed Captain Louis Edward Nolan conveyed, almost certainly mistakenly, the order that the Light Brigade—that is, a lightly armed cavalry brigade without heavy weapons—was supposed to charge into a cul-de-sac surrounded by Russian artillery in order to prevent them from taking their weapons with them in the orderly retreat they had begun the day before. Nolan apparently misconstrued a gesture of his commanding officer, and he sent the Light Brigade into the wrong terrain.

What gripped the English reading of the disaster, and what gripped Tennyson's imagination, was the gallantry of the soldiers, who knew they were riding toward almost certain death. They actually overran some of the Russian positions, under extraordinary fire, before retreating, losing as many men in the retreat as in the charge. More than "six hundred" (l. 4) charged, and nearly half were casualties, with 118 killed outright, including Nolan, who therefore could never be called upon to explain his message. He and the leader of the brigade, Lord Cardigan, rode very courageously, however.

Tennyson's poem is outraged at the "blunder" that sent these men to their deaths. The magnitude of the blunder is measured by the magnitude of the courage that its victims showed. That courage is memorialized in the propulsive rhymes and rhythms of the poem. The poem itself is in dactylic meter, the form appropriate for elegies. Tennyson said it was "founded on the phrase 'Some one had blundered.'" The blunder and the charge go together, in the sound of the poem as in the event it relates.

The poem's power is generally considered jingoistic: It depicts the gallantry of the English no matter who is ranged against them, blundering officers or Russian enemy. Tennyson published it in the *Examiner* on December 9, and the poem was subsequently distributed to English soldiers, whose morale it cheered. It continued to do so in subsequent years. It is certainly not a militaristic poem, but its energies helped the military and the nation gear itself up for the single-minded pursuit of military goals. We can see the poem as at once regretful and admiring, and understand it as an example of the dangers not of transmuting admiration and violence into poetry, but of the reverse process, where the poetry encourages the admiration of courage and the violence that sets it off.

See also VICTORIAN POETRY.

BIBLIOGRAPHY

Armstrong, Isobel. *Victorian Poetry: Poetry, Poetics and Politics.* New York: Routledge, 1993.

Bloom, Harold. *Poetry and Repression: Revisionism from Blake to Stevens.* New Haven, Conn.: Yale University Press, 1976.

Buckley, Jerome Hamilton. *Tennyson: The Growth of a Poet.* Boston: Houghton Mifflin, 1965.

Kilham, John. *Critical Essays on the Poetry of Tennyson.* New York: Barnes and Noble, 1960.

Kincaid, James R. *Tennyson's Major Poems: The Comic and Ironic Patterns.* New Haven, Conn.: Yale University Press, 1975.

Ricks, Christopher B. *Tennyson.* New York: Macmillan, 1972.

Rowlinson, Matthew. *Tennyson's Fixations: Psychoanalysis and the Topics of the Early Poetry.* Charlottesville: University Press of Virginia, 1994.

Tucker, Herbert. *Tennyson and the Doom of Romanticism.* Cambridge, Mass.: Harvard University Press, 1988.
Woodham Smith, Cecil Blanche Fitz Gerald. *The Reason Why.* New York: McGraw-Hill, 1954.

CHARTISM See COOPER, THOMAS.

"CHARTIST CHAUNT" THOMAS COOPER (1877)

According to *Poetical Works,* which THOMAS COOPER published in 1877, "Chartist Chaunt" was one of a number of "smaller prison rhymes," as opposed to what he called his "prison rhyme" pure and simple, his long and much-noticed (though perhaps not much read) "Purgatory of Suicides." Cooper was imprisoned from 1842 to 1845 on a somewhat trumped-up charge of incitement to riot, and in prison he wrote his most stirring Chartist poetry, of which "Chartist Chaunt" is now the most-anthologized. As a movement, Chartism may be seen as in the line of radical and sometimes visionary poetry produced by and on behalf of the English working class and most closely associated with WILLIAM BLAKE, though it is unlikely that Cooper knew of Blake, even later in his life—he certainly never mentions him in his autobiography. But Cooper was, like Blake, an autodidact who thought that the self-education of the working class could change the world; in Cooper's case (as in Blake's), much of that education was in the poetry of John Milton; indeed, Cooper knew several books of *Paradise Lost* by heart.

Cooper's poetry shows that he has taken some of Milton's prosody to heart, even though the "Chartist Chaunt" is nothing at all in style like *Paradise Lost.* (It may most nearly resemble the choral odes in Milton's *Samson Agonistes.*) In particular, he uses surprising enjambment and vocative to teach a lesson that focuses on the unexpectedness of the poem's movement. For example, the last stanza unexpectedly enjambs across a clausal boundary, and we are not expecting to find out what it is that "kings render their defender"—that is, what it is kings give him. We think, rather, that kings will make their defender *into* something, or just simply create their own defender. The next line seems to be an antithesis, as though the poem will go on thus: "Though kings render their defender, / Titles, gold and splendour gay / *Belong to Labour, Virtue's neighbor . . .*"—the italicized words are not in the poem but indicate what we expect. And then we realize that we must *reject* titles, gold and splendour gay, not just reapportion them.

Who, then, is this singular "defender" of plural "kings"? It would be any movement that duped humans into defending the system of monarchy. This idea is partly forced by Cooper's difficulty in making plural verbs agree with what must be a singular direct object (he would have first considered *renders/defenders,* but that would allude to too specific *a* king, and he could not rhyme the plural *defenders* with a plural verb without the *s* at the end of the singular). But it turns out to be a stroke of serendipity, since it opposes one abstraction—the defender of kings—to the other abstractions that speak in the poem: Truth, Freedom, and Peace. These abstractions address the Chartist brethren, the workers, for whom the time of universal peace is near. The poem, on the other hand, addresses the upholders of the old, the "warrior gory" it names at l. 30.

It is this address that makes the poem a chant. The Chartist brethren sing this song about their revolutionary idealism, and they address it against those who would stand against them. So they sing *together,* not to each other but with each other. And what they sing about is what truth, freedom, and peace sing to them, since they themselves embody those attributes. The poem is by no means a great one, but it is certainly stirring and deserves to be remembered.

BIBLIOGRAPHY

Charlton, John. *The Chartists: The First National Workers' Movement.* Chicago: Pluto Press, 1997.
Cooper, Thomas. *Life of Thomas Cooper; Written by Himself.* London: Hodder and Stoughton, 1872.
Janowitz, Anne F. *Lyric and Labour in the Romantic Tradition.* New York: Cambridge University Press, 1998.
Thompson, Dorothy. *The Chartists.* London: Temple Smith, 1984.

CHILDE HAROLD'S PILGRIMAGE GEORGE GORDON BYRON, LORD BYRON (1812–1818)

The crucial fact about *Childe Harold's Pilgrimage* is that it is a poem. In many ways it is the archetypal first approximation of a romantic poem, both for LORD BYRON'S contemporaries and disciples and for an understanding of English ROMANTICISM's conception of the relationship between nature and literature. The question always to keep in mind about *Childe Harold* is why Byron would write a combination travelogue, political tract, autobiography, lamentation, and paean to nature as a poem, and why such a poem should be so spectacularly popular. These are the basic questions of romanticism.

Byron famously woke up to find himself famous after the publication of cantos I and II of *Childe Harold* when he was 24. Those cantos are more or less the poetic journal of a trip Byron took with friends (in particular his close confidant John Cam Hobhouse) through the regions of Europe not occupied by NAPOLEON BONAPARTE's French forces; the areas held by Napoleon were enemy territory for an Englishman. Accordingly, Byron traveled through Portugal, Spain, Malta, Albania, Greece, and Turkey, whose Ottoman Empire extended over Greece, and Byron would die championing the cause of Greek independence, the loss of which he laments in *Childe Harold.*

Indeed, the poem is about the meaning of freedom in all its forms—personal, political, poetic. In canto I, Byron joins with WILLIAM WORDSWORTH and with a host of others to heap scorn on the Convention of Cintra, the terms by which the British bureaucracy agreed to allow the French forces Admiral Arthur Wellesley had soundly defeated in Portugal in 1808 (a major incident in the Peninsular War against Napoleon) to leave Portugal and Spain with their loot intact. For Byron, Britain was on the right side of the Peninsular War, since Napoleon had come to represent conquest and tyranny. He accordingly celebrates Iberian resistance to Napoleon's superior forces, and throughout *Childe Harold's Pilgrimage* he takes the side of the conquered over their conquerors.

In particular, this takes the form of commitment to Greek independence, a cause for which Byron would later fight and die. In the poem, what he sees everywhere he goes is emptiness and loss. In Greece the loss is that of the glorious past and the great writers who belong to that past; in Albania it is the sublime emptiness of the wilderness. Everywhere it is the indifference of time and fate and nature to human ambition. Byron's predilection for battlefields (which he explicitly mentions in a footnote to canto III) is for them as a place in which the most intense passion and pain display their ultimate pointlessness.

It is this sense of pointlessness—to be found in the ultimate insignificance of poetry as well as of political power—that Byron finds everywhere. The work of the poem is to transmute that feeling into one of freedom. Harold, who barely exists in the poem (he was originally to be called Burun, the old spelling of the Byron family name), is attempting to escape his own past by leaving England for the wastes of ocean and of a fabulous elsewhereness. He is Byron reduced to his own poetic perception, judgment, and feeling, "The wandering outlaw of his own dark mind" (III, l. 20). Indeed, Byron sees him as a kind of avatar by whose creation he can transform his nothingness into "A being more intense," by an apprehension of that very nothingness, "feeling still with thee"—his fictional avatar Harold—"in my crush'd feelings' dearth" (III, ll. 47–54).

All experience testifies to the nothingness that affords Byron the intensity of its own apprehension: "There is a very life in our despair" (III, l. 298). The final defeat of Napoleon at Waterloo, the battlefield Byron visits in canto III (and describes in a passage that will incite WILLIAM MAKEPEACE THACKERAY's great Waterloo scene in *Vanity Fair*), the later autobiographical projection he undertakes in his praise of "the self-torturing sophist, wild Rousseau" (III, l. 725; cantos III and IV are significant influences on PERCY BYSSHE SHELLEY's *The TRIUMPH OF LIFE,* which also contains a memorable account of the French philosopher Jean-Jacques Rousseau, perhaps the first romantic) all lead to the placement of nature above any human significance. As Byron explains in one of his many footnotes, which are essential to the poem's integrity, when describing the scenery of the Alps where Rousseau set his novel *Julie:* "If Rousseau had never written, nor lived, the same associations would not less have belonged to such scenes. He has added to the interest of his works by their adoption; he has shown his sense of their beauty by the selection; but they have done that for him which no human being could do for them" (note to III, l. 940).

This is a telling claim. When canto III of *Childe Harold* came out, Wordsworth complained about Byron (who, like Shelley, is often talking about the still-living Wordsworth when he refers to Rousseau) that his hymn to nature was derived from "TINTERN ABBEY." There is much justice in this claim. Byron had described himself in canto II as the child of nature, as "Her never-wean'd, though not her favour'd child" (II, l. 328). If we take Wordsworth to be her favorite child (as he himself often claimed), then we can see that Byron's relationship to nature is not quite Wordsworthian. For Wordsworth, it is nature that instills within him his vocation as a poet, even if in the end he can transcend nature and plumb the depths of his own soul. Indeed, it is that exploration of selfhood that makes poetic vocation greater and deeper than the experience of nature that catalyzes it. But for Byron, nature is greater than the poet who celebrates her. Poetry is our trivial human way of recording our experience of nature. However, nature is all in all. (Shelley's "MONT BLANC," written during the summer he and Byron both visited the mountain and the surrounding regions, is a kind of rebuttal of this conclusion.)

The odd and paradoxical effect of *Childe Harold* is that it testifies to the most important fact about Byron as a poet: Unlike any of the other romantics, he did not imagine being a poet as a transcendent fact. His refusal of such a claim is part of his greatness, but it is a refusal nonetheless. In comparing himself with Napoleon and with Rousseau, he is acknowledging the ultimate triviality of what he is doing, even while using the language of overweening pride. His poetry is more fully about nature than that of any other romantic poet, because it is least about the depths of selfhood. Of course, Byron's overwhelming and intoxicating personality can be felt in every page he writes. But he refuses to go deep, and this refusal returns us to the nature and freedom from self that he found in nature. Poetry is for Byron a means, and not an end: a means to finding freedom finally in the nature it celebrates. It is this fact—most palpable in *Childe Harold*—that displays both Byron's greatness and his limitations. Those limitations are the very subject of his poetry; they are what make it great, and they are also where he finds the freedom to be overwhelming and intoxicating, a freedom he preferred to the implacable demands of the uncompromising poetic vocation of the other romantics.

BIBLIOGRAPHY

Addison, Catherine. "Ottava Rima and Novelistic Discourse." *Journal of Narrative Theory* 34, no. 2 (2004): 133–145.

Bloom, Harold. *The Visionary Company: A Reading of English Romantic Poetry*. Garden City, N.Y.: Doubleday, 1961.

Duffy, Edward. *Rousseau in England: The Context for Shelley's Critique of the Enlightenment*. Berkeley: University of California Press, 1979.

Hazlitt, William. *Spirit of the Age; or, Contemporary Portraits*. London: Oxford University Press, 1970.

Saintsbury, George. *History of English Prosody, from the Twelfth Century to the Present Day*. New York: Russell & Russell, 1961.

Thorslev, Peter Larsen. *The Byronic Hero: Types and Prototypes*. Minneapolis: University of Minnesota Press, 1962.

"CHILDE ROLAND TO THE DARK TOWER CAME" ROBERT BROWNING (1855)

This is often thought to be ROBERT BROWNING's greatest poem. As a New Year's resolution in 1852, Browning attempted to write one poem a day, and "Childe Roland to the Dark Tower Came" was one of those poems. (He kept the resolution up for three weeks or so.) The poem's power is due in part to its mysteriousness: No one can say with certainty what the Dark Tower is, why Roland makes his way to find it, what has happened to the rest of his band, or whether his quest ends in failure or success. Many later writers, from Hart Crane to Stephen King (in his Dark Tower sequence of novels) have tried to solve the mystery of Browning's poem.

The fact that the poem induces such responses is a possible clue to its meaning. A "childe" is a candidate for knighthood, so that Roland's quest is in part a quest for what Harold Bloom calls poetic election, for entrance into the company of knights, which here will mean poets. The company of poets most relevant to Childe Roland consists of William Shakespeare, where Browning found his title and central goal; John Milton, who in *Paradise Lost* compares the sublime ruined archangel Satan to a dark tower, as Bloom points out in a dazzling interpretation of the poem; and PERCY BYSSHE SHELLEY, Browning's favorite poet, who uses Milton's image in *Julian and Maddalo* to give us the image of a madhouse in Venice in which the truth about human experience is ultimately to be found. To find the Dark Tower is in a sense to find the meaning of the tower and the meaning of the quest *for* the tower. All three coincide there, and so we know, in a sense, what the Dark Tower symbolizes: It symbolizes the meaning of the poem that it also makes mysterious.

This deep and powerful circularity is already implied by the relation of title to poem: The last line of the poem is the same as its title, and suggests that both Roland and the poem have achieved a perspective on their assigned quests which enables them to say that Childe Roland to the Dark Tower came. The poem not only recounts a quest—it *is* one: the quest for the Dark Tower.

Browning takes his line from Shakespeare's *King Lear,* as the parenthetical note under the title indicates: "(See Edgar's Song in Lear)." Seeing Edgar's song will do very little good, however: Edgar has disguised himself as a madman, and part of his madness is to sing snatches and fragments of nonsense. One of these is the line that gives the poem its title, but nothing in Lear explains the *meaning* of the line.

Edgar is perhaps quoting a lost poem or ballad; or Shakespeare is making it sound as though he is quoting a lost poem or ballad. So it is as though Browning has assigned himself the task, after the fact, of writing the poem that Edgar quotes from. In a reversal typical of the theme of Browning's poem, he turns Edgar's line into a quotation by providing the original.

This is a formidable task, for what Browning has to do is to write a poem adequate to his inspiration: the powerful and mysterious line that he knows from the play. Nothing would be more absurd than to explain the Dark Tower away; Shakespeare's line relies on its mystery, and Browning wishes to preserve that mystery. But it can feel as though *any* explanation would explain the mystery away.

The speaker of the poem, Roland, has to decide whether to follow the advice of the cripple who points his way to the Dark Tower. He suspects the cripple is setting a trap by pointing him in the direction of "that ominous tract, which all agree / Hides the Dark Tower." This line is paradoxical, and the paradox is one that characterizes the poem as a whole: The cripple misleads Roland by pointing him in the *right* direction. (The word *tract,* while referring to a topographical area of land, also means *book,* so that in a sense the ominous tract is *King Lear,* in which Edgar's strange and eerie line is hidden in plain sight.)

Roland acquiesces in the cripple's deceit because he hopes now to end his fruitless quest. He wishes, as he puts it, to "be fit" to *fail,* as all his companions have failed, and the paradoxical language of the poem can be found in the question of whether Roland can succeed at failing. If he does succeed, then he will enter the company of his disgraced comrades, Giles and Cuthbert and the rest of "the Band" who have searched for the tower. And somehow the Dark Tower comes to symbolize the failure of those who go out in search of it—for everyone is there when Roland finally arrives, all those who have failed in their quest, and they are all there to see his failure. And it seems he *has* failed: The tower is a spectacular anticlimax, squat, brown, "blind as the fool's heart." A Freudian reading would see it, and probably rightly, not as the phallic symbol one might have expected, the erect embodiment of manhood and knighthood, but as its excremental opposite, the loss of anything that might count as success.

And yet Roland somehow feels the sublimity of the moment that fails so spectacularly. There is nothing for him to rely on in the outside world: Not only are his audience and "the lost adventurers, my peers" unable to ratify his quest, but even the goal of that quest has been evacuated of all meaning and substance. For Roland, through a kind of slingshot effect characteristic of the SUBLIME, this spectacular confrontation with nihilism becomes a sublime confrontation with the void. Roland follows through the poem's paradoxical logic by undoing the difference between success and failure. In remaining "dauntless" in the face of a kind of transcendental failure, Roland measures his power by the extent of that failure. But it has to be real failure for his power to be at all meaningful, and so his success is fundamentally paradoxical.

Thus, the last lines of the poem rely heavily on the ambiguity of the phrase "And yet:"

> And yet, dauntless the slughorn to my lips a set,
> And blew: *Childe Roland to the Dark Tower came.*

What he can ultimately mean by this we cannot know, and one could say that the paradoxical success of the poem is that it fails to give more content to Edgar's line than it had in *King Lear,* and thereby succeeds in preserving and intensifying its mysterious power.

BIBLIOGRAPHY

Bloom, Harold. *A Map of Misreading.* New York: Oxford University Press, 2003.

———. *Poetry and Repression: Revisionism from Blake to Stevens.* New Haven: Yale University Press, 1976.

Browning, Robert. *Essay on Percy Bysshe Shelley.* London: Published for the Shelley Society by Reeves and Turner, 1888.

DeVane, William C. *A Browning Handbook.* New York: Appleton-Century-Crofts, 1955.

Langbaum, Robert Woodrow. *The Modern Spirit: Essays on the Continuity of Nineteenth- and Twentieth-Century Literature.* New York: Oxford University Press, 1970.

Raymond, William O. *The Infinite Moment, and Other Essays in Robert Browning.* Toronto: University of Toronto Press, 1965.

"CHILDHOOD" WILLIAM BARNES (1858)

THOMAS HARDY rightly saw WILLIAM BARNES as an intensely Wordsworthian poet. There was a characteristic and persistent difference, though. Unlike WILLIAM WORDSWORTH, Barnes tended to see the world not only from the point of view of the grown and nostalgic child, but also from that of the parent thinking of the experiences of his own children—experiences that his retrospective memory allowed him to understand. "Childhood" is one of Barnes's great poems on the subject, saturated with his trademark simplicity and directness while constructed with great delicacy, sophistication, and subtlety.

It starts out in the Wordsworthian mode, a kind of translation of the opening of the INTIMATIONS ODE ("There was a time when meadow, grove and stream . . .") into the Dorset language whose simplicity and directness Barnes used so powerfully. "At that time" life was hopeful and gay, and all seasons of joy were welcome.

The second stanza seems to extend the celebration of the first, but it is subtly different in the perspective it takes: that of someone who knows the truth of the world as opposed to its appearance to the child, for whom it is new. Barnes contrasts how the world "seemed" to the way it actually is. The houses seemed tall, but are not; the brook seemed wide but is narrow; and "time, that do vlee, did goo slow" (l. 11). This line is particularly important: The slowness of the days of youth was illusory even then. And yet he does not say, "time, that do vlee, did *seem* slow." Rather it *went* slowly, because time itself is a mode of seeming. When it goes slow, the world seems permanent; when it flies, the world's permanence flies with it. Compare the last lines of Barnes's "Slow to Come, Quick A-Gone": "Though slow did seem to us the peäce / O' comen days a-head, / That now do seem as in a reäce / Wi' aïr-birds to ha'vled."

This may seem a somewhat comforting thought, but in fact it is the opposite: Even the world of seeming itself is fleeting. There is no recourse to be had even in illusion, since the nature of illusion is unstable, and (to put it perhaps a little gnomically) illusion, too, is just an illusion, swept away by the hastening days of time. The third stanza makes the point more explicit, since the way the children inherit their world is "Vrom others that own'd 'em avore" (l. 20). The world's apparent permanence, even then, requires defending from the fact that children recognize that they inherit from those who are no longer children.

This does not derogate from their happiness, but it is the origin of the adult understanding that the last stanza expresses. The children are happy when "They have elders a-liven to love em" (l. 26), but the elders must undertake the toil and pain and knowledge of their own mortality, as well as that of the children they protect. The poem ends in beautifully balanced melancholy, the love of the elders expressed in the protection they offer the children. The "cwold blowen storm" does not prevent them from loving the children—it makes that love more precious because they know how short the time it will last.

After reading the poem, the full meaning of the title becomes clear. "Childhood" means not only the childhood of the speaker (as it would in Wordsworth), but that of those now children while the speaker is an adult. In an odd way, Barnes is more clear-sighted about anticipating the experience that *other* children will have than Wordsworth or even SAMUEL TAYLOR

COLERIDGE (see "FROST AT MIDNIGHT"), and a poem like this achieves the kind of tender clear-sightedness to be found in some of WILLIAM BLAKE's deceptively simple lyrics.

BIBLIOGRAPHY

Allingham, William. *William Allingham: A Diary.* Edited by H. Allingham and D. Radford. Introduction by John Julius Norwich. New York: Penguin, 1985.

Hardy, Thomas. *Thomas Hardy's Personal Writings: Prefaces, Literary Opinions, Reminiscences.* Edited by Harold Orel. London: Macmillan, 1990.

Levy, William Turner. *William Barnes: The Man and the Poems.* Dorchester, England: Longmans, 1960.

Parins, James W. *William Barnes.* Boston: Twayne Publishers, 1984.

Scott, Leader *The Life of William Barnes: Poet and Philologist, by his Daughter, Lucy Baxter ("Leader Scott").* 1887. Reprint, St. Clair Shores, Mich.: Scholarly Press, 1971.

"CHILD IS FATHER TO THE MAN, THE"

GERARD MANLEY HOPKINS (published 1918) This triolet, a lively and lovely parody of WILLIAM WORDSWORTH's "MY HEART LEAPS UP," was first announced as being by GERARD MANLEY HOPKINS in ROBERT BRIDGES's edition of his poetry; Hopkins had sent it to him as a newspaper clipping having published it under the pseudonym of Bran. The poem has had a long afterlife, both official, since it is of great interest to formalist critics of poetry; and subliminal, since the famous line that Hopkins takes as his title from Wordsworth's poem is often quoted and remembered through Hopkins's slight misquotation. Hopkins is parodying the last three lines of the lyric, the lines Wordsworth sets as an epigraph to his INTIMATIONS ODE: "The child is father of the man / And I could wish my days to be / Bound each to each by natural piety." (Hopkins, quoting from memory, changes *of* to *to*).

What Wordsworth meant by the line is that the sensibilities, perceptions, understanding, and mindset toward the world established in childhood will determine the rest of a person's life. One of the things it will determine is whether the adult wishes to stay faithful to his or her childhood perception of the world; and such faith is a good indicator that the perceptions of childhood were *accurate*—that is, morally and aesthetically right. Wordsworth means the word *father* figuratively.

But Hopkins's speaker is clueless and therefore the victim of a triolet. The triolet is a strict form (a version of it can be seen in LEIGH HUNT's "Jenny Kissed Me") and a difficult one to make interesting: it is eight lines long, rhymed *abaaabab,* with the first and second lines repeated verbatim as the last two lines, and the first line also repeated verbatim as the fourth line. Hopkins's speaker begins by quoting and then responding uncomprehendingly to Wordsworth's line: How can a child be the father of a man? Not understanding Wordsworth's deep metaphor, he assumes corruption of the text. That assumption is couched in a line that lightly parodies ROBERT BROWNING, himself a powerful and ambivalent reader of Wordsworth (see, for example, "The Lost Leader"). But it is everyone else who *can* "suck sense"—that is, understand—Wordsworth's line; only Hopkins's pedantic speaker cannot. He repeats the line in a tone of ridiculing exasperation, which shows the impressive way that the poem manages the dramatic play of tones, and then he corrects it to the more sensible but completely trivial statement "The man is father to the child." One reason *we* know this is not what "the poet did write" (besides its triviality) is that it would not rhyme in the original (Wordsworth rhymes *man* with *began*). It does rhyme in Hopkins, though, with his speaker's complaint that "the words are *wild.*" The triolet then ends with a second exasperated repetition of the supposedly senseless lines, but this time it is triumphant, as though the meaninglessness of the received lines is now self-evident.

The poem shows Hopkins's wonderful touch and his ability, not often appreciated, to master a wide range of tones. It also represents a serious piece of poetic criticism, since essentially it shows that Wordsworth is the opposite of trivial. Wordsworth always courts the danger of being trivialized by his readers, but the trivialization that Hopkins's speaker undertakes shows what struck Hopkins as really original about Wordsworth, and the poem is a tribute to both of them.

BIBLIOGRAPHY

Bridges, Robert. Preface to *Poems of Gerard Manley Hopkins.* Edited with additional poems, notes, and a biographical introduction by W. H. Gardner. New York: Oxford University Press, 1948.

Gardner, W. H. *Gerard Manley Hopkins (1844–1889): A Study of Poetic Idiosyncrasy in Relation to Poetic Tradition.* New Haven, Conn.: Yale University Press, 1949.

———, ed. Introduction to *Poems and Prose of Gerard Manley Hopkins.* Harmondsworth, Middlesex: Penguin, 1963.

Hartman, Geoffrey. *The Unmediated Vision: An Interpretation of Wordsworth, Hopkins, Rilke, and Valery.* New Haven, Conn.: Yale University Press, 1954.

Hopkins, Gerard Manley. *Gerard Manley Hopkins: Selected Letters.* Edited by Catherine Phillips. New York: Oxford University Press, 1990.

Miller, J. Hillis: "Gerard Manley Hopkins." In *The Disappearance of God: Five Nineteenth-Century Writers,* 270–359. Cambridge, Mass.: Belknap Press of Harvard University Press, 1963.

White, Norman. *Hopkins: A Literary Biography.* New York: Oxford University Press, 1992.

"CHIMNEY-SWEEPER, THE" WILLIAM BLAKE **(1789, 1794)** The two chimney-sweeper poems in WILLIAM BLAKE's SONGS OF INNOCENCE AND OF EXPERIENCE belong to the explicitly paired poems in the two books. In most of these pairings, the later song mounts a fiercer and more overt critique of the forces that have brought innocence into the disaster of experience than does the earlier song. But for just this reason the earlier song tends to be subtler, and the contrast between them also suggests that one of the losses in the move from innocence to experience is that of the subtlety—and the understanding by others that subtlety depends on—that characterizes the *Songs of Innocence.*

This contrast is particularly true in the "Chimney-Sweeper" songs. Both purport to be in the voice of a child chimney sweeper. Chimney sweepers, or sweeps, were particularly egregious examples of the child labor endemic to England at the start of the Industrial Revolution; children were used because they were small enough to scramble up and down the poisonously soot-choked chimneys they cleaned. They would go around advertising themselves with their cries. In both poems Blake makes those cries of "Sweep sweep!" into lisps, to derive the grim irony by which they call out, "Weep weep!"

The latter version, in being explicit, is psychologically less creditable. The poem puts into the child's mouth words that he could never say and indeed could not think. He *is* happy, he says, and *does* dance and sing; and part of what is heartbreaking is the fact that he does not know how heartbreaking he is. But of course, this means he cannot say it, as he does in the poem. The "Experience" version of the song speaks *for* the chimney sweep but does not show him, nor does it give us a representation of him, as the "Innocence" version does. The "Experience" version tells us how to understand the "Innocence" version and offers a kind of interpretation of it. But the interpretation it offers is itself affected by experience and is partial in the sense that it only attends to the bitterness of the situation, not the sweetness of the sweeps themselves.

Before turning to the "Innocence" version, it should be noted in passing that the two sweeps cannot be the same person, since in the earlier poem the sweep's mother has died (and his father has sold him into labor), while in the later song the sweep's parents are both at church. This is a grim and bitter piece of irony: The form of their piety comes at the cost of genuine love and duty. Blake's critique of the established Church of England is as clear here as it is in the "Experienced" version of "Holy Thursday" and, especially, "London." Both "Chimney-Sweeper" poems deplore parental nontenderness, but their lack of tenderness differs. In the later poem the parents are less devastated by poverty than by an illusion which they must bear some responsibility for complying with and therefore sustaining.

The "Innocence" version of the poem also criticizes hypocritical piety, but in a subtler and far more devastating way, a way that its speaker is not aware of. It is just because he is not aware of the way what he says is bound to affect any decent adult reader that this version is so powerful. The child sweep accepts with an angelic mildness all the horrors that he has experienced, though he does not know that they *are* horrors. (Charles Dickens will produce the same effect in novels such as *Oliver Twist.*) His song ends with a chilling moral: "So if all do their duty, they need not fear harm." The moral is chilling because it is false: He believes a false promise made by the self-serving adult authorities who exploit the children's trust and hope.

The tone with which the child describes himself and his fellow sweeps is matter of fact, from the poem's first line. That mothers die is a sad truth he already knows—for him the only question is when. More strikingly, he accepts it as an equivalent truth that fathers sell their children (into apprenticeship), as though this, too, is a natural fact and not a social disgrace. Part of what makes him so winning, and so heartbreaking is that he displays no self-pity: Whatever sorrow he shows is for his fellow-sweep Tom Dacre. Again, in describing Tom, he is matter-of-fact about the way Tom's lamblike hair has been shorn away, and we are to think (though the child does not) of another song of innocence, "The LAMB," which represents Christ as a childlike innocent. He comforts Tom, just as he himself deserves comforting, and his comfort seems to stay with Tom, who has a wonderful and telling dream. The chimneys, we find, are actually coffins—which is Blake's point, though the child himself does not make the connection. An angel comes and sets the sweeps free. Tom's dream shows him to be as generous as the speaker is himself: They want freedom for their friends, for all the sweeps, and they want the love of their friends.

The real depth of the poem is in the representation of the angel, who is by no means a figure of whom we should think well. It turns out the angel has not really freed the sweeps but has given them a vision of *future* reward. If they are good, they will be granted joy. But in this context, being good means being docile—obeying the social authorities that command the sweeps to their labor. This is why the angel offers the chillingly ambiguous promise that if the sweeps behave, they will have God for a father. Because we remember that God should already be a father, we recall how the poem represents fathers: ". . . my father sold me." The song (though not its singer) represents God as being just as evil or greedy or cruel a father as the sweep's father, and what the sweep thinks is a promise is in fact a threat. It is not a threat the sweep has to understand: All he has to understand is that he should do his duty *now* in order to hope for a reward that will only come *later*. And the dream sent by the angel, or by the church, or by religious authority in general, works: The sweeps awaken before dawn to go back to their horrendous work.

The speaker explains their ingenuous willingness to work with the moral already quoted, but it is worth noticing what the implicit converse of the moral is: "Harm will come to those who do not do their duty." We see that the threat of harm or violence is what ultimately keeps the sweeps, and the poor, in line. They do not realize that it *could* be otherwise: They think the authorities are protecting them from the harm with which they are, in fact, both causing and threatening them.

BIBLIOGRAPHY

Bloom, Harold. *Blake's Apocalypse: A Study in Poetic Argument.* Ithaca, N.Y.: Cornell University Press, 1970.

———. *Poetry and Repression: Revisionism from Blake to Stevens.* New Haven, Conn.: Yale University Press, 1976.

Damrosch, Leopold. *Symbol and Truth in Blake's Myth.* Princeton, N.J.: Princeton University Press, 1980.

Erdmann, David V. *Blake, Prophet against Empire: A Poet's Interpretation of the History of His Own Times.* Princeton, N.J.: Princeton University Press, 1977.

Fry, Northrop. *Fearful Symmetry: A Study of William Blake.* Princeton, N.J.: Princeton University Press, 1974.

Gilchrist, Alexander. *Life of William Blake, with Selections from His Poems and Other Writings.* Totowa, N.J.: Rowman and Littlefield, 1973.

Hollander, John. "Blake and the Metrical Contract." In *From Sensibility to Romanticism,* edited by Frederick Hilles and Harold Bloom, 293–310. New York: Oxford, 1965. Reprinted in John Hollander, *Vision and Resonance: Two Senses of Poetic Form.* New Haven, Conn.: Yale University Press, 1985, 187–211.

Ostriker, Alicia. "Desire Gratified and Ungratified: William Blake and Sexuality." *Blake: An Illustrated Quarterly* 16 (1982–83): 156–165.

Raine, Kathleen. *Blake and Antiquity.* Princeton, N.J.: Princeton University Press, 1977.

Thompson, E. P. *Witness against the Beast: William Blake and the Moral Law.* New York: Cambridge University Press, 1993.

CHRISTABEL SAMUEL TAYLOR COLERIDGE **(1797, 1800)** According to the preface to *Lyrical Ballads* (1798) SAMUEL TAYLOR COLERIDGE and WILLIAM WORDSWORTH agreed to divide their contributions to the joint volume, with Coleridge writing the "supernatural poems" and Wordsworth the natural ones—the scenes of everyday life. Coleridge's contributions included *The RIME OF THE ANCIENT MARINER,* and he meant to include *Christabel* in the second edition

(1800) but had not completed the poem; therefore, it was not published for another 16 years. Even then, like "KUBLA KHAN," it was only a fragment of a larger whole that Coleridge claimed to have fully thought through, but which he never completed.

Lyrical Ballads is remembered for its revolutionary poetry of normal human life, and it might at first seem—as it seemed to Wordsworth—that the supernatural poems would be out of place, or at least detract from the extraordinary originality of the book. But Coleridge's concern was not with supernatural incidents but with ordinary human response to such incidents and with the philosophical and psychological conclusions that can be drawn from such a response. *The Rime of the Ancient Mariner* is the greatest single poem in this mode, but *Christabel* is a close second. The story it tells hardly gets anywhere, but the psychological depths it probes show how deeply Coleridge plumbed his own mind.

Like William Shakespeare, Coleridge was deeply attuned to the experience of fatherhood. That is to say, he was highly sensitive to the ways fathers would become arbitrarily tyrannical, even with a full knowledge, veiled from their children, of how wrong their behavior was. As "poets of childhood" (PERCY BYSSHE SHELLEY on Wordsworth), Coleridge and Wordsworth were both deeply aware of what their own children's experience might be, a theme Wordsworth made explicit in his "Anecdote for fathers" and Coleridge in "FROST AT MIDNIGHT." We can trace in the two years between "Frost at Midnight" and the conclusion to the second part of *Christabel* the sensitivity of Coleridge's self-examination, as his son Hartley grew into his fourth year.

That conclusion is itself one of the deepest and most philosophical romantic lyrics. Its function in the poem is to explain Sir Leoline's Lear-like overreaction to Christabel's dislike of Geraldine. He explodes at Christabel at the end of part 2—but why? He feels "dishonoured" (l. 642) by his daughter's treatment of Geraldine and leaves with her, presumably to court and marry her. But it is Coleridge's deep psychological insight that the courtship he pays Geraldine is a displaced response to his daughter and not simple attraction to the seductress.

The conclusion to part 2 describes rage as an excess of love. This fact of human psychology is itself an aspect of human woe. We love what is hurt and therefore will rage sometimes in order to cause hurt, that we may love. The description of the relation of father and child there—the father's eyes are filled with light (l. 661)—is repeated by Wordsworth five years later in the INTIMATIONS ODE, where he describes the light Coleridge darts at his young son ("with light upon him from his father's eyes" [Intimations Ode, l. 89]). The conclusion to part 2 of *Christabel* laments that the depth and intensity of love might manifest itself only within the mode of pain. But this is a generalized insight within ROMANTICISM: Guilt, pain and loss are the modes and avenues of intensity that belong to us within the fallen world, and they are more intense than the things lost (see, for a Wordsworthian version of the conclusion to part 2, his "SURPRISED BY JOY").

The conclusion to part 2 can help to give a general account of the theme of the poem. Of course, it belongs to the kind of psychological study that Wordsworth and Coleridge found or thought they found in the ballads in Thomas Percy's *Reliques of Ancient English Poetry* (1765), a study of what Sigmund Freud would analyze under the name of the uncanny. But the uncanny needs explaining, and Coleridge offers more of an explanation in *Christabel* than do the ancient ballads it imitates. (The meter of *Christabel,* which Coleridge thought a new invention, actually goes back to the oldest kinds of English versification, as he must somehow have subconsciously felt.) For the love which goes awry in the conclusion to part 2 might be seen as going awry throughout the course of the poem.

Christabel (as will Madeline in JOHN KEATS's "The EVE OF ST. AGNES," which is a kind of happy revision of *Christabel*) has gone outside the safe and sacred precincts of the castle she lives in to perform a prayer for the knight to whom she is betrothed. She has dreamed of him, and somehow that dream has caused her anxiety. She does not know what is making her anxious, but we can guess that there is some frustrated sexual source: He is far away and she misses him, and therefore she sneaks away from her father's castle to pray for him by a giant oak, a symbol of his strength if not overtly phallic.

The important point is that the poem conjures up Geraldine as its response to Christabel's prayer, and if we imagine that Christabel is somehow dreaming the whole thing (see line 253), Geraldine (with her story of abduction by five warriors) would represent her own sexual anxiety, as well as being a source of that anxiety. In anxiety dreams, the same figure can represent how the dreamer feels and what the dreamer fears, because if that fear is externalized it can be denied or ascribed to someone else—in this case to Geraldine. There is no question that Geraldine is a source of sexual anxiety, since whatever nameless horror she strikes up in Christabel, and in the reader, derives from her nakedness: "Behold! her bosom and half her side—/ A sight to dream of, not to tell!" (ll. 252–253). Whatever it is that Christabel sees, she sees it after she has herself undressed and lain down in her loveliness (ll. 237–238).

What are we to imagine of Geraldine? On one level she is a witch, or spirit of evil, a "thing unblest" (l. 529), which is why she cannot cross the threshold without Christabel's aid (ll. 129–132). It is traditional—Coleridge would have known this most vividly from book 1 of Edmund Spenser's *The Faerie Queene*—that witches turn out to have bodily markings when stripped naked, particularly serpents' tails. The tail itself is phallic, and certainly one suggestion here is that Geraldine turns out to be male, or to have male organs. She should parallel the innocent Christabel, but she turns out to be the male sexuality that threatens her. The threat may be a specific and terrifying one: that exposure to male sexuality gives a maiden male sexual organs, makes her male or more male. This seems to be what has happened to Geraldine and what may therefore happen to Christabel by Geraldine's contagion. Therefore, Bracy will dream of Geraldine as a phallic serpent coiled around the dove the baron has named Christabel after his daughter. The serpent is phallic, and Bracy describes it "Swelling its neck" (l. 554), but so, too, does the dove swell her own neck, in a kind of involuntary sympathetic fear of the serpent's swelling.

It would be far too simple, however, to call Geraldine male. Rather, she might better be thought of as Christabel's vision of female corruption or contamination by male sexuality. This is an important issue for Christabel, whose sense of the dangers of sexuality go back to the beginning of her life, since her mother died in childbirth. Christabel feels that her mother is a guardian spirit to her, and apparently so, too, does Geraldine. Geraldine tries to second Christabel's wish for her mother's presence but is immediately brought up short by that invisible spirit (ll. 203–206). She responds by asserting her own power—but a power which is temporary and will last however long the trial that the poem makes Christabel undergo will last.

The death of her mother is clearly the most important fact in Christabel's life, and it governs her responses to everything else. But it is also important because of her father's reaction to the death of his wife and because of the despair and bitterness her death causes him. Geraldine can seduce him so easily because for him she represents a substitute for the dead woman. But Christabel's aim is life, whereas Sir Leoline's seems to be the dead past, and while he may be fooled by Geraldine, Christabel is not. In an odd way, she represents the triumph of love over its own corruption by the sorrows of life, and this is why Bracy the Bard takes her side, enraging Sir Leoline.

This reading of the poem helps to explain one of its notable and powerful features (which it also shares with book 1 of *The Faerie Queene*)—namely, the sympathy the poem shows Geraldine. For she represents less the malevolent principle that the plot requires of her than the uncertainty and anxiety of both Christabel and her father. If there were not something genuinely sympathetic about her, she could not be of such importance to Christabel's own thinking and sense of herself.

What would have happened had Coleridge completed the poem? We can be sure that Christabel would have eventually been vindicated and won her father's heart back, as Cordelia does in Shakespeare's *King Lear*. But we can see already that she wins even in the fragment that Coleridge completed: Her father's fury comes from the love he feels for Christabel, and the love he feels ultimately signals Christabel's triumph, as well as the triumph of life and hope over despair and death.

BIBLIOGRAPHY

Bate, Walter Jackson. *Coleridge.* New York: Macmillan, 1968.

Bloom, Harold. *The Visionary Company: A Reading of English Romantic Poetry.* Garden City, N.Y.: Doubleday, 1961.

Brisman, Leslie. *Romantic Origins.* Ithaca, N.Y.: Cornell University Press, 1978.

Coleridge, Samuel Taylor. *Selected Poems.* Edited by William Empson and David Pirie. Manchester, England: Fyfield, 1989.

Frank, Robert H. *Passions within Reason: The Strategic Role of the Emotions.* New York: Norton, 1988.

Freud, Sigmund. "The Uncanny." In *The Standard Edition of the Complete Psychological Works of Sigmund Freud* Vol. 17. London: Hogarth Press, 1953–1974, 219–256.

Janowitz, Anne. *England's Ruins: Poetic Purpose and the National Landscape.* Cambridge, Mass.: Blackwell, 1990.

Lowes, John Livingston. *Road to Xanadu: A Study in the Ways of the Imagination.* New York: Houghton Mifflin, 1930.

Parker, Reeve. *Coleridge's Meditative Art.* Ithaca, N.Y.: Cornell University Press, 1975.

Swann, Karen. "'Christabel': The Wandering Mother and the Enigma of Form." *SIR* 23, no. 4 (Winter 1984): 533–553.

CLARE, JOHN (1793–1864) It is only at the beginning of the 21st century that John Clare is finally getting his due. He was known in his lifetime as the "Peasant Poet" because of the life of manual and farm labor that he led as a village boy from Northhamptonshire in central England, and yet he was pretty much an autodidact. He became celebrated for his first book, published in 1820, when he was 26. Clare had read some of the major 18th-century poets but was most familiar with the ballads, songs, and folktales that comprised a large part of local oral and aural culture. He was an incessant and incessantly gifted writer, and his 1820 book *Poems Descriptive of Rural Life and Scenery* was published by John Taylor, who was also the publisher of (among others) JOHN KEATS; Clare in some sense exemplifies Keats's sense of being an outsider as well as his poetic theories.

When his book was published, Clare was celebrated as a kind of real-life example of WILLIAM WORDSWORTH's theories of poetry as the real language of real, primarily rural, people. But this was the high point of his career: He never managed to survive as a writer, and with a large family to feed, including perhaps some illegitimate children, he continued to work as a laborer as well as a writer. It is conventional to lament the toll this took on him as he eventually had a psychotic breakdown and was confined, first voluntarily and then permanently, to a lunatic asylum, where he continued to write poetry in a style highly indiosyncratic as to spelling and punctuation but nonetheless intense and profound.

In his madness, Clare believed himself at different times to be various of the great poets of his day. He thus represents JOHN KEATS's idea of the poetical character, so open to the world that he or she registers and responds to the pressure of everyone else's character, which overwhelms his or her own (see the account of Keats's letters in this volume). The extreme openness to impingement from the outside world, in the mode of both ideas and perception, also made Clare the extraordinary poet that he was. He observed nature with near-Darwinian subtlety and grace, and he conveyed the astonishment of what he saw. The intense subjectivity of what Keats called the egotistical sublime in Wordsworth makes the latter's nature poetry a kind of projection of a massively powerful and so massively protected self. Clare is the opposite sort of poet: The nature he describes is accurate in a way that it could not be if he were not enraptured by unknown and unexpected detail. Wordsworth remembers; Clare sees. In this way he was also something of a forerunner of the pre-Raphaelite poets, who were also intensely oriented toward detail and to GERARD MANLEY HOPKINS's journals. Clare, however, was struck by the detail even more for its own sake. Part of the reason for his revival in the 21st century is that he may be seen as the first of the poets that literary ecologists have become so interested in: those who preserve a record of the world in all its wonder and variety, and whose observations seek value only in the true detail of nature.

See also "I AM," "MOUSE'S NEST."

BIBLIOGRAPHY

Bate, Jonathan. *John Clare: A Biography.* London: Picador, 2003.

Chirico, Paul. *John Clare and the Imagination of the Reader.* New York: Palgrave Macmillan, 2007.

Martin, Frederick. *The Life of John Clare.* London: Macmillan, 1865.

CLOUGH, ARTHUR HUGH (1819–1861)

Arthur Hugh Clough became close friends with MATTHEW ARNOLD and Arnold's brother Thomas when he was a prize student at Rugby School, where Arnold's father was headmaster. They stayed friends for life, first at Rugby and then at Oxford University, and Arnold describes him memorably in "The SCHOLAR-GIPSY" and in his elegy for Clough, "THYRSIS." Clough was also a close friend and confidante of Carlyle and of Ralph Waldo Emerson, who was more or less his host when he tried living in Boston in the early 1850s. Clough had lived in the United States before. Born in England, he and his family moved to Charleston, South Carolina, when he was a toddler, but he moved back a few years later to attend school in England.

At Oxford, Clough was attracted by the uncompromising intellectual power of John Henry (later Cardinal) Newman to a more skeptical and radical view of the Anglican Christianity in which he had been brought up. Clough's intellectual power always probed and questioned the things that were presented to it, and indeed that intellectual power is the signal characteristic of his poetry. (It was one of the things that made Arnold so admire him.) Unlike many of Newman's disciples, Clough did not end up converting to Roman Catholicism; he became an atheist instead, skeptical of all religious doctrine.

This could hardly be said to be liberating for Clough, since in his poetry he saw that atheism requires a kind of willingness to face the true lack of meaning in the order of the universe, which is itself strenuous and painful. Clough was politically radical, and he went with Ralph Waldo Emerson to see the revolutions of 1848 in Paris. Following this, he went to Rome, where he lived during the short-lived Roman Republic and its fall to the French and restoration of Pope Pius IX. He describes these events memorably as the background to the unflinchingly realistic story he tells in his greatest long poem, *AMOURS DE VOYAGE,* drafted in Rome in 1849 but not published till 1858, and then in the United States. Following this, he worked on the fragments that comprise his psychological drama *Dipsychus* (double soul), which he never finished.

In 1852 Clough moved to Boston but could not find permanent and steady employment, despite Emerson's aid. However, friends procured him a position in London, at the Education Office, enabling him to marry in June 1854. By this time he had been translating as well as writing poetry, but his health was not good, especially after his mother died in 1860, and he went abroad to the Mediterranean in 1861, where he met ALFRED, LORD TENNYSON and his wife. There he read Tennyson some of the poetry he was working on at the time, from a long narrative poem called *Mari Magno* (after a line of the Roman poet Lucretius's about danger on the great sea, but punning in its subject, the great and dangerous sea of marriage; Tennyson had already proved an admirer of some of Clough's earlier poetry).

Clough contracted malaria in Florence shortly thereafter and died at the age of 42, leaving Arnold distraught and what might have been his greatest work unfinished. But what he did write was of great and original value, startlingly clear-sighted and unsentimental. Arnold at his best could sometimes sound like Clough, but Clough sustained it through very long meditative passages which sometimes seem to anticipate the great American poet Wallace Stevens.

See also "NEW DECALOGUE, A"; "SAY NOT THE STRUGGLE NAUGHT AVAILETH."

BIBLIOGRAPHY

Clough, Arthur Hugh. *Oxford Diaries of Arthur Hugh Clough.* Edited by Anthony Kenny. New York: Oxford University Press, 1990.

Cunningham, Valentine. Headnote to selection from Clough in *The Victorians: An Anthology of Poetry & Poetics.* Malden, Mass.: Blackwell, 2000, 442.

Hofmann, Michael. "Arthur Hugh Clough: 1819–1861." *Poetry* 187, no. 6 (March 2006): 495–496.

Kenny, Anthony. *Arthur Hugh Clough: A Poet's Life.* New York: Continuum, 2005.

Sutherland, Gillian. *Faith, Duty, and the Power of Mind: The Cloughs and Their Circle, 1820–1960.* London: Cambridge University Press, 2006.

COLERIDGE, HARTLEY (1796–1849)

Named after the philosopher David Hartley, whom his father SAMUEL TAYLOR COLERIDGE was reading intensely in the 1790s, Hartley Coleridge was burdened throughout his life by his child-star turn in his father's great poem "FROST AT MIDNIGHT" (and probably in the conclusion to part 2 of *CHRISTABEL*), and in WILLIAM WORDSWORTH's most important single poem, probably the most important single poem of ROMANTICISM, the INTIMATIONS ODE. In that last poem, Hartley appears as "A six years' Darling of a pygmy size" (l. 86) who nevertheless is the "best philosopher" who "read'st the eternal deep, / Haunted forever by the eternal mind" (ll. 110, 112–113) and knows those truths "Which we are toiling all our lives to find" (l. 116). And yet this six-year-old is headed the wrong way, toward conventional adulthood, and this is Wordsworth's central lament.

True, the depiction of Hartley in the earlier "Frost at Midnight" is somewhat otherwise: The "babe so beautiful" (l. 48) who lies beside his father as he composes the poem is to have a life of Wordsworthian attunement to the spirit of nature: He will "see and hear / The lovely shapes and sounds intelligible / Of that eternal language, which . . . God / Utters" (ll. 58–61). But as Hartley himself says in a note on the "DEDICATORY SONNET TO S. T. COLERIDGE," he wrote to prefix the 1833 collection of his own poems: "Poets are *not* prophets," and the life his father hoped for the infant Hartley was not to work out.

Hartley Coleridge was brilliant but oppressed by the expectations and achievements (and also failures) of his great elders. He tried to make a living as a writer, and his poetry and essays are lovely and sometimes powerful. But he was morbidly introspective and fearful of inner exposure (he frequently wrote in the essayistic persona he called "a whimsical Old Bachelor acquaintance of mine") and never freed himself from his legacy, which included his inheritance of his father's addictive personality. He was, however, well-loved by his friends and a successful if itinerant teacher and schoolmaster. His best poems are moving expositions of the pressure constituted by his elders' love and expectation and admiration. In "Long time a child," one of his most moving poems, we get the other side of the Wordsworthian and Coleridgean cult of childhood: Rather than experiencing his continuity with his early self as Wordsworthian "natural piety" (see "MY HEART LEAPS UP"), Hartley Coleridge discovers himself old but unfit for age: "But sleep, though sweet, is only sleep; and waking / I waked to sleep no more; at once o'er taking / The vanguard of my age, with all arrears / Of duty on my back. . . . For I have lost the race I never ran." That last line is a reference both to Psalms and to the Intimations Ode ("Another race hath been, and other palms are won" [l. 204]—but poets are not prophets and Hartley lived and died a disappointment to himself, and yet a moving figure, both as an example of a figure ruined by parental over-identification and as poet.

BIBLIOGRAPHY

Bloom, Harold. *The Visionary Company: A Reading of English Romantic Poetry*. Garden City, N.Y.: Doubleday, 1961.

Coleridge, Derwent. *Poems by Hartley Coleridge With a Memoir of His Life by His Brother*. 2 vols. London: E. Moxon, 1851.

Coleridge, Hartley. *Essays and Marginalia*. London: E. Moxon, 1851.

Griggs, Earl Leslie. *Hartley Coleridge: His Life and Work*. London: University of London Press, 1929.

Pomeroy, Mary Joseph, Sister. *The Poetry of Hartley Coleridge*. Washington, D.C.: Catholic University of America, 1927.

COLERIDGE, MARY ELIZABETH (1861–1907) Mary Elizabeth Coleridge was descended from SAMUEL TAYLOR COLERIDGE's brother, and like her illustrious great-grand uncle, she was a writer of both prose and poetry. In her lifetime she was better known for her novels and also for her volunteer work teaching working women in London, both lecturing at the Working Women's College and tutoring them individually. She lived with her parents all her life, dying suddenly at 45 of appendicitis.

ROBERT LOUIS STEVENSON thought very highly of Coleridge's fiction, but it was ROBERT BRIDGES, her elder by 17 years, who encouraged her to publish her poetry. She did, in a private edition, under the pseudonym Anodos (Greek for "the roadless one"), taken from the name of the main character in George MacDonald's fantasy novel *Phantastes* (1858)—not wishing to dishonor S. T. Coleridge's poetry, as she thought, by publishing under the same name. Her poetry is fascinating and original, but it is inevitably haunted by that of her illustrious forebear, whose mode of imagination she shared. You can hear echoes or allusions to Samuel Taylor Coleridge's poems in some of hers, as in "A Moment" (1896), where the moment of sunset that the poem describes could be straight out of *The RIME OF THE ANCIENT MARINER*—for instance, the repetition of *stormy* in the lines "The stormy sun was going down / In a stormy sky," whose form recalls the *Rime*'s "As idle as a painted ship / Upon a painted ocean."

One of Coleridge's best poems is the eerie "The Witch" (1896), which essentially retells the story of her ancestor's unfinished *CHRISTABEL* in 21 lines. In that poem, a strange and apparently needy woman begs for help from the narrator, who accedes to her strong solicitation, "Oh, lift me over the threshold, and let me in at the door." Readers of *Christabel* will remember that Christabel had to help Geraldine over the threshold as well, in conformity with the superstition that witches and evil spirits cannot cross a threshold unaided. Christabel deeply rues her aid, and so, too, does the speaker of "The Witch," whose life will never be the same again since the presence of the witch has forever put out the fire in her hearth.

The poem is therefore an allegory of love: The witch is something like the death of love or the truth of its inadequacy. This represents a reading of *Christabel* in which Geraldine would be the truth of the sexuality that Christabel wishes to idealize. Mary Coleridge's narrator knows what has happened to her and realizes that the time of idealization is over. This is the theme of many of her poems, including the grim complaint in "He Knoweth Not That the Dead Are Thine'" (1896), in which she complains that her lover's indifference is murderous; and the deeply subtle "Shadow" (1897), where the radiance of love also means that the darkness it contrasts is all the stronger.

Although she had a sense of humor, Coleridge's best poems are dark and sad, their whimsical conceits made to emphasize a revelation of the disappointing truths of life and the limited compensations of whimsy. While not a major poet like CHRISTINA ROSSETTI (who was perhaps the most important single influence on her poetry), at her best Coleridge certainly bears comparison with Rossetti, especially in her beautiful and eerie poem "L'Oiseau Bleu" (1897).

BIBLIOGRAPHY

Bloom, Harold. *The Visionary Company: A Reading of English Romantic Poetry*. Garden City, N.Y.: Doubleday, 1961.

Bridges, Robert. "The Poems of Mary Coleridge." *Cornhill Magazine* 23 (1907): 594–605.

Gilbert, Sandra, and Susan Gubar. *Madwoman in the Attic: The Woman Writer and the Nineteenth-Century Literary Imagination*. New Haven, Conn.: Yale University Press, 2000.

Parker, Reeve. *Coleridge's Meditative Art*. Ithaca, N.Y.: Cornell University Press, 1975.

COLERIDGE, SAMUEL TAYLOR (1772–1834)

The essayist William Hazlitt's famous description of first meeting the central thinker of English ROMANTICISM is unexcelled. Hazlitt's essay, "My First Acquaintance with Poets,") was written a quarter of a century later. It recalls the day when he was 20 and Samuel Taylor Coleridge six years older. Coleridge arrived to take charge of a Unitarian congregation near where Hazlitt's father was also a Dissenting minister, and the previous Unitarian minister went to pick him up at the coach station, but he "could find no one at all answering the description but a round-faced man in a short black coat . . . who seemed to be talking at a great rate to his fellow-passengers." Could this possibly be Coleridge? "The round-faced man in black entered and dissipated all doubts on the subject by beginning to talk. He did not cease while he stayed; nor has he since, that I know of."

Coleridge was the greatest of talkers and most restless and voracious of readers and thinkers among the romantics, yet his intellectual life may be ultimately the most tragic of them all. It was not that he died terribly young or terribly badly. But his prodigious talent was also his most fatal flaw, a flaw he would analyze in comparing NAPOLEON BONAPARTE's "commanding genius" to WILLIAM WORDSWORTH's "absolute genius." Commanding genius, like his own, turned out never to be enough. Coleridge could not find a single vocation to which he could devote all his fantastic talents, and to the extent that his deepest vocation was poetry (and not the more general and all-encompassing aesthetic imagination that for him comprehended poetry, art, psychology, religion, and the creation and existence of the universe), that vocation was hobbled and hindered by the tremendous shadow cast by his closest friend and greatest of romantic poets, Wordsworth. A crushing sense of failure, which was an inevitable concomitant of talents so great as to seem almost absolute, brought about physical infirmity for Coleridge, necessitating the addictive drugs that aggravated his misery in a vicious circle that would haunt him his whole life. The capacities he recognized in himself also led him to superhuman expedients, but expedients they were. As a result, some of his critical work, though brilliant and original, is nevertheless highly derivative in some of its formulations from the German idealist philosophers (Immanuel Kant and Friedrich Schelling in particular) who were his contemporaries, and who played much the same role as simultaneously enabling and blocking figures for his philosophical work as Wordsworth did for his poetry.

Coleridge always had grand ambitions. In the early 1790s, during the period of French revolutionary ferment—the dawn in which (as Wordsworth said) it was bliss to be alive, and in which to be young was very heaven—Coleridge and his friend ROBERT SOUTHEY conceived the idea of a utopian community, which they called a pantisocracy, to be established on the banks of the Susquehanna River in Pennsylvania. The collapse of this utopian scheme (partly impossible due to Coleridge's somewhat irresponsible debts) led him to try to support himself by founding a political magazine called *The Watchman,* where much of his important early prose is to be found. (LORD BYRON, too, would attempt to influence the culture in which he wrote his poetry through founding his own magazine; the magazine culture of romanticism was central to the circulation and publication of its central works.)

Having heard of Wordsworth through an acquaintance with his older brother and through reading his poetry, Coleridge went to visit him in Dorset (where William and his sister Dorothy were living) in summer 1797. They became close friends, though later a terrible argument would strain that friendship to the breaking point. The quarrel, which occurred 10 years later, seems to have been instigated by what was probably a hallucination on Coleridge's part that he saw his friend in bed with Wordsworth's sister-in-law Sara Hutchinson, with whom Coleridge was in love, and whom Wordsworth later tried to protect from Coleridge's miserable projections of feeling. Coleridge's great poem "DEJECTION: AN ODE" was originally written as a verse letter to Sara Hutchinson.

In the earlier, happier times, however, Wordsworth and Coleridge wrote a great deal of poetry in each other's company. (For more on their relationship, see the entry on Wordsworth.) Coleridge wrote some of his greatest lyrics during this halcyon period, and he and Wordsworth decided to publish a book together, anonymously, naming it *Lyrical Ballads.* This most important single book of poetry published in the last two centuries appeared in 1798, with augmented editions appearing in 1800 and 1802. Though there is a reasonable separation in authorship, each poet more or less wholly responsible for individual poems, they edited each other's works; suggested lines, ideas, and even stanzas to each other; and together founded modern poetry.

In winter 1798–99 Coleridge visited Germany, where he learned the language and began to read German philosophy. On his return, he moved with his family to live as neighbors to Wordsworth and (eventually) Southey at Grasmere, near Keswick in the Lake District—whence the appellation of the three poets as the LAKE POETS. Coleridge's restless erotic yearnings led to an unhappy family life, and this unhappiness was aggravated by illness and addiction to opium used both as analgesic and as inspiration. Finally, in 1804 Coleridge thought that a trip to Malta would help him recover; on shipboard he learned of basic navigational errors he had made in *The RIME OF THE ANCIENT MARINER,* which he revised accordingly). while he was away, Wordsworth wrote his greatest long poem, *The PRELUDE,* as a kind of autobiographical narrative explicitly addressed to Coleridge; anxiety on Coleridge's behalf is one of the running themes of the poem.

After Coleridge returned to England in 1806, he listened to Wordsworth read *The Prelude* aloud to him (over a period of about two weeks) and then composed an awed and somewhat ambivalent poem about the experience, "To William Wordsworth." But though he was still to publish some of his unfinished work, the period in which Coleridge wrote his greatest poems was over. (Exceptions to this statement may be found in some of his journals, where intense unfinished nightmarish phantasmagorias derived from what the author and addict Thomas DeQuincy would call "the pains of opium" are to be found; see "LIMBO.") Coleridge now worked very hard editing another journal, *The Friend,* and then eventually he wrote *Biographia Literaria* (1817), in which his most extended autobiographical, critical, and philosophical work is to be found. This volume is important not least for its account of Wordsworth's poetry and the frank though thoughtful admiration Coleridge displays there. He also makes the most influential argument in the history of English criticism for organic form (in which everything is naturally related to everything else in a poem), which he calls "multeity in unity," and for the nature of the poetic imagination (a grand "repetition in the finite mode of the infinite *I am*") as opposed to mere fancy. (For more on this topic, see IMAGINATION.) The task of writing this Herculean book necessitated more opium, and Coleridge, like De Quincy, never recovered from the addictions that haunted his life.

Nevertheless, he and Wordsworth resumed their friendship, and Coleridge, now an aging lion surrounded by the most brilliant writers and thinkers of the day, settled into a happier late middle age than might have been anticipated. Through it all, he never stopped talking.

See also CHRISTABEL, "FROST AT MIDNIGHT," "KUBLA KHAN."

BIBLIOGRAPHY

Bate, Walter Jackson. *Coleridge.* New York: Macmillan, 1968.

Bloom, Harold. *The Visionary Company: A Reading of English Romantic Poetry.* Garden City, N.Y.: Doubleday, 1961.

Brisman, Leslie. *Romantic Origins.* Ithaca, N.Y.: Cornell University Press, 1978.

Christensen, Jerome. *Coleridge's Blessed Machine of Language.* Ithaca, N.Y.: Cornell University Press, 1981.

Coburn, Kathleen. *Experience into Thought: Perspectives in the Coleridge Notebooks.* Toronto: University of Toronto Press, 1979.

Coleridge, Samuel Taylor. *Biographia Literaria.* London: Oxford University Press, 1954.

———. *Selected Poems.* Edited with an introduction, textual commentary and notes by William Empson and David Pirie. Manchester, England: Fyfield, 1989.

Empson, William. Introduction to *Coleridge's Verse: A Selection.* New York: Schocken Books, 1973.

Halmi, Nicholas. *Genealogy of the Romantic Symbol.* New York: Oxford University Press, 2007.

Holmes, Richard. *Coleridge.* New York: Pantheon, 2000.

Hughes-Hallet, Penelope. *The Immortal Dinner: A Famous Evening of Genius and Laughter in Literary London, 1817.* New York: Viking, 2000.

McFarland, Thomas. *Coleridge and the Pantheist Tradition.* Oxford: Clarendon Press, 1969.

Parker, Reeve. *Coleridge's Meditative Art.* Ithaca, N.Y.: Cornell University Press, 1975.

Swann, Karen. "'Christabel': The Wandering Mother and the Enigma of Form." *SIR* 23, no. 4 (Winter 1984): 533–553.

Woodring, Carl. *Politics in the Poetry of Coleridge.* Madison: University of Wisconsin Press, 1961.

COOK, ELIZA (1812–1889)

On July 18, 1854, to great fanfare, a monument to THOMAS HOOD was unveiled in Kensal Green Cemetery, where he had been buried nine years earlier. Monckton Milnes (a friend of ALFRED, LORD TENNYSON's who had recited his work to Robert Peel, the prime minister, thereby obtaining him a pension a year after Peel had visited Hood and granted *him* a pension as well) delivered the address, and everyone admired the statue, which had as one of its inscriptions "He sang the 'Song of the Shirt.'"

Sitting next to Mrs. Milnes was the striking 42-year-old Eliza Cook, dressed in mannish attire, as was her custom, her hair cut short and parted on the right. According to a contemporary, the fugitive American slave William Wells Brown, after the unveiling of the statue "a rush was made to get a view of Eliza Cook, as being the next great novelty after the monument, if not its equal" (*The American Fugitive in Europe*). Brown himself would later dine with Cook, Dickens, and others sympathetic to the plight of enslaved persons in America, and he wrote passionately on behalf of liberation, reform, and respect for laborers and the poor.

Hood wrote with similar aims, his "SONG OF THE SHIRT" being one of the leading poems of English radicalism. Cook, too, was such a writer. In fact, it was her visit to the Kensal Green Cemetery and the outraged poem that she wrote about the lack of any fitting monument for Hood ("Poor Hood") that induced the English public to subscribe to the erection of the monument that Milnes inaugurated. Her poem had this effect because she was one of the most popular poets in English at the time.

Cook wrote in intelligent defense, one might say, of the pieties of Victorian sentimentalism that later audiences were taught to look down on. Her intelligence comes from her sense of what the world is really like, a sense that also sparked her passionate commitment to social justice. In such poems as her most popular one, "The OLD ARM-CHAIR," she gives a lovely account of the depth and density of domestic experience; in her more political poems, such as "A Song for the Workers," she shows herself a passionate advocate for reform (in this case of the maximum working hours an employer could require).

Cook was herself the ninth and youngest child of a working-class father, a worker and trader in metals. Her family could not afford to send her to school, so she learned at home and was encouraged by her mother to write poetry. Her mother died when she was 15, but her influence lasted, and Cook became one of the most popular writers of the age. She edited her own journal, and for a time *Eliza Cook's Journal* was more popular than Charles Dickens's famous *Household Words*.

Cook was probably a lesbian (deeply in love with the actress Charlotte Cushman), but she was still popular because she spoke and wrote so well about and on behalf of the ordinary experience she felt her own life to exemplify. Her poetry is still refreshing today, partly because it is candid and engaging without ever being self-pitying. Her sense of human pleasures is wide-ranging and therefore communicates itself widely in her poetry as well (which accounts for her popularity). Her thinking is quite complex, but its expression is beautifully lucid, and her poems afford the pleasure not so much of deep thought (like those of many of the minor Victorians) as that of frank and justified enthusiasm for the pleasures of economic, social, and natural life.

BIBLIOGRAPHY

Brown, William Wells. *The American Fugitive in Europe. Sketches of Places and People Abroad.* New York: Sheldon, Lamport & Blakeman, 1855.

Faderman, Lillian. *Surpassing the Love of Men: Romantic Friendship and Love between Women from the Sixteenth Century to the Present.* New York: Morrow, 1981, 222–223.

COOPER, EDITH EMMA

See FIELD, MICHAEL.

COOPER, THOMAS (1805–1892)

Thomas Cooper was one of the two or three most important Chartist poets. Chartism was a radical movement in the 1830s and 1840s that sought representation of the English working class in Parliament and in the nation's political economy. The general movement of revolution in Europe in 1848 was represented in England by Chartists' violent resistance and agitation and by the police's violent suppression, after which it waned in importance. While radical, however, Cooper was essentially nonviolent, even though he was imprisoned for two years on somewhat trumped-up, and certainly overreactive, charges of inciting violence. He thought of himself as an "independent Chartist" and broke with the Chartist leader Feargus O'Connor, partly because O'Connor had had his mind poisoned by an enemy of Cooper's in the fraught internal struggles within the movement. O'Connor also conceived a scheme for buying land for working people to live on and to own, like modern-day workers' cooperative housing. This proved financially ruinous, as Cooper saw, and his resistance to O'Connor's plans made the break between them complete. Cooper took no more official part in the movement after that. A few years later he renounced free thinking (in 1856) and converted to Christianity, having himself baptized in 1859 while being still committed to socialism. He lectured tirelessly on religion and labor for the next two decades.

Cooper was the son of a dyer and himself became a shoemaker while teaching himself literature and memorizing huge tracts of poetry, including much of Milton's *Paradise Lost*. He devoted himself to the great project of working-class self-education, and to the Chartist movement. (The famous six points defining that movement included universal suffrage and the secret ballot, a radical demand that aroused wrath in the aging, reactionary, and cantankerous WILLIAM WORDSWORTH.) Arrested in 1842 for his participation in riots against the government, Cooper wrote what he called his "prison rhymes," including an endless and much-talked-about poem called *The Purgatory of Suicides,* dedicated to the Scottish essayist Carlyle. Through it he became friends with Carlyle and members of his circle. Charles Dickens read the poem in manuscript and said he admired it; Carlyle was less encouraging, though he said he found "a dark Titanic energy struggling there," with "indisputable traces of genius in it." The energy was the energy, Carlyle acutely observed, of real life, and not of poetic artifice, and he quoted Friedrich Schiller's important reminder that "life is a serious thing." Cooper rightly saw the seriousness of the praise and the encouragement that Carlyle was offering: that he should make real life better through his work. His poetry showed his capacity to do just that.

Although Cooper broke with Chartism as led by O'Connor, he continued to be faithful to the working-class politics he advocated. His 1872 autobiography is a stirring account of a radical and astonishing life in the 19th century, at a time when everything seemed possible. Cooper maintains his freshness and energy throughout, most especially, perhaps, when he thinks back on the years of Chartism, the working-men's associations and classes he participated in and taught, the Chartist hymnbooks and anthologies that he sought to put together while editing various Chartist journals, and attempting to give to the lower classes the sense of completion and depth within life that the combination of art and labor could offer.

See also "CHARTIST CHAUNT."

BIBLIOGRAPHY

Charlton, John. *The Chartists: The First National Workers' Movement.* Chicago: Pluto Press, 1997.

Cooper, Thomas. *Life of Thomas Cooper; Written by Himself.* London: Hodder and Stoughton, 1872.

Janowitz, Anne F. *Lyric and Labour in the Romantic Tradition.* New York: Cambridge University Press, 1998.

Thompson, Dorothy. *The Chartists.* London: Temple Smith, 1984.

CORY, WILLIAM JOHNSON (WILLIAM JOHNSON) (1823–1892)

William Johnson (who added Cory to his name when he was 50) is now largely remembered for one poem, "They told me, Heraclitus," which appears in the expanded version of Francis Turner Palgrave's *Golden Treasury of the Best Songs and Lyrical Poems in the English Language.* Cory was educated at Eton College and King's College, Cambridge University, where he won scholarships and prizes. He then became a teacher at Eton (the exclusive boys' school in Windsor, arguably the best in the world, both then and now), where he wrote textbooks that were used for decades. He was a beloved teacher; his loyal students included ROBERT BRIDGES as well as A. P. Primrose, who would become prime minister two years after Cory's death. However, a scandal forced his resignation from Eton. It seems to have had something to do with his homosexuality, most probably his tolerance of adolescent homoeroticism; at any rate, he left at age 49 and went to Madeira, where he married and changed his last name to Cory.

Cory is as good a poet in Latin as in English; his English poetry is distinguished by authority and verbal brilliance, with exquisite control of prosody and tone. Much of it is in the more technically difficult mode of light verse, such as the wittily melancholy "Hersilia," which imagines the future of women's education at Cambridge: In time they will be as disappointed as the men who preceded them were with their ordinary lives after their world-changing hopes as undergraduates.

Being a schoolmaster, Cory was able to affect (with ample justice) the tone of Victorian authority that is one of the great markers of minor VICTORIAN POETRY. It is a marker of the minor school because it is more self-assured than searching; but justified self-assurance is often what we wish from an author into whose hands we put ourselves, and Cory does not disappoint. "They told me, Heraclitus" is powerful because it has this tone: There is melancholy but also firmness in the account it gives of death and its limits. The poem is Cory's apparently improvised translation, for his pupils, of an epigram by the Greek scholar Callimachus (*Epigrams* II), who lived in the third century B.C.E. Callimachus wrote many of those epigrams to young men that he loved, which would make his work particularly congenial to Cory. This one is to a dead friend, Heraclitus (not to be confused with the Greek philosopher from two centuries earlier) of Halicarnassus in Caria, in the southwest of modern Turkey; the nightingales are his poems, which sing even after his death. Callimachus (known for the purity of his style) laments the death of his friend by addressing not the living person who reported the death but the dead friend himself.

The meter of the poem is what gives it its power in the end. It is in iambic heptameter—that is, seven feet to the line, with a medial pause in every line except the second and the last. That pause, or caesura, does the work of a stressed syllable and divides the line in two, as though it is stumbling on a sigh. The last line (which echoes a line in ALGERNON CHARLES SWINBURNE's "HYMN TO PROSERPINE") asserts with authority that death cannot take away Heraclitus's poetry, which is so alive that he can still imagine himself talking to his dead friend. That line does not pause: It simply balances and so refutes the claim that death takes everything away. The repetition of the word *take,* as the concluding rhyme of the poem, makes the assertion all the more final: Death is as unimportant in the end as those who told him of Heraclitus's death, since the poetry will live on.

BIBLIOGRAPHY

Benson, Arthur C. Biographical introduction in *Ionica,* by William Cory, xi–xxxii. London: George Allen, 1905.

Callimachus. *Poems of Callimachus.* Translated with introduction, notes and glossary by Frank Nisetich. New York: Oxford University Press, 2001.

MacKenzie, F. Compton. *William Cory: A Biography.* London: Constable, 1950.

CRABBE, GEORGE (1754–1832) George Crabbe was a kind of counterweight to all the great poets of his time. In his old age, WILLIAM WORDSWORTH called him "the driest of poets," and rated him as the diametrical opposite of the young ALFRED, LORD TENNYSON, but Tennyson also loved Crabbe (as the great Oxford classicist Benjamin Jowett noted with some wonder) and his "sledge-hammer lines," as did EDWARD FITZGERALD, who wrote a preface to his poetry. Crabbe is remembered today largely due to Benjamin Britten's operatic adaptation of "PETER GRIMES," one of the tales in his 1810 collection of character studies, *The Borough.*

Crabbe's poetic style is both old-fashioned and inelegant: He wrote in the heroic couplets he learned, more or less as a voracious but autodidactic reader, from Alexander Pope and the mid-18th-century poets who followed him. But Pope and John Dryden, who invented and glorified the heroic couplet, wrote in an urbane style that had to do with urbane 18th-century Augustan culture; upper-class city and country-house life; and the interests of politicians, aristocrats, and intellectuals. Crabbe (somewhat like his almost exact contemporary, WILLIAM BLAKE) came from a far poorer background—his father was a fisherman who liked the mathematical puzzles published in a magazine, whose poetry pages he gave to his young son—and he had a far poorer education. He trained as an apothecary and as a surgeon, and eventually he supported himself as a clergyman when given livings by various aristocratic patrons who had them in their gift. The first and most intellectually impressive of his patrons was Edmund Burke, perhaps the central aesthetic and political thinker of the 18th century in England. Burke's treatise on the SUBLIME was of great importance to ROMANTICISM, and thus Crabbe (who outlived Blake, PERCY BYSSHE SHELLEY, JOHN KEATS, and LORD BYRON) forms a large part of the link between 18th-century, romantic, and even Victorian tastes. Burke arranged for publication of Crabbe's collection *The Library* in 1781, after which Crabbe remained a mid-level respectable figure for the rest of his life, meeting and forming friendships with such writers as THOMAS MOORE and Sir WALTER SCOTT.

The result of Crabbe's background in manual labor was that he had a sense of what real life among the rural poor was like, both as a member of this class and as someone who ministered to its heartaches, as surgeon and as somewhat reluctant clergyman. Whatever romanticizing of this life less thoughtful readers of Wordsworth derived from his poetry, Crabbe's work made vivid the remorseless, grinding difficulties of the world and society he depicted. Crabbe's tales, as he called them, are interesting for their brutal realism, not for their well-made plots. Their point (again recalling Wordsworth, in this case "SIMON LEE") is that this is what life really is like among the poor. Wordsworth and Crabbe were both writing against the kind of airy descriptions to be found in Thomas Gray, and here again we can see in Crabbe an important feature in the transition to romantic thinking. But his tales had further repercussions. Despite FitzGerald's remark that Crabbe had no imitators, THOMAS HARDY's fiction (and probably also his poetry with its intense and stiff unloveliness) is clearly influenced by Crabbe; and indeed, Hardy is reported to have said that "his earliest influence in the direction of realism was obtained from

Crabbe's work." Crabbe was never much in fashion, and never will be, but his unyielding, unlyrical, staunch grimness will always attract readers and continue to influence other writers.

BIBLIOGRAPHY

Chamberlain, Robert. *George Crabbe.* New York: Twayne Publishers, 1965.

Huchon, René. *George Crabbe and His Times, 1754–1832: A Critical and Biographical Study.* Translated by Frederick Clarke. London: J. Murray, 1907.

New, Peter. *George Crabbe's Poetry.* London: Macmillan, 1976.

Pollard, Arthur. *Crabbe: The Critical Heritage.* London: Routledge, 1972.

"CRADLE SONG AT TWILIGHT" ALICE MEYNELL (1895)

This beautiful, eerie poem is one of ALICE MEYNELL's many works about the relationship of adult to child. It is a good example of the almost uncanny austerity she shows in her thinking about maternity, one of her central themes in both her poetry and critical writing. (Two decades later she would write her book-length essay on *Mary, Mother of Jesus.*) As is frequently the case in Meynell's poetry (see, for example, "The MODERN MOTHER"), the speaker is crucial despite the fact that the poem seems to be written in a detached style, without a first-person pronoun in it. That detachment of style is part of the poem's theme, however, and not just an attitude toward its theme.

Thus, the title tells us for whom the song is written: It is essentially a song to be sung by a woman trying to rock a child to sleep. As with all lullabies, certainly all English lullabies from John Skelton (ca. 1460–1529) on, the rhythm is for the child but the meaning is for the adult. That adult is very different from the personified Night whom she wishes would seal up the child's wakefulness in sleep. Both Night and the child are failing, in relation to each other, to do what the adult wants them to do. We can say that this adult is the mother herself, since she so contrasts with Night—that is to say, the mother is the speaker of the poem. She is estranged from what she most wants for the child—his sleep—and from what he is insisting on now, his own wakefulness. And she is estranged from the girlish, unmaternal Night, more interested in her own adventures than in the child's. Her relation to all is as alien as the alien eyes she attributes to Night.

The poem requires a little bit of parsing. Slender (or girlish) Night is too young a nurse to lull the child to rest, because she wishes to fly to pleasures of her own and not hold the child firmly and warmly to her breast. (Meynell is probably remembering one of her favorite passages from Christopher Marlowe's "Hero and Leander," where Cupid, thinking of Hero as being like his mother Venus, "laid his childish head upon her breast, / And with still panting rock'd there took his rest.") Because she cannot lull him to sleep, he is jolly but wide awake. He plays with her while she wishes he would sleep so she could undertake some erotic adventure with "other playfellows." Her alien eyes keep an unmaternal fondness for that adventure, and it is the word *alien* in the last line that is so striking. Night is strange and alien, and so, therefore, is the speaker, who can produce the poem of Night's strangeness; and yet that woman is the mother, brought into all the strangeness and self-denials of the vocation of motherhood that comprise Meynell's constant theme.

BIBLIOGRAPHY

Badeni, June. *The Slender Tree: A Life of Alice Meynell.* Padstow, Cornwall, England: Tabb House, 1981.

Leighton, Angela. "Alice Meynell." In *Victorian Women Poets: Writing against the Heart,* 244–265. Charlottesville: University Press of Virginia, 1992.

Meynell, Alice. *Prose and Poetry.* Centenary vol. Edited by Frederick Page, et al. London: J. Cape, 1947.

Meynell, Viola. *Alice Meynell: A Memoir.* London: J. Cape, 1929.

CRISIS LYRIC

See INTIMATIONS ODE.

"CROSSING THE BAR" ALFRED, LORD TENNYSON (1889)

ALFRED, LORD TENNYSON wrote "Crossing the Bar" when he was 80, three years before his death, but at his request it always appears last in any edition of his poetry. It is a conscious farewell, one that looks death in the face and hopes to find there the face of Christ. This was the hope that animated *IN MEMORIAM A.H.H.,* where he begins with an address to Christ as Immortal Love, whose face we cannot see but whom we embrace through faith. Now on the verge of death, he hopes to meet his pilot face to face, a hope that had originally rounded out the last section of the manuscript version of *In Memoriam,* where he has faith that he will "look on those we loved / And That which made us, face to face." Indeed, "Crossing the Bar" is in many ways an application of *In Memoriam* to himself, as he now follows ARTHUR HENRY HALLAM into the dark from which he wished so passionately to rescue him in his earlier elegy.

Thus, at the beginning of *In Memoriam,* Tennyson addresses the "Fair ship, that . . . sailest the placid ocean-plains / With my lost Arthur's loved remains" (IX, ll. 1–3), and he asks the ship to bring Hallam home through the night until Phosphor, the "star of dawn" as Tennyson glossed it, glimmers on his arrival. Phosphor presides as both evening and morning star over *In Memoriam;* now, in "Crossing the Bar," Tennyson sets *out* to sea under the light of "Sunset and evening star" (l. 1). As with Hallam's return, his journey outward into the dark is one in which he prays for the sea to be calm—here that would be because it is at high tide—and full of the substance that will bear him on beyond "Time and Place."

Presiding over the poem is PERCY BYSSHE SHELLEY's elegy for JOHN KEATS, *ADONAIS.* At the end of that poem, Shelly describes how his bark or boat is "borne darkly, fearfully afar" (compare Tennyson's "The flood may bear me far" [l. 14]) while "the soul of Adonais, like a star" acts as a beacon for him. By alluding to *Adonais,* Tennyson can invoke the double spirit of both Keats and Shelley—that is, of elegist and mourned figure—which enables him to imagine rejoining Hallam in the way *Adonais* joins his two great precursors. Keats had desired to pass beyond the world where men "sit and hear each other moan," as the sandbar of Tennyson's title might moan if the water were too low, and "to cease upon the midnight with no pain" in words that anticipate Tennyson's hope to die with the same gentle elision of the bar, the boundary, or "bourne" (l. 13), between life and death. The word echoes *Hamlet* as well, where death is "that undiscovered country from whose bourne / No traveler returns," but Tennyson manages an astonishing and Shelleyan delicacy here which sets up the climax of the poem. For once the flood bears him far from "the bourne of Time and Place" (l. 13), he will be beyond space itself. And yet the image of being far beyond "Time and Place" is a spatial image, so that space becomes the form of its own undoing.

It is because space can represent even being far beyond the limits of space (again, the image is the same as that at the end of *Adonais*) that Tennyson can hope for the eminently special experience of seeing another's face. That face is both Hallam's and God's, and perhaps somewhere behind this poem is ultimately the story in Genesis of Jacob crossing not the bar but the river Jordan to see his brother again after 14 years. They embrace, and Jacob weeps, as he says, to see his brother's face so clearly before him as though it were the face of God. It is fitting that Tennyson's last words should once again find some way to imagine the divinity of the human face ("the human face divine" as John Milton calls it) transcending the material facts of this world's time and place.

BIBLIOGRAPHY

Armstrong, Isobel. *Victorian Poetry: Poetry, Poetics and Politics.* New York: Routledge, 1993.

Bloom, Harold. *Poetry and Repression: Revisionism from Blake to Stevens.* New Haven, Conn.: Yale University Press, 1976.

Buckley, Jerome Hamilton. *Tennyson: The Growth of a Poet.* Boston: Houghton Mifflin, 1965.

Kilham, John. *Critical Essays on the Poetry of Tennyson.* New York: Barnes and Noble, 1960.

Kincaid, James R. *Tennyson's Major Poems: The Comic and Ironic Patterns.* New Haven, Conn.: Yale University Press, 1975.

Ricks, Christopher B. *Tennyson.* New York: Macmillan, 1972.

Rowlinson, Matthew. *Tennyson's Fixations: Psychoanalysis and the Topics of the Early Poetry.* Charlottesville: University Press of Virginia, 1994.

Tucker, Herbert. *Tennyson and the Doom of Romanticism.* Cambridge, Mass.: Harvard University Press, 1988.

"CUCHULAIN'S FIGHT WITH THE SEA" ("THE DEATH OF CUCHULAIN")

WILLIAM BUTLER YEATS (1893, 1925) This poem, originally published in 1893 under the title "The Death of Cuchulain," was later revised and retitled "Cuchulain's Fight with the Sea." The original was part of WILLIAM BUTLER YEATS's great volume *The Rose* (1893), and it began his sequence of poems and plays about the great warrior Cuchulain, who fought for King Conchubar. Yeats meditated on and retold the story of Cuchulain until the end of his life, and it is one of the masterful images that he describes in his retrospective poem "The Circus Animal's Desertion."

In *The Rose,* this poem follows on "FERGUS AND THE DRUID," in which the legendary pre-Christian King Fergus tells how he has given his kingdom over to the all-practical Conchubar, who is not tormented with the burdens of office because he is not tormented with the burdens of poetry or of dreaming. Cuchulain is one of Conchubar's men, and in Yeats's imagination he has something of the same relationship to Conchubar as Achilles does to Agamemnon in Homer's *Iliad.* (It should be noted that Yeats knew the classical myths before he knew the Irish ones, and that he referred again and again to the stories and literature of the Trojan War.)

The story as told in "Cuchulain's Fight with the Sea" takes a little puzzling out, but it is easy to do so, and the story is an old one. Yeats wants us to puzzle it out, though—to enter into the legendary world that he describes and to feel our way about until we come to know it. Once we do puzzle it out, we will understand the plot as follows.

Emer, Cuchulain's wife, is dyeing weblike clothing, while her husband is far off with Conchubar. Her activities, and the coming of a swineherd, are an ironic recollection of the faithful and loving Penelope and the swineherd who shelters Odysseus when he returns at the end of the *Odyssey,* as well as a recollection of Agamemnon's unfaithful wife Clytemnestra, who murders her husband when he returns home from the Trojan War. But she most fully derives from Medea, who kills her own children in an act of revenge against her unfaithful husband, Jason.

Emer has set the swineherd to look for Cuchulain's return; he tells her that Cuchulain has been wildly successful in battle but has been unfaithful to her: "With him is one sweet-throated like a bird." (Yeats's last account of Cuchulain will have him taking on the form of his archaic, birdlike soul, among the other dead who "had changed their throats and had the throats of birds," as he puts it at the end of "Cuchulain Comforted.") Here we enter the disastrous land of poetry, since the raiment Emer is dyeing is a "web" that she casts upon the floor. This act makes her a kind of spider, symbol of the weaver of dreams (that the Protestant Anglo-Irish poet Edmund Spenser had written of in "Muiopotmos"), and her web one of the webs of sorrow that has wrapped Fergus round in "Fergus and the Druid."

Emer's revenge is swift: She goes to her son, a cowherd, and sends him on a mission to battle. (Here Yeats is taking up the tradition of English and Scottish ballads, particularly the ballads about the hapless Edward, sent by his mother to kill his father.) He must kill a man, and he has the ability to do so because he is the strongest warrior in the world. He has inherited this strength from his father, who his mother says is now no longer preeminent because he is old and worn out. The son does not know whom he is to fight, but he trusts his mother's knowledge since "He who made you bitter made you wise."

Emer sends her son to the Red Branch camp where Conchubar and his men are staying, "Between wood's rim and the horses of the sea"—also the place of Fergus in "Who Goes with Fergus." "The horses of the sea" are a metaphor for the whitecaps of the waves, but the metaphor will become, importantly, half-literalized later on in the poem. The son is to answer no challenges once he gets there, except at the point of a sword, and so he goes to where Conchubar and Cuchulain are feasting, and Conchubar is singing Cuchulain's praise. We still do not know, and neither does he, that Cuchulain is the cowherd's father, but we begin to guess that Cuchulain is the figure Emer resents for being with the sweet-throated one, partly because his sweetheart is at his side, partly because Cuchulain is the object of the same extreme praise that the swineherd has uttered.

We switch now to Cuchulain's point of view. He hears the sound of the man who has come, hears his singing, and sends to know who he is. Conforming to his mother's command, the young man refuses to tell the messenger who challenges him, and so Cuchulain comes to ask him himself, respecting an oath that has bound him since childhood: that he must not give his name unless forced, and must challenge all those who refuse to give their names and force them to do so. Emer knew this of him and therefore sent her son with this particular task.

Cuchulain challenges the young man, but reluctantly: His face reminds Cuchulain of one he loved—although he does not know it he is recognizing Emer in his own son's countenance. The young man does not yield, and they fight until Cuchulain mortally wounds him, at which point he is compelled to give his name:

> "Speak before your breath is done."
> "Cuchulain I, mighty Cuchulain's son."
> "I put you from your pain. I can no more."
> While day its burden on to evening bore,
> With head bowed on his knees Cuchulain stayed;

Cuchulain has killed his own son, the son that challenged him without recognizing him in order to be worthy of his father. This is Emer's revenge: that he should know what he has done only when it is too late to prevent it. His knowledge comes from force, and the force kills his son. All he can do is mourn, as Achilles mourns for Patroclus, and like Achilles, what follows mourning will inevitably be revenge.

Conchubar, the subtle and practical king, sees that Cuchulain's rage will be ungovernable when he rejects the comforts of the young woman for whom he has betrayed Emer. Cuchulain will brood on the tremendous guilt of his betrayal of both wife and child, and he will recognize in his brooding that it was Conchubar who had arranged the seduction, in order to entice Cuchulain to follow him. He has attempted to entice him again by sending the maid to Cuchulain after the death of his son, and we recognize now that Conchubar's song of praise to Cuchulain's glory has been part of his campaign of flattery. But now he recognizes that Cuchulain will see the truth, and so he turns to the suggestive magic of the Druids:

> Then Conchubar, the subtlest of all men,
> Ranking his Druids round him ten by ten,
> Spake thus: "Cuchulain will dwell there and
>   brood
> For three days more in dreadful quietude,
> And then arise, and raving slay us all.
> Chaunt in his ear delusions magical,
> That he may fight the horses of the sea."
> The Druids took them to their mystery,
> And chaunted for three days.
>   Cuchulain stirred,
> Stared on the horses of the sea, and heard
> The cars of battle and his own name cried;
> And fought with the invulnerable tide.

The delusions magical are also delusions poetical. They make possible the images Yeats so loved, and the image that he loved perhaps most of all: a man fighting against the sea. These delusions are chanted in Cuchulain's ear, so their power is essentially the power of poetic imagery, and the Druids' mystery, their three-days chanting as Cuchulain mourns, is the mystery of poetry as the young Yeats conceived it. Now "the horses of the sea" are literalized for him, and he fights against them, crying his own name.

His own name—but is he addressing himself? Far more probably, he is addressing the bearer of that name he has just discovered and killed: "Cuchulain I, mighty Cuchulain's son." In his madness he still knows the source and reasons for his grief: the death of his son, who has shown by his youth and courage in his final battle with his father that he was worthy of him. Cuchulain cannot defeat the sea, but he can attempt the impossible. In his early poetry, Yeats persistently saw the subject of poetry as some sad figure's impossible attempt to provoke and achieve a response from a sublimely indifferent natural world. He famously said: "We make out of the quarrel arguments with others, rhetoric, but of the quarrel with ourselves, poetry." Cuchulain represented for Yeats, early and late, the impossible argument with himself and with the world he created but could not command.

BIBLIOGRAPHY

Bloom, Harold. *Yeats*. New York: Oxford University Press, 1970.

Ellmann, Richard. *Yeats: The Man and the Masks*. New York: Norton, 1978.

Grossman, Allen R. *Poetic Knowledge in the Early Yeats: A Study of* The Wind Among the Reeds. Charlottesville: University Press of Virginia, 1969.

Maddox, Brenda. *George's Ghosts: A New Life of W. B. Yeats.* London: Picador, 1999.
Rosenthal, M. L. Introduction to *Selected Poems and Three Plays of William Butler Yeats.* New York: Collier, 1986.
Vendler, Helen. *Poets Thinking: Pope, Whitman, Dickinson, Yeats.* Cambridge, Mass.: Harvard University Press, 2004.
———. *Yeats's Vision and the Later Plays.* Cambridge, Mass.: Harvard University Press, 1963.

"CYCLAMENS" **MICHAEL FIELD (1893)** The poet MICHAEL FIELD—a pen name for Katherine Bradley and Edith Cooper—excelled in intense and revelatory description, and the things Bradley and Cooper liked describing most were flowers and works of art. The cyclamen that they see here are interesting partly because of the erotic suggestion of their form. All flowers are literally erotic, since they are meant to attract the carriers of pollen in order to further their sexual reproduction. But some flowers look more erotic than others, and it is these that Field (as we should call the speaker of the poem) likes to describe, from "Irises" to roses to the cyclamen here.

Cylcamen may range in color from white to purple, but they are generally pink. The way their five petals join, together with their whiteness, gives them the erotic suggestiveness to which Field responds. The eros is a difficult one, suggestive of repression, more perhaps on the part of the Victorian society at large that disapproved of Bradley and Cooper's relationship as quasi-incestuous lovers, than on their own part; but the difficulty must necessarily be internalized as part of the intensity of their relationship with each other.

In a sense, this internalization is what the poem is about. The cyclamen are "terribly white" (l. 1), whiter than expected or hoped for. And that whiteness draws Field's attention to the whiteness of the world around him. It is winter, it is night, the ground is covered with snow, and the sharpness of the cold is suggested by the great description of how "The sky is cut by the winter light" (l. 4). Although he does not say so, this certainly suggests that the "handful of cyclamen" are in a cut glass bowl or vase, with the sharpness of the still life suggesting the sharpness of the winter, which suggests in turn the chiselled sharpness of the still life from which it derives.

That sharpness is the opposite of the erotic softness and the pleasure it would promise that is usual in a flower poem. Here erotic intensity is turned against the possibility of erotic fulfillment. Warmth becomes cold, the lissome becomes the chiseled, the soft becomes the cutting.

As they often did in their poetry, Bradley and Cooper use the singularity of their speaker—Michael Field—as a way of expressing the great and perennial poetic theme of erotic frustration in a particularly striking way. That frustration is endemic to the human condition, but also to the specifics of their own relationship. Field is alone, which means that in some sense even together they are alone, in a state of rigid, sharp-edged anhedonia, or inability to feel pleasure. That rigidity is the mark of intensity ("terribly white"), and that intensity is the intensity of their love for each other and their desire for each other. The poetry and the composite poet come out of this desire, out of the fact that it is inevitably painful and hurtful as well as pleasurable and healing. Thus, Field alone, struck as he is to the heart by the cyclamen, is like Bradley and Cooper together, the erotic flowers there and in their possession and ken, but still experienced in a mode of intensity as potentially painful as it is sometimes pleasurable (as in the springtime poem "IT WAS DEEP APRIL").

BIBLIOGRAPHY

Avery, Simon. "Michael Field." In *The Literary Encyclopedia.* (June 13, 2003). Available online. URL: http://www.litencyc.com/php/speople.php?rec=true&UID=1521. Accessed on March 1, 2008.
Castle, Terry, ed. *The Literature of Lesbianism: A Historical Anthology from Ariosto to Stonewall.* New York: Columbia University Press, 2003.
Moore, T., and D. C. Sturge. *Works and Days, from the Journal of Michael Field.* London: J. Murray, 1933.
Prins, Yopie. *Victorian Sappho.* Princeton, N.J.: Princeton University Press, 1999.
Sturgeon, Mary. *Michael Field.* London: G. G. Harrap, 1922.
White, Christine. "'Poets and Lovers Evermore': The Poetry and Journals of Michael Field." In *Sexual Sameness: Textual Differences in Lesbian and Gay Writing,* edited by Joseph Bristow, 26–43. New York: Routledge, 1992.

"CYNARA" ERNEST DOWSON (1891) The motto of this poem is "Non sum qualis eram bonae sub Regno Cynarae," which tells us that Cynara is the name under which Dowson represents a lost love. The motto (see MOTTOES) is from Horace (*Odes* 4, ll. 3–4) and may be translated, "I am not as I was under the reign of good Cynara"—that is, when Cynara governed his thoughts to the exclusion of all else. ("Cynara" is what the poem is usually called, but its motto is, in fact, its title.) Dowson's poem is remembered now for two phrases: "gone with the wind" (l. 13) and the refrain "I have been faithful to thee, Cynara! In my fashion."

Since that last line was made into a song by Cole Porter ("Always True to You in My Fashion," which also quotes the words "gone with the wind"), it has been nearly impossible to assess how seriously to take the poem. Dowson's contemporary and friend WILLIAM BUTLER YEATS had some contempt for it, but that may have been because he found ridiculous what might have been instead ambivalence between real seriousness and a kind of inevitable acknowledgement that the seriousness the poem might desire to express is structurally impossible. The poem's subject is central enough—that of "an old passion" and the desolate feeling it causes. But we can tell from the poem that its nostalgia is partly the regret of someone who has changed. He is not what he was when he was wholly passionate about Cynara. Those days are gone, and it is hard to make credible a superseded passion. Either he loves her and will remain true to her, or his love for her has faded and he cannot make a powerful case for his own desolation.

The poem risks, and perhaps deliberately courts, parody in using passionate language about superseded feelings. We might be able to call the poem a serious self-parody on Dowson's part: He understands that the desperate dissipation he has sunk into now has something to do with not liking the loss of a passionate attitude toward life, and that therefore the poem is substituting passionate language for the passion he knows he has lost. He is desolate not because of his desperate love for Cynara, but because the time of life in which he could experience desperate love is over.

Such an interpretation has the merit of finding considerable subtlety in a poem that is so vividly exaggerated. It is excessive because it is compensating for a sense of emptiness in life. It is overstated because there is nothing to feel passionate about any more. It is unsubtle because the losses that it records are losses of subtlety within feeling as well. The speaker has had no true love after Cynara, only bought companionship, but Cynara is no longer a true love either, and the desolation of not loving succeeds that of loving and is in some ways even harder to bear.

Much depends, of course, on what happened between him and Cynara. Did she die? (Not her real life model, Adeleide Flotinowicz.) Did she spurn him? (If so, why would he need to justify his faithfulness? Or is he trying to make her jealous?) Did he leave her, and does he now tenderly and self-pityingly nurse self-inflicted wounds? The fact that we do not know allows us to say simply that the poem registers a desire to write a passionate poem, even a Horation ode, but a failure to be the kind of person with sufficient passion to write that poem. It is a tribute more to poetry than to Cynara, a tribute which marks what is loved by how far short it comes of the poetry it emulates.

BIBLIOGRAPHY

Plarr, Victor. *Ernest Dowson, 1888–1897: Reminiscences, Unpublished Letters and Marginalia.* London: E. Mathews, 1914.

Swann, Thomas Burnett. *Ernest Dowson.* New York: Twayne Publishers, 1965.

Yeats, W. B. *Autobiography of William Butler Yeats: Consisting of Reveries Over Childhood and Youth, The Trembling of the Veil, and Dramatis Personae.* Garden City, N.Y.: Doubleday Anchor Books, 1958.

D

"DANNY DEEVER" RUDYARD KIPLING (1890) "Danny Deever" was RUDYARD KIPLING's breakthrough poem, the first of his *Barrack-Room Ballads,* and, in its use of dialect and ballad form, an astonishing innovation. The power of its story and language was apparent even to writers as temperamentally different as T. S. Eliot and OSCAR WILDE (who describes a similar execution a few years later in the Kipling-influenced "BALLAD OF READING GAOL").

Such admiration is well-deserved. Kipling undertakes a kind of new version of WORDSWORTH and COLERIDGE's *Lyrical Ballads* with the *Barrack-Room Ballads,* poems that speak for and also to the enlisted men on whose sacrifices and iron endurance the British Empire and its (self-asserted) civilizing mission relied, just as Wordsworth and Coleridge had sought to write poetry in "the natural language of natural men," as Wordsworth put it. The relation of soldiers and sailors to the state they served raises interesting and difficult issues of power and oppression. The enlisted men were mainly lower class and poor and lived lives of considerable misery, even as they were instruments of Victorian hegemony. For Kipling, as for many others from Edmund Burke and Jane Austen on, sympathy for the downtrodden would mean sympathy for both the soldiers and for those they conquered or policed, which is why Kipling likes stories of reconciliation between the British soldier and the "native" he interacts with ("GUNGA DIN" and "THE BALLAD OF EAST AND WEST.") Poems such as "Danny Deever" and "Tommy" are more about the experience and status of the soldiers alone, and the indifference or contempt they sometimes experience from the social betters they protect ("makin' mock o' uniforms that guard you while you sleep," as Tommy puts it).

What makes "Danny Deever" a masterpiece is not only its language but its form. The poem takes place in dialogue between the "colour-sergeant" of a battalion in India and the men he is leading, all personified in the allegorical name "Files-on-Parade," which means the rank-and-file formation that the soldiers take up on the parade ground where Danny Deever's hanging takes place. We find out what is happening by overhearing three different speakers, of whom the colour-sergeant is really the only one we could call a single and particular person.

Files-on-Parade wants to know why the bugles are blowing, and the sergeant answers that they are being called to the parade ground. Files notices that the sergeant is (despite being a colour-sergeant) white as a sheet, which he acknowledges: "I'm dreadin' what I've got to watch." That acknowledgment—the act of acknowledgement—is central to the poem. Deever is being executed for having shot a battalion-mate, but the sergeant has no sense of complacency with respect to his authority. He is as appalled as he knows Files-on-Parade will be when the latter finds out what is going on. It is here that the third voice comes on, the voice of the ballad itself. The narrative gives way to a sort of chorus (or what would be a chorus in a barracks-room bawdy song), in which we now find out what is about to happen: "For they're hangin' Danny Deever."

Who is that "they"? The same agency that the men comprise, the discipline and order and group existence of the army. The men are not hanging him, but all the men of the battalion, from Files-on-Parade to the colour-sergeant, to Danny Deever himself, are experiencing the shared situation that their common discipline and status and position imposes on them. Kipling takes very seriously the group identification and comradeship of the soldiers, a comradery scorned by the people they protect but intensified by the discipline they undergo together. In writing poetry (like "Danny Deever") that shows the impersonal voice of the poem itself arising from the voices of these oppressed common soldiers, Kipling could expand both the range of poetic relevance and the dignity of the poor (again like Wordsworth) because that dignity rose to the level of the most authoritative, because most fateful, poetic diction.

BIBLIOGRAPHY

Ayers, Roger. Notes on "Danny Deever." Available online: URL: http://www.kipling.org.uk/rg_deever1.htm. Accessed 27 February 2009.

Eliot, T. S. *A Choice of Kipling's Verse.* London: Faber and Faber, 1941.

"DARK ANGEL, THE" LIONEL JOHNSON (1893)

This tormented poem, probably LIONEL JOHNSON'S greatest, first appeared in *The Second Book of the Rhymers' Club,* the anthology put out by the London club comprising Johnson, WILLIAM BUTLER YEATS, ERNEST DOWSON, and a number of other decadent poets of the 1890s. The Dark Angel first of all represents the source of a conflict Johnson feels between the religion that he hopes will save him and a forbidden desire—the desire that tortures him with what it offers as delight (l. 12).

Although the poem is not explicit about the desires that its speaker attempts to withstand, one does not need to know Johnson's biography to see that what is torturing him are homosexual longings. The Dark Angel, from the start, is an angel of "aching lust" (l. 1), and what it lusts for is the end of penitence. This is a striking idea and should be taken seriously. The angel lusts not for sex but for sex without remorse. Against this Johnson wishes to preserve the sense of remorse, which suggests that the sin has already taken place (probably just in his soul, which is where the angel does its dark and subtle violence). It is convenient to Johnson's hopes to imagine that the angel is set against remorse, but it is easy to see that the Dark Angel is the allegory of remorse: remorse for the thoughts and desires that Johnson has had.

He acknowledges as much by the fourth stanza, when he says that it is the angel himself who turns the gracious muses into furies. This recognition makes it possible for the poem (and its speaker's psychology) to develop. The angel sexualizes the whole world—indeed renders the whole world a field for masochistic sexuality. This version of the world is far more effectively charged than the innocence it displaces. What could goodness now offer that matches the pleasure of the torments that oppose it?

The Dark Angel alludes to one of the angels in Shakespeare's sonnet 144, "Two loves I have of comfort and despair." Although the dark angel there is female, she is part of a love triangle which includes the fair young man ("the better angel"), and the poem is one of polymorphous sexuality and mediated desire. In "The Dark Angel" Johnson similarly converts the Dark Angel into an agent for salvation. It is resisting temptation that will allow the speaker to attain to a salvation as strangely intense as the sexual desire he is resisting. He sees the angel himself as doing part of the work of salvation (which for Johnson meant salvation within Roman Catholicism). He does what God bids him do, which is to use the energy of temptation to drive Johnson to the salvation of a God commensurate with that energy.

The great last lines of the poem transcend anything that the Dark Angel has been able to offer. But the angel (like the angel Jacob wrestles with in Genesis) is the condition for that transcendence, and in this way the "flames of evil ecstasy," which make "all things of beauty burn" (ll. 15–16)—that is, make beauty itself into a flame (as in Dante's *Paradiso*)—are the way to God, and in this way the great obsessions of Johnson's soul—beauty and art, homosexual desire, and salvation in the Catholic Church—may all be reconciled with each other, so that he may find himself (in Wallace Stevens's phrase) more truly and more strange.

BIBLIOGRAPHY

Barker, George. *Jubjub Bird, or, Some Remarks on the Prose Poem & a Little Honouring of Lionel Johnson.* Warwick, England: Greville Press, 1985.

Cevasco, G. A. *Three Decadent Poets: Ernest Dowson, John Gray, and Lionel Johnson: An Annotated Bibliography.* New York: Garland, 1990.

Pittock, Murray, ed. *Selected Letters: Lionel Johnson.* Edinburgh: Tragara Press, 1988.

Yeats, W. B. *Autobiography of William Butler Yeats: Consisting of Reveries over Childhood and Youth, The Trembling of the Veil, and Dramatis Personae.* Garden City, N.Y.: Doubleday Anchor Books, 1958.

"DARKLING THRUSH, THE" **THOMAS HARDY (1900)** "The Darkling Thrush" is one of THOMAS HARDY's characteristic poems of bleak despair over the world, natural and emotional. It is the last poem of the 19th century, or at least the last one to be discussed in this book, written on the last day of the century, December 31, 1900 (remember that centuries begin January 1, 01, and end December 31, 00). Because it is December, the gloomy weather of the day, which is described in the poem, can stand for the century itself—both the one coming to an end and the one about to start.

The day is characteristically gray (see "NEUTRAL TONES" for a similar evocation of grim weather, from 37 years earlier). The question the poem implicitly poses—and the question landscape and ambience always poses in Hardy, in both his poetry and his novels—is the extent to which the mind is brought low by the exterior grimness of weather and therefore of the surrounding world, of life, versus the extent to which we see in the surrounding world a reflection of our own moods and emotions.

"The Darkling Thrush" not only raises this question but perhaps despite itself answers it. For most of the poem, the landscape and the mood it is correlated with are indeterminate as to cause and effect. The features of the landscape seem to represent the corpse of the 19th century, gruesomely leaning out of its coffin, perhaps through rigor mortis. But it may be that the grimness of the century is the grimness of the passing of all time and the hopelessness of trying to impose human meaning on an unforgiving and indifferent natural process.

We can get some hint that not everyone may feel as grim as Hardy does through the fact that he is alone at the coppice gate: All other people have "sought their household fires," and while the landscape is inimical to them, it may be that the interior lives of their homes have compensatory pleasures. On the other hand, the fact that everyone sees nature as inimical might mean that Hardy is seeing the truth of the world, not imposing his own depression onto it. Indeed, he goes on to say "*every* spirit upon earth / Seemed fervourless as I."

The poem is partly about the use or point of writing poetry in so bleak and inhuman a universe. The land itself seems to be an allegory about the pointlessness of poetry: "The tangled bine-stems scored the sky / Like strings of broken lyres."

The broken lyres mean the breaking of the instrument of lyric poetry, the AEOLIAN HARP that SAMUEL TAYLOR COLERIDGE and WILLIAM WORDSWORTH saw as the emblem for the poetic mind's relation to nature, and that Hardy's favorite poet, PERCY BYSSHE SHELLEY, tried to imagine as a metaphor for the forest of autumn and then himself in the climax of "ODE TO THE WEST WIND."

And yet the thrush—like the 60-year-old Hardy, "aged . . . frail, gaunt, and small"—pours its soul abroad in "such ecstatic sound," recalling JOHN KEATS's description of the nightingale singing in "such an ecstasy" in "ODE TO A NIGHTINGALE." To that song Keats has listened "darkling," while "half in love with easeful death." *Darkling* is Keats's word as much as it is also John Milton's, from whom he derives it; in *Paradise Lost* Milton describes how he listens as the nightingale "sings darkling." The word means "in the dark," but Hardy wants it to mean "headed toward darkness." The "darkling thrush" of the title refers both to him, listening darkling, and the bird, singing darkling.

But we can see that the grimness of the poem is Hardy's and not the world's. The logic of the poem is to some extent self-refuting. It goes like this: Why should I not be bleak when the world around me is so demonstrably unvaried in its grimness? How can the thrush sing in such circumstances?

But the thrush *is* one of the circumstances, and therefore it contradicts the argument that the world is one of unvarying grimness. The hopelessness that the poem and perhaps the poet recognize is one within the human spirit, not the natural world. The thrush is singing a "happy good-night air" to the day, and not certainly to the century. There is hope in and for the natural world, but no hope that the poet can see for himself.

BIBLIOGRAPHY

Bloom, Harold, ed. *Thomas Hardy.* New York: Chelsea House, 1987.

Clements, Patricia, and Juliet Grindle, eds. *Poetry of Thomas Hardy.* London: Vision Press, 1980.

Hardy, Thomas. *Thomas Hardy's Personal Writings: Prefaces, Literary Opinions, Reminiscences.* Edited by Harold Orel. London: Macmillan, 1990.

Kramer, Dale, ed. *Cambridge Companion to Thomas Hardy.* New York: Cambridge University Press, 1999.

DARLEY, GEORGE (1795–1846) Born the same year as JOHN KEATS, George Darley, along with JOHN CLARE and THOMAS LOVELL BEDDOES, belonged to the group of three extraordinary minor romantic poets whose great work came just after that of Keats, the youngest of the great romantics, and whose power and originality were dedicated to the pursuit of one aspect of the new poetry that they loved so deeply. Darley was deeply influenced by both Keats and PERCY BYSSHE SHELLEY, and also by his intense reading of Elizabethan and Jacobean drama and poetry. He affected an antiquarian style (like Keats and like his friend and admirer CHARLES LAMB)—effectively enough that one of the very few of his compositions to be well-known in the 19th century, "IT IS NOT BEAUTY I DEMAND," was a poem that Francis Turner Palgrave included in the *Golden Treasury of English Songs and Lyrics,* believing it an anonymous 17th-century poem.

Darley was born in Dublin and moved to London when he was 26 to try to become a writer. He wrote a book of somewhat overwrought tales, *Labours of Idleness,* interesting for their style, their rural settings, and some of their descriptions of Ireland, and including as epigraphs or MOTTOES some of his own compositions, ascribed, like Sir WALTER SCOTT's, to anonymous sources. He also wrote criticism for various magazines, and became friends with Lamb and Beddoes. SAMUEL TAYLOR COLERIDGE also came to admire some of his poetry. But Darley tended to be very solitary, partly as a result of a terrible stammer that made social life extremely painful to him.

Unable to support himself entirely through his literary work, and trained as a mathematician, Darley also wrote a series of textbooks on mathematics and on astronomy that are both penetrating and gracefully written. He also edited an edition of the plays of the 17th-century team Francis Beaumont and John Fletcher, and he continued to write criticism, in which he demanded as much of others as of himself, and which was therefore often very harsh. He wrote a verse drama and some other long compositions, but his greatest work was *Nepenthe,* a long, unfinished poem whose first two cantos he had privately (and badly) printed for his friends. "The PHOENIX" is the most widely anthologized portion of this poem. After his death, Darley was largely forgotten, despite the efforts of some of those who had appreciated the intensity of his work, such as the playwright Mary Russell Mitford, whose 1852 *Recollections of a Literary Life* championed her favorite writers, Darley among them, and Richard Garnett, until the end of the 19th century; and early in the 20th century, ROBERT BRIDGES devoted a series of essays to him which led to Darley's revival.

Darley's poetry is intense, beautiful, strange, and resourceful. He was an amazing rhymer, combining Keatsian word-painting in a way that often anticipated ALFRED, LORD TENNYSON, with Shelley's sense of motion and metamorphosis—all in a language and style that owes much to Elizabethan poetry. No doubt Darley's taste for long rhyme sets, which are almost observed from the outside and marveled at by a poem's speaker, such as the one in *Nepenthe,* derives from the experience of hunting for different words while stuttering in his own speaking. Further, his gifts as a mathematician also gave him a sense of the ways repeated and self-differentiating elements could be brought together into a beautiful poetic architecture.

See also ROMANTICISM.

BIBLIOGRAPHY
Abbott, Claude Colleer. *The Life and Letters of George Darley, Poet and Critic.* London: Oxford University Press, 1928.
Bridges, Robert Seymour. "George Darley." In *Collected Essays, Papers, &c., of Robert Bridges.* Vol. 2, 187–188. London: Oxford University Press, 1927–36.
Brisman, Leslie. "George Darley: Bouyant as Young Time." In *Romantic Origins,* 182–223. Ithaca, N.Y.: Cornell University Press, 1978.
Simmel, Georg. "Eros, Platonic and Modern." In *On Individuality and Social Forms,* edited by Donald N. Levine, 235–248. Chicago: University of Chicago Press, 1971.

"DEDICATORY SONNET TO S. T. COLERIDGE" HARTLEY COLERIDGE (1832) This poem to his father, SAMUEL TAYLOR COLERIDGE, was at the head of the only edition of HARTLEY COLERIDGE's poetry published in his lifetime, *Poems,* published by his friend and patron F. E. Bingley in Leeds in 1833. The book is the first of a planned two-volume set but volume 2 never came out. Hartley had had a disappointing life: He was a skillful (though by no means a great) writer—brilliant, erudite, and charming. He inherited much of his father's great intellectual power, but also his father's intemperance, and while relations between him and his father were always good, he was inevitably a source of sadness to the elder poet. This volume came out when Hartley's other projects had more or less failed, and one can see from its dedication the desire to prove that his life had not entirely disappointed his father's hopes.

Those hopes are most famously articulated in the elder Coleridge's great poem "FROST AT MIDNIGHT," written as the infant Hartley lay asleep beside him. That poem ends with a prophetic blessing on Hartley (ll. 44–74), which Hartley now summarizes here in the sonnet's octet, and which he quotes in the sestet: "I 'wandered like a breeze'" (l. 9). This quotation alters the tenses of "Frost at Midnight," where Coleridge's beautiful prayer-prophecy predicts: "But *thou,* my babe! shalt wander like a breeze" (l. 54). What was future then is past now. In a note to the sad posthumous version of the poem published by his brother Derwent in an edition of Hartley's complete poems in 1851, Hartley quotes the relevant passage from his father (ll. 54–62) and adds: "As far as regards the *habitats* of my childhood, these lines, written at Nether Stowey [in Somerset in the southwest of England, where the Coleridges lived before moving north to the Lake District], were almost prophetic. But poets are *not* prophets." That is to say, they are not prophets because the glorious and better future that Samuel had predicted for Hartley did not come true, and because he, too, was a poet, none of his own plans or prophecies came to fruition.

Nevertheless, in the sonnet itself, given to his father the year before the latter died, Hartley does present the fruits of his life and of his father's love. There is the book, and there is the childhood his father wanted him to have and that he *did* have. His years may be sadder now, a point he makes gracefully and simply by alluding to the kinds of poems in the volume itself—those recollecting childhood and those that describe the "passions of [his] sadder years" (l. 11). But even if they are sadder now, he did have the life his father wanted him to, and it is notable that he attaches no blame to the burden of his father's expectations. Rather, he tries here to reassure his father that those expectations were sweet and enabling. And judging by the poetry itself, in the end they probably were.

BIBLIOGRAPHY
Bloom, Harold. *The Visionary Company: A Reading of English Romantic Poetry.* Garden City, N.Y.: Doubleday, 1961.
Coleridge, Derwent. *Poems by Hartley Coleridge with a Memoir of His Life by His Brother.* 2 vols. London: E. Moxon, 1851.
Griggs, Earl Leslie. *Hartley Coleridge: His Life and Work.* London: University of London Press, 1929.

"DEFENCE OF GUINEVERE, THE" WILLIAM MORRIS (1858) This is the title poem in WILLIAM MORRIS's first book, published when he was 24. As a book title, it suggests that Morris is taking as his task the defense of those accused by a self-righteous and violent scrupulosity in a world where violence reigns and moralism is one of its disguises. The background of the story, as it is for ALFRED, LORD TENNYSON's *Idylls of the King*), is Sir Thomas Malory's 15th-century *Morte d'Arthur,* printed by William Caxton, whom Morris took as a precursor when he started the Kelmscott Press (he reproduced Caxton's type as well). Tennyson's first Arthurian poem, "MORTE D'ARTHUR," written 16 years earlier, was his own version of the Malory story, which was one of Morris's favorite books. The title of Morris's poem, as opposed to his book, refers to Guinevere's defense of herself against Sir Gauwaine's accusations of adultery with Sir Lancelot.

Morris's Arthurian poems owe much to *The Faerie Queene* by Edmund Spenser (who also relied on Malory as a source) in the conscious antiquarianism of the style. But Morris puts that antiquarianism to quite different uses: We expect the tone of Spenser but we get instead something like a mixture of ROBERT BROWNING and the grim modernism of EMILY BRONTË's novel *Wuthering Heights.* The poem is written in terza rima, an extremely difficult form in which the middle line of each tercet provides the first and third rhymes for the next tercet. (For more on the form, see PERCY BYSSHE SHELLEY's *The TRIUMPH OF LIFE* and "ODE TO THE WEST WIND" and Browning's "THAMURIS MARCHING.") In Malory, Guinevere's adultery with Lancelot, greatest of Arthur's knights, is one of the catalysts and one of the excuses for the internecine battles that lead to the destruction of his kingdom. In Morris, Gauwaine is the villain in the confrontation in which Guinevere defends herself against his accusations.

The context is this: Gauwaine and his knights have surprised Lancelot and Guinevere alone together. Lancelot has killed most of them and escaped, but Gauwaine imprisons Guinevere and is about to have her executed. Most of the poem consists of her answering his accusations against her, and this gives Morris the chance to describe an intense and now-detached relationship to a past whose brilliant radiance is matched only by its distance. That past includes Guinevere's youth and great beauty, her first sight of Lancelot, their first kiss, which is neither chaste nor unchaste, and a previous incident when she was accused of adultery by Sir Mellyagraunce. Lancelot challenged the latter to trial by combat, gave him tremendous odds, fought half-unarmed, and (while Guinevere stood chained to the stake at which she would be burned if Lancelot lost) killed her accuser. Her recollection of this moment has what might be the finest description in the poem: her strange and abstract meditation on what the fire in which she would be burned would look like against the wavering heat of the summer's day (ll. 216–217).

Guinevere's, or Morris's, hard clinical, accurate vision also leads to the strange psychological acuity the poet specialized in, when Guinevere accuses Gauwaine of essentially imitating his brother Agravaine, who had beheaded their mother when she was accused of adultery. Guinevere recognizes, as Guawaine attempts not to, that his animus against her is displaced anger at both his own mother and his brother for killing her (ll. 151–157).

At the end of the poem, as in Malory, Lancelot returns to rescue Guinevere, but Morris has no interest in this, and so the poem ends. His interest is, rather, in the tight focus on the intense half-hour of the scene (l. 37) in which time essentially stops (see "The HAYSTACK IN THE FLOODS"), and the mind loses itself in detail. His accomplishment here is to blend the most scrupulous attention to the hardest-edged detail with a credible warning that Guinevere will haunt anyone who kills her. The haunting will not be vague but will be in the details as well, just as the poem haunts in *its* details.

The closest analogue to Morris's style here is that of the Italian poet Dante's *Divine Comedy* and the sacred poems by Morris's friend DANTE GABRIEL ROSSETTI. We can see that the terza rima is an allusion to Dante, who invented the form for his great poem. Accordingly, we are meant to think of the Arthurian story in the *Inferno* (the first part of the *Divine Comedy*), in which Paulo and Francesca describe the adultery that they began when reading together, the book itself being a kind of Sir Galahad (Lancelot's son), bringing them together. Morris achieves something like Dante's combination of hard-edged detail and extreme emotional intensity, kept almost rigidly within the isometric opposition of forces.

BIBLIOGRAPHY

Kinna, Ruth. *William Morris: The Art of Socialism.* Cardiff: University of Wales Press, 2000.

Kirchhoff, Frederick. *William Morris: The Construction of a Male Self, 1856–1872.* Athens: Ohio University Press, 1990.

Thompson, Paul Richard. *Work of William Morris.* New York: Viking Press, 1967.

"DEJECTION: AN ODE" SAMUEL TAYLOR COLERIDGE (1802) "Dejection" is one of SAMUEL TAYLOR COLERIDGE's greatest poems, and one of the greatest crisis lyrics of English ROMANTICISM. It is in a sense Coleridge's answer to WILLIAM WORDSWORTH's INTIMATIONS ODE, as well as to Wordsworth's "TINTERN ABBEY," a kind of reworking of his own "FROST AT MIDNIGHT," within a present crisis of more momentous scale than the meditative musings of the earlier poem. But "Dejection" is a meditation as well, and as with "Frost at Midnight," the time that passes during the meditation is central to its progress. For the nature of time—that is, the nature of the way life discloses itself to the mind, not all at once but piecemeal and unexpectedly over time—is part of what the poem broods about.

This is true as well in its primary source, the first four stanzas of the Intimations Ode, which Wordsworth read aloud to Coleridge, and indeed stanza 6 of "Dejection" begins with a direct quotation of the opening of the Intimations Ode: "There was a time when . . ." Furthermore, Wordsworth was once more obviously both subject and addressee of the poem. First addressed as a verse letter to Sara Hutchinson, with whom Coleridge was in love (she would become Wordsworth's sister-in-law; for more on the vexed relationship among Coleridge, Wordsworth, and Hutchinson, see the entry on Coleridge), he reframed it as a poem addressed to Wordsworth, whose poem "Lucy Gray" he alluded to in lines 117–125 when he wrote, in manuscript, of the "tender lay" that "*William*'s self had framed" (italics added). He changed *William* to the irrelevant *Otway* when he reframed the poem yet again and addressed it to the "Lady" who stands in relation to "Dejection" as Dorothy Wordsworth does to her brother at the end of "Tintern Abbey." It should be noted that Wordsworth, too, returns the interchange of influence when in the later parts of the Intimations Ode he describes Coleridge's son HARTLEY COLERIDGE at age six as an actor as well as a "mighty prophet," which echoes Coleridge's address to the storm: "Thou Actor, perfect in all tragic sounds! / Thou mighty poet . . . !" (ll. 108–109).

But Coleridge's poem has something of a different agenda from Wordsworth's (though the two make perfect companion pieces for an understanding of the romantic movement the two poets inaugurated). Wordsworth resolves the crisis he suffers over the course of the Intimations Ode by a more intense subjectivity, whereas Coleridge finds a way out of the subjectivity whose loneliness and solitude has oppressed him to the point of despair. It is worth outlining the stages of the poem and the account it gives of the poet's relation to the world.

We begin with a quotation from one of the ballads that so influenced Wordsworth and Coleridge to write *Lyrical Ballads* (1798) together—a ballad that prognosticates a storm on the basis of the near-supernatural clarity that allows one to see the disk of the old moon as a shadow within the crescent of the new. (PERCY BYSSHE SHELLEY used this image very powerfully in *PROMETHEUS UNBOUND*.) It is not stormy yet; rather, the weather is oppressive and frustratingly sluggish, and Coleridge wishes for some storm to break the corresponding sluggishness of his own soul, in hopes of something that "Might startle this dull pain" which oppresses him, the "grief without a pang . . . stifled, drowsy, unimpassioned . . . Which finds no natural outlet, no relief, / In word, or sigh, or tear" (ll. 20–24). Here, too, he is thinking about the "timely utterance" that gave Wordsworth "relief" in the Intimations Ode. He looks at the world around him and it does not move him, despite the beautiful description he is able to give of it. In the poem's most famous line, he describes how he can see all the excellently fair things of the world: "I see, not feel, how beautiful they are" (l. 38).

This leads Coleridge to a meditation about what gives the world meaning and power over the soul—the meaning and power he can no longer feel. The answer is that feeling itself does so. The external universe is simply an "inanimate cold world" (l. 51); whatever soul it has derives from the soul observing it and projecting its own light and life onto it. The light of the world is cast by the soul that looks on it, and its vitality is a reflection of the looker's joy.

But what would the looker be joyful about? The answer he will give in stanza 6 comes down to the feeling of youth, or what the essayist William Hazlitt would later call "the feeling of immortality in youth." However, before we get there, we can give an even more self-contained answer: Joy is what we feel at the thought of being wedded to the joyous world, but because the joy of the world is a reflection of the joy we feel, we turn out to be joyful because our joy suffuses the world.

Thus, in stanza 6 the very fact that this joy does not rely on the world at all, but is a self-sustaining power, makes possible the very fact of poetic vocation: "There was a time when, though my path was rough / This joy within me dallied with distress" (ll. 76–77). This is Coleridge's version of Wordsworth's account in "RESOLUTION AND INDEPENDENCE" of how poets begin in their youth in gladness and take pleasure even from the thoughts of the despondency and madness that one day will become all too real for them. Joy insulates the soul from the sorrow it can explore with transcendent élan.

But it is real sorrow, real "distress," that the soul dallies with, and in stanza 6 Coleridge recollects how he discovered that the joy he thought belonged to him was strangely not his at all. His hope was not of any reality he could actually possess, any outside world that would sustain him. It was, rather, home in something unpossessable; it seemed so but was not, because it was not real.

It is at this point in the poem that Coleridge effects a major though subtle transformation. The outside world cannot give the soul what it wants because the only thing the soul wants is, in fact, a projection from the soul. But now this comes to mean not the sheer emptiness of the outside world or its complete inanimate inertness. Rather, the outside world is *more* independent of the mind than Coleridge had hoped—or so he now asserts. But earlier he had lamented that it was *not* independent of the mind and its moods.

Now his failure to feel joy becomes a kind of self-infecting self-mutilation. Having been overly passionate, he has withdrawn too much from passion and love and feeling and imagination, thus stealing away everything that nature herself would endow him with. But this means, it turns out, that nature is real, that there is such a thing as "the natural man" (l. 90).

The subtle but saving ambiguity by which this poem progresses is captured in the wonderful rebuke of "Reality's dark dream" (l. 95). Is reality just a dream, and a dark one (the way hope is a delusive mine in Samuel Johnson's line about being "condemned to Hope's delusive mine")? Or is reality the saving truth, with the dark dream opposed to it being the thoughts that would drive him away from reality. The second interpretation takes over and displaces the first, both in point of meditation and in the reality of the surrounding environment in which Coleridge is pursuing the meditation, for he has not noticed that the storm has now arisen. He turns from reality's dark dream to reality itself, to "listen to the wind, / Which long has raved unnoticed" (ll. 96–97). Reality has been working away all along, and now he hears its immensities and hears as well the gentleness that reminds him of poetry itself (in this case, as noted, "Lucy Gray")—of poetry which derives from the reality it embraces.

The storm Coleridge had hoped would save him in stanza 1 has finally come, and now he can embrace a reality that transcends the emotions he would project onto it. This leads him to the great moment of all Coleridgean hope and salvation, the sense that this feeling is shared by others, that the soul is not alone but surrounded by "blesséd creatures" (*"The RIME OF THE ANCIENT MARINER"*) or sung to by an Abyssinian maid ("KUBLA KHAN"), or part of a transcendent emotional reality shared by others—Sara Hutchinson, Wordsworth, the Lady to whom the last version of the ode is addressed. He blesses her (as William had Dorothy) with the very sense that she belongs to the world he perceives, not as part of his perception, not therefore as part of his self-centeredness but as another perceiver of that world, another mind, something that simultaneously embraces the intensities of subjectivity and relieves them through the sense that the self is not alone in the world, that there are other selves to bless (as he blesses the Lady at the end of the poem), and that this very fact is what makes others blessed.

BIBLIOGRAPHY

Bate, Walter Jackson. *Coleridge*. New York: Macmillan, 1968.

Bloom, Harold. *The Visionary Company: A Reading of English Romantic Poetry*. Garden City, N.Y.: Doubleday, 1961.

Brisman, Leslie. *Romantic Origins*. Ithaca, N.Y.: Cornell University Press, 1978.

Christensen, Jerome. *Coleridge's Blessed Machine of Language.* Ithaca, N.Y.: Cornell University Press, 1981.
Coburn, Kathleen. *Experience into Thought: Perspectives in the Coleridge Notebooks.* Toronto: University of Toronto Press, 1979.
Coleridge, Samuel Taylor. *Biographia Literaria.* London: Oxford University Press, 1954.
———. *Selected Poems.* Edited by William Empson and David Pirie. Manchester, England: Fyfield, 1989.
Empson, William. Introduction to *Selected Poems.* Edited by William Empson and David Pirie, 13–100. Manchester, England: Fyfield, 1989.
Halmi, Nicholas. *Genealogy of the Romantic Symbol.* New York: Oxford University Press, 2007.
Holmes, Richard. *Coleridge.* New York: Pantheon, 2000.
Hughes-Hallet, Penelope. *The Immortal Dinner: A Famous Evening of Genius and Laughter in Literary London, 1817.* New York: Viking, 2000.
McFarland, Thomas. *Coleridge and the Pantheist Tradition.* Oxford: Clarendon Press, 1969.
Parker, Reeve. *Coleridge's Meditative Art.* Ithaca, N.Y.: Cornell University Press, 1975.
Swann, Karen. "'Christabel': The Wandering Mother and the Enigma of Form." *SIR* 23, no. 4 (Winter 1984): 533–553.
Woodring, Carl. *Politics in the Poetry of Coleridge.* Madison: University of Wisconsin Press, 1961.

"DIFFUGERE NIVES" A. E. HOUSMAN (1897)

This faithful adaptation of Horace's Ode 4.7 was not published until after A. E. HOUSMAN's death. On one memorable occasion he read it aloud. After his death, Dora Pym (who studied classics at Cambridge and later taught it) wrote to the London *Times* with a reminiscence of Housman's lectures on classical poetry. At noon, at the end of every lecture, he invariably "folded his papers and left the room," without looking at anyone in the audience. In May 1914, she wrote, he came to lecture on Horace's ode about the melting of the snow and the return of spring. The trees outside "were covered with blossom" as he analyzed the ode, which "he dissected with the usual display of brilliance, wit, and sarcasm" so notable in his critical writings. "Then, for the first time in two years he looked up at us, and in quite a different voice said: 'I should like to spend the last few minutes considering this ode simply as poetry.' Our previous experience of Housman would have made us sure that he would regard such a proceeding as beneath contempt. He read the ode aloud with deep emotion, first in Latin and then in an English translation of his own. 'That', he said hurriedly, almost like a man betraying a secret, 'I regard as the most beautiful poem in ancient literature' and walked quickly out of the room." Pym goes on to say that she and her fellow students felt that they had seen something "not really meant" for them—that they had seen into some truth that Housman sought to keep hidden. One of them said he was afraid that Housman was going to weep.

It would have been a truth that perhaps Housman expressed most fully in his poetry. The anecdote is notable because it suggests what motivated his own poetry: the beauty of the poetry he had read. It is not a rare thing for a poet to be inspired by the poetry he or she has read; what matters is what poetry the poet takes inspiration from later. Horace is notable for his plangent melancholy; the beauty that Housman found in the poem was just the same as the loveliness he found in the cherry blossoms in "LOVELIEST OF TREES." It was the beauty of the desperately ephemeral, of the blossoms on the trees outside as he lectured.

In a famous story, the Argentinian writer Jorge Luis Borges imagines someone trying to rewrite *Don Quixote* word for word, but meaning something different by it from what Cervantes meant. This is what Housman does here. Horace's poem, for example, describes how we, too, come where pious Aeneas, wealthy Tullus, and Ancus are, and like them we become dust and shadow. Housman's version is subtly different—just as Borges's verbatim *Quixote* is subtly different: "Come *we* where Tullus and where Ancus are, / And good Aeneas, we are dust and dreams" (ll. 15–16 in both). We will be dust and dreams because that is all they are. Aeneas was for Housman a fiction only, while for the Romans in Horace's time he was accepted as the real and heroic founder of Rome. Aeneas is Housman's dream, but we, too, will become dreams as well. (This sentiment might be compared with the great moment in LORD BYRON's *DON JUAN* in which he says, "I've heard Troy doubted; / Time will doubt of Rome.")

Housman's adaptation is about the distance between Horatian times and his own. Everything that Horace says has come true for Horace. There is no connection between the present and that distant past except the heartbreaking beauty of the poem itself, "the most beautiful poem in ancient literature." The beauty of its modern adaptation is in the demonstration of its own ephemerality. Horace, it is true, *does* have an heir, unlike the poem's Torquatus. What his heart has felt, all the more intensely because of its evanescence, is the evanescence itself. Torquatus for Housman might be a name for EDWARD FITZGERALD, whose *The RUBÁIYÁT OF OMAR KHAYYÁM* recommends the Horatian pleasures of drinking and love. But Housman is a connoisseur and inheritor of the ephemerality that Horace felt, and so what he inherits is the feeling but also the knowledge that it cannot be truly inherited, kept, or owned. We can see this most clearly, perhaps, in Housman's telling alteration of the end of the poem. Horace had written that Theseus himself was not strong enough to break the fetters of his dear Pirithoüs (when the two were tricked into putting themselves into the hands of the gods of the underworld). Housman insists on the "love of comrades," which is partly a defensive explanation warning away from an erotic interpretation of Theseus's affection for Pirithoüs, but more importantly an acknowledgement that Horace is his own comrade here. Which of the two is Theseus and which is Pirithoüs is finally an irrelevant question. The eternal separation between the two is what counts, so that each is either. Housman is living, while Horace is dead forever; and equally, Horace will live forever, even after Housman's death. And yet they are comrades, Horace and Housman.

Housman's poem is thus better thought of as a demonstration of the truth of its original than as a translation. Its beauty is in its failure to be as beautiful as Housman conceived Horace to be, when Horace's beauty was itself an evocation of the inevitable failure of the human spirit.

BIBLIOGRAPHY

Gardner, Philip, ed. *A. E. Housman: The Critical Heritage.* New York: Routledge, 1992.

Highet, Gilbert. *Classical Tradition: Greek and Roman Influences on Western Literature.* New York: Oxford University Press, 1957.

Richards, Grant. *Housman: 1897–1936.* New York: Oxford University Press, 1942.

"DIRCE" WALTER SAVAGE LANDOR (1831) This is a lovely four-line epigram or pseudo-epitaph devoted to an unknown, probably imaginary woman. Or it might be better to say that it is devoted to a *generic* woman—that is to say, to someone who can only be memorialized now to those who do not know her and must instead imagine her, as WILLIAM BUTLER YEATS said in an elegy of his own, as being as beautiful as their own first loves.

Elegies are generally of two types: those that attempt to particularize the virtues of the person being mourned, of which John Milton's *Lycidas* and PERCY BYSSHE SHELLEY'S *ADONAIS* are the great examples in English; and those that lament that death has rendered the dead person irretrievable even to the memory of the living. The second kind of elegy tends to be shorter, more in the mode of an epitaph on a tombstone, and it expresses the sorrow of the elegist more than preserving or capturing the essence of the departed. Landor's "Dirce" is a perfect example of this kind. It only names *Dirce* (pronounced "Dir-Chay") in the second line. Her name is italicized, in conformity with older usage when all proper names were italicized, but the effect is one almost of a third-person signature: Now we know whom this elegy is about, but we did not before then, since it is not addressed to Dirce; and in a sense we still do not because she is hidden under a Greek pseudonym (again like Lycidas/Edward King, and Adonais/JOHN KEATS). (The Greek mythological figure Dirce, unfilial but persecuted daughter of Antiope, is irrelevant here.)

The "Stygian set" of the first line represents the shades of the dead who have died at the same time as Dirce and are being ferried across the river Styx to the Underworld, or land of the dead. Notice that they are entirely anonymous, which sets the tone of the poem's treatment of the dead. They have a kind of spectral presence still, but it is plural and generic, and it is this generic sense that they give to being dead, which affects our sense of Dirce as well. And yet her own vividness, at least to her elegist, is such that she resists the Stygian tide toward an emptied-out generality, and even the ferryman of the dead, Charon, may come to a kind of life or wish for life in seeing her beauty. The poem reminds us that Charon is old, that death has been around for a long time, and that life and love and youth must occur in the forgetfulness of death. Dirce's beauty is such that it might almost defeat death by awakening desire in Charon. And yet this is the beauty of a shade, not a living being; death (as Romeo said of Juliet) has had no power yet upon her beauty. But the truth is nevertheless the sad and universal truth that she is a shade, like the others in the Stygian set, and that Charon will never see her as she was alive and will never forget that he is old and that she is dead.

BIBLIOGRAPHY

Butler, Marilyn. *Romantics, Rebels, and Reactionaries: English Literature and its Background, 1760–1830.* New York: Oxford University Press, 1982.

Hazlitt, William. *Spirit of the Age; or, Contemporary Portraits.* London: Oxford University Press, 1970.

Super, R. H. *Walter Savage Landor: A Biography.* New York: New York University Press, 1954.

"DIRGE IN WOODS" **GEORGE MEREDITH (1870)** GEORGE MEREDITH's poetry almost always seems easier than his novels, but close inspection will show it is as subtly and unexpectedly composed as his prose. The poet and critic Arthur Symons justly said of Meredith: "He reasons in pictures, every line having its imagery, and he uses pictorial words to express abstract ideas. . . . He disdains common rhythms, common rhymes, and common language . . . to give human warmth to arguments concerning humanity." "Dirge in Woods" exemplifies this judgment. One of Meredith's most famous poems, it combines qualities of sound and sense to convey the experience of muted bewilderment that the poem expresses about the course of human life. The poem *sounds* like a dirge—that is, it is full of a kind of monotone of undifferentiated sadness, like the sound of the trees swaying in the woods that it takes as its simile.

We might first ask who or what kind of being the speaker is. Clearly, the moral of the poem is that "even we" humans will drop and die like the fruits of the tree; but the poem is also a kind of articulation of the sound of the trees. We project into that sound our own sense of mortality, and this process by which we hear the woods speaking with our own voice—hear them speaking *for* us—is crucial to the structure of the poem. This is because what the poem laments, what we hear the trees saying, is that they *do not* speak for us. Life continues, and we drop *like* the fruits of the tree, but what we drop *away from* is the analogy with the processes of life. The analogy describes our separation from the possibility of analogy itself, because analogy is the tree and so analogy is life.

One can see how this happens in the subtlety with which Meredith uses the analogical imagery. The pine tree drops its dead, but the dead so described are not fruits but the needles that form the floor of the pine forest. The analogy in line 13—"*like* the fruits of the tree"—is not an analogy to anything in the poem, but rather to the fact that pine needles *also* drop. In any event, the pine needles on the trees are not the poem's metaphor for life. Life is presented as metaphor, and the metaphor is that it rushes by overhead "as the clouds the clouds chase."

The repetitions of "Overhead, overhead," and "the clouds the clouds" give the poem the sound of a dirge, but the clouds do not rhyme. They do not belong to the vertical repetition of sound that goes down the right margin, as in the rhyme of *dead* and *overhead.* The clouds are inaccessible—they belong to another world from that of the pine needles or mosses or fruit on the floor of the forest. Moreover, they always did; or at least at this time they belong to a region of the sky that it is unimaginable we ever belonged to it. That is the burden of the poem's dirge.

It should be noted that the title and much of the poem is a melancholy allusion to PERCY BYSSHE SHELLEY's "ODE TO THE WEST WIND," where the wind itself is the "Dirge of the departed year," and where Shelley can think of himself as borne up like a cloud and even of the possibility of outstripping the wind's speed. Meredith's poem is a sad revision of Shelley's, or a sad song of the impossibility of writing a poem like Shelley's.

BIBLIOGRAPHY

Bernstein, Carol L. *Precarious Enchantment: A Reading of Meredith's Poetry.* Washington, D.C.: Catholic University of America Press, 1979.

Neil, Roberts. *Meredith and the Novel.* New York: St. Martin's Press, 1997.

Symons, Arthur. "George Meredith as a Poet." In *Figures of Several Centuries.* London: Constable and Company, 1916, 91–97.

"DIVIDED" JEAN INGELOW (1863) This poem shows both the virtues and the far-less-important vices of JEAN INGELOW's poetry. It is beautifully descriptive, and more important, it puts its descriptions to powerful and novel use. Unfortunately, it tends to be too descriptive, going on too long for the moving story that it tells, and its ending is unconvincing and even slightly incoherent, though that very fact may have the odd effect of making it more moving than it would otherwise be, as wishfulness supplants more aesthetic criteria.

In his well-known parody of the poem, "Lovers, and a Reflection" (1872), CHARLES STUART CALVERLEY makes great fun of Ingelow's endless description of the weather, a word he sees as providing a convenient though stultified rhyme. Like any good parodist, Calverley is attacking the poem on one of its strong points: the way it makes meaning of the natural description of which it first seems to be over-enamored.

Ingelow's poem begins by describing a remembered walk she (or her speaker) took with her beloved. The memory is an intense one because the day was beautiful, and nature seemed to celebrate all around them. The poem's progress consists in the way this naturalistic description gradually shifts into metaphor. (In this we can see Ingelow reversing the direction of a similar shift in ALFRED, LORD TENNYSON's *IN MEMORIAM A.H.H.*, where nature is discovered more and more to be not a metaphor but a brute and brutally indifferent reality.) Where does the shift occur?

Retrospectively, we can see it beginning in the fourth quatrain, at the end of the first section. The speaker and her beloved are walking, and they walk "till the purple dieth" (l. 13). The word *till* can indicate either time or place—*we walked until the beautiful day faded*, or *we walked until we had gone beyond the place where the purpled foxglove was growing*. And yet this distinction is not a complete one: The walk through space takes time, and time is marked by changes in our perception of the outside world. The poem here is still in the present tense, but it is about to shift into the past, and we come to feel, retrospectively again, that the present tense is a mapping of time into space and not a true present.

As the great German thinker Georg Simmel said, space is at once the condition and the symbol of our relationship to each other; so, too, is the changing relationship the two of them have to the space they walk through as their walk lasts longer and longer; it is a condition of their being together and a symbol of how their being together changes over time. What changes is that they find themselves on opposite sides of a little beck (a brook or rill), which still makes the land beside it green and fresh as the rest of the landscape becomes more barren. That rill is more obviously metaphorical than the landscape that preceded it: They are growing older, but they still have hope, memory, and a sense of a continuous stream of beauty that will last into the future as it flows into the sea. But the beck also divides them, in a way that is not consistent with its first metaphorical use. The beck does not provide an *analogy* of the progress of human life and memory. Rather, it gradually takes on a second *metaphorical* significance: It is what divides them in the journey of life (even as it allows, perhaps, for some hope to remain within memory). Not only does space give way to time, but the way space attempts to characterize time—as continuous with the past, making the past available and present—gives way as well, to a different metaphor by which time divides (hence the title), and space is the metaphor for that division. The metaphor itself divides, and this very fact is a metaphor for what happens in the course of life.

The poem goes on about this burgeoning division for perhaps too long, though it is very beautiful and some will wish it longer still. It then ends, as noted, with an unconvincing and awkward resolution—unconvincing partly because there is no reason that the man on the other side should love the speaker more than she loves him. This claim is meant as praise, but it unfortunately also functions as censure. That very awkwardness speaks to her hope that something yet remains, that their love can survive the dissolution even of the metaphor that describes it. And this makes the poem very moving, despite itself. We know it would be absurd to build a bridge across the river now, but her attempt to save the metaphor, to find such resources in it, draws attention to the way she has had to endure the sadness of the loss of a literal world and literal love. Thus, the world around her becomes more and more a metaphor of its own remoteness as a place to live in pure and present happiness.

BIBLIOGRAPHY

Caesar, Terry. "'I Quite Forget What—Say a Daffodilly': Victorian Parody." *ELH: English Literary History* 51, no. 4 (Winter, 1984): 795–818.

Ince, Richard Basil. *Calverley and Some Cambridge Wits of the Nineteenth Century.* London: G. Richards and H. Toulmin at the Cayme Press, 1929.

DOBELL, SYDNEY (SYDNEY THOMPSON DOBELL) (1824–1874) Sydney Dobell is now somewhat unjustly neglected. As a poet and critic, he thought well and hard about the psychology of the poetic or lyric subject—the obsession of so much romantic poetry—when confronted with history. The grandson of a radical and primitivist Unitarian, and the descendant of Quaker nonconformists, Dobell was educated by his parents and instilled with their passionate idealism. This came partly through his reading of LORD BYRON, who died just two weeks after Dobell was born. He memorized *MANFRED* as a youth and followed Byron in his passionate political idealism. His first major work, *The Roman* (published in 1850 under the not very clever pseudonym of Sydney Yendys), was written in favor of Byron's cherished cause of Italian liberation from the Hapsburg Empire after the failure of the 1848 revolutions; it impressed the great Italian revolutionary Giuseppe Mazzini, who had been the leader of the short-lived Roman Republic and who wrote to Dobell to praise it.

Dobell also corresponded with Charlotte Brontë, whose work he admired, and was friends with many of the most important literary figures of the day, including ALFRED, LORD TENNYSON; ROBERT BROWNING; the English essayist and critic John Ruskin; and the Scottish essayist and historian Thomas Carlyle. His most ambitious work was also perhaps his biggest mistake: the poem *Balder,* published in 1854, about a Manfred-like student attempting to write a poem about the revolutionary apocalypse. In a poem about a poet, a poet can indulge any excess, and Dobell did, which the next year provoked a merciless parody by WILLIAM EDMONDSTOUNE AYTOUN called *Firmilian,* about the emotional life of a mass murderer. Aytoun's subtitle was *The Student of Badajoz. A Spasmodic Tragedy,* and the term *spasmodic* stuck for the school to which Aytoun relegated Dobell and his friend Alexander Smith (as well as some others). Originally a term applied by Carlyle to Byron, it refers to poetry that becomes so self-involved in its own intensity as to be able to accede to any emotional excess at any moment. In his preface to *Balder,* Dobell uses the term approvingly, and this is what gave Aytoun his opening.

Dobell, meanwhile, moved to Edinburgh to seek medical treatment for his wife, and there he became friends with Smith and eventually Aytoun. When the Crimean War began the next year, he and Smith collaborated on a book of sonnets about the war, some of which are very powerful. The next year, Dobell published another book called *England in Time of War,* which contains his most powerful verse. Committed to peace and liberty, he treats the horrors of war unflinchingly and with great psychological acuity—the kind of acuity that the gothic excesses of *Balder* were meant to frame, as they more or less do in the fiction of the Brontës. One of Dobell's great strengths was in the evocation of intense stress through the psychology of recourse to detailed natural description.

Dobell spent the last years of his life in ill health, especially after being injured by a bad fall which may have brought on epilepsy. His critical reputation has not been major, but *England in Time of War* was admired by his contemporary DANTE GABRIEL ROSSETTI, and it is uncannily relevant in modern times. Indeed, much of Dobell's technique anticipates modern poetic thinking about representation of psychic turmoil through objective correlatives, and he is due for a revival.

See also "BOTANIST'S VISION, THE"; "NUPTIAL EVE, A"; "WOUNDED, THE."

BIBLIOGRAPHY

Boos, Florence S. "'Spasm' and Class: W. E. Aytoun, George Gilfillan, Sydney Dobell, and Alexander Smith." *Victorian Poetry* 42, no. 4 (2004): 553–583.

Dobell, Sydney. *The Life and Letters of Sydney Dobell.* Edited by E. Jolly. London: Smith, Elder & Co., 1878.

Preyer, Robert. "Sydney Dobell and the Victorian Epic." *University of Toronto Quarterly* 30 (January 1961): 163–178.

Westwater, Martha. *The Spasmodic Career of Sydney Dobell.* Lanham, Md.: University Press of America, 1992.

DODGSON, CHARLES LUTWIDGE See CARROLL, LEWIS.

DOLBEN, DIGBY MACKWORTH (1848–1867) Toward the end of his life, the novelist Henry James read ROBERT BRIDGES's edition of Digby Mackworth Dolben's poetry, published nearly 50 years after Dolben's death. Bridges was Dolben's cousin, and he and his close friend GERARD MANLEY HOPKINS were four years ahead of Dolben at Oxford University, where all three came under the influence of the religious and particularly the Anglo-Catholic revival (led by JOHN HENRY NEWMAN [later Cardinal Newman]) that would eventuate in Hopkins's conversion and priesthood. Dolben only met Hopkins once, but they had a profound effect on each other, and Hopkins (who may have fallen in love with him) was profoundly moved by his death, apparently of a stroke, while he was trying to save his tutor's son from drowning on a hot July day. In a 1913 letter, James wrote: "The disclosure and picture of the wondrous young Dolben have made the liveliest impression on me."

James (who had been born five years before Dolben) had mixed feelings about Dolben's religiosity. He objected to the doctrine but agreed with Bridges that (as James paraphrased it) "no *equally* young case has ever given us ground for so *much* wonder (in the personal and aesthetic connection)." He wondered would Dolben's "'ritualism' have yielded to more life and longer days and his quite prodigious, but so closely associated, gift have yielded *with* that (as though indissolubly mixed with it)?" This was an extremely shrewd insight on James's part, who must have seen in Dolben something of a kindred spirit—an aesthete whose intense homoeroticism was as much bound up with the aesthetic as with the personal; as we'll see, James called his aesthetic power "almost abnormal," a kind of rogue instinct in the person who would otherwise be amenable to Victorian socialization. Dolben (like Hopkins) sublimated much of this homoerotic instinct to religious longing, and James saw the danger in such a connection to Dolben's future as a poet, fearing that the piety would overwhelm the daring.

Bridges had gone some way toward trying to disguise Dolben's erotic predilections (changing names and pronouns) and explaining away what obviously needed explaining. WILLIAM JOHNSON CORY, who had been Dolben's teacher at Eton, knew better, especially when Dolben was asked to leave for a few months, ostensibly because of his religiosity but almost certainly because of some embarrassing erotic relationship. Dolben's best poems are intense, wistful, Keatsian, and astonishingly assured laments over the impossibility of love. They mostly seem to have been about his schoolmate Martin Gosselin, later to become a Roman Catholic himself and to be a major diplomat in the British service, representing Britain at the Vatican among many other places. (After his death in 1905, his widow would not allow access to his diary). Some resemble what WILLIAM WORDSWORTH called JOHN KEATS's poems, "pretty pieces of paganism," but some might bear comparison as much to the Italian artist Caravaggio as to Keats—for example, the beautiful poem "Christ, for whose only Love I keep me clean." The titular line needs no explication, but it is worth noticing the poem's motto (see MOTTOES), or epigraph, from the biblical *Song of Solomon*: "Osculo oris sui osculetur me," *let him kiss me with the kisses of his mouth*. The poem ends by describing by beholding "God and man made one by Mary's kiss" (l. 46) at the birth of Jesus; but the man to whom Jesus joins is essentially every man, Dolben included, and he was able to see and reconcile all versions of union between man and Christ.

Dolben died before converting, and it may be that James was right to fear that his talent could not have survived his adolescence; but James also wondered, "would a big development of inspiration and form have come!" In the end, Dolben is a perfect doomed Jamesian youth and we may give James the last, subtly suggestive word: "Moreover it is just as we have him . . . that he so touches and charms the imagination—and how instinctive poetic mastery was of the essence, was the most rooted of all things, in him, a faculty or mechanism almost abnormal, seems to me shown by the thinness of his letters compared with the thickness and maturity of his verse. But how can one talk, and how can he be anything but wrapped, for our delightful uncertainty, in the silver mists of morning?—which one mustn't so much as want to breathe upon too hard, much less clear away."

See also "AFTER READING AESCHYLUS"; "LEAN OVER ME—AH, SO—LET FALL"; "ONE NIGHT I DREAMT THAT IN A GLEAMING HALL."

BIBLIOGRAPHY

Bridges, Robert. *The Poems of Digby Mackworth Dolben.* New York: Oxford University Press, 1911.

———. *Three Friends: Memoirs of Digby Mackworth Dolben, Richard Watson Dixon, Henry Bradley.* Westport, Conn.: Greenwood Press, 1975.

Cohen, Martin, ed. *Uncollected Poems of Digby Mackworth Dolben.* Reading, England: Whiteknights Press, 1973.

Cunningham, Valentine. Headnote to selection of Dolben in *The Victorians: An Anthology of Poetry & Poetics,* 901. Malden, Mass.: Blackwell, 2000.

Dolben, Digby Mackworth. *The Poems and Letters of Digby Mackworth Dolben, 1848–1867.* Edited by M. Cohen. Amersham, England: Avebury, 1981.

James, Henry. *Letters of Henry James.* New York: Charles Scribner's Sons, 1920.

White, Norman. *Hopkins: A Literary Biography.* New York: Oxford University Press, 1992.

DON JUAN GEORGE GORDON BYRON, LORD BYRON (1818–1824) *Don Juan* (pronounced, LORD BYRON insisted, with a pure English accent, to rhyme with "new one" and "true one") is nowadays regarded as Byron's crowning achievement and his greatest long poem. Unlike the Satanic self-dramatizing that was the source of his fame in the 19th century, in *MANFRED* and *CHILDE HAROLD'S PILGRIMAGE* especially, *Don Juan* shows Byron at his most self-aware, and the voice of the poem is very close to the voice of his letters. In fact, in one of those letters, to his friend Douglas Kinnaird, his expression of self-delight with the first two cantos captures that voice perfectly: "As to Don Juan, confess, confess—you dog and be candid—that it is the sublime of *that there* sort of writing—it may be bawdy but is it not good English? It may be profligate but is it not life, is it not the thing? Could any man have written it who has not lived in the world?—and tooled in a post-chaise?—in a hackney coach?—in a gondola?—against a wall?—in a court carriage?—in a vis a vis—? on a table?—and under it?"

The poem is full of vitality, but as everywhere in Byron vitality, it is a response to an intensely pessimistic view of life and of the world. Byron's energies, as the essayist William Hazlitt noted in a review of *Don Juan* written days before Byron's death, are directed against the listlessness and despair that would otherwise drag him down. Hazlitt conceded Byron's skill but rebuked him for using that skill only to shock, as Hazlitt thought. Powerful and gripping pieces of writing give way to moments of sudden and hilarious deflation, and Hazlitt complained that this meant Byron was using the powerful moments only parodically, rather than with any ambitious poetic intent.

Against Hazlitt we should cite PERCY BYSSHE SHELLEY's view that *Don Juan* was Byron's greatest work. Their difference in point of view may come down to a difference in critical evaluation of the purpose and procedure of *Don Juan.* Byron's hilarity is indeed a response to grimness of vision, but as such a response it also measures that grimness. The mocking, rollicking style of the poem displays a kind of gallantry in the face of despair, and that gallantry is impressive.

It is a poetic gallantry as well: The poem itself bears witness to its author's endless inventiveness. Many of Byron's rhymes are outrageous, but Byron's spirited gaiety in forming them is part of the point. As Hazlitt rightly said of *Don Juan,* "It is a poem written about itself." And it is: Byron is constantly commenting on it—not only on the rhymes, but on his process of composition, what he thinks of the poem or its characters, where or how the narrative might unfold next. But this very fact shows the extent to which the poem's manic energies are their own reward, and the only reward to be had in the midst of the gloominess of human life.

Don Juan is written in ottava rima, an Italian eight-line stanza form that rhymes *abababcc.* It was used for both comic and serious work in Italian, and both Ludovico Ariosto (1474–1533) and Torquato Tasso (1544–95) wrote their great epics in the form. Their English translators followed suit in the 16th and 17th centuries, but it never took hold, partly because in English multiple rhymes are hard to come by (Italian rhymes much more easily). The main legacy of ottava rima in English was the heroic couplet derived from the last two lines of the stanza (the *cc* rhymes), which sum it up and give it epigrammatic point. John Dryden's and Alexander Pope's heroic couplets, which Byron so much admired (see *Don Juan*'s first poetical commandment: "Thou shalt believe in Milton, Dryden, Pope" [1. 205, 1]), derive from Edward Fairfax's translation of Tasso. But Byron's most direct model was John Hookham Frere's 1817 imitation of the 15th-century comic poet Luigi Pulci, *Whistlecraft*; Byron was captivated by Frere's poem and wrote his own comic poems *Beppo, The Vision of Judgment,* and *Don Juan* in the form. After Byron, it more or less took hold. Shelley, who encouraged Byron to continue the poem after he had read the first cantos, tried his own hand at ottava rima with a somewhat different tonality in his translations of the Homeric hymns and in his great poem *The Witch of Atlas,* and later poets such as Kenneth Koch and Anthony Burgess would write verse novels in the form.

The first two cantos of the poem were published in 1819. Byron decided to hold back the wonderful prefatory note and the verse mock dedication to ROBERT SOUTHEY, refusing to attack him anonymously (it was the custom to publish anonymously).

Only after the preface and long dedication are we introduced to Juan, who in many respects is like Byron, in many respects not. Juan is not a figure whom Byron treats with great psychological subtlety. He is passive, the seduced rather than the seducer, attractive for his beauty and his sweetness. Although sexually experienced (after canto I), he is fundamentally an innocent (rather like Henry Fielding's Tom Jones) and therefore attractive to innocent women, whom he never corrupts. His most important relationship is with Haidée in the second, third, and fourth cantos, and the narrator says of their love that it was innocent though illicit: "Yet they were happy—happy in the illicit / Indulgence of their innocent desires" (III.13, ll. 1–2), since they were essentially "children still / And children still should they have ever been" (IV.15, ll. 1–2) if the world was not what it was.

But this means that, unlike Byron, they are not fitted for the world. For Byron's own attitude in the poem is not innocent. Rather, it might be described as a kind of dashing and daring ruefulness. His most tender moments are for the innocence of his characters when they *are* innocent; but that is an innocence that he has passed beyond. One mode of that superseded innocence is a belief (for him) in the importance of poetry such as his own earlier and much more transcendently ambitious *Childe Harold's Pilgrimage.* He no longer believes this (see canto XI, stanza 55), and makes fun of the time when he was ambitious to be reckoned as "The grand Napoleon of the realms of rhyme" (XI.55, l. 8). Time has changed ambitions that were "once romantic to burlesque" (IV.3, l. 8). Part of what makes *Don Juan* so great is its author's realism.

That realism is gallant, though, and not despairing or at least not just despairing. The poem's most famous lines are probably the closest thing it contains to a moral: "Let us have wine and women, music and laughter, / Sermons and soda water the day after" (II.178, ll. 7–8). This is not a serious moral because the moral is that seriousness leads finally to despair. The point, as Byron adds, is that "Man being reasonable must get drunk" (II.179, l. 1), a pun meaning it is reasonable to get drunk *because* reason is unbearable and drunkenness is how to escape it.

EDWARD FITZGERALD's magnificent version of *The RUBÁIYÁT OF OMAR KHAYYÁM* insists repeatedly on the same point. While this is the final truth of human life—that reason does not lead to some transcendent truth, and that this is liable to make reason despair—it is not the only truth in the poem, nor is the poem contemptuous of idealism. The same radical idealism that would lead Byron to join the rebellion for Greek independence from Turkey (in addition to contributing large sums of money, he was made a commander and died in the field of a fever) led him to similar commitments in his poetry and in particular in *Don Juan.* (For similar sentiments about Greek independence, see Shelley's verse drama *Hellas* as well.) One of the most beautiful moments in *Don Juan* is the interpolated song in the third canto, "The Isles of Greece," which looks backwards to Greece's idealized past to despair about her present but to build hopes for her future.

Byron's politics were in fact similar to William Hazlitt's (though Hazlitt suspected Byron's flair for dramatizing himself). Hazlitt disliked Byron's insults of WILLIAM WORDSWORTH, his strictures on SAMUEL TAYLOR COLERIDGE, and his utter contempt for Southey, but it is important to see that Byron felt as he did about the LAKE POETS because of their conversion to the Tory party, to which, in Byron's view, they abased themselves in order to win sinecures from the government in power. Byron's poetic models are Milton, Dryden, and Pope, and his model of a political poet is Milton in particular, who "closed the tyrant-hater he begun" (from *Don Juan*'s dedication). Byron would never convert politically as the Lake Poets did, although in accusing them of being motivated only with an eye to patronage, he perhaps neglected their genuine commitment to the views they espoused.

This does not mean that *Don Juan* is only parody. Parody provides its basic tonality, but it does so only because for Byron parody was the form that was adequate to the strange and irreconcilable varieties of life. Virginia Woolf called Byron's form an "elastic shape which will hold whatever you choose to put into it" (quoted by Addison), and Byron manages an amazing number of different tones within *Don Juan*.

One of the most impressive scenes in *Don Juan*, and perhaps the scene that shows the poem's powers, intentions, and origins most fully, is the grueling shipwreck recounted in canto II. Juan has left the scandal of his affair with Julia to travel to Italy, but the waves that cause the hilarious seasickness at the start of his journey turn into a dreadful and endless storm. The comic expectations that the poem has established and met so far contrast with an extraordinary sense of the duration and grimness of the storm, the wreckage, and the privation in the marooned lifeboat it causes; we keep expecting relief, both narrative and comic, and instead things go from bad to worse. Since ottava rima is so fitted to comic verse, the way Byron uses it for this grim and tragic tableau of the "dim desolate deep" (2.49, l. 7), without ever losing a sense of gallows humor, shows the sheer power of his technical skills (like writing a serious limerick). This section is in some ways a conscious and acknowledged rewriting of the similar nautical disasters in Coleridge's *The* RIME OF THE ANCIENT MARINER, which also works by using a somewhat discrepant form for serious purposes.

In addition to grimness, which has the energy but not the delight of the hilarious sections of *Don Juan*, Byron manages tenderness, love, regret, asperity, satire, and interpolated lyric. In a perhaps unparalleled fashion the poem contains and combines every kind of literary emotion or feeling. It is indecorous, in the technical as well as informal sense of the word: It does not keep to literary decorum (not confining itself to one genre) but tracks all the different moods or modes of life itself. For this reason, it might be more easily compared to the variety of tone typical of the novel and not poetry. But it *is* a poem, all its great effects are poetic effects, and while it may not be the most intense work of poetry written in the 19th century, it certainly combines more varieties of intensity than any other 19th-century work, and does it splendidly. It is a fit tribute to Byron and the capacious and various vitalities of his own personality.

BIBLIOGRAPHY

Addison, Catherine: "Ottava Rima and Novelistic Discourse." *Journal of Narrative Theory* 34, no. 2 (2004): 133–145.

Bloom, Harold. *The Visionary Company: A Reading of English Romantic Poetry*. Garden City, N.Y.: Doubleday, 1961.

Duffy, Edward. *Rousseau in England: The Context for Shelley's Critique of the Enlightenment*. Berkeley: University of California Press, 1979.

Hazlitt, William. *Spirit of the Age; or, Contemporary Portraits*. London: Oxford University Press, 1970.

McGann, Jerome. *Don Juan in Context*. Chicago: University of Chicago Press, 1976.

Saintsbury, George. *History of English Prosody, from the Twelfth Century to the Present Day*. New York: Russell & Russell, 1961.

Thorslev, Peter Larsen. *The Byronic Hero: Types and Prototypes*. Minneapolis: University of Minnesota Press, 1962.

DOUGLAS, LORD ALFRED (1870–1945)

Lord Alfred Douglas (nicknamed Bosie by his mother and universally known by that appellation) is best remembered now as OSCAR WILDE's young lover (16 years his junior), who described himself with the memorable phrase "I am the love that dare not speak its name" in "TWO LOVES." Douglas was beautiful and a talented poet, though not (like Wilde) a genius. His poetry is sensitively derivative of ALFRED, LORD TENNYSON (whom his boorish father, the ninth marquess of Queensberry, hated) and JOHN KEATS. Douglas brings out the latent gay sensibilities of their sensualism very frankly—in ways that would later prove seriously destructive to Wilde.

Wilde and Douglas were introduced in 1891 by LIONEL JOHNSON; they became lovers in 1892 when Douglas sought Wilde's help with a blackmailer. They genuinely loved each other, though Douglas was himself highly destructive in ways associated with his somewhat selfish narcissism—a character trait that many thought grew worse in his cantankerous later life, when he became (as Wilde had before him) a committed Roman Catholic and (unlike Wilde) homophobic and anti-Semitic.

Douglas's father, the marquess of Queensberry (who formulated the Queensberry rules of boxing), was a committed homophobe who held the gay socializing in which another son of his had engaged responsible for that son's accidental (or possibly suicidal) death during a shooting party. He left a card calling Wilde a sodomite at Wilde's club, where everyone could see it. Wilde (egged on by Douglas) sued Queensberry for libel, but the tables were turned when Wilde lost the case and was then tried and convicted of gross indecency. He was sentenced to two years of hard labor. Douglas appealed to Queen Victoria for mercy, but in vain.

On Wilde's release, he and Douglas became lovers again, traveling to the continent and living together in Italy and Paris. The marquess of Queensberry died early in 1900—perhaps of syphilis contracted during his arduous and varied heterosexual career—so that Wilde outlived his blustering bête noir by 10 months. He recorded with delight receiving Bosie and his brother Percy in Paris "in deep mourning and the highest spirits," a line that could almost have come out of his play *The Importance of Being Earnest.*

As a poet, Douglas excelled in sustaining a beautiful and intense aesthetic descriptiveness over long passages or through the architectonic of a sonnet. His poetry was about beauty as well as being very beautiful. But it was no more than that, and Douglas probably was best at fulfilling the vocation of being very young.

In prison, Wilde wrote the book that would be published posthumously under the title *De Profundis* (the name as well of an early poem of Douglas's, as well as one of Tennyson's). *De Profundis* paints an unflattering portrait of Douglas, but it is difficult to see where the truth lies. At any rate, he and Wilde reconciled, and we can hope that his love gave Wilde as much pleasure, in the end, as it caused him pain and suffering.

See also "REJECTED."

BIBLIOGRAPHY

Douglas, Alfred Bruce, Lord. *Oscar Wilde and Myself.* New York: Duffield and Co., 1914.

Ellmann, Richard. *Oscar Wilde.* New York: Knopf, 1988.

Harris, Frank. *Oscar Wilde: His Life and Confessions.* Garden City, N.Y.: Garden City Publishing Co., 1932.

Whittington-Egan, Richard, "Oscar Wilde: A Centennial Wreath of Memories." *Contemporary Review* (November 1, 2000). Available online. URL: http://www.encyclopedia.com/doc/1G1-68157978.html. Accessed on January 27, 2008.

Wilde, Oscar. *De Profundis.* In *Complete Works of Oscar Wilde.* New York: HarperCollins, 1989.

"DOVER BEACH" MATTHEW ARNOLD (1867)

"Dover Beach" is MATTHEW ARNOLD's most famous poem, as well as one of the standard poems in all Victorian canons. It was written sometime between 1848 and 1851 but not published till 1867, when Arnold had essentially ceased writing poetry. In the preface to the 1853 edition of his *Poems,* Arnold had said (following the German poet Friedrich von Schiller) that poetry is only justified if it gives its readers joy. (Arnold was also following his great master WILLIAM WORDSWORTH, who had notoriously asserted that poetry flows out of "the grand universal principle of pleasure, in which we live and move and have our being" [preface to *Lyrical Ballads*]). Arnold observed that such enjoyment does not require that poetry depicts joy, and indeed, tragedy seems to offer its spectator the deepest joy when the calamity it depicts is most terrible. This is a standard thing to note about tragedy, but it is perhaps more a critical than a poetic observation. The tragic writer may not mean to give joy but intensity. That such intensity has a component of joy for the spectator is a feature of human psychology (probably derived from the interest in each other's fate that is the human evolutionary inheritance) and not of a writer's explicit intention.

Arnold nevertheless understood the joy that even the most tragic writers can offer—for example, the

Greek dramatist Sophocles, who has heard the same "eternal note of sadness" (l. 14) that he himself hears in the lapping of the waves on the night when the poem is set. He knows that Sophocles has heard it because Sophocles has captured the sadness in his own tragedies; and those tragedies give Arnold pleasure to contemplate. Therefore, he can hear in the sound of the sea the literature he loves. This is part of Arnold's point: The world is a difficult and lonely place, and it does not keep the promises we in our youth think it makes. But in its depiction of the world as a lonely place, literature can console us and even give us joy in the representation of that loneliness.

Arnold's poem is less about Sophocles than about the English romantic poets (see ROMANTICISM) about whom he was so ambivalent, in particular JOHN KEATS and Wordsworth. Wordsworth was an obsession of Arnold's, and in his best poems he is more or less consciously trying to rewrite him. The scholar Harold Bloom has rightly identified "TINTERN ABBEY" as a source of "Dover Beach," which repeats the strains of that poem's "still, sad music of humanity." One can also hear Keats's "ODE TO A NIGHTINGALE" here, despite Arnold's stated disapproval of Keats. Where Arnold hears the same sea sounds that Sophocles did, he is really remembering Keats hearing "this passing night" the same nightingale voice that was heard in ancient days by emperor and clown, and that found a path through the "sad heart of Ruth" ("Ode to a Nightingale," ll. 64–66).

Such a thought is consoling, and what it consoles for is the loneliness of the world depicted in the last stanza. There Arnold is echoing William Shakespeare's *Measure for Measure* and the consolation the disguised Duke offers the condemned Claudio (a passage from which T. S. Eliot will derive his epigraph to "Gerontion.") Life, the Duke says, is not worth it, and the poetic representation of life's sorrowful emptiness is the only consolation that we may have. Arnold goes further, however, and also finds consolation in the possibilities of love.

How does the poem arrive at those possibilities? It is in the mode of a crisis lyric—that is to say, the kind of poem that Wordsworth wrote in the INTIMATIONS ODE as well as "Tintern Abbey." Through the poem the poet thinks himself out of despair and into consolation. The form that consolation takes in the romantics is one whereby a perceived loss of intensity in oneself over time is transfigured into a feeling of the intensity of loss. Arnold, however, has a more objective or general perspective than that of the high subjectivity that the romantic poets explore. If the poem was written in 1848, what Arnold is perceiving across the English Channel is a sense of the revolutions occurring on the continent, perhaps most notably for him in France. The world is a grim place not because we lose freshness but because it is a grim place. Its grimness consists in the fact that there is no possibility for human community or cooperation: no joy or love or light or certitude or peace or help from pain, to reproduce Arnold's list (no doubt influenced by the Bible's Book of Ecclesiastes as well as by Shakespeare).

Put more briefly, there is no human community. Ignorant armies clash by night (l. 37), and that night refers explicitly to the Greek historian Thucydides' account of the night battle of Epipolae between Athens and Syracuse, where no one could tell friend from foe (Arnold's father translated Thucydides), but more generally to the long night of human experience, the night in which we can hear the ebb and flow of human misery (l. 19). We hear it here in the north (on the English Channel) just as clearly as Sophocles heard it on the Aegean Sea.

This connection between Sophocles and our modern selves is essential to Arnold's hopes, both as poet and as the critic who promotes culture against the anarchy of the world (see also his account of the nightingale in "PHILOMELA"). The world is one of anarchy and misery, but that very fact joins or should join together all who understand this fact. The ignorant armies may not understand it—they represent anarchy, and the crucial word is *ignorant.* If they were not so, they might realize the community of sadness that we all share and the fidelity and love we should show one another in confronting this sadness.

The joy we take in great literature is the joy we take in love: not the joy of triumph or transcendence, but that of recognition. The world is a place (as Arnold repeats in all his great poems) where there is no love or real connection between us. We are all "enisl'd," as he says elsewhere. But literature shows that there is real love and connection in the discovery that others are alone just as we are, and this discovery is the way Arnold seeks to turn loss or despair into the poetic and literary gain offered by the common, even universal, recognition of this experience of loss and despair. In "Dover Beach" the woman he addresses will come to see the delusory world, but in doing so they will stand together and show their truth to one another.

BIBLIOGRAPHY

Arnold, Matthew. *Essays, Letters, and Reviews.* Collected and edited by Fraser Neiman. Cambridge, Mass.: Harvard University Press, 1960.

Bloom, Harold, ed. *Matthew Arnold.* New York: Chelsea House, 1987.

Dawson, Carl, and John Pfordresher, eds. *Matthew Arnold: The Critical Heritage.* New York: Routledge, 1995.

Trilling, Lionel. *The Moral Obligation to Be Intelligent: Selected Essays.* Edited by Leon Weiseltier. New York: Farrar, Straus, and Giroux, 2000.

DOWDEN, EDWARD (1843–1913) Like ANDREW LANG and A. E. HOUSMAN, Edward Dowden was a major scholar who wrote superbly crafted and exquisitely balanced poetry. Like Lang's (and unlike Housman's) work, Dowden's poetry is certainly minor, but it is the kind of minor poetry that offers just what the reader wants from it. Dowden does not change one's conception of poetry, which is one definition of what a major poet does, but he gives extremely good value: His poems are what they should be.

What they should be is essentially Keatsian (see KEATS, JOHN), and perhaps more essentially romantic. Dowden is now anthologized as a Keatsian poet, and already in 1900, in the major anthology *A Treasury of Irish Poetry in the English Tongue,* W. Macneile Dixon was calling him a Marvellian poet even as he quoted Keats to make his point. But Dowden could also sound sometimes like PERCY BYSSHE SHELLEY (whose biography he wrote), sometimes like WILLIAM WORDSWORTH, and his scholarship had the effect of making his internalizations of his models serious and deep.

Dowden's most important critical book is his study of William Shakespeare. *Shakspeare: A Critical Study of His Mind and Art* (1874) is a beautifully consistent characterization of Shakespeare's plays and of the sensibility which could write them. In general, Dowden was faithful to English poetry and to England, and despite living his entire life in Dublin (where he was professor of English literature at Trinity College), he was committed to English rule. Although he was a friend and mentor of WILLIAM BUTLER YEATS's (whose father, the painter Jack Yeats, had been his schoolmate), Dowden's political and poetic opinions incurred Yeats's strong disapproval. Dowden was somewhat notorious in Irish literary circles for (it was claimed) undervaluing the poetry of Samuel Ferguson (1810–86), who was his friend and neighbor. Ferguson had argued in a way that Yeats found congenial for an Irish heritage that would include Protestants like himself and Yeats (and Dowden) within an identifiable Irish tradition (a project the *Treasury of Irish Poetry* also furthers); but Dowden wanted nothing of this seperatism from England. Later, to Yeats's disgust, he was the only Irish writer Yeats approached who refused to write a letter of sympathy to OSCAR WILDE during Wilde's trial for gross indecency.

Dowden's poetry, then, can be seen as a kind of reconstitution of some of the most beautiful aspects of the English literary tradition. It shows genuine feeling for both language and life, and while its emotional tenor tends toward Eros, Dowden can be very funny as well.

One of the poems in the *Treasury* is called "Oasis" (from Dowden's 1876 book of *Poems*). In this poem he describes a moment of peace when he hears "Faint—oh so faint—some air I used to sing." This beautiful poem arises out of a memory of songs not his own that he loved long ago, and this seems an apt self-description on the part of the critic so acutely attuned to human sensibility and character.

See also "BURDENS," "TO JULY."

BIBLIOGRAPHY

Murphy, William M. "Yeats, Quinn, and Edward Dowden." In *John Quinn: Selected Irish Writers from His Library,* edited by Janis and Richard Londraville, 71–108. West Cornwall, Conn.: Locust Hill Press, 2001.

Yeats, W. B. *Autobiography of William Butler Yeats: Consisting of Reveries over Childhood and Youth, The Trembling of the Veil, and Dramatis Personae.* Garden City, N.Y.: Doubleday Anchor Books, 1958.

DOWSON, ERNEST (1867–1900) Except for WILLIAM BUTLER YEATS, the members of the Rhymers' Club, which included many of the most intense young English poets of the 1890s, are remembered more for single poems, even for single lines, than as poets. Yeats was ambivalent about this fact, as is clear, for example, in his 1914 poem "The Grey Rock," addressed to the "Poets with whom I learned my trade, / Companions of the Cheshire Cheese"—the Cheshire Cheese being the pub in London where they met. In that poem, Yeats praised those who "kept the Muses' sterner laws," writing only for the sake of art, never for money or praise or fame or political faction, and singled out two of those poets: "Dowson and Johnson most I praise" as those who have earned the right to "troop with those the world's forgot"—that is, those for whom poetic vocation is everything. In one of his prose autobiographies, Yeats recalled the ceremonious decorousness of the club's members to each other, even in their misery and poverty: "I think none knew as yet that Dowson, who seemed to drink so little and had so much dignity and reserve, was breaking his heart for the daughter of the keeper of an Italian eating house, in dissipation and drink; and that he might that very night sleep upon a sixpenny bed in a doss house."

The woman Yeats referred to was Adelaide Flotinowicz, to whom Dowson may have addressed his most famous poem, "Non sum qualis eram bonae sub Requo Cyharae" (see "CYNARA"). He fell in love with her—if it was love—when she was 11. It might be better to say that he fell in love with the idea of being in love with her: child, nurturer (she was a waitress in the Italian eating house of her father), and unattainable ideal. So this was a love for the aesthetics of melancholy unrequital, and she played a kind of telegraphic version of the role that Yeats's great love, Maude Gonne, played in his life.

As Yeats indicated, Dowson's commitment to the aesthetic (learned from the essayist and critic Walter Pater, confirmed by OSCAR WILDE and the artist Aubrey Beardsley, and also learned from the French decadents, in particular Charles-Pierre Baudelaire and Paul Verlaine) was central to his sensibility. Such a commitment, for him, involved a kind of melancholy sensuality (both his parents were suicides) where absinthe, love, the Catholicism to which he converted (as so many later Victorians did) and poetry were all facets of the same gem, all belonging to the short experience of "the days of wine and roses" ("Vitae Summa Brevis . . .", l. 5) to quote one of Dowson's aptest and most famous lines. The high aesthetics of Dowson's style makes his lines memorable even as his poetry can be excessive. T. S. Eliot could not get some of Dowson's lines out of his mind, he said, in particular the line to Cynara about how when night comes, "Then falls thy shadow," which is picked up in Eliot as the refrain "Falls the shadow" in "The Hollow Men." Along with "I have been faithful to thee, Cynara! In my fashion," and "gone with the wind" (both also from "Cynara"), the other lines quoted above form a considerable portion of the lines of English poetry most familiar to speakers of the language. This is all the more impressive because Dowson's life was so brief and his poetic output so small. He died at 32, virtually homeless as well as impoverished and ruined by drink, but as Yeats said he had earned the right "to troop with those the world's forgot," even as it remembers their words.

BIBLIOGRAPHY

Adams, Jad. *Madder Music, Stronger Wine: The Life of Ernest Dowson, Poet and Decadent.* New York: St. Martin's Press, 2000.

Bizot, Richard. "Pater and Yeats." *ELH: English Literary History* 43 (1976): 389–412.

Cevasco, G. A. *Three Decadent Poets: Ernest Dowson, John Gray, and Lionel Johnson: An Annotated Bibliography.* New York: Garland, 1990.

Plarr, Victor. *Ernest Dowson, 1888–1897: Reminiscences, Unpublished Letters and Marginalia.* London: E. Mathews, 1914.

Swann, Thomas Burnett. *Ernest Dowson.* New York: Twayne Publishers, 1965.

Yeats, W. B. *Autobiography of William Butler Yeats: Consisting of Reveries over Childhood and Youth, The Trembling of the Veil, and Dramatis Personae.* Garden City, N.Y.: Doubleday Anchor Books, 1958.

DREAM OF GERONTIUS, THE See NEWMAN, JOHN HENRY.

E

"EIGHTEEN HUNDRED AND ELEVEN" ANNA LAETITIA BARBAULD (1812) "Eighteen Hundred and Eleven" is ANNA LAETITIA BARBAULD's longest poem, a pointed satire at what she regarded as the dreadful conditions in England that year, and indeed in that period. The battles of 1812 in both Europe and North America were yet to come, but they were on the horizon; NAPOLEON BONAPARTE, the "Despot" of line 9, was plundering and annexing much of Europe, including parts of Germany and Poland, and coming into the inevitable conflict with Russia that would lead to his disastrous invasion. Although Britain had been more or less at war with France since the French Revolution, its behavior during Napoleon's leadership had always left idealists disgusted, first for its opposition to the liberation that the crowned heads of Europe feared from France's example, and then, conversely, for its caution in not being sufficiently involved in opposition to Napoleon's imperial designs. This was partly due to and aptly symbolized by the fact that the English king, George III, was mad, a condition she alludes to in her lament that "wasted realms enfeebled despots sway" now that the Genius or guardian spirit which had blessed England has departed (l. 244; see John Milton's *Lycidas,* l. 183). (Eight years later, PERCY BYSSHE SHELLEY would echo Barbauld in his sonnet "England in 1819" and call George III "An old, mad, blind, despised, and dying King.")

Barbauld had lived through the American War of Independence and now saw America as the hope of the future and the place where the freedom lost in Europe would be supreme. Despite the British desire to subdue and contain the United States, Barbauld saw that country as on the side of liberation and the true inheritor of England's idealism, and much of the poem is a paean to a future in which America would fulfill the promise of Britain's greatest traditions and ideals. In some sense, this prophecy has come true—that is to say, America and the American literary and political tradition did inherit the mantle of democracy and democratic idealism from Britain, and it honored those ideals. (For a later, more questionable version of this hope, see RUDYARD KIPLING's "The White Man's Burden.") Barbauld's vision, however, is stronger than prophecy, since it is a grim satire on the future of Britain, a foretelling of the time when it would all be picturesque ruins visited by Americans as Britons now visit Rome.

This vision was a very striking and disturbing one, and we can see in it the origin of a tradition of dystopian fantasies of the future, perhaps most famous in the novelist H. G. Wells's *The Time Machine*; but it was a direct influence on the novelist Mary Shelley's *The Last Man* and on the historian Thomas Babington Macaulay's 1840 vision (in an article) of a New Zealander coming to sketch the ruins of London. Barbauld derives her version of England's decline from Rome's (probably from Edward Gibbon's monumental and inescapable *Decline and Fall of the Roman Empire*). Every item of contemporary civilization is derived from Rome, but Rome itself fell into despotism and barbarism and is now only in ruins. Barbauld foresees the same fate for England and the removal of civilization to America.

This is perhaps the inevitable cycle of history: As LORD BYRON will write in *DON JUAN*: "I've stood upon Achilles' tomb, / And heard Troy doubted; time will doubt of Rome" (IV.101, ll. 7–8), presumably when London has become a ruin like Rome is now. But Barbauld's intent is to awaken England to a sense of the dangers of complacency combined with chaos, a warning we would do well to heed today, and perhaps in all ages. She does this through an astonishing and graceful catalog of the central and stunning achievements of English culture and science, achievements by which the moderns rival the ancients, but achievements which she now sees celebrated more in America than in England. America now will be as great as England, unless England herself can return to what she once was. What Barbauld explicitly wants is not perfectly clear, though in her catalogue of English heroes, Lord Nelson, who defeated the French at Trafalgar, features prominently. We can say that she wants England to return to its true self, and that would include alliance with the progressive forces the world over, and especially America (both North and South), where the idealism she credits England as originating will now flourish. Not the least of the credit that should go to Barbauld is the extent to which the alliance between England and the United States has been a net force for political progress in the world, more ambiguously it is true, but essentially in just the way she was urging.

BIBLIOGRAPHY

Armstrong, Isobel. "The Gush of the Feminine: How Can We Read Women's Poetry of the Romantic Period?" In *Romantic Women Writers: Voices and Countervoices,* edited by Paula R. Feldman and Theresa M. Kelley, 13–32. Hanover, N.H.: University Press of New England, 1995.

Armstrong, Isobel, and Virginia Blain, eds. *Women's Poetry in the Enlightenment: The Making of a Canon, 1730–1820.* New York: St. Martin's Press, 1999.

Barbauld, Anna Letitia. *Poems, 1792.* New York: Woodstock, 1993.

Keach, William. *Arbitrary Power: Romanticism, Language, Politics.* Princeton, N.J.: Princeton University Press, 2004.

Mellor, Anne K. *Romanticism & Gender.* New York: Routledge, 1993.

Stabler, Jane. *Burke to Byron, Barbauld to Baillie, 1790–1830.* New York: Palgrave, 2001.

Wordsworth, Jonathan. *Bright Work Grows: Women Writers of the Romantic Age.* Washington, D.C.: Woodstock Books, 1997.

ELIOT, GEORGE (MARY ANN EVANS) (1819–1880)

If all we knew of George Eliot was her poetry, we would regard her as a heartbreakingly minor talent—heartbreaking because her poetry demonstrates her extraordinary intelligence; her philosophical subtlety and force; her powerful depth of psychological insight; her intense and unconventional moral commitment; and her profound linguistic gift for description, exposition, and condensation. She had everything the greatest poet ought to have except for the talent of combining meaning with memorable expression within the poetic form to which she was committed. In her language, everything fits, but there are few surprises or delights, and the almost total lack of linguistic surprise relegates her to the rank of less-important poets.

Eliot was therefore not the best poet among the great novelists of 19th-century England. WILLIAM MAKEPEACE THACKERAY perhaps, GEORGE MEREDITH beyond doubt, and THOMAS HARDY absolutely were superior. But she was perhaps the greatest novelist. Her novels are masterpieces of morality, of the examination of the human character through incessant psychological explanation and verisimilitude. That psychology both derives from and contributes to an intensely moral vision of one's duty to others, a duty that includes accurately judging how well *they* fulfill their duty to others. Eliot was a strict and demanding moralist, of a near-Kantian type (part of the fruits of her intense reading in philosophy), despite her highly unconventional life.

She was born Mary Ann Evans on November 22, 1819, and her closest relation was her older brother Isaac (see "BROTHER AND SISTER"), who was four years her senior. Her teachers saw her gifts early and encouraged her in prodigious reading and the writing of poetry. She also had a strong philosophical bent and read, translated, and commented on a great deal of continental philosophy, most notably Ludwig Feuerbach. She was influenced by free-thinking friends in

England and ceased attending church, appalling her father and siblings. She acquiesced to her father's wishes for a time, but after his death she ceased going altogether. One of the hallmarks of her poetry (as of her novels) is the way it treats morality from a point of view that does not contemplate an afterlife (see "O MAY I JOIN THE CHOIR INVISIBLE" and, among many other examples, her lyric translation of an old Spanish song "Sweet Evenings Come and Go, Love"); morality must commit itself entirely to this world.

Living in London, Evans became assistant editor of the *Westminster Review* (its official editor had been her lover). After a couple of years, she met and fell in love with the philosopher and critic George Henry Lewes, who was in an open marriage with a woman who eventually had four children by another man. Lewes eventually renounced his wife but did not divorce her, and Eliot began living with him. Her siblings refused to meet her thereafter, and the loss of her friendship with Isaac was a particularly hard blow. Lewes encouraged her to write fiction, and she eventually began publishing under the pen name George Eliot, the first name being a tribute to Lewes. From the intensity of her psychological depiction of female characters, Charles Dickens recognized that she was a woman, and this was soon an open secret.

Throughout her life, Eliot wrote poetry, often of a fragmentary kind. She wished to sound Shakespearean, but her greatest influence, both as poet and novelist, was WILLIAM WORDSWORTH, and she often sounded like a Wordsworth who had read as much philosophy as SAMUEL TAYLOR COLERIDGE had, but who had been partly ruined by its didactic flavor.

The fragmentary form of much of Eliot's writing suggests the extent to which poetry was for her a resource for thought, to be remembered as intense fragmentary passages and not as whole poems. Accordingly, she tried to write poetry that was a resource for thought as well. She followed Sir WALTER SCOTT in inventing epigraphs, or MOTTOES, for the chapters of her books, and ascribing them to old works or by speech prefixes to notional plays. What mattered was the moment or passage, which in her novels she assimilated to her own story. Her poems—at least the less narrative ones (for some of them are badly versified stories)—are better when assimilated to her great power as a prose writer, but they are too stark and didactic when they stand alone. Nevertheless, there is some pathos in the intensity with which Eliot wishes to express her moral feelings, communicate them to others, and infect others with them, and her poems are certainly more serious as well as more competent (if less witty) than those of other minor poets.

We owe Lewes a debt of gratitude for turning Eliot toward fiction, which made her spectacularly famous and beloved in her day. All the great men of the time visited her (women avoided the imputation of scandal that such a visit would entail), and her novels were widely read and highly influential. Lewes himself died somewhat unexpectedly in 1878, and after a year of mourning, Eliot accepted the proposal of marriage made to her by Johnnie Cross, 20 years her junior. When she was married, her brother immediately reconciled with her, calling her "my dear sister." Alas, the reconciliation would be relatively brief since she died suddenly a few months later at the age of 61, on December 22, 1880. It would have cheered her to see her wish to live on as a moral force fulfilled, especially in her greatest novel, *Middlemarch*. That her poetry is of a lesser order might have bothered her but need not bother us, given the greatness of her novels. Her poetry is still a considerable achievement, both for the light it throws on the novelist and for the intelligence and plangency of its best moments.

BIBLIOGRAPHY

Bodenheimer, Rosemarie. *The Real Life of Mary Ann Evans: George Eliot, Her Letters and Fiction.* Ithaca, N.Y.: Cornell University Press, 1994.

Bonaparte, Felicia. *The Triptych and the Cross: The Central Myths of George Eliot's Poetic Imagination.* New York: New York University Press, 1979.

Haight, Gordon. *George Eliot: A Biography.* New York: Oxford University Press, 1968.

———, ed. *The George Eliot Letters.* New Haven, Conn.: Yale University Press, 1954.

Hertz, Neil. *George Eliot's Pulse.* Stanford, Calif.: Stanford University Press, 2003.

Woolf, Virginia. "George Eliot." *Times Literary Supplement* (November 20, 1919). Available online. URL: http://digital.library.upenn.edu/women/woolf/VW-Eliot.html. Accessed on April 5, 2008.

EPIGRAPHS See MOTTOES.

"EVE OF ST. AGNES, THE" JOHN KEATS (1819) This is one of JOHN KEATS's best-loved poems, with a wonderfully happy ending. Keats wrote it in late January 1819 (St. Agnes Day is January 21, and Keats seems to have started composition a few days before that). It is a story about warmth and love triumphing over winter cold (much as the cricket remembers summer days in the midst of winter in Keats's sonnet on "On the Grasshopper and the Cricket"). As the poem explains, if a young woman performs the right rituals, she should dream of her future lover on St. Agnes Eve, and this is what Madeline, the heroine of the poem, seeks to do.

In several ways, this poem is an anticipation of the great odes Keats would write three months later, in particular the first of them, "ODE TO PSYCHE." The narrative voice of the poem is besotted with the sensual beauties it records; the recording eye of the narrative is mesmerized by the richness of what it sees. Although there is no first-person narrator—that is to say, no first-person pronoun in the narrative—the poem itself feels highly voyeuristic, just as the "Ode to Psyche" will. Voyeurism in Keats is characteristically a pure pleasure: It does not tend to contain any masochistic sense of frustration, since the Keatsian poet gives himself over entirely to the rich pleasures of looking. In "Ode to Psyche," the figures he gazes at are Psyche and Cupid. Here they are Madeline and Porphyro.

The narrator's voyeurism, or scopophilia—love of looking—is mirrored in Porphyro himself. All he wants to do is gaze at Madeline; at least, this is what he thinks he wants to do, and he asks Angela to help him "That he might gaze and worship all unseen" (l. 80). But vision in Keats achieves a peak of sensuality, so that just gazing merges imperceptibly with sexual fulfillment, at least for Porphyro, and to be added to gazing and worshipping all unseen is a hope to "Perchance speak, kneel, touch, kiss—in sooth such things have been" (l. 81).

The story the poem recounts is a simple one, and all the pleasure of the poem is in the feeling of repletion with the telling. It is a cold St. Agnes Eve, but Madeline's father is having a winter ball for all his clan. The young beaux are all interested in Madeline, but she is interested only in going to sleep, so she can dream of her lover-to-be. Keats is no doubt recollecting SAMUEL TAYLOR COLERIDGE's recently published *CHRISTABEL,* which shares many plot similarities with *The Eve of St. Agnes,* including the way it begins with a young girl dreaming of her distant lover. Madeline finally retires, headed for bed; in the meantime, young Porphyro, who loves her and whom she hopes to dream of, has arrived at the castle, hoping to catch a glimpse of her.

We are in the same situation as that of the Capulets' ball in William Shakespeare's *Romeo and Juliet:* All of the people at the ball are his sworn enemies, Madeline's father most of all. But such is Porphyro's love that he must see her, and the only person willing to give him aid is the old crone Angela, who loves him as well as Madeline. Angela is, of course, an avatar of the Nurse in *Romeo and Juliet.* She guides Porphyro to Madeline's room, where Madeline falls asleep, not knowing he is there. He gazes upon her and upon the beauty of the scene which gilds her own loveliness, and he plays her "an ancient ditty, long since mute, / In Provence called 'La Belle dame sans mercy,'" or "The beautiful, pitiless woman." This is a dialogue by Alain Chartier from 1424, but it seems better to assume that the poem Porphyro sings is in fact Keats's poem of the same title, to be written three months later (see "LA BELLE DAME SANS MERCI"). That is to say, it is a poem in conformity with the Keatsian atmosphere of things, including the evocativeness produced by love's elusiveness. The later poem will echo this poem's sense of nightmare and loss: Madeline wakes up from a dream of Porphyro to the real thing, but she remembers the dream as being more beautiful. (Here we might recall one of Keats's dictums about the poetic IMAGINATION: "The imagination may be compared to Adam's dream: he awoke and found it truth." Keats there refers to Adam waking up to find his dream of Eve come true in John Milton's *Paradise Lost.* Here the truth is not quite so beautiful as the dream.

Consequently, Porphyro must enter Madeline's dream instead, which is to say enter the true land of fairy even within the fairyland in which the poem is set. In the poem's most notoriously sensual stanza, Porphyro, "Etheral, flushed, and like a throbbing star," is described as "melting" into her dream, blending with it in "solution sweet." That merging with her dream is sexual and yet is also the triumph of scopophilia, since he is merging with a visual world that she already sees. Nevertheless, in the real world they are in danger, and so he wakes her and they make their escape, in language again reminiscent of *Christabel,* of the scene where Christabel leads Geraldine into her father's castle. But Porphyro and Madeline are heading outward, into the kind of purely evocative place that Keats feels debarred from in his odes—the "fairly lands forlorn" of "ODE TO A NIGHTINGALE," for example. Here their escape is rendered through its opposite: the coldness and death and *time* that are inherent in the world from which they escape. They succeed in doing what Keats always wants to do: to be elsewhere, to experience the elsewhere *as* elsewhere. All the people in the world they leave behind die, but they somehow live, since they disappear into some fabulous beyond of love and happiness.

The sensuality of this world is the promise of that other one, and the imagination, which can imagine that sensuality, is the imagination that can take pleasure in Madeline and Porphyro's absence at the end of the poem. They are now in a dream world, or we are, and the ability to enter or exit that world is highly attractive and beautiful; it is an ability that the seductive beauty of the poem comes close to matching in its own right.

BIBLIOGRAPHY

Bate, Walter Jackson. *John Keats.* Cambridge, Mass.: Harvard University Press, 1963.

Bloom, Harold. *Poetry and Repression: Revisionism from Blake to Stevens.* New Haven, Conn.: Yale University Press, 1976.

———. *The Visionary Company: A Reading of English Romantic Poetry.* Garden City, N.Y.: Doubleday, 1961.

De Man, Paul. *The Rhetoric of Romanticism.* New York: Columbia University Press, 1984.

Dickstein, Morris. *Keats and His Poetry: A Study in Development.* Chicago: University of Chicago Press, 1971.

Flesch, William. "The Ambivalence of Generosity: Keats Reading Shakespeare." *ELH: English Literary History* 62, no. 1 (Spring 1995): 149–169.

McFarland, Thomas. *The Masks of Keats: The Endeavour of a Poet.* New York: Oxford University Press, 2000.

Stillinger, Jack. *The Hoodwinking of Madeline, and Other Essays on Keats's Poems.* Urbana: University of Illinois Press, 1971.

Wasserman, Earl. *The Finer Tone: Keats' Major Poems.* Baltimore: Johns Hopkins Press, 1953.

F

"FAIRIES: A NURSERY SONG, THE" WILLIAM ALLINGHAM (1849) This is probably now WILLIAM ALLINGHAM's most famous poem, and its opening lines are familiar to everyone. The subtitle, "A Nursery Song," tells you that the *we* the speaker refers to is the nursery-rhyme *we,* the community of those who learn to think as the rhyme says because it invites them into that community—that is, the community of human beings, and in particular those who like rhymes like these.

What makes this nursery song so evocative? It describes the little men—the fairies or leprechauns of Allingham's native Ireland—as mischievous and a little frightening. They populate the Irish countryside, everywhere, and the catalogue of the places they haunt is a catalogue of remote and attractive Irish locales: "the airy mountain"; "the rushy glen"; and, more sublimely, access to the place of "the gay Northern Lights" (l. 28). This list of places they live and that "we" cannot go allows us to range in imagination over all of Ireland, from the mountains to the "rocky shore."

The little men are not malicious, but they are inhuman. They belong to a world that does not recognize the human because it is more archaic and more elemental than human life. But the song is about our being able to imagine them, which is to say about the way the human singer and his human auditors can make Ireland the subject of their imagination. We can be there through poetry, and through the kind of narrative tradition that ballads enshrine and that poems like this allude to. That is, we can be in the place that represents pure poetry, the Ireland of the imagination and not of reality. WILLIAM BUTLER YEATS's 19th-century poetry learned this tone and aspiration, as he acknowledged, from Allingham.

The range of this poetry is as great as that of any poetic tradition. The little men may be free of malice (though not of mischievous revenge), but they can cause great sorrow nonetheless—sorrow of which they are themselves unaware. Bridget is a changeling, stolen for seven years before she is returned. In those seven years she finds that her friends are gone, and she dies of sorrow. The fairies, knowing nothing of death, imagine that she is asleep, and so they take her back "lightly." But we know the sorrow as much as the lightness.

The sorrow is the sorrow of adulthood—that is, of time and change and death. Bridget's friends are gone because they have grown older, not because they are dead. But in another sense this means that her childhood is dead, or at least so transitory as to be a matter of great sorrow. Her friends are gone, which means essentially that because they are grown up, they do not believe in fairies any more—nor, consequently, in poems like this, where the fairies' realm in Ireland is named in evocative admonition. As in much of Allingham, growing up means loss of poetic faith. But here the loss of faith becomes the proof of it: Bridget's sorrow is *caused* by the fairies and not by disbelief in them; or, to unpick the poem's schematic logic, the little men cause our sad disbelief in them. So our disbelief proves that they exist, and it shows Ireland to be a place of hidden but omnipresent poetry and poetic delight.

BIBLIOGRAPHY

Allingham, H., and E. Baumer Williams, eds. *Letters to William Allingham.* London, 1911.

Allingham, William. *William Allingham: A Diary.* Edited by H. Allingham and D. Radford. London: Macmillan & Co., 1907.

Hill, George Birkbeck, ed. *Letters of Dante Gabriel Rossetti to William Allingham, 1854–1870.* London: T. Fisher Unwin, 1897.

FALL OF HYPERION, THE See *HYPERION* AND *THE FALL OF HYPERION.*

"FELICIA HEMANS" LETITIA ELIZABETH LANDON (1838) LETITIA ELIZABETH LANDON's elegy on FELICIA HEMANS appeared in 1838. Hemans had died three years earlier, in Dublin, of tuberculosis. Like all poetic elegies, this poem is more or less an elegy for the self as well, who in another's fate now weeps for her own (to paraphrase a line from PERCY BYSSHE SHELLEY's *ADONAIS*), and indeed Landon died, a probable suicide, the year this elegy appeared. Hemans was for her a kind of role model or mirror image: a wildly popular poet whose poetry transmuted grim or difficult experience into beauty.

The poem is shot through with echoes of other poets, from William Shakespeare to LORD BYRON and especially WILLIAM WORDSWORTH, whose words Landon always had resonating in her mind. Thus, the first line of "Felicia Hemans" confirms that this is an elegy for the self as well, since it alludes to the great passage in Byron's *DON JUAN* that begins: "No more—no more—Oh! never more on me / The freshness of the heart can fall like dew" (canto I, l. 214). Where Byron had applied this lament to his own loss of youth and spirit, Landon officially applies it to Hemans but also therefore, as is traditional in the elegiac form, to her survivors, including Landon herself. The first 32 lines contain explicit reference to Hemans, her life, her work (including her translations), and her reputation, especially in North America, where she was extremely popular.

Most notable in those lines is a very quick encomium to poetry itself, derived from Landon's thinking about Hemans's translations from Italian and Castilian poetry: "A general bond of union is the poet, / By its immortal verse is language known, / And for the sake of song do others know it" (ll. 21–23). Poetry is what makes us care about other languages. The desire for song motivates us to the deepest communion with what is foreign and strange. (This is an idea that Landon also explores in "SAPPHO'S SONG.") This means that poetry itself is a kind of muse of language, inspiring us to master foreign tongues.

The second and longer part of the poem is more obviously an elegy for the self. There Landon writes quite powerfully about the experience that leads to poetry, in language reminiscent of Shelley's in *JULIAN AND MADDALO.* Poets learn in suffering what they teach in song, and Landon makes us recognize that this is true of Hemans, and of herself as well: "We say that song is sorrowful, but know not / What may have left the sorrow on the song" (ll. 41–42). The beauty of poetry is the sorrow it expresses, sorrow that wakes a sympathetic emotion in its audience. But the sorrow is real, even if we register mainly its beauty in tempered version in song. To this Landon specifies the particular aptitude for feeling sorrow that she thinks female poets have, women (supposedly) being more sensitive and empathic (ll. 49–64). More temperamentally suited to be poets, they are also more temperamentally likely to be balked by the sexism whose cruelty they feel all the more powerfully because of their poetic sensibility. Poets and women alike share in this acute sensitivity, and therefore women poets are especially alert to the sorrow which elicits poetry.

If poetry derives from suffering, it is also possible that it soothes the pain it makes the poet feel. This is the burden of the last stanza. Hemans finds in her poetry, as we do, something to comfort her for the harshness of existence. And now that she is dead, what remains of her is just the soothing and comforting poetry that she has written, the sorrow it derives from her being now at peace. The idea of poetic vocation as committed to the song that survives the sorrow that gives rise to it runs deep in Landon's work and makes it possible to see why the "cruel sneer and harsh reproach" uttered "by careless tongues and by ungenerous words" (ll. 57–58), which became her constant lot, would lead her to death the same year that this elegy appeared. (Prior to Landon's death, ELIZABETH BARRETT BROWNING had written a poem on Hemans and dedicated it to Landon's poem.)

BIBLIOGRAPHY

Greer, Germaine. *Slip-Shod Sibyls: Recognition, Rejection and the Woman Poet.* London: Viking, 1995.

Lawford, Cynthia. "Diary." *London Review of Books* (September 21, 2000). Available online. URL: http://www.lrb.co.uk/v22/n18/lawf01_/html. Accessed on March 29, 2008.

———. "'Thou shalt bid thy fair hands rove': L. E. L.'s Wooing of Sex, Pain, Death and the Editor." *Romanticism on the Net* 29–30 (February–May 2003). Available online. URL: http://www.erudit.org/revue/ron/2003/v/n29/007718ar.html. Accessed on March 30, 2008.

Mellor, Anne K. "Exhausting the Beautiful." In *Romanticism and Gender,* 107–143. New York: Routledge, 1993.

"FERGUS AND THE DRUID" WILLIAM BUTLER YEATS (1892) "Fergus and the Druid" is characteristic of the poems that WILLIAM BUTLER YEATS wrote about Fergus, the Red Branch King. Like "WHO GOES WITH FERGUS?" it is a poem describing Yeats's poetic commitments and desire in the phase of his poetry that coincided with the last decades of the 19th century. In this poem, we get Fergus's point of view rather than that of his followers, and as with "The SAD SHEPHERD," we find that the poet's attitude toward Fergus's followers, depicted in "Who Goes with Fergus?" as paralleling their attitude toward Fergus, here is paralleled by Fergus's attitude toward himself or his world or the world of which he is the emblem. "Fergus and the Druid" is important as depicting, almost offhandedly, the beginning of a series of events which culminates with CUCHULAIN'S FIGHT WITH THE SEA, the next poem in Yeats's 1893 book *The Rose.*

The poem is a dialogue between Fergus and the Druid he has been pursuing, much as Telemachus pursues Proteus in Homer's *The Odyssey.* Fergus is a poet figure for Yeats—

> . . . the proud dreaming king who flung the crown
> And sorrow away, and calling bard and clown
> Dwelt among the wine-stained wanderers in the
> deep woods . . .
>
> ("The Secret Rose," ll. 19–21)

That praise should help to see the profundity that compensates for the loss Fergus complains about in "Fergus and the Druid."

Fergus follows the Druid, a figure somewhere between a priest and a genius loci, a spirit of the place or landscape into which Fergus pursues him. (This pursuit is reminiscent of PERCY BYSSHE SHELLEY's "Alastor," and Shelley was one of Yeats's central influences.) Like Telemachus, Fergus at last compels the Druid to take on his own "human shape," but in that shape he turns out to be "A thin grey man half lost in gathering night" that is half absorbed and still being absorbed into the endless and insubstantial surround. The Druid himself describes his own "body trembling like a wind-blown reed," words that anticipate the title of Yeats's next book, *The Wind among the Reeds* (in which "The Secret Rose" appears).

In answer to the Druid's question, what does he want?, Fergus reports that he has given his kingdom up to Conchubar (this is a strong departure from the actual tradition; see more in the entry on "Who Goes with Fergus?"), and that he has "laid the crown / Upon his head to cast away my sorrow" (words echoed in "The Secret Rose").

But despite flinging sorrow away, Fergus is still burdened with sorrow and despair. (The word *burden* is one that Yeats liked to pun on, meaning both a heavy weight and the hypnotic repetitiousness of poetic refrain; see the entry on "The Sad Shepherd.") The Druid then offers him a kind of Pandora's box, an ambiguous "bag of dreams" that will wrap him round. Fergus opens the bag and everything—or perhaps nothing—changes:

> Fergus. I see my life go drifting like a river
> From change to change; I have been many
> things—
> A green drop in the surge, a gleam of light
> Upon a sword, a fir-tree on a hill,
> An old slave grinding at a heavy quern,
> A king sitting upon a chair of gold—
> And all these things were wonderful and
> great;
> But now I have grown nothing, knowing all.
> Ah! Druid, Druid, how great webs of sorrow
> Lay hidden in the small slate-coloured thing!

As always in these entries, I quote Yeats's final revisions. The most important revision was the first, also in 1892. In that revision, the last three lines of the poem replace these:

> But now I have grown nothing, being all:
> The sorrows of the world bow down my head,
> And in my heart the daemons and the gods
> Wage an eternal battle, and I feel
> The pain of wonds, the labour of the spear,
> But have no share in loss or victory.

The first version laments the insubstantiality of poetic dreams. He has *been* all, but not really, and therefore has become nothing. There is a reminiscence here of Keats's comparison and contrast between poetry and dreaming in *The Fall of Hyperion* (see HYPERION AND THE FALL OF HYPERION) and of Keats's account of the poetical character in a Letter on the Chameleon Poet, where he says, "The poet is the most unpoetical of all things. . . . He has no nature." Fergus, too, has become everything and nothing and now laments his retreat from the real world of real action. For Yeats, this lamentation is poetry itself, since the real world of real action is ultimately evanescent, insubstantial, no more real than its report in the words that memorialize it.

And so the somewhat pat complaint of the first version gives way to the far greater and more memorable revision. In that revision, the first thing to notice is that *being* gives way to *knowing*. The trade-off is not between "being all" and being nothing, but "knowing all" and therefore being nothing. Like Shakespeare's anti-Irish Richard II (another dreamy poet-king who abdicated to a relative and whose summary of human life—"Little man, with nothing pleased / Till he be eased with being nothing"—Yeats echoes in these lines), Fergus comes to the knowledge of truth, and that knowledge is that no *facts* endure. "All things pass away," as he will later put it.

This knowledge is the province of poetry. So the second version of the poem no longer has Fergus uttering a complaint to himself, an expression of lamentation about where he has ended up. Rather, he speaks here to the Druid, who has given him the "little bag of dreams." The Druid has known what will happen, has indeed warned Fergus that the dreams will wrap him round. Fergus, far from blaming the Druid for the gift, has joined him now within the knowledge of insubstantiality that the poet records. He has become like the Druid, also someone who has been all and has grown nothing. What Fergus has not known when he has known all is what it is like to be nothing, but now he does, and this is a state and a knowledge that he can share with the Druid.

It is this shared knowledge that makes possible the poem's extraordinary last line: "The small slate-coloured thing" is the bag of dreams. It is slate-colored because it is grey like the Druid, and it verges on the insubstantiality it harbors. The reader's initial puzzlement when confronted with the line is part of the point: It is enigmatic, and yet its meaning becomes inevitable, and that enigmatic inevitability is what Fergus—and Yeats—is describing. Yeats somehow expects us to know what the line means or alludes to, what the small slate-colored thing is, as Fergus expects the Druid to know what it means or alludes to.

The Druid will know, of course, because he has given Fergus the bag of dreams and the webs of sorrow it contains. But why should we know? The implication is that this knowledge is the ultimate or deepest knowledge of human life and human experience. Webs of sorrow lie hidden in all human lives, and we come to recognize that this is so, just as Fergus has come to recognize that this is so. To know everything about life is to know how great the webs of sorrow are. This knowledge is the knowledge that poetry affords, and it is also the emotional intensity that poetry can communicate. That, at any rate, is the moral of "Fergus and the Druid," and the inspiration and moral of all of Yeats's early poetry, a moral he returned to at the end of his career.

BIBLIOGRAPHY

Bloom, Harold. *Yeats*. New York: Oxford University Press, 1970.

Grossman, Allen R. *Poetic Knowledge in the Early Yeats: A Study of The Wind among the Reeds*. Charlottesville: University Press of Virginia, 1969.

Rosenthal, M. L. Introduction to *Selected Poems and Four Plays of William Butler Yeats*, xix–xliv. New York: Scribner, 1996.

Vendler, Helen. *Poets Thinking: Pope, Whitman, Dickinson, Yeats.* Cambridge, Mass.: Harvard University Press, 2004.
———. *Yeats's Vision and the Later Plays.* Cambridge, Mass.: Harvard University Press, 1963.

FIELD, MICHAEL (KATHARINE HARRIS BRADLEY [1846–1914], and EDITH EMMA COOPER [1862–1913]) Katharine Bradley and Edith Cooper published most of their poetry under the collaborative pseudonym of Michael Field, a name that combined their nicknames for each other. Bradley (born Catherine) was Cooper's aunt and more or less raised her niece after her elder sister became an invalid in 1865, when Cooper was three years old. The extreme closeness between the two was intellectual and emotional, and eventually they became lovers and lived together for the rest of their lives. Bradley nursed Cooper through her death by cancer, just as she had cared for her as a child, hiding the fact that she had cancer herself; she died just a few months after her niece did.

Bradley studied both at the Collège de France and Cambridge University; later, when Cooper was a teenager, the family moved to Bristol, where the two of them studied classical languages and literature at University College. In 1875, Bradley published a volume of poetry under the male pseudonym of Arran Leigh, a kind of tip of the hat to ELIZABETH BARRETT BROWNING'S "AURORA LEIGH," but one made more in honor of ROBERT BROWNING than in memory of Elizabeth, whom Bradley and Cooper did not rate as highly as most of their contemporaries did. Later, both women published a volume together, with Cooper taking the name Isla Leigh to Bradley's Arran.

They first took the singular name Michael Field, based on the nicknames they had among their friends, for the verse dramas which they undertook, in imitation of William Shakespeare and of the great Jacobean collaborative dramatists Francis Beaumont and John Fletcher. Robert Browning was very impressed by Field, and he continued to praise and admire them when Bradley wrote him with the truth in 1884. Their friendship is reflected in Michael Field's elegy "The Burial of Robert Browning," printed in Edmund Clarence Stedman's central *Victorian Anthology* (1895), which more or less summed up the age. Despite the fact that friends and luminaries such as OSCAR WILDE, WILLIAM BUTLER YEATS, ALGERNON CHARLES SWINBURNE, GEORGE MEREDITH, and especially LIONEL JOHNSON continued to admire their work, Michael Field's reputation plummeted when his works' true authorship became known.

Bradley and Cooper were not explicitly "out" as a lesbian couple, but Browning's affectionate description of them as his "two dear Greek women" referred both to their aesthetic commitments to the purity of a Greek lyric form (in their lyrics perhaps more than in their drama) and to their correlative commitment to the kind of ancient Greek sexual freedom that smiled on same-sex relationships. Indeed, they describe their 1889 book *Long Ago* as "an extension of Sappho's fragments into lyrics," in imitation of "the one woman who has dared to speak unfalteringly of the fearful mastery of love." Likewise, in a beautiful 1893 poem, "Why Are Women Silent?" (from *Underneath the Bough*), they compare Sappho with CHRISTINA GEORGINA ROSSETTI as women whose intense poetry derives from the painfulness of their love. This move was a daring one since in 1885 Henry Wharton had just translated Sappho for the first time with the proper (feminine) pronouns for her lovers.

Bradley and Cooper continued to use Michael Field as a pseudonym for several more years, but finally they decided to published anonymously since their joint authorship so clashed with the romantic and Victorian sense of singular poetic subjectivity. Close to it as they were, Bradley and Cooper were probably the most impressive challenge to that idea, especially in the amazing and graphically descriptive poetry that they wrote in which the sensibility of the describer is indicated through the intensity of description. Much of this poetry has a Paterian sheen, most obviously the recreation of the Mona Lisa of which the essayist Walter Horatio Pater had written so memorably, although in addition to Pater (who admired them), the essayist Ruskin (with whom Bradley had a friendship) and Oscar Wilde were strong influences.

After the death of Cooper's father in 1899, she seems to have begun a move toward religious conversion (Bradley had avowed herself an atheist in the 1870s), and in 1907, after the death of their beloved dog Whym Chow, Cooper, like so many of the most important minor Victorian poets, converted to Catholicism. Bradley followed suit, and at the end of their lives they published two books, written separately, both attributed to Michael Field. These late devotional poems are nevertheless consistent with their earlier poetry in the near-erotic intensity of their visual descriptions of Christ and Mary. Their devotion to God did not in the end preclude a devotion to each other, either as lovers or as poets.

See also "CYCLAMENS," "IT WAS DEEP APRIL," "NOON."

BIBLIOGRAPHY

Avery, Simon. "Michael Field (1846–1914)." *The Literary Encyclopedia* (June 13, 2003), Available online. URL: http://www.litencyc.com/php/speople.php?rec=true&UID=1521. Accessed on March 14, 2008.

Castle, Terry, ed. *The Literature of Lesbianism: A Historical Anthology from Ariosto to Stonewall.* New York: Columbia University Press, 2003.

Moore, T., and D. C. Sturge. *Works and Days, from the Journal of Michael Field.* London: J. Murray, 1933.

Prins, Yopie. *Victorian Sappho.* Princeton, N.J.: Princeton University Press, 1999.

Sturgeon, Mary. *Michael Field.* London: G.G. Harrap, 1922.

White, Christine. "'Poets and Lovers Evermore': The Poetry and Journals of Michael Field." In *Sexual Sameness: Textual Differences in Lesbian and Gay Writing,* edited by Joseph Bristow, 26–43. New York: Routledge, 1992.

FITZGERALD, EDWARD (EDWARD PURCELL) (1809–1883) Edward FitzGerald is now remembered for one poem: his translation, or rather adaptation, of *The* RUBÁIYÁT OF OMAR KHAYYÁM. That poem was first published anonymously in 1859 after *Fraser's Magazine* had rejected some of its stanzas a few years earlier, and it went unsold at a shilling a copy for a year or so. When the publisher reduced the price to a penny, a friend of DANTE GABRIEL ROSSETTI's and the explorer Richard Burton's found it and bought several copies, and it began circulating. ALGERNON CHARLES SWINBURNE was an admirer as well, and in its later revised, expanded, and sometimes reconstructed editions, it came to be one of the most popular poems ever written, certainly the most popular English translation. FitzGerald had published other translations as well, of the great Spanish playwright Pedro Calderón de la Barca in particular, but nothing else matches the *Rubáiyát.*

FitzGerald was born Edward Purcell, but his father took Edward's mother's name when she came into her immense fortune in 1819. He grew up in France for a while and then in England, and attended Trinity College, Cambridge University, where he became very close friends with WILLIAM MAKEPEACE THACKERAY. He had no great literary ambitions but wished rather to live a life of Epicurean idleness like that which he would eventually praise in the *Rubáiyát,* a life he could afford given the wealth he had inherited from his mother. He published a few works of a literary bent, including his first translations and a poem that CHARLES LAMB admired, but essentially devoted himself to reading and not to writing, except for the extraordinary letters to the friends he was so devoted to, ALFRED, LORD TENNYSON and the Scottish essayist Thomas Carlyle among them. That devotion often had a strong erotic component, and throughout his life FitzGerald would enjoy the company of athletic young men, including Edward Cowell, who taught him Persian and introduced him to some of the Persian poet Omar Khayyám's quatrains. He also numbered among his friends Bernard Barton (1784–1849), the Quaker poet who was a friend of Lamb, and eventually ROBERT SOUTHEY. On his deathbed Barton elicited a promise from FitzGerald to marry Barton's daughter Lucy; he did so in 1856, but their marriage was unhappy and they separated after less than a year. Harold Bloom has speculated that FitzGerald wrote the the *Rubáiyát* partly in response to the unhappy marriage; at any rate, he began his translation in 1856, three years before its publication.

After the poem finally met with its extraordinary success, FitzGerald revised it several times, and eventually (against his wishes) his name came out as its author. He also translated some more Calderón, as well as some of the ancient Greek tragedies. After FitzGerald's death, his letters were published, in one of which he wrote of the death of ELIZABETH BARRETT BROWNING, "Mrs. Browning's Death is rather a relief to me, I must say: no more Aurora Leighs, thank God! A woman of real genius, I know; but what is the upshot of it all? She and her Sex had better mind the Kitchen and their

Children: and perhaps the Poor: except in such things as little Novels, they only devote themselves to what Men do much better, leaving that which Men do worse or not at all." This incurred ROBERT BROWNING's wrath, expressed in his bitter and grotesquely witty poem "Lines to Edward FitzGerald." The letter, however, was less a document of active sexism than of complete lack of interest in women, and perhaps there was a kind of identification with Elizabeth Barrett Browning and with other poets he thought of as being affably minor, as he thought of himself.

FitzGerald may have felt the same way about WILLIAM BLAKE, whose power he was among the first to recognize, but who also comes in for his general genial severity, as when in 1833 he wrote to his friend W. B. Donne, "I have lately bought a little pamphlet which is very difficult to be got, called *The Songs of Innocence,* written and adorned with drawings by W. Blake (if you know his name) who was quite mad, but of a madness that was really the elements of great genius ill-sorted: in fact, a genius *with a screw loose,* as we used to say." For FitzGerald, genius was best when it went together with pleasure, and it was to the intoxicating and even erotic pleasures of literature and friendship that he devoted himself.

BIBLIOGRAPHY

FitzGerald, Edward. *Letters & Literary Remains of Edward FitzGerald.* Edited by William A. Wright. New York: Macmillan, 1889.

Hollander, John. "Paradise Enow." In *Edward FitzGerald's The Rubáiyát of Omar Khayyám,* edited by Harold Bloom, 165–191. Philadelphia: Chelsea House, 2004

Martin, Robert Bernard. *With Friends Possessed: A Life of Edward FitzGerald.* Boston: Faber and Faber, 1985.

Terhune, A. M. *The Life of Edward FitzGerald, Translator of The Rubáiyát of Omar Khayyám.* New Haven, Conn.: Yale University Press, 1947.

"FROST AT MIDNIGHT" SAMUEL TAYLOR COLERIDGE (1798) "Frost at Midnight" is one of SAMUEL TAYLOR COLERIDGE's most beautiful poems, It belongs to the genre he called "conversation poems" (in the subtitle to "The Nightingale")—that is, poems in the style of a person talking to a listener, perhaps himself, but even so following the explanatory impulses and digressions of social speech. (Coleridge derived the mode from the 17th-century poet George Herbert.) Coleridge, we know, was a great talker (as the essayist William Hazlitt recounted in "My First Acquaintance with Poets"), and here we see him talking seriously to himself and perhaps just as seriously to his child.

In the poem, Coleridge is up late on a cold but still winter night in the cottage that he shares with his young son HARTLEY COLERIDGE. The rest of the family is asleep, and he considers the beautiful frost that settles on the house and seems to increase the sense of calm and peace within it. Its secret ministry is the way it bestows this calm without any sort of personification, any sense of obligation conferred at all.

Hartley is asleep at his side as Coleridge meditates, adding to the sense of calm, but the calm itself is oddly vexing. Meditation has no object; the extreme stillness of the night prevents Coleridge from having to think of any particular thing, so it takes itself as the object. This image of meditation vexed by calm is one that WILLIAM WORDSWORTH will borrow for the opening of *The PRELUDE,* where the "correspondent breeze" within the poet that responds to the gentle breeze of the outside world becomes "a tempest, a redundant energy / Vexing its own creation" (1850 version, ll. 37–38). Stillness becomes paradoxically redundant, a characteristic romantic theme that has to do with the strange doubling of self-reflection. Subjectivity meditates on its own strange, uncharacterizable perspective, and that meditation on the void of selfhood seeks to understand the subjectivity it thereby creates. (This has often been aptly compared to the simile of an eye trying to see itself seeing, and not only what it sees.) Thought is related to the world it thinks about through an undefinable subjectivity, half-creating the world it perceives, as Wordsworth would put it in "TINTERN ABBEY." That poem is highly influenced by "Frost at Midnight," and its version of this self-sustained vexation appears at the start when he describes how the "wild secluded scene" that he sees gives rise to "thoughts of more deep seclusion" ("Tintern Abbey," ll. 6–7). In both Coleridge and Wordsworth, this vexation could become wild indeed, although never perhaps as ungovernably as in the poetry of JOHN CLARE, most observant of the natural world among the romantics, who called this aspect of subjectivity the experience of being the "self-consumer" of his own woes (see "I AM").

Indeed, it should be noted that this self-reflective meditation is finally absorbed into Coleridge's thinking about the form of the poem itself. In its original version, Coleridge imagined "tomorrow's warmth" when the whole house would be awake again and Hartley would fly to his mother's arms. That ending is beautiful, but not so beautiful as its omission, which allows the poem to end with a return to the vision of frost that sets him thinking about it and about how Hartley will think about it. Coleridge explained the deletion of the last lines in one of his famous marginalia: "The six last lines I omit because they destroy the rondo, and return upon itself of the poem. Poems of this kind of length ought to lie coiled with its tail round its head." True though, as a poetic principle the omission of the last six lines allows us to understand another feature of the poem, the extent to which it shifts, as all poetry (no matter how spontaneous) must shift, from expression to the reminder of a past attitude or thought. Hartley grows, and "Frost at Midnight" simultaneously becomes the place where Coleridge remembers him as the beautiful babe in the stillness of the evening. Futurity is there still in the extraordinary blessing that ends the poem, but not chronology—not the next day and the day after that, but the suspended and privileged time in which the whole blessed future may be felt in the instant.

That is to say that the afterlife of the poem is one in which it becomes itself an object of meditation, meditation expressed in the way Coleridge further abstracts, idealizes, and aims at the essence of the remembered scene. That kind of abstraction, idealization, and essentializing is what the poem is about anyway, so this is another dimension in which the poem lies coiled with its tail round its head: It becomes a way for the poet to remember it and to remember what he felt about the poem itself as he wrote it, not only *when* writing it but *by* writing it. And this is the subject of the poem, which is characteristic of the deep and subtle ways of thinking about the past that Wordsworth and Coleridge were experimenting with when they composed *Lyrical Ballads* (1798).

The stillness is such that even the flame in the grate does not move, but there is something that does (like the last red leaf dancing on the treetop in CHRISTABEL), the *stranger* or film of not-quite consumed material that he sees fluttering there despite the otherwise extreme stillness. (Convection currents caused by the fire heating the air are what make the film flutter.) The 18th-century poet William Cowper, in *The Task,* which Coleridge is thinking about in this poem, also describes the "sooty films that play upon the bars" (book 1, l. 292), but he relates them to a somewhat more anxious superstition than Coleridge does. Cowper describes them as forecasting the arrival of an unknown, perhaps dangerous, person, but Coleridge thinks the stranger a "companionable form." It is a companion to the self-inducing vexation he himself feels, and as such a form it can become a thing whereon to project and therefore calm his oddly serene restlessness. It is a toy in which thought believes itself reflected, interpreted by the mood of the perceiving spirit, but the self-reflexivity we have noticed also works now *between* mind and world as the film itself makes thought a toy (l. 23)—that is, guides the thought that had projected itself onto the film.

It guides Coleridge's thought to memory, and so we move from the midnight in which the poem begins to the time during his school days in London when he would watch the film on the grate and daydream about the stranger it was supposed to foretell. In a footnote for the poem, Coleridge understands *stranger* to mean an "absent friend." Why is an absent friend called a stranger? Because the friend's absence is more fundamental than accidental difference in location; the absence is partly about the way that life itself changes and friends become memories. (See, for example, CHARLES LAMB's "The OLD FAMILIAR FACES" and GEORGE ELIOT's "BROTHER AND SISTER.") Now he is at school, but the stranger makes him think of life at home, in his "sweet birthplace," and of how he used to fall asleep there to the sounds of the church bells. He most wished at school that the stranger would turn out to be his sister Ann (ll. 42–43), his elder by five years, to whom he was extremely close. It is therefore important to know that Ann died of consumption in 1791, and that in remembering her, Coleridge is mourning for her too. She has become a stranger indeed, absent forever.

Note then that from the midnight in which this meditation begins, Coleridge recalls another time (his school days) when he longed for a still earlier time (his early childhood) that was connected with an earlier time yet (the place of his birth), and where he would be lulled into dreams still further removed from the present. All these different moments can be seen as made discontinuous by "Frost at Midnight" or antithetically as being brought into perfect continuity. For if the memory of any moment in life is a memory of what one was remembering at that moment, then memory is the center of human experience and not a sign of being separated from it. At midnight Coleridge is remembering his memories, and so the present, too, is part of the experience of memory.

But who is the stranger now that the *stranger* on the grate portends? In some sense it is Hartley, the sleeping babe, having the dreams that Coleridge used to have when he fell asleep in his sweet birthplace. Coleridge is awake, but he can remember sleep and also experience it with intense vicarious happiness in seeing Hartley there, in the present. Thus, childhood returns as Coleridge shifts his thoughts of the past to thoughts of the present, the beautiful babe lying next to him; and Ann returns, perhaps, in the love that he feels for her in memory and for Hartley in the present. It is in that present that he utters the beautiful blessing for Hartley's future, a blessing that will allow Hartley to participate from all perspectives in the beautiful continuities of memory that the frost performs as its secret ministry.

BIBLIOGRAPHY

Bate, Walter Jackson. *Coleridge.* New York: Macmillan, 1968.

Bloom, Harold. *The Visionary Company: A Reading of English Romantic Poetry.* Garden City, N.Y.: Doubleday, 1961.

Brisman, Leslie. *Romantic Origins.* Ithaca, N.Y.: Cornell University Press, 1978.

Coleridge, Samuel Taylor. *Selected Poems.* Edited by William Empson and David Pirie. Manchester, England: Fyfield, 1989.

Frank, Robert H. *Passions within Reason: The Strategic Role of the Emotions.* New York: Norton, 1988.

Freud, Sigmund. "The Uncanny." In *The Standard Edition of the Complete Psychological Works of Sigmund Freud,* 219–256. London: Hogarth Press, 1953–74.

Janowitz, Anne. *England's Ruins: Poetic Purpose and the National Landscape.* Cambridge, Mass.: Blackwell, 1990.

Lowes, John Livingston. *Road to Xanadu: A Study in the Ways of the Imagination.* New York: Houghton Mifflin, 1930.

Parker, Reeve. *Coleridge's Meditative Art.* Ithaca, N.Y.: Cornell University Press, 1975.

Swann, Karen. "'Christabel': The Wandering Mother and the Enigma of Form." *SIR* 23, no. 4 (Winter 1984): 533–553.

G

"GARDEN OF PROSERPINE, THE" ALGERNON CHARLES SWINBURNE (1866) In ALGERNON CHARLES SWINBURNE's 1866 volume *Poems and Ballads,* this poem comes well after "HYMN TO PROSERPINE." It is thematically connected to the hymn, but all of Swinburne's poems are thematically connected, and "The Garden of Proserpine" looks forward to "A Forsaken Garden," to be found in *Poems and Ballads: Second Series,* published 12 years later. The Garden of Proserpine contrasts with two other great gardens in English poetry: John Milton's Garden of Eden and Edmund Spenser's Garden of Adonis in *The Faerie Queene.* Milton and Spenser had both compared their respective gardens to the "fair field / Of Enna, where Proserpine gathering flowers, / Herself a fairer flower by gloomy Dis / Was gathered, which cost Ceres all that pain / To seek her through the world" (*Paradise Lost,* 4, ll. 268–272). In Ovid's original, Dis or Pluto, god of the underworld, abducts Proserpine and makes her queen of the world of the dead. Ceres, goddess of grain ("corn," that is wheat, in l. 76), obtains Prosperpine's cyclical return to the upper world for half the year, during which grain grows and is harvested, before her return to the underworld brings winter on.

Swinburne also has ALFRED, LORD TENNYSON's "TITHONUS" in mind in his evocation of the peace that dying would bring. The garden of Proserpine is a place of such peace. Swinburne presents it as a place so subdued and so close to a narcotic unchangingness that the consciousness which experiences Proserpine's garden is at the extreme verge of its own attenuation. "Here where the world is quiet," everything that gives content to life seems only "the doubtful dream of dreams" (ll. 1, 4). The distance from earthly life is trebled: In the underworld as he imagines and longs for it, the memory of life is like the doubtful memory of a dream which itself contains a dream of life. The experience of peace and calm is one approaching the loss even of that experience.

The total loss of experience would not in itself be peaceful. What is peaceful is the never-ending easeful death that the garden promises. It is in this way that it contrasts with the gardens of Eden and Adonis, which are both environments of life. Spenser's Garden of Adonis is the place where all living things, pulsing toward birth, take on life's intense informing structures and enter into the world. And Milton's Eden is, of course, the place of creation as well as the place of sin and of the destructive doom of exile. Swinburne prefers the opposite, the metamorphosis into languor and inertness at the transitioning point where death and life are neighbors. This is, of course, characteristic of his poetry, and characteristically it takes the form of a desire to merge with the sea-mother. Proserpine is a mother figure like the sea, and the Garden of Proserpine feels as much as though it is underwater as underground. Swinburne sets himself here his perennial poetic task, which is to write a poem that does not move onward but builds up its own hypnotic resonances and conveys to both author and reader the peace that it describes.

He does this, as ever, through repetition and rhyme, as well as through content. The poem is written in 12 eight-line stanzas that rhyme *ababcccb*. Notice that the *b* and *c* rhymes are triple, lulling us even more through the repetition of the sounds, especially given the short trimeter lines. (Trimeter is three feet to the line; as usual in English poetry, the feet are iambic, but much shorter than the more or less standard iambic pentameter.) Many of the rhymes are repeated from stanza to stanza—manifestly in the repetition of *whither* (or *wither*) and *thither*, and more subtly in the large number of rhymes ending on a final *-er* sound. Swinburne's control of poetic form and music rivals Tennyson's and Spenser's, and "The Garden of Proserpine" presents a good example of that control. The hypnotic quality of the rhyme derives not only from its repletion but also from the careful distribution of feminine and masculine rhymes (as they are called). Feminine endings have an extra unstressed syllable at the end of a line; masculine endings conclude on a stressed syllable. In this poem, each stanza has exactly the same form even as regards the distribution of such endings. The *b* rhymes are all masculine, the *a*'s and *c*'s all feminine. The form, accordingly, of each stanza is *fmfmfffm*. The effect is that the more punctual masculine ending gives a sense not of finality but of fade-out. The poem attunes us to feminine endings, and even where they do not come, we feel a kind of metrical rest (like a musical one), rather than a full stop. The fact that the masculine rhymes are drawn out through their third repetition in the eighth line of each stanza contributes to this experience as well.

Spenser treats the forms in his Garden of Adonis as allegories of (among other things) poetic form. Swinburne wishes to produce a poetic form that verges on formlessness—that is, the residual form of the formless—and this is what he achieves in his repetitive rhyme and meter. Spenser's garden is all about the world of sowing and reaping that Swinburne's speaker finds shelter from in the Garden of Proserpine. He watches the green fields that Proserpine sponsors growing, but he takes no interest in the reaping and sowing that is a feature of the drive toward life. He wants to settle into sleep, and it is sleep that Proserpine offers.

The poem is essentially hypnagogic (the state we are in just as we fall asleep), or even thanatagogic (the state we are in if dying were like falling asleep). Its hypnagogic merging of all things into one can be felt in the great line "We are not sure of sorrow" (l. 73). Is that a fact about this world or the underworld? The answer is: both. In this world we cannot even hang onto sorrow as a way of defining ourselves, and in the underworld that is one of the ways we can feel the unimportance of any of the intense experiences of this world: love, hope, fear, grief. In the Garden of Proserpine, we can look forward to the fact that "Today will die to-morrow" (l. 75), a line that captures perfectly the languid sense of being on the verge of death and being able to experience death as a pleasant future that will never quite come—will only come tomorrow and never today. Swinburne sustains the moment of metamorphosis or transition, nearly as well as his great master PERCY BYSSHE SHELLEY does in his late lyrics, and he does it through the very nature of his poetic form, since the rhymes and endings are always looking forward to their own fading but not-quite-faded echoes.

BIBLIOGRAPHY

Louis, Margot Kathleen. *Swinburne and His Gods: The Roots and Growth of an Agnostic Poetry*. Kingston, Ont.: McGill-Queen's University Press, 1990.

McGann, Jerome J. *Swinburne: An Experiment in Criticism*. Chicago: University of Chicago Press, 1972.

Rutland, William R. *Swinburne: A Nineteenth Century Hellene*. Oxford: Blackwell, 1931.

"GHOST OF FADON, THE" JOANNA BAILLIE **(1821)** The story of William Wallace (d. 1305), the great Scottish hero (portrayed by Mel Gibson in the movie *Braveheart*) who was sometime friend and sometime foe of Robert the Bruce, survives in the long series of 15th-century Scottish poems written by Blind Harry. In writing a poem about an incident from Wallace's adventures, JOANNA BAILLIE is placing herself at the end of a tradition that extends from Blind Harry through, most recently, Sir WALTER SCOTT (who alluded to him frequently). Thus, in a sense she would be a direct poetic as well as biological descendant of Wallace's. Like Scott, she retells elements of Scottish legend in a consciously historical style, one which relishes the intensity and simplicity of the language and form it emulates. (WILLIAM WORDSWORTH, too, as he tells us in *The PRELUDE,* had considered devoting an epic to Wallace.)

In *Blind Harry's Wallace,* Wallace and his men have been repulsed in an attack on an English garrison, in their attempt to free Scotland from Southron (English) domination. They escape but are pursued with bloodhounds, and the English attempt to encircle them. One of Wallace's men, Faudon (spelled "Fadon" by Baillie) is malingering, attempting, it seems to Wallace, to slow them down so that they may be captured. (When Wallace was finally captured in 1305 through another betrayal, he underwent an agonizing execution at the hands of Edward I.) Wallace suddenly turns on Faudon and beheads him, using the blood to confuse the bloodhounds, and they escape to "Gask's deserted ancient hall" (l. 1), which is where Baillie's poem begins—just as Blind Harry seems to offer a kind of dream sequence.

In Blind Harry's account, there is little doubt of Faudon's guilt, but Baillie is interested in the psychological torment that Wallace undergoes. Like Wordsworth and SAMUEL TAYLOR COLERIDGE, she wants to blur the line between natural and supernatural occurrences. The supernatural may in fact be a kind of psychological fugue, or it may be the truth that sustains the natural world. At any rate, in her story, Wallace and his men are in the castle, exhausted. All they have to eat, if anything, is whatever Fadon ("yon varlet," l. 37) may have brought with him, supplied by the English.

Wallace is not sure that he did the right thing in killing Fadon. His impetuous action now appears to him in a light like that of the Ancient Mariner's killing the albatross in Coleridge's *The RIME OF THE ANCIENT MARINER*: "I needs must rue / That stroke so rashly given: / If he to us were false or true, / Is known to righteous heaven" (ll. 81–84). The men hear the noise of trumpets everywhere and search out their source. Wallace is left alone, where the reduplicated ghost of Fadon first loses his head and then seems to confront him everywhere. Wallace can only throw himself out of a window and is lost in a spell of horror, till he hears the sound of trumpets—living foes, he thinks, who would be much better than the dead. But it turns out his own men are returning, and Wallace stands relieved but also shattered, much like the mariner at the end of his journey.

What are we to make of this? Is it a guilt-induced hallucination or a real event? We might ask the same thing of the mariner's adventure and conclude that the difference may not make much of a difference. But we might say that if Fadon is real, then his treachery is confirmed, since he now shows himself in his true loyalties. But if he is a hallucination, then it is his innocence that oppresses Wallace. The moral consequences of the difference matter, and that is where the subtlety of Baillie's poem lies.

BIBLIOGRAPHY

Baillie, Joanna. *Dramatic and Poetical Works of Joanna Baillie.* London: Longman, Brown, Green, and Longmans, 1851.

Forbes, A. "'Sympathetic Curiosity' in Joanna Baillie's Theater Of The Passions." *European Romantic Review* 14, no. 1 (January 2003): 31–48.

Henry, the minstrel. *Acts and Deeds of the Most Famous and Valiant Champion Sir William Wallace, Knight of Ellerslie.* Written by Blind Harry in the year 1361. Together with Arnaldi Blair Relationes. (Edinburgh, 1758). Gale Group, *Eighteenth Century Collections Online.* Available online. URL: http://galenet.galegroup.com/servlet/ECCO. Accessed on January 5, 2008.

McMillan, Dorothy, ed. *The Scotswoman at Home and Abroad.* The Association for Scottish Literary Studies, ASLS Annual 29 (1999). Republished, Glasgow: Association for Scottish Literary Studies, 2000. (Contains excerpts from Baillie's unpublished "Memoir written to please my nephew, William Baillie," and "Recollections written for Miss Berry," both in English archives.)

Wordsworth, Jonathan. *Ancestral Voices: Fifty Books from the Romantic Period.* New York: Woodstock, 1996.

GOBLIN MARKET **CHRISTINA GEORGINA ROSSETTI (1859)** CHRISTINA ROSSETTI claimed that "Goblin Market" was extemporized in a single day. She also called it a children's poem, and for her it probably was since, like her romantic antecedents, she saw childhood as a time of unparalleled intensity and experience. Indeed if any single romantic poem can be said to be behind *Goblin Market,* it is WILLIAM WORDSWORTH's "NUTTING," also a sexualized coming-of-age poem in which intensity of feeling for nature climaxes in an unexpected sexuality which reverses into a sense of guilt and loss.

Clearly, the poem is about the experience of sexuality, and it also seems clear that the sexuality in the poem centers on same-sex eroticism. The poem is about as daring as can be imagined, and it is proto-Freudian in its evocation of dread, loss, anxiety, and sin in a context where two sisters (Lizzie and Laura) are sharing an experience of the awakening of desire. As with Freud, the stages of sexual desire go from a generalized friendship to intense and intensely singular sexual self-discovery; to its opening out into same-sex, half-individual sexual interplay between the sisters who are not one person but not quite two, either; to a more "mature" sexuality which can lead to the venerated states of marriage and motherhood. Rossetti is interested in all these stages and sees their persistence even as they develop.

The goblin men who offer Lizzie and Laura their wares offer a panoply of fruits from the tree of knowledge. Laura succumbs to their offerings, giving up (as in a ghost story) a curl of her hair for the forbidden fruits they offer. Their friend Jeanie has done this before them, with the result that she "who for joys brides hope to have / Fell sick and died / In her gay prime" (ll. 314–316). The *for* in the line is ambiguous: She may have received sickness and death instead of the joys brides hope to have (and this is the obvious reading); or it may be that she experienced the sexuality that brides hope to experience as joy as sickness and death instead. These are not necessarily mutually exclusive readings. One may be a metaphor for the other, and we can say that the awakening of sexuality transforms itself from excitement to dread—a dread that makes it the harbinger of age and death (both Jeanie before her and now Laura grow conspicuously gray as a result of eating the fruit).

The two readings of the poem—the metaphorical and the literal—would correspond to two attitudes toward the story it tells: the adult's and the child's, respectively. For the child, sexuality threatens death, real death, the utter change marked by sexuality and the adulthood it begins. Of course this is not real death from our point of view, but it is from the child's. The onset of sexuality is also the onset of the realization of mortality. When we are old enough to be sexually aware, we are old enough to understand that we will die. This is why the tree of knowledge introduces Adam and Eve to both sex and death. In "Goblin Market" the goblin men stand for both.

How much is sex worth? For Laura, as for Adam and Eve, it is worth death, but only when they do not yet know what death is. Metaphorically, from the point of view of the adult who can look back retrospectively, the intimation of mortality is the fact that the overwhelming primacy of sexual excitement is so ephemeral. The experience displaces every other experience, but only for a very brief period, and then the greatest experience of childhood—the first entry into sexuality—comes to an end, and its ending means the death of childhood and the beginning of death.

The end of the poem makes much of this clear: Lizzie and Laura are mothers now "With children of their own; / Their mother-hearts beset with fears" (ll. 545–546), and the time in which the bulk of "Goblin Market" is set is now called "Those pleasant days long gone / Of not-returning time" (ll. 550–551). So those days *were* pleasant, even in their intensity and terror. The fears of the mothers are different: less intense but far deeper. Notice that the mothers talk to the children about their own experiences—the experiences recorded in the poem. The poem is a children's poem in the same way that Laura's tales about the haunted glen and the goblin men are tales for the children. The children are being fortified against the coming loss by the knowledge that their mothers survived that loss by staying true to their own sisterhood—that is, the childhood relationship that endures beyond childhood.

It would be a mistake, however, to think the poem is only about sexuality. It is about every sort of childhood intensity, from sexuality to nature to language. The goblin men are noteworthy for their "iterated jingle" (l. 234)—that is, for the possibilities they offer in the very mode of poetry like "Goblin Market." (For other poems that metaphorize the prolixity of rhyme in fascinating ways, see the entries on ROBERT SOUTHEY's

"The CATARACT OF LODORE" and ROBERT BRIDGES's "LONDON SNOW"). Poetry arises out of a sense that the world's repetitions are ever novel and every energizing, but what makes it great—at least for the romantic tradition Rossetti is writing in—is the way it records the loss of novelty and energy in the very language which had promised so much and delivered so little. "Goblin Market" may be a children's poem, but like everything the children hear, it is sung by the goblin men, the inevitable emblems of age and death. The recompense, if there is one, is joy, love, tenderness, and fear for subsequent generations of children, and the poem's half-happy ending is one which makes it possible to reimagine the richness of the world through children who still feel it that way.

See also ROMANTICISM.

BIBLIOGRAPHY

Carpenter, Mary Wilson. "'Eat Me, Drink Me, Love Me': The Consumable Female Body in Christina Rossetti's *Goblin Market*." *Victorian Poetry* 29 (1991): 415–434.

Gilbert, Sandra M., and Susan Gubar. "The Aesthetics of Renunciation." In *The Madwoman in the Attic: The Woman Writer and the Nineteenth-Century Literary Imagination*. New Haven, Conn.: Yale University Press, 1979, 539–580.

Michie, Helena. *Sororophobia: Differences among Women*. New York: Oxford University Press, 1992.

"GOD'S GRANDEUR" GERARD MANLEY HOPKINS (1877) For GERARD MANLEY HOPKINS, as for his great predecessor, the 17th-century poet-priest George Herbert, God offered two different but correlated aspects: grandeur and love. "God's Grandeur" depicts Hopkins's characteristic focus on nature and the natural world. Although the poem does very little of the intense cataloguing of other sonnets such as "The WINDHOVER" and "PIED BEAUTY," it imagines nature in a similar way and allows two striking images to do the work of that imagination: the image of God's grandeur flaming out "like shining from shook foil" (l. 2) and that of gathering "ooze of oil / Crushed" (ll. 3–4) The world is charged with God's grandeur so that it is saturated with it. So intense is the charge that it can be felt in all its awesome suddenness at any and every moment. The idea behind the imagery of the second line is that shining itself flames out from shook foil. It is not that God shines as shook foil does, but that even the shining that shook foil makes vivid flames out, and it is therefore part of the way God's grandeur flames out. The simile becomes a synecdoche—an example of itself.

This poem should be compared to Hopkins's "BINSEY POPLARS" (written two years later), which forms a kind of pendant to it. Both poems depict human beings' depredation on nature. Indeed, the repetitions in line 5—"Generations have trod, have trod, have trod"—adumbrate the similar destructive repetition in the later poem, where the poplars are described as "All felled, felled, all are felled" (l. 3). The treading Hopkins complains of is one which reduces the world simply to predictable routine—the very opposite of grandeur. His line depicts the monotony he laments: The three *have trods* form three perfect and therefore monotonous iambs, bulking out the iambic pentameter line. They ruin the spontaneity and grandeur of poetry, just as the generations ruin the spontaneity and grandeur of the embodiment of God's grandeur, nature.

What destroys it all is the toil that is Adam's curse in the Book of Genesis ("In the sweat of thy brow shalt they labour . . ."). Humans tend too much to make that toil a vocation, or to impose it on others, instead of feeling how the world is charged with the grandeur of God. But God's grandeur consists in the fact that despite all the human insults it suffers, "nature is never spent."

This seems to be a naturalistic observation, but it is in fact the introduction of the sonnet's second theme. Nature is never spent because the Holy Ghost takes care of all of us, and nature represents that care. The coming of night to the west itself means also the recurrence of dawn in the east. This is a natural observation, but it is soon turned supernatural, as the coming of dawn is felt to be the intervention of the Holy Ghost. The Holy Ghost "broods" (as in John Milton's *Paradise Lost*) over the "bent world" (l. 13). The world is bent because we are all perverse sinners and we have so despoiled God's grandeur. The physical effect of our spoliation is a metaphor for our own "bent" condition. And still the Holy Ghost (or third person of the divine trinity, the "comforter," as Jesus calls him in the Gospel of John) bends over us as well in order to protect and solace us. His wings (the wings of the dove) turn out to be bright, spread as they are beyond the cone of night the earth casts behind itself. That unexpected brightness is the counterweight to the plodding tread upon the earth—that is, the counterweight to the monotonous poetic stance that would not understand the grandeur of God. The Holy Ghost does not so much represent God's grandeur as his life, his forgiveness for what we ignore in the grandeur. We know we ignore too much, but that knowledge sends us humbly to God in the end, and he comforts and broods over us until the next day offers a new beginning.

BIBLIOGRAPHY

Bridges, Robert. Preface to *Poems of Gerard Manley Hopkins.* Edited with additional poems, notes, and a biographical introduction by W. H. Gardner. New York: Oxford University Press, 1948.

Gardner, W. H. *Gerard Manley Hopkins (1844–1889): A Study of Poetic Idiosyncrasy in Relation to Poetic Tradition.* New Haven, Conn.: Yale University Press, 1949.

———. Introduction to *Poems and Prose of Gerard Manley Hopkins.* Harmondsworth, Middlesex, England: Penguin, 1963.

Hartman, Geoffrey. *The Unmediated Vision: An Interpretation of Wordsworth, Hopkins, Rilke, and Valery.* New Haven, Conn.: Yale University Press, 1954.

Hopkins, Gerard Manley. *Gerard Manley Hopkins: Selected Letters.* Edited by Catherine Phillips. New York: Oxford University Press, 1990.

Miller, J. Hillis. "Gerard Manley Hopkins." In *The Disappearance of God: Five Nineteenth-Century Writers,* 270–359. Cambridge, Mass.: Belknap Press of Harvard University Press, 1963.

White, Norman. *Hopkins: A Literary Biography.* New York: Oxford University Press, 1992.

"GOD'S JUDGMENT ON A WICKED BISHOP" **ROBERT SOUTHEY (1799)** This is one of ROBERT SOUTHEY's most anthologized pieces, and it was a major influence on ROBERT BROWNING's "The Pied Piper of Hamelin," which has pretty completely replaced it in the popular imagination. Browning's poem depicts a perennial myth, an implacable army of rats taking revenge against evildoers. Both stories are originally medieval and associated with Norse myths; indeed, the Pied Piper has been seen as an avatar of the god Odin. The story Southey based this poem on is about the origin of the name of the Mouse Tower at Bingen, Germany, on the Rhine River. He found it in *Coryat's Crudities,* the strange and fascinating travel book published by the English traveler Thomas Coryat originally in 1611 and reprinted in 1776.

Southey's poem belongs to the large set of "ballads and metrical tales" that he later collected as "the desultory productions of a man sedulously employed upon better things," but even then he had to acknowledge that these poems were in fact the ones that "pleased those readers whom the author was most desirous of pleasing." "God's Judgment" is typical of many of those ballads in the combination of a kind of rollicking grimness with a moral that justifies it, and it vindicates the readers who take pleasure in it.

The bishop of Hatto (891–913) was notorious for his indifference to the poor; however, the story of the mice or rats who took their revenge upon him is several centuries later. As in the original Pied Piper story, the rats are a kind of uncanny return of the souls of the poor, now turned into an implacable revenging army. Southey, like his close friend and brother-in-law SAMUEL TAYLOR COLERIDGE, has a sure sense of the form of the gothic ballad. The harvest has failed, and the rich bishop has no desire to grant his grain to the poor. He burns them alive instead, grotesquely comparing them to rats whose raids on the grain have now been stopped.

Southey follows the gothic model in describing the consequences of Hatto's action from his own point of view. After he kills the poor, we want to see him punished: What makes the poem effective is that we vicariously experience the horror that overwhelms him. We do not recognize or identify with the rats but with the human they attack, and yet we feel vindicated in his punishment.

Probably the best moment of the poem is the bishop's horror the next morning, when he sees the rats have eaten his own portrait out of its frame. It is fascinating that Southey has him recognize, before we do, the danger he is in and the mode that revenge will take. He attempts to escape a fate that we do not yet quite know but will discover when he fails to do so. The attack of the rats is as inevitable as it is surprising, and the ballad communicates its inexorablity with great skill and strange gusto.

BIBLIOGRAPHY

Brewer, Ebenezer Cobham. *Brewer's Dictionary of Phrase and Fable,* s.v. "Hatto." New York: Harper and Row, 1989.

Bromwich, David. "Of the Mule Breed." *London Review of Books* (May 21, 1998):

Butler, Marilyn. *Romantics, Rebels, and Reactionaries: English Literature and Its Background, 1760–1830.* New York: Oxford University Press, 1982.

Coryat, Thomas. *Coryat's Crudities: Reprinted from the Edition of 1611. To Which Are Now Added, His Letters from India, &c. and Extracts Relating to Him, from Various Authors: Being a More Particular Account of His Travels (Mostly on Foot) . . . Than Any Hitherto Published.* London: W. Cater [etc., etc.], 1776.

De Quincey, Thomas. *Recollections of the Lakes and the Lake Poets.* Edited by David Wright. Harmondsworth, England: Penguin, 1970.

Guerber, H. A. *Myths of Northern Lands: Narrated with Special Reference to Literature and Art.* New York: American Book Co., 1895.

Hazlitt, William. *Spirit of the Age; or, Contemporary Portraits.* London: Oxford University Press, 1970.

Perry, Seamus. "Southey's Genius for Repression," *London Review of Books* (January 24, 2006):

Storey, Mark. *Robert Southey: A Life.* New York: Oxford University Press, 1997.

"GONE IN THE WIND" JAMES CLARENCE MANGAN (1842) This beautiful poem of despairing wisdom purports to be (in its last stanza) the work of one "Abul-Namez," presumably translated by JOHN CLARENCE MANGAN for the *Dublin University Magazine.* Of course, the attribution is not to be taken seriously; indeed, the author's putative name might be a kind of Irish French for "Name him Abul," or possibly "Son of the Name," perhaps with some hint of the joke called an Irish Bull. But the poem is more serious than its humorously deflating signature. It is not a translation but rather an imitation of a Persian mode, and it might be technically described as a *ghazal.* (For another example of a ghazal in English, see ALFRED, LORD TENNYSON's slightly later "NOW SLEEPS THE CRIMSON PETAL, NOW THE WHITE.") In Persian poetry (and in the Arabic and Urdu poetry it influenced), the *ghazal* is a form written in rhymed couplets, with the second line of each couplet ending with the same repeated rhyme word. The last line is supposed to contain the name of the author (which Tennyson did not do, but which this poem supposedly does).

"Gone in the Wind" is a *ghazal* despite being written in quatrains because each *pair* of lines can be counted as one single, long line. The rhymes still work, and this is because, like a kind of double-*ghazal,* there is only one rhyme in the poem—the rhyme on the word *wind.* Mangan finds 16 different rhymes for wind (a possible 17th might be derived from the one repetition, since *blind* is used once as a noun and once as an adjective). Technically, the poem is extraordinary, its form being essential to the struggle with formlessness that it retells.

The poem itemizes all that has been lost with the wind ("gone with the wind" is how ERNEST DOWSON may remember this in his version of this *ubi sunt* theme), from the throne of Solomon to the latest pleasures of ordinary life. Where are the snows of yesteryear? Even the poem that records the passing of all things swept away by the great wind of time will not last. For the poem itself cannot last any more than any other glory—Solomon's or Babylon's: ". . . the garlands I bind / (Garlands of song) are but gathered, and—strewn in the wind" (ll. 31–32).

Note the deep hilarity of Mangan's wit, characteristic of his poetry. The garlands of song are bound by the parenthesis that protects them from the rush of chaos, but the interrupting dash of the very same line makes of them what it does of everything: disorder and oblivion.

We could say, therefore, that the form is not only characteristic of a certain style of melancholy distance, the Persian poem standing as an entirely decontextualized fragment for an Irish audience. It also represents an attempt to establish a bulwark against the chaotic motion that cannot be halted. The repeated rhymes are a kind of resistance to the winds of time, as though the poem could bind the garlands by the harmonies of its reiterated rhyme as well. But of course it cannot, and what will inevitably triumph is the thing that every end word in the poem rhymes with, the wind itself. All that will be left of "Abul-Namez" is his empty name, and the words that name that emptiness.

BIBLIOGRAPHY
Joyce, James. "James Clarence Mangan." In *Occasional, Critical, and Political Writing*, 55–60. Oxford: Oxford University Press, 2001.
Lennard, John. *But I Digress: Parentheses in English Printed Verse*. New York: Oxford University Press, 1991.
Shannon-Mangan, Ellen. *James Clarence Mangan: A Biography*. Dublin: Irish Academic Press, 1996.
Yeats, William Butler. *Uncollected Prose*. Vol. 1. Edited by John P. Frayne. London: Macmillan, 1970–75.

"GOOD NIGHT" See "SONG (GOOD NIGHT)"

"GOSSIPPING" LETITIA ELIZABETH LANDON (1841) LETITIA ELIZABETH LANDON was at her best in the short blank-verse poems published posthumously after her (probable) suicide in 1838. The object of much attention as a poet, she became as well the subject of notoriety, scandal, and vicious gossip, especially regarding her amorous adventures. The gossip may have exaggerated their extent, asserting as factual some things that were possibly only a kind of intellectual flirtation, although recent evidence has shown that much of it was certainly true. In poems such as "Gossipping" and "The MARRIAGE VOW," Landon speaks with a kind of controlled fury about the murderous pressures she feels in her own life. In some sense she is talking to herself, but she is externalizing that talk into blank-verse strictures on the viciousness of the situations described.

Landon learned this mode, as so many of her other modes, from WILLIAM WORDSWORTH. "Gossipping" owes much in its form and tone to the blank-verse fragments (some, it would later transpire, drawn from *The PRELUDE*) that Wordsworth published as intensely focused observations in his various volumes of collected poetry. "Gossipping" has a deceptive title, although the deception is perhaps more ours than an intended reader's since it is not clear that there *is* an intended reader besides Landon herself for the poem. Literature generally refers to gossip as a more or less harmless pastime, a way for people to interact with each other through a shared interest in the same social world that the writer is depicting. Real-life gossip is different, and Landon is original in her insistence on the destruction that real-life gossip can cause: "Alas the misery that such inflict" (l. 7). (In this she is somewhat like WILLIAM MAKEPEACE THACKERAY in his novel *Vanity Fair*.)

The "spiders of society" (l. 1) are the gossips themselves, "who delight in the ingenious torments they contrive" (l. 11). The poem's conceit is to describe gossip as a spider's web in which one finds oneself trapped. The web is that of social interaction ("networking" we would now say, and Landon would appreciate the idiom). Once caught in the net, its victims find themselves unable to extricate either their reputations or their lives.

The conceit is a reasonably powerful one, but its originality transcends the somewhat obvious idea that one can be trapped and tormented in the web of gossip. It allows for the ambiguity of the observation "A word, a look, have power to wring the heart" (l. 8), in which it may be that the gossips exchange words and looks with each other, or that gossip elicits, from those who have heard it, words or looks at the victim, who realizes what other people are thinking. Those words may be full of empathy and pity and so may wring the heart through their tenderness as much as in the other reading through their cruelty. The difference—this is Landon's grim disclosure—does not matter.

But there is one even subtler feature of the poem: the description of the beauty of the web glittering in the sun (l. 4). Spider webs are beautiful in the sun when covered with dew, but they work only when they are invisible. As Landon knew, they are not supposed to lure because they are not supposed to be seen. But she suggests that she *was* lured by the web, attracted by its beauty.

How so? The poem shows considerable self-knowledge on her part. Whatever dalliances she entered into she knew were risky. Perhaps she also saw benefits to her reputation too. To be known as beautiful, alluring, and sexy was also to court publicity. She was attracted to the web, she suggests, because she thought the gossip would benefit her. She might also have flirted with false gossip to draw attention away from the truth of her relation with her patron, editor, and lover, William Jerden. Once she discovered that she could not master the web she was caught and rolled around in, it was too late to do anything about it except, finally, to be destroyed.

BIBLIOGRAPHY

Greer, Germaine. *Slip-Shod Sibyls: Recognition, Rejection and the Woman Poet.* London: Viking, 1995.

Lawford, Cynthia. "Diary." *London Review of Books* (September 21, 2000). Available online. URL: http://www.lrb.co.uk/v22/n18/lawf01_/html. Accessed on March 29, 2008.

———. "'Thou shalt bid thy fair hands rove': L. E. L.'s Wooing of Sex, Pain, Death and the Editor." *Romanticism on the Net* 29–30 (February–May 2003). Available online. URL: http://www.erudit.org/revue/ron/2003/v/n29/007718ar.html. Accessed on March 30, 2008.

Mellor, Anne K. "Exhausting the Beautiful." In *Romanticism and Gender,* 107–143. New York: Routledge, 1993.

GREENWELL, DORA (1821–1882) Born in Greenwell Ford, northern England, on December 6, 1821, Dora Greenwell was an early Victorian feminist, probably a lesbian although her sexual desires were highly sublimated and took the form of passionate and devoted friendships with other women. She was equally devoted to God, whom she saw as the kindest of fathers comforting her for her reluctance regarding erotic life. Her best-remembered poetry is devotional, sometimes to her friends but always to God. Her mode is similar to that of her Anglican poetic forebear George Herbert (1593–1633). One of her poems became part of the Methodist hymnbook.

Her disposition toward shyness did not make Greenwell any less fierce in her writing or her agitation for social reform. Her father's bankruptcy in 1847 tutored her in hardship. She became a schoolmistress in order to aid the family and also began to publish poetry and write both political and theological essays. After her father's death in 1854, Greenwell and her mother returned to Durham, where she had been born. She was to live with her mother until the latter's death 17 years later (when Greenwell was 50). She numbered among her close friends CHRISTINA ROSSETTI and the social reformer and feminist Josephine Butler. She worked with the poor and with prisoners and wrote feminist essays advocating women's suffrage. Her 1864 essay "Our Single Women" is the most famous of these, slyly resisting the "angel in the house" concept of women's duty as devotion to married love that would become so associated with COVENTRY PATMORE. In this essay, Greenwell seems to concede male superiority but suggests that women will be more and more necessary to the great project of social reform, and that single women can do for society what hitherto married women have been expected to do for the home.

After her mother died, in 1871 Greenwell moved to London to be near her brothers, and she continued to write poetry and to publish both essays and biographies. Her reformist positions, her religious fervor, and her aesthetic stances are all aspects of the same extraordinary capacity for introspective intensity. She understood, one might say, shyness on a metaphysical level (see "A SCHERZO [A SHY PERSON'S WISHES]," which describes all the depths on which one might never guess a shy person meditates). The poor and outcast, the imbecile, the unmarried—all of these were avatars of shyness, of a relationship to the world that was hesitant, fearful, and too often ignored. But Greenwell thought God did not ignore the shy and thought that the lesson of religion was to imitate God in this attention and care for them, and in one way or another she devoted her extraordinary talents to such care. This devotion would perhaps include her attention to poets such as ELIZABETH BARRETT BROWNING, 15 years her senior, whom she met once but whose poetry was of extraordinary importance to her (see "TO ELIZABETH BARRETT BROWNING" AND "TO ELIZABETH BARRETT BROWNING IN 1861"). For Greenwell, Barrett was not a shy outcast but one who was devoted to the shy and outcast and could make their lives better even if they knew her only through her poetry. Greenwell was on both ends of this experience and knew its importance and depth.

BIBLIOGRAPHY

Chase, Karen. *The Spectacle of Intimacy: A Public Life for the Victorian Family.* Princeton, N.J.: Princeton University Press, 2000.

Cunningham, Valentine, ed. Note on Dora (Dorothy) Greenwell. In *The Victorians: An Anthology of Poetry & Poetics,* 518–519. Malden, Mass.: Blackwell, 2000.

Dorling, William. *Memoirs of Dora Greenwell.* London: J. Clarke, 1885.

Mason, Emma. *Women Poets of the Nineteenth Century.* Tavistock, Devon, England: Northcote House Publishers, 2006.

"GROWING OLD" MATTHEW ARNOLD (1867)

MATTHEW ARNOLD published this poem when he was 45, though it was probably written two or three years before that. He was certainly not old yet, but obviously old enough to be anticipating the experience. The poem is in seven stanzas, fierce but conversational at the same time, in a strict blank-verse form, alternating iambic trimeters with pentameters. The alternation allows for a kind of internal dialogue, with both sides converging on the same grim conclusion; the effect is a little bit like that of Sapphic stanzas, which Arnold may be very loosely adopting and adapting. The seven stanzas correspond very vaguely to the famous "seven ages of man" speech from William Shakespeare's *As You Like It* (2.7), a correspondence we only notice at the beginning of the seventh stanza, with its reference to the "last stage of all" of human life.

The poem is a controlled exposition of subjective experience—that of growing old. Its rhetorical questions, and the answers that they sometimes evoke, get progressively grimmer in the course of the poem. The exposition is powerful because it offers a truth that a young and therefore ideal reader could never have imagined. Such a reader would think of old age as like his or her own experience but in a different, weaker body. The youth conceives of old age as a kind of permanent masquerade. Arnold acknowledges this aspect of old age in the first stanza, where he describes old age as a loss of beauty, but the second stanza begins his powerful refutation of the youthful idea of old age. There the contrast between strength and bloom is one that the younger Arnold could never have expected since he could have no idea, when he "dreamed" (l. 12) of old age, what it would be like to feel "strength decay" (l. 7). We thought we would only lose the bloom of youth, but we lose far more than that. Does he remember what he expected in his youth when he corrects the misapprehension that we would lose only the bloom? Or is this an imaginary youth—a youth distorted by old age's imagination of it, just as old age is distorted by youth's anticipation? There is no perspective from which to answer this question. But the power of the second stanza consists in the fact that there need be no such perspective. The experience of old age is a perpetual shock that it is not youth, not even something that can imagine itself as a version of youth.

The grimness of the poem is palpable in the third stanza's echo of Macbeth's complaint that "My way of life / Is fall'n into the sear, the yellow leaf / And that which should accompany old age, / As honour, love, obedience, troops of friends, / I must not look to have" (*Macbeth,* 5.3). Arnold no more than Macbeth can look to have an ideal and happy old age (the old age that ROBERT BROWNING had celebrated in "Rabbi Ben Ezra," to which this poem may be seen as a kind of response.)

One may hope, a hope blasted in the fourth stanza, for the sight of meaningfulness that Moses was given of the Promised Land before he died (in the Bible's Book of Deuteronomy), but we don't in fact feel "The years that are no more." Having refuted Browning in the previous stanza, here Arnold refers to the refrain in ALFRED, LORD TENNYSON'S "TEARS, IDLE TEARS," where "the years that are no more" lend intensity to the present.

All this grim description reaches a climax in the sixth stanza, where it almost feels as though the ferocity of complaint will lead to the very emotion that the stanza reports is absent. That stanza's plain pessimism is one of the greatest things Arnold ever did. The account of the empty festering of remembrance, without any emotion attached to that memory, sounds absolutely true and absolutely without self-pity.

Had the poem ended here, it might have been near perfect. It would not have been *quite* perfect, however, since the last line of the stanza would have sounded too melodramatic as the last line of the poem. Accordingly, Arnold added one more stanza, but this actual last stanza blights the poem. He complains of the world's approval of the old and desiccated man and its disapproval of the living youth. The complaint may be legitimate enough, but it is a pat irony with which to end this grim and lucid poem, and it does contain an element of self-pity. He blames the world for the experience of old age, but it is no one's fault but time's or God's. It would be easier to blame the world, because then the grim conclusion might not be felt to be a necessary one. But it is—this is what the first six stanzas make us feel—and while we can understand and even excuse the last stanza, we cannot embrace it.

BIBLIOGRAPHY

Arnold, Matthew. *Essays, Letters, and Reviews.* Collected and edited by Fraser Neiman. Cambridge, Mass.: Harvard University Press, 1960.

Bloom, Harold, ed. *Matthew Arnold.* New York: Chelsea House, 1987.

Dawson, Carl, and John Pfordresher, eds. *Matthew Arnold: The Critical Heritage.* New York: Routledge, 1995.

Trilling, Lionel. *The Moral Obligation to Be Intelligent: Selected Essays.* Edited by Leon Weiseltier. New York: Farrar, Straus, and Giroux, 2000.

H

HALLAM, ARTHUR HENRY (1811–1833)

It is conventional to say (as, for example, Valentine Cunningham does in his headnote on Arthur Henry Hallam in *The Victorians: An Anthology of Poetry & Poetics,* which he edited) that the most important single event for Victorian poetry was the sudden death of Arthur Henry Hallam of a cerebral aneurysm in Vienna on September 15, 1833, while traveling through Europe with his father. ALFRED, LORD TENNYSON, his best friend, heard of his death a few weeks later, and the prolonged mourning and sorrow for Hallam formed the basis of Tennyson's greatest work, the book-long elegy *IN MEMORIAM A.H.H.* as well as Tennyson's obsessive interest in Arthurian legend—one Arthur prefiguring and standing in for another—and such poems as "TITHONUS" and "ULYSSES," which Tennyson said he wrote while mourning Hallam's death even more deeply than in *In Memoriam.*

Hallam was a younger contemporary of Tennyson's at Cambridge University. He was generally thought of as the most brilliant mind of his generation (and his talk helped form the lifelong political views of his classmate, the future Whig prime minister William Henry Gladstone); as an undergraduate, he wrote poetry that is still impressive for its descriptive power and (in the sonnets) elegance of phrasing and construction. More important than his poetry, though, were his poetic views. He began as a disciple of LORD BYRON but became converted to PERCY BYSSHE SHELLEY and JOHN KEATS, and at last to the still-living WILLIAM WORDSWORTH. His poetic ideas affected and supported Tennyson's own as a poet. In particular, Hallam's championing of Keats helped Tennyson feel justified in his own highly Keatsian early poetry. Hallam and Tennyson, like a latter-day Wordsworth and SAMUEL TAYLOR COLERIDGE, were going to publish a book of poems together, but Hallam's father (a notable Whig historian) forbade it; so Tennyson published his own book, which Hallam reviewed in a long and interesting article, once again helping to promote the taste by which Tennyson would be judged.

Hallam was in love with Tennyson's sister and engaged to be married to her (so that both could look forward to a completed domestic sphere). His early death was therefore disastrous not only for his elegist but for the whole Tennyson family. It is this more general disaster that allows *In Memoriam* its sense of both general grief and the acknowledgment by the mourner that he is not alone in the world in feeling grief for the death of his friend, and that the other grievers are also people to love and to engage.

See also "SCENE IN SUMMER, A."

BIBLIOGRAPHY

Cunningham, Valentine, ed. *The Victorians: An Anthology of Poetry & Poetics.* Malden, Mass.: Blackwell, 2000.

Gladstone, William. *Arthur Henry Hallam.* Boston: P. Mason and Co., 1898.

Hallam, Arthur Henry. *The Love Story of 'In Memoriam': Letters from Arthur Hallam to Emily Tennyson*. London: Eyre and Spottiswoode, 1916.

———. *The Poems of Arthur Henry Hallam: Together with His Essay on the Lyrical Poems of Alfred Tennyson*. Edited by Richard Le Gallienne. New York: Macmillan and Co., 1893.

HARDY, THOMAS (1840–1928) It is as a novelist that Hardy is mostly remembered today, but he was also one of the most significant of the late Victorian and early modern poets. Poetry was always Hardy's first literary vocation, and he turned to fiction first of all to support himself (preferring fiction to the architecture he had been trained for and had practiced creditably). The distinction between his novelistic writing and his poetry is in one sense vivid but in another minimal. Hardy's novels are (as he said) influenced by a poetic tradition that he learned from GEORGE CRABBE and WILLIAM WORDSWORTH. Crabbe's rural tales gave him a sense of what he could do in fiction and also showed how poetry and a realistic depiction of the lives of the rural poor could go together, a lesson also taught by Wordsworth (whose work influenced so many of the descriptive passages of the Victorian novelists, especially GEORGE ELIOT's and Hardy's).

If Hardy's novels respond to the possibilities of a counter-lyrical tradition in English poetry, his poems are often stunningly, powerfully, and intentionally prosaic (here, too, he follows in Crabbe's footsteps). We can say they are prosaic because Hardy was not in love with nature and therefore not in love with a style that clothed nature in a beauty in which he did not believe. Like so many of his Victorian contemporaries (in particular ALFRED, LORD TENNYSON and ROBERT BROWNING), Hardy had learned from the new geology (which he understood intimately as an architect and as the son of a stone cutter, knowledge importantly thematized in two novels, *Jude the Obscure* [1895] and *A Pair of Blue Eyes* [1873]) and from Charles Darwin's *On the Origin of Species* (which came out just when Hardy was turning 19) that nature was not the benevolent mother figure that it was so often a comfort to imagine. A poem like "Nature's Questioning" (published in 1898 and, Hardy remarked, often quoted against him) shows him feeling questioned about the nature of God by the "dull, constrained, and worn" faces of natural objects. He has no answer as to why they all live in a world of pain, but considers that God may be an imbecile, or dying, or pursuing a plan indifferent to the sufferings of the living pawns who are part of his strategy, or that we may come "of an Automaton / Unconscious of our pains," which would make God and natural selection two names for the same blind workings out of the laws of nature. In 1888, when asked by the Reverend A. B. Grosart how to reconcile the hideous violence to be beheld in nature with the idea of an omnipotent and good God, Hardy replied: "Mr. Hardy regrets that he is unable to suggest any hypothesis which would reconcile the existence of such evils as Dr. Grosart describes with the idea of omnipotent goodness," and he referred Grosart to the works of Darwin and to such contemporary evolutionists as Herbert Spencer (who coined the term *survival of the fittest*).

"Nature's Questioning," while a grim poem, is not completely nihilistic. While Hardy had no use for God, he did have a use for others, for fellow sufferers of God's indifference or imbecility or death or nonexistence—the questioners who asked him about why they found themselves in this world of woe. This means that Hardy did personify nature, or maybe it would be better to say that Hardy accepted that the world he lived in was one that was *given* to him, but not by a benevolent God. There is consciousness in the world, and therefore experience and suffering; and there are sufferers in the world. In a retrospective poem written when he was 86 Hardy ventriloquized nature as saying to him as a child what she had repeated ever since: "I do not promise overmuch / Child; overmuch; / Just neutral tinted haps and such." In the poem, she tells him that many have loved her desperately (and here Hardy may be thinking of Wordsworth), while others have loved her with serenity and others have shown her contempt—it does not matter which, since everyone dies. We might be able to sum up Hardy's poetic vocation as the simultaneous sense that in the end nothing matters, but that this is a fact that matters to all living beings, all fellow sufferers.

Hardy had been writing poetry since the 1860s, but he did not publish his first volume, *Wessex Poems,* until 1898, after he had given up writing novels. His second volume appeared in 1901, and his last (and perhaps best) was the posthumous *Winter Words.* Those poems, at their considerable and frequent best, are unflinching in their portrayal of natural suffering, both physical and psychological, and in their sense that poetry matters, not because it cures affliction but because it is part of the mutual communication among fellow sufferers.

See also "DARKLING THRUSH, THE"; "LAST SIGNAL, THE"; "NEUTRAL TONES."

BIBLIOGRAPHY

Bloom, Harold, ed. *Thomas Hardy.* New York: Chelsea House, 1987.

Clements, Patricia, and Juliet Grindle, eds. *Poetry of Thomas Hardy.* London: Vision Press, 1980.

Ebbatson, Roger. *The Evolutionary Self: Hardy, Forster, Lawrence.* Totowa, N.J.: Barnes and Noble, 1982.

Hardy, Thomas. *Thomas Hardy's Personal Writings: Prefaces, Literary Opinions, Reminiscences.* Edited by Harold Orel. London: Macmillan, 1990.

Kramer, Dale, ed. *Cambridge Companion to Thomas Hardy.* New York: Cambridge University Press, 1999.

Sherman, G. W. *The Pessimism of Thomas Hardy.* Rutherford, N.J.: Fairleigh Dickinson University Press, 1976.

Stevenson, Lionel. *Darwin among the Poets.* Chicago: University of Chicago Press, 1932.

"HARP THAT ONCE THROUGH TARA'S HALLS, THE" THOMAS MOORE (1834) This is probably THOMAS MOORE's most famous song today. Moore wrote in Sir WALTER SCOTT's mode, and like Scott, Moore's writing was more nostalgic than politically agitating. But Irish political discourse is highly literary and highly attuned to a nostalgia for Irish freedom—for the "language of the outlaw," including the outlaw's literary language, as the novelist James Joyce had a character in *Ulysses* (1922) put it—and so the nostalgia that was largely (though not entirely) aesthetic in Scottish literature by the beginning of the 19th century was (and would be through WILLIAM BUTLER YEATS, Joyce, and beyond) still perceived by the English as dangerous in Irish literature. (Joyce loved Moore, both for his words and for his music.) Indeed, Moore had been an associate of the United Irishmen, in particular of Robert Emmett, his contemporary at Trinity College, Dublin, which had only recently begun allowing Catholics like them to attend. He was ambivalent enough about their attempted rebellion that he escaped their disastrous fate. But he alluded to Emmet's last words—"Let no man write my epitaph" (Emmet was executed in 1803)—in his 1808 song about Emmet, "Oh! Breathe not his name." There he says that the Irish weep in secret over their lost leader, and that their weeping "shall keep his memory green in our souls."

"The Harp that once through Tara's Halls" was therefore perceived as a dangerous song to the British rule of Ireland. Despite the fact that Moore himself was a genial and successful member of English society, his early commitment to Irish freedom remained. The hill of Tara was the ancient seat of the kings of Ireland before English conquest. It was the abode of the Irish gods (like Mount Olympus in Greek mythology) and the place where Saint Patrick converted the Irish to the Catholicism the English would attempt to suppress. Now, under English domination, the harp of the ancient Irish bards hangs mute, just as the ancient Scottish harp hangs mute in the opening of Scott's *The Lady of the Lake.* Those days are over, and to suppress Ireland's poets is to suppress Ireland's spirit, which is essentially that of its ancient bards.

The poem holds out hope, though, since the harp is silent but not broken. (In fact, Irish harpers were still playing in Belfast, but at the end of the 18th century Irish Catholic poets began writing in English, and poets such as Moore knew the melodies but not the language of the Irish poets.) Occasionally at night a sob ("throb," l. 14) may be heard from it, to show that Freedom still lives even if at present she wakes seldom. That sob may come from the wind—the harp is perhaps a version of the AEOLIAN HARP, as it is in Scott—or it may come from some secret resisting musician who dares to play a chord and only a chord. The latter possibility would refer to the poem itself—that is, to Moore himself. He is the inheritor of the great tradition, attenuated to these poor Irish melodies. But they do show, even in their attenuation, the indignity and sorrow that has befallen Ireland, and they preserve the bare possibility that Ireland's great poets will rise again. Yeats will be one of them, and we may say that the Tories were right to fear Moore since his example would eventually lead to the Irish literary revival of which Yeats was so luminous a light.

BIBLIOGRAPHY

Colum, Padraic. Introduction to *Anthology of Irish Verse*, 3–20. New York: Boni and Liveright, 1922.

Nolan, Emer. *Catholic Emancipations: Irish Fiction from Thomas Moore to James Joyce*. Syracuse, N.Y.: Syracuse University Press, 2007.

Schirmer, Gregory A. *Out of What Began: A History of Irish Poetry in English*. Ithaca, N.Y.: Cornell University Press, 1998.

White, Terence De Vere. *Tom Moore: The Irish Poet*. London: Hamilton, 1977.

"HAWORTH CHURCHYARD" MATTHEW ARNOLD (1855) Haworth Churchyard is where Anne, Charlotte, and EMILY BRONTË are buried. On December 21, 1850, Arnold had met Charlotte Brontë at the house of his friend Edward Quillinan in Ambleside in the Lake District, where she had come with the novelist Harriet Martineau, with whom she was staying. (Brontë thought his religious opinions were vague and unsettled.) Quillinan, "Wordsworth's son-in-law" (l. 6), died the next year, and Arnold wrote an elegy for him (collected in the same 1885 volume as this poem). When Martineau lay ill in 1855, Arnold composed "Haworth Churchyard" as a tribute to her and as an elegy for all the Brontë sisters. Emily and Anne had died almost unknown in 1848 and 1849, respectively, but Charlotte had achieved great fame before she succumbed on March 31, 1855.

From antiquity on, and in English from John Milton's "Lycidas" to ALFRED, LORD TENNYSON's contemporaneous *IN MEMORIAM A.H.H.*, elegy is a mode of poetic self-reflection. The poet sees in the death of other poets a portent of his or her own death. Death provides the material but also foreshadows the failure of poetry. To be a poet is to aspire to immortality, and the elegist seeks immortality through the elegy itself. But the elegy by which the poet announces his or her presence is also an acknowledgement that such a wish is vain. In attempting to come to grips with the death of another poet, elegists also struggle with their own mortality and the use or meaning of the poetry they write.

Arnold's elegy is dactylic—that is, it is written in the meter that the classical elegists used. It is a difficult and somewhat unnatural meter in English, but that means it can have the tone of pained and melancholy stateliness, as it does here. It is saturated with death: the death of all those who were alive four years earlier—Quillinan, his father-in-law WILLIAM WORDSWORTH (who died in early 1850), and Brontë—and the still living but now ailing Martineau. Quillinan's house had been the place of repair for many other poets, including the dying Sir WALTER SCOTT (l. 23), who wrote some lines in the visitor's album there; Wordsworth described the scene very movingly in a note to his poem "Yarrow Revisited." Four years ago, nevertheless, the house was a place of hope. But now all is changed, and the last of the Brontë children is dead.

After the tribute to Martineau, Arnold turns to the north in Haworth. The grim recognition is that Charlotte Brontë is unlike Harriet Martineau since she cannot hear or register his lamentation; she is dead. But he imagines her sisters greeting her in the grave, an idea he must derive from Emily Brontë's *Wuthering Heights* (1847), since it is in the grave that Heathcliff and Catherine finally reunite. The thought leads to Arnold's extraordinary encomium on Emily as the most fiery and passionate writer since LORD BYRON, and in particular his response to what Charlotte said was Emily's last poem, "NO COWARD SOUL IS MINE," which stirred his soul like a trumpet calling to battle.

Arnold followed this poem with an epilogue, in which the Muse rebukes him and says that the quiet he wished for the Brontës will never be theirs. They will be "Unquiet souls" (epilogue, l. 10), suffering the "unquiet slumbers" that Emily Brontë spares Catherine and Heathcliff, "the sleepers in that quiet earth," at the end of *Wuthering Heights*. They will be part of the endless fermentation of life and death. Note that the Muse's rebuke is a *recovery* and a gain for both the living and the dead: The dead will not be reduced to inert matter, and now he knows that the Muse hears him, and comes, and corrects him, which is just what he wants as a poet.

BIBLIOGRAPHY
Arnold, Matthew. *Essays, Letters, and Reviews.* Collected and edited by Fraser Neiman. Cambridge, Mass.: Harvard University Press, 1960.
Bloom, Harold, ed. *Matthew Arnold.* New York: Chelsea House, 1987.
Dawson, Carl, and John Pfordresher, eds. *Matthew Arnold: The Critical Heritage.* New York: Routledge, 1995.
Trilling, Lionel. *The Moral Obligation to Be Intelligent: Selected Essays.* Edited by Leon Weiseltier. New York: Farrar, Straus, and Giroux, 2000.

"HAYSTACK IN THE FLOODS, THE"

WILLIAM MORRIS (1858) WILLIAM MORRIS's 1858 volume *The Defence of Guinevere* contains some of the most austerely powerful poems of the entire Victorian era (see VICTORIAN POETRY). "The Haystack in the Floods" is probably the best-known of these poems, and with good reason. Especially in the context of the resurgent near-medieval violence in many parts of the 21st-century world, it is striking to see a 19th-century poem examine that violence with as much severe lucidity as Morris achieves here. His narrative style in this poem is what will come to be known as hard-boiled, anticipating no one so much as the 20th-century American crime writer Dashiell Hammett (author of *The Maltese Falcon*).

"The Haystack in the Floods" contradicts any notion that the Pre-Raphaelite obsession with the way medieval art represented the world shows nostalgia for some more gorgeous and relation to detail. The detail in this poem is all very grim and underscores the persistent refusal of the brute material facts in the world to cohere into some order or meaning beyond themselves.

The poem narrates an invented, fictional account of the death of Robert de Marny, a real knight who was part of the English-Gascon army that defeated the French at the battle of Poitiers on September 19, 1356, one of the major battles of the Hundred Years' War. (The fact that the Gascons and English were allies explains the reference in line 47 to the safety to be found beyond the Gascon frontier.) Robert was from Marny, in Essex, England; accordingly, his battle cry is "St. George for Marny" (l. 61). But of his real death nothing is known; even less was known when Morris enlisted him for the poem, since Morris may have thought it possible he died in 1356, which we now know he did not.

Morris opens the poem from the point of view of Robert's beloved French mistress Jehane, who is traveling with de Marny and his men through hostile country in order to return to the safety of Gascony (in southwest France). They are nearly there when they come upon Godmar, who, because his castle is near the Gascon frontier, had thought it expedient to declare allegiance to the English forces. But he has apparently betrayed them since, probably in the battle of Poitiers from which he has escaped with a squad of 30 of his men. Both Jehane and Godmar are fictional.

The breathtaking power of the poem derives partly from its detached and elliptical style and partly from the fact that it is from Jehane's point of view. The first line is an example of free indirect style, of the sort that novelists were practicing more and more frequently in the 19th century—for example, Jane Austen and HENRY MAKEPEACE THACKERAY. The question that opens the poem is Jehane's question. Its understatement is its power, and the rest of the poem will explain the reasons for an understatement that we do not yet quite perceive. All we know is that Jehane and her lover must part, and without even the farewell that might give the parting a meaningful aspect. It is true that we know Robert is slain from the fourth line, but not that he is slain in battle, nor indeed that the two of them are not alone.

We find out that Jehane has ridden through the rain and muck with de Marny, sitting her horse astride like a male rider (and not sidesaddle, as women still rode in the 19th century). She is weeping as they ride (l. 14), but we find this out in the most casual manner, since the rain mixes with her tears. It turns out that her lover is leading his men, but that they are close to insurrection (l. 20) as he promises that they are near safety.

Morris's handling of the narrative's architecture is extremely powerful. We think the introduction is over at the end of the first verse paragraph (l. 5), but it turns out that the story proper does not start until the end of the second (l. 31). Both paragraphs end with the crucial line which will be repeated at the end of the poem describing how Robert will die "Beside the haystack in the floods." The first time it appears, it is made to rhyme with the subsequent line, conforming to the form of the poem, which is in tetrameter couplets (with the odd triplet), a somewhat medieval-sounding hybrid form. But in its second appearance, as in its last, the title rhyme remains austerely unrhymed, conveying the feeling of incompletion of their inability to kiss. *Rhymes* kiss, but he dies instead beside the unrhymed haystack in the floods.

Most of the subsequent verse paragraphs have a similar feel, ending in mid-line. The poem's abrupt and clinical style comes from these obstacles to rhyme even in the middle of rhyming lines. Their presence sets up the similar effect of the full but unrhymed line at the end of the poem.

The poem's elliptical style may necessitate some plot summary here. Because of the sodden, flooded grounds (even the haystacks are flooded), Robert and his band have no way of avoiding Godmar, who lies in ambush. Robert, who has fought well against the odds at Poitiers, calls on his men to fight against Godmar's larger squad, but Jehane sees already what will happen: His men will betray Robert to Godmar, and Jehane will have no choice but to return to Paris to be tried and convicted of treachery or even witchcraft (like Joan of Arc) at the Chatelet prison. And this indeed is what they do: After the amazing detail of Robert beating his thumb (impatiently) upon his sword-hilts (ll. 65–66), his men bind him and yield him to Godmar.

Godmar offers Jehane Robert's life if she will sleep with him; otherwise Robert will die before the rain ends. She refuses, but he gives her an hour to change her mind, reminding her that death as a witch awaits her if she returns to Paris (she'll either prove her innocence, uselessly, by drowning in a trial by water, or be burned as a witch if she does not sink). She dismounts and lies down on a wet heap of hay to think it over. The poem declines to tell us what she thinks, and indeed it may be wrong to say that she thinks anything since she enters what we would now call a catatonic state, dissociated from the impossible world around her, but with no other world to go to. After the hour is up, she refuses Godmar again. Robert, knowing he is about to be murdered, tries to kiss her, but Godmar jerks his head away and more or less beheads him. The description of violence sustains the dissociated feeling of Jehane's point of view, and it is all the more powerful for that. Godmar sends her back to Chatelet and her death, but he is unable to terrify her, since the violence she has seen and catalyzed has already subjected her to such horror that nothing worse can befall her, making her in a sense invulnerable to any other threat or punishment.

The severe understatement of the last two lines of the poem, ending the narrative as abruptly as it has begun, captures Jehane's strange, almost demonic tone and makes of the poem one of the most uncannily unsentimental evocations of violence in all of Victorian literature.

BIBLIOGRAPHY

Kinna, Ruth. *William Morris: The Art of Socialism.* Cardiff: University of Wales Press, 2000.

Kirchhoff, Frederick. *William Morris: The Construction of a Male Self, 1856–1872.* Athens: Ohio University Press, 1990.

Thompson, Paul Richard. *Work of William Morris.* New York: Viking Press, 1967.

HEMANS, FELICIA (1793–1835)

As WILLIAM WORDSWORTH makes clear in one of his last great poems, "Extempore Effusion upon the Death of James Hogg," the first years of the 1830s were a bad time for his poet friends. James Hogg himself died in 1835; SAMUEL TAYLOR COLERIDGE and CHARLES LAMB had died a year earlier, and Sir WALTER SCOTT and GEORGE CRABBE in 1832. They were old (though not as old as Wordsworth, as he laments); but the great sorrow he expresses there is over the untimely death of Felicia Hemans, who was only 41: "Mourn rather for that holy Spirit, / Sweet as the spring, as ocean deep; / For Her who, were her summer faded, / Has sunk into a breathless sleep" (ll. 37–40). Hemans had been a wildly popular poet, and continued to be so for many years later. In addition to Wordsworth's elegiac stanza, LETITIA ELIZABETH LANDON wrote an elegy (see "FELICIA HEMANS"), as did ELIZABETH BARRETT BROWNING.

In his preface to "Extempore Effusion," Wordsworth characterizes Hemans in a lovely and affectionate way: ". . . there was much sympathy between us, and, if opportunity had been allowed me to see more of her, I should have loved and valued her accordingly; as it is,

I remember her with true affection for her amiable qualities, and, above all, for her delicate and irreproachable conduct during her long separation from an unfeeling husband, whom she had been led to marry from the romantic notions of inexperienced youth." That husband, Captain Alfred Hemans, had abandoned Felicia and her five children when she was barely 25, and she was compelled to support her family and her mother by writing. Wordsworth laments this in his preface: She had to write "so frequently and so much, that she was compelled to look out for subjects wherever she could find them, and write as expeditiously as possible." Those subjects include translations from the Portuguese poet Luiz Vaz de Camoẽs; historical legends, especially of the lives of women; exotica set in North America (where one of her brothers had settled, and where one of her sons would eventually go to live); elegies on public figures; and many sentimental poems—poems at which she excelled. Indeed the critic Francis Jeffrey (whom Hemans visited) praised these most of all and thought that they might survive when Wordsworth and Coleridge were forgotten.

There is considerable debate on the merit of Hemans's poetry, which often tends to the obvious, even to doggerel. But at its best, it is subtly and finely sentimental—that is to say, it is sensitive and touching. It's not surprising that she should have been so admired in the Victorian era, since her poetry often has a proto-Victorian feel to it, in particular praising women for heroism in the domestic as well as the public sphere. Hemans knew all too well the strenuous, heartbreaking difficulties and responsibilities of motherhood, and her poems recording the achievements of women, feminist as many of them are, anticipate the achievements that COVENTRY PATMORE would praise in his "Angel in the House" sequence. Her feminism was essentially conservative, her politics Tory (which led PERCY BYSSHE SHELLEY to expostulate with her when they were both teenagers and he had read her first publications), but she had a brilliant mind and was a never-less-than competent poet, often a very moving one, even if some of her poetry might seem embarrassing now for being overly moving.

See also "CASABIANCA"; "HOMES OF ENGLAND, THE"; "SECOND SIGHT."

BIBLIOGRAPHY

Armstrong, Isobel. *Victorian Poetry: Poetry, Poetics and Politics*. New York: Routledge, 1993.
Armstrong, Isobel, and Virginia Blain, eds. *Women's Poetry in the Enlightenment: The Making of a Canon, 1730–1820*. New York: St. Martin's Press, 1999.
Southey, Robert. *Life of Horatio, Lord Nelson*. London: Society for Promoting Christian Knowledge, 1851.
Sweet, Nanora. *Felicia Hemans: Reimagining Poetry in the Nineteenth Century*. New York: Palgrave, 2001.

HENLEY, WILLIAM ERNEST (1849–1903) Henley is now widely remembered in the United States for only one poem, "INVICTUS," with its famous boast that the poet is "bloody but unbowed," "the master of his fate," and "the captain of his soul." But Henley is far a better and more subtle poet than this one example tends to show, and probably his best work is the sequence of poems he published in 1875 in *Cornhill Magazine* called *In Hospital*. Henley was in the Royal Infirmary in Edinburgh for nearly two years, receiving treatment on his right leg, which was threatened with amputation. His left leg had been amputated in his late teens, and when his right leg started showing signs of morbidity, he went to Edinburgh to seek the treatment of Joseph Lister, the great and charismatic promoter of antiseptic cleanliness (after whom the antiseptic-turned-mouthwash Listerine is named). There he underwent Lister's treatment and his right leg was saved. In the months of enforced idleness he spent in Edinburgh's Royal Infirmary, he read and wrote an enormous amount. The great man of letters Leslie Stephen (Virginia Woolf's father) edited *Cornhill* and came to visit him one day, along with ROBERT LOUIS STEVENSON, who hit it off with Henley immediately; they remained close friends, and Stevenson's Long John Silver, with his wooden leg, is based on Henley. (They would have a falling out later, since Henley made it too clear that he did not like Stevenson's wife.) Henley also met his wife-to-be at the infirmary. (They had one daughter, who died at the age of five, but who so struck J. M. Barrie that he based Wendy in Peter Pan on her and her toddler pronunciation of the word *friendly*.)

Henley's poetry has been aptly called the poetry of counterdecadence. The decadent poets, OSCAR WILDE in particular, rejected the ugliness of the industrialized world for a kind of pure aesthetic alternative. Henley, in the mode of the painter James McNeil Whistler, whom he championed (he was also the first and most important English supporter of Rodin, who did some sculptures of him), saw beauty in the urbanized world. His contribution as a poet is something like what he himself sees as the French romantic artist Eugène Delacroix's contribution as a painter: the beautiful representation of modern and often ugly things. Henley's portraits in poetry of the people he meets at the infirmary—Lister, other staff (especially nurses), other patients, visitors, the living, the dying—are striking and powerful, as are the meditations on life, death, beauty, and illness. Henley is unflinching, and because he is unflinching, he can see the aesthetic possibilities of the most unlikely subjects and how aesthetic presentation does honor to those subjects in their accurate portrayal. This is the mode Henley would sustain in all his best poetry throughout his life. In addition, he is a metrical experimentalist, most strikingly in the poems written in strong ballad meter but without rhyme.

Following his release from the Royal Infirmary, Henley became an editor (he published WILLIAM BUTLER YEATS, who found his advice helpful) and critic. He wrote his worst poetry at the end of his life, jingoistic propaganda for the Boer War, but he was always a subtle and impassioned critic and writer. His best poetry still seems strikingly novel and fresh, as though he had come up with a workable compromise between PRE-RAPHAELITISM and decadence.

BIBLIOGRAPHY

Buckley, J. H. *William Ernest Henley; a Study in the "Counter-Decadence" of the Nineties.* Princeton, N.J.: Princeton University Press, 1945.

Williamson, Kennedy. *W. E. Henley: A Memoir.* London: H. Shaylor, 1930.

HENRY, JAMES (1798–1876) When editing *The New Oxford Book of Victorian Verse,* the critic Christopher Ricks discovered the poetry of James Henry, whose self-published books were relegated to dusty shelves in the Cambridge University library. (Ricks noticed him first of all because of the far more famous novelist Henry James.) Ricks published several of Henry's poems in his anthology, and other anthologists (most notably Valentine Cunningham and Danny Karlin) picked up on this and published some of the same poems as well as others. Then, in 2002, Ricks edited and introduced *Selected Poems of James Henry,* a volume that will probably secure Henry's place as a considerable minor poet of the Victorian era.

Henry was already remembered for his classical scholarship, having been obsessed with the Roman poet Virgil from an early age. He grew up as a Protestant in Dublin and was essentially an atheist, or, as he preferred to say, a pagan, and Virgil was his bible and constant study. Trained as a physician—apparently he was a good one, and certainly a kindly and helpful presence—he devoted his spare time to his study of Virgil. In 1845 his mother left him enough money to retire as a physician and fully dedicate himself to his Virgilian studies. That same year, he published his translation of the first two books of the *Aeneid* (or, as he calls it, *Eneis*), into blank iambic pentameter.

The translation is somewhat stiff but very powerful, with extensive notes that fill up most of the page. One of those notes explains Henry's metrical practices. Unlike Virgil's previous translators, who attempted to make the *Aeneid* fluid in English and lost Virgil's meaning and intent, Henry "adopted therefore precisely the reverse principle, and proposed to myself, not the easy, and frequently performed, task of adapting Virgil to the English language and rhythm, but the difficult and never before attempted one, of adapting the English language and rhythm to Virgil." He conceded—or perhaps insisted—that this practice gave his lines "a stiff or foreign air," but it would be more accurate to say that Henry developed instead a far more subtle and flexible ear for the metrical possibilities of English than more apparently mellifluous poets.

In particular, Henry's poetry is notable for the rhythmical subtlety with which he counterpoints the metrical matrix (often trochaic tetrameter, as in "ALBUM MUTOR IN ALITEM," otherwise iambic pentameter) with the natural rhythms of the English words that fill up the line. Henry gets several dimensions of stress into a single line, and he almost always does so in a way that conveys the psychological subtlety of conflict or richness or surprise of the situation that he is observing in the poem.

Henry, his wife (who died young), and his daughter spent what eventually stretched out to 25 years collating and comparing all the important manuscripts of the *Aeneid* in Europe. The result is one of the best and most influential commentaries on the poem ever written, one whose teachings all subsequent editions have assimilated and absorbed. At the same time, he wrote poetry about the countries and customs he and his daughter encountered. Some of them are oddly like poems by Henry's contemporary, also a classical scholar and philologist, WILLIAM BARNES, though they did not seem to know each other. Barnes and Henry both took great delight in the surprising things they noticed, and they put these surprises into their poems. Neither of them thought of trying to become great as poets; rather, they *used* poetry to make the world a little clearer and more surprising. For Henry, that surprise almost always had a formal element in it, in the way that normal speech could be wrested a little bit away from its normality by a notation (often with unnerving accent marks) of a different possible rhythm or stress, coexisting with the natural and conversational emphasis. This gives to language and its users a particularity and an entitlement to particular respect that they might not otherwise have. Henry is great at inculcating that respect, both through and for his poems.

Henry's daughter died suddenly, at 42, shortly after his publication and dedication of the first volume of his commentary on the *Aeneid* to her (one that acknowledged her virtual coauthorship). He died four years later at 78, and the rest of his commentary was published posthumously.

See also "I SAW IN DRESDEN ON A WINDY DAY"; "OUT OF THE FRYING PAN, INTO THE FIRE."

BIBLIOGRAPHY

Cunningham, Valentine, ed. *The Victorians: An Anthology of Poetry and Poetics.* Malden, Mass.: Blackwell, 2000.

Henry, James. *Selected Poems of James Henry.* Edited by Christopher Ricks. New York: Handsel, 2002.

Ricks, Christopher, ed. *The New Oxford Book of Victorian Verse.* New York: Oxford University Press, 1987.

Rogoff, Jay. "First Fruits." *Southern Review* 40, no. 3 (2004): 602–628.

"HOMES OF ENGLAND, THE" FELICIA HEMANS (1827) This is one of FELICIA HEMANS's most famous poems (it was parodied by the 20th-century playwright Noël Coward), probably exceeded only by "CASABIANCA." It is a lovely, if sentimental, valentine to English domestic culture at all levels—the kind of life Hemans herself wished for but was more or less debarred from as an abandoned wife scrambling to make a living. The poem is in five stanzas, each beginning with an interjection naming something about the homes of England, each preceded with a different adjective: *stately; merry; blessed; cottage;* and finally, *free, fair.* The artfulness in the poem derives from the fact that these adjectives are not all of the same order but are made to seem equivalent, even synonymous. Thus, *blessed* is an adjective that would apply to all of them, and the third stanza begins with what is essentially an assertion that every home in England is blessed (l. 17), just as the second stanza suggests that they are all "merry" (l. 9). But, of course, not every home is "stately" (l. 1), and in particular the "stately homes" (as the cliché term the poem inaugurates has it) are to be distinguished from the "cottage homes" (l. 25). The "hut and hall" (l. 34) correspond to the cottages and stately homes, respectively.

The poem is a late version of the Horatian "country house" poem begun by Ben Jonson (1572–1637) in England (with "To Penshurst") and continued by Robert Herrick (1591–1674) and Andrew Marvell (1621–78). But where those poems celebrate the unusual beauty and peace that a perfect and deeply studied combination of art and nature makes possible, Hemans means to extend and generalize the celebration. Thus, the middle-stanzas adjectives apply to both the stately homes and the cottage homes: They all share in merriness and blessedness.

What makes the link between the two extremes convincing is Hemans's deft shifts in perspective. The stately homes of the first stanza are seen from the outside, as part of the natural landscape. The second stanza brings us inside the home, here limned with a proto-Victorian sensibility, and we feel welcomed to the home in general. So we have had two experiences now, that of landscape and that of indoor happiness, and they are linked: Though the poem begins with an exterior, we are not kept from an interior, one which might or might not be that of the stately homes.

The third stanza brings us to a vision of the outside world again, but now we have that vision more or less the way we would have it from inside, through the windows, as it were, as we hear both the hush and the churchbells and feel the breeze. Finally, the fourth stanza brings us to the outside landscape again, now filled as beautifully with "cottage homes" as the first was with stately homes. They all belong to a similar kind of rural painting, the sort of thing that John Constable (1776–1837) was famous for. And this is what the last stanza celebrates in its widest perspective—the whole landscape and the familiar interiority that makes the hearts reared there love the landscape in which the homes are scattered. The last line, in which Hemans celebrates how "the child's glad spirit loves / Its country and its God" (ll. 39–40) makes *country* refer to both landscape and state.

This is the ideological work the poem does, as the opening motto, or epigraph (see MOTTOES), from Sir WALTER SCOTT's *MARMION* makes clear: "Where's the coward that would not dare / To fight for such a land?" (IV, ll. 633–634). Scott puts this sentiment in the mouth of the Scottish minstrel who follows the English Lord Marmion against Scotland but nevertheless admires the sublimity of his enemy's encampment. The irony in *Marmion* that Hemans alludes to is that the beauty of the encampment will be destroyed by the very war that it might spur its admirers to undertake: that beauty should have encouraged peace and not war. That peace is Hemans's object as well, and one adroit way she suggests it is to make the celebration of Scottish landscape into that of England—not least by rhyming (and thus allying) the motto with her own poem, *England* picking up the *land* at the end of the quotation.

BIBLIOGRAPHY

Armstrong, Isobel. *Victorian Poetry: Poetry, Poetics and Politics*. New York: Routledge, 1993.

Sweet, Nanora. *Felicia Hemans: Reimagining Poetry in the Nineteenth Century*. New York: Palgrave, 2001.

"HOME THOUGHTS, FROM ABROAD"

ROBERT BROWNING (1845) ROBERT BROWNING is rarely thought of as a Keatsian poet—it was really ALFRED, LORD TENNYSON who inherited the mantle of JOHN KEATS—but "Home Thoughts, from Abroad" shows a deep understanding of Keats's mode. We could describe that mode as a kind of deferred sensuality, an intense recollection or fantasy of sensuality so great that it conveys the immediate experience of sensation better than sensation itself could. The poem by Keats that Browning echoes most directly here is on "ON THE GRASSHOPPER AND THE CRICKET": Browning, delighted in having us hear the songs of spring, points out, "That's the wise thrush," just as the earlier poetic naturalist identified the chirping behind the stove: "This is the cricket."

The similarity is not one of sound alone. Browning gives what is essentially a special version of Keats's temporal juxtaposition. Keats imagines summer in the midst of winter; then he further imagines winter from the perspective of the summer he has just evoked, in order to have his imagined cricket think again of summer. The series of meditations acts as a kind of evocative *still,* purifying memory and desire of any materiality that would interfere with the sense of pure and ideal evocation. So, too, does Browning imagine springtime in England while he is in Italy. The beautiful specificity of his vision of April in England is a kind of ode to the rich intricacy of descriptive language. The efflorescent language, tumbling into longer and longer lines like the vegetation it describes, stands in for the natural beauty it evokes from the distance of Italy—the distance also of the fact that (as it turns out) Browning probably wrote these lines in high summer or early fall, and not during April at all. "England—now" (l. 8) is England in the poem, not England in reality.

The second part of the poem, with its evocation of May rather than April, confirms that the poem is about how much more pleasure evocation gives than actuality. For even if the poem's narrator is speaking in April, the second stanza is about the coming May, and about how beautiful that evanescent season is. It is evanescent, but its beauty comes in part from its carelessness—that of the thrush's "first, fine careless rapture" (l. 16). It is careless of the fact that this is a season of carelessness, which cannot possibly last: that is part of its beauty. And for Browning in Italy, the fine, careless rapture is an imagined thing, and all the finer for that.

The contrast with the "gaudy melon-flower" (l. 20) that he has before him in Italy shows the vital pleasure of the idealized imagination of England. No real place could match this ideal pleasure of memory rewritten as distance and immediacy at once. Nature really does not offer the play and pleasure that Browning describes here—it offers instead merely gaudy melon-flowers. But poetry does offer that play and pleasure, perhaps most often when it is imagining nature, as Keats did and as Browning does here.

BIBLIOGRAPHY

Bloom, Harold. *A Map of Misreading.* 2nd ed. New York: Oxford University Press, 2003.

———. *Poetry and Repression: Revisionism from Blake to Stevens.* New Haven, Conn.: Yale University Press, 1976.

Browning, Robert. *Essay on Percy Bysshe Shelley.* London: Published for the Shelley Society by Reeves and Turner, 1888.

DeVane, William C. *A Browning Handbook.* New York: Appleton-Century-Crofts, 1955.

Langbaum, Robert Woodrow. *The Modern Spirit: Essays on the Continuity of Nineteenth- and Twentieth-Century Literature.* New York: Oxford University Press, 1970.

Raymond, William O. *The Infinite Moment, and Other Essays in Robert Browning.* Toronto: University of Toronto Press, 1965.

HOOD, THOMAS (1799–1845) In his *Roundabout Papers,* (in an 1863 essay entitled "On a joke I once heard from the late Thomas Hood," WILLIAM MAKEPEACE THACKERAY describes his old friend Thomas Hood, who had died nearly two decades earlier: "I quite remember his pale face; he was thin and deaf, and very silent; he scarcely opened his lips during the dinner, and he made one pun." Hood worked incessantly, despite the fact that his health was bad from his early youth. He was popular, mainly as a humorous writer, and famous for his puns. Thackeray, in fact, does not repeat the joke of his essay's title (although he does repeat another, made on Hood's deathbed), partly because he thinks that Hood is essentially a serious writer, even when most manic and most hilarious.

What Thackeray meant by Hood's seriousness was his care and concern for the poor. Both Thackeray and Hood contributed to the satirical magazine *Punch,* but Hood was always essentially a radical, while Thackeray was a Tory, so his praise is all the more striking. (*Punch* itself began as a radical journal.) Hood's later sentimental but deeply moving poems about the London poor, such as "The SONG OF THE SHIRT" and "The BRIDGE OF SIGHS" influenced some of his readers in both England and America to good intentions and others to good works. They are written in a tone of light verse, but their content turns out to be oriented to a highly painful reality. The light verse, where Hood learned his brilliant facility for the sharp use of language, is itself perfect in its kind, and it is no wonder that he was such a popular writer (and editor) for *Punch,* the *New Magazine,* and his own *Hood's Magazine.* Hood's work was both entertaining enough and socially effective enough that when he was dying, the prime minister, Robert Peel, came to visit him to announce that he was being given an honorary (Civil List) pension of 100 pounds per year. Peel wrote to him personally before the visit and told him how much he liked his work, all of which Peel had read.

Hood had started out as a serious poet only, writing beautiful Keatsian poetry (such as "ODE: AUTUMN") while making the acquaintance of the various contributors to *London Magazine,* where he worked on the staff from 1821 to 1823; coworkers included CHARLES LAMB, WILLIAM HAZLITT, THOMAS DE QUINCEY, JOHN CLARE, and HARTLEY COLERIDGE. SAMUEL TAYLOR COLERIDGE admired Hood's work as well. (Lamb wrote an elegy to a baby of the Hoods, who died the day it was born.) He also became friends with John Hamilton Reynolds, JOHN KEATS's friend; they published a volume together, and later Hood married Reynolds's sister Jane.

Hood had very bad luck, both as to money and as to health. Bankruptcy forced him to move to Ostend, Belgium, where his health deteriorated still further; eventually he moved back to England, where he died shortly after. Even on his deathbed, he labored indefatigably, writing some of his best-known work like "The Song of the Shirt" and "The Bridge of Sighs." At ELIZA COOK's instigation, a monument praising "The Song of the Shirt" was erected at his grave at Kensal Green.

BIBLIOGRAPHY

Hood, Thomas. *Memorials of Thomas Hood: Collected, Arranged, and Edited by His Daughter, with a Preface and Notes by His Son. Illustrated with Copies from His Own Sketches.* London: E. Moxon, 1860.

———. *Poetical Works of Thomas Hood, with a Critical Memoir by William Michael Rossetti.* New York: G. Routledge, 1874.

Shillingsburg, Peter L. *William Makepeace Thackeray: A Literary Life.* New York: Palgrave, 2001.

Thackeray, William Makepeace. *The Roundabout Papers.* London: Smith, Elder, & Co., 1879.

HOPKINS, GERARD MANLEY (1844–1889) In 1874, eight years after his conversion to Roman Catholicism and six years after burning his early poetry and joining the Society of Jesus (he would be ordained as a priest in 1877), Gerard Manley Hopkins was studying theology and spending much time immersed in Welsh culture at Saint Beuno's College in Wales. (He notes in "The WRECK OF THE DEUTSCHLAND" that this is where he was the night the ship was wrecked in the mouth of the Thames.) He had been teaching poetry the year before and was particularly interested in prosody and in the complexity of the interactions of stress, quantity, and rhyme—interests that derived from his training as a classicist at Oxford University, where he had been an undergraduate. Greek and Latin poetry use a quantitative meter—one that varies the length of a syllable or set of syllables (two shorts can be roughly equal to a long)—whereas English poetry relies not on length but on stress or beat. In Wales, Hopkins was struck both by the beauty of the Welsh landscape and by its language; he learned enough to be able to compose poetry in Welsh (as he had in Latin before, even translating two songs from William Shakespeare into Latin).

The rules of the Welsh poetic system called *cynghanedd* are complex, but they rely on the interplay of very strict alliteration (the same consonants in the unstressed syllables leading to a stress being repeated in the same order at the beginning and end of a line), assonance, stress, rhyme, and caesura (or pause) within the line. The rhymes are sometimes between rhymes but more often internal, and sometimes rhymes are balanced by alliteration, so that the experience of completion that a triple rhyme gives an English reader or hearer will find a counterpart in rhyme followed by consonantial patterning. Perhaps the closest analogue to great Welsh poetry in English is to be found in Hopkins's verse.

Hopkins wrote some poems in Welsh, more to study the language, which he felt to be of a piece with the landscape. The concatenation of forms was for Hopkins the way that God impressed himself into the world, through what he called *instress,* a pressure that carried presence into its perception by the soul. Concatenations also concatenate, so that language and natural landscape are both modalities of instress. Hopkins's amazing descriptions of natural landscape make his prose journals utterly fascinating.

In 1875, when the *Deutschland* went down in the Thames and five persecuted nuns aboard it drowned, the rector at Saint Beuno's suggested the tragedy as a fit subject for poetry. As Hopkins put it, echoing Othello, he took the hint and wrote his first great poem, the powerful expression of the things he had been thinking about for the last seven years. The poetry proved too difficult for his contemporaries, although his friend ROBERT BRIDGES and his old teacher R. W. Dixon found Hopkins's work profound. (Bridges, who had kept copies of the poems that Hopkins had burned, was his great champion, publishing almost the entirety of Hopkins's poetic production in 1918, nearly 30 years after his death.) From then on, Hopkins continued to write until his early death from typhus in Dublin, but he had no interest in publication, sending his poems to Bridges and Dixon but not seeking worldly notice.

In 1884, Hopkins went to University College Dublin to take up a position as professor of Greek literature. He felt isolated as an Englishman in an Irish nationalist environment, and he also knew he was not a good teacher. Consequently, he grew more and more depressed. This was reflected in the gloom of his poems of the time, what Dixon called the "terrible sonnets" or the "sonnets of desolation." He eventually recovered, and his earlier poems are sufficiently continuous with his later work as to make it clear that his desolating depression was an intensification of the kinds of thoughts and perceptions that always haunted him. He had become a Catholic under the tutelage of JOHN

HENRY NEWMAN (and against his parents' wishes), partly because of his feeling for both the beauty and the distress of the world (a feeling that was also both a sublimation and an acknowledgement of the homosexuality and masochism that he consciously recognized in himself). Official church teaching was thomist—that is, it sought universal system, truth, and essence. But Hopkins discovered the writings of the great medieval philosopher Duns Scotus (ca. 1266–1308), who insisted on what he called the *haecceity,* or *thisness,* of things in the world. Hopkins felt justified by Scotus in his interest in the details of the world and their manifold and intense interactions with each other. All things were a kind of stress, including language, and that stress was from God manifesting himself in myriad ways. The absence of God in the "terrible sonnets" is another indication of the intensity manifested by his presence. Hopkins's great late poem "THAT NATURE IS A HERACLITEAN FIRE AND OF THE COMFORT OF THE RESURRECTION" uses the idea of fire to account for the world's various and always self-discrepant intensities, all of it coming together to be "immortal diamond."

Hopkins's great formal innovation in poetry was the discovery or reinvention of SPRUNG RHYTHM, which involves a condensation and interpenetration of linguistic entities—stress, rhyme, alliteration, and, even more important, syntax—beyond anything seen before (although there is some analogue to Hopkins's syntax to be found in ROBERT BROWNING's knottier poems). These prosodical discoveries are not primarily formal: They *are* what the poems are about, the compacted density and stress of God's omnipresence. Hopkins wanted the perception of this poems to be an experience like the experiences they recorded—an experience of language akin to the experience of the natural world or of psychic distress they represented. They are analogous to what they record: Ultimately, they are analogous to *themselves.*

That self-similarity or self-analogy is at the heart of Hopkins's poetic practice. He uses portmanteau coinages and forces words into places they do not ordinarily fit (using verbs—such as *achieve* in "The WINDHOVER"—for nouns and nouns for verbs, for example). His syntax and grammar, like his lexical coinages, press things close together, to the point of making them collapse into each other. Their basic separateness is one of the elements that he forces together with the others, and all of this enormous heterogeneity within extreme compactness is for Hopkins the actuality of the presence of God, everywhere, and not just a metaphor for it. His poetry is ultimately of praise, even in its darkest despair, and what it praises is the way everything in the world, no matter how desolate it might appear, is charged with an intensity that it was his vocation to see as divine.

See also "AS KINGFISHERS CATCH FIRE"; "BINSEY POPLARS"; "CARRION COMFORT"; "CHILD IS FATHER TO THE MAN, THE"; "GOD'S GRANDEUR"; "I WAKE AND FEEL THE FELL OF DARK, NOT DAY"; "NO WORST, THERE IS NONE"; "PIED BEAUTY"; "SPRING AND FALL."

BIBLIOGRAPHY

Bridges, Robert. Preface to *Poems of Gerard Manley Hopkins.* Edited by W. H. Gardner. New York: Oxford University Press, 1948.

Gardner, W. H. *Gerard Manley Hopkins (1844–1889): A Study of Poetic Idiosyncrasy in Relation to Poetic Tradition.* New Haven, Conn.: Yale University Press, 1949.

———. Introduction to *Poems and Prose of Gerard Manley Hopkins.* Harmondsworth, Middlesex, England: Penguin, 1963.

Hartman, Geoffrey. *The Unmediated Vision: An Interpretation of Wordsworth, Hopkins, Rilke, and Valery.* New Haven, Conn.: Yale University Press, 1954.

Hopkins, Gerard Manley. *Gerard Manley Hopkins: Selected Letters.* Edited by Catherine Phillips. New York: Oxford University Press, 1990.

Miller, J. Hillis. "Gerard Manley Hopkins." In *The Disappearance of God: Five Nineteenth-Century Writers.* Cambridge, 1963, 270–359.

White, Norman. *Hopkins: A Literary Biography.* New York: Oxford University Press, 1992.

"HOUND OF HEAVEN, THE" **FRANCIS THOMPSON (1890)** "The Hound of Heaven" is God the hunter, as he is conceived in this ode by the Catholic poet FRANCIS THOMPSON. This is perhaps the last great ode in English, a distinguished inheritor of the romantic ode inaugurated by WILLIAM WORDSWORTH's INTIMATIONS ODE. The romantic ode is a poem of crisis that seeks in a desperate expression of passion some way to come through the extraordinary experience that is its occasion. For Thompson, that occasion is the sense that God is hunting him, pursuing him through the universe. The poem is a cry of protest against God's inescapable and overwhelming love, and the power of its language is pitched to the tremendous divinity that its language struggles against.

Why does Thompson struggle against God? We could read the poem as a kind of vocational autobiography. The very passion raised against God suggests that subordinating himself to God's love feels the opposite of poetic vocation. Indeed the poem is a kind of recapitulation of Thompson's passionate reading, so that the vocabulary of the ode is derived from Wordsworth (preeminently), from Thompson's favorite among the romantics, PERCY BYSSHE SHELLEY, from whose "ODE TO THE WEST WIND" he derives not only structure and content of the poem but also the vocabulary (as in the word *skyey* in line 31, echoing the "skiey speed" of the wind in Shelley's poem), and from JOHN KEATS (whose "ODE TO A NIGHTINGALE" Thompson is almost certainly remembering in ll. 16–24). But all the passion of his evasion of God is more than met by God's even more tremendous pursuit of him.

Even more important to the thinking of the poem than its romantic forebears is the poetry of the metaphysical poets, particularly of George Herbert (1590–1630). Herbert's poetic speaker consistently represents himself as frightened of God and seeking to escape him, much as Thompson does here. The speaker's very fear and evasion of God is a sign of the intensity of God's presence in his life. In Herbert, as in Thompson, that intensity is not a mark of the soul's *loss* (as it is in Wordsworth), but of the soul's need for God. The Herbert poems most behind "The Hound of Heaven" are "The Collar," whose title puns on the anger (choler) its speaker feels at his obligation to be loyal to God, an obligation he seeks to evade, and "The Pulley," where humanity's "repining restlessness" will eventually toss us to God's breast. For Herbert, as for Thompson, the bitter ambivalence of our relation to God shows that we take him seriously. Part of that seriousness is anger and anxiety that we are more serious about God than he is about us or about our seriousness. And then the moment of salvation, for both poets, comes when they recognize that God is even more passionately committed to them than they are to their own anxieties and emotions about God.

All of which is to say that the overwhelming energy of the poem is derived from a belief in something commensurate with that energy. The panic of the poem flips over into the energy of salvation. Only love could have the power that so frightens the speaker, and to realize that the nature of love is to be so fearful is to realize that the fear and desperation that are essential to the poetic vocation are also signs of the love for God, which initially understands itself as panicked flight from God. You cannot escape panic, which constitutes the very form of the attempt to escape it; but if the experience and expression of panic (that is, poetry) turns out to be the love that it seeks to escape, then poetic vocation and God's love turn out to be not at odds but versions of each other. (This is the burden as well of Thompson's great essay on Shelley.)

HOUSMAN, A. E. (ALFRED EDWARD HOUSMAN) (1859–1936) A. E. Housman was near perfect in his speciality, poetry of exquisite observation and nostalgia for a world as exquisite as the poems themselves. For many years, no one knew that Housman was a poet. He trained in the classics and became one of the most important classicists of his time, specializing in textual scholarship and acid and witty book reviews, first as professor of Latin at University College, London, and then at Cambridge University. (He could also have chosen to be professor of Greek.) And yet Housman had famously (and shockingly) failed his final examinations, for reasons that might have had to do with his arrogance or with his hidden and anxiety-provoking homosexuality, which led him to avoid the spotlight. He worked as a civil servant in the patent office in London, as did Moses Jackson, the athletic young man who seems to have been the great (and unrequited) love of Housman's life. For a while, Housman shared rooms with Jackson and his younger brother, for whom he wrote an elegy when the latter died young. In the meantime he began publishing articles on textual criticism. Their brilliance and mordancy was such that eventually he was appointed to his professorship at University College.

In the mid-1890s, especially in 1895, Housman wrote an extraordinary number of powerful poems, publishing them in 1897 under the title *A Shropshire Lad*. He had never been to Shropshire, but it was for him the far country that he sought in literature and to which he found some relation in his poetry. That poetry is inflected with his classical learning—that is, his classical sense of purity of diction and timeless simplicity of poetic emotion (a mode he learned especially from the Roman poet Horace). Nevertheless, he could be timely, and one of his poems from the period, "OH WHO IS THAT YOUNG SINNER," responds with bitter satire to the trial and imprisonment of OSCAR WILDE for "gross indecency." There but for the grace of God might have gone the young Housman, had he conducted himself in the Wildean manner, a manner exactly opposite to his own. Nevertheless, the shocking persecution of Wilde for his homosexuality drew both protest and defensiveness from Housman.

Housman was to publish two more books of poetry in his lifetime (both in the 20th century), and his poetic output is small. Nevertheless, it is almost all of very high quality Despite his protest over Wilde's treatment, it is perhaps unsurprising that Housman's tastes as well as his politics were conservative. That conservatism served his poetry well (even if it led to some bad topical poems) since it made him into a kind of scrupulously careful idealizer of a past that derived its attraction for those who live in the present from its very remoteness in time. Housman understood that remoteness and wrote poems that responded to its elusiveness—poems that at their best are as haunting and beautiful as the best poetry of his time.

See also "DIFFUGERE NIVES"; "INTO MY HEART AN AIR THAT KILLS"; "LOVELIEST OF TREES"; "ON WENLOCK EDGE"; "'TERENCE, THIS IS STUPID STUFF.'"

BIBLIOGRAPHY

Gardner, Philip, ed. *A. E. Housman: The Critical Heritage*. New York: Routledge, 1992.

Highet, Gilbert. *Classical Tradition: Greek and Roman Influences on Western Literature*. New York: Oxford University Press, 1957.

Richards, Grant. *Housman: 1897–1936*. New York: Oxford University Press, 1942.

HUNT, LEIGH (1784–1859) Leigh Hunt is a sort of supernode (as social-networking theorists call them) among the great writers of the first half of the 19th century. He is remembered most vividly as the model for Harold Skimpole in Charles Dickens's *Bleak House*, the parasitically innocent character who first charms and then horrifies all those around him with his open but finally venal insistence that he is "a perfect child" in all financial and social matters and will therefore rely on the kindness of others without feeling any obligations of his own. Dickens denied that any of Skimpole's negative characters were based on Hunt, but certainly his nearly criminal financial naïveté—is drawn from life: One day he left an envelope containing 100 pounds on a table after being shown how to cash a check from his publishers, and his wife, thinking it scrap paper, threw it into the fire. Hunt was sometimes so poor that he did not know where his or his family's next meal was coming from. But his connections, including Dickens, found ways of raising money for him—Dickens put on a benefit play, for example.

The American author Nathaniel Hawthorne also had a sense, but an entirely admiring one, of Hunt's childlike qualities which he described in his sketch "Up the Thames": "He was a beautiful old man. In truth I never saw a finer countenance, either as to the mould of features or the expression, nor any that showed the play of feeling so perfectly. It was like a child's face in this respect." Ralph Waldo Emerson, too, admired him, and was charmed by his company and the delicacy of his presence. Hunt was friendly with, and often the dependent of, such people as LORD BYRON, THOMAS CARLYLE, WILLIAM MAKEPEACE THACKERAY, and Thomas Babington Macauley. Everyone knew him, Queen Victoria admired his work, and even those whom his courageous political principles caused to resent him came to find his kindness and candidness irresistible. (One wonders whether Dickens resented finding so perfect a Dickensian innocent in real life, as though Hunt competed with his own fictional characters).

Hunt had been the center of things from an early age. He was a poet, political journalist, and a critic. He founded and published the *Examiner*, and when he was arrested for insulting the prince regent in its pages, he refused to apologize and spent two years in jail, still editing the journal. PERCY BYSSHE SHELLEY wrote him a letter of praise; eventually, he and Hunt became friends, and when Hunt met JOHN KEATS, it was Shelley who introduced them. Hunt also was the first critic to write insightfully and sympathetically of them, in the *Examiner,* even as he was also writing poetry himself, as in the contest he had with Keats on the subject of "The Grasshopper and the Cricket" (see "ON THE GRASSHOPPER AND THE CRICKET").

Hunt was by no means a great poet, but he was skillful enough and moving enough to make his poetry often seem magical, and insightful enough to admire his great friends' poetry. He was also committed to older poetic forms (even as he admired the innovations of the romantics), and his critical work influenced the forms that others wrote in. In particular, his defense of the heroic couplet affected the use of a version of this form in Shelley. As a much-loved, highly ingenuous supernode, Hunt probably did more toward reconciling opposing poetic factions with each other than any other person of his age, and (for better or worse) made possible much of what we now think of as the canon of early 19th-century poetry—providing the praise and the theory and the critical analysis that brought out what was essential to modern poetry in its infancy.

See also "RONDEAU."

BIBLIOGRAPHY

Dart, Gregory. "Cockneyism." *London Review of Books* (December 18, 2003). Available online. URL: www.lrb.co.uk/v25/n24/dovt01/_html. Accessed March 16, 2009.

Holden, Anthony. *The Wit in the Dungeon: A Life of Leigh Hunt.* London: Little, Brown: 2005.

Hunt, Leigh. *Autobiography of Leigh Hunt.* London: Oxford University Press, 1928.

———. *The Selected Writings of Leigh Hunt.* 6 vols. Edited by Robert Morrison and Michael Eberle-Sinatra. London: Pickering and Chatto, 2003.

Jones, John. "How Did He Get It Done?" *London Review of Books* (September 22, 2005)

Mahoney, Charles. Introduction to "Leigh Hunt, *Later Literary Essays.*" In *Selected Writings of Leigh Hunt.* Vol. 4, edited by Michael Erbele-Sinatra and Robert Morrison, xi–xxvi. London: Pickering and Chatto, 2003.

Roe, Nicholas. *Fiery Heart: The First Life of Leigh Hunt.* London: Pimlico, 2005.

"HYMN TO INTELLECTUAL BEAUTY"

PERCY BYSSHE SHELLEY (1816) "The Hymn to Intellectual Beauty" is often read in conjunction with "MONT BLANC," written at about the same time in summer 1816, when PERCY SHELLEY was in Switzerland. The two poems have many things in common, but "The Hymn to Intellectual Beauty" is far less dramatic, making a very powerful philosophical point very beautifully rather than enacting or demonstrating it. It is also far more autobiographical, in the sense that in it, Shelley gives an account of the origin of his poetic vocation, and of its relationship to his political radicalism.

The "intellectual beauty" of the title is a platonic formulation. Intellectual beauty belongs to the transcendent realm of the forms, which we know or remember purely through the mind and not through earthly experience. Earthly experience, however, can prompt us to remember the beauty we have known—including the earthly experience of reading WILLIAM WORDSWORTH'S INTIMATIONS ODE, which centers on the idea that in childhood we remember most fully the realm of ideas from which we descend at birth into the lower natural world around us. This poem is also strongly influenced by Wordsworth's "TINTERN ABBEY," especially in its evocation of a spirit inhabiting everywhere the world that it transcends. For Wordsworth, this comes to a kind of pantheism, with all that this also implies of a belief in "God who is our home" (Intimations Ode, l. 65). Shelley is resolutely an atheist, however, and he criticizes Wordsworth under a thin veil of generalization in the third stanza, where he says that "the name of God, and ghosts and heaven" (l. 27) is the record of the vain endeavor of sages (like SAMUEL TAYLOR COLERIDGE) and poets (like Wordsworth) to personalize the experience of poetic vocation that they feel.

We know that it is an experience of poetic vocation from Shelley's own account of how he searched for ghosts as a boy. What he found instead was the intimation of intellectual beauty itself. It is this, the Greek philosopher Plato says in the *Symposium,* that attracts our love. Shelley—first translator into English of the *Symposium* (under the title *The Banquet*)—renders the Greek philosopher Socrates' creed this way: "Love is that which thirsts for the beautiful, so that Love is of necessity a philosopher, philosophy being an intermediate state between ignorance and wisdom."

It is, in fact, this intermediate state that Shelley prefers to the satisfaction of thirst for the beautiful. Intellectual beauty is "Dear, and yet dearer for its mystery" (l. 12). That is to say, it gives the human mind a sense of imminent power and greatness, but a sense also of moving toward that power, not reposing in it. It is for this reason that Shelley says, in the poem's most beautiful simile, that it is nourishment to human thought "Like Darkness to a dying flame" (l. 45). The fact that the flame is dying causes (or at least contributes to) the darkness, and yet that darkness intensifies the beauty of the flame itself. Shelley uses a similar image in his *A Defence of Poetry* (1821): ". . . the mind in creation is as a fading coal which some invisible influence, like an inconstant wind, awakens to transitory brightness." The transitory nature of the brightness is part of its beauty, which is made more intense by its elusiveness.

It is not that beauty is itself elusive. Rather, it is that the human mind cannot sustain contact with it. It is important to see that this is not because intellectual beauty actually does exist in a platonic heaven that earthbound humans cannot quite attain to, even if we have intimations of it. To think this would be to repeat the mistake of sage and poet who imagine that beauty as being far beyond our human capacity to reach.

For Shelley, however, it is finally in the mind that poetic impulse toward beauty resides. But the impulse toward beauty is also the beauty it seeks. Like most of the other romantic and post-romantic poets—for example, Coleridge in "KUBLA KHAN" or ROBERT BROWNING in "CHILDE ROLAND TO THE DARK TOWER CAME"—Shelley is after the elusive principle of inspiration itself. Inspiration fills the mind with a sense of possible discovery, but what counts is the moment of inspiration and not the discovery it might lead to. Therefore, poetry at its most intense becomes an attempt to recapture inspiration, an attempt that is bound to experience itself as loss rather than achievement, as darkness rather than light. But the loss itself can be transformed into an achievement, if it is felt intensely enough. To be capable of feeling the decline of beauty is to be capable of a more intense apprehension than the beauty itself offered. This is how darkness nourishes a dying flame, an image Shelley probably alters from the progressive darkening in William Shakespeare's sonnet 73 ("In me thou seest the glowing of such fire / As on the ashes of his youth doth lie"). The last stanza shows (like Shakespeare) the decline of day and of the year, but it is in that decline that harmony, solemnity, serenity, and luster become all the more beautiful.

These are all images and vectors that will recur in Shelley, again and again: The "deep autumnal tone, sweet though in sadness" of "ODE TO THE WEST WIND"; the residual intensities of such late lyrics as "Lines: Music When Soft Voices Die" and "LINES WRITTEN IN THE BAY OF LERICI," both of which pick up the idea of beauty fading "Like memory of music fled" (l. 10). Here, though, as in the philosophical analysis of the SUBLIME given in "Mont Blanc," Shelley may be said to still believe in the powers of the human mind to live within the intensity of its own loss, rather than to feel the loss as deeper than the gain it offers. Later, he will not think the exchange, inevitable though it is, worth the price it exacts.

See also ROMANTICISM.

BIBLIOGRAPHY

Bloom, Harold. *Genius: A Mosaic of One Hundred Exemplary Creative Minds.* New York: Warner, 2002.

———. *Shelley's Mythmaking.* New Haven, Conn.: Yale University Press, 1959.

———. *The Visionary Company: A Reading of English Romantic Poetry.* Garden City, N.Y.: Doubleday, 1961.

Burke, Kenneth. *Grammar of Motives.* Berkeley: University of California Press, 1969.

Chernaik, Judith. *The Lyrics of Shelley.* Cleveland: Press of Case Western Reserve University, 1972.

Duffy, Edward. *Rousseau in England: The Context for Shelley's Critique of the Enlightenment.* Berkeley: University of California Press, 1979.

Hogle, Jerrold E. *Shelley's Process: Radical Transference and the Development of His Major Works.* New York: Oxford University Press, 1988.

Keach, William. *Shelley's Style.* New York: Methuen, 1984.

Leavis, F. R. *Revaluation: Tradition & Development in English Poetry.* New York: Norton, 1963.

Leighton, Angela. *Shelley and the Sublime: An Interpretation of the Major Poems.* New York: Cambridge University Press, 1984.

Notopolous, James A. *The Platonism of Shelley: A Study of Platonism and the Poetic Mind.* Durham, N.C.: Duke University Press, 1949.

Quinney, Laura. *The Poetics of Disappointment: Wordsworth to Ashbery.* Charlottesville: University Press of Virginia, 1999.

Wasserman, Earl. *Shelley: A Critical Reading.* Baltimore: Johns Hopkins Press, 1971.

———. *Subtler Language: Critical Readings of Neoclassic and Romantic Poems.* Baltimore: Johns Hopkins Press, 1968.

"HYMN TO PROSERPINE" ALGERNON CHARLES SWINBURNE (1866) This is one of ALGERNON CHARLES SWINBURNE's most Shelleyan poems, anti-Christian in its language and its aesthetics, but, like some of the work of PERCY BYSSHE SHELLEY, still preserving a hope that Christianity, too, might take its place as the source of an intensely aesthetic rather than moral vision.

As all commentators on the poem note, the Edict of Milan legalized Christianity in 313 C.E., in the names of the Roman emperor Constantine the Great, who took it seriously, as well as of his rival Licinius, who violated it. Twelve years later, after Licinius's death, Constantine convoked the Council of Nicaea, in which the bishops of the church established the tenets of the religion. This establishment of the official doctrines of Christianity, along with Constantine's convenient but momentous conversion, spelled the end of the religions of Greece and Rome, and of serious belief in the classical myths.

There was, however, a reversal toward those religions, when Julian the Apostate (331–363) became emperor. He was a nephew of Constantine, but his religion was a variety of the Neoplatonism that would later be so dear to WILLIAM BLAKE and to Shelley (the latter represents himself under the name Julian in *JULIAN AND MADDALO: A CONVERSATION* [Maddalo is LORD BYRON]). Julian was assassinated by a Christian, and his last reported words are "Vicisti, Galilaee"—"Thou hast conquered, Galilean," which Swinburne uses as the epigraph, or motto, to the poem (see MOTTOES). The Galilean is, of course, Jesus of Galilee, whose religion will now henceforth be preeminent.

The speaker of "Hymn to Proserpine" is a pagan, a devotee of the old religion, lamenting the replacement of the old gods by the new. (This is the theme as well of JOHN KEATS's *Hyperion* poems, though Keats's gods are entirely pagan.) It is therefore appropriate that Swinburne's hymn is to Proserpine, the queen of the dead, since now, as he says, he has lived long enough. (The opening words are a quotation of Shakespeare's Macbeth, about to be superseded by the lawful kings of Scotland.) Prosperine is a figure to whom Swinburne returns often (see "The GARDEN OF PROSERPINE"). She represents a woman lost to death, since she has been spirited away by Pluto, or Dis, god of the underworld, when gathering flowers. Edmund Spenser and John Milton both have extraordinary evocations of "Proserpin' gathering flowers," as Milton puts it, and how she "herself a fairer flower by gloomy Dis / Was gathered, which cost Ceres all that pain / To seek her through the world" (*Paradise Lost,* 4, ll. 269–272). Milton, too, is reciting the displacement of Proserpine by the story of Eden in his poem, but what seizes the imagination is Milton's evocation of the myth that his own story subsumes.

Proserpine—at least in Swinburne's reading of Milton—is gathered into the death of her own mythology. Her abduction from Earth means the supersession of the religions in which she features so prominently. Swinburne's hymnist calls upon her, therefore, because all that she represents is dead, and she is queen of the dead. This lends her a kind of second lease on being—not quite the second lease on life that the six months in the upper world the myth allows her has meant (spring, planting, growth, harvest), but a second way of representing the world mythologically. She is the myth that represents the supersession of her own mythology.

That mythology is a sweet one; indeed, it is the mythology on and in which the verbally sensuous poetry, which Swinburne wrote better than anyone else, thrives. Swinburne tends to use the sensuous resources of poetry, its hypnotic repetitions and rhythms, as a way of preparing a kind of easeful death for the soul. The "Hymn to Proserpine" is replete with repletion itself—repletion of rhyme, of anaphora (sonorous repetition), of rhythm. Its extremely long lines are meant to demonstrate the compelling sound counters of dactylic hexameter, the most common Greek and Latin meter for both epic and (somewhat modified) elegiac poetry. Swinburne's own sense of English rhythm tends to come to the fore as the poem proceeds, however, and its rhythm is more anapestic (short, short, long), two unstressed syllables followed by a stress, than dactalyic (long, long, short), a stressed syllable followed by two unstressed ones. The lines have many internal rhymes as well, which has the effect of shortening them but also of making their final words even more prominent. None of this is to be taken as a defect in the poem: rather, it shows how Swinburne was naturally absorbed in enriching the qualities of sounds.

As almost everywhere in Swinburne's poetry, the best image for the hypnotic, death-vectored fullness that he expresses so powerfully is the sea—see, for example, the famous lines about the maternal sea in "The TRIUMPH OF TIME." Here, time itself is a sea, the foam of the present swept into the past (l. 49); the future that brings Christianity is itself just another wave in the sea. "Hymn to Proserpine" acknowledges the coming of Christianity, but not its superiority to the sealike waves of time on which it comes and which will eventually carry it away. Venus, goddess of love, is born of the sea (l. 78), and this renders her closer to the truth imaged as the sea itself than the coming of her replacement Mary can possibly be.

"Hymn to Proserpine" has the structure of an elegy, but in reverse. The mode of the greatest English elegies, from Milton's *Lycidas* to Shelley's *ADONAIS* to ALFRED, LORD TENNYSON's *IN MEMORIAM A.H.H.,* is to use absence against itself. The dead person is absent from the world; therefore, that world is empty and poor, and so it is better that he is not here, in a world of death (which *his* death represents) but elsewhere, in what must be a world of life. Swinburne, however, uses the *presence* of death as a return to Proserpine. Because Christianity has conquered, the old gods are dead. But that means that they are the gods of the dead, and Proserpine is their queen. She is more fair than all—than Venus *and* Mary—because she offers the beauty of death against the restless and bitter mutability of life. It is therefore with the dead past, and hymning the gods of the dead, that the devotees of the great Greek and Roman deities can find the complete peace of sleep and death. Death is present here, now, with the triumph of Christianity, and therefore the presence of Christianity means that Proserpine is present, too, and she is still the greatest goddess of all. The death of pagan faith proves the pagan faith in death.

The poem does not end in triumph but with an achieved sense of the relation of death and beauty, a relation it is the poet's vocation to trace and express.

BIBLIOGRAPHY

Louis, Margot Kathleen. *Swinburne and His Gods: The Roots and Growth of an Agnostic Poetry.* Kingston, Ont.: McGill-Queen's University Press, 1990.

McGann, Jerome J. *Swinburne: An Experiment in Criticism.* Chicago: University of Chicago Press, 1972.

Rutland, William R. *Swinburne: A Nineteenth Century Hellene.* Oxford: Blackwell, 1931.

HYPERION AND THE FALL OF HYPERION JOHN KEATS (1819) Toward the end of 1818, JOHN KEATS began writing the poem called *Hyperion.* He abandoned it in April 1819 and diverted the intense creative energy of that poem into the writing of the great odes of April and May. In late July he took *Hyperion* up again, now as the *Fall of Hyperion,* reworked parts of it, and gave the narrative an astonishing and crucial first-person frame. By September, however, when he may have begun suspecting the presence of the tuberculosis that had killed his brother and would kill him less than a year and a half later, he abandoned the poem for good. As in the spring, that later and definitive abandonment finds a correlate in a different sort of poem—his last great ode, "TO AUTUMN," written just two days before he announced his intention to give up *The Fall of Hyperion.* In a letter to his friend J. M. Reynolds in which he described his composition of "To Autumn," he said of his dissatisfaction with the *Hyperion* project that "there were too many Miltonic inversions in it—Miltonic verse cannot be written but in an artful or rather artist's humour. I wish to give myself up to other sensations."

The odes record what Keats was describing here as "other sensations," but it might nevertheless be better to see the *Hyperion* poems and the odes as essentially continuous in their interests, themes, and anxieties. The year 1819 was Keats's annus mirabilis, and what he did in that year constitutes a single and singular creative blossoming worth studying on its own.

The first poem, *Hyperion,* intends to tell the story of the last battle between the fallen Titans and the Olympian gods who have displaced them. John Milton's *Paradise Lost* had reworked and reinterpreted the ancient myth of the battle between the earth and the sky gods as one between Satan and his rebel angels and the angels loyal to God. Milton describes the fallen Satan as being "in bulk as huge / As whom the fables name of monstrous size, / Titanian or Earth-born, that warred on Jove." In classical mythology, the Olympian gods usurped the throne of their father Saturn and the other Titans, themselves the usurping children of Heaven and Earth. *Paradise Lost* again refers to the usurpations and fate of "Saturn: he from mightier Jove, / His own and Rhea's son, like measure found; / So Jove usurping reigned." (In *Paradise Lost,* Jove is sometimes mapped onto Satan, as here, and sometimes onto God.) The Titans, like the fallen angels, attempt to regain their throne, and if he had finished it, Keats's poem would have described the last definitive battle in which the sky gods defeated the earth-born Titans.

Keats begins *Hyperion* with a repaganization of the story that Milton had Christianized in *Paradise Lost.* Now it is Saturn who is fallen and who, barely recovered from disaster, holds council with the other fallen Titans. One of them, however, still holds his place, though insecurely: Hyperion, the god of the sun. It is important to note that this Hyperion is not to be identified with Apollo (as he is in many myths). Apollo is one of the Olympian gods and will replace Hyperion in the course of the poem. But he is now, in Keats's rendition of the story, a youth who does not know his own fate or vocation. He lives alone, full of hope and longing, but he does not know for what. The story Keats is telling might have some affinities with Milton's *Paradise Regained,* in which Jesus is in a somewhat similar position. But its more immediate parallel is the Homeric stories about the youthful Achilles, whom his mother disguised as a girl in order to try to keep him from being enlisted for the Trojan War in which he would die. Odysseus comes and finds him, just as Mnemosyne, the goddess of memory, comes to reveal his birthright to the young Apollo in book 3 of *Hyperion.* That birthright includes not only the sun but also poetry. Apollo is the god of poetry, and the implication is that poetry originates with the displacement of the unpoetic Titans. Indeed, the fallen Oceanus, urging the other Titans not to resist the law of aesthetic progress by which they have been displaced, asserts that "'tis the eternal law / That first in beauty should be first in might" (2, ll. 228–229), and it is with the Olympian gods that true aesthetic beauty arrives. So Cybele reports to the other Titans, since she has heard all nature singing the arrival of "Apollo, young Apollo."

Mnemosyne, the mother of the muses but not a muse herself, is one of the Titans but has declared her loyalty to the young Olympians, and in particular to Apollo, who will be allied with the muses. Keats abandoned the poem, perhaps within 300 lines of finishing it, at the point where Apollo feels how the knowledge that Mnemosyne has brought him "makes a god of me." He "shrieks" at the transformation which will soon result in the displacement of the uneasily sublime Hyperion himself, but then the poem breaks off.

Keats's publisher, John Taylor, included *Hyperion* as a fragment in the 1820 edition of Keats's poems, against his own wishes, with a note saying that Keats had abandoned it because of the vicious reviews given to his *Endymion.* Keats wrote in a copy of the book, "This is a lie," but it helped give rise to the story that those reviews hastened his death, mentioned sympathetically by PERCY BYSSHE SHELLEY in his elegy for Keats, *ADONAIS,* and somewhat unsympathetically by LORD BYRON in *DON JUAN.* It was this edition of the poems that was found open in Shelley's pocket when his body was recovered from the sea in which he had drowned.

Hyperion and *The Fall of Hyperion* may be collated to give some sense of where the later poem was going, since Keats abandoned rewriting the second at a passage partway through the first book of *Hyperion* (1, l. 216), although some later passages have already been incorporated. The major innovation of *The Fall of Hyperion* is the appearance of the Keatsian narrator. Keats had been reading the Italian poet Dante, in Henry Francis Cary's translation and then in the original, and retells the story of being guided through another world with himself as a witness (within a dream) to the events he recounts. As with Dante himself—who supposedly undertakes the arduous journey through the worlds he describes—Keats's narrator is a significant character, perhaps the major character, and not just a device for registering what he sees. Indeed, he is as major a figure as he is in the first-person odes. As in "ODE TO PSYCHE," he has a dream vision of the gods of antiquity and of their displacement by younger and more beautiful deities: Psyche in the ode and Apollo in *The Fall of Hyperion.* For Keats, beauty is youth and youth beauty, and so the rise of youth is the rise of beauty. The question, as in the odes, is always what he himself will be identified with: the declining Titans, whose fate is too close to that of human mortality, or the rising gods who, like the nightingale ("ODE TO A NIGHTINGALE") and the figures on the urn ("ODE ON A GRECIAN URN") are not born for death?

Keats the narrator does not know, and one aspect of his ignorance is that he does not know whether the dream he reports is that of a true poet or not. Indeed, he says that he will never know this, for its truth will only be determined after his death. In the dream, he finds himself surrounded with the residue of astonishing plenty—the image he will recapitulate in "To Autumn"—and he drinks from what turns out to be a poisoned or drugged cup, much like the cup of nepenthe that Circe tempts her victims with in Homer's *The Odyssey,* and that Milton has his lecherous Comus offer all comers in the masque he wrote on chastity. Keats drinks from the cup and then has a vision of a nearly abandoned temple, where Moneta serves as priestess.

It is essential to a fuller understanding of the poem to know that Moneta is another name for Mnemosyne, whom we know from the first version. In this version it is Keats who shrieks (l. 126) and thereby gives himself enough awareness to complete the hard task of climbing up the stairs of the temple. In spite of himself, he subsequently calls upon Apollo, and when he does, Moneta gives him, Keats, some variation on the visions that in the first version she has given to the young Apollo. Keats is now brought to see the events that the original poem recounts, and he is clearly identified with the youthful god of poetry, more explicitly than in the first version. Moneta herself has declined past all aging, and her beautiful decay suggests again that poetry must take over from a memory that is closely approaching complete disappearance.

That this should happen may not be inappropriate. Keats's poetic vocation is one whereby he luxuriates in the beautiful fables of antiquity, regretting a past when (as he puts it in "Ode to Psyche") everything was haunted, when fairy lands were not forlorn ("Ode to a Nightingale"). But all turns on the balance between memory and belief. The pleasure of the stories is a pleasure in fiction, not in belief, which is why, in different ways, both in *The Fall of Hyperion* and in "Ode to Psyche," Keats erects a temple in the mind (as he puts it in the latter poem).

Rightly read, therefore, *The Fall of Hyperion* tells the story of its own supercession. Apollo, and Keats, no longer believe in the Titans. They wish to give themselves up to other sensations—and the myths are a part of the setting of these sensations. The temptation to deify and sacralize poetry was a temptation Keats was keen to resist. But poetry was the only mode by which he could cope with his more and more pressing fear of paralysis, suffocation, and death (a fear vividly depicted in the scene in which he nearly fails to climb the stairs in *The Fall of Hyperion*). The two modes of resistance are Hyperion's and Apollo's. Hyperion seeks epic power, but Apollo seeks the transparent lucidity of the upper world. Moneta points the lesson in her praise of those who are *not* visionaries, like the narrator of the *Hyperion* poems: "They are no dreamers weak, / They seek no wonder but the human face; / No music but a happy-noted voice" (ll. 162–164).

This is indeed a critique of Milton and of Miltonic poetry, but it is also a context for the kinds of poetry of sensation that Keats explores in the odes. The odes and the *Hyperion* poems are two sides of the same coin. Both are poems about the relationship of local sensation to the deepest and most disturbing questions about how we come to find ourselves where we are, able to participate in the heartbreakingly transient fullness of the local world and experience. And each kind of poem finds itself merging with its counterpart, as Keats considers the intense self-discrepancy which is as much a part of poetry as of life.

BIBLIOGRAPHY

Bate, Walter Jackson. *John Keats.* Cambridge, Mass.: Harvard University Press, 1963.

Bloom, Harold. *Poetry and Repression: Revisionism from Blake to Stevens.* New Haven, Conn.: Yale University Press, 1976.

———. *The Visionary Company: A Reading of English Romantic Poetry.* Garden City, N.Y.: Doubleday, 1961.

Chandler, James. *England in 1819: The Politics of Literary Culture and the Case of Romantic Historicism.* Chicago: University of Chicago Press, 1998.

De Man, Paul. *The Resistance to Theory.* Minneapolis: University of Minnesota Press, 1986.

———. *The Rhetoric of Romanticism.* New York: Columbia University Press, 1984.

Dickstein, Morris. *Keats and His Poetry: A Study in Development.* Chicago: University of Chicago Press, 1971.

Flesch, William. "The Ambivalence of Generosity: Keats Reading Shakespeare." *ELH: English Literary History* 62, no. 1 (Spring 1995): 149–169.

McFarland, Thomas. *The Masks of Keats: The Endeavour of a Poet.* New York: Oxford University Press, 2000.

Sperry, Stuart. *Keats the Poet.* Princeton, N.J.: Princeton University Press, 1994.

Stillinger, Jack. *The Hoodwinking of Madeline, and Other Essays on Keats's Poems.* Urbana: University of Illinois Press, 1971.

Wasserman, Earl. *The Finer Tone: Keats' Major Poems.* Baltimore: Johns Hopkins Press, 1953.

I

"I AM" **John Clare (1846)** John Clare actually has two well-known poems on the same theme, or perhaps they should be regarded as variations of the same poem: a sonnet and a slightly longer poem. Both are complaints of the soul's reduction by the world to its barest essence, what philosophers call the Cartesian Cogito ("I think therefore I am,") from the French philosopher René Descartes or the German philosopher Immanuel Kant's "transcendental unity of apperception." Clare may be thinking of Descartes (as Kant was); he is certainly thinking of the same issue which is the central one in ROMANTICISM of subjectivity thrown upon its own resources in a world that it discovers is alien to the self. In romanticism this discovery comes as an event in human life, one that the major romantics from William Blake to John Keats modeled on the Fall of humanity from Eden. They followed the 17th-century poet John Milton in psychologizing the Fall, treating it as a universal human *experience,* an *event* in everyone's life, and not simply as a universal human fact. We all discover the fact that we are fallen, and the moment of this discovery is the moment when we relive the Fall. The romantics secularized this psychological event, treating the Fall as the discovery of the otherness of the world, one of the signal features of which is the mortality of the self. The great exemplary text is William Wordsworth's Intimations Ode.

Clare is in that tradition, and his "I am" poems are intense and concentrated versions of the perception of this fall. The longer, 18-line version of the poem—published by Frederick Martin, Clare's first biographer, in his life of Clare in 1865—is the more optimistic. It is a crisis lyric, and like the great crisis lyrics it alludes to and to some extent approaches in power, it manages some resolution of the crisis that elicits it. That crisis is the extreme and existential solitude Clare feels (partly due to his having been confined for life to a mental asylum after a series of breakdowns), forsaken by friends and disappointed in all erotic hope. (A slightly different version of the poem was first published right after his death in the *Annual Report of the Medical Superintendent of Saint Andrews,* where Clare had been an inmate.) He longs for a place where human society has never been; he longs for a place where he would not find himself obsessed with erotic desire and tenderness, "A place where woman never smiled or wept" (l. 14); smiling and weeping are both the causes of his love and the ensuing disappointment and despair. The depth of that despair may be measured by Clare's metaphors, as when he compares the restive apparitions of his woes to "shadows in love's frenzied stifled throes" (l. 5)—that is, the shadows thrown up by the motions of sexual desire and actual intercourse. But the metaphors extend further, to include all human commerce, and the worst of it is that those whom he loves best are those from whom he feels most alienated. He has discovered the absolute and unbreachable limits of human contact, and it is for this reason that they are even "stranger," even more foreign to him, than the rest. All that is left to him is the sense of bare being within the noise of nothingness (he is remembering William Shakespeare's famous speech in *Macbeth* about sound and fury signifying nothing here).

The poem's deep paradox is that Clare feels solitary and wants solitude; bane and hope are indistinguishable. Here, too, we may mark a Wordsworthian feel to the poem, and see the Wordsworthian way this allows for a resolution to the crisis. The solitude he contemplates is one in which he will no longer be the "self-consumer" of his woes, no longer consuming a self reduced only to the experience of woe, but one in which he will feel the presence of God. God's presence, however, means only a sense of peace, a sense that the solitude of the world does not mean emptiness but refuge or harbor. The poem gives a strong sense of the metaphysical comfort that Clare took from his intense and expert naturalism, the feeling of the world of grass and sky as a place of rest and as a home.

The sonnet version of the poem (if it is right to speak of it as a "version") does not end with the same hopeful tone. It, too, is Wordsworthian, seeing the earth as a prison, as Wordsworth does in the Intimations Ode, and as a place that debases the soul. Clare is recalling the boast of Milton's Satan that "The mind is its own place, and in itself / Can make a heaven of hell, a hell of heaven," and recalling the way that boast is punished by Satan's internal realization that he himself is hell, that he carries hell within him (l. 254–255). Clare also thought he could disdain the bounds of place and time and travel like Milton's narrator between earth and heaven. As in the longer version of the poem, he seeks Wordsworthian solitude as a place to achieve self-sufficiency. Here, too, he has been disappointed in love and flees from "passion's dream." But the flight does him no good at all, for even in solitude he "peruses" strife, and that strife can only be internal—the strife within his own mind. All his hopes of self-sustaining power, hopes which sound a great deal like the SHELLEYan hopes of such poems as "THE TWO SPIRITS" and "ODE TO THE WEST WIND," are blasted, and there is no place for him to escape his own tormented soul. The longer poem had found a final and elemental solace being itself, in "the repetition in the finite mind of the eternal act of creation in the infinite I AM," as Clare's friend SAMUEL TAYLOR COLERIDGE defined the primary IMAGINATION. But the sonnet sees even that being—even the fact that "I am"—as a burden. He knows only that "I am—that is all," and to say that is all is not an anticlimax but a way of saying that the burden, which everything is, is all concentrated in the bare act of being, from which no being can successfully escape.

BIBLIOGRAPHY

Bate, Jonathan. *John Clare: A Biography*. London: Picador, 2003.

Chirico, Paul. *John Clare and the Imagination of the Reader*. New York: Palgrave Macmillan, 2007.

Martin, Frederick. *The Life of John Clare*. London: Macmillan, 1865.

"I DO NOT LOVE THEE" See NORTON, CAROLINE.

IMAGINATION Especially in ROMANTICISM, the imagination is a vexed and ill-defined concept, but a central one. An important strain of romanticism sees the poetic imagination as set against the empirical reality of the given world. The world as understood by empirical science lacks the depth, density, and meaning that the mind can put into it, or that (in another mode) transcends it. WILLIAM BLAKE's poem "Mock on, Mock on" ends with a central expression of this doctrine as he disparages the reductive scientism of the 17th- and 18th-century scientist Isaac Newton and the Greek philosopher Democritus (ca. 460–ca. 370 B.C.E.)

> The Atoms of Democritus
> And Newton's Particles of Light
> Are sands upon the Red Sea Shore
> Where Israel's tents do shine so bright.

The idea of the imagination that the romantics praised may be traced back at least to William Shakespeare's *A Midsummer Night's Dream,* where Theseus describes the poet, the lunatic, and the lover as being made up entirely of imagination. Imagination, then, allows you to transcend the ordinary things of this world, and ascribes to poetry a visionary status.

The classic doctrine of the romantic imagination is outlined by SAMUEL TAYLOR COLERIDGE in *Biographia*

Literaria (1817), where he distinguishes among three faculties: the fancy, the primary imagination, and the secondary imagination. What we tend to call artistic imagination is what Coleridge names the secondary imagination: the ability of human beings, poets especially, to imagine things never seen or thought of before. The primary imagination is more primordial, more the work of some transcendent power, and Coleridge defines it, in a famous phrase, as "the repetition in the finite mode of the infinite *I Am*." The *I Am* there is an allusion to what God said to Moses from the burning bush when Moses asks who he can say has sent him. God's response (Exodus 3:14) is: "I AM THAT I AM: and he said, Thus, shalt thou say unto the children of Israel, I AM hath sent me unto you." Coleridge contrasts the creative ("esemplastic") power of the imagination with the much weaker operation of the fancy, which he sees as the ability of the mind to recombine and reconstruct in a kind of mental collage images that it already has ready to hand, rather than creating new images.

Coleridge's passionate praise of the imagination marks him as a romantic poet. The idea of the imagination's relation to poetry had gained great currency in the 18th century, and its ground note was given by Mark Akenside's long poem *The Pleasures of the Imagination* (1744). At the head of that poem, Akenside gives a concise account of the prevailing preromantic view:

> The pleasures of the imagination proceed either from natural objects, as from a flourishing grove, a clear and murmuring fountain, a calm sea by moon-light; or from works of art, such as a noble edifice, a musical tune, a statue, a picture, a poem. In treating of these pleasures, we must begin with the former class; they being original to the other; and nothing more being necessary, in order to explain them, than a view of our natural inclination toward greatness and beauty, and of those appearances, in the world around us, to which that inclination is adapted. This is the subject of the first book of the following poem.
>
> But the pleasures which we receive from the elegant arts, from music, sculpture, painting, and poetry, are much more various and complicated. In them (besides greatness and beauty, or forms proper to the imagination) we find interwoven frequent representations of truth, of virtue and vice, of circumstances proper to move us with laughter, or to excite in us pity, fear, and the other passions.

For Akenside, artists, especially poets, are those who are peculiarly fitted to producing the effects described in this account. The freedom of the imagination could nevertheless become a source of anxiety for 18th-century poets and critics, just because creativity in many of the great 18th-century poets seemed to be close to madness (examples include William Collins, William Cowper, and Christopher Smart). This prompted the greatest critic of the age, Dr. Samuel Johnson, to express his fears about "the dangerous prevalence of the imagination" which, if unchecked, could lead to madness.

The romantic poets tended to praise the intensity that Dr. Johnson feared, and what for him was dangerous was for them thrilling. The imagination allowed access to a world transcending the normal world. It was a revolutionary principle in an age of revolution, and for romanticism throughout Europe, the young NAPOLEON BONAPARTE was felt to be the incarnation of imagination (which is how the German philosopher G. W. F. Hegel and, initially, the composer Ludwig van Beethoven both thought of him). Britain did not experience the revolutionary ferment that took place on the continent, and consequently the English romantics tended to see the imagination as an inner faculty, especially after their disenchantment with Napoleon.

Coleridge's distinction between imagination and fancy was not one that other poets tended to follow, however, and Coleridge drew it partly because he wanted to go beyond the philosophical accounts of the imagination that he found in philosophers, particularly in Kant. In philosophical contexts, the imagination is simply the faculty of mind that handles images, makes coherent pictures in the mind, and turns the world into a mental object that the mind can handle. But Kant himself aimed at a transcendental philosophy, and it was this soaring aspiring aspect in Kant that Coleridge wished to pick up.

WILLIAM WORDSWORTH, to some extent, followed Coleridge, whom he tended to acknowledge as the theorist of the romantic movement they were founding. In the division that he made of his own poetry in 1815, he distinguished between "poems of the fancy" and "poems of the imagination" (there are five other basic categories as well). It is not clear why some poems fall into one or another of these categories, but we may say that in general the poems of the fancy tend to praise natural objects for their freshness and beauty, whereas the poems of the imagination are deeply and powerfully introspective. Perhaps the most important of them are "TINTERN ABBEY," The LUCY POEMS, and the part of *The PRELUDE* about the Winander Boy, excerpted as "There was a Boy. . . ." These are poems of the imagination because they do not tell a reader how to think about or see some natural object; instead, they express the poet's own most intense thinking about the issue they take as their topic.

Wordsworth's most famous employment of the term *imagination* comes in *The Prelude,* when he describes his own sudden access of a baffling inspiration:

> Imagination!—lifting up itself
> Before the eye and progress of my song
> Like an unfathered vapour, here that power,
> In all the might of its endowments, came
> Athwart me. I was lost as in a cloud,
> Halted without a struggle to break through,
> And now, recovering, to my soul I say
> "I recognise thy glory". In such strength
> Of usurpation, in such visitings
> Of awful promise, when the light of sense
> Goes out in flashes that have shewn to us
> The invisible world, doth greatness make abode,
> There harbours whether we be young or old.
> Our destiny, our nature, and our home,
> Is with infinitude—and only there;
> With hope it is, hope that can never die,
> Effort, and expectation, and desire,
> And something evermore about to be. (1805 version, 6, ll. 525–542)

Imagination is a place of shadowy greatness, of hauntings (visitings) and usurpation, and when we have an excess of imagination, we see that our world is not the empirical or scientific reality that surrounds us, but infinity. Imagination is a power of infinite suggestiveness, and it offers itself to the visionary faculty, but as the very limit of the visionary. It offers us a glimpse of the invisible world, but only a glimpse.

The term was also of some importance to JOHN KEATS, who characterized it in a letter as an extraordinarily powerful mental or poetic faculty: "The Imagination may be compared to Adam's dream: He awoke, and found it truth." Keats was referring to the creation of Eve as John Milton recounts it in *Paradise Lost.* When Adam woke up from the sleep God had put him under to remove his rib, he found that the Eve he had dreamt of really existed.

Keats also, though far more implicitly, contrasted imagination with fancy, which seems to be its servant. "Fancy" is crucial to at least two of Keats's great poems, "ODE TO A NIGHTINGALE" and "ODE TO PSYCHE." In "Ode to a Nightingale," the disappointed speaker complains that "the fancy cannot cheat so well, As she is feigned to do." Fancy will not quite distract one from the realities of ordinary life. But the "gardener Fancy," in the "Ode to Psyche," is able to breed (mental) flowers infinitely within the mind. His mental temple to Psyche is replete "With all the gardener Fancy e'er could feign / Who breeding flowers, will never breed the same."

Since romanticism, the term *poetic imagination* has become something of a cliché, but it was the romantics who created the cliché in its fullest and richest sense.

See also SUBLIME, THE.

BIBLIOGRAPHY

Bloom, Harold. *The Visionary Company: A Reading of English Romantic Poetry.* Garden City, N.Y.: Doubleday, 1961.

Coleridge, Samuel Taylor. *Biographia Literaria.* Edited by J. Shawcross. London: Oxford University Press, 1968.

Richards, I. A. *Coleridge on Imagination.* New York: Routledge, 2001.

Scarry, Elaine. *Dreaming by the Book.* New York: Farrar, Straus, and Giroux, 1999.

INGELOW, JEAN (1820–1897) Jean Ingelow was one of the most popular poets of her time, especially in the United States, where her second volume of poetry, *Poems,* made her famous in a series of editions following its original publication in 1863. John Greenleaf Whittier published several of her more Tennysonian poems in his 1890 anthology *Songs of Three Centuries,* and indeed, ALFRED, LORD TENNYSON was an admirer of Ingelow, as was CHRISTINA GEORGINA ROSSETTI.

The poems Whittier published include Ingelow's famous ballad "The High Tide on the Coast of Lincolnshire (1571)," written in mock 16th-century rural diction and set in the region where she (and Tennyson) grew up. The poem tells of a sudden tide that breaks down a seawall in the town of Enderby and drowns a woman who is tending her cows at nightfall. The speaker of the ballad is the woman's mother-in-law, who hears her calling the cows and then sees her desperate son's agony at her loss in the flood. The poem is not so much about the events it recounts as about the songs that are the background of life as a ballad may recount it and which the ballad then justifies by exemplifying. In "The High Tide on the Coast of Lincolnshire," these songs are the relics of the disaster: The poem ends with the son remembering all that is left of his wife and two children, her song to the cows at twilight, which he now repeats. It is such songs that Ingelow liked, and she liked singing them: They are the residue of a self-annihilating story and achieve timelessness through a context of decontextualization.

This aspect of Ingelow's work makes her similar to Christina Rossetti, whose admiration for Ingelow was not untinged by rivalry. Rossetti is the greater poet, but the similarities are there, including a deep interest in child readers. Neither poet had children of her own (Ingelow was deeply secretive about whatever sexual life she had, though a very few hints have survived), but this meant that they could write for an idealized childish audience—an audience that would consist of readers such as they were when they were children. Ingelow (who lived to an advanced age and wrote an enormous amount) was highly successful in this vein, and much of her popularity was as a children's writer. This should not in any way detract from her power: Children are the purest and most unbiased of readers, unburdened by personal history or calcified personality, which is what childless poets remember about their own early childhood. It is the purity of audience that elicits the songlike purity of the best moments in Ingelow's verse, and at its best it well deserves the admiration of great poets like Tennyson and Rossetti. It continues to give the purest form of poetic pleasure, thus succeeding in its central aspiration to songlike timelessness.

See also "DIVIDED."

BIBLIOGRAPHY

Armstrong, Isobel. *Victorian Poetry: Poetry, Poetics and Politics.* London: Routledge, 1993.

Leighton, Angela. *Victorian Women Poets: Writing against the Heart.* Charlottesville: University of Virginia Press, 1992.

Lewis, Naomi. "A Lost Pre-Raphaelite." *Times Literary Supplement,* 8 December 1972, 1,487–1,488.

Preston, Harriet Waters. "Miss Ingelow And Mrs. Walford." *Atlantic Monthly* 56, no. 334 (1885); 230–242.

"IN JULY" EDWARD DOWDEN (1876) This sonnet is from a sequence entitled "From April to October" in EDWARD DOWDEN's 1876 book of *Poems.* The sequence forms descriptive responses to the changing seasons and atmospheres of the warmer part of the year. This poem is, perhaps, the most interesting in the sequence because it is self-contradictory. It is a poem in which the speaker explains why he is not writing any poems: the last two lines tell us that he is "too deep in joy's excess / For the imperfect impulse of a song" (ll. 13–14). Yet he is writing this poem—or at least the poem exists. How should that be?

We should note first of all the Keatsian or Tennysonian languor of the last line. To be "too deep in joy's excess" is Dowden's version of JOHN KEATS's "ODE TO A NIGHTINGALE," where Keats describes himself as "too happy in thy happiness" to wish to continue to deal with the world. Much of this poem (like much of Dowden) is shot through with Keats; he is thinking here of Keats's "TO AUTUMN," where the indolent flowers are also heavy with their own richness, as well as his sonnet "ON THE GRASSHOPPER AND THE CRICKET." Dowden also echoes ALFRED, LORD TENNYSON's famous line from "NOW SLEEPS THE CRIMSON PETAL, NOW THE WHITE" when he writes, "Now sleep the crystal and heart-charmid waves" (l. 9); as he also quotes Tennyson's "The LOTOS-EATERS." The poem is essentially a praise of indolence, of a perfection of sensory repletion that can abjure the imperfection of the poem itself. Somewhere behind it is John Milton's *Lycidas* (1638) with the eternal pastoral question, is it not better to simply take pleasure in the present than "strictly meditate the thankless Muse?"

But can a poem successfully praise the unpoetic sensual? Keats certainly attempted to, partly through the idea of being a chameleon and partly through the recognition that a life of sensation rather than of thought would finally leave no room for the poetic mind.

Dowden's solution in this near-perfect poem is more formal. It exists in the odd turn he gives to the form of the sestet of the Petrarchan sonnet. The octet (the first eight lines) are in standard form, rhyming *abbaabba*. But the sestet has an odd rhyme scheme indeed: *cdceed*. More explicitly, the last line completes a rhyme that has opened four lines earlier. This is the largest gap between rhymes in the poem, and indeed it would probably be impossible to hear in any poem. It is certainly rendered impossible to hear in this poem by the intentionally weak rhymes: *deliciousness / excess* (ll. 12–13), where the rhyming makes the very sense that the sonnet is rhyming start falling apart. (This is not the only poem where Dowden employs this eccentric rhyme scheme. He does it in "Seeking God," for example, where it is put to a somewhat similar use.)

The effect here is to make the last line sound unrhymed—just the effect that Dowden wants. The poem explains its own ending: It is unable to sustain the perfection of the scene it has just now described so perfectly. This has the odd effect of making the rest of the poem feel like the natural scene it mirrors, even as the last line sounds like a serious refusal to make a poem about it. The poem essentially breaks down into two parts, then: the last line and the 13 lines that precede it. The last line feels as though it does not rhyme and so separates out from the rest of the poem, which does rhyme. (Line 10, which presents the onset rhyme, *long*, does not feel unrhymed because onsets promise rhymes in the future, whereas last lines always have to be concluding rhymes.) The rest of the sonnet, then, is what the last line cannot hope to match, and yet its directness is just the natural description that a true statement of why he will not write poems would now require. Both parts of the poem act in odd concert to make the poem all the more convincing, and to solve the difficulty of praising the beauty of a present experience that needs no poem to memorialize it. This is a work of achieved directness and spontaneity, one of the most difficult (and beautiful) things to pull off in a poem. It typifies Dowden's style at its best.

BIBLIOGRAPHY

Murphy, William M. "Yeats, Quinn, and Edward Dowden." In *John Quinn: Selected Irish Writers from His Library*, edited by Janis and Richard Londraville, 71–108. West Cornwall, Conn.: Locust Hill Press, 2001.

IN MEMORIAM A.H.H. ALFRED, LORD TENNYSON (1850) *In Memoriam A.H.H.* is one of the great elegies in English; rivaled perhaps only by John Milton's *Lycidas*, PERCY BYSSHE SHELLEY'S *ADONAIS*, possibly Whitman's "When Lilacs Last in the Dooryard Bloom'd," and some short poems by Milton and WILLIAM WORDSWORTH. "A.H.H." is ARTHUR HENRY HALLAM—ALFRED, LORD TENNYSON'S closest friend for about five years and almost certainly, whether as a presence or an absence, the most important figure in Tennyson's life. King Arthur in Tennyson's "MORTE D'ARTHUR" and in *Idylls of the King* as a whole, as well as such characters as "ULYSSES" in scores of his other poems, are based on or influenced by Tennyson's memory of the other Arthur, Arthur Hallam. They met at Cambridge when Hallam (who was a year and a half younger than Tennyson) matriculated, and they stayed friends until Hallam's death of cerebral hemorrhage in 1833 at the age of 22, shortly before he was to marry Tennyson's sister Emily.

This biographical background indicates something unique about *In Memoriam* as an elegy: Unlike the other great English elegies mentioned above, Tennyson's elegy comes out of extreme and desperate personal feeling. Milton hardly knew *his* Cambridge colleague, Edward King; Shelley knew JOHN KEATS, but they were never close. ALGERNON CHARLES SWINBURNE'S elegy for Charles-Pierre Baudelaire, "AVE ATQUE VALE," is again addressed to someone important to Swinburne as a poet but not as a friend, a figure in the deepest core of his personal life. The biographical background therefore serves to underscore another feature of *In*

Memoriam: the length of time that Tennyson spent writing it and the intermittences of heart (as Proust would famously call them) that mark its unfolding.

In Memoriam comprises poems that Tennyson wrote over a period of more than 15 years. They were not intended as a single elegy, a single sequence that would aim from the start to develop and change in the course of its unfolding (see, for example, GEORGE MEREDITH's *MODERN LOVE*). Tennyson's laments are the laments of the moment, and the poem presents more a journal than a narrative of the experience of mourning and working one's way through grief. The poems certainly do not appear in the order that they were written, and it is interesting to note that section 59 was added in 1851 and section 39 in 1871. Both of these are odes to Sorrow, the personified grief that has replaced Hallam in Tennyson's life. He first addresses her in section 3, castigating her cruelty. But, of course, she is his own emotion and expresses his own fear about the meaninglessness of life. It will matter both to the poem and perhaps to the biography of the poet that he comes to a different relationship with sorrow from what he describes in section 3 as perhaps a vice in his blood, perhaps a "natural good," and takes her instead as friend and wife in 59. And yet in the last section added to the poem, 39, he accuses her "lying lips" of denying the possibilities of light. We can see this final addition as an expression both of late despair, nearly 40 years after Hallam's death, and of Tennyson's own mortality shadowing his life; and as part of the poem's architectonic arrangement, whereby he can feel sorrow late but place it early in a poem that ultimately has a saving movement—and in this way expositional time can overcome and offer solace for the depredations of real time.

In any case, what generally connects these poems is their subject and the poetic style, whose sound Tennyson felt harmonized with the grief he felt: They are all in the style he invented (or, as it happens, reinvented—since it had been used before), now called the "In Memoriam" stanza: tetrameter quatrains rhymed *abba.* The shortness of the lines and the strictness of the iambic rhythm makes the rhymes prominent. The stanzas have a marked tendency toward stasis, fixed on their inner, *b* rhymes and recurring to their opening *a* rhymes. Any movement forward takes labor, and this labor is the work that mourning must undertake in order to bear the heavy sorrows of loss.

One can see this from the start. The opening of *In Memoriam,* the section commonly called (in the critic A. C. Bradley's nomenclature) "The Prologue," Tennyson addresses Love, the son of God. Whether this son of God is to be identified with Jesus, whether this son of God *can* be identified with Jesus, is one of the poem's great mysteries. Love is immortal, but immortality turns out to designate a very long period of earthly time indeed. (For another example of a similar attitude toward immortality in Tennyson, see "TITHONUS.") In 1830 Charles Lyell (1797–1875) published the first volume of his revolutionary book *Principles of Geology,* in which he attempted through "an earnest and patient endeavour to reconcile the former indications of change with the evidence of gradual mutations now in progress." I quote this passage because it shows how Lyell, no less than Tennyson, saw the process of thought as also proceeding with a kind of geological slowness, as the mind slowly and gradually and with great patience changes imperceptibly from what it was to its contrary. It is just such a gradual change that *In Memoriam* charts, and it does so partly under the influence of Lyell, who was the first scientist to argue for what later came to be called "deep time," the idea that the earth was not thousands but millions and millions of years old. Lyell came to this conclusion through a consideration of the fossil record to be found in the various strata of rocks, and in particular from the fact that fossils of so many extinct species were recorded there. They were dead and gone indeed, and gone a long enough time ago to become part of the bedrock itself. These discoveries, so central to Charles Darwin's thinking, were shocking and depressing to Tennyson, contrasting as they did with the Christian idea that the fallen world was a temporary aberration to be redeemed by the son of God. In effect, we can say that Tennyson was confronted almost simultaneously with the death of Hallam and with the discovery that death lasts a very long time.

The implications offered by Lyell's geological insight are vivid from the opening of the prologue, where Tennyson invokes "immortal Love" as the maker of all things. That invocation is an echo of the 17th-century poet George Herbert's great "Love" (III), but here the nature of Love is highly ambiguous. The Greek philosopher Plato called love the offspring of plenty and poverty, and Love here may be divine fullness or human desperation to find something that will live when nothing does except for the Darwinian drive to reproduce. The sheerly biological features of this Love are to be seen in Tennyson's ascription to him of biological drives: "Thou madest Life in man and brute" (l. 6), where humans and animals are assimilated together.

This Love has also made Death, a chilling idea that should not be discounted too quickly. What does that mean? It means that life inevitably leads to death. To be born is to be fated to die. As in a famous line of Dante, love (*amore*) conducts always to death (*una morte*). The whole ambiguous and ambivalent anxiety of *In Memoriam* can then be felt in the lines that follow: "Thou madest Death, and lo, thy foot / Is on the skull which thou hast made" (ll. 7–8). It is too easy to read this as prophesying or celebrating the time when Death, too, shall die. For Love's foot is not on Death but on a skull—not on Death but on the dead, on the fossils buried in the accretions of time and life. Take the image as one of geological stratification, and it can seem very grim indeed: We all turn into skulls, left in the biblical dust which turns into real sandstone.

From the start, Tennyson attempts to use some of the geological perspective as a metaphor. The opening lines of the first section has him agreeing with the German poet and dramatist Johann M. Wolfgang von Goethe that people rise on "stepping-stones / Of their dead selves to higher things." The idea is given a geological twist in Tennyson: The death of the past stands for the rise of the living, as previous and lesser versions of the self are left to fossilize in the dust. Yet immediately (again in conformity with the antithetical style of the "In Memoriam" stanza, which can be thought of here as one step forward, two steps back, and then one step forward again), the speaker hesitates to forecast the future, which may be as dizzyingly empty as the past has become. Nature, as he will complain in poem 55, is "careful of the type . . . / careless of the single life;" and in the next poem, he must give up even that empty comfort (as geology shows) since even species come to an end, as Nature proclaims, "A thousand types are gone: / I care for nothing, all shall go." Love here turns out to be only this Nature, "red in tooth and claw" in the phrase this poem makes famous; for now it is Nature whom Tennyson makes say, "I bring to life, I bring to death." Spirit means only breath, she says, and breath ends. We live only in the present, and (as in "Tithonus") the emptied-out, mournful, vacant experience of the present here threatens to last forever. It is in this first poem that he feels how the empty hours scorn him as "the man that loved and lost," a phrase that will cadence and measure the trajectory of the whole work (so that in poem 27 he says, famously, that "'Tis better to have loved and lost / Than never to have loved at all," and he confirms this idea (when he gets engaged) in poem 85

The elegy, or set of elegies, does what Sigmund Freud called "the painful work of mourning." Tennyson sees the world as a world of absence where once it was a world of presence—the presence of Hallam. Every incident—but most particularly the three Christmas celebration sequences (beginning respectively at poems 28 in 1833, 51 in 1841, and 104 in 1837) that the poem describes—reminds him of an earlier incident in which Hallam was present. But sometimes he is reminded of the fact that he is taking some pleasure in the world, the kind of pleasure he used to take when Hallam was alive. The association of such pleasure with Hallam is both devastating and perhaps saving.

We can describe the process more or less like this: Tennyson feels the utter oppressiveness of the emptiness and vacuity of time that Lyell has so devastatingly demonstrated. Within all that, he feels the pain of his mourning for Hallam, a pain that may be sometimes intermittent but is always at the core of his being. The vastness of the emptiness he struggles against shows the vastness of the spirit of love, which can "whisper to the worlds of space / In the deep night, that all is well" (poem 126). The unimaginable hugeness of the worlds of nature, and the fact that love survives that unimaginability, becomes for Tennyson a sign, or hope, for transcendence and salvation—a transcendence and salvation by which he and Hallam will eventually be reunited.

The psychic movement of loss to its reversal as gain within human imagination is one that Tennyson learned from the romantics, particularly from Shelley in "MONT BLANC." But Tennyson knew, as they did not, just how much emptiness there is in the universe and how long it takes the mind to cope with it. His imaginative response and transcendence is one that he achieved through a lifetime of mourning—and this is what makes the poem so significant as an elegy.

In his review of Tennyson's poetry, Hallam had talked of the "fairy fineness" of Tennyson's ear and his strange "worship of beauty," but his death brings to Tennyson a vision "deeplier, darklier understood" (poem 129) It is that vision that he credits Hallam with teaching him, both by his presence and by his absence. In this way, Hallam's absence is part of the world itself—not the physical world but the world in all its dimensions and therefore, in the end, a sign of his presence or the hope of his presence.

BIBLIOGRAPHY

Armstrong, Isobel. *Victorian Poetry: Poetry, Poetics and Politics.* New York: Routledge, 1993.

Bloom, Harold. *Poetry and Repression: Revisionism from Blake to Stevens.* New Haven, Conn.: Yale University Press, 1976.

Buckley, Jerome Hamilton. *Tennyson: The Growth of a Poet.* Boston: Houghton Mifflin, 1965.

Kilham, John. *Critical Essays on the Poetry of Tennyson.* New York: Barnes and Noble, 1960.

Kincaid, James R. *Tennyson's Major Poems: The Comic and Ironic Patterns.* New Haven, Conn.: Yale University Press, 1975.

Ricks, Christopher B. *Tennyson.* New York: Macmillan, 1972.

Rowlinson, Matthew. *Tennyson's Fixations: Psychoanalysis and the Topics of the Early Poetry.* Charlottesville: University Press of Virginia, 1994.

Tucker, Herbert: *Tennyson and the Doom of Romanticism.* Cambridge, Mass.: Harvard University Press, 1988.

"IN SNOW" WILLIAM ALLINGHAM (1878) "In Snow" is as topical today as when it was written, in 1878. Throughout the latter half of the 19th century, Britain and Russia were engaged in constant conflict over Central Asia. The Crimean War of two decades earlier, the subject of ALFRED, LORD TENNYSON's great poem "The CHARGE OF THE LIGHT BRIGADE," was one of a number of such conflicts. In November 1878 the Second Afghan War began, as Britain attempted to control Afghanistan to counter Russian advances in Central Asia. RUDYARD KIPLING's "The BALLAD OF EAST AND WEST," written 11 years later, also details the central strategic importance the British ascribed to keeping control of Afghanistan and the Afghan frontier with what was then India, which was then governed by Britain (the raj). The British wanted to depose the emir of Afghanistan and put their own choice on the throne; the Russians supported a rival. Nearly two years later, a compromise was worked out, but in "In Snow," WILLIAM ALLINGHAM is writing at the violent start of the conflict.

The poem, a sonnet, is a good example of Allingham's subtle control of perspective, to be seen as well in "The FAIRIES: A NURSERY SONG" and "The BOY FROM HIS BEDROOM-WINDOW." He addresses an English mother, whom presumably he sees through a window in England; she is inside, holding her child on a snowy night. He imagines her imagining the snow and thinking of what it must feel like not to have access to the shelter her child has, and he imagines her thinking about the Afghan war, about the winter in Afghanistan where both war and winter hunt their prey—human beings.

The octet establishes the general feel of the way war seems. War, like winter, is everywhere. English children are dying in Afghanistan, even as their mothers are thinking about the winter in England. The grimness of war is its generality: The English mother's baby is safe, but only for now. Soon the child may be old enough to be like the "young soldier" of the sestet, the young soldier who can no longer "mind . . . *his* mother's parting syllables" (l. 11; emphasis in original). That young soldier comes out of nowhere and yet is completely convincing; it is as though the speaker has seen into the English mother's sad thoughts and perceived that she herself has seen something real and particular: an actual young soldier in the snow, whom they can seek to identify. His coat is red, so he seems English, a redcoat, and the poem a poem of national elegy or mourning. But the redness is blood, and the dead soldier, the peer of all other dead soldiers, turns out to be an Afghan.

The sonnet's last lines are bitterly ironic, as though the English need not mourn the dead Afghan youth. But he does, and so, presumably, does the mother he addresses. The youth is more important than the nationality. The Englishman who shot him is referred to in the poem merely as "the stranger." The youth is like all children, and the general fact of war is the way it kills children, and not the nationality of the dead.

BIBLIOGRAPHY

Allingham, H., and E. Baumer Williams, eds. *Letters to William Allingham.* London: Longmans & Co., 1911.

Allingham, William. *William Allingham: A Diary.* Edited by H. Allingham and D. Radford. London: Macmillan & Co., 1907.

Hill, George Birkbeck, ed. *Letters of Dante Gabriel Rossetti to William Allingham, 1854–1870.* London: T. Fisher Unwin, 1897.

INTIMATIONS ODE ("ODE: INTIMATIONS OF IMMORTALITY FROM RECOLLECTIONS OF EARLY CHILDHOOD")

WILLIAM WORDSWORTH (1802–1804) The Intimations Ode (as it is almost always called) is the single central work of British romantic poetry and widely regarded as one of the greatest English poems of any age. It belongs to, and is the greatest example, of the romantic genre called the "crisis lyric"—that is, a poem that articulates and responds to a moment of psychological or subjective crisis in the poet who writes it. The poem does not only record the crisis (although it certainly does that); it attempts to meet and resolve it. What this means is that whatever else the psychological crisis might be, the fact that poetry can address it means that it is a crisis about poetry and about poetic vocation, which is a true vocation, one that calls to the poet's whole soul. The difficulty is that the crisis is one of deep doubt about vocation, about whether poetry or whatever powers in the soul poetry responds to and expresses can do what the poet wants it to do; and so the poet in crisis begins saturated with doubt about the poetic means by which he or she would combat it.

For WILLIAM WORDSWORTH, poetry was the natural expression of the intensity of perception to be found in solitary communion with nature. That intensity of perception fills the mind capable of it, and it increases the depth at which that mind can think. Poetic vocation and thought arise from and cooperate with this deepening effect, so that the poet competes with the philosopher to find the "hiding places" of human thought and the sources of human experience.

The crisis begins as one of skepticism or doubt. Poetry should be, as it often is in lyrical ballads, SUBLIME in its simplicity, and therefore it should be true to the vivid and fresh perceptions of childhood. For this reason, Wordsworth sets the last lines of "MY HEART LEAPS UP" as a motto (see MOTTOES) to the Intimations Ode. That poem had claimed a continuity of feeling between the time "when my life began"; the present, "when I am a man"; and the future, "when I grow old"—a continuity that Wordsworth vows to preserve ("or let me die"). The last lines, which also serve as motto, assert that the child determines what the adult will be.

But this is just what the Intimations Ode begins by doubting. Its first words might be truncated to these central movements of thought: "There was a time . . . / It is not now as it hath been of yore." Everything is lost in that "But now" (much as Lucy is lost between the stanzas of "A Slumber Did My Spirit Seal" in the LUCY POEMS: "No motion hath she *now* . . ."). SAMUEL TAYLOR COLERIDGE was so impressed by the opening words, when Wordsworth read the beginning of the ode aloud to him (at the end of March 1802), that he repeated them at the opening of the climactic passage of his greatest crisis lyric, DEJECTION: AN ODE, which should be read in the context of the Intimations Ode. (The original version of "Dejection" was composed in April 1802.)

The time that is lost is one in which the world seemed illuminated by light from the heavens. "Celestial light" is a phrase from book 3 of John Milton's *Paradise Lost,* and also a phrase Satan uses in book 1 to describe what he has lost in falling from heaven. Milton himself, in the invocation to book 3, asserts that he has not lost access to that light, despite being physically blind, because of his own poetic and prophetic vocation. Wordsworth is not blind, but somehow he can no longer see the celestial light that used to seem to cloak the world.

The crucial word in the first sentence is *seem*. The world *seemed* appareled in celestial light, but it was not. Everything looks the way it did before, with the same loveliness it once had, but the loveliness is no longer celestial. Even the rainbow, which had been (in "My heart leaps up," where it provides the poem's epigraph) the sign of a covenant with himself and his own heart, no longer provides either natural piety nor even continuity, having declined to one of the lovely but essentially prosaic phenomena of the world: "The Rainbow comes and goes" (l. 9). The beauty of the world does not have the *force* that it did, and he can no longer see the things that he has seen. But the word *things* here does not mean *objects:* The objective world is unchanged. It is something more vague, "something that is gone" (l. 53).

However, the vagueness cannot be resolved, since what is gone is not something to be found in the objective world. Rather, it seems to be some capacity of subjective human feeling or responsiveness to the world. At least it seems that way in the first four stanzas of the ode, and in Coleridge's echo of them in "Dejection." There Coleridge writes of the lovely sights that surround him, particularly the moon: "I see them all, so excellently fair; / I see not feel how beautiful they are!" (ll. 37–38), which is a recollection of the second stanza of the Intimations Ode, especially "Waters on a starry night / Are beautiful and fair" (ll. 14–15). Grief has blighted the glory and the freshness that Wordsworth had once perceived in nature, and the poem begins with an effort to recover that freshness. Its first response to the sense of loss that it acknowledges is to try to overcome the jadedness of perception that has led to the loss, and stanzas 3 and 4 (until the very end) represent a strenuous effort of will to recover the celestial perceptions of childhood. One can see this in the *Now* with which stanza 3 begins, a *now* that is supposed to counterbalance the *nows* of loss in line 6 and in "A Slumber Did My Spirit Seal." The third stanza is a powerful, vital response to the dejection to which the previous stanzas testify, and it contains some of Wordsworth's greatest writing as he puts away his grief with an act of poetic will.

Stanza 4, accordingly, should be the stanza announcing recovery. Indeed, it echoes Coleridge's The RIME OF THE ANCIENT MARINER, where the Mariner's salvation begins when he spontaneously blesses the sea creatures he sees following the ship. Wordsworth achieves a moment of complete joy, and we may feel that he has managed to bind his days, each to each again; the act of creative concentration has bestowed this at once on the poem and on what the poem records and celebrates, helping him to weather the crisis and recover the perceptive and expressive responsiveness from which he had felt estranged. But then there comes the great dash that begins line 51: "—But there's a Tree, of many, one . . ." The tree, the field, the pansy all speak of something gone, and the recovery the poem has attempted is nipped in the bud. That line moved WILLIAM BLAKE, who ordinarily distrusted Wordsworth, to tears. We should understand that the tree is a naturalized and completely real version of the tree of knowledge of good and evil. The world speaks of what it lacks, and what it lacks is the delusory light of immortality we ourselves lent it in early childhood.

The end of the fourth stanza represents a very significant dead end. Wordsworth composed the first four stanzas of the Intimations Ode on March 27, 1802—the day after he had written "My heart leaps up." Indeed, we can see the third and fourth stanzas of the poem describing the process of writing "My heart leaps up" the previous day, and we can therefore measure the willfulness and anxiety ("Or let me die!") that the earlier poem seeks to counter. But the next day the poet acknowledges the failure of that attempt, and it is central to the seriousness of the Intimations Ode that Wordsworth stopped at the end of the fourth stanza and did not return to the poem *for nearly two years.* The sense of something gone is not momentary but deep, and it threatens to be permanent.

It is helpful to imagine Wordsworth baffled and without being able to make an effort to break through for two years—helpful to think of it as taking two years for him to work his way out of and through the crisis the poem records. When he returns to the poem, he returns from a different perspective to that of his earlier poetry and philosophy of inspiration. The Intimations Ode begins with a complaint that life is not what it was in childhood, with childhood as the ideal. But now in the fifth stanza, even childhood represents a decline: "Our birth is but a sleep and a forgetting" (l. 58). When he was much older, Wordsworth dictated comments on his poems to Isabella Fenwick, and in the "Fenwick note" to the poem, he says that he structured the rest of the poem on the Platonic myth of anamnesis (recalling to mind), or potential and partial recollection of a preexistent state. In his middle dialogues, especially *The Republic,* Plato sought to prove that the soul on earth is imprisoned in a lower and delusory world, and that its home is transcendent, whence it can contemplate the forms or ideas that are the only true reality. This world is an illusion, and all the beauty and order that we see in it or that we love in it is an incomplete survival of what we knew before birth but forgot when we were born. Childhood, then, is the time when we trail clouds of glory from that other world.

The soul that rises with us but has set elsewhere is Venus as the morning star. The morning star and the evening star never appear at the same time of year, and therefore it has set elsewhere, metaphorically by departing heaven. When Venus rises as the morning star, it is quickly overwhelmed by the light of common day, and while the splendid vision may attend us for the very first part of the morning, it will fade away very soon. (See PERCY BYSSHE SHELLEY's extension of this moment in his reworking of the Intimations Ode in *The TRIUMPH OF LIFE*). The earth looks beautiful to eyes that still reflect heavenly light, and what the opening stanzas of the ode had attested, the celestial light that the earth *seemed* appareled with, is now explained as light that comes from a source other than the common sun, the star that comes from another world and that is *within* us as the soul, illuminating what it sees.

But the soul can forget, even if there are still glimmerings of what is forgotten. In particular, what it forgets is that the beauty and freshness it sees on earth does not come from earth. The soul, paradoxically, has the native strength to ruin itself, as the story of the boy who is at strife with his own blessedness shows. (That boy is, in fact, based on Coleridge's son HARTLEY COLERIDGE, also the subject of his father's "FROST AT MIDNIGHT.") The boy sees light everywhere and so has no idea that he is pursuing a reflection or will of the wisp in giving himself wholly to the pleasures of earthly life. He is both an "Eye among the blind" (l. 111) and "blindly" (l. 125) striving against his own privilege. He is still close to heavenly perception, but he is headed the wrong way, and things are not yet dark enough for him to see that he is headed the wrong way.

Oddly enough, this fills Wordsworth with "joy" (l. 129)—the joy of his own grief at seeing the immensity of the boy's error. The man can see what the child cannot, which is how much there is to lose. "Something" is gone, but now he can take joy that there is still "something that doth live" (l. 130). They are, in fact, the same thing—a sense of blankness in this world that stands for what has been lost. The *discovery of loss* is the subject of the poem and also the solution to the crisis. The poem ends on a note of astonishing and difficult triumph, not because it ends in recovery but because it manages a powerful and radical transformation: It turns its original perception of a universal loss of intensity into the even greater intensity that belongs to the perception of loss. That formula—loss of intensity reversed to intensity of loss—is central to ROMANTICISM and to the romantic conception of the subject, and the Intimations Ode is both the greatest exposition and the greatest example of this transfiguration.

BIBLIOGRAPHY

Abrams, M. H. *Correspondent Breeze: Essays on English Romanticism.* New York: Norton, 1984.

———. *Natural Supernaturalism: Tradition and Revolution in Romantic Literature.* New York: Norton, 1973.

Alpers, Paul. *What is Pastoral?* Chicago: University of Chicago Press, 1996.

Barker, Juliet. *Wordsworth: A Life.* New York: Viking, 2000.

Bloom, Harold. *Poetry and Repression: Revisionism from Blake to Stevens.* New Haven, Conn.: Yale University Press, 1976.

———. *The Visionary Company: A Reading of English Romantic Poetry.* Garden City, N.Y.: Doubleday, 1961.

Bromwich, David. *Disowned by Memory: Wordsworth's Poetry of the 1790s.* Chicago: University of Chicago Press, 1998.

Brooks, Cleanth. *A Shaping Joy: Studies in the Writer's Craft.* London: Methuen, 1973.

De Man, Paul. *The Rhetoric of Romanticism.* New York: Columbia University Press, 1984.

Empson, William. *Seven Types of Ambiguity.* New York: New Directions, 1966.

Gill, Stephen. *William Wordsworth: A Life.* New York: Oxford University Press, 1989.

Hartman, Geoffrey. "The Question of Our Speech." In *The Geoffrey Hartman Reader,* edited by Daniel T. O'Hara, 321–347. Edinburgh: Edinburgh University Press, 2004.
———. *Wordsworth's Poetry, 1787–1814*. New Haven, Conn.: Yale University Press, 1971.
Hertz, Neil. *The End of the Line: Essays on Psychoanalysis and the Sublime*. New York: Columbia University Press, 1985.
Johnston, Kenneth. *Hidden Wordsworth: Poet, Lover, Rebel, Spy*. New York: Norton, 1998.
Levinson, Marjorie. *Wordsworth's Great Period Poems: Four Essays*. New York: Cambridge University Press, 1986.
Liu, Alan. *Wordsworth: The Sense of History*. Stanford, Calif.: Stanford University Press, 1989.
Moorman, Mary. *William Wordsworth: A Biography*. 2 vols. Oxford: Clarendon Press, 1957, 1965.
Pinch, Adela. *Strange Fits of Passion: Epistemologies of Emotion, Hume to Austen*. Stanford, Calif.: Stanford University Press, 1996.
Quinney, Laura. *The Poetics of Disappointment: Wordsworth to Ashbery*. Charlottesville: University of Virgnia Press, 1999.
Wolfson, Susan J. *Questioning Presence: Wordsworth, Keats, and the Interrogative Mode in Romantic Poetry*. Ithaca, N.Y.: Cornell University Press, 1986.

"INTO MY HEART AN AIR THAT KILLS"

A. E. HOUSMAN (1890) This is one of A. E. HOUSMAN's best-known and most moving lyrics. It is deceptively simple and therefore worth a little more explication than it often receives. We can tell right off that it is a poem about "lost content" (l. 5), about a sense that happiness and security and harmony with the world and with life are irrecoverable. As such, it is a distinguished descendant of its great forebear, WILLIAM WORDSWORTH'S INTIMATIONS ODE. But it is closer to Wordsworth's ode than many of its less subtle descendants. One does not need to know that Housman never set foot in Shropshire until he was an adult to see that the "far country" is *intrinsically* far. As in the French novelist Marcel Proust's sense of the evocativeness of the names of places he has never been, and the parallel evocativeness even of the names of places he has eventually come to see, as long as he can forget them or subordinate them to what they were before he visited, Housman's far country of Shropshire, or of the past—the far country of the Shropshire in which he was never a lad—owes its intense and melancholy beauty to its "impossibility" (Proust's word again).

One can see this in the precision of the poetic diction. "The land of lost content" (l. 5) is not the same thing as the *lost land of content* would be. The land itself is a place of loss, not a place that has been lost. Its hills are remembered, not forgotten, but their memory is itself, one might say, a memory of distance and absence and loss, not of presence and habitual fullness. It is a memory of the wistful experience of memory—hence the question: "What are those blue remembered hills?" This, again, is far different from the meaning to which one might naturally but wrongly adjust it: "Where are those hills now?" (This is the most plaintive of tropes, the *ubi sunt,* familiar in medieval Latin and more recently in the 15th-century French poet François Villon and in JOHN KEATS'S "TO AUTUMN": "Where are the songs of spring?") The speaker has been on those highways he can now see from afar, and to which he cannot return. That very idea means that the highways are not the thoroughfares they seemed, and he cannot return to the time when they were thoroughfares. Now the air that blows from that far country is one that kills and not one that revivifies or rejuvenates.

This poem registers the melancholy belief that happiness and intensity—especially poetic intensity—do not and cannot go together. The happiness that a poem can evoke is only a happiness lost. To be a poet is to want to recapture lost happiness and to succeed instead in an evocation of its loss. To read such a poem is to feel that evoked loss, and to write such a poem is to feel that poetry itself is such a region of evoked loss. This means that the far country of evoked loss in Housman's poem is not Shropshire, nor yet childhood, but poetry itself: the poetry within which he wishes to dwell (for example, that of Horace, Juvenal, and Manilius, Roman writers whom he edited), and for which he must substitute—paradoxically enough—poetic expression instead. Poetry expresses the intensity of its own distance from itself.

BIBLIOGRAPHY

Gardner, Philip, ed. *A. E. Housman: The Critical Heritage*. New York: Routledge, 1992.
Highet, Gilbert. *Classical Tradition: Greek and Roman Influences on Western Literature*. New York: Oxford University Press, 1957.
Richards, Grant. *Housman: 1897–1936*. New York: Oxford University Press, 1942.

"INVICTUS" WILLIAM ERNEST HENLEY (1875)

W. E. HENLEY's "Invictus" has become a kind of standalone poem, particularly popular in the United States, where it has become a sort of anthem of "death-before-dishonor" militant patriotism, in the tradition of Patrick Henry. It was part of President John F. Kennedy's cultivated campaign mythology that he was said to love the poem. The poem was not, in fact, much noted in Henley's own lifetime and only became an anthology piece later. But now its fame and its stirring and militant rhetoric have given it a life of its own, so that Oklahoma terrorist Timothy McVeigh could vividly distort this militancy when he recited it just before his execution.

But the poem, written by Henley in his mid-twenties when he was hospitalized for more than a year and at risk of amputation (one leg had already been amputated), is about psychological fortitude, not jingoistic posturing. The defiance that the poem certainly expresses is an internal and even an aesthetic defiance, befitting a poet whose capacities for intense aesthetic appreciation and discrimination were met by the horrors of death, poverty, and disease. Henley's poem is ambivalent about the very soul that it celebrates, for that soul's own experience of itself is one of darkness and distress.

To see this, notice how the poem simultaneously refuses and celebrates a sharp distinction between circumstances—the givens of the outside universe—and the soul mired in these circumstances. The gods write the scroll "charged with punishments" (l. 14)—the scroll not of the law but of fate; the gods also make strait the gate (l. 13: the allusion is to Matthew 7:14: "Strait is the gate, and narrow is the way, which leadeth unto life, and few there be that find it") that makes the possibility of heaven vanishingly small. Henley does not expect heaven or exemption from punishment, and in fact does not believe in heaven: The only thing beyond this dreadful place is the "Horror of the shade" (l. 10), and at best the gods *may* exist, but just as well may not (l. 3). Yet the gods (or the God) that have done this to him are also the gods that he thanks for his "unconquerable soul" (l. 4). Why?

Henley is a densely allusive poet (this is part of his aestheticism), and that last phrase is in fact highly allusive. The only precedents that Henley would have known for that phrase are from John Milton, Thomas Gray, and WILLIAM WORDSWORTH—indeed, these are practically the only precedents that exist for the use of the word *unconquerable* in a poem, and both Gray and Wordsworth are alluding to the famous Miltonic phrase in *Paradise Lost* where Satan declares that even though God has defeated him in battle and sent him to hell, even though "the field be lost / All is not lost" since he still retains his "unconquerable will . . . And courage never to submit or yield" (1.105–108). Henley is representing himself, more directly even than Gray and Wordsworth, as containing the virtues of Satanic resistance without the corresponding vices of Satanic ambition. (This is what McVeigh, genuinely devilish, failed to understand.) What is stirring about Satan is the way that he is the master of his fate, and we must understand that what Henley means by this is what Satan meant by it: not that he can control his fate, since it is, after all, *fate,* which by definition one cannot control, but that even his fate does not control *him.* He is the captain of his soul, and so is victorious in not capitulating to fate but remaining *invictus,* unconquered.

That this is not the Satanic and Byronic embrace of evil can be seen in the fact that he thanks the gods for the soul that allows him to resist their torments and bludgeonings. The unconquerable soul they have given him is again like Satan's soul, determined by *fate* (*Paradise Lost,* 1.116) to be immortal and so to suffer eternal punishment. The thanks that Henley offers to "whatever gods may be" (l. 3) are not thanks for a gift that they intended he should celebrate. They meant his unconquerable soul to be a source of torment to him, as it is to Satan, and so it is. But like Satan he celebrates that fact, celebrates the very unconquerability that is his lamentable fate, and so in celebrating it becomes its master.

BIBLIOGRAPHY

Buckley, J. H. *William Ernest Henley: A Study in the "Counter-decadence" of the 'Nineties.* Princeton, N.J.: Princeton University Press. 1945.

Cohen, Edward H. "Two Anticipations of Henley's 'Invictus,'" *The Huntington Library Quarterly* 37, no. 2 (February 1974): 191–196.

Rubin, Joan Shelley. *Songs of Ourselves: The Uses of Poetry in America.* Cambridge, Mass.: Harvard University Press, 2007.

Williamson, Kennedy. *W. E. Henley: A Memoir.* London: H. Shaylor, 1930.

"I SAW IN DRESDEN ON A WINDY DAY" JAMES HENRY (1856)

JAMES HENRY loved his cigars, as we know from "I am the pink of courtesy," his hilarious apology for smoking. "I saw in Dresden on a windy day" is more serious and more moving. Although Henry thought of himself as the opposite of a Wordsworthian poet, he might be seen here as noticing a Wordsworthian scene—but a scene far lighter in its meaning than those WILLIAM WORDSWORTH tended to describe in *his* sketches, and yet a scene ultimately as profound. Like Wordsworth in "SIMON LEE," Henry insists that he is telling "a plain fact, not a poet's story" (l. 3), by which he means he really did see what he says, and also that there is no allegory in the story he recounts. What he saw was a man and woman walking together in the wind, both of them weighed down with what they were carrying. The man was carrying his coat, and a gust of wind made him decide to put it on, but he dropped his cigar in doing so, and the woman picked the cigar up for the man. Henry calls her "compassionate" (l. 10) for doing so. The crucial thing is that her compassion does not take the form of self-sacrifice but of knowledge. She knows how unpleasant it is to lose the cigar, to have the pleasure of the smoke interrupted. Her compassion is her knowledge of him, the fact that she cares about him enough to know and knows about him enough to care.

The woman puts down her basket and helps the man with the coat while picking up the cigar and keeping it lit by puffing on it herself. This bit of business, as we may call it, would have been very unusual in 1856 when women did not smoke cigars, at least in public. But she knows too that the cigar will go out unless she keeps it going; so she does, and when they are ready to walk again, she hands him the cigar, and "Away they go, the man with his cigar / The woman with the man, well pleased and happy" (ll. 17–18). He is pleased with the cigar, and she is pleased with him. Note the analogical structure: Cigar is to man what man is to woman.

The worst reading here would be the vulgar-Freudian one which would see the cigar as phallic. (Even Sigmund Freud famously quipped that sometimes a cigar is just a cigar.) She has not succeeded in some imitative desire; she has made him happy, and she is happy that he is happy. And the cigar is for him now a kind of reminder of her compassion as well. He can move along smoking it, not only "happy" but also "well pleased" by how events have occurred. He is pleased by what she has done for him, and that makes the cigar stand for his love for her just as much as he represents *himself* to her, stands for her very love for him and happiness in their successful presence together. All this depth of intimacy is what Henry notices, leaving (as he says) the moral to us. He need not point the moral; he is well pleased and happy himself to have seen them.

BIBLIOGRAPHY

Cunningham, Valentine, ed. *The Victorians: An Anthology of Poetry and Poetics.* Malden, Mass.: Blackwell, 2000.

Henry, James. *Selected Poems of James Henry.* Edited by Christopher Ricks. New York: Handsel, 2002.

Ricks, Christopher, ed. *The New Oxford Book of Victorian Verse.* New York: Oxford University Press, 1987.

Rogoff, Jay. "First Fruits." *Southern Review* 40, no. 3 (2004): 602–628.

"ISOLATION: TO MARGUERITE" AND "TO MARGUERITE—CONTINUED" MATTHEW ARNOLD (1857)

Of Marguerite almost nothing is known. She was, apparently, a woman MATTHEW ARNOLD met in Switzerland on a visit there in 1848. We can guess from the paired poems he wrote to her that she was less devoted to him than he was to her. But we may guess more: that he preferred a kind of baffled devotion to actual love—that he wanted their love to be made impossible by distance and fate, and he wanted the two of them to share together in his love for that impossible love.

If this desire is to be inferred from the poems, it is partly because it is in keeping with Arnold's general sense of human communion as a communion of pessimism. The Marguerite poems certainly share that sense with poems like "DOVER BEACH" and "PHILOMELA," both of which echo these poems' obsession with the isolation of humans from each other. "Isolation: To

Marguerite" is the title of the first of the poems to Marguerite, and the word *isolation* is echoed by the first line of the second poem, "To Marguerite—Continued," which describes how we are all "in the sea of life enisled." *Enisled* is a rare word, constructed on the analogy of *enclosed,* and it means that we are cut off from one another, trapped in the islands of our own selfhood. (This is the opposite sentiment from John Donne's famous claim that "No man is an island.") *Isolation* has as its root meaning the Latin word *insula,* island. (The *n* dropped out, while an *s* was added to *island,* which makes *insula* an etymological source of the latter word as well.) Isolation and enforced separation or insulation is the experience Arnold cherishes and about which he complains. He cherishes it *because* he can complain about it, because it gives him matter for his poetry.

The first poem alludes to Shakespeare's famous sonnet (number 116) about how "Love's not love that alters when it alteration finds." Arnold and Marguerite have sworn to "be true to one another," as he says in "Dover Beach." Or at least, as in "Dover Beach," he thinks that he can make that vow more or less for her by being true to her. He never explicitly asserts that she has promised the same to him. But he has imagined that she would be as true to him as he was to her.

Clearly she was not, and he regards this as something that he ought to have known from his experience of the world before meeting her. The rest of the poem, while afflicted with genuine sadness, also displays Arnold's trademark fault of pompous self-absorption. He knows all too well the solitude of human life and human experience. The scales have fallen from his eyes, and the only joy he can take is in the "touch" (l. 32) of other lonely things. The shared communion of loneliness is all that makes up for that loneliness.

Even here, though, his pomposity gets the better of him, for he knows his loneliness, whereas he finds pleasure and companionship for his heart in the naive belief in love that other "happier men" (ll. 36–37) display. They are like him in being lonely but unlike him because they have not plumbed their loneliness to its depths. So he sees more deeply into the nothingness of human life than they do, although they share that nothingness with him. Thus, Arnold gets to eat his cake and have it, too.

The continuation of the poem in "To Marguerite—Continued" is far better. Arnold apportions less blame there and preens himself less on his own unparalleled melancholy. The first-person pronouns here are plural, not singular. Everyone mortal lives "*alone*" (l. 4; Arnold's emphasis); we are all enisled and separate from one another. A crucial Arnoldian touch comes at the end of the first stanza: We are islands, each one surrounded by the "shoreless watery wild," and those islands "feel the enclasping flow / And then their endless bounds they know" (ll. 3, 5–6). The islands have shores, but those are shores onto shorelessness. That this oxymoron is intentional can be seen from the fact that it is repeated in the phrase *endless bounds.* The bounds that isolate us are themselves unbounded.

This is the characteristic way that Arnold will attempt to reverse emptiness into a kind of secondary fullness, making what was void into the void itself. What we all share is the fact that we do not share anything. This is why the word *enisled* is picked up by the word *enclasping:* Arnold wishes to transform the one into the other.

What enclasps each island of mortality is the sea that enclasps them all. This sea is, of course, a sea of sorrow, "The unplumbed, salt, estranging sea" of the poem's great last line. But the sorrow is one we can all share. In the figurative or metaphorical conceit of the poem, on calm nights nightingales sing in the various islands (see also Arnold's "Philomela"), and the beauty of their songs may be heard from isle to isle. This is a vision of possible communion, made impossible by the sea between them. What is crucial, though, is that what the nightingales sing of is the despair of the islands' separation. Thus, the songs that make us so want to unite, so desire to feel "Parts of a single continent" (l. 16), are the plaintive anthems describing our separation from each other.

This fact could lead to a despairing paradox: What makes us want to join is only the fact of our separation. Were we joined, we would have no reason to want to remain so. This is why we can feel that Arnold preferred separation from Marguerite to the much tougher experience of living a real life with her. But it must be said we can also find hopefulness in the paradox. Our very isolation joins us and makes possible the joy-inspiring poetry that speaks of pessimistic things but transmutes them into art. Arnold's best moments in poetry are moments in which pessimism and despair are an achievement he can share with others, make others feel as he does, so that both he and his audience can find solace in that communal experience.

Needless to say, though, Marguerite is not part of that audience. She is only an excuse to address it.

BIBLIOGRAPHY

Arnold, Matthew. *Essays, Letters, and Reviews.* Collected and edited by Fraser Neiman. Cambridge, Mass.: Harvard University Press, 1960.

Bloom, Harold, ed. *Matthew Arnold.* New York: Chelsea House, 1987.

Dawson, Carl, and John Pfordresher, eds. *Matthew Arnold: The Critical Heritage.* New York: Routledge, 1995.

Trilling, Lionel. *The Moral Obligation to Be Intelligent: Selected Essays.* Edited by Leon Weiseltier. New York: Farrar, Straus, and Giroux, 2000.

"IT IS NOT BEAUTY I DEMAND" GEORGE DARLEY (1828) Francis Turner Palgrave put this poem in *The Golden Treasury of English Songs and Lyrics* as a 17th-century poem, and this is a significant fact about it. GEORGE DARLEY (like his contemporary THOMAS LOVELL BEDDOES and like JOHN KEATS) was attracted in poetry to the same kind of strangeness that would attract an anthologist like Palgrave. "It is not Beauty I Demand" is consciously archaic, influenced by William Shakespeare, both his sonnets (especially 130: "My mistress' eyes are nothing like the sun") and his songs, by Sir Philip Sidney's sonnet cycle *Astrophel and Stella,* and in another sense by the 17th-century poet Andrew Marvell. The attraction is the point: There is a sense in which it *is* beauty that Darley demands, but the beauty he demands is that of poetic language and of archaic poetic rhythm.

The poem is therefore an act of what in rhetoric is called *praeteritio*: the specification of what the speaker says he or she will not specify. It gives the impression, although it never says so explicitly, that the woman it refers to is in fact blazoned by all the attributes he says he does not seek. In fact, it never explicitly refers to her at all, but it is just this fact that allows us to know that it is about a particular person. Its emotional tonality is too rich for the poem to offer itself as mere quasi-platonic theory. There is someone whom it is about, and the poem praises that person. In fact, the praise consists in the very intuition that it *is* about someone. Only a real person could provoke this beautiful tribute, and only a person who was really beautiful could forego the praise of beauty on behalf of the more Sidneyan praise of soul. He does not demand beauty, but he gets it anyway, since she is beautiful.

The poem demands beauty, though: It demands the imagery that takes up 28 of its 40 lines. The beauty it demands is that of lyric imagery (of the sort to be found as well in the songs of LORD BYRON and PERCY BYSSHE SHELLEY), and what gives point and pungency and density to the imagery is the hint of danger there too. All the beauties catalogued might disguise some fatal harm; this is where Darley is closest to Beddoes. But that possible fatality is fascinating and explains not only why the speaker dwells on its details but also why the *poem* does. Because like all romantic poetry (see ROMANTICISM), indeed like most 19th-century poetry, one of the subjects of this poem is poetry itself, its conspicuously unfamiliar language, the fascination that poetry exercises, the subjectivity it plumbs. Poems aspire to the beautiful, but the beautiful to which they aspire is the beauty of poetry. They want to have something that they already *are* and so cannot have; or (put another way), the poet wants something that only a poem can have or be. Darley wants 17th-century poetry, and his poem records the desire and meets it (or awakens it) for *us* but not for him. He understands that this desire is akin to erotic desire and the way it wants more than it can possibly have, but he here treats erotic desire as an avatar for the desire for poetic beauty the poem expresses. Both are modes of communication with another subjectivity and the apparent religious end of the poem is in fact a platonic fantasy: that all these desires will be met in intellectual sympathy, his spirit and hers won to sympathetic union with the "intellectual beauty" (in Shelley's platonic phrase) to which they aspire.

BIBLIOGRAPHY

Abbott, Claude Colleer. *The Life and Letters of George Darley, Poet and Critic.* London: Oxford University Press, 1928.

Bridges, Robert Seymour. "George Darley." In *Collected Essays, Papers, &c., of Robert Bridges.* Vol. 2, 87–188. London: Oxford University Press, 1927–36.

Brisman, Leslie. "George Darley: Bouyant as Young Time." In *Romantic Origins,* 182–223. Ithaca, N.Y.: Cornell University Press, 1978.

Simmel, Georg. "Eros, Platonic and Modern." In *On Individuality and Social Forms,* edited by Donald N. Levine, 235–248. Chicago: University of Chicago Press, 1971.

"I TRAVELED AMONG UNKNOWN MEN" See LUCY POEMS.

"IT WAS DEEP APRIL" MICHAEL FIELD (1893)

Katharine Bradley and Edith Cooper knew that the admiration for their joint creation, MICHAEL FIELD, depended on its not being generally known that he was really two women writing in tandem. Some of their friends had known this for a while, and ROBERT BROWNING thought as highly of them as ever, but their reputation plummeted in the public eye after the truth became generally known in 1893. It is interesting to consider their poetry's relation to its audience's knowledge of who Michael Field was. The lyric *I* in their poems is sometimes meant to communicate a singular speaker to the reader. But in their later poetry, the fact that the *I* is actually the creation of two poets makes a difference for readers that the poems themselves exploit.

"It was deep April" is famous for its frankness, a frankness meant to be appreciated by some, but not all, of its readers. Its most famous lines declare how "My Love and I took hands and swore / Against the world, to be / Poets and lovers evermore" (ll. 4–6). The two women did make such a vow to each other and did more or less succeed in keeping it. By being poets and lovers, they could ignore the conventional judgments of the world (ll. 3, 10), which would disapprove of their relationship (both lesbian and more or less incestuous, since Bradley was Cooper's aunt). It was in poetry that they found a world other than that of conventional morality and judgment. (They thought of themselves as so intensely united as almost to be a single soul, comparing themselves favorably to the archetypal poet-couple, Robert and ELIZABETH BARRETT BROWNING.)

In the poem, the speaker's pledge is to join with the "fast-locked souls" who live with and devoted to Apollo, the god of poetry (ll. 11–12). Such souls (like "Shakspere" [l. 2], born April 23) are "fast-locked" because they are secure in their vocation (unlike the "timid souls" of line 9) and secure in each other. In a sense, for Bradley and Cooper, each was the other's vocation, and this poem describes how their vocation for love and their vocation for poetry were identical. It is in this vocation that they can be "Indifferent to heaven and hell" (l. 16), which is to say indifferent to any other idea of reward and punishment than that of love and poetry. (Bradley, at any rate, was an acknowledged atheist, at least until the end of the 19th century, and this poem explains her atheism, not her defiance of a heaven and hell in which she believed.)

It should be noted, however, that the poem, like so many of Michael Field's poems, is in the first-person singular. The speaker says, "*My* Love and I took hands," which is not the same thing as "*We* took each other's hands." The rest of the poem might feel as though it is in the first-person plural (partly because of the introductory complaint in l. 3), but it is actually in the infinitive construction, governed by what "My love and I . . . swore to be" and to do. That first person affords plausible deniability. The male Michael Field has a lover, and he and his lover swear to be poets. Even if Michael Field is discovered to be Bradley and Cooper, he is a fictional character referring to a fictional lover, someone precisely *not* a member of the couple he comprises.

And yet for them what the *I* would have meant is the sense that each would see herself and the other as being both the *I* and the love, and that beyond the deniability of the fact that they were lovers is the fact that they were so close that the *I* was a pronoun each could both say to the other and at the same time think of the other as being. The fellowship they feel with other poets is the fellowship that they feel with each other, written large and made universal.

BIBLIOGRAPHY

Avery, Simon. "Michael Field (1846–1914)." *The Literary Encyclopedia* (June 13, 2003). Available online. URL: http://www.litencyc.com/php/speople.php?rec=true&UID=1521. Accessed on March 14, 2008.

Castle, Terry, ed. *The Literature of Lesbianism: A Historical Anthology from Ariosto to Stonewall.* New York: Columbia University Press, 2003.
Moore, T., and D. C. Sturge. *Works and Days, from the Journal of Michael Field.* London: J. Murray, 1933.
Prins, Yopie. *Victorian Sappho.* Princeton, N.J.: Princeton University Press, 1999.
Sturgeon, Mary. *Michael Field.* London: G.G. Harrap, 1922.
White, Christine. "'Poets and Lovers Evermore': The Poetry and Journals of Michael Field." In *Sexual Sameness: Textual Differences in Lesbian and Gay Writing,* edited by Joseph Bristow, 26–43. New York: Routledge, 1992.

"ITYLUS" ALGERNON CHARLES SWINBURNE (1866)

ALGERNON CHARLES SWINBURNE's characteristic theme is immersion: immersion in the sea, in song and the hypnotic repetitions to which song is drawn, in myth, in thoughts of death, and in thoughts of maternal vastness. In his best poems, which is to say in his most extreme poems, these varieties of immersion are all brought together, so that every mode of poetic practice affords both poet and reader the consolatory beauty of such immersion, even as it demonstrates why it should be beautiful and why it should be consolatory. "Itylus" is a perfect example of Swinburne's practice.

The title is the first interesting thing about the poem. The story of Itylus is, in fact, the story of Philomela, of her sister Procne, and of her rape by Procne's husband Tereus. Its most famous and influential telling is in Ovid's *Metamorphoses* (book 6), where it explains the origin of the nightingale, the swallow, and the bird called the hoopoe as metamorphoses of these three characters. Procne, mother of Itylus, or Itys, desires to see her sister Philomela, and her loving husband King Tereus goes to conduct her back to his kingdom. However, he falls in love with Philomela, and when she resists his advances, he rapes her. To keep this violation secret, he cuts out her tongue so that she cannot report the crime, imprisons her, and tells his wife Procne that she has died. Philomela escapes imprisonment and finds Procne but cannot tell her story. Instead, she weaves a tapestry, picturing it, and the two women vow revenge on Tereus. That revenge, as is often the case in Greek and Roman myth, consists of killing Tereus's child, Itylus, who is Procne's son as well. (Swinburne's great verse drama *ATALANTA IN CALYDON* is also about a mother who ends up murdering her son, and he alludes to the story of Philomela there as well.) As they are about to do so, they are struck by his innocence and trust, but because of his resemblance to his father, they overcome their remorse and kill him anyway. Procne then serves his flesh to Tereus; Philomela enters and, finally understanding what has happened, Tereus storms after them. In the desperate violence of the pursuit, Procne turns into the roof-living swallow, Philomela into the woods-haunting nightingale, and Tereus into the hoopoe. The myth has long fascinated poets as accounting for the beautiful, plaintive, inarticulate song of the nightingale. Indeed, the name *Philomela* may be translated as "lover of sweet music."

That Swinburne would name the poem after Itylus, who is not even mentioned until the eighth stanza out of 10, shows the wishfulness with which he regards the attitudes of the two sisters, Itylus's mother and aunt. The poem is actually spoken by Philomela, and it is therefore in the voice of the nightingale, lamenting the endless sorrow she has caused. It is this lamentation that Swinburne, perpetual son of sorrow and of the sea, wishes to imagine on the part of the maternal generation, even as he wishes also to imagine the comforts of maternal oblivion. As in "The TRIUMPH OF TIME," the maternal sea is a place of both comfort and oblivion; what she offers is the comfort of oblivion.

That oblivion is first of all represented by the swallow, whose love for singing and for migration strikes Philomela as an emblem of her forgetfulness. For Philomela, the name *swallow* is one of the bird's most attractive features, offering a fantasy of being swallowed up by the sea or the spaces in which the nightingale cannot escape from herself. The question the nightingale Philomela first asks her sister the swallow, in the first stanza, is how she can still greet the spring. Philomela has seen the yearly cycle so many times before that she cannot find any hope in the world. Her words are a kind of reversal of PERCY BYSSHE SHELLEY's great poem ODE TO THE WEST WIND, in which the coming of winter portends the coming of spring as well. Although Swinburne loved Shelley, no such happy portents await the nightingale, since she knows that there is nothing new under the sun. But the nightingale also knows that the swallow is swallowed up by her own forgetfulness, or the oblivion of the past human life in which she has murdered her son.

Swinburne's poem is in part an answer to MATTHEW ARNOLD's "PHILOMELA," which mentions neither Itylus nor Procne. But like Arnold's poem, "Itylus" alludes strongly to the tradition of nightingale poems in English, from John Milton's comparison of himself as a blind poet to the hidden nightingale who "sings darkling," to SAMUEL TAYLOR COLERIDGE's conversation poem "The Nightingale," to JOHN KEATS's "ODE TO A NIGHTINGALE," to Shelley's description in *A Defence of Poetry* of the poet as a "a nightingale who sits In darkness and sings to cheer his own solitude." So, too, does Philomela in Swinburne's poem, and what she sings about is her solitude and the sorrow that overwhelms her.

Swinburne consistently uses hypnotic repetition and rhyme to convey this sense of engulfing sadness, and all the apostrophized addresses to the swallow, as well as all the rhymes on the word (*swallow* is rhymed in every stanza), convey this sense of being engulfed through sound and in sound. Philomela is explicit about this in the eighth stanza, when she describes how her heart "goes forth among the sea-gulfs hollow" (l. 47), which explains why she has used the Shelleyan metaphor "over my head the waves have met" (l. 39) which is also so central to *The Triumph of Time*. She sheds her song "upon bright and hollow," in Swinburne's beautiful image, but what she sings about is the impossibility of song and the impossibility of oblivion for herself like the oblivion her sister lives in. Hence, the swallow follows the cycle of the seasons, but the nightingale sings only through time, through spring and through night, merging all time into the engulfing duration of sadness.

Philomela sings about her sister's oblivion; she sings hoping to get her sister to cease her own oblivious singing for a space, on the wet roofs the swallow haunts (l. 50); she sings because she cannot forget the unchanging flower, so different from the flowers of spring, that the trustful, longing face of young Itylus presented to her (l. 53). His blood still cries out, "*Who hath remembered me, who hath forgotten*" (l. 58)—questions the last two lines of the poem answers. But more important, Philomela recognizes that what Itylus wants—what *Swinburne* wants from his maternal imaginings in his identification with Itylus—is for the difference of memory and forgetfulness to come undone. Rhyme's hypnotic repetitions pull toward oblivion; its meanings pull toward memory, and Swinburne's great achievement in poetry is the gorgeous, plangent combination of the two—the combination he ascribes to the beautifully intense song of the nightingale.

BIBLIOGRAPHY

Doggett, Frank. "Romanticism's Singing Bird." *Studies in English Literature, 1500–1900* 14, no. 4 (Autumn, 1974): 547–561.

Grossman, Allen. "Orpheus/Philomela: Subjection and Mastery in the Founding Stories of Poetic Production." In *The Long Schoolroom: Lessons in the Bitter Logic of the Poetic Principle,* 18–38. Ann Arbor: University of Michigan Press, 1997.

Louis, Margot Kathleen. *Swinburne and His Gods: The Roots and Growth of an Agnostic Poetry*. Kingston, Ont.: McGill-Queen's University Press, 1990.

McGann, Jerome J. *Swinburne: An Experiment in Criticism*. Chicago: University of Chicago Press, 1972.

Rutland, William R. *Swinburne: A Nineteenth Century Hellene*. Oxford: Blackwell, 1931.

"I WAKE AND FEEL THE FELL OF DARK, NOT DAY" GERARD MANLEY HOPKINS (1885) This is one of GERARD MANLEY HOPKINS's so-called terrible sonnets, or sonnets of desolation. It is the first of four Hopkins had written together on a single sheet of paper, which seem to be the poems he was referring to when he wrote his friend (and later editor) ROBERT BRIDGES, in a letter of September 1, 1885, "I shall shortly have some sonnets to send you. . . . Four of these came like inspirations unbidden and against my will. And in the life I lead now, which is one of a continually jaded and harassed mind, if in any leisure I try to do something I make no way—nor with my work, alas! but so it must be." This sonnet is to some extent self-explaining: It depicts an awakening from the long, dark night of the soul, but an awakening into horror not to be distinguished from the nightmarish dark it was supposed to end.

Hopkins explains in the second stanza that the hours of night actually mean years, indeed seem to mean his whole life up to this present moment, when he feels "the fell of dark." He awakens to it, and what he awakens to is a kind of portmanteau word, as though his ubiquitous concatenating and heaping up of nouns had collapsed into a single syllable. The noun *fell* is a kind of nominalization of the adjective *fell,* meaning evil or malevolent (as in its adjectival use in Hopkins's "NO WORST, THERE IS NONE," l. 8), but it also suggests that the dark which should rise has fallen even more claustrophobically on his soul, like the fell, or pelt, of some malicious animal. Dark is a creature from hell, which turns all feeling by a shortening of the vowel into its own fell horror.

The lament that is the poem is a cry out of the darkness. Hopkins compares those cries to "dead letters sent / To dearest him that lives, alas! away" (ll. 7–8), so that the written poems are pleas to Christ, who does not hear his prayers. Here, as everywhere, Hopkins should be compared to his great predecessor, the 17th-century metaphysical poet George Herbert. (The particular poem that Hopkins took to heart here is Herbert's "Denial" as well as his odd and grotesque poem "The Bag.") This Petrarchan sonnet makes its characteristic turn after the end of the octet, by following Herbert in finding God's silence and distance as itself a lesson directed at him and therefore a response. Like Herbert, whenever Hopkins cries out for God in his despair, the cry itself makes him take his despair as something that God knows about and intends (as at the end of "CARRION COMFORT," another sonnet of desolation). The intention, however painful, is better than God's indifference would be.

Thus, in the sestet Hopkins sees his despair as being "God's most deep decree" (l. 9). It is here that Hopkins's account of despair is most terrible and most psychologically plausible. He feels the despair of being trapped in his own selfhood, his own idiosyncrasy, forever. Other people—our friendship with them and our love for them—allow us an escape from the oppression of our own stale familiarity to ourselves. God is the most absolute receiver of such a love, such an escape. But God's decree is the reverse: The sheer gross materialism of the inescapable self, not the pure transcendental self of the German philosopher Immanuel Kant but the empirical self, condemned to be Hopkins forever with all his foibles and fears and specificities—what Hopkins captures in his amazing evocation of "the *sweating* self" (l. 14). He feels himself on the verge of eternal damnation: The only thing worse than being one's own sweating self in the moment of despair (the moment the poem is uttered) is to know that this will go on forever. This is the wholly negative, endlessly worsening version of the process of "selving" that he describes in "AS KINGFISHERS CATCH FIRE."

Most critics attempt to find Hopkins drawing a distinction between himself and the damned in hell here, but this is a misreading. The last word, *worse,* echoes the terrible and anguished beginning of "No worst, there is none," with its abyssal sense that the worse is always worsening. The experience of the eternity of sweating selfhood is an experience of eternal worsening, which is what the idea of damnation for eternity must always mean. The poem offers only the scantest hope that Hopkins will be rescued from this desolation, but the hope consists in his repudiation of the desolation of sour selfhood, his desire for rescue. This is a hope perhaps not to be distinguished from despair, since it is only a feeling of terror and a desire that things should be different, not even a tenuously confident anticipation that they will be. This is one of the darkest of all great poems.

BIBLIOGRAPHY

Bridges, Robert. Preface to *Poems of Gerard Manley Hopkins.* Edited by W. H. Gardner. New York: Oxford University Press, 1948.

Gardner, W. H. *Gerard Manley Hopkins (1844–1889): A Study of Poetic Idiosyncrasy in Relation to Poetic Tradition.* New Haven, Conn.: Yale University Press, 1949.

———. Introduction to *Poems and Prose of Gerard Manley Hopkins.* Harmondsworth, Middlesex, England: Penguin, 1963.

Hartman, Geoffrey. *The Unmediated Vision: An Interpretation of Wordsworth, Hopkins, Rilke, and Valery.* New Haven, Conn.: Yale University Press, 1954.

Hopkins, Gerard Manley. *Gerard Manley Hopkins: Selected Letters.* Edited by Catherine Phillips. New York: Oxford University Press, 1990.

Miller, J. Hillis. "Gerard Manley Hopkins." In *The Disappearance of God: Five Nineteenth-Century Writers,* 270–359. Cambridge, Mass.: Belknap Press of Harvard University Press, 1963.

White, Norman. *Hopkins: A Literary Biography.* New York: Oxford University Press, 1992.

"I WANDERED LONELY AS A CLOUD"

William Wordsworth (1804) This is one of William Wordsworth's most famous poems. Like many of Wordsworth's shorter poems, it is far more complex than it seems at first. Wordsworth was particularly good at interweaving several different temporal perspectives into a single poem, and since time and the changes it produces formed Wordsworth's central poetic preoccupation, his interweaving in this poem is of central importance.

The extent to which Wordsworth altered versions of events that were the origins of his poems should be noted here. We know from his sister Dorothy's journals that they were together when they saw the daffodils the poem celebrates. In her journal for April 15, 1804, she wrote: "I never saw daffodils so beautiful they grew among the mossy stones about and about them, some rested their heads upon these stones as on a pillow for weariness and the rest tossed and reeled and danced and seemed as if they verily laughed with the wind that blew upon them over the lake, they looked so gay ever dancing ever changing." Wordsworth waited two years to write the poem about that day, and in "I wandered lonely as a cloud," he reimagines it according to his poetic needs. The most obvious change, of course, is the speaker's loneliness, where in reality Wordsworth was with his sister. (Her hidden or unexpected presence should be compared with her surprising appearance at the end of "Tintern Abbey.")

The poem begins in the past tense and seems to be the present report of an incident just experienced. The speaker has been astonished by the sudden appearance, or at least his sudden awareness, of a host of daffodils. They put him in mind of the heavens at night—the stars in the milky way—as well as the waves of the lake by which they dance, and so they become a kind of center to the whole world of human experience: stars, sky (where the clouds and the breeze are active), earth, woods, and waters.

It is important to notice the loneliness of the wanderer in the opening line. This is not neediness but, rather, a sense of poetic selfhood as isolated and unlikely to find anything in the world that will comfort it or cheer its solitude. We discover in line 15—"a poet could not but be gay"—that the pleasure the sight of the daffodils affords him is not only unexpected, it may be something that he resists. He is "Surprised by Joy," and as in that poem, he may not quite wish to be.

But the daffodils do suddenly interrupt his reverie and fill him with joy. What he does not know is that the joy they afford him is related to his vocation as a poet. The poet is made gay by the company, either *because* or *in spite of* the fact that he is a poet, or both: the kind of melancholy attendant on being a poet may be just the sort of thing that will not sustain itself in the presence of the daffodils. As a poet, he is the type to gaze and gaze, but in his gazing he forgets that he is a poet: He is completely absorbed in the beauty and surprise of what he sees.

Notice that the poem could not end after the third stanza. The daffodils are not yet matter for poetry: He does not *think* ("I . . . little thought") that they are of any importance to him. The dramatic moment in the poem is the discovery that they *are* of importance, the discovery that he announces at the end of the third stanza and explains in the last.

The wealth the daffodils bring him is the wealth of thought and of memory. This is the second temporal perspective in the poem. Once he wandered and saw the daffodils but did not realize their importance. Later he did, those frequent times when the memory flashed upon his inward eye while he was lying on his couch either thinking much (pensive) or thinking little (vacant). The daffodils have brought something like the ebullience of the present into the courts of memory, so that the "loneliness" of the first stanza can become the *blissful* solitude of the last. It is *because* the memory fills his heart with pleasure that it can dance with the daffodils, and one of the things of which this dance is a metaphor is the poem that celebrates them. But the third temporal perspective is that of the poem itself, which tells how he remembers the daffodils involuntarily when he is *not* composing but lying on his couch. The poem records *this* event rather than the actual wandering that made this second event possible.

"I wandered lonely as a cloud" is often and rightly taken as an exemplification of Wordsworth's famous doctrine, expressed in his preface to *Lyrical Ballads* (1798), of poetry as "emotion recollected in tranquility." Here the emotion would be the poet's unexpected gaiety at seeing the daffodils, and the tranquility would be vacant or pensive moods when he suddenly remembers them. The fact that memories can surprise us with pleasure like this is what Wordsworth is noticing and celebrating.

The word *pleasure* in the second-to-last line is not one that Wordsworth uses lightly. In the preface to *Lyrical Ballads,* he says that the poet's purpose and vocation are the same thing: to give pleasure. That pleasure might derive from the description of painful things, but the description itself gives pleasure, and the contemplation and composition of the description gives the poet pleasure as well. Such pleasure is for Wordsworth the most important feature of human life and human dignity. He calls it "an acknowledgement of the beauty of the universe" and therefore praises and makes preeminent in man what he calls "the grand elementary principle of pleasure, by which he knows, and feels, and lives, and moves." As the American literary critic Lionel Trilling pointed out, this is a daring echo of Acts 17:28, where Paul tells the Athenians of God: ". . . for in him we live, and move, and have our being."

"I wandered lonely as a cloud" considers, then, the nature of the pleasure elicited by emotion recollected in tranquility. That pleasure seems to consist in burning the stages between the present and the past. It is a kind of recognition of the permanence of the past. Seeing the daffodils gives the poet a present-tense sense of gaiety, but he has no idea that this gaiety has a temporal dimension, that it will matter for the future. The future will have its moments of pensiveness and vacancy and be a time less of wandering than of worry or vacancy. The past may have been lonely but it was not a burden; the burden will come later, with experience, knowledge, and thought. The past is a time in which he thought little, but the later period is the time of pensive moods. And it is then that sometimes the daffodils will flash upon him and make him remember the past with the intensity of the present. But the intensity is, paradoxically, a function of the distance from the past—paradoxically, because in the past his heart had not danced with the daffodils; he gazed, without thinking. Now, however, in a time of thoughtfulness, he dances rather than gazes (now they *flash* upon that inward eye instead of being the object of long gazing), but that flash gives the poem the startling motion that leads to the alliterative dancing with the daffodils in the last line.

Like *pleasure,* the word *thought* is crucial in Wordsworth (see especially "Tintern Abbey" and the INTIMATIONS ODE. For Wordsworth, the greatest achievement of poetic thought occurs when it can combine with pleasure, and "I wandered lonely as a cloud" is one of Wordsworth's signal experiential and poetic successes.

BIBLIOGRAPHY

Abrams, M. H. *Natural Supernaturalism: Tradition and Revolution in Romantic Literature.* New York: Norton, 1973.

Alpers, Paul. *What Is Pastoral?* Chicago: University of Chicago Press, 1996.

Barker, Juliet. *Wordsworth: A Life.* New York: Viking, 2000.

Bloom, Harold. *The Visionary Company: A Reading of English Romantic Poetry.* Garden City, N.Y.: Doubleday, 1961.

Bromwich, David. *Disowned by Memory: Wordsworth's Poetry of the 1790s.* Chicago: University of Chicago Press, 1998.

Brooks, Cleanth. *A Shaping Joy: Studies in the Writer's Craft.* London: Methuen, 1973.

Gill, Stephen. *William Wordsworth: A Life.* New York: Oxford University Press, 1989.

Hartman, Geoffrey. "The Question of Our Speech." In *The Geoffrey Hartman Reader,* edited by Daniel T. O'Hara, 321–347. Edinburgh: Edinburgh University Press, 2004.

Hartman, Geoffrey. *Wordsworth's Poetry, 1787–1814.* New Haven, Conn.: Yale University Press, 1971.

Liu, Alan. *Wordsworth: The Sense of History.* Stanford, Calif.: Stanford University Press, 1989.

Moorman, Mary. *William Wordsworth: A Biography.* 2 vols. Oxford: Clarendon Press, 1957, 1965.

Pinch, Adela. *Strange Fits of Passion: Epistemologies of Emotion, Hume to Austen.* Stanford, Calif.: Stanford University Press, 1996.

Quinney, Laura. *The Poetics of Disappointment: Wordsworth to Ashbery.* Charlottesville: University of Virginia Press, 1999.

Wolfson, Susan J. *Questioning Presence: Wordsworth, Keats, and the Interrogative Mode in Romantic Poetry.* Ithaca, N.Y.: Cornell University Press, 1986.

"I WAS NOT FALSE TO THEE" See NORTON, CAROLINE.

J

"JABBERWOCKY" LEWIS CARROLL **(1855)**
"Jabberwocky" is LEWIS CARROLL's most famous nonsense poem, and like all his nonsense poetry, it is in part a meditation on the nature of poetry itself. Of its 167 words, its title and 41 other words are invented (some, like *chortle,* now assimilated into the English language). But their form is not arbitrary. In *Through the Looking Glass and What Alice Found There* (1872), "Jabberwocky" is one of the first things Alice finds, a poem in mirror writing that she can make nothing of until she holds it up to a looking glass. (Carroll had written and distributed the poem as a stand-alone bit of nonsense in 1855, when he was 23, in a private periodical he gave to his friends called *Mischmasch*). Later in the book, Humpty Dumpty explains many of the terms, especially those he calls "portmanteau words," in which "there are two meanings packed up into one word," like the French word *portmanteau* (luggage designed for coats and therefore not only a compound word but a compound thing). Consider the first stanza, repeated as the poem's last:

> 'Twas brillig, and the slithy toves
> Did gyre and gimble in the wabe:
> All mimsy were the borogoves,
> And the mome raths outgrabe.

Brillig, Humpty Dumpty informs us, means "four o'clock in the afternoon—the time when you begin *broiling* things for dinner." *Slithy,* he goes on, means "lithe and slimy" (and thus perhaps is a source for J. K. Rowling's Slytherin House); while *toves* "are something like badgers—they're something like lizards—and they're something like corkscrews; . . . also they make their nests under sun-dials," prompting Alice herself to guess that "'the wabe' is the grass-plot round a sun-dial, I suppose?" It is, says Humpty Dumpty, "because it goes a long way before it, and a long way behind it—," an idea that Alice completes, "And a long way beyond it on each side." *Mimsy* is also a portmanteau word, combining *flimsy* and *miserable.* Humpty Dumpty spells out a few more meanings, but of course, the gloss is of no use at all to understanding whatever is to be understood about the poem.

The main outline of the story "Jabberwocky" tells is reasonably easy to figure out. On a day in the world where the poem occurs, nature is pursuing its strange but consistent course, and a man warns his perhaps-too-eager son against the monster called the Jabberwock. The name of the Jabberwock differs slightly from that of the poem, and it is worth hazarding that the title refers to nonsense itself; it might be translated as meaningless jabber. The monster, then, would be a kind of embodiment of nonsense as meaninglessness. This is a conservative, paternal fear, but the son (like Carroll himself) is bolder, as befits folk heroes, and is willing to grapple with nonsense without fearing absolute chaos. His hunt for the Jabberwock is thus a kind of allegory or parallel to the composition of the poem itself.

The son seeks his foe and fails to find him, but then—again in standard folktale fashion (see ROBERT BROWNING'S "CHILDE ROLAND TO THE DARK TOWER CAME")—when he pauses in his pursuit, the thing he pursues suddenly appears "with eyes of flame." The son kills the monster (much as Saint George kills the dragon in the founding story of the birth of England, a myth known to every English schoolchild) and returns to his ecstatic father, who praises him extravagantly. The poem then ends with a repetition of its opening stanza; the world of nonsense has been preserved, beautiful and consistent, against the chaotic meaninglessness from which it is essential to distinguish it.

That nonsense is not meaningless is, in a sense, the point of the poem, and that all poetry has an element of nonsense—of sound determining sense rather than (as in normal expression) sense determining sound—is one of its corollaries. One way the poem makes this point is to show the way its form is consistent with the general structure of the English language. Everyone knows how to pronounce the nonsense words: that *brillig, slithy, gimble,* and *mimsy* are trochees (stressed-unstressed), like most two-syllable words in English, which fits them perfectly into the iambic meter; and everyone can see that *borogoves* and *Jabberwock* are pronounced with the same stresses as the everyday word *element.* Probably, too, everyone has trouble with the last line of the first and last stanzas, and comes to conclude that *outgrabe* is an iamb (the mirror image of a trochee), like *conclude.* We can also tell that *mimsy* is an adjective, as is *mome* (whose meaning even Humpty Dumpty is not sure of, though it might be a headless version of *from home*), and that *outgrabe* is a verb, and not only a verb but an irregular verb in the past tense. ("'Outgribing' is something between bellowing and whistling, with a kind of sneeze in the middle," Humpty Dumpty confirms.)

The poem, then, decomposes language to show the ways in which different streams of meaning combine, and those streams include not only parts of speech, important to all expression, but the metrical structure and vowel sounds that make us read the nonsense as prosody and not as mishmash. In an odd and intriguing way, one might say of "Jabberwocky" that it typifies a deep and persistent theme in 19th-century poetry, from JOHN KEATS to ALFRED, LORD TENNYSON to ALGERNON CHARLES SWINBURNE to GERARD MANLEY HOPKINS to WILLIAM BUTLER YEATS: the idea that the music or pure sound of the poetry can somehow metamorphose into a kind of emblem of meaning, and that poetic meaning can then arise in pursuit of this enticing emblem. The greatest, or at least longest, work to come out of this theory is the Irish novelist James Joyce's *Finnegans Wake* (1939), which raises the technique of "Jabberwocky" to sublime heights.

BIBLIOGRAPHY

Bloom, Harold, ed. *Lewis Carroll.* New York: Chelsea House, 1987.

Kelly, Richard. *Lewis Carroll.* Boston: Twayne Publishers, 1990.

Lehmann, John. *Lewis Carroll and the Spirit of Nonsense.* Nottingham, England: University of Nottingham Press, 1974.

"JENNY KISSED ME" See "RONDEAU."

JOHNSON, LIONEL (1867–1902) Johnson is now best remembered through WILLIAM BUTLER YEATS's memories of him, both in his autobiographies and in his elegy "In Memory of Major Robert Gregory," son of his close friend and patron Augusta, Lady Gregory. Of the friends "who cannot sup with us . . . Lionel Johnson "comes the first to mind, / That loved his learning better than mankind." (11, 17–18) Johnson, born in Kent, met Yeats in London. He had previously written a book on THOMAS HARDY, after spending a month walking through the Wessex countryside in which Hardy set his novels. He was a leading member of the Rhymers' Club, the center of the young aesthetic poetry circle of the 1890s. Johnson had been a pupil of the essayist Walter Pater's when he was a star student at Oxford University, and his poetry aspires to gorgeously Paterian intensities of feeling. For Johnson, as for OSCAR WILDE and A. E. HOUSMAN and a slew of other members of the decadent movement, much of that aesthetic feeling was connected to—and may have to some extent derived from the repression of—homosexuality. This was certainly true of Johnson, who was tormented by his own homosexual inclinations. (The 1912 *Dictionary of National Biography* entry on Lionel Johnson, by Campbell Johnson, coyly but unmistakably ends its account of his life by observing that "He was unmarried.") It was Johnson who introduced Wilde to LORD ALFRED DOUGLAS, who had been a student at Oxford with him, with disastrous personal consequences to both of them.

Johnson, like Wilde and the French novelist Marcel Proust, tended to sublimate homosexuality into religion or nationalism. For Proust this meant his own Judaism, for Wilde his Irish background. Johnson, famously drunk and filled with unbearable anxiety and desire (he could feel no "Delight untortured by desire," as he says in "The DARK ANGEL"), channeled them into a commitment to Roman Catholicism (to which he converted in 1891) and to Irish nationalism, which was part of his bond with Yeats. Yeats, like Wilde, was Protestant and sought a nationalism that would be based on Irish rather than religious culture, and we may say in part that Johnson became a Roman Catholic to become Irish. "Lambeth Lyric," one of his most entertainingly scathing poems is an indictment of the established church and what he called its revision of creeds "written by the Holy Ghost" (l. 9).

Johnson's best poem by far is "The Dark Angel," but all his poems are marked by a beautiful and subtle sense of language and imagery. His satirical poems can be very funny indeed; a lot of the humor comes out of the unexpectedness of the content, given the beauty of the form.

Johnson's death of a cracked skull following a fall in 1902 has been made into an emblem of the self-destructive drunken poet, not least by Yeats and the 20th-century American poet Ezra Pound. Probably he fell because of a stroke, not because he was drunk, but it is certain that he poisoned himself with extraordinary quantities of alcohol. He deserves to be remembered as a poet, drunk or sober, even if what made him drink were the torments that made him into a poet as well.

BIBLIOGRAPHY

Barker, George. *Jubjub Bird, or, Some Remarks on the Prose Poem; &, A Little Honouring of Lionel Johnson.* Emscote Lawn, Warwick, England: Greville Press, 1985.

Cevasco, G. A. *Three Decadent Poets: Ernest Dowson, John Gray, and Lionel Johnson: An Annotated Bibliography.* New York: Garland, 1990.

Pittock, Murray, ed. *Selected Letters: Lionel Johnson.* Edinburgh: Tragara Press, 1988.

Yeats, W. B. *Autobiography of William Butler Yeats: Consisting of Reveries Over Childhood and Youth, The Trembling of the Veil, and Dramatis Personae.* Garden City, N.Y.: Doubleday Anchor Books, 1958.

JOHNSON, WILLIAM See CORY, WILLIAM JOHNSON.

JONES, ERNEST (1819–1868) Ernest Jones was the most radical of the Chartist poets (see the entry on THOMAS COOPER, who became one of Jones's chief antagonists in the Chartism movement). His advocacy of violent revolution led to his imprisonment (along with many other Chartist leaders who were less radical than he was), where (again like Cooper) he wrote some of his most powerful poetry. Reports on Jones's personality differ wildly. It seems clear that he was a charismatic and principled man, but perhaps humorless; at least, he is represented this way by Charles Dickens in his unsympathetic portrait of him as the opportunistic agitator Stackbridge in *Hard Times* (1854). Jones was the editor (as a protégé of Feargus O'Connor) of the Chartist journal the *Northern Star,* where he also published many of his most ferocious poems. The ferocity of those poems is what gives them their power, and that power is a considerable one.

Jones was born affluent, and while always wildly romantic in his aspirations—as a writer and as a political figure—he was not drawn to radical politics until his own disastrous financial failure (as well as a failure to get his work published). It may be that this failure alerted him to the condition of the poor, so that his biography has something of the form of a proto-naturalist novel. At any rate, Chartism offered him both a political cause to which to devote his extraordinary energies and a literary context in which to publish his poetry. He had trained as a lawyer, and after his release from prison he practiced law, defending radical causes. He ran for Parliament three times and was on the verge of winning a seat when he died suddenly, a day after his 50th birthday.

His best poetry (for example, "The Factory Town") is fueled by the demonic energy of his outrage at the appalling conditions faced by the poor in England. His complaint in "The Song of the Low" that "We're far too low to vote the tax / But we're not too low to pay" makes vivid the reason behind the Chartists' central demand that they should be allowed to vote (and to stand for Parliament); it is because they cannot that they are essentially enslaved to the voting fraction of English society whose food they grow, whose cities they build, and whose wars they fight. (Compare poll taxes and racist measures taken to disenfranchise African Americans in the pre-civil-rights American South.)

Jones was a friend of the German socialists Friedrich Engels and Karl Marx, and also a friend to the British prime minister William Gladstone. His poetry is still powerful through the vividness of its depiction of the horrors of unregulated industrial conditions. WALTER SAVAGE LANDOR (also the model of a character in Dickens) called his poetry "noble: [Lord] Byron would have envied, [Sir Walter] Scott would have applauded." Jones in general seemed to have nobility of character, and while he may have been humorless and easy to hate, he was also principled, devoted, and easy to love.

BIBLIOGRAPHY

Charlton, John. *The Chartists: The First National Workers' Movement.* Chicago: Pluto Press, 1997.

Cooper, Thomas. *Life of Thomas Cooper; Written by himself.* London: Hodder and Stoughton, 1872.

Cunningham, Valentine. Headnote to selection of Jones in *The Victorians: An Anthology of Poetry and Poetics,* 478. Malden, Mass.: Blackwell, 2000.

Janowitz, Anne F. *Lyric and Labour in the Romantic Tradition.* New York: Cambridge University Press, 1998.

Thompson, Dorothy. *The Chartists.* London: Temple Smith, 1984.

JULIAN AND MADDALO: A CONVERSATION PERCY BYSSHE SHELLEY (1819)

This is one of PERCY BYSSHE SHELLEY's great achievements in both style and content. Its diction is very different from that of the extravagant high rhetoric of Shelley at his most visionary, as he himself noted in a letter to LEIGH HUNT (who, he expected, would publish the poem). This poem is written in a loose, relaxed urbane style, in open couplets (such as those Hunt was experimenting with and writing essays about) that are able to say anything and rise to any necessary height of passion and then relax again, without our ever feeling any jarring discrepancy in style.

The headnote, which is an integral part of the poem, briefly characterizes the two title characters. Maddalo is a pessimist: His amazing intellect endows him "with an intense apprehension of the nothingness of human life." He sees through all illusion and delusion and is intellectually, though not personally, bitter. Julian, the narrator, praises Maddalo for his personal kindness and decency, and for the pleasure of his company, seeing his pessimism as philosophical—no less real for that, but not poisoning friendship. Julian presents himself with more modesty, as someone who prefers hope to despair. These characterizations will reappear in the poem proper.

The poem was to be published anonymously, so that its fictional characters would be like the real characters they are based on—of the same *type.* But much of the story is a fiction, although based on real conversations and debates that Shelley and LORD BYRON had in the summer of 1819.

Julian's name is almost a homonym of "Shelleyean," and Julian, the narrator, is the Shelleyean character in the debate. Count Maddalo is based on Byron; the daughter Julian meets at the beginning and then again at the end is Byron's daughter Allegra (1817–22), who did not live until adulthood in reality; her death at age five, a few months before Shelley's own, was one of the greatest sorrows of her father's life. This poem was written when Allegra was two; however, Shelley's own daughter Clara, just a few months older than Allegra, had died a couple of week after her first birthday. Shelley began the poem shortly thereafter, and certainly some of the sadness to be felt there, as well as some of the hopes for Allegra, derives from this event.

The poem begins by recounting a particular conversation between Julian and Maddalo as they are riding horses on the Lido outside Venice (where Byron lived; the Shelleys were visiting for the summer). Despite its urbanity, the poem has a subtle structure, since the ride with Maddalo introduces its theme but also provides a significant piece of evidence for the argument they have. They love riding together; the ride is a "delight" (l. 14), and part of that delight is the conversation itself and the friendship it represents and sustains. Since what they talk about is the appropriateness of despondency, the pleasure of the conversation itself is an argument against despair. Their conversation, Julian tells us, is like that which John Milton recounts in *Paradise Lost* between the fallen angels, arguing philosophy. Shelley and Byron were both of the devil's party in *Paradise Lost,* but their conversation occurs in a much more beautiful place than hell: "bright Venice," by the sea and then at the amazing sunset, described by Julian for 80 lines (ll. 53–133; for more on Shelleyean description, see "MONT BLANC").

On their return to Venice, they see a bell tower, which Maddalo explains to Julian belongs to a mental asylum. The bell is ringing to call the inmates to prayer. Julian (as in the "HYMN TO INTELLECTUAL BEAUTY") is against religion and thinks it exacerbates the misery of the inmates, who might be free if they were not oppressed by superstitious dogma. He therefore takes the asylum as a sign of what might be easily overthrown to make universal freedom possible. Maddalo, of course, takes it as a symbol of the relentless misery of human life, since it indicates the despairing and irremediable madness within. He offers to take Julian to meet one of the inmates, whom he has been drawn to; Julian agrees, since each hopes to convince the other of the truth of his own point of view. It is before their departure the next day that Julian meets Maddalo's young daughter.

The madman whom they meet at the asylum provides an aria of despair for the middle of the poem. The language of his grief is highly poetic (which is why the poem can quote it at such length); indeed, it seems to comprise Shelley's own despairing fragments from the same period. Julian underlines an important doctrine of Maddalo's—probably his own as much as Byron's: "Most wretched men / Are cradled into poetry by wrong; / They learn in suffering what they teach in song" (11. 544–546).

What is crucial about the encounter with the madman is that he undercuts both their positions: the easy pessimism of Maddalo, the not much-more-difficult optimism of Julian. They both return from the visit shaken and appalled. In fact, Julian is so shaken that he leaves "bright Venice" for London, and he does not return for many years. When he does return, Maddalo's daughter has grown up, to be like one of "Shakespeare's women," sober, serious, deep, and accurate in insight. Hers is the mode with which the poem ends. She tells Julian the whole story of the madman and the woman he loved. She returned to him but then departed again, and now they have both died and are buried together. Julian asks for more of the story, but her reply indicates that the story itself is not important; more sadly, it indicates that telling a story, whether optimistic or pessimistic, is not important.

The poem therefore ends somewhat abruptly, with the story left untold, and with Julian feeling uncertain about the very idea of literature and literary vocation, much as Shelley did. The idea that literature could matter comes from a more innocent time of life, and finally what Julian tells is the story of that more innocent time when it felt as though literature could matter. The story is one of disappointment with the possibilities of literature.

That story is similar to the one WILLIAM WORDSWORTH tells in "RESOLUTION AND INDEPENDENCE," as does Shelley's wife, Mary Shelley, in her preface to the third edition of *Frankenstein.* It does not (necessarily) spell the end of a writer's life as a writer, but it may spell the end of the impulse that made him or her into a writer. And it is perhaps only at this point that writing can attain to the truly serious sobriety that the end of *Julian and Maddalo* depicts—when it registers disappointment with its own inspiration, and yet has nowhere else to go.

BIBLIOGRAPHY

Bloom, Harold. *Genius: A Mosaic of One Hundred Exemplary Creative Minds.* New York: Warner, 2002.

———. *Shelley's Mythmaking.* New Haven, Conn.: Yale University Press, 1959.

———. *The Visionary Company: A Reading of English Romantic Poetry.* Garden City, N.Y.: Doubleday, 1961.

Burke, Kenneth. *Grammar of Motives.* Berkeley: University of California Press, 1969.

Chernaik, Judith. *The Lyrics of Shelley.* Cleveland: Press of Case Western Reserve University, 1972.

Duffy, Edward. *Rousseau in England: The Context for Shelley's Critique of the Enlightenment.* Berkeley: University of California Press, 1979.

Hogle, Jerrold E. *Shelley's Process: Radical Transference and the Development of His Major Works.* New York: Oxford University Press, 1988.
Keach, William. *Shelley's Style.* New York: Methuen, 1984.
Leavis, F. R. *Revaluation: Tradition & Development in English Poetry.* New York: Norton, 1963.
Leighton, Angela. *Shelley and the Sublime: An Interpretation of the Major Poems.* New York: Cambridge University Press, 1984.
Notopolous, James A. *The Platonism of Shelley: A Study of Platonism and the Poetic Mind.* Durham, N.C.: Duke University Press, 1949.
Quinney, Laura. *The Poetics of Disappointment: Wordsworth to Ashbery.* Charlottesville: University Press of Virginia, 1999.
Wasserman, Earl. *Shelley: A Critical Reading.* Baltimore: Johns Hopkins Press, 1971.
———. *Subtler Language: Critical Readings of Neoclassic and Romantic Poems.* Baltimore: Johns Hopkins Press, 1968.

"JUMBLIES, THE" EDWARD LEAR (1871) The essayist and critic John Ruskin, always anxious about how he spent his intellectual time, said of EDWARD LEAR in 1886, "Surely the most innocent and beneficent of all books produced for [families seeking amusement] is *The Book of Nonsense,* with its corollary carols?—inimitable and refreshing and perfect in rhythm. I really don't know any author to whom I am half so grateful, for my idle self, as Edward Lear. I shall put him first of *my* hundred authors" [that is, the hundred books that he would recommend to the common reader instead of those recommended in a lecture by Sir John Lubbock]. Ruskin's wonderful comment, which thrilled Lear beyond measure, captures something important about nonsense verse in general and about Lear's in particular, something also captured in an early 20th-century manual on a reader for grade-school students. The manual of the *Elson Readers* says of "The Jumblies," that it "should be read for amusement and enjoyment only. It affords an interesting change from the more thoughtful selections in this book." Both these comments bring out the central component of *vicarious* pleasure to be found in reading nonsense verse. It is verse for children, or for one's own "idle self," and not the thoughtful and content-laden poetry that speaks to us adults directly. And yet such poetry enacts something crucial about the way much of the inheritance of ROMANTICISM works: the way it always suggests that the essence of poetry is always elsewhere, a meaning beyond the more responsible meanings of every day life. It is not only Ruskin and William Elson who have this attitude toward the poem. Donald Barthelme ends a wonderful story from the 1970s called "You Are Cordially Invited" with a dotty and charismatic old lady quoting "The Jumblies" to the more and more besotted young narrator as she drinks a toast to "Our noble predecessors . . . Their heads were, you know, *green* and their hands were blue and they went to sea in a sieve." And Lear is for the same reason a central presence in Joyce's *Finnegans Wake:* He suggests another possible world, not like this one, where we could live with the nonsense on more familiar terms, where we could be more familiar with it and with ourselves, perhaps.

This is why Ruskin and Elson imagine nonsense verse as appealing to an earlier, younger, more carefree version of themselves (even as Barthelme's narrator imagines a self he could never be but only admire). But this is just what this late poem is about. The Jumblies are not like us. Not unlike the First Spirit in PERCY BYSSHE SHELLEY's "THE TWO SPIRITS: AN ALLEGORY," we prudent adults warn the green-headed blue-handed Jumblies not to go to sea in a sieve of all things. But they do, and we anticipate, with some self-satisfaction, their disaster.

Going to sea in a sieve is an image of all human life. We sink. But the Jumblies do it happily. And indeed we come to realize that going to sea in a sieve is an image of starting out in life. That is what all of us do, and that is why all of us sink. But the Jumblies go places that we can only imagine—places that can only belong to the imagination. They can go there because they are children, and can live within imagination as we adults cannot. We can only imagine such a life. We know they are children because they return in the last stanza, "In twenty years or more. / And everyone said, 'How tall they've grown!'" But in their travels, in those 20 years, they have lived among marvels. The nonsense poem imagines these marvels as real. It imagines the imaginary as real. If this is nonsense, that is the point. But the Jumblies have gone there, and the wistfulness that we feel for not going with them (we only get the most enticing suggestions of their adventures), is the wistfulness that so much romantic poetry alludes to, sometimes with great intensity, sometimes with less. It is the wistfulness of thinking of another life, elsewhere and other than our life, a life which only poetry can intimate—far and few are the lands where the Jumblies live. They are *from* here, they return *to* here (when they reach maturity), but they *live* there, in those lands far and few of lost childhood. Ruskin is right to admire the perfection of Lear's poetry—the perfection of its rhythm means something like poetic perfection itself, perfection not carried by its ideas but by what makes it poetry. In Lear's nonsense verse, especially in a poem like "The Jumblies," which recognizes this fact, we are close to the very heart of all poetry.

BIBLIOGRAPHY

Elson, William Harris. *The Elson Readers, Book Three.* Chicago: Scott, Foresman and Co., 1920.

Ruskin, John. "Arrows of the Chace." In *The Works of John Ruskin.* Vol. 34, edited by T. E. Cook and Alexander Wedderburn, London, 1908.

K

KEATS, JOHN (1795–1821) John Keats is the most popular and least controversial of the romantic poets (see ROMANTICISM). One reason for this is the humility of his poetic persona: He criticized what he called the "egotistic sublime" in WILLIAM WORDSWORTH (who in turn called Keats's *Endymion* "a pretty piece of paganism" on one of the two occasions they met, when Keats recited part of it). This humility in someone who struck others as possibly a great poet did not impress them, at least not the other great poets, an unusual number of whom wrote about him in their poetry. WILLIAM BUTLER YEATS, who was highly sympathetic to Keats, nevertheless essentially thought him a failure: "I see a schoolboy when I think of him, / With face and nose pressed to a sweet-shop window, / For certainly he sank into his grave / His senses and his heart unsatisfied, / And made—being poor, ailing and ignorant, / Shut out from all the luxury of the world, / The coarse-bred son of a livery stablekeeper— / Luxuriant song" ("Ego Dominus Tuus" [1919]).

This takes with one hand what it grants with the other. Keats was indeed the son of a stablekeeper and did not have the education (whether at private school or at university) of the other great romantics (leaving the then-unknown WILLIAM BLAKE aside). Yeats agreed that "No one denies to Keats love of the world," but he doubted that Keats could fulfill that love with the ease that Keats claimed, rather than through the bleary-eyed wisdom and incessant toil in which Yeats took pride in engaging and complaining in his own poetic practice. But Keats famously thought (as he said in a letter) that "if Poetry comes not as naturally as the Leaves to a tree it had better not come at all." LORD BYRON, for whom poetry did come like leaves to a tree (but Keats thought *DON JUAN*, Byron's greatest work, to be just another "flash poem") had the same aristocratic disdain for Keats (the five-foot-tall Keats complained of him, "You see what it is to be six foot tall and a lord") that he had for most of his work; Byron lamented without much grief that Keats died when and as he did:

> John Keats, who was killed off by one critique,
> Just as he really promised something great,
> If not intelligible,—without Greek
> Contrived to talk about the Gods of late,
> Much as they might have been supposed to
> speak.
> Poor fellow! His was an untoward fate:—
> 'Tis strange the mind, that very fiery particle,
> Should let itself be snuff'd out by an Article
> (*Don Juan* XI, stanza 60).

The article Byron refers to is the vicious review of *Endymion* that had appeared in the *Quarterly Review* in autumn 1818, which PERCY BYSSHE SHELLEY also refers to explicitly in the preface to his elegy on Keats, *ADONAIS*. This was not the only vicious review that Keats received that month, and all the reviewers piled on with references to Keats's low-class "Cockney" origins. The "Cockney School" they named (the term is from an attack in *Blackwood's*) included LEIGH HUNT and the essayist William Hazlitt, and the epithet was motivated by political hatred for Hunt's liberalism (which had landed him in jail). As one of Hunt's closest friends, named by him as one of the most important rising poets, Keats was tarred by association. This all occurred as his brother Tom was dying of the tuberculosis that had killed his mother and that was to kill Keats himself two years later. He was already symptomatic, though he was still able to hope (despite some medical training) that he didn't have the disease. Thus, the reviews of *Endymion* came at a time of extreme stress in Keats's life, and Shelley was furious at the know-nothing vulgarians who attacked Keats; but, of course, the articles did not kill him, nor indeed cause him very much despair, comparatively speaking.

Shelley alone among the other great romantics had high praise for Keats (and it was because of Shelley's praise that Byron somewhat modified his own contempt). Shelley met Keats through Hunt, and though Keats was always suspicious of him, and of the resolutely unsensual poetry that Shelley wrote, Shelley invited Keats to Italy when (as Keats said) it was clear that another English winter would kill him. Shelley's poem *Adonais* is one of the great elegies of the English language. Even *Adonais,* though, treats Keats in an essentially Miltonic mode: The flowers that Adonais gathers cover over "the coming bulk of death," and Adonais, like the narrator of the poem and like its other romantic denizens, feel themselves the lost inhabitants of a fallen world.

This Miltonic mode (following the 17th-century poet John Milton) is central to romantic self-conception—the idea of subjectivity as confronting and constituting a fallen world—and it is what underwrites the similarity between Byron and Wordsworth and between Blake and Coleridge. But Keats is the romantic poet who was most suspicious of the Miltonic mode. He said that he gave up the great *Hyperion* poems (see HYPERION AND *THE FALL OF HYPERION*) because they were too Miltonic, and he preferred other sensations. *Sensation* is one of his characteristic words (in his great letters, themselves among the most important documents of poetic theory in the English language). Keats loved to evoke the outside world and not the intense subjectivity that found loss and distance in that world. Where Wordsworth would find himself in thought, in the self-sustaining intensity of thought, Keats lost himself in observation and in the self-dissolving thoughts that observation might elicit in him. He regarded this mode as Shakespearean, rather than Miltonic—Shakespearean in the way that the poet, as he put it, has no character, is a chameleon who enters into the character of all other things but has no character of his own. A more un-Miltonic sentiment cannot be imagined.

And yet Keats, too, is a romantic poet, and his similarity to the other five (Shelley and the four mentioned above) can be felt in the way he struggled with a Miltonic legacy that went very deep in him. He may have wanted to give himself wholly to the rich pleasures of the sensory world, but he was never able to do so completely; there was for him always a sense of separation, of subjectivity despite itself. In the great odes, he is always unable to lose himself in the contemplation of the object of the ode. He is always tolled back to his sole self. Even his praise of Shakespeare is a kind of acknowledgement of his inability to be sufficiently like Shakespeare—that is, to become (as he put it in his letters) a wholly allegorical figure, as opposed to a subjective one. The *Hyperion* poems imagine the young Apollo as able to achieve this freshness, but Keats and his own narrator in *The Fall of Hyperion* are much more like the falling and failing Titans of subjectivity than the rising gods of music.

Music was for Keats the sound of self-presence, beauty that refers only to itself and he is always evoking the songs that his speakers hear, but always at a distance: the unheard music of the Grecian urn ("ODE ON A GRECIAN URN"), the song of the nightingale ("ODE TO A NIGHTINGALE"), the music of autumn in his last great ode ("TO AUTUMN"). Correspondingly, Keats is famously a voyeur, observing the world into which he cannot entirely assimilate himself. He wished for easeful death, but there is no such thing, and the subjectivity his poetry works so hard to dissolve within the richness of sensation is what in the end makes his work far more than a pretty piece of paganism, or of any other kind of secure belief in the world. Pleasure in Keats is a foil for what it cannot efface. Pleasure in

Keats therefore becomes a Miltonic sign of loss, of what will be lost and is therefore already lost, and this is the "burden of the mystery" that Keats understood so deeply from Wordsworth and that made him a Miltonic and Wordsworthian poet after all. Yeats understands this when he remarks in "Ego Dominus Tuus" that despite the fact that Keats aimed at "deliberate happiness," "His art is happy, but who knows his mind?"

See also "BRIGHT STAR"; "EVE OF ST. AGNES, THE"; "ODE ON MELANCHOLY"; "ODE TO PSYCHE"; "ON FIRST LOOKING INTO CHAPMAN'S HOMER"; "ON SITTING DOWN TO READ KING LEAR ONCE AGAIN"; "ON THE GRASSHOPPER AND THE CRICKET"; "THIS LIVING HAND"; "WHEN I HAVE FEARS THAT I MAY CEASE TO BE."

BIBLIOGRAPHY

Bate, Walter Jackson. *John Keats.* Cambridge, Mass.: Harvard University Press, 1963.

Bloom, Harold. *Poetry and Repression: Revisionism from Blake to Stevens.* New Haven, Conn.: Yale University Press, 1976.

———. *The Visionary Company: A Reading of English Romantic Poetry.* Garden City, N.Y.: Doubleday, 1961.

Dickstein, Morris. *Keats and His Poetry: A Study in Development.* Chicago: University of Chicago Press, 1971.

Gittings, Robert. *John Keats.* Boston: Little, Brown, 1968.

———. *Mask of Keats: A Study of Problems.* Cambridge, Mass.: Harvard University Press, 1956.

Ricks, Christopher. *Keats and Embarrassment.* Oxford: Clarendon Press, 1974.

Vendler, Helen. *Odes of John Keats.* Cambridge, Mass.: Harvard University Press, 1983.

"KEITH OF RAVELSTON"

See "NUPTIAL EVE, A."

KIPLING, RUDYARD (1865–1936)

Rudyard Kipling was almost the exact contemporary of WILLIAM BUTLER YEATS, and for a time he was regarded as Yeats's great rival for the title of greatest British poet. Both won the Nobel Prize, but Kipling won it 16 years and a world war earlier, in 1907. Kipling is now out of favor with the modernist canon that champions Yeats, partly because of Kipling's frankly imperialist political views, especially after having observed some military action in the Boer War in 1900 in South Africa: it was here that he began his more militant championing of what he had already so notoriously called "the white man's burden" to police and administer the world. The 1899 poem of that title was addressed to the United States after it took control of the Philippines in the Spanish-American War (which also helped Kipling's friend Teddy Roosevelt to make his political fortune). What makes it slightly less objectionable than one might guess from its single famous line is that Kipling accepted that history was the chronicle of power devolving from older to newer civilizations, which then took up the burden of educating and civilizing still newer ones. The "white man" of the title refers to a historical period, when (for Kipling and others of his generation) the white, particularly English-speaking, race was charged with preserving the world from anarchy. This was not a permanent state of affairs but a historically contingent one, and Kipling certainly spoke as powerfully to his English audience of the experience and human reality of colonized peoples (in the India where he spent his childhood and then where he learned to be a writer) as any other white Anglo-Saxon writer of his time (cf. the extraordinary heroism of Gunga Din in the poem of that name).

Kipling also was a champion of the working class, and in particular of the working-class and ill-educated young men who constituted the British infantry. The novelist and critic George Orwell, in his 1945 review of T. S. Eliot's anthology of Kipling's verse, made the observation that Kipling became increasingly jingoistic in his work—brutally so, according to Orwell. But this did not prevent Kipling from being a poet whose extraordinary popularity had to be taken and respected on its own terms. In the view of many later critics, to scorn Kipling is to scorn all but elitist tastes; he was actually a marvelous craftsman, and many of his poems are genuinely deep. Had he died at 35, like so many of the poets born in the 1860s, he would be remembered now as a preternaturally precocious talent, able to tell compelling and powerful stories in both verse and prose, stories that showed the kind of well-rounded respect for all their characters to be found in the Victorian novel.

Kipling became very much out of tune with modernism, and yet Orwell and Eliot could not help respecting him and the powerful effects he could make available to the most naïve readers. His poetry speaks not only to but for its popular audience, dressing down authority in political struggles of the day (over soldiers' pensions, for example), and he always maintained faith with them, even as he moved from England to America (where he lived in Vermont) to South Africa and back to England. Kipling wrote what Orwell called "good bad verse," and Orwell conceded its necessity. We could say that, in general, good bad verse is probably more necessary than all but the greatest of poetry, and that we could less afford to lose Kipling's most compelling poems than those of greater poets.

See also "BALLAD OF EAST AND WEST, THE"; "DANNY DEEVER"; "RECESSIONAL."

BIBLIOGRAPHY

Bloom, Harold, ed. *Rudyard Kipling.* New York: Chelsea House, 1987.

Kipling, Rudyard. *Something of Myself, and Other Autobiographical Writings.* Edited by Thomas Pinney. New York: Cambridge University Press, 1990.

Orwell, George. "Rudyard Kipling." In *Kipling's Mind and Art,* edited by Andrew Rutherford, 70–84. Stanford, Calif.: Stanford University Press, 1964.

Eliot, T. S. "Rudyard Kipling." In *On Poetry and Poets,* 65–94. New York: Octagon, 1975.

"KITTEN, THE" JOANNA BAILLIE (1840) "The Kitten" is one of JOANNA BAILLIE's most justly admired poems. From the start, it mainly sustains a note of light verse as it describes all the tricks and wanton wiles of a kitten, that universally charming creature. The description is in the tradition of poems on pets, of which the 18th-century author Oliver Goldsmith's "Ode on the Death of a Favourite Cat" was the most famous for more than 150 years. The kitten in Baillie's work is the center of every household the poem imagines it; it organizes not only the description of the household but the household itself. It also organizes the poem that would like to describe it but must fail to do so, since poems cannot move with the same agility or vivacity as cats. But so infectious is its playfulness and its joy that the poem can catch the same antic spirit, and talk of "many a whirling somerset / (Permitted by the modern muse / Expression technical to use)" (ll. 38–40).

The first household the cat centers is that of the merry rustic faces surrounding the cottage hearth: the crone, the maid, and the child, who represent the three generations of a lifetime. The kitten is the same to all of them, as they are to the kitten. It is pure unheeding juvenility, bringing merriment everywhere it goes and receiving greater applause than poet or juggler could. But from here we move out to consideration of the sage, who will pause in his airy flights of poesy to smile at the kitten (ll. 65–72), as will both the lonely widow and the lonely maid (l. 73). The kitten tempers loneliness and increases jollity, and it can even soften the misanthropic heart of the proud or the damned.

This review of the possibilities of human life, all embraced under the aspect of spontaneous benevolence toward the kitten, is already impressive, but it is intensified by the poem's very grand two stanzas in which Baillie analyzes the reason the kitten affects us as it does. The kitten may make us feel safe in the domesticity it organizes, even as it reminds us of an outside world of lions and tigers from which we are safe. Or it may remind us instead of childhood, presenting "An emblem . . . Of tricky, restless infancy" (ll. 103–104). Whose infancy? Both our own and that of a younger generation, whom we disown when they have "To dull and sober mankind grown" (l. 108). This is genuinely sad. The kitten reminds us of what we loved in the children who have since grown up and become like us, as we were once like them. (Like many childless poets, ANNA LAETITIA BARBAULD for example, Baillie had an intensely sympathetic relationship to childhood, which she remembered from the inside.) But even the kitten is not immune to the passage of time, since it too will become "a cat demure" (l. 110), annoying those it used to delight. And yet, unlike adult humans, it will always be a reminder of what it once was.

This fact allows the poem its most subtle and moving turn, when Baillie anticipates its eventual death. Who will mourn it? It will be the children whose love it has reminded us of, and who will weep as they point out its grave (ll. 125–126).

BIBLIOGRAPHY

Baillie, Joanna. *Dramatic and Poetical Works of Joanna Baillie.* London: Longman, Brown, Green, and Longmans, 1851.

Forbes, A. "'Sympathetic Curiosity' in Joanna Baillie's Theater of the Passions." *European Romantic Review* 14, no. 1 (January 2003): 31–48.
McMillan, Dorothy, ed. The Association for Scottish Literary Studies, ASLS Annual Volume 29: 1999: *The Scotswoman at Home and Abroad,* Association for Scottish Literary Studies, Glasgow, April 2000 (contains excerpts from Baillie's unpublished "Memoir written to please my nephew, William Baillie," and "Recollections written for Miss Berry," both in English archives.)
Wordsworth, Jonathan. *Ancestral Voices: Fifty Books from the Romantic Period.* New York: Woodstock, 1996.

"KRAKEN, THE" ALFRED, LORD TENNYSON **(1830)** The kraken is a legendary monster described by Scandinavian sailors, said to be as horrifying as any creature from the myths of antiquity. (ALFRED, LORD TENNYSON refers to an 18th-century account of it given by Erik Pontoppidan, the bishop of Bergen, Norway.) There was much talk of various sightings of the animal in the 18th and 19th centuries; its real basis, if there is one, is probably the giant squid, which had not yet been discovered when Tennyson wrote his poem.

The poem should be read as skeptical, at least of the idea that humans ever encountered the creature. Rather, Tennyson uses the kraken for one of his many meditations on one of his own primary poetic tendencies: the love of languorous, unmoving, drawn-out description of imagined sensation. This was a primary mode throughout his career, and especially in his earlier poetry, from "MARIANA" to "The LOTOS-EATERS" to "TITHONUS" to *IN MEMORIAM A. H. H.*, the latter of which shows the persistence of mourning through the iterated sadness of its descriptions of the world.

In this sense we can see the creature as representing a focus for the description of its own fabulousness. It lives so deep under water that the living world might only be perceived there as the faintest of shadows. But the kraken does not perceive those shadows. It sleeps as it has slept, presumably from the beginning of time, and its sleep is "uninvaded" (l. 3), even by dreams. The kraken has no experience at all of the world in which it lives, but it allows Tennyson to imagine what that world might be like, including the darkest shadow there, the sleeping bulk of the kraken, whose life is just the dimmest shadow of life in our world.

The torpor Tennyson evokes is not beautiful, but it is hypnotic, and it is that tendency toward the hypnotic in his poetry that this poem explores and attempts to resist or to justify. The kraken's dreamless sleep is the abyss to which Tennyson's own poetical sensuality is attracted; and unlike JOHN KEATS, his single greatest influence, Tennyson does not seem to fear its richnesses and darknesses. But the kraken represents a limit to the pure luxuriousness that Tennyson so luxuriates in evoking—a limit in which sensual luxury goes unperceived, as the kraken lies "Battening upon huge seaworms in his sleep" (l. 12).

It is at this limit that Tennyson imagines its sudden and antithetical opposite. At the coming of the apocalypse, when (according to Revelations 8:8–9) one of the seven angels will cast a mountain of fire into the sea, destroying a third of its creatures, the kraken will roar into enraged and helpless awareness of its own destruction. (There is no reason to identify the kraken with the seven-headed beast that rises out of the sea in Revelation 13:1). The kraken lives therefore only to make possible the vision of his spectacular death. But the describing poet can imagine both his timeless state of being and the end of timelessness at the end of time, and both turn out to be facets of the perception made possible by Tennyson's attentive and vigilant propensity not toward drama but toward description.

BIBLIOGRAPHY

Armstrong, Isobel. *Victorian Poetry: Poetry, Poetics and Politics.* New York: Routledge, 1993.
Bloom, Harold. *Poetry and Repression: Revisionism from Blake to Stevens.* New Haven, Conn.: Yale University Press, 1976.
Buckley, Jerome Hamilton. *Tennyson: The Growth of a Poet.* Boston: Houghton Mifflin, 1965.
Kilham, John. *Critical Essays on the Poetry of Tennyson.* New York: Barnes and Noble, 1960.
Kincaid, James R. *Tennyson's Major Poems: The Comic and Ironic Patterns.* New Haven, Conn.: Yale University Press, 1975.
Ricks, Christopher B. *Tennyson.* New York: Macmillan, 1972.
Rowlinson, Matthew. *Tennyson's Fixations: Psychoanalysis and the Topics of the Early Poetry.* Charlottesville: University Press of Virginia, 1994.
Tucker, Herbert. *Tennyson and the Doom of Romanticism.* Cambridge, Mass.: Harvard University Press, 1988.

"KUBLA KHAN" ("KUBLA KHAN: OR, A VISION IN A DREAM. A FRAGMENT.")

SAMUEL TAYLOR COLERIDGE (1816) Along with *The Rime of the Ancient Mariner* "Kubla Khan" is one of SAMUEL TAYLOR COLERIDGE's two most famous and most-quoted-from poems. Originally written in either 1797 or 1798 (Coleridge claimed 1797), it was not published until 1816 (along with *CHRISTABEL*). The long note by Coleridge explaining the circumstances of its composition ought to be considered a part of the poem too. There he explains that he is publishing it at the behest of a great and celebrated poet—LORD BYRON, who had used his great fame to intervene with his own publishers on Coleridge's behalf—despite the fact that it is only a fragment. The reason it is a fragment, he says, is that the whole poem, which came to him in a dream after taking medicine for a slight indisposition, was some 300 lines long, and he began writing it down when he was interrupted by the famous and unnamed "person on business from Porlock." An hour later, he had forgotten almost the entirety of the rest of the poem.

The medicine Coleridge took was laudanum, a combination of opium and alcohol, and his addiction to it would intermittently but severely ruin his health and his ability to work over the next two decades. Thus, the poem was the fruit of an opium trance. Like so many of Coleridge's great poems, including *Christabel,* it presents itself as a fragment, but we may ask whether it really is a fragment of anything greater than itself. Without the interruption from Porlock, would there have been a complete, or at least a longer poem? Or is visitor from Porlock part of the story that the poem tells: the story that romantic poets tell so often of the fall into the mundane world from visionary heights, perhaps never to be regained?

In a 1955 essay on inspiration, writing in the romantic tradition, the great French critic Maurice Blanchot, observed that we usually think of inspiration as the pathway to literary work, but that, in fact, the work is a pathway that seeks to regain and to understand the inspiration that it has lost. Coleridge awakened from his reverie and tried to return to it in his poem. That return only half succeeded: As Coleridge notes in the preface, the poet sought "to finish for himself what had been originally, as it were, given to him" but failed. He quotes, and in a later revision misquotes, the Greek poet Theocritus: The misquotation may be translated as "I shall sing you a sweeter song tomorrow" (and not the originally correct "another day"), a subtle allusion to the quotation from the Roman poet's Virgil's own allusion to Theocritus in the *Eclogues* that WILLIAM WORDSWORTH put at the head of the 1807 publication of his INTIMATIONS ODE: "Paulo majora canamus" ("Let us sing of loftier things"). Coleridge says in his preface to "Kubla Khan" that this "'tomorrow is yet to come,'" which means both that it will never come and that it belongs to the futurity, which is just what poetic inspiration promises and where it promises to be found.

The question, then, is: To what extent is this what the poem is *about,* or to what extent is the preface in accord with the poem? Here we should look to poem's ending, to the dream vision that occurs *within* the poet's dream vision. If we take seriously the framing narrative presented by the preface, we have to say that Coleridge never did see the Abyssinian maid he describes in the last stanza. The poem came to him as a whole, and so while it may *be* an experience it does not represent other experiences external to itself. "All the images rose up before him as *things,* with a parallel production of the correspondent expressions, without any sensation or consciousness of effort," he says in the preface, so that what arose before him with such vividness includes not the Abyssinian maid *but the fragmentary memory of the Abyssinian maid.*

The full title of the poem should be recalled: "Kubla Khan: Or, A Vision in a Dream. A Fragment." That fragmentary vision or memory occurs in his dream; the maid not as present but as a lost vision is what has come to him in the opium reverie or dream. The poem which he claims came to him whole, unbidden, and utterly without effort included, in what turns out to be its climactic passage, an unfulfilled desire to revive just the sort of vision that the preface laments Coleridge has not been able to revive after the visit of the person from Porlock. For what the last stanza says is that if he could revive the vision of the maid, he could write—"with music loud and long"—a poem like the poem about Xanadu that he wishes to write now, and that he is failing to write. Remember that

that poem is not, in the fiction the fragment presents, the poem that we have or would have had without the interruption. Even in its unavailable finished state, "Kubla Khan" as it supposedly was at one time in Coleridge's mind would have been a poem about not being able to write the great poem of which he had a failing vision. And that is just what "Kubla Khan" *is*: It is a fragment of a poem about only being able to write a poetic fragment.

In this sense, the poem should be compared to other great romantic poems, in particular Coleridge's own "DEJECTION: AN ODE" and Wordsworth's Intimations Ode and *The PRELUDE,* which begins with Wordsworth lamenting that he is unable to write the poem that he wishes to write, and that *The Prelude* will exist to some extent, but only to the extent that the failure it recounts is real, and so it fails to be the poem he wishes to write. This is not an arid paradox but a deep and central element of the romantic conception of poetry: that what makes it haunting is an absence or phantom that can never be grasped or attained, and that this phantom is itself the spirit of poetry—that is, the "Spirit of Solitude" (as PERCY BYSSHE SHELLEY puts it in *Alastor,* his own reworking of "Kubla Khan").

We can therefore identify the maid with a dulcimer as the muse herself, the source of poetic inspiration. She appears to Coleridge in a vision, and her symphony and song gives him something not that he can keep but that he can attempt to revive. The half-memory of the music is what causes him to write; his writing is an attempt to bring that memory to an unattainable fullness. His poem is about the intense experience of trying to remember the intensity of a lost experience of poetry. Were he to succeed, he would return to the lost paradise of pure poetry or pure aesthetic experience; but there is no such paradise, even in the poetry of John Milton, because all aesthetic experience is predicated on loss. As the French poet Charles-Pierre Baudelaire will say, the only paradises are lost ones. Loss is the condition and, in fact, the substance of poetry, especially when the poetry laments loss. (For a later "demonstration" of this sense of being haunted by fragments of a nonexistent whole, see ROBERT BROWNING'S "CHILDE ROLAND TO THE DARK TOWER CAME.")

The preface of "Kubla Khan" gives a demonstration of this just in its account of the actual words that elicited the poem: the sentences from the book Coleridge was reading when he nodded off, Samuel Purchas's 1613 book of explorers' tales, *Purchas His Pilgrimage.* The passage from Purchas (which Coleridge quotes from memory) elicits the poem and is the fact behind the dream poem, a literal fact which, were the dream to recover, would be entirely deflating. We have the original words that sparked the poem; what makes it great is the way it forgets those words, even as it laments that forgetting. It becomes instead a poem about trying to recover them, or trying to recover how the soul felt in first responding to them. The soul hears "ancestral voices prophesizing war" (l. 30), not because the poem is about war but because it is about a tumult that can never be put to rest by the attainment of its object. The poet will always experience tumult, always hear the prophecies that give him or her no peace. Kubla Khan's creation of Xanadu is itself an image of the creation of the poem, the "miracle of rare device" (l. 35) that contains within it the unplumbable caverns and sunless seas of the parts of the mind that the mind cannot reach. (Coleridge is thinking of the Greek philosopher Plato here, but we may think of Sigmund Freud's similar invocation of the platonic myth of forgetfulness of all but dim intimations left to the soul.)

It is therefore telling that Coleridge invents a river, Alph, based probably on the Sicilian river Alpheus, which features prominently in classical mythology (particularly Ovid) but which, Coleridge knew, had no connection whatever with Xanadu or any other place frequented by Kubla Khan. The sacred river that runs through caverns measureless to man and all the way to the sunless lifeless sea of death is the alphabet (the word comes from *alpha* and *beta,* the first two letters of the Greek alphabet); so Xanadu is the creation of the letters that come together so mysteriously to make the poem. It is not a real place but a place that can only exist in the words that describe it, and not even there. The phantom that haunts the poet and makes him seek to follow the river does not lead him back to Xanadu, but, through it, to the poem that tries and fails to describe it.

BIBLIOGRAPHY

Bloom, Harold. *The Visionary Company: A Reading of English Romantic Poetry.* Garden City, N.Y.: Doubleday, 1961.

Brisman, Leslie. *Romantic Origins.* Ithaca, N.Y.: Cornell University Press, 1978.

Frank, Robert H. *Passions within Reason: The Strategic Role of the Emotions.* New York: Norton, 1988.

Freud, Sigmund. "The Uncanny." In *The Standard Edition of the Complete Psychological Works of Sigmund Freud.* Vol. 17, 219–256. London: Hogarth Press, 1953–1974.

Janowitz, Anne. *England's Ruins: Poetic Purpose and the National Landscape.* Cambridge, Mass.: Blackwell, 1990.

Lowes, John Livingston. *Road to Xanadu: A Study in the Ways of the Imagination.* New York: Houghton Mifflin, 1930.

Parker, Reeve. *Coleridge's Meditative Art.* Ithaca, N.Y.: Cornell University Press, 1975.

Swann, Karen. "'Christabel': The Wandering Mother and the Enigma of Form." *SIR* 23, no. 4 (Winter 1984): 533–553.

"LA BELLE DAME SANS MERCI" JOHN KEATS (1819) JOHN KEATS wrote this poem—or "ballad," as he called it—the same day that he started working on his "ODE TO PSYCHE," and it is worth thinking of the "Beautiful Lady without Mercy" and Psyche as related characters. The ballad is one of Keats's most mysterious poems, in part his answer to SAMUEL TAYLOR COLERIDGE's "KUBLA KHAN," whose mysteries it emulates. As with JOANNA BAILLIE's rewriting of Scottish ballads, Keats has an original in mind, a poem by Alain Chartier from 1424, as his friend LEIGH HUNT pointed out in a note accompanying the poem when it was published in the *Indicator* in 1820. Chartier's poem is about courtly love, though, and has nothing mysterious about it; rather, a cruel fair, as the term is, tells the man who loves her (quite reasonably) that she is not responsible for that love. Keats liked the title—and its "language strange"—and indeed had already referred to it four months earlier in "The EVE OF ST. AGNES," where Porphyro plays Madeline "an ancient ditty, / Long since mute, / In Provence called 'La belle dame sans mercy'" (ll. 291–292). Here he attempts a poem appropriate to that title.

Who is "La Belle Dame"? Keats meets a knight who is suffering from a sense of irremediable loss. The three opening quatrains comprise a first speaker's bridge into the story that the Knight at Arms tells in the remaining nine. He met a beautiful woman, a "fairy's child" (l. 14), who takes him to fairyland. "Fairyland" here means something like the land of the imagination (the land of Edmund Spenser's *The Faerie Queene,* which Keats loved), a place elsewhere. It is a place that must be elsewhere, since it is a land of pure evocation or imagination, and therefore it can exist only as its own evocativeness. This is a feeling Keats explores in his odes as well, from the haunted landscapes of "Ode to Psyche" to the far fields and times of which the nightingale ("ODE TO A NIGHTINGALE") sings, "far away" from this world, as well as the "fairy lands" that poem imagines, to the Greece depicted on the urn ("ODE ON A GRECIAN URN") to the very existence of melancholy as her own dissolution ("ODE ON MELANCHOLY"). It is for this reason that "La Belle Dame Sans Merci" provides a bridge: The speaker can only know of the fairyland in the knight's ballad. The form implies intense distance, the intensity of elusiveness. La Belle Dame herself is, then, a kind of muse of this evocation, like the vision of the Abyssinian maid in "Kubla Khan," who feeds the dreaming speaker on honeydew, like the "honey wild and manna dew" (l. 26) here. But he cannot possibly sustain this life of pure evocation. The meaning of his dream is not that she has somehow maliciously bewitched him (as Coleridge's Geraldine has bewitched *CHRISTABEL*), but that he is in thrall to the muse herself, who can never be anything but elusive. What she leaves is what she inspires: the very sense of loss, of a lost world or place or time or dream, that poetry records, most adequately when most evocatively promising what can only exist in the form of promise or memory, but never as actuality. It was this that so inspired the Pre-Raphaelites, to the extent that WILLIAM MORRIS could call it the seed from which all their poetry grew.

See also PRE-RAPHAELITE POETRY.

BIBLIOGRAPHY

Bate, Walter Jackson. *John Keats.* Cambridge, Mass.: Harvard University Press, 1963.

Bloom, Harold. *Poetry and Repression: Revisionism from Blake to Stevens.* New Haven, Conn.: Yale University Press, 1976.

———. *The Visionary Company: A Reading of English Romantic Poetry.* Garden City, N.Y.: Doubleday, 1961).

De Man, Paul. *The Rhetoric of Romanticism.* New York: Columbia University Press, 1984.

Dickstein, Morris. *Keats and His Poetry: A Study in Development.* Chicago: University of Chicago Press, 1971.

Flesch, William. "The Ambivalence of Generosity: Keats Reading Shakespeare." *ELH: English Literary History* 62, no. 1 (Spring 1995): 149–169.

McFarland, Thomas *The Masks of Keats: The Endeavour of a Poet.* New York: Oxford University Press, 2000.

Stillinger, Jack. *The Hoodwinking of Madeline, and Other Essays on Keats's Poems.* Urbana: University of Illinois Press, 1971.

Wasserman, Earl. *The Finer Tone: Keats' Major Poems.* Baltimore: Johns Hopkins Press, 1953.

"LAKE ISLE OF INNISFREE, THE" WILLIAM BUTLER YEATS (1890)

Published in *The Rose* in 1892, this is one of WILLIAM BUTLER YEATS's most famous poems. It describes his desire, intention, and expectation to return to the island of Innisfree, in County Sligo, Ireland (where his mother's family lived), and there to live alone, surrounded by the elemental and summer beauties of nature. The poem ultimately may be said to derive from the country-house tradition invented in the 17th century by Ben Jonson and his followers, especially Robert Herrick and Andrew Marvell: the idea that Yeats pursues of going to the country to be find peace and to be freed from all the petty and useless troubles and harassments of modern urban, commercial life.

This poem is one of Yeats's most beloved and most anthologized, and Yeats can be heard reading it at http://www.poets.org/poems/poems.cfm?prmID=1371. It is like most of his 19th-century poems in seeking a return to the simplicity of a kind of aristocratic version of rural Ireland. The poem is so popular because it perfectly conceives the possibility of escape. What the escape is from is finally announced in the penultimate lines: Yeats thinks of Innisfree "While I stand on the roadway, or on the pavements grey" of the city of Dublin. But he is not standing on the roads as he writes the poem, even fictionally, since he plans to "arise and go;" he is sitting and writing, and the poem announces the intention that he begins putting into action by articulating it, an action that is articulated by writing the poem. That is to say, the poem announces an intention that will be successfully completed.

Yeats can count on this success because he has been there before: He knows Innisfree and knows that it is a place of inner freedom (the suggestion is inevitable in the sound of the place name) and of peace. His anticipation that he "will have some peace there" shows by contrast what he does not have *here* under the pressures of commerce and society. The journey to Innisfree is therefore an instance of what the Danish philosopher Søren Kierkegaard called *repetition.* Kierkegaard defined repetition as "remembering forward," and the ability to repeat is an ability to preserve the past and bring it into the future. That past is real, but the future is somewhat idealized. We know Yeats will not really build a cabin or plant beans, but the fantasy of doing so is what the poem presents, and the poem is in fact the artifact, the work that Yeats builds.

That work and that building are important (and later Yeats would talk about the work of his own hands in the land and tower that he bought). The idea that work brings peace and tranquillity goes back to pastoral poetry, but Yeats is particularly thinking here of the Roman poet Virgil's *Georgics,* which give an account of beekeeping, when he anticipates the "bee-loud glade." The bees are also a recollection of JOHN KEATS's ode "TO AUTUMN," where they stand for an abundance that seems to go on forever. Indeed, we might see "The Lake Isle of Innisfree" as a kind of answer or pendant to "To Autumn," for reasons I will return to in a moment.

It is important to see what Yeats anticipates at Innisfree, and what he will therefore be free of: He relishes the idea of work, of peace, and also of solitude, since it is his intention to "live *alone*" when he gets there. The question might be asked, though, why the poem is prospective. We have already glanced at one reason: The poem feels successful because it achieves an attitude toward the future that looks sure to bear fruit. Being certain of future peace is in a sense the goal of every poem, but it is a very difficult goal to reach. But we can also say that the poem recognizes that the place to hear what Yeats hears is in Dublin, at least as much as in Innisfree. The poem is successful because it anticipates the future ultimately in the present tense; it feels the future in the instant or absorbs the future into the present. This occurs in the poem's last stanza of the poem, where are found the only lines in which Yeats describes himself in the present:

> I will arise and go now, for always night and day
> I hear lake water lapping with low sounds by the shore;
> While I stand on the roadway, or on the pavements grey,
> I hear it in the deep heart's core.

The future tense that has governed the poem in the opening lines of each stanza—"I will arise and go now," here and at the start, as well as "And I shall have some peace there," opening the second stanza—finally gives way to the present: "I *hear* lake water lapping . . . While I *stand* on the roadway, . . . I *hear* it in the deep heart's core."

These are not the first present tenses in the poem, though: The second stanza marks an advance from the first in describing how things *are* on the Lake Isle: "there peace comes dropping slow"; "There midnight's all a glimmer, and noon a purple glow / And evening full of the linnet's wings." These timeless present tenses (timeless because they describe different times of day simultaneously, characterizing how things are *there*) prepare for the more local but still permanent present tense of the last stanza and allow for the subtle gradation into that present-tense self-description: "I hear it in the deep heart's core." Remember that in the last stanza, he is not *currently* standing on the roadway, just as it is not *currently* midnight and noon and evening at Innisfree. But he is currently—continuously and always—hearing the continuous and unceasing lapping of the lake water.

In "To Autumn," Keats slowly manages a subtle gradation of present-tense repletion and even stagnation into an address toward the future. He escapes the paralysis of the present to find movement and freedom in what will come later. Yeats performs the opposite movement, as the pure anticipation of Innisfree becomes its presence even when it is absent: He hears the water now, while he is standing on the roadway or pavements of Dublin.

As in many of Yeats's early poems, he specifies hearing as the most important sense here. He hears the cricket sing (another Keatsian inheritance) and the lake water lapping. It is natural for a poet to favor the sense of hearing, and a poet like Yeats, who is intoxicated by the sensuous qualities of language, will be most likely to do so. Indeed, *The Rose* is full of poems about hearing, where the desire to hear is somehow met by the sounds of the poems which describe that desire (see "The SAD SHEPHERD," for example). In "The Lake Isle of Innisfree," the celebration of hearing is embodied in the poet's striking rhythmical subtlety and novelty.

Everyone feels the poem's ponderous sonorities. It is worth being specific, though. The first lines of each quatrain have exactly the same form: the 13-syllable line has a pause, or caesura, after the seventh syllable and then picks up with a further six syllables in iambic meter. The important juncture in these lines is the transition from the slightly irregular seven-syllable beginning to the highly regular six-syllable ending. The first seven syllables are also iambic, until one gets to the seventh syllable: *now* in the first and last stanzas, *there* in the second. Those syllables are stressed when we expect an alternating unstressed syllable, and this unexpected but strong stress gives the poem's sound its sense of substance. It is not only in the first lines that you can feel this sudden and weighty doubling of stress; the same is true of the building repetitions of *build there, have there,* and *peace there,* as well as *roadway* in the penultimate line.

These repeated stresses set up the unexpectedly short final lines of each stanza. In the first and second stanzas, the final lines are nine syllables long, substantially less than the 13 or more syllables of the other lines. They express a kind of achievement of the desire articulated earlier, a kind of resolution of sonorities, and again are highly parallel to each other, each ending with a prepositional phrase that sets two unstressed syllables, preposition and definite article, together: ". . . in the bee-loud glade"; "of the linnet's wings"; "in the deep heart's core."

Here, again, this is set up as a metrical template. The last line of the poem is shorter than the last lines of the first two quatrains. It is only eight syllables long and concatenates *three* stressed syllables: "deep heart's core," as a culmination of the great double stresses that stand for the long-lasting anticipations of Innisfree's unchanging, almost archetypal quality. This last line is where Yeats's sonority becomes most powerful, just where he responds most fully to the rhythmic sounds of "lake water lapping." The poem makes itself *heard* even as it describes its speaker's hearing. And it does so with a subtle ambiguity Yeats would use to fullest effect in "Among School Children": "I hear it in the deep heart's core" (note the *hear* in *heart*) may mean that he hears *with* his heart, or that the sound is already to be found *in* his heart and that now he hears what his heart contains.

Of course, the line means both things at once: Because his heart's core has taken and harbored the sound, he can hear what is in his heart's core. He is creator and perceiver simultaneously, which is exactly the attitude toward intention, expectation, and anticipation that the poem describes. He is going to Innisfree, and because he *is* going, he is already there, as a poet, and it is in the poem that we, too, can hear wave waters lapping.

BIBLIOGRAPHY

Anscombe, G. E. M. *Intention.* Cambridge, Mass.: Harvard University Press, 2000.

Bloom, Harold. *Yeats.* New York: Oxford University Press, 1970.

Grossman, Allen R. *Poetic Knowledge in the Early Yeats: A Study of the Wind among the Reeds.* (Charlottesville: University Press of Virginia, 1969.

Rosenthal, M. L. Introduction to *Selected Poems and Three Plays of William Butler Yeats.* New York: Collier, 1986.

Vendler, Helen. *Poets Thinking: Pope, Whitman, Dickinson, Yeats.* Cambridge, Mass.: Harvard University Press, 2004.

———. *Yeats's Vision and the Later Plays.* Cambridge, Mass.: Harvard University Press, 1963.

LAKE POETS This term refers to the poets WILLIAM WORDSWORTH, SAMUEL TAYLOR COLERIDGE, and ROBERT SOUTHEY, who lived near each other and spent much time together in the Lake District in England, in what is now called Cumbria (at the time Cumberland and Westmoreland). The term was first coined by Francis Jeffrey (1773–1850), the gifted and vituperative editor of the *Edinburgh Review* (1829–47) and was meant derogatorily. Jeffrey felt the Lake Poets were given to ridiculous self-indulgence, and he jeered at the way they combined philosophical intensity with a preference for what he regarded as the primitivity of rural life. In a memorable moment, he wrote of Wordsworth: "It may be that he has dashed his Hippocrene with too large an infusion of lake water, or assisted its operation too exclusively by the study of the ancient historical ballads of 'the north countrie.'" (Hippocrene, as in Keats's ODE TO A NIGHTINGALE, refers to the waters of the fountain of the Greek Muses) LORD BYRON picked up the taunt in his parodic dedication to *DON JUAN*:

> Bob Southey! You're a poet—Poet-laureate,
> And representative of all the race;
> Although 'tis true that you turn'd out a Tory at
> Last—yours has lately been a common case;
> And now, my Epic Renegade! what are ye at?
> With all the Lakers, in and out of place?
> A nest of tuneful persons, to my eye
> Like "four and twenty Blackbirds in a pye."

Byron, who also hated Jeffrey but was closer to his political views, regarded the Lake Poets, or Lakers, as having the relatively conservative politics that they had come to choose as consonant with the backward-looking conservatism of their rural environment. Byron was urbane and southern (Italy and Greece) in his outlook and dead set against the northernism of the Lake Poets.

The author Thomas De Quincey, (1785—1859) probably did most, however, to preserve the term in his great book *Recollections of the Lakes and the Lake Poets,* a highly sympathetic and powerful biographical and critical account, especially of Wordsworth. De Quincey, who was a city dweller, hated Wordsworth's rustic manners (he memorably described Wordsworth cutting the pages of a new book with a soiled butter knife) but knew that Wordsworth was the great poetic genius of the age. CHARLES LAMB also remembering of the Lake Poets, with great nostalgia a three-week trip he made to the Lake District to visit Coleridge and Wordsworth.

It is certainly true that the Lake Poets were opposed to the ferment of the urban environment. Wordsworth wrote a still-useful "Guide to the Lakes" (1810), and late in his life he lamented the coming of the railroads to the Lake District since it would make it easy for city dwellers to invade his beloved countryside. But the reason that the Lake Poets loved the Lake District and made it the subject or setting for much of their most memorable poetry was its beauty and the fact that there they could think of both poetry and of human experience in its most basic and elemental modes. The kind of poetry, and the kind of experience, to arise there would be timeless in the way that the 18th-century urbane poetry that the Lake Poets rebelled against could not. In fact, modern ecological movements originated in the poetry of nature and of "natural men" that the Lake Poets created, and that made possible an appreciation of nature picked up by the American writers Ralph Waldo Emerson (who knew Wordsworth and Coleridge) and Henry David Thoreau, and then by Theodore Roosevelt, an appreciation that continues to this day.

BIBLIOGRAPHY

Bate, Jonathan. *Romantic Ecology: Wordsworth and the Environmental Tradition.* New York: Routledge, 1991.

De Quincey, Thomas. *Recollections of the Lakes and the Lake Poets.* Edited by David Wright. Harmondsworth, England: Penguin, 1970.

Jeffrey, Francis. *On the Lake Poets.* Washington, D.C.: Woodstock Books, 1998.

LAMB, CHARLES (1775–1834)

As a writer, Charles Lamb is known mainly for his wonderful "familiar essays" as he called them, the *Essays of Elia* (the pseudonym is based on the first two letters of *Lamb*). Those essays are brilliant, mordant, often hilarious, and sometimes plangent accounts of the life of an ordinary person living in extraordinary times and among extraordinary peers. For Lamb's friends, particularly SAMUEL TAYLOR COLERIDGE (who was his older schoolmate and mentor at grammar school) and WILLIAM WORDSWORTH, were extraordinary, and Lamb himself *is* their peer—not as a great poet, nor as a major philosophical or literary thinker, but as the leading member of whatever a fit audience for their work would be.

Lamb's familiar essays are exquisite and exquisitely faithful accounts of ordinary human life. On the whole, he lived a more or less ordinary life (an extraordinary version of an ordinary life), working for the East India Company as a clerk for 33 years and never giving himself over to the passionate excesses of the great romantic poets (see ROMANTICISM). His contemporary Thomas De Quincey writes very shrewdly of "Elia": "The instances are many, in his own beautiful essays, where he literally collapses, literally sinks away from openings suddenly offering themselves to nights of pathos or solemnity in direct prosecution of his own theme. On any such summons, where an ascending impulse and an untired pinion were required, he refuses himself (to use military language) invariably." De Quincey was not saying anything Lamb did not already know, and indeed some of Lamb's essays are about the way his imagination always returns to the solid ground of the ordinary, often to ordinary sadness and disappointment. He is even more explicit in an 1802 letter to a friend describing a month-long vacation he took with his sister Mary in the Lake District, visiting Coleridge:

> We have clambered up to the top of Skiddaw, and I have waded up the bed of Lodore. In fine, I have satisfied myself that there is such a thing as that which tourists call *romantic,* which I very much suspected before: they make such a spluttering about it, and toss their splendid epithets around them, till they give as dim a light as at four o'clock next morning the lamps do after an illumination. . . . Oh, its fine black head, and the bleak air atop of it, with a prospect of moun-

tains all about and about, making you giddy; and then Scotland afar off, and the border countries so famous in song and ballad! It was a day that will stand out, like a mountain, I am sure, in my life. But I am returned (I have now been come home near three weeks; I was a month out), and you cannot conceive the degradation I felt at first, from being accustomed to wander free as air among mountains, and bathe in rivers without being controlled by any one, to come home and *work.* I felt very *little.* I had been dreaming I was a very great man. But that is going off, and I find I shall conform in time to that state of life to which it has pleased God to call me. Besides, after all, Fleet Street and the Strand are better places to live in for good and all than amidst Skiddaw. Still, I turn back to those great places where I wandered about, participating in their greatness.

It is not that Lamb lacked imagination. He was institutionalized in his youth, apparently after a fit of violent mania, and when he was 21 his much-older sister Mary suddenly attacked and killed their mother at the dinner table. Lamb agreed to care for Mary from then on, and he did, the two of them living what he called a relatively peaceful life of "double singleness," though Mary did have occasional bouts of mental illness.

Lamb's poetry is resolutely minor—the poetry of a person who does not feel that he is fulfilling his poetic vocation but regretting its unfulfillment. He may be said to be the greatest talent we know to have subordinated his talent to the tasks and demands of ordinary life. No one else has so well described the duties and disappointments of being ordinary from the inside; no one else who was so extraordinarily gifted has lived so resolutely ordinary a life—full of hilarity and wit (for which he was famous) and loved by all who knew him (despite some of the surprising barbs of his conversation), but conforming to the needs and desires of a world that had him living in Fleet Street and the Strand, and not amidst the beauty of Skiddaw.

See also "OLD FAMILIAR FACES, THE."

BIBLIOGRAPHY

De Quincey, Thomas. *Biographical Essays.* (Boston: Ticknor and Fields, 1866.

Flesch, William. "'Friendly and Judicious' Reading: Affect and Irony in the Works of Charles Lamb." *Studies in Romanticism* 23, no. 22 (1984): 163–181.

Lamb, Charles. *A Complete Elia: The Essays of Elia, together with The Last Essays of Elia.* New York: The Heritage Press, 1943.

Lucas, E. V. *Life of Charles Lamb.* New York: G.P. Putnam's Sons, 1905.

"LAMB, THE" WILLIAM BLAKE (1789) "The Lamb" and "The TYGER" (1794) correspond to each other in WILLIAM BLAKE'S *SONGS OF INNOCENCE AND OF EXPERIENCE.* "The Lamb" is a song of innocence, and it is spoken by a child, as we find in its last stanza. The child addresses the lamb and thinks about the gentleness and generosity of Christ, the lamb of God. Blake is uncannily good at representing the depths of childlike innocence. The child asks the lamb whether it knows who made it; the lamb is a perfect metaphor for a child who would think a lamb might wonder at its own creation and the gentleness of its created world—the stream and mead, the wool that clothes it, the voice with which it makes the vales echo. We understand, in the first stanza, all that we need to understand about the child just because the child thinks of the lamb as being like himself.

In the second stanza, the child answers the question, "who made thee?" The answer is one who calls himself a lamb and became a child, so that the metaphor whose use by the child is so touching and revealing now becomes justified or confirmed by the fact that the child has made the connection with Christ. He has made the connection for the same reason we do and that the poem does: that the child would see in the idea that the lamb represented him a deep and moving metaphor for the gentleness and mercy of God. And so the poem ends with the child blessing the lamb, or calling upon God to do so.

BIBLIOGRAPHY

Bloom, Harold. *Blake's Apocalypse: A Study in Poetic Argument.* Ithaca, N.Y.: Cornell University Press, 1970.

Frye, Northrop. *Fearful Symmetry: A Study of William Blake.* Princeton, N.J.: Princeton University Press, 1974.

Gilchrist, Alexander. *Life of William Blake, with Selections from His Poems and Other Writings.* Totowa, N.J.: Rowman and Littlefield, 1973.

Raine, Kathleen. *Blake and Antiquity.* Princeton, N.J.: Princeton University Press, 1977.

Thompson, E. P. *Witness against the Beast: William Blake and the Moral Law.* New York: Cambridge University Press, 1993.

"LA MORT D'ARTHUR"

See AYTOUN, WILLIAM EDMONDSTOUNE.

LANDON, LETITIA ELIZABETH (L.E.L.) (1802–1838)

In his autobiography, the editor William Jerden describes his first sight of the 3-year-old Letitia Elizabeth Landon in about 1815: "My first recollection is that of a plump girl bowling a hoop round the walks, with the hoop-stick in one hand and a book in the other, reading as she ran. The exercise was prescribed; the book was choice." Landon read voraciously and delighted in everything she read. Jerden edited the *Literary Gazette,* in which he published Landon's poems, and he helped her get her work published in other journals and in book form with *The Improvisatrice* (which quickly went through five editions after its publication in 1825). Jerden assiduously promoted Landon's poetry (sometimes embarrassingly), to the extent that she became one of the most popular poets of her day. Her popularity was of paramount importance to her because after her father's death in 1824, she became her family's main support.

Landon signed her poems "L.E.L." She did very well with her writing but had to write incessantly. Her fame made her an object of journalistic interest and of gossip, an experience she describes memorably and powerfully in her posthumous fragment "GOSSIPPING." Jerden's incessant promotion required her to embrace publicity, and to some extent she seems to have begun by relishing notoriety. She cut a daring figure in her poetry and also wrote flirtatious letters to some of her prominent male friends. The tabloids of the day began to hint knowingly of her sexual dalliances. There is no evidence that she actually did have all the affairs credited to her, and she was much stung by the gossip, which would eventually assert her involvement with Jerden, the painter Daniel Maclise (who did her portrait, which now hangs in the National Portrait Gallery), the novelist Edward Bulwer-Lytton, and others. But what stung her most was the claim that she and Jerden had had a child together; she complained furiously about this story.

So, too, have many of her critics in recent years. However, Cynthia Lawford showed in her 2001 Ph. D. dissertation for the City University of New York that Landon and Jerden had had three children together, and that Landon had courted the danger that eventually overwhelmed her. At any rate, the rumors reached the ears of John Forster, editor of the *Examiner* and 10 years her junior. They had been engaged, but he asked her to explain and refute the rumors. Having done so to his satisfaction, she then broke off the engagement.

In 1838 Landon married George Maclean, in what seems to have been more or less a marriage of convenience, at least to judge by the bitter, posthumously published fragment "The MARRIAGE VOW." Maclean was governor of Cape Coast Castle, in what is now Ghana, and they moved there. Seven months later, Landon died at her own hand of an overdose of prussic acid, perhaps accidental.

Landon's poetry shows lyrical skill as well as real thought and daring. Her best poems are heavily influenced by WILLIAM WORDSWORTH, whom she thoroughly understood, and her popularity was well-deserved, even as her victimization by scandalmongers was not.

See also "FELICIA HEMANS," "SAPPHO'S SONG."

BIBLIOGRAPHY

Greer, Germaine. *Slip-Shod Sibyls: Recognition, Rejection and the Woman Poet.* London: Viking, 1995.

Lawford, Cynthia. "Diary." *London Review of Books* (September 21, 2000). Available online. URL: http://www.lrb.co.uk/v22/n18/lawf01_/html. Accessed on March 28, 2008.

———: "'Thou shalt bid thy fair hands rove': L. E. L.'s Wooing of Sex, Pain, Death and the Editor." *Romanticism on the Net* 29–30 (February–May 2003). Available online. URL: http://www.erudit.org/revue/ron/2003/v/n29/007718ar.html. Accessed on March 30, 2008.

Mellor, Anne K. "Exhausting the Beautiful." In *Romanticism and Gender,* 107–143. New York: Routledge, 1993.

LANDOR, WALTER SAVAGE (1775–1864)

Walter Savage Landor was one of the most accomplished minor writers of the 19th century. His long life and career spanned ROMANTICISM: Only three years younger than his friend SAMUEL TAYLOR COLERIDGE and a year younger than his very close friend ROBERT SOUTHEY, he was born the same year as CHARLES LAMB, whom he outlived by 30 years. He lived through much of what we call the Victorian period, surviving ELIZABETH BARRETT BROWNING by four years and writing a wonderful encomium to her husband, ROBERT BROWNING, whose genius Landor recognized as early as 1845, when he was 70 and Browning 33; Landor ranked Browning with Geoffrey Chaucer and second only to William Shakespeare.

At the end of his life, Landor became the Brownings' neighbor in Italy and counted them as his close friends, whom he could rely on in his strange and fraught domestic circumstances. Although the great love of his life was the twice-married Sophia Jane Swifte (the Ianthe of many of his poems, including "PAST RUIN'D ILION," written over many years), he married Julia Thuiller, 19 years his junior, in 1811. They had four children, but Landor abandoned them in Italy (where they had gone to live in 1815 to avoid his debts) 24 years later, when he was 60, and returned to England. Twenty-three years after *that,* he returned to his wife for another year (it was then that Browning gave him support) and then abandoned her for good, at 84.

Landor, it will be obvious, was a very cantankerous person. The extravagance of his character is well captured by Charles Dickens in *Bleak House* (1853), where he appears as the character Boythorn. (LEIGH HUNT is Skimpole in that novel, and it is interesting to see how Dickens handles his two aging friends, survivors of the great generation of romantic poets.) The diarist Henry Crabb Robinson, who first met Landor in 1830 and reported his reputation as a man hard to stay on good terms with, said of Dickens's portrait that it accurately captured Landor's "fierce tones, tenderness of heart, and exaggeration in all his judgments." That outsized cantankerousness is the other side of Landor's aloofness to life: Early and late, his most powerful poems regard the world as fundamentally unworthy of the human spirit. This is evident in such a poem as the great elegy on "ROSE AYLMER," his close friend who died when Landor was 25, but the same sense that the world is unfit for human virtue and grace may be found in the poem he wrote on his 74th birthday, "Dying Speech of an Old Philosopher," in which he says, "I strove with none, for none was worth my strife."

Of course, Landor strove with many, but on some deep level he did not regard this strife as worthy of anything but momentary vehemence, intense because only momentary. What he says in "Dying Speech" is accurate: "Nature I loved, and next to Nature, Art," and it was in art, both poetry and prose (especially the remarkable *Imaginary Conversations* that are his greatest work), that he found a way to hold life at the proper distance. In the poetry, this can be seen in the classical chastity of his style (he wrote many of his greatest poems by drafting them in Latin and then translating them into English), which holds the relentless demands and disappointments of the world at just the right distance.

See also "DIRCE."

BIBLIOGRAPHY

Butler, Marilyn. *Romantics, Rebels, and Reactionaries: English Literature and its Background, 1760–1830.* New York: Oxford University Press, 1982.

De Quincey, Thomas. *Recollections of the Lakes and the Lake Poets.* Edited by David Wright. Harmondsworth, England: Penguin, 1970.

Hazlitt, William. *Spirit of the Age; or, Contemporary Portraits.* London: Oxford University Press, 1970.

Robinson, Henry Crabb. *Diary, Reminiscences, and Correspondence of Henry Crabb Robinson.* New York: Hurd and Houghton, 1877.

Storey, Mark. *Robert Southey: A Life.* New York: Oxford University Press, 1997.

Super, R. H. *Walter Savage Landor: A Biography.* New York: New York University Press, 1954.

LANG, ANDREW (1844–1912)

Andrew Lang was one of the most voraciously well-read, wide-ranging, and talented figures of his age. WILLIAM ERNEST HENLEY's lovely phrase about Lang, "the divine amateur," sums him up. He wrote articles in the *Encyclopedia Britannica* on crystal gazing (he was a spiritualist) as well as anthropological and mythological subjects. An early advocate of comparative anthropology, he was a novelist, a classicist, and a translator. Lang was born in Selkirk, south of Edinburgh, and was true to his Scottish literary heritage (his grandfather was a friend of Sir WALTER SCOTT's), in his poetry and in the collections of fairy tales that he put together in the course of many volumes named for the color of their covers and still in print today.

Lang went to Oxford University as an undergraduate, and there he attended MATTHEW ARNOLD's lectures (Arnold would later become a friend and patron); after his degree, he became a fellow of Merton College, Oxford. In 1874, while recuperating from a respiratory ailment, he went to France, where he met ROBERT LOUIS STEVENSON, also a convalescent and also from the border country in Scotland. Stevenson influenced Lang enormously and channeled his anthropological study into an interest in old and elemental forms, so that Lang became an important resister of the modernism on the horizon. He disliked THOMAS HARDY and Henry James and devoted himself instead, like the Pre-Raphaelites to whom he had been exposed as an undergraduate (see PRE-RAPHAELITE POETRY), to old and antique forms. Following the example of ALGERNON CHARLES SWINBURNE and DANTE GABRIEL ROSSETTI, he revived troubadour forms such as the ballade (see "BALLADE OF BLUE CHINA" and "ON CALAIS SANDS"), first in his book of translations *Ballads and Lyrics of Old France* (1872), which contains some classic translations of the group of 16th-century French poets known as the Pleaides poets, and then in his own poetry.

In 1875 Lang married an heiress and was able to resign his fellowship at Oxford and devote himself to his scholarship (especially classical and anthropological studies) and his writing. (Merton College made him an honorary fellow 15 years later.) Lang was a journalist and a writer of popular fiction (he collaborated with H. Rider Haggard, most famous for *She*), as well as a poet and scholar. He was also notoriously devoted to fishing, especially in the Border regions where he grew up, and to cricket: this was part of the life of the divine amateur that he led. He died in Banchory, Scotland, and was buried at St. Andrews.

Lang was a decidedly minor poet, but of the sort T. S. Eliot had in mind in his praise of Andrew Marvell over John Milton: that being a good poet is sometimes better than being a great poet. Lang's poetic talents were those of the sensitive revivalist. He wrote the kind of poetry he loved and gave the world more of it. He wrote it with the perfection not of the inventor but of one supremely well-studied in the art. His poems therefore aim not for profundity but for a kind of grand wit, which is itself a tribute to the richness and profusion of language. His one attempt at a serious long poem, *Helen of Troy* (1882), is polished but tedious, and we can be grateful that he knew his own strengths well enough to write the wonderful, witty verse that he did, poetry that makes its readers happy.

See also "SCYTHE SONG."

BIBLIOGRAPHY

Beerbohm, Max. "Two Glimpses of Andrew Lang." *Life and Letters* 1, no. 1 (June, 1928): 1–11.

Cocq, Antonius Petrus Leonardus de. *Andrew Lang, a Nineteenth Century Anthropologist.* Tilburg, Netherlands: Zwijsen, 1968.

Green, Roger Lancelyn. *Andrew Lang: A Critical Biography with a Short-Title Bibliography of the Works of Andrew Lang.* Leicester, England: E. Ward, 1946.

Gross, John. *Rise and Fall of the Man of Letters: Aspects of English Literary Life since 1800.* London: Weidenfeld & Nicolson, 1969.

Orel, Harold. *Victorian Literary Critics: George Henry Lewes, Walter Bagehot, Richard Holt Hutton, Leslie Stephen, Andrew Lang, George Saintsbury, and Edmund Gosse.* London: Macmillan Press, 1984.

Webster, A. Blyth. *Andrew Lang's Poetry, by A. Blyth Webster, being the Andrew Lang lecture delivered before the University of St. Andrews 20 October 1937.* London: Oxford University Press, 1937.

"LAST SIGNAL, THE" THOMAS HARDY (1886)

This poem is identified as a "moment of vision" (from his book *Moments of Vision*) that THOMAS HARDY had on the Winterborne Came path in Dorset, near where he lived, when he saw the coffin of WILLIAM BARNES, who had just died. Hardy read the poem at Barnes's funeral a few days later. It is a sad and moving elegy for one of the contemporary poets whom Hardy esteemed most. (He also wrote Barnes's obituary for the *Athenaeum* and later edited a selection of Barnes's poetry.)

Hardy's poetry is all in standard English, unlike Barnes's. He admired his fellow poet's dialect verse (dialect that he reproduced in the dialogue in his novels), and there is a sense in which "The Last Signal" is an elegy for that kind of poetry as well. One can see this in the strange but unobtrusive formal innovation in Hardy's elegy. It consists of three stanzas, all of which rhyme *abcb* (that is, the second and fourth line of each stanza rhyme). It takes much longer to see the internal rhyme that each second line gives to the last word of the first line in each stanza: *road/abode, east/least,* and *prime/time.* Hardy's lines are sluggish, sad, precise, and patient in mourning his friend. The poem keeps making false starts toward the kind of quick and spritely, almost balladic meter that Barnes was so good at, so that rhyme and meter we almost hear never ignites. Instead, we get the very long third lines and the sense that the poem is too heavy to take flight.

It is worth describing the scene. Hardy is walking along the path at sunset, depressed by the death of his friend, which has just occurred. He leaves his abode to think, as Barnes himself might have done, in some "yew-boughed" solitude. (Hardy, in his anonymous review of Barnes's 1879 edition of *Poems of Rural Life in the Dorset Dialect,* the last review Hardy ever wrote, praises Barnes's penchant for the "compound epithets" he here imitates; later he will describe Barnes as journeying on his "grave-way.") Looking eastward toward darkness, he sees a flash; it is Barnes's coffin, reflecting the last light of the setting sun.

Hardy takes this as a signal from Barnes himself, or he affects to take it that way. But does he really? The striking thing about this elegy—the thing that makes it characteristic of Hardy—is the way it goes against its own claims. It is a convention of elegy to imagine the dead person communicating with the living one final time. But such elegies are almost always written in the *second* person. The poet shows his or her belief in the survival of the dead by speaking back to him or her. There's something of this even in WILLIAM WORDSWORTH's great sonnet on the death of his daughter, "SURPRISED BY JOY," and a great deal of it in some of Barnes's own poetry to his dead wife, such as "The WIFE A-LOST." But Hardy does not use the second person. The chance reflection of the setting sun leads him to describe it as a signal from "my friend there." But it is to us, not to Barnes, that he describes the scene. It is by chance that Barnes's coffin signaled him, "As with the wave of his hand." But it was not a wave: It was something random and unmeaning, except that it meant Barnes's death and the loss of that deep friendship forever, while at the same time, it names him as a friend, a word whose understated severity is its power.

BIBLIOGRAPHY

Barnes, William. *Poems of Rural Life in Common English.* London: Macmillan and Co., 1868.

Bloom, Harold, ed. *Thomas Hardy.* New York: Chelsea House, 1987.

Clements, Patricia, and Juliet Grindle, eds. *Poetry of Thomas Hardy.* London: Vision Press, 1980.

Hardy, Thomas. "Barnes." In *Thomas Hardy's Personal Writings: Prefaces, Literary Opinions, Reminiscences,* edited by Harold Orel, 76–81. London: Macmillan, 1990.

Kramer, Dale, ed. *Cambridge Companion to Thomas Hardy.* New York: Cambridge University Press, 1999.

"LEAD KINDLY LIGHT"

See "PILLAR OF THE CLOUD, THE."

"LEAN OVER ME—AH SO,—LET FALL"

DIGBY MACKWORTH DOLBEN (ca. 1867) This is one of DIGBY MACKWORTH DOLBEN's most beautiful Keatsian poems—Keatsian in subject, in tone, and in erotic charge. The poem is somewhat ambiguous as to whom its speaker is identifying with—intentionally so, since it is one of the places where Dolben is exploring the nature and meaning of his own homoeroticism.

It can be read first of all as an appeal to the moon herself, the goddess Cynthia, who falls in love with the mortal boy Endymion, which is the subject of Keats's poem *Endymion.* The speaker addresses a woman whom he metaphorizes as the moon, her long dark hair falling about his face and neck in the imagined kiss he receives from her (ll. 1–2). He then would be the "new Endymion" (l. 8) whom she kisses, and he would experience the Keatsian joy of poetic power—of the sensual pleasure which itself is a metaphor for being touched by the lips of the Muse (l. 12), lips which kiss but also which speak the words of the poem they inspire. Thinking of JOHN KEATS, he declares his preference for beauty and youth, though transitory, to the old age that he saw in "an old man yesterday" (l. 13), an old man whom the poem pegs as being born before Keats himself was, though Keats has died a quarter of a century before Dolben's birth. He prefers the moment of intensity and love to length of life, thinking of Keats's fear of old age in "ODE TO A NIGHTINGALE," and he explicitly relates this intensity and love to poetic vocation in his repudiation of "a century / Of heavy years that trail the feet" (ll. 17–18)—that is, the poetic feet characteristic of what John Milton called "lame matter and wretched meter."

A second reading of the poem will acknowledge its homoerotic undertones. The flash of vision (see MOTTOES) that the poem derives from reads, "O, a moon face / In a shadowy place" Whose is the "moon face" that he desires? He addresses the moon in the second stanza, but it is not clear that the first stanza does. Rather, it may address the "new Endymion" (l. 8) who would be the boy that the speaker wishes would kiss him in this shadowy place, rather than the speaker himself. After all, Endymion is described in the poem as "The boy . . . with cheeks for ever round and fair" (ll. 9–10), and so the "moon face" may describe the new Endymion by whom the speaker wishes to be kissed. It is in the shadowy place that they can steal their embraces, even as he admires the beauty of the boy in the moonlight.

This is not to claim that the poem is a kind of coded homoerotic declaration. It is, rather, a declaration of eroticism pure and simple, of delight in love and in beauty of whatever origin or gender. It is "youth" that matters here—the youth of the face he wishes to kiss, the youth of the Keatsian poetry he wishes to write.

BIBLIOGRAPHY

Bridges, Robert. *Three Friends: memoirs of Digby Mackworth Dolben, Richard Watson Dixon, Henry Bradley*. Westport, Conn.: Greenwood Press, 1975.

Cunningham, Valentine. Headnote to selection of Dolben in *The Victorians: An Anthology of Poetry and Poetics,* 901. Malden, Mass.: Blackwell, 2000.

Dolben, Digby Mackworth. *The Poems and Letters of Digby Mackworth Dolben, 1848–1867*. Edited by Martin Cohen. England: Avebury, 1981.

———. *The Poems of Digby Mackworth Dolben*. New York: Oxford University Press, 1911.

———. *Uncollected poems of Digby Mackworth Dolben*. Edited by Martin Cohen. Reading, England: Whiteknights Press, 1973.

Najarian, James. *Victorian Keats: Manliness, Sexuality and Desire*. New York: Palgrave, 2002.

LEAR, EDWARD (1812–1888) Edward Lear is often compared to and ranked with LEWIS CARROLL as one of the two great nonsense poets of the 19th century. Both a children's poet and writer of nonsense stories, Lear provided whimsical illustrations to his own nonsense and was also a serious landscape painter who gave Queen Victoria drawing lessons; his illustrated journal of his travels in Greece and Albania is one of his great works. He was a close friend of ALFRED, LORD TENNYSON, some of whose poems he illustrated.

As a poet, Lear is best known for "The Owl and the Pussycat," since set to music and a staple of the nursery. The term *runcible spoon,* now used to refer to the serrated spoon used for eating grapefruit, was Lear's nonsense coinage in that poem. He also wrote "The Dong with the Luminous Nose" and "THE JUMBLIES" (they went to sea in a sieve). His poems are much less acerbic than Carroll's, and typically they will recount the nonsense travels of some strange and whimsical beings with a poignant edge of melancholy.

Lear is also remembered for his limericks. He did not invent this form, but he made it very popular and wrote more of them than anyone had hitherto. Unlike the familiar modern variety, which uses its last line to make an unexpected point, the 19th-century limerick tended to be a variant of the first or second line—for example:

> There was an old man who screamed out
> Whenever they knocked him about;
> So they took off his boots,
> And fed him with fruits,
> And continued to knock him about.

This earlier form of limerick tends toward nonsense rather than wit, since nothing *happens* in the last line, and it was a form at which Lear excelled.

Lear's work is sufficiently delightful, original, memorable, whimsical, and strangely poignant (perhaps because of his homosexuality in Victorian England, although he was an essentially happy man) to have been treated as a fecund source for many later writers. His lovely self-description, "How pleasant to know Mr Lear," was echoed by the 20th-century poet T. S. Eliot in his serious parody "How unpleasant to know Mr. Eliot," and some of his nonsense, especially about his famous cat Foss, is behind Eliot's *Old Possum's Book of Practical Cats* (1939). Lear's work is a major source for the imagery and language of James Joyce's vast dreamscape of a novel, *Finnegans Wake* (1939), some of whose characters are also based on Lear's. And even a postmodern writer such as the American Donald Barthelme has quoted "The Jumblies" in one of his short stories.

Lear might also be thought of as a kind of anticipatory parody of RUDYARD KIPLING. Another way to put this is to say that Kipling got some sense of the possibilities of exoticism at the limits of sense from Lear, so that a passage from "The Dong with a Luminous Nose" can sound like a Kipling poem:

> When the angry breakers roar
> As they beat on the rocky shore—
> When Storm-clouds brood on the towering
>   heights
> Of the Hills of the Chankly Bore . . .

Lear's consummate skill as a poet is deceptive, but along with Carroll he is one of the very few figures ever to write *memorable* nonsense poetry. The influence that he had on later writers shows that what is memorable about nonsense poetry might take one very close to what is memorable about all poetry.

BIBLIOGRAPHY

Byrom, Thomas. *Nonsense and Wonder: The Poems and Cartoons of Edward Lear*. New York: E. P. Dutton, 1977.

Hark, Ina Rae. *Edward Lear*. Boston: Twayne Publishers, 1982.

Lear, Edward. *The Complete Nonsense of Edward Lear*. Edited by Holbrook Jackson. London: Faber and Faber, 1947.

LEVY, AMY (1861–1889) Amy Levy has recently been rediscovered as one of the better minor poets of the late Victorian era. She was very well-known in her time, however. OSCAR WILDE thought her poetry showed genius, and WILLIAM BUTLER YEATS lamented her suicide at age 27. The notorious memoirist Frank Harris thought that her poetry perfectly expressed her sense of the uselessness of life and the smallness of the consolations it offers, but he agreed with his friend, the blind poet Philip Marston, that her poetry did not get one very far in coping with the despair it expressed. Harris and Marston, as well as Levy, liked quoting a line of ROBERT BROWNING's—"Dead! All's done with!"—which Levy made the refrain of a poem.

Harris's opinion of Levy and of Marston was the same: He was interested, as he put it, "by the sheer pathos of their unhappy fate and immitigable suffering." He went on to concede that "it was only later that I came to see that their poetic achievement, too, if not of the highest, was of real value and had extraordinary importance." Few people will remember Marston today, but the description of Levy is apt.

Levy was the first Jewish woman to attend Newnham College, Cambridge University, and indeed only the second Jewish woman ever at Cambridge. She returned home to London to help her parents and also to travel and write. Not believing in the religious doctrines of Judaism, nor any other religion, her tendency toward depression and despair comported well with her skepticism. In many of her poems, she describes the meaninglessness of death, if not of life, since death puts an end to all individuality and all being.

Levy was a radical feminist even before her days at Cambridge, and she frequented feminist circles. She was almost certainly in love with "Vernon Lee" (the writer Violet Paget) and possibly also with the South African author and political activist Olive Schreiner, and some of her most beautiful poems are poems of disappointed love. In addition to being a superb stylist, Levy had strong intellectual gifts, and her poems seek to reconcile their author to the world through both aesthetic and discursive stances. Indeed, she combines them, seeing in the sorrows she experienced a kind of promise for the depth and power of her art.

That art consisted not only of poetry but also of novels, and *Reuben Sachs* (1888) is still read today as an important and effective account of the Jewish experience in Victorian England. But it was in her poetry that Levy spoke most openly about herself and her sense of herself as in one way or another not quite assimilable to the world around her—"A LONDON PLANE-TREE" or "a minor poet," to cite two descriptions she also used as titles for volumes of poetry she published.

Levy's sense of exclusion and despair was exacerbated by the fact that she began going deaf in her 20s. She committed suicide in 1889 by breathing coal smoke, her prodigious talents largely wasted. But the poems she left behind demonstrate how much more she might have done.

See also "LONDON POETS," "TO VERNON LEE."

BIBLIOGRAPHY

Harris, Frank. *Frank Harris, His Life and Adventures: An Autobiography*. London: Richards Press, 1947.

Parejo Vadillo, Ana. *Women Poets and Urban Aestheticism: Passengers of Modernity*. New York: Palgrave Macmillan, 2005.

Scarry, Elaine. *Dreaming by the Book*. (New York: Farrar, Straus, and Giroux, 1999.

"LIFE! I KNOW NOT WHAT THOU ART" ANNA LAETITIA BARBAULD (1825) Francis Palgrave published a short version of this poem as the end of the third book of his *Golden Treasury of English Songs and Lyrics* (1861); it is his only selection from ANNA LAETITIA BARBAULD, now recognized as a major precursor of the romantics and one of the poets who helps make clear the relationship between the philosophical speculation of the 18th century and the intense subjectivity of ROMANTICISM. In the 19th century, "Life! I know not what thou art" was her most widely known poem, and it was part of an anthology of poems for children published in 1904. It is not known when this poem was written—certainly after the publication of Barbauld's first book of poems in 1773—and it has an end-of-life feel to it, which may be why it was published at the end of the 1825 volume of her poetry. However, given how long her life was, we can imagine the poem as having been written substantially earlier.

At any rate, this work broaches a central romantic theme. PERCY BYSSHE SHELLEY's great fragment *The TRIUMPH OF LIFE* ends with the Shelleyan narrator demanding, "What is life?"—the answer to which he seems always on the verge of getting. For Shelley as for Barbauld, as well as JOHN KEATS and WILLIAM WORDSWORTH, life is a never-ending process of asking a question and feeling that the answer is almost within reach. And if that *is* what life is, then the disclosure of its meaning will come as a sense of beginning, and not ending. A deep and powerful strain in romanticism renders one's past, one's discovery of being a subjective being in the world, as a promise of the future, when one will think one's way into the meaning of this discovery. For Barbauld, there was a religious aspect to this, but it might be better to say that romanticism took that religious sense of future disclosure and rendered it entirely a question of poetry—of poetic meditation and what it will discover. Wordsworth's word for this was *intimations*: Recollections of early childhood give us intimations of immortality (to allude to the full title of the INTIMATIONS ODE), not because we have a true memory of another world (Wordsworth made clear that he was using the platonic idea of recollection as a myth), but because plumbing the depths of memory will help us make contact with the truth whose home is thought itself.

What matters is the sense of futurity here. Keats expresses this in a letter in which he says that all poetic inspiration is oriented toward the future, "that face we *will* see." And Barbauld's sense that she will say "Good Morning" to life—that life is still to come in the discovery of its meaning whose search her poem inaugurates—may be taken as her version of the end of Shelley's "ODE TO THE WEST WIND"—"O Wind, if winter come, can spring be far behind?"

BIBLIOGRAPHY

Armstrong, Isobel, and Virginia Blain, eds. *Women's Poetry in the Enlightenment: The Making of a Canon, 1730–1820*. New York: St. Martin's Press, 1999.

Barbauld, Anna Letitia. *Poems, 1792*. New York: Woodstock, 1993.

Keach, William. *Arbitrary Power: Romanticism, Language, Politics*. Princeton, N.J.: Princeton University Press, 2004.

Palgrave, Francis Turner. *Golden Treasury of the Best Songs and Lyrical Poems in the English Language*. (London: Palgrave, 2000.

Wordsworth, Jonathan. *Bright Work Grows: Women Writers of the Romantic Age*. Washington, D.C.: Woodstock Books, 1997.

"LIMBO" SAMUEL TAYLOR COLERIDGE (1817) "Limbo" was one of the nightmarish poems that SAMUEL TAYLOR COLERIDGE wrote in his notebooks during one of the worst periods of his addiction to opium. Like Thomas De Quincey's account of "the pains of opium" in *Confessions of an English Opium Eater* (1822), "Limbo" depicts the horrendous, hallucinatory state of addiction and withdrawal, a state Coleridge struggled with for years. Coleridge described this horror as "positive negation" (l. 38)—not privation but, as he put it in "Ne Plus Ultra," the poem he put next in his notebook, the "Sole Positive of Night! / Antipathist of Light," and the "One permitted opposite of God" (ll. 1–4). Privation is mere purgatory compared to the hell of limbo. Limbo had meant (in Dante, for example) a between place for virtuous pagans, not in hell but not in salvation either; but for Coleridge it meant the absolute oppression of the positive negation, of the combination of the worst and most horrific aspects of the antitheses of positive and negative, a place that is of the terrible experience of "half-being" (l. 14), having enough being to apprehend the sheer nothingness that is its other half.

The poem is fascinating as a document of near madness on Coleridge's part; however, it should be stressed that this is not true madness but the oppressive sense of its possibility. Time and space themselves—the forms of apprehension that Coleridge understood from the German philosopher Immanuel Kant as the most basic intuitions of the human mind, are at the verge of becoming nonexistent. Limbo is a place of allegory where even the allegorical figures are oppressed by the place itself, so that space and time, which should in any allegory be our judges (whether we can appeal to them or not) are here "lank" and "scytheless."

Nevertheless, the poem's *poetic* interest is in its odd, hallucinatory beauty, in the central passage that begins with the wistful, longing description of lovely "Human Time" at line 19. The Old Man looks calm and at peace, but then it turns out that he is blind. What the old man represents or should be taken to represent is deeply ambiguous—not only to us but to Coleridge as well. He looks like Human Time, and perhaps he is an allegory of time as experienced by human beings, or perhaps he is an allegory of what time does to human beings. He is blind, and the beauty of his face that "seemeth to rejoice in" silent light has a beauty that we cannot assess and that Coleridge cannot either. The vision is a "lovely" one, like many of Coleridge's visions, but the question is whether its loveliness is as deceptive as many of Coleridge's visions are.

The vision the poem describes is a revision of the end of "FROST AT MIDNIGHT," where the beautiful icicles wrought by the cold are "Quietly shining to the quiet Moon" (l. 74). But that wholly beautiful vision is rendered inscrutable here, where the man "having moonward turned his face by chance / Gazes the orb with moonlike countenance" (ll. 23–24). The same interchange between two beacons of reflected light occurs here as in "Frost at Midnight," but the eeriness of this poem is partly due to the fact that this interchange constitutes the ambiguous limbo it conveys with such great and irresolvable power.

BIBLIOGRAPHY

Bloom, Harold. *The Visionary Company: A Reading of English Romantic Poetry*. Garden City, N.Y.: Doubleday, 1961.

Brisman, Leslie. *Romantic Origins*. Ithaca, N.Y.: Cornell University Press, 1978.

Frank, Robert H. *Passions within Reason: The Strategic Role of the Emotions*. New York: Norton, 1988.

Freud, Sigmund. "The Uncanny." In *The Standard Edition of the Complete Psychological Works of Sigmund Freud*. Vol. 17. London: Hogarth Press, 219–256.

Janowitz, Anne. *England's Ruins: Poetic Purpose and the National Landscape*. Cambridge, Mass.: Blackwell, 1990.

Lowes, John Livingston. *Road to Xanadu: A Study in the Ways of the Imagination*. New York: Houghton Mifflin, 1930.

Parker, Reeve. *Coleridge's Meditative Art*. Ithaca, N.Y.: Cornell University Press, 1975.

Swann, Karen. "'Christabel': The Wandering Mother and the Enigma of Form." *Studies in Romanticism* 23, no. 4 (Winter 1984): 533–553.

LINES: COMPOSED A FEW MILES ABOVE TINTERN ABBEY ON REVISITING THE BANKS OF THE WYE DURING A TOUR, 13 JULY 1798 See "TINTERN ABBEY."

"LINES: 'WHEN THE LAMP IS SHATTERED'" PERCY BYSSHE SHELLEY (1822) This poem belongs to the extraordinary series of intensely sad, delicately powerful late lyrics that PERCY BYSSHE

SHELLEY wrote under the spell of Jane Williams, the last of his passions. In particular, "Lines: When the Lamp is Shattered'" should be compared with "TO——— (MUSIC, WHEN SOFT VOICES DIE)," whose theme it in some ways reverses. "Music, when soft voices die" and Shelley's last lyric, "LINES WRITTEN IN THE BAY OF LERICI," are both about what lingers on when the beloved has left: thoughts of her, or a sense of her touch, or a sense that she fills the memory. This poem is a little closer to another of Shelley's late lyrics, "When Passion's Trance is Overpast," since both describe the end of an erotic relationship—the end of love.

That end does not come without regrets, even on the part of the person who no longer loves. (These poems are as much about Shelley's fading love for his wife, Mary, as they are about his new passion for Jane Williams.) "The torch of love," as the Second Spirit calls it in "THE TWO SPIRITS: AN ALLEGORY," has shattered, and its light has gone out. As Harold Bloom points out, the second line of the poem does not mean just that the light has died in the dust onto which the lamp, or its oil, has fallen; it also means that the light that animates the dust that humans are has gone out. When the lamp of love shatters, the light of the human soul, which had transfigured the dust of which we are made, now dies. When this happens, all the things that had made the beloved's presence seem to linger on (as Shelley describes them in the other lyrics) disappear. Now that the spirit is mute, we no longer echo the songs of love that we have heard, responded to, perhaps sung ourselves. Or, if a residuum remains, it is only that of the dirge.

The third and fourth stanzas are the poem's most breathtaking. As in "Music, when soft voices die," Shelley personifies love here, but it does not sleep on a bed of rose leaves: He leaves the well-built nest where he had once been at home. His leaving is that of the lover who has fallen out of love, and only the abandoned person is left.

As is usual in Shelley (by what he calls a "strange and natural antithesis" in *A Defence of Poetry* [1819]), love's abandonment of the home is also the opposite: He takes up permanent residence in the broken home. He has left the eagle's nest, or home where he once lived, and entered instead the frailest of all places, the place where love is reduced to love broken and heartbroken. For the irremediable experience of abandonment is one of the modalities of love. Love bewails human frailness and itself comes to experience love among those frailties. Love itself experiences the loss and despair of loving. The sadness with which the poem ends is that of a kind of faithfulness in love itself, when the lover has abandoned the love which allegorizes him, and all that is left is love itself.

A less complex way to put this would be to say that the abandoned person continues to feel and now suffers from the love that she felt before but that the lover no longer feels. But this would be to cast love in too wholly negative a light. The point is that the experience of love still persists, with all its intensity, perhaps even with more intensity, and its frailty is what elicits the reciprocating love of the person abandoned. She personifies or is loyal to the personification of love, as a substitute but also a concentration, of all that she had seen in the lost lover. Love's frailty is its grandness and loyalty, and what it finally evokes is the loyalty of the person lamenting the loss, not so much of love as of the lover.

See also "WHEN YOU ARE OLD."

BIBLIOGRAPHY

Bloom, Harold. *Genius: A Mosaic of One Hundred Exemplary Creative Minds.* New York: Warner, 2002.

———. *Shelley's Mythmaking.* New Haven, Conn.: Yale University Press, 1959.

———. *The Visionary Company: A Reading of English Romantic Poetry.* Garden City, N.Y.: Doubleday, 1961.

Burke, Kenneth. *Grammar of Motives.* Berkeley: University of California Press, 1969.

Chernaik, Judith. *The Lyrics of Shelley.* Cleveland: Press of Case Western Reserve University, 1972.

Hogle, Jerrold E. *Shelley's Process: Radical Transference and the Development of His Major Works.* New York: Oxford University Press, 1988.

Keach, William. *Shelley's Style.* New York: Methuen, 1984.

Leavis, F. R. *Revaluation: Tradition & Development in English Poetry.* New York: Norton, 1963.

Quinney, Laura. *The Poetics of Disappointment: Wordsworth to Ashbery.* Charlottesville: University Press of Virginia, 1999.

Wasserman, Earl. *Subtler Language: Critical Readings of Neoclassic and Romantic Poems.* Baltimore: Johns Hopkins Press, 1968.

"LINES WRITTEN IN THE BAY OF LERICI" **PERCY BYSSHE SHELLEY (1822)** PERCY BYSSHE SHELLEY wrote "Lines Written in the Bay of Lerici" (so entitled by its first editor) within a month, perhaps within a few days, of his death in 1822. It was written on the back of one of the manuscripts for his last, great, unfinished poem *The TRIUMPH OF LIFE.* A relatively short lyric, "Lines" shares some of the concerns and sense of imagery of *The Triumph of Life,* but it is also perhaps the last poem Shelley wrote about Jane Williams, the woman to whom his intense late lyrics are addressed. It was in the Bay of Lerici, north of Rome, that Shelley and Edward Williams (Jane's husband) drowned just days later.

It has been pretty conclusively determined in the last few decades that the full poem (at least the full surviving poem) begins with a kind of six-line induction that had been published as a separate poem; it is addressed to the moon ("Bright wanderer"). Shelley regards the moon as a kind of permanent symbol of transience and change, and he contrasts it with the absent beloved (Jane Williams). The induction is important (as well as beautiful) because it avoids any attempt to specify the time that the speaker of the poem is speaking it.

The poem itself will describe a kind of timeless aftermath to a moment of unalloyed intensity. The beloved leaves the speaker at just the moment when the moon has reached its zenith. We cannot know what time this is because we do not know what phase the moon has reached. But in a way, that is the point: We know where the moon is in the sky, not where the sun would be, and so it is as though we have entered into another time or trajectory of time, parallel to diurnal time but strange and incalculable. It is this other time that the rest of the poem seeks to sustain and even to arrest, to hold the moment of love and longing at its fullest without letting any of it evaporate. But given the very nature of that love and longing, this sustained moment cannot be maintained by force or will; it can only be a kind of exquisitely beautiful extension of its own description—just such a description that the poem undertakes. (For more on Shelley's deep vocation for description, see "MONT BLANC.")

The entry into a paradoxically transient timelessness, what Shelley calls "the time that is our own" (l. 30), begins with the way the moon itself hovers at its zenith rather than immediately beginning its decline. The description shows Shelley's typical combination of brilliance and delicacy: The moon is like a sleeping albatross (as Shelley knew, albatrosses sleep on the wing, hovering in the updrafts of the atmosphere), balanced on wings so light as to be comparable to light itself and therefore comparable to the moon, which will eventually seek its ocean nest when it sets. The interchange of the characters of comparison contribute to the whole atmosphere of hovering.

But the speaker is alone, even as he thinks over everything about his beloved's late presence. She has touched him, and the effect of her touch lingers, as though she is touching him still. He remembers her voice in the silence that it leaves, and her absence becomes the beautiful, time-transcending residue of her presence. The past and future are forgotten (l. 31).

But this experience cannot last, and now that she is gone—she who guarded him from the demon of despair and loneliness—that demon returns. This language might help illuminate some of the temptations to despair sung by the evil spirits in *PROMETHEUS UNBOUND.*

What are the thoughts that the demon brings? Shelley says that he dares not speak them, and we can hazard that they are related to the "thoughts which must remain untold" in *The Triumph of Life* (l. 21)—thoughts that cannot be shared with others and that must therefore have in them a component of absolute loneliness even as they also have a component of responsibility to someone else whom he would betray by telling them. At any rate, Shelley seeks to distract himself from that melancholy loneliness, again through intense description, now of the Bay of Lerici itself. It is as though having descended from his absorption in the vertical space of moon and sky and flight, he now arcs down to an absorption in the horizontal. He is doing the same thing as he has done in trying to preserve the memory of the departed woman by making the landscape stand for that memory, but now it is the pain of her absence with which he fills the landscape, attempting again through the beauty of his description to make that absence into the experience of timelessness itself.

But the modulation into loneliness is too great: He is left with the lingering melancholy of her absence and not the lingering joy of her very late presence. It is then that he turns to the beautiful, concluding image in the poem, as he notes a fisher with his lamp in the darkness. Fish will rise to the light of a lantern in the night (in Japan today the cormorant fishermen float burning paper lanterns on the dark waters to attract the fish). The fisher strikes them with his spear when they rise, and Shelley imagines the intense pleasure the fish take in their approaching nearness to the light. It is a pleasure that can never be consummated, and in that it is like Shelley's (presumably) impossible adoration of Jane Williams. The fish can never reach the lamp, but they can believe they are about to reach it. They can live the experience of timeless imminence *before* rather than *after* the peak of experience. Their happiness is complete, because the fisher kills them before their anticipatory pleasure has any chance of fading.

The last lines of the poem are unfinished, but we can know that life and peace are opposed there, and that the fish achieve peace in their worship of the delusive flame, even if they do not also maintain their lives. This is for Shelley a singular happiness, since they will never lose the peace he has lost. But it is worth seeing that such telling happiness is part of the beautiful landscape he is describing, as though the whole world is beautified by the intensity of his unfulfillable need. Everything is beautiful, and beauty stands for Jane or for the intense memory of her, so that Shelley can redirect his love for her to the landscape itself, but also feel that the beauty of the landscape is a version of his love for her.

BIBLIOGRAPHY

Bloom, Harold. *Genius: A Mosaic of One Hundred Exemplary Creative Minds.* New York: Warner, 2002.

———. *Shelley's Mythmaking.* New Haven, Conn.: Yale University Press, 1959.

———. *The Visionary Company: A Reading of English Romantic Poetry.* Garden City, N.Y.: Doubleday, 1961.

Chernaik, Judith. *The Lyrics of Shelley.* Cleveland: Press of Case Western Reserve University, 1972.

Keach, William. *Shelley's Style.* New York: Methuen, 1984.

Leavis, F. R. *Revaluation: Tradition & Development in English Poetry.* New York: Norton, 1963.

Notopolous, James A. *The Platonism of Shelley: A Study of Platonism and the Poetic Mind.* Durham, N.C.: Duke University Press, 1949.

Quinney, Laura. *The Poetics of Disappointment: Wordsworth to Ashbery.* Charlottesville: University Press of Virginia, 1999.

Wasserman, Earl. *Shelley: A Critical Reading.* Baltimore: Johns Hopkins Press, 1971.

"LOCHINVAR" SIR WALTER SCOTT (1808)

"Lochinvar" is a song extracted from Sir WALTER SCOTT's great narrative poem *MARMION.* It tells a story, not unlike that of the movie *The Graduate,* of a love that triumphs over a marriage ceremony as the dashing knight Lochinvar rescues his beloved from the very altar where she has been forced to pledge her vows to another man. He dances with her at her wedding feast, to the nervousness of all assembled, and then swings her onto his horse, and they ride away, never to be seen again. The poem is powerful and stirring and touches on the center of a romantic fantasy—that of love and escape from the pressures and fetters of real life. It is written in a swinging anapestic rhythm, which gives it the feeling of momentum, and what we would now call escape velocity, which makes it stirring.

In context, the poem is sung by the English wife of Sir Hugh the Heron, one of the Borderers who will be involved in the 1513 Battle of Flodden Field between Scotland and England that *Marmion* recounts. She is not interested in the wild and isolated life of a Borderer and has eagerly agreed to go to the Scottish court of King James IV, ostensibly as a hostage but in fact as a mistress. The song is one in which she, too, imagines the possibilities of escape, of a disappearance into the legendary world of song itself.

"Lochinvar" is certainly behind other, similar fantasies of escape, most notably perhaps JOHN KEATS's "The EVE OF ST. AGNES," where Porphyro and Madeline manage a similar (though less public) elopement. In Keats, their disappearance anticipates his own desire to die unseen and fade away into the forest dim (as he expresses it in "ODE TO A NIGHTINGALE"), and in the link from "Lochinvar" to "The Eve of St. Agnes" to the "Ode to a Nightingale," we can see what kind of escape it is that certain poems seem to offer. If we could lose ourselves in the poem, we could lose our relationship to the life that binds and burdens us.

The song belongs to a world that is not only fictional but becomes purely evocative. It is only in song that such a disappearance seems possible (which is why Keats feels its attraction in the nightingale's anthem). It is, of course, impossible, but that very impossibility is what gives the song its power. The song belongs to a region that is different from that of the real world, the region of the impossible. That is why it is important to stress the fact that "Lochinvar" is a fiction within a fiction, a story told by the fictional Dame Heron within the fictional story of *Marmion.* The first fiction could be real; it could be true in a possible world. But it is in *that* world that another and impossible world beckons. And yet the very fact that we feel it beckoning in the first possible but still fictional world seems to put us into some relationship to it. We meet it within what is fictional already, and so we meet it in a frontier zone (that of *Marmion*) between the evocative but impossible fictive and the real, and we feel halfway to that impossible fiction. The song promises what it can never deliver—except all that it promises is the promise itself and the poignancy and power of that promise. No one managed such beautiful songs better than Scott, and in some ways they are the most basic and most arresting examples of what we most want from poetry, and what we most wish we could get from it.

BIBLIOGRAPHY

Kerr, James. *Fiction against History: Scott as Storyteller.* New York: Cambridge University Press, 1989.

Lauber, John. *Sir Walter Scott.* Boston: Twayne Publishers, 1989.

Lincoln, Andrew. *Walter Scott and Modernity.* Edinburgh: Edinburgh University Press, 2007.

"LOCKSLEY HALL" (1842) and "LOCKSLEY HALL SIXTY YEARS AFTER" ALFRED, LORD TENNYSON (1886) When he was in his late 70s, ALFRED, LORD TENNYSON wrote a bitter sequel to his mainly optimistic "Locksley Hall." Now the speaker of the earlier poem returns as an old man to the fictional house of the title and complains to his grandson of the delusory nature of human progress. Most critics see the later poem as a recantation of the hopes the earlier one expresses, and while there is some justice to this judgment, it neglects the subtlety to be found in both poems. Tennyson's point in returning to "Locksley Hall" is to stress certain aspects already to be found in the earlier poem, while allowing some continuation of the hope the early poem managed to end with.

The later poem is valuable in itself but also for the light it sheds on the early poem, since Tennyson's sequel remains faithful to the story the early poem tells (indeed, lines 13–16 of the later poem were originally written for the earlier one but cut from it). We can judge the age of the speaker of "Locksley Hall" by the poem written 44 years after it was published and 50 years or so after it was begun in 1835 or so. The speaker of "Sixty Years After" is 80, which means that the speaker of "Locksley Hall" is 20, while Tennyson himself was in his early 30s when he finished the earlier poem. His speaker is therefore younger and more naïve than he is, and this difference matters because Tennyson was unusually interested in denying that "Locksley Hall" was autobiographical, even as he conceded that it was inevitably a reflection of his temperament. It probably also reflected his intense disappointment over the fact that the parents of Eva Baring forbade the romance developing between her and Tennyson: The speaker of "Locksley Hall" blames his beloved cousin Amy (note the suggestive mirroring in the vowels of their names) for submitting to her father's threats and her mother's "shrewish tongue" (l. 42).

Tennyson told his son Hallam that the frame for the dramatic monologue was given to him by Sir William Jones's late 18th-century translation of the *Moâllakât,* or "seven ancient Arabic prize poems," pre-Islamic works from the end of the sixth century that hang in Mecca. The first of them, by Amriolkais (as Jones transliterated his name) begins with a soldier stopping by the site where his lost beloved once had her tent, there to meditate upon his past love. His companions try to cheer him by reminding him both of other unhappy experiences he has gone through and of the great pleasures he has taken in his life, and he regains his spiritedness as he responds to them with reminiscences of those times. Tennyson's speaker muses alone, but the structure of the poem is more or less the same, and Tennyson directly adopts one of the couplets, written in the Arabic form called "long verse," into his own long lines: Jones's "It was the hour when the Pleiads appeared in the firmament, like the folds of a silken sash variously decked with gems" (verse 23) becomes Tennyson's beautiful image of seeing "the Pleiads . . . / Glitter like a swarm of fireflies tangled in a silver braid" (ll. 9–10). Like Amriolkais, he ends with a beautiful description of the coming of a cleansing storm.

The "long verse" in "Locksley Hall" is striking, consisting of trochaic hexameters with the last (unstressed) syllable omitted to yield a 15-syllable line, more or less like the very long lines of medieval poetry. The beat thus becomes extremely prominent and gives the poem a propulsive restlessness, partly because the ear hears the lines divide into two parts, the first of which ends on a weak syllable (after the fourth foot), which seems to await renewal in a recapitulation ending on a strong one. (ROBERT BROWNING used the same line, often to dazzlingly different effects—and in triplets, not couplets—in "A TOCCATA OF GALLUPI'S.")

The metrical timing is a kind of allegory of the poem's relation to history. Its speaker tells the story of the love between him and Amy, the catastrophe of her marriage to someone else, and the extreme disappointment this makes him feel. This leads (as in its source) to a retrospective lamentation for the days before these events when his life was full of hope and he "dipt into the future" (l. 119). He makes this the object of his lamentation because those hopes have been blasted. But the memory of the blasted hopes revives in him a sense of their vividness, and Tennyson gives a gorgeous, Shelleyan vision of a time when ships will take to the air and float argosies in the skies. (Tennyson was referring to lighter-than-air craft, and it seems likely that the modern writer Philip Pullman was thinking of these lines when he described the zeppelin and balloon travel that takes place in Lyra's world in *His Dark Materials* [1995–2000]). The vision is framed as lost optimism, but in fact its visionary energy rekindles the optimism it is supposed to memorialize. That future is still *in* the future; so the future is still a time of greatness, hope, and energy, and the speaker of Locksley Hall returns to his comrades, and to his commitment to them and to their common goals, refreshed and revived.

It is important to note that this recovery is one that places human society above individual experience. The poem's speaker complains that "The individual withers and the world is more and more" (l. 142), but in the end he sees that the experience of progress leads to better things, even if the individual can only be part of that experience for a lifetime. The minuteness of individual life in the vastness of time was an obsession of Tennyson's (as it was of many other people who had just learned from the geologist Charles Lyell the immense age of the earth and the loss of species that humans had never known; for more on this, and on Tennyson's response to evolution, see *IN MEMORIAM: A.H.H.*) "Better fifty years in Europe than a cycle of Cathay" (l. 184) means that adult human experience—the 50 years that remains of his three-score-and-ten—is always getting better, and that this is a good, not an evil. (The unpleasant disparagement of Asian culture here is in line with the German socialist Karl Marx's famous Eurocentric critique of what he called the "Asiatic mode of production.")

Well, 50 years in Europe may be good, but the later poem suggests that *60* years may be too many. We discover in the later poem how much its speaker got wrong in his youth. Amy does not raise her daughter, as he had imagined she would; both she and her son die in childbirth. Now, 60 years later, her husband (his rival) has also died. He repents his hatred for him: The widower has turned out to be a good man, and the speaker, who had loathed him, has now "come to love him" (l. 280). The irony of history is that Locksley Hall is now going to pass to the speaker's grandson (the poem's addressee), since his cousin Amy and her husband had no children.

The poem's speaker also gets wrong, or thinks he does, the vision of progress that he had celebrated. Now he sees progress as bringing war, immorality, poverty, disease, and death in the wake of industrialism and urbanization. He sees no reason to think that evolution, again an obsession of Tennyson's and here named explicitly, is progressive in a good sense. It simply intensifies what Charles Darwin called "the struggle for survival." And indeed, his grandson is late to the funeral obsequies at Locksley Hall because of a train wreck, the result of a vicious boy's sabotage (l. 215).

And yet the speaker of the later poem should also be credited for recognizing that age perennially complains of the way the world is going. The world leaves everyone bitter and behind, and yet in doing so it reconciles everyone to leaving it, and therefore he can end the poem with a kind of recapitulation of the optimism that he finds in the early poem. Now that optimism is for an afterlife, one that transcends the relentless march of geological and evolutionary time. No one knows what will become of the earth, but it is no longer on earth that the speaker sees his own future—or that of any individual—occurring. But life on earth does make it possible for him to forgive, forget, and love those he hated or spurned or could not foresee as a youth. If the individual withers and the world advances more and more, the experience of this withering allows each of us an eventual exit from the demands and oppressions of progress, through the acceptance of each other and of hopes of another world to come. That, at any rate, is how Tennyson manages to make the second poem recapitulate the first and transmute bitterness to hope.

BIBLIOGRAPHY

Armstrong, Isobel. *Victorian Poetry: Poetry, Poetics and Politics.* New York: Routledge, 1993.

Bloom, Harold. *Poetry and Repression: Revisionism from Blake to Stevens.* New Haven, Conn.: Yale University Press, 1976.

Buckley, Jerome Hamilton. *Tennyson: The Growth of a Poet.* Boston: Houghton Mifflin, 1965.

Jones, Sir William. Translation of Amriolkais. In *Arabian Poetry for Indian Readers,* edited by W. A. Clouston. 1881. Reprint, London: Darf, 1986.

Kilham, John. *Critical Essays on the Poetry of Tennyson.* New York: Barnes and Noble, 1960.

Kincaid, James R. *Tennyson's Major Poems: The Comic and Ironic Patterns.* New Haven, Conn.: Yale University Press, 1975.

Ricks, Christopher B. *Tennyson.* New York: Macmillan, 1972.

Rowlinson, Matthew. *Tennyson's Fixations: Psychoanalysis and the Topics of the Early Poetry.* Charlottesville: University Press of Virginia, 1994.

Tucker, Herbert. *Tennyson and the Doom of Romanticism.* Cambridge, Mass.: Harvard University Press, 1988.

"LONDON" JOANNA BAILLIE (1790) One useful aspect of JOANNA BAILLIE's poetry (minor as it is in comparison with her drama) is the way it provides a helpful reference point for considering the transition from the late 18th-century poetry of sensibility to the literature of ROMANTICISM. Baillie's most influential literary work was in verse drama, where she had great success and influence, but her poetry too is original and accomplished. "London" should be compared with the 18th-century loco-descriptive (derived from the landscape) poetry whose tradition it extends, from Sir John Denham's "Cooper's Hill" (1642) to John Dyer's "Grongar Hill" (1726) to Thomas Gray's magnificent and highly influential proto-romantic "Ode on a Distant Prospect of Eton College" (1747).

The poem is written mainly in couplets, introduced by a set of 16 irregularly rhymed lines. These irregular rhymes do much to mute the over-conspicuous feel of the couplets that follow, and Baillie's couplets anticipate the couplet's romantic reinvention, as undertaken by PERCY BYSSHE SHELLEY, JOHN KEATS, and LEIGH HUNT. Here Baillie is already experimenting with expanding the possibilities of the heroic couplet as practiced from John Dryden to the end of the 18th century, with its pointed and end-stopped lines, and already showing how the couplet can be brought into conformity with John Milton's injunction that the musical quality of poetry comes from the way the sense is "variously drawn out" from line to line.

This is an appropriate form for the piece of description that comprises the poem, the assimilation of the great city of London, as viewed from Hampstead Heath (where Baillie lived), to the natural landscape. Such description anticipates WILLIAM WORDSWORTH's great sonnets on the sight of London (for instance, "Composed on an Evening of Extraordinary Beauty"), and eventually the kinds of cityscapes that William Turner and Claude Monet would paint. Where description of nature in heroic couplets tended to use their artful balance as a way of showing nature's own, Baillie's enjambed lines do not balance the city against the natural world around it but merge the city with that world. She does this through her imagery as well, not only using metaphors and similes from nature to describe the city but using a language that would be literally but uninterestingly true if she had not already been able to make it read metaphorically. Thus, she describes the tall buildings of London, like Saint Paul's Cathedral, as rising "With more than natural height" (l. 19), as though the building were a part of nature and not *in fact* a more than natural edifice. But we accept this impressive description because we have already accepted that London is a part of nature—but a very impressive part.

In her much-debated "Introductory Discourse" to the publication of her first *Plays on the Passions,* Baillie had written of the central importance of human interest to any description of nature. Human apprehension is at the center of all poetic passion. "London" might be taken as making the same statement in poetry. She looks at the city, and thinks (in the last stanza) of the traveler seeing the city at night and hearing "the flood of human life in motion," that flood itself being "the voice of a tempestuous ocean" (ll. 45–46). All of this makes the traveler think of how the city displays humans in relation to the natural universe, and therefore how humans themselves, in their millions and their generations, stand for the awe-inspiring natural facts of time and eternity. In this mode, as in many others, Baillie is an important precursor to Wordsworth.

BIBLIOGRAPHY

Baillie, Joanna. *Dramatic and Poetical works of Joanna Baillie* London: Longman, Brown, Green, and Longmans, 1851.

Forbes, A. "'Sympathetic Curiosity' in Joanna Baillie's Theater of the Passions," *European Romantic Review* 14, no. 1 (January 2003): 31–48.

McMillan, Dorothy, ed., The Association for Scottish Literary Studies, ASLS Annual Volume 29: 1999: *The Scotswoman at Home and Abroad,* Association for Scottish Literary Studies, Glasgow, April 2000 (contains excerpts from Baillie's unpublished "Memoir written to please my nephew, William Baillie," and "Recollections written for Miss Berry," both in English archives.)

Wordsworth, Jonathan. *Ancestral Voices: Fifty Books from the Romantic Period.* New York: Woodstock, 1996.

"LONDON" WILLIAM BLAKE (1794) "London" is one of the grimmest of WILLIAM BLAKE's songs of experience (see *SONGS OF INNOCENCE AND OF EXPERIENCE.* Like "The TYGER" and the "experienced" version of "Holy Thursday," this is one of the comparatively few songs that seem to be written in Blake's own voice. The tone is one of reproach so severe that it defeats even sardonic irony. But it must be kept in mind that such reproach is partial—paradoxically, because it is so total as to affect the speaker himself and to jaundice his own view. Although he can see how terrible the world is, Blake is not exempt from the famous "mind-forg'd manacles" (l. 8) he sees binding everyone everywhere.

What are those manacles? They are, first of all, a metaphor for oppression that people could cast off if they wished to. The manacles do not have material reality, although they have material consequences. But because people's minds, as well as their bodies, are enslaved, they are unlikely to cast the off the manacles. Their slavery and oppression goes deeper than material life can reach, although it is a consequence of the materialism and greed of the enslaving interests—the rich and the government. And everyone is enslaved: The speaker sees "marks of weakness, marks of woe" in "every face" he meets (ll. 3–4). The poem's repetitive fury—*chartered, mark, every, cry*—seems to leave no out at all.

Indeed, the poem does not make room for the happiness of innocence that the Songs of Innocence have treated so touchingly. The infants in "London" cry with fear, and the chimney sweepers' cry is one of pain, not simply (as in the "innocence" version of "The CHIMNEY-SWEEPER") meant as the announcement of their availability. The speaker of "London" may be correct in what he hears in these cries, but that is not the only thing to hear in them. Blake himself declares that poetic vision means seeing beyond the material world, the world of the senses, and not becoming enslaved to the oppression that it shows one everywhere. In his book *The Marriage of Heaven and Hell,* he has the sublime Satanic figure who represents him ask: "How do you know but ev'ry Bird that cuts the airy way, / Is an immense world of delight, clos'd by your senses five?" (plate 6). The speaker of "London," then, while accurate, must also be regarded as partial, as himself unable to break his own mind-forged manacles.

There is reason for his despair, however. The London he describes is real, and the oppression and misery that it contains ubiquitous. The statesman Edmund Burke, who famously defended what he called "the chartered rights of Englishmen," was violently opposed to the French Revolution (for which Blake had great hopes, as his 1791 prophetic poem *The French Revolution* attests). Against perfect liberty Burke set the materialistic rights of property, and it was these rights, enshrined in the charters—both the laws and the documents of ownership—that Blake saw as oppressive.

The defense of these charters required the courage and blood of soldiers (l. 11) who might otherwise find no way to survive. The churches of London, parts of the established Church of England, supported the government's policies and did so at the expense of the poor; here Blake refers in shorthand to his Chimney-Sweeper poems when he writes of how the sweeps' cries appalled the churches that were blackening the children around them (who remove the black soot from the chimneys) with their indifference to the misery of the children and the poor ("London," ll. 9–10). The children—perhaps like the nurse in the "experienced" version of "The NURSE'S SONG," or perhaps like her charges as she sees them—become harlots even in their youth (l. 14), not only unsympathetic to their own illegitimate children who interfere with the only way they can survive, but to all the infants of the city.

Their "curse" is an expression of bitterness, but also a physical state—both sexuality (menstruation, as Harold Bloom argues) and the woes that attend it within the vast hypocrisy of London as well as venereal disease: the plague with which they blight marriage. The "marriage hearse" of the poem's last line interprets what should be a joyful occasion as a deadly one: The groom will transmit to his wife the venereal disease he has become infected with through his consorting with prostitutes, even as he abandons the prostitutes to their own fate. The newlywed couple are going to their graves or are going to procreate children who will repeat the dreadful experience of life in London. The poem's vision of London is bitter and hopeless.

But what are we to make of the speaker? In many ways he is an aspect of Blake, in the mode of the biblical prophets Isaiah and Ezekiel whom he so much admired and who blasted the Israelites from the wilderness or the dungheap. Blake makes the connection explicit in *The Marriage of Heaven and Hell* when he describes a fancy of dining with Isaiah and Ezekiel: "I then asked Ezekiel why he eat dung, & lay so long on his right & left side? he answer'd, 'the desire of raising other men into a perception of the infinite; this the North American tribes practise, & is he honest who resists his genius or conscience. only for the sake of present ease or gratification?'" The bitterness of tone in "London" is therefore not the last word. Its purpose is to demonstrate the baseness to which humanity has fallen, not in order to promote despair but to provoke change. Thus, Isaiah, the other prophetic denunciator of his people, whom Blake imagines dining with him and Ezekiel, asserts the power and truth of his chastising vision when Blake asks him how he dared to assert he spoke on behalf of God: "I saw no God, nor heard any, in a finite organical perception; but my senses discover'd the infinite in every thing, and as I was then perswaded, & remain confirm'd, that the voice of honest indignation is the voice of God, I cared not for consequences but wrote."

The important thing to see here is that an assertion of the stark and oppressive limitations of the material world is not the last but the first step toward speaking with the voice of God about the infinite in everything. Those who would charter the city and the river are those who impose weakness and woe everywhere, and those who resist the determinate limitations of the material and financial world are those who can transcend human weakness for the transcendence offered to visionary power, hope, and love. Far from turning their backs on the world, Blake thinks such prophets, among whom he includes himself, will change it.

BIBLIOGRAPHY

Bloom, Harold. *Blake's Apocalypse: A Study in Poetic Argument.* Ithaca, N.Y.: Cornell University Press, 1970.

———. *Poetry and Repression: Revisionism from Blake to Stevens.* New Haven, Conn.: Yale University Press, 1976.

Damrosch, Leopold. *Symbol and Truth in Blake's Myth.* Princeton, N.J.: Princeton University Press, 1980.

Erdmann, David V. *Blake, Prophet against Empire: A Poet's Interpretation of the History of His Own Times.* Princeton, N.J.: Princeton University Press, 1977.

Fry, Northrop. *Fearful Symmetry: A Study of William Blake.* Princeton, N.J.: Princeton University Press, 1974.

Gilchrist, Alexander. *Life of William Blake, with Selections from His Poems and Other Writings.* Totowa, N.J.: Rowman and Littlefield, 1973.

Hollander, John. "Blake and the Metrical Contract." In *From Sensibility to Romanticism,* edited by Frederick Hilles and

Harold Bloom. New York: Oxford, 1965. Reprinted in John Hollander, *Vision and Resonance: Two Sense of Poetic Form,* 293–310. New Haven, Conn.: Yale University Press, 1985.
Raine, Kathleen. *Blake and Antiquity.* Princeton, N.J.: Princeton University Press, 1977.
Thompson, E. P. *Witness against the Beast: William Blake and The Moral Law.* New York: Cambridge University Press, 1993.

"LONDON PLANE-TREE, A" AMY LEVY (1889) AMY LEVY loved London and loved writing poems describing the city and the details of her life there. "A London Plane-Tree," which gives the last book of her poems its title, is about how much she loves London. She loves it for its plane trees, and she loves it because she is a kind of plane tree herself, thriving where other trees fail to thrive, and preferring the town to the country. (London plane trees are notable for their bark, which absorbs pollution and sheds periodically.)

The title of the book *A London Plane-Tree* picks up on the title of her 1883 book, *A Minor Poet,* which is also tactfully self-referential. Why should Levy regard herself as like the tree, aside from her love for London? As a Jew among Christians, a female and feminist among largely male poets, a lesbian among heterosexuals, and a disbeliever among believers, she felt an enormous difference between herself and her compatriots.

The poem itself is deceptively simple. It consists almost entirely in description of the plane tree, but it is important to see that its describer, Levy herself looking at it from her garret window, is as much rooted to the spot as the tree she looks at. She sees it in all weathers and all seasons, budding and blowing (or blooming) as well as shedding its bark. The weathers and times that she sees the plane tree are less cyclical than urban. The important and twice repeated phrase *city breezes* (ll. 10, 16) are in contrast to phrases like *spring* or *autumn breezes.* The city breezes are like seasonal ones, but they are a function of place, not of time. This transformation is the important one for the poem, and it captures the urban experience that Levy wishes to express.

The last stanza contrasts what "others" do with what the plane tree does. But it is not at first clear what *others* contrasts with: the plane tree or Levy herself. The answer is, of course, both. Other trees, and other poets, may scorn the town, but neither the plane tree nor Levy does. The plane tree has "listened to the voice / On city breezes borne" (ll. 15–16). That last phrase is the most mysterious of the poem. What is this voice of the city? Where does it come from; what does it say?

In some sense, it represents the voice of the poet herself, singing to the plane tree; it also represents the voice of the city as a kind of living entity, an entity whose life the plane tree both perceives and represents, as does Levy herself. This combination of perception and representation means, then, that the voice is the voice of the muse, and the muse is the city that inspires Levy. *City breezes* is almost an oxymoron, but here it means that poetry itself is an artificial and urban activity, not a natural and rural one, even if it sometimes presents itself that way. It is in the city that poetry can flourish, and this is what a poem like this insists. Poetry may describe the country beautiful, but it is an artificial, social, urban activity, and therefore its very conditions deserve some poetic account as well. This is what Levy frequently tries to give, and she has never done so with a lighter touch than in this poem.

BIBLIOGRAPHY

Parejo Vadillo, Ana. *Women Poets and Urban Aestheticism: Passengers of Modernity.* New York: Palgrave Macmillan, 2005.
Scarry, Elaine. *Dreaming by the Book.* New York: Farrar, Straus, and Giroux, 1999.

"LONDON POETS" AMY LEVY (1889) AMY LEVY combined extraordinary poetic gifts with an equal intellectual subtlety. "London Poets," whose motto (see MOTTOES) is "(*In Memoriam*)," is one of the sonnets where this combination can be seen most clearly. It depicts Levy's melancholy view of life with impressive restraint.

Levy was preeminently a London poet, as is made clear by the title poem of *A London Plane-Tree,* her last book, in which "London Poets" and "A LONDON PLANE-TREE" appear. Like John Milton's elegist to the dead Lycidas, she walks through London mourning the poets who are dead and anticipating that she, too, will one day receive an elegist's tribute. The London poets walked the same streets that she is walking, through all the seasons of the year, their thoughts haunted by despair. Although she need not say so, this means that she is projecting her own thoughts onto them, universalizing them. This universalization is not, however, mere projection: It is a definition of the poetic vocation, which is to turn despair into art (see "TO VERNON LEE"). Therefore, the dead poets (l. 8), just because they were poets, must have experienced the despair that she, too, is feeling. Levy seeks in poetry some communion with others who feel and understand what she does. Such communion, for a poet, comes in both reading and writing, expressing herself and understanding the expression of others.

What is crucial for Levy, though, is that the fact that these poets are dead places a limit on their communion, since as she says repeatedly in her poetry, the dead are truly gone, without even enough existence remaining to them for us to say they once existed (this is an interated theme in *A London Plane-Tree*). This is the recognition that comes at the turn from the octet (in this Petrarchan sonnet) to the sestet.

But the fact that they are dead also allows for some possibility of comfort or consolation—the comfort that Levy would soon seek in suicide. The sorrows of the dead poets seemed real to them, as hers does to her. But now that sorrow is entirely gone, the shadow of a dream; the past is gone forever into nothingness. And this is her consolation for the future: that some day she will be dead and her sorrows, too, will become "half-forgotten breath" (l. 12).

This would be enough to say, but the real subtlety in the poem comes from the way Levy actually says this. Having imagined communion with poets of the past, she now imagines a poet of the future, walking the same streets. It is this poet who will "soothe his woe supreme" (l. 13) with a thought of poets of the past, namely, poets like her. She does not say *she* is soothing her woes by thinking of the past poets. Rather, she soothes them by thinking of the future poet who will recognize her death as the promise of a still more future consolation, when the future poet is dead. She tells us how she feels, but almost entirely vicariously, describing the poets and readers of both past and future. As her future readers, then, we can also count on eventual consolation of the sort she promises herself here: the peace of nonexistence, which poetry can foreshadow.

BIBLIOGRAPHY

Parejo Vadillo, Ana. *Women Poets and Urban Aestheticism: Passengers of Modernity*. New York: Palgrave Macmillan, 2005.

Scarry, Elaine. *Dreaming by the Book*. New York: Farrar, Straus, and Giroux, 1999.

"LONDON SNOW" ROBERT BRIDGES (1880)

ROBERT BRIDGES wrote "London Snow" while he was working out some of his prosodical theories; in both theory and practice, he was heavily influenced by his close friend and correspondent GERARD MANLEY HOPKINS. "London Snow" contains a toned-down version of some of Hopkins's SPRUNG RHYTHM (which is the prosody of Hopkins's greatest poetry, all of it sent to Bridges, who later edited and published it). Its form is mainly syllabic (as Bridges would call it), rather than iambic, although there is not any regularity in the number of syllables per line in the poem.

Bridges was working out a system of prosody that was based on the parameters of both number of stresses in a line and the number of syllables in the line, with the latter subordinated to the former. He did not think that stresses should come at regular intervals. For Bridges, it was the irregularity of stress that made it possible for poetic lines to escape monotony and reinforce whatever it was that they were saying. He and Hopkins had discussed John Milton's *Paradise Lost* (1667) at length; indeed, in the late 1880s, Bridges would publish the first sketch of his theory of Milton's prosody. In his 1893 book on the subject, Bridges memorably describes *Paradise Lost* as "an attempt to keep blank verse decasyllabic by means of fictions." Those fictions had mainly to do with managing words and pauses so they looked like elisions. But for Bridges and Hopkins, what determined the form of the line were the stressed syllables, and there was considerable looseness in the unstressed syllables that framed them. (It should be noted that Bridges regarded Milton as perhaps the greatest of English metrists; he thought that Milton needed the fictions to allow himself to believe he was not innovating as much as he was.)

In a journal letter to his friend and teacher D. W. Dixon, Hopkins analyzed "London Snow" as an example of sprung rhythm (December 22, 1880; the section on Bridges is from January 14, 1881). Hopkins wrote that, unlike him, Bridges treated sprung rhythm "in theory and practice as something informal and variable without any limit but ear and taste." For Hopkins, this allowed too much slackness to the play of unstressed syllables, and he thought Bridges did not pay sufficient attention to them as primarily embodying the *relation* of stresses to each other, or to their distance from each other. The difference in their styles therefore was one in which Bridges's lines tended to become long and leisurely, where Hopkins's tended to be extremely pressured and compact, the stresses barely held apart by the unstressed syllables. This is not to say that Hopkins did not admire "London Snow." He wrote to Bridges on October 26, 1880, that it was "a most beautiful and charming piece. It is charmingly fresh, I do not quite know what is like it." But he went on, "The rhythm, as I told you, is not quite perfect," and later he suggested ways of making the stresses more prominent by getting rid of unstressed syllables—which shows how his metrical tendencies tended to the converse of Bridges's.

In the book on *Paradise Lost,* Bridges wrote that he had "avoided as far as possible entering even upon the borderland between prosody and poetry." But in his poetry he did enter that borderland, using his rhythms to convey the impression the poem sought to give its readers—in this case, the impression of snow falling and drifting all over London. Indeed, it would be right to see "London Snow" as an impressionist poem, a kind of verse experiment not unlike the contemporaneous paintings of James Whistler and Claude Monet.

This is best seen, first, by considering the end words of the lines, all of which rhyme. The plurality of those words are gerundives (verbal adjectives), or words ending in *–ing.* The *ing* is not what rhymes: rather, it is the stressed syllable that precedes it which rhymes, as in *flying* and *lying* (ll. 1, 3). But the *–ing* words continue through line 21, sifting downward through the poem like snowflakes. (It is possible that Bridges was influenced here by ROBERT SOUTHEY's grand prosodical experiment in "The CATARACT OF LODORE [1820].") Not by accident is the last of these gerundives the word *snowballing* (l. 21); it rhymes "falling" and "calling" (ll. 17, 19), as though now the snow has piled up sufficiently to be thought of as a mass.

These multisyllabic words, ending on an unstressed syllable, brings to notice the play of other such words, all the words ending *–er,* such as *wonder* and *asunder* (ll. 23, 27), which seem to rhyme, but do not, with *number, encumber,* and *slumber* (ll. 32, 34, 36). We might say that their assonance is to rhyme what an unstressed syllable is to a stressed one: a kind of attenuation of the bright or vivid form. Thus, too, the *–en* endings in *even* and *seven* (ll. 8, 10) get picked up again at the end of the poem by *unspoken* and *broken* (ll. 35, 37), the original words now so far back in the poem as to offer only the faintest echo at the end.

We have only examined last syllables here, but it is the internal unstressed syllables that do most of the poem's muting, muffling, and blurring, softening work. The number of stresses per line varies, as in Hopkins, but the variation for Bridges is a function of the cushioning effect of the unstressed syllables. The stresses do not stand out, as they do in Hopkins; their outlines are softened by the lulling sift of unstressed syllables around them.

"London Snow" is an answer to Hopkins's more relentless ideas about sprung rhythm. It is a mild polemic against what Bridges thought of as Hopkins's extremism (even as he was lost in admiration for his friend's genius), and therefore, like so much of 19th-century poetry, it should be regarded as in part an *ars poetica,* a commentary on poetry itself. The descriptions of the snow are also descriptions of poetic effect (as impressionist paintings are depictions not only of their objects but of the way their very colors depict objects). It is both the snow and the uncounted, unregularized unstressed syllables that are "Silently sifting and veiling" what they cover, "Hiding difference, making unevenness even" (ll. 7–8). In a beautiful (and gently Shelleyan) line, Bridges describes how the snow "lay in the depth of its uncompacted lightness" (l. 11), and it is just that quality of being *uncompacted* that he contends for in this poem, against Hopkins's intense compaction.

Hopkins was by far the greater poet, but it is interesting to see what effects a poet whose supersubtle ear was formed by the more standard canon of English poetry could draw from Hopkins's sprung rhythm, and in general what he could make make of it. Bridges made much of it, and a poem like "London Snow" could be said to prepare the rest of the audience for English poetry for some of the prosodical innovations that Hopkins would put to such different use.

BIBLIOGRAPHY

Bridges, Robert. *Milton's Prosody*. Oxford: Clarendon Press, 1893.

Gross, Harvey. *Sound and Form in Modern Poetry*. Ann Arbor: University of Michigan Press, 1996.

Guerard, Albert. *Robert Bridges: A Study of Traditionalism in Poetry*. Cambridge, Mass.: Harvard University Press, 1942.

Hopkins, Gerard Manley. *Gerard Manley Hopkins: Selected Letters*. Edited by Catherine Phillips. New York: Oxford University Press, 1990.

Ritz, Jean-George. *Robert Bridges and Gerard Hopkins: A Literary Friendship*. London: Oxford University Press, 1960.

"LOTOS-EATERS, THE" ALFRED, LORD TENNYSON (1832) "The Lotos-Eaters" represents one of ALFRED LORD TENNYSON's most extended experiments in, and demonstrations of, the sensual nature of poetry. Tennyson—heavily influenced by JOHN KEATS—was interested in testing the limits of poetic expression, and thus, more than most poets, he wrote poems about the nature not so much of poetry but of poems themselves. How richly can a poem elaborate its own particular and specific means of producing pleasure? The kind of poetry at which Keats and Tennyson excelled was loved because of its gorgeous and sensual descriptive powers, not because of the exciting story it had to tell, nor even because of the insight into the struggles of the human soul that it afforded. Both Tennyson and Keats did afford such insight, but both were interested in the means of dwelling on human experience, of lingering, with a sustained intensity, on the mind's experience of the world.

"The Lotos-Eaters" is based on a 15-line episode in Homer's *The Odyssey*, in which Odysseus and his men travel through the land of the lotos-eaters (lotus eaters) as they attempt to return home from the Trojan War. As Odysseus tells the story to his host, King Alcinous:

> I was driven . . . by foul winds for a space of nine days upon the sea, but on the tenth day we reached the land of the Lotus-eater, who live on a food that comes from a kind of flower. Here we landed to take in fresh water, and our crews got their mid-day meal on the shore near the ships. When they had eaten and drunk I sent two of my company to see what manner of men the people of the place might be, and they had a third man under them. They started at once, and went about among the Lotus-eaters, who did them no hurt, but gave them to eat of the lotus, which was so delicious that those who ate of it left off caring about home, and did not even want to go back and say what had happened to them, but were for staying and munching lotus with the Lotus-eaters without thinking further of their return; nevertheless, though they wept bitterly I forced them back to the ships and made them fast under the benches. Then I told the rest to go on board at once, lest any of them should taste of the lotus and leave off wanting to get home, so they took their places and smote the grey sea with their oars. (*The Odyssey*, translated by Samuel Butler)

Homer treats the land of the lotus-eaters as a place his audience would have heard about, and he does not dwell on its description. But for Tennyson, the very languorousness of the idea of the endless pleasurable drowsiness conferred by the lotus's narcotic suggested an endlessly pleasurable, seemingly endless languorous poem. (A more recent source also would have been Keats's "TO AUTUMN," where the figure of Autumn is represented as "drowsed with the fume of poppies . . . hour by hour.")

The opening of Tennyson's poem has been justly praised:

> "Courage!" he said, and pointed toward the land,
> "This mounting wave will roll us shoreward
> soon."
> In the afternoon they came unto a land
> In which it seemed always afternoon.
> All around the coast the languid air did swoon,
> Breathing like one that hath a weary dream.
> Full-faced above the valley stood the moon;

And like a downward smoke, the slender
stream
Along the cliff to fall and pause and fall did seem.

Note that the poem diverges from Homer in being told in the third person, where Homer has Odysseus tell the story in the first person. We will not get Odysseus's efficient rejection of the pleasures of the lotus, but Tennyson's interest is in its languid and luxurious sensual qualities. And then we will get the song of the Lotos-Eaters themselves.

The poem begins with a moment of intense emotion—Odysseus's cry to courage in the midst of danger and potential shipwreck. We plunge, as Horace said the epic must do, in medias res, right into the middle of the action. But the action peters out into the endless afternoon of the land of the Lotos-Eaters. Tennyson manages the transition by two interesting formal features. The first is the *rime riche* of the first and third lines. *Rime riche* means rhyming a word on itself or its own homonym, and it is generally avoided in English poetry as leading to a sense of stasis. Rhyme tends to propel poems onward: For every dove there is some love, for all fears there are tears, each onsetting rhyme anticipating a varying resolution. But with *rime riche* we do not move onward; we linger or idle. Tennyson called this effect of repetition "lazier" than a differing rhyme would be, and the same sense of enervated torpor can be felt in the repetition and extension of the idea of the afternoon. They come to the land of the Lotos-Eaters at a particular time, the afternoon, but that time comes to feel like an eternity since it is a land where it seems to be always afternoon. This repetition mimics the repetition of the word *lotus* in Homer: "They started at once, and went about among the *Lotus*-eaters, who did them no hurt, but gave them to eat of the *lotus,* which was so delicious that those who ate of it left off caring about home, and did not even want to go back and say what had happened to them, but were for staying and munching *lotus* with the *Lotus*-eaters without thinking further of their return" (the Greek is much more compressed, so the repetition is more obvious).

The first five stanzas of "The Lotos-Eaters" are written in Spenserian stanzas, the form invented in the late 16th century by Edmund Spenser for *The Faerie Queene* and much imitated in the 19th century, especially by PERCY BYSSHE SHELLEY (in *The Revolt of Islam* and *ADONAIS*), Keats, and WILLIAM WORDSWORTH. The rhyme scheme of the stanza itself tends to be languorous: *ababbcbccc.* Note what this means: Of the nine lines in the stanza, there are four *b* rhymes and three *c* rhymes, and the couplet that seems to end the first half of the stanza also begins the second half and tends to make the stanza slow down and linger around its own sounds. The last line of the Spenserian stanza is always an Alexandrine—that is to say, a 12- and not a 10-syllable line, so that it has one extra poetic foot—which further slows the line down. At the end of the first stanza, one can sense the extra syllable, perhaps, in the repetitions of "to fall and pause and fall," a line which would be much more rapid without the pause that it both describes and enacts.

The second and longer part of the poem is an irregular choric song (like a Greek chorus), sung by Odysseus's sailors. Its irregularity is appropriate to the slackness induced by the lotos, and it enables Tennyson to use all the resources of repetition and intense sensuality to follow the flow of sound and sense wherever it takes him. The intense beauty of the land of the Lotos-Eaters is clearly an allegory for the intense beauty of poetry itself. The poem is about poetry—about what it can do, the meaning of what it can do, and its relevance. What Odysseus might say against poetry is that it makes one content with a kind of sensual quietism, a luxurious indulgence in melancholy and dream. In fact, Spenser had offered a similar warning, which Tennyson wants us to remember, in the first book of *The Faerie Queene,* where the allegorical figure of Despayre offers much the same feeling of "port after stormie seas, death after life" to the questing knight whom he tempts. What Tennyson notices is that Despayre's temptation is the most beautiful passage in the first book, and therefore that poetry seems strangely wedded to the pleasures of despair.

It is not necessary to derive a moral from "The Lotos-Eaters," which seems more about the fact that poetry attempts to offer some consolation for the difficulties and essential painfulness of human life. That pleasure may be just reading "The Lotos-Eaters," or writing it, without more than the poem itself as a goal. At any rate, this poem anticipates the idea of art as the perfection of pleasure that would be the goal of OSCAR WILDE ("all art is perfectly useless," as he says in the preface to his novel *The Picture of Dorian Gray*). It is also a major source—as is, of course, Tennyson's "ULYSSES"—for James Joyce's great novel *Ulysses* (1922), which has an entire chapter based on the Lotos-Eaters passage in *The Odyssey,* but a chapter heavily indebted to Tennyson. In "The Lotos-Eaters," we have Tennyson attempting to write a kind of pure poetry.

BIBLIOGRAPHY

Armstrong, Isobel. *Victorian Poetry: Poetry, Poetics and Politics.* New York: Routledge, 1993.

Bloom, Harold. *Poetry and Repression: Revisionism from Blake to Stevens.* New Haven, Conn.: Yale University Press, 1976.

Buckley, Jerome Hamilton. *Tennyson: The Growth of a Poet.* Boston: Houghton Mifflin, 1965.

Kilham, John. *Critical Essays on the Poetry of Tennyson.* New York: Barnes and Noble, 1960.

Kincaid, James R. *Tennyson's Major Poems: The Comic and Ironic Patterns.* New Haven, Conn.: Yale University Press, 1975.

Ricks, Christopher B. *Tennyson.* New York: Macmillan, 1972.

Rowlinson, Matthew. *Tennyson's Fixations: Psychoanalysis and the Topics of the Early Poetry.* Charlottesville: University Press of Virginia, 1994.

Tucker, Herbert. *Tennyson and the Doom of Romanticism.* Cambridge, Mass.: Harvard University Press, 1988.

Woodham Smith, Cecil. *The Reason Why.* New York: McGraw-Hill, 1954.

"LOVELIEST OF TREES" A. E. HOUSMAN (1895) A. E. HOUSMAN's great theme is the ephemerality of life. He called Horace's ode on the passing of time the most beautiful poem of ancient literature (see "DIFFUGERE NIVES"), and the most beautiful poems in *A Shropshire Lad* share that theme. This is particularly evident in "Loveliest of trees," the second poem of the volume. Written in May or June 1895, it describes the cherries that are all too briefly in bloom. (Easter in 1895 occurred on April 14, and at the end of March Housman had just turned 36, just past the midway point of the "threescore years and ten" [l. 5] allotted to human life).

To stress how much older Housman is than the speaker is not mere pedantry: The discrepancy highlights the fact that the speaker both describes the cherries in bloom and that he is not, in fact, seeing them now but plans to do so. The cherry "now" is lovely and hung with blooms, but the speaker resolves that he "will go" to see what he is presumably not actually seeing but only intending to see. His description can anticipate what he will see because he has seen them before; but that means that the time he came to really *see* them before—the time when Housman himself was 20, say—is in the past and over, and the cherry blossoms stand (as in Japanese prints) for their own ephemerality. Housman is always haunted, and always echoing, a line from a song of Shakespeare's: "Youth's a stuff will not endure."

The whiteness of the blossoms first means the Easter colors of purity and renewal that are appropriate to the spring holiday. The renewal promised is a recovery from winter and the passing of time that it represents. The poem beautifully balances the sense of the ephemerality of a lifetime with the beauty of the moment. Its central lines lament that "to look at things in bloom / Fifty springs are little room" (ll. 9–10). Fifty years is not much time, especially since there is so much to see. What there is to see is the "things in bloom," so that their blooming is so full and so extensive that they easily take up the 50 years allotted their appreciator.

This idea allows the speaker to turn the tables on the passage of time. The beauty of the blossoms is so intense and at the same time so widespread that everything that life can have to offer is present all at once. The 50 years remaining are telescoped into the present moment; as they will be every spring for the next 50. The cherry blooms promise endless store of spring and loveliness; they are so charged with transience that the transience itself becomes overwhelmingly present to the speaker, here now and here every year for the rest of time.

All of this can be seen, perhaps, in the marvelous repetition of the word *now.* The cherry is the loveliest of trees: That is a truth "now"; the cherry "now" in spring is hung with blossoms; while hung with blossoms, the cherry is "now" the loveliest of trees. All these *nows* point to the moment of the tree's blossoming beauty. But *now* is repeated as a word about where the speaker is in *his* life: "Now, of my threescore years and ten, / Twenty will not come again" (ll. 5–6). The *now* that points to a particular moment in his own history is coordinated with the more ephemeral and yet more eternal *now* of the cherry's blossom. The cherry turns his precise fixing of how much his life is over into the eternal renewal of its own *now*.

The cherry is therefore "hung with snow," which is a metaphor at once for the whiteness of the blossoms and the winter encroaching on the speaker's life. The metaphor shows that the blossoms can make snow metamorphose into bloom. We read the last word of the poem as a metaphor; we forget the real snow that the blossoms replace. The poem's achievement, and the cherry's, is to make snow into a metaphor of the blossom's beauty, and to make us forget the winter the cherries announce the end of, at least for this year of our three score and 10.

BIBLIOGRAPHY

Gardner, Philip, ed. *A. E. Housman: The Critical Heritage.* New York: Routledge, 1992.

Highet, Gilbert. *Classical Tradition: Greek and Roman Influences on Western Literature.* New York: Oxford University Press, 1957.

Richards, Grant. *Housman: 1897–1936.* New York: Oxford University Press, 1942.

"LUCIFER IN STARLIGHT" GEORGE MEREDITH (1883) This poem first appeared in GEORGE MEREDITH's 1883 book *Poems and Lyrics of the Joy of Earth,* and it is worth considering what makes it a poem about such joy. The language is SUBLIME but a little difficult, rendered somewhat easier by the story that it recounts. But it is difficult to say what that story is: Lucifer is Satan, and this is Satan after the fall consequent upon his rebellion against God, "the old revolt from Awe" (l. 10) whose memory still pains him. That revolt is recounted in John Milton's *Paradise Lost* (1667), as well as Satan's corruption of humanity through the temptation and seduction of Adam and Eve told in the Bible. Satan corrupts them by breaking through the bound of hell, or at least the physical place of hell, to come to earth. Now, in Meredith's poem, he takes another flight from hell and into the Dantesque dominions of starlight (every book of Dante's *The Divine Comedy* ends with the word *stars*) to attempt again some measure of the freedom Milton depicts him as seeking. In this he fails.

The confusion arises, however, because the poem so strongly alludes to the original and only mention of Lucifer in the Hebrew Bible. The prophet Isaiah intones a rebuke: "How art thou fallen from heaven, O Lucifer, son of the morning! . . . For thou hast said in thine heart, I will ascend into heaven, I will exalt my throne above the stars of God: I will sit also upon the mount of the congregation, in the sides of the north: I will ascend above the heights of the clouds; I will be like the most High." (The whole passage, Isaiah 14: 12–17, deserves study.) This has usually been interpreted, for example by Milton, as the unfallen angel Satan's rebellion in heaven against God; but there is no reason to suppose this was Isaiah's intention. Note that Lucifer seeks to ascend into heaven, so that he is not an angelic denizen of that realm. Rather, he is the morning star; his name means light-bearer, and Isaiah's image is of the way the morning star, rising just before sunrise, is overwhelmed by the sun it seeks to outpace and outshine. Meredith's Lucifer is similarly motivated, rising from the night, seeking the heights above the clouds, sitting in the sides of the North, over the Arctic.

Meredith is characteristically describing Lucifer's ambitions as looking to some now remote and inaccessible place of aspiration up (see also "DIRGE IN WOODS"). This is what he reads Isaiah as describing: not Satan's original fall from heaven, nor yet his return to earth to engineer humanity's fall from Eden, but a sense of hopelessness doubly estranged from those earlier moments and modes of possible participation. He interprets Isaiah this way for two related reasons. The first may be explained through Harold Bloom's theory of "the anxiety of influence." By treating the original story of the fall of Satan (more accurately) as describing an event that occurs *after* the story told in *Paradise Lost,* Meredith makes his later poem a truer recounting of the original biblical verses than anything Milton did. He connects his poem back to Isaiah's prophecy, and simultaneously he makes Isaiah's prophecy an account of Satan's last defeat, the one that comes after *Paradise Lost* and that had to wait for Meredith to render as poetry.

Meredith is thus able to give an account of all human experience, especially that of human sinners hugging a specter or ghost of repose—the sleep that is a false and not a true experience of peace. Like the fallen spirits who have lost paradise because of Satan's revolt in *Paradise Lost,* we are the prey of Satan's "hot pride" here on earth. But Satan's sublime flight, which makes the earth seem a little thing in the space of his motion, is itself rendered trivial by the stars he cannot affect in the slightest. They move according to the unalterable law of the universe, the Newtonian laws of motion that Satan cannot conceive of matching. Satan's view of law is willful, individuated, and so ultimately petulant. But what God has created is far above individual vanity or self-interest: He has created the very laws of the stars. Satan, appropriately to Lucifer as the morning star, is *not* a true star but a planet (l. 8). He can only attain a middle rank, before sinking back to his own domain. As with Dante's Paradise, which trumps the realms of Hell and Purgatory that come before it, the ancient God-created Heaven is entirely beyond the reach of Satan.

But it is not beyond the reach of humans—in Dante or in Meredith. The second reason that Meredith has Isaiah alluding to the time and situation of fallen humanity is that in this way his prophecy can be applied to us. We live in prophetic times, and while Satan's situation might be hopeless, ours is not.

For what is the brain of heaven but the laws that humans have discovered about celestial motion? The motion of the stars is somehow part of the harmony of celestial or heavenly thought, but it is also the harmony of our thought, the order that human astronomy finds and explains in the heavens and the order in our *own* brains that awes us. We are like the universe in contemplating the ancient motion of the stars. Indeed, that motion is a metaphor for poetic form; or perhaps we could say that poetic form (like the sonnet that is this poem's form), with its orderly motions and returns, turns out to be a metaphor for the unalterable law of God.

It should be noted that Meredith may indeed be writing a song of the joy of earth, if we take that joy to be a kind of naturalist's joy (like Meredith's friend THOMAS HARDY's) in the observation of the real world. We might then consider that Meredith's poem seems to allude to the transit of Venus across the face of the sun, which occurs twice a century and which had just occurred on December 6, 1882. (Oliver Wendell Holmes wrote a poem about watching it from the Boston Common; the next transit is to occur in 2012.) Lucifer does turn into "a black planet" (and not the luminous star-like object it usually appears to be) during the transit of Venus. But it is hopeless against the sun, and the unalterable laws of its motion are entirely predictable. Meredith found in this a way of making modern astronomy the fulfillment and triumph of the human "rage for order" (in the 20th-century American poet Wallace Stevens's famous phrase) that is the subject and substance of poetry.

BIBLIOGRAPHY

Bernstein, Carol L. *Precarious Enchantment: A Reading of Meredith's Poetry.* Washington, D.C.: Catholic University of America Press, 1979.

Bloom, Harold. *The Anxiety of Influence: A Theory of Poetry.* New York: Oxford University Press, 1997.

Neil, Roberts. *Meredith and the Novel.* New York: St. Martin's Press, 1997.

Symons, Arthur. "George Meredith as a Poet." In *Figures of Several Centuries,* 83–89. London: Constable and Company, 1916.

LUCY POEMS WILLIAM WORDSWORTH (1800 and 1801) The Lucy poems are a series of five poems by WILLIAM WORDSWORTH about an unknown, perhaps unreal young woman named Lucy (who is *not* Lucy Gray in the poem of that title). The poems are: "Strange fits of passion have I known," "She dwelt among the untrodden ways" (memorably parodied by HARTLEY COLERIDGE), "Three years she grew," "A slumber did my spirit seal," and "I traveled among unknown men." Wordsworth wrote the first four during his trip to Germany with his sister and with SAMUEL TAYLOR COLERIDGE in 1799 and added them to the 1800 (second) edition of *Lyrical Ballads.* The last was probably composed in 1801 and partly reflects on his absence from England during that trip.

The Lucy poems are extraordinary for the power that their restraint makes felt. We know so little of Lucy because the poems tell us so little about her. Unlike most poems of mourning, they do not memorialize or eulogize her, nor do they seek to preserve a sense of her life in a world after her death. They mourn her more completely than that since what they are about is her *absence* rather than her presence. In some ways they typify the radical change in the purpose of poetry that Wordsworth was bringing about. They *express* rather than describe emotion, and what they express is the extent to which the experience of loss may be inexpressible. The austere simplicity of the Lucy poems stands for depth of feeling, not lack of it.

This is perhaps best seen in the amazing understatement of the last lines of "She dwelt among the untrodden ways":

> She lived unknown, and few could know
> When Lucy ceased to be;
> But she is in her grave, and, oh,
> The difference to me.

He describes the difference as a blank but all-encompassing fact. Everything is different, although there is no way to make that difference palpable since Lucy's existence was not important as the public world counts importance. This poem, and the Lucy poems in general, plumb private experience in an unprecedented way.

It is worth quoting the most famous of the Lucy poems in full:

> A slumber did my spirit seal,
> I had no human fears:
> She seemed a thing that could not feel
> The touch of earthly years.
>
> No motion has she now, no force;
> She neither hears nor sees;
> Rolled round in earth's diurnal course,
> With rocks, and stones, and trees.

What happens in the intense blank space between the first and second stanzas is that Lucy dies. The transition—the "difference"—is everything: the difference between life and death but also between the past and past-tense verbs of the first stanza and the present tense of the second, the difference between the speaker's perspective in the first ("my spirit," "I had," "she *seemed*") and Lucy's nonperspective (since she is dead) in the second.

The word *now* in line five is a central word in Wordsworth's poetry: It consistently registers how things have changed for the speaker from a past which was better in certain ways than the present. (See INTIMATIONS ODE.) In the first stanza, she *seems* to be an immortal thing; in the second stanza, she is literally a thing, rolled round like other things: rocks, stones, trees. The second stanza *literalizes* the mildly metaphorical language of the first, and that literalization spells death. Lucy seemed not to be able to feel before; now she literally cannot sense anything: "she neither hears nor sees." The earthly years have become the physical movement of the planet, whose material substrate she has joined.

The last word of the poem is deeply and powerfully ambiguous, in a way typical of Wordsworth. Is the reference to "trees" at the end a hopeful one, indicating the possibility of renewed life? Or do trees now belong to the same category as rocks and stones—that is, the category of what is *not* alive—so that life itself no longer counts? The question may have an answer, but it may also be the case that Wordsworth confronts himself (and us) with the question in order to help us gauge the depth and uncertainty of his grief. The Lucy poems, and in particular "A slumber did my spirit seal," show all of Wordsworth's power in miniature, without any diminution of his strength.

See also "NUTTING."

BIBLIOGRAPHY

Abrams, M. H. *Natural Supernaturalism: Tradition and Revolution in Romantic Literature.* New York: Norton, 1973.
Bloom, Harold. *Poetry and Repression: Revisionism from Blake to Stevens.* New Haven, Conn.: Yale University Press, 1976.
———. *The Visionary Company: A Reading of English Romantic Poetry.* Garden City, N.Y.: Doubleday, 1961.
Bromwich, David. *Disowned by Memory: Wordsworth's Poetry of the 1790s.* Chicago: University of Chicago Press, 1998.
Brooks, Cleanth. *A Shaping Joy: Studies in the Writer's Craft.* London: Methuen, 1973.
De Man, Paul. *The Rhetoric of Romanticism.* New York: Columbia University Press, 1984.
Empson, William. *Seven Types of Ambiguity.* New York: New Directions, 1966.
Hartman, Geoffrey. *Wordsworth's Poetry, 1787–1814.* New Haven, Conn.: Yale University Press, 1971.

Johnston, Kenneth. *Hidden Wordsworth: Poet, Lover, Rebel, Spy*. New York: Norton, 1998.
Levinson, Marjorie. *Wordsworth's Great Period Poems: Four Essays*. New York: Cambridge University Press, 1986.
Liu, Alan. *Wordsworth: The Sense of History*. Stanford, Calif.: Stanford University Press, 1989.
Moorman, Mary. *William Wordsworth: A Biography*. 2 vols. Oxford: Clarendon Press, 1957, 1965.
Pinch, Adela. *Strange Fits of Passion: Epistemologies of Emotion, Hume to Austen*. Stanford, Calif.: Stanford University Press, 1996.
Quinney, Laura. *The Poetics of Disappointment: Wordsworth to Ashbery*. Charlottesville: University Press of Virginia, 1999.
Wolfson, Susan J. *Questioning Presence: Wordsworth, Keats, and the Interrogative Mode in Romantic Poetry*. Ithaca, N.Y.: Cornell University Press, 1986.

"LWONESOMENESS" WILLIAM BARNES (1863)

This poem, about lonesomeness, is in the voice of a woman, so it is clearly not WILLIAM BARNES himself speaking. But it is close enough: The sadness as well as the possibility of sharing emotion that are so central to his poetry means that his "characters" understand each other. It is part of their shared experience of a shared world—the natural surround that is for Barnes at once stability and a measure of a person's own changing trajectory toward sadness and sorrow. But the fact that others share this experience is consoling, and Barnes's poetry offers itself as part of that consolation.

There are two possible sources for this poem. One is Henry Howard, earl of Surrey's great 16th-century poem "Ye Happy Dames," which is spoken by a woman whose love is on a dangerous sea journey, and which is remembered for its immortal line, "Lo, what a mariner love hath made me" (a line ROBERT SOUTHEY quoted in his poetry). The other is the Horatian tradition of poems of invitation, picked up most notably by Ben Jonson (though Barnes is probably thinking more of Horace than of Jonson). Here a woman is lamenting the absence of her brother, who is presumably in the navy, on ship in stormy November seas. (William Miles Barnes, Jr., born 1840, was not a sailor; he might have been traveling, however.) She is keeping house for her father, and we can tell that he is no company for her because he is too downcast by his widowhood. (It may be that the father stands for Barnes himself, whose grief over the death of his wife 11 years earlier was to last the rest of his life; his own daughters were now in their 20s and 30s.) We know that he is a widower because we know the woman's mother has died: She is in a place where she is out of pain, free from the fair of cold and rain in "her now happy hwome" (l. 22). The mother's home is happy, but her daughter's is not. She is doing her work, alone, in the declining November weather in the oppressively empty house. But the poem is not a poem of despair, since it can invite a friend in a similar situation to come and share her work in the empty house, "Vor company" (l. 28).

The poem's beautiful directness at the end, which is what makes it so moving, is made possible by mutual understanding. Neither woman has anything to hide from the other. They understand each other fully—the world they live in and the emotions of this world. And in that understanding there is comfort and love. The speaker offers love, and part of that offer is the pure and candid way she expects (rightly) that the woman she is inviting over will accept that friendship with the same candidness. There is no defensiveness there. Invitation poems are very hard to write, just because it is the nature of an invitation to be defensive, to prepare for rejection. But there is no such preparation here, and there need be none. The imperatives, with their slight and wonderful variation, are those of pure love: "Now do" (l. 28); "Do come" (l. 30). The very way the woman expects that her friend will understand her repeated directness and respond to it and come is that love's sign. Probably we can see Barnes seeing in the daughter an image of what he loved in his wife. At any rate, the speaking voice of "Lwonesomeness" is hauntingly wonderful.

BIBLIOGRAPHY

Levy, William Turner. *William Barnes: The Man and the Poems*. Dorchester, England: Longmans, 1960.
Parins, James W. *William Barnes*. Boston: Twayne Publishers, 1984.
Scott, Leader. *The Life of William Barnes: Poet and Philologist, by his Daughter, Lucy Baxter* ("Leader Scott") 1887. Reprint, St. Clair Shores, Mich.: Scholarly Press, 1971.

M

"MAD GARDENER'S SONG, THE" LEWIS CARROLL (1889) "The Mad Gardener's Song" comes from LEWIS CARROLL's story *Sylvie and Bruno,* where it appears as a series of verses that the gardener breaks into in the course of the narrative, whenever a likely word or phrase drifts by. It stands alone as a poem, however, and it is one of Carroll's greatest pieces of nonsense verse. Like all Carroll's nonsense (see "JABBERWOCKY"), it is partly about the nature of poetry, the limits of meaning and of form, and the relationship between them.

The poem is worth considering for its expression of hidden psychological content. As Harold Bloom points out, the suggestible man who keeps having his wishful visions corrected seems to hope for some escape from domesticity and the oppression of married life. The elephant playing on a fife gives way to a letter from his wife—where is she? What freedom does their clearly temporary separation give him?—to which he reacts despairingly, even without opening it. That opening disappointment is echoed at the close when his hope that he might turn out to be the pope, preeminently unmarried, is disappointed again, leaving him without hope. Given Carroll's own bachelorhood and his chaste but intense interest in young girls, especially Alice Liddell, marriage with a grown woman seems to represent for Carroll the opposite of the imaginative freedom afforded by his nonsense verse.

What is finally striking about the poem, though, is the extent to which it takes its own form as its theme. Here is the last stanza, to which I have already alluded:

> He thought he saw an Argument
> That proved he was the Pope:
> He looked again, and found it was
> A Bar of Mottled Soap.
> "A fact so dread," he faintly said,
> "Extinguishes all hope!"

An argument that might prove the mad gardener or his poetic stand-in was the pope would be an argument that he was up to the standards of that other famous gardener and rhymer, the 18th-century poet Alexander Pope. Pope was perhaps the most skilled rhymer in English poetry, and all his rhymes adhered to the central rule of the heroic couplet that he excelled in: They made an antithetical point of contrast. Rhymes represent arbitrary and accidental connections between words, and the skill of the poet is to render those connections meaningful (as the 20th-century scholar William K. Wimsatt persuasively argued). It was this at which Pope excelled.

Nonsense verse seems to take the opposite tack: It can follow the illogical logic of any arbitrary rhyme. And yet this is not so: its juxtapositions have to be striking, which means they have to be motivated, and the mere fact of rhyme is not enough. Carroll solves this problem through his triple rhymes, where the third rhyme connects the nonsensical juxtaposition of the first two. This stanza is of the same form as the other eight. Note that its rhyme scheme is *xaxaxa,* (where only the even-numbered lines rhyme). In this case, the nonsensical connection between the pope and a bar of soap is noted with an absence of "all hope" that comments on the first two rhymes.

"The Mad Gardener's Song" does this throughout, each stanza having the same form. The even lines rhyme, and the odd lines are also connected to each other, forming a stable template that persists throughout the poem. Each stanza begins with what its hallucinating protagonist "thought he saw." The third line of each stanza is the same as well: "He looked again, and found it was . . ." Carroll's *was* is the truth that reverses what the man in the poem thought he *saw.* Throughout, truth is the palindrome, or reversal, of wishful fantasy. And in each case, he pronounces judgment in the fifth line, which always ends with the speech tag "he said."

I note these regularities because they help to disguise the remarkable fact that the most striking words in the poem are not rhyme words. Take the first two stanzas, for example:

> He thought he saw an Elephant
> That practised on a fife:
> He looked again, and found it was
> A letter from his wife.
> "At length I realize," he said,
> "The bitterness of Life!"
>
> He thought he saw a Buffalo
> Upon the chimney-piece:
> He looked again, and found it was
> His Sister's Husband's Niece.
> "Unless you leave this house," he said,
> "I'll send for the Police!"

It takes examination to realize that *Elephant* and *Buffalo* are not rhyme words; they seem preeminently the kind of words that nonsense seeks to rhyme, as later on *Rattlesnake, Kangaroo,* and *Albatross* will as well. The most whimsical and vivid images are not effects of the accidents of rhyme but of the free play of Carroll's imagination. Rhyme brings him back to earth: the letter from his wife, his sister's husband's niece, and so on, all turn out to be the truth that undercuts the extravagant fiction. And it is this that causes him to make a bitter comment linking the arbitrariness of the rhymes.

As a logician, Carroll was highly interested in the interplay of seemingly arbitrary statements. (One of his most famous logical puzzles requires making sense of the near-impossible concatenation of many different statements.) In the penultimate stanza of "The Mad Gardener's Song," the man he sings about thinks he's found his way to a garden, or perhaps out of one:

> He thought he saw a Garden-Door
> That opened with a key:
> He looked again, and found it was
> A Double Rule of Three:
> "And all its mystery," he said,
> "Is clear as day to me!"

The "Rule of Three" is an antique term for calculating proportions: Given three quantities, a, b, and c, find the fourth when a is to b as c is to this fourth. The "Double Rule of Three" refers to the calculation of proportions when the quantities are variable rather than given as constants in the simple Rule of Three. But in the poem, the "Double Rule of Three" must refer to the form of the poem itself, with its triple rhymes in each two-times-three-equals-six–line stanza, and its three-to-the-second-equals-nine stanzas. The deflatingly pedantic double rule of three also becomes a kind of description of the poem's logical nonsense or nonsensical logic, and the Man who sees that the door through which he might escape is a double rule of three also sees that the poem itself, with all its intricate formal puzzles, is the garden into which he might escape, once he has the key.

BIBLIOGRAPHY

Bloom, Harold, ed. *Lewis Carroll.* New York: Chelsea House, 1987.

Kelly, Richard. *Lewis Carroll.* Boston: Twayne Publishers, 1990.

Lehmann, John. *Lewis Carroll and the Spirit of Nonsense.* Nottingham, England: University of Nottingham Press, 1974.
Wimsatt, William K. "One Relation of Rhyme to Reason." In *The Verbal Icon,* 153–168. Lexington: University of Kentucky Press, 1967.

"MAGNA EST VERITAS" COVENTRY PATMORE **(1879)** This is the 12th poem in the series making up the first book of COVENTRY PATMORE's late multivolume work *The Unknown Eros* (1877). As with his long narrative poem *The Angel in the House* (1854), the poems are less a sequence than a series, and here each one captures the feeling of the poet at the moment that he wrote it. By its placement, we can assign this poem to a time about five years after the death of Patmore's beloved wife (the model for some of the poems of *The Angel in the House*). Although remarried, and a convert to Catholicism, Patmore's grief was deep, long-standing, and often verged on despair. That despair is the other side of his too easily criticized sentimentality, and he is never less sentimental than he is here.

The title is a famous biblical tag, actually from the Apocrypha, 1 Esdras 4:41. The Vulgate Bible has it as "Magna est veritas et prævalet," which the King James Bible translates as "Great is Truth, and mighty above all things." Patmore prefers the more obvious (though more modern) translation that he himself gives: "The truth is great, and shall prevail" (l. 9), which is a slight but common—and, in this instance, telling—misquotation since it casts into the future tense what is originally in the present.

The speaker is sitting in a bay to which he has walked in order to be alone, "far from the huge town" (l. 5), and he is thinking about the meaning—or the meaninglessness—of the natural process and natural life that he sees before him. He sounds very much like Patmore's friend ALFRED, LORD TENNYSON in *IN MEMORIAM A.H.H.* here, struck with the meaninglessness of life itself. The bay is full of life, the tides come and go twice a day, but the glad ocean is purposeless, which might mean pleasantly idle (it is glad, after all) or might mean meaningless and pointless. The speaker comes to see the ocean and reflects on his own unimportance, in a line whose placement beautifully balances it between transcendence and nihilism: "For want of me the world's course will not fail" (l. 7). He may be talking about his absence from the town, which is insignificant to the business he is now not interested in, being intent on larger things; or it might be that this is the lesson that he learns from watching the life and tides of the bay—that it is all meaningless and that his death will not have an iota of importance.

This line makes possible the transition to the bitter hopelessness of the last lines. The lie that is the working of the world shall rot, or perhaps the working of the world will eventually, as it must, bring the lie to rot. Therefore the truth will eventually prevail—will defeat the lie and extend itself everywhere. But the last line takes away all sense of triumph from this triumph: The truth shall prevail "When none cares whether it prevail or not," either because it will take so long that we will all be dead, or, even more powerfully, because the truth that will eventually prevail is the fact that we will all be dead. From this perspective, the lie that will finally rot is the very statement that the truth is great and shall prevail. It will prevail only in destroying the idea that it can prevail. This is not a paradox, though it may sound as though it verges on one, but a grim fact.

The poem is extraordinarily modern in tone, prosody, and substance; indeed, it may be a source for Wilfred Owen's famous World War I poem, "Dulce et Decorum Est," which also ironizes the Latin tag that provides its title. "Magna est veritas" also shows the greatness to which Patmore could sometimes aspire, especially when being most searingly honest about his experiences of loss.

BIBLIOGRAPHY

Champneys, Basil. *Memoirs and Correspondence of Coventry Patmore.* London: G. Bell and Sons, 1900.
Gosse, Edmund. *Coventry Patmore.* New York: Charles Scribner's Sons, 1905.
Hopkins, Gerard Manley. *Further Letters of Gerard Manley Hopkins, including His Correspondence with Coventry Patmore.* 2nd rev. ed. Edited by C. C. Abbott. New York: Oxford University Press, 1956.
Page, Frederick. *Patmore: A Study in Poetry.* Hamdon, Conn.: Archon Books, 1970.
Weinig, Mary Anthony. *Coventry Patmore.* Boston: Twayne Publishers, 1981.

MANFRED **George Gordon Byron, Lord Byron (1817)** Like Percy Bysshe Shelley's *Prometheus Unbound* (1820), which it heavily influenced, *Manfred* is a verse drama written under the shadow of the German poet and dramatist Johann Wolfgang von Goethe's *Faust* (part 1, published in 1808; in part 2, completed in 1832, Goethe alludes to Lord Byron, who had died eight years earlier; in general, Goethe was an admirer of the much-younger Byron). Like *Faust* (which Byron had read in a French translation), *Manfred* is what Shelley would call a "lyrical drama"—that is, a play whose intensities are both the context and the product of intense lyrical passages which can stand alone but which stand alone *best,* one might say, in the drama they characterize. The mode is a kind of modernization of Greek tragedy (from whose choral odes lyric developed), of the sort that John Milton had begun in English in *Samson Agonistes* (1671). But in *Manfred* and *Prometheus Unbound,* the lyrics characterize the intensity of the protagonist's experience. He has lived in such a way that his world has become intense and full of subjective despair, so much so that it is saturated with the lyricism that remains when all worldly power has become useless or impotent.

For Manfred, this despair comes out of the remorse he feels for an all-but-named crime committed with his beloved, Astarte. That crime is, of course, incest, as the play hints very broadly and with surprising good humor. (See, for example, the interruption at act 3, scene 3, line 47 and the black comedy of the misunderstanding at 3.3, lines 15–18. Byron was rumored—and the rumors were true—to have had incestuous relations with his older half sister Augusta, and it is part of his Byronic verve that he would flirt with the issue in *Manfred.*) *Manfred* is like *Faust* in beginning with a chant of despair about the emptiness of human knowledge. Manfred laments that "Philosophy and science, and the springs / Of wonder, and the wisdom of the world, / I have essay'd . . . / But they avail not" (1.1, ll. 13–17), echoing Faust, whom we first see complaining, "I've learned, alas, philosophy, / Legal skill, and medicine—/ And, what's worse, theology—/ All through heated discipline, / Which leaves me still the fool I was" (*Faust,* part 1, ll. 354–358). But Faust's response to this is to learn black magic, and his sin (selling his soul to the devil) is still to come. Manfred's, whatever it is, has already occurred. Unlike Goethe, Byron has no wish to dramatize the fall of the soul. Rather he is interested in what comes after this fall. He depicts the anguish and courage of a psyche who feels infinite remorse but no fear: "the innate tortures of that deep despair / Which is remorse without the fear of hell" (3.1, ll. 70–71).

As important to *Manfred* as *Faust* is William Shakespeare's *Hamlet,* which Byron's verse drama echoes everywhere. Byron emulates Shakespeare's portrayal of the depth and intensity of the human soul. It is the soul's own capacity for pain and regret that shows its depth, and it is the soul's own capacity to embrace that depth that shows its greatness.

In the first edition of *Manfred,* Byron's publisher left out his last line: "Old man! 'tis not so difficult to die" (3.4, l. 151). Byron was furious, regarding that line as the point of the poem. The question throughout *Manfred* has been whether he should be regarded as mortal or immortal. Mortals are capable of a knowledge that immortals lack (a theme Shelley will take up in *Prometheus Unbound*): the meaning of death. Manfred is able to embrace his own mortality, and in doing so he transcends the immortality that is the human birthright. This makes him one of Byron's most stirring heroes and also allows Byron to avoid the dangers of self-infatuation, which he always courted in his serious poetry. Manfred's remorse is real enough.

BIBLIOGRAPHY

Bloom, Harold. *The Visionary Company: A Reading of English Romantic Poetry.* Garden City, N.Y.: Doubleday, 1961.

Duffy, Edward. *Rousseau in England: The Context for Shelley's Critique of the Enlightenment.* Berkeley: University of California Press, 1979.

Hazlitt, William. *Spirit of the Age; or, Contemporary Portraits.* London: Oxford University Press, 1970.

Saintsbury, George. *History of English Prosody, from the Twelfth Century to the Present Day.* New York: Russell & Russell, 1961.

Thorslev, Peter Larsen. *The Byronic Hero: Types and Prototypes.* Minneapolis, University of Minnesota Press, 1962.

MANGAN, JAMES CLARENCE (1803–1849) In 1903, the Irish biographer and editor D. J. O'Donoghue, who had written a biography of James Clarence Mangan six years earlier, put together, for the first time, a collection of Mangan's poems. A year earlier, the 20-year-old James Joyce had lectured on Mangan, comparing him to PERCY BYSSHE SHELLEY in praising him as one of the greatest of Irish poets, badly underestimated in his own country and abroad. (This lecture [minus the references to Mangan] is the origin of much of the celebrated aesthetic theory in Joyce's *Portrait of the Artist as a Young Man* [1916].) WILLIAM BUTLER YEATS would also call Mangan a poet of the first rank. But it was only in the 20th century that he began to rise out of the obscurity into which misfortune, poverty, and drunkenness had consigned him, and only in the last decade has a reasonably complete edition of his works, culled from an enormous quantity of writing, been assembled.

Mangan was the impoverished son of a brutal father. When his father died, Mangan supported his mother and siblings, partly as a scrivener but largely on his own writings. He wrote an enormous amount of poetry for various Dublin periodicals, especially nationalistic ones. His own political commitments were to Irish nationalism, which helped make him a hero to Yeats later on, but when he had to, he wrote for fiercely unionist journals as well. Early on, he apparently became addicted to drink and to opium, and he had a reputation as a difficult, eccentric, half-mad Irish bard, in the Byronic mode he admired.

One particularly astute comment of Joyce's on Mangan understands his poetry to be rendered all the more powerful and intense by the relentless incomprehension he suffered in daily life: "Mangan, however, is not without some consolation, for his sufferings have cast him inwards, where for many ages the sad and the wise have elected to be. When someone told him that the account which he had given of his early life, so full of things which were, indeed, the beginnings of sorrows, was wildly overstated, and partly false, he answered—'Maybe I dreamed it.'"

Joyce thought that Mangan's excesses "saved him from indifference" and made him the great and internally exiled poet that he was. Of Mangan's talent and intensity there can be no doubt. He wrote in a wide variety of modes, from comic verse (see "TWENTY GOLDEN YEARS AGO" to serious evocations of the harshness of life; translated contemporary German poetry freely (his one possible foray out of Ireland was to Germany, and his German was fluent), usually improving on the original; and claimed to have translated Irish and "Oriental" poetry, such as "GONE IN THE WIND," much of which he made up. He had a wry sense of himself in his poetry and a wry sense of the relentless assault of reality on human hopes and the human spirit. He was taken by later nationalistic writers to represent the results of Ireland's oppression, and also the mode by which the Irish would resist that oppression; as the author and playwright Samuel Beckett would later put it, "When you are in the last ditch, there is nothing left but to sing."

In 1849 Mangan did fall into a ditch in a drunken state; malnourished and ill with cholera, he was hospitalized. He refused to stay in the hospital, however, and died shortly after leaving it. None of his troubles seems to have induced self-pity or mawkishness in his work. His intelligence was always intensely self-aware despite having had a far greater acquaintance than most with the dreadful aspects of the human condition.

BIBLIOGRAPHY

Joyce, James. "James Clarence Mangan." In *Occasional, Critical, and Political Writing.* Oxford, 53–60. Oxford University Press, 2001.

Shannon-Mangan, Ellen. *James Clarence Mangan: A Biography* Dublin: Irish Academic Press, 1996.

Yeats, William Butler. *Uncollected Prose.* 2 vols. Edited by John P. Frayne. London: Macmillan, 1970–1975.

"MARIANA" ALFRED, LORD TENNYSON (1830) "Mariana" is one of ALFRED, LORD TENNYSON's earliest poems of extended static enervation, a mode he would explore throughout his career. As a poet, he was attracted to shadow and repetition (as he has the narrator of *The PRINCESS* say), to the hypnotic sense of a world saturated with an unchanging melancholy or languorousness. The exploration of this state was also for Tennyson a way of exploring the human experience of time—of its vastness (which Charles Lyell discovered in his geological investigations and which shocked Tennyson on Lyell's 1837 publication of his *Principles of Geology*) and of its evanescence, which makes only the present moment real.

How can the continuously cresting standing wave of the present moment give a sense of the stasis that Tennyson found so attractive? In poetic style, the atmosphere of that stasis is conveyed through repetition, especially of poetic refrain; sometimes through anaphora, or the repetition of the same word through various positions in the poetic line; and sometimes through *rime riche,* or the repetition of a word instead of its rhyme (since a true rhyme requires a different onset: *afternoon / laughter soon* is a true rhyme; *afternoon / afternoon* is not). These modes may be seen in the heavily rhymed *ghazals* that Tennyson wrote, for example "NOW SLEEPS THE CRIMSON PETAL, NOW THE WHITE."

Poetic style correlates with the human experience that a poem depicts, and it may be said that Tennyson chose experiences to describe that were consonant with the style he found so attractive, or that the style was appropriate to the human experience closest to his own. In human experience (as opposed to poetic depiction), the sense of time and timelessness come together through present anticipation of the future based, perhaps, on a synthesizing sense of the past. Thus, in "TITHONUS," the title character wrongly believes that he will age forever, and at every moment that belief contains all the despair that eternal aging would bring with it.

Mariana, similarly, as we know from *Measure for Measure,* is not doomed to live abandoned on the moated grange forever. In William Shakespeare's comedy, she has been seduced and abandoned by the horrendously self-righteous Angelo, and she lives alone "in the moated grange," as Tennyson summarizes her description in the first scene of act 3. This is where Tennyson places her as she repeats with just enough variation to make the unchanging despair of her life felt, her constant refrain: "I am aweary, aweary . . . I would that I were dead!" What we know, which she does not, is that Angelo will be forced to marry her in the end, and that he, too, will come to see this as a happy ending, as (arguably) she does.

The litany of despair that she recites here, though, feels permanent to Mariana, and it affords Tennyson the time and leisure for his intense, hypnotic description of her melancholy world and the melancholy passage of time within that world. For Tennyson, the feeling of the future in the instant means that the instant can offer the experience of eternity, even if for Mariana it is the experience only of despair. For Tennyson, it is not despair but timelessness. There are ghosts everywhere, ghosts of her own memory that she does not see or hear, but that he does.

This way of inhabiting a world that the central figure in that world cannot inhabit (see "The KRAKEN") is something particularly alluring to Tennyson, since he can assimilate description to a more general, spread-out, dispersed consciousness. The ability to be everywhere within the saturated world being described allows for an escape from the oppression of instantaneous and unchanging consciousness. This was an escape that JOHN KEATS, Tennyson's greatest model, never managed: His movements toward freedom were far more assertions of his own individual desires. But Tennyson, in his beautifully dreamy poems, can stay "All day within the dreamy house" (l. 60)—the dream itself rather than as identified with the undreaming and despairing Mariana. She is part of the dream, but he and his poem are everywhere within it.

BIBLIOGRAPHY

Armstrong, Isobel. *Victorian Poetry: Poetry, Poetics and Politics.* New York: Routledge, 1993.

Bloom, Harold. *Poetry and Repression: Revisionism from Blake to Stevens.* New Haven, Conn.: Yale University Press, 1976.

Buckley, Jerome Hamilton. *Tennyson: The Growth of a Poet.* Boston: Houghton Mifflin, 1965.

Kilham, John. *Critical Essays on the Poetry of Tennyson.* New York: Barnes and Noble, 1960.

Kincaid, James R. *Tennyson's Major Poems: The Comic and Ironic Patterns.* New Haven, Conn.: Yale University Press, 1975.

Ricks, Christopher B. *Tennyson.* New York: Macmillan, 1972.

Rowlinson, Matthew. *Tennyson's Fixations: Psychoanalysis and the Topics of the Early Poetry.* Charlottesville: University Press of Virginia, 1994.

Tucker, Herbert: *Tennyson and the Doom of Romanticism.* Cambridge, Mass.: Harvard University Press, 1988.

MARMION Sir Walter Scott (1808) *Marmion* is subtitled *A Tale of Flodden Field.* Flodden was one of the most famous battles in English history. James IV, king of Scotland, invaded Northumberland in England in August 1513, partly in support of France, which perennially allied with Scotland against its inveterate enemy, England. England was supporting Italy against French invasion on the continent, and James thought that its forces at home would be relatively weak. James had a huge army—the army so stirringly described in *Marmion*—but England won the battle, which took place on September 9, 1513, under the command of Henry Howard, earl of Surrey (father of the poet). James was killed in battle, as *Marmion* recounts.

The subtitle, *A Tale of Flodden Field,* indicates that Sir Walter Scott's interest is not in the history but in a story for which the historical events provide a stirring and sometimes sublime background. That background is the Border country, a region unto itself where the distinction between England and Scotland mattered far less than that between the Borderers and the nations to which they nominally belonged. (William Wordsworth's 1796 verse drama *The Borderers* is interested in much the same dynamic.) It was this wild region that interested Scott, because of the austere ethics of the barren marches, in particular the laws of hospitality that are so central to Homer as well. Indeed, his first-person narrator, the minstrel figure he had already used to frame *The Lay of the Last Minstrel,* reminds us that "Mine is a tale of Flodden Field, / And not a history" (V.34, ll. 21–22). And indeed it is. Its central figures are Marmion himself, Constance, Clare, and de Wilton, as well as Marmion's two loyal and squabbling followers, Fitz-Eustace and Blount, and they are all fictional, "Unnam'd by Hollinshed or Hall" (VI.38, l. 1,155), the two great historians of the times.

Marmion (like Homer's Odysseus) is an ambiguous hero. He enters with a kind of grandeur that gradually pales as we discover the various elements of his past (one that seems in some ways to anticipate the behavior of Lord Byron), and in particular his abandonment of his first love, Constance, who, in a vain attempt to keep his love, helps him to frame de Wilton for treason so as to court Clare, de Wilton's betrothed. Constance is immured at the start of the poem, but out of revenge and a desire for justice, she tells the truth, exculpating de Wilton before bravely facing her horrible death, and the truth eventually comes out. (The whole of de Wilton's history is given in Canto VI.)

Nevertheless, Marmion—not wholly unlike Shakespeare's Macbeth—behaves with great courage and verve in the battle at Flodden Field where he, too, is killed. The description of the battle showcases Scott's amazing combination of archaic and balladic style with stunning visual evocativeness. We have seen such evocation in the poem's early account (later explained) of Marmion's tilting with an apparent ghost. Now, in the battle, the Scottish forces "fire their tents"—that is, burn all their moveables so as to produce a cloud of thick black smoke out of which they come charging against the English in a silence as uncanny as their invisibility (VI, stanza 25). The description here evokes, as it is meant to, one of the sublimest scenes in *The Iliad,* when Aphrodite covers the whole battlefield with mist in order to protect the Trojans from the Achaians.

Homer is relevant to *Marmion* overall because the poem is about courage and war more than it is about heroism and triumph. Both sides are dauntless, both sides sublime. In such a poem, an ambiguous hero such as Marmion must die; given his past, we cannot praise or admire him if he lives. But death evens everything out (as when Hector dies in *The Iliad*), and the manner of his death, urging his companions on, allows him his sublime courage and explicitly allies him to the doomed Roland of French legend. Scott's (or his minstrel's) epitaph for Marmion asks us not "to speak presumptious doom" on him but to say "'He died a gallant knight / With sword in hand, for England's right'" (VI, stanza 37).

It should be noted that *Marmion* contains some famous set-pieces, most notably the Dame Heron's "soft, yet lively, air" (V.11, l. 311) "Lochinvar" (V, stanza 12), which tells a story paralleling that of Marmion but with a happy ending.

BIBLIOGRAPHY

Kerr, James. *Fiction against History: Scott as Storyteller.* New York: Cambridge University Press, 1989.

Lauber, John. *Sir Walter Scott.* Boston: Twayne Publishers, 1989.

Lincoln, Andrew. *Walter Scott and Modernity.* Edinburgh: Edinburgh University Press, 2007.

"MARRIAGE VOW, THE" LETITIA ELIZABETH LANDON **(1841)** This 10-line poem, like "GOSSIPPING," belongs to LETITIA ELIZABETH LANDON's posthumously published literary remains. It seems to have been written following her disastrous marriage to George Maclean, undertaken as an escape from the terrible scandals that were plaguing her in London. Seven unhappy months later, she would be found dead at their house in Africa (where Maclean was governor of Cape Coast Castle in present day Ghana), probably a suicide.

"The Marriage Vow" would seem to support the idea that Landon was a suicide, since it prefers the funeral service, "read above the open grave" (l. 7) to the marriage service. The reason for this preference is in the fact that marriage vows bind their "victim," the woman who is forced to make them. (That forced vows are nevertheless binding is one of the grim lessons of Dante's *Paradiso* in his *Divine Comedy*.) Her will is bound in one way, in that it does not have freedom to pursue its objects any more. But in another and deeper way, it is not bound but helpless. She is not prevented from wanting what she nevertheless cannot have. The only way to prevent the will from desiring is death, and this ending to the will's chaffing under the victim's restraint will feel like rest. The helplessness and the sense of the cruelty of fate that the poem expresses is clearly autobiographical.

The idea that if the heart "Annuls the vow while speaking" it (l. 5) is less binding is an old and famous one in classical literature, dating to Euripides' *Hippolytus* in the fifth century B.C.E.—a play about adulterous desire. But in Victorian England, the heart's or will's truth are overborne by the requirements of social convention. Landon was certainly still in love with William Jerden, her patron and the married father of her three children, when she married Maclean, and she saw all possibilities of happiness blocked.

The poem is impressive for the fierce dispassionate tone of its blank verse (an attitude learned from WILLIAM WORDSWORTH). If it expresses self-pity, the tone is not lugubrious but instead an achievement in grim clear-sightedness. Because it is unsparing of itself, or of Landon herself, it is entitled to puncture the hypocrisy of the worthies whose social codes forced her into this unhappy marriage. The clergyman reading the service should know better; the society controlling women through marriage should know better.

Such complaints are therefore not only about her own situation, but about the prudish conventions of Victorian morality, which made Landon's alliances with Jerden (preeminently), and with the other men with whom she was rumored to be involved, so shocking. Jerden's marriage, too, was an unhappy one, and if the strictures had not been so tight, the victims would have been far fewer in number.

Like GEORGE ELIOT's MOTTOES and epigraphs, Landon's blank-verse relics are often meant to read like fragments from a play. Thought of that way, "The Marriage Vow" is clearly the speech of a doomed character, one who has no hope left in this life. Landon's control in presenting such a character is highly impressive. But, of course, it did not prevent her from being doomed herself.

BIBLIOGRAPHY

Greer, Germaine. *Slip-Shod Sibyls: Recognition, Rejection and the Woman Poet*. London: Viking, 1995.

Lawford, Cynthia. "Diary." *London Review of Books* (September 21, 2000). Available online. URL: http://www.lrb.co.uk/v22/n18/lawf01_/html. Accessed on March 28, 2008.

Lawford, Cynthia: "'Thou shalt bid thy fair hands rove': L. E. L.'s Wooing of Sex, Pain, Death and the Editor." *Romanticism on the Net* 29–30 (February–May 2003). Available online. URL: http://www.erudit.org/revue/ron/2003/v/n29/007718ar.html. Accessed on March 30, 2008.

Mellor, Anne K. "Exhausting the Beautiful." In *Romanticism and Gender*, 107–143. New York: Routledge, 1993.

"MEMORABILIA" ROBERT BROWNING **(1855)** The title is plural and refers to the two memorabilia, or things worthy of remembrance, that the poem itemizes: contact with PERCY BYSSHE SHELLEY and an eagle feather. In his youth, ROBERT BROWNING worshipped Shelley, the figure he addressed as "Suntreader" in his poem "Pauline," and Shelley was always central to his sense of what poetry was and could be. One might say that even the 17th-century poet John Milton came to Browning as Shelley's Milton—that the whole of

English literature came to Browning at first through Shelley's tutelage.

The poem begins with awe of a mediated sort: Browning meets someone who has talked to Shelley. (This actually happened in a bookshop; the man who had met Shelley laughed at Browning's astonishment.) Browning imagines that such a meeting would have been the signal event of his life, the only memory worth preserving. Indeed, to express his amazement, he echoes Milton's *Paradise Lost,* where the rebel angels regard God's decree apotheosizing his Son as a "strange point and new." So, too, is the single degree of separation from Shelley. But the person who had met Shelley laughs at this supposition, and at Browning's astonishment. His contact with Shelley should prove that Shelley is as human as everyone else, and that only an idealist who had never met the real person would think as Browning does.

Browning responds with an anecdote, but it would be better to understand that the last two stanzas of the poem are *not* a response to the person who met Shelley. Browning turns aside to brood, and what he broods on is the parallel scene in which he found a Shelleyan eagle feather. The moment he found the feather, and the feather itself, are all that matter. He does not locate the feather in the world but sees it as marking a place or event where the world falls away. And he falls away with it: All that matters is the feather, and the "miles round about" are *blank,* in his astonishing word—blank in memory as in importance.

The eagle feather is Shelleyan, but it is not Shelley—neither a symbol nor a metaphor for him. It is, rather, *like* Shelley in being indifferent to the triviality of the world. The person who met Shelley remembers him as involved in the world, speaking and conducting business, "living before" and after, just like himself. But Browning is moved to turn away from just this engagement and to identify himself with a moment of intense solitude. Not that he is not "living before" and after; since the same man who mentions having met Shelley could also mention having met Browning; perhaps Shelley's response to something he said moved him to laughter as well. But in the mind, Browning goes elsewhere, to the place where he knows Shelley to reside and where the man cannot conceive of following him.

Where he goes is to the great understatement, both as regards expression and as regards meter, that ends the poem. "I forget the rest" means that he keeps only one memory, and that this memory does not turn into an anecdote. But it also means that his poem is not turning into an anecdote. Rather, the thought of Shelley is a thought that allows Browning a full sense of himself as transcending anecdote for a moment of poetic intensity. The last line is intentionally and paradoxically powerful because it is an understatement, in the mode of WILLIAM WORDSWORTH's "But O! The difference to me" at the end of "She Dwelt among th'Untrodden Ways." There is nothing more for Browning to say, which means that he has internalized his own impulse to poetic expression just as much as he has internalized Shelley's. This is a major poetic gain, since he no longer speaks or writes to please anyone, but rather puts what matters in his poetry inside his breast, and cherishes it there.

BIBLIOGRAPHY

Bloom, Harold. *A Map of Misreading.* New York: Oxford University Press, 2003.

DeVane, William C. *A Browning Handbook.* New York: Appleton-Century-Crofts, 1955.

Langbaum, Robert Woodrow. *The Modern Spirit: Essays on the Continuity of Nineteenth- and Twentieth-Century Literature.* New York: Oxford University Press, 1970.

Raymond, William O. *The Infinite Moment, and Other Essays in Robert Browning.* Toronto: University of Toronto Press, 1965.

MEREDITH, GEORGE (1828–1909) George Meredith is best remembered now as the author of novels that are quite funny but nearly impossible to read; he is one the important second-rank Victorians. What makes him impossible to read is the wildness of his language, exceeding even the American, Herman Melville. In an era when style inflected storytelling as much as it would for the modernists (for example, James Joyce and William Faulkner), Meredith's style was among the wildest. This was partly because of his hatred for Charles Dickens and Dickens's sentimentality. Style in Dickens was a kind of process of familiar ritual, of a language capacious enough to register all eccentricity in unique terms of affection for each eccentric. Meredith and his peers in the PRE-RAPHAELITE POETRY movement were as alert to the intricacy and variety of detail as Dickens was—perhaps more so—but their response was not so much affectionate as probing, rather like the Darwinian naturalist who would be seen slightly later in THOMAS HARDY. Meredith was among the earliest to patronize Hardy, who always admired Meredith, even when others found him excessive, by Victorian standards, which is saying a lot. In his elegy for Meredith, "George Meredith," Hardy wrote of Meredith's language as "trenchant" but "kind," and described how his language lived on, not for its own beauty and power but because he was "one of those whose wit can shake / And riddle to the very core / The falsities that Time will break" (*riddle* here, appropriately, means both "puzzle" and "shoot full of holes"). It is for this reason that his "strong words" will continue to "wing on" through the world's "vitiate air."

Meredith (like Hardy) began as a poet. He made himself part of the circle of Thomas Love Peacock (PERCY BYSSHE SHELLEY'S close friend) after becoming friends with his son. He subsequently married Peacock's older, widowed daughter, Mary Ellen Nicolls, when he was 21 and she was seven years older. The marriage was miserable, partly because of the horrible poverty in which they lived, and she left him for the Pre-Raphaelite painter Henry Wallis (whose portrait of Meredith posing as the dead poet Thomas Chatterton is his most famous painting. Meredith wrote about this miserable experience, both in poetry and in fiction; it is the source of his most important poetic work, the quasi-sonnet sequence *MODERN LOVE*. Comparison of that poem (written shortly after Mary Ellen had died in 1861) to the overheated but compelling novel *The Ordeal of Richard Feverel* (published in 1859, while she was still alive) shows the extent of Meredith's probing and unsparing analysis (both of his own desires and of hers) as well as the discipline that writing in poetry imposed upon his language. That discipline hardly makes him a euphonious poet.

Hardy is relevant here, too: Language of subtle but uncompromising strength and directness is fitted to poetic form in such a way that it cannot quite lose itself in the inarticulate excess to be found in the fiction. (Hardy sustained this language in his novels as well, but Meredith would not.) The discipline of form is one of the things that makes Meredith a Pre-Raphaelite poet: It is always the details that curb the centrifugal force of his language, and the details are (like the self-analysis) unsparing. As a novelist, Meredith is fascinating and unruly; as a poet, he is equally fascinating, but the compression of all his energy into so much narrower a scope makes the poetry all the more intellectually and psychologically intense.

See also "DIRGE IN WOODS," "LUCIFER IN STARLIGHT."

BIBLIOGRAPHY

Bernstein, Carol L. *Precarious Enchantment: A Reading of Meredith's Poetry*. Washington, D.C.: Catholic University of America Press, 1979.

Neil, Roberts. *Meredith and the Novel*. New York: St. Martin's Press, 1997.

Symons, Arthur. "George Meredith as a Poet." In *Figures of Several Centuries*, 83–89. London: Constable and Company, 1916.

MEYNELL, ALICE (ALICE CHRISTIANA GERTRUDE THOMPSON MEYNELL) (1847–1922) Alice Meynell, born Alice Christiana Gertrude Thompson, was one of the most fascinating of the Victorian minor poets, although she might just as well be called an early modernist. She was born in Barnes, near London, but spent much of her early life in Italy. She and her sister Elizabeth (who later became famous as Elizabeth, Lady Butler, the painter of military scenes, were educated by her father, and they were fluent in Italian.

Although Meynell had been raised as an Anglican, that Anglicanism was apparently of a character and intensity that made it possible for the entire family to convert more or less independently to Catholicism. Meynell's mother converted a few years before Meynell herself did, in 1868, being received into the church by one Father Dignam, a Jesuit priest who seems to have fallen in love with Meynell as she had with him. He had himself posted elsewhere, an event that filled her with a sense of loss, and which she records in her poem "RENOUNCEMENT," published in her well-received first book *Preludes* (1875), which ALFRED, LORD TENNYSON, whom she had recently met, had encouraged her to publish. COVENTRY PATMORE, who had himself converted to Catholicism three years before Meynell did, was one of the book's admirers, as was the essayist and critic John Ruskin, who singled out "Renouncement" for praise.

Preludes and the moral stance it evinced drew the attention of a Catholic journalist five years Alice's junior, Wilfred John Meynell. They married in 1877 and eventually had eight children (one of whom died in infancy), to whom they tended to give Shakespearean names, especially from *Twelfth Night* (Viola, Olivia, and Sebastian). Motherhood was one of the major themes of Alice Meynell's poetry and was a personal experience in which the necessities and intensities of renunciation reached their zenith.

Meynell contributed to various journals, and she helped her husband edit the *Weekly Register* and also a monthly, *Merry England,* for which she wrote much material. She published books of essays and literary criticism, a wonderful anthology of English poetry in 1893, and an augmented collection of poetry in 1902. She moved in the most august Catholic literary circles and was apparently very popular in them. Patmore fell in love with her, which eventually led to a fallout with him (she published an important anthology of his verse, however). So, too, did FRANCIS THOMPSON. Her charisma extended more widely as well, to people like GEORGE MEREDITH.

Meynell was a suffragette and a pacifist, a position she maintained throughout the First World War. One of her most powerful, and still-relevant, poems, "Parentage," is written against Britain's (or anyone's) involvement in the wars at the turn of the 20th century. It takes as an epigraph, and issue with, Caesar Augustus's pronouncement that those who did not have children were "slayers of the people." No, she says, the slayers of the people are those who do since these children will be sent to their deaths in war. The mother who bears the child also bears the fact that she is sending her child to his death in the British Empire's wars.

See also "CRADLE SONG AT TWILIGHT"; "MODERN MOTHER, THE."

BIBLIOGRAPHY

Badeni, June. *The Slender Tree: A Life of Alice Meynell.* Padstow, Cornwall, England: Tabb House, 1981.

Leighton, Angela. "Alice Meynell." In *Victorian Woman Poets: Writing against the Heart.* Charlottesville: University Press of Virginia, 1992: 244–265.

Meynell, Alice. *Prose and Poetry.* Edited by Frederick Page, et al. London: J. Cape, 1947.

Meynell, Viola. *Alice Meynell: A Memoir.* London: J. Cape, 1929.

MICHAEL WILLIAM WORDSWORTH (1800)

"Michael" appears in the second edition of *Lyrical Ballads,* the volume WILLIAM WORDSWORTH wrote with SAMUEL TAYLOR COLERIDGE, and it is one of his most original and intense explorations of the relations between narrative, environment, and human psychology. It is always important to remember that Wordsworth was one of literature's most profound analysts of the soul—both his own and others. The egotism and self-regard for which Wordsworth is much disparaged had a counterpart in his great NEGATIVE CAPABILITY (to use the phrase of JOHN KEATS, who thought Wordsworth deficient in it)—that is, his ability to enter fully and intensely into the experience of the figures he sketched and whose stories he told in *Lyrical Ballads* and other poems of the same period (some of which were later assimilated into *The PRELUDE* and *The Excursion:* see, for example *The RUINED COTTAGE*). Wordsworth wrote to the radical Whig politician Charles James Fox that *Michael* was "written with a view to show that men who do not wear fine clothes can feel deeply."

The feelings he intended to depict in the character of Michael were at odds with each other: "parental affection and the love of property." This phrase is often quoted in accounts of the poem, making it sound like a clash between true love and greed, but that is not what Wordsworth meant. He meant that Michael has achieved a true feeling of "home and personal and family independence," as he wrote to his brilliant and urbane self-educated friend Thomas Poole (one of the great benefactors of Nether Stowey, where he was Coleridge's neighbor). Michael achieves this at 40 and risks losing it at 80 because of the financial disaster suffered by a nephew. Believing that he can save both his lands and his relationship with the descendants he would leave those lands to, he agrees to allow his beloved son Luke to work in the city for another kinsman. The story is told very rapidly: Luke is at first successful and diligent but then grows dissolute and corrupt and disappears. Michael continues to work on the sheepfold that he and Luke were just beginning to construct when Luke had to leave, but he dies leaving it unfinished. His wife survives him for three years and then his lands are sold off after all, so all his sacrifice was for nothing.

All that remains of Michael's property is "a straggling heap of unhewn stones!" (l. 27). The insistent exclamation point shows the depth of feeling that this little object signifies. It tells a tale, "A story—unenriched with strange events" (l. 19), and this is a crucial aspect of Wordsworth's attitude. As with "SIMON LEE," where the speaker fears he will disappoint the reader with the seeming triviality of the tale, the story here seems trivial only because it resembles life itself. Most of it is given to telling of the intense joy that Michael feels in the birth and growth of his son Luke, who is described in capital letters as "Boy" and "Child" and regarded as semidivine, as Wordsworth always regards the children reared as lovers of nature. The story (as already noted) is an old and perennial one, a staple of moral literature: The innocent child of nature is corrupted by the city and comes to a tragic ending.

But Wordsworth's story is anything but standard. In the standard story, the city brings out corruption already present in germ in the child; we know this because of the child's eagerness to travel to that world, thus being attracted to corruption. Luke is eager, too, but his eagerness is innocent. He weeps to part and would, in the end, have as happily stayed home. His corruption and Michael's bad decision to send him to the city are not the manifestations of some particular flaws in their character but of the sorry facts of socioeconomic life and poverty that are the constant and oppressive lot of men who do not wear fine clothes. Capable of poverty when attuned to nature, they are forced into the artificialities of debt and urban life, which kills their spirit.

Yet they leave behind their stories—and the primary story they leave behind, as with the similar story of Margaret in *The Ruined Cottage,* is of their participation in the natural scene and scenery. Their story is the inevitable and unidealized story of all people, no matter how much they are lovers of the woods: decline, decay, and death. Nature is not an alternative to this story; it is, rather, the background against which it plays out, a background whose beauty is intensified by contrast with the way every human ceases feeling at home in the natural world, and therefore in any world. But this loss of belonging is itself the most significant aspect of the natural world. It is what makes nature uncanny and inhuman—what gives it whatever it has of transcendence. In the end, nature is the record of the lives of those expelled from it, a series of monuments like the unhewn stones of the abandoned sheepfold. It offers and then later withdraws the peace of its own indifferent and eerie and exalting forgetfulness of the things it records, their exile from nature becoming the very matrix of nature itself.

Michael is famously subtitled *A Pastoral Poem*—that is, a poem about shepherds, which traditionally appealed to sophisticates imagining a longing for a simpler life. The shepherds in Wordsworth's poem are real, and while they are part of the natural background for any traditional pastoral, they are also as excluded as any person, perhaps more than any person, from the fantasy of belonging to nature, in which the consumers of traditional pastoral indulged. The suffering that arises from the failure of their attempts to sue for peaceful terms by which to live with the natural world they love is the record that gives substance and form to that world.

BIBLIOGRAPHY

Abrams, M. H. *Correspondent Breeze: Essays on English Romanticism.* New York: Norton, 1984.

———. *Natural Supernaturalism: Tradition and Revolution in Romantic Literature.* New York: Norton, 1973.

Alpers, Paul. *What is Pastoral?* Chicago: University of Chicago Press, 1996.

Bloom, Harold. *The Visionary Company: A Reading of English Romantic Poetry.* Garden City, N.Y.: Doubleday, 1961.

Bromwich, David. *Disowned by Memory: Wordsworth's Poetry of the 1790s.* Chicago: University of Chicago Press, 1998.

Hartman, Geoffrey. *Wordsworth's Poetry, 1787–1814.* New Haven, Conn.: Yale University Press, 1971.

Johnston, Kenneth. *Hidden Wordsworth: Poet, Lover, Rebel, Spy.* New York: Norton, 1998.

Liu, Alan. *Wordsworth: The Sense of History.* Stanford, Calif.: Stanford University Press, 1989.

Moorman, Mary. *William Wordsworth: A Biography*. 2 vols. Oxford: Clarendon Press, 1957, 1965.

Pinch, Adela. *Strange Fits of Passion: Epistemologies of Emotion, Hume to Austen*. Stanford, Calif.: Stanford University Press, 1996.

Wolfson, Susan J. *Questioning Presence: Wordsworth, Keats, and the Interrogative Mode in Romantic Poetry*. Ithaca, N.Y.: Cornell University Press, 1986.

MODERN LOVE GEORGE MEREDITH (1862)

In 1849, when he was 21, GEORGE MEREDITH married Mary Ellen Nicolls (1821–61), the daughter of the novelist and poet Thomas Love Peacock (who was then in his 60s). Nicolls was the mother of a-five-year old girl; her husband had drowned a few months after their marriage. She was seven years older than Meredith, and they were a brilliant couple, each an intellectual match for the other, which made for intense passion but also for rivalry. In 1858 Mary abandoned Meredith for Henry Wallis, a minor Pre-Raphaelite artist, whose most famous painting (to be found most recently, for example, on the cover of Peter Ackroyd's novel *Chatterton* [1996]) is of the death by suicide of the despairing boy-poet Thomas Chatterton (1752–70), who was such an important exemplary figure to the romantics (see ROMANTICISM and PRE-RAPHAELITE POETRY). Wallis painted it in 1856, and Meredith was the model for Chatterton.

Modern Love is a sonnet, or pseudo-sonnet, sequence completed after Mary's death in 1861. Sonnets need not be 14 lines long, but Meredith wrote this in a new form, consisting of four Shakespearean quatrains for a total of 16 lines per sonnet. (The prefatory sonnet appended to the 1892 edition is in the conventional form.) *Modern Love* expresses great bitterness and grimness about the possibilities of love. It is innovative not only in form but in language, style, and narrative presentation. Nevertheless, it takes as its context—as the background against which it displays its innovations—the traditional sonnet sequence in English, most notably Sir Philip Sidney's *Astrophel and Stella* (1581), Spenser's *Amoretti* (1595), and William Shakespeare's sonnets. It is like these predecessors in expressing the speaker's woes, anxieties, and disappointments. He is in love with a woman whose love he cannot plausibly hope to have. The general situation is that which sonnet sequences usually depict: the indifference of the "cruel fair." In Sidney, to take the greatest example, the cruel fair is (conformably to the genre of courtly love poetry) a woman already married who therefore cannot think to take a lover—or at least the lover imagines that this will be her response. But Meredith rings a Shakespearean change on this theme. The cruel figure here is one who has become indifferent to him. It is a break-up sequence (as perhaps Shakespeare's sonnets are as well). The woman he addresses the sonnets to herself turns away to a lover, leaving him bereft and bitter. The sonneteer is not the other man: He is the jealous husband.

The sequence is further complicated by the appearance of a fourth figure—another woman to whom the husband turns, more out of an attempt to get even with his wife than out of true passion or love. Yet this woman also has a real personality, and the sequence must acknowledge her own claims. The situation is intense (as befits the novelist Meredith was) and charged with narrative possibilities. Meredith includes the narrative, too (much as Sidney does), or at least as much of it as is necessary to prevent a reader from imagining that the sequence is simply the expression of his own bitterness. For the speaker of *Modern Love* is presented with a great deal of irony by the sequence itself, and we are not simply supposed to take his side, even if he (the speaker, not Meredith) seems to expect us to. (In this, too, Meredith is writing in Sidney's mode.)

The irony is palpable from the multiple perspectives the sonnet takes on the husband. It begins in the third person, with its great first line: "By this he knew she wept with waking eyes" (sonnet 1, l. 1) Note that it is not Meredith but the *speaker* who is speaking of himself in the third person. He is trying to dissociate himself from his own emotion—from his jealousy and despair—by imagining the situation from a distance. But he cannot sustain that distance: The pose of distance itself betrays the deep involvement it seeks to deny. He cannot sustain it, and so in the third sonnet he switches, momentarily, into the first person. The language and setup make this transition happen fairly imperceptibly, because the third stanza begins by turning to the man, the adulterous lover whose suspected liaison with the wife torments the husband. The male pronouns refer to him, so we do not even notice that he switches to the first person in line 10, and yet that line justifies that very shift: "See that I am drawn to her even now!"

He cannot help his own involvement, and it is interesting to see the different modulations of self-pity depending on the pronoun—depending, that is, on whether the speaker identifies himself more with the self-pitying or the self to be pitied. The latter makes him somewhat more appealing in the end, because it makes him one of the figures of the story less than the figure who judges authoritatively from beneath the third-person mask. He dons that mask a few more times in the next few sonnets, but by the time we get to sonnet 9, we will find that the poem remains pretty consistently in the first person thenceforward.

A more important reason to prefer the first-person formulation is that the rest of the poem becomes more or less an elegy for the death of love. It might be regarded as Meredith's version of ALFRED, LORD TENNYSON's *IN MEMORIAM A.H.H.* The world that the speaker describes is shockingly the same world as it was before love died, just as Tennyson finds the world unchanged from the way it was before ARTHUR HENRY HALLAM died. And yet everything has changed for the speaker, and the outside world, or nature's cruel indifference to this change, accentuates it (see sonnet 13, for example). He has made himself vulnerable by loving too much, and now he discovers that all that is left is his own vulnerability and loss. That might allow him a consolation like *In Memoriam*'s famous claim that "'Tis better to have loved and lost / Than never to have loved at all." But the death of love—unlike the death of the beloved—includes within the grief that it brings the terrible possibility that the love was never real. In sonnet 12, the speaker says that he would be "content" (l. 11) if he could know that the past was real. But he cannot know even that.

If this were all that *Modern Love* depicted, we might regard it as a grand example of a known type of sonnet sequence. But it subsequently becomes far more interesting, from the 14th sonnet on. Here Meredith picks up a theme hinted at in Sidney and Shakespeare: the idea that the anguished poet might, in fact, be the person trifling with the affections of the woman he depicts as the cruel fair. For in sonnet 14 we discover that the speaker has found himself interested in another woman. Is this intentional? Or despite himself? It is both: He wishes to find himself interested in someone else despite himself, because he can blame his wife for that as well—and he does. For the fact that the wife has been adulterous does not mean, we discover, that she does not love him. But it gives him an excuse for not loving her.

This is the deep self-knowledge that Meredith evinces in the sequence, even though his speaker does not have it. The wife's adultery has liberated the husband, enabled both self-righteousness and self-pity, and allowed him complete freedom of action. He cannot wrong her—so he thinks—because it is she who has wronged him. He is the one who betrays the relationship more fundamentally than she ever did. He becomes monstrous, countering her expressions of need for him with evidence of her unfaithfulness (as he does immediately in sonnet 15). Indeed, he admits, again with some huffiness, that he could willingly "hurt her cruelly" (sonnet 19, l. 6)

This is not to deny that he experiences real pain from the failure of their relationship. Breaking up with her is not easy. But he wishes to make the pain her fault, which it is not, exactly or entirely. The depiction of pain is nevertheless one of the subtle glories of the sequence: the sense of regret, of longing for a more innocent past. And then they have to playact in various painful ways since their estrangement from each other is not public yet. One might see in these depictions of their last days of keeping up appearances a foreshadowing of the kind of novel Henry James would write (partly under Meredith's influence), or a recollection of the novelist Samuel Richardson's Lovelace in *Clarissa* (1748), as, for example, in sonnet 27, in which he boastfully confesses that he "must be flattered," and in sonnet 28, where he feels "the promptings of Satanic power" in his relationship to the other woman.

The crucial thing to see about the sequence is that it is in his power to rescue and revive the love gone bad, but he refuses to do so. He uses the other woman—the "lady" he sometimes addresses—as a way out of the marriage, although he has no love for this lady. (*Lady* always refers to the other woman, and the venomously formal *madam* refers to the wife.)

The tragedy, which the speaker wants to imagine is his own, is in fact the wife's. The sequence opens with her feigning sleep as she weeps for the sorrow she has allowed to enter into her life; it recurs to this opening when it represents the husband waking her up, filling her with love till he shows her the evidence of her adultery; it recurs again to sleep when he manages to sleep in the same bed as his wife at a Christmas party at a country house and almost relents from the psychic banishment he has imposed upon her (sonnet 23), and finally ends when she is disappointed in her hopes after she had "believed his old love had returned" (sonnet 49, l. 3), and poisons herself, so that the motif of sleep turns into that of death: "About the middle of the night her call / Was heard, and he came wondering to the bed. / 'Now kiss me, dear! It may be, now!' she said. / Lethe had passed those lips, and he knew all" (sonnet 49, ll. 13–16). He knows what he has done, and she knows that the only way to win his love back is by dying, and so she does.

Does this penultimate sonnet, and the last conclusive sonnet that follows it, represent Meredith's regret for his treatment of Mary? Perhaps after her death he allowed his bitterness to modulate into honesty, or into self-recrimination. At least it led to extraordinary, and genuinely modern, psychological insight.

BIBLIOGRAPHY

Bernstein, Carol L. *Precarious Enchantment: A Reading of Meredith's Poetry*. Washington, D.C.: Catholic University of America Press, 1979.

Bloom, Harold. *The Anxiety of Influence: A Theory of Poetry*. New York: Oxford University Press, 1997.

Neil, Roberts. *Meredith and the Novel*. New York: St. Martin's Press, 1997.

Symons, Arthur. "George Meredith as a Poet." In *Figures of Several Centuries*, 83–89. London: Constable and Company, 1916.

"MODERN MOTHER, THE" **ALICE MEYNELL (1900)** This is one of many poems by ALICE MEYNELL about the experience of maternity. Herself the mother of nine children (one of whom died in infancy) and a suffragette, she felt very intensely the most profound commitment to what might be described as the calling of motherhood, a calling as demanding and perhaps as terrifying as any in the Catholic religion she had converted to at 21. "The Modern Mother" handles with great economy and compression a complex play of perspective. It describes a mother's feeling for her child, a feeling of which one of the largest components is the child's intuition of and response to the mother's feeling. The poem, written when Meynell was 53, probably alludes to her youngest son, Francis (1891–1975), who was nine years old when it was written—the poem alludes to the mother's "nine years' love" (l. 10; Francis would later become a distinguished publisher, and founder of the Nonesuch and Pelican Presses.) The speaker, who never uses the first person, is aware that she is not to be independent and therefore separate from her child. It is a painfully self-limiting vocation, then: The moral demands it makes consist in a kind of abnegation that can never turn itself into fullness or triumph.

But the very painfulness of the situation has its own rewards. The poem describes the kiss the nine-year-old gives his mother. The speaker's breast is "misgiving" (l. 3) probably because she does not know or trust in the success of her love. But it is just the fact that she is feeling these misgivings that elicit her son's beautiful, spontaneous act, running to succor her just because he needs her, and succoring her by needing her. The speaker had thought the most she could hope for was "A little tenderness" (l. 7).

Or perhaps not even that. In lines and thought that echo one of Meynell's favorite poets, George Herbert (1593–1633; an Anglican priest popular with Catholic writers and one whom she would have read in her deeply Anglican youth), she acknowledges the depths of hopelessness that are part and parcel of the vocation of motherhood. For the mother who gives life also thereby gives death, and if she gives peace, she also brings distress. The most she might hope for from the child she has brought into this vale of tears, therefore, might be forgiveness. The fact that this is the most she might hope for is part of what makes this world a vale of tears.

But the child loves her, unconditionally and passionately, and love triumphs over the very separateness which is its condition and which makes it necessary and makes its triumph so precious. The triumph is inevitably ephemeral. He will age, just as she has aged and entered into "this dusk of days" (l. 20). But he forgives her that, too, and in doing so lights up the dusk.

BIBLIOGRAPHY

Badeni, June. *The Slender Tree: A Life of Alice Meynell.* Padstow, Cornwall, England: Tabb House, 1981.

Leighton, Angela. "Alice Meynell." In *Victorian Woman Poets: Writing against the Heart*, 244–265. Charlottesville: University Press of Virginia, 1992.

Meynell, Alice. *Prose and Poetry.* Edited by Frederick Page, et al. London: J. Cape, 1947.

Meynell, Viola. *Alice Meynell: A Memoir.* (London: J. Cape, 1929.

"MONT BLANC" **PERCY BYSSHE SHELLEY (1816)** On July 21, 1816, PERCY BYSSHE SHELLEY, his companion Mary Godwin (who would subsequently marry him), and her half sister Claire Claremont, first saw Mont Blanc, the tallest mountain in Europe. The sight impressed them mightily, so much so that Mary Shelley set the central scene of her novel *Frankenstein* (1818), in which the monster confronts Victor Frankenstein for the first time, on a glacier in the mountains, which she has Frankenstein describe at great length. Percy, too, was stunned by the landscape, and he wrote one the greatest poems of the romantic era (see ROMANTICISM) in response to the experience.

The fiction by which "Mont Blanc" proceeds is that its speaker is addressing the mountain, responding spontaneously to the vision. This is not true, of course, but neither is it altogether false. Shelley's immediate response to Mont Blanc (preserved in a letter to the novelist and poet Thomas Love Peacock) was one of awe, not unlike that which he depicts in the poem, and we can see the few weeks that he took to complete it as an attempt to make the awe he felt as poetically palpable as he could.

The result is as SUBLIME as the mountain it describes. Indeed, "Mont Blanc" may be the great English poem of the sublime, at once a literary or aesthetic experience and an experience of the natural world. Poems that aim at sublimity often do so through a description of landscape (the natural sublime) in language elevated enough to be adequate to the landscape described (the literary sublime). The match between the poem and the landscape it describes can seem obvious. But for Shelley, it is highly problematic, because his view of the sublime is so close to the German philosopher Immanuel Kant's (whom he had read in Latin).

For Kant the sublime was an experience that arose in the mind overwhelmed by a natural landscape and then suddenly recovered a sense of its own power. In the experience of the sublime, said Kant, we feel empirically very small, but just that feeling makes us feel the grandeur of our own minds, able to take in and transcend the very external thing that makes us feel so small. The experience of the sublime is therefore double-sided: The grandeur of what we perceive first makes us feel very small, and then we rebound so that we feel in touch with what is absolutely great in our own souls.

It is this double experience that "Mont Blanc" explores. The poem is subtitled "Lines written in the Vale of Chamouni," the valley from which Shelley's party explored the mountain. And yet the poem begins not with a description of the mountain but with a philosophical claim about the relationship between the mind and the world. To understand the dramatic tension in the poem, it is important to see that the first stanza declares itself as not about the mountain at all, nor about the River Arve, whose source is Mont Blanc, but about the mind itself. But, of course, to say that the first stanza declares itself as not about the mountain means that in some sense it is, since denials are always about what is being denied.

At any rate, what the first stanza says is that the outside world, the world of *things,* is essentially inert until it is perceived by the mind. (This is an idea that WILLIAM WORDSWORTH partially explores in "TINTERN ABBEY," and "Mont Blanc" is in part an explicit response to that poem, especially at lines 37–39.) The universe is always the same, but the perceiving or adverting mind has the power to dissolve the things it perceives into the flow of thought. Thought is therefore a more basic, fluid medium than the physical objects it thinks about, and the flow of the universe through the mind is made possible by the mind's own fluidity. And yet it may be, the poem almost immediately recognizes, that the mind is, in fact, simply the passive recipient of the universe's grandeur. The key to the poem is to understand that the thinking mind is imaged in two ways in the opening stanza. It is both the region through which the perceptible universe flows, and it is a tributary stream to the riparian flow of the universe through the mind. If there are two ideas of the mind competing here, there are two versions of what is beyond human thought: the static external universe itself and the dynamic universe which has subjected almost the entire perceptual apparatus of the human mind to its own power, assimilating it to the external world and leaving only the weakest thought available to an independent human soul ("The source of human thought" [l. 5]).

The question, then, is which has priority, the universe or the mind? This question is almost immediately, and significantly, reframed as the question of which has priority—the *mountain* or the mind? For the universe may be taken to be a weak though grandly named mental abstraction. But the mountain is not abstract: It is concrete and overwhelming, "piercing the infinite sky" of abstraction itself (l. 60). That is to say, its magnitude is such that it is a finitude that overwhelms any abstract concept of the infinite that the human mind might oppose to it. The first reframing of the question suggests that it is the universe that has priority.

The second stanza begins the struggle proper, as we might call it, between mind and mountain. That struggle occurs as Shelley, champion of the mind, attempts to justify one reading of the first stanza, the reading whereby the mountain is a figure—a simile or metaphor—for the structure of the mind. For it is the mind that perceives similes and metaphors: Analogy is a mental operation, not a fact of the outside world. The word *Thus* that begins the second stanza of the poem is a word asserting the priority of the mind's power of analogy to the world analogized; that is to say, Shelley attempts to make the mountain an image of the mind, which would thereby have priority.

But the simile takes over the thing it is supposed to clarify. The description of the mountain overwhelms the use to which it is supposed to be put. The mountain assumes priority over the mind that attempts to describe it; thus, an appositional phrase that works semantically to specify some aspect of the ravine takes over lines 12–19, and the rest of the stanza shows the mountain entirely governing what should have been an account of the human mind. The mind does put in an appearance, finally, at line 34, but it is now entirely overawed by the mountain. Shelley seems to see in the landscape an image of his own mind, but in that very image his mind is only a minute element in the landscape.

Description is the poem's crucial activity. The mountain seems to compel description, but description is an activity of the mind, and accordingly, in the third stanza Shelley attempts, not to resist the magnetism of the mountain in order to concentrate on describing the mind instead, but to match the mountain through the sublimity of his own verbal description. In round three of their struggle for mastery, or what Shelley sees as their struggle for mastery, he gives himself over to a verbal description that will rival the thing it describes.

This tactic initially works—after all, it is Shelley, unexcelled in verbal sublimity, who is doing the describing. The mountain is enlisted at last to a kind of human project just through its grandeur, which overawes everything mean about the human spirit but ratifies everything morally good, everything on the side of moral freedom, repealing "large codes of fraud and woe" (l. 81). The mountain's voice is not understood by all, but it is understood by those who feel and respond to its greatness, so that the power to describe that greatness—the poem's power to do this—is what makes the mountain part of human significance. But just this sense of the meaning of the mountain's grandeur misses its transcendent indifference to the living world, and in the fourth stanza, the fact that the mountain is indifferent to all the description of the third becomes manifest. It does not change, even as our interpretations of it might. The power it embodies "dwells apart in its tranquility / Remote, serene, and inaccessible" (ll. 92–93), and scornful of human power (l. 103). And it appears that by the end of this most sublime of stanzas, the human attempt to match the mountain has failed.

Therefore, the last stanza seems to concede everything to the mountain, which "yet gleams on high" (l.

127), engaged in its own eerily beautiful, indifferent play. It is in this stanza that the poem finally achieves the sudden reversal that Kant saw as the experience of the sublime. Everything about the mountain, everything the human mind concedes to the mountain in being unable either to avoid describing it or to produce an adequate description, is suddenly recognized as the power of the human imagination, but for which the inhuman and eerie silence and solitude of the mountain would be nothing at all, mere vacancy. The mountain's sublimity belongs to the mind that perceives it, and the more overwhelming the mountain seems, the more overwhelming is the imagination that can project this overwhelming power onto it.

BIBLIOGRAPHY

Bloom, Harold. *Genius: A Mosaic of One Hundred Exemplary Creative Minds.* New York: Warner, 2002.

———. *Shelley's Mythmaking.* New Haven, Conn.: Yale University Press, 1959.

———. *The Visionary Company: A Reading of English Romantic Poetry.* Garden City, N.Y.: Doubleday, 1961.

Burke, Kenneth. *Grammar of Motives.* Berkeley: University of California Press, 1969.

Chernaik, Judith. *The Lyrics of Shelley.* Cleveland: Press of Case Western Reserve University, 1972.

Duffy, Edward. *Rousseau in England: The Context for Shelley's Critique of the Enlightenment.* Berkeley: University of California Press, 1979.

Ferguson, Frances. "What the Mountain Said." In *Romanticism and Language,* edited by Arden Reed, 202–214. Ithaca, N.Y.: Cornell University Press, 1984.

Hogle, Jerrold E. *Shelley's Process: Radical Transference and the Development of His Major Works.* New York: Oxford University Press, 1988.

Keach, William. *Shelley's Style.* New York: Methuen, 1984.

Leavis, F. R. *Revaluation: Tradition & Development in English Poetry.* New York: Norton, 1963.

Leighton, Angela. *Shelley and the Sublime: An Interpretation of the Major Poems.* New York: Cambridge University Press, 1984.

Notopolous, James A. *The Platonism of Shelley: A Study of Platonism and the Poetic Mind.* Durham, N.C.: Duke University Press, 1949.

Quinney, Laura. *The Poetics of Disappointment: Wordsworth to Ashbery.* Charlottesville: University Press of Virginia, 1999.

Wasserman, Earl. *Shelley: A Critical Reading.* Baltimore: Johns Hopkins Press, 1971.

———. *Subtler Language: Critical Readings of Neoclassic and Romantic Poems.* Baltimore: Johns Hopkins Press, 1968.

MOORE, THOMAS (1779–1852) Thomas Moore is now best remembered for his *Irish Melodies* (see "The HARP THAT ONCE THROUGH TARA'S HALLS"), which he published in a series of 10 volumes between 1808 and 1834; the music was adapted from Irish songs by Sir John Stevenson. Moore, born in Dublin and a Roman Catholic, made his name in London as a singer as well as a poet, and the *Irish Melodies* continued this lyric and quasi-patriotic mode in him. He had come to London because Dublin was too backward and straitlaced for his poetic exuberance. In London, he studied law and became acquainted with the aristocracy, including the prince of Wales, later the prince regent, who for a while supported the long struggle for Catholic suffrage. When the prince's support cooled, Moore lampooned him, earning him friendship with the liberal opposition polemicist, editor, and writer LEIGH HUNT, who was a friend of so many of the major poets of the day.

When Moore was 24 he was given a government post in Bermuda, but he left the job's administration to an underling whose eventual embezzlement of thousands of pounds was to leave Moore in financial difficulties for the second half of his life. He returned to England (via the United States and Canada) and continued writing poetry. LORD BYRON had made fun of him in his satire "English Bards and Scotch Reviewers" (and mentions him again in *DON JUAN*). As was characteristic of Moore, this led to a deep friendship between the two, and Moore's biography of Byron, to which are appended some letters and journals, was the first and most important of the posthumous accounts of Byron's life.

Moore was most famous for his romance *Lalla Rookh* (1817), written in the wake of Byron and Sir WALTER SCOTT. Byron (also writing in Scott's mode) had published several tales set in the East (which he had visited himself), most notably *Lara* (1814); Scott had written tales of the Border country in England (for example, *MARMION*). Moore wrote in that tradition, where gorgeous strangeness combines with lyricism in a way that, while not entirely original, certainly provides what people want from popular poetry. Like Scott, Moore could allude to issues closer to home—the relationship of Ireland to England, for instance—by setting them in a notional and fantastical Orient.

Moore wrote popular poetry of a very high quality, and the 20th-century writer James Joyce, who had a beautiful singing voice himself, loved Moore's *Irish Melodies.* Byron's *Hebrew Melodies* (1815) are directly influenced by Moore, and a large tradition of poetry as song (the word that WILLIAM BUTLER YEATS consistently used to describe his own poetry) can be traced to Moore's combination of originality with a tradition of timeless and impersonal lyricism. His songs and poems are still widely popular today and have achieved the status they claimed for themselves, songs whose author very few people know, but which are all the more powerful for being timeless and anonymous.

BIBLIOGRAPHY

Colum, Padraic. Introduction to *Anthology of Irish Verse.* New York: Boni and Liveright, 1922, 3–20.

Nolan, Emer. *Catholic Emancipations: Irish Fiction from Thomas Moore to James Joyce.* Syracuse, N.Y.: Syracuse University Press, 2007.

Schirmer, Gregory A. *Out of What Began: A History of Irish Poetry in English.* Ithaca, N.Y.: Cornell University Press, 1998.

White, Terence De Vere. *Tom Moore: The Irish Poet.* London: Hamilton, 1977.

MORRIS, WILLIAM (1834–1896) Everyone knows William Morris now, primarily from his wallpaper and textile designs, endlessly repeated these days in wrapping paper and scarves. In addition to his design work, Morris was a political writer (socialist), book designer and printer, dyer and weaver, painter, prose romancer, and poet, and if his poetry is least remembered now, that is because his other qualities were so prominent. But Morris's poetry is exceedingly powerful and makes him (along with DANTE GABRIEL ROSSETTI) one of the two or three most important of Pre-Raphaelite poets (see PRE-RAPHAELITE POETRY). Morris's works belongs to three different periods: his early, intense lyrics in the book *The Defence of Guinevere and Other Poems,* published in 1858 when he was only 24; the later *Earthly Paradise* (1868–70), a consciously Chaucerian retelling of many of the world's great myths; and the strange retelling of some of the Icelandic legends he was interested in (and helped translate) in *Sigurd the Volsung and the Fall of the Niblungs* (1876), an immense narrative in rhymed 14-line couplets (more or less) which was Morris's own favorite, an opinion shared these days by Harold Bloom.

Morris's interest in medievalism—the stories of Guinevere and of the Hundred Years' War (see "THE HAYSTACK IN THE FLOOD"), the Chaucerian tales of *The Earthly Paradise,* the Icelandic retelling of *Sigurd*—began with his intense reading of Sir WALTER SCOTT when he was a child (Scott, too, excelled in historical romance, both in prose and verse); and then continued with his equally intense reading of JOHN KEATS and ALFRED, LORD TENNYSON when he and his friends were undergraduates. Probably the most important work that Morris did by way of influencing other poets was such early poetry as "The DEFENCE OF GUINEVERE." In that poem, Morris achieved an immensely powerful analytical intensity of style, a detached account of violence, notable for its unsparing and unsentimental realism. This was to be a hallmark of all of Morris's poetry, but it is found most starkly in his early poetry. (Here, too, he learned something of immense importance from Tennyson, especially the unsentimental Tennyson of some of the *Idylls of the King*).

Morris's life was genuinely utopian, which is to say that he put into practice his utopian political ideals, learned from John Ruskin and from Karl Marx (he collaborated with Friedrich Engels and with Marx's daughter Eleanor Marx Aveling). Those ideals involved every aspect of human interaction with the world, from crafts to architecture to poetic composition. Morris was immensely talented in every one of these fields and at spreading his enthusiasm and the taste he formed and furthered. His intense and bitterly undemonstrative early poetry is probably the most surprising aspect of his unparalleled vitality and force.

BIBLIOGRAPHY

Kinna, Ruth. *William Morris: The Art of Socialism.* Cardiff: University of Wales Press, 2000.

Kirchhoff, Frederick. *William Morris: The Construction of a Male Self, 1856–1872.* Athens: Ohio University Press, 1990.

MacCarthy Fiona. *William Morris: A Life for Our Time.* London: Faber, 1995.

Thompson, E. P. *William Morris: Romantic to Revolutionary.* New York: Pantheon, 1977.

Thompson, Paul Richard. *Work of William Morris.* New York: Viking Press, 1967.

"MORTE D'ARTHUR" ("THE DEATH OF ARTHUR") ALFRED, LORD TENNYSON (1842)

This poem, whose title ALFRED, LORD TENNYSON would later translate in the collection of Arthurian poems called *Idylls of the King* (1856–85) as "The Passing of Arthur" (and not, as here, "The Death of Arthur") is the first part he wrote of that long book, and certainly the best. It first appears as one of a series of poems told during a Christmas holiday and framed by the narrator's introduction and conclusion. This work begins and ends with the narrator (Tennyson), a Parson Holmes, a poet named Everard Hall, and their host, Francis Allen, speaking by the fireside on Christmas Eve. In the introductory poem, "The Epic," Francis Allen tells Tennyson about the long poem in 12 books about King Arthur that Everard Hall wrote at Cambridge and then consigned to the fires as what Hall now calls "faint Homeric echoes, nothing-worth, / Mere chaff and draff, much better burnt" (ll. 39–40), which is Tennyson's sly self-deprecation, and interesting in the way it shows that he was already thinking about the possibility of an epic poem about King Arthur (a work not unrelated to Edmund Spenser's The *Faerie Queene* [1590, 1596]). Francis, however, has saved part of the manuscript, the 11th book, which tells of the death of Arthur, and now prevails upon Hall to read it aloud.

The source of Tennyson's story is mainly Sir Thomas Malory's 15th-century digest of Arthurian legends in his *Morte Darthur* (book 21, chapters 3–5). Arthur has just fought his last battle with the his nephew, the treacherous Mordred. Mordred is dead but has mortally wounded Arthur, and the rest of Arthur's knights, except Sir Bedivere and Sir Lucan, have died as well, so it is the end of Camelot, and Arthur is to die. (Sir Lucan dies aiding him to move.)

Tennyson tells the story as a kind of cross between the Bible's Book of Job and an epic by Homer, offering the lulling calm of Homeric repetition, with much allusion to William Shakespeare, especially the play *Hamlet,* mixed in. *Hamlet* is crucial to his thinking, because "Morte d'Arthur" is one of his poems of unslakable grief. The Arthur that mattered most to him, now and throughout his life, was ARTHUR HENRY HALLAM, his closest friend and the object of his greatest love, and the figure memorialized with such pain in *In MEMORIAM A.H.H.* Hallam, who was to have been Tennyson's brother-in-law, had died in 1833 at age 22, and Tennyson's grief was lifelong. "The Death of Arthur" is, then, a poem of mourning, and in fact also a poem of wish fulfillment. Everard Hall seems a version of the ever-ardent Hallam, and the lost epic with its one relic saved from flame seems to express the relation of Hallam's potential work to Tennyson's own. Sir Bedivere, who serves the dying Arthur, seems another version of Tennyson himself, who must dedicate himself to the truth of his own mourning, and his lament, "Ah! My Lord Arthur, whither shall I go?" (l. 226) is a cry from Tennyson's own heart. (Malory's original runs: "Ah my lord Arthur, what shall become of me, now ye go from me and leave me here alone among mine enemies?")

Arthur is a Christ-like figure, and his promised return is what most comforts both Sir Bedivere and Tennyson himself. (In Malory there is no such promise, only some uncertainty about whether Arthur's body is ever found.) Tennyson's hope for heaven was primarily a hope to see the dead again, not to lose them forever. For him, Christmas and the bells that ring at the end of the poem (in its full version) promises that possibility, essential to his hopes in the future. Indeed, in the poem's concluding segment, he dreams of Arthur's return after hearing Hall's recital. He dreams that "there came a bark that, blowing forward, bore / King Arthur, like a modern gentleman / Of stateliest port," and everyone cries with joy that Arthur has returned, this time for good (ll. 344–346). Tennyson's fantasy is that in poetry, at least, he can arrest and perhaps reverse the passage of time away from life and companionship, or at least hasten its return. As in "ULYSSES," where Hallam is represented as "the great Achilles, whom we knew," Tennyson's hope is that the figure reduced to its pure evocation in literature can survive, *through* memory and literature, and come alive again. This means preferring legend to relic; hence, Bedivere must throw the sword away, since it is only through love, and therefore through the minds of those who do love, that we can hope to see the dead again.

See also AYTOUN, WILLIAM EDMONSTOUNE.

BIBLIOGRAPHY

Armstrong, Isobel. *Victorian Poetry: Poetry, Poetics and Politics.* New York: Routledge, 1993.

Bloom, Harold. *Poetry and Repression: Revisionism from Blake to Stevens.* New Haven, Conn.: Yale University Press, 1976.

Buckley, Jerome Hamilton. *Tennyson: The Growth of a Poet.* Boston: Houghton Mifflin, 1965.

Kilham, John. *Critical Essays on the Poetry of Tennyson.* New York: Barnes and Noble, 1960.

Kincaid, James R. *Tennyson's Major Poems: The Comic and Ironic Patterns.* New Haven, Conn.: Yale University Press, 1975.

Ricks, Christopher B. *Tennyson.* New York: Macmillan, 1972.

Rowlinson, Matthew. *Tennyson's Fixations: Psychoanalysis and the Topics of the Early Poetry.* Charlottesville: University Press of Virginia, 1994.

Tucker, Herbert: *Tennyson and the Doom of Romanticism.* Cambridge, Mass.: Harvard University Press, 1988.

MOTTOES (EPIGRAPHS) Mottoes, or epigraphs, are the short quotations found at the beginning of some poems; they can also grace title pages or chapter headings. Mottoes are often apt quotations from other works—for example: WILLIAM WORDSWORTH's quotation of Virgil starting off the INTIMATIONS ODE, SAMUEL TAYLOR COLERIDGE's of "the Ballad of Sir Patrick Spens" at the head of "DEJECTION: AN ODE," and ALFRED, LORD TENNYSON's quotation of Horace that leads off his "Parnassus." Sometimes they are from the poet's own earlier work (Wordsworth also quotes "MY HEART LEAPS UP" at the beginning of the Intimations Ode); they are sometimes in a foreign (usually classical) language, such as PERCY BYSSHE SHELLEY's Greek motto to *ADONAIS,* sometimes in the language of the poem; and sometimes, perhaps most interestingly, they are made up and falsely ascribed. Thus, Sir WALTER SCOTT often quoted from what he calls an "old play," and Tennyson and GEORGE ELIOT followed suit. Their interest derives from the way they represent a poetic facet—that which can appear out of context and which may in fact be better out of context or can only exist out of context. When asked why he did not extend his invented mottoes into full works, Scott replied, "Nothing so easy, when you are full of an author, as to write a few lines in his taste and style; the difficulty is to keep it up—besides, the greatest success would be but a spiritless imitation, or, at best, what the Italians call a *centone* from Shakespeare." The spirit, then, is in the quasi-anonymity of the motto, the sense that what one is getting is what survives and transcends context, so that it is like perceiving the mystery of poetry itself.

Mottoes have an interesting history, arising from two different sources. It was the practice of preachers to assemble texts for sermons by gathering related biblical quotations on some spiritual or doctrinal point. These quotations took on an out-of-context authority and were often treated on their own. A bit later, the French and Italian interest in coins and medals led to a great interest in devices and emblems, first used on pennants and shields in battle and then codified in coats of arms but also in iconographic representations such as publishers' colophons. These related icons usually had mottoes, and the great motto theorists of the 16th and 17th centuries made it a point of aesthetic skill to have the quotations mean something different on the emblem than they meant in their original context. Thus, the choice of a good motto was highly artful, as the choice of a good text for a sermon was artful for a preacher.

In the early 18th century, essay writers, notably Joseph Addison (1672–1719) and Richard Steele (1672–1729) in the *Spectator,* began affixing mottoes to their essays. Ann Radcliffe (1764–1823) did the same in her gothic fiction, placing mottoes at the heads of chapters, and their gothic feel came partly from a sense of unmoored and inhuman spookiness. The English romantic poets followed this practice, but not as much as the French romantics did. Through the French, mottoes became widespread throughout the 19th century, and they continue to be ubiquitous today. In English, throughout the 19th century, mottoes were more often used for prose than for poetry, but they allowed for a contrast of the poetic with the prosaic, a contrast that underlines and makes palpable the extent to which 19th-century poetry is about the distinction between the poem and its context, and this distinction mirrors the subjectivity that is the glory of 19th-century English poetry.

BIBLIOGRAPHY

Gennette, Gerard. *Paratexts: Thresholds of Interpretation*. New York: Cambridge University Press, 1997.

Jackson, Kevin. *Invisible Forms: A Guide to Literary Curiosities*. London: Picador, 1999.

Praz, Mario. *Studies in Seventeenth-Century Imagery*. 2 vols. London: The Warburg Institute, 1939–1947.

Price, Leah. *Anthology and the Rise of the Novel from Richardson to George Eliot*. New York: Cambridge University Press, 2000.

Russell, Daniel S. *The Emblem and Device in France*. Lexington, Ky:. French Forum, 1985.

Segermann, Krista. *Das Motto in der Lyrik: Funktion und Form der "ipigraphe" vor Gedichten der französischen Romantik sowie der nachromantischen Zeit*. Munich: Fink, 1977.

"MOUSE'S NEST" JOHN CLARE (ca. 1832)

"Mouse's Nest" shows JOHN CLARE at his most delightful and most disarming. Clare probably knew more about the details of nature than any other of the romantic poets, even those most devoted to the service of nature, and it is part of the naturalism of this poem that one cannot tell from the poem alone whether Clare is remembering Robert Burns's famous "To a Mouse" or not (he is: he was always compared to Burns as the "peasant poet"). He was a laborer in the fields from an early age, and when he obtained more leisure, first because of his success and then because of the forced inaction of his confinement for insanity, he could continue his intense, naturalist's scrutiny of the natural world around him.

The plot of "Mouse's Nest" is almost trivial—but not for the mouse. Clare is walking the fields and finds a ball of grass. He pokes at it, and the sudden motion that he sees makes him think he has a chance to catch a bird, but it turns out to be a mouse's nest; the mouse bolts, the brood she is nursing still attached to her. Pure curiosity makes Clare look for her where she has gone, and once again she bolts, this time leaving her young behind. At this point, the important fact, deceptively understated in a subordinate clause, is that he goes away to leave the mouse alone. He has recognized that she has left her brood not in order to escape the danger that he represents, even while abandoning them to it, but in order to distract his attention from them. This act of courage and self-sacrifice is enough for him, and he knows that she is returning to her nest and her brood, and that the disaster his story might have meant for her does not occur.

It is striking to compare Clare to WILLIAM WORDSWORTH here. Wordsworth's observer-narrators tend to be both central and more or less invisible. They are the center of their own brooding, and the natural world is a catalyst for this brooding. (This is what LEWIS CARROLL parodied in Wordsworth in "The Knight's Song," or "A-sitting on a Gate.") Wordsworth may have the knowledge of a naturalist, but he does not convey it. He is interested in nature, even in mountains, but not in mice. The kind of Clare poem that "Mouse's Nest" exemplifies beautifully focuses on a natural object. Clare himself is important to the poem—he disturbs the mouse, his observation harries it, he finally leaves it in peace—but he is important not as a central subjective intelligence for whom all this has taken place. He is, rather, another natural being. It is not that Clare is uninterested in the great romantic question of isolated subjectivity—consider his "I AM" poems. But Clare's accurate view of the human subject also recognizes him as a natural being akin to the mouse, and so he goes away from the mouse, not with some other intense subjective focus to pursue but as a natural being moving around in nature. We know this from the wonderful last two lines which describe the world around Clare, the world of which he is a very small part, neither a major presence nor an absence but simply a denizen, like the mouse and like everything else.

BIBLIOGRAPHY

Bate, Jonathan. *John Clare: A Biography*. London: Picador, 2003.

Chirico, Paul. *John Clare and the Imagination of the Reader*. New York: Palgrave Macmillan, 2007.

Martin, Frederick. *The Life of John Clare*. London: Macmillan, 1865.

"MUSIC, WHEN SOFT VOICES DIE"

See "TO ———."

"MUSICAL INSTRUMENT, A" ELIZABETH BARRETT BROWNING (1862) This poem shows ELIZABETH BARRETT BROWNING at her most authoritative but also at her subtlest. Like much 19th-century poetry—written under the influence of ROMANTICISM, which took poetic vocation as its subject—"A Musical Instrument" is partly about the nature of poetry itself. The poem narrates a kind of Ovidian story about how Pan invented the flute, the pipes that he plays on, which have been associated with pastoral poetry from antiquity.

The form of the poem is hypnotically repetitious. It is written in seven stanzas of six lines each. The first line of all but one of these stanzas ends with the words "the great god Pan," the second with a reference to "the river" where he fashions the reed into the pipe he plays on. The third line rhymes with "Pan," for a total of five different rhymes in five stanzas; the rhyme "man" appears twice, and "Pan" rhymes with itself once, and significantly. The fourth and fifth line of each stanza form a unique and unrepeated couplet, and then the sixth and final line of each stanza repeats the reference to "the river" that the third line introduces.

The plot of the poem is simple: Pan, the goat-footed god of satyrs, sexuality, and shepherds (and source of our word *panic,* which is what he can produce in sentient beings) comes to the river "Spreading ruin and scattering ban." He does this because he splashes into the river to tear out a reed, thus disturbing the natural order of things, breaking and killing the golden lilies, muddying the waters, and scaring away the beautiful dragonfly that was hovering there. He does this in order to take a reed, strip it of its signs of life, dry it out, and turn it into a shell of its living self, notched with holes so that it becomes a pipe. Pan is triumphant about his depredations, declaring this to be the only way "To make sweet music," which he plays on the pipe.

Then comes the anomalous stanza mentioned above:

> Sweet, sweet, sweet, O Pan!
> Piercing sweet by the river!
> Blinding sweet, O great god Pan!
> The sun on the hill forgot to die,
> And the lilies revived, and the dragon-fly
> Came back to dream on the river.

Pan's music is so sweet that the first line of the stanza changes from the typical nine-syllabled "What was he doing, the great god Pan," to the intense, all-stressed five syllable repetition of his sweetness. (The number of stresses is always five, but here there are no unstressed syllables.) The sweetness of his music comes from the harm he caused at the river. Poetry, on this reading, seems to compensate for the harm it causes and derives from through its own sweetness: The sun shines, the lilies revive, even the dragonfly returns.

But the compensation is false: The true gods, unlike the satyr Pan, recognize the cost and pain of this creation. Pan stands for a relentlessly cloying sweetness, but at the expense of the "reed which grows nevermore again / As a reed with the reeds of the river." The repetition of the word *reed* here contrasts subtly with the repetitions of *sweet* and *Pan* in the previous stanza: The reeds are not or should not be aggregated into a kind of pounding insistence but simply live at a proper and humane distance from each other, as companions but not as purveyors of a corrupt sweetness. Browning is thinking here of Pascal's definition of the human being as "a thinking reed." What makes poetry is the destruction of the everyday life that makes us human: It is pain and also sexuality.

Browning shared the Victorian distrust of sexuality and of the pain it could bring. The sweetness that the priapic Pan produces with his phallic pipe is the piercing sweetness of orgasm, expressed in the iterated cries "Sweet, sweet, sweet, O Pan!" This sexuality is, for Browning, what makes a human "half a beast" and not the transcendent being that the "true gods" represent. The reed becomes a phallic symbol and not the chaste companion of the other reeds in the river. The same human tendency that leads to poetry leads to sexual abasement and beastliness, and this Swiftian conclusion is a painful one. The sweetness of poetry is also what should make us distrust it. Poetry always risks being close to degradation.

BIBLIOGRAPHY

Armstrong, Isobel. *Victorian Poetry: Poetry, Poetics and Politics.* New York: Routledge, 1993.

Bloom, Harold. *A Map of Misreading.* New York: Oxford University Press, 2003.

Bristow, Joseph, ed. *Victorian Women Poets: Emily Bronte, Elizabeth Barrett Browning, Christina Rossetti.* Houndsville, Basingstoke, England: Macmillan Press, 1995.
DeVane, William C. *A Browning Handbook.* New York: Appleton-Century-Crofts, 1955.
Donaldson, Sandra, ed. *Critical Essays on Elizabeth Barrett Browning.* New York: G. K. Hall, 1999.
Mason, Emma. *Women Poets of the Nineteenth Century.* Tavistock, Devon, England: Northcote House Publishers, 2006.

"MY DAYS AMONG THE DEAD" ROBERT SOUTHEY (1818) This is one of ROBERT SOUTHEY's best-known poems, partly because of its inclusion in Francis Palgrave's *Golden Treasury of English Songs and Lyrics* (1869)—an unsurprising choice on Palgrave's part because the poem is about collecting and admiring the literary works of the dead. The poem displays Southey's characteristic strengths as well as weaknesses: the strengths that made him poet laureate (after Sir WALTER SCOTT refused the honor) and the weaknesses that made him an object of derision for younger poets such as LORD BYRON and PERCY BYSSHE SHELLEY.

Southey was a considerable and influential historian and one of the most intensely bookish of poets (the author Thomas De Quincey called him "the most industrious of all literary men on record," and the essayist Hazlitt criticized the way "Study serves him for business, exercise, recreation") The range and detail of his writing testify to his vast library and the learning he accumulated through his obsessive reading. His friends ascribed the mental breakdown of his later years to overwork. "My Days among the Dead" shows that Southey had something of a sense of this propensity and the dangers it might incur.

In the poem, he passes his days among the dead (we would now write the first line as "My days among the dead are passed"), which is to say that he spends his days in his study, surrounded by the great books of the past, "The mighty minds of old" (l. 4). His study is so crammed with their works that he sees them wherever he looks.

The great first line suggests Southey's awareness that there is something deeply unnatural about this experience, that it is contrary to an affirmation of life. Where WILLIAM WORDSWORTH, his friend and fellow member of the LAKE POETS, had urged the scholar to "quit your books" in "The Tables Turned" (ca. 1800) since book learning is "a dull and endless strife," devoted to the study of "barren leaves," Southey takes a perverse pride in just this soil and strife. Life is ephemeral, but the dead are eternal, and therefore spending his days with them is a way of making a difficult commitment to the aspect of eternity and not that of time.

The dead offer some escape from the reality of daily life, and while Southey seems to be offering a symmetry of "weal" and "woe" in the second stanza, it is clear that the weal comes from the possibility of spending his days with them, while the woe whose immediacy he escapes in devoting himself to his books is the woe of real life. It is for this reason that the poem modulates the variation of its first line as it does: His days are passed among the dead; his thoughts are only with the dead (l. 13); and finally, most shockingly, his hopes are with the dead (l. 19). This is a Southeyan version of Wordsworth's striking claim that he "dares to hope" for some benefit from the future in "TINTERN ABBEY," but Southey's hopes are the expressions of despair. He will be with the dead "anon," and there is nothing to be done about it, except to hope that he will be remembered as they are.

The human problem (and the poem's virtue) is that Southey does not think of the dead as living, the way poets of far greater vitality, like Wordsworth or Byron, do; he thinks of the living as already just about dead, himself first and foremost. Thus, the trust he has that his name will not perish communicates no joy or relief but, rather, a sense that an unperishing name—the most one can hope for—means very little indeed: It is the name of someone already all but dead.

BIBLIOGRAPHY

Bromwich, David. "Of the Mule Breed." *London Review of Books* (May 21, 1998). Available online. URL: www.lrb.co.uk/v20/n0/brom01_.html. Accessed March 16, 2009.
Butler, Marilyn. *Romantics, Rebels, and Reactionaries: English Literature and its Background, 1760–1830.* New York: Oxford University Press, 1982.
De Quincey, Thomas. *Recollections of the Lakes and the Lake Poets.* Edited by David Wright. Harmondsworth, England: Penguin, 1970.
Hazlitt, William. *Spirit of the Age; or, Contemporary Portraits.* London: Oxford University Press, 1970.

Perry, Seamus. "Self-Management." *London Review of Books* 28, no. 2 (January 26, 2006). Available online by subscription. URL: www.lrb.co.uk. Accessed March 16, 2009.

Storey, Mark. *Robert Southey: A Life.* New York: Oxford University Press, 1997.

"MY HEART LEAPS UP" WILLIAM WORDSWORTH (1802) This poem is probably WILLIAM WORDSWORTH's most famous lyric of the "natural piety" which he believed one owed to nature—to the natural world that tutors and succors the unjaded human heart and gives it the joys of solitude, joys sometimes SUBLIME and sometimes beautiful. Wordsworth says in *The PRELUDE* that he grew up fostered "by beauty and by fear," and by the sublime as well, and the rainbow is one of the few natural phenomena that exemplify both the sublime and the beautiful, the awe-inspring as well as the harmonious. The poem, short as it is, combines the emotions appropriate to both: the spontaneous gladness that Wordsworth feels in perceiving the beauty of the rainbow, but also the deeply sworn vow to feel this way forever, "or let me die" (l. 6). Death is present in the poem, not only as a penalty Wordsworth risks but as the end of the sequence the poem goes through: being a boy, being a man, growing old, after which would come death, the avoidance of which he swears by.

The poem should obviously be compared to "I WANDERED LONELY AS A CLOUD," where his "heart with pleasure fills / And dances with the daffodils." Wordsworth wrote that poem two years later, but in both the sudden appearance of some dazzling natural phenomenon fills him with immediate joy but also sets him reflecting on the passage of time and the emotional vicissitudes that passage brings with it. Beneath those vicissitudes is a continuity. He keeps faith with the spontaneity of nature and therefore keeps faith with himself and with his sense of nature's truthfulness to him. The rainbow, sign of God's covenant with Noah, is for him a symbol of a covenant and commitment to stay the same till he dies.

But it may sound as though there is something wishful, even anxious about the poem. The spontaneity it asserts should not need assertion. There is a hint of fear here that his heart may *not* continue to leap up; he wants to feel that his whole life will be continuous with its earliest, most intense, least skeptical phase, but he cannot be sure that this is true. The idea that "The Child is father of the Man" (l. 7), which GERARD MANLEY HOPKINS memorably parodied in his triolet "The CHILD IS FATHER TO THE MAN, betrays a strong desire to feel that he need not worry about what he is, in fact, worrying about: that the rainbow no longer really awakens such ebullience in him. And indeed, in the INTIMATIONS ODE, Wordsworth would write of how the coming and going of the rainbow no longer moved him, since he no longer felt continuous with his own childhood self. Nevertheless, he set the last three lines of "My heart leaps up" as an epigraph, or motto (see MOTTOES), to the Intimations Ode, with the purpose of showing the relation to nature characteristic of childhood but so fragile in adulthood. The question in Wordsworth, here as always, is whether spontaneity of response or pensive and considered meditation conduces to great poetry the emotion or the tranquility of its recollection (to use the famous terms of the preface to *Lyrical Ballads* [1798]). He *could* wish his days to be bound each to each, but perhaps they are not so bound; perhaps, indeed, such a wish would come true only at the expense of the unmet desires and the loss his greatest poem's lament.

BIBLIOGRAPHY

Abrams, M. H. *Natural Supernaturalism: Tradition and Revolution in Romantic Literature.* New York: Norton, 1973.

Bloom, Harold. *The Visionary Company: A Reading of English Romantic Poetry.* Garden City, N.Y.: Doubleday, 1961.

Bromwich, David. *Disowned by Memory: Wordsworth's Poetry of the 1790s.* Chicago: University of Chicago Press, 1998.

Empson, William. *Seven Types of Ambiguity.* New York: New Directions, 1966.

Hartman, Geoffrey. "The Question of Our Speech." In *The Geoffrey Hartman Reader,* edited by Daniel T. O'Hara, 321–347. Edinburgh: Edinburgh University Press, 2004.

———. *Wordsworth's Poetry, 1787–1814.* New Haven, Conn.: Yale University Press, 1971.

Liu, Alan. *Wordsworth: The Sense of History.* Stanford, Calif.: Stanford University Press, 1989.

Pinch, Adela. *Strange Fits of Passion: Epistemologies of Emotion, Hume to Austen.* Stanford, Calif.: Stanford University Press, 1996.

Quinney, Laura. *The Poetics of Disappointment: Wordsworth to Ashbery*. Charlottesville: University Press of Virginia, 1999.

Wolfson, Susan J. *Questioning Presence: Wordsworth, Keats, and the Interrogative Mode in Romantic Poetry*. Ithaca, N.Y.: Cornell University Press, 1986.

"MY LAST DUCHESS" ROBERT BROWNING (1842) "My Last Duchess" is ROBERT BROWNING's most famous dramatic monologue. The form, which Browning perfected, is based on Shakespearean soliloquy (as is made more or less explicit in "SOLILOQUY IN A SPANISH CLOISTER"): A single character speaks, but within a dramatic situation that can be worked out through an attentive reading. The genius of the form, which Browning also used in many other poems—including "Andrea Del Sarto," "A TOCCATA OF GALUPPI'S," and most notably in the 12 monologues by 11 speakers making up the book-length *The RING AND THE BOOK*—is in the way characters can be made to impart information they do not know they are imparting, and may not know at all.

This latter is not true of "My Last Duchess," whose speaker, the duke of Ferrara, knows the truth about what he has done very well indeed. In this case Browning actually gives the prefix *Ferrara* to the speech, although this is not his usual practice. The speaker is based on the 16th-century duke Alfonso II of Ferrara, whose young wife Lucrezia died after three years of marriage. Here he is negotiating with the agent of a count (historically the count of Tyrol, though Browning simplifies the situation slightly) to marry the count's daughter. The poem represents an incident of crafty courtesy during these negotiations: The Duke is showing his art collection to the agent, and they come to a curtained painting whose curtain he draws. The fact that he does so indicates the courtesy he is showing his guest. The painting is of his dead wife, "My last Duchess," since he intends for there to be a next one. He is very proud of the painting, in which his late wife looks very beautiful. The Duke has exquisite taste and can point out the most subtle touches of the painting, including "the faint / Half-flush that dies along her throat" (ll. 18–19). What we come to learn, overhearing him talk, is that he has had her killed (and perhaps the painter, Fra Pandolf, as well), which is why he is now free to marry the count's daughter.

One important question in the poem is how much Ferrara knows he is communicating. Certainly he knows that he has used his power to thwart his wife and is telling the emissary this. He presents himself as justifiably jealous of his wife's relationship with the painter, as well as justifiably irritated in general with her indiscriminate attitude toward the things she took an interest in. The painter was one of those things, but so were the other inoffensive pleasures of life: a bough of cherries, sunset, her white mule. Ferrara voices his contempt for her unaristocratic enthusiasm for these things; eventually he had her silenced: "Then all smiles stopped together."

What is not clear is the extent to which Ferrara knows himself. Is he jealous of her relationship with the painter? He certainly imagines that something went on between them, when he says that everyone who has seen the painting

> . . . seemed as they would ask me, if they durst,
> How such a glance came there; so, not the first
> Are you to turn and ask thus. Sir, 'twas not
> Her husband's presence only, called that spot
> Of joy into the Duchess' cheek: perhaps
> Frà Pandolf chanced to say, "Her mantle laps
> Over my Lady's wrist too much," or "Paint
> Must never hope to reproduce the faint
> Half-flush that dies along her throat"; such stuff
> Was courtesy, she thought, and cause enough
> For calling up that spot of joy. . . .

We know that he does imagine this because he was sure to be present for the painting—he did not trust them to be alone together—and because he thought he saw more than she did into the painter's motivations. And he also thinks that he can read the expression of those who view the paintings, who do not dare to voice their thoughts. Like Leonato in William Shakespeare's *A Winter's Tale*, Ferrara thinks the fact that no one suggests anything untoward about the depiction of his wife is a sign that they do not *dare* to broach the terrible subject.

But we do not know the extent to which he is really jealous, and the extent to which he is using jealousy as a convenient excuse. The most chilling moment in the poem is the subtle rhetorical turn he uses to justify his actions. A rhetorical question leads to an obvious answer, but because the answer is obvious and not argued for, it becomes unexpectedly ambiguous:

> . . . Who'd stoop to blame
> This sort of trifling? Even had you skill
> In speech—(which I have not)—to make your will
> Quite clear to such an one, and say, "Just this
> Or that in you disgusts me; here you miss,
> Or there exceed the mark"—and if she let
> Herself be lessoned so, nor plainly set
> Her wits to yours, forsooth, and made excuse,
> —E'en then would be some stooping; and I choose
> Never to stoop. . . .

Ferrara's hilarious assertion that he has no skill in speech is, of course, belied by this very passage. The trick behind it is this: Because we all agree that blaming the innocent and trifling behavior of the duchess would be beneath him, we agree with him for not blaming her, not saying just what "disgusts" him in her actions. But it turns out that not blaming means doing something far worse than blaming, because for Ferrara *blaming* means speaking to her of displeasure; not speaking means commanding her death. It does not mean what it should—indifference, let alone trust; it means a rage that nothing less than her death can assuage.

But the question still remains of how much of this Ferrara wants the count's emissary to know. When he says that he wants to marry the count's daughter for herself, we know that it is actually for her dowry—he practically says so. And he regards her, chillingly, as an "object"—that is, both an objective and a possession (like the works of art that he shows his visitor). Does he know that he is saying this? He might if part of the point between the two men is a kind of Machiavellian knowledge of how things work. The duke is staking out a clear position within the negotiations: he will offer the count alliance with a 900-year-old name as long as the count assures an ample dowry as well as continued support. But the alliance also means—and this is perhaps what Ferrara wants to make clear—that he will have his daughter as a kind of hostage. He expects the count to continue his munificence and is confident that the alliance will be worth it to the count.

The one thing we can be sure that Ferrara does not appreciate is his last Duchess herself. He feels sufficiently justified in his treatment of her not to see that to *our* eyes, or to the eyes of any impartial observer (which the emissary may not be), the dead woman is wonderful: spontaneous, loving, appreciative of the natural world and of unassuming objects in a way that comes closer to her heart than any appreciation of his art objects comes to his. With all his subtlety and acquisitiveness, he has lost not only the capacity for pleasure but the capacity to recognize innocence and guilelessness. He lives within a realm of guile, and while guile itself may be part of the way he seeks to present himself—while he may be paradoxically open about being guileful—he has lost all sense of what true frankness and candor would be. But just because he has lost it, he communicates that sense to us.

"My Last Duchess" is a poem that many people do not realize is written in rhyming couplets. The conversational tone is so natural, the style so urbane, that none of the artificial diction that rhyme usually seems to force on a poet mars this poem. The hiddenness of the rhyme is essential to its point. Its beauty and ease—and the fact that the speaker (who has no "skill in speech") does not recognize the form he conveys—makes of the rhyme a kind of allegory of the dead woman. It is there, conveyed by what the duke says, lovely and graceful, though without the duke's knowledge. But Browning knows, and we know.

BIBLIOGRAPHY

Bloom, Harold. *A Map of Misreading.* New York: Oxford University Press, 2003.

———. *Poetry and Repression: Revisionism from Blake to Stevens.* New Haven, Conn.: Yale University Press, 1976.

DeVane, William C. *A Browning Handbook.* New York: Appleton-Century-Crofts, 1955.

Langbaum, Robert Woodrow. *The Modern Spirit: Essays on the Continuity of Nineteenth- and Twentieth-Century Literature.* New York: Oxford University Press, 1970.

Raymond, William O. *The Infinite Moment, and Other Essays in Robert Browning.* Toronto: University of Toronto Press, 1965.

N

NAPOLEON BONAPARTE (1769–1821)

One of the world historical figures chained to the chariot of life in PERCY BYSSHE SHELLEY's *The TRIUMPH OF LIFE* is Napoleon Bonaparte, perhaps the single most towering figure of the 19th century. His rise and fall obsessed the Western world. As a French general, "first consul" (the Roman title he revived when he became the most powerful person in France), and emperor, he came close to conquering the whole of Europe and much of the Mediterranean. In the course of his career, he invaded, among other territories, Egypt, Italy, Spain, Portugal, Austria, present-day Germany, and (most disastrously) Russia. At one point he was also on the verge of invading England, which was, with Russia, the power most responsible for his containment and fall.

Napoleon was the center of all political discourse for the first decade and a half of the 19th century and an object of obsession in all the arts. Think of Jacques-Louis David's famous painting of Napoleon crossing the Alps; Ludwig van Beethoven's *Emperor* Concerto and *Eroica* Symphony; Pyotr Ilich Tchaikovsky's *1812 Overture*; G. W. F. Hegel's stunned illumination on the nature of what he called Absolute Spirit and its desires when Napoleon marched below his window at Jena; and, preeminently, the great literary works that took Napoleon and his ambitions as central themes. The French author Stendhal, the Russian novelist Lev Tolstoy, WILLIAM THACKERAY (who met him as a child when Napoleon was in his final exile in St. Helena) and LORD BYRON set climactic scenes on Napoleonic battlefields. The war in *War and Peace* is the war of Napoleon against Russia.

For the English romantics (see ROMANTICISM), Napoleon was the most prominent example of their exploration of the dialectic between freedom and power. Liberation seems to require power—that is the power that manifests itself as prophetic and revolutionary, since to be prophetic is to prophesy that everything will change utterly, that the order of things or of the mind's relation to things will undergo revolutionary upheaval. But power also seems to mean power *over* one's inferiors. Romantic aspiration always means something close to the aspiration of John Milton's Satan (*Paradise Lost*), where freedom means greatness and greatness means superiority to every other being, so that freedom becomes transformed into oppression.

The first generation of romantics saw in Napoleon a model and a warning. WILLIAM BLAKE painted him grasping the sun and moon but chained to the earth. SAMUEL TAYLOR COLERIDGE called Napoleon a "commanding genius" in an analysis of the distinction between that term and "absolute genius." WILLIAM WORDSWORTH was prompted to write the sonnets that became his most frequent mode by reading Milton and writing a Miltonic lament, as early as 1801, on Bonaparte's yielding to the temptations of power. Coleridge's "absolute genius" would be Wordsworthian—freedom within one's own soul rather than freedom mediated by externalities such as power over others. But Wordsworth himself, under the influence of Coleridge, internalized the idea of Napoleonic grandeur as found most fully not in political power but in nature and in the human mind, which transcended the very nature to which it ascribed such grandeur. Wordsworth compared Napoleonic greatness to mountain greatness, explicitly in *The Excursion* and implicitly (as the scholar Alan Liu has argued) in *The PRELUDE*.

For the younger romantics, Napoleon might be compared but also contrasted with Prometheus, the central symbol of revolutionary heroism in both Shelley and Byron (and perhaps in Mary Shelley as well). Byron analyzes Napoleon at some length in *CHILDE HAROLD'S PILGRIMAGE*, where he describes his tour of Waterloo (Napoleon's final loss), having earlier given a powerful account of Napoleon's titanic ambition: "*there* hath been thy bane; there is a fire / And motion of the soul which will not dwell / its own narrow being, but aspire / Beyond the fitting medium of desire" (III, ll. 371–374). (Sir WALTER SCOTT rightly suspected that Byron continued to harbor admiration for Napoleon, as in the quasi-identification he testifies to in these lines, as well as in *DON JUAN*, where he affects amusement at his reputation as "the grand Napoleon of the realms of rhyme" [XI, stanza 55, l. 8]; *Don Juan* represents, Byron says, his defeat and displacement from his status as the world's leading poet). What Byron says of Lambro in *Don Juan* applies as well to Napoleon: a sense of the wrongs suffered by his country "had stung him from a slave to an enslaver" (*Don Juan* III, stanza 53, l. 8). So, too, had Napoleon been a Republican hero early on, offering liberation to the subjects of the European monarchies before making himself the would-be greatest monarch of the age and putting his relatives on the thrones of the countries he had rendered dependencies.

Both Shelley and Byron drew on the legend of Prometheus in seeking to imagine a liberating hero for humanity who would embody all the idealism that Napoleon once seemed to represent, without that idealism turning into its own opposite through pride. Shelley's great "Lines on Hearing the News of the Death of Napoleon" has Mother Earth speaking of Napoleon much as she speaks of Prometheus in his *PROMETHEUS UNBOUND*. In the preface to that poem, Shelley contrasts Prometheus with Satan, who is not, he says, "exempt from the taints of ambition, envy, revenge, and a desire for personal aggrandizement, which, in the Hero of *Paradise Lost*, interfere with the interest. The character of Satan," he goes on, and he may still be speaking of Napoleon, "engenders in the mind a pernicious casuistry which leads us to weigh his faults with his wrongs, and to excuse the former because the latter exceed all measure." For the revolutionary aspirations of the romantic poets, Napoleon was, like Milton's Satan, both a visionary example and formidable warning, showing both the sublimity and the tremendous collapse of idealism that the human soul is capable of reaching and of suffering.

BIBLIOGRAPHY

Asprey, Robert. *The Reign of Napoleon Bonaparte*. New York: Basic Books, 2002.

———. *The Rise of Napoleon Bonaparte*. New York: Basic Books, 2001.

Bloom, Harold. "Napoleon and Prometheus: The Romantic Myth of Organic Energy." *Yale French Studies* 26 (1960): 79–82.

Liu, Alan. *Wordsworth: The Sense of History*. Stanford, Calif.: Stanford University Press, 1989.

NEGATIVE CAPABILITY This was a phrase coined by JOHN KEATS in a letter to his brothers dated December 21, 1817 (when he was 22 years old). The passage that the phrase comes from is worth quoting at greater length:

> . . . it struck me what quality went to form a Man of Achievement, especially in Literature, and which Shakespeare possessed so enormously—I mean Negative Capability, that is, when a man is capable of being in uncertainties, mysteries, doubts, without any irritable reaching after fact and reason—Coleridge, for instance, would let go by a fine isolated verisimilitude caught from the Penetralium of mystery, from being incapable of remaining content with half-knowledge. This pursued through volumes would perhaps take us no further than this, that with a great poet the sense of Beauty overcomes every other consideration, or rather obliterates all consideration.

The passage is helpful both to an understanding of Keats's attitude toward William Shakespeare, whom he took as a model more than any other poet, and of his persistent stance toward the various inspirations and subjects of his odes. Negative capability is what SAMUEL TAYLOR COLERIDGE lacked: the ability to let poetry be suggestive rather than conclusive.

Juxtaposing other passages from Keats's letters helps to provide a context for this one. In a letter to J. H. Reynolds six months later, Keats wrote:

> . . . axioms in philosophy are not axioms until they are proved upon our pulses. . . . This Chamber of Maiden Thought [where poets begin their poetic life] becomes gradually darken'd and at the same time on all sides of it many doors are set open—but all dark—all leading to dark passages—We see not the balance of good and evil. We are in a Mist—We are now in that state—We feel the "burden of the Mystery." To this point was Wordsworth come, as far as I can conceive when he wrote "Tintern Abbey" and it seems to me that his Genius is explorative of those dark Passages.

The phrase "burden of the Mystery" is taken from "TINTERN ABBEY," and Keats's praise of WILLIAM WORDSWORTH here contrasts with his rebuke of Coleridge for not being able to accept the mystery *as* mystery, for insisting on attempting to plumb its depth. The burden is that life should remain a mystery, that at best we will achieve half-knowledge.

But for Keats, such half-knowledge is the source and price of beauty. Accepting things by halves (as in "ODE ON A NIGHTINGALE" and its account of being "half in love with easeful death") means allowing their genuine strangeness and eerie beauty to remain strange and eerie. It is the condition of poetic power, as in *The Fall of Hyperion* (see HYPERION AND *THE FALL OF HYPERION*), whose narrator bears until he is "rotted half" the load of eternal quietude, before he can begin his quest. But, contrariwise, it allows for grace and insight: "Sleep and Poetry" defines the grace of poesy as "might half-slumbering on its own right arm."

The "other consideration[s]" that are overcome by the sense of beauty are those considerations of truth which Coleridge could not help himself from seeking out. For Keats, perhaps, the only truth that matters is beauty, so that the famous last lines of "ODE ON A GRECIAN URN" would subsume truth to beauty in both formulations: Beauty by itself is truth, and truth is to be found in beauty. You need know nothing more, whereas Coleridge always attempted to know more.

One other contextual letter: A month before the "negative capability" letter, Keats wrote to his friend Benjamin Bailey: "I am certain of nothing but of the holiness of the Heart's affections and the truth of Imagination—What the imagination seizes as Beauty must be truth—whether it existed before or not—for I have the same idea of all our passions as of love: they are all, in their sublime, creative of essential beauty. . . ." Negative capability gives the imagination the ability to search out mysteries, doubts, and uncertainties without transforming them into their opposite: solutions, assurance, and certainties. It is in this half-light that poetry and the mysteries of poetry reside, and the ability to explore this half-light is what Keats consistently praised in Shakespeare (who could, he said, get into the experience of any character) and Wordsworth, and always attempted to do himself. Perhaps the best illustrations of this attempt at negative capability in Keats's own work is in *The Fall of Hyperion* and in his odes.

See also "ODE ON MELANCHOLY," "ODE TO PSYCHE," "TO AUTUMN."

BIBLIOGRAPHY

Bate, Walter Jackson. *Negative Capability: The Intuitive Approach in Keats.* New York: AMS Press, 1976.

Bloom, Harold. *A Map of Misreading.* New York: Oxford University Press, 2003.

Flesch, William. "The Ambivalence of Generosity: Keats Reading Shakespeare." *ELH: English Literary History* 62, no. 1 (Spring 1995): 149–169.

Spurgeon, Caroline Frances Eleanor. *Keats's Shakespeare: A Descriptive Study Based on New Material.* London: Oxford University Press, 1929.

NEPENTHE See DARLEY, GEORGE; "PHOENIX, THE."

"NEUTRAL TONES" THOMAS HARDY (1867)

"Neutral Tones" is one of THOMAS HARDY's earliest poems. Although remembered primarily as a novelist,

Hardy regarded himself as a poet, and by 1898, when he published *Wessex Poems and Other Verses,* he had stopped writing novels and started publishing the poetry he had been writing for more than 30 years. "Neutral Tones" comes from 1867, Hardy's 27th year, but even at that age (and certainly by 58), he had a grim and despairing view of the possibilities of life and of love.

"Neutral Tones" is a powerfully despairing poem. Like all of Hardy's poetry, it does not recommend itself by its mellifluousness but by an intensity that overrides the usual virtues of poetry—sonority, cadence, harmonious word choice. The neutral tones the poem describes are also the tones of Hardy's own poetry. In a much later poem, "He Never Expected Much," written when he was 86, Hardy has the world of reality tell him:

> "I do not promise overmuch,
> Child; overmuch;
> Just neutral-tinted haps and such,"

which is the sum of what life has meant. The word *neutral,* therefore, had a stable meaning throughout Hardy's career, and meant something like leached of intensity or possibility or promise.

"Neutral Tones" is striking in the way its meaning trumps its structure. The structure is one of an old memory of love, recalled in a bitter or disillusioned future (and yet Hardy was only 27!). The last stanza is set in the present of the poem:

> Since then, keen lessons that love deceives,
> And wrings with wrong, have shaped to me
> Your face, and the God-curst sun, and a tree,
> And a pond edged with grayish leaves.

Since the time the poem describes, the poet has learned the lessons of how love deceives. The sun and the pond are both neutral in tone, cheerless and leached of life, and so is the whole world. But if you read only this last stanza, you would think it was preceded by stanzas of illusory but convincing hopefulness. The first three stanzas are just as bitter and hopeless as the last, however:

> We stood by a pond that winter day,
> And the sun was white, as though chidden of God,
> And a few leaves lay on the starving sod,
> —They had fallen from an ash, and were gray.
>
> Your eyes on me were as eyes that rove
> Over tedious riddles solved years ago;
> And some words played between us to and fro—
> On which lost the more by our love.
>
> The smile on your mouth was the deadest thing
> Alive enough to have strength to die;
> And a grin of bitterness swept thereby
> Like an ominous bird a-wing. . . .

He is recollecting a winter day that he stood with the woman to whom the poem is addressed, with a *white* sun and gray leaves on the "starving sod." Hardy is recollecting, by contrast, William Shakespeare's sonnet 73:

> That time of year thou mayst in me behold
> When yellow leaves, or none, or few, do hang
> Upon those boughs which shake against the cold,
> Bare ruin'd choirs, where late the sweet birds sang.
> In me thou seest the twilight of such day
> As after sunset fadeth in the west,
> Which by and by black night doth take away,
> Death's second self, that seals up all in rest.
> In me thou see'st the glowing of such fire
> That on the ashes of his youth doth lie,
> As the death-bed whereon it must expire
> Consumed with that which it was nourish'd by.
> This thou perceivest, which makes thy love more strong,
> To love that well which thou must leave ere long.

In both poets, the fact that there are "a few leaves" left helps to point out the bleakness of the landscape. In Shakespeare the trees of the first quatrain end up providing the kind of fuel that the fire of the third quatrain burns into ashes. But in Shakespeare the bleakness of winter, of time, and of life elicit a reaction on the part of the beloved, who loves Shakespeare all the more strongly because time and life are short. In contrast, Hardy compresses the images, so that the gray leaves he describes in the first stanza have fallen from an ash; it is they who lie on the sod, as the embers of Shakespeare's fire lie on the ashes of the wood they have burned. By such compression he indicates that there is no compensatory movement, or equal and opposite reaction, to the bleak ineluctability of time.

The past that "Neutral Tones" evokes, the contrast that does not contrast with the present, refers to yet an earlier past, the past of "years ago," when his presence was somehow still a riddle to the poem's addressee—which is to say, it was still an exciting mystery. And yet it was not even that, since the riddles solved years ago were "tedious." The speaker cannot console himself with the idea that once things were better. The love—and he does call it love—between them was always something desiccated and hopelessly empty.

They had argued at the pond, and that argument had drawn a smile from her which Hardy describes in one of his greatest lines: "The smile on your mouth was the deadest thing / Alive enough to have strength to die" (ll. 9–10). The smile dies, but it is a smile that already represents the deadness of all things, of the world where life means only the power to die. This is the past that Hardy recollects when he writes the poem, a past in which even then the only past they could recollect was a tedious and pointless one. And when he comes to publish the poem, that endless series of pointless pasts simply displays another increment. In 1898 (the year of the poem's publication), he recalls how in 1867 he recalled a past in which he and she recalled a past in which she found the riddles of love already tedious.

And yet, as we have noted, the last stanza somehow declares itself a contrast to the stanzas that precede it, and one might ask to what extent it displays a telling self-knowledge. Is the world so blighted for Hardy now that this blight infects a past that *once was different* but now no longer *is*? Can the present infect the past? That seems to be the claim of the poem: that bitterness and disappointment can reach a level where they change the nature of what has happened—change it in reality, so that love now will have never mattered or counted. (This is the lesson as well of Hardy's great last novel, *Jude the Obscure* [1895].) When did this terrible change begin? It was at the pond, on the winter day that the poem describes.

BIBLIOGRAPHY

Bloom, Harold, ed. *Thomas Hardy*. New York: Chelsea House, 1987.

Clements, Patricia, and Juliet Grindle, eds. *Poetry of Thomas Hardy*. London: Vision Press, 1980.

Hardy, Thomas. *Thomas Hardy's Personal Writings: Prefaces, Literary Opinions, Reminiscences*. Edited by Harold Orel. London: Macmillan, 1990.

Kramer, Dale, ed. *Cambridge Companion to Thomas Hardy*. New York: Cambridge University Press, 1999.

"NEW DECALOGUE, A" ARTHUR HUGH CLOUGH (1862) ARTHUR HUGH CLOUGH had a talent very rare in a serious poet, that of excelling in comic poetry or light verse as well. The demands of comic verse are very different from those of serious poetry. The former requires absolute lightness of touch, and its effect depends on a marvelous sense of *coincidence* between an urbane and witty way of putting things and perfect poetic form. Serious poetry must always insist on the relevance of its own formal properties (from the Spenserian stanzas to free verse) as conveying part of its meaning. All serious poetry, whatever else it communicates will also communicate *why* it is poetry. Light verse, by contrast, must affect a fine indifference to its poetical qualities, as though they came about effortlessly and spontaneously. This does not mean that light verse does not have anything to say about its own form; on the contrary, it says a lot about its form just because the form is not absorbed as in serious verse into the very fiber of its meaning.

Clough's rare talent derived from his highly informed urbanity—the urbanity that made him just as much at home in abstruse philosophy as in vers de societé (witty, light verse). "A New Decalogue" is an example of the second sort of verse making, but even so, it has the seriousness of great parody. It reiterates the Ten Commandments from a point of view that imagines itself modern, knowing, worldly, and primarily economic. This is the Decalogue under the conditions of modern industrial capitalism and the economic relations it governs.

The poem proper consists of 20 lines, each odd line more or less repeating the corresponding original commandment, and each even line offering a succinct explanation or qualification for that commandment. The smooth, even oily, rhyming couplets turn the sublime original list of prohibition into a depiction of facile balance. Why only one God, as the first commandment enjoins? Because two are too expensive. The second commandment prohibits the worship of graven images; the New Decalogue agrees, with the exception of currency. This addendum has the effect of changing the meaning even of the repetition of the original commandment, which now is made into an expression of contempt for any human aesthetic culture except the worship of money. It becomes a rejection of art, not a rejection of false gods; indeed, it requires the worship of the false god of money. The other eight commandments are revised in a similar mode, the sixth being most famous: "Thou shalt not kill, but need not strive / Officiously to keep alive" (ll. 11–12). In other words, every man for himself.

The way these maxims of selfishness are couched in a variation of the language of the original Decalogue shows the hypocrisy of the pseudo-Christians of the time whom Clough so roundly condemns in his poetry, the hypocrisy that finally made him an atheist. A bitter epilogue to the poem, found only in one manuscript, summarizes the New Testament summary of the Decalogue: Love God—that is, be pious—and you need not show any generosity to your neighbor. Clough's rejection of this ethic is urbane but firm, as befits the seriousness even of his comic verse.

BIBLIOGRAPHY

Clough, Arthur Hugh. *Oxford Diaries of Arthur Hugh Clough.* Edited by Anthony Kenny. New York: Oxford University Press, 1990.

Hofmann, Michael. "Arthur Hugh Clough: 1819–1861." *Poetry* 187, no. 6 (March 2006): 495–496.

Kenny, Anthony. *Arthur Hugh Clough: A Poet's Life.* New York: Continuum, 2005.

Sutherland, Gillian. *Faith, Duty, and the Power of Mind: The Cloughs and Their Circle, 1820–1960.* London: Cambridge University Press, 2006.

NEWMAN, JOHN HENRY (CARDINAL NEWMAN) (1801–1890)

As a poet, John Henry Newman—Cardinal Newman from 1879 to his death—is remembered now mainly for some hymns, including (most famously) "Lead Kindly Light" (see "The PILLAR OF THE CLOUD"). His influence on VICTORIAN POETRY is far more vast, however. Newman was the intellectual father of the tide toward conversion to Catholicism in so many Victorian intellectuals, including, most prominently among poets, GERARD MANLEY HOPKINS; other important Catholic poets included ALICE MEYNELL and COVENTRY PATMORE. Newman had begun as an evangelical Christian but was led more and more (under the intellectual influence of his teachers, friends, and colleagues at Oxford University) to the view that there could be only one true Christian Church; that church, however, might have several branches, including Eastern Orthodoxy, the Roman Catholic Church, and English Anglicanism (this view, called Anglo-Catholicism, would be the one that T. S. Eliot would eventually take). Newman sought to argue that the central creed of the Anglican Church, the 39 articles of the 16th century, was not essentially Protestant—that is, a protest against the Roman Catholic Church—but compatible with it.

The Anglican Church was the state church of Britain, and Newman saw the church as becoming more secularized during the various reforms of the 19th century, a tendency against which he protested very strongly, seeing the world hastening everywhere toward atheism. He began to think that any schism was bad, and that the branching of the church into three parts, which he had initially imagined would allow for reconciliation of the Anglican Church in which he was ordained with a larger catholic faith that would also include Roman Catholicism, was unworkable. Thus, in 1845 he converted to Roman Catholicism, and he soon became a priest and eventually, in old age, a cardinal. He certainly accepted and indeed rejoiced in polemical argument about theological and religious matters; he thought such argument was good for the church, but that it should occur *within* the church and not between schisms or sects.

Newman saw the church as having "it in charge to rescue human nature from its misery, but not simply by raising it on its own level, but by lifting it up to a higher level than its own. She recognizes in it real moral excellence though degraded, but she cannot set it free from earth except by exalting it towards heaven. It was for this end that a renovating grace was put into her hands, and therefore from the nature of the gift, as well as from the reasonableness of the case, she goes on, as a further point, to insist, that all true conversion must begin with the first springs of thought, and to teach that each individual man must be in his own person one whole and perfect temple of God, while he is also one of the living stones which build up a visible religious community" (*Apologia Pro Vita Sua,* 1866). The visible religious community is the one church, though each individual is treated as an individual, not merely as a cog in the wheels of the church.

For this reason, Newman was intensely interested in individual human experience, and his long poem *The Dream of Gerontius* (1865) is a kind of modern *Everyman* (the 15th-century morality play), describing the immediate after-death of the soul of the old man who gives the poem its title (*gerontius* means "old man"; compare T. S. Eliot's 1920 poem "Gerontion.") In *The Dream of Gerontius,* Newman wrote his own counter-poem, partly out of the tradition of the English mystery plays, partly out of Greek tragedy, partly out of Dante's great Catholic work *The Divine Comedy* (whose *Paradiso* Newman echoes in particular), and largely out of the transformation of Greek tragedy into lyric drama by the 17th-century poet John Milton, the German poet and dramatist Johann Wolfgang von Goethe, LORD BYRON, and PERCY BYSSHE SHELLEY; it is against these last four poets. In the poem, Gerontius, led by his guide and guardian angel, has a vision of the dizzying perspectives of time and void that the soul faces in dying and in going to judgment. That experience rebukes the claims made by the romantic version of Milton (as well as the Protestant version) for the meaning of rebellion and self-reliance as against what Milton's and Newman's rebel angels assert as the slavish worship of a vain God, and Gerontius instead learns that the most intense lyricism (here Newman is trying to rewrite Shelley's *PROMETHEUS UNBOUND*, itself a revision of Dante) comes in a perspective of God himself. It is fascinating that Gerontius cannot *see* (so this is not really a vision); rather, he has a kind of faith that is less visionary than Shelley's but is therefore supposed to be deeper. Among the conversations he has with his guardian angel are some that accept the possibility of the truth of Darwinian evolution Newman seems willing to accept (just as the Roman Catholic Church now accepts it) as compatible with faith—that is, with matter that slowly works its way up to humanity and the possibility of salvation.

Charles Darwin's *On the Origin of Species* had been published in 1859, the same year that Newman wrote *The Dream of Gerontius.* THOMAS HARDY concluded that Darwin made a belief in a kind God untenable. It is important to realize that they started from the same observations to come to different conclusions. Hardy saw in the blind mechanism of the world proof that God was at best imbecilic, dying, feckless, immoral, nonexistent. Newman saw the world as missing what only God could supply. "Arguments in proof of a God, drawn from the general facts of human society and the course of history," he admits in his autobiography, *Apologia Pro Vita Sua* (1866), "do not warm me or enlighten me; they do not take away the winter of my desolation. . . . The sight of the world is nothing else than the prophet's scroll, full of 'lamentations, and mourning, and woe.'" The world has almost nothing to demonstrate "a superintending design," and "great powers or truths, the progress of things" occur through "blind evolution . . . as if from unreasoning elements, not towards final causes." All human experience, "the greatness and littleness of man, his far-reaching aims, his short duration, the curtain hung over his futurity, the disappointments of life, the defeat of good, the success of evil, physical pain, mental anguish, the prevalence and intensity of sin, the pervading idolatries, the corruptions, the dreary hopeless irreligion, that condition of the whole race, so fearfully yet exactly described in the Apostle's words, 'having no hope and without God in the world,'—all this is a vision to dizzy and appal; and inflicts upon the mind the sense of a profound mystery, which is absolutely beyond human solution."

That last hope is what Hardy could not accept, but what some of Newman's great Catholic followers did accept: the desolation, as he called it, of Gerard Manley

Hopkins's "terrible sonnets" also derives from visions to "dizzy and appall," and out of those visions comes poetry that faces the depths of human desolation and despair. This is often great religious poetry, but it is often (as in the case of Hardy) simply great poetry, religious or not, because both sides agree that the desolation is real. The absence of God, whether it stands for the mystery of his presence *elsewhere,* as Newman believed, or is a genuine absence, is among the most powerful and devastating of human experiences. Whether one accepts Newman's solution or not, his courage and seriousness in articulating the profundity of the mystery made possible poetry that would plumb its depths still further—poetry that addressed the very heart of the human condition.

BIBLIOGRAPHY

Block, Ed., Jr., ed. *Critical Essays on John Henry Newman.* Victoria, B.C.: University of Victoria, 1992.

Ker, Ian, and Alan G. Hill, eds. *Newman after a Hundred Years.* New York: Oxford University Press, 1990.

Newman, John Henry. *Apologia Pro Vita Sua.* New York: Penguin, 1994.

Roberts, Noel Keith. "Newman on the Argument from Design." *New Blackfriars* 88, no. 1,013 (2007): 56–66.

"NO COWARD SOUL IS MINE" EMILY BRONTË (1846)

Charlotte Brontë, EMILY BRONTË's older sister, said that these were the last lines she wrote, but they are dated in the manuscript January 2, 1846, well over two years before her death and a year before she published her great novel *Wuthering Heights.* In fact, this is the second-to-last poem she wrote; afterward, she turned to the novel.

Even if written some two and a half years before Brontë's passing, the poem nevertheless anticipates death's approach, and Charlotte's sense that Emily felt her death was near is probably accurate. The tuberculosis that would kill all four of the surviving Brontë children—Charlotte (1816–53), Branwell (1817–48), Emily (1818–48), and Anne (1820–49)—had already killed their two elder sisters, and the presence of disease and death was palpable in Haworth parsonage (as is obvious from Emily's novel *Wuthering Heights* as well). It is therefore no wonder that Brontë should define God as "Being and Breath" (l. 27).

That breath is within her. The poem is radical in its conception of God as "within my breast" (l. 5), so that her soul or spirit (whose root meaning is "breath") breaths with God's. She perceives him *in* and *as* an interchange with her own soul; it is not a coward soul because God is there. She knows that he is there because of the tremendous meaning of life.

In independent conformity to the German philosopher Immanuel Kant's exposition of the SUBLIME, Brontë first registers the vastness of the world, a vastness that risks giving meaning to the terrors of death. All these things—"earth and moon / And suns and universes"—might cease to be. Death can entirely annihilate the material world and may threaten the coward soul with fear of such annihilation. But the lesson the soul takes from the very vastness of the world at risk—vastness registered in the metaphors the poem uses, such as the "boundless main" and the "eternal years"—is that the thought of death cannot possibly encompass the things it threatens. The sense of infinity must therefore come from elsewhere, from the soul and from God. The power we are tempted to ascribe to death is a power that it cannot have, since death is entirely negative. He has no power and no might to render even the least atom void. Therefore, the power we ascribe to death really comes from God, which is to say also from the soul's perception of the sublimity it fears.

The grandness of Brontë's soul comes from the grandness of the life it opposes to death. And it comes as well for recognizing just that: that its own grandness is opposed to death. This is how it recognizes the God resting within and the life within which it rests. Her capacity to perceive the reality of life means that she perceives that life alone is real, and that it consists in her capacity to perceive its reality. This is what it means to perceive God, or infinity, or the meaning of the soul, and she converts the terrifying annihilation of death into as momentous an affirmation of being and breath.

BIBLIOGRAPHY

Barker, Juliet. *The Brontës.* New York: St. Martin's Press, 1994.

Bristow, Joseph, ed. *Victorian Women Poets: Emily Brontë, Elizabeth Barrett Browning, Christina Rossetti.* Houndsville, Basingstoke, England: Macmillan Press, 1995.

Gezari, Janet. "'Fathoming Remembrance': Emily Brontë in Context." *ELH: English Literary History* 66, no. 4 (1999): 965–984.

Homans, Margaret. *Women Writers and Poetic Identity: Dorothy Wordsworth, Emily Brontë, and Emily Dickinson.* Princeton, N.J.: Princeton University Press, 1980.

Mason, Emma. *Women Poets of the Nineteenth Century.* Tavistock, Devon, England: Northcote House Publishers, 2006.

"NOON" MICHAEL FIELD (1893) One of the fascinations of knowing that MICHAEL FIELD is a pseudonym for the aunt-niece couple of Katharine Bradley and Edith Cooper is in how it affects one's reading of individual poems. Field liked to describe "his" solitary experiences, and "he" did so with great sensitivity and deftness. (Henceforth, the quotes will not be used when referring to the masculine Field.) "Noon" is a good example of such description.

It is summer, and Field is dazzled by what he sees at the height of the day. The fullness of summer and of noon are mirrored in the bed of flowers opening to the blaze of day. The summer heat is such as to overwhelm any sense of absence within the scene, despite the fact that it is void of any other human being. The flowers grow on a "waste bed," which means that no one is interested in them, and no one cares for them, but the "triumph of the sunshine" (l. 3) is such that they need no other care nor other sponsoring presence. They represent the fullness of the summer's light and heat. Their solitude has a highly positive attraction, since it is a solitude from which nothing is missing.

It is somewhat surprising to discover at the end of the second tercet that the scene is not entirely solitary since Field himself is there, and the foreground of the scene lies at his feet. But he does not interfere much with the sense of solitude in the scene, just because it *is* a scene and therefore something that is observed by someone. At first it appears that he does not have to observe himself: He is the observer, not the observed, and what he observes is the fullness of nature at its estival peak.

And yet the third stanza has a further surprise. All the beauty that had filled out the previous lines, making the triple rhymes themselves stand for the completeness of the scene, falters a little in the last line of the third stanza (l. 9). Repeated rhymes mean plenitude, but that plenitude is not quite given any more in description, since the descriptive sentence ends before the last foot of the line. Field pieces out the line, and the rhyme, with an infinitive, which (again surprisingly) leads to an enjambment into the fourth and final stanza: "To think . . ." Thought always stands for absence in 19th-century poetry, and Field—a highly Keatsian poet—is almost certainly remembering the end of JOHN KEATS's sonnet "WHEN I HAVE FEARS THAT I MAY CEASE TO BE," where plenitude gives way to the absence in which he will "stand and think." Field thinks of the unshared solitude of the scene, of the fact that no one but him is aware of it.

The last line of the poem is weakened by an unfortunately maudlin conclusion. But it should not be taken quite seriously (in fact, its weakness may signal its falsity), since Field is of course *not* alone looking at the scene so vividly defined by the light. For the poets he comprises, Bradley and Cooper, are together, of course, and what they see is what they describe to each other in writing the poem.

But perhaps this stands for a further solitude, that of their own relation with respect to the rest of the ignorant or disapproving world. Flower and fern might stand for us readers, blind to Bradley and Cooper's life together, a life that they could only share through the singular pseudonym. But the poem, in thus perhaps privately contradicting the public meaning of its last stanza, succeeds as a communication between them, where the scene is shared, a communication we can now overhear through the accidents of biographical disclosure. Here John Stuart Mill's definition of lyric as overheard conversation becomes almost literally true, and it is verified through the poem's intensive lyrical power.

BIBLIOGRAPHY

Avery, Simon. "Michael Field (1896–1914)." *The Literary Encyclopedia* (June 13, 2003). Available online. URL: http://www.litencyc.com/php/speople.php?rec=true&UID=1521. Accessed on March 14, 2008.

Castle, Terry, ed. *The Literature of Lesbianism: A Historical Anthology from Ariosto to Stonewall.* New York: Columbia University Press, 2003.

Moore, T., and D. C. Sturge. *Works and Days, from the Journal of Michael Field.* London: J. Murray, 1933.

Prins, Yopie. *Victorian Sappho.* Princeton, N.J.: Princeton University Press, 1999.
Sturgeon, Mary. *Michael Field.* London: G.G. Harrap, 1922.
White, Christine. "'Poets and Lovers Evermore': The Poetry and Journals of Michael Field." In *Sexual Sameness: Textual Differences in Lesbian and Gay Writing,* edited by Joseph Bristow, 26–43. New York: Routledge, 1992.

NORTON, CAROLINE (CAROLINE ELIZABETH SARAH SHERIDAN, LADY CAROLINE STIRLING-MAXWELL) (1808–1877)

The granddaughter of the Irish playwright Richard Brinsley Sheridan, Caroline Norton, later Lady Caroline Stirling-Maxwell, is largely remembered now for a handful of poems. These include her entry in the expanded edition of the *Golden Treasury of English Songs and Lyrics*—the witty but also emotionally insightful poem "I do not love Thee." She was famous in her day, however, as an extremely successful writer, comparable to LORD BYRON, and then also as the exploited wife of a grasping and selfish husband, George Chapple Norton, who commandeered her considerable earnings and set in motion a scandal when he sued a political opponent for adultery with her. He sought both money and political advantage, but the charges were ludicrous, and he gained neither. The incident, however, was sufficiently notorious for Charles Dickens and GEORGE MEREDITH both to fictionalize it in their novels. In the end, the dreadful way she was treated and her highly effective campaign for women's claims to economic rights led eventually to the signal event of the passage of the Married Women's Property Act (1882), which laid the foundations for modern women's suffrage and equality under the law.

Norton's best-remembered poems come from her youth, before the troubles and disaster that would encompass so much of her time and energy. One could say that "I do not love Thee" is an early version of the Carly Simon song "You're so vain," with its chorus "You're so vain, you probably think this song is about you." Similarly, "I do not love Thee" is a love poem whose very existence contradicts the assertion of its titular first line. If she did not love him, she would not have to write a poem saying so.

A slightly more subtle poem in this vein is "I was not false to thee" (written around 1830, when Norton was 21 or 22), which depends on what the philosopher Paul Grice called implicature. Why does she repeat this assertion at the beginning and end of each of the poem's three stanzas? Because *he,* the addressee of the poem, *has* been false to her. The contrast is a more or less obvious one; what is not obvious is how the poem will puzzle over the fact that she is upset and he is not. Should that go without saying? After all, he betrayed her, and she is upset about the betrayal. But the speaker (not Norton herself, whose own misadventures were still largely in the future) is surprised that she is the one showing the signs that she expects him to show. This is because she expects him to be suffering pangs of guilt and remorse for his betrayal of her, which would, in some sense, compensate for his behavior. What the poem depicts, then, is the psychologically acute insight that it is not the infidelity that she sees as a betrayal, but his indifference to the infidelity. She still loves him, which is why she evinces all the signs of sorrow and shame when he does not. It is as though she is both trying to do it *for* him, and aware in a way which shows that she *does* feel for him what he fails to feel for her, that her love and her attempt to compensate for his indifference is useless. Caring about the grief of the one you love is enough. She wants him to grieve over the grief he has caused her, and each can then love the other for what his or her grief signifies. But he does not, and so she knows the relationship is over, although she still hopes that he will come to regret it some time in the future. Such emotional paradoxes as these are at the heart of Norton's best poems.

BIBLIOGRAPHY

Price, Richard. *British Society, 1680–1880: Dynamism, Containment and Change.* New York: Cambridge University Press, 1999.
Staves, Susan. *Married Women's Separate Property in England, 1660–1833.* Cambridge, Mass.: Harvard University Press, 1990.

"NO WORST, THERE IS NONE" GERARD MANLEY HOPKINS (1885)

This is one of GERARD MANLEY HOPKINS's "terrible sonnets," or "sonnets of desolation" as they later came to be called. (For more on them, see the entry on "CARRION COMFORT," whose final version Hopkins drafted on the same sheet of paper as the surviving draft of this poem.) The gnomic and anguished first line echoes Edgar's great speech in William Shakespeare's *King Lear* when, at the opening of act 4, he comes to realize that there is no bottom to despair, that part of what makes it despair is that it is itself the abyss that makes it despair—the "cliffs of fall" (l. 9) are themselves the fall, not just the place from which there is a danger of falling. On seeing his blinded father, Edgar takes back his claim that things can get no worse: "O gods! Who is't can say I am at the worst? / I am worse than e'er I was. . . . And worse I may be yet: the worst is not / So long as we can say, This is the worst" (4.1). Pain prepares one for pain, despair for more despair.

One can think of this poem as verging on a refutation or bitter repudiation of "Carrion Comfort," a kind of rebuttal written in the margin of the same page on which that poem appears. Some of the vocabulary is strikingly the same. "Carrion Comfort" describes Christ's "wring-world right foot" (l. 6), but here it is the pangs that perpetually accelerate the wildness of their wringing of their victim (l. 2; see also the ninth stanza of "The WRECK OF THE DEUTSCHLAND"). The Comforter, the Holy Ghost or Paraclete (Greek for "comforter" or "consoler"), who finally intervenes in "Carrion Comfort" is absent here (l. 3), as is the Virgin Mary (l. 4), whom he had earlier wished to think of as present as the air itself (in his poem "The Blessed Virgin compared to the Air we Breathe"). Even the lulls in the torments only show the ferocity of their renewal. It should be noted that here, as in "The WINDHOVER," Hopkins employs split rhyme, but the split here (on "ling-/ering" between lines 7 and 8) shows how the lull is only that of an enjambment before Fury's next blow.

The sestet returns to allusive memorials of *King Lear* in its great and memorable metaphor of the mind's mountains and "cliffs of fall / Frightful, sheer, no-man-fathomed" (ll. 9–10). Edgar had described the fall from the cliff he had led his blind father to in terms that Hopkins borrows, in particular the description at that dizzying height of how "half-way down / Hangs one that gathers samphire, dreadful trade!" (4.7). The cliffs of fall are "no-man-fathomed" because no man could survive the fall, nor even endure the falling long.

The poem offers what looks like a potential way out, via a kind of reversal of the logic of the SUBLIME: the idea that our small durance protects us from "that steep or deep" (l. 12) because we are too small and limited and short-lived to perceive the abyss in all its terrifying magnitude. But this is the only "comfort" (l. 13) the poem offers, and it is a far cry from the comfort Hopkins had hoped for from the Comforter. Indeed, it is the suicidal comfort of death which "serves in a whirlwind" (l. 13). Life will end with death and with it despair will end as well, offering perhaps a permanent lull akin to the diurnal lull that ends each day as it dies with sleep. But this shelter—the same that Edgar's father seeks in (as he believes) throwing himself off the cliff his son has described—is only suicide, that is, the carrion comfort he had refused in the earlier poem. It may be that he is rescued from suicide only by the sleep that gives him a moment to pause, but that means that sleep itself is a kind of mini-suicide, one that he suffers every day. Small wonder that these were called the "sonnets of desolation."

BIBLIOGRAPHY

Bridges, Robert. Preface to *Notes in Poems of Gerard Manley Hopkins.* Edited by W. H. Gardner. London: Oxford University Press, 1918, 94–101.

Gardner, W. H. *Gerard Manley Hopkins (1844–1889): A Study of Poetic Idiosyncrasy in Relation to Poetic Tradition.* New Haven, Conn.: Yale University Press, 1949.

———, ed. Introduction to *Poems and Prose of Gerard Manley Hopkins.* Harmondsworth, Middlesex, England: Penguin, 1963.

Hartman, Geoffrey. *The Unmediated Vision: An Interpretation of Wordsworth, Hopkins, Rilke, and Valery.* New Haven, Conn.: Yale University Press, 1954.

Hopkins, Gerard Manley. *Gerard Manley Hopkins: Selected Letters.* Edited by Catherine Phillips. New York: Oxford University Press, 1990.

Miller, J. Hillis. "Gerard Manley Hopkins." In *The Disappearance of God,* 270–359. Cambridge, Mass.: Belknap Press of Harvard University Press, 1963.

White, Norman. *Hopkins: A Literary Biography.* New York: Oxford University Press, 1992.

"NOW SLEEPS THE CRIMSON PETAL, NOW THE WHITE" ALFRED, LORD TENNYSON (1847) This is one of ALFRED, LORD TENNYSON's most famous lyrics, widely anthologized and loved. It is one of the songs from *The* PRINCESS: *A* MEDLEY, a long narrative poem with many intermittent songs. In part 7, the Prince, who has attempted to win his betrothed but militantly antimale Princess Ida, is lying wounded after a battle with her and her followers. He is hovering in a kind of half-sleep, not certain if he is beholding her or not. Then he becomes aware that the dreamy mood is not his alone: "Deep in the night I woke: she, near me, held / A volume of the Poets of her land; / There to herself, all in low tones, she read" (*The Princess,* part 7, ll. 158–160). She reads to herself, but he overhears it, so he is aware of what she is feeling. She is feeling what he is now telling, the lovely anonymous love song that she reads.

The song itself is in the form of a ghazal (originally a Persian form, though it was also used for Arabic and Urdu poetry). The rules of the ghazal vary in strictness, but generally they are erotic poems written in couplets, with the end word of the second line always the same; they usually mention flowers and often name the poet in the last line. In "Now Sleeps," Tennyson adapts these rules and gets the spooky, timeless beauty the form aims at perfectly. He does so partly because he is writing in what is already (for an English poet) an exotic form. Tennyson said, "I don't read Persian" (unlike his friend EDWARD FITZGERALD, whose *RUBÁIYÁT OF OMAR KHAYYAM* is a translation from the Persian), and it is just because he did not that the ghazal's inaccessible origin within a strange poetic language can lend the form just the beautiful, evocative strangeness that Tennyson aims for.

That evocative, irresolvable distance and difference, at the heart of so much of Tennyson's greatest poetry, can be felt as well in the fact that the poem is written for a woman's point of view (that of the princess), although the poet who wrote the poem she reads aloud—in a sense Tennyson himself—might be a man. At any rate, the form of the ghazal contributes to its beauty. The dreamy repetitions of the couplet-ending *me* mark the amorous intensifications of the poem, and so, too, do the repetitions of the word *Now* at the beginning of the stanza. It is always *Now* in the eternal moment the poem, or its speaker, seeks to sustain.

It is night, the petals of the flesh-colored flowers (crimson and white) are laid to sleep, and in the stillness of the night the speaker bids her beloved to wake. The wakefulness is almost no different from sleep (especially since the Princess is reading this in low tones, as she sits by the Prince's bed). The stillness grows more hushed and rich under the aspect of her own central stillness. The beautiful line "Now lies the Earth all Danaë to the stars" captures the mood perfectly. In Greek mythology, Zeus impregnated Danaë as "a shower of golden stars"; but here the stars do not fall but shine, and it is the gold of their light alone that constitutes the still, intense eroticism of the scene. So, too, does the speaker want an intensification of the stillness of the scene so great that the beloved may be lost in it, in the speaker, and in the poem itself.

The kind of decontextualized lyric Tennyson aims for here is self-descriptive. The kind of love the poem describes is also the kind of love it evokes, so that love *for* the poem is a metaphor for the love in the poem. This both Prince and Princess feel, within the poem that contains both this poem and them.

BIBLIOGRAPHY

Armstrong, Isobel. *Victorian Poetry: Poetry, Poetics and Politics.* New York: Routledge, 1993.

Bloom, Harold. *Poetry and Repression: Revisionism from Blake to Stevens.* New Haven, Conn.: Yale University Press, 1976.

Buckley, Jerome Hamilton. *Tennyson: The Growth of a Poet.* Boston: Houghton Mifflin, 1965.

Kilham, John. *Critical Essays on the Poetry of Tennyson.* New York: Barnes and Noble, 1960.

Kincaid, James R. *Tennyson's Major Poems: The Comic and Ironic Patterns.* New Haven, Conn.: Yale University Press, 1975.

Ricks, Christopher B. *Tennyson.* New York: Macmillan, 1972.

Rowlinson, Matthew. *Tennyson's Fixations: Psychoanalysis and the Topics of the Early Poetry.* Charlottesville: University Press of Virginia, 1994.

Tucker, Herbert: *Tennyson and the Doom of Romanticism.* Cambridge, Mass.: Harvard University Press, 1988.

"NUPTIAL EVE, A" ("KEITH OF RAVELSTON") SYDNEY DOBELL (1856) This poem consists of an introduction in which we see a young woman sitting and singing, and then the ballad that she sings, often published separately as "Keith of Ravelston." The separate version appeared in the expanded edition of Francis Palgrave's *Golden Treasury of English Songs and Lyrics* and was a great favorite of DANTE GABRIEL ROSSETTI's. However, it is in no way harmed by the introduction, which gives it some context.

The poem originally appeared in SYDNEY DOBELL's 1856 volume *England in Time of War,* when he was close to despair over England's disastrous participation in the Crimean War. The speaker sees a happy maid in Scotland (where Dobell was living) some June night, free of the sorrow that is general in this "year of war and death" (l. 2). She sings almost randomly, somewhat like WILLIAM WORDSWORTH's "Solitary Reaper," who sings to herself in solitary and beautiful melancholy and the speaker reports her song. Because, in Dobell's beautiful phrase, "the sorrow of the air" (l. 19) is everywhere, her song must be a sorrowful one, even though neither she nor the speaker understand it. It is in the form of a ballad, much like the kinds that Sir WALTER SCOTT invented, about a Scottish clan leader, Andrew Keith of Ravelston. The Keiths were a real clan in Ravelston, but the source of whatever legend the poem retells is either nonexistent or lost in the mists of time, though it has something of the feel of *Macbeth* about it.

We do not know what curse pursues the line of the Keiths of Ravelston, or of Andrew's descendants. The ballad describes the endless refrain of a mourning ghost, who kept her mother's kine (cattle) and now keeps *their* ghosts as well. As with the framing narrative, the sorrow of her song is prior to the events that cause it; it is part of the general air of sorrow in Britain. What we know is that she was singing one day when Andrew Keith of Ravelston and his henchmen rode by one beautiful morning. Since then she has been singing the sorrows of his line. It is not clear whether he has hurt her or raped her; or whether this was the moment in which some other disaster was foretold for him, and this disaster would haunt him and his line forever henceforth, or whether he fell in love with her and she refused him. The obscure generic formulae of ballads make it immaterial which of these, if any, was the beginning of his sorrow. What matters is that the sorrow continues still: The ghost of the young woman is still there singing her sad refrain.

The ballad's sadness now infects the young woman who sings the frame narrative, also absorbed into this obscure sorrow, and the speaker who sees and hears her. The poem as a whole, like her ballad within it, is about finding a proper expression for the sadness of Britain's situation, but it is also about the sense that Britain is cursed with some obscure sorrow that the Crimean War embodies.

See also "WOUNDED, THE."

BIBLIOGRAPHY

Boos, Florence S. "'Spasm' and Class: W. E. Aytoun, George Gilfillan, Sydney Dobell, and Alexander Smith." *Victorian Poetry* 42, no. 4 (2004): 553–583.

Dobell, Sydney. *The Life and Letters of Sydney Dobell.* Edited by E. Jolly. London: Smith, Elder & Co., 1878.

Preyer, Robert. "Sydney Dobell and the Victorian Epic." *University of Toronto Quarterly* 30 (January 1961): 163–178.

Westwater, Martha. *The Spasmodic Career of Sydney Dobell.* Lanham, Md.: University Press of America, 1992.

"NURSE'S SONG" WILLIAM BLAKE (1789, 1794) The Nurse's songs in *SONGS OF INNOCENCE AND OF EXPERIENCE* are among the subtlest of the paired poems from the two books. The contrast is the grim one that WILLIAM BLAKE was intent to draw in all of his pairings, between the idea of life given to the hopefulness of youth and the discovery of what life really is, or at least what it seems to be once one experiences the greed, venality, bitterness, jealousy, and sadism of the adult world.

More explicitly than most of the other contrasts between the two sections or states of mind, the Nurse's songs show how the world of experience is self-creating, self-amplifying, and self-reinforcing. This is because the two poems give two different points of view of one world—that of innocence, first from the perspective of the innocent nurse, then from that of the experienced one. These perspectives are themselves not straightforward in the poem: The real perspectives we get are those of the children and then the adolescents themselves. But first we have to consider the poems in their surface presentation; we will return later to the question of *who* imagines that surface.

The situation described in both poems is easily summarized: A nurse is watching her charges at play and reflecting on what she is watching. In the "Innocence" version, the children have a voice of their own, since they resist the nurse's injunction that they come in as darkness falls, and she agrees to let them play a little bit longer. The "Experience" version only gives the nurse's words.

This difference in an otherwise parallel structure is significant and focuses our attention on what the nurse is saying and, in the "Innocence" version, what she accepts from the children. In the "Experience" version, she makes it clear that the words *Day* and *Night* stand for times of life, also describable as *Spring* and *Winter*—that is, innocence and experience. Therefore, the children in the "Innocence" version who cry that "It is yet day" (l. 9) are essentially telling us that they are still children, that they have not yet entered the fallen world of experience. They do not know that they are saying this; they *show,* through their love of the day and the sports of day, that they belong to the innocent daytime of life. The nurse in "Innocence" allows them more time to play and expects and encourages the idea that night is only a time of rest in a world of unchanging innocence (since the morning will "appear in the skies" [l. 8] the next day).

The far more cynical nurse of the "Experience" version of the poem also treats day and night as both real and metaphorical. Where in "Innocence" actual day and night all occur under the aspect of day—we could say they are the day and night of springtime—in "Experience" actual day and night occur under the aspect of night: They are the day and night of winter. In "Innocence," even night is innocent; in "Experience," even day is a time of immoral waste, and of sexual secrecy and manipulation.

The important thing to note, then, is that it is the figure of the nurse who represents innocence in one poem and experience in the other. Her view of the children as innocent in the first version gives way to a view of children as experienced in the second. The two views of the children say more about the nurse than about the children; and perhaps we could go a little farther to note that the children have a reality, since they speak, in the "Innocence" version but not in the "Experience" version; and therefore, Blake never concedes that children could be corrupt from the start. It is only the doctrine of cynical experience that would imagine that they could—the doctrine of original sin and total depravity, which Blake rejects.

The poems are somewhat more complicated than this, though, especially in the play of voices. Because it is the nurse who represents the perspectives of both innocence and experience, we are faced not only with two different accounts of innocence (the "Innocence" version and the "Experience" version); we are also faced with two different accounts of experience—that of the *Songs of Innocence* and that of *Songs of Experience.* For the nurse, at least by contrast to the children, is experienced in both: She is not herself a child but the experienced authority who takes care of the children.

The nurse in *Songs of Innocence* is more like Blake himself than her counterpart in the *Songs of Experience.* She loves the children and loves observing their play. She is exempt from a sense of jealousy; more centrally, perhaps, she is exempt from a sense of time. She does not recall her youth as her counterpart from "Experience" will: She feels the joy of the children in the present moment, and loves it in the present moment. She sees children as children, and as children only.

Her experienced counterpart sees children as secret and conniving, as presenting themselves as innocent when they are not. For the experienced nurse, time is central. She is at once resentful of the fact that the time of youth has fled (see "The ANGEL") and too cynical to admit there ever was such a time; for her, innocence is deceit and disguise.

Which is true? One way of asking this is to ask: Is it the same nurse in both poems? How could it be? One way is to say that the nurse, like the children, and like everything else in the two conditions, is understood and presented through the respective filters of innocence and experience. Here we touch on the extreme and astonishing subtlety of Blake's diptych, for who would *see* the nurse as innocent? Who would imagine and give voice to that perspective? The answer is: not the nurse herself, but the children thinking about what she thinks about them. The innocent nurse is a product of innocent children; the experienced nurse is a product of experienced children—that is, of adolescents.

This leads to the lovely, Blakean consequence, that the innocents see somewhat more clearly than the experienced, or at least see truths that the experienced cannot. They can see, as the innocent nurse does, the innocent joy of the children. We know, through a kind of self-sustaining circle, that their joy is innocent—because their idea of the nurse is the innocent nurse. The experienced nurse (and the older children) cannot see this, and their blindness is a loss, not only of feeling but also of truth.

It is a truth that it takes a further insight to recover: the insight of the poet himself, who can see both innocence and experience, and can understand each fully without being blinded by the experience that is skeptical of innocence. This is, in a sense, Blake's whole project in a nutshell.

BIBLIOGRAPHY

Bloom, Harold. *Blake's Apocalypse: A Study in Poetic Argument.* Ithaca, N.Y.: Cornell University Press, 1970.

———. *Poetry and Repression: Revisionism from Blake to Stevens.* New Haven, Conn.: Yale University Press, 1976.

Damrosch, Leopold. *Symbol and Truth in Blake's Myth.* Princeton, N.J.: Princeton University Press, 1980.

Erdmann, David V. *Blake, Prophet against Empire: A Poet's Interpretation of the History of His Own Times.* Princeton, N.J.: Princeton University Press, 1977.

Fry, Northrop. *Fearful Symmetry: A Study of William Blake.* Princeton, N.J.: Princeton University Press, 1974.

Gilchrist, Alexander. *Life of William Blake, with Selections from His Poems and Other Writings.* Totowa, N.J.: Rowman and Littlefield, 1973.

Ostriker, Alicia. "Desire Gratified and Ungratified: William Blake and Sexuality." *Blake: An Illustrated Quarterly* 16 (1982–83): 156–165.

Raine, Kathleen. *Blake and Antiquity.* Princeton, N.J.: Princeton University Press, 1977.

Thompson, E. P. *Witness against the Beast: William Blake and The Moral Law.* New York: Cambridge University Press, 1993.

"NUTTING" WILLIAM WORDSWORTH (1800)

"Nutting" was written in 1799 and was part of the second (1800) edition of *Lyrical Ballads,* which WILLIAM WORDSWORTH wrote with SAMUEL TAYLOR COLERIDGE. In manuscript, "Nutting" was preceded by an address to a friend named Lucy, who is nutting (gathering nuts) now as he did then. The structure is therefore something like "TINTERN ABBEY": He sees in someone else a reminder of himself at that age, and for that person he can be an anticipation of what she will be at his age. In the published version, his friend does not appear until line 54 as the "dearest maiden" the poem addresses—much as Wordsworth's sister Dorothy does not appear in "Tintern Abbey" until its last movement. In the excised portion, the friend's name is Lucy, and it is likely that this is the same as the Lucy of the LUCY POEMS. She comes slightly more into focus here than in those poems, and perhaps that was intentional on Wordsworth's part, not giving her the specificity that "Nutting" would have lent her in the manuscript version.

If "Nutting" connects with "Tintern Abbey" and the Lucy poems, it also has strong affiliations with *The PRELUDE,* of which it was originally intended to be a part. Wordsworth decided to publish it separately, but it shares obvious features with some of the great episodes of *The Prelude.* Like "Tintern Abbey," it is about returning to nature with an enhanced and chastened sense of both nature's gifts and its limitations, but it goes beyond "Tintern Abbey" in recollecting an intense experience of guilt even in the times of innocent youth it recounts. The guilt is that of depredation (as in the egg-stealing scene in *The Prelude*): He pillaged and destroyed the woods that made him so happy. This is, in a sense, Wordsworth's version of the shooting of the albatross in Coleridge's *The RIME OF THE ANCIENT MARINER* (whose central moment, the arbitrary shooting of the albatross, was Wordsworth's suggestion)—the wanton destruction of natural life followed by an unaccustomed and emotionally deepening feeling of guilt.

Here that destruction and guilt are sexualized. Some critics have seen the ravaging of the landscape as a fantasy of rape, or have seen in rape a metaphor for Wordsworth's sudden, thoughtless, guilt-inducing relation to the woods. But it is more correct to see the scene as masturbatory (as in the American poet Robert Frost's "Birches" [1916], which it strongly influenced). The wanton self-involved destruction of the edenic natural scene gives way to knowledge—the sense of there being another being there besides the speaker. He transcends his own egocentrism, and this story of the fall into knowledge as leading to the transcendence of self-involvement will be repeated again and again in Wordsworth, especially in the poems already mentioned. Now he can sympathize with the pain of others, and this is a gain: He now knows that there is a spirit in the woods, and he knows of the gentle maid whom he addresses that she, too, exists, and that she, too, may come to know that there is a spirit in the woods.

BIBLIOGRAPHY

Abrams, M. H. *Correspondent Breeze: Essays on English Romanticism.* New York: Norton, 1984.

Alpers, Paul. *What Is Pastoral?* Chicago: University of Chicago Press, 1996.

Barker, Juliet. *Wordsworth: A Life.* New York: Viking, 2000.

Bloom, Harold. *The Visionary Company: A Reading of English Romantic Poetry.* Garden City, N.Y.: Doubleday, 1961.

Bromwich, David. *Disowned by Memory: Wordsworth's Poetry of the 1790s.* Chicago: University of Chicago Press, 1998.

Brooks, Cleanth. *A Shaping Joy: Studies in the Writer's Craft.* London: Methuen, 1973.

De Man, Paul. *The Rhetoric of Romanticism.* New York: Columbia University Press, 1984.

Hartman, Geoffrey. *Wordsworth's poetry, 1787–1814.* New Haven, Conn.: Yale University Press, 1971.

Levinson, Marjorie. *Wordsworth's Great Period Poems: Four Essays.* New York: Cambridge University Press, 1986.

Liu, Alan. *Wordsworth: The Sense of History.* Stanford, Calif.: Stanford University Press, 1989.

Pinch, Adela. *Strange Fits of Passion: Epistemologies of Emotion, Hume to Austen.* Stanford, Calif.: Stanford University Press, 1996.

Quinney, Laura. *The Poetics of Disappointment: Wordsworth to Ashbery.* Charlottesville: University Press of Virginia, 1999.

Wolfson, Susan J. *Questioning Presence: Wordsworth, Keats, and the Interrogative Mode in Romantic Poetry.* Ithaca, N.Y.: Cornell University Press, 1986.

O

"ODE: AUTUMN" **THOMAS HOOD (1822)** THOMAS HOOD wrote his beautiful ode on autumn when he was 23. It should be read as an elegiac tribute to JOHN KEATS, four years his senior, who had died the year before (and whose death evoked mention by LORD BYRON as well as PERCY BYSSHE SHELLEY's great elegy *ADONAIS*). Hood echoes Keats everywhere in the poem and might be said to be attempting to exercise his own poetic power in the mode of sheer evocative beauty that Keats handled so well. This would not be Hood's mode in his later writing, and it is striking to see how perfectly he could do it.

Autumn here is personified as a male figure surrounded by the forlornness of the season he represents. The sounds that Keats scattered with such profusion through his poetry—birdsong, insect whirrings, lambs bleating—are absent here in the silent scene, and we realize that the silence represents a kind of universal mourning for Keats's death. Thus, Hood echoes the great final question of Keats's ode "TO AUTUMN"—"Where are the songs of spring?"—when he asks, "Where are the songs of Summer?" (l. 9). The songs of summer, as well as "the pride of summer" (l. 23) and "the sweets of Summer" (l. 34), are gone with Keats; "the swallows" that gather in the last line of his "To Autumn" "all have winged across the main," and what is left is the empty world in which all that remains is "the long gloomy Winter" (l. 29).

The second half of the ode introduces yet another personification—not that of Autumn, who is male (see line 4; I think this was an accurate interpretation of Keats's own personification in "To Autumn"), but of the female "Autumn melancholy" (l. 36), who sighs with sadness, reckoning up the number of "the dead and gone," primarily the dead poets. Her language naturally echoes that of Keats's "ODE ON MELANCHOLY" (including that ode's references both to Psyche and Proserpina), but it is as though she has been left behind by him. Keats's Melancholy comes in the spring, but the Autumn melancholy is, one might say, more accurate or more in tune with the world around it, or perhaps a feature of the world and not of the mind.

Most like the "Ode on Melancholy," though, is the turn from first- to second-person address in the final stanza. Now the poem calls on its addressee to go and sit with her, much as Keats's ode called on his young reader to sit with his angry beloved and gaze into her eyes, because her beauty will die—just as the rose is doomed with her own beauty in Hood (l. 56). This last stanza is also the most beautiful and original of Hood's poem. There still remains enough flora to make her bower, but this is because "there is enough of withered everywhere" (l. 52); her bower is made of the withered. Therefore, there is enough sadness left over to mourn the fact that all that is left is sadness and mourning.

Thus, we could say that the poem is the record of its own sadness, or that sadness records itself in poetry. This was what Hood most aspired to in his early, Keatsian poetry.

BIBLIOGRAPHY

Hood, Thomas. *Memorials of Thomas Hood: Collected, Arranged, and Edited by His Daughter, with a Preface and Notes by His Son. Illustrated with Copies from His Own Sketches.* London: E. Moxon, 1860.

———. *Poetical Works of Thomas Hood, with a Critical Memoir by William Michael Rossetti.* New York: G. Routledge, 1874.

Shillingsburg, Peter L. *William Makepeace Thackeray: A Literary Life.* New York: Palgrave, 2001.

Thackeray, William Makepeace. *The Roundabout Papers.* London: Smith, Elder, & Co., 1879.

"ODE: INTIMATIONS OF IMMORTALITY FROM RECOLLECTIONS OF EARLY CHILDHOOD" See INTIMATIONS ODE.

"ODE ON A GRECIAN URN" JOHN KEATS (1819) "Ode on a Grecian Urn" is one of the great odes that JOHN KEATS wrote in 1819 and is perhaps Keats's most famous poem. All the odes treat the relation of human mortality to something eternal, the eternal having some relation to the durability of art. Keats's odes are in the tradition of WILLIAM WORDSWORTH's great INTIMATIONS ODE, which was also the great model for some of PERCY BYSSHE SHELLEY's greatest lyrics. Shelley and Keats learned from the Intimations Ode the idea that an ode could be a way to think through a difficult imaginative realization and come to some resolution about it. The odes of the romantic poets are probably the single most influential genre for the subsequent history of poetry in English.

Keats spent a lot of time in the British Museum, and in other exhibitions of ancient art; in particular, he was struck by the Elgin Marbles (the Parthenon friezes and sculptures that Lord Elgin had arranged to bring to England, an appropriation of Greek heritage that continues to be a source of irritation between the Greek and the British governments). It is thought that the urn of Keats's title was included among the artifacts accompanying the original display of the Elgin Marbles. However, no particular urn has been successfully identified as the one that Keats is referring to, and it is doubtful that he had a particular one in mind. Rather, his imaginary urn was a sort of symbol for the great art of antiquity, art that had lasted long enough for its relationship to time to be vividly different from that of a mortal human being. The question that such art raises, then, is: What can art do for human beings? Is it helpful or not, and why? The more general question that all the odes ask is how to feel about discovering our ephemeral condition when face to face with the vastest reaches of time.

This ode ends with the resonant and justly famous but difficult lines: "Beauty is truth, truth beauty,—that is all / Ye know on Earth, and all ye need to know." The urn points this moral, but what exactly is the moral? The example of beauty the poem considers is, of course, the urn itself, and the possible truth that the poem utters is the moral: Beauty is truth, truth beauty. So in one way the poem is a demonstration of its own claim: The urn *is* beautiful and *does* assert that the only truth it can offer is its own beauty, down the ages.

But the question is whether this beauty is enough—or whether Keats thinks that it is enough. Here it is instructive to see that the ode changes attitude toward the urn that it is considering. At first, the speaker is amazed at the beauty and expressiveness of the work of art. It is important to see that he contrasts it with poetry ("our rhyme") as though poetic speech were as ephemeral as the human beings speaking it, whereas plastic art may be eternal. But that eternity comes at the price of stasis, even paralysis. The urn lasts forever, but nothing changes in it. The unheard melodies may be sweet, and the lovers depicted on the urn forever young, but they will never get what they want. They are frustrated by their own immortality, frozen and unchanging.

We can mark the distance the speaker's attitude toward the urn travels by his switch from thinking of the urn as showing a love "forever warm and still to be enjoy'd" (l. 26) to his accusation that it is a "Cold pastoral" (l. 45), a picture of warmth, but drained of the warmth and light it depicts.

The beauty of the urn stands in sharp contrast to the life it transcends, but it sends Keats back to the intensity of life. We can see this by noting the obvious fact that we are asked to consider the possibility that the urn is a symbol for the poem (for any poem that aspires to greatness, as this one does). But the urn says nothing like what the poem says: that the world is a place where old age wastes the generations, that we are left frustrated and poor in our relation to love, that we are mortal and not immortal. We know these things not by somehow identifying with the transcendent quality of the urn but by failing to do so. We return to life instead, and the lesson the urn teaches is not the lesson that it means to: Beauty is truth, truth beauty. Instead, it teaches us the truth that we cannot know more than this, (this is "all ye know" and all we *can* know) and that therefore our lives are not fulfilled and cold but (paradoxically) unfulfilled and warm.

All of Keats's great odes (including "Ode on Indolence,") tell something like this story: that the eternal is suffocating, airless, static, and frozen, and that life is ephemeral but warm. Art that aims only at beauty, like the urn, shows that only beauty is transcendent. But art that aims at thought—like Keats's poetry ("Upon the shore / Of the wide world I stand and think," he wrote in his sonnet "WHEN I HAVE FEARS THAT I MAY CEASE TO BE")—shows that thought is sorrowful but deep, and that its depth makes for an art more human and humane than the inhuman coldness of the urn. The urn offers its friendship to everyone and therefore to no one, ignoring the disasters and devastations of the humans it turns away from as it "remains" indifferent. So the truth it offers is that it does not offer transcendence—"that is all ye know on earth" means that we do not know very much, and not knowing very much is the human condition that we can conceive, and a poetry like Keats's can conceive, but the urn cannot. It throws Keats back upon life.

See also "ODE ON MELANCHOLY," "ODE TO A NIGHTINGALE," "ODE TO PSYCHE," "TO AUTUMN."

BIBLIOGRAPHY

Bloom, Harold. *Poetry and Repression: Revisionism from Blake to Stevens.* New Haven, Conn.: Yale University Press, 1976.

———. *The Visionary Company: A Reading of English Romantic Poetry.* Garden City, N.Y.: Doubleday, 1961.

De Man, Paul. *The Rhetoric of Romanticism.* New York: Columbia University Press, 1984.

McFarland, Thomas. *The Masks of Keats: The Endeavour of a Poet.* New York: Oxford University Press, 2000.

Vendler, Helen Hennessy. *Odes of John Keats.* Cambridge, Mass.: Harvard University Press, 1983.

Wasserman, Earl. *The Finer Tone: Keats' Major Poems.* Baltimore: Johns Hopkins Press, 1953.

"ODE ON MELANCHOLY" JOHN KEATS **(1819)** This is one of of the great odes JOHN KEATS wrote in 1819, most of them in May but with a final coda "TO AUTUMN" in September. To contemporary sensibilities, parts of "Ode on Melancholy" seem overwrought, but it shows Keats thinking through the relationships between art, life, and death and the characteristic way he thought through these relationships. Keats at his best thought aesthetically, or used his sense of beauty, in both nature and art, as a guide to direct his thought.

The word *melancholy* literally means "black bile" and names a condition—according to the theory of "humors" that prevailed in Galenic medicine until the 17th century—in which choler or bile predominates, leaving the sufferer liable to anger, despair, and hatred of self and of others. Keats (who had medical training) had read the great work on melancholy, Richard Burton's *Anatomy of Melancholy* (1621), a literary monument in its own right. Burton addressed all aspects of the disorder, from suicidal despair to a kind of self-pleasing bittersweet sense of the sadness of the world—the more modern sense that we tend to give it. That modern sense is to be found in "Il Penseroso" (1631), one of John Milton's pair of poems on two attitudes toward life. The pensive one who is the speaker of that poem prefers melancholy to mirth, feeling (as Keats will) that melancholy offers the profounder pleasures of thought to the person who is brought to melancholy by thinking itself rather than indulging merely in the pleasures of sensation, as L'Allegro, or the high-spirited one, does. We might describe the distinction between melancholy and mirth in Milton as one between deep-spiritedness and high-spiritedness.

The odes of 1819 (including the September poem "To Autumn") are all characterized by a greater or lesser feeling of melancholy—a feeling that the beauties they respond to are achingly ephemeral. The plaintive song of the nightingale fades (that "'most musical, most melancholy' bird," as SAMUEL TAYLOR COLERIDGE called it, quoting Milton for the first four words) in "ODE TO A NIGHTINGALE"; the context of feeling the urn modulates in "ODE ON A GRECIAN URN" is one of "woe"; and even "ODE TO PSYCHE," which is probably the most purely joyous of the odes, imagines that joy in terms of moaning over a semi-sorrowful and very rich estrangement from the scene of joy. The indolence whose siren song Keats hears in "Ode on Indolence" is just the aspect of melancholy that he tries to resist here. This is because melancholy is itself an aesthetic feeling that might conduce to the desire for easy, painless suicide. In "Ode to a Nightingale," Keats had described himself as "half in love with easeful death," his poetry itself ("many a mused rhyme") calling upon death "to take into the air my quiet breath" (ll. 52–54). The temptation to death, as a kind of aestheticized and perfected indolence, is something that Keats consistently feels, and also consistently represented himself as heroically resisting, most powerfully in *The Fall of Hyperion* (see HYPERION AND *THE FALL OF HYPERION*).

The first stanza of "Ode on Melancholy" begins with a gesture of that resistance: "No, no! go not to Lethe." Lethe (source of the English word *lethal*) is the only pleasant river in the classical underworld, the river of forgetfulness. What it offers is the oblivion of pain and sorrow. To forget is to be freed of all sense of loss and to live lapped in an eternal present (what ALFRED, LORD TENNYSON represented in one of his most Keatsian poems, "The LOTOS-EATERS"). The idea of Lethe is a perfect one for the melancholy sensibility, as offering something like the pleasure of melancholy without the motive to try to transcend that self-indulgent indolence: recollection of all that is lost in being in love with death. What Lethe will drown is "the wakeful anguish of the soul," and the ode suggests that this wakeful anguish is what is most important, rather than what one should try to escape. (Compare this with Keats's fear in "Ode to a Nightingale" that if he dies he will not be able to hear the nightingale sing.)

"Ode on Melancholy" is written in the second person. Unlike the second persons of the other odes (Psyche, the nightingale, the urn, autumn), the *you* it addresses is not the subject of the ode; it is, first of all, the aspect of Keats's own mind that he is trying to resist. But the second-person address also gives a sense of the universality of melancholy and its various temptations. All of us would be inclined to go to Lethe if we could, and we need to be warned against this. The speaker's expression of belief in the universality of melancholy is itself a sign of the melancholy he describes; it is the nature of melancholy to affect how we see the whole world.

The first line of the poem had originally been a response to a cancelled first stanza, which survives in only one manuscript. That stanza imagines one going to seek the personified Melancholy in a kind of odyssey to the underworld: "Though you should build a bark of dead men's bones / And rear a phantom gibbet for a mast . . . certes you would fail / To find the Melancholy—whether she / Dreameth in any isle of Lethe dull." The whole stanza is quite grotesque and suggests that the violence of suicide will not allow one to reach Melancholy's abode. She does not dream indolently away on an isle of the river Lethe; she is to be found in this world only—which is part of the melancholy truth she presides over.

To experience melancholy fully turns out to require vigilance and alertness, not drowsiness. This ode is the best exemplification of the NEGATIVE CAPABILITY that Keats discusses in his letters. He wants simultaneously to be lost in the aesthetic emotionality of melancholy and to be sufficiently detached from that experience to be able to appreciate its every aspect. The shades who would interact "too drowsily" may be lost in some indolent melancholy, but they cannot appreciate what they are lost in. Keats instead wants to experience melancholy in this world.

Accordingly, the second stanza of the poem describes what the right reaction to a sudden access of melancholy should be, which is to become absorbed in the very melancholy that one projects onto everything one sees in the world. Melancholy falls "Sudden from heaven like a weeping cloud" (l. 12): it falls not quite like rain but like the cloud itself that weeps rain, so that the weeping, melancholy cloud and its own tears are cloudily merged. Thus, too, should we merge with the outside world that we view in so melancholy a fashion. The cloud "fosters the droop-headed flowers all" (l. 13), which is to say not that they thirsted for the rain and now perked up, but that they are the flowers characterized by their own droopiness, the narcissi whose origin Keats's great favorite poet Ovid recounts in his *Metamorphoses* when he retells the myth of Narcissus. The rain of melancholy intensifies the pleasure of self-indulgent or narcissistic sadness, so that Keats asks his addressee to "glut thy sorrow," which does not mean to counter sorrow but to satisfy what it wants: the beautiful pleasure of sorrow itself.

That pleasure is a pleasure which belongs to love and to joy as well, and it intensifies their experience. The addressee is asked to feel even the melancholy of the vehement and nonmelancholy emotions that others feel. If his mistress is angry at him, he is to transcend that anger with the thought that this, too, is life and therefore ephemeral, and therefore shot through with transient preciousness. Rightly considered, melancholy should make everything precious. In feeding "deep, deep upon her peerless eyes (l. 20), the addressee is glutting his sorrow as he did on the morning rose, taking pleasure in the sorrow that he brings to a peak.

The third stanza makes this explicit. The mistress "dwells with Beauty—Beauty that must die" (l. 21). And so, too, does Melancholy: the feminine pronoun is ambiguous and refers both the mistress and to Melancholy. She is not to be found in Lethean islands but with Beauty in this world; hence, she is the very center and principle of what makes the aesthetic so precious. She dwells also with Joy; the fact that his fingers are "ever at his lips / Bidding adieu" (l. 22) imagines a kind of eternity in the ephemeral. Joy is always what is about to disappear, and that moment when joy is about to disappear is therefore its culmination, its transcendence into a timeless and utterly transient instant. Transience and timelessness are reconciled, but under the rubric of transience. This is why Pleasure aches, and why Melancholy has her shrine even in the midst of the temple of Delight.

The experience of pleasure is that of bursting the grape (Keats is also referring to sexual climax here (l. 29). The fact that pleasure is brief intensifies it and makes sadness an integral part of joy. To take pleasure in the experience of the transience of pleasure, rather than to rebel against this fact, is to be seduced by melancholy, to become one of the trophies in her shrine within the temple of Delight.

The last line is somewhat, and *appropriately,* obscure, but it is clarified, perhaps, if we remember the "weeping cloud" of line 12. To be placed among the "cloudy trophies" of Melancholy is to be absorbed into her in just the way that will fulfill our desire for longing, for the unfulfillable, the desire we experience when we experience Melancholy. That desire is the desire also to write languorously and at length about Melancholy, to capture her within the aesthetic of a poem that can only fulfill itself by failing to do so. We can therefore say that for Keats, Melancholy is one of the names of the Muses.

BIBLIOGRAPHY

Bloom, Harold. *Poetry and Repression: Revisionism from Blake to Stevens.* New Haven, Conn.: Yale University Press, 1976.

———. *The Visionary Company: A Reading of English Romantic Poetry.* Garden City, N.Y.: Doubleday, 1961.

De Man, Paul. *The Rhetoric of Romanticism.* New York: Columbia University Press, 1984.

Empson, William. *Seven Types of Ambiguity.* New York: New Directions, 1966.

McFarland, Thomas. *The Masks of Keats: The Endeavour of a Poet.* New York: Oxford University Press, 2000.

Vendler, Helen Hennessy. *Odes of John Keats.* Cambridge, Mass.: Harvard University Press, 1983.

Wasserman, Earl. *The Finer Tone: Keats' Major Poems.* Baltimore: Johns Hopkins Press, 1953.

"ODE TO A NIGHTINGALE" JOHN KEATS (1819) This is one of JOHN KEATS's great odes, written in spring 1819 and all on more or less related themes. Those themes include the connections among beauty, poetry, melancholy, and death. Keats's sense of beauty is both natural and aesthetic, but the arts that he responds to in the odes do not include poetry. Thus, we may perceive in the odes Keats's attempt to determine what place poetry has in relation to the beauty offered by nature and art, and therefore what place the poet has in relation to that beauty. Keats's imagination has rightly been seen as deeply voyeuristic. He *looks* at the things that fill him with a sense of beauty, but he knows that he cannot touch them. To take one example, in "ODE ON A GRECIAN URN," the scene on the urn is depicted but unavailable to him, and what it depicts is a past and future from which he will, as a mortal being not an aesthetic object, necessarily be absent.

This is why in Keats, beauty is the mother of death. His "Ode to a Nightingale" is perhaps the clearest example of this pattern in his poetry, and it represents as well a crisis lyric in which he must strive to overcome the desire to die with which the beauty of the nightingale's song fills him. But, more subtly, he must overcome the fear of death that beauty instills in him as well: the sense that the worst thing about death is the loss of contact with beauty it will bring.

The poem begins powerfully and unexpectedly with a deep sigh of lamentation (connecting it to the "ODE ON MELANCHOLY," which Keats was about to write). He feels as though he has taken poison, which is not quite the same as feeling that he wants to take it. He does not actively want to die; he does not actively want *anything,* and it is just that feeling which he is expressing. Death for him means forgetfulness, since he feels that he is sinking Lethe-ward; the river Lethe, as he knew from John Milton more than anywhere else, is the underworld's river of forgetfulness, which offers balm and relief from all the pains of life. To feel that he is sinking Lethe-ward is to desire forgetfulness; we will find out in the third stanza that what Keats desires is forgetfulness of the fragility of life and youth and love, as exemplified by the recent death of his brother.

The real surprise comes in the second half of the first stanza: The reason Keats feels so sad is because he is listening to the beautiful and happy song of the nightingale, who is anticipating the coming of summer. Keats may be remembering Jessica's great line in William Shakespeare's *The Merchant of Venice:* "I am never merry when I hear sweet music." At any rate, the beauty of the nightingale's song of summer makes him sad, and it makes him sad because it is happy and because, paradoxically, it makes him happy. He is "too happy," and that excess of happiness knows itself as unsustainable; it knows its excess, we might say, more than it knows its happiness, and it knows that the final meaning of excess is the void it leaves behind. (Several months earlier, Keats had nursed his tubercular brother Tom through his last illness. The nightingale sings in "full-throated ease" [l. 10], whereas, we know, Keats was suffering a chronic sore throat that spring, and would probably have seen in it the incipient signs of the consumption that would eventually kill him, too.) He is happy for the nightingale, and the nightingale represents—as in Ovid and supremely in Milton's invocation to book 3 of *Paradise Lost*—the singer and poet. But Keats cannot identify himself with the nightingale; the song pierces him to the soul and yet it is a song from which he is distanced, as much as from the scene on the Grecian urn.

Accordingly, he wants the experience of a lighter intoxication, one that can make him feel part of the world and not achingly separate from it. The poem's second stanza imagines a kind of simple belonging to the "poetry of earth" (as Keats puts it in "ON THE GRASSHOPPER AND THE CRICKET"), so that he might be with and like the nightingale, and not its earthbound hearer. He would then fade away into the natural scene, and this desire to fade away recalls him to the poem's central melancholy: that it is not nature but just that desire which is really at the center of his soul. Nature is an escape from the lamentable life depicted in the fourth stanza, not an end in itself, or at least any nature he can imagine joining will not be an end in itself.

The fourth stanza tries to reconcile the desire to join with nature to the poetic vocation that makes it impossible for Keats to give himself over simply to the intoxications of wine he had imagined in the second stanza. He will fly to the nightingale, not through the means of the wine-god Bacchus but through poetry itself, and he sets out to do so in the lines that follow, in the beautiful catalogue of flowers that he sets forth. It is important and characteristic of Keats that this catalog is of flowers that he cannot see but can guess at from their scents. One sense replaces another; he thinks of what they look like and thereby tries to reconcile beauty with the intimation of beauty that can only be felt in its absence. It was that melancholy intimation of beauty without its possession that the poem began by lamenting; here he tries to overcome the gap between that intimation and presence through his characteristic use of synesthesia. Synesthesia combines or merges the experience of different senses, and one way to overcome the sense of beauty as being visual, and therefore distant and only available in the frustrating mode of voyeurism, is to turn beauty into something close by and sensual through the psychological mechanism of synesthesia. (The 17th-century philosopher John

Locke had described the sense of sight and hearing as operating at a distance, whereas the other three senses, including smell, require intimate contact of the body with the thing perceived.)

The synesthetic absorption or assimilation of the beauty of the nightingale's song seems as though it might lead to a successful assimilation of beauty, and Keats listens "darkling," just as Milton describes the nightingale who "sings darkling" in the invocation to books of *Paradise Lost.* Where WILLIAM WORDSWORTH had felt loss at the sight of the pansy at his feet in the INTIMATIONS ODE (ll. 54–55), Keats guesses the presence of the flowers at his own (l. 41) and so makes them part of his sensory experience, not a sign for thought (*pansy* means "thought") and the separation that thought implies. Keats here seems to achieve his desire to "live of sensation rather than thoughts" (letter to Benjamin Bailey, November 22, 1817) and to be part of the embalmed darkness around him.

But that embalmed darkness spells death, as Keats comes to realize in the next stanza. The fullest experience of synesthesia, or of absolute plenty, means a merging with the world so complete as to leave him no space to breathe. This is a recurrent theme in the Odes, perhaps most worked out in his later ode "TO AUTUMN" (written in September 1819). Here it seems "rich to die" (l. 55), and what he is in love with is "easeful Death" (l. 52). But he realizes that this is deceptive, that death is the cessation of the beauty that leads toward death. The song of the nightingale is so beautiful that it makes death seem beautiful, but death would mean that he could no longer hear its song. He would not be closer but farther away from beauty, a senseless sod unable to hear the bird's song. Thus, here too, the poem is at an impasse, since neither life nor death seem able to reconcile Keats with the overpowering but inaccessible beauty of the song of the nightingale.

It is in the seventh stanza that Keats does find a way out, by pursuing the logic of the bird's repletion with life. The fact that it was not born for death, that the nightingale's song has been heard (as the Grecian urn has and will be seen) in other ages allows him a sense of community with the other human beings who have heard that song. ("Ode on a Grecian Urn" does not treat this theme.) In particular, he is able to think of the Bible's Ruth, following Naomi after the death of her husband and standing amid the alien corn. Ruth does not belong to the world, but the communion that Keats cannot have with the nightingale he can have with her, another alien in an alien world. This is what poetry can do from afar through pure aesthetic experience, which is always its burden and its vocation. Poetry is written in words and thoughts, rather than in sensation, and the temptation to pure feeling, which returns at the end of stanza 7 with the idea of "magic casements" (l. 69) is what poetry has to resist and what Keats *does* resist when he hears his own word, *forlorn* (ll. 70–71).

Here he is drawn back to his own solitude, but it is not a solitude too luxuriously rich with the beauty it cannot quite grasp; it is the solitude of the poet who hears the nightingale's song and returns to himself and to the possibility of wakefulness in a world that had been too rich with sleep. He may be sleeping still—he does not know (though we do)—but he is no longer giving himself over to the temptations of sleep and death. Rather, he has become a chronicler of forlornness, able to breathe in the thinner air of thought, and in that air to write poetry not overwhelmed by pure sensation.

BIBLIOGRAPHY

Bloom, Harold. *Poetry and Repression: Revisionism from Blake to Stevens.* New Haven, Conn.: Yale University Press, 1976.

———. *The Visionary Company: A Reading of English Romantic Poetry.* Garden City, N.Y.: Doubleday, 1961.

De Man, Paul. *The Rhetoric of Romanticism.* New York: Columbia University Press, 1984.

Empson, William. *Seven Types of Ambiguity.* New York: New Directions, 1966.

Flesch, William. "The Ambivalence of Generosity: Keats Reading Shakespeare." *ELH: English Literary History* 62, no. 1 (Spring 1995): 149–169.

Fry, Paul. *The Poet's Calling in the English Ode.* New Haven, Conn.: Yale University Press, 1980.

McFarland, Thomas, *The Masks of Keats: The Endeavour of a Poet.* New York: Oxford University Press, 2000.

Vendler, Helen Hennessy. *Odes of John Keats.* Cambridge, Mass.: Harvard University Press, 1983.

Wasserman, Earl. *The Finer Tone: Keats' Major Poems.* Baltimore: Johns Hopkins Press, 1953.

"ODE TO PSYCHE" JOHN KEATS (1819) This was probably the first of the great odes that JOHN KEATS wrote in 1819, most of them in May but with a final coda in "TO AUTUMN," written in September. The odes share a sufficient number of elements so as to be almost describable as variations on each other. They are about the possibilities and also the limitations of the imagination's self-transcendence within a world that seems fragile and transient, and they are about the soul's yearning for beauty while experiencing doubt of what constitutes beauty itself, thus signaling beauty's inherent ephemerality. "Ode to Psyche" is probably the happiest of the odes, the one in which the elusiveness of beauty—and of the love it stands for—is most resolved into an image of happiness and peace. Unlike the cold pastoral of "ODE ON A GRECIAN URN," the aching sense of unfulfilment of "ODE ON MELANCHOLY," or the forlorn sorrow of "ODE TO A NIGHTINGALE," Keats's "Ode to Psyche" ends with warmth and love.

In a letter, Keats described the poem just after completing it as "the first and only one with which I have taken even moderate pains." He explained some of the mythological background as well: "You must recollect that Psyche was not embodied as a goddess before the time of Apulieus the Platonist who lived after the Augustan age, and consequently the Goddess was never worshipped or sacrificed to with any of the ancient fervour—and perhaps never thought of in the old religion—I am more orthodox than to let a hethan Goddess be so neglected." By "Apulieus" Keats meant Apuleius, author of the great classical novel *The Golden Ass,* which recounts the tale of Cupid and Psyche among its many stories.

Psyche was a mortal who fell in love with a young man she did not know to be the god Cupid because she never saw his face, since he insisted on coming only in the dark. Every night she left the window (or casement) open for him. Cupid hid his identity because his mother, Venus, was jealous of Psyche. Her sisters, also jealous of her, induced her to surprise her unknown lover by suddenly lighting a lamp. In doing so, she scalded Cupid with hot oil from the lamp. He ran from her, but eventually Zeus took pity on her and transformed her into a goddess, the last of all the Olympians. Finally, Psyche and Cupid were married.

Keats also knew from his trusty guide to mythology, *Lemprière's Classical Dictionary* (1788), that *Psyche* meant "soul," and the word only later became personified as the spouse of love. Their offspring in Apuleius is Voluptas, or that most Keatsian of beings, Pleasure; thus, we could say the most fundamental allegorical interpretation of the myth is that the cause of pleasure, and therefore of poetry, is the soul in love, or perhaps in love with love.

This certainly seems to be the attitude of the ode's narrator toward Cupid and Psyche. The ode is addressed to Psyche, even as it describes her. The speaker will tell her secrets into her own "soft-conchèd ear" (l. 4), and the whirling shape of the ear to which he alludes can be an image for the way the address of the poem curves back in on itself: He speaks to his own creation of that creation, creating it in speaking it. This will be the gesture made by the entire ode as Keats builds a temple for Psyche in his mind—in his own soul or psyche, which is where she can live.

Unlike "Ode to a Nightingale," this ode evinces no anxiety about whether its speaker is awake or asleep. It begins by raising the question, even as "Ode to a Nightingale" ends with the same question. For the nightingale poem, to awaken is to awaken into a world of sorrow, but "Ode to Psyche" displays Keats in his more confident relation to sleep and to the truth of the imagination that comes to him in dreams. Poets, he will say in the preamble to *The Fall of Hyperion* (see HYPERION AND *THE FALL OF HYPERION*), tell their dreams, and in a famous letter he tells us (alluding to the 17th-century poet John Milton), "The Imagination may be compared to Adam's dream: he awoke and found it truth." To see Psyche with awakened eyes is to know her reality, but to dream of her may also be to know her reality, since that reality is mental anyhow. In this sense, the most important line in the poem is the line where Keats declares his poetic vocation in relation to his vision (external or internal) of Psyche: "I see, and sing, by my own eyes inspired" (l. 43).

The narrator tells his story: He was wandering through a forest and suddenly saw two fair, winged creatures, lying together in the forest. There is a subtle allusion to the myth of Acteon here, torn to pieces for having spied on Diana (goddess of chastity) at her bath. But Psyche and Cupid are not Diana. They are themselves at the border of sleep and wakefulness; they are resting after making love, but also, therefore, before making love again, since they are "ready still past kisses to out-number" (l. 19). The speaker recognizes the boy—love—but has to ask who the woman is and to answer himself.

"Ode to Psyche" is one of the most explicit documents of Keats's love of looking. He persistently represents himself as someone filled with pleasure at the contemplation of the world's beauties and as reporting and sharing that (sometimes melancholy) pleasure with others. (Consider, for example, the setup of "WHEN I HAVE FEARS THAT I MAY CEASE TO BE.") But Keats is a great poet, not because of his descriptions but because of the way he finally reacts to what he describes, the way his desire to be lost in the world that he sees (as what he calls the "chameleon poet") finally affects his own deepest interior life.

In this context, what would it mean for him to recognize Psyche? She is his own mind, or a possibility available to his own mind, in a transcendent world of beauty and of love. It's not that he identifies with her; she is not himself. Rather, she is what he imagines would be the soul of poetry in a world still magical with poetical possibility—the world of classical mythology, which saw poetic meaning in everything. This is the time of "the fond believing lyre, / When holy were the haunted forest boughs, / Holy the air, the water, and the fire" (ll. 37–39).

Psyche was made a goddess "too late" for those times, but that means she is still bright now, when all the other Olympian gods have faded into antiquity. (This is the burden as well of the *Hyperion* poems, which Keats began, abandoned, and then recommenced after writing the odes.) She is the mind's true love for those poetic things which have lost their power to otherwise haunt the world. The fact that she—or Keats—was born too late to inhabit a poetry-haunted world is both a loss and a gain for Keats. The loss is that of a sense of the world Keats greatly desires to have, a place where poetry is everywhere. Such a world is Keats's vision of happiness, and in his other poems he tends to imagine it as a world to be found only in dreams. This is the world where Psyche would feel at home, which is to say that the poetic mind would be at home among the Homeric gods. Keats (as "ON FIRST LOOKING INTO CHAPMAN'S HOMER" can show), wants nothing more than to feel wonder and to feel at home in that wonder.

The gain, however, is that Psyche could only come to exist after the supercession of the other gods, since she is a mortal who falls in love with them, not a mortal placed under their sway or accepted into their ranks. A mortal—like Psyche, like Keats—can only fall in love with the gods when they no longer exist or are no longer an object of religious superstition (superstition for which Keats always expressed contempt). Therefore, the proper place for Psyche's temple—a temple to the mortal mind in love with the faded immortals—is in the mind; therefore, Keats says that this is where he will build his temple for her. That temple is the poetic imagination, filled with the flowers that "the gardener Fancy" feigns—flowers that are more beautiful than any on earth.

The midnight Keats proposes for his worship for Psyche (l. 45) is like the midnight he imagines conducting to easeful death in "Ode to a Nightingale" (l. 56), where the thoughts of death also are ornamented with imagined flowers (ll. 41–50). In "Ode to Psyche," though, it is the mind and the imagination, not death, that yields happiness. The "magic casements, opening on the foam / Of perilous seas, in faery lands forlorn" of the nightingale ode (ll. 69–70) are here casements "ope at night / To let the warm Love in" (ll. 66–67).

Forlornness and love are two sides of the same coin, and in both the world is made something other than ordinary, something poetic. "Ode to Psyche" gives the happy side of this equation, with the anticipation of the coming of Cupid or Love. Psyche's torch is already lit, not to discover who Cupid is (she knows that already) but because the myth is over, and what remains is the bright love and bright poetry it inspires.

BIBLIOGRAPHY

Bate, Walter Jackson. *John Keats.* Cambridge, Mass.: Harvard University Press, 1963.

Bloom, Harold. *Poetry and Repression: Revisionism from Blake to Stevens.* New Haven, Conn.: Yale University Press, 1976.

———. *The Visionary Company: A Reading of English Romantic Poetry.* Garden City, N.Y.: Doubleday, 1961.

De Man, Paul. *The Rhetoric of Romanticism.* New York: Columbia University Press, 1984.
Empson, William. *Seven Types of Ambiguity.* New York: New Directions, 1966.
Flesch, William. "The Ambivalence of Generosity: Keats Reading Shakespeare." *ELH: English Literary History* 62, no. 1 (Spring 1995): 149–169.
Fry, Paul. *The Poet's Calling in the English Ode.* New Haven, Conn.: Yale University Press, 1980.
McFarland, Thomas, *The Masks of Keats: The Endeavour of a Poet.* New York: Oxford University Press, 2000.
Vendler, Helen Hennessy. *Odes of John Keats.* Cambridge, Mass.: Harvard University Press, 1983.
Wasserman, Earl. *The Finer Tone: Keats' Major Poems.* Baltimore: Johns Hopkins Press, 1953.

"ODE TO THE WEST WIND" PERCY BYSSHE SHELLEY (1819) "Ode to the West Wind" is one of PERCY BYSSHE SHELLEY's two or three most famous poems. It displays the combination of furious energy, plangency, passion, and hope that is at the center of his poetry, and the struggle between an idealism that would reject the inevitable facts of life and the facts themselves as they become progressively more restrictive.

Shelley's version of an autumn ode should be contrasted to JOHN KEATS's "TO AUTUMN" (also written in autumn 1819), which is about things coming to a halt. In Keats, things slow down, become still and breathless; in Shelley, everything picks up speed, the wind in particular. This partly reflects a difference in environs. In a note, Shelley wrote that "this poem was conceived and chiefly written in a wood that skirts the Arno, near Florence, and on a day when that tempestuous wind, whose temperature is at once mild and animating, was collecting the vapours which pour down the autumnal rains." It is the tempestuous wind that affects Shelley—a natural object that threatens to engulf and overcome his idealizing mind. The west wind should be compared in this regard to the mountain in "MONT BLANC." In these poems of confrontation with a potentially overwhelming natural world, the poem itself represents an attempt to come to terms with an overwhelming and superhuman exterior reality. Shelley offers the most intense imaginative response possible to a natural world indifferent to imagination.

In this ode, as in Keats's "To Autumn," the first gesture of engagement is the invocation—the address, or apostrophe, of the oddly energetic abstraction with which the poem attempts to come to terms. This address is in the vocative, as though autumn or the wind *could* be addressed, could hear an address. The poem opens with an endlessly elaborated description of the being it is addressing, as does "To Autumn," with its series of appositional descriptions of the season, and "Mont Blanc" (in its second stanza), where the address to the mountain turns into a description that returns to an address.

Indeed, the first three of the ode's five sonnet-stanzas are an invocation and a "prayer" (as Shelley will call it in the fourth stanza at line 52), but the prayer is an intensely self-referential one: He prays that the wind will hear his prayer so that he will be heard. Of course, a prayer to be heard is often an ellipsis for the granting of the prayer. To be heard means to be acknowledged and to have the justice of one's request accepted. But Shelley does not mean to go that far. For him, the hearing of the prayer would mean that the wind acknowledges the very existence of the petition that is the poem. The poem would address the wind in terms harmonious with the wind's. It does this through the fierceness of its petition. The very wildness of the wind is a wildness the poem seeks to match, and Shelley's prosody is as rapid, total, and unstoppable as the wind it describes and invokes.

The poem is written in the terza rima form that the Italian poet Dante Alighieri had invented for his *Divine Comedy* (1321), a form much harder in English than in Italian and of which Shelley is the supreme English exponent. (See especially Shelley's great Dantesque poem *The* TRIUMPH OF LIFE.) Terza rima is a form committed to onwardness. The middle line of each tercet provides the frame for the next tercet, so every middle line lays out a template for another stanza. Once a terza rima poem gets started, it becomes a formal difficulty to stop it. Dante did so by ending each canto of the *Divine Comedy* with a kind of quatrain, the middle line of the last tercet rhymed by just one more line. Shelley, in "Ode to the West Wind," leaves out the middle line in what would be the fifth tercet of each stanza, so that they become terza rima sonnets that end on a kind of intensified climax. The form follows the poem's content in doing so, since the concluding couplet of each stanza (a closing which readers have learned to recognize from Shakespearean sonnets) moves from an amassing description of the infinite phenomenon of the wind's power to the poet's culminating petition:

> Wild Spirit, which art moving everywhere;
> Destroyer and preserver; hear, oh hear!

What is it that he wants the wind to hear? He discovers the answer to this question as he goes along. And what he discovers is what he has nevertheless known from the start: He wants the wind to hear him, whatever he says. He wants to participate in its essence, to be a being that can make itself heard by the wind. And yet, to be heard he must have something to say, and what it turns out he has to say is that his petition should be heard.

We finally see this when the poem moves into powerful lamentation in the fourth stanza. That stanza represents the decline that is at the heart of the romantic fall into consciousness. ROMANTICISM treats the present moment—the moment of adulthood, of the regret and loss that poetry delineates—as a moment when the subjective self uttering the poem discovers how much he or she has lost of a once unself-conscious relationship to the transcendent or celestial powers of the natural world. WILLIAM WORDSWORTH's INTIMATIONS ODE is the classic exemplar of this account of the fall into consciousness or self-consciousness, and "Ode to the West Ward" is a Shelleyan version of the Wordsworthian story. In the fourth stanza we hear how fallen from his boyhood self Shelley has become:

> If I were a dead leaf thou mightest bear;
> If I were a swift cloud to fly with thee;
> A wave to pant beneath thy power, and share
>
> The impulse of thy strength, only less free
> Than thou, O uncontrollable! If even
> I were as in my boyhood, and could be
>
> The comrade of thy wanderings over Heaven,
> As then, when to outstrip thy skiey speed
> Scarce seem'd a vision; I would ne'er have
> striven
> As thus with thee in prayer in my sore need.
> Oh, lift me as a wave, a leaf, a cloud!
> I fall upon the thorns of life! I bleed!
>
> A heavy weight of hours has chain'd and bow'd
> One too like thee: tameless, and swift, and
> proud.

The penultimate line of this sonnet refers overtly to the Intimations Ode, where Wordsworth describes the fate of all humans:

> Too soon thy soul shall have her earthly freight,
> And custom lie upon thee with a weight
> Heavy as frost, and deep almost as life.

The loss of unself-conscious imaginative power or intensity is what the wind now represents to Shelley. In his boyhood, he was like the wind; now that similarity has been reduced to a mere vision, but also to a visionary possibility.

In this stanza we hit upon an exemplary Shelleyan moment: the sense of intensity by contrast. As in "THE TWO SPIRITS: AN ALLEGORY," *ADONAIS,* and "Mont Blanc," the condition for perceiving the speed and power of the wind is precisely its difference from the perceiver. The wind's "skiey speed" (l. 30) is a speed that only one on earth, feeling its speed by contrast, can notice. Dead leaves and clouds, just as much as self-confident boys sure of their dinner (as the American poet Ralph Waldo Emerson said), can match the speed of the wind, but the earthbound adult is able to perceive the wind and the nature of its wildness, speed, and pride. And it is *only* that adult who has the impulse, reason, and perception to strive with the wind—whose need is as sore, as intense, as the thing that it measures by its need.

At this point, we can summarize the poem's 75 lines fairly succinctly: O wind, hear me. If I were still my boyish self I would not need to ask you to hear my question. But if you blow through me strongly enough, your movement and my perception of that movement will make me into the trumpet of a prophecy. Similarly, at the end of *A Defence of Poetry* (1821), Shelley wrote his famous definition of poets: "Poets are the hierophants of an unapprehended inspiration, the mirrors of the gigantic shadows which futurity casts upon the present, the words which express what they understand not, the trumpets which sing to battle and feel not what they inspire: the influence which is moved not, but moves. Poets are the unacknowledged legislators of the World." The intensity that exists in the relationship between what moves and what does not move, between "skiey speed" and falling on the thorns of life, or (in "The Two Spirits: An Allegory") between being a spirit of air and a dreaming spirit of earth, is what makes it possible for Shelley to be a poet—that is, in the ode, the trumpet of a prophecy.

And that prophecy is the prophecy of spring. If the Autumn wind announces winter, winter in its turn means that spring will come, and this is the prophecy that Shelley is able to make. It is one that integrates or reconciles the dynamic antitheses of speed and earthbound awe. The wind's wildness is so great, the intensity it figures and the contrast it embodies so powerful, that it can mean and indeed climax in its own self-transcendence as spring, which is to say as the prophecy that its antithetical celebrant, Shelley himself, can utter. Because of the extent of his sense of self-loss, represented by the wind, he, more than anyone, can feel and celebrate and strive with the wildness of the wind, and it is the power of this feeling that enables the visionary poem in which he celebrates it.

BIBLIOGRAPHY

Bloom, Harold. *Genius: A Mosaic of One Hundred Exemplary Creative Minds.* New York: Warner, 2002.

———. *Shelley's Mythmaking.* New Haven, Conn.: Yale University Press, 1959.

———. *The Visionary Company: A Reading of English Romantic Poetry.* Garden City, N.Y.: Doubleday, 1961.

Burke, Kenneth. *Grammar of Motives.* Berkeley: University of California Press, 1969.

Chernaik, Judith. *The Lyrics of Shelley.* Cleveland: Press of Case Western Reserve University, 1972.

Duffy, Edward. *Rousseau in England: The Context for Shelley's Critique of the Enlightenment.* Berkeley: University of California Press, 1979.

Hogle, Jerrold E. *Shelley's Process: Radical Transference and the Development of His Major Works.* New York: Oxford University Press, 1988.

Keach, William. *Shelley's Style.* New York: Methuen, 1984.

Leavis, F. R. *Revaluation: Tradition & Development in English Poetry.* New York: Norton, 1963.

Leighton, Angela. *Shelley and the Sublime: An Interpretation of the Major Poems.* New York: Cambridge University Press, 1984.

Notopolous, James A. *The Platonism of Shelley: A Study of Platonism and the Poetic Mind.* Durham, N.C.: Duke University Press, 1949.

Quinney, Laura. *The Poetics of Disappointment: Wordsworth to Ashbery.* Charlottesville: University Press of Virginia, 1999.

Wasserman, Earl. *Shelley: A Critical Reading.* Baltimore: Johns Hopkins Press, 1971.

———. *Subtler Language: Critical Readings of Neoclassic and Romantic Poems.* Baltimore: Johns Hopkins Press, 1968.

"OH WHO IS THAT YOUNG SINNER"

A. E. HOUSMAN (1895) In May 1895 OSCAR WILDE was convicted of gross indecency for his homosexual liaisons and sentenced to two years of hard labor. Wilde's behavior had been reckless—not his sexual behavior so much as his prosecuting his lover Lord ALFRED DOUGLAS's father, the marquess of Queensberry, for libel when Queensberry publicly accused him of being a sodomite. The outcry against Wilde's imprisonment was loud, but so was the insistence that an example be made of him, and Wilde was convicted for activities that were, though widely condemned, known to occur among English boys and men—of all classes.

A. E. HOUSMAN himself experienced great homoerotic longing (in particular for his Oxford classmate Moses Jackson), and he felt more vividly than most the terrible injustice of the persecution and prosecution of Wilde. He was proud of the fact that a friend memorized and recited some poems from *A Shropshire Lad* to the imprisoned Wilde.) He wrote "O who is that young sinner" at the end of the summer of 1895, though he did not publish it in his lifetime; his brother Laurence included it in a memoir written after Housman's death. Laurence was hesitant to publish it because he knew that the poem would be seen as Housman's acknowledgement of his own homosexuality, as indeed it was. But because Housman had not given his brother explicit instructions not to publish it, as he had with a few other poems, Laurence did release it.

The full title of this poem is sometimes given as "Oh who is that young sinner with the handcuffs on his wrists?" It is written in strong quasi-comic dactylic verse, with 15 syllables per line—the mode of some of RUDYARD KIPLING's ballads and of many a drinking song. It takes the form of an absurd denunciation of Wilde (the young sinner) for the color of his hair—that is, for a natural fact that is no more a matter of choice than it is one of any genuine significance outside of arbitrary social disapproval. The poem manifests considerable bitterness, and it is not perfectly clear how far we should see that bitterness as extending. The last line can be read in two not-quite-consistent ways. The poem is a parody, which means that what its speaker seems to be saying is literally absurd and appalling. Of course, the speaker is parodic: It is his words that are appalling if we do not recognize the parody, and their absurdity is what makes it parody. What those words say is that the poor young sinner deserves to suffer because, after all, the color of his hair is damnable. If there is anyone to blame, it is God, who made him what he is. (This is a Calvinist God, who predestines the elect and the damned.) Cursing God is a recipe of death (most famously in the Book of Job), so that the literal meaning of the poem's words lays none of the blame on society (it is not our fault but God's) and encourages the young sinner to curse God and therefore die.

But taken more seriously, it is God that the poem is cursing, and in full voice. God has allowed the persecution of Wilde to take place; God has so constructed human beings that some have homoerotic impulses, and some seek to kill those with such impulses. This was an idea that Housman took seriously, as another 1895 poem, this one published in *A Shropshire Lad,* makes clear. In "Shot? so quick, so clean an ending," Housman (or his speaker) praises a young man for shooting himself rather than giving in to his homosexual desires. The praise is very serious indeed, lauding him for getting clear of the world "Undishonoured, clear of danger, / Clean of guilt" (ll. 23–24). Housman's praise of the young suicide has been wrongly seen as stern disapproval of any indulging of homosexual inclinations, and therefore Housman would also have disapproved of those inclinations in himself. But it is better to say that the disapproval is of a moral code that made suicide the only possible manifestation of bravery in the young man's life. It *was* brave, as Housman says in the poem, for the lad to take his own life (l. 2), but to praise the young man's courage and loyalty is not to praise what he was courageous about or loyal to. God (or morality) gives an opportunity for self-denial and courage, but the nature of that opportunity is terrible and makes it appropriate to curse God. The situation is genuinely tragic, but the fault is all on the side of those who put the young in the category of sinners.

BIBLIOGRAPHY

Ellmann, Richard. *Oscar Wilde.* New York: Knopf, 1988.

Gardner, Philip, ed. *A. E. Housman: The Critical Heritage.* New York: Routledge, 1992.

Harris, Frank. *Oscar Wilde, His Life and Confessions.* Garden City, N.Y.: Garden City Publishing Co., 1932.

Highet, Gilbert. *Classical Tradition: Greek and Roman Influences on Western Literature.* New York: Oxford University Press, 1957.

Richards, Grant. *Housman: 1897–1936.* New York: Oxford University Press, 1942.

Wilde, Oscar. *De Profundis.* New York: Putnam, 1909.

"OLD ARM-CHAIR, THE" ELIZA COOK **(1837)** It could be said of ELIZA COOK that she was popular because her sentimentality was so in keeping with the atmosphere of Victorian sentimentality generally, but that would both simplify and patronize a complex, subtle, interesting cultural commitment on the part of the Victorians, in addition to undervaluing Cook's real poetic talents. "The Old Arm-Chair" is the poem she is most associated with, and it is worth considering the merits that made it so popular with Victorian readers.

There is, first of all, the wonderful and refreshing opening: "I love it, I love it." Cook *knows* she is being corny, and happily so—who, she asks, is to chide her for it? At the end she repeats the sentiment with somewhat more defiance: "Say it is folly, and deem me weak, . . . But I love it, I love it" (ll. 29–31), In this sense the poem is partly a defense of Victorian sentimentality, and accordingly, Cook undertakes to explain why she treasures it so much: It is because "a mother sat there" (l. 9). The indefinite article is the sign of the sentimental, generalizing the very idea of motherhood (as ALICE

MEYNELL and COVENTRY PATMORE did at a far more subtle level) so as to make it a cultural point of reference that everyone will imagine everyone else will accept.

But the mother who sat there, and who is the motive of Cook's love for the chair, was her own mother, as the second stanza begins to make clear. As a child, she lingered by the chair her mother sat in and learned the things that made her what she is now (at age 24, when Cook wrote the poem). We are thus given a sense of the mother's influence precisely in the tone of the child she educated—largely alone. Poetic tone and the poetic personality it bespeaks thus becomes a fitting tribute to the mother.

Part of what we would praise the mother for is the way the growing child turns outward from her own interests to that of the aging mother in the third stanza. The years roll on, but the mother continues to show her love and bless her child; and the child loves her not because she is the one blessed but because the mother is blessing her. She loves that fact about her mother. It is in this stanza that somewhat to our surprise—so delicately is it handled—we become aware that the reason the obviously empty chair is now the object of Cook's love is that the mother has died: "Years roll'd on, but the last one sped" (l. 22). It is in that very armchair that her mother died (Cook's mother died when Cook was 15).

The last stanza, therefore, is a reprise in which Cook insists on the right to her own sorrow. Why put this in a poem? Because the right to that sorrow is a right that all people will recognize. She insists once again on the generalization of the experience and of the sentiment as she uses the indefinite article again at the end of the poem: "I love it, I love it, and cannot tear / My soul from a mother's old arm-chair" (ll. 31–32). Her mother has become impersonal with death and therefore like every other mortal mother. However, the sentimentality of her attachment to the chair and to her mother's memory is justified by the fact that we are dealing with the deepest questions of life and death.

See also VICTORIAN POETRY.

BIBLIOGRAPHY

Faderman, Lillian. *Surpassing the Love of Men: Romantic Friendship and Love between Women from the Sixteenth Century to the Present.* New York: Morrow, 1981.

"OLD FAMILIAR FACES, THE" CHARLES LAMB (1798) This is CHARLES LAMB's most famous poem, and indeed the only poem for which he is remembered. Francis Palgrave included it in his *Golden Treasury of English Songs and Lyrics,* and it has been a popular favorite since the 19th century. It is not hard to see why: Like much of Lamb's essayistic work, the poem is saturated in a nostalgia that everyone is susceptible to feeling.

The poem's structure is more subtle than appears at first sight, but that subtlety is probably what most people respond to in it. Every stanza ends with the same phrase: "old familiar faces." But the phrase goes from being the subject of a repeated refrain in the first three stanzas to being a direct object in the next three; the final, seventh stanza returns to the refrain of the first three. This shift makes possible a turn to severe self-criticism that can harmonize with an unchanging undertone of regret within the poem. This may be particularly noted in the fourth stanza of the poem, where Lamb's description of himself as an ingrate turns out to be ratified by the poem itself: "I left my friend abruptly,"—why?—"to muse on the old familiar faces." He prefers the silent and melancholy thought of what he has lost than the presence of the very thing that he misses and laments. He addresses the same friend in the sixth tercet, lamenting that he is not a brother so they could lament the old familiar faces together, but even here the wish for such a lamentation is one that imagines it as occurring in the first-person singular—"*we*" might talk of the faces taken from "*me.*"

The poem is in love with its own sorrow, and this is what speaks to a reader's own experience when he or she indulges the desire to read a poem of this sort. It is this which makes its own self-reflection so enticing to a reader's melancholy moods. The way the poem likes its own melancholy strikes a chord in a reader in the mood for such a poem. But this does not mean the melancholy is not real. The lost love of the third stanza is a wistfully recurrent figure in Lamb's *Essays of Elia* (1823, 1833), the wife he could never have once he had committed his life to caring for his insane sister. The great tragedy of Lamb's life was his sister's sudden psychotic murder of their mother, and although Mary

Lamb never again became violent, she made the literary and erotic ambitions of her brother things that could only be imagined in the mode of regret.

The form of the poem is noteworthy, being written in a kind of loose dactylic rhythm. Each line is 11 syllables long, which gives the poem a feel of lamentation too informed for the kind of verse whose formal perfection is a demonstration of the success of its ambitions. But it is also too tight for prose, and thus it has a kind of litany-like or dirge-like quality. That odd but fascinating rhythm contributes to the atmosphere of justifiable self-indulgence that the poem cultivates and allows the reader to cultivate as well.

BIBLIOGRAPHY

Flesch, William. "Friendly and Judicious Reading: Affect and Irony in Charles Lamb." *Studies in Romanticism* 23 (1984): 163–181.

McFarland, Thomas. *Romantic Cruxes: The English Essayists and the Spirit of the Age.* New York: Oxford University Press, 1987.

Monsman, Gerald Cornelius. *Confessions of a Prosaic Dreamer: Charles Lamb's Art of Autobiography.* Durham, N.C.: Duke University Press, 1984.

"O MAY I JOIN THE CHOIR INVISIBLE"

GEORGE ELIOT (1874) GEORGE ELIOT was a novelist, and her novels' narrators tended to be ironic moralists. The typical narrator was usually male, or at least conventionally so, and approved of the passionate morality of some of the characters while disapproving of the venality and selfishness of others. But he tended to be somewhat aloof, somewhat too experienced to be able to give himself over wholeheartedly to other characters' pure, moral impulses. Eliot rarely wrote her novels in her own passionate voice. The exception is in the invented chapter MOTTOES, or epigraphs, where she would cite (as Sir WALTER SCOTT had done before her) fragments from nonexistent texts that often said what she wanted to say. "O May I Join the Choir Invisible" might be regarded as a soliloquy from a nonexistent play, one in which a character expresses a deep moral commitment in the face of her nonbelief in the existence of an afterlife.

Eliot's idea of an afterlife is skeptical and wishful. If there *were* one, she tells us in "BROTHER AND SISTER," she would like to be born a little sister there, so as to relive her own purely happy childhood. She wants what this world can give. But as the motto to *this* poem shows, she disbelieves in the afterlife, following instead the Roman orator Cicero's intense Lucretian skepticism about existence after death. The epigraph is from one of Cicero's letters to his friend Atticus, part of his correspondence about the great loss of his life, that of his daughter Tullia. He wishes to set up a monument to her, no matter how painful it will be in the life that remains to him, because "that long time, in which I will not be, moves me more than this scant one." That long time is for Eliot when she will be invisible but when she will live again in the minds of those who remember her generosity and rectitude. This is her version of WILLIAM WORDSWORTH's praise of "that best portion of a good man's life, / His little, nameless, unremembered acts / Of kindness and of love" ("TINTERN ABBEY," ll. 33–35).

It is important to see that the immortals in this poem are dead. They do not exist as minds or as conscious being, but only in the memory or influence they have on other minds. This desire is a generous desire. To be the kind of person who finds value in being remembered with gratitude by others, even when that gratitude can do one no good at all because one no longer exists, is already to have the attitude toward others tending to lead to the generosity and rectitude Eliot desires. But the yearning to be such a person is not yet the virtue that she yearns for (unlike in the church she left, where the *desire* for salvation is itself the sign of salvation). Wanting to be good is not enough: One must be good, help others, love justice, and do mercy.

Still, the poem has something of the self-sustaining structure of religious faith and desire, even as it justifies literature as a moral calling, because if it moves readers to rectitude and generosity, both by its eloquence and by its passion, it will itself do what Eliot seeks to do. She will then live in the minds of others not merely as a great writer, but in the poem that inspires others to human generosity and justice.

BIBLIOGRAPHY

Bodenheimer, Rosemarie. *The Real Life of Mary Ann Evans: George Eliot, Her Letters and Fiction.* Ithaca, N.Y.: Cornell University Press, 1994.

Bonaparte, Felicia. *The Triptych and the Cross: The Central Myths of George Eliot's Poetic Imagination.* New York: New York University Press, 1979.
Haight, Gordon. *George Eliot: A Biography.* New York: Oxford University Press, 1968.
———, ed. *The George Eliot Letters.* New Haven, Conn.: Yale University Press, 1954.
Hertz, Neil. *George Eliot's Pulse.* Stanford, Calif.: Stanford University Press, 2003.
Woolf, Virginia. "George Eliot." *Times Literary Supplement* (November 20, 1919). Available online. URL: http://digital.library.upenn.edu/women/woolf/VW-Eliot.html. Accessed on April 5, 2008.

"ON A DEAD CHILD" Robert Bridges (1880)

This is one of several poems written in SPRUNG RHYTHM that ROBERT BRIDGES composed after reading his friend GERARD MANLEY HOPKINS's poem "The WRECK OF THE DEUTSCHLAND." Hopkins did not like this poem at all. He wrote to Bridges that the rhythm was worse than in "LONDON SNOW" and that the poem itself "is worse, indeed *it is* Browningese, if you like; as for instance 'To a world, do we think, that heals the disaster of this?' or something like that. You are certainly less at your ease in spring rhythm" (letter of October 26, 1880). What Hopkins disliked in Bridges's sprung rhythm was its large accumulations of unstressed syllables. For Hopkins, stress was all that mattered, and he tended to avoid unstressed syllables whenever possible. Regarding line 22 from "On a Dead Child," which he slightly misquotes in his letter, he apparently objected to the lilting rhythms the unstressed syllables apply to the parallel phrases, and to the fact that they are *made* parallel by some poetic inversion of the kind ROBERT BROWNING practiced.

For Bridges, the great advantage of sprung rhythm was not in the intensification of stress but in the flexibility it allowed in the extensive distribution and concatenation of *unstressed* syllables. Despite Hopkins's strictures, "On a Dead Child" is a beautiful poem, justly praised as one of Bridges's best and widely anthologized. It captures a tone of mourning in the quietly drawn-out sighs of its unstressed syllables. Its last line provides a kind of brief for its style, and for the way it deploys and arranges its unstressed syllables to emphasize the stressed ones. The 15 syllables of that line—"And the things we have seen and have known and have heard of, fail us"—break down into five groups of three syllables each. The first three are exactly parallel anapests: "And the things," "we have seen," "and have known." The fourth is almost parallel, especially to the third: "and have heard." But, of course, the word *of* belongs to this phrase as well, and it is almost as though the anapest has a feminine ending. But it also begins the last three-syllabled group, which is, in fact, an amphibrach, the middle syllable *fail* being the stressed one. (An amphibrach is a metrical foot consisting of a stressed syllable between two unstressed syllables.) But we are conditioned to hearing the anapests, and the way the final *f* in the unstressed *of* merges (over the comma) with the initial *f* in *fail* (softening it to the /v/ sound it has in *of*) causes the word *fail* itself to falter, and the stress fails as well—a perfect example of the things we have seen and have known and have heard of, and which fail us.

That sadness of tone matches the sadness of content: The child has just died, and the speaker is there, arranging the boy's body in the coffin for his vigil and viewing. The corpse is so lifelike as to remind the speaker of the life that is gone. (The experience the poem recounts may well be from Bridges's work as a physician, where he showed extraordinary conscientiousness and empathy for the sick and dying, and for their survivors.) The poem's sadness is manifest, but the last two stanzas are tricky. Bridges expresses the hope—a hope he is not sure of having ("do I think")—that the child's soul has gone to a better world "that rights the disaster of this" world (l. 22). But he does not know, and his last stanza is remarkable in applying equally to the child's (and everyone else's) experience of dying and to the human experience of being born in *this* world. "Our hopes avail us" little (l. 25) whether directed at our own future or at the future of the dead child. We are unwilling and embarked alone, both on our dying and on our lives. The things we have seen and have known and have heard of might be the things of this life, or they might be the things we once knew in a platonic or Wordsworthian prenatal residence in the ideal world. But we do not know, and the death of the child stands for the universal lack of knowledge and of confidence, which makes us unsure that either his soul or our own will survive. The immense sadness and realism of the vision is matched by the sadness of the poem's tone, its prosody muted and dark and slow.

BIBLIOGRAPHY

Bridges, Robert. *Milton's Prosody*. Oxford: Clarendon Press, 1893.

Gross, Harvey. *Sound and Form in Modern Poetry*. Ann Arbor: University of Michigan Press, 1996.

Guerard, Albert. *Robert Bridges: A Study of Traditionalism in Poetry*. Cambridge, Mass.: Harvard University Press, 1942.

Hopkins, Gerard Manley. *Gerard Manley Hopkins: Selected Letters*. Edited by Catherine Phillips. New York: Oxford University Press, 1990.

Ritz, Jean-George. *Robert Bridges and Gerard Hopkins: A Literary Friendship*. London: Oxford University Press, 1960.

"ON CALAIS SANDS" ANDREW LANG (1891)

This was one of ANDREW LANG's best-known poems. Despite its serious subject matter, it is not quite serious because it is a dreamy demonstration of poetic form and tone, rather than a document of horror and regret. Its wit makes its ending at once inevitable and surprising, thereby manifesting some of the arbitrariness of the comic. Nevertheless, its sound and tone were melancholy enough to make it the source of one of the greatest poems of the First World War, John McCrae's "In Flanders Fields" (1915). McCrae, in fact, most fully achieved the sadness that Lang explored.

Lang's poem is a ballade (like his "BALLADE OF BLUE CHINA"), a troubadour form revived in the second half of the 19th century by ALGERNON CHARLES SWINBURNE and DANTE GABRIEL ROSSETTI. The ballade consists of three stanzas (of eight or 10 lines each) with only three or four different rhymes throughout the whole poem, followed by a half-stanza envoi, all four stanzas ending with the same last line or refrain. A difficult but effective form, it fascinated poets like Lang and Swinburne because of the play of tonality it required. For the repetition to work, both rhyme-sound and refrain must shift in meaning. (Some of the rhymes can be repeated, but this will only work if the meaning of the homophones changes.) In modern poetry, this often makes possible broad comic effect through the use of puns (as in Phyllis McGinley's hilarious but also moving and melancholy "Ballade of the Lost Objects" [1953]), and Lang did use it for light verse. But "On Calais Sands" is sadder than that: It is a poem about the contrast of life and death, a contrast brought out in the change in meaning of the repeated refrain, or change in attitude that the reader brings to the repeated refrain.

Dueling was illegal in England and on the Continent, but in England it was prosecuted in the second half of the 19th century, whereas in France it was tolerated until the 20th century. Therefore, Englishmen went to Calais, just a short boat ride across the English Channel, where they dueled on the shores to settle their differences. (The novelist Anthony Trollope's characters regularly went to France or the Netherlands to duel.)

In Lang's poem, the first stanza sets the scene: a beautiful dawn on the shore. We do not yet know that the poem will be anything but description; the beauty of the morning suggests gaiety and not tragedy. But this is the point: The natural world is indifferent to human absurdity, and this indifference underscores the absurdity.

The second stanza effects a transition between the flashing beauty of the scene and the violence that will culminate in the third. The duelists are part of the beauty, their rapiers catching the dazzling play of sunlight. But by the end of this stanza, one man has been killed. It is important to note that the victor stands "mournful" (l. 15); this has not been a duel between good and evil, with the victor being one or the other, but between two youths over what must be a trivial matter. We know that the dead youth is as appealing as the living from the third stanza: His lips have never said, "Nay" (l. 21), which means he has always sought to please, and he has even accepted the duel out of the candidness of his heart.

The end of the third stanza chillingly telescopes love and death together, an effect that melancholy refrain and repetition are particularly suited to produce (see THOMAS LOVELL BEDDOES's "The PHANTOM WOOER"). The sea will now dally with the hands of the once living, beautiful, perfumed boy. This image both prepares us for and distracts us from the worst blow in the envoi: the woman who awaits the return of the youth in vain. He will never return. He is colder than the sands themselves, not literally but in the sense that the poem registers his death, and the poem's own ending, as utterly final—unlike the ebullient natural scene, and the love it might represent, with which the poem began and which the duelists, out of some mistaken point of honor, were too proud to heed. The poem is not, of course, about the sadness of its characters, but an exposition of the possibilities of its own form, as life gives way to endless repetition and death, on Calais sands.

BIBLIOGRAPHY

Beerbohm, Max. "Two Glimpses of Andrew Lang." *Life and Letters* 1, no. 1 (June,1928): 1–11.

Cocq, Antonius Petrus Leonardus de. *Andrew Lang, A Nineteenth-Century Anthropologist.* Tilburg, Netherlands: Zwijsen, 1968.

Green, Roger Lancelyn. *Andrew Lang: A Critical Biography with a Short-Title Bibliography of the Works of Andrew Lang.* Leicester, England: E. Ward, 1946.

Gross, John. *Rise and Fall of the Man of Letters: Aspects of English Literary Life since 1800.* London: Weidenfeld & Nicolson, 1969.

Orel, Harold. *Victorian Literary Critics: George Henry Lewes, Walter Bagehot, Richard Holt Hutton, Leslie Stephen, Andrew Lang, George Saintsbury, and Edmund Gosse.* London: Macmillan Press, 1984.

Webster, A. Blyth. *Andrew Lang's Poetry, by A. Blyth Webster, being the Andrew Lang lecture delivered before the University of St. Andrews 20 October 1937.* London: Oxford University Press, 1937.

"ONE NIGHT I DREAMT THAT IN A GLEAMING HALL" DIGBY MACKWORTH DOLBEN (ca. 1867) Here DIGBY MACKWORTH DOLBEN wrote a very short sonnet sequence (a Victorian vogue). "One night I dreamt" is only four sonnets long, and while each may be read as an independent poem, all four deserve to be read as a sequence. They chronicle a relationship more or less from the moment that it is clear that it cannot last—a relationship the speaker regrets.

The sonnets are clearly if subtly homoerotic, and the reason that the love they describe cannot continue is that the "boyish friendship" (3, l. 1) appropriate (in the tacit understanding of aristocratic Victorian culture) to school days at Eton and Oxford must yield to marriage and the normative demands of heterosexuality (see ALFRED, LORD TENNYSON'S *IN MEMORIAM A.H.H.*) Dolben himself found in an intense but somewhat affected religiosity an outlet for the intensities that he also experienced as homoeroticism (and the last sonnet of this sequence should be compared with his beautiful poem about Christ and his human birth, "Christ, for whose only Love I keep me clean"). Here that religion is itself a faithfulness to the addressee of the sonnets.

The first sonnet recounts a dream in which the beloved (certainly Dolben's schoolmate Martin Gosselin) is surrounded by "a starry ring" (l. 5) of angelic forms that sing for him. The beloved challenges the speaker to sing, too, but when he does, he produces only "a piercing discord" (l. 12), prompting the beloved to laugh at him and causing him to wake up in "great bitterness" (l. 14). We can identify the starry ring as that of the women to whom the beloved will now turn, his boyish days over; and we can note that what marks those boyish days as being over is the change in voice that the speaker experiences: He is no longer a beautiful boy with a boy's voice; he loses that voice as he becomes a young man.

In the second sonnet, the speaker accepts the fact that he must be one of a number of rivals for the beloved's affections, even as he remembers that the "ideal west" (l. 10), the later part of the day that comes with adulthood, was once the place where youth could find the blessings of love.

The third sonnet is the most openly bitter. Its first words echo what the beloved must have said to him, that theirs was "A boyish friendship" (l. 1). But the speaker denies this, instancing his faith and love even after many years. Particularly noteworthy are its concluding couplet, which at least allows for the erotic residuum of masochistic intensity (also to be found in Dolben's religious poems), even if the beloved will not reciprocate as he has during their boyhood.

The last sonnet says more or less what the others do (and what Dolben's poem "Christ, for whose only Love I keep me clean" does)—that it is a privilege to at least be able to attend upon the sovereign he was once so close to. That sovereign is clearly male here, addressed as "my king" in the first line. The homoeroticism of the poem is deniable through the idea that the poem is addressed to Eros, the god of love, but that denial would be very weak indeed. It relies only on the idea that love can express itself through allegory. But the very announcement that love can express itself through allegory is here an allegory itself, namely of the fact that it *must* express itself through allegory because it is homoerotic—what Lord ALFRED DOUGLAS would later call "the love that dare not speak its name."

BIBLIOGRAPHY

Bridges, Robert. *The Poems of Digby Mackworth Dolben.* New York: Oxford University Press, 1911.

———. *Three Friends: Memoirs of Digby Mackworth Dolben, Richard Watson Dixon, Henry Bradley.* Westport, Conn.: Greenwood Press, 1975.

Cohen, Martin, ed. *Uncollected Poems of Digby Mackworth Dolben.* Reading, England: Whiteknights Press, 1973.

Cunningham, Valentine. Headnote to selection of Dolben in *The Victorians: An Anthology of Poetry & Poetics.* Malden, Mass.: Blackwell, 2000, 901.

Dolben, Digby Mackworth. *The Poems and Letters of Digby Mackworth Dolben, 1848–1867.* Edited by M. Cohen. Amersham, England: Avebury, 1981.

"ON FIRST LOOKING INTO CHAPMAN'S HOMER" JOHN KEATS (1816) This is perhaps JOHN KEATS's most famous sonnet and his most quoted poem. In the early 17th century, George Chapman, a contemporary of William Shakespeare and a playwright, had translated the Greek poet Homer into just the kind of language that Keats reveled in when reading Shakespeare and Edmund Spenser. Keats had no classical education, and while he loved the classical myths and wrote many poems on classical subjects, he could not read them in the original. Chapman's Homer gave him a sense of what he was missing.

The sonnet is typical of Keats in that it describes the kind of literary experience that his conscious and committed vocation as a poet made him regard as a fit subject for poetry. He describes himself more or less as Odysseus, traveling through various realms and having memorable adventures in all of them. Like Odysseus's, these adventures are primarily literary (for Keats because they are literature), and so we can understand the opening lines as metaphors for the reading Keats has done, in poems by "bards" who have declared "fealty to Apollo" (l. 4). These "realms of gold," especially those near the "western islands" where he has been (ll. 1, 3) stand for the imaginative worlds of the literature he has read—primarily British literature (the literature of the "western islands"), especially Spenser, Shakespeare, and Milton—all three of whom retold classical myths. But he had never read Homer, or never read a version of Homer that conveyed to him the epic poet's greatness, until now.

In following up its Homeric conceit, the poem treats Homer as one of his own hero-kings or gods, a cross between Agamemnon or Menelaus and Zeus himself. Keats has never entered into Homer's world until now, and the end of the octet of this Petrarchan sonnet has him hearing Chapman's language and being transported by it to Homer's demesne.

The sestet describes the experience, and it is crucial to note how Keats manages his similes. Reading Homer is like having a contemporary experience similar to that of finding a new planet (as had been done most recently a generation earlier) or of discovering not only a new continent but a new ocean, as the conquistadors did when they first saw the Pacific. The simile points in two directions and puts Keats squarely in the middle. On the one hand, the limits of Homer's world are pretty much the Straits of Gibraltar, whereas Keats knows infinitely more than Homer and his contemporaries did. Like Milton invoking Galileo and his telescope in *Paradise Lost,* Keats can allude to contemporary astronomy in ways that place the moderns above the ancients. But on the other hand, no modernity can claim to outvie poetry as the setting of absolute novelty and transcendent discovery. One need not see Uranus for the first time, nor discover the Pacific (as Balboa, not Cortez, did) to have an experience of commensurate magnitude. Reading Homer will do. (F. Scott Fitzgerald, who loved Keats, was thinking of this moment at the end of *The Great Gatsby.*)

Keats had praised NEGATIVE CAPABILITY as essential to the poet. This poem ratifies in him the chameleon-like ability to experience anything: what it was like reading Homer, what it is like discovering a new world (like both the astronomer and Cortez). The ancients and the moderns are all more or less confined by their respective ignorance of each other's freshness and novelty. But Keats can experience both, and in this poem he declares that capacity.

The poem ends with a typically Keatsian hush, and we can understand that hush here to be a silence induced by the negative capability that is his triumph (rather than the smothering claustrophobia it sometimes threatens to mean for him, as in "ODE ON A GRECIAN URN" and "TO AUTUMN"). The wild surmise is the moment of poetic creation or influx, the moment when the mind understands the unprecedented and is in its silence aware that it will be able to express its own wonder—as Keats does in this poem.

BIBLIOGRAPHY

Bate, Walter Jackson. *John Keats*. Cambridge, Mass.: Harvard University Press, 1963.

Bloom, Harold. *Poetry and Repression: Revisionism from Blake to Stevens*. New Haven, Conn.: Yale University Press, 1976.

———. *The Visionary Company: A Reading of English Romantic Poetry*. Garden City, N.Y.: Doubleday, 1961.

De Man, Paul. *The Rhetoric of Romanticism*. New York: Columbia University Press, 1984.

McFarland, Thomas. *The Masks of Keats: The Endeavour of a Poet*. New York: Oxford University Press, 2000.

Wasserman, Earl. *The Finer Tone: Keats' Major Poems*. Baltimore: Johns Hopkins Press, 1953.

"ON SITTING DOWN TO READ *KING LEAR* ONCE AGAIN" JOHN KEATS (1818)

This is one of several great sonnets that JOHN KEATS wrote in the winter of 1817–18, and it should be compared in particular with "WHEN I HAVE FEARS THAT I MAY CEASE TO BE," written at the same time and to which it is a kind of pendant. In his sonnets, Keats was experimenting with both Shakespearean and Petrarchan forms, and although this one is about William Shakespeare, there is significance in the fact that it is Petrarchan (where "When I have fears" is Shakespearean).

The Petrarchan sonnet divides into an octet and a sestet and generally changes direction after the octet, which is what it does here. The octet describes the experience of a kind of aesthetic rebuke that Keats receives from Shakespeare. This is a common theme for Keats, especially in the sonnets: The Elgin Marbles make his spirits fail ("ODE ON A GRECIAN URN"); George Chapman's translation of Homer fills him with awe (ON FIRST LOOKING INTO CHAPMAN'S HOMER); *King Lear* makes him feel the triviality of the kind of poetry he had been aspiring to—the kind of poetry he turns away from as well in "When I have fears." That poetry is one of sensual pleasure, the pleasure of language and of a happy plot, of the type that we associate in Keats with "The EVE OF ST. AGNES." This is what he calls "golden-tongued Romance" (l. 1), or the "high romance" in line 6 of "When I have fears." That romance is the "Queen of far-away," a siren or muse of evocativeness who makes him feel that poetry is elsewhere and inspires him to write the poetry that will carry him elsewhere. Thus, too, he wishes to follow the nightingale in "ODE TO A NIGHTINGALE" and fade far away with her into the forest dim. But *King Lear* is of another order, and now he will close the Spenserian romances he so loves to imitate and "assay" the absolutely serious poetry of Shakespeare, bracing and SUBLIME and tragic.

So says the octet, but there is a turn in the sestet that too often goes unnoticed. It begins as an apostrophe to Shakespeare, praising him, but then it turns into the expression of his intention to go "through the old oak forest" (l. 11)—that is to say, Keats calls on Shakespeare to aid him in his journey through the forests of romance. The fire he alludes to in the penultimate line seems something out of Ludovico Ariosto or Edmund Spenser (as at the end of book 3 of Spenser's *The Faerie Queene*), although it will also mean the fire of death and the fire that threatens to destroy all books. But Keats emphasizes the first of these meanings, which is to say that the fire that consumes him will be that of the *desire* that the last word of the poem reveals as its subject. Thus, Shakespeare is transfigured into a marvelous, Merlin-like figure who inhabits the world of romance to which he seems to be opposed. Keats makes romance overcome its Shakespearean critique, or he subsumes that critique into an element of romance. (It helps, too, that the phoenix, the bird that arises out of its own ashes, is an allusion to Shakespeare's nondramatic poem "The Phoenix and the Turtle.") All of this clarifies the subtlety hidden by the title, and which we may expand a little bit like this: "On sitting down to read *King Lear* once again, I wrote this sonnet-romance instead."

BIBLIOGRAPHY

Bate, Walter Jackson. *John Keats.* Cambridge, Mass.: Harvard University Press, 1963.

Bloom, Harold. *Poetry and Repression: Revisionism from Blake to Stevens.* New Haven, Conn.: Yale University Press, 1976.

———. *The Visionary Company: A Reading of English Romantic Poetry.* Garden City, N.Y.: Doubleday, 1961.

De Man, Paul. *The Rhetoric of Romanticism.* New York: Columbia University Press, 1984.

Flesch, William. "The Ambivalence of Generosity: Keats Reading Shakespeare." *ELH: English Literary History* 62, no. 1 (Spring 1995): 149–169.

McFarland, Thomas, *The Masks of Keats: The Endeavour of a Poet.* New York: Oxford University Press, 2000.

Wasserman, Earl. *The Finer Tone: Keats' Major Poems.* Baltimore: Johns Hopkins Press, 1953.

"ON THE GRASSHOPPER AND THE CRICKET" JOHN KEATS (1986)

"On the Grasshopper and the Cricket" is one of JOHN KEATS's most delightful sonnets. Like his sonnet "On the Nile," it was written in competition with his close friend LEIGH HUNT in December 1816, when Keats was visiting Hunt. They took 15 minutes to write their sonnets.

In general theme, the sonnets are similar enough and probably reflect the conversation that led up to the game of writing the sonnets. The grasshopper represents the songs of summer (as in Aesopian fables about the ant and the grasshopper), and the cricket represents those of winter. All this Hunt's sonnet makes clear:

To the Grasshopper and the Cricket

Green little vaulter in the sunny grass,
Catching your heart up at the feel of June,
Sole voice that's heard amidst the lazy noon,
When even the bees lag at the summoning
brass;
And you, warm little housekeeper, who class
With those who think the candles come too
soon,
Loving the fire, and with your tricksome tune
Nick the glad silent moments as they pass;
Oh sweet and tiny cousins, that belong
One to the fields, the other to the hearth,
Both have your sunshine; both, though small,
are strong
At your clear hearts; and both were sent on
earth
To sing in thoughtful ears this natural song:
Indoors and out, summer and winter,—Mirth.

Hunt's sonnet, while lovely and evocative, is nothing like a great poem, and it shows Keats's genius by contrast. Hunt makes clear the similarities between grasshopper and cricket: Both stand for the natural songs of mirth, which are preserved summer and winter. Hunt makes summer and winter part of a generalized human weather.

Keats, on the other hand, was one of the great poets of weather, and of the changing seasons. For Keats, the natural world was much more specific, more localized, and much fuller of sensual richness. He would write that poetry had better come like leaves to a tree, and the quick spontaneity of this sonnet shows him to have fulfilled his own definition of the poet. It is worth remembering that the sonnet was written in December, despite or perhaps motivating the wonderful evocations of summer in the octet. (This is a Petrarchan sonnet, divided into octet and sestet; in such sonnets there is usually, as here, a turn or switch in emotional direction or quality with the sestet.) As is typical of Keats, one experiential condition—that of winter—leads his imagination to an intense evocation of the contrary or complementary condition, in this case summer. (See "ODE TO A NIGHTINGALE," where the speaker in a bower imagines the nightingale in the free air and thinks of the bird's immortality in contrast to his own frailty.) The effect of this evocation of summer's heat and the pleasure of "cooling trees" is to turn winter into a further evocation. In the midst of winter, Keats evokes summer, and then from that evocation of summer he gets us back to winter, but now from the perspective of summer heat. Here the cricket sings (as the crickets will sing in "TO AUTUMN," Keats's greatest poem about the saving evocativeness of change of season), its song "in warmth increasing ever," so that passion becomes a kind of metaphor for weather (and not the more obvious converse).

The warmth of the song stands for the warmth of the stove behind which the cricket sings, and that warmth, in the midst of winter, is so comfortable that someone sits by it and drowsily dreams of the soporific heat of summer, with which the poem has opened, and the cricket's song reminds the dreamer of the grasshopper. As with Hunt, cricket and grasshopper come together to stand for the same "poetry of earth," but for Keats this is not because they are two examples of the same thing. It is because each evokes the other, and the play of evocation is what gives poignancy to the sensual fullness of experience, or fullness to poignancy. For at the end of the poem, we discover that its opening is the dream whose impetus the end describes: the play of evocations by which winter evokes summer, which evokes the beauties of winter, "when the frost / Has wrought a silence," which wraps one around with a drowsiness in which one dreams of summer and can therefore write a sonnet like "On the Grasshopper and Cricket."

BIBLIOGRAPHY

Bate, Walter Jackson. *John Keats.* Cambridge, Mass.: Harvard University Press, 1963.

Bloom, Harold. *Poetry and Repression: Revisionism from Blake to Stevens.* New Haven: Yale University Press, 1976.

———. *The Visionary Company: A Reading of English Romantic Poetry.* Garden City, N.Y.: Doubleday, 1961.

De Man, Paul. *The Rhetoric of Romanticism.* New York: Columbia University Press, 1984.

Flesch, William. "The Ambivalence of Generosity: Keats Reading Shakespeare." *ELH: English Literary History* 62, no. 1 (Spring 1995): 149–169.

McFarland, Thomas. *The Masks of Keats: The Endeavour of a Poet.* New York: Oxford University Press, 2000.

Wasserman, Earl. *The Finer Tone: Keats' Major Poems.* Baltimore: Johns Hopkins Press, 1953.

"ON WENLOCK EDGE THE WOOD'S IN TROUBLE" A. E. HOUSMAN (1896) One way of understanding A. E. HOUSMAN's singular form of melancholy is to compare it to JOHN KEATS's. In "ODE TO A NIGHTINGALE," Keats compares his experience hearing the nightingale now to the experience of those who heard its song in ancient days, suggesting thereby a continuity in human feeling and affection. It is this continuity that MATTHEW ARNOLD also stresses in his more Keatsian poems, even as he regrets the discontinuity imposed by his belonging to a later age and a more northern clime. In this comparison between the ancients and the moderns, Housman is perhaps more fully on the side of the moderns, despite or rather because of his own vocation as a classicist. Housman was a connoisseur of the ephemeral in all things, and the great remoteness in time of the classical poetry he loved was an element in that love. The Roman poet Horace's melancholy sense of the ephemeral is verified for Housman by the distance imposed by time, so that Housman has an even more intense apprehension of this melancholy. He knows, from an experience Horace could not have had, the experience of Horace's distance, how elusively remote the most beautiful and moving poetry can be, how tenuous is the link between the past and the present. (For more on this issue, see the entry on Housman's adaptation of Horace's "DIFFUGERE NIVES.")

"On Wenlock Edge" is characteristic of many of the poems in *A Shropshire Lad* in the way it combines attention to the present moment with a sense of the immensity of time. Wenlock Edge is a feature of the Shropshire landscape, as are the Wrekin hill and the River Severn. A strong wind is agitating all of Shropshire, shaking and bending the trees and sending their leaves onto the river. "The wood's in trouble" on Wenlock Edge (l. 1) in the sense that it is physically troubled by the gale; this is the literal meaning of the word *trouble* as turbulence, familiar from the phrase "troubled waters."

But its literal meaning also makes it a metaphorical correlative for Housman looking on at the landscape, as it was for the Roman whose onetime "trouble" has been trivialized to ashes at the end of the poem (l. 19). Housman thinks of how long these woods and this landscape have been here. The woods are the same and not the same. They have changed because time has passed and one generation of living things has succeeded another. But the wind is still the same wind (l. 7), so that the trouble is felt to be more permanent than its instances.

The wind swept through another wood because centuries ago, in Roman times (when the city of Viroconium, which Housman names here as Uricon, was to be found in Shropshire), it was not Housman who saw the wind agitating the forest but some Roman. They were about as different, which means about as similar, as the woods of their two ages were. The same blood warmed them, the same thoughts hurt them. Housman is almost offhanded at describing the thoughts that hurt him (l. 12), but we can say that they are thoughts both of mortality itself and thoughts that are individuated (thoughts of love, say). Nevertheless, they lead to thoughts of mortality, since no matter how individuated the thoughts, there is nothing original in human thinking. In the end we all experience, fear, desire, and suffer the same things.

It turns out that those thoughts, no matter how troubling, are also the signs of life, imaged in the life of the forest that Housman gazes on. But this momentarily saving consideration—that thinking, no matter how painful, means that one is alive—is itself brought up short by the recollection that now the Roman and all that troubled him are gone—turned into shades and ashes (as Horace also put it).

Housman sees the woods and knows that the Roman who once saw them, and who once was hurt by thoughts the same as his, is gone. Did the Roman also have *that* thought? In a sense it does not matter what the answer to this question is; it is enough that the poem has posed it. That melancholy thought—that all who feel the life of the gale, and the life that its melancholy brings, must die—allows Housman some escape from whatever other melancholy thoughts are hurting him. All thought is in the end about the discontinuity of time, but Housman says and laments this more plainly than the Roman before him, whether Horace or a townsman of Uricon. That is the difference between them: that he explicitly says and knows that it is not a saving difference.

BIBLIOGRAPHY

Gardner, Philip, ed. *A. E. Housman: The Critical Heritage.* New York: Routledge, 1992.

Highet, Gilbert. *Classical Tradition: Greek and Roman Influences on Western Literature.* New York: Oxford University Press, 1957.

Richards, Grant. *Housman: 1897–1936.* New York: Oxford University Press, 1942.

"OUT OF THE FRYING PAN, INTO THE FIRE" JAMES HENRY (1854)

This is one of JAMES HENRY's iambic meditations. Although he tended to write his lighter verse in trochees, even when engaged in what seems a slightly more serious form, his touch is very light, as the title makes obvious. The genre here is one that Henry perhaps derived from LORD BYRON's "Darkness," that of a dream vision of hell.

Here Henry dreams of an afterlife in which he is judged by God, and at first the poem seems to be an expression of religious awe. But it is quite the reverse. God questions him accusingly, but the question is a horrid and near-unanswerable one: "Wherefore / Wast thou as I made thee?" (ll. 16–17). The dreamer is not being accused of failing to live up to his own divine origins; he is not accused of having *fallen* into sin. Rather, he is accused of being just as he was created by God. God has made him as he is and is now punishing him for being the limited and flawed being that God made him. This is Henry's summary of Christian moral doctrine: that God punishes us for being the human beings he made us to be. (Henry was resolutely anti-Christian.)

Unable to answer the accusation, the dreamer finds his soul plunged to a hell which owes something of its description to *Paradise Lost* but more to its author, Dante. For the hell he finds contains all the great minds of the history of the world. The dreamer ironically says that they were all miscalled *good*—he knows this because God has placed them in hell and has even had to set aside some of heaven's territory in order to find room to incarcerate them. This causes the cherubim (the unfallen angels) to rebel against God's bureaucratic solution to the problems caused by infinite damnation, and so God has to establish martial law in heaven. This is an amazing conceit, one that the great 20th-century critic William Empson will ascribe to Milton, but which never had been made explicit before Henry.

It is at this point that the dreamer wakes up to find himself in Germany. He has fallen asleep at an inn, but now the innkeeper wakes him up to obtain the information required of travelers: his name, age, birthplace, religion, origin, and destination. He must also pay a fee in order to be registered with the state, so that we begin to see that the afterlife Henry has dreamt of is much like the bureaucratic state of the Victorian era. There is one difference, though. In this world, Henry can pay his sixpence and be left alone. He is not branded a spy or felon or disturber of the peace just through his existence. If the innkeeper is not particularly friendly, it does not matter; he will leave Henry alone.

We now see that the frying pan and the fire of the title refer respectively to this life, and the afterlife. In this life, people may be unpleasant and greedy, but that is all they are. There is none of the absurd and self-righteous moralism that marks the God of the afterlife. Henry is a connoisseur of the tolerable, and he likes this world just because it is tolerable.

BIBLIOGRAPHY

Cunningham, Valentine, ed. *The Victorians: An Anthology of Poetry and Poetics.* Malden, Mass.: Blackwell, 2000.

Henry, James. *Selected Poems of James Henry.* Edited by Christopher Ricks. New York: Handsel, 2002.

Ricks, Christopher, ed. *The New Oxford Book of Victorian Verse.* New York: Oxford University Press, 1987.

Rogoff, Jay. "First Fruits." *Southern Review* 40, no. 3 (2004): 602–628.

"OZYMANDIAS" Percy Bysshe Shelley (1817)

"Ozymandias" is one of Percy Bysshe Shelley's best-known poems, primarily perhaps because of its deftly ironic structure and because of the moral that it points: that the mighty will certainly fall. He wrote it in a sonnet contest with his friend Horace Smith, the subject being the inscription on a pedestal on which only the legs remain, as described by a much-quoted account given by the first century B.C.E. Greek historian Diodorus Siculus, more than 1,000 years after the death of Ozymandias himself. Leigh Hunt published both versions in his radical journal the *Examiner,* Shelley's on January 11, 1819, and Smith's three weeks later.

Ozymandias is the Greek name for the Egyptian pharaoh Rameses II (who opposed Moses and, as recounted in the Book of Exodus, would not let the children of Israel depart in the 13th century B.C.E.). He was one of the most powerful of Egyptian rulers, and Diodorus Siculus's account is a parable of the fall of pride and might. Shelley picks up that moral and extends it, partly in keeping with his radical critique of autocratic power.

The frame Shelley gives the sonnet is integral to its power. The speaker does not describe what he has seen, but what the traveler says to him. Ozymandias is thus rendered remote in space as well as in time. The speaker is in some sense the opposite of Ozymandias, which is to say, the opposite of Ozymandias's singularity. He is nondescript, part of the more democratic plurality and not identified with the autocratic tyrant.

The traveler's account may be a little bit hard to decipher. He has seen just the legs of the statue still standing; in the sands of the desert nearby, the shattered head of the statue is half-buried. Nevertheless, you can see the proud expression of the face, a pride that does not know itself brought low because the statue is stone and therefore lifeless. The expressions outlive the hand that created them—that is to say, the hand of the sculptor who made the statue and whose heart fed on the praise and approval of the tyrant. Nevertheless, it is the hand of the sculptor that still can direct our attention, three thousand years later, to the artefact he has sculpted. The hand and heart of the artist continue to speak to the observer's empathy and understanding, even as the statue he has created has come to grief and absurdity. That hand is absent, unlike the legs and visage of the statue, but somehow still more living than the dead stone that survives it.

The great irony of the poem is, of course, in its last lines. Ozymandias's inscription—"Look on my Works, ye Mighty, and despair" (l. 11)—once referred to the extraordinary buildings and other works around the statue. Now all that surrounds it are the lone and level sands. The despair that the mighty will come to feel, therefore, is not that of their inability to match the might of Ozymandias, but that of the *pointlessness* of matching his might, since the result, eventually, will be the same oblivion that has covered over Ozymandias's works as well.

The mighty should despair because their might will do them no good at all in the long run. What does matter is the report of the present moment, the interest the nearly anonymous audience to the parable takes in it. Might will do no good at all. What matters is the experience of the people now alive, not interested in power but in life. For a similar moral from a similar perspective, "Ozymandias" should be compared to those moments in LORD BYRON'S *DON JUAN* where he accepts that all things will pass away. What matters is action in the present, not vain building for an unknown future.

BIBLIOGRAPHY

Bloom, Harold. *Genius: A Mosaic of One Hundred Exemplary Creative Minds.* New York: Warner, 2002.

———. *Shelley's Mythmaking.* New Haven, Conn.: Yale University Press, 1959.

———. *The Visionary Company: A Reading of English Romantic Poetry.* Garden City, N.Y.: Doubleday, 1961.

Hogle, Jerrold E. *Shelley's Process: Radical Transference and the Development of His Major Works.* New York: Oxford University Press, 1988.

Keach, William. *Shelley's Style.* New York: Methuen, 1984.

Leavis, F. R. *Revaluation: Tradition & Development in English Poetry.* New York: Norton, 1963.

Notopolous, James A. *The Platonism of Shelley: A Study of Platonism and the Poetic Mind.* Durham, N.C.: Duke University Press, 1949.

Quinney, Laura. *The Poetics of Disappointment: Wordsworth to Ashbery.* Charlottesville: University Press of Virginia, 1999.

Smith, Horace. *"Ozymandias," Poets' Corner.* Available online. URL: http://www.theotherpages.org/poems/2001/smith0101.html. Accessed on June 1, 2008.

Wasserman, Earl. *Shelley: A Critical Reading.* Baltimore: Johns Hopkins Press, 1971.

———. *Subtler Language: Critical Readings of Neoclassic and Romantic Poems.* Baltimore: Johns Hopkins Press, 1968.

P

"PAST RUIN'D ILION" WALTER SAVAGE LANDOR (1831) This is one of WALTER SAVAGE LANDOR's many poems to Ianthe—that is, to Sophia Jane Swifte, the great (and consummated) love of his life. During most of Landor's pining for her, Swifte lived abroad in Paris with her second husband, a departure that he memorialized in "Absence" (which begins "Ianthe! you resolve to cross the sea!"). He had first met her in 1803. The name Ianthe is a partial anagram of her real name, the *ian* picking up letters from both her first and middle names.

In this poem, Landor, who wrote in a classical mode, often composing first drafts in Latin before translating them into English, is here writing in the Horatian tradition. The Roman poet Horace first promised his beloved immortality in his verse since, as he said, life was short and art long. In English literature, this tradition is expressed most famously in William Shakespeare's sonnets, particularly numbers 18 ("As long as men may breathe or eyes can see / So long lives this, and this gives life to thee"), 55, and 107. Landor, however, is also thinking of Edmund Spenser's sonnet sequence *Amoretti* in some of the Ianthe poems, especially in the poem "Well I remember how you smiled," in which she rebukes him for writing her name upon the sand. He replies that her name will live forever in his verse, as had Spenser in the 73rd sonnet of *Amoretti*.

Both Spenser and Landor engage in an interesting paradox, though, which is that they do not accurately name their beloveds (nor, of course, does Shakespeare in his sonnets). Landor says that "men / unborn shall . . . find Ianthe's name again," but if they do so it will be in a book like this and not in his verse. This allows him his characteristic combination of passion and aloofness from things in this world. In "Past Ruin'd Ilion," Landor shows his usual subtlety in the interaction of literal and metaphorical, or in the way that the literal story of a poem becomes a metaphor for what the poem is doing. Helen and Alcestis survive the stories they are central to, because Helen returns to Menelaus and Alcestis is rescued from the grave by Hercules. Verse tells the story of their survival, but also they survive in the verse that tells their story, so that their survival *in* the story is a metaphor for their survival *through* the story. Landor promises Ianthe the same thing, since the sad anticipation of oblivion and death is material for a poem like this one. Beauty fades and glory passes, but he still assures her that "One name, Ianthe, shall not die" (l. 12).

That last line is very delicately poised between assurance that *this* is the poem that Ianthe will survive in and a veiled threat (characteristic of the bargain that eternizing poets seek to make with those they would seduce) that hers might *not* be the name that will survive. It all depends on whether we read—or whether *she* reads—"Ianthe" as a vocative or an apposition. Is he saying, "One name—that is to say the name *Ianthe*—shall not die?," as we might think at first? This would be characteristic of the way Landor subtly names the subjects of his poems, as in "DIRCE." Or is he saying instead, "One name, O Ianthe, shall not die," in which case he might be calling upon her to volunteer the name she hopes will live by requiting his passion and desire? In a sense, it is both, but because it is both, she survives, or a version of her name survives, no matter what she does, as a function of the greatness of his love and the greatness of the poetry that expresses it.

BIBLIOGRAPHY

Butler, Marilyn. *Romantics, Rebels, and Reactionaries: English Literature and its Background, 1760–1830*. New York: Oxford University Press, 1982.

De Quincey, Thomas. *Recollections of the Lakes and the Lake Poets*. Edited by David Wright. Harmondsworth, England: Penguin, 1970.

Hazlitt, William. *Spirit of the Age; or, Contemporary Portraits*. London: Oxford University Press, 1970.

Super, R. H. *Walter Savage Landor: A Biography*. New York: New York University Press, 1954.

PATMORE, COVENTRY (COVENTRY KERSEY DIGHTON PATMORE) (1823–1896) Coventry Patmore is now best remembered as the stalking horse of Virginia Woolf's attack on Victorian sexual piety and morality, when she disparaged the idea of the Victorian wife as "the angel in the house." The phrase is the title of a long series of works by Patmore, in four volumes, written between 1854 and 1862. Their titles give some sense of the trajectory they trace: *The Angel in the House, The Espousals, Faithful Forever*, and *The Victories of Love*. They represent the wife—more or less *his* wife, the writer Emily Augusta Patmore (née Andrews)—as the object of the kind of poetic sequences that the poets of the English Renaissance, from Sir Thomas Wyatt to William Shakespeare and beyond, addressed to unattainable beloveds. Patmore's point was that the angel of the house is herself so far beyond men as to be unattainable, but so pure and kind as nevertheless to serve her inferiors. She is therefore the victim of a kind of sentimental oppression on the part of the men who worship her or think they worship her. Her perfection is expressed in her faithful service to them.

These poems are not mawkish, however, and there is much to be said about Patmore's originality in turning the resources of the sonnet sequence to marriage. His sentimentality is everywhere, but it is the obverse of a certain lucid grimness in his vision and in his work. He does not describe marriage as in any way the embodiment of the kind of bliss that one gets, for example, in the novels of Charles Dickens. Life with others is difficult and unsure, and women in particular bear the burden of trying to negotiate these difficulties.

Patmore was himself an austere figure, and part of the power of his work consists of his representation of a certain Victorian stance: the ability to speak with complete unblinkered and untempered authority about how the world, and human life within the world, really is. This is one of the characteristic stances that the Victorian era enjoyed in its leading literary lights. Britain had seemed to itself to have settled things, to have authority over space, time, and knowledge. This illusion was soon to be exploded, but it made possible an authoritative tone in Victorian authors who represented themselves as having unprecedented omniscience, merging narrative, psychological, historical, critical, and scientific certainty in a way that was peculiarly modern. Patmore wrote with this tone, and it makes his grimmer poetry seem all the more accurate in its grimness.

Perhaps it was a feature of Patmore's austerity that when his wife, Emily, died in 1862, after bearing six children, he converted to Catholicism, leaving the more sociable and gregarious doctrine of the Church of England behind. He remarried in 1864, although perhaps that marriage, to Marianne Caroline Byles, was unconsummated; and then again, after Byles's death, to Harriet Georgina Robson, who had been a governess in the household. (Patmore's early poetry was often sexually explicit, and it would be wrong to regard him in any way as a prude.) In the years after Emily's death, he wrote his greatest poetry, published in the various editions of *The Unknown Eros* between 1868 and 1886. (Some, it must be admitted, are highly political and distasteful in their invective.)

Patmore was admired early in life by the Pre-Raphaelites (see PRE-RAPHAELITE POETRY), to whose journal the *Germ* he contributed. Later, he counted ALFRED, LORD TENNYSON as a friend, and after Patmore's conversion to Catholicism, he and GERARD MANLEY HOPKINS, who admired him, became friends and correspondents. In many ways, Coventry Patmore is the epitome of one major strand of the Victorian character, and he shows not only how sentimental but how tough-minded it could be.

See also "MAGNA EST VERITAS"; "TOYS, THE."

BIBLIOGRAPHY

Champneys, Basil. *Memoirs and Correspondence of Coventry Patmore.* London: G. Bell and Sons, 1900.

Gosse, Edmund. *Coventry Patmore.* New York: Charles Scribner's Sons, 1905.

Hopkins, Gerard Manley. *Further Letters of Gerard Manley Hopkins, Including His Correspondence with Coventry Patmore.* 2nd rev. ed. Edited by C. C. Abbott. New York: Oxford University Press, 1956.

Page, Frederick. *Patmore: A Study in Poetry.* Hamdon, Conn.: Archon Books, 1970.

Weinig, Mary Anthony. *Coventry Patmore.* Boston: Twayne Publishers, 1981.

"PEACE: A STUDY" CHARLES STUART CALVERLEY **(1866)** "Peace" is typical of CHARLES STUART CALVERLEY's light verse (at which he excelled). Unlike serious poetry on similar themes, one of the points of light verse is not to show what is unique about something that might seem generic, but to present the generic in a unique way. In "Peace" a worn-out clerk is taking his first holiday in 40 years from his job in the financial district of London. The clerk is recognizable as a good-hearted Dickensian laborer—someone like Wemmick in Charles Dickens's *Great Expectations*—but he also bears a resemblance to CHARLES LAMB. Lamb had visited WILLIAM WORDSWORTH and SAMUEL TAYLOR COLERIDGE in the Lake District, but he felt more at home in London, and not among the sublimities of the Lakes, which he acknowledged.

The clerk here has gone to Caermarthen Bay, in Wales, and he, too, is having a more or less Wordsworthian vacation. In feeling the salt spray from the ocean and hearing the children's voices on the sands, he reminds us of Wordsworth's great vision in the INTIMATIONS ODE of being able, now matter how far inland one is, "to see the children sport upon the shore / And hear the mighty waters rolling evermore" (ll. 166–167). He also reminds us of the romantic idea of transcendence in general. He laughs with joy, and again that joy is Wordsworthian, a "joy too deep for tears" (see the last line of the Intimations Ode), but not a joy that is the pure object of romantic contemplation. For the sights and sounds are somewhat distracting, and the bandanna he puts around his ears presumably mutes them. We know he is sensitive to sound because the *bandanna* is opposed to the summer *bands* in Camden Hill that would be playing discordantly near his door, one the extremely popular music of the great opera composer Guiseppe Verdi, the other the music-hall jingles of Alfred Glenville Vance. The poem puts them together because of the alliteration of their names, in order to make sure that sound will not be an echo of sense but, rather, of dissonance.

One of the lovely things about this poem is that it is hard to say who the joke is on. The clerk has taken pains to go on vacation far away from the City and from Camden Hill, but what he does is more or less what he would have done at home anyhow. Calverley, who loved and translated the Roman poet Horace, might have meant this poem as a mild and light exposition of Horace's famous dictum: "Who crosses seas can view a different part of the heavens but will not change the environment of his own mind." Horace meant (as John Milton's Satan knew in *Paradise Lost*) that one cannot escape from oneself. But the nice thing about the situation here is that the clerk does not *want* to escape from himself. He is happy to be reading his newspaper with slightly different sounds and textures and weather about him than he would have at home. He *is* at peace, and his laughter is genuine.

BIBLIOGRAPHY

Auden, W. H. Introduction to *W. H. Auden's Book of Light Verse,* xxii–xxx. New York: New York Review of Books, 2004.

Babington, Percy L. *Browning & Calverley; or Poem and Parody.* (London: John Castle, 1925.

Ince, Richard Basil. *Calverley and Some Cambridge Wits of the Nineteenth Century.* London: G. Richards and H. Toulmin at the Cayme Press, 1929.

"PETER GRIMES" GEORGE CRABBE **(1810)** "Peter Grimes" is the 22nd of the 24 "letters," or chapters, that make up *The Borough,* GEORGE CRABBE's series of narratives of life in a country town. "Peter" is the best-known, partly because its grim and strange originality was recognized in the middle of the 20th century by the composer Benjamin Britten, who turned it into his best opera.

The story is written in heroic couplets, Crabbe's almost invariable mode. Crabbe was born in 1754, earlier than WILLIAM BLAKE, and knew Edmund Burke and Dr. Samuel Johnson, who admired and corrected his verse, especially his first long poem, *The Village.* He wrote in their mode, the style inherited from John Dryden and Alexander Pope and that WILLIAM WORDSWORTH condemned as vicious and artificial in inaugurating the revolution that would be English ROMANTICISM. Wordsworth complained, in the preface to *Lyrical Ballads* (1798) as well as the great set of *Essays upon Epitaphs* (1810), that the couplet rendered everything it observed or asserted to sharp antithesis, sometimes brought to paradox for its own sake, and that the natural language of real people and real passions was not at all like this. But Crabbe, too, wrote about real people, or at least not about the idealized "types" to be found in most 18th-century poetry, and for this reason he deserves to be regarded as a romantic. Indeed, the delightful WINTHROP MACKWORTH PRAED wrote a beautiful inscription to his future wife to accompany a gift of Crabbe's poems in which he compared Wordsworth and Crabbe: "Brethren they are, whose kindred song / Nor hides the right, nor gilds the wrong" ("To Helen: with Crabbe's poems, a Birthday Present," 1837).

Peter Grimes is a poor and sadistic fisherman, and the poem is a character study of the psychological depths of a fundamentally bad person. Its plot is simple but contains one enigma. Peter is the vicious drunken son of a widowed, hardworking father, a man like most of the poor but more or less honest laborers of the borough (of whom the self-effacing narrator is one as well). After his father dies, Peter seeks to keep enough funds, by fishing and filching, to enjoy his life; his enjoyments seem to consist of alcohol and sadism. To further both, he essentially buys a series of apprentices, slaves in all but name, from the workhouses; his abuse and neglect of them lead to their deaths. After the death of the third, he can find no other apprentices, and he spends the second half of the poem thinking about his grim and lonely situation. He might be compared to Charles Dickens's Scrooge, except without the redemption. Or he might better be compared to SAMUEL TAYLOR COLERIDGE's mariner (in *The RIME OF THE ANCIENT MARINER*), who is harassed by an unassuageable guilt that will haunt him and those who meet him through his death. "Peter Grimes" might be called a version of Coleridge's ballad written in heroic couplets. But where the mariner has killed an albatross, Grimes is directly responsible for the deaths of three young boys. (The mariner's responsibility for the deaths of his shipmates is indirect.)

Once the young boys can no longer be replaced, Grimes begins thinking about what he has done, or about what the world he has made, and that his very existence helps to characterize, is like. Again, we might anticipate the kind of novelistic exploration that Fyodor Dostoyevsky will undertake, especially in *Crime and Punishment* (1866). Crabbe was probably thinking of the guilt of a figure like Claudius in William Shakespeare's *Hamlet,* since much of Peter Grimes alludes to *Hamlet,* to the return of Hamlet's father as a ghost in particular. (The MOTTOES, or epigraphs, of the Peter Grimes story, usually not reprinted in anthologies, are from similar moments in Shakespeare: Richard III describing the nightmare in which those he murdered returned to haunt him, and Macbeth complaining of Banquo's return.) As with Claudius—and this is perhaps the central insight of "Peter Grimes"—guilt is not sufficient punishment to redeem the guilty soul. Where the mariner's guilt caused him to bless the innocent living creatures he saw in the track of the ship, no such blessing is forthcoming from Peter Grimes. He is sufficiently tormented to draw sympathy from the women who before had hated him for what he had done to the boys; he is "A lost, lone man, so harras'd and undone, / Our gentle females, ever prompt to feel, / Perceived compassion on their anger steal" (ll. 256–258). But their compassion does him no good at all since he must struggle with his sense of self-ostracization. He has done what excludes him forever from the community, and if they are able to forgive him, there is a deep sense in which he knows himself unforgivable. It is at this point that he descends, as the argument of the poem puts it, into madness, but it is a madness in which he is haunted by the crimes he has committed—a madness, that is to say, that has its origin in a guilty conscience.

What is not entirely clear is how much he is guilty of. His sadism and neglect has certainly led in one way or another to the deaths of his three charges. But are his sins of commission? Is there anything the community does not already know? In particular, how did the second and third boy die? We do not know how the second boy drowns—and the poem tells us that only Peter Grimes will ever know. It might be an accident, or it might be some sadistic act brought to its ultimate conclusion. And the death of the third boy is obscure as well. (These obscurities appealed to Britten, who liked operas about ambiguous guilt.) What we do know is that in his last moments he "clung affrighten'd" to Peter's knee, which might mean that Peter is not entirely a monster, at least in the boy's eyes, since he had been looking to Peter for protection.

At any rate, after this, Peter's madness leaves him no rest. He sees on earth what he fears he will see after death, and his death itself recollects that of Hamlet. In Shakespeare's play, the ghost of the father, which has haunted Peter as well as Hamlet, told Hamlet that a description of the country after death would freeze his young blood; and when Hamlet died, he echoed the ghost, saying that he *could* tell of what he now saw, but that fell Death was too swift for him. Similarly, as Peter dies he looks upon the horrors that he sees around him in his madness, and his dying words are "Again they come." Will he go to hell? Or will he find peace? Is he haunted by conscience or by some supernatural agency? In a sense, the distinction is ultimately unimportant: Hell is his own conscience, and whether a supernatural hell exists or not, what Crabbe has done has been to depict the hell that one's own unpardonable guilt can create. In this he shows extraordinary psychological insight, of a sort more usually associated with romanticism than with the heroic couplet.

BIBLIOGRAPHY

Chamberlain, Robert. *George Crabbe.* New York: Twayne Publishers, 1965.

New, Peter. *George Crabbe's Poetry.* London: Macmillan, 1976.

Pollard, Arthur. *Crabbe: The Critical Heritage.* London: Routledge, 1972.

"PHANTOM WOOER, THE" Thomas Lovell Beddoes **(1849–1850)** This is one of Thomas Lovell Beddoes's most eerie poems. It is characteristic of his strange and haunting poetry, of the poetry that he wrote and the poetry that obsessed him as well. Beddoes was obsessed with Percy Bysshe Shelley, in particular with the other-worldly strain in Shelley, and this is in that mode.

The poem's ghost entices the lady to death; whether or not she follows him is not specified in the poem, but we can assume she does. The poem has something of the form of a warning in the burden or refrain that ends both stanzas—the note of such wooers is sweet but poisoned—and the *tone* of that warning is that of posthumous experience. Everyone whom the phantom wooer loves—that is to say, everyone who hears the phantom wooer—is already on the verge of following. This is because in some sense the phantom wooer is a part of one's own mind, or his song is a song of one's own hearing. We can see this because the song comes from the vision of the snakes nesting and lying in the skulls. The lady sees or thinks of those things, and in doing so she hears the song that comes to her soul from her soul.

The warning *is* a posthumous one, since Beddoes committed suicide in 1849, perhaps a year after composing the poem. The words of the wooer are those of a siren; they are enticing beyond the luring words of human love, and they woo the soul itself (ll. 4–5). What are these luring words? The poem is perhaps ambiguous, since they may either be the center of the refrain—"die, oh! die."—or they may be the entire second stanza, addressed as it is to the "Young soul."

There is no indication that the second stanza is spoken by a different speaker than the first, except that it is addressed *to* the young soul, while the first only refers to it. But these may not be the same souls; what we learn about the first may have the effect of making us feel what we hear the second stanza saying to *us*. In fact, the poem must work this way when you think about it: The haunting and hypnotic song has to draw us into its atmosphere, and we, too, have to feel the temptation of suicide.

The power of the temptation is real, its account of death beautiful. That beauty is the only reason for the poem to exist, and so the phantom wooer is in some sense the muse and instigator of poetry. We can say, then, that what Beddoes found in poetry, and in Shelley in particular, was something that he found so haunting as to feel like a wooing to an idealism indistinguishable from despair. The phantom wooer is poetry itself, or at least the strain of poetry that Beddoes loved best, wrote best, and came closest to articulating what he hoped to get, if not from life, then from death.

BIBLIOGRAPHY

Bradshaw, Michael. *Resurrection Songs: The Poetry of Thomas Lovell Beddoes.* Burlington, Vt.: Ashgate, 2001.

Freud, Sigmund. *Beyond the Pleasure Principle.* Translated by James Strachey. New York: Liveright, 1961.

Wolfson, Susan J., and Peter J. Manning. *Selected Poems of Thomas Hood, Winthrop Mackworth Praed and Thomas Lovell Beddoes.* London: Penguin, 2000.

"PHILOMELA" MATTHEW ARNOLD (1853)

This poem alludes to the classical myth of the origin of the nightingale. In the version MATTHEW ARNOLD followed—and in contrast to the far more familiar Ovidian version, which writers from William Shakespeare to ALGERNON CHARLES SWINBURNE (see "ITYLUS" for a brief summary of nightingale poems in English) took as their background—Tereus, king of Daulis, lusted after his wife Procne's sister, Philomela. He therefore cut out Procne's tongue, hid her away, and reported her as dead, thus freeing him to marry Philomela. Procne, however, wove her story into a tapestry ("the too clear web" of the poem's line 21), which she arranged to have delivered to her sister, and the two of them took revenge by killing Itylus, son of Procne and Tereus, and serving his body as meat to his father. When Tereus found out the truth, he sought to kill the two sisters, but all three were metamorphosed—Procne into a swallow, Philomela into a nightingale, and Tereus into a lapwing. (Arnold's version of this myth can be found in *Classic Myths in Literature and Art,* by Charles Mills Gayley.) In "Philomela," Arnold, as is typical, has in mind both a poetic situation and the moral it serves. And as is typical, the poetic situation is more interesting than the moral. The moral is pointed for a silent young woman, Eugenia, who corresponds to the addressee of "DOVER BEACH," the woman who will receive the moral for us. They are listening to the nightingale sing, and Arnold is remembering, like JOHN KEATS in his great "ODE TO A NIGHTINGALE," where the nightingale comes from, and where else its song may be heard. This nightingale is heard in a very particular and explicit London, not a vague outdoors, as in Keats. The specificity of modern London is linked by the nightingale to ancient Greece. Arnold's point is twofold: The modern city can be as barbarous, in particular in its treatment of its poor and defenseless, as Tereus himself was, but the recovery and devotion to the sweetness and light of Hellenism, as represented by the greatest classical myth on the origin of song, can help mollify and change the cruelty of the present moment.

It is therefore central to the moral of the poem that the nightingale should afford this connection to the past. It ultimately ennobles "this English grass" (l. 17) to have Philomela here. Easily the best part of the poem, which probably influenced WILLIAM BUTLER YEATS's "Leda and the Swan," is the description of "the feathery change" the "fugitive" nightingale feels come over her at the moment of her metamorphosis (l. 24). This metamorphosis has nothing to do with the story of the myth, only with the experience of finding oneself in the world, embodied, and not in control of one's own fate. It is therefore that the nightingale song is "Eternal passion! / Eternal pain!" (ll. 31–32). The beauty of the bird's song is like the beauty of the myths and mythmakers it recollects. But it is also the beauty of making the connection with myths that themselves describe perennial human experience, which literature itself, embodied in the singing bird, has always and will always describe.

BIBLIOGRAPHY

Arnold, Matthew. *Essays, Letters, and Reviews.* Collected and edited by Fraser Neiman. Cambridge, Mass.: Harvard University Press, 1960.

Bloom, Harold, ed. *Matthew Arnold.* New York: Chelsea House, 1987.

Dawson, Carl, and John Pfordresher, eds. *Matthew Arnold: The Critical Heritage.* New York: Routledge, 1995.

Murray, Alexander S. *Manual of Mythology: Greek and Roman, Norse and Old German, Hindoo and Egyptian Mythology.* New York: Scribner, 1874.

Trilling, Lionel. *The Moral Obligation to Be Intelligent: Selected Essays*. Edited by Leon Weiseltier. New York: Farrar, Straus and Giroux, 2000.

"PHOENIX, THE" George Darley (1835)

In its fullest form "The Phoenix" comprises (ll. 167–215) George Darley's 1,750-line poem *Nepenthe,* whose narrator describes, in a mode that combines both John Keats (as in the *Hyperion* poems) and Percy Bysshe Shelley (as in *Alastor* and *The Triumph of Life*), the visions that he sees after falling into a reverie on a hot summer's day. He has been snatched away like the Greek mythical hero Ganymede and has awakened to find himself by the "Incense Tree" (l. 1, l. 147) where the phoenix has its nest. The first 16 lines were anthologized in 1922 by Padraic Colum in his groundbreaking *Anthology of Irish Verse.* Robert Bridges, in an essay on Darley, had also commented on those lines, and this gave new life to the almost-forgotten Darley. He had been championed in the mid-19th century by the novelist and playwright Mary Russell Mitford, who had corresponded with him and knew him by reputation from mutual friends such as the Scottish essayist Thomas Carlyle. She excerpted the poem, as the *Oxford Anthology of English Literature* would later print it, in volume 3 of her *Recollections of a Literary Life* (1852), but despite her advocacy, and that of the scholar Richard Garnett 35 years later, Darley was almost wholly forgotten. *Nepenthe* was not published in full until 1897.

As printed by Mitford and the *Oxford Anthology,* "The Phoenix" comprises lines 147–215 of the first of *Nepenthe*'s two cantos. The break is a reasonable one since near the end of "The Phoenix's" three sections, when the speaker sips the phoenix's "amber blood" (l. 58–l. 205), a new vision is introduced as a result of this new intoxicant. It starts off with a conscious echo of William Shakespeare's nondramatic poem "The Phoenix and the Turtle," in very similar meter, which begins, "Let the bird of loudest lay / On the sole Arabian tree / Herald sad and trumpet be / To whose sound chaste wings obey." (Shakespeare's meter is technically what is called acephalous—that is, it lacks the first unstressed syllable that Darley's fully iambic tetrameter has, as in the *O* that begins section 3 of Darley's poem; you could put an *O* at the beginning of every line in Shakespeare's poem without harming the metrical sense.) From *The Tempest* we know that this tree is the tree the phoenix lives in; Sebastian says "that in Arabia / There is one tree, the phoenix' throne; one phoenix / At this hour reigning there" (3.3.22–24). In Shakespeare's poem, the phoenix has disappeared with the dove, its great love, but Darley represents himself as seeing the phoenix despite the fact that she makes her nest into a "sight high from spoiler men" (l. 11–l. 158)—that is, a sight that men cannot see (including Shakespeare) but that he in his vision can.

In mythology the phoenix is a bird that lives as the unique example of its kind. There is only one phoenix at a time, and indeed, there may only be one phoenix ever. Every half a millennium it dies in flame but returns to life out of its own ashes. Keats, who was never far from Darley's mind, imagined his own poetic rebirth by being granted "new Phoenix wings to fly at my desire" ("On Sitting Down to Read *King Lear* Once Again"). Darley here imagines the death of the phoenix. Among the "mountainless green wilds" of Arabia (l. 13–l. 160), in a world where all is clear to her and nothing hidden, "Here ends she her unechoing song," because there is no other phoenix to reply to her. Darley's song *is* an echo of the phoenix's, but an echo, like his sight of her, which is permissible only because in the fiction he is entirely absorbed into observation and not interaction. This is what gives him access to the astonishingly beautiful vision of the phoenix gazing at the sun.

This second part of the poem about the "self-born" (l. 12–l. 159) bird owes as much to John Milton's *Samson Agonistes* (1671), with its evocation of "that self-begotten bird, / In the Arabian woods embost, / That no second knows nor third." Darley's phoenix, like Milton's Philistines (see *Samson,* where God has "urged" the Philistines "on with mad desire / To call in haste for their destroyer"), calls upon her own "destroyer" (l. 6) the sun, which will dissolve her in flame and bring her back to life. He sees her dissolve and then in the last movement of this part of *Nepenthe* moves to sip the sap of the "Incense Tree," as though to be literally influenced by the blood of the tree—not of knowledge or of life, but—of beauty. The poem is the result of this influence.

BIBLIOGRAPHY

Abbott, Claude Colleer. *The Life and Letters of George Darley, Poet and Critic.* London: Oxford University Press, 1928.

Bridges, Robert Seymour. "George Darley." In *Collected Essays, Papers, &c., of Robert Bridges.* Vol. 2. London: Oxford University Press, 1927–36, 187–188.

Brisman, Leslie. "George Darley: Bouyant as Young Time." In *Romantic Origins,* 182–223. Ithaca, N.Y.: Cornell University Press, 1978.

"PIED BEAUTY" GERARD MANLEY HOPKINS (1877)

"Pied Beauty" is one of GERARD MANLEY HOPKINS's most accessible poems of praise of God (in this case through the praise of "dappled things" [l. 1]) that was part of his tormented vocation as a poet and Catholic priest. Hopkins was a formidable naturalist, and his descriptions of the world around him, in his journals, are striking both for the probing curiosity they evince and for their accuracy of depiction. This sense of detail is central to "Pied Beauty," where the very title suggests that God is in the details, in the different manifestations that beauty can take.

Hopkins's attention to detail derives from his slightly older precursors of PRE-RAPHAELITE POETRY, and as with them, it is both subject and allegory for his own poetic practice. His eccentric and anachronistic mode is built up on the accretion of stresses throughout a line. "Pied Beauty" is built on a four-stress line, each line containing an indefinite number of unstressed syllables, or "outrides," as Hopkins called them. They make the stresses more prominent and also more sudden, since they do not come at regular intervals. The stresses, too, are not mere monosyllables in a line, since Hopkins tends to treat a conglomeration of stressed syllables as one stress (like "coal chestnut falls" [l. 4] and the accent-marked "all trades" [l. 6]). All of this tends to make the play of stresses itself an instance of the pied beauty—the dappled, scattered, clotted, bursting irregularity—that the poem celebrates. Hopkins's metrics not only seem to echo the sense, they *are* the sense that the poem seeks to convey.

This is true of all of Hopkins's instressed poems (of which "The WINDHOVER" is probably, as Hopkins himself felt, the greatest). What is fascinating about "Pied Beauty" is the way stress also has a semantic function. The piedness of the beauty that Hopkins is praising consists in the way nature is replete with sudden and arresting juxtaposition. This juxtaposition is conveyed in the poem both through the accretion of stress and other prominent sound qualities such as assonance and alliteration (both combined in the self-describing metaphor "couple-colour" [l. 2]) and through the metaphors that make such accretion possible. Hopkins's characteristic mode of metaphor (and of its somewhat distant cousin simile) is to compress the tenor and vehicle into a compound noun or compound phrase.

Take the phrase "Fresh-firecoal chestnut-falls" (l. 4), from which we get the idea that the newly fallen chestnuts seen in autumn are of a color like that of glowing coals in a grate. The coals themselves are "fresh," mainly because they are being compared to the fresh chestnuts but also because they are bright with the fire they fuel. The accumulation of stresses fuses the terms that serve as metaphors for each other, even as it also evokes a different relation among those terms; the chestnuts will be roasted in the fire, into which they are already practically falling. (We are reminded of roasted chestnuts in contrast with the notably "fresh" chestnuts that fall spontaneously from the tree.)

The poem might be said to describe this procedure in its own coupled words of "couple-colour" (l. 2). It is a catalogue, originally derivable from the Book of Job, of all the varieties of things that God has wrought—a catalogue like those to be found contemporaneously in the American poet Walt Whitman, and not unlike some of the accretionary poems of ROBERT BROWNING. But it is also a catalogue that includes itself within it, or at least catalogues the effects of the catalogue. Poets produce catalogues, but in this case God produces the juxtapositions (like the "rose-moles" on the trout (l. 3), where *rose* is far more noun than adjective), compacting all of nature into its own variety. The catalogue does not just list God's creation: the catalogue is his mode of creation and beauty, the overflow of his own beauty, which contains all things within itself, as though he is the compacted stress that includes all the others, everything Hopkins would ever be tempted to list as part of the beauty of the world.

BIBLIOGRAPHY

Bridges, Robert. Preface to *Poems of Gerard Manley Hopkins.* Edited by W. H. Gardner. New York: Oxford University Press, 1948.

Gardner, W. H. *Gerard Manley Hopkins (1844–1889): A Study of Poetic Idiosyncrasy in Relation to Poetic Tradition.* New Haven, Conn.: Yale University Press, 1949.

———, ed. Introduction to *Poems and Prose of Gerard Manley Hopkins.* Harmondsworth, Middlesex, England: Penguin, 1963.

Hartman, Geoffrey. *The Unmediated Vision: An Interpretation of Wordsworth, Hopkins, Rilke, and Valery.* New Haven, Conn.: Yale University Press, 1954.

Hopkins, Gerard Manley. *Gerard Manley Hopkins: Selected Letters.* Edited by Catherine Phillips. New York: Oxford University Press, 1990.

Miller, J. Hillis. "Gerard Manley Hopkins." In *The Disappearance of God,* 270–359. Cambridge, Mass.: Belknap Press of Harvard University Press, 1963.

White, Norman. *Hopkins: A Literary Biography.* New York: Oxford University Press, 1992.

"PILLAR OF THE CLOUD, THE" ("LEAD KINDLY LIGHT") JOHN HENRY NEWMAN (1833)

JOHN HENRY NEWMAN wrote this poem—better known now as the hymn "Lead Kindly Light"—when he was desperate to return to England from a trip to the Mediterranean that he had made with his friend R. H. (Richard Hurrell) Froude's father. Newman spent some time in Rome brooding about what he regarded as the corruption of all the Christian churches, Catholic as well as Anglican. His encounters with various Catholic ceremonies left him thoughtful and confirmed his wish to begin what he thought of as a second Reformation in England, one that would return the English church to her first-century roots. As he says in the opening chapter of his 1864 autobiography *Apologia Pro Vita Sua,* of which the composition of "The Pillar of the Cloud" is the climactic event, he did not yet think of leaving the Church of England: "still I ever kept before me that there was something greater than the Established Church, and that was the Church Catholic and Apostolic, set up at the beginning, of which she was nothing but the local presence and organ" (*Apologia Pro Vita Sua,* pp. 31–32).

In May 1833 Newman fell ill in Sicily, where he had gone in a kind of feverish impatience. He became delirious, and his servant asked for instructions lest he should die; in his delirium he replied, in words that he later affected to find puzzling and mysterious, "I shall not die. I shall not die, for I have not sinned against the light."

At least in his autobiographical account of his own progress toward conversion, these words should be seen as introducing "The Pillar of the Cloud," with its famous first line, "Lead, Kindly Light, amid the encircling gloom." Newman wrote the actual hymn (as he tells us with accelerating haste in the last paragraph of that opening chapter) on June 16, while becalmed on an orange boat from Palermo to Marseilles, the first boat he could get to return to England. He arrived in England on a Tuesday, which allowed him to hear John Keble preach his sermon complaining against "national apostasy" that Sunday, July 14, 1833—the event that Newman considered the beginning of the Oxford movement, which affected so many people's relations to the Church of England and in so many cases eventuated (as at length with Newman) in their conversion to Roman Catholicism.

It is after his conversion to Roman Catholicism that Newman recounts the writing of the hymn two decades earlier, and, therefore, as a Roman Catholic that he wants to see the hymn as testifying to God's leading him to conversion. The title refers us to the story of the pillar of cloud by day and pillar of fire by night, covered by which the Lord led the children of Israel through the desert, in Exodus 13:21–22. This would more or less make Newman one of the chosen people devoted to the Lord, and perhaps even the very Moses of English Romanism that he more or less became.

Nevertheless, the hymn itself, as composed in 1833, has very little that is sectarian in it. It is more in the mode of the 17th-century poet George Herbert's personal self-denials and cries to God. Only by giving up a sense of one's own arrogant control of life ("I loved to choose and see my path" [l. 9]), can one put oneself wholly in God's power and trust him at every step.

This trust allows for a return of some primordial sense of happiness in the world, as the last line tells us. We have seen and loved the angel faces that the light will lead us back to. Whatever they are, angels or loved ones (as in WILLIAM WORDSWORTH'S "SURPRISED BY JOY"), the sense of return is what the poem offers as joy and hope. (Again, Herbert's "The Flower" [1633] is somewhere behind this poem.) The juxtaposition of the hymn with Newman's delirious assertion that he did not sin against the light helps make sense of its near-universal promise, and also of Newman's conception of sin. We are all sinners, but perhaps we have not sinned against the light. As long as we still love, as long as we wish to be led back to our own innocence and the angel faces we have loved, even if we have lost them awhile, we have hope and will not die. It is no wonder that this became one of the most popular hymns ever written.

BIBLIOGRAPHY

Block, Ed., Jr., ed. *Critical Essays on John Henry Newman.* Victoria, British Columbia: University of Victoria, 1992.

Ker, Ian, and Alan G. Hill, eds. *Newman after a Hundred Years.* New York: Oxford University Press, 1990.

Newman, John Henry. *Apologia Pro Vita Sua.* New York: Penguin, 1994.

"POLLY BE-EN UPSIDES WI' TOM"

WILLIAM BARNES (1841) This is from the first volume of *Poems in the Dorset Dialect,* published when WILLIAM BARNES was 40 and well before the death of his wife, Julia. Barnes's life had not been without tragedy, but a sea change came over his poetry—over the sense of the world conveyed in his poetry—at her death in 1852. The earlier poetry (it matters that he was younger, too) is less concerned with the passage of time (though he was already writing very plangently about that), and more about local pleasures. Some of Barnes's most delightful poems are reminiscent of Shakespearean songs in their perfectly pitched ambitions, and this is one of them.

The poem—as is not infrequent for Barnes—is spoken by a woman, Polly, who is flirting with Tom. Like Beatrice and Benedick in William Shakespeare's *Much Ado about Nothing,* they are teasing each other, and we can tell what they feel for each other better than they can, at least better than each can about the other. Notice how much we can tell about them and the world they live in from Polly's own account of the incident. She has found Tom's coat and smock under one of the trees that he must be working (since they are pollarded, or pruned so as to produce thicker branches). Probably she has gone out to see whether she can see him. His labor is difficult—he works all day at it (l. 9)—and it has made him hot, which means that the weather is warming up and it is probably spring. She sabotages his smock and coat, and she and her friends ("we" in l. 12) laugh at his discomfiture. She may be there with her friends, but he knows it is she who has done it and comes after her. She teases him and goes running away, but he vows he will catch her "an' be my match" (l. 26). By this he means she will not be able to defeat him; but we know that they are matched for a longer time than that.

Polly makes it safely to her room, and looks to make sure that Tom is still there—which, of course, he is. We then find that all her antics were revenge for *his:* He had teased her, whipped her horse so as to throw her, and slipped itchy horsehair down her neck. The poem ends there, with her rebuking him for doing all those things, and that ending is marvelous. We might expect some stanza of reconciliation. But the point is that it is the anecdote and not some moral or resolution that Polly is delighting Tom. She loves thinking about what she has done to him, and what he has done to her, and what she has said to him as a result. The pleasure is in the interaction, and in the replay of the interaction, and we can feel perfectly it does not point beyond itself, but only offers itself as a pleasure. In other, sadder, later poems, like "LWONESOMENESS," Barnes will still manage this pure pleasure of the local moment, a pleasure that is really hard to achieve in poems but one that we can share when reading Barnes.

BIBLIOGRAPHY

Levy, William Turner. *William Barnes: The Man and the Poems.* Dorchester, England: Longmans, 1960.

Parins, James W. *William Barnes.* Boston: Twayne Publishers, 1984.

Scott, Leader. *The Life of William Barnes: Poet and Philologist, by his Daughter, Lucy Baxter* ("Leader Scott"). 1887. Reprint, St. Clair Shares, Mich.: Scholarly Press, 1971.

PRAED, WINTHROP MACKWORTH

(1802–1839) Winthrop Mackworth Praed was one of the best comic poets of the 19th century, and he is still to be found in anthologies of light verse, such as the various Oxford anthologies edited by W. H. Auden, Kingsley Amis, and John Gross. Praed went to Eton College, were he established a library that is still part of the school's collection, and then on to a brilliant career at Cambridge University. The philosopher and economist John Stuart Mill mentions Praed as a political presence in his *Autobiography*.) He was a Tory member of Parliament (the Tories tended to be more conservative or traditionalist than the more liberal Whigs) and died of tuberculosis, at age 37.

As a writer of comic verse, Praed owed a great deal to LORD BYRON. He represented himself with a great deal of panache; indeed, he dedicated a book of satirical verses, *Trash,* to someone who beat him in a parliamentary election, much as Byron had dedicated *DON JUAN* to ROBERT SOUTHEY, whom he loathed. Praed was not primarily a poet, though, and therefore his poetry is more the expression of a deeply witty interest in the form itself than a mode of self-expression. The same may be said of all light verse, at least all verse when it is being light. Praed was fond of the rhetorical use of zeugma, a kind of witty self-deflation through the use of two different objects for a verb or preposition and turning the governing, doubly used word into a kind of pun that (in light verse) juxtaposes the high with the low. For example, in a New Year's poem, "Twenty-Eight and Twenty-Nine," Praed writes that nothing will change in the new year:

> Still Beauty must be stealing hearts,
> And Knavery stealing purses;
> Still cooks must live by making tarts,
> And wits by making verses:
> While sages prate, and courts debate,
> The same stars set and shine;
> And the world, as it rolled through
>   Twenty-eight,
> Must roll through Twenty-nine.

Wits live by making verses, and verse is therefore witty, not deeply self-expressive. A little later in the poem, Praed harkens back to the way Alexander Pope used zeugma ("Britain's statesmen oft the fall foredoom / Of foreign tyrants and of nymphs at home") for knowingly jaded social comment: "And jokes will be cut in the House of Lords, /And throats in the county Kerry."

Praed's wit flatters a reader that he or she is similarly experienced in the ways of the world, similarly above the fray. Light verse does not try to change the world but to characterize its predictability in unpredictable ways. In this sense Praed is rather more like the romantic novelist and poet Thomas Love Peacock (1785–1866) than Byron, but his poetry is also a tribute to Byron and Byron's own scornful attitude. Praed could not have agreed with Byron's political radicalism, but he admired the other man as a poet from his own early youth. His serious poems often have a verse of Byron's as epigraph (see MOTTOES), and his comic poems refer to Byron by name in addition to imitating him.

One can speculate that Praed excelled in comic poetry because he could not write serious poetry that ultimately transcended the hackneyed. His serious poetry is technically proficient but jejune, but just those sorts of lines work best as a foil for wit in comic poetry, and since Byron also was powerful as a comic poet, Praed learned the art from him.

BIBLIOGRAPHY

Amis, Kingsley, ed. *New Oxford Book of Light Verse.* New York: Oxford University Press, 1978.

Auden, W. H. *Oxford Book of Light Verse.* (Oxford: Oxford University Press, 1938.

Gross, John. *Oxford Book of Comic Verse.* New York: Oxford University Press, 1995.

Hudson, Derek. *A Poet in Parliament: The Life of Winthrop Mackworth Praed.* London: J. Murray, 1939.

Wolfson, Susan J., and Peter J. Manning. *Selected Poems of Thomas Hood, Winthrop Mackworth Praed and Thomas Lovell Beddoes.* London: Penguin, 2000.

PRELUDE, THE WILLIAM WORDSWORTH (1850)

The Prelude is WILLIAM WORDSWORTH's greatest long poem and one of the three or four greatest long poems in English; its only rival as a serious philosophical poem is John Milton's *Paradise Lost* (1667). The title *The Prelude* is not Wordsworth's but was assigned to the poem when it was published shortly after his death in 1850; he always called it the poem on the growth of his own mind, and sometimes also the "poem to Coleridge," the "friend" it is addressed to (1805 version, l. 55; he read the whole work aloud to SAMUEL TAYLOR COLERIDGE in 1807). Bits and fragments of it were published in his lifetime, as well as associated fragments, such as "NUTTING," that were originally meant for the poem but took on a life of their own. But Wordsworth would not allow the publication of the whole since he conceived it as the antechamber (his word) to the great philosophical work he was trying to write, *The Recluse*. The only other complete part of that work is *The Excursion,* which Wordsworth did publish in his lifetime, in 1814.

Wordsworth begun working on *The Prelude* in 1798, the year of *Lyrical Ballads*; it was then a much shorter autobiographical poem, not unlike "Nutting" or "TINTERN ABBEY," though with many more narrative episodes; it was eventually published in the late 20th century as the two-part *Prelude 1798–99*. After drafting this poem, and conceiving *The Recluse* (which he was already talking about in 1798), Wordsworth went back to it and eventually, in 1805, had a complete version of the poem, the one commonly referred to as the 1805 *Prelude* and generally, though not universally, preferred by scholars and critics. After this, and particularly after the publication of *The Excursion,* Wordsworth periodically revised *The Prelude,* and the version most readers knew from his death until 1926 was the 1850 version, which includes his last revisions, more or less completed by 1838. (The 1805 *Prelude* has 13 books and the 1850 14, but that is mainly a matter of Wordsworth's division of the original 10th book into two.)

Although the revisions represent Wordsworth's final decisions about how he wanted the poem to be read (he knew that it would be published posthumously), Wordsworth's final decisions were not always his best ones. In 1805 he was at the height of his poetic powers; 10 years later, he had very few good poems left in him, and his example in later life was regarded as a warning by later poets (for example, WILLIAM BUTLER YEATS, who cautioned young poets to remember "Wordsworth at eighty.") One major difference between the younger and the older Wordsworth is that later in life Wordsworth became a more or less orthodox Anglican, and he revised his poems to make them more explicitly religious in their piety. The worship of nature that he acknowledged in "Tintern Abbey" he later denied, asserting instead a worship of the God of nature. Thus, the revisions in *The Prelude* that tend to make it more orthodox and pious falsify the time of life in which he wrote it, and they falsify as well the time of life that the poem is about.

Other revisions are stylistic, but the scholar Jonathan Wordsworth (an Oxford professor who was a descendant of William Wordsworth's brother) convincingly showed that the increased elegance of the language of the 1850 version comes at the price of simplicity, directness, and power. The following discussion focuses on the 1805 version, but the general points apply to the 1850 version as well, unless otherwise noted.

The poem is essentially a spiritual autobiography of the sort pioneered by St. Augustine. It is an account of how the poem's speaker—Wordsworth himself—got to be where he is when the poem opens, when he starts speaking or writing it. The longer versions of the poem begin with what Wordsworth later in the poem called its "glad preamble" a kind of ode to the beautiful, renovating, natural air of freedom that will allow him to rejoin with nature and begin to write his great work. "Oh there is blessing in this gentle breeze," he begins in the present tense, returning to the country he loved after being, as he puts it, pent in the city whose dehumanizing features will be the subject of book 7. The movement of thought is the same as that of "Tintern Abbey": He returns to a place of imaginative freedom and wealth, promising the solitude and renovation that he had missed in London.

But it turns out that in the narrative *The Prelude* relates, the present-tense "glad preamble" is not, in fact, the start of *this* poem, spoken in full voice, but another spontaneous composition that he is recalling now. He is recalling it because it turned out to be a failure. He has been in the city for so long, separated for such a time from the sources of the powerful feeling that ought to lead to the spontaneous overflow of poetry (to allude to his language in the preface to *Lyrical Ballads*), that he is "not used to make / A present joy the matter of my song" (1, ll. 1.55–56). He is unused to present joy and therefore unused to writing poetry at all, at least poetry about joy, and so he cannot capture the gladness that he feels, and the poem disperses into straggling sounds and then utter silence (1, ll. 106–107). He tries to put a brave face on this moment of poetic failure, preferring the experience of joy to the attempt to represent it in a poem. But the joy itself is not simply or fundamentally the joy of nature but the joy that nature affords in giving him the material for poetic composition. Wordsworth's vocation is that of a poet. He loves nature because he is a poet, even if he believes that he is a poet because he loves nature. At least, he may have believed this in 1799 when the "glad preamble" was composed. WILLIAM BLAKE shrewdly complained to the diarist Henry Crabb Robinson that "I fear that Wordsworth loves nature," but by the time of the 1805 *Prelude* and the contemporaneous INTIMATIONS ODE, Wordsworth thought of nature as a potential distraction from his truest poetic destiny.

For this reason, the "glad preamble" represents the poetry Wordsworth could not write, and the rest of *The Prelude* is couched as an attempt to analyze how he came to this impasse. *The Prelude* is therefore a paradoxical work, paradoxical in the deep and saving sense that the great romantic poems tend to be, since it is the record of its own failure. But the failure carries with it more power than any success could. The loss of self-identity and security in the world of childhood and of nature leads to an apprehension of intensity measured by that loss, which yields poetry far deeper than satisfaction possibly could.

Wordsworth represents this as an internalization and secularization of the fall of humanity, and of the rebel angels, in Milton's *Paradise Lost.* Indeed, the passage where he describes the failure of the glad preamble echoes two crucial passages in *Paradise Lost.* He says that it was a beautiful evening and so "my soul / Did once again make trial of the strength / Restored to her afresh" (l, ll. 101–103), which echoes the argument to book 9 of *Paradise Lost,* where Eve decides to work alone because she is "desirous to make trial of her strength;" whereupon Satan spies her and tempts her to eat the apple and fall. This connection has not, to my knowledge, been noted before. After Wordsworth's own fall into a kind of self-discrepant self-consciousness (figured in his sense of distance between himself and his earlier self, so that he now seems to himself two consciousnesses [2, ll. 32–35]), he resists and then embraces his fate with the words *Be it so.* These are perhaps Satan's most famous words in *Paradise Lost,* when he gives himself over to the defiant love of his own destiny despite anything God can do to him. The fall leads to grandeurs—those associated with the SUBLIME—greater than the place from which they fell.

Thus, the original version of *The Prelude* opens with the stark, unanchored words signifying a discovery of loss: "Was it for this . . . ?," only far this, that he had the intense experiences of childhood and youth that he had—where *this* means something like the "common" world around all of us. These lines reappear at line 271 in book 1, and here the context is clear: *this* means that the sources of his poetic power seem gone, but it will turn out that this sense of loss is, in fact, a greater source of power than what was lost.

Such, at least, is the hope of *The Prelude,* and its most interesting and intense passages are those where it achieves the sublime. The autobiography Wordsworth relates—his tutelage by nature, his residence in London, his journey to France, his experience of the French Revolution—is a fascinating one, but what it comes to in the last analysis is an account of what made him able to perceive the sublime in nature and to render the sublime in his poetry. For Wordsworth, the two are related as a sense of what he calls "the host of shadowy things" where "darkness makes abode." There, he says, "visionary power / Attends upon the motions of the winds / Embodied in the mystery of words" (5, ll. 619–624). The great passages of *The Prelude*—the boat-stealing scene (1, ll. 372–426); the Simplon Pass episode, while crossing the Alps (6, ll. 549–572); the analysis of the "spots of time" (11, l. 257) whose loss and intense memory fill the mind with power; the climbing of Snowdon, which is the climax of the book (13, ll. 1–65)—all manifest what Wordsworth called the "obscure sense / Of possible sublimity" (2, ll. 336–337) at the heart of all his perception and all his greatest poetry. *The Prelude* is among the greatest, indeed, by Wordsworth or by any other poet writing in English.

BIBLIOGRAPHY

Abrams, M. H. *Correspondent Breeze: Essays on English Romanticism.* New York: Norton, 1984.

———. *Natural Supernaturalism: Tradition and Revolution in Romantic Literature.* New York: Norton, 1973.
Alpers, Paul. *What Is Pastoral?* Chicago: University of Chicago Press, 1996.
Barker, Juliet. *Wordsworth: A Life.* New York: Viking, 2000.
Bloom, Harold. *Poetry and Repression: Revisionism from Blake to Stevens.* New Haven, Conn.: Yale University Press, 1976.
———. *The Visionary Company: A Reading of English Romantic Poetry.* Garden City, N.Y.: Doubleday, 1961.
Bromwich, David. *Disowned by Memory: Wordsworth's Poetry of the 1790s.* Chicago: University of Chicago Press, 1998.
Brooks, Cleanth. *A Shaping Joy: Studies in the Writer's Craft.* London: Methuen, 1973.
De Man, Paul. *The Rhetoric of Romanticism.* New York: Columbia University Press, 1984.
Empson, William. *Seven Types of Ambiguity.* New York: New Directions, 1966.
Gill, Stephen. *William Wordsworth: A Life.* New York: Oxford University Press, 1989.
Hartman, Geoffrey. *Wordsworth's Poetry, 1787–1814.* New Haven, Conn.: Yale University Press, 1971.
Hertz, Neil. *The End of the Line: Essays on Psychoanalysis and the Sublime.* New York: Columbia University Press, 1985.
Johnston, Kenneth. *Hidden Wordsworth: Poet, Lover, Rebel, Spy.* New York: Norton, 1998.
Levinson, Marjorie. *Wordsworth's Great Period Poems: Four Essays.* New York: Cambridge University Press, 1986.
Liu, Alan. *Wordsworth: The Sense of History.* Stanford, Calif.: Stanford University Press, 1989.
Moorman, Mary. *William Wordsworth: A Biography.* 2 vols. Oxford: Clarendon Press, 1957–1965.
Pinch, Adela. *Strange Fits of Passion: Epistemologies of Emotion, Hume to Austen.* Stanford, Calif.: Stanford University Press, 1996.
Quinney, Laura. *The Poetics of Disappointment: Wordsworth to Ashbery.* Charlottesville: University of Virgnia Press, 1999.
Wolfson, Susan J. *Questioning Presence: Wordsworth, Keats, and the Interrogative Mode in Romantic Poetry.* Ithaca, N.Y.: Cornell University Press, 1986.
Wordsworth, Jonathan, Michael C. Jaye, and Robert Woof. *William Wordsworth and the Age of English Romanticism.* New Brunswick, N.J.: Rutgers University Press, 1987.

PRE-RAPHAELITE POETRY

Pre-Raphaelitism is a term that originally and primarily (as the allusion to Raphael implies) applies to painting. The Pre-Raphaelite Brotherhood (who often initialed their paintings PRB) was formed by several painters in 1848, notably William Holman Hunt, John Everett Millais, and DANTE GABRIEL ROSSETTI. (Hunt is now best known for his painting of GEORGE MEREDITH, a Pre-Raphaelite fellow traveler in poetry, posing as the dying 18th-century poet Thomas Chatterton; Hunt subsequently eloped with Meredith's wife.) Rossetti's younger brother, the editor and critic William Michael Rossetti, wrote many of the prose defenses of the movement in their journal *The Germ,* in which their younger sister CHRISTINA GEORGINA ROSSETTI published her first poetry. William Rossetti insisted on the intellectual content of the Pre-Raphaelite movement, so it is not surprising that the movement would manifest itself in poetry as well as in painting (and Dante Gabriel Rossetti, like WILLIAM MORRIS a later Pre-Raphaelite, was an incomparably better poet than he was a painter, though as a painter he was very good).

To give a definition of Pre-Raphaelite poetry (whose practitioners include, arguably, poets as different as Meredith and WILLIAM BUTLER YEATS, ALGERNON CHARLES SWINBURNE and THOMAS HARDY) is notoriously more difficult than to describe pre-Raphaelite painting. Perhaps we should start by noting their commonality, as in Virginia Woolf's remark about Christina Rossetti's poetry, that her "eye, indeed, observed with a sensual pre-Raphaelite intensity that must have surprised Christina the Anglo-Catholic." William Rossetti's book-length essay on *Preraphaelitism* (1851) insisted on minute observation of nature. The Italian artist Raphael (1483–1520) and his followers produced the kinds of paintings that we take in as wholes, where structure, grouping, and form subordinate vision and detail to "a Raphaelesque standard of form and sentiment." The Rossettis knew the botanist Charles Lyell (father of the geologist who revolutionized the history of the world and whose work was the foundation for Charles Darwin's; Lyell Sr. was also the godfather of Dante Gabriel Rossetti), and they belonged to a movement emphasizing very careful and detailed naturalism, whether in science, in art, or in poetry. (Nature poetry, as WILLIAM WORDSWORTH wrote it, was not naturalistic in this sense, but precursors to Victorian naturalism may be found in his contemporaries, particularly CHARLOTTE SMITH and JOHN CLARE, as well as in *The Loves of the Plants,* by Charles Darwin's grandfather Erasmus Darwin.)

Details matter and form new ways of seeing the world. The Pre-Raphaelite painter, William Michael Rossetti said, seeing clearly, eyes open, "will come across groups of endless variety, consistency, and interest, which by rights do not compose at all," a phrase that might almost appear in Darwin's *On the Origin of Species*. The Pre-Raphaelites, while painting recognizable scenes (from the Bible, from mythology, from legends, from their own compositions, as in Dante Gabriel Rossetti's "The BLESSED DAMOZEL") always engaged in "minute study" in order to follow their principle "which contemplates the rendering of nature as it is." This principle derived from their creed, which was "truth; which in art means appropriateness in the first place; scrupulous fidelity in the second." Although William Rossetti disagreed with much that the essayist and critic John Ruskin had to say in his 1853 lecture on Pre-Raphaelitism, they were at one in seeing in the movement a return to the depiction of truth as more important than compositional beauty. Ruskin lamented of the followers of Raphael that any such "modern painter invariably thinks of the grace and beauty of his work first, and unites afterwards as much truth as he can with its conventional graces." For both of them, Pre-Raphaelitism placed accuracy above beauty, at least that painterly beauty which is a mere matter of convention.

Perhaps the best poem to illustrate this creed is Dante Gabriel Rossetti's "The WOODSPURGE," which ends with a kind of botanical description of the flower. That description is what the 20th-century poet T. S. Eliot would call "an escape from personality," a way of handling intense grief by fixating on a detail of the world. The speaker *handles* his grief by putting all his soul into "minute study," and the poem *expresses* his grief by showing how the speaker handles it. It is therefore no paradox to learn that Rossetti was uninterested in botany and natural history; the details are only interesting insofar as they engage with the adverting mind, with the eyes that see them *as* details, and not as symbols of the larger meaning which is the mind's preoccupation. Thus, William Rossetti noted in his account of the Pre-Raphaelite creed of truth, to elaborate on the idea of "scrupulous fidelity," the artist also had to be "true to himself. . . . His work must be individual too—expressive of *me* no less than of *not-me*." Thus, for Pre-Raphaelite artists, "there is nothing but watchfulness, study, and self-reliance," which makes their subject "nature, as interpreted by their own eyes and feelings."

Detail in painting is imitative. In poetry it is both imitative ("The Woodspurge hath a cup of three") and prosodical: the foregrounding of sound, meter, rhyme, rhythm, repetition. The attention to detail in all its forms is what links the otherwise disparate poetry of the spare Hardy with the lush Swinburne, of the sensual Christina Rossetti with the hard William Morris, of the passionately anguished Dante Gabriel Rossetti with the clinical detachment of Dante Gabriel Rossetti. In all these poets there is a sense of the intense self-reliance that William Michael Rossetti insisted on: scrupulosity sustained even through the most intense emotional upheaval, scrupulosity being what allows the poet to face that upheaval. Pre-Raphaelite poetry, while more inchoate as to its rules than painting was, is the more important movement. Pre-Raphaelite painting was certainly a significant precursor to modernism, but without Pre-Raphaelite poetry, it is doubtful that modern poetry would have evolved at all.

BIBLIOGRAPHY

Bloom, Harold, ed. *Pre-Raphaelite Poets*. New York: Chelsea House, 1986.

Rossetti, William Michael, arr. and ed. *Ruskin: Rossetti: Preraphaelitism; Papers 1854 to 1862*. 1899. Reprint, New York: AMS Press, 1971.

Ruskin, John. "Pre-Raphaelitism." In *Lectures on Architecture and Painting, delivered at Edinburgh, in November, 1853*, 159–201. New York: Wiley, 1890.

Stevenson, Lionel. *Pre-Raphaelite Poets*. New York: Norton, 1974.

PRINCESS: A MEDLEY, THE ALFRED, LORD TENNYSON (1847)

The Princess is best remembered for the beautiful songs it contains—and ALFRED, LORD TENNYSON would have been more or less happy about that. The songs are framed by a story, and the story itself is framed by the sort of device that Tennyson had already used (a fact *The Princess* alludes to obliquely) in "MORTE D'ARTHUR" (1842), which is read out in the course of a conversation between some friends. The "medley" of the subtitle of *The Princess* refers to the mode of composition that takes place *in* the poem: A group of friends improvise succeeding sections of the narrative as they sit together. Tennyson and his own friends actually did this at Trinity College, Cambridge University. Here the story they tell about women who wish to found their own university refers to the contemporary discussion on educational opportunities to women at the great universities, which was the cause of much high feeling, reflected in the debate that leads to the medley. (WILLIAM JOHNSON CORY's "Hersilia" [1891] takes a lovely and good-humored look at the same issue a few decades later, when he sees a young woman who is a Cambridge "blue," just as "Arthur, Alfred, Fitz," and the poet-speaker himself were.) Appropriately, therefore, women contribute to the medley as well, but mainly what they contribute are the songs between the poem's seven divisions (these were added in the 1850 edition of the poem).

The story told is a kind of reversal of William Shakespeare's *Love's Labour's Lost.* A group of women, led by Princess Ida, forswear the company of men (one is a young widow with a child), in order to throw off their subjugated status and aspire to higher attainments. The prince who narrates the story has been betrothed to Ida, but he finds that she is absent and refuses to see him. In a series of fairy-tale improbabilities highly reminiscent of JOHN KEATS's "THE EVE OF ST. AGNES," he and his companions disguise themselves as women and learn the situation. Inevitably, they are found out (the widow is the sister of one of the prince's companions), and a Spenserian battle ensues. (One of the sources of *The Princess* is book 5 of Edmund Spenser's *The Faerie Queene* [1596].) The prince loses and lies close to death, and the princess, who is caring for him in his semiconscious state, is struck through with the pity appropriate to the gentler sex. As he awakens, he understands the change in her that has ensued, and after some discussion, they both agree that each sex is fulfilled by the other, and that it beseems men to be gentler as it does women to be more fully educated; but that women's nurturing, and therefore their fundamentally maternal instinct, is nevertheless not to be denied, since it is their greatest, gravest, and most cherished impulse, the care of the child being the most important duty of a person's personal life. On this understanding, the prince will seek to help her attain equal rights. Having come to this agreement, they can live happily ever after. (The Gilbert and Sullivan operetta *Princess Ida* is based on *The Princess.*)

When we return to the poem's main storytelling frame, the narrator tells us that he was assigned to write up and poeticize the story, and that the songs of the women moved him to agree to their equal rights.

The tale is entertaining, its technique brilliant, and its debate liable to engage contemporary readers, but the glory of *The Princess* is its songs. Several of these are far more famous than the poem whence they derive. This is appropriate, because the real poetic point of the narrative of *The Princess* (as opposed to its somewhat uninteresting polemical point) is to make it possible to present the songs without the kind of context that would explain them and therefore explain away their power. One central feature of romantic and postromantic poetry is the desire to find or write a poem pure in itself, like the anonymous ballads that Thomas Percy had collected in his *Reliques of Ancient English Poetry* (1765) and that WILLIAM WORDSWORTH, no less than Sir WALTER SCOTT, was obsessed by and often sought to imitate. Scott's "PROUD MASIE," a mad song in a novel of his, is an example of this pure, out-of-context song, as are many of the beautiful songs that THOMAS LOVELL BEDDOES and JOANNA BAILLIE interpolated into their own verse dramas.

The 20th-century poet Kenneth Koch wrote (in a poem) "Around songs, everything becomes a play," and this is the attitude that Tennyson and his peers took to the songs they were trying to write. A way to put this is to say that the narrative of *The Princess,* far from providing a context for the songs, makes it possible for the songs to have no context. Tennyson himself said, "The child is the link through the parts, as shown in the Songs (inserted 1850), which are the best interpreters of the poem." He was referring specifically to the songs inserted in 1850 (and sung, therefore, by the women of the frame), but he might have been referring to all of them. The songs are deeply related to the child: They are rightly understood as essentially unacceptable to the everyday world of adult society and its narratives, essentially *other* to that world. The interpolated songs are about children, both living and dead, and consequently about their decontextualized, unparalleled importance, and all of the songs stand for that decontexualization. The children and the songs are metaphors for one another. They solicit human attention outside of any wider calculation or negotiation. They are not parts of anything; they are wholes in themselves. The speaker acknowledges that in the frame, at the end, when he says of the women singing them that "perhaps they felt their power, / For something in the ballads which they sang, / Or in their silent influence as they sat, / Had ever seem'd to wrestle with burlesque, / And drove us, last, to quite a solemn close" (ll. 3,196–3,200).

One aspect of Tennyson's poetic vocation is his feel for the intensity that true poetic language exemplifies, and the attention it solicits is directed to the same part of us that can and should be attentive to the fragile, endangered, lost, or dead. The prince himself is the appropriate hero for the poem since he is destined to fulfill the prophecy of his house where none can "know / The shadow from the substance, . . . that one / Should come to fight with shadows and to fall" (ll. 247–249). Not knowing the shadow from the substance, grappling with shadows, is what the poem shows the hero doing, but it is also an image for writing the poem itself. Skeptical when she heard of what Tennyson was doing, ELIZABETH BARRETT BROWNING wrote to ROBERT BROWNING, "Now is not the world too old and fond of steam, for blank verse poems, in ever so many books, to be written on the fairies?" This is a fair question, but *The Princess,* or at least its beautiful songs, are a fair answer: It is just because the industrialized and modernized world contextualizes everything and makes everything part of economic life that the voice of a kind of pure poetry, ephemeral and self-decontextualizing, is most needed.

For comments on individual songs, see "NOW SLEEPS THE CRIMSON PETAL, NOW THE WHITE" "TEARS, IDLE TEARS"; and "SPLENDOUR FALLS, The."

BIBLIOGRAPHY

Armstrong, Isobel. *Victorian Poetry: Poetry, Poetics and Politics.* New York: Routledge, 1993.

Bloom, Harold. *Poetry and Repression: Revisionism from Blake to Stevens.* New Haven, Conn.: Yale University Press, 1976.

Buckley, Jerome Hamilton. *Tennyson: The Growth of a Poet.* Boston: Houghton Mifflin, 1965.

Kilham, John. *Critical Essays on the Poetry of Tennyson.* New York: Barnes and Noble, 1960.

Kincaid, James R. *Tennyson's Major Poems: The Comic and Ironic Patterns.* New Haven, Conn.: Yale University Press, 1975.

Ricks, Christopher B. *Tennyson.* New York: Macmillan, 1972.

Rowlinson, Matthew. *Tennyson's Fixations: Psychoanalysis and the Topics of the Early Poetry.* Charlottesville: University Press of Virginia, 1994.

Tucker, Herbert. *Tennyson and the Doom of Romanticism.* Cambridge, Mass.: Harvard University Press, 1988.

***PROMETHEUS UNBOUND* PERCY BYSSHE SHELLEY (1820)** On its title page, PERCY BYSSHE SHELLEY called *Prometheus Unbound* a "lyrical drama." Lyric poetry has become a genre of its own, and indeed, it is now the primary genre for poetry, while drama, once universally written in poetry, has become an almost universally prose form since the Restoration. It was not always this way; lyric poetry developed out of the odes sung by the choruses in ancient Greek plays. In a sense, lyric is intense expression out of context, which focuses the attention of both the poet and the reader or hearer on the emotional experience rather than on the story of which that experience would be a part. Drama could always find some place for lyric, but its focus on plot and on the interaction between characters make it not particularly hospitable to the intense subjectivity into which lyric naturally developed. Some of the greatest dramatists, such as William Shakespeare and Ben Jonson, interspersed their plays with beautiful lyrics, but in the history of English poetical forms, the distinction between the genres is nearly total (partly because in Europe, lyric survived from ancient to modern times, whereas drama had to be reinvented), and indeed, it is responsible for the quality of lyric as we now love it.

Some poets have attempted to reintegrate the forms. John Milton's *Samson Agonistes* (1671) is a precursor—a closet drama that focuses more on the expression of intense feeling than on plot. Nineteenth-century English literature is littered with abandoned attempts to reintegrate the two forms. Among the romantics, one can mention WILLIAM WORDSWORTH, JOHN KEATS, SAMUEL TAYLOR COLERIDGE, and THOMAS LOVELL BEDDOES. But the only poets who did anything truly great in this mode were Shelley and LORD BYRON, largely because they took the German poet and dramatist Johann Wolfgang von Goethe (1749–1832) rather than Shakespeare or Milton as their model. Byron's *MANFRED* is the earlier drama in the vein of part I of Goethe's *Faust* (part II was written after the deaths of Byron and Shelley), but *Prometheus Unbound* is incomparably the greater.

Because lyric is about one person's subjective experience, while drama is about external interactions between different people, the most important thing we should understand from Shelley's somewhat contradictory designation of *Prometheus Unbound* is that the poem is the visible and external exposition—an allegory—of an interior and psychological dynamic. The two modes are fused thematically as well: The more dramatic aspect of the poem is about the power relations between those who have power to hurt and those who are subject to that power; the more lyrical aspect is about the experience of subjectivity itself, especially the most intense such experience, which belongs to human mortality.

Readers who come to *Prometheus Unbound* for the plot are inevitably disappointed, though there is certainly a plot. Jupiter, who has ruled over the universe for close to a million years has attempted all that time to wrest from the Titan Prometheus the secret that will end his reign. That secret is of no particular interest in itself; like the apple Eve eats in Milton's *Paradise Lost,* its main interest is its self-symbolism: It stands for itself. In *Prometheus Unbound* the secret is that Jupiter's marriage to Thetis will lead to the birth of the son who will dethrone him—Demogorgon. But there is no dramatic development that turns Demogorgon into Jupiter's enemy. Rather, his birth stands for the fact that Prometheus has not revealed to Jupiter the fact that he should not allow Demogorgon to be born. His birth stands for his birth—that is, it stands for Jupiter's fall, and nothing external actually seems to motivate that fall. Rather, as Demogorgon says, the hour of his fall has come.

Jupiter does fall, and the friends of Prometheus—his consort Asia and her sisters Panthea and Ione—celebrate the universal freedom to love that the world's liberation from tyranny inaugurates. They celebrate with the Spirit of the Hour that brings Jupiter to his fate; with Mother Earth; with the Spirit of the Earth, which propels the planet through the universe; with the Spirit of the Moon, in love with the Spirit of the Earth; and with all things brought to happiness by the jubilant overcoming of tyranny and the triumph of love.

Because it is a drama, we are entitled to ask the first plot question of all drama: Why is this happening *now*? What causes the events the drama discloses? How do things come to the dramatic pass that the drama displays? *Prometheus Unbound* is written almost entirely in lyric—lyrics of despair and lyrics of celebration. Why should this be the time for lyrics of celebration to occur? The answer is that there is one dramatic action in *Prometheus Unbound,* and perhaps only one; everything else follows from it. That action is the opening of the play: Prometheus seeks to recall the curse he pronounced on Jupiter aeons ago. The word *recall* (act 1, l. 59) means both recollect and revoke. Prometheus can no longer recollect the curse, and that very forgetfulness sketches the beginning of his gesture of revocation. He ceases resisting Jupiter's power with opposing power and instead regrets the hatred with which he has met Jupiter's hatred.

The whole world, laboring under Jupiter's tyranny, finds hope in the force of Prometheus's resistance to Jupiter. But this hope for revenge is vindictive and, like Prometheus's hatred, is itself the evil that Jupiter feeds on. We could say that just as Demogorgon stands for the fact that it is now time for Demogorgon to unseat Jupiter, Jupiter himself stands for the hatred he provokes in Prometheus and his followers. We know this because it is the Phantasm of Jupiter who pronounces the curse (1. 262 ff), and that phantasm is introduced as one of the shadows, phantoms, or mirror images in the world of death of all the forms of the living, gods, and powers of the upper world. But the phantoms in the realm of death are the projections of the mind that sees them, like the Magus Zoroaster whom Earth instances (act 1, ll. 191–218). We know this because the Phantasm of Jupiter says to Prometheus the very words that he is also repeating. Prometheus becomes Jupiter, while the image of Jupiter speaks the words of Prometheus. Jupiter is the emanation of Prometheus's hatred for Jupiter, and so Prometheus has cursed himself.

In this he is like Milton's Satan ("the Hero of *Paradise Lost,*" as Shelley notoriously calls him in the preface to *Prometheus Unbound*), to whom Shelley explicitly compares and contrasts Prometheus. The contrast is in Prometheus's "being exempt from the taints of ambition, envy, revenge, and a desire for personal aggrandisement, which in the Hero of *Paradise Lost,* interfere with the interest." Is Prometheus exempt from the taint of revenge? Not entirely, but even when he curses Jupiter his curse is far more in the mode of Jesus' attitude toward Satan in *Paradise Regained* than Satan's attitude toward God in *Paradise Lost.* He curses Jupiter with the agony of remorse (act 1, l. 287), "when thou must appear to be / That which thou art internally" (act 1, ll. 298–299). Since Prometheus is now feeling remorse—for what? for cursing Jupiter with the agony of remorse—Jupiter as his image and emanation is now suffering the curse itself. He suffers it because Prometheus no longer intends revenge—because he is the remorse that Prometheus feels or the part of Prometheus that cannot bear for Prometheus to feel remorse for Jupiter.

But why and how does Jupiter take power to begin with? Asia gives the backstory in a long and crucial speech in act 2 (2.4.32–109). There she describes how Prometheus gave Jupiter the strength to overthrow the tyranny of Kronos, or Saturn (also the subject of Keats's *Hyperion* poems [see *Hyperion and The Fall of Hyperion*]). Shelley puns on his name, a near homonym of Chronos (as in "chronology"), when Asia says that time was the shadow of Saturn's throne. Time is an "envious shadow" (2.4.34) because it envies the transcendence of love or (to say what turns out to be the same thing) because all beings are subject to the envy produced by the scarcity that time names. Jupiter reigns instead of Saturn but is as envious as Saturn has been. No power or agency lasts: again, Jupiter's very being is the manifestation of his own resentment over the fact that he will fall. Power feels only the frustration of its desire, and so "to be / Omnipotent but friendless is to reign" (2.4.47–48). To be omnipotent is to be friendless because even omnipotence cannot achieve the impossible escape from the envious shadow of time.

Here it is important to see that Jupiter stands for human dissatisfaction with the world, and that this dissatisfaction has two sources, one of which is inevitable, the other unfortunate but not, Shelley hopes, the necessary consequence of the first. Life is painful for two reasons: first, that we are heir to all the inevitable heartache and natural shock of being mortal beings, heir at last to mortality itself; and second, that power oppresses us. The most crucial analytic phrase in *Prometheus Unbound,* repeated throughout the play, is "self-contempt." Power is the embodiment of the self-contempt that we are prone to as frail and mortal beings. We are oppressed by self-contempt, we oppress others in order to escape our own self-contempt, and so they are oppressed by our own self-contempt as we are oppressed by theirs and as they are oppressed by their own. As Asia's speech has shown, the desire for power arises and is the manifestation of a denial of human mortality and death. It is the poor substitute for eternal love, which is why the "omnipotent" is friendless. Accepting, like Job or the Jesus of Milton's *Paradise Regained,* love even in the absence of eternity is the triumph that *Prometheus Unbound* celebrates. Prometheus himself is immortal, but as an allegorical figure his endurance—suffering woes which Hope thinks infinite and forgiving wrongs darker than Death or Night (4.570–571)—stands for the endurance of mortal beings. It is not his immortality that counts for us but the immortal way he shows us how to face our own mortality. But because we can never overcome our own mortality, we can never be fully confident that we can overcome the perennial temptation to tyranny—as Demogorgon warns again and again.

This returns us to the relation between lyric and drama with which we started, a relationship that is also allegorized in *Prometheus Unbound.* As drama, it is about the interactions between immortal beings. But as lyric, it treats those interactions as allegorical of the human psyche. The triumph of Prometheus is, then, the triumph of the lyrical over the dramatic, a triumph confirmed by Shelley's decision, pretty much after completing a full draft of the work, to add its fourth act, which constitutes a sustained and astonishing lyric celebration. The play itself is an attempted demonstration that the sheer subjective intensity of lyric can stand up to the far more efficacious *action* of drama, and that the intensity of lyric can save us from the self-contempt which is the engine of dramatic—that is, mutually oppressive—interaction. Jupiter, then, stands for action and self-contempt, and Prometheus for lyric, and the work is the proof of its own argument.

BIBLIOGRAPHY

Bloom, Harold. *Genius: A Mosaic of One Hundred Exemplary Creative Minds.* New York: Warner, 2002.

———. *Shelley's Mythmaking.* New Haven, Conn.: Yale University Press, 1959.

———. *The Visionary Company: A Reading of English Romantic Poetry.* Garden City, N.Y.: Doubleday, 1961.

Duffy, Edward. *Rousseau in England: The Context for Shelley's Critique of the Enlightenment.* Berkeley: University of California Press, 1979.

Hogle, Jerrold E. *Shelley's Process: Radical Transference and the Development of His Major Works.* New York: Oxford University Press, 1988.

Keach, William. *Shelley's Style.* New York: Methuen, 1984.

Leighton, Angela. *Shelley and the Sublime: An Interpretation of the Major Poems.* New York: Cambridge University Press, 1984.

Notopolous, James A. *The Platonism of Shelley: A Study of Platonism and the Poetic Mind.* Durham, N.C.: Duke University Press, 1949.

Quinney, Laura. *The Poetics of Disappointment: Wordsworth to Ashbery.* Charlottesville: University of Virgnia Press, 1999.

Wasserman, Earl. *Shelley: A Critical Reading.* Baltimore: Johns Hopkins Press, 1971.

———. *Subtler Language: Critical Readings of Neoclassic and Romantic Poems.* Baltimore: Johns Hopkins Press, 1968.

"PROUD MASIE" SIR WALTER SCOTT (1818)

"Proud Masie" is one of Sir WALTER SCOTT's best-known quasi-ballads, written in the pure, sad, grim form of the Border ballads he loved (lately collected by Thomas Percy in his *Reliques of Ancient English Poetry* (1765); the collection and publication of these ballads was of immense importance to the early romantics). Its story, like that of all the ballads, is simple enough: Masie has been too proud to give her love to any of those who would have loved her, and now she learns that her fate is to be a kind of lonely, natural exemplar of pride, brought low and unloved into the grave.

Part of the purity of ballad form, which Scott gets so well, is the introduction of speech without speech tags. We know that Masie addresses the robin from what she says, not from a report of who says it. This is typical of the form, because ballads deal with elemental figures, and what they say is appropriate to who they are, each speech appropriate to each speaker alone. There is no hint of surprise, and hence nothing surprising, in the tone of the ballad when Masie addresses the robin, nor when the robin answers her. When shall I marry, she asks, and the robin that it will be when the pallbearers carry her to the graveyard.

There is nothing unclear about the answer, and we must not understand Masie to be puzzled when she poses her next question: Who will make up the bridal bed? The answer is: the sexton who will dig the grave. Masie asks the question only to get the answer. She contributes, as the figures in ballads do, to the unfolding of the ballad, so that their anonymous speakers and near-anonymous characters are all on the same level.

Contributing to this tone is the fact that the alternation between speakers, and between question and answer, ceases as we go from third to fourth stanza: the robin finishes the ballad, and the welcome she attributes to the owl feels in a strange way like a real one. This is not surprising, given the context of the ballad: It is a mad song sung by the dying Madge Wildfire in Scott's novel *The Heart of Midlothian* (1818). In that book, Madge Wildfire, a sad madwoman, has stolen the baby fathered by her seducer with someone else after he abandons her, and the mother has been accused of murder. The truth comes out before she dies. She dies at the end of chapter 22 of volume 2 of the novel, singing snatches of ballads and mad songs. This is the last one she sings: "Again she changed the tune to one wilder, less monotonous, and less regular. But of the words, only a fragment or two could be collected by those who listened to this singular scene." After she sings it, she falls asleep and dies. Scott modeled Madge on a real person, Feckless Fannie, a strange vagrant of his neighborhood. He also modeled her on William Shakespeare's Ophelia and the mad songs she sings just before her death—songs of disappointed love and of abandonment by Hamlet.

I mention this context mainly to give reasons to transcend it. Scott's first ambition was to be a poet, and when he turned to the novel, overawed by LORD BYRON, he nevertheless was driven by a lyric as much as by a narrative desire. He wrote "Proud Masie" not because he needed a mad song in *The Heart of Midlothian;* the fact that Madge's listeners can only make out "a fragment or two" of the song show that it is in itself irrelevant to the plot. Rather, one might almost say that Scott wrote *The Heart of Midlothian* as a place to put "Proud Masie" (as well as a number of other snatches of poetry), and that the eerie anonymity achieved by the poem has precedence over the context that seems to explain it.

See also MOTTOES.

BIBLIOGRAPHY

Kerr, James. *Fiction against History: Scott as Storyteller.* New York: Cambridge University Press, 1989.

Lauber, John. *Sir Walter Scott.* Boston: Twayne Publishers, 1989.

Lincoln, Andrew. *Walter Scott and Modernity.* Edinburgh: Edinburgh University Press, 2007.

R

"RECESSIONAL" RUDYARD KIPLING (1897)

This poem is remembered mainly by the quasi-biblical line it left to the English language: "Lest we forget," subsequently a favorite for military tombstones. RUDYARD KIPLING wrote it for Queen Victoria's diamond jubilee in 1897, celebrating the 60th anniversary of her reign. But as its title should indicate (a recessional is the exit of the clergy and choir from the church at the end of a service, the converse of the opening processional), the poem is far from being naively jingoistic. Kipling, in an autobiographical account, said that with the queen's jubilee arrived "a certain optimism that scared me" (*Something of Myself*, p. 159). He was scared most immediately because of the disastrous skirmishes in South Africa that would eventually lead to the Second Boer War in 1902 (where the British soldiers would sing "Recessional" to celebrate the taking of Pretoria). On the weekend of the New Year 18 months earlier, Leander Starr Jameson, a British administrator, led a raid into Afrikaans territory designed to spark a revolt against the Boers by their British workers. (The primary struggle between the British and the Boers was over the control of the diamonds and gold that had been discovered in the region). Jameson failed, many British workers were killed, and Jameson himself was imprisoned. Kipling admired Jameson (and had him in mind when he wrote his later poem "If—") and was depressed by the failure of the raid, which contributed to the "uneasiness" he felt "at the back of his head" about what he was hearing about Britain's imperialistic experiences abroad. The celebration of the jubilee, which was enormously impressive, was also perhaps blind to these troubles abroad, and so he wrote "Recessional," a poem not very celebratory but "more in the nature of a *nuzz ur-wattu* (an averter of the Evil Eye)" (pp. 159–160).

It is worthwhile noting that the poem accuses the British, the first person plural of its chorus, of having the "heathen heart" that trusts to military might and not to God, and forgets the enormous cost borne by the men who do the fighting. That the *bien-pensant* British are the heathens is a telling point, and one that puts the pressure on them to recall, not their ambitions for imperial domination, but, rather, the gratitude that they owe to those who defended Britain in the past, however temporarily. (Kipling is probably thinking of the great story the Greek historian Herodotus tells of the Persian King Xerxes weeping when he saw his millions of soldiers assembled for battle, to think that every one of them would be dead and forgotten in a hundred years.) Kipling's jingoism is complex and takes the form of establishing and praising a culture of grateful memory of sacrifice (the obligation to such memory is at the heart of all his greatest poems). You can see this in "Recessional" in the repeated reasons that the poem calls upon God's aid: God is there "lest we forget" those who have come before us to make our current world possible. We must remember not our power but the sacrifice and devotion that made it possible. We do not thank God for his goodness to us but for allowing us to remember what we owe to each other and to our predecessors (again, his immediate reference is Jameson). God is a power in the poem, but his is the power of memory, not of might. We want him with us so that we can remember those whom he was with before. God is a medium and a means, not an end, in the poem. What we remember is the past, before the current dying fall that the empire is experiencing at Victoria's jubilee. Not that Kipling was imagining that the empire was about to fall. Rather he was taking Victoria's imminent departure as a reminder that to be an empire is to face its fall: "Our navies melt away . . . [and] all our pomp of yesterday / Is one with Nineveh and Tyre." Empires fall and so we should all remember those who fell for us and are falling for us even now (the soldiers and sailors to whom Kipling was always devoted), and God's blessing upon us is not the blessing of security so much as of gratitude. The world as Kipling was troubled by it was a world of very fragile standing, that military might would do nothing to secure, and it is this sense of the world that makes this poem a powerful and necessary countercurrent to the jingoism of the jubilee that both attracted and troubled Kipling.

BIBLIOGRAPHY

Kipling, Rudyard. *Something of Myself and Other Autobiographical Writings.* Edited by Thomas Pinney. New York: Cambridge University Press, 1990.

"REJECTED" LORD ALFRED DOUGLAS (1899)

George MacBeth calls "Rejected" Lord ALFRED DOUGLAS's "one good poem," which is either too harsh or too kind. The poem is at any rate an interesting one, and (as with "TWO LOVES") the interest is not entirely biographical. Douglas and his lover and unintentional victim OSCAR WILDE were both attracted to Catholicism—oddly, given their sexual and aesthetic commitments. But they both saw in Catholicism (to which Douglas later converted) a religion that took such things seriously, even if it disapproved of them. The pleasure that Douglas earlier took in the experience of shame is here transfigured into the more obvious masochism of being bound up by the cords of iron wire made of his desire. The desire and the punishment it elicits are both strangely pleasurable for Douglas.

Apollo in the poem is clearly Wilde, and we understand the speaker to be in the position of Hyacinth, the beautiful boy Apollo pursued and who was transformed (as the Roman poet Ovid described in his *Metamorphoses*) into the flower. Hyacinth is parted from Apollo, and in "Rejected" he regrets this. The allusion is particularly pointed since one of the pieces of evidence that did a lot of harm to Wilde during his trial for obscenity was a letter that he wrote the 16-years younger Douglas in January 1893, in which he said, "Your slim gilt soul walks between passion and poetry. I know Hyacinthus, whom Apollo loved so madly, was you in Greek days." Douglas had left this letter in some clothes that he gave to another young man, who then blackmailed Wilde with it; Wilde refused to pay, and eventually the letter was produced in court.

After Wilde's release from prison, he and Bosie (Douglas's universally used nickname) had a fairly mercurial relationship, which lasted until Wilde's death. This poem, undoubtedly from a low point in that relationship, depicts Bosie's despair at losing Wilde (Wilde had treated him harshly in some of his prison writing) and his attempts to make amends for that despair through piety. Wilde is represented as the beautiful god Apollo—the god sacred to Bosie's greatest influence, JOHN KEATS (see especially *HYPERION* AND *THE FALL OF HYPERION*). The opening of "Rejected" is also a kind of gay recapitulation of Keats's "LA BELLE DAME SANS MERCI," where the lady leaves the ailing knight while he sleeps, so that he wakes up in the despair of his abandonment. Apollo leaves Hyacinth here because Hyacinth has been unable to sustain the courage of his aesthetic and erotic convictions; his weakness destines him to be left behind. He seeks solace in Christ as a substitute for Apollo, but he cannot give up the desires, even as they have been made into cords to bind him. Hyacinth becomes his own pagan sacrifice and seeks Apollo, but Apollo still rejects him, and now he is left alone in the world, "lost in the mist / Of the things that can never be" (ll. 49–50). Wilde has escaped with his integrity, and never faltered as Douglas has; but Douglas still, at least at this point, prefers his despairing love for Wilde to the demands and consolations of the church.

The poem seems more final than the relationship it records, and it is in that finality that we can see its quality. It is a powerful evocation of loneliness and comfortless despair, of desire that survives dejection and still must assert itself, no matter how hopelessly.

BIBLIOGRAPHY

Douglas, Alfred Bruce, Lord. *Oscar Wilde and Myself.* New York: Duffield and Co., 1914.

Ellmann, Richard. *Oscar Wilde,* New York: Knopf, 1988.

Harris, Frank. *Oscar Wilde. His Life and Confessions.* Garden City, N.Y.: Garden City Publishing Co., 1932.

Whittington-Egan, Richard. "Oscar Wilde: A Centennial Wreath of Memories." *Contemporary Review* November 1, 2000. Available online. URL: http://www.encyclopedia.com/doc/1G1-68157978.html. Accessed on January 27, 2008.

"REMEMBRANCE" EMILY BRONTË (1846)

"Remembrance" is a fascinating poem, both as a precursor to EMILY BRONTË's famous novel *Wuthering Heights* (1847) and in its own right. The original manuscript, dated March 3, 1845 (when Brontë was 26), had as its title "R. Alcona to J. Brenzaida." Rosina Alcona and Julius Brenzaida were characters in the imaginary world of Gondal, which Emily and her younger sister Anne invented and peopled with characters and narratives (this was one of the two imaginary worlds that the Brontë siblings invented and explored). It took its present form with the 1846 publication of *Poems by Currer, Ellis, and Acton Bell* (Charlotte, Emily, and Anne Brontë).

The imaginary provenance and unlikely dating (15 years earlier, when the addressee had died [l. 9], the real Emily would only have been 11) make it clear that this does not depict—or if it does, only in a highly mediated fashion—a true loss on Emily's part, but the poetic imagination of such a loss. Much of it is more or less standard issue: the sense of unappeasable loss, the memory of a time that cannot possibly be reclaimed, and the risks entailed in such a memory: The speaker "dare not indulge in memory's rapturous pain" (l. 30) lest she lose all contact and agency within the world. But the extraordinary moments are the ones where she sees—as Catherine and Heathcliff do in *Wuthering Heights*—that loss brings one into deeper regions than possession could possibly have offered. The poem is an earlier version of Catherine's impassioned avowal to Nelly about Heathcliff, "If all else perished, and HE remained, I should still continue to be; and if all else remained, and he were annihilated, the universe would turn to a mighty stranger: I should not seem a part of it. . . . My love for Heathcliff resembles the eternal rocks beneath: a source of little visible delight, but necessary. Nelly, I AM Heathcliff! He's always, always in my mind: not as a pleasure, any more than I am always a pleasure to myself, but as my own being" (*Wuthering Heights,* chapter 9).

Heathcliff is alive when Catherine says this, but its truth even beyond the grave is confirmed when, despite her death, she and Heathcliff continue to haunt each other. So, too, the speaker of "Remembrance" can describe an existence strengthened without the aid of joy, cherished, she implies, because it lacks joy (ll. 23–24)—that is, the "visible delight" that Catherine abjures, an existence sustained in opposition to the emptiness of the world that does not contain her dead lover. She can say, like Catherine saying, "I am Heathcliff," that his tomb is "already more than mine," which carries her identification with him or with his state to hyperbolic extremes.

These moments are extraordinary and make this into a very nearly great poem, and they make us take seriously (as *Wuthering Heights* will do preeminently) the speaker's conversation with the dead. She speaks to a man who has been dead for 15 years and seems not haunted by him but able to sustain the intensity of relations with him. This is because they have both given up the joy of life but maintained, over the boundary of life and death, the bare existence of a life deprived of joy and which must therefore exist since only what exists can be deprived of joy. Brontë will repeat this logic in "NO COWARD SOUL IS MINE"; it is the logic of the SUBLIME, whereby the increased intensity of affect produced by loss ratifies the sheer existence of what has been lost rather than denying that existence. For Brontë, this was literature's primary quality.

BIBLIOGRAPHY

Barker, Juliet. *The Brontës.* New York: St. Martin's Press, 1994.

Bristow, Joseph, ed. *Victorian Women Poets: Emily Bronte, Elizabeth Barrett Browning, Christina Rossetti.* Houndsville, Basingstoke, England: Macmillan Press, 1995.

Gezari, Janet, "Fathoming 'Remembrance'; Emily Bronte in Context." *ELH: English Literary History* 66, no. 4 (1999): 965–984.

Homans Margaret. *Women Writers and Poetic Identity: Dorothy Wordsworth, Emily Brontë, and Emily Dickinson*, Princeton, 1980.

Mason, Emma. *Women Poets of the Nineteenth Century*. Tavistock, Devon, England: Northcote House Publishers, 2006.

"RENOUNCEMENT" ALICE MEYNELL (1875)

"Renouncement" is one of ALICE MEYNELL's most famous poems, although it is not one of her best. Even so, it has considerable merit, enough so that the essayist and critic John Ruskin singled it out for praise when it was published in her first book of poems, *Preludes*. "Renouncement" foretells Meynell's later literary career and the very fine poems to follow. She wrote it after her 1868 conversion to Catholicism, following instruction from a Father Dignam. He received her into the church but later asked to be posted elsewhere because of the intense mutual attraction between them.

"Renouncement" is a sonnet (a Petrarchan one with octet and sestet), the canonical form of the love poem, whether requited or unrequited. In this case it is not clear that a difference can be drawn between the two kinds of love. Meynell's intensity as a poet and thinker was addressed to the experience of radical separation from others, an experience not attenuated but exacerbated by love. It would be far too easy to speculate that Meynell's attraction to Catholicism was in fact an attraction to Father Dignam; it would almost certainly be more correct to say that her attraction to him was a confirmation of her attraction to Catholicism, the self-sacrificing and self-abnegating Catholicism that was for her the most direct route to spiritual intensity. (It was this commitment that she most admired in her close friend and admirer COVENTRY PATMORE.)

Whose renouncement does the title refer to? It is obviously Meynell's own, since she begins with the self-breaking injunction to herself, "I must not think of thee." But it is the poem's addressee as well: He has had to renounce her just as she has had to renounce him, and what they still have together is the painfulness of their mutual renouncement.

She must not think of him, but thoughts of him are everywhere. She suppresses those thoughts, and that very suppression gives an erotic charge to the whole world, since every thing she does or feels hides thoughts of him that she must keep in check. In the sonnet's sestet, she turns from wakefulness to sleep. There she knows that she will not be able to help dreaming about him. But in dreams she is alone, and not with him, so it is in dreams that she can complete the reconciliation of prohibition and desire that has begun with the eroticization of the whole waking world.

This reconciliation is very delicately managed by the poem. The speaker is "tired yet strong" in the poem's first line—tired from resisting her impulses so strongly. The reward of that tiredness is the rest that comes after the "whole day long" (l. 8) is over and "sleep comes" (l. 9). Then she can dream of him, and when she does, all the negatives—"I must not," "I must stop short," and so on—are reversed into the joyousness of the last line's "I run, I run." There is an internal rhyme here marking the contrast with the way "I *shun* the thought" (l. 2) of him. "I run, I run, I am gathered to thy heart" is a remarkable line, partly because it has an additional syllable, with the word *am* being the interloper. But the line itself gathers up and gathers her up at its ending. Meynell had extraordinary delicacy of ear (as can be seen in the strictures of the preface and notes to the anthology of poems she put out in 1893, *The Flower of the Mind*) and knew exactly what she was doing. In dreams and poems, she can run, the meter itself will falter and then regather, and her renunciation can inspire the possibilities of its expression, of its expressive address to the absence she has embraced. Her faith is a way of keeping faith with him, just as the intensity of her renunciation is a way for her to keep faith with the intensity of her faith.

BIBLIOGRAPHY

Badeni, June. *The Slender Tree: A Life of Alice Meynell*. Padstow, Cornwall, England: Tabb House, 1981.

Leighton, Angela: "Alice Meynell." In *Victorian Woman Poets: Writing against the Heart*, 244–265. Charlottesville: University Press of Virginia, 1992.

Meynell, Alice. *Prose and Poetry*. Edited by Frederick Page, et al. London: J. Cape, 1947.

Meynell, Viola. *Alice Meynell: A Memoir*. London: J. Cape, 1929.

"RESOLUTION AND INDEPENDENCE"

William Wordsworth (1802) One of William Wordsworth's most parodied poems (Lewis Carroll's "A Sitting on a Gate" is the most famous parody), "Resolution and Independence" is also one of his greatest. Throughout his life, Wordsworth insisted on this poem's centrality to his work, and it is worth considering why that should be.

The poem is a narrative (a true one) in which Wordsworth describes his meeting with an old leech gatherer, who tells him about his solitary and difficult trade. The poem is essentially a narrative of its speaker's psychological trajectory, from gaiety to despondency to perception—a perception that both makes possible the psychological insight the poem displays and sees a way to get beyond or behind that psychology.

The narrative begins with an evocation of a natural scene. It is in the present tense, although in the poem's third stanza, we will find that this is a retrospective anecdote. The vividness of the present tense is part of the point, though, as the poem begins with a sense of natural renovation. After the night storm, "now the sun is rising calm and bright" (l. 3). The scene prompts a mood in Wordsworth that makes him open to seeing it as lightly allegorical: He feels fresh and therefore able to respond to its beauty and freshness. In general, for Wordsworth the natural scene will be an appropriate allegory for the mental mood that makes him able to respond to it and feel it as meaningful—a mood that derives from the scene itself.

That renovation, then, is one Wordsworth feels, too, like the little animals sporting in the scene. But then he experiences a purely human reaction: the mood, as he puts it elsewhere, when pleasant thoughts bring sad thoughts to the mind. He starts out being "happy as a boy" (l. 18), but we can perceive the reasons for that happiness: "My old remembrances went from me wholly / And all the ways of men, so vain and melancholy" (ll. 20–21). This tells us that he is not generally happy, since he is no longer a boy, and that his remembrances and the ways of men he now experiences are melancholy ones. He is not thinking about any of this, but as in the Intimations Ode, a thought of grief comes to him. He is not sure why, but we can say that for Wordsworth, human experience is or eventually comes to be always an experience of *relationship* to what is different from the self-coincident present. That relationship can be to the past, through memory; to others, through kindness and love; or to one's own moods, so that the pure self-sufficiency of happiness will always be aware of what is different from it. Wordsworth is an extraordinary chronicler of psychological experience, and we notice how he chronicles it here: He becomes aware of the "Dim sadness" (l. 28) that suddenly comes upon him and the nameless blind thoughts that surround him.

The poem's third psychological movement begins here. Having soared into a good mood because of the beautiful morning, and then sunk into despondency for reasons he cannot quite understand, Wordsworth makes an effort to recover his good cheer by reminding himself of the beauties and joys that surround him, and his relationship to "these blissful creatures" (l. 32) of the earth. But now he sees the contrast between this mood and what may come in the future since it has already come in the past: "there may come another day to me—/ Solitude, pain of heart, distress, and poverty" (ll. 34–35).

He knows this may happen because it has happened to the other poets he thinks of as his peers: Robert Burns, Thomas Chatterton, Samuel Taylor Coleridge. He experiences a crisis of poetic vocation, since the vocation of a poet, certainly of the romantic poet for whom vocation becomes a central issue (see romanticism), is to take and give pleasure through the intense description of the world and of human experience, a description whose intensity tends to be a function of the sadness it can recognize and record as central to the human condition. Poets choose such a vocation in the glory of their own youthful strength, not recognizing that the "gladness" that allows them to see all things, even sorrow, as joyful will turn into its own opposite: "We Poets in our youth begin in gladness; / But *thereof* come in the end despondency and madness" (ll. 48–49; emphasis added). Despondency and madness come *because* of the gladness in which the poets begin. They embrace an experience which will eventually defeat them, as it defeats everyone.

It is now that Wordsworth meets the leech gatherer, an old man who represents a future old age that the poet has not dreamt of. His otherness, or dissimilarity, to Wordsworth—the seriousness and opacity and difference that embodies—is total. He is patient, knowledgeable, and uncanny—almost a part of nature, but a different nature from what the young Wordsworth had seen at the beginning of the poem. It is not that he knows more; he knows differently. He makes Wordsworth understand that he does not have a clue about nature or living in nature or time or age or life. Nor do his friends, who have somehow lost their way and not seen clearly what the leech gatherer knows, not gone as deeply as the leech gatherer has gone. The leech gatherer is, for the speaker, a kind of "apt admonishment" (l. 112). Yet Wordsworth does not quite see the aptness at first. He tests this old man against his fears and finds that he still has them (l. 116), and so he seeks comfort from the old man, asking him the famous (much-parodied) question: "'How is it that you live, and what is it you do?'" (l. 119).

That question, we must recall, means: How can you stand old age? What do you do to reconcile yourself to it? This is the question Wordsworth wants the leech gatherer to answer. But the desire for an answer is his mistake, of which the leech gatherer represents the admonishment. The leech gatherer is absorbed into the troubling uncanniness of nature, rather than trying to explain it. He shows how human loneliness can be part of nature's loneliness, how humans can be a deeper part of the deeper aspects of nature—the sublime and uncanny aspects—than the jocund, young appreciation of nature that the poets in their youth were celebrating. What Wordsworth sees is that he does not yet see everything there is to being human. The leech gatherer has gone where the poet cannot yet imagine going; therefore, he recognizes the shallowness of the arrogance in which he thought he understood the melancholy of human life. There is more there than he can know, more than he has the capacity to know. Whatever it is that nature means, the leech gatherer and the old age he represents is part of that meaning, and so, too, is Wordsworth. He will be part of the meaning, rather than its interpreter or recipient, and if he can understand that, at least, then his poetry will be truer to nature (as it was) than that of any of the other poets who simply sought to praise or lament the pleasures and sorrows nature provides the human spectator. Wordsworth confronts the otherness of nature, and therefore of human nature, here in a way far deeper than he had done before.

BIBLIOGRAPHY

Abrams, M. H. *Correspondent Breeze: Essays on English Romanticism.* New York: Norton, 1984.

———. *Natural Supernaturalism: Tradition and Revolution in Romantic Literature.* New York: Norton, 1973.

Bloom, Harold. *The Visionary Company: A Reading of English Romantic Poetry.* Garden City, N.Y.: Doubleday, 1961.

Bromwich, David. *Disowned by Memory: Wordsworth's Poetry of the 1790s.* Chicago: University of Chicago Press, 1998.

De Man, Paul. *The Rhetoric of Romanticism.* New York: Columbia University Press, 1984.

Empson, William. *Seven Types of Ambiguity.* New York: New Directions, 1966.

Gill, Stephen. *William Wordsworth: A Life.* New York: Oxford University Press, 1989.

Hartman, Geoffrey. *Wordsworth's Poetry, 1787–1814.* New Haven, Conn.: Yale University Press, 1971.

Liu, Alan. *Wordsworth: The Sense of History.* Stanford, Calif.: Stanford University Press, 1989.

Moorman, Mary. *William Wordsworth: A Biography.* 2 vols. Oxford: Clarendon Press, 1957–1965.

Pinch, Adela. *Strange Fits of Passion: Epistemologies of Emotion, Hume to Austen.* Stanford, Calif.: Stanford University Press, 1996.

Quinney, Laura. *The Poetics of Disappointment: Wordsworth to Ashbery.* Charlottesville: University Press of Virginia, 1999.

Wolfson, Susan J. *Questioning Presence: Wordsworth, Keats, and the Interrogative Mode in Romantic Poetry.* Ithaca, N.Y.: Cornell University Press, 1986.

RIME OF THE ANCIENT MARINER, THE

SAMUEL TAYLOR COLERIDGE (1798, 1800) *The Rime of the Ancient Mariner* is SAMUEL TAYLOR COLERIDGE'S most popular poem. It opened the 1798 first edition of *Lyrical Ballads,* where it first appeared; Coleridge revised it for the 1800 edition and undertook further revisions later, after his sea voyage to Malta (where he went to recover his health), revisions that include the wonderful marginal glosses. Nevertheless it would probably be better to see the different versions of the poem as essentially true to the same vision and to regard them as presenting that vision with the slight stereoscopic differences that allow us to see depth.

In chapter 14 of his intellectual quasi-autobiography, *Biographia Literaria* (1817), Coleridge describes how he and WILLIAM WORDSWORTH decided to split the writing of *Lyrical Ballads* so that Coleridge would do the so-called supernatural poems and Wordsworth the entirely naturalistic ones. The idea was that Wordsworth would treat natural events as though they had the special interest that ballads had traditionally found in the supernatural; while Coleridge would do the converse, which is to say he would treat supernatural events as they would be experienced by psychologically real human beings. Both procedures would meet in the attention they focused on the reactions, psychological and expressive, to be represented (as Wordsworth put it in the preface to the 1800 volume) by "fitting to metrical arrangement a selection of the real language of men in a state of vivid sensation." For Wordsworth, the vividness of sensation would be communicated by intensity of language in the naturalist poems; for Coleridge, the intensity of language would reflect the vividness of sensation that the supernatural elements would necessarily produce, but it was the sensation of real people and not its supposed supernatural occasions that was the source of the poetic language. Thus, he wrote in perhaps the most famous passage in *Biographia Literaria,* "it was agreed, that my endeavours should be directed to persons and characters supernatural, or at least romantic, yet so as to transfer from our inward nature a human interest and a semblance of truth sufficient to procure for these shadows of imagination that willing suspension of disbelief for the moment, which constitutes poetic faith."

In a letter to Wordsworth about the 1800 edition of *Lyrical Ballads,* which Wordsworth had just sent him, CHARLES LAMB had foreshadowed just this language in a deeply insightful comment on the poem: "I am sorry that Coleridge has christened his Ancient Marinere, a Poet's Reverie; . . . What new idea is gained by this title but one subversive of all credit—which the tale should force upon us—of its truth!" He goes on, "For me, I was never so affected with any human tale. After first reading it, I was totally possessed with it for many days. I dislike all the miraculous part of it; but the feelings of the man under the operation of such scenery, dragged me along like Tom Pipe's magic whistle. . . . the Ancient Marinere undergoes such trials as overwhelm and bury all individuality or memory of what he was—like the state of a man in a bad dream, one terrible peculiarity of which is, that all consciousness of personality is gone" (letter dated January 30, 1801). This comment is perhaps the single best thing ever said about the poem. The Ancient Mariner is a man reduced to his simple, bare essence, and that essence is simply the obsessive memory of what brought him to this extremity.

Coleridge later said that ANNA LAETITIA BARBAULD complained of the poem that it had no moral. He replied that he thought "the poem had too much: and that the only, or chief fault, if I might say so, was the obtrusion of the moral sentiment so openly on the reader as a principle or cause of action in a work of such pure imagination. It ought to have had no more moral than the *Arabian Nights'* tale of the merchant's sitting down to eat dates by the side of a well and throwing the shells aside, and lo! a genie starts up and says he *must* kill the aforesaid merchant *because* one of the date shells had, it seems, put out the eye of the genie's son" (*Specimens of the Table Talk of the Late Samuel Taylor Coleridge* [1835]). This is just what Lamb admired about the poem, the sense that it gives, through supernatural means, of being thrown into the world of mortality and loss for obscure and even impenetrable reasons. On one level—this might be the extent to which the poem might seem to have too much of a moral—the reason seems evident: the mariner is guilty of shooting the albatross. But how much of a sin can that be? What is sinful about it is its apparent randomness. He never explains why he shot it, only that after shooting it, everything went wrong.

Why did he shoot it? One reason is that Wordsworth suggested it, giving Coleridge the idea as the central plot point of the poem. This is not a facetious answer: To be alive is to have a story to tell, and to have a story to tell is to be able to point to some moment of arbitrary and shocking deviation from the expected and the norm. The Ancient Mariner himself does not know why he shot the albatross, just as the Wedding Guest cannot make sense of his sudden change of demeanor. Nothing in his character or in his story prepares us for the moment; nothing in his character or in his story has prepared *him* for it. He has done so with the same unremarkable thoughtlessness of the merchant throwing the shells (the pits) of the dates aside, and it is therefore part of his experience of being thrown into the world of mortality and loss that he is also thrown into the world of *guilt*.

The remarkable thing about the poem is its analysis of a sense of guilt without a corresponding sense of willful wrongdoing. The mariner is saturated with guilt—but it is important to see that the main content of his guilt is guilt for the *punishment* that he has brought down on the entire crew. He is guilty because he is being punished, more than he is being punished for his guilt.

The importance of this moral and psychological insight may be underscored by its reappearance in a poem that might at first seem very different—Wordsworth's INTIMATIONS ODE. There Wordsworth sees as the saving moment the sudden sense within the self of "high instincts before which our mortal nature / Did tremble like a guilty thing surprised" (ll. 145–46). Unfounded guilt is the way the mind preserves a sense of itself as in the world but not of the world. In the psychological lexicon of ROMANTICISM, it is the original sin of subjectivity itself—that is, a sense of being different from the world that demands one be a part of it. Guilt registers our failure to be a part of the world.

This is why the Ancient Mariner can make the Wedding Guest feel guilty as well. The mariner ends his tale by saying that he recognizes the person he must tell it to. But what has the Wedding Guest done? He desires to be part of the social world, to belong to it fully and happily. There is no albatross in his past. But the mariner's tale fills the guest with fear and wonder and makes it impossible for him to feel unquestioningly of the world any more. He has been submitted to the eeriness of whatever poetic impulse corresponded in Coleridge's mind to the guilt in the mariner's.

If the story had a simple moral, it would be that the mariner's unconscious impulse of love and pity is saving. He blessed the "happy living creatures" unawares because some kind saint took pity on *him* as well. But it is one of the central puzzles of the poem that this blessing turns out not to be nearly enough. It is the beginning of penance and redemption, but not the end. In fact, the end never comes. The return of the wind, the return to harbor, the subsequent years—none free him of the eternal burden of repeating his tale when he sees a person somehow like himself. The beauty of the blessing and of the impulse to bless does not restore him to his original state. Rather, it sustains itself as a sense of movement toward love in a world that is hostile to love. The world's hostility to love is what makes its creatures suffer, and the love that seeks to counter that hostility can never ignore or transcend the world's suffering.

Here, too, *The Rime of the Ancient Mariner* foretells the Intimations Ode, in which Wordsworth also feels a sudden and, he hopes, saving impulse of love toward the "blessed creatures" (l. 36) that surround him. But the impulse would not be saving if blessing were enough. Wordsworth needs to feel that the world is a world of loss, and what he and the Ancient Mariner have in common is the realization that all the living creatures in it are similarly thrown into it without orientation, bearing, or hope of escape from the burden of subjectivity. Both poems are about the irremediable discovery of the weight of this burden on all human beings, and the intensity of insight this discovery brings. The poem shares the insight even as it shares the burden, in Coleridge with the Wedding Guest. It is not too much to say that Coleridge hopes, perhaps rightly, that the Wedding Guest is Wordsworth himself, profoundly affected by the poem and surprised in his mortal nature by his own high instincts.

See also "KUBLA KHAN."

BIBLIOGRAPHY

Bate, Walter Jackson. *Coleridge*. New York: Macmillan, 1968.

Bloom, Harold. *The Visionary Company: A Reading of English Romantic Poetry*. Garden City, N.Y.: Doubleday, 1961.

Brisman, Leslie. *Romantic Origins*. Ithaca, N.Y.: Cornell University Press, 1978.

Coleridge, Samuel Taylor. *Selected Poems*. Edited by William Empson and David Pirie. Manchester, England: Fyfield, 1989.

Frank, Robert H. *Passions within Reason: The Strategic Role of the Emotions*. New York: Norton, 1988.

Freud, Sigmund. "The Uncanny." In *The Standard Edition of the Complete Psychological Works of Sigmund Freud,* 17: 219–256. London: Hogarth Press, 1953–74.

Janowitz, Anne. *England's Ruins: Poetic Purpose and the National Landscape.* Cambridge, Mass.: Blackwell, 1990.
Lowes, John Livingston. *Road to Xanadu: A Study in the Ways of the Imagination.* New York: Houghton Mifflin, 1930.
Parker, Reeve. *Coleridge's Meditative Art.* Ithaca, N.Y.: Cornell University Press, 1975.

***RING AND THE BOOK, THE* ROBERT BROWNING (1869)** In 1860, as he recounts in book 1 of *The Ring and the Book,* ROBERT BROWNING came across a book in yellow covers, mainly printed but with manuscript additions, that preserved the record of a Roman murder trial and its outcome during the winter of 1698. The case had been a scandal in its day but entirely forgotten in the century and a half since. One of Browning's themes, and one of the spurs and sparks to his IMAGINATION, is the evanescence of the most intense experience, which disappears with the lives of those who live it (see, for example, "A TOCCATA OF GALUPPI'S"), unless a later imagination like Browning's can somehow reanimate the dead past through its own passionate attention and projection. The case related in the yellow book was a perfect example and a perfect subject for Browning.

The story of *The Ring and the Book* is told in 12 books (as is John Milton's *Paradise Lost,* the greatest of long poems in English, though *The Ring and the Book* certainly is not crushed by the comparison). In the first, Browning both tells how he found the book and then summarizes the story it tells and that he will retell. The printed part of the yellow book consisted of the documents that were gathered together to try Count Guido Franceschini for the murder of his wife Pompilia and her parents during the Christmas holidays, on January 2, 1698. Browning has read the book avidly and gives a synopsis of his story. Guido, a bankrupt nobleman from Arezzo, had arranged with the 14-year-old Pompilia's mother to marry her for the dowry she provided, while he would supply the family with nobility. (This is a theme Browning treats as well in "MY LAST DUCHESS.") The marriage was atrocious and miserable for poor Pompilia, and for her strikingly elderly parents as well. All lived in Guido's house in Arezzo, but he so deprived them of food and recreation that eventually they could stand it no longer; they abandoned Pompilia and returned, penniless, to Rome.

Guido was the worst of husbands, but he had not quite won a victory for his own tyrannous usurpation of Pompilia's dowry and inheritance, as he had thought, since Pompilia's parents turned out not to be her parents. Violante, who had arranged the marriage of her "daughter" Pompilia with Guido, now confessed to her husband Pietro and to the world that she had not had a surprising pregnancy at 50, but had bought the infant Pompilia from a prostitute in order that Pompilia might make it possible for Violante and her husband to inherit a small estate that he had in usufruct and that would otherwise go to some nephew or cousin of his. Her confession deprived Guido of the estate that he would have controlled if he and Pompilia had a child to inherit from her "father" Pietro.

The unpleasant and unloving Guido now found himself with a wife he did not love, a wife who did not love him, and none of the dowry he expected would prop up his ruined household in Arezzo. He treated her with tyrannous cruelty, at least in the Browning version, which is certainly morally accurate, though it just as certainly exaggerates—in Shakespearean fashion—the leading characteristics of the main players in the drama. Pompilia appealed to various temporal and spiritual authorities who, friends of Guido's, took his side. Finally, she determined to escape him and return home to Rome, and she appealed to a young priest, Giuseppe Caponsacchi, to help her escape. Browning presents Caponsacchi as in love with Pompilia but motivated by what Henry James would call "a virtuous attachment." The truth may be less ideal but ultimately no more blameworthy: Guido produced letters between Caponsacchi and Pompilia as evidence of an adulterous liaison between them, but she said that she was illiterate and forced by Guido to trace written characters she could not understand; later evidence (unavailable to Browning) suggests that in fact she could read and that therefore Guido *may* have been telling the truth about the letters. Nevertheless, his tyrannous oppression was such as to justify any steps Pompilia took to escape him, and she and Caponsacchi made their way nearly to Rome before Guido caught up and surprised them a day's journey from the city. (Italy at the time was not a unified country, and therefore arrival at Rome would put Pompilia outside of the Aretine jurisdiction that had ruled against her in her earlier appeals against her husband.)

After a series of hearings, Pompilia (who turned out to be a month or so pregnant; in Browning's version, at any rate, Guido was the father) was sent to a convent, the priest Caponsacchi was forced to leave Rome for three years, and Guido was sent back home. But the convent sickened Pompilia, and she was allowed to return to the house her parents had moved to on the outskirts of Rome, where she gave birth to a son eight months later, just before Christmas (a coincidence that Browning uses to good symbolic purpose). Guido, meanwhile, hired four ruffians to return with him to Rome, and on January 2 they gained entry to the house and stabbed and killed Pietro and Violante; Pompilia, mortally wounded, survived long enough to give evidence but died shortly thereafter. The baby survived, but his ultimate fate (after the first year or so of his life) is unknown. Guido and his minions were caught trying to return to Arezzo, and they were brought to trial in Rome. Roman trials then were not done orally; rather, transcripts of the interrogation of the various principals were submitted to the court, as were the arguments made by the prosecutor and the defense; and the documents were printed up and bound together (the yellow book was one of these bound copies), upon which the court read through them and rendered judgment. In Guido's case, they found him guilty (as he obviously was); he claimed benefit of clergy on doubtful grounds (as a minor officiant in the church) but the elderly Pope Innocent XII confirmed the death sentence, and Guido and his henchmen were publicly executed on February 22, 1698.

The power of the poem is in the 10 different points of view (in addition to Browning's own and some minor ones that he reports) presented by the dramatic monologues that make up the poem's 12 books. The first and last books are in Browning's own voice, as he tells the story of his discovery of the story and the imaginative hold it laid on him. The middle 10 books are in the voices of those present during the events recounted. The first three books are three different versions of "what everyone is saying": the worldly knowledge of which half of Rome is complacently certain, the exactly opposed worldly knowledge of which the other half of Rome is equally certain, and a kind of fine and worldly-wise dismissal of both these positions by an equally complacent aristocrat who is even less idealistic

If the vividness of representation of character is Shakespearean, so, too, is the intense empathy with which Browning is able to enter into the points of view and the experiences of the major actors in the events. We first get the testimony of Guido himself, who has been tortured for evidence. He represents himself as a person of extreme goodwill who has been cheated both by the Comparini (Pompilia's parents) and then by Pompilia herself in partnership with Caponsacchi. Much of the evidence—which we know already from the gossip of the Romans—is accurate, and it is hard not to accept that the smoke Guido points to is evidence of fire. He seems a reasonably harmless, aging gentleman forced into a violence he would never otherwise be capable of by a conspiracy of enemies, fate, and extreme emotional pressure.

The priest Caponsacchi speaks next and gives a powerful and moving account of Pompilia's purity and the desperation of her plight, as well as of the shifts and wiles through which Guido and his servant attempted to implicate them for adultery. (Had Guido succeeded, he could have kept her dowry and she would have no appeal from his cruelty.) Caponsacchi makes it clear that he is in love with Pompilia—spiritually, not sexually—and sets up her introduction as a paragon of purity in the next book.

Pompilia's dying monologue is the simplest and most straightforwardly beautiful in the book, and she fully justifies everything that Caponsacchi has said about her. Her version of the story is very close to his, and it makes Guido's inability or refusal to appreciate her all the more damning. She dies at peace with herself and with God, and even at peace—for her part—with Guido, whom she pities but does not hate.

Following the speeches of these principals of the drama, the lawyers speak: first, Guido's defender, who represents him as a cuckolded husband forced to an extremity that was as foreign to him as can be imagined; then the prosecutor, who concedes that Pompilia cannot have been as pure as she has presented herself but argues, overwhelmingly, that Guido's response was excessive. What is interesting about the lawyers' briefs is the likability of Guido's defender, Hyacinthus de Archangelis, himself the father of a nine-year-old boy he dotes on; and the cynicism of Pompilia's advocate, prosecuting Guido though he does not think nearly as well of Pompilia as he ought to. (Later on, it will transpire, he tries to loot her estate on behalf of a convent that has hired him to lay claim to the possessions of fallen women, so he will argue that she was an adulteress.)

Both advocates having spoken, the case is referred at last to Pope Innocent XII, the speaker of book 10. The pope wryly laments that no one will remember the incidents he is judging, "No bard describe in verse how Christ prevailed / And Satan fell like lightning" (10, ll. 670–671). He has read through all the documentation of the events which led to the killing of Pompilia and her two parents by Guido Franceschini, and now he gives judgment, based (as he says) on the documents he has read of the interrogations of the principal witnesses.

The elderly pope gives his judgment in one of the philosophically richest and most powerful monologues in English literature. He confirms Guido's execution, hopeful that it may jar him to true repentance. He knows the unlikeliness of this because the triumph of the church he heads has resulted in its worldly wisdom. It is no longer a place for idealists (like Caponsacchi himself) but for hankerers after power. The pope foresees with some hope a time when the authority of the church will be so challenged by science that it will become again a place for faith alone; thus, Browning makes him more or less prophesy the coming of Charles Darwin and the challenge that the materialist theory of evolution mounted to theology. The pope celebrates this challenge—one that Browning was considering contemporaneously in "CALIBAN UPON SETEBOS," which explores a theology based on an examination of a Darwinian struggle for survival. If the world really does turn out to be a rat race in which the most ruthless fulfill their worldly ambitions, the comfort and the consolation the church offers will be attractive only to idealists and those in need of true spiritual comfort, rather than to the careerists who infest it now. The thinking here can be put into interesting juxtaposition with ALFRED, LORD TENNYSON's similar crisis, as recounted in *IN MEMORIAM A.H.H.*

After the pope has confirmed Guido's sentence, we get his last desperate monologue as he awaits execution, and the striking thing about it is how closely he mirrors the pope's thinking about the corruption of the church. Guido expected that corruption to help him, and he is shocked by the pope's confirmation of the sentence. The pope has wanted him to repent, as he understands, but he absolutely refuses. He describes himself in all his Satanic or Darwinian selfishness and (paradoxically) takes moral exception to the application of morality to his case. It turns out that only he and the pope see things clearly; the difference between them is, finally, that the pope believes in the teachings of Christ and the primitive church, and Guido does not.

This last monologue of Guido's is an extremely powerful document of the fear of death, specifically of execution, and bears comparison to that of Claudio awaiting execution in William Shakespeare's *Measure for Measure*. At the end, Guido finally does crack, and in great anxiety and horror he calls upon Pompilia to try to save him—finally valuing her correctly. So perhaps he is saved in the end—*perhaps*—and the pope is vindicated.

The Ring and the Book is one of the longest poems in English, even by Browning's standards, and also one of the greatest. It is a near-total exploration of character in a social world where the stakes are nevertheless mortal and the thinking that goes into considering those stakes therefore profoundly philosophical. It treats the depths of human character when confronted with other human characters and when confronted with the facts of life—of nature, faith, and humanity—and it shows Browning, both by precept and example, thinking as deeply as the moral lesson of the poem would have us think.

BIBLIOGRAPHY

Bloom, Harold. *A Map of Misreading*. New York: Oxford University Press, 2003.

DeVane, William C. *A Browning Handbook*. New York: Appleton-Century-Crofts, 1955.

Gest, John Marshall. *The Old Yellow Book: Source of Browning's The Ring and the Book, a new translation with explanatory notes and critical chapters upon the poem and its source.* Boston: Chipman Law Publishing Co., 1925.

Langbaum, Robert Woodrow. *The Modern Spirit: Essays on the Continuity of Nineteenth- and Twentieth-Century Literature.* New York: Oxford University Press, 1970.

Parker, Derek. *Roman Murder Mystery: The True Story of Pompilia.* Gloucestershire, England: Sutton, 2001.

Raymond, William O. *The Infinite Moment, and Other Essays in Robert Browning.* Toronto: University of Toronto Press, 1965.

ROMANTICISM The classic essays on romanticism tend not to define the term but to survey the manifold and unsuccessful attempts to define it. In English poetry, however, we can give a more or less historical definition: Romanticism is a movement that can be dated as beginning with WILLIAM WORDSWORTH and SAMUEL TAYLOR COLERIDGE's *Lyrical Ballads* of 1798 and that is still continuing today, despite reactions and countermovements which begin almost immediately and which are highly relevant to any consideration of Victorian and modern literature. (Although romanticism includes all of WILLIAM BLAKE's major poetry, beginning more than a decade prior to *Lyrical Ballads,* Blake's obscurity limited his influence on other major writers for a good half century.)

Paradoxically, though, these reactions can themselves be regarded as highly romantic in nature—partly, perhaps, because one very general but still useful early (1825) definition of romanticism is, in the words of the French dramatist and politician Ludovic Vitet (1802–73), "Protestantism in arts and letters" (quoted in Furst, *European Romanticism*). Protestantism was a protest against the fetters of the past (even romanticism itself)—against rule and convention, as Vitet realized—and therefore was also an analogue to the Protestant Reformation. In this sense, romanticism is the analogue in the literary sphere of the freedom brought by the Enlightenment in the political, moral, and philosophical world—according to Vitet, "the right to enjoy what gives pleasure, to be moved by what moves one, to admire what seems admirable, even when by virtue of well and duly consecrated principles it could be proved that one ought not to admire, nor be moved, nor enjoy." Wordsworth, too, spoke of his object in *Lyrical Ballads* as giving pleasure to his readers, rather than conforming to rules: "There will also be found in these volumes little of what is usually called poetic diction . . . because the pleasure which I have proposed to myself to impart is of a kind very different from that which is supposed by many persons to be the proper object of poetry." That pleasure is Protestant in its deference to the judgment and poetic conscience of the individual soul: "[T]his necessity of producing immediate pleasure . . . is an acknowledgment of the beauty of the universe, an acknowledgment the more sincere because it is not formal, but indirect; . . . it is a homage paid to the native and naked dignity of man, to the grand elementary principle of pleasure, by which he knows, and feels, and lives, and moves" (preface to *Lyrical Ballads,* 1800).

Romanticism is therefore to be defined negatively, perhaps, as a principled protest against classicism. Since the French were the earliest to identify it as a movement, we can recur to the incisive definition one of the great French romantics, Victor Hugo, who (in the preface to his 1830 play *Hernani*) wrote, "Romanticism, so often badly defined, is . . . viewed wholly under its militant aspect, nothing but liberalism in literature . . . a literary liberty [which] is the daughter of political liberty." The philosopher John Stuart Mill was one of the earliest purveyors of the term in English, but again he was describing French literature when he wrote in 1837:

> The stateliness and conventional decorum of old French poetic and dramatic literature, gave place to a licence which made free scope for genius and also for absurdity, and let in new forms of the beautiful was well as many of the hideous. Literature shook off its chains, and used its liberty like a galley-slave broke loose; while painting and sculpture passed from one unnatural extreme to another, and the stiff school was succeeded by the spasmodic. This insurrection against the old traditions of classicism was called romanticism: and now, when the mass of rubbish to which it had given birth has produced another oscillation in opinion the reverse way, one inestimable result seems to have survived it—that life and human feeling may now, in

> France, be painted with as much liberty as they may be discussed, and, when painted truly, with approval.

Mill's account shows the extent to which romanticism was central to Victorian literary attitudes, even as the heyday of what came to be called high romanticism came to an end in England with the beginning of the Victorian period. Indeed, the Victorian parody of the continued influence of romanticism identified what it called the "spasmodic school" of poetry (see the poems of DIGBY MACKWORTH DOBELL for examples of what WILLIAM EDMONSTOUNE AYTOUN ridiculed under that name).

These quotations show the extent to which romanticism is regarded as a revolutionary rejection of the past—of Mill's classicism—which might be regarded as the literary equivalent of the French Revolution. Indeed, the first generation of English romantics were admirers of the French Revolution before its descent into destruction and terror. For this reason as well, the romantics saw NAPOLEON BONAPARTE as a Promethean figure who promised liberty but ended up besotted with despotic power. Wordsworth, who celebrated the death of the French revolutionary Robespierre in *The PRELUDE*, nevertheless began that work with an ode to liberty. For the English romantics, that liberty was at once a break with Enlightenment rationalism and (as we have seen) a continuation of the Enlightenment's intensely humanistic project of rejecting religious superstition and arbitrary law on behalf of the human soul's freedom and primacy.

It is important not to make the mistake that some critics fall into of thinking of romanticism as essentially an irrational egotism. Romanticism is far more the inheritor of Enlightenment ideas than their displacer. It shares with the Enlightenment an intense focus on the powers of the human mind. For Enlightenment philosophers, that focus was often on its rational and analytic powers, whence the flowering of modern science. But such Enlightenment figures as the philosophe Jean-Jacques Rousseau paid equal or greater attention to the mind's subjective experience. Rousseau's *Confessions* (1769) as well as his novel *Julie* (1761) were forerunners of intense influences on (respectively) such works as Wordsworth's *The Prelude*, LORD BYRON'S *CHILDE HAROLD'S PILGRIMAGE*, and PERCY BYSSHE SHELLEY'S *The TRIUMPH OF LIFE*. In Immanuel Kant and the German idealists, and in Coleridge, much of whose work is uncomfortably close to plagiarism of the idealists, the relationship between its objective and subjective powers is central to a philosophical account of the mind. Kant saw that relationship forming in the faculty of judgment, of which aesthetic judgment was the most vivid example. The half-creation, half-perception of the world which takes place in judgment is the theme of romanticism, explicitly in such poems as Wordsworth's "TINTERN ABBEY" and Shelley's "MONT BLANC." Sometimes the difference between subjective and objective attitudes manifested itself as a sense of self-division within the soul, a sense that could be traced back to the philosophy of John Locke (1632–1704), which was repugnant but therefore powerfully influential, to such figures as Blake and Wordsworth.

Self-division, solitude, subjective longing—all of these are aspects of the subjectivity which romanticism took as its starting point and theme (in part inheriting it from the more sentimental mode of 18th-century sensibility, though sensibility was far more an overtly social phenomenon than romanticism). Because of its intense interest in subjectivity as well as its rejection of superstition, it is possible to see romanticism as a kind of religious sensibility without religious belief. The soul, or self, experiences itself as fallen in a fallen world (often represented as the world of childhood or the world most closely present in childhood). In Romanticism, by rejecting the doctrines of religion—that the biblical Fall is punishment for some derogation from a state of grace—the soul also rejects the consolations of religion; accordingly, it has no hope of salvation except within itself and its own experience. That salvation is therefore primarily aesthetic and philosophical (the distinction between the two is one of emphasis, which is why so many romantic poems are so intensely philosophical). The romantics took to heart Satan's claim in John Milton's great 17th-century work *Paradise Lost* (the poem most essential to the English romantics) that "The mind is its own place and in itself / Can make a Heaven of hell, a Hell of heaven (1, l. 254)." Our sense of ourselves as fallen, as having a destiny and home "with infinity," as Wordsworth says, makes the finite world a negative measure of our own subjective intensity. When this intensity is represented as a claim to greatness of soul, it can look egotistical; but what counts is the intensity of experience measured by the failure as well as by the intermittent success of the outside world at matching it.

This intermittent success tends to come with a sense of the grandeur of nature, which is why so much great romantic poetry is about nature in its most intense aspects: those of beauty, solitude, and most of all, the SUBLIME. Nature's wildness, partly imaged in ruined castles and abbeys, which had been a staple of gothic fiction in the 18th century were particularly appropriate settings for romantic thought. But nature is itself a projection—it is the place the mind makes of it, as in the last two lines of Shelley's "Mont Blanc," where it is the human mind's imaginings that transfigure vacancy into silence and solitude.

The general mode of a romantic poem is one of crisis—a crisis that leads to its own solution. The very fact of crisis is a sign that the intensity of feeling and thought at risk is still there. Romantic poets worry about the loss of intensity that seems the inevitable course of human experience, but they reimagine that loss of intensity as the intensity of loss. Loss becomes, as the 20th-century literary critic Paul de Man put it somewhat skeptically, "shadowed gain." The gain for the soul is in its apprehension of its own capacity to measure its losses, and therefore to rise above them. Loss within the soul comes to be figured as the loss of poetic vocation. The poetry inspired by this loss is a sign that poetic vocation is intensified in its own undoing, rather than dissipated—for a while at least. Romanticism reimagined poetry as an intense analysis of human subjectivity, and in doing so it lent splendor to the universal human experience of loss and decline. What more can poetry do?

See also VICTORIAN POETRY.

BIBLIOGRAPHY

Abrams, M. H. *Natural Supernaturalism: Tradition and Revolution in Romantic Literature*. New York: Norton, 1973.

Bloom, Harold. *The Visionary Company: A Reading of English Romantic Poetry*. Garden City, N.Y.: Doubleday, 1961.

———, ed. *Romanticism and Consciousness: Essays in Criticism*. New York: Norton, 1970.

Brown, Marshall. *Preromanticism*. Stanford, Calif.: Stanford University Press, 1991.

Deane, Seamus. *French Revolution and Enlightenment in England, 1789–1832*. Cambridge, Mass.: Harvard University Press, 1988.

De Man, Paul. *The Rhetoric of Romanticism*. New York: Columbia University Press, 1984.

Furst, Lilian, ed. *European Romanticism: Self-Definition: An Anthology*. London: Methuen, 1980.

Lovejoy, Arthur. "On the Discrimination of Romanticisms." *PMLA* (journal of the Modern Language Association) 39, no. 2 (June 1924): 229–253.

McGann, Jerome. *The Romantic Ideology: A Critical Investigation*. Chicago: University of Chicago Press, 1983.

Mill, John Stuart. "Armand Carrel." In *Dissertations and Discussions*. Vol. 1. 237–308. Boston: Holt, 1882.

Quinney, Laura. *The Poetics of Disappointment: Wordsworth to Ashbery*. Charlottesville: University Press of Virginia, 1999.

"RONDEAU" ("JENNY KISSED ME")

LEIGH HUNT (1838) "Rondeau," also known as "Jenny Kissed Me," is one of LEIGH HUNT's most popular poems. It is not hard to see why: It combines the light touch he could sometimes manage to perfection with a melancholy that never risks descending into bathos. The poem was originally published in the *Monthly Chronicle* as "Nelly kissed me," but this would have been to avoid making it into merely an occasional piece when the occasion gave rise to so wonderful a poem.

"Jenny" was Jane Welsh Carlyle, married to the essayist and historian Thomas and one of the most brilliant and intimidating women in Britain. Hunt had had influenza, and when he told her that he was better, she spontaneously leapt up and kissed him—not the sort of thing she generally did. Hunt was so struck by her action that he wrote the poem.

Hunt titles this a rondeau, but technically that it is not what it is. In fact, it is much closer to the light-verse form of a triolet, but somewhat looser since a triolet uses only two end rhymes and repeats the first line (the *rentrement*) two more times. Both the rondeau and the triolet are poems that round on themselves, though, and that is what this one does. Such poems are hard to write (and therefore wonderful when written well) because the repeated line has to sustain freshness even though it has been repeated. In Hunt's poem, this is managed through the sense of wonder that the repetition expresses. The tone also conveys the wonder, partly through Hunt's technical skill.

Hunt was an important theorist of poetic form, and "Rondeau" is a splendid example of its possibilities. The poem is written in perfect trochees, a form that tends toward over-rhythmical monotony (as all the parodies of Henry Wadsworth Longfellow's *Hiawatha* show). But in Hunt's hands, the trochees allow for unusual surprise of emphasis. *Who* kissed him? Jenny. *What* did she do? Kissed him. The moment is for him a moment of wonder, and time itself will not be able to falsify this fact. The fact itself is what is valuable, not what it led to, nor what it arose from. The moment is what amazes him, and the repeated emphasis of the moment and of the trochees that preserve the moment also preserve the amazement. Whatever happens, he will be able to remember this moment.

Whatever happens—that is, all the ways in which life and love can go wrong. The speaker has been weary and sick (Hunt had just recovered from influenza) and he will be again. While the poem asserts that it is worth everything that the destructive powers of time can demand from him, it also acknowledges that time absconds with all the sweet things and sweet people of life (including Jenny herself). But against the passage of time is the single moment, repeated in the surprising last line.

Its surprise is a metrical surprise. The form has been in trochaic tetrameter, with the odd lines tailless, ending on the seventh-syllable stress, and the even lines all trochees, containing eight syllables. The form is very prominent, and it makes the rhymes prominent as well. We therefore *expect* the last line to read something like this: "Still it is true that Jenny kissed me." But instead we get the moment that is the only one that counts, simple and direct and pure, and the shortest line in the poem: "Jenny kissed me." That is what we are to remember forever: not who she was, or what he hoped from her, or why she kissed him, but just that she did and that this made him happy.

BIBLIOGRAPHY

Edgecombe, Rodney Stenning. *Leigh Hunt and the Poetry of Fancy*. London: Associated University Presses, 1994.

Roe, Nicholas, ed. *Leigh Hunt: Life, Poetics, Politics*. New York: Routledge, 2003.

Thompson, James R. *Leigh Hunt*. Boston: Twayne, 1977.

"ROSE AYLMER" **WALTER SAVAGE LANDOR** **(1806)** The opening of "Rose Aylmer" is perhaps WALTER SAVAGE LANDOR's most famous line: "Ah, what avails the sceptred race!" Rose Aylmer was a young Welsh woman, the daughter of Henry, Baron Aylmer, and Landor knew the family during the years after he moved to Wales in 1796 to work and write. Rose lent him the book on which he based his first important poem, the epic *Gebir* (now largely forgotten), about the Arabian hero who founded Gibraltar. She died in India in 1800 at the age of 21, and Landor's elegy is, like most of his great short lyrics, powerful not because it is personal but because it is general. We can feel that the poem is not about the loss of someone the speaker is in love with but a lament over what the American poet Ralph Waldo Emerson called the unhandsomeness of the human condition. It is no wonder that CHARLES LAMB, who also felt the world as a place of lost friendships and relationships (see "The OLD FAMILIAR FACES") was always quoting this poem.

"The sceptred race" are, of course, the British, who controlled the seas and had extended their empire to India in the wake of British commercial interests there, in particular the East India Company (where Lamb had worked). Aylmer's presence in India as a British subject afforded her no immunity from the vicissitudes of life; nor did her being a child of God created in his image, endowed, that is, with "the form divine" (l. 2). She was perfect in every way, but none of this could avail her. What is her elegist to think about the meaning of human life when its most eloquent promises are unfulfilled? She has no special meaning to him, as she would if he were in love with her, and therefore she cannot be the gain that a lost love is to any poet for whom poetry is the record of the intensity of the loss he or she has suffered. Rather, she stands for the world that Landor would be a poet in, and one could describe the poem as an allusion to a crisis of vocation: What avails anything in this world, whether earthly power or the divine power of poetic form (as the conceptual pun in the second stanza would describe it)?

But the poem—in a style that we recognize as central to ROMANTICISM—is to some extent the answer to the critical question it raises. The question is so pressing that even acknowledging it appropriately, as the poem does, requires the poet to consecrate a night of memories and sighs to the work that the poem is doing, the work of memorializing Rose Aylmer in a world in which her virtues and graces were no proof against death. The grim antithesis between weeping and seeing in the sixth line therefore receives a kind of internal resolution: What he cannot see in this world he must weep for, and his weeping will be in this world, in the form of the poem itself.

BIBLIOGRAPHY

Butler, Marilyn. *Romantics, Rebels, and Reactionaries: English Literature and Its Background, 1760–1830*. New York: Oxford University Press, 1982.

Hazlitt, William. *Spirit of the Age; or, Contemporary Portraits*. London: Oxford University Press, 1970.

Super, R. H. *Walter Savage Landor: A Biography*. New York: New York University Press, 1954.

ROSSETTI, CHRISTINA GEORGINA

(1830–1894) Christina Rossetti may well be England's greatest female poet. She is certainly one of the greatest of Victorian poets and one of the most original. Her most canonical piece now is *GOBLIN MARKET*, an extraordinary poetic experiment in the great Pre-Raphaelite insight into the relationship of such decorative elements as rhyme, rhythm, assonance, and repetition to the deepest needs of human psychology under pressure (see PRE-RAPHAELITE POETRY). In her beautiful and artful centenary essay on Rossetti, the 20th-century author Virginia Woolf aptly quotes ALGERNON CHARLES SWINBURNE and the great critics George Saintsbury and Sir Walter Raleigh on Rossetti's astonishing clarity of word choice, before going on to apostrophize Rossetti herself: ". . . your eye, indeed observed with a sensual pre-Raphaelite intensity that must have surprised Christina the Anglo-Catholic. But to her you owed perhaps the fixity and the sadness of your muse."

Rossetti was the youngest of the four Rossetti siblings and two years younger than her brother DANTE GABRIEL ROSSETTI, who illustrated *Goblin Market* when it came out. Her brother William Michael Rossetti was a great critic and editor, both of PERCY BYSSHE SHELLEY and, after her death, of Christina's own poetry. She shared with her brothers a near-perfect sense of language and of the different modes by which it could be imitative. Unlike Dante Gabriel, however, she was extremely prudish, at least in her personal life, and devoted, as Woolf observed, to the Anglo-Catholicism that was a strong movement within Victorian society at the time, derived from the "tracts" written by the theologian Edward Bouverie Pusey and his followers. (For more on this, see the entry on JOHN HENRY NEWMAN). Woolf also observed how trivial these commitments were in the attempt to understand Rossetti as a poet, because she was a poet first and foremost. It is in this mode that she should be understood (like her rival JEAN INGELOW) as a Pre-Raphaelite poet; in fact, she contributed poetry to the magazine put out by the Pre-Raphaelite Brotherhood, *The Germ*.

What always comes back in Rossetti's poetry is the intense prosody, the seemingly trivial decoration that trumps everything. At least, it *seems* trivial: This is why her contemporaries could think that *Goblin Market* was a children's poem, when it is actually a poem about obsessive repetition and longing, the repetition of the soul and also the residue of all sexual desire. Similarly, in a poem like "Passing Away" (1862) what finally counts are the rhymes (all of them the same, rhyming on /*ay*/) and the speaker's persistent last word, *Yea*, not only in response to the world and to her own soul but to God himself.

Woolf ended her essay by describing how much of Rossetti she knew by heart, without ever reading her systematically or completely. No better characterization of her poetry can be given. It is as though she wrote nursery rhymes for adults: words that haunt and seem both inevitable and strange, but that she made fully hers, and that she *knew* she had made fully hers.

See also "SONG" ("WHEN I AM DEAD, MY DEAREST").

BIBLIOGRAPHY

Battiscombe, Georgina. *Christina Rossetti: A Divided Life*. London: Constable, 1981.

Jones, Kathleen. *Learning Not to Be First: The Life of Christina Rossetti*. New York: St. Martin's Press, 1992.

Marsh, Jan. *Christina Rossetti: A Literary Biography*. London: Jonathan Cape, 1994.

Stevenson, Lionel. *Pre-Raphaelite Poets.* New York: Norton, 1974.

Thomas, Frances. *Christina Rossetti.* London: Virago Press, 1994.

Woolf, Virginia. "'I Am Christina Rossetti,'" In *The Second Common Reader,* 214–221. New York: Harcourt, Brace, 1932.

ROSSETTI, DANTE GABRIEL (1828–1882)

Dante Gabriel Rossetti was one of the most important members of the Pre-Raphaelite movement, which began (and was most coherent) as a school of painting (see PRE-RAPHAELITE POETRY). Like the Pre-Raphaelite WILLIAM MORRIS (with whose wife, Jane, Rossetti was to have a long-standing affair) and like WILLIAM BLAKE (whose poetry Rossetti was one of the first to appreciate; Rossetti gave advice on the poetry to Alexander Gilchrist in his history-changing biography of Blake), Rossetti was a poet-painter, and his painting commitments affected the nature of his poetry. It should also be noted that Rossetti was the godson of the botanist Charles Lyell and therefore the "godbrother," so to speak, of Charles Lyell the younger, the geologist whose studies were so earth-shattering for ALFRED, LORD TENNYSON, and (through Charles Darwin) for much of the Victorian sense of the material world and its origin.

Like so many of his contemporaries, Rossetti was interested in natural history, but that interest was intensely ambivalent, since it drew the mind away from the idealisms that haunted him as well: the work of the medieval Italian poet Dante (whom Rossetti adored and translated) and medieval literature in general, as well as the idealism of passionate romantic love, to which Rossetti gave himself over in copious and destructive quantities. He was probably most destructive of all to the painter and model Elizabeth Siddal (whom he married); she committed suicide (partly probably as a result of depression after the birth of a stillborn child), and Rossetti placed a manuscript volume of his poetry in her grave. Seven years later, in a typically and emblematically macabre incident in his life, he received permission to exhume her corpse, since he now wanted those poems for the collection he would print the next year.

As a poet, Rossetti was influenced by JOHN KEATS, PERCY BYSSHE SHELLEY, and his older friends Tennyson and ROBERT BROWNING, whose interest in painting made Rossetti admire him all the more. Many of Rossetti's most famous poems are what the scholar John Sparrow called "visible words"—poems that appear as writing in paintings, most famously "The BLESSED DAMOZEL." As a painter, Rossetti was committed to extreme and gorgeous detail, and the meaning of that commitment can be understood in his poetry. It is passionate and gives signs of the paranoia that would haunt him later in his life in the way that passion expresses itself through a powerful obsession with detail. The best example of this is probably "The WOODSPURGE" (1856), in which "perfect grief" leaves him with the intensely observed botanical knowledge that he devotes his attention to in order not to think about things that hurt him more: "One thing then learnt remains to me,—/ The woodspurge has a cup of three" (ll. 15–16). Rossetti is in some ways the 20th-century American poet Elizabeth Bishop's closest precursor.

Rossetti was roundly abused for the sexuality of his poetry, which is intense. It is also oddly clinical: given over so wholly to passion, he consistently steps back in his poetry to observe that passion, just as he does the woodspurge. The notorious poem "Nuptial Sleep" (1869) is a kind of rewriting of Keats's "ODE TO PSYCHE," with the male lover waking in wonder from a postcoital sleep to see the woman sleeping there. But the sleep itself is strange: The lovers' "dreams watched them sink" (l. 10) into sleep in which they are utterly separated from each other, and this is a separation which Rossetti can never overcome. Keats's voyeuristic interest becomes in Rossetti the impossibility to get beyond observation: Something within him is always alert, watching himself sink, perhaps, but always observant, of every detail, so that sex and the sleep that follow it are part of the details of the scene, and not something to which he wholly belongs. It is not that he does not feel passionately—he does. But no passion contents him wholly or helps overcome human separation, and the painterly and even botanical obsessing with observation is the final attitude, defensive and solitary and grimly sad, to be found in Rossetti's poetry. Everything else comes to fruition, he says in "Autumn Idleness"

(1867), "While I still lead my shadow o'er the grass, / Nor know, for longing, that which I should do" (ll. 13–14).

Thus, in what Harold Bloom calls Rossetti's greatest poem, *"The Stream's Secret"* (1869), Rossetti laments the fundamental impossibility of love and imagines the impossible, Keatsian "darkling close embrace" that would somehow replace his relentless vision of the "worshipped form and face . . . Round which so oft the sun shone clear, / With mocking light and pitiless atmosphere" (ll. 116–119). But that hour is never to come, and her face (the poem is about Jane Morris) will always be "soul-sequestered."

BIBLIOGRAPHY

Ash, Russell. *Dante Gabriel Rossetti.* New York: H. N. Abrams, 1995.

McGann, Jerome J. *Dante Gabriel Rossetti and the Game That Must Be Lost.* New Haven, Conn.: Yale University Press, 2000.

Rossetti, Dante Gabriel. *Correspondence of Dante Gabriel Rossetti.* Edited by William E. Fredeman. Rochester, N.Y.: D. S. Brewer, 2002.

Stevenson, Lionel. *Pre-Raphaelite Poets.* New York: Norton, 1974.

RUBÁIYÁT OF OMAR KHAYYÁM, THE

EDWARD FITZGERALD (1859) EDWARD FITZGERALD is now remembered only for this poem, which went through many editions and five revisions in his lifetime (the last was posthumous) because of its vast popularity. It is related to the verses that it allegedly translates, but since the word *rubáiyát* (plural of *rubáí*) means "quatrains" it is better to see the translation as a kind of adapted anthology of the Persian poet Omar Khayyám's original verses or at least of their sentiments. The Rubáiyát stanza form is rhymed *aaba,* which is to say that it turns in on itself with a certain inevitability, at least in FitzGerald's hands. He introduced it into English and treated it with considerably more regularity than it had in Omar Khayyám's Persian (which FitzGerald had read in the original). The one unrhymed line feels as though it is setting out toward the realm of some other possibility from the one the stanza lays down, but it quickly arcs back and returns, confirming and consolidating the rhymes of the first two lines. FitzGerald himself describes the form in his preface: "The original Rubáiyát . . . are independent Stanzas, consisting each of four Lines of equal, though varied, Prosody; sometimes all rhyming, but oftener (as here attempted) the third line suspending the Cadence by which the last atones with the former Two." Most of FitzGerald's poem has some source in the original, but the ordering, which follows a trajectory from morning to night, is his own.

The Rubáiyát stanza is the appropriate form for the beautiful poetry FitzGerald writes. The poetry is all about the ephemerality of life, and it consists of a kind of pessimistic hedonism. The fact that it is a translation of 700-year-old poetry adds to its tone. Omar Khayyám (ca. 1048–1122) was a great Persian mathematician and astronomer of the 11th and 12th centuries, when Persia was one of the pinnacles of civilization, but he was not a great poet. Omar as the speaker in FitzGerald's version surveys everything that has passed away and sees no permanence in any achievement, just as FitzGerald sees Omar as long dead, and we begin to see him as long dead as well. (FitzGerald echoes some aspects of the narrator of BYRON's *DON JUAN.*) But the ephemerality of things—for example, the Bird of Time on the Wing (stanza 7)—is not a cause only of despair; it makes the present moment all the more beautiful.

The best way to intensify this beauty is through wine, both metaphoric and literal. FitzGerald himself summarized the moral of the poem for Tennyson as "Drink—for the Moon will often come round to look for us in this Garden and find us not." Wine and the tavern that offers it make possible a relation to the fleeting present in which its fleetingness becomes part of its purity. What makes the ephemerality of the present melancholy to the sober is the fact that we are aware of all that is gone and all that is going. But the intoxicated forget past and future and in a sense may be said to identify with the fleeting present. They are all present to it and able, therefore, to feel the annihilation of the past and their own nonexistence in the future as irrelevant, thus making the past and future irrelevant. All that matters is the present. This central but difficult insight is clarified by the poem's refusal to praise *either* ant or grasshopper (in the standard opposition). Both "those who husbanded the Golden Grain / And those who flung it to the Winds like Rain" (stanza 15) are equally dead and gone, and the hedonists who lived in the present are no happier or more successful than the antlike husbanders of grain. But this is a reason *for* hedonism. The future, in which the present will be the past, does not matter, nor does the present matter to the future. The only goal, therefore, is to achieve the momentary timelessness of the vine.

This is the lesson of the little fable of the vessels, which FitzGerald entitled *Kuza-Náma,* or "tale of the pots," in the first edition (stanzas 69–76 in that edition). In the fasting month of Ramazán, the pots in the potter's shop are discussing philosophy, considering the perennially human question of the purpose and meaning of their own existence. The potter is their creator, and they are thinking of him theologically. Such thought has the moral and eschatological dimensions of human theology, as they wonder about what reward or punishment they will undergo and who is responsible—they or the potter—for whatever qualities they have.

But the reason the potter formed the vessels was not for the ultimate end of their own existence but for their capacity to hold wine. The timeless present that the poem so promotes as the only counter to the abysses of past and future is a present that has to do with the very purpose of the vessels, which is to hold the wine. That purpose is our purpose: We, too, should be filled with wine, just as the vessels should be.

The vessels, however, hold wine for our benefit—but also for their own; the wisest of them murmurs of the pleasure it takes in being moistened by "the old familiar Juice" (1859 edition, stanza 65). So, too, the wine we drink and which intoxicates us also makes us intoxicating to be with, as friends or lovers or poets. It is in this sense that wine is a metaphor for what can make the present a pure and timeless pleasure. What are perhaps the poem's most famous lines makes the metaphorical relationship clear: "A book of Verse underneath the Bough, / A jug of Wine, a loaf of Bread—and Thou / Beside me singing in the Wilderness—/ Oh, Wilderness were Paradise enow!" (1879 final edition, stanza 12).

The "book of Verse" is intoxicating, too, and is the one way that the present can be more than momentarily timeless. The pleasure of poetry is momentary but also a pleasure that can record its own commitment to the momentary, which is what the idea of translating and resuscitating this poetry must have meant to FitzGerald. *The Rubáiyát of Omar Khayyám* was FitzGerald's explicit counter to his friend ALFRED, LORD TENNYSON'S *IN MEMORIAM A.H.H.,* which found only despair in the absolute fading away of all things in time and finally set its hope on eternity. FitzGerald, perhaps more persuasively, sets all his hope on the present moment.

BIBLIOGRAPHY

FitzGerald, Edward. *Letters and Literary Remains of Edward FitzGerald.* Edited by William Aldis Wright. New York: Macmillan, 1889.

Hollander, John. "Paradise Enow." *Yale Review* 86, no. 3 (1998): 128–139.

Martin, Robert Bernard. *With Friends Possessed: A Life of Edward FitzGerald.* Boston: Faber and Faber, 1985.

Terhune, A. M. *The Life of Edward FitzGerald, Translator of The Rubáiyát of Omar Khayyám.* New Haven, Conn.: Yale University Press, 1947.

RUINED COTTAGE, THE **WILLIAM WORDSWORTH (1799)** *The Ruined Cottage,* in its present form, was not published until the mid-20th century. It exists in several manuscript versions, of which Manuscript D has become more or less the canonical version; however, Wordsworth eventually revised it as the second half of book 1 of *The Excursion* (1814), where it is certainly the best part of that monumental failure. In *The Excursion,* the figure of the Old Man, the Pedlar Armytage (the man from whom the narrator hears the story of Margaret), becomes the Wanderer who is the central guiding figure there—in essence Virgil to Wordsworth's Dante.

It is instructive to compare the end of the Old Man's story in *The Excursion* to its ending in *The Ruined Cottage.* Both end with him describing a kind of catharsis, as—calm of mind, all passion spent—he leaves the ruins where Margaret died: "I turned away / And walked along my road in happiness" (1, ll. 955–956). In the later version, this conclusion makes sense, since he is secure that she died feeling "The unbounded might of prayer," and had "her soul / Fixed on the Cross" (ll. 936–937). Because the Wanderer's "meditative sympathies repose / Upon the breast of Faith" (ll. 954–955) he has faith that she died knowing how "consolation springs, / From sources deeper far than deepest pain" (ll. 937–938). As the 20th-century critic Jonathan Wordsworth (William Wordsworth's collateral descendant) urged, the turn to faith in Wordsworth's poetry by the time he published *The Excursion* can be marked in revisions, mainly for the worse (as in the 1850 version of *The PRELUDE*), of the poems that he wrote in the strange intensity of his 20s.

If it is not faith in salvation, what is it that brings happiness to the Old Man in the original version? The answer has something to do with Nature's indifference to the suffering of human beings. This indifference is not coldness but a kind of self-sufficiency on her part. No matter what disasters occur—disasters that affect human beings living in the natural landscape, or (as in "NUTTING") disasters that affect Nature herself, it is her signal property not to take notice of them. It is not that Nature is unconscious, and therefore necessarily unconscious of suffering. Rather, Nature is the place of pure meditation (l. 524), where meditation means something like an intense and humanly indifferent alertness to her own presence. This is what makes Nature eerie rather than merely beautiful. In *The Excursion,* this meditation is reimagined in the dictum that the enlightened human spirit's "meditative sympathies repose / Upon the breast of Faith" (ll. 954–955), but no such appeal to faith, nor even to the human spirit, appears in *The Ruined Cottage.*

The disasters in *The Ruined Cottage* are socioeconomic. Robert, Margaret's husband, has suffered along with everyone else the failure of two harvests in a row. His loss of livelihood transforms him from a paragon of devoted industry into the image of erratic and frightening unemployment. Knowing and regretting this, he eventually signs up with the British militia for the bounty money (what we would call a signing bonus) they offer, leaving Margaret lonely and despairing. The Old Man charts the stages of her further decline and eventual death, following that of her younger child.

How can this lead to his happiness at the end? The answer is partly in the fact that the Old Man warns against taking pleasure in stories of suffering like that of Margaret, what he calls wanton and "Vain dalliance with the misery / Even of the dead" (ll. 223–224). But Wordsworth does not take pleasure in her story. He feels sorrow and sympathy for her, and in doing so he comes to suffer himself. Because he (like the Old Man) has in some sense become a fellow sufferer, any comfort or consolation he discovers is legitimate. He needs them, just as she would have needed them, and now the Old Man offers to him what he feels himself, that ruin, change, and grief are simply idle dreams, the passing shows of being.

It is impossible for Margaret to take solace in the meditative indifference of nature to her suffering. But it is possible for those who sympathize with her story to transmute the interest at the heart of that sympathy to meditation on it and then to meditation on nature, which is itself nothing but meditation without sympathy. This is an achievement of consolation that can do Margaret no good at all, but it is the characteristic mode of Wordsworth's early achievement, as one might call it, of an uncanniness of poetic originality, self-sufficiency, and solitude that takes human suffering seriously but goes further into what it takes to be the still deeper realm of poetic meditation. In Wordsworth's INTIMATIONS ODE, this is the "joy" that comes from an adequate and adequately powerful understanding of loss, the soothing thoughts that spring out of human suffering. *The Ruined Cottage* may be more severe still in placing the mind's apprehension, that its meditations are the same as nature's, above all human illusion.

BIBLIOGRAPHY

Abrams, M. H. *Natural Supernaturalism: Tradition and Revolution in Romantic Literature.* New York: Norton, 1973.

Alpers, Paul. *What is Pastoral?* Chicago: University of Chicago Press, 1996.

Barker, Juliet. *Wordsworth: A Life.* New York: Viking, 2000.

Bloom, Harold. *The Visionary Company: A Reading of English Romantic Poetry.* Garden City, N.Y.: Doubleday, 1961.

Bromwich, David. *Disowned by Memory: Wordsworth's Poetry of the 1790s.* Chicago: University of Chicago Press, 1998.

Gill, Stephen. *William Wordsworth: A Life.* New York: Oxford University Press, 1989.

Hartman, Geoffrey. *Wordsworth's Poetry, 1787–1814.* New Haven, Conn.: Yale University Press, 1971.
Levinson, Marjorie. *Wordsworth's Great Period Poems: Four Essays.* New York: Cambridge University Press, 1986.
Liu, Alan. *Wordsworth: The Sense of History.* Stanford, Calif.: Stanford University Press, 1989.
Moorman, Mary. *William Wordsworth: A Biography.* 3 vols. Oxford, England: Clarendon Press, 1957.
Wolfson, Susan J. *Questioning Presence: Wordsworth, Keats, and the Interrogative Mode in Romantic Poetry.* Ithaca, N.Y.: Cornell University Press, 1986.

S

"SAD SHEPHERD, THE" William Butler Yeats (1885) "The Sad Shepherd" belongs to William Butler Yeats's early period as a poet, which pretty much coincides with the last two decades of the 19th century. During this period he wrote poems about poetic desire, about the desire to be a poet, and about the desire of the poems' figures to live in poems and to be their subjects. These are not different desires but forms of the same commitment to a pure sense of otherworldly poetic vocation. As mentioned in the entry on Yeats, he returned to an analysis of this desire in his last poems, where he describes his own vicarious sense of desire for what his protagonists desire—"what cared I that set him on to ride, / I, starved for the bosom of his fairy bride?"

The sad shepherd—the ancient emblem of the pastoral poetry in which poets express their desire to be pure poets by living like shepherds and composing as they watch their sheep—is the man "whom Sorrow named his Friend" (l. 1) and because he and "his high comrade Sorrow" (l. 2) are companions, he belongs already to the poem to which he desires to belong. He wishes to be part of the world that he is already a part of, and that is constituted by its plangent strangeness so that his estrangement from it is the way he belongs to it. And this is the way Yeats belongs to it as well: The sad shepherd is a figure midway between Yeats and the stars on their pale thrones who govern the singing world of the poem.

It should be noted that "The Sad Shepherd" is a companion poem to "The Song of the Happy Shepherd," and that the two open Yeats's 1889 book *Crossways.* They relate to each other not as opposites but as complements or facets of the same jewel, much as William Blake's *Songs of Innocence and of Experience* complement rather than contradict each other. Ultimately, the sad shepherd and the happy shepherd do not differ from each other; for Yeats—and this is perhaps his central lesson—poetic sadness is a form of poetic happiness.

The shepherd seeks to tell his story, first to the stars, then to the sea, and then to the dewdrops, but all ignore him. (His procedure is somewhat reminiscent of that of the title character in Blake's "The Book of Thel," which Yeats knew very well.) The shepherd then decides not to attempt to arouse a response any more from the estranged others of his sorrowful world, but to listen instead for his own echo in the sound of the shell that he finds. (The shell may also be reminiscent of the episode of the dream of the Arab that William Wordsworth recounts in *The Prelude.*) This is the moment of poetic vocation: it does not matter who listens to his story, but only that he tell it, and that he hears the echo of its telling.

Despite the fact that Yeats's poetry, early and late, often seems profoundly still—Harold Bloom calls him the great poet of the refrain, that is, of repetition—it turns out in this poem that his thinking has progressed through his interaction with the stars, sea, and dewdrops, the last especially:

> . . . in a far-off, gentle valley stopping,
> Cried all his story to the dewdrops glistening.
> But naught they heard, for they are always listening,
> The dewdrops, for the sound of their own dropping.
> And then the man whom Sorrow named his friend
> Sought once again the shore, and found a shell,
> And thought, *I will my heavy story tell*
> *Till my own words, re-echoing, shall send*
> *Their sadness through a hollow, pearly heart;*
> *And my own tale again for me shall sing,*
> *And my own whispering words be comforting,*
> *And lo! my ancient burden may depart.*

He will listen to his own words as the dewdrops have listened to the sound of their own dropping, and it will not matter that the shell has a hollow heart. His burden is that of sorrow, but also it is poetry itself, since *burden* also means poetic refrain. His ancient burden will become part of the world he hears and listens to. But even the song to the shell fails him, or seems to fail him:

> Then he sang softly nigh the pearly rim;
> But the sad dweller by the sea-ways lone
> Changed all he sang to inarticulate moan
> Among her wildering whirls, forgetting him.

What comes back is his own inarticulate moan, changed to the pure sound of the landscape, like that of the stars, sea, and dewdrops. The shell forgets him, but that forgetting is also the way he merges with the world from which he feels rejected. Being forgotten is a sign of success as much as it is one of failure: He has become part of the beautiful soundscape whose beauty and strangeness he can neither master nor command, but which has absorbed him. As with "FERGUS AND THE DRUID" and "Cuchulain's Fight with the Sea," being and knowing are in a strange and always eerily discrepant relationship, and poetic success is to lose oneself, to be absorbed by and made part of that infinite discrepancy.

BIBLIOGRAPHY

Anscombe, G. E. M. *Intention.* Cambridge, Mass.: Harvard University Press, 2000.

Bloom, Harold. *Yeats.* New York: Oxford University Press, 1970.

Rosenthal, M. L., ed. Introduction to *Selected Poems and Four Plays of William Butler Yeats,* xix–xliv. New York: Scribner, 1996.

Vendler, Helen. *Poets Thinking: Pope, Whitman, Dickinson, Yeats.* Cambridge, Mass.: Harvard University Press, 2004.

———. *Yeats's Vision and the Later Plays.* Cambridge, Mass.: Harvard University Press, 1963.

"SAPPHO'S SONG" LETITIA ELIZABETH LANDON (1824) This song is part (ll. 141–160) of LETITIA ELIZABETH LANDON's long poem *The Improvisatrice,* published when Landon was 22 but completed several years earlier. An old tradition has it that Sappho, perhaps the greatest of Greek lyric poets, threw herself to her death in the Aegean Sea from the Leucadian cliff on the Isle of Lesbos after being rejected by the youth Phaon. Landon's probable suicide 14 years later makes this poem a little uncanny in retrospect, but its chief interest is in her beautiful sense of the relation of song or poetry to emotion, a subject to which she would return in her elegy on "FELICIA HEMANS."

Here Landon imagines Sappho taking a farewell of her lute, or lyre, the instrument to which lyric poetry (*lyric* derives from *lyre*) was sung. (Sir Thomas Wyatt, the great 16th-century poet who introduced the sonnet into English, has a similar poem, usually entitled "To his Lute," which ends "My lute, be still, for I have done.") Sappho addresses the lute as the source of the emotion that is now driving her to suicide, for which she is putting her lute aside: We are to picture this as occurring on the edge of the cliff. Landon delicately fills in the emotional coloring of Sappho's character when she has her regret the harshness with which she blames the lute (ll. 5–8), which is as innocent as she feels herself to be in loving Phaon.

The question this second thought raises is whether poetry or emotion has priority in human life. One of the eerie and powerful insights of ROMANTICISM's major poets was that poetry expressed emotion but also enticed young people into the difficult and harsh emotional life of the poet. In "RESOLUTION AND INDEPENDENCE," WILLIAM WORDSWORTH describes the foolhardy commitment to grim or tragic experience that poets in their youth feel strong enough to embrace, and the deeply troubling, but poetical, result of this embrace when the grim experience becomes fully real to them. To be committed to poetic vocation is to be committed to the sorrow that poetry transmutes into song.

Although Sappho attempts explicitly to deny this in the next stanza (while Landon herself will essentially admit it in her elegy on Hemans), that stanza accepts the second part of the two-step movement. "It was not song that taught me love, / But it was love that taught me song" (ll. 11–12), Sappho says. But what that means is that her poetic vocation—which was to *learn* song—required her to fall in love. So we might say that the chiasmatic lines (*chiasma,* a very useful term of poetic analysis, describes a semantic form that goes *abba,* here song-love-love-song) show that song requires the experience of love. The experience itself is real—that is her point—and when she learns love, she also learns song and all the sorrows that it requires from the singer.

That sorrow is real, enough to cause Sappho to put song aside and die, even as she sings a song about the end of song. She dedicates her lute and her wreath to Apollo, the "sun-god" of line 17, a truer love perhaps than Phaon, whom she refuses to name (l. 16). But still she dies, in the hope that the only part of her to survive will be her songs themselves, without the pain that was their origin.

BIBLIOGRAPHY

Greer, Germaine. *Slip-Shod Sibyls: Recognition, Rejection and the Woman Poet.* London: Viking, 1995.

Lawford, Cynthia: "'Thou shalt bid thy fair hands rove': L. E. L.'s Wooing of Sex, Pain, Death and the Editor." *Romanticism on the Net* 29–30 (February–May 2003). Available online. URL: http://www.erudit.org/revue/ron/2003/v/n29/007718ar.html. Accessed on March 30, 2008.

Mellor, Anne K. "Exhausting the Beautiful." In her *Romanticism and Gender,* 107–143. New York: Routledge, 1993.

"SAY NOT THE STRUGGLE NAUGHT AVAILETH" **ARTHUR HUGH CLOUGH (1855)** At the end of "THYRSIS," his elegy on ARTHUR HUGH CLOUGH, MATTHEW ARNOLD imagines his dead friend adjuring him to go on, not to give up but to search for the light, which may be anywhere, until he dies. Here Clough's most famous lines are similarly exhortatory, demanding optimism and hope in the midst of despair. Just as truly as Clough's lines might dissuade Arnold from despair, they are also intended to dissuade Clough himself from the despair to which he might otherwise give in. That is to say, we should read the poem less as a bit of wise moralistic advice for those who might need it than as directed toward Clough himself, toward his own proclivity to say that the struggle has not been worth it.

Clough had become a skeptic about the meaning of all human life—skeptical enough, at any rate, that the poem's opening line is one countering a real temptation in his thought. The rest of the poem is similarly self-therapeutic. It has some real chance of success because of the subtlety and power of its imagery. Clough's urbane skepticism can be seen in his taste for antithesis—that is, for multiple and often mutually canceling perspectives that prevent any adherence to a specific doctrine. Here the antithesis allows for hope, rather than despair, because the existence of either requires the dialectic balance of the other. This usually means that all hope will be met with despair, but here Clough reverses the direction of the sequence—"If hopes were dupes, fears may be liars" (l. 5)—so that the very fact that hope turned out to be hollow might suggest that fear is hollow, too.

We can see in the hypothetical Clough's own sense that his hopes were dupes. Nevertheless, he continues onward, attempting to exemplify the courage that he urges. We may feel that the persuasiveness of these stanzas is somewhat weak. The image of the tide's imperceptible but mighty return, which is the ideal of the third stanza, might remind us of what Clough's friend Ralph Waldo Emerson said, that as one gets older, the ebb is sure and certain, but the flow is fitful, unexpected, and transitory.

Clough is nevertheless seeking a natural illustration of the antithetical movement that will balance his despair with future compensations. The last stanza is more convincing than the previous one because it acknowledges that a huge part of hopelessness comes from the fact that we cannot know what the truth of our lives is. The "eastern windows" (l. 13), reminiscent of William Shakespeare's *Romeo and Juliet,* look out upon the sunrise. The sun's rise is so slow that the watcher cannot take it as a sign of hope. But were he to look westward, he would see that "the land is bright," presumably because the sun is angled in such a way that its nearly horizontal beams can illuminate the land farther west first. The last line is a metaphor as well, of course: The sunset land, which we approach through time—the direction we head in during our lives—is bright even if it seems dark here at the dawn itself. Darkness is the condition for brightness, and the poem concludes with a cautious optimism just because it does not deny everything that would make that optimism cautious, including the imminent sunset and death that will end everything. Given that, it is at least permitted to notice that the sunset land is bright now.

BIBLIOGRAPHY

Clough, Arthur Hugh. *Oxford Diaries of Arthur Hugh Clough.* Edited by Anthony Kenny. New York: Oxford University Press, 1990.

Hofmann, Michael. "Arthur Hugh Clough: 1819–1861." *Poetry* 187, no. 6 (March 2006): 495–496.

Kenny, Anthony. *Arthur Hugh Clough: A Poet's Life.* New York: Continuum, 2005.

"SCENE IN SUMMER, A" ARTHUR HENRY HALLAM (1831) In his introduction to the collection of ARTHUR HENRY HALLAM's poetry he edited and published in 1893, Richard Le Gallienne ended by quoting from this poem. It shows Hallam at his very best, writing in deeply subtle Wordsworthian blank verse. Hallam, in a review of ALFRED, LORD TENNYSON, had compared his friend to JOHN KEATS and PERCY BYSSHE SHELLEY, but he had also singled out the still-living WILLIAM WORDSWORTH as the object of his particular praise, and it seems clear that Hallam would have been a Wordsworthian poet. (Le Gallienne called Wordsworth Hallam's genius loci, citing the places in his poetry where Hallam mentions Wordsworth by name, as when he praised "TINTERN ABBEY" in a poem of his own.) Le Gallienne emphasized Hallam's talent at blank verse, which Hallam put to the same meditative uses that Wordsworth and SAMUEL TAYLOR COLERIDGE had developed for it (out of their reading of George Herbert's 17th-century poetry, so influential on Coleridge's "conversation poems").

Enjambed blank verse works for meditation because it never feels as though it is headed toward some predetermined end. It is at the other end of the spectrum from the closed heroic couplet of the 18th century, where every line heads toward end-stop and every other line heads toward a highly prescribed ending: line, rhyme, grammatical unit, thought. Heroic couplet is about balanced antithesis, whereas blank verse with the lines variously drawn out (in John Milton's famous formulation) is about following a thought wherever it goes. The thoughts one follows this way are thoughts that themselves follow a sinuous and wandering pathway, like that of nature itself—which is how Wordsworth and Coleridge employed it. There is always something unexpected to see in nature, and yet something harmonious; that is the lesson that Wordsworth and Coleridge—and here Hallam—mean to teach.

This is, of course, an effect of meditation (Isaac Newton saw nature very differently). Nature, as the meditative mind considers it, thus becomes a kind of representation of the movement of blank verse itself, and this is what Hallam perceived. Indeed, in his review of Tennyson, Hallam thought even Wordsworth was sometimes misled by his philosophical bent, commenting quite astutely that "a man, whose reveries take a reasoning turn, and who is accustomed to measure his ideas by their logical relations rather than the congruity of sentiments to which they refer, will be apt to mistake the pleasure he has in knowing a thing to be true, for the pleasure he would have in knowing it to be beautiful, and so will pile his thoughts in a rhetorical battery, that they may convince, instead of letting them glow in the natural course of contemplation, that they may enrapture."

This is just what Hallam does in this poem. The bench he is sitting on as he writes "Winds an accordant curve" to the old wall he sits beneath (ll. 2–4). The beauty of the summer scene he contemplates harmonizes with the poetry that describes it. The scene is made up of beautifully patterned boundaries—the leaves, the lawns, the wall, the shade cast by the elms. The end of the poem brings the whole aggregation together, in a perfectly balanced description that is the summer echo of the end of Coleridge's "FROST AT MIDNIGHT." The fitful wind twirls the leaves (of the coming fall), hurries the butterflies and gnats (of the passing summer) about, and makes the trees sway. We know this because its gusts alter the bound of the elms' shadows which are the boundary or "majestic line" (l. 22) between shade and light. The shadow and the light seem to divide the dominion of the day, but let us not forget that it is the winds that determine their dominion. The beauty is the beauty of a present that is at once fixed and passing, which reminds us how transitory is the moment, the *now* of the first line, which Hallam would have wished to share with Tennyson but which is passing, despite the beautiful ending's evocation of "the abundant light" (l. 23).

A final word: One might say that a poem written more or less as a letter to Tennyson should not bear this kind of close reading. But it is just *because* it was written to Tennyson, the most important person in Hallam's life as Hallam was the most important person in his, that it should. This is Hallam at his most ambitious and most judicious best, and it gives a sign of what he might have become as a poet had he lived.

BIBLIOGRAPHY

Gladstone, William. *Arthur Henry Hallam.* Boston: P. Mason and Co., 1898.

Hallam, Arthur Henry. *The Poems of Arthur Henry Hallam: Together with His Essay on the Lyrical Poems of Alfred Tennyson.* Edited by Richard Le Gallienne. New York: Macmillan and Co., 1893.

"SCHERZO (A SHY PERSON'S WISHES), A" DORA GREENWELL (1867)

This poem sheds some light and delight on DORA GREENWELL's more serious devotional poetry. A scherzo is a short musical piece in very quick ¾ time (often but not always part of a longer piece); it means "joke" in Italian and is marked by rapid gaiety. Greenwell wants both meanings here—the quickness and the funniness. Who is the shy person? Greenwell herself seems to have been very shy, although quite fearless in her writing, so the joke is partly at her own expense. But this makes her the joker as well, and most of the poem is from the joker's point of view. And we can say that the last line then turns tables on the joker.

The poem is very deftly done. It is a catalogue of the delights that a shy person can appreciate which a coarser and more boisterous sensibility would miss, and the delights are really lovely, permitting access even to the place "where the secret of beauty shows" (l. 14). Greenwell may be thinking of some of the fairy songs found in the works of William Shakespeare, especially Puck's in *A Midsummer Night's Dream* (the impetus for another poem of hers with the same title as Shakespeare's play) and Ariel's in *The Tempest.* The important thing to note about the catalogue is that the pleasures the shy person proposes herself are not secondary or unassuming pleasures. True, she begins by listing places of retirement, seclusion, shelter, and tiny inconspicuousness (the innermost heart of a peach; hidden with the fern-seed; in the woodbine's horn). But the lines describing these desires—she wants to be "With things that are hidden, and safe, and bold, / With things that are timid, and shy, and free" (ll. 9–10)—both end with surprising words: *bold* and *free.* All of this is a way of "Wishing to be" (l. 11)—not only wishing to be *with* these things, but just wishing to be, to exist fully.

After that short line, which provides a kind of turn in the poem's movement, the catalogue aims at far greater sublimity, and Greenwell starts desiring Shelleyan delights, wishing (as PERCY BYSSHE SHELLEY did in the "ODE TO THE WEST WIND") to be with things that are "Chainless, and tameless, and proud" like "wind in its sleep [and] the wind in its waking" (ll. 18–20; Greenwell is echoing Shelley's account of himself as being like the wind, "Tameless and swift and proud").

The last line seems to deflate the poem's genuine grandeur. It turns out to be the fantasy of a shy person who would imagine any escape at all from the social pressures of the party she is attending. So the poem seems to be making fun of its fantasist—and yet we could also say that it is just this kind of teasing that the last line repudiates. It is the people *in* "this room" who make fun of the kinds of reveries that Greenwell gives herself to, and we are quite in sympathy, not only with her desire to mingle with the beautiful and the SUBLIME, but also to escape those who turn such a desire into a joke.

It should be noted that this is an essentially comic version of an attitude Greenwell takes in her more serious devotional poetry—the idea she articulates in "The Sick Child," for example, that the child's inability to join in happily with its fellows is finally what allows for the joy brought by the comfort of God. Greenwell's God, like Greenwell herself, understands the sensitivity and emotional depths of the reticent and shy, and she devotes herself to those who cannot boisterously press their own way through the world.

BIBLIOGRAPHY

Cunningham, Valentine, ed. Note on Dora (Dorothy) Greenwell in *The Victorians: An Anthology of Poetry & Poetics,* 518–519. Malden, Mass.: Blackwell, 2000.

Dorling, William. *Memoirs of Dora Greenwell.* London: J. Clarke, 1885.

Mason, Emma. *Women Poets of the Nineteenth Century.* Tavistock, Devon, England: Northcote House Publishers, 2006.

"SCHOLAR-GIPSY, THE" MATTHEW ARNOLD (1853)

"The Scholar-Gipsy" is MATTHEW ARNOLD's version of JOHN KEATS's "ODE TO A NIGHTINGALE," a poem which haunted Arnold's imagination in ways he wished he could deny. Perhaps this was because he felt that Keats took too much pleasure in a kind of hopelessness, which Arnold sought to counter with the moral "high seriousness" he thought Keats lacked. He began his 1880 introduction to an anthology selection of Keats's poetry by quoting John Milton's doctrine (from "Of Education" [1644]) that poetry should be "simple, sensuous, impassioned," and he conceded that Keats was sensuous; the question was "whether he is ever anything else." And in a letter to ARTHUR HUGH CLOUGH written at roughly the same time as "The Scholar-Gipsy" (October 28, 1852), Arnold's judgment was even harsher, when he complained of those who "think that the object of poetry is to produce exquisite bits and images—such as Shelley's *clouds shepherded by the slow unwilling wind* [from PERCY BYSSHE SHELLEY's *PROMETHEUS UNBOUND*], and Keats passim: whereas modern poetry can only subsist by *its contents;* by becoming a complete magister vitae as the poetry of the ancients did: by including, as theirs did, religion with poetry, instead of existing as poetry only. . . . [T]he language, style, and general proceedings of a poetry which has such an immense task to perform, must be very plain and direct and severe."

This is the plainness and severity that Arnold attempted in his own poetry. "The Scholar-Gipsy" is a beautiful example of Arnold's ambivalence about the exquisiteness of Keatsian poetry. It should be noted that the poem is addressed to Clough (which makes possible its recapitulation in "THYRSIS," Arnold's elegy for Clough); Clough is the shepherd Arnold addresses in the first line. The structural strangeness of that address, in the context of the whole poem, gives a clue to Arnold's investment in it. Arnold addresses Clough as "Shepherd" because he is thinking of Milton's conceit, in *Lycidas* (1637), of university life as being like a pastoral, the students working and studying in pastoral simplicity and intensity. But Arnold does not represent *himself* as a shepherd; rather, he is the poet *imagining* a pastoral and representing himself as imagining it. He is too serious to dally with the false surmise that the pastoral world might be true.

It is the Scholar Gipsy himself who might belong to another life, or another way of being. That figure (whose legend Arnold explains in a note to the poem: his poverty forced him to leave Oxford and join a company of Gypsies whose lore he learned) shares many attributes with Keats's nightingale, especially in lines 211–230. Arnold imagines the Scholar Gipsy leading a life like the nightingale, or like its auditor, Keats himself, when he encourages the legendary student to "listen with enchanted ears . . . to the nightingales" (ll. 219–220). The Scholar Gipsy can do this because he has escaped the weariness, fever, and fret of our life—an escape which Arnold can only envy. But he and Clough know that the Scholar Gipsy is an idealized figure, and that he serves as a foil for the serious experiences that the two 19th-century poets can measure by contrast. Clough, who knows the world, represents the complement to the Scholar Gipsy, who does not.

This helps explain the beautiful but strange final image in the poem. The Scholar Gipsy is compared to the Tyrian trader (he has already been compared to the Tyrian queen, Dido), who escapes the conquest of the

Greeks and brings his wares to the Iberian shores, where the inhabitants are too shy to appear to those they trade with. He sails the "magic foam" (Keats) "through sheets of foam" (l. 248 of "The Scholar-Gipsy") to bring some image to the dark Iberians. And who are they? Oddly, they would be Arnold and Clough, trafficking in poetry and rejecting the pure conquest of unpoetic reason, but not allying entirely with the Tyrian gipsy either. They treat his wares at once warily and as of great preciousness, and the ending makes possible an image whereby the modern poets take on the legendary elusiveness of the Scholar Gipsy while attributing that elusiveness to their sense of the world as a harsh and dangerous place. The beautiful final image (from the Greek historian Herodotus) does manage at the same time to be "plain and direct and severe," and yet to preserve the poetry that matters. The Scholar Gipsy and those he negotiates with are both aspects of poetry, and the poetry that Arnold seeks to write must accommodate both of them—both Keats (and WILLIAM WORDSWORTH and the German poet Johann Wolfgang von Goethe) and the real and uncompromising world that Arnold thought was anathema to them.

BIBLIOGRAPHY

Arnold, Matthew. *Essays, Letters, and Reviews.* Collected and edited by Fraser Neiman. Cambridge, Mass.: Harvard University Press, 1960.

Bloom, Harold, ed. *Matthew Arnold.* New York: Chelsea House, 1987.

Dawson, Carl, and John Pfordresher, eds. *Matthew Arnold: The Critical Heritage.* New York: Routledge, 1995.

Trilling, Lionel. *The Moral Obligation to Be Intelligent: Selected Essays.* Edited by Leon Weiseltier. New York: Farrar, Straus, and Giroux, 2000.

SCOTT, SIR WALTER (1771–1832) Sir Walter Scott is now remembered primarily as a novelist, most famously as the author of *Ivanhoe* (1819) and *Waverly* (1814), historical fictions set in the Border regions of England and Scotland that came to be known as the "Waverly novels." Until recently, Scott's poetry was a staple of school memorization: some of that poetry comprises long narratives, such as *MARMION*; some of it is ballad-like, giving a narrative itself or appearing within longer narratives, such as "PROUD MASIE"; and some of it is even more fragmentary, such as the invented MOTTOES, or epigraphs, that Scott set at the heads of some of the chapters of his fiction, and of which he said that it was easier to invent the telling piece of poetry that he wanted, and give it a vague or fictional ascription, than to quote it from someone else.

Scott's literary education was wide-ranging and somewhat haphazard. Though he did read the classics in Latin, he also read James Macpherson's forged farrago of ancient forms and fragments, *The Works of Ossian* (1765), and Thomas Percy's great *Reliques of Ancient English Poetry* (1765), the most important anthology of ballads in history. After doing some eerie translations of the German poet Johann Wolfgang von Goethe, particularly of "The Erl-King," while working as a lawyer, Scott began gathering ballads himself, eventually publishing his own collection, *Minstrelsy of the Scottish Border,* in 1802.

Thus, Scott's poetic taste was for the tone of ancient anonymity, a poetry of place and tradition, not of subjective self-expression. No poet is better than Scott at these tones and effects. If ROMANTICISM often seems to be the deepest self-examination of subjective experience, it matters also what that experience is *of.* For Scott, as for WILLIAM WORDSWORTH and SAMUEL TAYLOR COLERIDGE, it is the experience of poetry itself, and Scott's work is in line with what those poets were doing in *Lyrical Ballads* (1798), which also influenced him in the early 1800s, when he joined the extended literary and social network of the leading poets of the day. Scott's poetry was wildly successful for a time, but eventually its sales fell off, and he concentrated on the historical novels, declining the poet laureateship, which went to ROBERT SOUTHEY. The classical archaeologist William Gell liked Scott's Scottish pronunciation of *beat,* which so embodied his Scottish sense of language and of self. Gell asked Scott at the end of his life why he had stopped writing poetry. "Because Byron *bet* me . . . he *bet* me out of the field in the description of the strong passions, and in deep-seated knowledge of the human heart, so I gave up poetry. . . ." (quoted in Lockhart, p. 351). The Byronic work Scott refers to here is the LORD BYRON of *CHILDE HAROLD'S PILGRIM-*

AGE—that is, the highly and morbidly self-conscious romantic poet. In terms of ambition and talent, Scott thought Byron to be the greatest poet in over a century, and yet Byron's notion of what poetry should do, of the figure that the poet cuts in the poetry, was the very opposite of Scott's. It is unquestionably true that Byron is the greater poet, but Scott's poetry is perfect in its way, far more perfect than the novels, which, while great, are sometimes ponderous. They are the equivalent for a literate audience of the balladry and minstrelsy that haunted Scott as a child, and that haunt his poetry still.

See also "LOCHINVAR."

BIBLIOGRAPHY

Johnson, Edgar. *Sir Walter Scott: The Great Unknown.* 2 vols. New York: Macmillan, 1970.

Lauber, John. *Sir Walter Scott.* Boston: Twayne Publishers, 1989.

Lincoln, Andrew. *Walter Scott and Modernity.* Edinburgh: Edinburgh University Press, 2007.

Lockhart, J. G. *Memoirs of the Life of Sir Walter Scott.* Philadelphia: Carey, Lea, and Blanchard, 1838.

Sutherland, John. *The Life of Walter Scott: A Critical Biography.* Cambridge: Blackwell, 1995.

"SCYTHE SONG" ANDREW LANG (1888)

"Scythe Song" is a beautiful poem and typical of ANDREW LANG's sheer talent at tone and at being able to write just the kind of poem that he most loved reading. This is Lang's great quality. Andrew Marvell's 17th-century Mower Poems (four pastorals published in 1681) are among the most perfect of their kind, a combination of depthlessness and melancholy that feels elemental and not ponderous. Lang's interest in fairy tales speaks to the same impulse. In "Scythe Song" it is almost as though he has written another Mower Poem.

But not quite, as the title shows just what he is doing. This is not the actual song of the scythe or of the mowers who handle it; it is a song about the song of the scythe, addressed to the mowers and therefore addressed, in a sense, to Marvell. Appropriately, it is onomatopoeic, which is to say that the song of the scythe and the song about the scythe merge in the sounds that they make. This merging of things is what the scythe does; the soft, hushed fall of the clover and grass is about the passing away of difference into a lulling unity.

Behind the poem (as behind Marvell's Mower Poems) is the great line from the Book of Isaiah, "All flesh is grass" (40:6), quoted by Peter in the New Testament (1 Peter 1:24). Flesh will be cut down by time and his consuming sickle, as Edmund Spenser put it in *The Faerie Queene* (1596), and the truth of this fact is an unavoidable one: Marvell's mower Damon says that death is a mower too.

But what Lang and Marvell do is to try to make that grim prophecy into a kind one. The mowers are blithe in Lang's poem, not threatening, and the sound of the scythe is soothing. Time here does not slaughter but sings a lullaby (l. 13), and the song and the mowing are the same thing. It is the song of the scythe, not the song of the mowers, that Lang's song repeats. The wooshing sound lulls to sleep, and the poem renders dying into a kind of falling asleep.

The sounds of the poem reconcile the reader to its content, since the fact that such content can be conveyed in so peaceful a way is what the poem shows. "Scythe Song" ought to be compared to those other evocations of "easeful death" which influence it, JOHN KEATS's "ODE TO A NIGHTINGALE" and ALFRED, LORD TENNYSON's "The LOTOS EATERS." They make repetition into a lullaby. But Keats and Tennyson were major poets, among the greatest of all time, and inevitably moved beyond the allurements of sound that they felt. Lang was a minor poet and knew it, and therefore, paradoxically, he was more perfect in one of the aspects of poetry that major poets cannot afford to succumb to: the pure lullaby of sound that gives content and allows a minor poet to be happy and at peace in his or her own poetry.

BIBLIOGRAPHY

Beerbohm, Max. "Two Glimpses of Andrew Lang." *Life and Letters* 1, no. 1 (June 1928): 1–11.

Cocq, Antonius Petrus Leonardus de. *Andrew Lang, a Nineteenth Century Anthropologist.* Tilburg, Netherlands: Zwijsen, 1968.

Green, Roger Lancelyn. *Andrew Lang: A Critical Biography with a Short-Title Bibliography of the Works of Andrew Lang.* Leicester, England: E. Ward, 1946.

Gross, John. *Rise and Fall of the Man of Letters: Aspects of English Literary Life since 1800*. London: Weidenfeld & Nicolson, 1969.

Orel, Harold. *Victorian Literary Critics: George Henry Lewes, Walter Bagehot, Richard Holt Hutton, Leslie Stephen, Andrew Lang, George Saintsbury, and Edmund Gosse*. London: Macmillan Press, 1984.

Webster, A. Blyth. *Andrew Lang's Poetry, by A. Blyth Webster, being the Andrew Lang lecture delivered before the University of St. Andrews 20 October 1937*. London: Oxford University Press, 1937.

"SECOND SIGHT" FELICIA HEMANS (1830)

FELICIA HEMANS's sentimentality achieves real if intermittent power because of the grim streak that runs through it. "Second Sight" is a good example of this mode of her poetry. It opens with a motto, or epigraph (see MOTTOES), from the contemporaneous playwright Charles Maturin (1782–1824) to the effect that no one who ever prophesizes grief turns out to be wrong. Maturin's formulation is significant to our understanding of the work that Hemans's poem is doing. He says that the heart inspired by grief will prophesize correctly, but that means that grief is first, not prophecy. The prophesizing heart is itself full of grief, and the prophecy, true though it might turn out to be, is a *sign* of sadness in the prophet; it is caused by that sadness rather than causing it. The prophet's heart is sad and therefore anticipates sad endings, but it has no more knowledge than anyone else about the future.

This is the central idea that Hemans explores in the poem. It is an address to "friends," which is to say she needs an audience for the prophecy she is about to utter—an audience of those who live in the present, and not in the future she will predict. She needs them because she needs friends, all the more so because she is afflicted with the "mournful gift" (l. 1) of sadness. As the motto shows, that gift is not supernatural in any way; it takes no great acuity to make the predictions that she does, all of which boil down to the idea that everything vanishes, that all present pleasures are ephemeral.

Ought one to forget that fact? Are her reminders morally, humanly, or aesthetically useful? We can say that the self-description in the poem is of a person who sees the skull beneath the skin, who sees horror or sadness everywhere because she is sad herself. But what motivates the self-description? Is she attempting to make everyone else sad, too? How is this poem an act of friendship, addressed as it is to her friends?

The speaker is sad about being sad, which is why she calls her gift mournful. She cannot appreciate the present moment because she knows her sad predilection for meditating on the time when that moment will be over. And yet it is not the case that she does not love things in the present moment. She does not just live in the barren future that will destroy it. For her, mournfulness registers the importance of the fading fairness of the present. She would not be sad if she did not value the things that are so fragile and ephemeral.

This is the point of the poem. In his masterpiece *Faust* (1808–32), the German poet and dramatist Johann Wolfgang von Goethe (whose work Hemans knew extremely well) has Faust deny that he will ever say to the fleeting moment, "Stay, thou art so fair." But it is just this that Hemans wants from the moments superseded as quickly as they are catalogued in "Second Sight:" She wants them to pause, not disappear forever so swiftly. In wanting the moments to stay, she gives us a sense of the beauty whose fragility and evanescence she laments in the poem.

We can say, therefore, that Hemans's sense of the beauty of the moment is far more intense than that of those who surround her. Thus, the poem understands sadness as a mode by which the beauty of things may be perceived. Their beauty is in their transience, and it is sadness that can understand such transience. She appreciates all the things she seems to be undermining in the poem, more than the friends she addresses otherwise would, because she takes their fragility seriously. In doing so, she makes them subjects of her poems (including this one), and not the inconspicuous background that others who do not have her mournful gift generally ignore.

So the poem is characteristically romantic (see ROMANTICISM): It is a declaration of the character of poetic vocation, and it offers that vocation as compensation for the things that poetry has to deal with. It is in the same mode as WILLIAM WORDSWORTH's "TINTERN ABBEY," also addressed to a friend. She knows that happiness is hollow, but she knows also that it is real happiness, and that if it is hollow, what makes it hollow makes it deep as well. This is what belongs "to all deep souls" (l. 34).

That depth is not the same as a genial confidence that all will be made right in heaven. The last line does not offer the moral it seems to, since the seemingly conventional appeal to heaven turns out instead to mean the sense of mournful depth that belongs only to poets. This is PERCY BYSSHE SHELLEY's heaven—the inspiration to truth, not to salvation.

BIBLIOGRAPHY

Armstrong, Isobel. *Victorian Poetry: Poetry, Poetics and Politics.* New York: Routledge, 1993.

Sweet, Nanora. *Felicia Hemans: Reimagining Poetry in the Nineteenth Century.* New York: Palgrave, 2001.

"SHE DWELT AMONG THE UNTRODDEN WAYS"

See LUCY POEMS.

SHELLEY, PERCY BYSSHE (1792–1822)

Poets imagine their readers, and one way to describe or interpret a poem is to consider the implied reader the author anticipates—perhaps a previous or more naive or younger version of himself or herself, or perhaps someone very different who can be converted into an avatar of the poet's present self or some previous self. Percy Bysshe Shelley is the last person WILLIAM WORDSWORTH would have imagined as his greatest reader—and yet that is what Shelley was. His poetry is widely different in style and content from Wordsworth's, but no one took more deeply to heart Wordsworth's lesson of the world's evanescence or of the freshness of the mind that perceives the world, nor the intensity and subtlety of the loss that evanescence produces, nor the sense that this loss is the very center and heart and content of poetic vocation. Wordsworth (1770–1850) was a generation older than Shelley, and by the time Shelley came into his own, Wordsworth's poetry had more or less deteriorated into the middle-aged crankiness of *The Excursion* (1814). Upon reading *The Excursion* when it was first published, Shelley wrote his sonnet "To Wordsworth," a lamentation about Wordsworth's political and poetic apostasy (as LORD BYRON would call it), and his wife, Mary Shelley, wrote in her journal the simple verdict, "He is a slave." Shelley would never be a slave, partly because he always kept the vision of Wordsworth before his mind. His later judgment on Wordsworth, in *Peter Bell the Third* (written in 1819), his anticipatory parody of Wordsworth's odd fantasy *Peter Bell,* is that Peter/Wordsworth was "a kind of moral eunuch" who "touched the hem of Nature's shift, / Felt faint, and never dared uplift / The closest all-concealing tunic" (ll. 313–317).

The best way to understand Shelley is as a Satanic reader of Wordworth, much as he was an avowedly Satanic reader of John Milton's *Paradise Lost* (he regarded Satan as the undoubted hero of that poem). *Paradise Lost* is about the "loss of Eden," and the defiant soul's response to that loss; Wordsworth's poetry is about the loss of the secular Eden of childhood. That loss is cause for weeping, but the recompense that Wordsworth believed made up for it was a discovery of the soul's own humanity. For Shelley, the recompense was instead, one could say, a discovery of the soul's visionary power, its capacities for experiencing the sublimity that is a feature not of the unconscious strength of childhood but of a loss of that strength—what the German philosopher Immanuel Kant would call empirical strength or power. As a boy, as Shelley says in "ODE TO THE WEST WIND," it "Scarce seem'd a vision" to outstrip the wind's speed (ll. 50–51); as an adult, visionary power and striving with the wind in his "sore need" (l. 52) are synonymous experiences. To feel the power one has lost, one has to lose it; but with that loss comes recognition that this power is one's own power in its most essential and inward form. The best introduction to Shelley's vocation for sublimity (see SUBLIME, THE) is the end of "MONT BLANC," where he sees that all the overwhelming sublimity of the natural world is the projection of the adverting mind viewing its own sublimity.

The tunic that Peter/Wordsworth was unable to uplift is the veil of so many of Shelley's poems: the veil that separates life from death and makes the natural world seem the only one. Beyond that veil is the realm of the imagination in which the soul finds its full intellectual power. For Shelley, that power is connected with his radicalism: The region beyond the veil is the region where souls can or should be able to see or perceive each other's indescribable beauty. The best way to understand Shelley's commitment to poetry is to see that it is always a communicative act; it is the act of communication between souls, whose presence to each other is ratified by each soul's capacity to perceive and take flame from the beauty that is its recognition of this universal capacity: "Each are mirrors of / The fire for which all thirst," as he says in *ADONAIS,* his elegy to JOHN KEATS.

There is nothing naive about Shelley's attitude, in poetry or in politics. He explicitly states at the beginning of *PROMETHEUS UNBOUND,* for example, that the poetic and half-utopian vision of that poem has nothing to do with practical political action, as many of his critics have also assumed. Rather, it gives the *motive* for practical political action, a motive we could summarize by saying that the lyrical intensities of the work intimate the depth and intensity of the human capacity for love and for suffering. Shelley believed in a kind of universal elite, and if his commitment and espousal of this demand led to much suffering—the consequences, for example, of his embrace of free love, whose early result was his elopement with Mary Godwin (daughter of the radical political philosophers Mary Wollstonecraft and William Godwin), which played some role in the eventual suicide of his first wife, Harriet Westbrook, with whom he had also eloped—it also manifested itself in the princely generosity that he showed to all around him. This was so much the case that his best friend, the misanthropic Byron (memorably depicted in *JULIAN AND MADDALO: A CONVERSATION*) could say in several letters, a month after Shelley had drowned, that the world was "brutally mistaken about Shelley, who was, without exception, the *best* and least selfish man I ever knew. I never knew one who was not a beast in comparison" (letter to John Murray, August 3, 1822). "The world was ill-naturedly, and ignorantly, and brutally mistaken," Byron wrote THOMAS MOORE a few days later, in seeing Shelley as selfish and cruel when he expected the same generosity of soul and selflessness in everyone else.

The Shelleys were close to Lord Byron and lived together with him and Mary Shelley's half sister (and Byron's lover) Claire Claremont on Lake Geneva after Byron had left England for good. Following his former wife Harriet's suicide in 1816, and his failure to gain custody of the children they had had together, Shelley also left England permanently. Despite his close friendship with Byron, he lived a life of increasing unhappiness. The death of his three-year-old son William after that of two babies, and a near-fatal miscarriage by Mary, erotic longing, loneliness, political despair—all combined to make the older Shelley a markedly pessimistic poet, writing of life as a sea of agony and "Stanzas written in Dejection," as one of his titles has it, though he was more committed to political and spiritual emancipation than ever, and more generous than ever. He invited the tubercular and dying Keats, who was no friend to him (though their mutual friend LEIGH HUNT had introduced them), to Italy to try to save him from the English winter; after Keats's death he wrote his great elegy *Adonais,* set in part in the Protestant cemetery in Rome where Shelley, too, would soon be buried. Even his apparently optimistic poems, like *Prometheus Unbound,* were written under the shadow of mortality, in this case the death of his son William, which seems to have stimulated Shelley to write the strange and ambiguous fourth act of that play.

Shelley's last poems are his greatest: the late lyrics of despair that he wrote, mainly to and about Jane Williams, with whose common-law husband he would drown in a storm off Leghorn on July 8 of 1822; as well as *Adonais* and the great, unfinished *The TRIUMPH OF LIFE,* the manuscript of which contains some of the lyrics as well. *Triumph* is a Dantesque poem written in the terza rima Shelley had experimented with for many years. That poem, no less than *Alastor,* written seven years earlier, is a response to Wordsworth and Wordsworthian reticence about nature. In *Alastor* the Wordsworthian narrator, whose heart, dry as summer's dust, burns to the socket (to adapt Shelley's epigraphic quotation from Wordsworth), fails to match the Shelleyan Poet's daring, which leads him to death, but only after bringing him through all strangeness and gorgeousness. By the time of *The Triumph of Life,* in which Wordsworth appears as the French philosopher and confessional lover of nature, Jean-Jacques Rousseau, Shelley was able to acknowledge Wordsworthian loss, and the sense that poetry is not a recompense for such loss.

Shelley and Wordsworth are certainly the two greatest poets of English ROMANTICISM. In many ways, they seem like opposite figures: Wordsworth is sober where Shelley is visionary. But each was a radical experimentalist. Shelley was far more brilliant in his experimentation, and his prosody was unexcelled by any later poet. But it is prosody in service of Wordsworthian themes of loss and sadness, and the brilliance and inventiveness of his poetry bring out just how far Wordsworthian disappointment with the course of life could extend, both into the platonic realms of idealism (Shelley was the first person to translate the Greek philosopher Plato's *Symposium* into English, as well as parts of the Dutch Jewish philosopher Benedict de Spinoza) and into the "intense inane" (as Shelley called the cosmological vacuum which transcends human hope).

See also "HYMN TO INTELLECTUAL BEAUTY," "LINES: 'WHEN THE LAMP IS SHATTERED,'" "LINES WRITTEN IN THE BAY OF LERICI," "OZYMANDIAS," "TO ———," "TWO SPIRITS: AN ALLEGORY."

BIBLIOGRAPHY

Bloom, Harold. *Poetry and Repression: Revisionism from Blake to Stevens*. New Haven, Conn.: Yale University Press, 1976.

———. *Shelley's Mythmaking*. New Haven, Conn.: Yale University Press, 1959.

———. *The Visionary Company: A Reading of English Romantic Poetry*. Garden City, N.Y.: Doubleday, 1961.

Keach, William. *Shelley's Style*. New York: Methuen, 1984.

Holmes, Richard. *Shelley: The Pursuit*. London: Weidenfeld and Nicolson, 1974.

Quinney, Laura. *The Poetics of Disappointment: Wordsworth to Ashbery*. Charlottesville: University Press of Virginia, 1999.

Wasserman, Earl. *Shelley: A Critical Reading*. Baltimore: Johns Hopkins Press, 1971.

"SHE WALKS IN BEAUTY" LORD BYRON (1814) Byron is the greatest poet for whom poetry is not the major vocation of life, for whom poetry is in some ways ancillary to other vocations. Where Milton thought of his political life as an achievement of the left hand, and poetry as his most important commitment, Byron's political commitments and his social life were more important to him than being a poet, a fact that he is quite entertaining about in *DON JUAN*. But this is not to say that he did not take poetry as seriously as the other great poets: He had attention and vocation to spare, and if poetry is only one of the things he devoted himself to, that devotion was certainly as strong in him as in almost any other poet. It just was not a totalizing vocation.

This fact and this separation between poetry and life is what gives his exquisite lyrics and the perceptions they express their shimmering quality. "She walks in Beauty" is exemplary in this regard, and it is worth noting the mildly perfect ways the poem's diction is surprising. The poem could be taken as a reworking of WILLIAM WORDSWORTH's great lyric, "The Solitary Reaper" (published 1807), which is also framed as a poem of wonder at the sight of a woman moving in an alien aura of her own making. In the case of the reaper, it is the song that she is singing in Scots; in Byron the lady walks partly in the aura of the *Hebrew Melodies* to which Byron imagines his lyrics being set. "She walks in Beauty" is the first poem in the volume, and although it is about Byron's cousin's wife, Lady Anne Horton, it is also about the unattainable spirit that can only be thought about in song.

We can say this because, in Byron, the aura she walks in is Beauty itself. The woman is not beautiful, since beauty surrounds her. She is not its source; rather, beauty is her medium. And the beauty in which she walks is not dazzling but "like the night," so that somehow her own beauty is set off by contrast with the darker beauty through which she walks. All that restraint means, in the end, that there is nothing sexual about Byron's praise of her beauty. It harmonizes with the understatement that makes it lovely and serene and an object of contemplation. This is what makes the last line so convincing: Her beauty is innocent because it is the sort of beauty that a poem has—that *this* poem has. The apprehension of her beauty does not belong (as it usually would for Byron) to life and erotic desire; it belongs to whatever subtlety and tact the idea of a poetic lyric implied to him. Subtlety and tact underscore the fact that Byron is so perfect at poetry—perfect without obsession. He can convey the sublime mildness of her beauty because of the sublime mildness of his poetic vocation, and the perfection of the lyric derives from the fact that it is in no way a sign of vocation or bid for greatness but the expression of pure pleasure in the lady's beauty, without any ulterior motive.

"SIMON LEE" ("SIMON LEE: THE OLD HUNTSMAN") William Wordsworth (1798)

"Simon Lee" appeared in the original (1798) edition of William Wordsworth and Samuel Taylor Coleridge's *Lyrical Ballads,* and it is something like that book's poetic manifesto. The 1798 edition came without the later prose preface and supplementary essays, which would have that function from 1800 on. "Simon Lee" is first and foremost a ballad: It tells a story, as the line that sometimes precedes the poem makes clear in alluding to "an incident in which he was concerned." The poem has a long windup before coming to this incident: Simon Lee's vigorous youth, his present old age and inevitable decrepitude, and the feeble courage with which he and his wife continue to try to keep themselves alive.

That introduction is a good setup for the incident it promises, but then comes the surprise. Wordsworth addresses the patient reader (l. 65) who has been waiting for the anecdotal payoff. But he says there will be no such thing, at least not compared to what the conventions of the genre of the ballad or narrative poem might have led the reader to expect. Instead, Wordsworth tells us that there is "a tale in every thing" (l. 68)—that is, the unexceptional incidents of an ordinary or natural life are fit matter for poetry. Here the incident is this: The speaker, vigorous as Simon Lee once was, removes the root that Simon Lee had such trouble cutting at a single blow. Simon Lee bursts into tears of gratitude, and this leaves the speaker filled with ambivalence.

Why? What leaves him mourning Simon Lee's gratitude? It is sympathy with Simon Lee, but a sympathy perhaps with a feeling that Lee himself does not have. The speaker mourns the fact that Simon Lee has become so old and enfeebled, so fallen from his youthful and vigorous self, that he must be grateful for the simplest of aid. But he mourns even more that Simon Lee no longer has the strength or the connection with his younger self even to lament this fact. His gratitude is genuine and simple, and so he becomes an element of the tale, and not someone capable of understanding it.

This means that the story of Simon Lee is a story about losing the capacity even to understand one's own suffering. The nature of the human suffering to which Wordsworth took it as his task to give poetic expression is that the poetical beings who populate his poetry do not know that they are poetical beings. Tragic poetry, then, becomes understood as the record of the decay in our ability to understand tragic poetry. There is a tale in everything, and the tale is that of human loss. The ability to perceive a tale in everything means that Wordsworth, and the ideal reader, are fully committed to their own humanity, and this means as well that they are living in a world of inevitable mutability and loss. Wordsworth is not mourning himself in this poem (as he may perhaps in the Intimations Ode and "Tintern Abbey"), but he is mourning the human condition, even as he praises the fact that it is only by embracing the human condition in oneself that one is capable of the great act of mourning.

BIBLIOGRAPHY

Abrams, M. H. *Natural Supernaturalism: Tradition and Revolution in Romantic Literature.* New York: Norton, 1973.

Bloom, Harold. *The Visionary Company: A Reading of English Romantic Poetry.* Garden City, N.Y.: Doubleday, 1961.

Bromwich, David. *Disowned by Memory: Wordsworth's Poetry of the 1790s.* Chicago: University of Chicago Press, 1998.

Hartman, Geoffrey. *Wordsworth's Poetry, 1787–1814.* New Haven, Conn.: Yale University Press, 1971.

Liu, Alan. *Wordsworth: The Sense of History.* Stanford, Calif.: Stanford University Press, 1989.

Pinch, Adela. *Strange Fits of Passion: Epistemologies of Emotion, Hume to Austen.* Stanford, Calif.: Stanford University Press, 1996.

Quinney, Laura. *The Poetics of Disappointment: Wordsworth to Ashbery.* Charlottesville: University Press of Virginia, 1999.

"SLUMBER DID MY SPIRIT SEAL, A" See Lucy poems.

SMITH, CHARLOTTE TURNER (1749–1806)

Three decades after Charlotte Turner Smith's death, William Wordsworth wrote, in a note to one of his poems, that she was "a lady to whom English verse is under greater obligations than are likely to be either acknowledged or remembered. She wrote little, and that little unambitiously, but with true feeling for rural nature, at a time when nature was not much regarded by English Poets; in point of time her earlier writings preceded, I believe, those of Cowper and Burns." Wordsworth was an enthusiast for Smith's poetry when he was an undergraduate, paid his respects to her in 1791 when he was 21 (they hit it off, and she wrote him letters of introduction to her friends in France, where he was bound), and quoted from her in his early poem in couplets, "An Evening Walk." SAMUEL TAYLOR COLERIDGE also admired her work, especially her sonnets, which were her primary claim to fame in the 18th century.

Smith was unlucky in her financial connections. Born Charlotte Turner, she was raised first by her aunt (with whom she remained close) after her mother's death, when she was a toddler, and her father's subsequent departure for the Continent. Her aunt brought her up in London, a city she did not like, and when her father returned, they remained there, in ticklish financial circumstances, although her father encouraged her education and paid for tutors. He remarried, partly for the dowry his second wife provided, and accepted a proposal for his daughter's hand when she was just 15, no doubt anticipating further financial stability. But, in fact, the 21-year-old Benjamin Smith would prove to be feckless, and eventually Charlotte Smith joined her husband in debtor's prison.

Smith was far more financially responsible than her husband, and one of the ways that she supported her family was by writing, first poetry and then novels. She was regarded as the finest sonneteer of her time; in later work, she would follow William Cowper (1731–1800) and James Thomson (1700–1748) in composing in blank verse. Wordsworth gave her priority over Cowper in the invention of the kind of poetry of natural description at which she was unexcelled (and which may be seen in all its glory in *BEACHY HEAD*); such poetry of nature is one of the major ways that she became a forerunner to and major exponent of early ROMANTICISM. Smith's early lessons in drawing made her alert to the minute details of the scenes that she described, and she had a powerful gift for the communicative possibilities of spatial relationships. She also incorporates quotation into her poetry with great verve and style, manifesting a sense of what can be conveyed by the relationship thus established between the original text quoted and the poem quoting it.

Smith also wrote novels to support her many children (a number of whom died young, to her heartbroken sorrow) while her husband was in and out of debtor's prisons. Her own difficult experiences made her sympathetic to the radical movements sweeping across Europe in the wake of the French Revolution, though later she would recoil at its excesses. This sympathy for the downtrodden is evident in all her work and is another aspect of her poetry that makes her a major forerunner not only of Cowper but of Wordsworth himself. She is probably the single most important poet among the generation just older than Wordsworth who influenced him in ways that were to make him the central figure of romanticism.

BIBLIOGRAPHY

Aikin, John. *An Essay on the Application of Natural History to Poetry*. 1777. Reprint, New York: Garland Pub., 1970.

Fletcher, Loraine. *Charlotte Smith: A Critical Biography*. New York: St. Martin's Press, 1998.

Labbe, Jacqueline M. *Charlotte Smith: Romanticism, Poetry, and the Culture of Gender*. New York: Palgrave, 2003.

Smith, Charlotte. *The Poems of Charlotte Smith*. Edited by Stuart Curran. New York: Oxford University Press, 1993.

Johnston, Kenneth, ed. *Romantic Revolutions: Criticism and Theory*. Bloomington: Indiana University Press, 1990.

Quinney, Laura. *Poetics of Disappointment: Wordsworth to Ashbery*. Charlottesville: University Press of Virginia, 1999.

Zimmerman, Sarah MacKenzie. *Romanticism, Lyricism, and History*. New York: State University of New York Press, 1999.

"SO, WE'LL GO NO MORE A-ROVING"

LORD BYRON (1817) This is one of BYRON's handful of exquisite lyrics, songs of the refined regret that is one of his signal modes. Like PERCY BYSSHE SHELLEY's late lyrics, Byron's are characterized by a sense of afterglow, the dying reverberation of an experience or of a time of life that is now over. This is preeminently true in "We'll go no more a-roving," which is spoken from a vantage of age. The wonderful "So" that begins the poem catches all its tone of the casual inevitability of time. It needs no explanation: The future tense of the conclusion, repeated in lines 1 and 11, shows that we are entering into that future or lateness of life. The rest of the poem is in the present tense, but the present to which it refers is merely the present that is fading away, becoming the past or the last relics of the past: "*still as* loving," "*still as* bright," the *still* indicating the subtle evanescence of the speaker's relation to the things that remain what they once were.

For just this reason, we can say that the beauty of the poem corresponds to the beauty it regrets. The heart is still as loving, the Moon still as bright, the night made for loving, and so on, but this is now something that the speaker knows rather than experiences directly. Because he knows it, the poem knows it, and can say it. So the beauty resigned finds a kind of compensation in its lyric representation. That return is in an inevitably melancholy mode because it is now only representative of the youthful energy that is gone. The poem, of course, is referring to the waning of erotic life. "The sword outwears its sheaf" (l. 5) is a frankly sexual image, but the erotic sense goes deeper than that: "the soul wears out the breast." In both cases, desire comes up against the end of the speaker's capacity to meet its demands. He feels the desire, but does not have the energy to pursue it. What he now discovers is the difference between desire and energy, which had once seemed to be the same thing. Desire without energy, so that it is still love, but "Love itself" must have rest.

Discovering that distinction is what allows the poem its beauty, which is all the more lovely for the disinterested attitude it now takes. The beauty now becomes a matter of pure representation, something the poem offers rather than something that life offers. To the extent that we could call this poem a song, in the sense that Byron and Shelley gave to that word (a sense not unlike WILLIAM BLAKE's), it makes an appearance in the world: the song sung after the time of erotic pursuit is over. (This is the sense that the classicizing duo would have learned from Homer: "the gods did these things so that men should sing about them afterwards.") So the poem/song represents another way that beauty can be in the world: not only in erotic pursuit but in beautiful songs of regret and nostalgia. The song is as beautiful as the experiences it purifies and laments, but beautiful in a different way from them, which is both its success and its loss.

"SOLILOQUY IN A SPANISH CLOISTER"

ROBERT BROWNING (1842) "Soliloquy in a Spanish Cloister" is a hilarious dramatic lyric (*Dramatic Lyrics* was the title of the book the poem first appeared in) with some serious insight into the relations of human beings with each other and with God. The obvious first reading is the right one: The speaker or soliloquizer is a monk in a Spanish cloister who is full of resentment and disgust for his goody-two-shoes colleague Brother Lawrence. The poem begins with a famous growl of disgust, and the disgust is all at Lawrence's mincing and self-satisfied ways (as the speaker views them to be). He cannot stand Lawrence's benign commitment to his half-holy hobby of growing fruits and flowers. The hatred Lawrence provokes in the speaker is ludicrously out of proportion to the significance so mild and meek a figure could possibly bear.

And it is just this that disgusts the speaker. He is quite able to imitate Lawrence, which he does several times, for his and our delectation. Lawrence imagines that everyone around him is interested in just the little things that he likes talking about: the Latin name for parsley, the weather, the flowers he is growing. He is utterly without irony, utterly without suspicion, utterly guileless. The speaker knows this, though at one point he tries to believe something else: that Lawrence is in fact as sexually aroused by the sultry women they can see outside the neighboring convent telling stories and washing their hair as he is. But he knows that Lawrence is not: His eye really is "dead" (l. 30).

Part of what is great, and also telling, about the poem is the speaker's sarcastic use of *we*, when he is ventriloquizing Lawrence's prissiness. That ventriloquization, of course, is just what ROBERT BROWNING is doing in his *Dramatic Lyrics*: showing the possibilities of seeing other points of view, of *getting* differences of perspective and interest. We are not to admire the speaker of this poem. He is intolerant and mean (and sabotages the things that Lawrence loves, nipping his flowers in secret). He imagines escaping Satan's or Belial's grip, but just the fact that he is imagining this suggests the dramatic irony: that his hatred will damn him. And yet he has a fantastic vitality that Lawrence lacks. And the reason he hates Lawrence is that Lawrence lacks it. That vitality is what the poem trades in. We readers (including Browning) may be on Lawrence's side, but we are not like Lawrence. We, too, *get* the speaker, in a way that Lawrence never could. Lawrence trades in vegetables, but Browning and the speaker both see more than those they make fun of. It would probably be correct to say, not that the speaker is in any way a hero (after all, he is prissy himself about some things, like the absurd way he makes his mealtime activities into religious symbols), but he is fully human, and being fully human partly means parodying others—parodying them when they seem to deserve parody by not being parodists themselves.

"SONG" THOMAS LOVELL BEDDOES (1825–1828) THOMAS LOVELL BEDDOES's death-besotted poems are always beautiful, and this "Song" is exemplary. Beddoes is the extreme continuator of one strand in PERCY BYSSHE SHELLEY, the poet he most revered. It is a strand that we may find as well in Despayre's astonishing temptation to suicide in Edmund Spenser's *The Faerie Queene* (1696) and that comes to Beddoes through some of the temptations to despair in Shelley's *PROMETHEUS UNBOUND*, his favorite book, which his own *Death's Jest Book* sought to emulate, and through Shelley's late lyrics. This song is sung by the avenger Isbrand (act v, scene iv), disguised as the jester in *Death's Jest Book*. The Shellyan strand is the one in which beauty and death are brought close together through their affinity for an intense lyricism—a lyricism that takes itself as subject and makes both beauty and death images of itself—that is, of lyricism. JOHN KEATS, too, sometimes came close to this mode (as in his description in "ODE TO A NIGHTINGALE" about having been "half in love with easeful death"), but for Beddoes it was essential to what he thought poetry was, what haunted him in poetry, and what he tried to do in writing it. We cannot imagine that Keats would ever have committed suicide, but Beddoes was at times wholly in love with death, which for him had the visage of the pure aestheticism of rhyme and refrain—that is, of the hypnotic repetition that Sigmund Freud saw as the manifestation of what he called the death instinct.

There can be no pure aestheticism in poetry, however, since the material of poetry is language and the condition of language is meaningfulness. What Beddoes did, however, was to write poems about the meaning of refrain, and "Song" is one of the most beautiful of these. Adam and Eve are crows. Whom are they named by? They know their names, but that means they know how to speak, and so they are not real crows but the crows of the poem, the crows which the poem can imagine as the bearers of pure unchangingness. Carrion crows, they eat the dead, and that means that (again like Keats's nightingale) they are not themselves born for death but to be witnesses to the eternity of death. They sup on kings' marrow, because (as William Shakespeare repeated in his plays) it is the fate of kings to die, but the crows who are on the side of death will not die.

The crows are given human personalities, though, which is to say that they stand for a relation to unchangingness that is Beddoes's in the repetition that marks the poem. Adam is the crow of Cairo (pronounced as an iamb, to rhyme with *crow*) because of the rhyme; and it is therefore because of rhyme that Cleopatra the great Egyptian queen can come in. After death, nothing changes, and it is the rain in the poem that stands for that unchanging repetition of things. Adam's words to Eve are tender, though not kind. They live together in this pure aesthetic life of rain and refrain, and the way they drink and make their life merry is through the pure repetition of that refrain to each other. The poem is typical of Beddoes in moving seamlessly from a first descriptive stanza into an example of the thing described (see "The PHANTOM WOOER"), so that the strange joy the poem describes is the strange joy ghostly but palpable in its own words and prosody.

BIBLIOGRAPHY

Bradshaw, Michael. *Resurrection Songs: The Poetry of Thomas Lovell Beddoes*. Burlington, Vt.: Ashgate, 2001.

Wolfson, Susan J., and Peter J. Manning. *Selected Poems of Thomas Hood, Winthrop Mackworth Praed and Thomas Lovell Beddoes*. London: Penguin, 2000.

"SONG (GOOD NIGHT)" JOANNA BAILLIE **(1836)** JOANNA BAILLIE published her play *The Phantom* (written a few years earlier) in 1836, in the three-volume set of her dramatic work called *Miscellaneous Plays*. One of her three plays on Scotland, it is subtitled "A Musical Drama," and it is musical partly because it contains so many songs. Baillie, like her friend and literary influence Sir WALTER SCOTT, liked the Shakespearean tradition that interpolated out-of-context songs or ballads into a narrative because they were beautiful in their own right. (One of the characters in *The Phantom,* hearing another sing, praises her in these terms: "Thou singest sweetly, ay, and sadly too, / Even as it should be sung.") Many of Scott's greatest poems appear within his novels, and the same is true of many of Baillie's works. ALFRED, LORD TENNYSON did the same within his long narrative poem *The PRINCESS: A MEDLEY*; and THOMAS LOVELL BEDDOES's unfinished masterpiece *Death's Jest-Book* is a repository of his songs.

The Phantom contains a number of songs, all intensely evocative of the legendary Scottish past that Baillie was so interested in exploring. "Good night" is sung by travelers, accompanied by a piper, arriving at the house where they are to spend the night. It is a beautiful example of the kind of song that Baillie excelled in, with its repeated refrain—"Good night! Good night!"—rhyming on different onsets. Baillie uses refrain in the right balladic style to bring everything to the same eventual conclusion. Here that conclusion can be summarized in the line "Sweet sleep be with us, one and all!" (l. 19), where the sweetness of the sleep, and of the nighttime in which we all sleep, is partly composed of the fact that in sleep all are equal partakers of an elemental human pleasure. That line rings a lively change on a line of blessing in the previous stanza, where the song itemizes: "The lady in her curtain'd bed, / The herdsman in his wattled shed, / The clansmen in the heather'd hall / Sweet sleep be with you, one and all!" (ll. 13–16). There is in sleep no difference between any of these different kinds of people, and no difference either between those who wish good night—sweet sleep be with *you*—and those who are the objects of the wish—sweet sleep be with *us*.

The effect that Baillie aims at here is rather like that of the end of William Shakespeare's *A Midsummer Night's Dream,* where parting and friendship are not opposed to each other but are entirely reconciled. In wishing each other good night, we all betake ourselves to our rest mutually, and while we separate, we do so anticipating the same communal experience of sleep. This is a very hard tone to pull off, and Baillie does it admirably. It works in the play, which is about the final triumph of friendship, because it works as a song, where it so beautifully evokes mutual trust and sympathy.

BIBLIOGRAPHY

Baillie, Joanna. *Dramatic and Poetical Works of Joanna Baillie.* London: Longman, Brown, Green, and Longmans, 1851.

Forbes, A. "'Sympathetic Curiosity' in Joanna Baillie's Theater of the Passions." *European Romantic Review* 14, no. 1 (January 2003): 31–48.

"SONG" ("WHEN I AM DEAD, MY DEAREST") CHRISTINA ROSSETTI **(1848)** Virginia Woolf, apostrophizing Christina Rossetti, praises "the fixity and the sadness of your muse." The idea of fixity is crucial here. Rossetti's muse is sad because she will not give herself over to sensual pleasure. She will not attempt to satisfy desires that her religious convictions deny her, and so she remains fixed in the emotional experience of a longing that cannot be fulfilled. This experience, as Woolf saw, lends Rossetti's poetry its tonal qualities, the sense of the intensity of poetry as what you have when the intensity of fulfillment is not to be had.

So even though "When I am dead, my dearest" enjoins its addressee—the man it is impossible for the speaker to have a relationship with—not to sing sad songs, this song already is a sad song, but a song like the nightingale's that should be heard under the rubric of "as if" (l. 11), since we cannot know the speaker's pain or even know that we cannot know it. We could perhaps say that it is sadness without pain, that is to say, that the poem reconceptualizes sadness (this is Woolf's point), not as the result of a missed possibility, of something that could be otherwise (she *could* be alive, though she now will be dead), but as an inherent and fixed state. Her death will not change anything about the way things are. The grass will be wet with rain and dewdrops and does not need the voluntaristic wetness of his tears.

It is because of the fixity and sadness of her muse that it makes no difference if he remembers her or not. Those lines, at the end of the first stanza, may seem bitter, but part of the point of the poem is that they are not. The difference between remembering and forgetting cannot be a difference for her, neither when she is dead (since presumably she will now know), nor even now in advance, since it will make no difference even now whether he mourns her or not.

It turns out that it is not the fact that she will, like the speaker in JOHN KEATS's "ODE TO A NIGHTINGALE," be simply a clod of earth that will make her indifferent to her addressee's mourning. She will not hear the nightingale (l. 11), she will not perceive anything, but she will dream through the twilight, although whether dreaming here means consciousness or unconsciousness is perfectly ambiguous. (Rossetti, like Keats, is thinking of the Duke's exchanges with Claudio about the nature of death in Shakespeare's *Measure for Measure,* act 3, scene 1). Unlike him, who can make memory or forgetting an act of will (though there is a slight ambiguity there, with *wilt* in lines 7–8 verging on turning into an indicative future tense), she will remember or forget by chance. Love and sadness are not for her acts of will but experiences of spirit, and it is that experience that this poem, and almost all of her great poems, captures.

"SONG OF THE SHIRT, THE" THOMAS HOOD (1843) Although first published anonymously in the Christmas issue of *Punch* in 1843, "The Song of the Shirt" might have seemed a title suggesting THOMAS HOOD's trademark humor. *Punch* was just over two years old at the time, and it was still in its radical phase (it would become the more genial forerunner to the *New Yorker* a few years later), and in fact Hood's humor was always Dickensian (although he anticipated Charles Dickens). Like Dickens, he could use it to disarm resistance to his scathing social critique, of which this poem is a central and effective example.

The polemicist Douglas Jerrold, perhaps *Punch*'s most important writer at the time, reported the event that led to "The Song of the Shirt," the widely discussed case of a desperately poor widowed mother arrested for pawning some of her master's (or boss's) goods, for which bail was set at two pounds. It came out that her weekly wage was seven shillings, an amount her master thought provided a good living. This would be very roughly equivalent in U.S. terms in 2005 to $40–50 a week, with a week (as the poem makes clear) consisting of considerably more than 40 hours. Even at a time of extremely low wages, the discovery that people were living in the kind of squalor this testimony implied was shocking to many, and Hood's poem responded to and helped amplify that shock.

This is one reason that "The Song of the Shirt" is widely considered one of Hood's most important poems (although the German socialist Friedrich Engels had some contempt for it as overly sentimental). It had the Dickensian effect of being a goad to the reformation and improvement of the treatment of the poor in England. It did so partly because of the way it humanized the poor—Dickens's stock-in-trade as well—by giving voice to their perspective and experience. This was a mode Hood learned from the early romantics, especially WILLIAM WORDSWORTH, who would similarly give a voice to the rural laborers and rural poor of the Lake District. Hood (who was an outlier in the Wordsworth circle when he became a deputy editor of *London Magazine*) gave voice to the urban poor instead, and in doing so he made his readers aware of those they saw every day.

"The Song of the Shirt" is in Hood's characteristically strong meter, here highly appropriate to the rhythmic motion and complaint of the seamstress. The framing stanzas, first and last, abstract that rhythm as "stitch! stitch! stitch!" whereas the singing woman beats it out as "Work—work—work!" The difference is that the framing stanzas attend not only to what she says but to what she does: Her work is stitching, and even if she were not complaining, the endless repetitive stitching would still be a fact. The first and last stanzas are almost identical, another mode of repetition, and in both stanzas, the worst irony is perhaps that the woman plying her needle and thread in order to clothe the rich is herself a woman sitting in unwomanly rags. These rags concentrate the force of the powerful psychological images in the poem and metaphors in the poem: that her stitching is so incessant as to invade her dreams; that it is so exhausting that she is metaphorically stitching her shroud; and that this metaphor holds no fears for her because death cannot be worse than this life.

The last stanza adds one extra line, the poem's hope that "The Song of the Shirt" could "reach the rich" who have no idea at what human cost their clothing is made. (This is, of course, still an issue today.) The word *rich* is brilliantly rhymed with *stitch* so that the appeal the poem made to the readers of *Punch* must have struck them with particular force. In "The Song of the Shirt," the tone does begin to reach the rich, and in Hood's time, some of them, at least, began to do something about it.

BIBLIOGRAPHY

Hood, Thomas. *Memorials of Thomas Hood: Collected, Arranged, and Edited by His Daughter, with a Preface and Notes by His Son. Illustrated with Copies From His Own Sketches.* London: E. Moxon, 1860.

———. *Poetical Works of Thomas Hood, with a Critical Memoir by William Michael Rossetti.* New York: G. Routledge, 1874.

"SONG OF THE STYGIAN NAIADES"

THOMAS LOVELL BEDDOES (1851) Harold Bloom calls this poem, written about 1835, "exquisite and menacing," a phrase that might apply to most of Beddoes's strange and haunting lyrics. This one is probably harder to analyze than most, but it is worth the effort since it is a perfect example of what Beddoes does best, which is to produce a background song to the eerie fatality of his visions.

The Stygian Naiades are the river nymphs or spirits native to the river Styx, in Beddoes's astonishing conceit. Styx is one of the four great rivers of Hell, and the worst one of all since to pass over the Styx is to be confined to the underworld forever. The idea of *that* river presided over by Naiades is wholly original to Beddoes. (Somewhere in the back of his mind, probably, was the "fierce Naiad" in PERCY BYSSHE SHELLEY's "ODE TO THE WEST WIND.")

The poem is framed by an anonymous question of which only the answer is important, but the form of the question means that the describer is part of the world of beings hypnotically external to each other. This is a mode that ALFRED, LORD TENNYSON, who admired Beddoes intensely, shared with him and might have learned from him. In the poem, the Naiades sing to one another of the doings in Hell, where Pluto and Proserpine are king and queen. These doings, in Beddoes's IMAGINATION, parallel those of Jupiter and Juno (Zeus and Hera) in the upper world, which is to say that the king of the gods of the dead wishes to philander, while his queen wishes to stop him. We learn that Proserpine plucks flowers in Hades, much as she did in the story of her abduction, told by the Roman poet Ovid and related by the 16th-century poet Edmund Spenser and most beautifully by John Milton in *Paradise Lost* (1667). In Hades she plucks flowers as a sign of anger and grief; like Ophelia in William Shakespeare's *Hamlet,* she plucks the flowers appropriate to her emotions, "wet with tears, Red with anger, pale with fears" (ll. 2–3). What she is sad, angry, and fearful about is the fact that her husband returns from earth every night with a new beautiful maiden—that is, every night, such a maiden dies, but we are seeing this from the point of view of those in Hell watching Pluto bring her there. He does so for the same reason that he abducted Proserpine herself, which is erotic desire.

Pluto, too, is subject to the rule of love, the fly of Beelzebub (lord of the flies), whom mortals call "Cupid, Love, and Fie for shame" (l. 18), depending on their morality and on the situation. Beelzebub is more an attributive name than a figure in the poem; he is not Pluto but is, rather (we might say), the proper name for what we sometimes call Cupid, but which is an abstraction, namely, Love. Beelzebub, too, is an abstraction, and we might say that he represents the relationship between love and death, or the way that love leads in the end to love of death.

The second stanza makes this clearer. Here the phrase "A great fly of Beelzebub's" (l. 34) is a direct object of the verb *fix,* whereas in the first stanza it is the subject of that verb. That is, in the first stanza, the fly fixes among the Stygian reeds; in the second, it is fixed there by the poet's thought. The poet's thought would shame Pluto himself, because it sees through him, and sees that he, too, is prey to love—the love of death of which poetry alone can think (for Beddoes) and of which Pluto is not lord and master but only a representation.

BIBLIOGRAPHY

Bradshaw, Michael. *Resurrection Songs: The Poetry of Thomas Lovell Beddoes.* Burlington, Vt.: Ashgate, 2001.

Wolfson, Susan J., and Peter J. Manning. *Selected Poems of Thomas Hood, Winthrop Mackworth Praed and Thomas Lovell Beddoes.* London: Penguin, 2000.

"SONG OF WANDERING AENGUS, THE" WILLIAM BUTLER YEATS (1899)

"The Song of Wandering Aengus" is from WILLIAM BUTLER YEATS's 1899 volume *The Wind among the Reeds.* Like much of Yeats's 19th-century poetry, it is at once a beautiful evocation of an otherworldly strangeness and a brief for the poetry that evokes that strangeness. That is because the strangeness itself is that of poetry, and the world poetry evokes is itself a poetic world.

The last lines of "The Song of Wandering Aengus" have become famous because they provide the epigraph and title (in their last five words) to Ray Bradbury's classic science fiction collection *The Golden Apples of the Sun* (1953):

> And pluck till time and times are done,
> The silver apples of the moon,
> The golden apples of the sun.

"The golden apples of the sun" refer in Yeats to the classical story of the garden of the Hesperides, whence it was one of the labors of Hercules to steal the apples of the sun. ALFRED, LORD TENNYSON had also written about the Hesperides, and evokes something of the same atmosphere in his poem of that name. Like Tennyson, Yeats was less interested in the classical story than in the patina of myth, legend, and strangeness of the idea. In "The Song of Wandering Aengus," Yeats invents a story about an Irish god—or in this case a demigod since he seems to be a prey to the longings of a mortal being.

The story is a simple one of metamorphosis: Aengus tells his story, in which a fish that he catches turns into a beautiful woman who then disappears, rather like JOHN KEATS's "LA BELLE DAME SANS MERCI." Aengus tells how he continues to wander in search of her (hence the title), and the song that he sings is the song of his vocation, which is the search and the song of the search.

It is central to the poem to see that it finds what it seeks, since what it seeks is not the "glimmering girl" but the search itself, the *glimmering* more than the *girl.* We know this because the reason Aengus has gone into the woods is that "a fire was in my head" (l. 2). He is ardent before he catches the fish that turns into the object of desire. She is the creation of his desire, rather than its cause. His journey to the hazel wood has the same goal as WILLIAM WORDSWORTH's in "NUTTING" (where Wordsworth, too, pulls down hazel branches)—a sense of unappeasable longing that in ROMANTICISM is always figured as a longing for an irreducible otherness, an unpossessable proximity, sometimes called nature, sometimes an erotic partner, sometimes the past, sometimes immortality (as in Wordsworth's great INTIMATIONS ODE). This ardency is why the second stanza recurs to the flame with which the poem opens:

> When I had laid it on the floor
> I went to blow the fire a-flame,
> But something rustled on the floor,
> And someone called me by my name:
> It had become a glimmering girl
> With apple blossom in her hair
> Who called me by my name and ran
> And faded through the brightening air.

He went to blow *the* fire a-flame, and the only fire he has referred to is the fire in his head. All this, it should be noted, takes place at night; it was still dark, and the moths and stars were still out, when he caught the silver fish, and it is because it is night that she is glimmering. She glimmers in the night and like the night, because like La Belle Dame, she is a figure of night. (This effect can also be seen in WILLIAM BLAKE's strange, great poem "The Mental Traveller.") She is a figure of night, and she disappears in the day, as she fades through the brightening air (recollecting the "shape all light" in PERCY BYSSHE SHELLEY's *The TRIUMPH OF LIFE,* a poem Yeats may have known by heart).

Yeats, following Shelley, likes images where it is not clear which is cause and which is effect: Is the air brightening because she is running through it? Or is she fading because the air is brightening? We may suspect, in the end, that it is the latter (since the stars are already flickering out when he goes out to fish), but Aengus will not permit us to say so. He wants to blur the distinction between the two, which is why the poem ends as it does. The apples of the moon and sun, the moon and sun themselves, are metaphors for the woman as well as contexts for her. The moon presides over the nighttime, and its silver is the silver of the "silver trout" that turns into the girl. The apples, of both sun and moon, are the fruition of the "apple blossom in her hair."

When Aengus imagines his timeless, eternal future with her, what he is imagining is sharing a relationship *with* her that is like his relationship *to* her. He can be with her without losing the sense of mystery that is her reason for being (or his reason for summoning her out of the night)—the "heart mysteries" that Yeats will later name as the things that drove his poetry in "The Circus Animals' Desertion." That mystery is absorbed by the world at large, the "long dappled grass" (l. 21) and the endlessness of "time and times" (l. 22). This creation of a mysterious world, or success in making a legendary and timeless Irish landscape absorb the burden of the poetic mystery, was Yeats's unceasing goal in his 19th-century poetry, and "The Song of Wandering Aengus" may be its most complete expression.

BIBLIOGRAPHY

Anscombe, G. E. M. *Intention.* Cambridge, Mass.: Harvard University Press, 2000.

Bloom, Harold. *Yeats.* New York: Oxford University Press, 1970.

Grossman, Allen R. *Poetic Knowledge in the Early Yeats: A Study of The Wind among the Reeds.* Charlottesville: University Press of Virginia, 1969.

Rosenthal, M. L., ed. Introduction to *Selected Poems and Three Plays of William Butler Yeats,* xix–xliv. New York: Scribner, 1996.

Vendler, Helen. *Poets Thinking: Pope, Whitman, Dickinson, Yeats.* Cambridge, Mass.: Harvard University Press, 2004.

———. *Yeats's Vision and the Later Plays.* Cambridge, Mass.: Harvard University Press, 1963.

SONGS OF INNOCENCE AND OF EXPERIENCE WILLIAM BLAKE (1789, 1794)

Songs of Innocence and of Experience contain WILLIAM BLAKE's best-known and most widely read works, including what is perhaps his most famous poem, "The TYGER." The book, beautifully and delicately illustrated by Blake, has been vastly influential, determining, for example, the opening poems in WILLIAM BUTLER YEATS's book *The Rose* (1893), which contrasts "The Song of the Happy Shepherd" with "The SAD SHEPHERD:" (The second Song of Innocence is called "The Shepherd.") The contrast, and the very idea of the song, harkens back to Blake.

The title itself has had an enormous effect on ways of thinking about poetry. *Songs of Innocence*—the title of the first part, which appeared by itself in 1789—might seem a fairly innocuous title, like the famous *Songs and Sonnets* which begin the full title of *Tottel's Miscellany* (1557; Shakespeare has Falstaff refer to it that way). But the idea of *Songs of Experience* (added to the *Songs of Innocence* in a new volume in 1794) was peculiarly modern; it led eventually to such titles as Bertolt Brecht's "Ballad of ill-gotten gains" in *The Threepenny Opera* (1928), but it is more radical still because of the difficulty of understanding the idea that there should be such things as songs of experience. The idea of the songs is something like the idea of innocence. Experience does not sing (although sorrow might), since the idea of experience might be that it no longer believes in song.

But for Blake there is more than irony in the title. That all things should be in some sense poetic—should long for poetic expression, long to sing—is one of his central tenets. The songs of experience also indicate the possibility that in experience there is still some fundamentally saving innocence that may not recognize itself but is still there, still attracted toward the love and life which for Blake constituted holiness. Conversely, the idea of *Songs of Experience* might mean that songs themselves are not the sure symptom and symbol and expression of incorruptibility we might wish them to be, so that the songs of innocence do not protect or immunize their singers from corruption as we would wish them to do.

Another way to put this point is to say that the *Songs of Innocence,* even when they appeared alone, are far from being expressions of naïveté, later corrected by an older Blake with the *Songs of Experience.* The very idea of songs of innocence is an idea that comes from a no-longer-innocent perspective. This is clear throughout the *Songs of Innocence,* for example in "The NURSE'S SONG" and "The Little Black Boy." As these poems indicate, the truly innocent do not recognize their innocence because, by the very nature of that innocence, they have had no experience to the contrary. But the title alone of the volume is enough to make the point. *Songs of Innocence* as a title means, in one respect, "songs of those still innocent," though innocence will never last long. To recognize innocence, as the title and entitler does, is to recognize that it is fleeting.

This can be seen in the introductory poem. Some of the poems in "Innocence" and "Experience" form obvious diptyches, and we consider other paired poems in the two parts of the book elsewhere (see the pairings of the two versions of "The Nurse's Song," "The CHIMNEY-SWEEPER," "The LAMB" and "The Tyger"). Here we will take the inaugural poems as exemplary. *Songs of Innocence* opens with this subtle introductory verse:

> Piping down the valleys wild,
> Piping songs of pleasant glee,
> On a cloud I saw a child,
> And he laughing said to me:
>
> "Pipe a song about a Lamb!"
> So I piped with a merry chear.
> "Piper, pipe that song again;"
> So I piped: he wept to hear.
>
> "Drop thy pipe, thy happy pipe;
> Sing thy songs of happy chear:"
> So I sung the same again,
> While he wept with joy to hear.
>
> "Piper, sit thee down and write
> In a book, that all may read."
> So he vanish'd from my sight,
> And I pluck'd a hollow reed,
>
> And I made a rural pen,
> And I stain'd the water clear,
> And I wrote my happy songs,
> Every child may joy to hear.

The speaker meets the laughing angelic child, and both the songs he pipes—"songs of pleasant glee"—and the child's response seem to speak for purity and innocence. The child wants to hear more from the piper and then *weeps* to hear the song. Why does he weep? The piper believes that it is "with joy," but even if it is, the joy seems to be the joy of relief or return to innocence from a more experienced, bleaker perspective, not the simple, innocent joy that one would expect a child in the *Songs of Innocence* to exemplify.

The child asks the piper to write the songs down, and then he vanishes. Why? Partly perhaps because he grows up; at any rate, he cannot sustain the presence of eternal innocence. He asks the piper to write the songs down in order to record what otherwise would not last: childhood glee is ephemeral. Writing the songs down requires something other than the innocent piping that the speaker delights in. It requires the *hollow* reed and, as well, that the clear water be stained. Every child may *hear* these songs read aloud—the children cannot read, but the piper can, and so, too, can those the child considers: "sit thee down and write / In a book, that all may read . . ." Those who read will therefore read aloud to those who can only hear but will rejoice to hear these songs. But their hearing, like the piper's writing, is mediated by the less-innocent position of the writers and performers of the song. Those who can read or write are no longer innocent, since the innocent children *hear* the songs, rather than reading them. And the angelic child who vanishes is the most knowledgeable of all: What he knows is that a child's form is no guarantor of protection from experience. The weeping child shows both the value and the fragility of innocence.

This introductory song has a pendant, or counterweight, in the introductory song to the *Songs of Experience.* There the singer is not the piper but the "bard / Who present, past, & future sees." He has seen God walking in the Garden of Eden after the Fall of humanity, and therefore the *Songs of Experience* begin with an account of the end of innocence with the eating of the fruit of the tree of knowledge. The bard is the one who calls upon the fallen earth to return to what she was before she fell. That return is not a return to ignorance but to hope and assurance of life, rather than the perpetual fear she now lives under. The beautiful last stanza assimilates experience (represented as nighttime) to the possibilities of a transcendent innocence that understands, accepts, and transmutes sin, sorrow, and experience itself:

> "Turn away no more;
> Why wilt thou turn away?
> The starry floor,
> The wat'ry shore,
> Is giv'n thee till the break of day.'

The simplest way to read this, and one consonant with those interpretations of Blake that see the "starry floor" and "wat'ry shore" as cause for regret and as symbols of psychic and spiritual oppression, is to take them instead as beautiful forerunners of the day that is coming. It is night, perhaps, but at night the stars and waters are a token of the coming of the morning.

"Earth's Answer" (to this appeal) in the next poem in the *Songs of Experience* shows the grim reading of the starry floor as a place of "starry jealousy," and the "wat'ry shore" as a prison. But even that idea of them can be read in the more properly Blakean style: that even jealousy and prison can be transmogrified in the imagination into something beautiful, starlike and shorelike. Earth's answer shows the extent to which the soul is oppressed by experience. But the very fact that she must make an answer—that the introduction to the *Songs of Experience* by itself does not offset the introduction to the *Songs of Innocence*—shows both the deeper, more ubiquitous nature of experience and the fact that the negativity of experience is in some sense false and contrived, preserved by the earth's insistent fearfulness rather than overcome through the spirit of hope.

See also "LONDON"; "ANGEL, The."

BIBLIOGRAPHY

Bloom, Harold. *Blake's Apocalypse: A Study in Poetic Argument.* Ithaca, N.Y.: Cornell University Press, 1970.

———. *Poetry and Repression: Revisionism from Blake to Stevens.* New Haven, Conn.: Yale University Press, 1976.

Damrosch, Leopold. *Symbol and Truth in Blake's Myth.* Princeton, N.J.: Princeton University Press, 1980.

Erdmann, David V. *Blake, Prophet against Empire: A Poet's Interpretation of the History of His Own Times.* Princeton, N.J.: Princeton University Press, 1977.

Fry, Northrop. *Fearful Symmetry: A Study of William Blake.* Princeton, N.J.: Princeton University Press, 1974.

Gilchrist, Alexander. *Life of William Blake, with Selections from His Poems and Other Writings.* Totowa, N.J.: Rowman and Littlefield, 1973.

Ostriker, Alicia. "Desire Gratified and Ungratified: William Blake and Sexuality." *Blake: An Illustrated Quarterly* 16 (1982–83): 156–165.

Raine, Kathleen. *Blake and Antiquity.* Princeton, N.J.: Princeton University Press, 1977.

Thompson, E. P. *Witness against the Beast: William Blake and The Moral Law.* New York: Cambridge University Press, 1993.

"SONG: WOO'D AND MARRIED AND A'"

JOANNA BAILLIE (1822) While publishing her highly popular and much admired plays from 1798 onward, JOANNA BAILLIE was also writing poetry, which she eventually published (in 1840) in an expanded version of her 1790 volume *Fugitive Verses.* "Woo'd and Married and A'" is subtitled "Version taken from an old song of that name." The song, sometimes also called "The Runaway Bride," describes more or less the same situation as Baillie's version: A young girl is to be married but is too "proud and saucy" to tolerate the poverty of both her wedding and her married life, and she complains of her fate. She is rebuked by her mother, father, brother, and sister, and implored by her husband to try to be happy with the absurdly little that they will have.

Baillie's version is both more accessible to the English (rather than Scots) reader, and it is wittier. Like her friend Sir WALTER SCOTT (see, for example "PROUD MASIE,") she wants to give a literate audience a sense of the feel of the Scots ballads, with their spirited and exuberant rhythms. Where the original simply repeats the rebuking chorus—"An was nae she very weel aff, / That was woo'd and married and a'?"—Baillie rings changes on it, giving the original at the end of her first stanza and then putting versions of it into the mouths of the bride's interlocutors. These changes turn the song from a jig (which it was originally) into a kind of balladic narrative. The bride comes out looking beautiful but feeling resentful because she is to be married in borrowed finery. Her mother rebukes her, with some wisdom but some silliness as well: She says that her daughter will be happier to earn her clothing than to get it as a gift, but also that she is lucky "to be woo'd and married at a!" (l. 24).

Her father is more tender, and sadder to lose her. For him she is still a girl, and he feels displaced by her husband, who will have to be "half daddy" to her since she is so young. Her pride is evidence of her youth and therefore something he loves about her, and while he celebrates her marriage, he also weeps to lose her: "I'm baith like to laugh and to greet, / When I think o' her married at a'!" (ll. 35–36; *greet* means to cry).

The third variation is her husband's, who shows his wiliness through his more or less sincere flattery. We are already disposed to like him because her father does; the father recognizes that he is marrying for love, and Johnny confirms it. She is wealth enough for him—she is herself a dowry. He therefore hopes that she does not "grieve to be married at a'" (l. 48).

The last stanza seems to foretell a happy ending as she looks at him and blushes and smiles. But suddenly she takes off like a cat or a hare, Johnny presumably in pursuit, and "thinks herself very weel aff, / To be woo'd and married at a'!" (ll. 59–60), which is either bitter or happy, since she knows that he will follow her. The tone of the poem is ultimately so full of the pleasure of its own language that we like her for the same reason that Johnny likes her and that she likes herself, and that she is glad that he will chase her. He will be a good man, like her father, whereas she will not become stern and censorious like her mother, and so the poem ends happily.

BIBLIOGRAPHY

"Woo'd And Married And A'" (original song). Available online. URL: http://cityofoaks.home.netcom.com/tunes/WoodAndMarriedAndA.html. Accessed July 2, 2008.

Baillie, Joanna. *Dramatic and Poetical Works of Joanna Baillie.* London: Longman, Brown, Green, and Longmans, 1851.

Forbes, A. "'Sympathetic Curiosity' in Joanna Baillie's Theater of the Passions." *European Romantic Review* 14, no. 1 (January 2003): 31–48.

SONNETS FROM THE PORTUGUESE

ELIZABETH BARRETT BROWNING (1850) ELIZABETH BARRETT BROWNING wrote this wildly popular sonnet sequence, most famous for its penultimate sonnet—"How do I love thee? Let me count the ways" (sonnet 43)—during ROBERT BROWNING's courtship of her in 1845 and 1846. She only showed him the poems in 1849, three years after their marriage and elopement, and published them, at his insistence, in her 1850 collection of *Poems.* The title is often mistaken as suggesting that the poems are translations of some Portuguese collection of sonnets (like their friend EDWARD FITZGERALD's *The RUBÁIYÁT OF OMAR KHAYYÁM,* from the Persian). Although the title is intentionally misleading, the mistake it fosters has an element of truth in it. Robert loved Elizabeth's 1844 poem "Catarina to Camoens," which is a fictional farewell, spoken when she is dying, by the real lady Catherina de Athaide to the great Portuguese poet Luis Vaz de Camoens (1524–80), who had made her the lady of some of his love poems. Their relationship was broken up, and she died in 1556. Robert's admiration for the poem made Elizabeth frame herself as Catarina (who also sang), filled with admiration and love for the Camoens of her day, Robert. She would therefore be the Portuguese, the woman writing these sonnets for the poet she loved and admired, and who loved and admired her in turn. (As in her poem, in which she follows a story whereby Catarina gives a ribbon from her hair to Camoens, Elizabeth describes giving a lock of her own hair to Robert in sonnet 18.) The obscurity of the title helps to maintain some deniability that the sonnets describe her relationship to Robert, but that is just what they do describe.

The sonnets are striking, then, as a kind of poetic autobiography of Elizabeth's feeling for Robert in his insistent and passionate courtship. She had been an invalid for years, and unexpectedly she had found passionate love. What is striking about the sonnets is the difference in attitude they take from most sonnet sequences. The standard sequence, from the 14th-century poet Petrarch in Italian and from the 16th-century poets Sir Thomas Wyatt and Sir Philip Sidney in English (and William Shakespeare preeminently) is one of complaint that the beloved does nor reciprocate the sonneteer's love. This is often couched in terms of a kind of astonishment: Given how much I love you, why don't you love me back? But *Sonnets from the Portuguese* displays an opposite attitude: astonishment that someone like Robert Browning *does* love her. They register the surprise—the constantly defeated skepticism—that he should love her, and that she should be able to count on his love.

The sonnets also tell, but more incidentally, of the domestic happiness Elizabeth had to give up in order to elope with Robert. She had love at home, and her evocations of this love are moving, particularly her comfort in "Home-talk and blessing and the common kiss / That comes to each in turn" (sonnet 35, ll. 3–4). Of course, her home life was not what it had been two decades earlier: Her mother died when Elizabeth was 22, definitively ending the pleasures of childhood that had pretty much ceased for her at 14 when she was struck by the debilitating illness that would make her an invalid before Robert met her.

But meet her he did, and he struck her as both a great poet and abundant recompense for all that her elopement with him made her give up. Sonnets 33 and 34 provide a particularly striking account of this unlooked-for happiness after she had lost an older contentment in the world. He calls her by the same pet name she "used to run at, when a child" (33, l. 2) to take joy in the company of whatever beloved person called her—primarily her mother. Now those beloved persons are dead (33, l. 7). When he calls her, she first imagines that she has resuscitated a way of feeling love that she lost in early childhood. If he calls her by the same name, she will answer "With the same heart" (33, l. 14). But in the next sonnet, she sees that this is not so. When she was young, she left play to see someone she loved, and both activities were pleasurable and life-enhancing. Now, when she is called (by him), she is interrupted in the grave thoughts that the death of all those other loved ones have evoked in her. But the result of this is that he is not, like his earlier avatars, one loved thing among others but everything to her, not "a single good, but all my good" (34, l. 12). Her love of him is the concentration and essence of all love she has felt before.

The Shakespearean background to these sonnets is not to be found in Shakespeare's sonnets but in *Antony and Cleopatra,* which Elizabeth echoes in her sonnet 26. Robert is unimaginably more wonderful than she could ever have fantasized, which is just what Cleopatra tells Dolabella about Antony. She is wonderstruck by the love she could never have hoped for: "God's gifts put man's best dreams to shame" (l. 14).

The most famous of these sonnets, as has been noted, is the penultimate one, number 43. Throughout the sequence, Elizabeth recognizes, with some uneasiness, that she loves Robert more than she loves God. This is the burden of the second sonnet already, where she declares that their love is stronger than any contrary obstacle God might erect to it, even death. The somewhat excessive claim of that second sonnet is beautifully tempered in the second to last. She loves him as far as her "soul can reach, when feeling out of sight / For the ends of Being and ideal Grace" (ll. 2–3). Her love is a human love, and she loves him when she is fully human, not when her soul seems on the verge of transcending the human. It is the humanity of this love that is so moving here and at the end allows her the prayer to God, or at least the hope that he will allow their love to survive even their deaths.

One of the technical achievements of *Sonnets from the Portuguese* is its use of enjambment. Browning writes sentences far longer than most sonnets tolerate. Her rhymes come in the middle of sentences that go on and on. The effect is one of great urbanity chastened by the sadness and love that she has been brought to feel. (It should be noted how different her tonality is from Robert's.) We could call the style one of chastened enjambment and recognize in it a formal counterpart to her hope that even death will be an enjambment in the progress of their love, and not an end-stop. Certainly it is the sense of conversation, of saying what needs to be said, unhurriedly and seriously, that the enjambment helps us to feel, and to feel as well the depth of their love for each other and the hopes that they have for its endurance.

BIBLIOGRAPHY

Armstrong, Isobel. *Victorian Poetry: Poetry, Poetics and Politics.* New York: Routledge, 1993.

Bloom, Harold. *A Map of Misreading.* New York: Oxford University Press, 2003.

Bristow, Joseph, ed. *Victorian Women Poets: Emily Bronte, Elizabeth Barrett Browning, Christina Rossetti.* Houndsville, Basingstoke, England: Macmillan Press, 1995.

DeVane, William C. *A Browning Handbook.* New York: Appleton-Century-Crofts, 1955.

Donaldson, Sandra, ed. *Critical Essays on Elizabeth Barrett Browning.* New York: G. K. Hall, 1999.

Mason, Emma. *Women Poets of the Nineteenth Century.* Tavistock, Devon, England: Northcote House Publishers, 2006.

SOUTHEY, ROBERT (1774–1843) Robert Southey is remembered today mainly as a kind of butt, or straight man, in the poetry of LORD BYRON and in anecdotes involving the far greater romantic poets Byron, SAMUEL TAYLOR COLERIDGE, and PERCY BYSSHE SHELLEY. He is remembered—but not by name—by any child who hears or tells the story of "Goldilocks and the Three Bears," which Southey essentially wrote in its present form (except that the Goldilocks character is an old woman in his original version); and he is remembered as well by anyone who has read or heard LEWIS CARROLL's parody "You are old, father William," which lampoons Southey's pious original.

Southey was not always thus. He was widely celebrated in his own time, becoming poet laureate in 1813. His youth was ardently revolutionary: He was expelled from Westminister School for his radical views on education (he was against flogging), and he was a staunch supporter of the French Revolution, that touchstone of 1790s radicalism. In 1793 he wrote a tragedy sympathetic to Wat Tyler, the leader of the Peasant's Revolt in the 14th century, as well as an epic on Joan of Arc, French challenger of English authority and the aristocratic elites who wielded it. Southey and Coleridge planned to set up a utopian proto-communist society, which they called a pantisocracy, on the banks of the Susquehanna River in Pennsylvania. Southey met Coleridge June 1794, when Coleridge (who had gone to Cambridge University) visited Oxford; Coleridge immediately fell under Southey's powerful intellectual influence, and due at least in part to that influence, he married Sara Fricker (in October 1795), the younger sister of Southey's wife-to-be, Edith (they were married a month later).

After the stillborn death of the schemes for pantisocracy, Coleridge and Southey became somewhat estranged. Southey's somewhat envious bad review of *Lyrical Ballads* (1798), which Coleridge wrote with WILLIAM WORDSWORTH, did not help matters, but when Southey's first daughter died in infancy in 1802, Coleridge urged him to move to Keswick in the Lake District. There Southey lived for the rest of his life as one of the LAKE POETS. When Coleridge went to Malta to attempt to recuperate from his addiction to opium (the maguffin, more or less, of Wordsworth's *The PRELUDE*), Southey had Coleridge's wife (his own sister-in-law) and children in his care at Keswick, at a time when he had very little money. In Keswick, as well, he came to know Wordsworth and Sir WALTER SCOTT, who in 1813 would decline the poet laureateship and engineer its grant to Southey. Scott also arranged for Southey to become a reviewer for the *Quarterly Review,* the Tory answer to the more radical *Edinburgh Review* under the direction of Francis Jeffrey, who had trashed Southey's earlier poetry.

In the prefatory verses to *DON JUAN,* Byron called Southey an "epic renegade," and there is justice in the indictment, since he did end up "a Tory at / Last," as Byron says, rhyming scornfully on the fact that Southey had become poet laureate. Southey maintained that his political convictions never changed throughout his life, and this may be so. He had spent several months in Portugal and had rebelled against what he saw as the intolerance of Catholicism, even as he loved the people he knew there. His later political stances—against NAPOLEON BONAPARTE as a corrupt inheritor of the French Revolution who invaded Portugal, and against emancipation for Ireland—led him to a defense of England and of orderly government in England.

In 1812 the 20-year-old Shelley visited Southey in Keswick. An enthusiast for Southey's more exotic epics, he intended to explore the various mythologies behind the world's great religions, in order to give a sense of evocative romantic background set in other cultures, religions, worlds, in the mode the 16th-century poet Edmund Spenser. Apparently the meeting was less than successful from Shelley's point of view, since it largely consisted of Southey reciting his own work to the youthful acolyte. Shelley's own early Spenserian epic, *The Revolt of Islam* (1817), owes much to Southey's influence, as does *Alastor* (1815), but the visit apparently was not much of a success, Southey being much more interested in himself than in Shelley. Later, he would round on Shelley's atheism and radical politics and help destroy Shelley's personal reputation in England, to the latter's great harm. (Southey had been scandalized by coming upon a visitor's inscription book in the Alps where Shelley had signed his name and, under destination, had written *L'Enfer*—hell—and he spread the scandal upon his return to London.)

Southey's self-righteous politics and his complacency, as well as the general inferiority of his poetry to that of his great contemporaries, make him into one of literature's also-rans. He suffered from Alzheimer's disease for the last years of his life, to the great sadness of his devoted friends and family. That sadness speaks to Southey's great personal qualities—his love for his children (and general proto-Dickensian defense of children from the harm done them by adults, whether teachers or industrialists) and his great generosity to his friends. Southey also wrote some important and influential historical work, like his biography of Lord Nelson, which was much more widely read and influential than any of his poetry. Despite some recent attempts to revive his reputation (most notably that of Oxford University's Marilyn Butler), Southey's position in literary history is that of the figure in ROMANTICISM who stood for everything that romanticism defined itself as against.

See also "BATTLE OF BLENHEIM, THE"; "CATARACT OF LODORE, THE"; "GOD'S JUDGMENT ON A WICKED BISHOP"; "MY DAYS AMONG THE DEAD."

BIBLIOGRAPHY

Bromwich, David. "Of the Mule Breed." *London Review of Books* (May 21, 1998). Available online. URL: www.lrb.co.uk/v20/n10/brom01_.html. Accessed March 16, 2009.

Butler, Marilyn. *Romantics, Rebels, and Reactionaries: English Literature and Its Background, 1760–1830.* New York: Oxford University Press, 1982.

De Quincey, Thomas. *Recollections of the Lakes and the Lake Poets.* Edited by David Wright. Harmondsworth, England: Penguin, 1970.

Hazlitt, William. *Spirit of the Age; or, Contemporary Portraits.* London: Oxford University Press, 1970.

Perry, Seamus. "Southey's Genius for Repression." *London Review of Books* (January 24, 2006). Available online by subscription. URL: www.lrb.co.uk. Accessed March 16, 2009.

Storey, Mark. *Robert Southey: A Life.* New York: Oxford University Press, 1997.

"SPLENDOUR FALLS, THE" ALFRED, LORD TENNYSON (1850) ALFRED, LORD TENNYSON's long narrative poem *The PRINCESS: A MEDLEY* contains a number of songs, and rather than providing a context for those songs, the poem provides a place for them to be readable out of context. Indeed, the Prince, the poem's hero, is haunted by phantoms and is therefore liable throughout to lose his sense of context and fall into communion with a world of shadows. Like Sir WALTER SCOTT, JOANNA BAILLIE, THOMAS LOVELL BEDDOES, ROBERT BROWNING, and GEORGE ELIOT, and like all those so interested in the epigraph (see MOTTOES), Tennyson has a sense of the power of a certain kind of intense lyric poetry as existing in its evocativeness.

For Tennyson, that evocativeness is like the evocativeness of the past or of love or of faith. The question is whether the thing evoked could ever live up to what it haunts us with in its absence. This was a pressing question for Tennyson, since he wanted to believe that he could have the kind of faith, love, or happiness whose loss in so intensely felt. The question goes to the heart of Tennyson's sense of vocation, since it makes all the difference whether the intensity of lyric is a metaphor for something more basic, say the moment of full and clear presence and restitution, or whether love, faith, and memory are themselves instead metaphors for poetry, for the evocativeness that belongs to lyric and which can never be matched by the thing for which it longs.

"The Splendour Falls" is one of the songs inserted in *The Princess*'s seven sections three years after its 1847 publication. It comes between the third and fourth sections, just before "TEARS, IDLE TEARS" (part of the original poem), and is close in feeling to that song, a kind of spatial version of the earlier poem's temporal longing. In 1848 Tennyson had gone to hear the astonishing echoes at a location called the "Eagle's Nest," near Killarney in Ireland. Someone blew a bugle, and he heard eight different echoes of it.

He treats those echoes here as the evocation of distance. The place is beautiful, suggestive of ancient legend, and wherever one is within it, it is its distances that matter. The wild echoes go flying, and the poem makes them self-describing as they "answer . . . dying, dying, dying" at the end of each stanza. The echoes are versions of Tennyson's aural obsession with rhyme and with repetition—of words, lines, and refrains.

The essence of the echo is to be formed by its own dying. Echoes are not the original sound but its evocation as it dies away. Echoes are the sound made by the dying of sound, and their relation to rhyme makes it possible to describe the evocativeness of the song as consisting in its own transience—that is, in the way it dies away. Tennyson said of "Tears, idle tears" that he sought to capture the sense of "abiding in the transient." The same is true here, and the question remains for him whether what is transient can be made to abide or whether the only place to abide, and only for a time, is in what is inevitably transient. "The Splendour Falls" hopes for the latter, in imagining echoes that will not "faint" but "roll from soul to soul / And grow for ever and for ever" (ll. 14–16). That would be a way of imagining how the transient abides, under the sign of a permanent love. But it might be that this is itself only another evocative wish, one which the "echoes answer, dying, dying, dying."

BIBLIOGRAPHY

Armstrong, Isobel. *Victorian Poetry: Poetry, Poetics and Politics.* New York: Routledge, 1993.

Bloom, Harold. *Poetry and Repression: Revisionism from Blake to Stevens.* New Haven, Conn.: Yale University Press, 1976.

Buckley, Jerome Hamilton. *Tennyson: The Growth of a Poet.* Boston: Houghton Mifflin, 1965.

Kilham, John. *Critical Essays on the Poetry of Tennyson.* New York: Barnes and Noble, 1960.

Kincaid, James R. *Tennyson's Major Poems: The Comic and Ironic Patterns.* New Haven, Conn.: Yale University Press, 1975.

Ricks, Christopher B. *Tennyson.* New York: Macmillan, 1972.

Rowlinson, Matthew. *Tennyson's Fixations: Psychoanalysis and the Topics of the Early Poetry.* Charlottesville: University Press of Virginia, 1994.

Tucker, Herbert. *Tennyson and the Doom of Romanticism.* Cambridge, Mass.: Harvard University Press, 1988.

"SPRING AND FALL" GERARD MANLEY HOPKINS (1880) This is one of GERARD MANLEY HOPKINS's most accessible poems, but its ending is often misread. It is addressed to Margaret, "a young child," as the subtitle indicates. Goldengrove would be a house and its grounds, and Margaret is a denizen, perhaps the daughter, of the house. It is fall (the poem is dated September 7), and Goldengrove is "unleaving"—losing its leaves. Hopkins makes us see these leaves as ubiquitous and beautiful, saturated with autumn's gold, through the name he gives the house, which suggests something considerably richer and mellower than the "yellow leaf" that Shakespeare's Macbeth complains "his way of life has fallen into," or the "yellow leaves, or none, or few" to which Shakespeare compares his own "time of year" and time of life in his sonnet 73. Shakespeare (as ever), and in particular sonnet 73, is in Hopkins's mind as he writes this poem, and the word *unleaving* is recalled from the disquieting pun at the end of Shakespeare's sonnet, when the young man "must leave ere long" the thing that he loves—that is, depart from the life that the unfolding and finally fallen leaves show to be entirely ephemeral.

Margaret is a child, which is to say that she, with her fresh thoughts, represents the springtime of life (as the title makes clear), but she can still care for the leaves. Their ephemerality makes them like "the things of man" (l. 3), and therefore Margaret's grief is over what humans lose and grieve for. The third line is complex in that it suggests that grief is human, even though it is also human to become indifferent to such grief. Margaret can *only* care for them because of her fresh thoughts, even though her fresh thoughts should make her indifferent to the falling leaves, which have nothing to do with her.

Hopkins laments, observing Margaret, what happens to humans as they grow older. They lose that sense of grief and mourning that Margaret has; they become cold and indifferent, and Hopkins forecasts such a future for her, too. He does not singularize it; rather, he talks about what happens to "the heart" (l. 5), even when the entire world decays. "Wanwood" (l. 8) means that even the wood of the trees from which the leaves are shed will fall, rot, and decay, piecemeal but also turned into meal and mulch. (For this idea of decay extending even to the substrate which holds the things that decay, see also George Herbert's "Church Monuments," where the gravestones that name the dust buried beneath them crumble into dust as well; the 17th-century poet-priest Herbert was a poet Hopkins probably knew by heart.)

We discover in line 9 that the utterance that this poem mimics is, in fact, more or less heard by Margaret: To his assurance—not the comforting one he in his middle age might think it is—that she will learn to cease weeping, she weeps all the harder. "You will weep and know why" is not a future but a present tense: "You insist on weeping, and on knowing why you weep." It is at this point that he shifts into a more serious discussion with her, by saying that reasons for weeping are human emotions. What all weeping comes from is human sorrow, and neither the mouth nor the mind need be able to describe it. Poetry, that is to say, may not be up to the expression of this sorrow's content.

But that does not matter: Margaret mourns for her own human condition, including the fact that she will indeed come to such sights when she is older. Margaret weeps because the falling of the leaves is a metaphor for the time when she will no longer weep about such things. Her weeping means not self-pity but a kind of abnegation from her own self. Although critics tend to read the last line as something of a rebuke to her, her mourning for herself is in fact the best part of her, the part that makes her deserve salvation.

Behind this poem is PERCY BYSSHE SHELLEY's "ODE TO THE WEST WIND," with its reversal of the sequence of fall and spring. Here, too, Margaret's spring, and sorrow's, are a response to the fall. She is young, but she is weeping for what will become of her when she is old, and so the freshness of her youth is not thoughtless but full of a deep, pensive, saving melancholy. This is because it is the *result* of her own knowledge of what will become of her later self, and as the result of this knowledge, we can say that morally it comes after what it laments will come later chronologically.

BIBLIOGRAPHY

Bridges, Robert. Preface to notes in *The Poems of Gerard Manley Hopkins.* Edited by W. H. Gardner, 94–101. New York: Oxford University Press, 1948.

Gardner, W. H. *Gerard Manley Hopkins (1844–1889): A Study of Poetic Idiosyncrasy in Relation to Poetic Tradition.* New Haven, Conn.: Yale University Press, 1949.

———, ed. Introduction to *Poems and Prose of Gerard Manley Hopkins.* Harmondsworth, Middlesex, England: Penguin, 1963.

Hartman, Geoffrey. *The Unmediated Vision: An Interpretation of Wordsworth, Hopkins, Rilke, and Valery.* New Haven, Conn.: Yale University Press, 1954.

Miller, J. Hillis. "Gerard Manley Hopkins." In *The Disappearance of God,* 270–359. Cambridge, Mass.: Belknap Press of Harvard University Press, 1963.

White, Norman. *Hopkins: A Literary Biography.* New York: Oxford University Press, 1992.

SPRUNG RHYTHM

SPRUNG RHYTHM This is GERARD MANLEY HOPKINS's term for his most characteristic and idiosyncratic poetic mode. Hopkins seemed to define it as organizing lines around stressed syllables. In sprung rhythm, the poetic foot always starts on a stressed syllable and may be one to four syllables long; other unstressed, or "slack," syllables may also cluster around the strongly stressed ones, but it is only stress that counts. The most important consequence of this theory for Hopkins's own poetry was his feel for a poetic foot that might be a single syllable long: No alternation of any sort is required between stressed and unstressed syllables, as would be required in what Hopkins called "running meter"—that is, the received iambic and sometimes trochaic meter of English poetry.

In Hopkins's poetry, the accumulation of stresses can produce moments of great intensity, as in the sonnet "The Windhover." There such lines as "Brute beauty & valour & act, oh, air, pride, plume, here / Buckle!" and "& blue-bleak embers, ah my dear, / Fall, gáll themsélves, & gásh góld-vermílion" pile up stresses without pausing for breath. The accent marks in the last line show Hopkins making sure that the stresses are not neglected, and they tend to match up as well with assonance and alliteration: *Brute beauty; pride, plume; blue-bleak; Fall, gáll; gash gold.* To write in sprung rhythm is to hunt for stresses and therefore to tend to go to Anglo-Saxon one-syllabled nouns and adjectives; thus, one becomes a kind of poetic cataloger of the intense and bristling variety of the world (which is one of the affinities between Hopkins and the American poet Walt Whitman, whom he admired).

Hopkins, one of the central theorists of prosody in English literary history, confirmed the percussive nature of this meter in a letter of 1879, when he wrote: "[T]he word Sprung which I use for this rhythm means something like abrupt and applies by rights only where one stress follows another running, without syllable between." Later, he wrote of some kinds of poetry in which "the stresses come together and so the rhythm is sprung." Hopkins invented the name, in an 1877 letter to ROBERT BRIDGES, his friend, fellow poet, critic, and editor, using it to describe the meter of "The WRECK OF THE DEUTSCHLAND": "I do not of course claim to have invented sprung rhythms but only sprung rhythm; I mean that single lines and instances of it are not uncommon in English. . . . The choruses in Samson Agonistes are intermediate between counterpointed and sprung rhythm. In reality they are sprung."

Hopkins was more modest in a preface he wrote for possible publication of his poems six years later, where he again defined the sprung form as a rhythm based on stresses but claimed that he had rediscovered the rhythm of classical and early English poetry, in particular the medieval poem *Piers Plowman,* probably by William Langland. SAMUEL TAYLOR COLERIDGE, who did not know that he was reinventing the prosody of Old English, also wrote a stress-based meter in *CHRISTABEL* (under the influence of the ballad meter of Thomas Percy's *Reliques of Ancient English Poetry* [1765]). But Hopkins was more radical still (if not quite so great a poet) in allowing for one syllable feet and in also making, as he often did, a series of stresses into one stress by the way he crammed them together.

In the 1877 letter to Bridges, Hopkins asked, "Why do I employ sprung rhythm at all? Because it is the nearest to the rhythm of prose, the least forced, the most rhetorical and emphatic of all possible rhythms." But to say that it is close to prose is not to say that it is close to speech, which Hopkins also liked to claim. Rather, it shares with considered rhetoric a sense that rhythm should sustain pressure rather than dissipate it, as it does in what Hopkins called "running meter."

Hopkins did not write only in sprung rhythm and, in fact, noted that the kind of counterpoint between expectation and actualization that is characteristic of much of the most mellifluous English poetry is impossible in sprung rhythm. It is nevertheless his most memorable mode, and no one succeeded better than he. WILLIAM BUTLER YEATS, later in life, experimented with it, and in our own day, it can be seen in poets such as Paul Muldoon. But Hopkins is unexcelled in its use.

BIBLIOGRAPHY

Bridges, Robert. Preface to Notes in *The Poems of Gerard Manley Hopkins,* edited by W. H. Gardner, 94–101. New York: Oxford University Press, 1948.

Gardner, W. H. *Gerard Manley Hopkins (1844–1889): A Study of Poetic Idiosyncrasy in Relation to Poetic Tradition.* New Haven, Conn.: Yale University Press, 1949.

———, ed. Introduction to *Poems and Prose of Gerard Manley Hopkins.* Harmondsworth, Middlesex, England: Penguin, 1963.

Hollander, John. "Blake and the Metrical Contract." In *From Sensibility to Romanticism,* edited by Frederick Hilles and Harold Bloom, 293–310. New York: Oxford, 1965. Reprinted in John Hollander, *Vision and Resonance: Two Senses of Poetic Form.* New Haven, Conn.: Yale University Press, 1985, 187–211.

"STANZAS FOR MUSIC" GEORGE GORDON BYRON, LORD BYRON (1815) This is one of LORD BYRON's most exquisite lyrics rivaling the late lyrics of PERCY BYSSHE SHELLEY. It originally appeared in Byron's *Hebrew Melodies* (1815), and the idea of the poem as sung or spoken to music is part of the atmosphere it evokes.

The poem is essentially about its own evocativeness. It is not clear, nor need it be, whether the poem's addressee is a real person or not. The title suggests that the poem is generic, about the magical atmosphere that the poem and the music together seek to create. But it could be that a real person elicits the poem, and makes its speaker feel the magical atmosphere, and therefore the title is part of his response.

At any rate, the poem's movement is its secret. The form of the analogy is given in lines 3–12, and it is very subtle. It may be roughly paraphrased: *Your sweet voice is like the sound of music on water when the waves calm down and the moon is reflected in the mild ripples of a peaceful and gently swelling sea.* Note, though, that it is very hard to tell, in the poem, what is being analogized to what. The addressee's voice is like music on the waters, but it is not perfectly clear whether her voice is like music that seems to cause the calm of the water or whether, like music, her voice seems to cause the calm:

> And like music on the waters
> Is thy sweet voice to me:
> When, as if its sound were causing
> The charmed ocean's pausing,
> The waves lie still and gleaming,
> And the lull'd winds seem dreaming:
>
> And the midnight moon is weaving
> Her bright chain o'er the deep;
> Whose breast is gently heaving,
> As an infant's asleep: . . .

We cannot tell, in line 5, whether "its sound" refers to the sound of music, in the vehicle of the simile, or to the sound of her voice, the tenor of the simile. That is to say, we cannot tell whether the adverb *When,* at the start of the line, is still part of the analogy (your voice sounds like music heard when . . .) or whether it reports the conditions that prompt the analogy (when the waves pause and I hear your voice, it is like music). The reason for the ambiguity is the nesting of analogy: Your voice is *like* music when something occurs *as if* it were something else. There are two similes here, and we cannot tell whether they are parallel or hierarchical.

The difference leads to a difference in the linkage between the two stanzas. The second stanza—lines 9–12—might describe the actual night that they are together: All this is happening as I hear your voice; the moon is there, the deep is there. Or they might extend the simile of the first stanza: Your voice is like the ocean's pausing when the waves are still and the winds are at rest and the moon is reflected in the water.

The last lines of the poem do not clarify this question but sustain it:

> So the spirit bows before thee,
> To listen and adore thee;
> With a full but soft emotion,
> Like the swell of Summer's ocean.

The word *So* in line 13 can mean either a marker of simile—*thus, in this way, in such a manner*—or it can mean *therefore, for the reason.* His spirit bows before her *as* the ocean pauses to the sound of music; or, *because* of the beauty of the atmosphere, the place, the ambience, or her voice, his spirit bows before her, and it does so, to use a final, cycling analogy, like the ocean that is part of the ambience.

A way to see the ambiguity here is to notice that the poem can be read as definitely implying that the two lovers are within sight of the waters, but it can also be read as a simile for his feelings when they are together, even in the heart of the city. Both readings are consistent.

But we should not see this ambiguity as requiring us to make a stark distinction. Rather, the way the two meanings flow into and around and from each other is part of the poem's magic atmosphere. Its subtlety and delicacy does not ask us to make a choice, nor does it confront us with one. Her voice makes the all-embracing sense of atmosphere possible, so that she may be real or not; the place may be by the sea or not; the items of the poem may be figurative, or they may be real. Her voice dissolves the real into the figurative and the figurative into the real, and this dissolution is what the poem celebrates. Note that this is one of the points the analogy makes: He hears the music *because* the water, which would otherwise drown it out, is calm; but he imagines the converse—that the water is calm *because* of the music it pauses to hear. The reversal of cause and effect becomes a reciprocal interchange, and that reciprocal interchange is just the simile for love that the poem offers.

One should not dismiss the very tactful sexual imagery in the poem. The "swell" of summer's ocean is erotic (what isn't in Byron?); the poem is about how the erotic and the subtle and magical and languorous can all merge. Therefore, one should also note the lovely, unexpected surprise of the first lines of the poem:

> There be none of Beauty's daughters
> With a magic like thee; . . .

Logically, this means that the addressee is not one of Beauty's daughters. This could mean that she is not beautiful or, more likely, that she is not a *daughter* of beauty. In that case, the pronoun I have been using is wrong, and the poem is addressed to a beautiful man, not a beautiful woman. Byron was certainly bisexual, and again, part of the poem's subtlety and beauty is that even the addressee's sex is, at best, ambiguous. But ambiguity—unlike in most poetry—here does not mean anxiety but love and the way the soul and its ambience merge within a genuine erotic relationship. The poem itself is like music on the waters.

BIBLIOGRAPHY

Bloom, Harold. *The Visionary Company: A Reading of English Romantic Poetry*. Garden City, N.Y.: Doubleday, 1961.

Hazlitt, William. *Spirit of the Age; or, Contemporary Portraits.* London: Oxford University Press, 1970.

Saintsbury, George. *History of English Prosody, from the Twelfth Century to the Present Day.* New York: Russell & Russell, 1961.

Thorslev, Peter Larsen. *The Byronic Hero: Types and Prototypes.* Minneapolis: University of Minnesota Press, 1962.

STEVENSON, ROBERT LOUIS (1850–1894)

Robert Louis Stevenson was born in Edinburgh; a sickly child, he spent much time thinking and inventing imaginary words and stories, and he was much taken with Scottish literature. One of his first publications was an essay on Robert Burns in which he praised the freshness of Burns's writing in the Scots dialect (in which Stevenson also wrote some poetry) "while the English language was becoming daily more pedantic and inflexible." Like WILLIAM WORDSWORTH and SAMUEL TAYLOR COLERIDGE, Stevenson saw Burns as a proto-romantic poet, inaugurating the tradition of ROMANTICISM to which Stevenson, too, belonged even in the late Victorian period. He particularly praised Burns not for having "'discovered' Nature" but for having "discovered poetry—a higher and more intense way of thinking of the things that go to make up nature, a higher and more ideal key of words in which to speak of them," all of this, moreover, communicated in "a direct, speaking style." Like Burns and his Scottish predecessors, there was in Stevenson the power to say what he wished to say "definitely and brightly" (Stevenson, *Familiar Studies of Men and Books,* 71–73).

Stevenson is best known now—by adults, at least—for his adventure stories, like *Treasure Island* (1883) and *Kidnapped* (1886), but also by one book of poetry, the superb *Child's Garden of Verses* (1885). This is not his only book of poetry, though, and his *Songs of Travel* (1895) sustains comparison with that book, not only as to quality but as to theme. The best way to think of Stevenson's poetry is to compare it with the kind of poetry written for children by LEWIS CARROLL and EDWARD LEAR. Carroll and Lear wrote for children, over whose shoulders adults could read, appreciate, love, and admire. Stevenson wrote not only for children but for anyone who once was a child. We might say that to fully appreciate a Carroll poem, one has to be a child (despite the subtle jokes that the child would not get), and that his poems remind adult readers of a pure childish delight in language. But to fully appreciate a Stevenson poem, one has to be an adult, remembering childhood and perhaps projecting that memory onto the child over whose shoulder we may be reading. This idea is explicitly thematized in "To Any Reader," the last poem in *A Child's Garden of Verses,* and it can be seen in a non-childhood context in a poem like "I will make you brooches" (in *Songs of Travel*), which anticipates the time when the present moment will be remembered nostalgically, so that it can be felt nostalgically now, even as it is happening.

Stevenson was a poet of vicarious experience; indeed, all his writing had a strongly vicarious base, since he was an extremely sickly child (see "The Land of Counterpane" in *A Child's Garden of Verses*) as well as a sickly adult, tubercular (apparently), traveling widely for his health and supporting himself through incessantly brilliant and incessantly exhausting writing. The vicarious experience of childhood gives plangency to his poetry, the sense that absence and time haunt self-presence, which can only be a memory or an anticipation, never a direct experience.

BIBLIOGRAPHY

Chesterton, G. K. *Robert Louis Stevenson.* New York: Dodd, Mead, 1928.

Maixner, Paul. *Robert Louis Stevenson: The Critical Heritage.* London: Routledge, 1981.

Stevenson, Robert Louis. *Familiar Studies of Men and Books.* New York: Scribners, 1905.

"STRANGE FITS OF PASSION HAVE I KNOWN" See LUCY POEMS.

SUBLIME, THE The sublime is a central category of aesthetics in ROMANTICISM. It was a major topic of aesthetic theory in the 18th century, especially in England and Germany, but its inauguration as a topic was due to the translation by Nicolas Boileau (1636–1711) of Longinus's third-century treatise *Peri Hypsos* (Of elevation) into French in 1674. The word *sublime* is Boileau's translation of Longinus's *height,* or *elevation,* and it stuck.

The beautiful had been a perennial object of aesthetic and philosophical interest, from Plato onward. But the sublime is something different, and what that difference is was interesting, first of all, to Longinus, then to Boileau, and then to the 18th-century theorists and philosophers (Edmund Burke, Hugh Blair, Immanuel Kant, and Georg Wilhelm Friedrich Hegel especially) and the 19th-century poets who followed them. Boileau coined the famous phrase "je ne sais quoi" (literally, "I do not know") to describe what made something sublime—something powerful, perhaps overwhelmingly so, but not conformable to some preexistent category, like that by which we think of beauty as harmonious (for example).

We have to distinguish between two aspects of the sublime in order to see what was novel about the modern account of it. Longinus's treatise was about *style* in writing. He collected and considered passages that filled the soul with exaltation (the "elevation" of his title), passages which might interrupt the reader's unfolding experience of the work in which they appeared to stand alone in their power. For Longinus, such passages characterized Homer especially, as in Ajax's great prayer for light in the *Iliad* after the gods have suddenly blinded them with mist and darkness: "O father Zeus—draw our armies clear of the cloud, / give us a bright sky, give us back our sight! / Kill us all in the light of day at least" (17.645, translated by Fagles, treated by Longinus at 9.9). It is not for life but light that Ajax prays; Longinus compares this passage to the opening of the Book of Genesis and the creation of light as the first of things. The sublime is not a question of language, though it may be, but of greatness of soul, and so Longinus writes that "the silence of Ajax in the Underworld is great and more sublime than words" when Ajax turns away from Odysseus in the *Odyssey* (11.543). One definition Longinus gives, therefore, is that "Sublimity is the echo of a great soul" (9.2), and it finds an echo in its perceiver, as can be seen by how even the father of the gods, Zeus, responds to Ajax's prayer for light, "So he prayed / and the Father filled with pity, seeing Ajax weep, / He dispelled the mist at once." (*Iliad* 17.728–730, Fagles translation) For this reason, the central hallmark of the experience of the literary sublime, and the insight most quoted from Longinus, is that it is "as if instinctively, our soul is uplifted by the true sublime; it takes a proud flight, and is filled with joy and vaunting, as though it had itself produced what it has heard" (7.2).

That elevation of soul is what obsessed the modern theorists and poets. It was an elevation that Longinus ascribed to the power of writing—that is, to the description of the world and the people in it—but that the moderns ascribed to the power of the world itself, as well as to that of writing. Ajax's silence would be sublime in reality as well as in Homer's invention of it. Light itself was sublime. Alexander Pope famously said that Longinus was the great sublime he drew, the critic inspired with a poet's fire by all the muses (*Essay on Criticism,* 3.675–680), a description which captures both the sense of the sublime as occurring in exalted *response* to what is perceived and the idea that what can be perceived is an object in the real world—Longinus himself and not just the purely textual literature that exalts its readers.

The turn to the natural sublime characterized its 18th-century theorists, most importantly Edmund Burke (1729–97). His *Philosophical Enquiry into the Origin of Our Ideas of the Sublime and Beautiful* (1757) carefully distinguished between the two terms and between the aesthetic responses they elicited. The beautiful, according to Burke, produces pleasure pure and simple. The pleasure is one of the perception of harmonies. The mind perceives beautiful objects in a way that does not cause anxiety but, rather, allows it to use its faculties serenely and naturally. Beauty is a matter of smoothness, proportion, and gradation.

The sublime, on the other hand, does not procure pleasure but *delight*. Delight is, for Burke, by no means a synonym for pleasure. Although it is more intense than pleasure (in common parlance as well), that intensity comes from the fact that the sublime is associated with pain, danger, and anxiety, but not pleasure. The experience of the sublime is one of intense relief. It is associated with scenes like those of the Alps or the Grand Canyon because our first, instinctive response is one of fear. We perceive altitudes or depths that could kill us; then we recall that our vantage point is one of comparative safety—they could kill us, but they will not. Delight is the exalting relief that we feel: We have been overwhelmed with some vehement negative passion, and we have recovered. The thrill of the sublime is that of danger courted and overcome. It is not a positive pleasure but a more intense and delighting experience of danger survived.

The sublime is therefore associated with obscurity, fear, uncertainty, speed, and similar experiences. But how does it work in literature? For Burke, sublime literature first of all depicts scenes of sublimity and therefore shows the way (in Longinus's terms) in which the writer's soul has been exalted by what he or she has seen or imagined. But in a fascinating coda to the book, a section called "How Words Influence the Passions," Longinus talks about how literature can be the origin of the sublime and not only its recorder. There is a kind of literature that defeats the reader's imagination and threatens the psyche's self-confidence, much as sublime natural phenomena do. For Burke, the great English writer of the sublime was John Milton, who could turn a natural description into a sublime one through the sudden and overwhelming force of his language, which defeats the *representational* abilities of his readers but not their *cognitive* abilities. Burke's example of the type of transformation that Milton makes his language undergo is a profound one: "To represent an angel in a picture, you can only draw a beautiful young man winged: but what painting can furnish out anything so grand as the addition of one word, 'the angel of the Lord'?" Painting cannot do it, but literature can fill one with the exaltation of the unrepresentable.

Burke's idea of the sublime overshadows the great philosophical treatment that the German philosopher Immanuel Kant gave it in *The Critique of Judgment* (1790). For Kant, too, the beautiful is harmonious, in particular in harmony with the mind's perceptive faculties. But the sublime defeats those faculties, and Kant described it as occurring in a double movement. We perceive something that exceeds our powers of sensory intuition or imitative representation. We are blocked and baffled and suddenly feel ourselves to be as nothing compared to the natural world. From this sense of being overwhelmed, the mind shifts to its transcendental aspirations, its fundamental commitment not to the "empirical world" where we are very little, but to the world of our imagination, which transcends the empirical and in which our minds participate. We are awestruck by the unmeasurable power of some object in the outside world, but we have the inner resources to measure absolute magnitude or power. The world may be bewilderingly large, but it is finite; the mind can conceive of the infinite, which is its proper home. Thus, as WILLIAM WORDSWORTH said, "Our destiny, our nature, and our home, / Is with infinitude—and only there" (*The* PRELUDE, 1805 version, book 6, ll. 538–539) in a passage that describes his response to an experience of blockage, of being caught in a mist in his writing, much like the mist that Ajax prayed to Zeus to dissipate.

The sublime in nature sends the mind back to its own "supersensible destiny," as Kant called it, and shows how we transcend the world that seems to trap us. The loss of power *within* the world leads to a gain of power in our relation *to* the world. This is the central and perennial theme of romanticism, to be found in all of Wordsworth's and SAMUEL TAYLOR COLERIDGE's great philosophical poetry (Coleridge translated and often plagiarized Kant); in PERCY BYSSHE SHELLEY (see "MONT BLANC," for example); and in their greatest Victorian followers, especially ROBERT BROWNING and, in America, Ralph Waldo Emerson, Walt Whitman, and Emily Dickinson. Loss leads to a perception of intensity, and that perception is what gives rise to poetry, both in the poet writing it and in the reader reading it. The intensity of the romantic sublime and its precursors, especially Milton, is one of the greatest glories of English literature.

BIBLIOGRAPHY

Bloom, Harold. *Agon: Towards a Theory of Revisionism.* New York: Oxford University Press, 1982.

Burke, Edmund. *Philosophical Enquiry into the Origin of Our Ideas of the Sublime and Beautiful.* Notre Dame, Ind.: University of Notre Dame Press, 1968.

De Bolla, Peter. *The Discourse of the Sublime: Readings in History, Aesthetics, and the Subject.* New York: Blackwell, 1989.

De Man, Paul. *The Rhetoric of Romanticism.* New York: Columbia University Press, 1984.

Hartman, Geoffrey. *Wordsworth's Poetry, 1787–1814.* New Haven, Conn.: Yale University Press, 1971.

Hertz, Neil. *The End of the Line: Essays on Psychoanalysis and the Sublime.* New York: Columbia University Press, 1985.

Hegel, G. W. F. *Aesthetics: Lectures on Fine Art.* 2 vols. Translated by T. M. Knox. Oxford: Clarendon Press, 1974–75.

Kant, Immanuel. *The Critique of Judgment.* Translated by Werner S. Pluhar. Indianapolis: Hackett Pub. Co., 1987.

Monk, Samuel Holt. *The Sublime: A Study of Critical Theories in XVIII-Century England.* Ann Arbor: University of Michigan Press, 1960.

Weiskel, Thomas. *The Romantic Sublime: Studies in the Structure and Psychology of Transcendence.* Baltimore: Johns Hopkins University Press, 1986.

"SURPRISED BY JOY" WILLIAM WORDSWORTH (1815) "Surprised by Joy" is one of WILLIAM WORDSWORTH's greatest sonnets, a memorial to his dead daughter Catherine, who had died at three years old in June 1812. He had previously described her in a lovely poem written in the year before her death, "Characteristics of a Child Three Years Old," which included her ability to surprise him with her unexpected spontaneity:

> Light are her sallies as the tripping fawn's
> Forth-startled from the fern where she lay couched;
> Unthought-of, unexpected, as the stir
> Of the soft breeze ruffling the meadow-flowers
> . . . (ll. 15–18)

In "Surprised by Joy," what is unexpected is his forgetting her absence, but that unthought-of thought returns, and brings back with it all the pain of loss.

Wordsworth wrote more sonnets than any other form of poem, and some of his most memorable poems are in sonnet form. This one owes much to John Milton's last sonnet (number 23), even as it displays a striking and devastating originality. Milton's sonnet describes a dream of his late wife, Katherine Woodcock:

> Methought I saw my late espoused saint
> Brought to me, like Alcestis, from the grave,
> Whom Jove's great son to her glad husband gave,
> Rescu'd from death by force, though pale and faint.
> Mine, as whom wash'd from spot of child-bed taint
> Purification in the old Law did save,
> And such as yet once more I trust to have
> Full sight of her in Heaven without restraint,
> Came vested all in white, pure as her mind;
> Her face was veil'd, yet to my fancied sight
> Love, sweetness, goodness, in her person shin'd
> So clear as in no face with more delight.
> But Oh! as to embrace me she inclin'd,
> I wak'd, she fled, and day brought back my night.

Part of the point and power of Milton's sonnet is that he *never saw* Katherine Woodcock, because he was blind when he met her. In the poem, his dream is as much a wishful dream of himself, as someone who can see, as it is a dream of his dead wife, whom he thinks he can see. Day brings back his night, both literally and metaphorically, since he wakes to discover that he is blind and she is dead.

"Surprised by Joy" also describes a moment in which the speaker forgets the death of the person he loves and then remembers it again with a painfulness made all the sharper by its momentary absence. He is surprised because he had forgotten, in his grief, the joy that he felt before Catherine's death; now he forgets that she is dead, as we know from the fact that he turns to her to share his joy. The joy he wishes to share is the joy of not remembering that she is dead, but the desire to share it reminds him that she is dead.

The poem is strikingly addressed to the dead Catherine: "I turned to share the transport, Oh with whom, / But thee, . . .?" That mode of address, the apostrophe to the absent person, briefly treats her as though she was alive and could share the transport of intense joy the poem describes, and describes her as being unable to share. She is gone forever, and he apologizes to her for forgetting this, for forgetting that there is no way to apologize to her just because she is gone.

As in Milton's sonnet, her heavenly face is what Wordsworth most desires to see, and what he now knows he never will. The "years unborn" contrast with his daughter, born and now dead, and all that is left to be born is the parade of years. The great, self-rebuking question "How could I forget thee?" partly answers itself. "Love, faithful love, recalled thee to my mind" he says, but that might mean that love has caused him to forget as well as to remember her death. Love makes him wish to think she is still alive for him somehow, still able to be addressed by his poem.

Love itself is partly personified here ("faithful love"), and in that personification is something like a dream or half-image of the dead girl. But her forgotten absence simply intensifies the shock of its recollection: "That thought's return / Was the worst pang that sorrow ever bore." Now it is the thought of her death that returns, and not Catherine, and to recollect her death is nearly to reexperience it.

But not quite, and one of the things the poem mourns is that even its grief eventually loses intensity. Recollecting her death is the worst pang he has felt since her death, but it is not quite as awful as her death itself was. It represents a slight attenuation of that pang. The fact that such attenuation is possible, that he can be blind (like Milton) to his loss even for a moment, is itself a cause of pain. And for Wordsworth, this second-order pain—pain about the nature and mutability of even the most intense human experience (see the INTIMATIONS ODE)—contributes to the intensity it mourns and regrets. But, inevitably, if attenuation is the source of pain, then pain itself must be seen as becoming attenuated. It is this fact that the poem mourns so movingly: It mourns the fact that even mourning comes to an end.

It is strange but typically Wordsworthian that the most plangent part of his work should be its recognition of the ephemerality of the plangent, the powerlessness of mourning, Mourning is even powerless to memorialize itself in the poem that describes it accurately, and Wordsworth is desperately aware that "the hiding places of his power" (*The* PRELUDE) close when he approaches. To quote a poem of Thomas Gray's, which Wordsworth cites in the preface to *Lyrical Ballads,* he weeps the more because he weeps in vain. The vanity of weeping is what Wordsworth recognizes as both the ultimate limitation to what poetry can do—it cannot bring the dead back even if it attempts the two extremes of either forgetting or addressing the dead—and the saddest fact of the experience of one's own experience, a fact to which only poetry is adequate. In many ways, "Surprised by Joy," perhaps Wordsworth's most moving poem, is also the most concentrated example of the aspirations and bafflements that he records in his greatest poetry. It ought to be compared to "TINTERN ABBEY," *The Prelude,* and the Intimations Ode as one of the greatest documents of the romantic crisis lyric.

BIBLIOGRAPHY

Barker, Juliet. *Wordsworth: A Life.* New York: Viking, 2000.

Bloom, Harold. *Poetry and Repression: Revisionism from Blake to Stevens.* New Haven, Conn.: Yale University Press, 1976.

———. *The Visionary Company: A Reading of English Romantic Poetry.* Garden City, N.Y.: Doubleday, 1961.

Bromwich, David. *Disowned by Memory: Wordsworth's Poetry of the 1790s.* Chicago: University of Chicago Press, 1998.

Gill, Stephen. *William Wordsworth: A Life.* New York: Oxford University Press, 1989.

———. *Wordsworth's Poetry, 1787–1814.* New Haven, Conn.: Yale University Press, 1971.

Johnston, Kenneth. *Hidden Wordsworth: Poet, Lover, Rebel, Spy.* New York: Norton, 1998.

Liu, Alan. *Wordsworth: The Sense of History.* Stanford, Calif.: Stanford University Press, 1989.

Moorman, Mary. *William Wordsworth: A Biography.* 2 vols. Oxford: Clarendon Press, 1957, 1965.

Pinch, Adela. *Strange Fits of Passion: Epistemologies of Emotion, Hume to Austen.* Stanford, Calif.: Stanford University Press, 1996.

Quinney, Laura. *The Poetics of Disappointment: Wordsworth to Ashbery.* Charlottesville: University Press of Virginia, 1999.

SWINBURNE, ALGERNON CHARLES (1837–1909) The most striking thing about Algernon Charles Swinburne's poetry is the overwhelming richness of his language, which tends to make people either love or hate his poetry. Those who hate it think the language gets in the way of any idea, emotion, perspective, passion, or stance that the poetry embodies or expresses; those who like it think the language is part of the sensuous intensity of experience.

Swinburne belongs to the PRE-RAPHAELITE POETRY movement (at one point he participated in the micro-utopian scheme of lodging with GEORGE MEREDITH and DANTE GABRIEL ROSSETTI), a movement that can most generally be characterized (as William Michael Rossetti said) as a commitment to perceptive truth. Therefore, according to the Pre-Raphaelites, perception must be scrupulously accurate, not only to the outside world but to the experience of the perceiver of that outside world. Perception is double-sided: It fronts both world and the mind, and the poet or painter who reproduces perception expresses thereby both the world perceived and the mind that perceives it.

For the more sensual Pre-Raphaelites, CHRISTINA ROSSETTI and Swinburne in particular, the perceived world included the effects of language, both on the level of sound and on that of meaning. But language is also the deepest matrix of responsive perception, which is to say the active and focused perception that the Pre-Raphaelites cultivated and that is issued in expression. Language is the plane on which the two sides of perception join: It belongs to the world, and it belongs to the self.

One way to think this through is to think through the relationship of sound and sense. Sound is a fact of nature whose effect is almost purely mental (there is almost no real poetic beauty, despite endless sentimental claims to the contrary, in hearing poetry in a language one does not know); sense, to continue the paradox, while it seems to imply mind through the fact that it is *meaningful,* is nevertheless essentially defined as its picturing a *fact,* some truth about the outside world. The merging of sound and sense is a merging of perception of the world with the emotional tonality that perception takes in the mind.

Another, and related, way to think through this relationship between the perceived world and the perceiving and self-perceived self within language is to consider, as Swinburne did incessantly, the relationship of figurative to literal language. Literal language describes things as they are; figurative language describes the mind's take on things and shows how the mind perceives them. We are accustomed (very wrongly) to think that there is only a difference in degree between simile and metaphor, but in fact the difference is one of kind. Metaphors are *figurative;* stars are not foam. Similes are *literal;* stars are *like* what the word foam *literally* designates. Generally, poets use simile to compare the literal to the figurative, and in doing so, they tend to keep the two separate. Simile shows what a purely figurative assertion might look like but sustains the literal separation between the objects of comparison.

Swinburne, on the other hand, was a master at the far harder task of allowing for ambiguity between the literal and figurative in metaphor. In *ATALANTA IN CALYDON,* for example, Althaea praises her doomed son Meleager for being fearless and courageous in battle, even "in the green blossom of they life / Ere the full blade caught flower" (ll. 560–561). The "blade" here is the somewhat metaphorical blade of the flowering grass. (Swinburne might have known that this was its original meaning, applied to weapons only later, which furthers the shuttle between literal and figurative that is so central to his technique.) It would flower, but how does it "catch flower"? Things burst into flower throughout the poem, and usually that means something like a sudden blaze of bright light, as in the amazing description of Castor and Pollux as "Fair flower-like stars on the iron foam of fight," where they are both warriors surfing the battle and the glittering of the iron blades themselves in the sunlight during the battle. Althaea has already said that she cannot identify all the warriors present to hunt the boar because the blades of their weaponry dazzle her sight. So now we can say that Meleager is both the metaphorical blade of grass that will catch a literal flower—that is (within the metaphor), the blade will bloom—and that his blade will catch flower from the sun that shines on the hunt as well as from the blood that will spatter it.

This is a typical effect in Swinburne, what he calls the "flower-like mixed with flowers" earlier in the poem, and it is the kind of effect that governs all his beautifully repetitious poems. It is most obvious, perhaps, in his double sestina "The Complaint of Lisa," where again we can trace the adventures of the word *sun-flower* to see the interplay within it between simile (usually referring to the speaker, Lisa) and metaphor (as when it refers to the King). The most prominent of words to balance between the literal and the figurative in Swinburne is probably the *brand* in *Atalanta in Calydon,* which will sometimes be used figuratively and literally in close proximity; when Swinburne gives it prominence at the end of a line (for example, l. 1,911) he gets a sestina-like fatalism into the feeling of the poem.

We can summarize by saying that in Swinburne, the world presents similes which the mind absorbs as metaphor, so that the world itself becomes significant as the figurative world of the perceiver. It also becomes what characterizes the perceiver because she interacts with it, first and most intensely as its perceiving subject. There is fatalism to this: There is play in the movement between literal and various figurative uses of the word, but only at the expense of the word following us everywhere and fully characterizing what we can feel or know or perceive.

The double-bladed perception of language conduces to one logical extreme of Pre-Raphaelitism, a sadomasochistic relationship to language and to the world. The world for Swinburne, as for most poets, is a painful place. As a poet, it is his vocation both to perceive the world and therefore to measure up to it, and as a poet, he does this through language. He speaks to the world the language that converts its similes into metaphors and returns those metaphors to the world. Similitude becomes transformation, encroachment, obliteration of difference between the perceiving self and the perceived world. This is what Sigmund Freud would argue the so-called death instinct aimed at, an instinct that manifests itself as aggression and repetition.

Repetition and aggression aim at the same thing: the abolishment of the difference between the me and the not-me. Indeed, aggression is marked by repetition, by the excesses of punishment or pain that it embraces, so that punishment and pain are no longer instrumental to some end of self-preservation. This is how Swinburne's insistent and characteristic imagery of peaceful death by drowning as being embraced by the sea and by darkness is connected to imagery that is apparently its opposite of sharpness and brightness and pain. Repetition swaddles pains, and is beautiful because of the pain it swaddles.

Swinburne is the best exemplification of Freud's theory of the death instinct. His poetic form and insistent meter, as well as his figurative matter, find their most intense theme in his sadomasochistic poetry. Swinburne was flogged as a child at Eton, and he wrote poetry (often surreptitiously) about flogging with excited fascination throughout his life. Probably the best of these poems is the still-shocking "Anactoria," spoken by the Greek poet Sappho to or against a lover of hers (Swinburne was a superb classicist, and was always classicizing in his poetry). Spoken *to* or *against* Anactoria—the point in Swinburne is to eliminate the difference between the two prepositions, which is to say to eliminate the difference between pain and pleasure. To recur to the Pre-Raphaelite language of perception, the pleasure of cultivating perception culminates in the capacity to be intensely open to pain itself, so that loss and gain, hurt and ecstasy, are two versions of the same intense alertness, not only to the world but to one's most exquisitely responsive perceptions of the world. It is this build-up of intensity in Swinburne that comes out as the controlled perversity of his theme, his obsessive repetitions, and his prosody. We could say that in Swinburne there is some of the same religious intensity that characterized so many of his contemporaries, but without any of the doctrine or belief, so that where they overlap is in a sense of poetry as the intense substitute for intense absence. (The chorus in *Atalanta in Calydon* beginning at line 1,038 provides another good example of this attitude.)

Swinburne was a vivid and outrageous social presence through much of his life, interested in sex, interested in drink (which ruined him and essentially turned him into an invalid), interested in literature (he wrote one of the best early books on WILLIAM BLAKE)—interested in everything. The one great fact for Swinburne was that language is how we interact with others, even with sexual partners, and how we bridge the gap, both ways, between the self and the world. He converted the object world—the self—into language, and therefore brought language to the most extreme experience, on every level, that it could possibly be, both for himself and for his readers.

See also "AVE ATQUE VALE"; "GARDEN OF PROSERPINE, THE"; HYMN TO PROSERPINE"; "ITYLUS"; "TRIUMPH OF TIME, THE."

BIBLIOGRAPHY

Bragman, Louis J. "The Case of Algernon Charles Swinburne: A Study in Sadism." *Psychoanalytic Review* 21 (1934): 59–74.

Castle, Terry. "Always the Bridesmaid." *London Review of Books* (September 30, 1999). Available online. URL: www.lrb.co.uk/v21/n19/cast01_.html. Accessed March 17, 2009.

Prins, Yopie. *Victorian Sappho.* Princeton, N.J.: Princeton University Press, 1999.

TAYLOR, ANN See TAYLOR, JANE.

TAYLOR, JANE (1783–1824) is now best remembered for "The Star," a poem most people recognize by its first line—"Twinkle, twinkle little star"—and which they assume is an anonymous song. Jane and her sister Ann (1782–1866) were raised and educated by ambitious parents, and they published poems even as children. In 1806, when Jane was 21, the two sisters published the wildly popular *Rhymes for the Nursery,* which went through scores of editions. It is there that "Twinkle, twinkle, little star" appears. Since very few people know the whole poem, we quote it in full:

Twinkle, twinkle, little star,
How I wonder what you are.
Up above the world so high,
Like a diamond in the sky.

When the blazing sun is gone,
When he nothing shines upon,
Then you show your little light,
Twinkle, twinkle, all the night.

Then the trav'ller in the dark,
Thanks you for your tiny spark,
He could not see which way to go,
If you did not twinkle so.

In the dark blue sky you keep,
And often thro' my curtains peep,
For you never shut your eye,
Till the sun is in the sky.

'Tis your bright and tiny spark,
Lights the trav'ller in the dark:
Tho' I know not what you are,
Twinkle, twinkle, little star.

It is hard not to hear the tune when reading the poem, but the poem was not set to Wolfgang Amadeus Mozart's music until 1860. Reading it as a poem, we notice that it is in trochaic tetrameter, one variation of the kind of ballad meter that WILLIAM WORDSWORTH and SAMUEL TAYLOR COLERIDGE learned from Thomas Percy's *Reliques of Ancient English Poetry* (1765) and put to such good effect in *Lyrical Ballads* (1798). It may be wrong to try to get the poem to make perfect sense—it is a "rhyme for the nursery," after all—but Jane Taylor knew a lot about the physical world. No star could cast enough light to illuminate the path of a traveler, so this "shiny spark" must orient him, and therefore the star is probably the North Star. This fits with the idea that the star never sets, since the North Star is always visible in the Northern Hemisphere. If this is so, it must peep through her curtains when they are moved by a draft or on clear nights, since the North Star never changes its orientation toward any window on Earth.

LEWIS CARROLL might have doubted this consistency when he parodied this poem in *Alice in Wonderland* (1864). This is what the Mad Hatter tells Alice that he had to "sing" at a concert given by the Queen of Hearts:

> Twinkle, twinkle, little bat!
> How I wonder what you're at!'
>   Up above the world you fly,
> Like a teatray in the sky.
>   Twinkle, twinkle—

Carroll is imagining in Alice a different kind of child and a different kind of nursery from that promulgated by the Taylors, and interestingly enough, this was while Ann was still alive.

Some other poems by Jane and Ann are remembered, most notably "Dance little baby, dance up high."

BIBLIOGRAPHY

Carroll, Lewis. *The Annotated Alice: Alice's Adventures in Wonderland & Through the Looking Glass.* Edited and annotated by Martin Gardner. New York: Norton, 2000.

Opie, Iona, and Peter Opie, eds. *Oxford Dictionary of Nursery Rhymes.* New York: Oxford University Press, 1997.

Taylor, Ann. *Autobiography and Other Memorials of Mrs. Gilbert (formerly Ann Taylor).* Edited by Josiah Gilbert. London: H. S. King, 1876.

"TEARS, IDLE TEARS" ALFRED, LORD TENNYSON (1847) This is one of the most famous songs from ALFRED, LORD TENNYSON's long narrative poem *The PRINCESS.*. In the poem's context, the song is sung in public at the Princess's command to pass a brief interval in the arduous studies she and her women are undertaking, and one of her maids then sings it. The maid brings herself to weep, and the Princess responds disdainfully that her maid's sadness comes only out of the sweetness and vagueness of the song (part 4, l. 46) sung by a destructive siren of idleness.

What the Princess disdains, Tennyson attempts: the poetry of pure evocation, or even the evocation of evocation itself. The idleness the Princess deplores is what the poem is explicitly about—the idleness of the tears it indulges in. The pleasure of remembering "the days that are no more" is that of feeling estranged from them but close to them as well. How can that be? Because the rememberer weeping over the lost days is himself or herself now completely in contact with the distance or estrangement of the past. The tears are idle because they can do nothing to bring the past back; but they are idle, too, because the past does not belong to the world of present business; it belongs to a kind of sublime idleness as well, since there is nothing for the past or its memory to do. This, then, is what it is possible to share with the past: the idleness born of the fact that we are distanced from it.

The song is in blank verse, but like Tennyson's other blank-verse songs and poems, a kind of dreamy repetition takes the place of rhyme (see especially "NOW SLEEPS THE CRIMSON PETAL, NOW THE WHITE," also from *The Princess*). That repetition here is of the phrase "the days that are no more" at the end of each stanza. The memory of those days arises from the present, in particular from "looking on the happy Autumn-fields" (l. 24). Tennyson wrote the poem during autumn at Tintern Abbey, and he may have been thinking of his dead friend ARTHUR HENRY HALLAM, the subject of *IN MEMORIAM A.H.H.,* who was buried nearby. But he may also have been thinking of WILLIAM WORDSWORTH's great assertion in the INTIMATIONS ODE that "a single field" that he had looked upon spoke to him "of something that was gone." The very presentness of the present, without a hint of the past anywhere, puts one in mind of the past and how completely it is gone. The present, then, becomes the place for these idle tears because the present speaks of past by not speaking of it. The repetition of sorrow in the present moment is a way of keeping the sorrowful present going, idly, in contact with the idle past.

Tennyson talked of the feel of the song as "the sense of the abiding in the transient." The transient of the presence is known by the transience of the past, but the abidingness of the past, and therefore of a present that gives itself over to idle memories of the past, consists just in the way that idleness never gets anywhere and will therefore never resolve its sorrow. Tennyson does not want resolution but sorrow, and the beautiful, evocative, hypnotic repetitions of the poem convey that perfectly.

BIBLIOGRAPHY

Armstrong, Isobel. *Victorian Poetry: Poetry, Poetics and Politics.* New York: Routledge, 1993.

Bloom, Harold. *Poetry and Repression: Revisionism from Blake to Stevens.* New Haven, Conn.: Yale University Press, 1976.

Buckley, Jerome Hamilton. *Tennyson: The Growth of a Poet.* Boston: Houghton Mifflin, 1965.

Kilham, John. *Critical Essays on the Poetry of Tennyson.* New York: Barnes and Noble, 1960.

Kincaid, James R. *Tennyson's Major Poems: The Comic and Ironic Patterns.* New Haven, Conn.: Yale University Press, 1975.

Ricks, Christopher B. *Tennyson.* New York: Macmillan, 1972.

Rowlinson, Matthew. *Tennyson's Fixations: Psychoanalysis and the Topics of the Early Poetry.* Charlottesville: University Press of Virginia, 1994.

Tucker, Herbert. *Tennyson and the Doom of Romanticism.* Cambridge, Mass.: Harvard University Press, 1988.

TENNYSON, ALFRED, LORD (1809–1892)

The great Oxford classicist Benjamin Jowett (translator of a still standard edition of Plato) was prompted by his friendship with and admiration for Alfred, Lord Tennyson to jot down characterizations of him, thinking him to be like Socrates, a kind of outrider astonishingly sympathetic to the average or ordinary person. "Not a man of the world (in the ordinary sense) but a man who had the greatest insight into the world, and often in a word or a sentence would flash a light," Jowett wrote, and described as well how "at good things he would sit laughing away—laughter often interrupted by fits of sadness." Tennyson thought his biography of little interest. The interruptions of sadness, or, better, the unworldliness that would sometimes make itself palpable when he was with friends is the true source and subject of his poetry.

The narrator of Tennyson's *The* PRINCESS describes his susceptibility to strange trancelike states where he lives and moves in a world of shadows. Those shadows continually appear, with strange and persistent beauty, in Tennyson's work. As to the trance states, it can be noted that Tennyson did have some sort of breakdown in his 30s, and that his father and brothers were also notable for their sometimes morbidly melancholic dispositions. For Tennyson, that melancholia was hard to distinguish from his lifelong mourning for ARTHUR HENRY HALLAM, his closest friend (and best critic), engaged to be married to his sister but dead of a cerebral hemorrhage at 22.

Tennyson hoped his life would be of even less interest than it was, and he wanted to be remembered only for his works, as (his examples) William Shakespeare and Jane Austen were. And indeed, almost all that is relevant to his poetry can be found *in* his poetry. The ruling event of his life was the death of Hallam, which gave rise to the great elegy *IN MEMORIAM A.H.H.* (one of the three or four great elegies in all of English literature, and by far the longest of them), published 17 years after Hallam's death, as well as such poems as "ULYSSES"; "TITHONUS"; and, of course, all the Arthurian poems in which one ideal and idealized Arthur stood for another. This is not to say that Tennyson spent his life in morbid misanthropy—quite the reverse, as Jowett made clear. He remained close to his brothers, especially Charles, who was also a poet; to his wife Emily, a deep critic of his poetry; and to his children (the death of his son Lionel at age 32 in 1886 is part of the impetus to "Locksley Hall Sixty Years After," in which the narrator has a conversation with his grandson, which mirrors Tennyson's relation to Lionel's young sons, then ages seven and eight). (See "LOCKSLEY HALL" AND "LOCKSLEY HALL SIXTY YEARS AFTER.")

Tennyson was probably always disposed to melancholy, but the occasions for that melancholy in his life combined to give his poetry its characteristic feel. The death of Hallam coincided for him with his reading of Charles Lyell's *Principles of Geology* (1830–33), which showed how the fossil record established the unimaginable antiquity of the earth, while also showing how much of past life was gone forever, even as new life evolved and passed away. Late in life, as a motto (see MOTTOES) to his poem "Parnassus," Tennyson quoted Horace's boast at the end of book 3 of the Odes that he had written poetry that would outlast bronze monuments and time itself, an assertion Tennyson could see was vain because "Astronomy and Geology, terrible Muses," overshadow all human achievement, even poetry. The vastness of time and space crush human pretension to understanding the universe or to any importance within it. For Tennyson, the insignificance of life underlined the permanence and meaninglessness of death, in particular the death of his beloved Hallam. How could poetry afford any consolation or any defense against this fact?

Tennyson's answer, in the late "Parnassus" as well as in the relatively early poem *In Memoriam,* is to achieve a simultaneous double perspective, a combination of JOHN KEATS (his most important poetic influence) and the 13th- and 14th-century Italian poet Dante Alighieri (perhaps his favorite poet); "Parnassus" concludes: "If the lips were touch'd with fire from off a pure Pierian altar, / Tho' their music here be mortal need the singer greatly care? / Other songs for other worlds! the fire within him would not falter; / Let the golden Iliad vanish, Homer here is Homer there." For Keats, the eternal was opposed to the present-tense intensity of immediate experience; part of what is immediately experienced is the ephemerality of experience. In Tennyson, the turn to the immediate and ephemeral was a constant propensity, and his poetry, with its haunting repetitions and trancelike extensions of the momentary is an attempt not to fix the ephemeral but to make it last a little longer. For Tennyson, poetic form and its elaborations, made as beautiful as possible ("ornate," his critics, like Walter Bagehot, said), was what helped to make the mortal music last.

The other perspective is one from beyond all height, above all time. The very vastness of the universe and its antiquity allow for a kind of Dantesque ascent to a perspective where all this vastness, far from dwarfing the soul, gives it a sense of tremendous spiritual extent. As a mortal human being ("Homer here"), Tennyson can nevertheless be "here at times a sentinel / Who moves about from place to place, / And whispers to the vast of space / Among the worlds, that all is well" (*In Memoriam,* section 127).

Tennyson's inheritance from the romantics (see ROMANTICISM) was his sense of poetry as a vocation, which made it possible to survive the world's alienness. Tennyson endured some poverty to pursue his vocation, before being made poet laureate upon the death of WILLIAM WORDSWORTH in 1850. Another sign of the seriousness of his vocation was his reluctance to publish. What poetry did for him—even in the occasional and public pieces that are now so much out of favor but that made him so beloved to the British public during his lifetime—was to make him see how the ephemeral flower in the crannied wall could last a little longer in poetical meditation, and how that meditation could help the soul understand and cope with the vastness of God and humanity.

See also "CHARGE OF THE LIGHT BRIGADE, THE"; "CROSSING THE BAR"; "KRAKEN, THE"; "LOTOS-EATERS, THE"; "MARIANA"; "MORTE D'ARTHUR"; "NOW SLEEPS THE CRIMSON PETAL, NOW THE WHITE"; "SPLENDOUR FALLS, THE"; "TEARS, IDLE TEARS."

BIBLIOGRAPHY

Armstrong, Isobel. *Victorian Poetry: Poetry, Poetics and Politics.* New York: Routledge, 1993.

Bloom, Harold. *Poetry and Repression: Revisionism from Blake to Stevens.* New Haven, Conn.: Yale University Press, 1976.

Buckley, Jerome Hamilton. *Tennyson: The Growth of a Poet.* Boston: Houghton Mifflin, 1965.

Kilham, John. *Critical Essays on the Poetry of Tennyson.* New York: Barnes and Noble, 1960.

Kincaid, James R. *Tennyson's Major Poems: The Comic and Ironic Patterns.* New Haven, Conn.: Yale University Press, 1975.

Ricks, Christopher B. *Tennyson.* New York: Macmillan, 1972.

Rowlinson, Matthew. *Tennyson's Fixations: Psychoanalysis and the Topics of the Early Poetry.* Charlottesville: University Press of Virginia, 1994.

Tennyson, Hallam Tennyson, Baron. *The Life and Works of Alfred, Lord Tennyson.* London: Macmillan, 1899.

Tucker, Herbert. *Tennyson and the Doom of Romanticism.* Cambridge, Mass.: Harvard University Press, 1988.

"'TERENCE, THIS IS STUPID STUFF'"

A. E. HOUSMAN (1895) This is one of A. E. HOUSMAN's most famous poems, but it is often remembered as more comic than it actually is. The "Terence" of its first line is the fanciful name that Housman gave himself as speaker of *A Shropshire Lad,* which was originally to be called *The Poems of Terence Hearsay.* The whimsy such a name suggests is subtle: Terence is a little estranged from the world, or from happiness, and much of what he knows, he knows as hearsay and must take on faith. But what he takes on faith is what he has heard and now can say—the idea of poetry. The comedy of the Latin dramatist Terence (ca. 186–ca. 159 B.C.E.), to whom Housman alludes, is very humane and psychologically forgiving in its depiction of character. That humanity comes not from lived experience among the characters he depicts but from his reading in Greek comedy, which he imitates and adapts brilliantly—he hears (or reads) and then says (or writes). These all seem important characteristics for a model for Housman, for whom literature was a way into an imagined Shropshire, rather than a way to recollect it.

In this poem, Housman gives an account of his estrangement from the bare, particular, untrammeled experience of present pleasures, his own included. His critics (ll. 1–14) think his stuff is stupid because they see that he takes pleasure in the present—in his eating and drinking. But he is not what the philosopher Harry Frankfurt calls a "wanton"; he looks before and after and is not concerned only with present pleasures.

One of the striking things about the poem is how its lighthearted tone, with its lively iambic tetrameters (which often feel as though they are modulating out of even more ebullient trochaic rhythm, as in the opening line). Terence agrees with his friends' critique, or at least part of it, at the beginning of his response, where he acknowledges the strength of the hedonistic critique even of John Milton: "And malt does more than Milton can / To justify God's ways to man" (ll. 21–22). Part of the wit here is in the monosyllabic directness of "malt" as compared to the more tediously drawn out "Milton." Housman's allusion is to the opening of *Paradise Lost*, where Milton declares his ambition to "justify the ways of God to man" (book 1, l. 26). Housman (or Terence) continues by agreeing that pleasure makes life better, and this is partly because life—the sober life that poetry aims at in its tendency toward truth—is not very good. He sees the attractions of the kind of wine and song and present mirth praised by EDWARD FITZGERALD (an openly homosexual poet) in his *The RUBÁIYÁT OF OMAR KHAYYÁM*, and so recommends that one "Look into the pewter pot / To see the world as the world's not" (ll. 25–26)—that is, into the pot of beer, his version of the wine vessels that FitzGerald's Omar tirelessly and exuberantly praises.

The desire "To see the world as the world's not" is an aesthetic one. MATTHEW ARNOLD had said repeatedly that the function of criticism, or "critical effort," on all scales and in all modes of intellectual endeavor, was "to see the object as in itself it really is" (see, for example, Arnold's 1864 essay *The Function of Criticism at the Present Time*). As Harold Bloom has pointed out, OSCAR WILDE (with whose travails Housman sympathized; see "OH WHO IS THAT YOUNG SINNER") famously went beyond the essayist and critic Walter Horatio Pater, who said that first one must "know one's impression of the object as it really is," to put into an 1890 dialogue his dictum that "the primary aim of the critic is to see the object as in itself it really is not" (*The Critic as Artist*, 1890). And what malt and beer show is that God's ways to man are just—this is the world as the world is not.

But where wine allows Omar to greet the day with joy, seeing the world as it is not gives Terence a hangover. The world is the old world yet (l. 38), a world with some good but more ill. Refusing to acknowledge the ill makes us wake up in the muck, even if we have slept happily. But waking up in the muck allows Terence to wake up to the truth—and it is truth that his poetry is after.

Why should poetry seek truth? Terence asks himself the same question that Milton asked in *Lycidas* (1638): Why (as Milton says) strictly meditate the thankless muse? Milton asked this in the context of an elegy, for a friend and therefore in anticipation of his own elegy. In *Lycidas* he plucks the berries harsh and crude before they are ripened—and so, too, does Terence. The "stuff" (l. 49) he brings is not so good as ale, but is not stupid (or, like ale, stupefying) either: "Out of a stem that scored the hand / I wring it in a weary land" (ll. 51–52). Poetic vocation hurts the writer, but it will do good (as PERCY BYSSHE SHELLEY had said, poetry does good) to the reader he addresses "When your soul is in my soul's stead" (l. 56).

This is a crucial line, because it shows that what prompts this poem, and all the poems in *A Shropshire Lad*, is sadness—the "dark and cloudy day" (l. 58) which his time of life has become. Poetry offers a way of thinking about that dark and cloudy day and being truthful to it without retreating into the false pleasures of the deceptive and fleeting present. (That day contrasts with the night of drunkenness that Ludlow beer has made possible.) Somehow being trained for unhappiness allows one to face the world and its truth. This is the ambiguous point of the poem's famous closing anecdote about Mithridates, who inured himself to the poisons his murderers sought to use against him. Because of the immunity he developed, he survived into old age.

And yet the story does not quite seem apposite. The closing lines about Mithridates could form a separate poem (and are often excerpted). Why are they there? Perhaps only, and importantly, because the anecdote offers a literary pleasure. Instead of presenting a moral or a parable illustrating the point of the poem, it is a demonstration of the pleasure to be derived from old stories, from reading and seeing those stories in verse. This is not the pleasure of truth—truth has no pleasures—but the pleasure of poetry when it can be *consonant* with the truth. This is why it relieves some of the dismal distress with which the previous stanza ends. Poetry can modulate through all moods—from comic complaint to melancholy reflection to captivating anecdote. What allows this modulation is its respect for the truth about life, a truth that makes the poet sad but also gives him a solid foundation for every kind of description of the world—that is, a solid foundation for poetic vocation.

BIBLIOGRAPHY

Gardner, Philip, ed. *A. E. Housman: The Critical Heritage.* New York: Routledge, 1992.

Highet, Gilbert. *Classical Tradition: Greek and Roman Influences on Western Literature.* New York: Oxford University Press, 1957.

Richards, Grant. *Housman: 1897–1936.* New York: Oxford University Press, 1942.

THACKERAY, WILLIAM MAKEPEACE

(1811–1863) William Makepeace Thackeray is, of course, one of the great Victorian novelists, now most famous for *Vanity Fair* (1847–48). The title, from John Bunyan's *The Pilgrim's Progress* (1678), as well as a series of famous events in the novel, such as Becky Sharpe's ejection of Doctor Johnson's great dictionary from the carriage when she finally leaves the school she detests, show Thackeray's great and good-humored literary gusto. Born in India in 1811 (he saw the exiled NAPOLEON BONAPARTE on his journey to England as a child), he came from an affluent background (which he wrote about very winningly in some autobiographical essays); accumulated numerous gambling debts of the sort that he depicts in some of his more appealingly ne'er-do-well characters; and immersed himself in all kinds of literature as well as in the great works of the British historians, such as David Hume and Edward Gibbon. (That immersion can be seen in his historical novels, such as *Vanity Fair,* set during the Napoleonic Wars, and *The History of Henry Esmond* [1852], which begins during the English Civil War.) He also—perhaps surprisingly, given his own more conservative tendencies—was very taken with PERCY BYSSHE SHELLEY, whom he studied diligently. He knew EDWARD FITZGERALD as an undergraduate; wrote memorably about his close friend THOMAS HOOD; and was a literary antagonist of Charles Dickens, whose richly self-indulgent style the far-more-ironic Thackeray thought was overdone.

About 1838, the literary activity that had been a pleasant avocation for Thackeray became a necessity: His family was more or less bankrupt, and he had to make a living through writing. Adding to the pressure was the fact that his wife was an invalid, and that he had three daughters to support. This may help explain why Thackeray was notably alert to the experience of women, which he understood perhaps as well as or better than any male novelist of his time. He wrote in all sorts of genres, and his writing is always of a very high quality. He did not write very much poetry, but the poems he did write are marked by the same whimsically piquant humor that marks the narrative voice of his great novels: a sense of pure and delightful literary command. It is interesting to note that Thackeray's daughter Harriet was Leslie Stephen's first wife and therefore the mother of Virginia Woolf's step-siblings. Stephen, an author and critic, wrote the original *Dictionary of National Biography* entry on Thackeray.

See also "BALLAD OF BOUILLABAISSE."

BIBLIOGRAPHY

Peters, Catherine. *Thackeray's Universe: Shifting Worlds of Imagination and Reality.* London: Faber and Faber, 1987.

Ray, Gordon N. *Thackeray: The Age of Wisdom, 1847–1863.* New York: McGraw-Hill, 1957.
———. *Thackeray: The Uses of Adversity, 1811–1846.* New York: McGraw-Hill, 1955.
Shillingsburg, Peter L. *William Makepeace Thackeray: A Literary Life.* New York: Palgrave, 2001.
Thackeray, William Makepeace. *Roundabout Papers.* London: Dent and Sons, 1946.
Trollope, Anthony. *Thackeray.* London: Macmillan, 1936.

"THAMURIS MARCHING" ROBERT BROWNING (1875) "Thamuris Marching" is one of the three or four great poems in terza rima in English. Terza rima is a rhyme scheme in the form of interlocking tercets. Each tercet rhymes *aba*; the *b* rhyme in the middle line establishes the *a* rhymes for the next tercet, so that each stanza implies a subsequent one whose rhymes it gives. Each rhyme (after the very first) is triple, since the poem unfolds like this: *aba, bcb, cdc,* etc.; there are three *b* and *c* rhymes, and in the next tercet there will be two more *d*'s, and so on. The Italian poet Dante Alighieri (1265–1321) invented this pattern for his *Divine Comedy,* and it is a far more difficult form in English than in Italian because English has fewer rhymes. The great exponents of *terza rima* in English are PERCY BYSSHE SHELLEY, ROBERT BROWNING, WILLIAM BUTLER YEATS, and the American James Merrill (1926–95). When Browning was writing, his main example was Shelley, in particular the "ODE TO THE WEST WIND," written in terza rima sonnets (the final couplet leaves out the propelling middle line), and Shelley's greatest poem, though unfinished, *The* TRIUMPH OF LIFE. Shelley's example showed terza rima as a form that committed the poet to keep going on, projected further by each middle line's new onset rhyme.

Browning's "Thamuris Marching" is a terza rima song that appears as part of a long, late, near-unreadable narrative poem called *Aristophanes's Apology,* it comprises lines 5,188–5,264 of that poem. The song stands alone as a poem, and Browning loved reading it aloud. We need not dwell on the rest of the long poem, since its singer disapproves of the song but suddenly has an impulse to sing it anyway. A little context may be useful, though: Upon hearing of the death of Euripides (ELIZABETH BARRETT BROWNING's favorite Greek tragedian), Balaustion (a fictional character whose name means pomegranate in Greek) and Aristophanes, the most famous of the comic playwrights, are arguing about the merits, both poetic and civic, of the great tragedians, of whom Euripides was the last. Aristophanes recalls seeing Sophocles' (now lost) play on Thamuris, the one play in which Sophocles appeared on stage himself, as Thamuris. Aristophanes is moved by this memory to retell the story of Thamuris, despite disapproving of him. We know the story from Homer (as does Aristophanes, who cites him): In book 2 of the *Iliad,* Homer tells how Thamuris, a mortal from Thrace, had challenged the Muses to a singing contest—challenged, that is, the beings who claimed to be the divine inspiration of all song. He lost the contest, and the Muses "in their anger struck him maimed, and the voice of wonder / they took away, and made him a singer without memory" (2, ll. 594–600), memory itself being the first requirement for an oral poet like Homer and therefore being always figured as Mnemosyne, the mother of the Muses.

In this poem, the brilliant and sublime Thamuris, fearless of the wrath of divinity, is clearly a representation of Shelley, the precursor who for Browning most represented what it meant to be a poet. Browning did not think of Shelley as the greatest poet who ever lived; but he might be thought of as the greatest of *mortal* poets—that is, the greatest poet of ROMANTICISM, who challenged a place with those whose poetry came directly, we might put it, from the Muses (for example, Homer, Virgil, Dante, Shakespeare, and Milton), and who more or less asserted or acknowledged this (in Browning's reading of them). For Browning, Shelley's death was, if not "the first," certainly "the worst of woes" (l. 5,189). Aristophanes, on the other hand, has not risked all to be a poet and has survived "heart-whole, / no Thamuris" (ll. 5,162–5,163) into old age, much like Browning himself. But now he picks up Euripides' psalterion (an instrument like a zither, which Balaustion has inherited) and sings the song to Thamuris at the dawn of day and the dawn of poetry.

The song he sings is that of the moment when Thamuris is on his way to the competition with the Muses. He is full of SUBLIME energy, "gay and glad," energized by the brilliant youth of the morning, joining "the rush of air and light / And force: the world was of one joyous mind" (ll. 5,222–5,223). The earth is full of this rushing joy because it is dynamic, unlike the abode of the gods, which is eternal but comparatively static. As in ALFRED, LORD TENNYSON's "TITHONUS," heavenly dawn is beautiful but not fresh, an eternal repetition of what it always is, whereas this earthly dawn is utterly fresh and unprecedented. The price of freshness is that it cannot last. Neither Shelley (as he himself insisted in his preface to *Alastor*) nor Thamuris can be earth's poet long.

The Shelleyan references stress this—the reference to speed above all, but also to the fact that the season is autumn (as in "Ode to the West Wind") and not the spring that promises the length of the year to come. Browning is also remembering Shelley's account of how "long before the day / Was old, the joy which waked like Heaven's glance / The sleepers in the oblivious valley, died" (*The Triumph of Life,* ll. 537–539). The river Balura has not yet received its name—thrown lyre—which it will get when the defeated and broken Thamuris hurls his lyre into its waves. Now it rushes along namelessly but like the Arve, whose description in Shelley's "MONT BLANC" as "the breath and blood of distant lands" (l. 124) Browning echoes here. That river, which will very soon memorialize his failure, here is part of the general jubilation, or onward rush of things (an explicit allusion to Shelley's *The Triumph of Life,* where the chariot and the triumph roll onward on the storm of their own rushing splendor; note that Thamuris himself is coming from "triumph on to triumph" at l. 5,197). The river's sparkling, racing gaiety now makes Thamuris laugh, and he produces a simile that is the poem's thematic center: "Each flake of foam . . . Mocks slower clouds adrift in the blue dome" (ll. 5,206–5,208). The foam flakes are as nothing compared to the massive Olympian clouds, but they nevertheless mock the eternal they can image only for an instant. This, too, is the attitude of "Earth's poet" to the "Heavenly Muse."

"Thamuris Marching" is therefore a kind of pendant or happy version of Browning's greatest poem, "CHILDE ROLAND TO THE DARK TOWER CAME." When Thamuris, "predominating foremost of the band" (l. 5,340) arrives at the appointed site, "He saw, he knew the place" (l. 5,253), echoing Roland's assertion of triumph when he saw "the Band" waiting for him at the Dark Tower: "I saw them and I knew them all" (l. 202). Roland is dauntless, but Thamuris is joyful as he declares the start of the contest that will destroy him to see "Which wins—Earth's poet or the Heavenly Muse" (l. 5,264). Of course, the Heavenly Muse will win, but she will win as a poet of the heavens, not of the earth. Thamuris and Shelley are better as poets of the earth than she is, even if she is better as a muse of heaven than they are: "She sings for gods, not men," Aristophanes will say after "the song broke up on laughter" (ll. 5,265–5,268).

The last line of the song—"Earth's poet of the Heavenly Muse"—is the second line of a tercet and, accordingly and appropriately, does not rhyme, as the song breaks up. Terza rima will always fail to rhyme at the end, always leaving an unrhymed line (or suppressing it), so that to write a terza rima poem is at once to take on the self-propelling onwardness of the form and to know that the form will break up one way or another at its end. To do so (at least for Shelley and Browning) is therefore an act of defiance, knowing that the end will be bad, but nevertheless committing oneself to the energy of the way to that end.

BIBLIOGRAPHY

Bloom, Harold. *A Map of Misreading.* New York: Oxford University Press, 2003.

———. *Poetry and Repression: Revisionism from Blake to Stevens.* New Haven, Conn.: Yale University Press, 1976.

Browning, Robert. *Essay on Percy Bysshe Shelley.* London: Published for the Shelley Society by Reeves and Turner, 1888.

DeVane, William C. *A Browning Handbook.* New York: Appleton-Century-Crofts, 1955.

Langbaum, Robert Woodrow. *The Modern Spirit: Essays on the Continuity of Nineteenth- and Twentieth-Century Literature.* New York: Oxford University Press, 1970.

Raymond, William O. *The Infinite Moment, and Other Essays in Robert Browning.* Toronto: University of Toronto Press, 1965.

"THAT NATURE IS A HERACLITEAN FIRE AND OF THE COMFORT OF THE RESURRECTION" GERARD MANLEY HOPKINS (1888) This is one of GERARD MANLEY HOPKINS's later poems, written after the "terrible sonnets" or "sonnets of desolation" in which he had expressed such anxiety and grief. It is in part a poem that depicts recovery, a renewed sense of the haecceity, or "thisness," of the world (see "BINSEY POPLARS") following Hopkins's descent into an abyss of dark despair. The particularity of the world, he now recognizes, includes despair as well as the beautiful forms and "inscapes" by which he can know beauty. It contains the failure of beauty as well, the "fell of dark," since it is in that dark that the fire of the world can be seen most brightly.

The works of the Greek philosopher Heracleitus (ca. 540–ca. 480 B.C.E.) survive only in gnomic and powerful fragments. Often called the weeping philosopher, he is famous for his claim that "everything flows" and nothing remains. Heracleitus said that the substance of the world was fire, ever-changing and ever-consuming. This can be a nightmarish idea, but in Hopkins's hands it becomes instead one of the modes of celebrating Christ. For Hopkins (as for PERCY BYSSHE SHELLEY, whose *ADONAIS* always haunts Hopkins's poetry—"each are mirrors of / The fire for which all thirst"), fire stands not only for consumption and destruction but for an ever-renewed and kaleidoscopic freshness and beauty in creation, the "flaunting forth" of being that he praises at the beginning of the poem, and that we recognize as well from the title line of "AS KINGFISHERS CATCH FIRE," which this poem essentially rewrites in a more intense mode.

The greatest of these fires and sparks is the human being. But as a spark or star shining in darkness, the human soul is liable to becoming quenched in darkness, swept away by the universal flow of things—the experience whose horror Hopkins suffered and depicted three years earlier. In a letter to ROBERT BRIDGES, Hopkins described "That Nature is a Heraclitean Fire" as "a sonnet in sprung rhythm with two codas," although as Bridges remarked, it really has three (the stanzas comprising lines 15–24). The sonnet itself does not end but flows on, just as everything flows, including "man" and "his mark on mind" (l. 11), i.e., poetry. But the flow beyond the sonnet's natural limit leads to the comfort of the resurrection in the first of the codas (l. 16). The sonnet might have ended in despair, like some of the "terrible sonnets," but instead it goes on past its 14th line, and its very force converts everything that is inessential to the flash of fire itself. It celebrates the bonfire, or wildfire, of the world as the energy of God, the flame that allows the universal similitude by which "I am all at once what Christ is, since he was what I am" (l. 22; compare the account of what I call universal similitude with the entry on "As Kingfishers Catch Fire")—that is, poor, despairing, and mortal. But all that, too, is one of the flares of the fire. Fire joins and mates everything to everything else. Everything is fire, and its appearances are universal so that a joke or patch can be the matchwood that burns with the brilliance of the immortal diamond.

The diamond itself is fire; or, better, fire turns out to be an immortal diamond, the light of the "beacon" and "eternal beam" that shines across the speaker's deck. Here, again, Shelley's *Adonais* should be noted, since Hopkins echoes its closing lines, in which Shelley, too, is on a boat following an eternal beacon: "I am borne darkly, fearfully afar! / Whilst, burning through the inmost veil of heaven, / The soul of Adonais, like a star, / Beacons from the abode where the Eternal are" (ll. 492–495).

The idea that fire is a gem dissolved in ever-moving light is also Shellyan. It is a mistake to read this poem (as some do) as seeking to transcend the bonfire of creation: rather, it sees that the fire and diamond are one. The poem ends with the tautologous comparison that Hopkins had explored in "As Kingfishers Catch Fire," the assertion that "immortal diamond, / Is immortal diamond." The first diamond is the sum of things listed in the last line, the second is their essence, and that sum and essence are the same. Hopkins knew that a century earlier the greatest of all chemists, Antoine-Laurent Lavoisier, had shown that diamonds are chemically identical to charcoal, and he also knew that they could burn (this was discovered in 1771). But the burning of a diamond is just the way the universe "selves" or "justices" or "keeps grace" ("As Kingfishers Catch Fire"), just as the way the immortality of the world is the immortality of the fire out of which it is composed and the "pure ethereal stream" (as John Milton called it) of the light that it shines.

BIBLIOGRAPHY

Bridges, Robert. Preface to *Poems of Gerard Manley Hopkins*. Edited by W. H. Gardner. New York: Oxford University Press, 1948.

Gardner, W. H. *Gerard Manley Hopkins (1844–1889): A Study of Poetic Idiosyncrasy in Relation to Poetic Tradition.* New Haven, Conn.: Yale University Press, 1949.
———, ed. Introduction to *Poems and Prose of Gerard Manley Hopkins.* Harmondsworth, Middlesex, England: Penguin, 1963.
Hartman, Geoffrey. *The Unmediated Vision: An Interpretation of Wordsworth, Hopkins, Rilke, and Valery.* New Haven, Conn.: Yale University Press, 1954.
Miller, J. Hillis. "Gerard Manley Hopkins." In *The Disappearance of God,* 270–359. Cambridge, Mass.: Belknap Press of Harvard University Press, 1963.
White, Norman. *Hopkins: A Literary Biography.* New York: Oxford University Press, 1992.

"THEY TOLD ME, HERACLITUS" See CORY, WILLIAM JOHNSON.

"THIS LIVING HAND" JOHN KEATS (1820)

"This Living Hand" is often taken to be JOHN KEATS's last poem (although, in great depression, he stopped writing poetry a year before his death from tuberculosis). There is some evidence that Keats meant it for a speech in his play *Otto the Great,* but even if he did, the poem stands alone, and Keats conceived it as a unit that would stand alone. It is interesting to think of it as addressed to Fanny Brawne, the great unrequited love of Keats's life, but not with certainty. The addressee of the poem is at least someone that Wallace Stevens, most Keatsian of 20th-century poets, called the "interior paramour," or the idealized object of love.

All that matters is that the poem's addressee seems somewhat ghostly herself. Her ghostliness is not ghostliness to Keats; *he* knows whom he is addressing, But we cannot know, because he is now dead, "in the icy silence of the tomb," and therefore his knowledge has died with him. The fact is that because he is no longer alive, we cannot know whom he is addressing, so that his death renders her a phantom. And this is what the poem is about: She will be haunted and will be inextricably involved with death if he dies. He has died, and this has made her—again, within the poem itself—a phantasmal figure, just as the poem has predicted.

"This Living Hand" belongs to a tradition of poems that prophesy the regret a poet's survivors will have after his or her death, but Keats's version sings a subtle change on the theme. He says that the very poem he is writing will become uncanny after his death—that is to say, he prophesizes the effect of his own prophecy. WILLIAM BUTLER YEATS will later do something similar, probably under the spell of Keats, in his great poem "WHEN YOU ARE OLD."

What gives "This Living Hand" its eeriness is the gesture with which it ends. "See here it is—/ I hold it towards you." The hand he holds out, at the time of writing, is the hand that is "warm and capable / Of earnest grasping." He knows that it is capable of grasping because it is holding the pen with which he is writing the poem. At the end, he holds the hand out, but if he is holding it out, he is not writing. He has put down his pen. To *write* that he is holding it out proves that he is not.

In this way, the poem knows itself to be fundamentally posthumous. The hand that writes it is alive, but the hand the poem memorializes is necessarily dead. The question remains, though: Who is the *you* in the poem? She is, of course, the phantom beloved, but because she is a phantom, too, she gets out of the way of the poem's address, and thus, the *you* means the reader as well. The reader is haunted by the death of the poet, and by the way his death renders phantasmal those to whom he addresses the poem. Therefore, by an ineluctable logic, we are reminded of our phantasmal fates, of the fact that our own warmth and life are temporary, and that we, too, will end in the icy silence of the tomb, whether or not we extend our hands to Keats. "This Living Hand" is generally regarded as one of the most uncanny poems of all time, and here we can see why this is so.

BIBLIOGRAPHY

Bate, Walter Jackson. *John Keats.* Cambridge, Mass.: Harvard University Press, 1963.
Bloom, Harold. *Poetry and Repression: Revisionism from Blake to Stevens.* New Haven, Conn.: Yale University Press, 1976.
———. *The Visionary Company: A Reading of English Romantic Poetry.* Garden City, N.Y.: Doubleday, 1961.
De Man, Paul. *The Rhetoric of Romanticism.* New York: Columbia University Press, 1984.
Dickstein, Morris. *Keats and His Poetry: A Study in Development.* Chicago: University of Chicago Press, 1971.

Flesch, William. "The Ambivalence of Generosity: Keats Reading Shakespeare." *ELH: English Literary History* 62, no. 1 (Spring 1995): 149–169.

McFarland, Thomas, *The Masks of Keats: The Endeavour of a Poet.* New York: Oxford University Press, 2000.

Stillinger, Jack. *The Hoodwinking of Madeline, and Other Essays on Keats's Poems.* Urbana: University of Illinois Press, 1971.

Vendler, Helen Hennessy. *Odes of John Keats.* Cambridge, Mass.: Harvard University Press, 1983.

Wasserman, Earl. *The Finer Tone: Keats' Major Poems.* Baltimore: Johns Hopkins Press, 1953.

THOMPSON, FRANCIS (1859–1907)

Thompson was one of the intense and great Catholic poets who, like ALICE MEYNELL and COVENTRY PATMORE (both of whom he knew) and, most eminently, GERARD MANLEY HOPKINS, flourished in the second half of the Victorian era. To be a Catholic intellectual in Victorian England tended to mean living as a convert, apart from the ruling culture and religion—often under the influence of Cardinal Newman, the most influential of English converts to the Roman Catholic faith. For poets, the attraction of such conversion is often consonant with their attraction toward poetic intensity. Although not a convert himself (he was born Catholic), Thompson was in some ways the best exemplar of this contention. His parents and uncles had followed Newman to Catholicism before he was born, and so still he lived the semi-outcast life that was itself a paradoxical sign of vocation.

For Thompson the life into which he was born (as his parents' second but only surviving son) included consideration of the priesthood, which in the end he could not take up, and of medicine, whose close connection to human abjection he found too close to home. Abjection was both his theme and mode. Having failed to become a physician, he moved to London after his mother died, and there he became an opium addict, sometimes living in the most abject poverty, starving and homeless. That poverty was for him a strong reminder of what he calls (in "An Anthem of Earth") "The shunless fardel of the world." The material world is for him the place from which God is absent and, therefore, becomes the best sign and example of the need for God. To need God means, by his logic, that God is necessary, and what is necessary must exist, so the absence of God in the material world is a sign of his presence in the spiritual world.

This idea is a constant in Thompson's work, so that in his great essay on PERCY BYSSHE SHELLEY, the famous atheist whom Thompson defended to the last, he describes how the materialist science in which he was trained becomes so materialist as to suggest its own antithesis: "amidst material nature, where our dull eyes see only ruin, the finer eye of science has discovered life in putridity and vigour in decay, seeing dissolution even and disintegration, which in the mouth of man symbolize disorder, to be in the works of God undeviating order, and the manner of our corruption to be no less wonderful than the manner of our health." This idea is central to all of Thompson's poetry: that corruption too is wonderful; that putridity and life, vigor, and decay go together; that abjection and poetry are both signs of the spirit. Such a perspective allowed him to combine all his poetic and scientific interests: the sheer materialism of the world as given by science and as conveyed by the PRE-RAPHAELITE poets whom he loved (see, for example, DANTE GABRIEL ROSSETTI'S "THE WOODSPURGE") stood (as it stood for his great 17th-century forebears George Herbert and Richard Crashaw) for the absence that caused pain and compelled an urge toward transcendence. Thus in his great ode "To the Sinking Sun" he notes that the Sun never sets the same way twice (as the angle of Earth's axis with respect to the Sun changes day by day), so that its repetition shows the "grief of vicissitude but not / Its penetrant surprise." As for Patmore (and indeed ALFRED, LORD TENNYSON, also haunted by the newest and most shocking scientific discoveries), the material world for Thompson is a world of vicissitude, and the surprise has to be elsewhere—in a spiritual realm that transcends the material world.

Thompson's own life bears out his commitments, almost as in a fiction. A mysterious prostitute, almost the symbol of abjection, supported him and gave him a place to live. While homeless, he submitted some poems to Alice Meynell's journal (edited with her husband, Wilfrid). They were published and widely read, and the Meynells took him up. ROBERT BROWNING admired his work, and Patmore became a patron. The unknown prostitute vanished, so as not to interfere with the more promising route his life was taking. From then on, Thompson was a literary figure, with an audience, but never far from the abjection that he had known so intensely. He died penniless. Opium and disease haunted him for most of his life, a life devoted to a vocation for both abjection and transcendence.

See also THE HOUND OF HEAVEN.

BIBLIOGRAPHY

Boardman, Brigid M. *Between Heaven and Charing Cross: The Life of Francis Thompson.* New Haven, Conn.: Yale University Press, 1988.

Taylor, Beverly. *Francis Thompson.* Boston: Twayne, 1987.

"THREE YEARS SHE GREW"

See LUCY POEMS.

"THYRSIS" MATTHEW ARNOLD (1866)

"Thyrsis" is MATTHEW ARNOLD's elegy for ARTHUR HUGH CLOUGH who died suddenly of malaria in 1861, age 42. Clough and Arnold had been friends at Rugby School (where Clough was a pupil and Arnold's father was headmaster) and at Oxford University. "Thyrsis" is in the mode of John Milton's *Lycidas* (1638), and indeed, Arnold calls it a "monody," Milton's word for his own elegy, indicating a single solitary voice bewailing alone. The name is drawn from classical elegy, a tradition Milton followed as well. Milton's Lycidas was a fellow undergraduate, and Arnold follows Milton in imagining his undergraduate days as a pastoral in which he and Thyrsis "assay'd" their "shepherd pipes" (l. 35).

This is not the first time that Arnold imagined Clough as a shepherd, since in "The SCHOLAR-GIPSY," he depicts Clough as a shepherd busy at his work while Arnold himself rests and meditates on the legendary figure of the scholar gypsy, who stands for a timeless absorption in the best of a Wordsworthian, meditative, philosophical, poetic life. A note in "Thyrsis" refers us to "The Scholar-Gipsy," to which it acts as a kind of pendant, with Clough replacing the Gipsy Scholar himself.

However, he replaces him as an absence. In "Thyrsis," Arnold describes walking through the old haunts around Oxford where he and Clough used to talk of the "Our friend, the Scholar-Gipsy" (l. 29), the legendary 17th-century student who went to live with the Gypsies. Now he returns to think again of the times that are gone—the times, that is, when he and Clough were students together. Clough's absence now is like the Scholar-Gipsy's absence then. That absence is to be thought of more or less like Lycidas's at the end of Milton's elegy: They have become the geniuses of the place, the spirits whose absence means their absorption into the landscape that speaks of it.

Arnold's elegy, like all good elegies (but perhaps no great ones), is for himself, for the ephemerality of his own life. The landscape from which Clough is absent is one in which he can feel that his own absence has mattered very little and will matter very little when it is rendered permanent by death. The two crucial symbols in the poem are the tree that Arnold first misses and then sees, permanent even as the landscape is developed and changed; and the Scholar-Gipsy, who also turns out to be permanent in a way that ends up contrasting him with Clough and with Arnold.

The poem makes it appear that the rediscovery of the lost tree will stand for some recovery of memory and hope on the part of the poet. And indeed, the tree does stand for reassurance that the Gipsy-Scholar is still there (ll. 193–97). But Clough is not there; he has died elsewhere and is elsewhere now for good.

He is, in fact, in a place where the conventions of classical elegy are appropriate, as their absence is appropriate in England. Clough's absence and the Gipsy-Scholar's presence come to mean the same thing. He cannot be properly mourned in England because the classical gods whom elegies invoke, like Proserpine, know nothing of England (ll. 91–100). But since Clough died in Italy, Arnold's classical imitation can mourn him, while at the same time, England can be preserved, not as a place of mourning and of time overpast, but as a place in which the strange innocence and eternal youth of the Scholar-Gipsy can still be a beacon to poetic inspiration, as it was for Clough and Arnold. Thus, the elegy ends with Arnold's own paraphrase of Clough's famous poem "SAY NOT THE STRUGGLE NAUGHT AVAILETH," since the spirit to which both poets aspired still haunts the places they used to haunt, and the meaning of their own absence is converted to a sense that everything lovely and new about those places will continue to be as fresh as it ever was. Their deaths guarantee this freshness and help them to participate in it, if not as presences, like the Scholar-Gipsy, at least as tender and meaningful absences.

BIBLIOGRAPHY

Arnold, Matthew. *Essays, Letters, and Reviews.* Collected and edited by Fraser Neiman. Cambridge, Mass.: Harvard University Press, 1960.

Bloom, Harold, ed. *Matthew Arnold.* New York: Chelsea House, 1987.

Dawson, Carl, and John Pfordresher, eds. *Matthew Arnold: The Critical Heritage.* New York: Routledge, 1995.

Trilling, Lionel. *The Moral Obligation to Be Intelligent: Selected Essays.* Edited by Leon Weiseltier. New York: Farrar, Straus, and Giroux, 2000.

"TINTERN ABBEY" WILLIAM WORDSWORTH (1798) More properly called "Lines: Composed a Few Miles Above Tintern Abbey On Revisiting the Banks of the Wye During a Tour, 13 July 1798," this is one of WILLIAM WORDSWORTH's greatest poems, second perhaps only to the INTIMATIONS ODE in its influence and power. (In conversation, Wordsworth always called it "Tintern Abbey," and this natural abbreviation has persisted.) It is the last poem in the 1798 edition of the revolutionary book he wrote with SAMUEL TAYLOR COLERIDGE, *Lyrical Ballads.* The full title deserves attention since the poem is not a description of Tintern Abbey itself but of the River Wye (in South Wales, where he was on a walking tour with his sister), miles away from that beautiful relic.

The abbey itself was originally built in the 12th century, and its remains date from the 13th; it was abandoned after 1536 when England began its cataclysmic transition to Protestantism, and Henry VIII (and later Elizabeth I) seized, despoiled or destroyed Catholic religious holdings. (William Shakespeare alludes to such ruins in sonnet 73, where he talks of the "bare ruined choirs where late the sweet birds sang"). But for the 28-year-old Wordsworth, faith was to be found elsewhere, in the woods, not the abbeys, and faith was not in God but in nature or the spirit of nature. In the poem, Wordsworth knows where the abbey itself is because he is *revisiting* the banks of the River Wye; however, he is not returning to Catholicism but to an earlier version of his own soul and the worship of Nature that was and continues to be his (l. 153; Wordsworth was to regret this line afterward, and it should not be taken too literally; it is, rather, an indication of what he *does not* worship at this time, the personal or Christian God).

Wordsworth composed the poem on July 13, 1798, but he did not write it down for another few days, until he and his sister reached Bristol, so the thought that it records is the thought that he actually had on his return to the Wye. He had last been there in August 1793; now he has returned and can measure how much he has changed by how little the natural landscape has. He returns to hear "again / *These* waters," to see "*these* steep and lofty cliffs," to repose under "*this* dark sycamore." More important, perhaps, is that he is returning at "*this* season," which is to say that the place is the same and so is the time. The natural world is seasonal and essentially timeless, but human life is time-bound, not seasonal and cyclical but headed toward age and death.

The poem is about subjectivity and time—about what time does to subjectivity. The passage of time is felt through the relationship between memory and loss, through the memory of what has been lost. At the least, what has been lost is one's own earlier self. "Tintern Abbey" is directly influenced by Coleridge's "FROST AT MIDNIGHT" (gracefully alluding to it through the reference to the shining moon at line 135, to which compare the last lines of "Frost at Midnight"), and by the intense and melancholy reflections on the relationship of memory to present peace that is the heart of Coleridge's poem. Indeed, the structure of "Tintern Abbey" is fundamentally the same, ending with Wordsworth blessing his companion, as Coleridge had blessed his son HARTLEY COLERIDGE, with the prophetic wish that nature will be, for his sister, as imbued with a sense of spirit and life as it is for him.

The blessing and the wish are wonderful but melancholy; in both poems, they register the fact that such a sense of nature may not go without saying. Nature is *felt* to be or to contain a "motion and a spirit that impels / All thinking things, all objects of all thought, / And rolls through all things" (ll. 101–103; compare the opening of PERCY BYSSHE SHELLEY's "MONT BLANC," which begins with an overt allusion to this passage), but the world is half created by the senses and the mind that perceives it; therefore, the spirit of Nature may be a projection of the human mind. Indeed, the famous passage I have just quoted suggests just this (although usually this suggestion is unnoticed), since what the motion or spirit impels is all *thinking* things and all objects of *thought,* and if it rolls through all things, that is a motion that occurs in the mind and not necessarily in the world. This, too, is one of Coleridge's ideas in "Frost at Midnight," where "the idling spirit" interprets what it sees "By its own moods," seeking everywhere for a mirror of itself (ll. 20–22).

This is a serious issue for Wordsworth, more so than it was in Coleridge's poem, since "Tintern Abbey" is the first of Wordsworth's great crisis lyrics. Like the memory of childhood in the INTIMATIONS ODE (begun four years later), the return to the Wye forces Wordsworth to confront the distance between his present and his past self. This should be compared to the passage of *The* PRELUDE wherein he describes memory as giving him "two consciousnesses, conscious of myself and of some other Being" (book 2, ll. 32–33). In the intervening five years, he has changed; it is no longer what he calls "the hour of thoughtless youth" (l. 90) but a time of life in which he feels chastened and subdued by the earthly freight of living. When he was a child, nature was everything to him, but now he no longer feels this way—he no longer *can* feel this way. The very fact that nature reflects the mind means that its actual, unchanging, external physical attributes only determine what it no longer reflects. The place is exactly the same, but his "recognitions [are] dim and faint" (l. 59). Here we should give the word *recognitions* its full meaning of *thinking again.* He sees but no longer feels what he once did, and this fills him with "a sad perplexity" (l. 60). The fact that nothing has changed in the landscape measures how all the change he perceives is in himself.

"Tintern Abbey" tries to think this issue through, and it succeeds in such a way that Woodsworth can come to some resolution of the crisis. The thematic issues we have been considering are presented in an order that allows for this resolution. We can summarize the order this way: The place is just the same as it was, but the poet no longer feels as he did. He now thinks in terms of past and future as well, and so he *dares* to hope (l. 65), in that anxious and uncertain formulation, for some recompense. That recompense is the recompense of memory. Tintern Abbey no longer fills him with the joy he remembers it as filling him with. But he *does* remember, even if memory is a muted and attenuated experience, and so he dares to hope for future memories, both of the past and of the present—of the present because he thinks that "in *this* moment" there is food for future years, but that food is the memory he has now of the past. This is a movement toward further attenuation, however; the future is even further removed from the past, and memory weakens into a second-order memory of memory, since the past is already remote from the present.

Memories of memories are central to romantic melancholy, and also to the dynamic of recovery (see, again, the different levels of memory in Coleridge's "Frost at Midnight," and also Wordsworth's "Lines written in Early Spring," where he describes that "sweet mood when pleasant thoughts / Bring sad thoughts to the mind" [ll. 3–4]). For while the aching raptures of youth are over, they were also thoughtless. Nature was "all in all" to him then (l. 75), a line in which Wordsworth (as is typical) recalls John Milton's *Paradise Lost,* in which God foretells the time when he "shall be All in All" (book 3, l. 341; this is an echo of 1 Corinthians 15:28, but Wordsworth is clearly thinking of Milton—who also puts in a cameo perhaps as the "blind man" of line 24—and not what Milton is echoing). Now, however, Wordsworth is subdued by thought; he looks on nature not "as in the hour of *thoughtless* youth" but with a far augmented sense of human capacities and human depth. The costs and benefits of this deepened apprehension are the same and can be put simply: The price of thought is giving up thoughtlessness. But that price is an easier one to pay once Wordsworth realizes that it was all thought anyway, that the mind half created what it perceived always. Therefore, the memory of the present will not be an attenuated but an intensified memory as he thinks further on this moment in which he learned to start thinking about thought.

Woodsworth's sister Dorothy, whom he addresses in the poem's final movement, represents the gain offsetting future loss; she also allows him to carry forward even what has been lost into the present. For now Dorothy, like Hartley Coleridge, is the other consciousness, not lost but there with him, and the future he foretells for her (like the future Samuel Taylor Coleridge foretells for Hartley) is one in which she, too, will become more thoughtful, even as Woodsworth is now. But now both consciousnesses are there, and Dorothy represents both the present's past and the past's future, his own earlier raptures and his sense of what she will discover about herself and about him, even as he discovers the same about her, when she thinks back on this time as he has thought on his previous experience of the Wye. The present moment stands, therefore, both for the future and the past, and it links them each to each.

BIBLIOGRAPHY

Abrams, M. H. *Correspondent Breeze: Essays on English Romanticism.* New York: Norton, 1984.

———. *Natural Supernaturalism: Tradition and Revolution in Romantic Literature.* New York: Norton, 1973.

Alpers, Paul. *What Is Pastoral?* Chicago: University of Chicago Press, 1996.

Barker, Juliet. *Wordsworth: A Life.* New York: Viking, 2000.

Bloom, Harold. *Poetry and Repression: Revisionism from Blake to Stevens.* New Haven, Conn.: Yale University Press, 1976.

———. *The Visionary Company: A Reading of English Romantic Poetry.* Garden City, N.Y.: Doubleday, 1961.

Bromwich, David. *Disowned by Memory: Wordsworth's Poetry of the 1790s.* Chicago: University of Chicago Press, 1998.

Brooks, Cleanth. *A Shaping Joy: Studies in the Writer's Craft.* London: Methuen, 1973.

Empson, William. *Seven Types of Ambiguity.* New York: New Directions, 1966.

Gill, Stephen. *William Wordsworth: A Life.* New York: Oxford University Press, 1989.

Hartman, Geoffrey. *Wordsworth's Poetry, 1787–1814.* New Haven, Conn.: Yale University Press, 1971.

Johnston, Kenneth. *Hidden Wordsworth: Poet, Lover, Rebel, Spy.* New York: Norton, 1998.

Levinson, Marjorie. *Wordsworth's Great Period Poems: Four Essays.* New York: Cambridge University Press, 1986.

Liu, Alan. *Wordsworth: The Sense of History.* Stanford, Calif.: Stanford University Press, 1989.

Moorman, Mary. *William Wordsworth: A Biography.* 2 vols. Oxford: Clarendon Press, 1957, 1965.

Pinch, Adela. *Strange Fits of Passion: Epistemologies of Emotion, Hume to Austen.* Stanford, Calif.: Stanford University Press, 1996.

Quinney, Laura. *The Poetics of Disappointment: Wordsworth to Ashbery.* Charlottesville: University Press of Virginia, 1999.

Wolfson, Susan J. *Questioning Presence: Wordsworth, Keats, and the Interrogative Mode in Romantic Poetry.* Ithaca, N.Y.: Cornell University Press, 1986.

"TITHONUS" ALFRED, LORD TENNYSON (1859)

"Tithonus" is a kind of companion poem to ALFRED, LORD TENNYSON'S "ULYSSES," begun at about the same time in the early 1830s after the death of Tennyson's great friend and the fiancé of his sister Emily, ARTHUR HENRY HALLAM. It was not completed, however, for another quarter century, perhaps because the subject was too painful. Emily had said that, unlike Hallam, "none of the Tennysons ever die," and "Tithonus," like "Ulysses," is a story about survival in a world that has lost all freshness, hope, and even meaning or reason to survive.

The poem also alludes, appropriately enough, to a moment in the medieval Italian poet Dante's *Purgatorio,* the book of waiting, where Dante describes Aurora, the goddess of Dawn, as "the fair consort of Tithonus old" (Purgatorio 9, l. 1). She is fair, and he is old because he was a mortal, a Trojan youth. According to the Greek myth, Aurora fell in love with Tithonus, and Zeus granted her request that he be immortal. But she failed to request eternal youth, and so when Aurora's displaced handmaidens the Hours go to Zeus with their anger at Tithonus's usurpation of their rights to the ordering of time, the gift of immortality, like so many gifts of the gods, became a poisoned one. Tithonus will decay without falling, decay beyond the limits of any natural decrepitude, and there is no possibility of setting a limit to how old and frail and feeble he may become. He is like JOHN KEATS's Moneta in *The Fall of Hyperion* (see HYPERION AND *THE FALL OF HYPERION*), perhaps the poem most influential on "Tithonus"—doomed to a survival that can measure only the ever-increasing passages of loss. As for the ancient myth of Tithonus, insofar as it describes a timeless situation, we might see it as being about the relation of aging to the eternal freshness of the natural world—the thing that Emily Tennyson was lamenting.

Tennyson's version of the poem, like "Ulysses," belongs to the genre of crisis lyric—that is, it is a poem that thinks its way through to a solution of the crisis that elicits it—the death of Hallam and the desperate mourning that ensued. What the poem does is to make death into a good thing, part of the natural cycle that Tithonus, the speaker of this dramatic monologue, wishes he could still be part of. Emily felt the same way, but in a despairing mode. This poem makes death positive and meaningful, and not simply the cessation of meaningless suffering. The logic by which it does so is essentially this: Hallam died, which was terrible; his death made our survival terrible; therefore, survival beyond the terms of love and hope is terrible; and so death, as part of the natural cycle of love and hope, is desirable; and thus, Hallam's death is not terrible after all.

The poem begins with an evocation of the natural cycle, in a line that echoes (in Tennyson's revision) WILLIAM WORDSWORTH's *The PRELUDE,* in which he talks of "The immeasurable height of woods decaying, never to be decayed" (1850 version, book 6, ll. 624–625). For Wordsworth, life itself is immortal even as its individuals die, a point that Tennyson laments in his great elegy for Hallam, *IN MEMORIAM A.H.H.,* when he complains of Nature: "So careful of the type she seems, / So careless of the single life" (LV, ll. 7–8). There the single life is lost; here it survives and is not able to join with the rhythm of the type, the universal abstract types named by *the* woods, *the* swan, and *the* field, and the man himself, who comes and tills it and then lies beneath it.

Tithonus is consumed not by time or by death but by immortality itself. This is a reversal that again makes of time and mortality something to be desired, not lamented. The ever-renewed freshness and beauty of the dawn is something that the old no longer desire to see. The poem is a kind of mirror image, or negative, of Wordsworth's INTIMATIONS ODE, since it comes to reject the freshness of the dawn for an absorption into the rhythms of nature. Those rhythms include dying at the right time, and death is made into the natural fulfillment of a natural life, not its antithesis.

Dying at the right time is important for, as with Wordsworth, time is the central issue here. For Wordsworth, time measures the distance from an ideal past and the perception of that distance's permanence. The fall into time is the fall into the knowledge of death, and of the ephemerality of what seems like human permanence and human connection, with nature thought of as nurse or mother. For Tennyson, or at least for Tithonus, time is the name for the pressure of eternity, not ephemerality, for a future that will be endless and endlessly more bleak.

Yet there is a potentially happy ending to the poem. In the best-known versions of the myth, from the so-called Homeric hymns, the story of Tithonus is a story of metamorphosis. Eventually the gods take pity on him and turn him into a grasshopper (an insect that looks much like an old man). He returns to the natural world that he has lost; his fears of an endless future will not come to pass.

But this raises a further philosophical point, perhaps the deepest and most interesting point in the poem and the one that Tennyson brooded on throughout his life. How *could* fears of an endless future come to pass? The endlessness of his life can never *be* confirmed, and hence Tithonus's hesitation about what his fate will be. She is silent, and he can only guess at what will happen to him, but he can never know that his guess is right.

He can never know because, like all of us, he lives in the present; his experience is always of the present moment. We are, as the American poet John Ashbery says, always cresting into the present in a standing wave of arrival. Does this make Tithonus different from us, or similar? In any case, mortal or immortal, the experience of subjectivity is an experience of being time-bound. The natural cycle belongs to others, to nature and to the dead. "Tithonus" is a poem from the subjective point of view and ultimately Wordsworthian despite itself, since it describes what it means for any person to feel ultimately separate from the natural existence of what he or she loves.

BIBLIOGRAPHY

Armstrong, Isobel. *Victorian Poetry: Poetry, Poetics and Politics.* New York: Routledge, 1993.

Bloom, Harold. *Poetry and Repression: Revisionism from Blake to Stevens.* New Haven, Conn.: Yale University Press, 1976.

Kilham, John. *Critical Essays on the Poetry of Tennyson.* New York: Barnes and Noble, 1960.

Kincaid, James R. *Tennyson's Major Poems: The Comic and Ironic Patterns.* New Haven, Conn.: Yale University Press, 1975.

Ricks, Christopher B. *Tennyson.* New York: Macmillan, 1972.

Rowlinson, Matthew. *Tennyson's Fixations: Psychoanalysis and the Topics of the Early Poetry.* Charlottesville: University Press of Virginia, 1994.

Tucker, Herbert. *Tennyson and the Doom of Romanticism.* Cambridge, Mass.: Harvard University Press, 1988.

"TO ———" ("MUSIC, WHEN SOFT VOICES DIE") PERCY BYSSHE SHELLEY (1821)

This is one of PERCY BYSSHE SHELLEY's intensely beautiful late lyrics, almost certainly addressed to Jane Williams, the common-law wife of his friend Edward Williams. It belongs to a series of experiments in the delineation of the relationship of lyric to feeling that Shelley undertook in the last few months of his life, and which culminated in his great, not-quite-finished poem "LINES WRITTEN IN THE BAY OF LERICI." The experiment, or the motive to experiment, is essentially what the poem itself describes, the feeling that remains after the momentary climax of love or passion. John Milton had described, in *Paradise Lost* (1667), what he called "sweet, reluctant amorous delay"—that is, the heightening of erotic charge before it peaks. In "To ———," Shelley is interested in something symmetrical but vectored the other way: the love that remains after its culmination and which, because it is in decline, is inevitably tinged with sadness.

The content of that sadness is the sense that erotic feeling is over, but the presence of that sadness warrants that it is not over, since the sadness is a modality of the erotic feeling. Shelley presents this in starker but still exquisitely subtle form in what is probably a slightly earlier poem, "When Passion's Trance Is Overpast," which may be addressed to his wife Mary Shelley, instead of, or as well as, Jane Williams. There he expresses the wish that tenderness and truth could last—that the softness of feeling and dreaming could outlive the intense but brief moment of erotic climax. The climax he refers to is both momentary, in sexual consummation, and somewhat longer-lasting, but it is still brief—the experience of falling in love. But "Passion's Trance" ends with the pure lamentation and regret that "life and love" do not revive, and that once the trance is over, it is over for good, even if life and love at least leave regret in their wake. (That poem should be compared to LORD BYRON's "SO, WE'LL GO NO MORE A-ROVING.")

It is against this bleak conclusion that some of the other lyrics are written. They will themselves draw out the lingering sense of love, making the transient stay a little longer through the beauty of the lyric, which describes the dying beauty of love. "To ———" (a poem Shelley worked on with great care) describes this explicitly, even in the momentary difficulty it presents to grammatical parsing. The first stanza, examined closely, says that music vibrates in the memory even when the voices that have sung it have ceased, So, too, do the odors of faded violets still linger in the sensory memory.

The second stanza both parallels and extends the first stanza: As the violets fade and die, so do roses, but their petals may be heaped for the beloved's bed. This heaping cannot be literal—who sleeps on a bed of rose leaves? Rather, it is a kind of higher-level metaphor, a metaphor for *how* the other images of lingering memory are metaphors for the memory of love. This is what the concluding lines confirm: Love itself will slumber on in thoughts of the beloved even when she is gone, like the music and the violets. Love is half-personified here ("Lines: when the lamp is shattered"), and therefore stands not only for his love for her, lingering after her departure (perhaps back to her own husband, until their next assignation), but for her presence itself. Love personified is what remains of her person, and it slumbers on in his thoughts of her, merging in memory and dream.

It should be noted that another draft reverses the stanzas. The final effect is very much the same, since in either case the second stanza reads as a subtlization of the experience outlined in the first.

BIBLIOGRAPHY

Bloom, Harold. *Genius: A Mosaic of One Hundred Exemplary Creative Minds.* New York: Warner, 2002.

———. *Shelley's Mythmaking.* New Haven, Conn.: Yale University Press, 1959.

———. *The Visionary Company: A Reading of English Romantic Poetry*. Garden City, N.Y.: Doubleday, 1961.
Burke, Kenneth. *Grammar of Motives*. Berkeley: University of California Press, 1969.
Chernaik, Judith. *The Lyrics of Shelley*. Cleveland: Press of Case Western Reserve University, 1972.
Hogle, Jerrold E. *Shelley's Process: Radical Transference and the Development of His Major Works*. New York: Oxford University Press, 1988.
Keach, William. *Shelley's Style*. New York: Methuen, 1984.
Leavis, F. R. *Revaluation: Tradition & Development in English Poetry*. New York: Norton, 1963.
Notopolous, James A. *The Platonism of Shelley: A Study of Platonism and the Poetic Mind*. Durham, N.C.: Duke University Press, 1949.
Quinney, Laura. *The Poetics of Disappointment: Wordsworth to Ashbery*. Charlottesville: University Press of Virginia, 1999.
Wasserman, Earl. *Shelley: A Critical Reading*. Baltimore: Johns Hopkins Press, 1971.

"TO A LITTLE INVISIBLE BEING WHO IS EXPECTED SOON TO BECOME VISIBLE" ANNA LAETITIA BARBAULD (ca. 1795)

This lovely poem was written when ANNA LAETITIA BARBAULD was in her early 50s. It is striking but characteristic of her poetry for the graceful way an address to a child is made an expression of empathetic blessing on its mother as well as the child. The little invisible being is, of course, the baby in the mother's womb, soon to be born.

Barbauld's poems always provide an interesting perspective on that of the later romantics, whose work she foreshadowed but whose intense subjectivity she resisted, especially when or because it threatened to verge on egocentricity (see her 1797 poem "TO MR COLERIDGE"). Barbauld's sensibility and morality is characteristically 18th century in its commitment to what the philosopher David Hume called "general benevolence"—that is, to the social virtues of sympathy and altruism. "To a Little Invisible Being" should be compared to WILLIAM WORDSWORTH'S INTIMATIONS ODE in the way it treats earthly life. (Wordsworth admired Barbauld enough to have a copy of *Lyrical Ballads* sent to her when it was published in 1798.) Like Wordsworth's great ode, it is a brief for human sympathy, but unlike Wordsworth, Barbauld is fully committed to human sociability and not to the intense introverted solitude characteristic of Wordsworth. Thus, the poem seeks to hasten the birth of the child. What for Wordsworth is the origin of disaster is for Barbauld the beginning of awe at the created world, Wordsworth will regard the natural world as a prison house; for Barbauld, it is liberation from the captivity of the womb: "Haste, little captive, burst thy prison doors" (l. 29). The poem's view of nature is not the opposite of Wordsworth's, but one which he will think partial. Nevertheless, for both, the wonders of the natural world, especially when perceived with the eyes of childhood, are cause for celebration.

"To a Little Invisible Being" is essentially romantic on a deeper level: the way it empathizes with the human capacity for empathy. The poem stems from the sense that what is most human about a human being is the way he or she can feel the humanity of another. Barbauld was not a mother herself (though she adopted a niece), but she kept school and wrote spectacularly popular books for children, and this poem might be said to make the claim for the moral stance represented by understanding them so well. Although not a mother herself, what she understands is that the child, unknown but loved (l. 22), will be the mother's most intense interest, and that this maternal interest in the child is what will make it an empathetic being as well.

Love is self-sustaining: It springs from being the object of unconditional love, an object which will then devote unconditional love to others. Barbauld's poem not only urges this idea but is a demonstration of it since it so movingly shows her love for both mother and child; and while addressed to the child in order to be overheard by the mother whom it comforts and makes happy, the poem is also addressed to the general reader, brought into the circle of benevolence and empathy just by the fact that we find the poem so moving without having any selfish interest or stake in the human interactions it describes. This is probably what Wordsworth found most striking in Barbauld, and what he and SAMUEL TAYLOR COLERIDGE sought to do in their own way in *Lyrical Ballads*.

BIBLIOGRAPHY

Armstrong, Isobel. "The Gush of the Feminine: How Can We Read Women's Poetry of the Romantic Period?" In

Romantic Women Writers: Voices and Countervoices, edited by Paula R. Feldman and Theresa M. Kelley, 13–32. Hanover, N.H.: University Press of New England, 1995.

Armstrong, Isobel, and Virginia Blain, eds. *Women's Poetry in the Enlightenment: The Making of a Canon, 1730–1820.* New York: St. Martin's Press, 1999.

Barbauld, Anna Laetitia. *Poems, 1792.* New York: Woodstock, 1993.

Keach, William. *Arbitrary Power: Romanticism, Language, Politics.* Princeton, N.J.: Princeton University Press, 2004.

Mellor, Anne K. *Romanticism & Gender.* New York: Routledge, 1993.

Wordsworth, Jonathan. *Bright Work Grows: Women Writers of the Romantic Age.* Washington, D.C.: Woodstock Books, 1997.

"TO ANY READER" ROBERT LOUIS STEVENSON **(1885)** This is the last poem in ROBERT LOUIS STEVENSON's wonderful 1885 book *A Child's Garden of Verses.* The poem originally had two stanzas, and it now tends to be reprinted in its "fuller" version, but Stevenson published only the second stanza in his book, a decision that perhaps was right. Nevertheless, it adds depth to compare the two versions and to consider how the poem changes with the excision of the first stanza.

The poem as Stevenson printed it addresses "any reader," and we must recognize that the "you" of its first line refers to adults as well as to children, perhaps more to adults than to children. This is evident from the tight simile it offers: As our mother can see us playing by the garden trees, so we, too, can "look / Through the windows of this book" (ll. 2–3) at another child in another garden. The four elements of the simile may be schematized like this: Mother is to us *playing* as we *reading* are to a child. The two extremes are the parent and the child. The reader goes from one to the other, from the position of the child, playing around the garden trees, to that of the parent looking at the child. The simile is itself a little fable of growing-up. We grow up when we cease playing and start reading (or writing). Through the windows of the book, we can see the lost child, the "child of air" (l. 15)—Stevenson himself as a child, whose childhood is now remembered in the book. He cannot hear, because he is "far, far away" (l. 5) in another garden, the Eden of childhood, which is now only a memory. This poem should be compared with WILLIAM ALLINGHAM's "The BOY FROM HIS BEDROOM-WINDOW." The last lines are intensely moving because as in Allingham's poem, the *other* child—the child we see through the windows of this book—and our own childhood self—the child we were—are indistinguishable. They are both inaccessible to us—both what we are not. The most we can do, perhaps, is to write for them and take care of them.

The first stanza was published 22 years after Stevenson's death, and it is interesting for itself but much more directed towards the innocent child reader. There he imagines that child reading the book in the garden or in the house. She is already growing up, but this excised first stanza still considers reading as a pleasure of childhood and not of incipient loss of childhood. The first stanza celebrates the ways that children can enter secretly into the fantasy world of books, and it explicitly parallels Stevenson's own book to that of another, LEWIS CARROLL's *Alice Through the Looking Glass,* and to a story of Hans Christian Andersen's, "The Snow Queen." The first stanza is lovely, but the poem is much more moving without it because we become aware that the fantasy life of children is not a secret to adults but the secret *of* adults, who wish for nothing more ardently than to go through the looking glass back to the garden of childhood.

BIBLIOGRAPHY

Callow, Philip. *Louis: The Life of Robert Louis Stevenson.* London: Constable, 2001.

Jones, William B., Jr., ed. *Robert Louis Stevenson Reconsidered: New Critical Perspectives.* Jefferson, N.C.: McFarland, 2002.

Maixner, Paul, ed. *Robert Louis Stevenson: The Critical Heritage.* London: Routledge, 1981.

"TO AUTUMN" JOHN KEATS **(1819)** The last of the great series of odes that JOHN KEATS wrote in 1819, this one was composed on September 19 and therefore on the cusp of autumn rather than early summer, like the others. Although it is like the other odes in reflecting on human mortality and the passage of time, "To Autumn" is often regarded as having achieved a resolution and ending more reconciled to the nature of the world and of life.

In a letter to a friend written two days after the ode's composition, Keats described its genesis: "How beautiful the season is now—how fine the air. A temperate sharpness about it. Really, without joking, chaste weather. Dian skies. I never lik'd stubble fields so much as now—Aye, better than the chilly green of the spring. Somehow a stubble field looks warm—in the same way that some pictures look warm—this struck me so much in my sunday's walk that I composed upon it." The warmth that he describes here is like the "warm love" that he hopes for at the end of his "ODE TO PSYCHE," and it contrasts with the "cold pastoral" offered by the subject of "ODE ON A GRECIAN URN." Pictures and stubble fields look warm for Keats because they retain a sense of life; life is by definition transient, but that very transience leaves a sense of lingering warmth behind.

This is the theme as well of the famous first stanza of "To Autumn," which describes the way summer lingers on into the "warm days" of autumn, filling "all fruit with ripeness to the core" (l. 6) and making but "more, / And still more, later flowers for the bees, / Until they think warm days will never cease" (ll. 8–10). The stanza itself is strikingly quiescent, mellow and rich and, in the end, tending toward somnolence. It has no main verb. This is a fact easy to miss because of the accumulation of infinitives ("to load and bless") and gerundives and present participles ("conspiring," "maturing," "budding") that load the stanza down. But the languor of the stanza may verge on feeling oppressive, or on the sense of paralysis, of inability to move, which is prominent in many of Keats's poems, including "Ode on a Grecian Urn" and *The Fall of Hyperion* (see *HYPERION* AND *THE FALL OF HYPERION*).

It is not surprising that the first stanza should be subtly troubling: It is the task of a poem to see and confront a problem, and "To Autumn" does just that. The first stanza can seem a little airless, and the second stanza can confirm that sense, with the slow motion movement of the figure of Autumn (is it male or female?) and the oozings of the cider press. But the second stanza also keeps the first stanza from coming to a complete halt. The second turns the first into a kind of invocation—the invocation with which odes generally begin. All the appositions on "Season of mist" that pile up in the first stanza now become part of an 11-line vocative; so we can summarize the first two stanzas like this: "Season of mist and mellow fruitfulness, Who hath not seen thee oft amid thy store?"

This means that the speaker—for there is one, as there is in all the other odes—achieves a kind of breakthrough to voice in this stanza. The silence of the first stanza—the silence that Keats always finds threatening, whether it is the silence of the urn or of the nightingale in "ODE TO A NIGHTINGALE" or of Saturn in *The Fall of Hyperion*—gives way to the possibility of voice: the question that the speaker poses to the oppressively rich silent image of the season. Autumn in this stanza continues as a silent figure, but that silence is countered by the voice of the speaker (or of the poem itself) as it achieves its own power to confront the pressures of time.

In the third stanza, that voice finally wins out, and we move from the pictorial silence of the depiction of autumn in the first stanza to the songs and sounds of the season in the third. That third stanza also starts with a question, but the question is now about sound (and not the sight that the second stanza begins with: "Who hath not seen thee . . .?"). The songs of spring are, perhaps, something like the "chilly green of spring" that Keats disparages in his letter, but autumn, too, has songs, and those songs are the sounds that its denizens make: the gnats, the lambs, the crickets, the robin, and the swallows. They sing at sunset, as Keats follows the logic of Shakespeare's sonnet 73 ("That time of year thou mayest in me behold") to find in a smaller period of time—the evening of a particular day—a metaphor or analogy for the period of the year, so that evening is like autumn. But at evening, creatures sing, and the primary impression one takes away from the last stanza is one of airiness. The oppressive suffocation of the first two stanzas is relieved, and we feel that songs and the breath that makes them possible come only when the cloying overabundance of the first stanza is superseded.

It should be noted that the "full-grown lambs" are an allusion to the "young lambs" in WILLIAM WORDSWORTH'S INTIMATIONS ODE; Keats's odes in general are shot through with references to Wordsworth, as though Keats is trying to correct or surpass him. (See, for example, the entry on "Ode to a Nightingale.")

"To Autumn" is a poem that learns how to breathe, and learns that breath means that things are ephemeral, or perhaps it would be better to say that the ephemerality of things makes breathing and singing possible. Most of Keats's odes end with some relation to sound, but usually they tend toward silence (as in "The plaintive anthem fades" in "Ode to a Nightingale"). The world may say something to the poet, or to us, like the urn's "Beauty is truth, truth beauty," but it says it silently. "To Autumn," the last of Keats's odes, achieves the more rarified freedom of breath and song.

BIBLIOGRAPHY

Bate, Walter Jackson. *John Keats.* Cambridge, Mass.: Harvard University Press, 1963.

Bloom, Harold. *Poetry and Repression: Revisionism from Blake to Stevens.* New Haven, Conn.: Yale University Press, 1976.

———. *The Visionary Company: A Reading of English Romantic Poetry.* Garden City, N.Y.: Doubleday, 1961.

De Man, Paul. *The Rhetoric of Romanticism.* New York: Columbia University Press, 1984.

Dickstein, Morris. *Keats and His Poetry: A Study in Development.* Chicago: University of Chicago Press, 1971.

Flesch, William. "The Ambivalence of Generosity: Keats Reading Shakespeare." *ELH: English Literary History* 62, no. 1 (Spring 1995): 149–169.

McFarland, Thomas. *The Masks of Keats: The Endeavour of a Poet.* New York: Oxford University Press, 2000.

Stillinger, Jack. *The Hoodwinking of Madeline, and Other Essays on Keats's Poems.* Urbana: University of Illinois Press, 1971.

Vendler, Helen Hennessy. *Odes of John Keats.* Cambridge, Mass.: Harvard University Press, 1983.

Wasserman, Earl. *The Finer Tone: Keats' Major Poems.* Baltimore: Johns Hopkins Press, 1953.

"TOCCATA OF GALUPPI'S, A" ROBERT BROWNING (1847) The Italian composer Baldassare Galuppi (1706–85) is little remembered today but was of some importance in 18th-century music, especially in England, where he lived for several years, influencing musical theory and performance in a country with few great composers. ROBERT BROWNING has therefore not picked someone obscure for his clavichord player to address, but also not someone who has risen to the transcendent regions of artistic achievement. Like the imaginary piece the speaker plays, the composer is talented enough and accomplished enough to give rise to genuine emotional response in his interpreter without overwhelming him.

The speaker of the poem is presumably studying and playing the music, although he has other interests—especially the new and terrifying study of geology that led to such anguish in some of Browning's other poems (such as "CALIBAN UPON SETEBOS" and book 10 of *The RING AND THE BOOK*), and to even greater anguish in ALFRED, LORD TENNYSON'S *IN MEMORIAM A.H.H.* He imagines Galuppi telling him, "you know physics, something of geology" (l. 37), as well as mathematics, and assuring him that such scientific knowledge of nature does not challenge but reinforces the religious doctrine of the soul, because it shows the creator's depth and sober seriousness. This is a minority position, since the new geology (as Charles Lyell was formulating it in the 1830s) was challenging the idea of a benevolent God who had made humanity the center of his system. The discovery of geological scales of time and of the vastly remote extinction of thousands of species was a tremendous shock to Victorian beliefs, one that still reverberates today. Lyell himself, however, believed in a benevolent Creator, and so does Galuppi as the speaker interprets him. (From now on, everything I say about Galuppi should be understood as the speaker's interpretation of his music.)

Galuppi acknowledges the "extinction" (l. 39) of butterflies, but he assumes that human souls will triumph over the geological process. The line itself is more troubled, however: "Butterflies may dread extinction," but not the butterflies he means. He is using the word more or less as William Shakespeare's Hamlet uses it of Osric, to refer to the flighty and thoughtless lovers in Venice who take no care for the future. And yet his complaint of them is that they *do not* dread the extinction that the fossil record shows real butterflies (and every other sort of species) have suffered.

The really fascinating thing about the poem is the tension between Galuppi's interpreter and his own emotional responses to Galuppi's toccata. A toccata is a brilliant piece of keyboard music, showing off the virtuosity of composer and performer; in this case, it also shows off the virtuosity of the poet who can sustain these astonishing triple-rhymed tercets for 45 lines in trochaic octameter. It is almost impossible to write an emotionally serious poem in trochees in English since the sing-song sound of the meter (see Henry Wadsworth Longfellow's *Hiawatha*) overwhelms the poem's content. (Iambic poetry allows for much more metrical variation in the feet of the line, which preserves it from dullness.) Here the prominent rhythm sounds like the speaker's resistance to the music he plays, whose description in stanzas seven and eight hardly sounds like the tone of the poem (whose persistence is rhythmical, not harmonic as in line 24).

Galuppi *means* to tell his interpreter that Venice was trivial and worthless. The speaker is shocked by his discovery (or imputation) of this meaning. He thinks Galuppi is praising him for being indifferent to the ephemeral pleasures the toccata evokes in order to dismiss. But for the speaker, it is just those ephemeral pleasures that make the toccata so evocatively beautiful.

This, at any rate, is what he thinks at the end. But it is important to see that, as in much of Browning's greatest monologues, the speech *does* something for the speaker. It is dramatic because a drama occurs in the course of his speaking (here in the course of his struggle with Galuppi), and that at the end he projects his own first response onto Galuppi himself as he attains to a different and subtler one.

Thus, his first complaint is that Galuppi's old music brings almost no good at all. It simply tells us that "they lived once thus at Venice" (l. 5)—tells us something trivial about the butterflies dreading extinction. The speaker has never been out of England and is somewhat uncertain about his facts with respect to Venice, but nevertheless, and in spite of himself, he becomes enraptured by the end of the third stanza: "It's as if I saw it all" (l. 9).

What Galuppi permits him to see are the beauties of Venice, in particular the beauty of love. It is the nature of love that it is a commitment to the ephemeral, and it can even (as in Venice) be commitment to only the present moment. Galuppi's sevenths (chords that stretch nearly an octave) are "commiserating" (l. 21); his music evokes the plaintive, melancholy, happy conversations the lovers have, part of which is the question "Must we die?" (l. 20). The answer is that we must, and it is this that gives love its value in the moment—the value of the kisses.

The lovers heard Galuppi play, and the speaker at first scorns them for not hearing how melancholy his music is. But of course, it is melancholy because it evokes *them* so well, so the scorn, in one way well-placed, is wrong at a deeper level. They are the lovers, and they will die. If they are different from their musical chronicler, that difference discredits *him,* Galuppi, so that the speaker can surprisingly and yet convincingly call Galuppi's music "cold" (l. 33). It is the lovers who are warm. Galuppi's praise for the eternal verities of science and of the God who formed it are part of this cold song of the "ghostly cricket" (l. 34) who survives them. But the speaker only recalls the evocations of the dead. Perhaps none of their souls were left "when the kissing had to stop" (l. 40), as he imagines Galuppi sneering. But that is because they put all their souls into their kissing and their love.

The speaker is now left alone with Galuppi, and he still complains, as he did at the beginning of the poem. But the complaint has reversed into its opposite. Galuppi's meaning is not that they lived in Venice in a trivial way, different from the England of the 19th century, but that the wonderful way in which they lived then is all over. The speaker rejects his own condemnation for 18th-century Venice, imputing it to Galuppi, and instead he stands by his own love for the evocation with which Galuppi has made him fall in love. That love makes him somewhat Venetian as well. "Chilly and grown old" he may now be, but this in a sense gives him a youth that he did not have before—a youth that he derives from the toccata despite his belief that the toccata condemns it.

Every Browning poem about an artist provides an occasion for him to theorize about art. In this poem, the theory, one he embraces, recognizes that any interpretation of a poem will turn it into something the reader wants it to be, sometimes in spite of what the poet intends, or what the reader *thinks* the poet intends. What the poem can do is make it possible for the reader to be half a poet as well. (This is the small lesson of *The Ring and the Book* as well, with its enormous number of conflicting interpretations, each indicative of the interpreter, not the thing interpreted; and of "MY LAST DUCHESS," as well, where Ferrara interprets the painting according to his own somber and artificial lights.)

BIBLIOGRAPHY

Bloom, Harold. *A Map of Misreading.* New York: Oxford University Press, 2003.

———. *Poetry and Repression: Revisionism from Blake to Stevens.* New Haven, Conn.: Yale University Press, 1976.

DeVane, William C. *A Browning Handbook.* New York: Appleton-Century-Crofts, 1955.

Langbaum, Robert Woodrow. *The Modern Spirit: Essays on the Continuity of Nineteenth- and Twentieth-Century Literature.* New York: Oxford University Press, 1970.

Raymond, William O. *The Infinite Moment, and Other Essays in Robert Browning.* Toronto: University of Toronto Press, 1965.

"TO ELIZABETH BARRETT BROWNING" (1861) and "TO ELIZABETH BARRETT BROWNING IN 1861" (1867) DORA GREENWELL The second of these two poems was published in DORA GREENWELL's 1867 collection but was presumably written in 1861, after the publication of her collection of poems that same year, and prompted by ELIZABETH BARRETT BROWNING's death. In the 1867 collection, it follows the earlier poem Greenwell wrote to Browning in 1851, first published in the 1861 collection. The two sonnets, then, form a kind of diptych; the earlier one praises the living poet who makes Greenwell "'swoon for very joy'" (l. 8) and both undermines and gives poetic confidence to the younger acolyte; the second laments her death and is a kind of brief elegy denying that Browning *could* die, since her soul must transcend mortality.

The poems are interesting (and often extremely affecting) because they show both Greenwell's sense of what poetry can do and her own commitment to live vicariously through literature, in a way that she was temperamentally unsuited to in her personal life. She met Elizabeth Barrett Browning once, as the second poem informs us, but loved her intensely because of her poetry, not because of any emotional attachment. The second sonnet praises Browning for the way she "made the rose more red / More sweet each word by olden singers said / In sadness, or by children in their glee" (ll. 6–8). Poetry or art does not reproduce what we already feel: It intensifies feeling—increases the redness of the rose and the sweetness of the song.

This second claim is worth dwelling on for a moment. Greenwell praises Browning for making the poetry of the olden singers even sweeter than it was. This means that one of the things poetry can do is intensify the experience of—poetry. Rather than regarding this as a paradox, we should see that it is true. Poets are readers as well as writers, which is why Greenwell writes these sonnets to Browning: She, too, is a reader before being a writer. In this she follows Browning herself, who in her *SONNETS FROM THE PORTUGUESE* takes almost the same perspective on ROBERT BROWNING's poetry, inspired to write by poetry whose greatness is in part the fact that it does not seek to silence but to sustain those who are awed by it (see, for example, the third of those sonnets). Their reading, transmogrified into writing, lends splendor to the things they read. In essence, Browning is teaching Greenwell both how to see the world with the intensity that a poet does and how to read poetry as a poet does.

This is the theme of the first sonnet as well. Browning's poetry is so powerful that it would certainly silence Greenwell if it did not, paradoxically, have the reverse effect. Browning's poetic strength instills the nobler thoughts that makes it possible for Greenwell to sing and to survive the greatness of Browning's poems. This is the paradoxical formulation that the second poem to Browning generalizes. What it comes to is the idea that poetry has the power to give us the strength and understanding that we need to sustain the power of poetry.

It is interesting to note that the quoted phrase in the poem (which I alluded to above)—"'swoon for very joy'"—seems to be Greenwell's inaccurate quotation of a moment in Robert Browning's *Paracelsus* where he speaks of "shivering for very joy." It is not surprising that she would quote Robert, given that his (and her) love for Elizabeth Barrett Browning came first of all through the poems he (and she) admired, and also given the wistful jealousy that she would have had for Robert. By quoting him, she ends up putting herself in the position of both Brownings. Like Robert, she loves Elizabeth, and like Elizabeth, she feels incomparably inspired to her own writing by the poetry of the person she loves.

See also "SCHERZO (A SHY PERSON'S WISHES), A."

BIBLIOGRAPHY

Chase, Karen. *The Spectacle of Intimacy: A Public Life for the Victorian Family*. Princeton, N.J.: Princeton University Press, 2000.

Cunningham, Valentine, ed. Note on Dora (Dorothy) Greenwell in *The Victorians: An Anthology of Poetry & Poetics*. Malden, Mass.: Blackwell, 2000.

Dorling, William. *Memoirs of Dora Greenwell*. London: J. Clarke, 1885.

Mason, Emma. *Women Poets of the Nineteenth Century*. Tavistock, Devon, England: Northcote House Publishers, 2006.

"TO MR COLERIDGE" ("TO MR. S. T. COLERIDGE") ANNA LAETITIA BARBAULD **(1799)** This poem was published in the *Monthly Magazine* in 1799, but it was composed in 1797 when ANNA LAETITIA BARBAULD met the 25-year-old SAMUEL TAYLOR COLERIDGE on a visit to a mutual friend in Bristol. The previous year, Coleridge had expressed great admiration for her as one of the two great stylists in English. He already had a name, not as much as a poet (his great period began more or less the next year, although his early volume *Religious Musings* was already known) but as a rising Unitarian intellectual; his reputation is vividly portrayed in the essayist William Hazlitt's account of meeting him for the first time a few months later when he came to Shrewsbury to fill the position of Unitarian minister. Coleridge had been lecturing on religion and politics, editing *The Watchman,* and in general exploring and contributing to the philosophical and intellectual ferment that was bubbling throughout Europe. Barbauld, nearly 30 years his elder, had a more experienced and less speculative view of intellectual life. Her poetry in general, and "To Mr Coleridge" in particular, warns against getting lost in abstraction and metaphysical speculation. Her warning is particularly pointed because she felt that the issues that were to exercise the great poets of ROMANTICISM were real and central ones; but for her part, the way to engage with them was to commit oneself to social and civic life and avoid the temptations of extreme solitude and intense introspection.

Barbauld's warning to Coleridge shows just how impressive a young man he must have been, and how much she understood what was motivating him. It opens with an allusion to the Italian poet Dante's opening of the *Inferno*—"In the middle of the journey of our life"—and warns against the phantasmagoria that can tempt a deep and original thinker away from the real, moral world. It is impressive how well she describes these temptations, which clearly contain an autobiographical component. She has been there. His feet are "unpractised" (l. 2); hers are not, but they once were. She feels the charms of indolence and philosophy, which in a sense means that she feels the charms not only of the issues that will so obsess the romantic poets but also of the pseudo-Spenserian allegorical poetry that marks and mars so much mediocre 18th-century verse and that she herself was able to resist and overcome. This is to say that Barbauld gives a penetrating account of what might motivate a writer like Coleridge in particular, and the romantic movement in general, and shows how much it motivates her. Of her penetration, Coleridge was later to concede: "The more I see of Mrs Barbauld—that wonderful Propriety of Mind!—She has great acuteness, very great—yet how steadily she keeps it within the bounds of practical Reason. This I almost envy as well as admire—My own subtleties too often lead me into strange (though, God be praised) transient out-of-the-waynesses" (letter to John Prior Estlin, March 1, 1800).

Barbauld chose to publish the poem two years later, after the 1798 publication of *Lyrical Ballads,* which WILLIAM WORDSWORTH (the book's coauthor, with Coleridge) made sure was sent to her. Coleridge was responsible, as she would have known, for the supernatural poems in that volume, including *The RIME OF THE ANCIENT MARINER,* with which it opens, and she must have worried that he was still prey to the metaphysical speculations that, in fact, he would pursue with great intellectual power but some lack of direction for the rest of his life. The publication of the poem is thus a renewed appeal to him to return from the fairy lands of metaphysics to civic life.

We may be glad that Coleridge never did become as "sound" as Barbauld wanted him to be. But the poem probably has an afterlife within his productions, and Wordsworth's as well. "To Mr Coleridge" ends with a kind of parental or step-parental blessing on him (perhaps one might think her as setting herself up as Beatrice to his Dante), which Coleridge will echo in his blessing on HARTLEY COLERIDGE in "FROST AT MIDNIGHT," one of his greatest poems, and the poem to which Wordsworth was to respond in his still greater "TINTERN ABBEY."

BIBLIOGRAPHY

Armstrong, Isobel. "The Gush of the Feminine: How Can We Read Women's Poetry of the Romantic Period?" In *Romantic Women Writers: Voices and Countervoices,* edited by Paula R. Feldman and Theresa M. Kelley, 13–32. Hanover, N.H.: University Press of New England, 1995.

Armstrong, Isobel, and Virginia Blain, eds. *Women's Poetry in the Enlightenment: The Making of a Canon, 1730–1820.* New York: St. Martin's Press, 1999.

Keach, William. *Arbitrary Power: Romanticism, Language, Politics.* Princeton, N.J.: Princeton University Press, 2004.

Mellor, Anne K. *Romanticism & Gender.* New York: Routledge, 1993.

Wordsworth, Jonathan. *Bright Work Grows: Women Writers of the Romantic Age.* Washington, D.C.: Woodstock Books, 1997.

"TO THE EVENING STAR" WILLIAM BLAKE **(1769–1777)** "To the Evening Star" is perhaps the most beautiful of WILLIAM BLAKE's early poems, published in "Poetical Sketches" (1783) when he was 25, and all written between the ages of 12 and 21. (This poem is included here as the early work of one of the most major of romantic poets.) The poem is a kind of blank-verse sonnet, but even the term *blank verse* may insult its astonishing delicacy. The poem is in the form of a prayer to Venus, the star of evening, which sets shortly after the sun sets. (Venus will provide a consistent image in the romantic poets, especially for WILLIAM WORDSWORTH and PERCY BYSSHE SHELLEY.)

The speaker of the poem addresses Venus as the goddess of love. She lights her torch in the setting sun and smiles down, scatters her dew, and washes the dusk with her silver luminescence. Her presence is a benign one, but not in a benign world. After the afterglow of sunset, after Venus herself sets, true night will come, and just as Venus looks forward to the state of innocence in SONGS OF INNOCENCE AND OF EXPERIENCE, the night itself overshadows the state of experience. The wolf will rage and the lion, like "The TYGER," will glare through the "dun forest" (l. 12) of the night. These anticipations of grimness, however, make the ephemeral time of the evening star's presence all the sweeter, more intense and more beautiful. Her dew is sacred, and her influence protects those headed toward shelter from the night that is coming. Innocence is transitory, but it is all the more precious for that.

"To the Evening Star" derives its extraordinary subtlety and lightness of tone from its form. It does not rhyme but engages in surprising formal experiments in the way it enjambs its lines. It is rare—especially in a serious poem—to end a line with the word *the,* as this poem does in its fifth line. But the poise of the word at the end of the line enacts what it describes: the way the star draws the blue curtains of the sky as we draw our eyes back over the next line after the enjambment. Equally unusual are the lines that end with *on* (l. 8) and *with* (l. 11). The poem also substitutes a subtle but intense repetition for rhyme, so that Venus will "smile upon our evening bed" and also "smile on our loves" (ll. 4–5), the "evening bed" being the bed the "angel of the evening" would smile upon. Note that the word *evening* is used both as a noun and as an attributive adjective. So, too, are other repetitions grammatically varied: As each flower shuts its eyes "in timely sleep" (noun), the speaker prays that the star's west wind will "sleep on / The lake" (verb). The "silver dew" and the "silver" she will wash the dusk with represent a kind of resolution of adjective into noun, as though her silver is more permanent than the dew that first makes us aware of it. The dew itself goes from being silver ("thy silver dew" in line 6) to being sacred (l. 14), as the poem enacts Venus's blessing. And for this reason, the flowers that shut their "sweet eyes" can find security in Venus's open, "glimmering eyes" (ll. 7, 9).

Those eyes, in a beautiful phrase, "speak silence," so that Venus is the goddess and guardian of peace, her gentleness just exactly what will best preserve the gentleness she symbolizes. The paradox of speaking silence is a deep one: It makes silence not the absence of sound but the presence of a kind of achieved serenity, which is both what the prayer desires and the balance the poem maintains.

BIBLIOGRAPHY

Bloom, Harold. *Blake's Apocalypse: A Study in Poetic Argument.* Ithaca, N.Y.: Cornell University Press, 1970.
Damrosch, Leopold. *Symbol and Truth in Blake's Myth.* Princeton, N.J.: Princeton University Press, 1980.
Frye, Northrop. *Fearful Symmetry: A Study of William Blake.* Princeton, N.J.: Princeton University Press, 1974.
Hollander, John. "Blake and the Metrical Contract." In *From Sensibility to Romanticism,* edited by Frederick Hilles and Harold Bloom, 293–310. New York: Oxford, 1965. Reprinted in John Hollander, *Vision and Resonance: Two Senses of Poetic Form,* 187–211. New Haven, Conn.: Yale University Press, 1985.
Ostriker, Alicia. "Desire Gratified and Ungratified: William Blake and Sexuality." *Blake: An Illustrated Quarterly* 16 (1982–83): 156–165.
Raine, Kathleen. *Blake and Antiquity.* Princeton, N.J.: Princeton University Press, 1977.
Thompson, E. P. *Witness against the Beast: William Blake and the Moral Law.* New York: Cambridge University Press, 1993.

"TO VERNON LEE" AMY LEVY (1889) Vernon Lee was the nom de plume of Violet Paget (1856–1935), the novelist and critic, who was a friend of AMY LEVY's and with whom Levy was probably in love. This Petrarchan sonnet, like a large number of Levy's best poems, is a kind of wry account of her own tendency toward despair. (It was one of the four that Edmund Clarence Stedman (1833–1908), the great American anthologist of VICTORIAN POETRY, selected for his 1895 volume *Victorian Anthology.*) The poem takes as its theme—as despairing poems must if they are true poems—the question of why despair might seek expression within poetry. "To Vernon Lee" is impressive in the restraint both with which it approaches this question and with which it expresses its author's despair.

Levy recalls a time when she and Paget went seeking flowers in early spring, at Bellosguardo, near Florence, Italy. Indeed, most of the poem is a catalogue of flowers, of the form that John Milton undertook in *Lycidas* (1638) when he described the flowers that strew Lycidas's hearse; and that, in *Hamlet,* William Shakespeare had Ophelia utter as she brought flowers to her father's grave. We have no idea, however, that these are the allusions until the end of the poem. Rather, their search for flowers, scattering their route and filling its hollows, is a prefiguration and therefore a representation in the poem of the act of writing the poem. This is because the names of flowers have to fill their places in the poetic line perfectly: They must rhyme when rhyme is needed, and they must be metrically apt wherever they are placed in the lines. To write a poem cataloging flowers, therefore, requires the poet to search for the flowers that will arrange the poetic bouquet, and it is this that we can feel Levy doing.

Our sense that the poem is about the sweet and beautiful activity of collecting and arranging words in the poem is confirmed, after its "purples" fill its plots (ll. 3–4), by the conversation that Levy and Paget had. They spoke, we learn, about art and life, "And of the gifts the gods had given to each" (ll. 12–13). Since the flowers and their background have filled the rest of the poem, there is almost no time to find out what they had said about the gifts given to art and life. But it turns out there is an ambiguity in the line just quoted. *Each* turns out to refer not to art and life but to the two women and the gifts the gods gave them. To Paget came hope, to Levy despair.

This ending is not quite the simple trick of grimness it seems, though. It is important to see that Levy does describe despair as a "gift," and important to see as well that the ambiguity of *each* is a genuine one. Paget gets the gift that is valuable to life, which is hope. But Levy gets the gift valuable to art, which is despair. To search for flowers—of verse or of evil (as ALGERNON CHARLES SWINBURNE reminded his contemporaries in his elegy on Charles Baudelaire, "AVE ATQUE VALE"), is to do what is psychologically apt for one who despairs: to attempt to lose oneself in the task of form. It is therefore to be moved to what makes great art possible—the forms in which despair seeks to distract itself.

BIBLIOGRAPHY

Parejo Vadillo, Ana. *Women Poets and Urban Aestheticism: Passengers of Modernity.* New York: Palgrave Macmillan, 2005.
Scarry, Elaine. *Dreaming by the Book.* New York: Farrar, Straus and Giroux, 1999.

"TOYS, THE" COVENTRY PATMORE (1876) "The Toys" is probably COVENTRY PATMORE's most famous single poem, widely anthologized since its first reprinting in the Victorian expansion of Francis Turner Palgrave's *Golden Treasury of English Songs and Lyrics.* It combines Patmore's trademark sentimentality, dear to the heart of the Victorian common reader, with his strange and sometimes willfully blind intelligence, and it is brilliantly composed. The poem comes out of a tradition we recognize from WILLIAM WORDSWORTH's "Anecdote for Fathers" and the end of part 2 of SAMUEL TAYLOR COLERIDGE's *CHRISTABEL,* the parent expressing guilt for his overbearing treatment of his own child, to whom he realizes he may feel morally superior. "The Toys" probably refers to Patmore's youngest son, Henry (1860–83), who would predecease his father a few years after the poem's composition.

The poem is a sad one, from its first line, where the praise of the boy is in the tradition of the *senex puer,* the wise child. We find out why the boy is sad and why the father impatient at the same moment: "His mother, who was patient, being dead" (l. 6); the child will certainly be grave beyond his years (Henry was two when his mother, the writer Emily Augusta Patmore, died) and the father easily vexed in his sorrow. The father's heart is good, and he goes to comfort the child he had dismissed unkissed, lest he should still be awake. But the child is asleep, which tells us that he is not unused to sorrow. His eyelids are still wet, however, and the speaker adds to the tears as he (finally) kisses them away. Then he sees the set of things his son has so innocently collected—stones, shells, and coins. He has collected them, the father realizes, "to comfort his sad heart" (l. 21), and so the father comes now to understand that he is not alone in his sadness, but that his son shares it or even feels it more intensely.

Thus far, the poem is immensely moving, but then comes a turn that will not be to the taste of all readers. The speaker makes an application of the scene to his own relationship to God. Here Patmore's reading of the great 17th-century poet George Herbert becomes evident: He represents himself as Herbert did, as a child in the care of his father, God. His hope and prayer is that God will ultimately love him just as truly as he loves his own son, and will forgive him whatever infringements he makes on the rules, just as he is moved to forgive his own son.

We may feel that his own son is more or less forgotten in this illustration of the anecdote's moral. But this may be too severe a judgment. The thing that he would need God to forgive him for is just the harsh way he has treated his son. When he weeps, he knows that he loves his son, and this knowledge makes him realize that his own wrath is no more the final truth of his character than was his son's disobedience. His son, therefore, becomes the embodiment of the loving rebuke he hopes to get from God, the embodiment of forgiveness. If he, the father, is a child like his son, and God is a father, then the tonal hope of the poem is that God will be as loving and as forgiving as his son clearly is. One can imagine, and hope, that this poem itself was part of the way he expressed love and begged forgiveness from Henry (who we know loved his father dearly till the day he died).

BIBLIOGRAPHY

Champneys, Basil. *Memoirs and Correspondence of Coventry Patmore.* London: G. Bell and Sons, 1900.

Gosse, Edmund. *Coventry Patmore.* New York: Charles Scribner's Sons, 1905.

Hopkins, Gerard Manley. *Further Letters of Gerard Manley Hopkins, Including His Correspondence with Coventry Patmore.* 2nd ed. Edited by C. C. Abbott. New York: Oxford University Press, 1956.

Page, Frederick. *Patmore: A Study in Poetry.* Hamdon, Conn.: Archon Books, 1970.

Weinig, Mary Anthony. *Coventry Patmore.* Boston: Twayne Publishers, 1981.

TRIUMPH OF LIFE, THE **PERCY BYSSHE SHELLEY (1822)** Although unfinished and only properly edited in the 1960s, *The Triumph of Life* is regarded by many as PERCY BYSSHE SHELLEY's greatest poem, putting to use his characteristic imagery and intensity in undreamt of ways. The 20th-century poet T. S. Eliot, who did not like Shelley at all, said of this poem that it marked a new and impressive departure in his work, and this comment is supported by a general consensus that goes a little bit further. It is obvious that the poem is heavily influenced by the medieval

Italian poet Dante's *Divine Comedy,* whose terza rima rhyme scheme Shelley adopts and adapts with very great power in *The Triumph of Life.* He had already used it in a number of poems, as well as in his translation of the "Matelda gathering flowers" episode in Dante's *Purgatorio,* but in *The Triumph of Life* he sustains the form at much greater length while achieving new beauty and power. Dante also gets extended mention in the poem, although he does not actually appear.

Beyond that, there is disagreement, largely because the poem is unfinished. Shelley was in the midst of writing it when he drowned, and critics disagree about where it would have gone. It is Dantesque, but is Shelley taking as his model Dante's *Inferno,* with its population of the damned; or Dante's *Purgatorio,* which is a story with a happy ending for all those who must experience Purgatory. The horrors of Purgatory lead to a happy ending. They purge sin and leave the soul new, innocent, and ready to enter Paradise. Is that what Shelley had in mind? Would the poem have ended with the possibility at least of hope? Or is it a document of despair?

Certainly the poems were that Shelley was writing at the same time as *The Triumph of Life*—the late lyrics to Jane Williams and "LINES WRITTEN IN THE BAY OF LERICI," a poem written on the reverse side of one of *Triumph's* manuscript sheets. The title of the poem is nothing like optimistic—*triumph* is the kind of "triumphal pageant" (l. 118) that William Shakespeare's Cleopatra fears Octavius Caesar will lead her in through the streets of Rome to the jeers of its spectators. Shelley describes this as a spectacle of conquest, humiliation, and death: "when to greet some conqueror's advance / Imperial Rome poured forth her living sea . . . / When freedom left those who upon the free / Had bound a yoke which soon they stooped to bear" (ll. 112–115). Even those who jeer at the victims of the triumph will soon stoop to bear it, which is what happens in the poem. The French philosophe Jean-Jacques Rousseau is one of the major characters in the poem, where he gives an account of his own life and a prognostication of Shelley's; both stories are about turning from being a spectator to "actor or victim in this wretchedness" (l. 306). The trajectory of life within that wretchedness does not sustain the distinction between the two: Every triumphal actor soon becomes a victim, whose ranks include "all who have their age subdued / By action or by suffering" (ll. 212–122). All the despoilers of others are despoiled themselves (l. 235), the "heirs of Caesar's crime from him to Constantine" (l. 284), who have led others in triumph, are chained to the triumphal car, as is NAPOLEON BONAPARTE, whose rise and fall is one among thousands of similar careers (ll. 223–224).

The poem is not a political allegory of rise and fall, however. The conqueror who leads all others in triumph is Life herself, a dark form in the chariot that enchains or destroys all those it takes captive. And it takes everyone captive: It is easier to say who is not part of this "sad pageantry" (l. 176) than who is, since "All but the sacred few" who repudiated life as soon as born or refused every one of its gifts "till the last one / Were there" (ll. 128–134). The poem explains that the sacred few are the two great figures of "Athens and Jerusalem" (l. 134), which is to say Socrates and Jesus, figures whom Shelley revered but who were (for him) saints, not examples of the humanity they sought to teach and solace. As the 20th-century literary critic Paul de Man noted, they were not writers themselves but "fictions in the writing of others," and so ideal beings and not real ones. The Greek philosopher Socrates is the hero most of all, perhaps, of Plato's *Symposium,* or *Banquet* (as Shelley titled it in his translation of the dialogue, the first in English). But if Socrates is not to be found "mid the mighty captives . . . Nor mid the ribald crowd that followed them / Or fled before" (ll. 135–137) the same cannot be said of the philosopher who created his reputation, whom we see chained to the chariot itself being punished for giving himself to experiences of "joy and woe his master knew not" (ll. 254–255).

The experience of reality, the experience of being a real human being, is the experience that Shelley honored Rousseau and WILLIAM WORDSWORTH for as much as Plato. Rousseau, in fact, is more or less an avatar of Wordsworth here. Harold Bloom, in *Poetry and Repression,* says that Shelley uses the name Rousseau only because Wordsworth was "still, technically speaking, alive," and we shall see the justice of Bloom's identification. Rousseau's account in the poem of his own corruption and vanquishment at the hands of life echo that of WILLIAM WORDSWORTH's cautiously optimistic "spiritual autobiography" in the INTIMATIONS ODE—but without the optimism.

In the Dantesque scheme of the poem, Rousseau is Virgil to Shelley's Dante. Dante, too, is mentioned in the poem, as the poet who wrote the "rhyme" in which he told "in words of hate and awe the wondrous story / How all things are transfigured, except Love" (ll. 475–476), which reminds us that love leads just as easily to damnation as to salvation in *The Divine Comedy* and suggests Shelley's sense that Dante, though a great poet, the second among the "sons of light" that *ADONAIS* and *A Defence of Poetry* lists, was nevertheless corrupted by his own moral righteousness. Shelley discovers that he is not alone when he experiences a trance state after having been kept up all night by some "sad thought" which he must not tell us (but which echoes the thoughts he does not report in "Lines Written in the Bay of Lerici"—written, remember, on the back of one of the pages of a manuscript of *The Triumph of Life*). He sees the pageant of life and is horror-struck. He asks himself the questions that will appear in four variants across the poem—What am I seeing, and why is it happening? (ll. 178–179)—and is astonished that a Dantesque tree (as in the circle of the suicides in the *Inferno*) is not a tree but a human being who begins answering him. This is Rousseau, and his story is more or less a recapitulation of Shelley's own.

Like Shelley, Rousseau found himself where the Triumph passed, and he asked what it was that he was experiencing and why it was happening (l. 398). Rousseau's own guide is "a shape all light," and Rousseau's account of what happens next is a brilliant narrative device for foretelling Shelley's parallel future as well. What happens to man and guide is that a chariot, based on the mystical chariot in the Book of Ezekiel, as well as on the chariots from the Roman triumphs, blazes in the cold and blinding light of its own glory through the natural world and extinguishes even the light of the Sun in its own oppressive radiance. The Sun itself has extinguished the stars; the poem represents light and life not as signs of ideal happiness but as crushingly oppressive. The "shape all light" gives Rousseau a cup of Nepenthe, the same drink Circe gives her victims in Homer's *The Odyssey* and that Milton's villain Comus gives his prey (in *Comus*).

Rousseau takes the drink, and in describing what happens next, he gives an extraordinarily beautiful recapitulation of the Intimations Ode. The light of the chariot dims even the "shape all light," but she still seems to be present to him like "The ghost of a forgotten form of sleep" (l. 428) or like the "fairest planet," Venus, "whose light is like the scent / Of a jonquil when evening breezes fan it." He imagines ending the day as he "began it / In that star's smile" (ll. 418–420), but we know that this will not happen because Venus cannot be both morning and evening star. This is a fact that Shelley well knew, and one that Wordsworth knew as well in the Intimations Ode, where he used Venus as a metaphor of how "the soul that rises with us, our life's star / Hath had elsewhere its setting, and cometh from afar." As in the Intimations Ode, where it "fades into the light of common day," Rousseau's star is lost in the hideous light that supersedes it.

It is here that Rousseau gives the most terrifying description of the poem: how the masks of youth, eagerness, and desire drop from the form and countenance of all, leaving only misery and despair and populating the universe with the shadows of lost hope. These masks turn into vampire bats and lead to a vision of universal nightmare. We recall that the poem opens with "the mask of darkness" falling from the awakened earth (ll. 3–4); the end of the fragment shows that even its "joyous beginning," as the American literary critic M. H. Abrams calls it, is, in fact, vectored toward an ever-increasing horror that does not seem to promise any relief. If the mask of darkness is stripped away, one cannot anticipate the darkness of oblivion when one comes to the end of things. The tone of irremediable despair here is not unlike that of GERARD MANLEY HOPKINS's tone in "NO WORST, THERE IS NONE," and it suggests that, as with Hopkins and with Milton's Satan in the fourth book of *Paradise Lost* (frequently echoed in *The Triumph of Life*), the hell that Shelley equates life with is endless and endlessly worse.

Would the poem have found a way out of its own despair? The last lines repeat again a version of its structuring question: "'Then, what is life?' I said" (l. 543).

Every answer to that question begins a grimmer narrative than the one in which it is asked, and I see no reason to believe that Shelley would have retreated from the uncompromising vision of hopelessness already set out. Too many people suffer in *The Triumph of Life* for any happy ending to compensate for their suffering. The poem, while not as great as Dante, certainly bears comparison with *The Divine Comedy,* and it should be read as a rebuke of Dante's belief in God's justice. The grim moral for Shelley is that "God made irreconcilable / Good and the means of good" (ll. 231–232).

BIBLIOGRAPHY

Bloom, Harold. *Genius: A Mosaic of One Hundred Exemplary Creative Minds.* New York: Warner, 2002.

———. *Poetry and Repression.* New Haven, Conn.: Yale University Press, 1980.

———. *Shelley's Mythmaking.* New Haven, Conn.: Yale University Press, 1959.

———. *The Visionary Company: A Reading of English Romantic Poetry.* Garden City, N.Y.: Doubleday, 1961.

Burke, Kenneth. *Grammar of Motives.* Berkeley: University of California Press, 1969.

Chernaik, Judith. *The Lyrics of Shelley.* Cleveland: Press of Case Western Reserve University, 1972.

de Man, Paul. "Shelley Disfigured." In *The Rhetoric of Romanticism,* 93–124. New York: Columbia University Press, 1984.

Duffy, Edward. *Rousseau in England: The Context for Shelley's Critique of the Enlightenment.* Berkeley: University of California Press, 1979.

Hogle, Jerrold E. *Shelley's Process: Radical Transference and the Development of His Major Works.* New York: Oxford University Press, 1988.

Keach, William. *Shelley's Style.* New York: Methuen, 1984.

Leavis, F. R. *Revaluation: Tradition & Development in English Poetry.* New York: Norton, 1963.

Leighton, Angela. *Shelley and the Sublime: An Interpretation of the Major Poems.* New York: Cambridge University Press, 1984.

Derrida, Jacques. "Living On." In *Reconstruction and Criticism,* edited by Geoffrey Hartman, 62–142. New York: Continuum, 1979.

Notopolous, James A. *The Platonism of Shelley: A Study of Platonism and the Poetic Mind.* Durham, N.C.: Duke University Press, 1949.

Quinney, Laura. *The Poetics of Disappointment: Wordsworth to Ashbery.* Charlottesville: University Press of Virginia, 1999.

Wasserman, Earl. *Shelley: A Critical Reading.* Baltimore: Johns Hopkins Press, 1971.

———. *Subtler Language: Critical Readings of Neoclassic and Romantic Poems.* Baltimore: Johns Hopkins Press, 1968.

"TRIUMPH OF TIME, THE" ALGERNON CHARLES SWINBURNE (1866) Near the beginning of James Joyce's great novel *Ulysses,* a character looks out from the shore and asks, "Isn't the sea what Algy called it? Our great green mother." "Algy" is ALGERNON CHARLES SWINBURNE, and the reference is to Swinburne's most famous lines, "I will go back to the great sweet mother, / Mother and lover of men, the sea" (ll. 257–258), and these lines are central to the poem and the work that it does for its author. "The Triumph of Time" is one of a series of poems full of erotic despair that Swinburne wrote in 1866. The biographical source of the poem was probably the marriage of his cousin, Mary Gordon, to another, much older man.

For Swinburne, the sensory qualities of poetry had a kind of powerful narcotic effect, as they also often did in ALFRED, LORD TENNYSON. The poem presents itself as partly about narcotizing the despair that it narrates. Certainly, that despair is over the top and risks sounding like adolescent angst. The hyperbolic rhetoric and imagery are easy to parody, but it should be remembered that Swinburne is, in fact, taking refuge from a genuine calamity in poetic hyperbole. The vaguely mystical other-worldliness that poetry can evoke stands for an alternative to the common but grinding sorrows of this world. It is for this reason that Swinburne's poetry can be a source of solace to others as it was to him.

To find refuge in writing a poem that describes what the poet is taking refuge from will inevitably mean that the poem is about itself, about the way that it offers refuge. In "The Triumph of Time," that refuge is offered by the sea to which Swinburne repeatedly returns. The sea is all-embracing and vastly undiscriminating. This does not make it anything like kind or tender in Swinburne. Rather, it stands for the vastness of despair. Consider some of the ways that Swinburne characterizes it: "A barren mother, a mother maid" (l. 67); "Thou art subtle and cruel of heart, men say" (l. 290); "Thy lips are bitter, and sweet thine heart" (l. 298). Men are wrong to think the sea is cruel of heart, but of course, Swinburne invents that characterization as part of the general characterization of the sea that the poem expresses. The sea is bitter, cold, full of the dead, because it stands for the fact that everything human will vanish, including, preeminently, Swinburne's despairing, disappointed love.

That love is for him its own relic, the thing he keeps absolute faith with when all other faith is broken, since his beloved has left him and become indifferent to him. This is what makes the thought that this relic, too, will fade so bitter to him. But the heart of the sea is sweet because when he forgets himself, and when his hopes and dreams "vanish away and apart," he will no longer feel the intolerable bitterness of being abandoned by the woman he loves. Rather, he will be absorbed into abandonment itself, into its vastness, indifference, and generality, which is what the sea stands for. The love and time that humans experience are "swift and sad, being born of the sea" (l. 74), but the sea remains, "older than earth" (l. 301) when the hours of human life are done. The sea, then, stands for the solitude out of which we come and to which we return (saddened especially by the loss of love), and at the same time it stands for a comfort and solace in that solitude.

The way the sea comforts for the loneliness it represents parallels and images what the poem itself is doing. In the poem's ninth octet, Swinburne calls the sea "Mother" and then expresses the wish that "I would we twain were even as she. / Lost in the night and the light of the sea" (ll. 69–70). These lines are fascinating no matter how we resolve the ambiguity: "we twain" could stand for Mary and himself, who would be even as the sea; or the phrase could refer to the sea mother and himself, who would be even as Mary is. (It is on the shore of the sea that the poem is set in its first stanza, so Mary may by now have sailed off to her new life.) In either case, the sea is somehow being compared (in wish) to itself. We would that we, like the sea, were lost in the night and the light of the sea; or we wish that we (Swinburne and the sea) were lost (like Mary) in the night and the light of the sea. The sea is lost in itself, and this is a kind of emblem of the way the despairing poetry gets lost in the poetry itself.

It is for this reason that Swinburne describes the passage of time that they (he and the sea more likely than he and Mary) will love through as he does: "We shall hear, as one in a trance that hears, / The sound of time, the rhyme of the years" (ll. 309–310). *Rhyme* is an internal rhyme for *time* in l. 310, and the sound of time thereby modulates into the rhymes of the poem, as well as the narcotic melodious repetitions that characterize it and give solace to its author.

The "sound of time" alludes to the poem's ambiguous title. The triumph of time is not necessarily a good thing; rather, it is more probably time's triumph over Swinburne, and over his love. The title alludes to the Italian early Renaissance poet Petrarch's great poems, the *Trionfi,* and in particular to his "Triumph of Time," which is about what times does to all human beings. It alludes as well to PERCY BYSSHE SHELLEY's great poem *The TRIUMPH OF LIFE,* and indeed, Swinburne's poem is full of Shelley, especially *ADONAIS* and *The Triumph of Life.* The 48th stanza (the second to last) is a quick reprise of what the "shape all light" does to the character of Rousseau in *The Triumph of Life,* including the strange and idiosyncratic reference to the palms of the feet (l. 382). A couple of years after writing "The Triumph of Time," Swinburne said of Shelley, "He was alone the perfect singing-god; his thoughts words deeds all sang together." It was as though in going to Shelley, to poetry in general, and to the sea that Shelley drowned in while composing *The Triumph of Life* that Swinburne was, in his own poem, escaping into a purely mental sea of poetry, and taking solace in its sounds and repetitions.

A half century later, Sigmund Freud would describe the death drive (as he called it) as a desire to merge again with the oceanic, maternal feeling that was originally ours. Freud saw this drive as "Beyond the pleasure principle"—that is to say, a drive that did not have a sexual or erotic component. It is characterized by a compulsion to repeat, so that the psyche can be lost in the endlessness of repetition—a compulsion Swinburne amply and deeply yields to in "The Triumph of Time" through his hypnotic anaphoras and rhymes. Swinburne clearly anticipates Freud's insight. He does not eroticize the sea at all, despite his desire to "Close with her, kiss her and mix her with me"; rather, he eliminates eros, turning desire into love of death. He represents the sea as a place of oblivion and therefore escape from eroticism. Freud's famous dictum, that the poets were there before him, is amply confirmed by "The Triumph of Time."

BIBLIOGRAPHY

Louis, Margot Kathleen. *Swinburne and His Gods: The Roots and Growth of an Agnostic Poetry.* Kingston, Ontario: McGill-Queen's University Press, 1990.

McGann, Jerome J. *Swinburne: An Experiment in Criticism.* Chicago: University of Chicago Press, 1972.

Rutland, William R. *Swinburne: A Nineteenth Century Hellene.* Oxford: Blackwell, 1931.

"TURNSTILE, THE" WILLIAM BARNES (1859)

This is a subtle and sad poem, one of WILLIAM BARNES's most moving, and one of the best examples of the way Barnes describes how the unchanging landscape registers our changing relationship to it, or registers the fact that the human relationship to landscape is always changing as human life becomes more tenuous with aging and time. The turnstile (a gate that allows a person to pass through fences erected to keep livestock penned in) is on the road between the speaker's house and the church, and they go through it every Sunday on the way to church. They are now walking (probably not on the way to church) as the church bells ring the day after the funeral held for the speaker's son—essentially, Barnes's son Julius, his second child, who died in his third year. They can hear the bells ringing gaily that yesterday tolled for the child, and then they come upon the turnstile, and Barnes thinks of what had been his usual relationship to it on the way to church.

His wife, Julia (often called Jenny in Barnes's poetry), would go through first, followed by their eager daughter (this would have been Lucy), Barnes himself, and then Julius. Lucy would race through to be again at her mother's side, turning the stile so rapidly that Barnes would be wheeled through, and Julius, giddy with the pleasure, would shake it some more as its motion rushed him through. But yesterday, on the way to the funeral, there was no fourth to go through. Jenny went through "vull o' woe" (l. 28) in contrast to her earlier "winsome gait" (l. 18), and Julia followed her, not "A-skippen onward" (l. 20) as she used to but "A-walken softly" (l. 30) in mourning clothes. Then, after Barnes himself went through, there is no fourth": "He had noo little bwoy to vill / His last white eärmes, an' they stood still" (ll. 33–34). The little boy is dead, and seeing the turnstile now and always will remind him of that death.

The subtlety of the poem may be seen first of all in the way the turnstile stands for several different things simultaneously, and therefore appropriately stands for always-turning mutability. Empty-armed, it is like Barnes himself, his child taken from him: He sees in it the image of what he has become. It stands for a different time of life—the time that Julius went through it with such vitality. Nothing can be more moving than the memory of how the turnstile "sent us on our giddy child" (l. 27). But now, in 1859, not only is the child dead and gone, but so is the *us*. The parents are gone, too, at least Julia is, and so the parental unit is no more. Twenty years earlier, when they were mourning his death, the parents were still alive, and Julius, even though dead, was still alive in the fact that they *were* parents and were mourning him. But now Jenny is dead as well (she died in 1852; see "The WIFE A-LOST"), and that ghostly after-life he had in his parents' love is attenuating as well.

The turnstile has become the gateway out of life. It stands for a place in this world—a place of joy and love where the parents and the children were happy together. But just because of that, it stands for its own revolution into a symbol of absence. Those who have gone through it are gone. To be in the world and to go through the turnstile is to be mortal and to die, and the landscape—as is always true in Barnes—which had stood for presence and life imperceptibly (just through the fact of that imperceptibility) comes to stand for absence and death.

BIBLIOGRAPHY

Levy, William Turner. *William Barnes: The Man and the Poems.* Dorchester, England: Longmans, 1960.

Parins, James W. *William Barnes.* Boston: Twayne Publishers, 1984.

Scott, Leader. *The Life of William Barnes: Poet and Philologist, by His Daughter, Lucy Baxter* ("Leader Scott"). 1887. Reprint, St. Clair Shores, Mich.: Scholarly Press, 1971.

"TWENTY GOLDEN YEARS AGO" JAMES CLARENCE MANGAN (1840) In this poem, JAMES CLARENCE MANGAN, just turned 37, is remembering his lost youth—a loss more or less standard and therefore more or less simply evoked through the title, which provides the poem's repeated refrain. "Twenty Golden Years Ago" is characteristic of Mangan in various ways: There is the combination of light, good humor with genuine pathos over the passing of time, hope, and ambition; there is the winning incongruity of many of the regrets he juxtaposes; and there is the highly skilled and highly inventive use of rhyme. One of the things Mangan was particularly good at was surprisingly numerous rhymes on a single word (see "GONE IN THE WIND"). This is a talent that essentially requires great invention in coming up with ways of making the point one wants to make, as much as it requires inventiveness or resourcefulness in rhyming.

The poem's situation is that its speaker is taking shelter from a rainstorm and remembering the glory days when he was 20 years younger. Each stanza ends with the marveling recollection of how life was "twenty golden years ago," and this means every third-to-last line has to rhyme with *ago.* The first rhymes are not so difficult: *flow* and *low,* and the third adds *know* to the list. Because the stanza-ending refrain contrasts then and now, the rhymes will also tend to pair off around a contrast—how things are now compared with how things were then. Now, he watches the *flow* of the coffee; then, he drank alcohol (in truth, Mangan himself was drinking as much as ever); now, the fire is "dwindling *low*"; but back then, he had an interior fire burning within him to keep him satisfied; now, whether he is living he does not *know,* but he certainly "*was* alive / Twenty golden years ago" (ll. 23–24).

These antitheses are well-handled but somewhat sentimental. The poem becomes genuinely original in its modulation to a kind of self-parody. The wit and energy of that parody begin to suggest that whatever the loss of innocence in the last twenty years, there has been a gain in self-knowledge as well as understanding of the ways of the world. The next stanza, therefore, describes him as "Wifeless, friendless, flagonless, alone" (l. 25), which is funny when one pauses on the third word: He is complaining that he does not have enough to drink. All he has left, he says, is the muse, that is to say, his own poetry; but he used to live *en haut*—the high life—so it is the flagon he misses most.

The rest of the poem sustains the jaunty self-parodic mode and therefore undercuts the funny confession that he is "Sentimentalizing like Rousseau" (l. 54), in contrast to the "grand Byronian soul" he had 20 years ago. But, in fact, he is a lot more like the mature LORD BYRON now than he would have been 20 years ago, and like Byron, he ends the poem with his head aching from the work he has put into finding the "reluctant rhymes" he has dragooned into the poem. So, rather than to the grave, he chooses to go to bed. These were not his dreams 20 years ago, but neither was the death that is real to him now, which makes his not-quite-gallows humor real and vital to him as well.

BIBLIOGRAPHY

Joyce, James. "James Clarence Mangan." In *Occasional, Critical, and Political Writing,* 53–60. Oxford: Oxford University Press, 2001.

Shannon-Mangan, Ellen. *James Clarence Mangan: A Biography.* Dublin: Irish Academic Press, 1996.

"TWINKLE, TWINKLE, LITTLE STAR"

See TAYLOR, JANE.

"TWO LOVES" LORD ALFRED DOUGLAS (1894) This poem as a poem is a competent takeoff of JOHN KEATS, particularly of such poems as "ODE TO PSYCHE" and *The Fall of Hyperion* (see *HYPERION* AND *THE FALL OF HYPERION*). It is most notorious, however, for the famous phrase in its last line, "I am the love that dare not speak its name." Lord ALFRED DOUGLAS published the poem in an undergraduate literary magazine called by the Keatsian name of *The Chameleon* in December 1894, when he was 24 (Keats famously refers to the "chameleon poet" in his Letters). He and OSCAR WILDE were lovers, and the poem's publication made Douglas notorious. Everyone understood that the love that dare not speak its name was being contrasted with the self-styled "true Love" that fills "The hearts of boy and girl with mutual flame"—(1. 72) that is with mutual heterosexual love for each other. (The phrase *mutual flame* is taken from Shakespeare.) The personification of heterosexual love names the other love Shame, instead, and the shame that love would feel is the shame of perversion.

Partly as a result of this poem, Douglas's self-righteous, cruel, and overbearing father, the marquess of Queensberry, publicly accused Wilde of being a sodomite. Wilde felt that he had to sue him for libel and therefore essentially put himself on trial since Queensberry's defense was the truth of his claim. Wilde lost and was then arrested for his sexual behavior, put on trial, and eventually convicted of "gross indecency" and sentenced to two years of hard labor. Douglas's poem was used in evidence against Wilde, one of the purest examples of Wilde's doctrine of how life imitates art. The poem that lamented the shame the self-righteous promoter of heterosexual love imputed to same-sex love was thus used by one of the prosecutors, C. F. Gill, to do the same to Wilde.

Wilde's defense of the poem's sentiments is famous—and somewhat untruthful. At his trial, the cross-examination turned upon the word *shame* in this and another poem by Douglas, also published in *The Chameleon,* called "In Praise of Shame," which ends: "Of all sweet passions Shame is loveliest." Under cross-examination, Wilde asserted that *shame* here meant *modesty,* but it is better to understand it as almost its own antonym: the pleasure derived from feeling shame in one's own immodesty. "Two Loves" does not assert the same praise, but it comes from the same pleasure. For Bosie (as Douglas was known to all), aesthetic and erotic experience were very close to each other. The shame that since Genesis has been part of erotic life was aestheticized, lingered over for its own sake, or for the intensities of feeling it promoted. Wilde had famously asserted, in the preface to his novel *The Picture of Dorian Gray* (1891), that no moral demand could be put on the aesthetic: "There is no such thing as a moral or an immoral book." Shame as an aesthetic category, then, had nothing to do with morality.

Wilde responded to Gill's quotation of the poem in the cross-examination with a now-famous paeon to virtuous platonic love. If the response was not altogether truthful, it was not altogether false, either, since Wilde refused to see erotic love as discontinuous with all other pleasurable intensities of feeling—from friendship to art. Wilde and his friends and protégés insisted on the pure aesthetic qualities of even the most transgressive sexual acts (not very transgressive at all, by more liberal standards), while also making it impossible to ignore the erotic components of the highest aesthetic achievements. Douglas's poem is a poor imitation of Keats, but what it gets right in Keats is the eros that charges *his* poetry everywhere, and that it took people like Wilde and Douglas to recognize and explain.

BIBLIOGRAPHY

Douglas, Alfred Bruce, Lord. *Oscar Wilde and Myself.* New York: Duffield and Co., 1914.

Ellmann, Richard. *Oscar Wilde.* New York: Knopf, 1988.

Harris, Frank. *Oscar Wilde, His Life and Confessions.* Garden City, N.Y.: Garden City Publishing Co., 1932.

Whittington-Egan, Richard. "Oscar Wilde: A Centennial Wreath of Memories." *Contemporary Review* (November 1, 2000). Available online. URL: http://www.encyclopedia.com/doc/1G1-68157978.html. Accessed on January 15, 2008.

Wilde, Oscar. *Complete Works of Oscar Wilde.* New York: HarperCollins, 1989.

———. *Three Trials of Oscar Wilde.* Edited and introduced by H. Montgomery Hyde. New York: University Books, 1956.

"TWO SPIRITS: AN ALLEGORY, THE"

PERCY BYSSHE SHELLEY (1820) "The Two Spirits: An Allegory" is a powerful poem of PERCY BYSSHE SHELLEY's middle period, published posthumously. In it, some of his most basic themes may be seen with particular intensity. The poem takes the form of a dramatic dialogue between two spirits, one of earth and one of the air. Their form and their debate makes them kin to the various choruses of spirits in *PROMETHEUS UNBOUND,* Shelley's great verse play staging the debate between freedom and tyrannical prudence.

Like *Prometheus Unbound* (1820), "The Two Spirits" is about the relevance of lyricism—of the major Shelleyan impulse to poetry—in a world in which poetry seems extravagant and powerless. MATTHEW ARNOLD's libelous description of Shelley as "a beautiful and ineffectual angel beating his luminous wings in the void in vain" presents just the view that Shelley sought to counter.

The first spirit, the spirit of caution and prudence, is a kind of allegory of WILLIAM WORDSWORTH come to middle-aged conservatism—the Wordsworth Shelley condemns in his poetry from *Alastor* and "To Wordsworth" through *The* TRIUMPH OF LIFE. The second spirit is uncontrollable in his desire for transcendence, or rather for the experience of seeking transcendence. He flies with the lamp of love in his heart and flies to the regions of light to whose metaphoric sphere Shelley consistently assigned love.

In this he follows that earlier aspiring spirit, the Italian poet Dante Alighieri (1265–1321), a passage from whose *Divine Comedy* Shelley translated; and, more than this, the Greek philosopher Plato, especially the Plato of the *Phaedrus* and *Symposium,* the great dialogue on love, which Shelley was the first to translate into English. The idea of love that Shelley derives from Plato is the idea that it represents not the presence of transcendence but aspiration toward it. Shelley's early essay "On Love" calls it the feeling of "that powerful attraction towards all that we conceive, or fear, or hope beyond ourselves, when we find within our own thoughts the chasm of an insufficient void, and seek to awaken in all things that are, a community with what we experience within ourselves."

In Shelley's platonic conception, love is a kind of self-transcendence, and the idea of self-transcendence is crucial to Shelley. It is his version of the romantic self-discrepancy that haunts all romantic accounts of consciousness (see ROMANTICISM). In Shelley that self-discrepancy takes the form of a desire to transcend as well as to witness the power and intensity of that transcendence through or by way of contrast. The great line at the end of *ADONAIS,* "I am borne darkly, fearfully, afar," imagines a double perspective: that of where the speaker *is,* and that of a distant observer who sees how far away the speaker has been borne. (Adonais in heaven helps make the contrast, since the Keats figure achieves transcendence, by contrast with the narrator, who is fearfully distant but not transported upward.)

Here the figure who can calibrate the transcendence of the second spirit is, of course, the first. Although he will be slumber-bound on his dull earth, he is needed nevertheless to "mark" the moonlike flight of the second. And it is the first spirit who gets the beautiful description of the second spirit's flight with which the poem opens. Without the first spirit, we would have no sense of the second's intensity or wildness or power, a fact that the poem knows even if the second spirit does not.

The poem knows it best of all in the coda. There the positions represented by the two spirits have become somewhat assimilated and naturalized into the two legends (legends consistent with each other, it should be noted) that balance the end of the poem. As the first stanza of the coda has it, some believe the first spirit has been right about the second—that he has made himself the object of an endless and inescapable pursuit. The storm that the first spirit has predicted has come about, and the second spirit will never escape it.

But others say something different: that the lonely traveler sometimes hears whispers in the grim, unpeopled places where he must spend the night as he travels. The traveler is not the second spirit, but he perceives the second spirit, and hears the whispers of his presence. It is that traveler who dreams of his early love, so that the second spirit—the spirit of love—is what makes the traveler feel and recollect the intensity of first love. We love others because we feel the spirit of love: This is Plato's lesson, one that Shelley has learned and seeks to communicate.

The end of the poem is dazzling. The traveler wakes on the fragrant grass, as Adam does after he dreams of Eve's creation in John Milton's *Paradise Lost* (a scene itself borrowed from the dream Prince Arthur has of the Faerie Queene Gloriana in Edmund Spenser's epic). Keats had written, in a letter on the poetic IMAGINATION that would become very famous: "The imagination may be compared to Adam's dream,—he awoke and found it truth' (letter to Benjamin Bailey, November 22, 1817). Shelley's traveler, though, does not wake like Adam to see the woman he has dreamt of. He awakens to "find night day."

The poem finally depends on how one interprets the word *find* in that last line. Indeed, it depends on combining the two possible meanings of the word. A simplistically optimistic reading of the poem would take it that good had followed on loss or danger: The traveler awakens to discover that day has followed night (as spring will follow winter in Shelley's "ODE TO THE WEST

WIND"). A simplistically pessimistic reading, perhaps that of the first spirit, would take the ending to mean that the traveler is willfully self-deceptive. He does not find that the *time* is day but that *night itself* is day. This would be like a jury's finding an innocent person guilty—a *verdict,* and in this case a false one. But the proper meaning of the line is that the traveler, through the idealizing intensity of his apprehension, of his platonic and therefore transcendent dream, sees so intensely and with such visionary power that in rendering the verdict that night is day, as the first spirit might have it, he turns night into day, which is the second spirit's aspiration. In a sense, then, both spirits are right, which is what makes the idealism that the second spirit stands for so powerful, and so typical of Shelley.

BIBLIOGRAPHY

Bloom, Harold. *Genius: A Mosaic of One Hundred Exemplary Creative Minds.* New York: Warner, 2002.

———. *Shelley's Mythmaking.* New Haven, Conn.: Yale University Press, 1959.

———. *The Visionary Company: A Reading of English Romantic Poetry.* Garden City, N.Y.: Doubleday, 1961.

Chernaik, Judith. *The Lyrics of Shelley.* Cleveland: Press of Case Western Reserve University, 1972.

Hogle, Jerrold E. *Shelley's Process: Radical Transference and the Development of His Major Works.* New York: Oxford University Press, 1988.

Keach, William. *Shelley's Style.* New York: Methuen, 1984.

Notopolous, James A. *The Platonism of Shelley: A Study of Platonism and the Poetic Mind.* Durham, N.C.: Duke University Press, 1949.

Quinney, Laura. *The Poetics of Disappointment: Wordsworth to Ashbery.* Charlottesville: University Press of Virginia, 1999.

Wasserman, Earl. *Shelley: A Critical Reading.* Baltimore: Johns Hopkins Press, 1971.

"TYGER, THE" WILLIAM BLAKE (ca. 1794)

"The Tyger" is the terrifying pendant to "The LAMB" in WILLIAM BLAKE'S *SONGS OF INNOCENCE AND OF EXPERIENCE* as its climactic rhetorical question makes clear: "Did he who made the lamb make thee?" Like "The Lamb," it takes the form of an address to the animal that is the poem's subject, and as in the other poem, it asks the question, "Who made thee? Dost thou know who made thee?" The speaker of "The Tyger" is not a child, though, but a man overwhelmed by the fierceness that the tiger embodies. Where the lamb is an embodiment of gentleness, innocence, and trust, the tiger represents everything dreadful about life—about the forests of the night where we spend the half of our lives in which we are the prey of experience.

"The Lamb" alerts us to one important element of "The Tyger," which is the way the creature represents his creator. The creator of the lamb calls himself a lamb and is childlike. The creator of the tiger is dreadful. The poem gives us as much a bodily sense of the creator as of the creation: It is God's shoulder that provides the force to twist the sinews of the tiger's heart, so that we can see in those sinews the straining sinews that formed them. God's dread hand formed the tiger's dread feet, the dreadfulness of one making palpable the dreadfulness of the other.

The tiger's fierceness is so overwhelming that the stars themselves throw down their spears and water heaven with their tears. Within the context of the poem, this means that the celestial phenomena of starlight and rain reach us as a kind of cosmic response to the creation of the tiger. The animal then becomes pure representation: He represents God's power rather than being an actual element in the speaker's world.

This is evident in the famous change from the first to the last stanza, where the final question is altered from: "What immortal hand or eye, / Could frame thy fearful symmetry?" to "What immortal hand or eye, / *Dare* frame thy fearful symmetry?" The first question is addressed to the tiger, just as the child has addressed the lamb. But even though the rest of the poem continues to apostrophize the tiger, he feels less and less present as a separate being, becoming more and more an object of the speaker's own fierce contemplation. His final question is the culmination of his questions about God. It addresses the tiger only in form, but it is purely rhetorical.

The interesting thing about that rhetorical question is that its answer is not obvious. That is to say, the question may be rephrased as this: "Who but Jehovah himself could dare such a thing?" Or it may instead be rephrased this way: "*How* could any immortal, even Jehovah himself, dare frame such a creature?" The first question implies an answer in which the tiger represents the awe-inspring power of the creator. The second implies a different answer: the creator's willingness to create a world of inhuman ferocity.

Notice that unlike the lamb, the tiger is not blessed at the end of the poem, nor is he cursed. This is because he does not belong to the world he represents. He has become instead the sign, or avatar, of the world's ferocity, and perhaps a sign that that ferocity is intended by God and not just the random workings of nature.

In any case, it is worth considering the status of the lamb after reading "The Tyger." The rhetorical questions that end the penultimate stanza ask:

> Did he smile his work to see?
> Did he who made the Lamb make thee?

That last question is climactic and is put in a suggestive parallel with the question before it. The work at issue is the tiger, and so the smile lines up with the lamb, perhaps the most terrifying idea in the poem. But it need not be, since whatever doubt it casts on the gentleness or genuiness of God's smile, the lamb is immune to that doubt. "Did he smile his work to see?" might mean that God's smile is not one to trust. But the lamb does not represent the untrustworthiness of "The Tyger"'s God. It represents the still undeterred alternative to the tiger. That the creator of the lamb could also create the tiger is terrifying, but that means the lamb is still one of the irreducible terms in the representation of this terror, and that means that he resists and overcomes it, so that the lamb's power of salvation—or of innocence, truth, or hope—are just as much represented by the purely representational tiger as are their opposites. And remember that the lamb is real, in its poem, whereas the tiger is an imaginary vision.

BIBLIOGRAPHY

Bloom, Harold. *Blake's Apocalypse: A Study in Poetic Argument.* Ithaca, N.Y.: Cornell University Press, 1970.

———. *Poetry and Repression: Revisionism from Blake to Stevens.* New Haven, Conn.: Yale University Press, 1976.

Damrosch, Leopold. *Symbol and Truth in Blake's Myth.* Princeton, N.J.: Princeton University Press, 1980.

Erdmann, David V. *Blake, Prophet against Empire: A Poet's Interpretation of the History of His Own Times.* Princeton, N.J.: Princeton University Press, 1977.

Fry, Northrop. *Fearful Symmetry: A Study of William Blake.* Princeton, N.J.: Princeton University Press, 1974.

Gilchrist, Alexander. *Life of William Blake, with Selections from His Poems and Other Writings.* Totowa, N.J.: Rowman and Littlefield, 1973.

Hollander, John. "Blake and the Metrical Contract," In *From Sensibility to Romanticism,* edited by Frederick Hilles and Harold Bloom, 293–310. New York: Oxford, 1965. Reprinted in John Hollander, *Vision and Resonance: Two Senses of Poetic Form,* 187–211. New Haven, Conn.: Yale University Press, 1985.

Ostriker, Alicia. "Desire Gratified and Ungratified: William Blake and Sexuality." *Blake: An Illustrated Quarterly* 16 (1982–83): 156–165.

Raine, Kathleen. *Blake and Antiquity.* Princeton, N.J.: Princeton University Press, 1977.

Thompson, E. P., *Witness against the Beast: William Blake and the Moral Law.* New York: Cambridge University Press, 1993.

U

"ULYSSES" Alfred, Lord Tennyson (1833)

"Ulysses," a perennial favorite and one of Alfred, Lord Tennyson's greatest poems, appeared in the 1842 volume of *Poems* that made Tennyson's name. However, it was written at age 24, nine years earlier, after the death in 1833 of Arthur Henry Hallam, the most important single person in Tennyson's life, and the subject of his great elegy *In Memoriam A.H.H.* Tennyson himself said of "Ulysses" in a note that it "was more written with the feeling of [Hallam's] loss upon me than many poems in *In Memoriam,*" a formulation revised in a later note to read that it "gave my feeling about the need of going forward, and braving the struggle of life perhaps more simply than anything in *In Memoriam.*"

The main sources of the poem are book 11 of Homer's *Odyssey,* where Odysseus (Ulysses is the Latinized form of his name) goes to the underworld and has his future foretold by Tiresias the prophet (this is the scene also in which Ajax turns away from Odysseus, one of the touchstones in Longinus's description of the sublime); and the 26th canto of Dante's *Inferno,* where Dante is led by his guide Virgil to meet Ulysses and hear his story. There are also echoes of William Shakespeare's Ulysses in *Troilus and Cressida.* The Italian poet Dante Alighieri (1265–1321) had not read the ancient Greek poet Homer but only accounts of the Homeric epics; his Ulysses came largely from the Roman poet Virgil's *Aeneid.* Therefore, Tennyson is synthesizing two traditions and two sources, not simply adding a link in a chain.

In Homer, Tiresias tells Ulysses (as we will call him here for consistency) that he will return home to Ithaca, but that eventually he will make one more journey and die in a land so far from the world he knows that it will be entirely alien to him. Neither the *Odyssey* nor any other surviving work tell the story that was clearly known to Homer's audience, but Dante invented it. He has Ulysses gather his men together, perhaps in Ithaca (as Tennyson obviously thought) to make one final journey. The reason for this, he says in the English translation by H. F. Cary that Tennyson would have read at the time, was that he and his men "were not form'd to live the life of brutes / But virtue to pursue and knowledge high" (*Inferno* 26, ll. 116–117). His virtue is not Christian, and so Dante puts him in the hell he has visited in the classical myths. But his words are powerful and striking, especially the famous exhortation not to waste the little time that remains to them in "the brief vigil of our senses:" "questa tanto picciola vigilia / d'i nostri sensi ch'è del rimanente" (26, ll. 114–115; Cary translates: "the short remaining watch, that yet / Our senses have to wake").

Tennyson's poem is a dramatic monologue, spoken by Ulysses as he decides to leave the Homeric Ithaca to which he has returned and undertake the journey predicted for him by Tiresias. The two great authorities, Homer and Dante—or, within their respective fictions, Tiresias and Ulysses himself—disagree about how the story will end. In Homer, Ulysses will die "far from the sea" (*Odyssey,* 11, l. 154); in Dante,

Ulysses and his men are sucked down, perhaps straight to hell itself, in an Atlantic whirlpool (see line 62 of Tennyson's poem). Because it is a dramatic monologue, Tennyson's Ulysses need not know what will happen. But he knows what he is giving up: the kingdom he has reestablished, which he leaves to his son Telemachus to manage and rule. The arts of peace are more necessary than those of war, and Telemachus matters more to the rest of humanity than Ulysses now can. He is the last, or at least the latest, of the introspective romantic explorers—the internalized questers, as Harold Bloom calls the romantic poets embarked upon the seas of subjective experience. Telemachus will save the world; Ulysses seeks to save his soul, and to do so more or less disbelieving in the world's existence.

The crisis provoked by Hallam's death was for Tennyson a crisis about the meaningfulness of anything in the world. (This is a crisis that would be confirmed for him by contemporaneous geological discoveries about the extreme age of the world, and the almost complete disappearance of its former accepted forms and vitalities.) What is the purpose of going on in a world that comes to an end for the self when the self comes to an end? Why care about what survives you—son or city—when nothing will survive for long? "Ulysses" is a crisis lyric (which is described in the entry for the INTIMATIONS ODE). What can you do in a world become empty and poor, from which all possibility of meaningful interaction with another, all hope, has been removed?

Ulysses recognizes that there is nothing *in* experience worth the desire to experience it. The joys he has known turn out to be fugitive ones, their promises unfulfilled. What he wants is life, but he wants it not for its own sake but for something hauntingly elusive—in a way the ghost-memory of Hallam, to be compared and contrasted to the great Achilles, whose absence is what characterizes the world now. Where is meaning if its only bearer is gone? What kind of faith can Tennyson keep with the nonexistent? For Ulysses disbelieves in any afterlife (this is part of Dante's irony in making him speak in an afterlife), and this is a disbelief that Tennyson is close to feeling.

Does the poem resolve the crisis? It does not resolve it, but it copes with it, by offering poetry itself as the place where Hallam can be mourned and therefore throw his shadow. (This sense of poetry as a vocation for being haunted by poetry can also be seen in another Homeric poem of Tennyson's, "The LOTOS-EATERS.") The death of Hallam put Tennyson in Ulysses' position of hopelessness and indifference to human meaning. But the hopelessness and indifference themselves come from a sense of loss and are haunting rather than evacuated of all feeling. They haunt the way poetry haunts, and it is here, if anywhere, that Hallam is to be sought—not to be found, but at least to be an absence, if not a presence. For the meaninglessness of the world would mean that he would not even be an absence from the world. But he is, at least, an absence; he is a ghost or phantom in the poetic thinking and the poetic journey that Tennyson undertakes, and therefore to be found only in the poetry that mourns his loss.

BIBLIOGRAPHY

Armstrong, Isobel. *Victorian Poetry: Poetry, Poetics and Politics.* New York: Routledge, 1993.

Bloom, Harold. "The Internalization of Quest Romance." In *Romanticism and Consciousness: Essays in Criticism,* 3–24. New York: Norton, 1970.

———. *Poetry and Repression: Revisionism from Blake to Stevens.* New Haven, Conn.: Yale University Press, 1976.

Buckley, Jerome Hamilton. *Tennyson: The Growth of a Poet.* Boston: Houghton Mifflin, 1965.

Kilham, John. *Critical Essays on the Poetry of Tennyson.* New York: Barnes and Noble, 1960.

Kincaid, James R. *Tennyson's Major Poems: The Comic and Ironic Patterns.* New Haven, Conn.: Yale University Press, 1975.

Ricks, Christopher B. *Tennyson.* New York: Macmillan, 1972.

Rowlinson, Matthew. *Tennyson's Fixations: Psychoanalysis and the Topics of the Early Poetry.* Charlottesville: University Press of Virginia, 1994.

Tucker, Herbert: *Tennyson and the Doom of Romanticism.* Cambridge, Mass.: Harvard University Press, 1988.

V

"VAÏCES THAT BE GONE, THE" **WILLIAM BARNES (1841)** This beautiful early poem shows WILLIAM BARNES's abiding interest in the surrounding world, and in the changing relationship that human beings have to that world, even as it remains the same. Barnes's typical way of conveying the sense of the unchanging environment by which we measure our own changes is through the refrain. He handles refrain as well as any poet ever did. Here the refrain is about the "vaïces that be gone," and so it has the effect of serving as a kind of echo of those voices. The world stays the same, and one of the ways that it stays the same is in its distinction from a past in which the voices were. Now the surrounding world is the place from which they are gone. The world reminds us of what has departed from it—those now married, those now dead and gone (ll. 20–21).

As with the much-later "LWONESOMENESS," this poem is probably spoken by a young woman living at home with an aged parent. We learn in the first stanza that she goes out at evening as the birds are twittering and returning to their roosts. Their sounds remind her of the voices that are gone, and we feel her affection for the orchards around her because the voices were there. The voices, we learn in the second stanza, belong to her siblings, and they are the voices of all of them as children. The world is still the same: "There's still the tree that bore our swing, / An' others" (ll. 9–10), although the effect the children had on the landscape around them has been covered over. But the place is one that she regards with affection since it reminds her of the past.

It is in the third stanza that the poem becomes genuinely sad. It begins with a memory of the children's mother, vexed by the children's loudness, and we expect that she is just as much a part of the past and departed world as they are. But it turns out that she is still alive, still living in the same place as before. Only the children are gone—whether alive or dead, they are equally absent, since they have grown up. Now the mother wishes to be able to hear the voices that so annoyed her before, but her tears are useless.

So, too, is the speaker's sympathy. The mother's tears are useless since she can never have the voices in her ears again, and even the speaker cannot comfort her. They live in a kind of silence (again as in "Lwonesomeness") even though they are together, isolated from each other even though their experiences are similar. The greatest subtlety of effect in the poem is achieved in the fourth and last stanza, which nearly repeats the third stanza in its list of those who are gone, and in the description of the tears the speaker sheds this time, as her mother has in the previous stanza, missing about her own ears the voices that are gone. She and her mother share the same feelings, but that does not do them any good, because the vital human voices are gone.

And it is here that we find that what had looked like pleasant sauntering in the first stanza actually feels somewhat different: "I still do saunter out, wi' tears" (l.

30). This is a perfect example of the power Barnes derives by framing his poetry in dialect: The voices that are gone are voices that spoke in that dialect. Also, it is only in dialect that sauntering could reasonably be described as occurring as the saunterer wept. This poem is a particularly good and moving example of Barnes's superb control of his own evocations through the subtleties of his prosody and language.

BIBLIOGRAPHY

Levy, William Turner. *William Barnes: The Man and the Poems.* Dorchester, England: Longmans, 1960.

Parins, James W. *William Barnes.* Boston: Twayne Publishers, 1984.

Scott, Leader. *The Life of William Barnes, Poet and Philologist, by his Daughter, Lucy Baxter* ("Leader Scott"). 1887. Reprint, St. Clair Shores, Mich.: Scholarly Press, 1971.

VICTORIAN POETRY

"Victorian poetry" is a term that does not quite coincide with the reign of Queen Victoria—a reign that began with the death of her uncle, William IV, in 1837 and lasted until her own death some 63 years later on January 22, 1901. The great poets who wrote most or all of their work while she was queen (and later, starting in 1876, empress of India) include ALFRED, LORD TENNYSON, ROBERT BROWNING, ALGERNON CHARLES SWINBURNE, DANTE GABRIEL ROSSETTI, CHRISTINA ROSSETTI, MATTHEW ARNOLD, GERARD MANLEY HOPKINS, and A. E. HOUSMAN. Some of the poets we think of as major 20th-century figures began writing in the Victorian Age, most significantly, perhaps, WILLIAM BUTLER YEATS, but also THOMAS HARDY and RUDYARD KIPLING. The measure and historical importance of the Victorian period in literary history can be marked by the fact that WILLIAM WORDSWORTH, who had seen the French Revolution, was still writing a decade after Victoria became queen, while Yeats (who would live until the eve of the Second World War) had already published some of his most important books before she died.

Mention of Yeats and Kipling in the same sentence suggests a different way of defining the Victorian era: Kipling feels Victorian in a way that Yeats does not, and this is because Kipling's great poetry accepted as a fact of history Britain's Victorian-style preeminence in the world, whereas Yeats joined with the moderns to see how all that was solid melted into the air—in particular the air of World War I (1914–18), which changed everything. As a cultural phenomenon, the Victorian era might be said to have come to an end in August 1914. Indeed, at the end of the era thus defined, some of the most significant late Victorian writers, such as ALICE MEYNELL, began leading pacifist movements against the resurgent militarism and international violence that so characterized Europe in the first half of the 20th century.

Violence on the mechanized and global scale of the 20th century was one of the results of the seismic scientific and technological shifts that gave rise to the Industrial Revolution, which began in the 18th century and spread throughout Europe and North America. If we put the end of the Victorian era at the beginning of World War I, we can say that it begins a little before Victoria's accession, with the sudden and earthshaking discoveries of Victorian science. Tennyson and Browning, the two greatest Victorian poets, both took an intense interest in the revolutionary scientific discoveries of the day. The central and most revolutionary achievement of Victorian science was Charles Darwin's (1809–82) discovery of the mechanism of evolution, the "Origin of Species by Means of Natural Selection, or the Preservation of Favoured Races in the Struggle for Life," as the title page of the first edition of his book puts it. That book, generally known as *On the Origin of the Species*, appeared in 1859, the same year as EDWARD FITZGERALD's despairing celebration of the nothingness of human life in *The RUBÁIYÁT OF OMAR KHAYYÁM,* written partly in answer to Tennyson's *IN MEMORIAM A.H.H.* The first edition of *In Memoriam* had been completed 10 years earlier, so Darwin was not a shadow in Tennyson's early world. But his gigantic shadow was, in fact, first cast by the discoveries and systematic exposition of Charles Lyell (1797–1875) in his *Principles of Geology*, published in three volumes between 1830 and 1833—the year that ARTHUR HENRY HALLAM (A.H.H.), Tennyson's closest and most beloved friend, died at 22 of a cerebral hemorrhage. Lyell was one of the first to have an inkling of what has come to be called "deep time," the shocking, almost infinite antiquity of the world—an antiquity that suggested an equally shocking future stretching uniformly ahead forever. Since it was really only in the 18th century that astronomers began to be aware of the vastness of space (no one knew that other stars were also suns until then), the scientific revolution that began with the Enlightenment and accelerated throughout the Victorian era was one that severely undercut human belief in transcendentalist idealism. The universe suddenly appeared too big to transcend, and as Tennyson put it, the muse of astronomy, Urania, rebuked the muse of elegy and tragedy, Melpomene, who replied, "A touch of shame upon her cheek; / 'I am not worthy ev'n to speak / Of thy prevailing mysteries'" (*In Memoriam,* section 37, ll. 10–12).

For Tennyson, the death of Hallam was a catastrophic experience of the overwhelming of the human soul by an indifferent universe. Romantic poetry (see ROMANTICISM) had found a way to idealize human subjectivity as against the trash of mere empirical externality, but the cascading discoveries of science represented a kind of revenge on the part of the material world. In theory—romantic theory—the mind could transcend any world, no matter how great, because the world's greatness was only relative, and the mind traffics with absolutes (see, for example, PERCY BYSSHE SHELLEY'S "MONT BLANC"). But for the Victorians, the discovery of unimagined abysses showed that the world far outvied the mind when it came to IMAGINATION—nature's indifferent, inhuman imagination (personified in *In Memoriam*) made little of anything the human mind could offer from its own petty resources. *In Memoriam* and many other great Victorian poems struggled against this apprehension, but the struggle shows few of the transcendent and absolute victories to be found in the greatest romantic poets. (Browning's essay on Shelley explicitly contrasts the objectivity of contemporary poetry—an objectivity he also ascribes to William Shakespeare—to romantic subjectivity.)

Accordingly, it might be more correct to say that the Victorian era is the era of perhaps the greatest minor poetry ever written in English. "Minor poetry" is not meant as a belittling term: The Victorians wrote in an age when for the first time, perhaps, poets were realizing that with respect to the world around it, poetry could only *be* minor. Tennyson, again, imagining a critic of the intense grief he displays in *In Memoriam,* asks: "Is this an hour / For private sorrow's barren song, / When more and more the people throng / The chairs and thrones of civil power? / A time to quicken and to swoon, / When Science reaches forth her arms / To feel from world to world and charms / Her secret from the latest moon?" (section 21, ll. 13–20). Indeed, many still complain that Victorian literature marked the beginning of a general phenomenon of escapism which in the 20th century would become transmogrified into incessant television watching. (Victorian critics lambasted the widespread reading of novels in ways that the stern moralists of the second half of the 20th century lambasted the widespread *failure* to read novels instead of watching TV. These are really the same complaint.)

All of this means that Victorian literature in general and poetry in particular aimed at giving its readers pleasure. The Victorians could no longer quite believe—as Wordsworth had in the preface to *Lyrical Ballads* (1800)—that such pleasure could save the soul. The Victorians were the heirs of the romantics in many ways, not least in their sense that the pleasures of literature, difficult as they sometimes were, went as deep as the depth of the human soul. But for the Victorians, the human soul did not seem quite as deep as it did for their predecessors.

All of this is generalization, of course, but it is generalization that accounts for a range of Victorian reaction, from the insistence on the absolute accuracy to which human perception can attain, to be found in Arnold, to the counter-insistence on the primacy of subjective experience over any empirical accuracy, with which the essayist and critic Walter Horatio Pater countered Arnold, and which culminated in Wildean (see WILDE, OSCAR) aestheticism. It also accounts for Yeats's folkloric anachronizing on the one hand and the striking number of conversions to Catholicism, such as Hopkins's, on the other, offering an account of the soul fiercely capable of the same minute severity as any faith-challenging science. Further, it accounts for the triumphal shrewdness of such a champion of English industrial and economic achievement as Kipling.

What these poets almost all share is a sense of poetry as giving pleasure. Once the burden is taken off literary pleasure as the royal road to transcendence, pleasure can be regarded as an end in itself, and the Victorians could write the kind of poetry that gave a purer pleasure than the strongly individualized poetic self-assertions to be found in the romantics. (JOHN KEATS is a partial exception and a high influence on the Victorians, especially on Tennyson.) If one thinks of the kind of poetry that we remember without remembering or caring who wrote it, then this is the kind of poetry that the Victorians wrote. This can be seen as much in the vogue for highly sophisticated dramatic monologues—as with Browning and Tennyson, who were inventing characters, not speaking for themselves—as in the nonsense verse of LEWIS CARROLL and EDWARD LEAR. It is no accident that Francis Turner Palgrave's great and wildly successful anthology *Golden Treasury of English Songs and Lyrics* was a product of the Victorian age and ended with a few contemporary poems (Palgrave thanked Tennyson in his introduction), and that almost all its selections, from whatever age, *sound* Victorian.

The character of Palgrave's collection culled from various poets can be found in the kinds of collections that individual Victorian poets put together, such as ROBERT LOUIS STEVENSON'S *A Child's Garden of Verses*. Similarly, among Tennyson's most popular works were songs from the longer narrative works, such as the songs from *THE PRINCESS: A MEDLEY*, which themselves are contextless, songs *sung* by characters, not *spoken* by them. FitzGerald pointed out that the *Rubáiyát* was an anthology (published alphabetically in Persian), which he gave the form of an eclogue (pastoral poem)—so that even when placed into a consecutive form, it is the stanzas that had priority, not the story they told. Even Tennyson described *In Memoriam* as a collection of lyrics, not as a consecutive work (though it is that, too, of course). Swinburne was another impresario of the evocative (partly through his study of WILLIAM BLAKE'S *SONGS OF INNOCENCE AND OF EXPERIENCE*), and Yeats consistently described his poems as songs.

Idiosyncratic and unpredictable as so many of the Victorians were, they nevertheless wrote poems that people remember as poems rather than as the expressions of poets. They wrote poems that gave people pleasure as poems, and such pleasure is the most archaic and deeply rooted experience of poetry that any of us ever has. Thus, Melpomene, the muse of tragedy shamed by Urania's rebuke in *In Memoriam* states that as an earthly muse, she owns "but a little art / To lull with song an aching heart, / And render human love his dues," so that in the end her role is to intensify human experience, minor as it is compared to the transcendence where science and religion come together in the grandeur and immensity of the universe. She, on the other hand, ministering to purely human and earthly experience, has "darken'd sanctities with song" (section 37, l. 24).

None of this should suggest that Victorian poetry is cloying. Its intensity of grief and its apprehensions of despair rival those of any other poetic tradition or period. In fact, some of that intensity derives from a paradoxical acknowledgement of its uselessness. The idea that the human soul is minor, just as the poetry that soul expresses is minor, is a grim one—consonant with the Victorian insights of that greatest of analytic pessimists, Sigmund Freud. The PRE-RAPHAELITE POETRY can have the last word here: The absolutely minor pleasures of decorative beauty—scorned as unworthy of poetry by too many grander aspirants—became for them the devastatingly precise detail which undercuts any notion of transcendence. (They are the forebears of such modern great poets as Elizabeth Bishop.) All there is, in the end, is the world of detail, without the saving importance that might turn loss into gain, as it did for the romantics, that might make pleasure any more than decorative. It is the success of Victorian poetry that it preserves the importance of the decorative, gives us something to hang onto on earth when there is nothing that poetry can communicate that will bring us into heaven.

BIBLIOGRAPHY

Browning, Robert. *Essay on Percy Bysshe Shelley*. London: Reeves and Turner. 1888.

Hough, Graham Goulden. *The Last Romantics*. London: Duckworth, 1949.

Houghton, Walter Edwards. *Victorian Frame of Mind, 1830–1870*. New Haven, Conn.: Yale University Press, 1957.

Trilling, Lionel, and Harold Bloom. *Victorian Prose and Poetry*. New York: Oxford University Press, 1973.

Ricks, Christopher, ed. *The New Oxford Book of Victorian Verse*. New York: Oxford University Press, 1987.

W

"WASHING DAY" **ANNA LAETITIA BARBAULD (1797)** ANNA LAETITIA BARBAULD first published this poem anonymously in the *Monthly Magazine* (to which she often contributed). It is a fascinating and subtle poem that repays thought. "Washing Day" exemplifies the fascinating combination in Barbauld's poetry of 18th-century sociability, attention to social life in all its aspects, and the incipient romantic sensibility that was less interested in the thing described than in the subjectivity or mind of point of view of the describer. Its near mock-epic tone should be compared to many passages of WILLIAM WORDSWORTH's *The PRELUDE* and *The Excursion,* which it anticipates and may have influenced (both Wordsworth and SAMUEL TAYLOR COLERIDGE had the greatest admiration for Barbauld).

"Washing Day" is like Wordsworth's work in the way it takes a topic not commonly thought to be fit for serious poetry and treats it seriously. For both Wordsworth and Barbauld, such a treatment of this sort of topic (in some ways indebted to the 18th-century poet William Cowper's *The Task* but done more seriously and more subtly) represents everyday life and its real and exhausting incidents, labors, and difficulties as a fit subject for poetry because poetry should be about the real issues in life. Barbauld begins in something of the Shakespearean tone she gets from her epigraph (see MOTTOES): It is from Jacques's famous "Seven Ages of Man" speech in *As You Like It* and describes the sixth stage, when late middle age regresses precipitously toward both the appearance and the incapacity of adolescence. The joke is that the Muses are doing the same thing, becoming domestic and no longer inspiring poets with the sublimities of yore.

But for Barbauld, washing day is a serious subject, first of all because all human labor ought to be taken seriously. Washing day, which is about purification, is also about stress and tension, among the women doing the washing and within families on the days that women have to engage in this laborious chore. (This poem ought to be compared to THOMAS HOOD's even more grueling "The SONG OF THE SHIRT.") Barbauld is not only writing a brief for women's domestic labor, however; she shows washing day from the male point of view as well, not to ridicule men for their cluelessness but to show the effects of the division of labor between the sexes following the Fall. For her audience, there be nothing much new here except the treatment of the subject in a poetic form; but that treatment (not unlike the novels of Jane Austen) dignifies human experience and treats what Sigmund Freud would call the normal unhappiness of daily life as a fit subject for poetry.

It would be a mistake to see the poem as only about human labor, though. It is also about human joy, in particular the joys of childhood. Barbauld the adult knows the pains of washing day, but she can also remember its pleasures and the way she was thrown on her own resources as a child. The memory reminds her of other days and the happy indulgences she received then; of her grandmother's patience on washing day;

and then, finally, of her own pastimes, thinking about the adults and their activities from the perspective of the precocious child, and blowing bubbles. Those bubbles are like the bubbles of earth in Shakespeare's *Macbeth,* to which the end of the poem alludes—the fascinating ephemera of childhood and memory and poetry itself (this verse itself, as she says). Writing the poem is a way of being connected to the washing days of Barbauld's childhood, and of seeing the trivial things in life as its best portion. She shows why the muses, including her grandmother, eldest of forms, would have turned domestic: because it is there that you can come to know the real essence of the human being, from girl to grandmother.

BIBLIOGRAPHY

Armstrong, Isobel. "The Gush of the Feminine: How Can We Read Women's Poetry of the Romantic Period?" In *Romantic Women Writers: Voices and Countervoices,* edited by Paula R. Feldman and Theresa M. Kelley, 13–32. Hanover, N.H.: University Press of New England, 1995.

Armstrong, Isobel, and Virginia Blain, eds. *Women's Poetry in the Enlightenment: The Making of a Canon, 1730–1820.* New York: St. Martin's Press, 1999.

Barbauld, Anna Letitia. *Poems, 1792.* New York: Woodstock, 1993.

Keach, William. *Arbitrary Power: Romanticism, Language, Politics.* Princeton, N.J.: Princeton University Press, 2004.

Mellor, Anne K. *Romanticism & Gender.* New York: Routledge, 1993.

Stabler, Jane. *Burke to Byron, Barbauld to Baillie, 1790–1830.* New York: Palgrave, 2001.

Wordsworth, Jonathan. *Bright Work Grows: Women Writers of the Romantic Age.* Washington, D.C.: Woodstock Books, 1997.

"WHEN I HAVE FEARS THAT I MAY CEASE TO BE" JOHN KEATS (1818) This great sonnet contains the essence of JOHN KEATS's poetic thinking in miniature. Its candidness, subtlety, and beauty combine to give a sense of what his fears really are and what his sense of vocation finally means. The first line is consciously reminiscent of the 17th-century poet John Milton's sonnet on a similar subject, "When I consider how my light is spent," which Keats radically rewrites in a secular mode. Milton complains of his own blindness before he can complete the work his talents have fitted him for—indeed, before half his life is over. Keats's anxiety is not blindness but death itself. His mind is filled with poetic ideas, but he fears he may not have time to express them.

The image of Keats's pen *gleaning* his thoughts (l. 2) should be compared to the images of those other gleaners in his odes, Ruth in the "ODE TO A NIGHTINGALE" and autumn in "TO AUTUMN," as well as the narrator of *The Fall of Hyperion* (see HYPERION AND *THE FALL OF HYPERION*) who seeks to "glean [his] memory" (1. 467). The gleaners collect the residual richness of the autumn harvest, and Keats likes the idea because of the way it suggests that the world will be endlessly generous to its gleaners, even as the season approaches winter or death. Here, even though winter looms in his anxiety, it is still high summer in his thoughts, and his brain is full of wealth, which he would like to store up like grain in the books he imagines writing. Those books would be full of Spenserian story and fairy tale—indeed, the kind of work that ALFRED, LORD TENNYSON, Keats's great disciple and continuator, undertook in his long and high romances.

Keats's sense of poetic richness has never received a better description than his desire to trace the shadows of the symbols of night "with the magic hand of chance." Chance is magical, which is to say that it is adequate to the magical romances it would trace. The magical chance he means is the magical *rightness* of meter and, preeminently, of rhyme. Poets take two attitudes toward rhyme: the Miltonic attitude, which sees it as deforming expression due to arbitrary rules; and the Keatsian and Byronic attitude, which sees rhyme as part of the wonderful, surprising, spontaneous aptness of language to the things it would express. For Keats, who thought that poetry should come like leaves to a tree, the natural spontaneity of how rhymes occur to him is magical.

That magic is also erotic. The poem seems to have arisen out of a chance encounter: He sees a beautiful woman and is filled with both joy and sorrow—with the feeling he will also trace in his "ODE ON MELANCHOLY." She is part of the chance spontaneity of the world, granted for an instant like the flowers fancy breeds in the "ODE TO PSYCHE," "who breeding flowers will never breed the same" ("Psyche," l. 63).

It is only in the 12th line of the sonnet that we arrive at the main clause after all the subordinating *Whens.* When he fears, beholds, and considers these things, then he shifts into some profounder state of poetic vocation than that of the spontaneity he has described so far. He stands on the "shore / Of the wild world"—a beautiful phrase, reminiscent of William Shakespeare's *Antony and Cleopatra,* and an image that he recurs to frequently. He is "alone," thinking as he gazes out of the wide world into a wideness still greater (not unlike the darkness of Milton's phrase "this dark world and wide" in "When I consider"), and there the vital desires that have animated and energized his poetic vocation before him—fame as a poet, love for the fair creature of an hour, or for the possibility of love itself—sink into nothingness.

This is *not* what Keats fears. It is what counters his fears. What finally matters for him is the possibility of thought and not sensation, despite the desire famously expressed in his letter, "O! for a life of sensation rather than of thought." But thought is where he can feel, as it were, *free* of the sensations that make him cling to the profuse details of life, and therefore free of desire and free of the fear of loss. It is in thought and not in sensation that Keats finds within himself a vastness and a power adequate to the overall darkness and distance of the world. In that state, he no longer feels hurried on to write. Milton's sonnet ends with Patience enjoining him that "They also serve, who only stand and wait." Keats goes one better: He does not serve at all. Perhaps he stands and waits, but he does not wait for anything except for love and fame to sink into nothingness, after which only the waiting itself, without an object, which is to say thought itself, will remain. (Compare the "steadfastness" of "BRIGHT STAR," which comes to a similar, though more eroticized, conclusion.)

BIBLIOGRAPHY

Bate, Walter Jackson. *John Keats.* Cambridge, Mass.: Harvard University Press, 1963.

Bloom, Harold. *Poetry and Repression: Revisionism from Blake to Stevens.* New Haven, Conn.: Yale University Press, 1976.

———. *The Visionary Company: A Reading of English Romantic Poetry.* Garden City, N.Y.: Doubleday, 1961.

De Man, Paul. *The Rhetoric of Romanticism.* New York: Columbia University Press, 1984.

Empson, William. *Seven Types of Ambiguity.* New York: New Directions, 1966.

Flesch, William. "The Ambivalence of Generosity: Keats Reading Shakespeare." *ELH: English Literary History* 62, no. 1 (Spring 1995): 149–169.

McFarland, Thomas. *The Masks of Keats: The Endeavour of a Poet.* New York: Oxford University Press, 2000.

Vendler, Helen Hennessy. *Odes of John Keats.* Cambridge, Mass.: Harvard University Press, 1983.

Wasserman, Earl. *The Finer Tone: Keats' Major Poems.* Baltimore: Johns Hopkins Press, 1953.

"WHEN THE LAMP IS SHATTERED"

See "LINES: WHEN THE LAMP IS SHATTERED."

"WHEN YOU ARE OLD" WILLIAM BUTLER YEATS (1891) "When You Are Old" is WILLIAM BUTLER YEATS's free adaptation of one of the most famous sonnets to Hélène by the French renaissance poet Pierre de Ronsard (1524–84). Ronsard was the greatest of the French Renaissance poets known as the Pléiade, after the seven-starred constellation the Pleiades, and a favorite of the great 16th-century poet of Faeryland, Edmund Spenser. As always, originality within the context of an invented or reimagined archaic tradition is what counts in Yeats, and so it is instructive to compare Ronsard's original with Yeats's 12-line reformulation.

Ronsard's sonnet, "Quand vous serez bien vieille. . . ," may be translated as literally as is consistent with clarity as follows:

When you are old, at evening, by your candle
Seated by the fire, separating yarn and sewing,
You will say, singing my verses and marveling:
"Ronsard celebrated me in the days when I was
  fair.

Then no servants hearing this news,
All already half-asleep from the labor of the day,
Won't awaken at the sound of my name,
Blessing your name with immortal praise.

I will be below the earth, and a boneless
  phantom:
I will take my rest in the myrtle shades;
You will be an old woman, squatting by the
  hearth,

Regretting my love and your proud disdain.
Live, believe me, do not wait for tomorrow:
Gather today the roses of life.

Here is Yeats's version of the poem in full, to facilitate comparison:

When you are old and grey and full of sleep,
And nodding by the fire, take down this book,
And slowly read, and dream of the soft look
Your eyes had once, and of their shadows deep;

How many loved your moments of glad grace,
And loved your beauty with love false or true,
But one man loved the pilgrim soul in you,
And loved the sorrows of your changing face;

And bending down beside the glowing bars,
Murmur, a little sadly, how Love fled
And paced upon the mountains overhead
And hid his face amid a crowd of stars.

In the Yeats version, the woman is alone; she is full of sleep but takes down the very book in which this poem appears (*The Rose,* 1893) and reads this very poem. As with JOHN KEATS's "THIS LIVING HAND" (and Dorothy Fields's great Tin Pan Alley lyrics to "The Way You Look Tonight," which it certainly influenced), the poem describes the effect it will have in the future, when the *you* it addresses will have survived the poet who addresses her. Ronsard's beloved will remember all his poems but will not particularly refer to this one, since she recollects his celebrations of her beauty.

But Yeats's beloved will read this very poem. As in Ronsard's original, she will remember him and his love and her own departed beauty too late. But Yeats's poem is not a carpe diem poem (a poem urging the woman courted to seize the day since youth and beauty are fleeting; technically Ronsard's is a carpe florem—seize the flower—poem, the most famous example of which in English is Robert Herrick's "Gather ye rosebuds while ye may"). He does not love her for her beauty but for the mysterious "pilgrim soul in you," and for the sorrows that he sees in her now, in the time of writing. Far from chastising her for her pride, he sees in her sorrow that love for her, like all his poetic desire, is love for the impossible.

As with all of early Yeats, one theme of the poem is the nature of poetry itself. And for the early Yeats, the nature of poetry is the impossible desire to live poetically, to live within the literary space of poetry. That place is a place of sorrow and longing, because what poetry is about is unappeasable sorrow and longing—a pilgrimage (like Geoffrey Chaucer's) that can never attain its goal since its goal is the always-elsewhere impulse that makes people long to go on pilgrimages. Love for her is love for sorrow, and sorrow can never accept the salvation love offers because then it would no longer be sorrow. For Yeats, to be a poet is to be befriended by sorrow (as in "THE SAD SHEPHERD," where Yeats imagines himself as the shepherd "whom sorrow named his friend").

The closest he can come, therefore, is to imagine that her sorrow makes his love the true, sorrowing love of the poet, a love like that of Wandering Aengus (see "SONG OF WANDERING AENGUS, THE"), or of the Sad Shepherd. The discrepancy, the impossibility of mutual resolution of the tension between the love that loves sorrow and the sorrow too sad to be redeemed by love, can only be solved by poetry. He thinks of her *now,* and thinks of how, later, she will think of him and recognize *then* what she cannot recognize now. She will miss him, as now he misses her; she will feel the sorrow of love then as he feels it now; and all this will happen when she reads this poem, which becomes part of the impossible irresolvable poetic relationship it describes.

It should be noted that the personification of love here does not quite mean that Yeats is describing himself as Love, any more than he is describing her as Sorrow. Rather, Love despairs, so that it is the personification of the despair that it should ever attain its goal. (Late in life, Yeats personified love in the Crazy Jane poems: "Love has built his mansion in the place of excrement.") Love personifies the sorrow of Love. This is an idea that Yeats got from PERCY BYSSHE SHELLEY's great poem "LINES: 'WHEN THE LAMP IS SHATTERED,'" where Shelley personifies and addresses a fragile and defeated love:

O Love! who bewailest
The frailty of all things here,

Why choose you the frailest
For your cradle, your home, and your bier?

Its passions will rock thee
As the storms rock the ravens on high;
Like the sun from a wintry sky.
From thy nest every rafter
Will rot, and thine eagle home
Leave thee naked to laughter,
When leaves fall and cold winds come.

For Yeats, as for Shelley, the personification of love as lonely, vulnerable, and unsavable is the heart of poetry, the vocation of which is to love the sorrow of love and the pilgrim soul it loves.

BIBLIOGRAPHY

Anscombe, G. E. M. *Intention.* Cambridge, Mass.: Harvard University Press, 2000.
Bloom, Harold. *Yeats.* New York: Oxford University Press, 1970.
Grossman, Allen R. *Poetic Knowledge in the Early Yeats: A Study of The Wind among the Reeds.* Charlottesville: University Press of Virginia, 1969.
Vendler, Helen. *Poets Thinking: Pope, Whitman, Dickinson, Yeats.* Cambridge, Mass.: Harvard University Press, 2004.
Vendler, Helen. *Yeats's Vision and the Later Plays.* Cambridge, Mass.: Harvard University Press, 1963.

"WHO GOES WITH FERGUS?" WILLIAM BUTLER YEATS (1892) "Who Goes with Fergus?" one of WILLIAM BUTLER YEATS's most beautiful poems, is about the Red Branch King, whose story he told at somewhat great length in "FERGUS AND THE DRUID," earlier in his 1893 volume of poems, *The Rose.* The novelist James Joyce quotes the first three lines of the second stanza in *Ulysses* (1922), where he has Stephen Dedalus recollect his mother's obsession with "love's bitter mystery." Joyce first heard the lines at 17 in 1899 at a performance of Yeats's play *The Countess Cathleen.* The poem offers not an account of but an escape from the bitter mystery of love, into the dreams of fairyland.

Who will go drive with Fergus now,
And pierce the deep wood's woven shade,
And dance upon the level shore?
Young man, lift up your russet brow,
And lift your tender eyelids, maid,
And brood on hopes and fear no more.

And no more turn aside and brood
Upon love's bitter mystery;
For Fergus rules the brazen cars,
And rules the shadows of the wood,
And the white breast of the dim sea
And all dishevelled wandering stars.

Those who drive with Fergus will find in the dance and in the woods the kind of communion with the fairy-tale world that Yeats constantly sought to portray in his earlier (19th-century) poems. In all these expressions of desire, though, what Yeats desires is always an antithetical alternative to the experience he seeks to overcome. Thus, Stephen Dedalus's mother is right to focus on "love's bitter mystery": Only someone who brooded on the bitterness of love would seek to end that brooding. Fergus, the king who gave up his kingship to explore all the mysteries of the enchanted world, offers an alternative, one which offers us, or Yeats, a way to "turn aside" toward the demand not to turn aside. In 1899 Yeats called Fergus "the poet of the Red Branch Cycle [of Irish legends], as Osian was of the Fenian." Yeats added: "He was once king of all Ireland, and . . . gave up his throne that he might live in peace hunting in the woods" (*Variorum Poems*). Yeats got this story from a 19th-century reimagination of the Red Branch, or Ulster, stories, Irish folklore about legendary kings, and in fact it does not correspond much to the traditional tales. As Yeats later said, in a note to *The Wind Among the Reeds* (1899), "In the song in my early book, 'Who will drive with Fergus now?' . . . my imagination dealt more freely with what I did know than I would approve of to-day."

In the story, as told in some detail in "Fergus and the Druid," Fergus abdicates his kingship to Conchubar (who will have Cuchulain, one of Yeats's favorite heroes, as one of his men) in order to pierce the deep wood's woven shade himself. He abdicates his kingship over other humans, the Red Branch people in particular, but he gains instead the more poetic kingship that this poem celebrates. Now he rules the brazen cars, the chariots (in an echo from PERCY BYSSHE SHEL-

LEY'S "ODE TO THE WEST WIND") that carry him through his domain, and he rules shadows and the breast of the sea and the wandering stars themselves.

The stars he rules are wandering and disheveled, which means finally that they are not the fixed stars. Rather, they are comets—the stars named after the Greek word for hair, *comes;* "disheveled" literally means their hair is in disarray. The beauty and irregularity of the comets make them the most extravagant part of the astronomical dance, and they provide the model for those who will follow them. Fergus and his domain do not stand for regularity and law but for a wildness that transcends law, and which for Yeats was to be found in poetry and the poetic metamorphoses it makes possible.

BIBLIOGRAPHY

Anscombe, G. E. M. *Intention.* Cambridge, Mass.: Harvard University Press, 2000.

Bloom, Harold. *Yeats.* New York: Oxford University Press, 1970.

Ellmann, Richard. *Yeats: The Man and the Masks.* New York: Norton, 1978.

Grossman, Allen R. *Poetic Knowledge in the Early Yeats: A Study of The Wind among the Reeds.* Charlottesville: University Press of Virginia, 1969.

Rosenthal, M. L., ed. Introduction to *Selected Poems and Four Plays of William Butler Yeats,* xix–xliv. New York: Scribner, 1996.

Vendler, Helen. *Poets Thinking: Pope, Whitman, Dickinson, Yeats.* Cambridge, Mass.: Harvard University Press, 2004.

———. *Yeats's Vision and the Later Plays.* Cambridge, Mass.: Harvard University Press, 1963.

"WIFE A-LOST, THE" WILLIAM BARNES **(1863)** WILLIAM BARNES's wife Julia died in 1852 of breast cancer, and he missed her ever after. It is a measure of how deeply involved in each other's lives they were that he describes her, or her absence, in just the same terms as all other losses that are reflected in their absence from a nature essentially unaffected by their lack. This poem appears in *Hwomely Rhymes: A Second Collection of Poems in the Dorset Dialect* (1859), and THOMAS HARDY quotes it as an instance "of rare intensity [in] the expression of grief" in his review (the last book review that he wrote) of a collection of all of Barnes's volumes of dialect poetry. Hardy praises the "turn of thought in the sixth line of each stanza" as "particularly fine."

That turn represents the lost wife's entry into each stanza, followed by the speaker's iterated recognition that she is gone. He wants to hide from that recognition, but he cannot. Everything reminds him of it, even the places that should not. The first stanza has him leaving the house from which she is all too palpably absent to sit under the beeches. The place where he sits is one like that in a number of poems where he can be entirely alone, because it has always been a place in which he has been able to be alone. Her absence *there* is not significant, as it is in the house. But just the fact that she never came there is what her absence reminds him of. Or to put it another way, she used to be elsewhere when he was in the "lwonesome pleäce" (l. 3), but now she is nowhere.

The second stanza describes another escape from what they used to do together. Instead of walking side by side with her during the summer's heat, the speaker goes down to the colder place where the trees are dripping wet, and where she never came. The landscape itself has become a sad one, her absence (Persephone-like) affecting the world from which she is gone. And we see more clearly now that it is the entire world that her death affects—at least *his* entire world. This is made all the clearer by the great alteration of the stanza-ending burdens, or refrains, that comes at the end of the third stanza. He cannot stand eating alone at home, and so in his grief and mourning, he eats "A-vield upon the ground" and doesn't grieve to miss her now "As I at hwome do pine." The word *As,* which stands at the beginning of each last line to compare his solitary grief out of doors to the grief that he would have at home, becomes clarified here. It is not a conjunction meant to underline a contrast in states, as he might have hoped. It is not that he does not grieve here and does grieve at home; it is that the way he grieves here is different from the way he grieves at home. At home he pines, as though she could return home. Here his grief is more extensive, universal, and inescapable.

In his review, Hardy wisely printed only the first three stanzas of this poem, silently omitting the fourth, as though he had printed the whole poem. (He did this again, omitting the last stanza of a different poem, in a selection of Barnes's poetry he had made in 1918.) As a poem written by Barnes and edited by Hardy, the first three stanzas of "The Wife A-Lost" make a perfect poem. Barnes's fourth stanza, which is actuated by the idea of seeing his wife in heaven, is as hauntingly beautiful in its poetry as the first three, but it is the weakest of the poem. He, too, looks to join her in the world which is above this world of absence. The last stanza confirms the sense of worldwide loss in the first three, but it does so only by offering a hopeful contrast that may have been deeply helpful to Barnes's own despairing spirit, which weakens the poem. Nevertheless, even with that stanza, one can concur with the writer and anthologist Francis Turner Palgrave, who said of this poem, "One can hardly find a better example than this of the contrast between true feeling and sentimentalism." That feeling will include the confidence that Barnes's love will allow him to see his wife again.

BIBLIOGRAPHY

Hardy, Thomas. Review of *Poems of Rural Life in the Dorset Dialect. New Quarterly Magazine* (October 1879): 469–473. Reprinted in *Thomas Hardy's Public Voice: The Essays, Speeches, and Miscellaneous Prose,* edited by Michael Millgate, 17–27. New York: Oxford University Press, 2001.

Levy, William Turner. *William Barnes: The Man and the Poems.* Dorchester, England: Longman, 1960.

Parins, James W. *William Barnes.* Boston: Twayne Publishers, 1984.

Scott, Leader. *The Life of William Barnes: Poet and Philologist, by his Daughter, Lucy Baxter* ("Leader Scott"). 1887. Reprint, St. Clair Shores, Mich.: Scholarly Press, 1971.

WILDE, OSCAR (1854–1900)

Oscar Wilde is one of the most striking literary figures of the later 19th century, a sensation as much in our time as in his own. He is infinitely more important as a playwright, novelist, and critic, as well as a sheer cultural presence, than as a poet. But his poetry is not negligible, and parts of *THE BALLAD OF READING GAOL* bear comparison with some of the greatest moments in SAMUEL TAYLOR COLERIDGE. Wilde has been taken as something of an icon of gay aestheticism, a role suitable to his own ideals but also perhaps somewhat too limited in its perspective.

It would be best to regard Wilde as a disciple of the essayist and critic Walter Horatio Pater (1838–94). Pater had championed a high literary impressionism which was about human perception and its intensification within the aesthetic mode. (Wilde was a friend of both the essayist and critic John Ruskin and the artist James Whistler, and he served as the model for Bunthorne in Gilbert and Sullivan's operetta *Patience.*) In one of his dialogues, Wilde noted that "the primary aim of the critic is to see the object as in itself it really is not" (*The Critic as Artist;* for more on this issue, see the entry on A. E. HOUSMAN's "'TERENCE, THIS IS STUPID STUFF,'" which alludes to this line). "In itself" means as a part of gross reality; to see it differently is to see it as refracted through the aesthetic morality of the artistic mind, which (as Wilde says in the famous page-long preface to his novel *The Picture of Dorian Gray*) consists in "the perfect use of an imperfect medium." The imperfect medium is what the world gives us; the perfect use is what enables us to see the work as in itself it is not. Such perfect use is essentially on behalf of aesthetic perfection, and has no use beyond itself. As Wilde says in the last and summary sentence of the preface: "All art is quite useless."

This aestheticism is, for Wilde, a way of making life into art. Much of his aestheticism was sexual, and though he was married and had two children, he began exploring homosexuality in his early 30s (through the offices of his friend Robert Ross), perhaps feeling that gay dalliances were less adulterous than heterosexual alliances would be. He and his wife Constance grew sexually cooler toward each other after the birth of their second son, Vivian, in 1885, and Wilde began taking more delight in the company of younger men.

The great love of his life was Lord ALFRED DOUGLAS, with whom Wilde began an affair in 1892 when Douglas came to him for help with a blackmailer. Douglas was 16 years younger than Wilde, and Wilde loved him no less passionately for his beauty than for his mind. Douglas reciprocated and began writing poetry under Wilde's tutelage. One of those poems, "TWO LOVES," was used as evidence against Wilde in his 1895 libel suit against Douglas's father, John Sholto Douglas, the blustering, vulgar, and overbearing eighth marquess of Queensberry.

Queensberry had heard that his son and Wilde were lovers, and he provoked a conflict by leaving a card at

Wilde's club notoriously addressed to Wilde as someone posing as a sodomite (a word that Queensberry famously misspelled as "somdomite"). Wilde unwisely sued for criminal libel, and after he lost his case, he was himself put on trial for gross indecency. After two trials, he was found guilty and sentenced to two years' hard labor; from that experience comes *The Ballad of Reading Gaol*. Wilde was released in 1897 and died in 1900 of meningitis from an ear infection exacerbated by his treatment in prison.

The Ballad of Reading Gaol shows Wilde's interest in Catholicism, which probably also had an aesthetic component—or it might be said that his aestheticism had a religious component, as both religion and art intensified an otherwise grossly material human existence. Indeed, Wilde read the Italian Renaissance poet Dante Alighieri intensively in prison and refers to him in the *Ballad*. Wilde saw no contradiction between Catholicism and homosexuality, and he died, apparently in the Catholic faith, a few months after visiting the pope and obtaining his blessing. As with Judaism in the life of the French novelist Marcel Proust, Catholicism played something of a dissonant role in Wilde's life (including his aesthetic life), equivalent to his sexuality. In Wilde's case, his Protestant mother had had him baptized and brought up as an Irish Roman Catholic, in protest of the treatment of Catholic Ireland by its English overlords. Wilde's aestheticism had an important element of social protest in it, though he would have been the last to say so (or perhaps the first, depending on how one understands the epithet *social*), and his Catholicism, like his homosexuality, should be seen as part of the same commitment to refuse to accept the world as in itself it really is.

BIBLIOGRAPHY

Douglas, Alfred Bruce, Lord. *Oscar Wilde and Myself*. New York: Duffield and Co., 1914.

Ellmann, Richard. *Oscar Wilde*, New York: Knopf, 1988.

Harris, Frank. *Oscar Wilde, His Life and Confessions*. Garden City, N.Y.: Garden City Publishing Co., 1932.

Morrison, Paul. *The Explanation for Everything: Essays on Sexual Subjectivity*. New York: New York University Press, 2001.

Nunokawa, Jeff. *The Tame Passions of Wilde: Styles of Manageable Desire*. Princeton, N.J.: Princeton University Press, 2003.

Whittington-Egan, Richard. "Oscar Wilde: A Centennial Wreath of Memories." *Contemporary Review* (November 1, 2000). Available online. URL: http://www.encyclopedia.com/doc/1G1-68157978.html. Accessed on January 15, 2008.

Wilde, Oscar. *Complete Works of Oscar Wilde*. New York: HarperCollins, 1989.

Wilde, Oscar. *Three Trials of Oscar Wilde*. Edited and introduced by H. Montgomery Hyde. New York: University Books, 1956.

"WINDHOVER, THE" GERARD MANLEY HOPKINS (1877) GERARD MANLEY HOPKINS regarded "The Windhover" as his best poem. It combines all his characteristic and idiosyncratic intensities with extraordinary verve and power. Hopkins focuses simultaneously on poetic form and on what that form itself represents—what its physical power may be said to *embody*, which is the power of Christ, to whom the poem is dedicated. The second person of the Trinity, Christ is at once the God who "fathers-forth" the beauty of the world (as Hopkins was to put it a month or two later in "PIED BEAUTY") and the Son, the God who is forth-fathered and therefore like the world itself in his combination of all its attributes. Form is embodied in Hopkins because his poetic forms are all conceived as postures of the body in stress and in prayer. His distinction between "sprung" and "running" rhythm, for example (see SPRUNG RHYTHM), and his stress on *stress* as at once a linguistic, psychological, and physical or physiological experience, shows how form and its content are one, or how content under sufficient pressure turns into the form that conveys and addresses it.

The windhover itself shows in its bodily posture the same relation to the world that the poem attempts in describing the bird. (A windhover is a kestrel, a kind of falcon.) In the way he rides the air, he sustains his posture through matching and reciprocating all the motions of the world he addresses and the motions of the medium through which he addresses it, "the rolling underneath him steady air" (l. 3).

We can see Hopkins doing what he describes the bird as doing in his own prosody. The poem is sufficiently condensed that it is worth examining the first few lines. On the morning of Wednesday, May 30,

1877, Hopkins sees a windhover hovering in the wind and then flying freely against it. He calls the bird "morning's minion" (meaning morning's darling, from the French *mignon*). This particular morning he sees the representative of morning itself. The windhover negotiates the connection between the particular as Hopkins experiences it and the general form of morning that fathers-forth all these particulars. The windhover—like JOHN KEATS's nightingale in "ODE TO A NIGHTINGALE"—belongs to both realms. The windhover is the beloved of morning and the inheritor and heir of the kingdom of daylight; therefore, it is itself an avatar of Christ, dauphin of the Kingdom of God.

The broken rhyme on *king- / dom* is not unprecedented in Hopkins, and here it is doing significant work. It stresses the assonance between *king* and the first syllable of *minion,* establishing the poem's through-connection, syllable by syllable or stress by stress, each one picking up and finding some new facet of the last. And it also carries this connection across larger arcs, so that *king-* will rhyme with *wing, swing,* and *thing* in the octet of this Petrarchan sonnet.

Those rhymes are also near rhymes with the *-ing* endings of the *b*-rhymes in the octet: *riding, striding, gliding, hiding.* But, most significantly, the carrying over of *king- / dom* to the next line mimics the bird's self-sustained riding of the rolling air. It is as though the poem itself rides the unrolling of its lines, skates off when it wishes to, and rebuffs the wind. The poem represents how the bird's achievement and mastery stirs the poet to write these lines (l. 8).

The crucial word in the poem is the much-discussed *Buckle!* in line 9. The word means both the collapsing of everything under its own stress and the union or conjoinment of everything together. The word *dangerous* picks up on the first meaning, and *lovelier* on the second (l. 10). *Buckle* means both the breaking and the filling in of what is broken in the variegated continuities of the world. The poem itself buckles, but the windhover continues its flight, and this explodes into a revelation of its own fantastic power. The danger and the loveliness go together: They represent the incessant freshness and sustained unprecedentedness of God.

This is so despite the world's ancientness and the repetitiveness of the poetic form that represents it. "Shéer plod" (l. 12) refers both to ploughing the earth and the plodding of the poetic beat through its lines, the *sillions* (furrows) into which the earth is ploughed. But the sillions shine.

What is true of the earth is true of its cycles as well. The poem begins in the morning but is written at night, while Hopkins contemplates the embers in his fire and sees how they go from the compacted alliteration of the "blue-bleak" into the unexpected beauty of the "gold-vermilion." The word *gold* picks up from *gall* by way of *gash,* the way the embers break open, which itself rhymes on *fall* in one of Hopkins's linked pairs. The rhymed linkage in "Fall, gall" picks up from the alliterative linkage of "blue-bleak." The fall is the result of buckling: The coals cannot sustain themselves. It also represents the Fall of humanity, one of the central concerns of Hopkins's ministry as a Roman Catholic priest. But for Hopkins the buckling that leads to a fall also leads to the glory of the intense beauty, of which the fall turns out to be another version. It is Christ whom Hopkins addresses in the end with the interjection "ah my dear" (borrowed from George Herbert's great 17th-century poem "Love" [III]). He is dear because he is there, and we know he is there because the beauty linked everywhere in the world is the sign of his presence. He is present, then, even in the fall, making it beautiful and thereby redeeming it with the incessant intensity of his presence.

BIBLIOGRAPHY

Bridges, Robert. Preface to Notes to *The Poems of Gerard Manley Hopkins.* Edited by W. H. Gardner, 94–101. New York: Oxford University Press, 1948.

Gardner, W. H. *Gerard Manley Hopkins (1844–1889): A Study of Poetic Idiosyncrasy in Relation to Poetic Tradition.* New Haven, Conn.: Yale University Press, 1949.

———, ed. Introduction to *Poems and Prose of Gerard Manley Hopkins.* Harmondsworth, Middlesex, England: Penguin, 1963.

Hartman, Geoffrey. *The Unmediated Vision: An Interpretation of Wordsworth, Hopkins, Rilke, and Valery.* New Haven, Conn.: Yale University Press, 1954.

Hopkins, Gerard Manley. *Gerard Manley Hopkins: Selected Letters.* Edited by Catherine Phillips. New York: Oxford University Press, 1990.

Miller, J. Hillis. "Gerard Manley Hopkins." In *The Disappearance of God,* 270–359. Cambridge, Mass.: Belknap Press of Harvard University Press, 1963.

White, Norman. *Hopkins: A Literary Biography.* New York: Oxford University Press, 1992.

"WOODSPURGE, THE" DANTE GABRIEL ROSSETTI (1855) "The Woodspurge" is one of the best examples of PRE-RAPHAELITE POETRY. It describes an intense focus on accurate botanical detail, standing against any sort of generalization in description. That attention to detail—highly consistent with the focus on nature and natural history that in the 19th century characterizes both poetry (from CHARLOTTE SMITH'S *BEACHY HEAD* on to HOPKINS) and science (preeminently in Charles Lyell and Charles Darwin)—allows for an intensity that does not dissipate itself in large emotional projections. If WILLIAM WORDSWORTH describes the speaking face of nature, Rossetti looks only at "some ten weeds" (l. 10) and, finally, only at the woodspurge, a kind of groundcover that one would not ordinarily focus upon.

Why the focus on the woodspurge? That focus stands for the speaker's intense reticence—the reticence of pain and the consequent repulsion of the emotional depths at which the pain is felt. We know that the poem is a poem of grief: We know it from its last stanza. The crucial word in that stanza is "then," in line 14. He learned *then,* at that time of "perfect grief" not wisdom nor even the experience that memory would imply. He learned only one thing, that "The woodspurge has a cup of three," that is, a cupped flower formed of three petals.

Perfect grief is a precise phrase. Grief is characterized by its imperfection, its shocked disbelief in what it lacks, its mercurial emotional fluctuation. Perfect grief would be an oxymoron, therefore, but it is the oxymoron that Rossetti is describing here. It is grief that has nothing more to say, or think, or do. It is in this way that it has repressed all depth and become the pure observer of the outside detail, not the inner world of torment. So the scene that the poem commemorates is one we can now reconstruct with as much terseness as the poem itself insists on: In grim and complete hopelessness, the speaker with no place to wish to go walks around as the wind directs, then sits and looks at the grass. He does not close his eyes, which would be a last gesture of protest or refusal of how things are, but simply looks at the ground and sees in perfect and inhuman detail the natural object his eyes light upon.

Now writing the poem he remembers not the grief but the fact that he learned. And this indicates that the perfect and empty hopelessness that he experienced then was true: All that remains to him is what he learned about the woodspurge, and we can feel this in the extreme and rigid restraint of that which the poem embodies as well as records. The perfect grief he felt then was never countered, and it led him to write poems like this one, not a poem of recovery, but a poem continuous in its tone with the austere and stripped-down mode of perception that allowed him to see the woodspurge in such unsentimental detail.

Elizabeth Bishop and James Wright are probably the 20th-century poets who owe most to this poem or this kind of poem: not emotion recollected in tranquility, as Wordsworth said poetry should be, but emotion stripped away, so that the speaker's relation to the past is always in the perfect tense (hence *perfect grief*), and even the present tense seems perfect and cold in aspect.

WORDSWORTH, WILLIAM (1770–1850) William Wordsworth is generally regarded as the most important of the English romantic poets, not least by his greatest contemporaries and followers, WILLIAM BLAKE, SAMUEL TAYLOR COLERIDGE, LORD BYRON, PERCY BYSSHE SHELLEY, and JOHN KEATS. It was Wordsworth, under Coleridge's influence, who invented a revolutionary new way to think about poetry—about poetic diction and about the topics that poetry could take as its theme—which still persists today.

Wordsworth wrote a kind of intellectual autobiography in his poem *The PRELUDE* substantially completed in 1805 but not published until after his death in 1850. The poem underlines certain aspects of his life: the death of his parents when he was very young (his mother died when he was eight and his father when he was 13); his attendance of Cambridge University, where he was struck with awe by his great predecessors there, John Milton and Isaac Newton; and his tours of France and sojourn in London after graduation. The poem ostensibly describes the way he became a poet, "the growth of a poet's mind," as his executors' subtitle put it (neither subtitle nor title are Wordsworth's) when they published it posthumously.

Wordsworth had himself described the work in 1814 in his preface to *The Excursion,* part of the grand philosophical poem he intended, of which *The Prelude* would have formed the first part. He describes himself as having undertaken

> to record, in verse, the origin and progress of his own powers, as far as he was acquainted with them.
>
> That work, addressed to a dear friend, most distinguished for his knowledge and genius, and to whom the Author's intellect is deeply indebted, has been long finished; and the result of the investigation which gave rise to it, was a determination to compose a philosophical Poem, containing views of Man, Nature, and Society, and to be entitled the "Recluse"; as having for its principal subject the sensations and opinions of a poet living in retirement.
>
> The preparatory poem is biographical, and conducts the history of the Author's mind to the point when he was emboldened to hope that his faculties were sufficiently matured for entering upon the arduous labour which he had proposed to himself; and the two works have the same kind of relation to each other, if he may so express himself, as the Ante-chapel has to the body of a Gothic church.

The "dear friend" to whom Wordsworth addresses the poem is Samuel Taylor Coleridge, two years younger than Wordsworth. Though Coleridge had also been at Cambridge, they did not meet then. In June 1797 Coleridge, who was already showing astonishing promise as a writer and thinker, went on a walking tour of Dorset, where Wordsworth was living with his sister Dorothy. He had set up house with Dorothy after his return from France, and she lived with him until his death. Coleridge sought out Wordsworth, having seen in the older man's first publications the genius that his contemporaries missed, and the two hit it off immediately. Coleridge prevailed upon William and Dorothy to move to his neighborhood, some 25 miles away in Nether Stowey, and the rest is literary history.

Coleridge was enormously impressed by Wordsworth's interest in the impressions of everyday life and saw that this interest had powerful affinities with his own philosophical interests. These included what their contemporary, the German philosopher Immanuel Kant (whom Coleridge was to translate, often without acknowledgment) called the "structure of experience." Kant was interested in how the mind makes sense of the world, and Wordsworth's interest was similar. In the Wordsworthian view, it is not the interesting objects of the world but the mind that perceives them that is primary. As he puts it in "SIMON LEE," one of the *Lyrical Ballads*:

> O Reader! had you in your mind
> Such stores as silent thought can bring,
> O gentle Reader! you would find
> A tale in everything.

The perceiving mind has depths far greater, altitudes far higher, than anything the material world can offer, and one of the things that the mind perceives is *other minds.* Thus, Wordsworth's interest was in people in their most elemental and starkly human state, whether he was considering his own mind or those of others (like Simon Lee's).

Coleridge gave Wordsworth the encouragement he needed to continue his radical experiments in form. They saw each other daily for the next couple of years, and in 1798 they published *Lyrical Ballads,* one of the most important books in the history of English literature. The first edition was published anonymously, as was appropriate to a collection of ballads, even "lyrical" ones, consisting mostly of Wordsworth's poems, including some of his greatest (such as "TINTERN ABBEY") as well as some of Coleridge's most important work (including *The RIME OF THE ANCIENT MARINER*).

In 1799, after a trip to Germany with Coleridge, William and Dorothy Wordsworth moved to Grasmere in the Lake District (see LAKE POETS), the area where he would spend the rest of his life. There he saw Coleridge very frequently and wrote the preface to the 1800 edition of *Lyrical Ballads,* which contains some of Wordsworth's greatest critical writing on the nature of poetry. In particular, and in accordance with his idea that there was a tale in all experience, he called poetry "the spontaneous overflow of powerful feeling," written in "the natural language of natural men." Also in Grasmere, he began the series of powerful and dark works whose greatest examples are *The Prelude* and the INTIMATIONS ODE, by which he is entitled to be ranked with John Milton.

Indeed, Wordsworth courts that comparison in "Home at Grasmere," a poem that composes book 1 of *The Recluse,* where he writes of his own project in comparison to Milton's *Paradise Lost* (1667), where Milton also had prayed to the muse Urania for "fit audience though few":

. . . "fit audience let me find though few!"
So prayed, more gaining than he asked, the Bard—
In holiest mood. Urania, I shall need
Thy guidance, or a greater Muse, if such
Descend to earth or dwell in highest heaven!
For I must tread on shadowy ground, must sink
Deep—and, aloft ascending, breathe in worlds
To which the heaven of heavens is but a veil.
All strength—all terror, single or in bands,
That ever was put forth in personal form—
Jehovah—with his thunder, and the choir
Of shouting Angels, and the empyreal thrones—
I pass them unalarmed. Not Chaos, not
The darkest pit of lowest Erebus,
Nor aught of blinder vacancy, scooped out
By help of dreams—can breed such fear and awe
As fall upon us often when we look
Into our Minds, into the Mind of Man—
My haunt, and the main region of my song
(*The Recluse* 776–794)

Wordsworth's revolutionary power was to see all human experience as the experience of the Fall that Milton delineated in the story of Adam and Eve. To be human is to experience a loss of belonging to the world. Poetry, for Wordsworth, registers that loss, and in registering it comes partially to compensate for it.

The deepest expression of this claim is in the Intimations Ode, but it is everywhere in Wordsworth's great poetry. What Wordsworth sought to do in his poetry was to convert an experience of the loss of intensity—the intensity of one's relation to nature, to the outside world, to hopes or dreams or the future—into its own intensity—the intensity of loss. In *Paradise Lost,* Adam had spoken of what is known as the "happy fall": The fall of humanity makes possible the great experience of redemption. Wordsworth naturalized this idea, so that the fall of humanity from the celestial securities and wonders of childhood becomes itself an occasion for an experience more powerful than the experience relinquished: an experience *of* that relinquishment.

This is not a position that can be sustained, however. Loss is loss, and even if the experience of loss can flare up into pathos greater than what it memorializes, that pathos cannot last as loss becomes permanent and the poet becomes inured to it. Wordsworth realized this in some of his greatest late poems, especially the sonnet on the death of his three-year-old daughter, "SURPRISED BY JOY." But it is even clearer, perhaps, in the way his own poetic originality and power suffered a precipitous decline in the second half of his life. He remained in the Lake District for the rest of his life and was given various governmental sinecures and pensions, culminating in the poet laureateship in 1843 when his and Coleridge's friend and contemporary ROBERT SOUTHEY died. However, he wrote very little of lasting value after he turned 40 and almost nothing after 45. WILLIAM BUTLER YEATS admonished youthful poets to remember the example of William Wordsworth, "withering into eighty years, honoured and empty-witted," because he could not sustain the experience of "new bitterness, new disappointment," which gives rise to the intensity of the poetry (*Per Amica Silentia Lunae*) p. 50.

But at its greatest, Wordsworth's poetry is unsurpassed, and it makes possible all modern explorations of human subjectivity, in Marcel Proust as much as in Sigmund Freud, for example, as unfathomably dark, unfathomably deep, and correspondingly unfathomably powerful.

See also "I WANDERED LONELY AS A CLOUD"; LUCY POEMS; *MICHAEL*; "MY HEART LEAPS UP"; "NUTTING"; "RESOLUTION AND INDEPENDENCE"; *RUINED COTTAGE, THE.*

BIBLIOGRAPHY

Abrams, M. H. *Correspondent Breeze: Essays on English Romanticism.* New York: Norton, 1984.

———. *Natural Supernaturalism: Tradition and Revolution in Romantic Literature.* New York: Norton, 1973.

Alpers, Paul. *What Is Pastoral?* Chicago: University of Chicago Press, 1996.

Barker, Juliet. *Wordsworth: A Life.* New York: Viking, 2000.

Bloom, Harold. *Poetry and Repression: Revisionism from Blake to Stevens.* New Haven, Conn.: Yale University Press, 1976.

———. *The Visionary Company: A Reading of English Romantic Poetry.* Garden City, N.Y.: Doubleday, 1961.

Bromwich, David. *Disowned by Memory: Wordsworth's Poetry of the 1790s.* Chicago: University of Chicago Press, 1998.

Brooks, Cleanth. *A Shaping Joy: Studies in the Writer's Craft.* London: Methuen, 1973.

De Man, Paul. *The Rhetoric of Romanticism.* New York: Columbia University Press, 1984.

Empson, William. *Seven Types of Ambiguity.* New York: New Directions, 1966.

Gill, Stephen. *William Wordsworth: A Life.* New York: Oxford University Press, 1989.

Hartman, Geoffrey. "The Question of Our Speech." In *The Geoffrey Hartman Reader,* edited by Daniel T. O'Hara. 321–347. Edinburgh: Edinburgh University Press, 2004.

———. *Wordsworth's Poetry, 1787–1814.* New Haven, Conn.: Yale University Press, 1971.

Hertz, Neil. *The End of the Line: Essays on Psychoanalysis and the Sublime.* New York: Columbia University Press, 1985.

Johnston, Kenneth. *Hidden Wordsworth: Poet, Lover, Rebel, Spy.* New York: Norton, 1998.

Levinson, Marjorie. *Wordsworth's Great Period Poems: Four Essays.* New York: Cambridge University Press, 1986.

Liu, Alan. *Wordsworth: The Sense of History.* Stanford, Calif.: Stanford University Press, 1989.

Moorman, Mary. *William Wordsworth: A Biography.* 2 vols. Oxford: Clarendon Press, 1957, 1965.

Pinch, Adela. *Strange Fits of Passion: Epistemologies of Emotion, Hume to Austen.* Stanford, Calif.: Stanford University Press, 1996.

Quinney, Laura. *The Poetics of Disappointment: Wordsworth to Ashbery.* Charlottesville: University Press of Virginia, 1999.

Wolfson, Susan J. *Questioning Presence: Wordsworth, Keats, and the Interrogative Mode in Romantic Poetry.* Ithaca, N.Y.: Cornell University Press, 1986.

Yeats, William Butler. *Per Amica Silentia Lunae.* New York: Macmillan, 1918.

"WOUNDED, THE" SYDNEY DOBELL (1855)

SYDNEY DOBELL was obsessed with the Crimean War (1854–56), the struggle between the allied forces of Britain and France against Russia for control of the Crimean peninsula and in particular of Sevastopol, the Russian port on the Black Sea. Although the allies were eventually successful, the war was bloody and badly handled by the allies, and the English poets were often highly critical of the strategy that led to so many disasters of battle. The most famous of these critical works is ALFRED, LORD TENNYSON'S "The CHARGE OF THE LIGHT BRIGADE," with its repeated refrain "Someone had blundered." Dobell and his friend Alexander Smith published a book of *Sonnets on the War* (1855), of which "The Wounded" is probably the best. It combines more or less typical Victorian sentimentality with the grimness that sentimentality will often limn and which is its tough-minded other side.

We begin thinking that the poem is a sentimental anecdote about the importance of life and love even in the face of death. It is a dialogue between a surgeon on the battlefield and a wounded soldier. The surgeon warns the soldier that his body and life have been destroyed, that he cannot wish to live. This seems harsh, and we expect him to learn a lesson from the soldier who sees the possibilities of love and comfort even if, after amputation, he is left a "Poor branchless trunk" (l. 4); he could still rest his head upon his wife's or sweetheart's breast. He clings to life, in a strikingly reversed simile, as a soul might cling to heaven, treating the surgeon as a kind of St. Peter, or even God. He wants the surgeon's ministration, but even as he prays for them, he dies in the eighth line of the poem. Formally, this is shocking: We think the sonnet will be about their interaction, but it is not. We become aware at this moment, perhaps, that the surgeon is offering comfort and not hope to the man. "Thou canst not wish to live" is meant to sound like an offer of benign neglect, but in fact it is the surgeon's attempt to get the soldier to make his peace with the death so closely impending.

The sestet of the sonnet draws back, like a camera pulling back to show all the wounded who need the surgeon's ministrations, to the "cauldron vast of many-coloured pain" (as Dobell calls it in the last line of the previous sonnet, "The Army Surgeon," which gives the surgeon's point of view as he walks among the dying). Here he is speaking to them; one asks him not to work to spare him another day, but to go help someone who can be saved. Then we get the voices of six more wounded, most of them the same, in the astonishing line: "'Help,' 'help,' 'help,' 'help!'" That is all the wounded can say, unless they curse, or unless yet another points out, self-sacrificingly—but to what end?—that another soldier, one of the French allies, is wounded in another part of the field. Relevantly enough, the poem is (like Tennyson's) about the great courage and spirit and humanity of the soldiers who have been made cannon fodder by the incompetence and neglect of those who should be looking out for the interests of those in their charge.

BIBLIOGRAPHY

Boos, Florence S. "'Spasm' and Class: W. E. Aytoun, George Gilfillan, Sydney Dobell, and Alexander Smith." *Victorian Poetry* 42, no. 4 (2004): 553–583.

Dobell, Sydney. *The Life and Letters of Sydney Dobell.* Edited by E. Jolly. London: Smith, Elder & Co., 1878.

Preyer, Robert. "Sydney Dobell and the Victorian Epic." *University of Toronto Quarterly* 30 (January 1961): 163–178.

Westwater, Martha. *The Spasmodic Career of Sydney Dobell.* Lanham, Md.: University Press of America, 1992.

"WRECK OF THE DEUTSCHLAND, THE"

GERARD MANLEY HOPKINS (1876) It is with this great long poem that GERARD MANLEY HOPKINS, age 31, returned to his poetic vocation after eight years of the self-denial he thought his religious vocation and ordination as a Jesuit priest required of him. In a letter two years later (October 5, 1878) to his former teacher and great friend Richard W. Dixon, Hopkins explains why he broke poetic silence with this poem:

> . . . when in the winter of '75 the *Deutschland* was wrecked in the mouth of the Thames and five Franciscan nuns, exiles from Germany by the Falck [sic] Laws, aboard of her were drowned I was affected by the account and happening to say so to my rector he said that he wished someone would write a poem on the subject. On this hint I set to work and, although my hand was out at first, produced one. I had long had haunting my ear the echo of a new rhythm which now I realized on paper.

The new rhythm was too much for the editor of the Jesuit periodical *The Month,* and they did not print it; indeed, like most of Hopkins's great poetry, it did not appear till ROBERT BRIDGES's edition of 1918.

Hopkins's letter to Dixon expands a little on the context offered by the poem's dedication, "To the happy memory of the Franciscan nuns exiles by the Falck Laws drowned between midnight and morning of December 7, 1875." *Between midnight and morning* is the crucial phrase, since it is the long night of the soul they suffered that night that is Hopkins's concern, the experience into which he enters with extraordinary imaginative and prosodic intensity.

The Falk Laws were a series of edicts passed in Germany in the 1870s, officially at the behest of Adalbert Falk, the new minister of worship, but in fact at the behest of the German chancellor, Otto von Bismarck. The new German empire, as Bismarck was constituting it under Wilhelm I, had many more Roman Catholics than before, and Pope Pius IX had just promulgated the doctrine of papal infallibility, which Bismarck saw as a threat to temporal authority in all the European states, whether Catholic or Protestant. This gave rise to what became known as the *Kulturkampf,* or "culture struggle." Bismarck saw the Catholic Church (as represented also by France, defeated in the Franco-Prussian War of 1870) as Germany's main antagonist, and he sought to reduce the church to an arm of the state. (The Falk Laws applied in Prussia, not all of the newly united Germany, but Prussia was the great power within this kingdom and held it together while augmenting its territory to the south.) He did this partly because a Catholic political party was on the rise in Germany, and he saw that party as a fifth column, a danger to German imperial ambitions and the

Protestant state religion he was establishing. Under the Falk Laws, the Catholic Church was under the control of the state, and any church official owed fealty to Germany, not Rome. (The relevance of these political struggles to the new muscular Catholicism in England and the Home Rule movement in Ireland is obvious, and it is underlined in the last stanza of Hopkins's poem.) In 1872 Bismarck had the German branch of Hopkins's Jesuit Order dissolved. Most of the Catholic hierarchy, as well as their parishioners, rejected this incursion on their religious freedom. On May 31, 1875, Bismarck had a law passed that closed all the monasteries in Prussia and expelled their members—hence the emigration of the Franciscan nuns from Prussian Bremen to the United States.

The poem is in two parts, the first 10 stanzas comprising a personal address to God which shows the poet's communion with the terrible mastery of Christ through both beauty and suffering. (Hopkins was probably influenced by WILLIAM WORDSWORTH's account in *The PRELUDE* of growing up "fostered alike by beauty and by fear.") For Hopkins, these were related manifestations of the awe-inspiring, and the awe inspired was directed toward God. These first 10 stanzas intimate the deeply intense Ignatian (after Ignatius of Loyola founder of the Jesuit order) meditations that Hopkins would undertake in much of his later poetry, and they use much of the same vocabulary of wringing the spirit to submission. Particularly notable is the language of "stress" in the fifth and sixth stanzas. God's "mystery must be instressed, stressed," and that "stress felt" does not come out of his bliss, but is "a stress that stars and storms deliver" (ll. 39–45). The stars are "lovely-asunder" (l. 34)—that is, beautiful in their particularity; this is the language Hopkins will echo in "THAT NATURE IS A HERACLITEAN FIRE" when he describes the individual human shape shining in the universe as "disseveral, a star" (l. 14)—that is, both separate and joined (through the privative *dis-*, meaning *not*-several) to every other severed and joined shape of existence. Here the "lovely-asunder" stars are joined by the loveliness of their individuated existence in the night sky. They make themselves felt through *stress,* like the poetic stress of the poem, and carry themselves into the soul through their "instress," the pressure of their stress both on each other, creating out of the ensemble of each stressed particularity a lovely whole, and on Hopkins feeling the whole brought into himself by its manifold stresses and pressures, a whole to which he belongs like every other particular being.

Hopkins therefore belongs to the same world as the nuns the second and longer part of the poem praises. He vividly imagines the wreck and the terrible night of cold, fear, and solitude of those on the ship. He thinks of the sailors escaped to the rigging and unable to save the nuns below-decks, and then of one nun (generally called the "tall nun") who calls upon God in spite of the terrors they are undergoing. Stanza 18 is particularly important here since he addresses his own heart and his heart's responsiveness to what he imagines, indeed its "glee" at the intensity of the scene and of the poetic language that records it. His heart will "make words break from me here all alone" (l. 139), and he takes it that the glee he feels is that of God's mercy to him in teaching him to imagine the scene of the nuns' righteousness and passion. He will recur to his own relation to the scene in stanza 24, when he describes where he was, "under a roof," and "at rest" in Wales (l. 186). He is asunder from the scene but still part of it. He knows where he was when the nuns drowned, connected to them by the universal similitude that is for Hopkins the matrix and structure of what he called "inscape" (see "AS KINGFISHERS CATCH FIRE") and that makes the five of them comparable to the five wounds of Christ and the stigmata of the founder of their order, St. Francis. He is awed by what the tall nun he imagines as speaking for all of them says when she calls Christ to her, and he "christens her wild-worst Best" (l. 192). That is to say, through a kind of linguistic baptism underwritten by Christ himself (christening), Hopkins names the experience of pain and horror and the joy of joining with Christ, who is their "martyr-master" (l. 167), both master of all martyrs (and who has also mastered Hopkins in the poem's great first line) and the greatest of martyrs himself, weighing their fates in the pierced palms of his hands (l. 166).

For Hopkins, the nuns' martyrdom is the poetry's inspiration and the meditation that leads to it and leads him through his own "sweet skill" (as he says of Augustine in l. 78) to the love of Christ he sees in them. Thus, he describes himself again, in stanzas 27 and 28, writing the poem in an attempt to live up to his own vision. He is not like the tall nun he imagines; he is alone and writing, and therefore "other," but still he gathers "in measure her mind's Burden" and conveys through his own remarkable prosody the "beat of endragonéd seas" (ll. 215–216). Stanza 28, then, mimics its own hesitant composition (here Hopkins sounds most like his great contemporary ROBERT BROWNING), and he realizes that he cannot do justice to her in his poetry. But that means that only Christ can, and so he calls on Christ to "cure her extremity" (l. 222).

But what of the other nuns, who did not make it up on deck to call upon God? The remarkable 31st stanza asks and answers this question: They were rung into comfort (one of Hopkins's key words) and confession by the intercessory voice of the tall nun he has imagined on deck. And the stanza's prosody shows how this was so, turning what is asunder into a unified constellation. It should be noted that the very long last line starts with the word *Startle* (with its implicit allusion to the stars), though the necessities of printing will often make the line look like two. The rhymes in this stanza at first seem irregular, despite the presence of much homonymity: *for the* (l. 241) rhymes with itself (l. 243) and with *for thee* (l. 248). But the even rhymes seem less regular: *rest of them* (l. 242) rhymes beautifully with *unconfessed of them* (l. 244) but seems not to rhyme with *breast of the* (l. 246), which gravitates toward the *for the* rhymes; while *Providence* (l. 245) seems not to rhyme with *and* (l. 247). But then we notice the *startling* enjambments: *rest of them* does indeed rhyme with *breast of the / M(aiden)* (ll. 246–247); and *Providence* rhymes with *and / S(tartle)* (ll. 247–248). (In his later poetry, Hopkins showed a penchant for dividing words at their syllable endings in order to rhyme, most famously in "The WINDHOVER," which breaks *king-dom* up to rhyme *king-* with *wing*.) These rhymes also startle and to make the asunder a part of the general loveliness (see l. 34–35 "lovely-asunder starlight"), which brings together everything in its own particularity, even the fact of these things being asunder from each other. So, too, are these words sundered and "cured," just as the nuns are five separate beings and yet also joined together by the martyrdom of the one who calls to Christ, made into the "cinque-foil token" (l. 175) of Christ's own martyrdom. All of this draws Hopkins into its universal particularity—and Britain, too, he hopes, is drawn into the universal "throng" (l. 280), ruled and saved by and centered on the Lord.

Hopkins was to suffer terrible despair later in his life, but the meaning of that despair, as he understood it, is something he had already begun thinking through in his first great poem.

BIBLIOGRAPHY

Bridges, Robert. Preface to *Poems of Gerard Manley Hopkins,* edited by W. H. Gardner. New York: Oxford University Press, 1948.

Craig, Gordon. *Germany: 1866–1945* New York: Oxford University Press, 1978.

Gardner, W. H. *Gerard Manley Hopkins (1844–1889): A Study of Poetic Idiosyncrasy in Relation to Poetic Tradition.* New Haven, Conn.: Yale University Press, 1949.

———, ed. Introduction to *Poems and Prose of Gerard Manley Hopkins.* Harmondsworth, Middlesex, England: Penguin, 1963.

Hartman, Geoffrey. *The Unmediated Vision: An Interpretation of Wordsworth, Hopkins, Rilke, and Valery.* New Haven, Conn.: Yale University Press, 1954.

Hopkins, Gerard Manley. *Gerard Manley Hopkins: Selected Letters.* Edited by Catherine Phillips. New York: Oxford University Press, 1990.

Lowe, Charles. *Prince Bismarck: An Historical Biography.* New York: Cassell and Co., 1885.

Miller, J. Hillis. "Gerard Manley Hopkins." In *The Disappearance of God,* 270–359. Cambridge, Mass.: Belknap Press of Harvard University Press, 1963.

White, Norman. *Hopkins: A Literary Biography.* New York: Oxford University Press, 1992.

Y

YEATS, WILLIAM BUTLER (1865–1939)

In "The Circus Animals' Desertion" (1939), one of his last poems, William Butler Yeats wrote of the passions that constituted his early poetic vocation. In his stock-taking, the poet particularly alludes to "The Wanderings of Oisin," the long title poem of his first book, as well as an early play on Cuchulain, the Irish hero close to his heart from the beginning of his poetic career to the end of his life, and Countess Cathleen, subject of another play. The circus animals of the title refer, somewhat bitterly, to the poems that he has brought into the world—the gaudy shows that entertain by being exotic, as in the Roman prescription of bread and circuses to keep the masses happy. In this retrospective poem, Yeats is considering the nature and importance of the poetic vocation that was central to a life of very great variety and political as well as artistic activity.

That political activity became particularly public in the 20th century, which is somewhat outside the scope of this volume. Yeats was a passionate but skeptical partisan of Irish independence; he essentially supported the Easter Rebellion of 1916, bloodily suppressed by the British (in the midst of the First World War), and after the establishment of the Irish Free State, he served as a senator and involved himself at a fairly detailed level in the practical details of legislation and government. While he was a senator, he also won the Nobel Prize in literature, and he continued to write major poetry for the rest of his life. In the 1930s he was somewhat attracted to the strong, dictatorial leadership of Mussolini and the fascists, and it is not clear how his politics would have developed had he lived longer, but by then he was not seriously involved in political life any more, and perhaps he would have given vent to an irascible and bitter sense that the world was going to the dogs. At any rate, those later political strains had no practical effect, and very little effect on his poetry either.

Yeats's politics were vexed because of his own background. He was part of the elite Protestant Anglo-Irish minority, born in Dublin to John Butler Yeats, a lawyer who subsequently became a painter (one of the most famous portraits of Yeats was done by his father in 1900). Yeats's younger brother, Jack Yeats, was also a major artist—the most important Irish painter of the 20th century as well as an influential short story writer, who had a strong influence on such writers as James Joyce and Flann O'Brien. Yeats himself was committed to Irish independence, which was counter to the Protestant, pro-British position, but as a Protestant he was estranged from the Catholic resistance to British rule. When he was a young man, his father moved the family to London, so that now he was estranged again, as an Irish boy going to school in the capital of England.

Yeats resolved this conflict through aesthetic means—a commitment to the legendary and non-Christian past of Ireland and her folklore. In one of his autobiographical books, he wrote: "I had noticed that Irish Catholics among whom had been born so many political martyrs had not the good taste, the household courtesy and decency of the Protestant Ireland I had known, yet Protestant Ireland seemed to think of nothing but getting on in the world. I thought we might bring the halves together if we had a national literature that made Ireland beautiful in the memory, and yet had been freed from provincialism by an exacting criticism, a European pose" (*Reveries Over Childhood and Youth,* 1916). His early poems see in literature and in the archaic myths and legends which are the source of literature the possibility of a unified Irish heritage prior to, and at the same time more modern than, the sectarian differences between Catholic Ireland and Protestant England. His treatment of Oisin is a kind of case in point; Ossian was the hero of a great 18th-century forgery, in which the Scottish poet James MacPherson claimed to have found the manuscripts of a Celtic rival to Homer and the Bible. He published his translation, which was debunked in many quarters almost immediately but continued to attract a dwindling number of partisans through the mid-20th century. For Yeats, MacPherson would have been a dishonest version of what he sought to do: invent a literary past commensurate with the ambitions of the literary present. Yeats's efforts were fundamental to the resurgence of interest in this heritage, and many of his early poems take such legendary figures as Cuchulain, Conchubar, Aengus, and Fergus as their theme.

In "The Circus Animals' Desertion," he describes what it was about Oisin and Cuchulain (and the Countess Cathleen) that meant so much to him:

> What can I but enumerate old themes?
> First that sea-rider Oisin led by the nose
> Through three enchanted islands, allegorical
> dreams,
> Vain gaiety, vain battle, vain repose,
> Themes of the embittered heart, or so it seems,
> That might adorn old songs or courtly shows;
> But what cared I that set him on to ride,
> I, starved for the bosom of his fairy bride?
>
> And then a counter-truth filled out its play,
> The Countess Cathleen was the name I gave it;
> She, pity-crazed, had given her soul away,
> But masterful Heaven had intervened to save it.
> I thought my dear must her own soul destroy,
> Sop did fanaticism and hate enslave it,
> And this brought forth a dream and soon enough
> This dream itself had all my thought and love.
>
> An when the Fool and Blind Man stole the bread
> Cuchulain fought the ungovernable sea;
> Heart-mysteries there, and yet when all is said
> It was the dream itself enchanted me:
> Character isolated by a deed
> To engross the present and dominate memory.
> Players and painted stage took all my love,
> And not those things that they were emblems of.

The important thing to see here is the sense that Yeats had, from the beginning to the end, of literature as providing a mysterious otherworldly idea worth a wholehearted and complete conviction—what Yeats called perfection of the work rather than perfection of the life; it was not meaning, but what Yeats's contemporary Freud dismissed as the *manifest* (as opposed to latent) *content* of the dream that most captivated Yeats. Later in his career, this otherworldliness would lead to a serious, sustained, and often ridiculed involvement in mysticism, most famously expressed in *A Vision,* but in the 19th century his sense of otherworldliness was restricted to a gorgeous, powerful, and intensely lyrical rendition of Irish myths.

In 1891, along with such end-of-century poets as ERNEST DOWSON and LIONEL JOHNSON, Yeats formed the Rhymers Club, devoted to an intensely aesthetic idea of poetry, strongly influenced by the Pre-Raphaelites (see PRE-RAPHAELITE POETRY). Yeats's own literary background, he later wrote, owed most to this postromantic aesthetic and its attitude toward romantic forebears such as WILLIAM BLAKE and PERCY BYSSHE SHELLEY (both championed by the Pre-Raphaelites), rather than more solid, worldly figures such as WILLIAM WORDSWORTH and LORD BYRON. In *The Trembling of the Veil* (1922), Yeats describes his youthful apprenticeship:

> I was in all things pre-Raphaelite. When I was fifteen or sixteen my father told me about Rossetti and Blake and given me their poetry to read. . . .

> . . . I had made a new religion, almost an infallible church of poetic tradition, of a fardel of stories, and of personages, and of emotions, inseparable from their first expression, passed on from generation to generation by poets and painters with some help from philosophers and theologians. I wished for a world, where I could discover this tradition perpetually. . . . I had even created a dogma: "Because those imaginary people are created out of the deepest instincts of man, to be his measure and his norm, whatever I can imagine those mouths speaking may be the nearest I can get to truth." When I listened they seemed always to speak of one thing only: they, their loves, every incident of their lives, were steeped in the supernatural.

A few years later, in 1896, Yeats met the great love of his life, Maude Gonne, who refused his repeated proposals of marriage and who is the subject of much of his poetry for the rest of his life. In 1898 she married John Macbride. Though they separated a few years later, they were still married when Macbride was killed in the Easter rebellion, and Yeats memorializes him in his great poem on the rebellion, "Easter, 1916."

Under the tutelage of Augusta, Lady Gregory, who was one of the revivalists of Irish culture (in the Irish literary revival, to which Yeats was a major contributor), Yeats traveled Ireland and learned its culture. Starting in 1897 he spent much time at Lady Gregory's country house at Coole, which he wrotes about much later (1916) in "The Wild Swans at Coole."

Later in his career, as what he would call "a smiling sixty-years old public man," Yeats became critical of the high aestheticism of his 19th-century youth: "Without knowing it, I had come to care for nothing but impersonal beauty." But as "The Circus Animals' Desertion" shows, at the end of his life he saw in the poems that he wrote in the 19th century the stable center of his aesthetic and poetic vocation. Those poems had already made him an important figure by the turn of the century. In his great novel *Ulysses* (1922), James Joyce has Stephen Dedalus quote "WHO GOES WITH FERGUS?" Joyce's book takes place on June 16, 1904. A couple of years earlier, Yeats had collaborated in the founding of the Abbey Theatre in Dublin, still a going concern (although Yeats was to break with it), and he wrote a play for one of its first performances, in which Maude Gonne acted.

Yeats's 19th-century poetry is marked by a kind of absolute aesthetic purity that is, as he would later say, perfect in its sphere and shows the ultimate development of the pure aesthetic strain of ROMANTICISM. Such poems as "Who Goes with Fergus?" "FERGUS AND THE DRUID," "The SAD SHEPHERD," "The LAKE ISLE OF INNISFREE," "The SONG OF WANDERING AENGUS," "WHEN YOU ARE OLD," and "CUCHULAIN'S FIGHT WITH THE SEA" are central to any sense of his achievement, and to the things that poetry can do.

BIBLIOGRAPHY

Anscombe, G. E. M. *Intention.* Cambridge, Mass.: Harvard University Press, 2000.

Bloom, Harold. *Yeats.* New York: Oxford University Press, 1970.

Ellmann, Richard. *Yeats: The Man and the Masks.* New York: Norton, 1978.

Grossman, Allen R. *Poetic Knowledge in the Early Yeats: A Study of The Wind among the Reeds.* Charlottesville: University Press of Virginia, 1969.

Maddox, Brenda. *George's Ghosts: A New Life of W. B. Yeats.* London: Picador, 1999.

Rosenthal, M. L., ed. Introduction to *Selected Poems and Four Plays of William Butler Yeats,* xix–xliv. New York: Scribner, 1996.

Vendler, Helen. *Poets Thinking: Pope, Whitman, Dickinson, Yeats.* Cambridge, Mass.: Belknap Press of Harvard University Press, 2004.

———. *Yeats's Vision and the Later Plays.* Cambridge, Mass.: Harvard University Press, 1963.

Z

"ZILVER-WEED, THE" WILLIAM BARNES **(1861)** In his poetry, WILLIAM BARNES found in the worked and farmed and pollarded landscape around him signs of human life occuring within the landscape and eventually becoming absorbed by it—absorbed into death. (Compare ALFRED, LORD TENNYSON's "TITHONUS": "Man comes and tills the field and lies beneath . . .") Landscape was for Barnes a place of unchanging cycle, its permanence the foundation and bedrock of our sense of security in the world. But it also came to mean our own estrangement from the world: The landscape is permanent, but we are not. We can read signs of our impermanence in the landscape itself, in the way we alter it, but only temporarily. The grass that children trample down grows back when they too grow up (see, from 20 years earlier, "The VAÏCES THAT BE GONE": "long-leav'd docks to overgrow / The groun' we trampled beäre below" (ll. 11–12).

In "The Zilver-Weed," Barnes recalls the green where his children (he had seven) played, trampling down the silverweed with their steps. That weed never had to bloom—and that is because *they* were blooming, running and playing while their somewhat older (presumably) sisters were pruning an avenue of rose trees. It is worth remarking on the subtlety of Barnes's imagery: It is not that nature itself in some unified way represents the natural growth and natural participation of the children; rather, the roses represent them more than the profuse silverweed, which is negligible in the sense of needing no care. The roses are like the children, the silverweed like the world of natural vitality that they also display but to which as humans, growing up, they do not quite belong.

We see this in the Wordsworthian "But now" with which the second stanza begins. THOMAS HARDY had cited WILLIAM WORDSWORTH to explain the peculiar effect and power of Barnes's poetry, and you can see how often Barnes follows Wordsworth's characteristic rhythm: "There was a time . . . But now." Now the silver leaves are growing just fine, because there are no feet of girl and boy to beat them down in merry play anymore. Life continues, despite the absence of the children; indeed, it continues and blossoms *because* of the absence of the children.

But the roses that they have taken care of cannot survive their absence. The profusion of color with which they had covered the walls is gone. All the rose trees die, and their death foreshadows the aging and death of the maidens who have taken care of them. Barnes is probably thinking of the moment in John Milton's *Paradise Lost* (1667) when Adam drops the chaplet of roses he has made for Eve upon seeing that she has eaten the forbidden fruit. Few of the rose trees still stand, which at least means the sadness of neglect but also foretells the fall of everything that had made this a place of human happiness. It is a place of happiness still for the silverweed, but not for the humans who had once found joy there. This sense of the beauty and also the indifference of the natural world, even to those who had thought they had a natural home in the natural world, is one of Barnes's most powerful modes.

BIBLIOGRAPHY

Hardy, Thomas. Review of *Poems of Rural Life in the Dorset Dialect. New Quarterly Magazine* (October 1879): 469–473. Reprinted in *Thomas Hardy's Public Voice: The Essays, Speeches, and Miscellaneous Prose,* edited by Michael Millgate, 17–27. New York: Oxford, 2001.

Levy, William Turner. *William Barnes: The Man and His Poems.* Dorchester, England: Longmans, 1960.

Parins, James W. *William Barnes.* Boston: Twayne Publishers, 1984.

Scott, Leader. *The Life of William Barnes: Poet and Philologist, by his Daughter, Lucy Baxter* ("Leader Scott") 1887. Reprint, St. Clair Shores, Mich.: Scholarly Press, 1971.

APPENDIX I

GLOSSARY

accent The STRESS on one or another syllable, especially when poetry is read aloud.

accentual verse A system of VERSE throughout at least a portion of a poem that depends on a certain fixed number of stresses in a line of poetry; this system, however, allows for any number of unstressed syllables.

allegory Extended metaphor or symbol with at least two levels of meaning, a literal level and an implied, figurative level; an allegorical narrative tells a story and at the same time suggests another level of meaning.

alliteration Repeating consonant sounds at the beginnings of words.

allusion Making reference to something or someone, usually in an indirect manner.

anapest A metrical foot consisting of two soft stresses followed by a hard stress. See METER.

anaphora A word or phrase that is repeated at the start of successive lines of poetry.

apostrophe A turn away from the reader to address another listener.

assonance Repetition of like vowel sounds, often in stressed syllables in close proximity to each other.

ballad A narrative in VERSE; the form derives from a narrative that was sung.

blank verse Unrhymed IAMBIC PENTAMETER.

cadence The rhythm in language, a pattern that can lend a musical order to a statement.

caesura A pause within a VERSE line, usually at approximately mid point.

canon A term originally derived from the Roman Catholic Church having to do with church law, this term also refers to a body of literature that is generally accepted as exhibiting what is best or important in terms of literary art.

collagist poetry Poetry that employs the organizing element of collage or the bringing together of disparate material to create a new statement or vision.

conceit Not unrelated to the term *concept,* an unusual supposition, analogy, metaphor, or image, often clever.

connotation Meaning that is implied rather than stated directly as in DENOTATION.

consonance Repetition of identical consonant sounds, within the context of varying vowel sounds.

couplet Two VERSE lines in succession that have the same END RHYME. When the two lines contain a complete statement in themselves, they are called a closed couplet. See also HEROIC COUPLET.

dactyl A metrical foot consisting of a hard stress followed by two soft stresses.

denotation The literal meaning of a word or statement, the opposite of CONNOTATION.

diction Word choice, the actual language that a writer employs.

dimeter A VERSE line consisting of two metrical FEET.

dramatic monologue An address to an interlocutor (another potential speaker) who is not present; a dramatic monologue has only one actual speaker.

elegy A poem mourning someone's death.

ellipsis Part of a statement left out, unspoken.

end rhyme A rhyme at the end of a VERSE line.

end-stopped A VERSE line that pauses at its end, when no ENJAMBMENT is possible.

enjambment A VERSE line whose momentum forbids a pause at its end, thus avoiding being END-STOPPED.

epic A long poem that, typically, recounts the adventures of someone in a high style and diction; classically, the adventures include a hero who is at least partially superhuman in makeup or deed, and the events have special importance in terms of the fate of a people.

epigram A brief, witty statement, often satiric or aphoristic.

epithet A word or phrase that characterizes something or someone.

eye rhyme Agreement of words according to their spelling but not their sound.

feet See FOOT.

feminine ending A VERSE line that ends with an extra soft stress.

feminine rhyme The rhyming of two words in more than a single syllable.

figurative language Language that employs figures of speech such as IRONY, HYPERBOLE, METAPHOR, SIMILE, SYMBOL, METONYMY, etc., in which the language connotes meaning.

foot A configuration of syllables to form a METER, such as an IAMB, TROCHEE, ANAPEST, DACTYL, or SPONDEE. A line of one foot is called a MONOMETER line, of two feet a DIAMETER line, of three feet TRIMETER, of four TETRAMETER, of five PENTAMETER, of six HEXAMETER, etc.

free verse Poetry lacking a metrical pattern or patterns; poetic lines without any discernible meter.

haiku A Japanese lyric form consisting of a certain number of syllables overall and in each line, most often in a five-seven-five syllabic line pattern.

half rhyme A form of CONSONANCE in which final consonant sounds in neighboring stressed syllables agree.

heroic couplet Two successive lines of END-RHYMING IAMBIC PENTAMETER.

hexameters A VERSE line consisting of six metrical FEET.

hyperbole An exaggeration meant to emphasize something.

iamb A metrical FOOT consisting of a soft stress followed by a hard stress.

iambic pentameter A five-FOOT line with a preponderance of IAMBIC FEET.

image Language meant to represent objects, actions, feelings, or thoughts in vivid terms.

internal rhyme A RHYME within a poetic line.

masculine rhyme A RHYME depending on one hard-stressed syllable only.

metaphor An implicit comparison, best when between unlike things, made without using the words *like* or *as*.

meter An arrangement of syllables in units called FEET, such as IAMB or TROCHEE, and in numbers of feet to make a pattern, such as IAMBIC PENTAMETER; the syllables can be hard- or soft-stressed according to the type of FOOT or pattern to be employed.

metonymy The substitution of a word that represents an association with, proximity to, or attribute of a thing for the thing itself; this figure of speech is not unlike SYNECHDOCHE.

monometer A VERSE line consisting of a single metrical foot.

occasional verse VERSE written to celebrate or to commemorate a particular event.

octave An eight-line stanza of poetry, also the first and larger portion of a SONNET. See OCTET.

octet An eight-line stanza of poetry. See OCTAVE.

ode A lyric poem usually in a dignified style and addressing a serious subject.

onomatopoeia A word or phrase whose sound resembles something the word or phrase is signifying.

oxymoron A phrase or statement containing a self-contradiction.

paradox A statement that seems to be self-contradictory but contains a truth that reconciles the contradiction.

pastoral A poem that evokes a rural setting or rural values; the word itself derives from the Latin *pastor,* or "shepherd."

pentameter A VERSE line consisting of five metrical FEET.

persona The speaker in a poem, most often the narrator; the term is derived from the Latin word for "mask."

personification Attributing human qualities to an inanimate entity.

prosody The study of versification; the term is at times used as a synonym for METER.

quatrain A four-line stanza of a poem, also a portion of a SONNET.

rhetorical figure An arrangement of words for one or another emphasis or effect.

rhyme Fundamentally, "agreement," the term specifically indicates the sameness or similarity of vowel sounds in an arrangement of words; there can be END RHYME, INTERNAL RHYME, EYE RHYME, HALF RHYME, FEMININE RHYME, etc.

rhyme scheme The arrangement of END RHYMES in a poem, indicated when analyzing a poem with the letters of the alphabet, such as, for a poem in successive COUPLETS, AA, BB, CC, etc.

rhythm A sense of movement created by arrangement of syllables in terms of stress and time.

sestet A six-line stanza of poetry, also the final large portion of a SONNET.

sestina A 36-line poem broken up into six SESTETS as well as a final stanza of three lines, the six words ending the first sestet's lines appearing at the conclusions of the remaining five sestets, in one or another order, and appearing in the final three lines; these repeated words usually convey key motifs of the poem.

simile A comparison using the word *like* or *as.*

slant rhyme A partial, incomplete RHYME, sometimes called a *half, imperfect, near* or *off rhyme.*

sonnet A poem of 14 lines, traditionally in IAMBIC PENTAMETER, the RHYME SCHEME and structure of which can vary. There are two predominant types of sonnets: the English or Shakespearean, which consists of three QUATRAINS and a final COUPLET, usually with a rhyme scheme of ABAB CDCD EFEF GG; and the Italian or Petrarchan sonnet, often with an initial OCTAVE rhyming ABBA ABBA and a concluding SESTET rhyming CDECDE. However, it is important to keep in mind that sonnet rhyme schemes can be very different from the above.

spondee A metrical FOOT comprised of two hard stresses.

sprung rhythm Lines or STANZAS made up of a preset number of hard syllabic stresses but any number of soft stresses; the effect is a rhythmic irregularity.

stanza A group of lines of poetry.

stress The emphasis when reading a poem accorded to a syllable.

strophe A STANZA, or VERSE paragraph in a prose poem, derived from classical Greek drama.

syllabic verse Poetry that employs a set number of syllables in a line, regardless of STRESS.

symbol A figure of speech that means what it says literally but also connotes a secondary meaning or meanings, and which usually conveys a concept, motif, or idea.

synecdoche A figure of speech in which a part of something is meant to signify the entirety of the thing, such as a hand that is meant to suggest a sailor whose hands are used in sailing a ship (as in "all hands on deck"). See METONYMY.

synesthesia The mingling or substitution of the senses, such as when talking about a sound by mentioning a color.

tanka A Japanese VERSE form consisting of five lines, with the first and third line each containing five syllables and the rest of the lines each containing seven.

tercet A three-line STANZA grouping.

terza rima Poetry comprised of TERCETS and an interlocking RHYME SCHEME: ABA, BCB, CDC, etc.

tetrameter A VERSE line of four metrical FEET.

tone A poet's manifest attitude toward the subject expressed in the poem.

trimeter A VERSE line of three metrical FEET.

trochee A metrical FOOT consisting of a hard STRESS followed by a soft stress.

trope A figurative or rhetorical mechanism, and at times a motif.

verse A line of poetry or at times a synonym for *poetry* or *poem*.

vers libre FREE VERSE.

villanelle A 19-line poem made up of six STANZAS—five TERCETS and a final QUATRAIN—with the first tercet employing an ABA RHYME SCHEME that is then replicated in the following tercets as well as in the final two lines of the quatrain. In addition, the first and third lines are repeated in lines 6, 12, and 18, and 9, 15, and 19, respectively. The poem's first and third lines, and their subsequent iterations, carry a special thematic weight, and the poem's motifs are brought together in the concluding quatrain.

voice Not unlike the poem's PERSONA, a sense of a personality or speaker's diction, point of view or attitude in a poem; voice can also simply refer to a poem's speaker.

APPENDIX II

SELECTED BIBLIOGRAPHY

Abbott, Claude Colleer. *The Life and Letters of George Darley, Poet and Critic.* London: Oxford University Press, 1928.

Abrams, M. H. *Correspondent Breeze: Essays on English Romanticism.* New York: Norton, 1984.

———. *Natural Supernaturalism: Tradition and Revolution in Romantic Literature.* New York: Norton, 1973.

Adams, Jad. *Madder Music, Stronger Wine: The Life of Ernest Dowson, Poet and Decadent.* New York: St. Martin's Press, 2000.

Adams, James Eli. *Dandies and Desert Saints: Styles of Victorian Masculinity.* Ithaca, N.Y.: Cornell University Press, 1995.

Adams, James Eli, and Andrew H. Miller, eds. *Sexualities in Victorian Britain.* Bloomington: Indiana University Press, 1996.

Alpers, Paul. *What Is Pastoral?* Chicago: University of Chicago Press, 1996.

Armstrong, Isobel. "The Gush of the Feminine: How Can We Read Women's Poetry of the Romantic Period?" In *Romantic Women Writers: Voices and Countervoices,* edited by Paula R. Feldman and Theresa M. Kelley, 13–32. Hanover, N.H.: University Press of New England, 1995.

———. *Victorian Poetry: Poetry, Poetics and Politics.* New York: Routledge, 1993.

———. *Women's Poetry in the Enlightenment: the Making of a Canon, 1730–1820,* Isobel Armstrong and Virginia Blain, eds. New York: St. Martin's Press, 1999.

Ash, Russell. *Dante Gabriel Rossetti.* New York: H. N. Abrams, 1995.

Badeni, June. *The Slender Tree: A Life of Alice Meynell.* Padstow, England: Tabb House, 1981.

Barker, Juliet. *The Brontës.* New York: St. Martin's Press, 1994.

———. *Wordsworth: A Life.* New York: Viking, 2000.

Bate, Jonathan. *John Clare: A Biography.* London: Picador, 2003.

———. *Romantic Ecology: Wordsworth and the Environmental Tradition.* New York: Routledge, 1991.

Bate, Walter Jackson. *Coleridge.* New York: Macmillan, 1968.

———. *John Keats.* Cambridge, Mass.: Harvard University Press, 1963.

———. *Negative Capability: The Intuitive Approach to Keats.* New York: AMS Press, 1976.

Bentley, G. E., Jr. *William Blake: The Critical Heritage.* London: Routledge Press, 1975.

Bernstein, Carol L. *Precarious Enchantment: A Reading of Meredith's Poetry.* Washington, D.C.: Catholic University of America Press, 1979.

Block, Ed., Jr., ed. *Critical Essays on John Henry Newman.* British Columbia: University of Victoria, 1992.

Bloom, Harold. *The Anxiety of Influence: A Theory of Poetry.* New York: Oxford University Press, 1997.

———. *Genius: A Mosaic of One Hundred Exemplary Creative Minds.* New York: Warner, 2002.

———. *Map of Misreading.* New York: Oxford University Press, 2003.

———. *Poetry and Repression: Revisionism from Blake to Stevens.* New Haven, Conn.: Yale University Press, 1976.

———, ed. *Pre-Raphaelite Poets.* New York: Chelsea House, 1986.

———. *Romanticism and Consciousness: Essays in Criticism.* New York: Norton, 1970.

Bloom, Harold, et al. *Deconstruction and Criticism.* New York: Seabury Press, 1979.

———. *The Visionary Company: A Reading of English Romantic Poetry.* Garden City, N.Y.: Doubleday, 1961.

Bodenheimer, Rosemarie. *The Real Life of Mary Ann Evans: George Eliot, Her Letters and Fiction.* Ithaca, N.Y.: Cornell University Press, 1994.

Bonaparte, Felicia. *The Triptych and the Cross: The Central Myths of George Eliot's Poetic Imagination.* New York: New York University Press, 1979.

Bradshaw, Michael. *Resurrection Songs: The Poetry of Thomas Lovell Beddoes.* Burlington, Vt.: Ashgate Press, 2001.

Brisman, Leslie. *Romantic Origins.* Ithaca, N.Y.: Cornell University Press, 1978.

Bristow, Joseph, ed. *Victorian Women Poets: Emily Brontë, Elizabeth Barrett Browning, Christina Rossetti.* Houndsville, Basingstoke, England: Macmillan Press, 1995.

Bromwich, David. *Disowned by Memory: Wordsworth's Poetry of the 1790s.* Chicago: University of Chicago Press, 1998.

Brooks, Cleanth. *Shaping Joy: Studies in the Writer's Craft.* London: Methuen, 1973.

Brown, Andrew. *The Aeolian Harp in European Literature, 1591–1892.* Cambridge: Bois de Boulogne, 1970.

Brown, Marshall. *Preromanticism.* Stanford, Calif.: Stanford University Press, 1991.

Buckley, Jerome Hamilton. *Tennyson: The Growth of a Poet.* Boston: Houghton Mifflin, 1965.

———. *The Victorian Temper; A Study in Literary Culture.* Cambridge, Mass., Harvard University Press, 1969.

Burke, Kenneth. *A Grammar of Motives.* Berkeley: University of California Press, 1969.

Butler, Marilyn. *Romantics, Rebels, and Reactionaries: English Literature and its Background, 1760–1830.* New York: Oxford University Press, 1982.

Byrom, Thomas. *Nonsense and Wonder: The Poems and Cartoons of Edward Lear.* New York: E. P. Dutton, 1977.

Callow, Philip. *Louis: The Life of Robert Louis Stevenson.* London: Constable, 2001.

Castle, Terry, ed. *The Literature of Lesbianism: A Historical Anthology from Ariosto to Stonewall.* New York: Columbia University Press, 2003.

Chamberlain, Robert. *George Crabbe.* New York: Twayne Publishers, 1965.

Chandler, James. *England in 1819: The Politics of Literary Culture and the Case of Romantic Historicism.* Chicago: University of Chicago Press, 1998.

Charlton, John. *The Chartists: The First National Workers' Movement.* Chicago: Pluto Press, 1997.

Chase, Cynthia. *Decomposing Figures: Rhetorical Readings in the Romantic Tradition.* Baltimore, Md.: Johns Hopkins University Press, 1986.

Chase, Karen. *The Spectacle of Intimacy: A Public Life for the Victorian Family* Princeton, N.J.: Princeton University Press, 2000.

Chernaik, Judith. *Lyrics of Shelley.* Cleveland, Ohio.: Press of Case Western Reserve University, 1972.

Chesterton, G. K. *Robert Louis Stevenson.* New York: Dodd, Mead, and Co., 1928.

Chirico, Paul. *John Clare and the Imagination of the Reader.* New York: Palgrave Macmillan, 2007.

Christensen, Jerome. *Coleridge's Blessed Machine of Language.* Ithaca, N.Y.: Cornell University Press, 1981.

Coburn, Kathleen. *Experience into Thought: Perspectives in the Coleridge Notebooks.* Toronto: University of Toronto Press, 1979.

Cocq, Antonius Petrus Leonardus de. *Andrew Lang, a Nineteenth-Century Anthropologist.* Tilburg, the Netherlands: Zwijsen, 1968.

Colley, Linda. *Britons: Forging the Nation, 1707–1837.* New Haven, Conn.: Yale University Press, 1992.

Damrosch, Leopold. *Symbol and Truth in Blake's Myth.* Princeton, N.J.: Princeton University Press, 1980.

Dawson, Carl, and John Pfordresher, eds. *Matthew Arnold: The Critical Heritage.* New York: Routledge, 1995.

De Bolla, Peter. *The Discourse of the Sublime: Readings in History, Aesthetics, and the Subject.* New York: Blackwell, 1989.

De Man, Paul. *The Resistance to Theory.* Minneapolis, Minn.: University of Minnesota Press, 1986.

———. *The Rhetoric of Romanticism.* New York: Columbia University Press, 1984.

Deane, Seamus. *French Revolution and Enlightenment in England, 1789–1832.* Cambridge, Mass.: Harvard University Press, 1988.

DeVane, William C. *A Browning Handbook.* New York: Appleton-Century-Crofts, 1955.
Dickstein, Morris. *Keats and His Poetry: A Study in Development.* Chicago: University of Chicago Press, 1971.
Donaldson, Sandra, ed. *Critical Essays on Elizabeth Barrett Browning.* New York: G.K. Hall, 1999.
Donner, Henry Wolfgang. *Thomas Lovell Beddoes: The Making of a Poet.* Oxford: Blackwell, 1935.
Duffy, Edward. *Rousseau in England: The Context for Shelley's Critique of the Enlightenment.* Berkeley: University of California Press, 1979.
Durand, Ralph. *A Handbook to the Poetry of Rudyard Kipling.* London: Hodder & Stoughton, 1914.
Ebbatson, Roger. *The Evolutionary Self: Hardy, Forster, Lawrence.* Totowa, N.J.: Barnes and Noble, 1982.
Edgecombe, Rodney Stenning. *Leigh Hunt and the Poetry of Fancy.* London: Associated University Presses, 1994.
Ellmann, Richard. *Oscar Wilde.* New York: Knopf, 1988.
———. *Yeats: The Man and the Masks.* New York: Norton, 1978.
Empson, William. *Seven Types of Ambiguity.* New York: New Directions, 1966.
Engell, James. *Creative Imagination: Enlightenment to Romanticism.* Cambridge, Mass.: Harvard University Press, 1981.
———. *Forming the Critical Mind: Dryden to Coleridge.* Cambridge, Mass.: Harvard University Press, 1989.
Erdman, David V. *Blake, Prophet against Empire: A Poet's Interpretation of the History of His Own Times.* Princeton, N.J.: Princeton University Press, 1954.
Faderman, Lillian. *Surpassing the Love of Men: Romantic Friendship and Love Between Women from the Sixteenth Century to the Present.* New York: Morrow, 1981.
Ferguson, Frances. *Wordsworth: Language as Counter-spirit.* New Haven, Conn.: Yale University Press, 1977.
Fletcher, Loraine. *Charlotte Smith: A Critical Biography.* New York: St. Martin's Press, 1998.
Frosch, Thomas R. *Shelley and the Romantic Imagination: A Psychological Study.* Newark, N.J.: University of Delaware Press, 2007.
Fry, Paul H. *The Poet's Calling in the English Ode.* New Haven, Conn.: Yale University Press, 1980.
———. *Wordsworth and the Poetry of What We Are.* New Haven, Conn.: Yale University Press, 2008.
Frye, Northrop. *Fearful Symmetry: A Study of William Blake.* Princeton, N.J.: Princeton University Press, 1947.
———. *A Study of English Romanticism.* Brighton: Harvester, 1983.
Furst, Lilian, ed. *European Romanticism: Self-Definition: An Anthology.* London: Methuen, 1980.
Gardner, Philip, ed. *A. E. Housman, the Critical Heritage.* New York: Routledge, 1992.
Gilbert, Sandra, and Susan Gubar. *The Madwoman in the Attic: The Woman Writer and the Nineteenth-Century Literary Imagination.* New Haven, Conn.: Yale University Press, 2000.
Gilchrist, Alexander. *Life of William Blake, with Selections from His Poems and Other Writings.* Totowa, N.J.: Rowman and Littlefield, 1973.
Gill, Stephen. *William Wordsworth: A Life.* New York: Oxford University Press, 1989.
Gittings, Robert. *John Keats.* Boston: Little, Brown, 1968.
———. *Mask of Keats: A Study of Problems.* Cambridge, Mass.: Harvard University Press, 1956.
Gladstone, William. *Arthur Henry Hallam.* Boston: P. Mason and Co., 1898.
Gosse, Edmund. *Coventry Patmore.* New York: Charles Scribner's Sons, 1905.
Green, Roger Lancelyn. *Andrew Lang, a Critical Biography with a Short-Title Bibliography of the Works of Andrew Lang.* Leicester, England: E. Ward, 1946.
Greer, Germaine. *Slip-Shod Sibyls: Recognition, Rejection and the Woman Poet.* London: Viking, 1995.
Griggs, Earl Leslie. *Hartley Coleridge: His Life and Work.* London: University of London Press, 1929.
Grigson, Geoffrey. *The Harp of Aeolus: And Other Essays on Art, Literature & Nature.* London: Routledge, 1948.
Gross, Harvey. *Sound and Form in Modern Poetry.* Ann Arbor: University of Michigan Press, 1996.
Gross, John. *Rise and Fall of the Man of Letters: Aspects of English Literary Life since 1800.* London: Weidenfeld & Nicolson, 1969.
Grossman, Allen. *The Long Schoolroom: Essays in the Bitter Logic of the Poetic Principle.* Ann Arbor: University of Michigan Press, 1997.
Grossman, Allen R. *Poetic Knowledge in the Early Yeats; a Study of* The Wind Among the Reeds. Charlottesville: University Press of Virginia, 1969.
Guerard, Albert. *Robert Bridges: A Study of Traditionalism in Poetry.* Cambridge, Mass.: Harvard University Press, 1942.

Guyer, Sara Emilie. *Romanticism after Auschwitz.* Stanford, Calif.: Stanford University Press, 2007.
Haight, Gordon. *George Eliot: A Biography.* New York: Oxford University Press, 1968.
Halmi, Nicholas. *Genealogy of the Romantic Symbol.* New York: Oxford University Press, 2007.
Hark, Ina Rae. *Edward Lear.* Boston: Twayne Publishers, 1982.
Harris, Frank. *Frank Harris, His Life and Adventures: An Autobiography.* London: Richards Press, 1947.
Hartman, Geoffrey. *The Unmediated Vision: An Interpretation of Wordsworth, Hopkins, Rilke, and Valery.* New Haven, Conn.: Yale University Press, 1954.
———. *Wordsworth's Poetry, 1787–1814.* New Haven: Yale University Press, 1971.
Hertz, Neil. *The End of the Line: Essays on Psychoanalysis and the Sublime.* New York: Columbia University Press, 1985.
———. *George Eliot's Pulse.* Stanford, Calif.: Stanford University Press, 2003.
Highet, Gilbert. *Classical Tradition: Greek and Roman Influences on Western Literature.* New York: Oxford University Press, 1957.
Hogle, Jerrold E. *Shelley's Process: Radical Transference and the Development of His Major Works.* New York: Oxford University Press, 1988.
Holden, Anthony. *The Wit in the Dungeon: A Life of Leigh Hunt.* London: Little, Brown, 2005.
Holmes, Richard. *Coleridge.* New York: Pantheon, 2000.
———. *Shelley: The Pursuit.* London: Weidenfeld and Nicolson, 1974.
Homans, Margaret. *Women Writers and Poetic Identity: Dorothy Wordsworth, Emily Brontë, and Emily Dickinson.* Princeton, N.J.: Princeton University Press, 1980.
Hough, Graham Goulden. *The Last Romantics.* London: Duckworth, 1949.
Houghton, Walter Edwards. *Victorian Frame of Mind, 1830–1870.* New Haven, Conn.: Yale University Press, 1957.
Huchon, René. *George Crabbe and His Times, 1754–1832: A Critical and Biographical Study.* Translated from the French by Frederick Clarke. London: J. Murray, 1907.
Hudson, Derek. *A Poet in Parliament: The Life of Winthrop Mackworth Praed.* London: J. Murray, 1939.
Hughes-Hallet, Penelope. *The Immortal Dinner: A Famous Evening of Genius and Laughter in Literary London, 1817.* New York: Viking, 2000.
Ince, Richard Basil. *Calverley and some Cambridge Wits of the Nineteenth Century.* London: G. Richards and H. Toulmin at the Cayme Press, 1929.
Jackson, Kevin. *Invisible Forms: A Guide to Literary Curiosities.* London: Picador, 1999.
Janowitz, Anne. *England's Ruins: Poetic Purpose and the National Landscape.* Cambridge, Mass.: Blackwell, 1990.
Janowitz, Anne F. *Lyric and Labour in the Romantic Tradition.* New York: Cambridge University Press, 1998.
Jeffares, A. Norman. *A New Commentary on the Poems of W. B. Yeats.* Stanford, Calif.: Stanford University Press, 1984.
Johnson, Edgar. *Sir Walter Scott: The Great Unknown.* 2 vols. New York: Macmillan, 1970.
Johnston, Kenneth. *Hidden Wordsworth: Poet, Lover, Rebel, Spy.* New York: Norton, 1998.
———, ed. *Romantic Revolutions: Criticism and Theory.* Bloomington: Indiana University Press, 1990.
Jones, Kathleen. *Learning Not to Be First: The Life of Christina Rossetti.* New York: St. Martin's Press, 1992.
Jones, William B., Jr., ed. *Robert Louis Stevenson Reconsidered: New Critical Perspectives.* Jefferson, N.C.: McFarland, 2002.
Keach, William. *Arbitrary Power: Romanticism, Language, Politics.* Princeton, N.J.: Princeton University Press, 2004.
———. *Shelley's Style.* New York: Methuen, 1984.
Kelly, Richard. *Lewis Carroll.* Boston: Twayne Publishers, 1990.
Kenny, Anthony. *Arthur Hugh Clough: A Poet's Life.* New York: Continuum, 2005.
Ker, Ian, and Alan G. Hill, eds. *Newman after a Hundred Years.* New York: Oxford University Press, 1990.
Kerr, James. *Fiction against History: Scott as Storyteller.* New York: Cambridge University Press, 1989.
Kilham, John. *Critical Essays on the Poetry of Tennyson.* New York: Barnes and Noble, 1960.
Kincaid, James R. *Tennyson's Major Poems: The Comic and Ironic Patterns.* New Haven, Conn.: Yale University Press, 1975.
Kinna, Ruth. *William Morris: The Art of Socialism.* Cardiff: University of Wales Press, 2000.
Kirchhoff, Frederick. *William Morris: the Construction of a Male Self, 1856–1872.* Athens: Ohio University Press, 1990.

Kramer, Dale, ed. *Cambridge Companion to Thomas Hardy.* New York: Cambridge University Press, 1999.

Labbe, Jacqueline M. *Charlotte Smith: Romanticism, Poetry, and the Culture of Gender.* New York: Palgrave, 2003.

Langbaum, Robert Woodrow. *The Modern Spirit; Essays on the Continuity of Nineteenth- and Twentieth-Century Literature.* New York: Oxford University Press, 1970.

Lauber, John. *Sir Walter Scott.* Boston: Twayne Publishers, 1989.

Leavis, F. R. *Revaluation: Tradition & Development in English Poetry.* New York: Norton, 1963.

Lehmann, John. *Lewis Carroll and the Spirit of Nonsense.* Nottingham: University of Nottingham Press, 1974.

Leighton, Angela. *Shelley and the Sublime: An Interpretation of the Major Poems.* New York: Cambridge University Press, 1984.

———. *Victorian Women Poets: Writing Against the Heart.* Charlottesville: University of Virginia Press, 1992.

Lennard, John. *But I Digress: Parentheses in English Printed Verse.* New York: Oxford University Press, 1991.

Levinson, Marjorie. *Wordsworth's Great Period Poems: Four Essays.* New York: Cambridge University Press, 1986.

Levy, William Turner. *William Barnes: The Man and the Poems.* Dorchester, England: Longmans, 1960.

Lincoln, Andrew. *Walter Scott and Modernity.* Edinburgh: Edinburgh University Press, 2007.

Liu, Alan. *Wordsworth: The Sense of History.* Stanford, Calif.: Stanford University Press, 1989.

Louis, Margot Kathleen. *Swinburne and His Gods: The Roots and Growth of an Agnostic Poetry.* Kingston, Ont.: McGill-Queen's University Press, 1990.

Lovejoy, Arthur. "On the Discrimination of Romanticisms." *PMLA* 39, no. 2 (June 1924): 229–253.

Low, Donald A. *Robert Burns: The Critical Heritage.* London: Routledge, 1974.

Lowes, John Livingston. *Road to Xanadu; a study in the ways of the imagination.* New York: Houghton Mifflin, 1930.

Lucas, E. V. *Life of Charles Lamb.* New York: G. P. Putnam's Sons, 1905.

MacCarthy, Fiona. *William Morris: A Life for Our Time.* London: Faber, 1995.

MacKenzie, F. Compton. *William Cory: A Biography.* London: Constable, 1950.

Maddox, Brenda. *George's Ghosts: A New Life of W. B. Yeats.* London: Picador, 1999.

Mahoney, Charles. *Romantics and Renegades: The Poetics of Political Reaction.* New York: Palgrave Macmillan, 2003

Maixner, Paul, ed. *Robert Louis Stevenson: The Critical Heritage.* London: Routledge, 1981.

Marchand, Leslie A. *Byron: A Portrait.* New York: Knopf, 1970.

Markus, Julia. *Dared and Done: The Marriage of Elizabeth Barrett and Robert Browning.* New York: Random House, 1995.

Marsh, Jan. *Christina Rossetti: A Literary Biography.* London: Jonathan Cape, 1994.

Martin, Frederick. *The Life of John Clare.* London: Macmillan, 1865.

Martin, Robert Bernard. *With Friends Possessed: A Life of Edward FitzGerald.* Boston: Faber and Faber, 1985.

McFarland, Thomas. *Coleridge and the Pantheist Tradition.* Oxford: Clarendon Press, 1969.

———. *The Masks of Keats: The Endeavour of a Poet.* New York: Oxford University Press, 2000.

———. *Romantic Cruxes: The English Essayists and the Spirit of the Age.* New York: Oxford University Press, 1987.

McGann, Jerome. *Byron and Romanticism.* New York: Cambridge University Press, 2002.

———. *Don Juan in Context.* Chicago: University of Chicago Press, 1976.

——— *The Romantic Ideology: A Critical Investigation.* Chicago: University of Chicago Press, 1983.

McGann, Jerome J. *Dante Gabriel Rossetti and the Game That Must Be Lost.* New Haven, Conn.: Yale University Press, 2000.

———. *Swinburne: An Experiment in Criticism.* Chicago: University of Chicago Press, 1972.

McGuirk, Carol. *Critical Essays on Robert Burns.* New York: G. K. Hall, 1998.

Mellor, Anne K. *Romanticism and Gender.* New York: Routledge, 1993.

Mermin, Dorothy. *Audience in the Poem: Five Victorian Poets.* New Brunswick, N.J.: Rutgers University Press, 1983.

———. *Elizabeth Barrett Browning: The Origins of a New Poetry.* Chicago: University of Chicago Press, 1989.

Michie, Helena. *Sororophobia: Differences among Women.* New York: Oxford University Press, 1992.
Miller, J. Hillis. *Disappearance of God: Five Nineteenth-Century Writers.* Cambridge, Mass.: Harvard University Press, 1975.
Monk, Samuel Holt. *The Sublime: A Study of Critical Theories in XVIII-century England.* Ann Arbor, Mich.: University of Michigan Press, 1960.
Monsman, Gerald Cornelius. *Confessions of a Prosaic Dreamer: Charles Lamb's Art of Autobiography.* Durham, N.C.: Duke University Press, 1984.
Moorman, Mary. *William Wordsworth: A Biography.* Oxford: Clarendon Press, 1965.
Morrison, Paul. *The Explanation for Everything: Essays on Sexual Subjectivity.* New York: New York University Press, 2001.
Najarian, James. *Victorian Keats: Manliness, Sexuality and Desire.* New York: Palgrave, 2002.
Neil, Roberts. *Meredith and the Novel.* New York: St. Martin's Press, 1997.
Nestor, Pauline. *Female Friendships and Communities: Charlotte Brontë, George Eliot, Elizabeth Gaskell.* New York: Oxford University Press, 1985.
Notopolous, James A. *The Platonism of Shelley: A Study of Platonism and the Poetic Mind.* Durham, N.C.: Duke University Press, 1949.
Nunokawa, Jeff. *Tame Passions of Wilde: Styles of Manageable Desire.* Princeton, N.J.: Princeton University Press, 2003.
Page, Frederick. *Patmore: A Study in Poetry.* Hamdon, Conn.: Archon Books, 1970.
Parejo Vadillo, Ana. *Women Poets and Urban Aestheticism: Passengers of Modernity.* New York: Palgrave Macmillan, 2005.
Parker, Reeve. *Coleridge's Meditative Art.* Ithaca, N.Y.: Cornell University Press, 1975.
Peters, Catherine. *Thackeray's Universe: Shifting Worlds of Imagination and Reality.* London: Faber and Faber, 1987.
Phillips, Catherine. *Robert Bridges: A Biography.* New York: Oxford University Press, 1992.
Pinch, Adela. *Strange Fits of Passion: Epistemologies of Emotion, Hume to Austen.* Stanford, Calif.: Stanford University Press, 1996.
Pollard, Arthur. *Crabbe: The Critical Heritage.* London: Routledge, 1972.
Pomeroy, Mary Joseph, Sister. *The Poetry of Hartley Coleridge.* Washington, D.C.: Catholic University of America, 1927.
Price, Leah. *The Anthology and the Rise of the Novel from Richardson to George Eliot.* New York: Cambridge University Press, 2000.
Prins, Yopie. *Victorian Sappho.* Princeton, N.J.: Princeton University Press, 1999.
Quinney, Laura. *Literary Power and the Criteria of Truth.* Gainesville: University Press of Florida, 1995.
———. *The Poetics of Disappointment: Wordsworth to Ashbery.* Charlottesville: University Press of Virginia, 1999.
Raine, Kathleen. *Blake and Antiquity.* Princeton, N.J.: Princeton University Press, 1977.
Rajan, Tilottama. *Dark Interpreter: The Discourse of Romanticism.* Ithaca, N.Y.: Cornell University Press, 1980.
Ray, Gordon N. *Thackeray: The Age of Wisdom, 1847–1863.* New York: McGraw-Hill, 1957.
———. *Thackeray: The Uses of Adversity, 1811–1846.* New York: McGraw-Hill, 1955.
Raymond, William O. *The Infinite Moment, and Other Essays in Robert Browning.* Toronto, Ont.: University of Toronto Press, 1965.
Redfield, Marc. *The Politics of Aesthetics: Nationalism, Gender, Romanticism.* Stanford, Calif.: Stanford University Press, 2003.
Richards, Grant. *Housman: 1897–1936.* New York: Oxford University Press, 1942.
Richards, I. A. *Coleridge on Imagination.* New York: Routledge, 2001.
Ricks, Christopher. *Keats and Embarrassment.* Oxford: Clarendon Press, 1974.
Ricks, Christopher B. *Tennyson.* New York: Macmillan, 1972.
Ritz, Jean-Georges. *Robert Bridges and Gerard Hopkins 1863–1889: A Literary Friendship.* New York: Oxford University Press, 1960.
Roe, Nicholas. *Fiery Heart: The First Life of Leigh Hunt.* London: Pimlico, 2005.
———, ed. *Leigh Hunt: Life, Poetics, Politics.* New York: Routledge, 2003.
Rowlinson, Matthew. *Tennyson's Fixations: Psychoanalysis and the Topics of the Early Poetry.* Charlottesville: University Press of Virginia, 1994.
Russell, Daniel S. *The Emblem and Device in France.* Lexington, Ky.: French Forum, 1985.
Rutland, William R. *Swinburne: A Nineteenth-Century Hellene.* Oxford: Blackwell, 1931.
Said, Edward. *Culture and Imperialism.* New York: Knopf, 1993.

Saintsbury, George. *History of English Prosody, from the Twelfth Century to the Present Day.* New York: Russell & Russell, 1961.
Scarry, Elaine. *Dreaming by the Book.* New York: Farrar, Straus and Giroux, 1999.
Schirmer, Gregory A. *Out of What Began: A History of Irish Poetry in English.* Ithaca, N.Y.: Cornell University Press, 1998.
Segermann, Krista. *Das Motto in der Lyrik: Funktion und Form der "épigraphe" vor Gedichten der französischen Romantik sowie der nachromantischen Zeit.* Munich: Fink, 1977.
Shannon-Mangan, Ellen. *James Clarence Mangan: A Biography.* Dublin: Irish Academic Press, 1996.
Sherman, G. W. *The Pessimism of Thomas Hardy.* Rutherford, N.J.: Fairleigh Dickinson University Press, 1976.
Shillingsburg, Peter L. *William Makepeace Thackeray: A Literary Life.* New York: Palgrave, 2001.
Sperry, Stuart. *Keats the Poet.* Princeton, N.J.: Princeton University Press, 1994.
Spurgeon, Caroline Frances Eleanor. *Keats's Shakespeare: A Descriptive Study Based on New Material.* London: Oxford University Press, 1929.
Stabler, Jane. *Burke to Byron, Barbauld to Baillie, 1790–1830.* New York: Palgrave, 2001.
Staves, Susan. *Married Women's Separate Property in England, 1660–1833.* Cambridge, Mass.: Harvard University Press, 1990.
Stevenson, Lionel. *Darwin among the Poets.* Chicago: University of Chicago Press, 1932.
———. *Pre-Raphaelite Poets.* New York: Norton, 1974.
Stillinger, Jack. *The Hoodwinking of Madeline, and Other Essays on Keats's Poems.* Urbana: University of Illinois Press, 1971.
Storey, Mark. *Robert Southey: A Life.* New York: Oxford University Press, 1997.
Sturgeon, Mary. *Michael Field.* London: G. G. Harrap, 1922.
Super, R. H. *Walter Savage Landor: A Biography.* New York: New York University Press, 1954.
Sutherland, Gillian. *Faith, Duty, and the Power of Mind: The Cloughs and Their Circle, 1820–1960.* London: Cambridge University Press, 2006.
Sutherland, John. *The Life of Walter Scott: A Critical Biography.* Cambridge: Blackwell, 1995.
Swann, Karen. "'Christabel': The Wandering Mother and the Enigma of Form." *SIR* 23, no. 4 (Winter 1984): 533–553.
Swann, Thomas Burnett. *Ernest Dowson.* New York: Twayne Publishers, 1965.
Sweet, Nanora. *Felicia Hemans: Reimagining Poetry in the Nineteenth Century.* New York: Palgrave, 2001.
Swinburne, Algernon Charles. *William Blake: A Critical Essay.* New York: Dutton, 1906.
Terhune, A. M. *The Life of Edward FitzGerald, Translator of the Rubáiyát of Omar Khayyám.* New Haven, Conn.: Yale University Press, 1947.
Thomas, Frances. *Christina Rossetti.* Hanley Swan, England: Self Publishing Association, 1992.
Thompson, Dorothy. *The Chartists.* London: Temple Smith, 1984.
Thompson, E. P. *William Morris: Romantic to Revolutionary.* New York: Pantheon, 1977.
———. *Witness against the Beast: William Blake and the Moral Law.* New York: Cambridge University Press, 1993.
Thompson, James R. *Leigh Hunt.* Boston: Twayne, 1977.
Thorslev, Peter Larsen. *The Byronic Hero: Types and Prototypes.* Minneapolis, Minn., University of Minnesota Press, 1962.
Trilling, Lionel. *The Liberal Imagination: Essays on Literature and Society.* New York: New York Review Books, 2008.
———. *Matthew Arnold.* New York: Columbia University Press, 1949.
Trollope, Anthony. *Thackeray.* London: Macmillan, 1936.
Tucker, Herbert. *Tennyson and the Doom of Romanticism.* Cambridge, Mass.: Harvard University Press, 1988.
Vendler, Helen. *Odes of John Keats.* Cambridge, Mass.: Harvard University Press, 1983.
———. *Poets Thinking: Pope, Whitman, Dickinson, Yeats.* Cambridge: Harvard University Press, 2004.
———. *Yeats's Vision and the Later Plays.* Cambridge, Mass.: Harvard University Press, 1963.
Wasserman, Earl. *The Finer Tone: Keats' Major Poems.* Baltimore, Md.: Johns Hopkins University Press, 1953.
———. *Shelley: A Critical Reading.* Baltimore, Md.: Johns Hopkins University Press, 1971.
———. *Subtler Language: Critical Readings of Neoclassic and Romantic Poems.* Baltimore, Md.: Johns Hopkins University Press, 1968.
Weinig, Mary Anthony. *Coventry Patmore.* Boston: Twayne Publishers, 1981.
Weinstein, Mark A. *William Edmondstoune Aytoun and the Spasmodic Controversy.* New Haven, Conn.: Yale University Press, 1968.

Weiskel, Thomas. *The Romantic Sublime: Studies in the Structure and Psychology of Transcendence.* Baltimore, Md.: Johns Hopkins University Press, 1986.

Westwater, Martha. *The Spasmodic Career of Sydney Dobell.* Lanham, Md.: University Press of America, 1992.

White, Norman. *Hopkins: A Literary Biography.* New York: Oxford University Press, 1992.

White, Terence De Vere. *Tom Moore: the Irish Poet.* London: Hamilton, 1977.

Wolfson, Susan J. *The Questioning Presence: Wordsworth, Keats, and the Interrogative Mode in Romantic Poetry.* Ithaca, N.Y: Cornell University Press, 1986.

Woodring, Carl. *Politics in the Poetry of Coleridge.* Madison: University of Wisconsin Press, 1961.

Wu, Duncan. *Companion to Romanticism.* Oxford: Blackwell, 1998.

———. *Wordsworth: An Inner Life.* Oxford: Blackwell, 2002.

Wordsworth, Jonathan. *Ancestral Voices: Fifty Books from the Romantic Period.* New York: Woodstock, 1996.

———. *Bright Work Grows: Women Writers of the Romantic Age.* Washington, D.C.: Woodstock Books, 1997.

Zimmerman, Sarah MacKenzie. *Romanticism, Lyricism, and History.* Albany: State University of New York Press, 1999.

INDEX

Note: **Boldface** page numbers indicate main entries.

D

E

F

G

N

O

P

T